Exploring Marriages & Families

SECOND EDITION

Karen Seccombe

Portland State University

PEARSON

Boston   Columbus   Indianapolis   New York   San Francisco   Upper Saddle River
Amsterdam   Cape Town   Dubai   London   Madrid   Milan   Munich   Paris   Montreal   Toronto
Delhi   Mexico City   Sao Paulo   Sydney   Hong Kong   Seoul   Singapore   Taipei   Tokyo

Editor in Chief: Dickson Musslewhite
Publisher: Charlyce Jones Owen
Program Manager: Seanna Breen
Editorial Assistant: Maureen Diana
Marketing Manager: Brittany Pogue-Mohammed
Marketing Assistant: Karen Tanico
Project Manager: Fran Russello
Procurement Manager: Mary Fischer
Procurement Specialist: Diane Peirano
Design Interior: Irene Ehrmann
Digital Media Project Manager: Claudine Bellanton
Senior Art Director: Blair Brown
Art Director: Maria Lange
Cover Designer: iEnergizer Aptara Limited
Manager, Rights and Permissions: Carolyn Cruthirds
Photo Researcher: Carolyn Arcabascio/PreMediaGlobal
Cover Art: Fuse/Getty Images
Full-Service Project Management: Mohinder Singh/Aptara®, Inc.
Printer/Binder: Courier Companies, Inc.
Text Font: Sabon LT Std 10.5/12

Credits appear on page 551, which constitutes an extension of the copyright page.

Library of Congress Cataloging-in-Publication Data

Seccombe, Karen
    Exploring marriages & families/Karen Seccombe, Portland State University.—Second edition.
      pages cm
    ISBN-13: 978-0-13-380777-6
    ISBN-10: 0-13-380777-0
    1. Marriage.   2. Families.   3. Parent and child.   I. Title.
    HQ503.S377 2015
    306.8—dc23   2013045421

10 9 8 7 6 5 4 3 2 1

PEARSON

ISBN 10:   0-13-380777-0
ISBN 13: 978-0-13-380777-6

Brief Contents

Contents

Part IV   Family Strengths, Challenges, and Reorganization

Chapter 11
Family Stress and Crisis: Violence among Intimates   308

Chapter 12
The Process of Divorce   343

Preface

Marriages and Families is my favorite course among the many I have taught over the past twenty years. Students crave information about love, sex, dating, relationships, marriage, and children. However, they tend to see these issues in individualized terms, which makes the course a constant challenge to teach.

My goal, therefore, is to offer students a fresh perspective—*one that places individual relationships in their social context so that students can more fully understand why they make the choices they do.* Throughout the text, I illustrate the ways in which historical, cultural, social, and political factors influence our personal experiences, beliefs, privileges, constraints, and choices. Our likelihood of marrying, bearing children, or divorcing; our family values, lifestyles, and opportunities; and our health and well-being (and stressors upon them) are all influenced by these structural factors. With a strong focus on theory and research, a celebration of diversity, a rich look at how history shapes both our present and future, an emphasis on family resilience and empowerment, and an emphasis on assessment and engaging visual presentation (including video segments for each chapter opening), this introductory text helps students make more informed decisions about their relationships by better understanding the social context in which they live and the relevance of social science to their lives.

I introduce the following key themes in the opening chapter, provide provocative examples of each throughout subsequent chapters, and revisit the themes in the concluding chapter: (1) the best way to truly understand families is to link micro- and macro-level perspectives; (2) families are not monolithic or static, but ever-changing; and (3) social science theory and research help us understand families and relationships.

The Best Way to Truly Understand Families Is to Link Micro- and Macro-Level Perspectives

Although all of us experience relationships and family life as individuals, we will not understand these experiences without an appreciation of the social environment in which they happen. Our relationships are shaped in large part by our culture and elements of social structure, including our statuses (i.e., race, ethnicity, social class, gender, and sex) and our institutions (i.e., the economy, religion, and the political system). Thus at every appropriate opportunity in the text, the relationship between macro-level factors and micro-level personal choices, experiences, opportunities, and constraints is highlighted. For example, social structure may influence who is considered an appropriate mate, how we communicate with our partners, our sexual experiences, benefits that accrue from marriage, the division of household labor between husbands and wives, decisions about children and childrearing, and our likelihood of divorcing and repartnering.

Families Are Not Monolithic or Static, but Are Ever-Changing

People construct families to meet their needs for warmth, companionship, economic cooperation, and as a way to raise children. Therefore, families take many different forms that continue to evolve, sharing historical, cultural, and subcultural differences in family life. The text suggests there is not one "right" type of family—one size does not fit all—and each chapter celebrates the diversity of families in the United States and around the world. For example, extensive coverage of topics such as gay and lesbian families, cohabitation, single parents, racial and ethnic differences in family structure and interaction, and social class differences are fully integrated throughout the text. Also included are documented changes in relationships and families advanced by technology, such as cell phones, laptops, and networking sites like Facebook and Twitter. These technologies have changed the way people meet, communicate, and carry on their daily lives.

Social Science Theory and Research Help Us Understand Families and Relationships

Everyone holds "common sense" opinions about families based on personal experience or information filtered through the mass media, peers, or parents. However, a scientific perspective can provide a more objective and factual window on the world, and can help us form opinions, develop our values, and make sound personal choices. Theories and methods of social research are introduced in Chapter 1. Each subsequent chapter provides solid theoretical grounding in key issues, demonstrates the value of research, and includes the most recent quantitative and qualitative interdisciplinary scholarship available. Finally, the boxed feature *Why Do Research?* illustrates how family scientists conduct research, the methods they use, the dilemmas they face, and how conclusions of research champion common sense perceptions about families. Students sometimes complain that research is "dry," but I have done my best to show that it isn't.

What Is New in This Edition

Overall:

- Includes specific learning objectives in each chapter
- Updated with 2013 statistics whenever possible
- Incorporates the most recent scholarship in the leading family journals
- More user-friendly writing style
- Greater attention to racial and ethnic minorities and differences across groups
- Increases coverage of same-sex couples
- Greater use of theory throughout
- Clearer comparisons of macro- and micro-level factors that influence families
- Additional personal narratives to help students grasp the concepts

Chapter 1

- Revises discussion of China's one-child policy
- Updates information about the movement to increase minimum wage
- Clearer distinction between qualitative and quantitative research

Chapter 2

- Discussion of "gender apartheid" in Saudi Arabia
- Suggests greater caution about overgeneralizing
- Expands coverage of the ways in which video games and television shows teach gendered roles
- Updates information about the race and ethnic composition of the U.S.
- Clarifies differences between first and second generation Hispanics
- Elaborates on the intersection of ethnicity, race, class, and gender

Chapter 3

- Expands coverage of singlehood, including how intersections affect the experience of singlehood
- Reviews research on cross-sex friendships
- Updates discussion of online dating

- Increases coverage of cohabitation and effects of cohabitation on children
- Highlights new data on same-sex partner households

Chapter 4
- Increases coverage of biochemical approaches to love
- Presents the positive aspects of an arranged marriage on relationships
- Expands coverage of controlling behavior, including stalking
- Highlights research on break-ups

Chapter 5
- Greater attention to the portrayal of sex in the popular media
- Updates discussion of the double standard, including how both males and females view the double standard
- Provides the latest data on teen pregnancy and births
- Expands coverage about the hook-up sexual culture among young adults
- Updates research on sex and the elderly
- Broadens discussion of STIs

Chapter 6
- Expands coverage of social media sites
- Updates research about sex differences in communication

Chapter 7
- Updates marriage trends
- Expands coverage about interracial and interethnic marriage
- Reviews the research about marriage across social class boundaries
- Expands coverage of the "marriage premium," and compares it to the benefits that accrue to cohabitors
- Incorporates the most recent data about marital satisfaction

Chapter 8
- Updates fertility patterns in the U.S.
- Expands coverage of infertility
- Includes new information about the history of adoption
- Provides new information about transracial adoption
- Elaborates on the transition to parenthood

Chapter 9
- Introduces the importance of computers as an agent of socialization
- Provides information on spanking
- Expands coverage on fathering
- Updates statistics on teen parenting
- Expands discussion of grandparents raising grandchildren

Chapter 10
- Updates trends on women's labor force participation
- Revises discussion on the recession to reflect where we are in 2014
- Expands discussion of health insurance and health care reform
- Expands coverage on family chores and the division of household labor
- Updates and increases coverage about childcare

Chapter 11

- Greater international coverage
- Updates data using the National Intimate Partner and Sexual Violence Survey and the National Crime Victimization Survey
- Expands coverage of stalking
- Includes new information about violence in same-sex relationships

Chapter 12

- Clarifies how divorce data are collected and the ways in which collection has changed
- Expands coverage of alimony
- Updates discussion on joint physical custody
- Greater attention to the plight of children

Chapter 13

- Introduces the differences in women's downward mobility after divorce by social class
- Includes new data about cohabitation after divorce
- Expands coverage of stepfamilies
- Compares the sense of family obligation between biological and stepfamilies

Chapter 14

- Updates changing demographics
- Includes new information about the increase of young adults living with their parents
- Expands coverage of same-sex elderly couples
- Discusses the macro- and micro-level reasons that the age at retirement is increasing
- Further coverage of health issues such as Alzheimer's Disease and long-term care

Chapter 15

- Greater coverage of telecommuting jobs
- Expanded analysis of the Earned Income Tax Credit
- Introduce Child Tax Credit

Visual Style and Assessment Tools

Many college students today are *visual learners*, reading more websites, magazines, graphic novels, emails, and text messages than ever before. They learn and absorb information differently, thriving in an environment awash in information technology, where fast delivery and visually rich presentations are expected.

Professors, myself included, have been challenged by students' seeming disinterest in traditional textbooks. Many perceive textbooks as boring, outdated, and irrelevant. They find the material too intimidating to master. Many would rather consult Google, a study partner, or a classmate rather than struggle with their textbook if they have a question.

This text has been designed with these concerns in mind. Based on a sound scholarship, the text is written in a conversational tone to help grab and hold students' attention. Each chapter begins with an engaging video from our *Exploring Families* video series (found on **www.mysoclab.com**) and opening vignette about a couple or family whose story illustrates the chapter's main ideas. The video is then recalled at the end of the chapter as students answer questions applying what they have learned.

Graphs, charts, and tables are attractively designed to deliver key information quickly and engagingly. Students can easily become overwhelmed with data. The tables and graphs here are not simply add-ons; rather, they are fully integrated within the text itself and are strategically designed to help students process information more efficiently. Key points are specifically identified in each visual so that students are not left wondering, "What am I supposed to learn from this chart?"

The flow of each chapter is easy to follow, and includes a variety of assessment tools for students. They can test their knowledge and apply the information they have learned to their own lives. Each chapter begins with important learning objectives, and then moves to more specific questions, which are repeated in the margin within the chapter and answered in the **Chapter Review**. Self-reflection questions and **Questions That Matter** can be found peppered throughout the chapter in the margins, as well as at the end of the boxed features (**What Do You Think?**). The **Getting to Know Yourself** boxed feature contains self-assessment tests and inventories students can take on their own time. The last paragraph of each chapter (**Bringing It Full Circle**) asks students to think critically about what they have learned and apply it to the *Exploring Families* video from the chapter opener. (All of these features, and more, are explained in detail in the next section of the Preface.)

My overall goal is to present the material in a lively and appealing format, with 15 chapters to grab and retain students' attention as they work through their Marriages and Families course.

- For professors, this text is grounded in solid theory and research.
- For students, it is accessible, relevant, and engaging.
- For both, the text captures the compelling relationship and family issues of our time.

Pedagogical Features

The features in each chapter are specifically designed to make learning easier and more rewarding, and to highlight the themes of the text:

Opening Vignette and Video Clip

Grabbing students' attention immediately. Each chapter begins with a compelling personal narrative and accompanying video clip (found in our *Exploring Families* video series on **www.mysoclab.com**) that chronicles an individual's or couple's experience that is relevant to the chapter. Students can identify with these real stories; they bring the material to life, revealing the micro- and macro-level connections in our relationships while stimulating students' critical evaluation of the material. Questions appear at the end of each video that feed directly into the MySocLab Gradebook, allowing the videos to be assigned as homework assignments. Instructors also have access to a wealth of additional video samples in MySocLab they can choose from to match their teaching preference. Examples of vignettes and video clips include a couple describing the benefits of their arranged marriage; a young couple discussing their decision to cohabit; insights into the double standard from both a male and a female perspective; a moving account of an international adoption; how one family juggles work and family responsibilities; a heroic confrontation of intimate partner violence; a young woman's painful remembrance of her parents' divorce; and the story of caring for a frail elderly parent while also carrying for a young child at home. Vignettes and video clips use humor, emotion, and curiosity to engage students and immediately draw them into the chapter. A **Video Discussion Guide** available on MySocLab provides multiple-choice and critical-thinking questions to promote further review of the *Exploring Families* videos and chapter themes.

Questions That Matter

Allowing students to measure their understanding. Each chapter contains 12–15 questions drawn from the learning objectives of the chapter. These questions identify the key points of the chapter and allow students to test and measure their degree of understanding of the material. Detailed answers to these questions are provided at the end of each chapter in the Chapter Review.

Questions for Reflection

Encouraging students to form and analyze their own opinions. Provocative critical thinking questions are strategically placed in the margins throughout the chapters to challenge students to think about controversial issues, form opinions, and analyze the factors that shape their opinions. This feature integrates all three themes, so that students think about macro–micro linkages, diversity, and how research findings can challenge our "common sense" ideas. Students are encouraged to use the information in the text to help them reflect on their own lives, take a stand, and to defend their position.

Key Terms and Glossary

Keeping students organized. To help students better retain important information, key terms and concepts appear in boldface within the chapter text, and a marginal definition is included for reinforcement. Key terms are repeated again at the end of the chapter in the Chapter Review and a full glossary concludes the book.

Boxed Features

Tying It All Together: Factors That Shape . . .

Explicitly identifying the macro and micro links. Students often have difficulty identifying the importance of culture and social structure and how these influence personal relationships. This feature highlights the first theme by explicitly identifying macro- and micro-level influences on our marriages, families, and close relationships. Students benefit from the insights of each perspective and their interrelationship. Within each chapter, this feature shows how culture, history, social institutions, and social status shape personal choices and constraints, including sexual scripts; dating and mate-selection practices; the decline in marriage rates; the division of household labor; and the decision to have a child.

Policy and You: From Macro to Micro

Connecting social structure to our personal lives. This feature, supporting the text's first theme, critically examines programs or policies designed to strengthen families and focuses on how social structure creates specific needs within families, and how social policy can address those needs. Chapters include specific examples of "best practices," here in the United States and abroad, to show students what is happening and what is *possible*. Examples include maternity and family leave policies in the United States compared with other developed nations; the history of domestic partnerships and issues surrounding same-sex marriage; budgeting choices families living in poverty must make; and a look at family allowances available in more than 80 countries to help families with the costs of raising children.

My Family

Relating personal narratives that reveal how macro-level factors shape our micro-level experiences, choices, and constraints. Family narratives bring the material alive for students. These boxes allow students the opportunity to see all three text themes in action: the effect of social structure on families, the diversity of family experience, and the importance of systematic research. Examples of this feature include stories of delaying marriage; living in a stepfamily; dating violence; growing up poor; and the experience of being widowed at a young age.

Diversity in Families

Showing the diversity of experience around the world, and within our own country. This feature illustrates a variety of diverse family experiences and traditions, and emphasizes the text's second theme: families are not monolithic or static, but ever-changing. Examples include stories of social class differences in the way parents socialize their children; teaching children about racism; sex trafficking of children; patriarchy and divorce laws in Egypt; and father-headed single families.

Why Do Research?

Demonstrating the relevance of research. Bolstering the text's third theme, students learn the logic behind quantitative and qualitative research. All chapters are grounded in research, and include many articles, books, and reports published in 2013 and 2014. This box offers specific theoretical or methodological insights so that students can better evaluate research findings and see the relevance to their lives. For example, students will read about the distinction between correlation and causation by using the example of successful men who were raised by single parents. Specific methodologies are highlighted, such as content analysis to see how adoption is portrayed in college textbooks or how art can be used to understand children's views of divorce. In addition, the feature shows how research findings can challenge our stereotypes, such as whether women are really more talkative than men.

Getting to Know Yourself

Employing self-tests and inventories that allow students to assess their own attitudes and compare their opinions with others. This feature includes fun and engaging self-tests so that students can identify their own opinions, and compare themselves to others. Self-tests include both adapted classic scales as well as newly created self-tests, such as ones that assess attitudes toward divorce, sex differences in communication styles, and attitudes toward homosexuality. These self-tests can be taken individually or completed in class to springboard discussion.

Bringing It Full Circle

Revisiting and reinforcing student learning. Each chapter's concluding section revisits the opening narrative and *Exploring Families* video clip, and prompts students to think critically about it in the context of what they have learned in the chapter. For example, the opening story in Chapter 12, "The Process of Divorce," presents a child's view of her parents' divorce. In the *Bringing It Full Circle* feature, we return to this case, and pose several questions that draw on the chapter content.

- How would you describe Melanie's experiences with the different stations of her parent's divorce: emotional, legal, economic, co-parental, community, and psychic?

- Because the research shows that children do better if they remain in close contact with their noncustodial parents, should children like Melanie be required to stay with their fathers even if they don't really want to?
- Do you think that Melanie's family had a "good divorce"? Explain your answer.
- If you or someone close to you divorced, how would you explain it to your child? Would you focus only on micro-level issues, or would any macro-level issues be relevant?

Chapter Review

Engaging and detailed question-and-answer format. Each chapter concludes with a series of answers that summarize the important concepts introduced in the *Questions that Matter* located in the margins throughout the chapter. The Chapter Review also contains a list of key terms and instructions on additional assets and videos students can access on **www.mysoclab.com**.

Supplements

Instructor's Manual and Test Bank

Each chapter in the Instructor's Manual includes the following resources: Chapter Summary, Chapter Outline, Learning Objectives, Critical Thinking Questions, Activities for Classroom Participation, Key Terms, and a Video User's Guide. A grid opens each chapter that correlates the detailed chapter outline to its corresponding video. Designed to make your lectures more effective and to save preparation time, this extensive resource gathers useful activities and strategies for teaching your Marriage and Family course.

The Test Bank, written by Karen Seccombe, contains more than 1400 questions. Each question is organized by its corresponding Learning Objective and classified according to Bloom's Taxonomy. An additional feature, currently not found in any other Marriage and Family test bank, is the inclusion of rationales for the correct answer in the multiple-choice questions. The rationales help instructors reviewing the content to further evaluate the questions they are choosing for their tests and give instructors the option to use the rationales as an answer key for their students.

This second edition Test Bank has been developed thoroughly in response to market feedback. It has also been analyzed by a developmental editor and a copy editor in order to ensure clarity, accuracy, and delivery of the highest-quality assessment tool.

MyTest

This computerized software allows instructors to create their own personalized exams, to edit any or all of the existing test questions, and to add new questions. Other special features of this program include random generation of test questions, creation of alternate versions of the same test, scrambling question sequence, and test preview before printing. For easy access, this software is available within the instructor section of the MySocLab for *Exploring Marriages & Families* by Seccombe, or at **www.pearsonhighered.com**.

PowerPoint Presentations

The PowerPoint presentations for Exploring Marriages & Families are informed by instructional and design theory. You have the option in every chapter of choosing from any of the following types of slides: Lecture & Line Art and/or Special Topics PowerPoints. The Lecture PowerPoint slides follow the chapter outline and integrate images from the textbook. The Special Topics PowerPoint slides allow you to integrate rich supplementary material into your course with minimal preparation time. In addition, all of the PowerPoints are uniquely designed to present concepts in a clear and succinct manner that allows you to customize them with your own clip art or color ideas. They are available to adopters at **www.pearsonhighered.com.**

MySOCLab™

MySocLab is an easy-to-use online resource that allows instructors to assess student progress and adapt course material to meet the specific needs of the class. This resource enables students to diagnose their progress by completing an online self-assessment test. Based on the results of this test, each student is provided with a customized study plan, including a variety of tools to help him or her fully master the material. MySocLab then reports the self-assessment results to the instructor as individual student grades as well as an aggregate report of class progress. Based on these reports, the instructor can adapt course material to suit the needs of individual students or the class as a whole.

The Pearson e-Text version of Exploring Marriages & Families include both an audio and text versions of the text.

MySocLab includes several exciting new features. Social Explorer provides easy access to census data from 1790 to the present. You can explore the data visually through interactive data maps. MySocLibrary contains numerous original source readings with discussion questions and assessment exercises.

Writing Space provides writing opportunities in response to essay and short answer questions that can be graded through MySocLab.

Contact your local Pearson Education representative for ordering information, or visit **www.mysoclab.com.**

Acknowledgments

This book has been a long journey, and, fortunately for me, I have had support every step of the way. Thank you to everyone who helped to make this dream a reality. First and foremost, there is my family, husband Richard and daughters Natalie (age 13) and Olivia (age 11), who provided zany distractions and steadfast love that both drove me nuts and kept me grounded. Although many authors write of the sacrifices their families made, I think writing this book actually enhanced our lives. What a great way to combine theory, research, and practical experience. For example, I know Richard really appreciated all that I learned in writing the chapter on communication!

I also want to thank my friends and academic colleagues who provided their ideas, listened to mine, and challenged me to do my best work. Karen Pyke, with her keen insights and generous heart, always invigorates me intellectually and keeps me moving forward. Mentors Gary Lee, Kathy Kaiser, and Manley Johnson sparked my intellectual curiosity about families.

Then, of course, there are many friends who, at first blush, had nothing to do with this book but helped me more than they will ever know. I thank Cordie Tilghman and Ali Cook, who took me to movies, discussed *other* books at our book club, or shared glasses of wine in cool Portland venues when I needed a break. I am genuinely grateful to the entire Oregon Episcopal School community for providing Natalie, Liv, and our whole family with a safe harbor.

Many reviewers took time from their busy schedules to provide important feedback. I want to thank the following reviewers for their suggestions:

Henry Borne, *Holy Cross College*

Sandra Caron, *University of Maine*

Dr. Lloyd Ganey, *College of Southern Nevada*

James Guinee, *University of Central Arkansas*

Linda Lotz, *Santa Fe College*

Ana Lucero-Liu, *Calilfornia State University, Northridge*

Muketiwa Madzura, *Normandale College*

Erin Olson, *Dordt College*

Janice Purk, *Mansfield University*

Meena Sharma, *Henry Ford Community College*

Also, thanks to the families and couples featured in the *Exploring Families* video series for graciously sharing their stories with us: Becca, Taylor, Meghan, Jono, Rati, Subas, Kayla, Chris, Scherazade, Roderick, Tracey, Juan, Cassandra, John, Karen, Betsy, Jayla, Henry, Fred, Lisa, Chris, Christopher, Shannon, Melanie, Jane, Daneen, Jim, Connor, Kate, Lindsay, Jamie, Amy, Sophie, Alain, Hugo, and Noe. These are real people telling their stories, not actors, and I appreciate their willingness to open their lives and allow us to learn from them.

I also appreciate the tremendous help I received from my friends at Pearson: Charlyce Jones Owen (Publisher); Seanna Breen (Program Manager); Fran Russello (Project Manager); Maureen Diana (Editorial Assistant).

Now, to the readers—faculty and students alike—if you have questions or comments, please send them my way. I want to hear from you: seccombek@pdx.edu.

All my best,

Karen Seccombe

About the Author

Karen Seccombe is a proud community college graduate (Go Citrus!) and a first-generation college student. She is now a professor in the School of Community Health at Portland State University, located in Portland, Oregon. She received her B.A. in sociology at California State University, Chico; her M.S.W. in health and social welfare policy from the University of Washington; and her Ph.D. in sociology from Washington State University. Karen is the author of *"So You Think I Drive a Cadillac?": Welfare Recipients' Perspectives on the System and Its Reform* (Pearson); *Families and Their Social Worlds* (Pearson); *Just Don't Get Sick: Access to Healthcare in the Aftermath of Welfare Reform*, with Kim A. Hoffman (Rutgers University Press); and *Families in Poverty* (Pearson). She is a fellow of the National Council on Family Relations, and a member of the American Sociological Association and the Pacific Sociological Association, where she has held elective offices.

Karen lives in the San Juan Islands, located off the coast of Washington with her husband Richard, a health economist, her thirteen-year-old daughter, Natalie Rose, her eleven-year-old daughter, Olivia Lin, and her two Australian Shepherds, Stella and Bart. In her spare time, she enjoys hiking with her family near their cabin in the Oregon Cascades, kayaking and cycling in the San Juan Islands, and exploring the kid-friendly attractions in Portland and Seattle, of which there are many.

Why Study Families and Other Close Relationships?

Listen to Chapter 1 on **MySocLab**

LEARNING OBJECTIVES

Identify the different definitions of "family" and their implications	**1.1**
Describe the functions of families	**1.2**
Recognize the link between micro-level and macro-level perspectives on families	**1.3**
Assess the ways that families are always changing	**1.4**
Summarize the importance of social science theory and research	**1.5**

What is a family? This seems a fairly simple question, but it can have a surprisingly complex answer.

Throughout this text, you'll meet people in different types of relationships: married couples, cohabiting couples, same-sex couples, and stepfamilies, to name just a few. Let's introduce a few of these families to you now.

Are Betsy and Karen a family?

👁 **Watch** on **MySocLab**
Video: *What is a Family?*

Becca is a 31-year-old single mother of 7-year-old Taylor. Raised in poverty, homeless as a young adult, she has struggled successfully to overcome the odds against her. She is no longer homeless, has completed her degree in community college, and is a loving mother to Taylor. Becca has no relationship with her mother and other relatives. Unfortunately, Becca had to give up a son for adoption before she had Taylor. Today, Becca and Taylor have a good relationship with him and his adoptive family. Are Becca and her mother *family*? Are Taylor and her half-brother *family*?

Melanie, a young woman in her twenties, was devastated by her parents' divorce when she was 10 years old. Like other children whose parents divorced, she harbored dreams that they would one day get back together, even though both parents remarried other people. She had little use for her stepparents at the time, but finally realized that her parents would never remarry when her father and his wife had a baby together. Are Melanie and her stepparents family? Are her half-brother and her mother family?

Meghan and Jonathon—"Jono" as he is called—are a young couple happily in love. They have lived together for a couple of years, and both think they will probably get married someday, even though there has been no explicit discussion of marriage. They believe it's important for her to finish her education first and begin her career. Are Meghan and Jono a family?

Tracey and Juan, unable to have biological children, adopted two beautiful children from Colombia. Juan was born in Colombia and still has family there, so it seemed a natural place to pursue adoption. Tracey and Juan have some information on the birth mother of their son John, but know virtually nothing about the birth mother of their daughter Cassandra. The adoptions are closed—there will be no contact with either birth mother. So, are John and Cassandra's birth mothers part of the family?

Karen and Betsy have been together for 13 years. They talked early on about wanting to raise children together. Today they have two children: Henry, 8, and Jayla, 3. Karen gave birth to Henry, and although Henry's father doesn't live close by, he still plays a role in Henry's life. Jayla was adopted and came to them just before her first birthday. Are Karen and Betsy a family? Are Betsy and Henry a family? Are Henry's father and Jayla a family?

Becca, Melanie, Meghan, Jono, Tracey, Juan, Karen, and Betsy represent some of today's families. The number of "traditional" two-parent heterosexual families has declined, while the number of non-traditional families is on the rise. Together we'll examine these trends, look at their causes, and discuss their implications.

What is a *family*? Who would guess that such a commonly used word could generate disagreement? We all probably come from some kind of family. Students of all ages crave information about families, including love, sex, relationships, marriage, and children. Unfortunately, most students have a very individualized view of these issues. They tend to emphasize personal choices without focusing on the broader social, cultural, and historical conditions that shape these choices. This chapter will show you how our personal experiences are shaped by the social structure in which we live. To do this, we introduce you to the latest in research and theory. Be prepared not only to learn "fun facts" to share with your friends, but also be ready to open yourself up to new ways of thinking about the world and your place in it.

How Do We Define Family?

Welcome to the study of families! This text takes you on a journey of personal self-discovery and greater social awareness. We'll learn about love and dating, cohabitation and marriage, parenting, aging families, divorce and remarriage, families and work, and family crises. Like all journeys, we'll encounter bumps along the road—issues like miscommunication, jealousy, economic problems, discrimination, violence, and other stressors. However, we'll also encounter sources of strength that help families cope with these stressors—education, legislation to help families, and cultural change that has led to greater acceptance of diversity in family life.

Today, we're surrounded by child-free married couples, multigenerational families, unmarried adults who cohabit and who sometimes have children, step-parents whose stepchildren live with them only part-time, and gay and lesbian partnerships. These types of living arrangements are increasing, while the more traditional type of family—husband, wife, and children all living together—is declining in numbers (Lofquist, Lugaila, O'Connell, & Feliz, 2012; Vespa, Lewis, & Kreider, 2013).

With such a variety of relationships, how can we define *family*? Some people believe that a couple must be married legally to be considered a family. Others think that children must be present—certainly, you've heard people ask, "So, when are you going to start a family?" They mean, of course, "So, when are you going to have children?" And still others believe that gay and lesbian partners don't really qualify as a family regardless of their level of commitment to one another.

Legal versus Social Science Definitions

How would you define *family*? With all these different possibilities, it's important to stop and reflect on your own views for a moment. The feature box *Getting to Know Yourself: How Do You Define Family?* gives you a chance to think about your definition, and then perhaps, compare it to the way other people think.

The U.S. Census Bureau defines a *family* as two or more people living together who are related by birth, marriage, or adoption. Heterosexual or

1.1 Identify the different definitions of "family" and their implications

Questions That Matter

1.1 How does this text define *family,* and how does it differ from a legal perspective?

1.2 Why is the definition of *family* so important?

👁 **Watch** on **MySocLab**
Video: *Judith Stacey: How a Family is Defined*

What is a family? Opinions differ. Let's see what you think. Please answer how you think regarding each statement. There are no right or wrong answers here, just your opinions. Your answers can include:

1 = Yes; 2 = Unsure; 3 = No

_____ **1.** Elian and Rosa have been living together for two years, but are not married, nor have they seriously discussed marriage. Are they a family?

_____ **2.** Jake and Tina have a child together, but they live in separate cities and see each other about once every month or two. Are they a family?

_____ **3.** Soolyn and Tran are married and have two young daughters. Are they a family?

_____ **4.** Jonathan and Patrick have been together for almost a year, and spend all their time together. They each have their own place to live, but Patrick has his house up for sale, and as soon as it sells, he'll move in with Jonathan. Are they a family?

_____ **5.** William and Jenica have cohabited for seven years and have no children. Are they a family?

_____ **6.** Janie, Helen, and Rachel live with a man who is legally married to only one of them, yet all three women consider themselves married to him, a practice known as *polygamy*. Are they a family?

_____ **7.** Hannah, 16, ran away from her parents' home last summer and has been living on the streets. She has since met up with a group of runaway and homeless youth. Together they beg or steal food, and some of the young people prostitute themselves to earn money for the group. They take care of one another. Are they a family?

_____ **8.** Corey, 8, has lived in four different foster homes since he was taken away from his drug-addicted and violent parents when he was 3. He has lived in his current foster home for 2 years and has a good relationship with the family in which he lives. His foster parents treat him just like they treat their other children. He does not know how much longer he will stay there, but hopes it is for a long time. Are they a family?

_____ **9.** Dee has five children fathered by five different men. She has never been married. The fathers rarely if ever pay child support and only a few come around sporadically to see her or their child. Are Dee and her children's fathers a family?

_____ **10.** Lucas and Emma are a married couple who are firmly committed to not having children. Are they a family?

Tally your answers. The lower the score, the broader your definition of family. The higher your score, the more narrow your definition of family. Compare your answers with others. How do you compare?

WHAT DO YOU THINK?

1. What is your score? Do you have a broad or narrow definition of family, or are you somewhere in between?

2. Where do you think your views have come from? Do they reflect the values of your parents, your culture, or your peers? Which of these influences is the strongest, and why?

homosexual unmarried partners are excluded from this definition. The U.S. government continues to use this traditional definition as the basis for many social programs and policies. However, many people object to the Census Bureau's definition because it excludes groups who consider themselves to be families. They argue that government should expand its definition of *family* because it doesn't adequately reflect the reality of the rich diversity of family life in our society today (Boss, Doherty, LaRossa, Schumm, & Steinmetz, 1993 (reprinted 2008); Lloyd, Few, & Allen, 2009; Trask & Hamon, 2007). If people believe they are a family, these feelings shouldn't be ignored because of rigid definitions.

The leading scholarly journal about families, published by the National Council on Family Relations, changed its name from *The Journal of Marriage and the Family* to *The Journal of Marriage and Family* (deleting the second *the*), reflecting the growing recognition that families come in many forms. This text also opts for a broader, more inclusive definition, proposing that a **family** is a relationship by blood, marriage, or affection, in which members may cooperate economically, may care for children, and may consider their identity to be intimately connected to the larger group. It can include a **family of orientation**, which is the family that you are born into, and a **family of procreation**, which is the family you make through marriage, partnering, and/ or parenthood.

This text includes **fictive kin** in its definition of family. *Fictive kin* are nonrelatives whose bonds are strong and intimate, such as the relationships shared

family: A relationship by blood, marriage, or affection, in which members may cooperate economically, may care for children, and may consider their identity to be intimately connected to the larger group.

family of orientation: The family that you are born into.

family of procreation: The family you make through marriage, partnering, and/or parenthood.

fictive kin: Nonrelatives whose bonds are strong and intimate.

among unmarried homosexual or heterosexual partners, or very close friends. Fictive kin can provide important services and support for individuals, including financial assistance or help through life transitions (Heslin, Hamilton, Singzon, Smith, & Anderson, 2011). Nonetheless, fictive kin are routinely passed over for critical benefits that more traditional family members have come to expect, such as health insurance or tax advantages.

Why Are Definitions So Important?

Why should we care about the definition of a *family*? How society defines a family has important consequences with respect to rights, including access to a spouse's or partner's Social Security benefits, pensions, and health insurance (Employee Benefit Research Institute, 2013; Human Rights Campaign, 2013). For example, unmarried partners can't file jointly on federal taxes. Many employer health insurance plans cover only a worker's spouse and dependent children. Unmarried partners may be excluded completely from coverage. Therefore, if an unmarried couple with one employed partner has children, the children may be covered under the employed parent's health insurance plan, but the partner may be excluded. These decisions involve billions of dollars in employer and government benefits and affect millions of adults and children each year, as shown in the feature box "Policy and You: From Macro to Micro." In addition, special membership discounts to a wide variety of organizations are available to families, but not to people who are roommates or friends.

There are many different kinds of families, including traditional married couples, same-sex couples, and even fictive kin.

One clear way in which societal definitions of *family* affect our individual relationships can be seen in our marriage laws. In most places around the country, unmarried adults in long-term, committed relationships are routinely denied important benefits, such as spousal health insurance or dental care, bereavement leave, relocation benefits, or the benefit of filing joint tax returns or receiving Social Security. Unmarried adults, homosexual and heterosexual, face numerous obstacles simply because they lack the legal status of marriage. These obstacles affect the security and well-being of millions of families.

However, employers are recognizing that denying benefits to partners in committed relationships may be not only unjust, but also bad for business. In 1982, the New York City weekly *The Village Voice* became the first employer to offer "domestic partner benefits." Since that time, more than 9,300 employers have chosen to offer domestic partner benefits to an employee's unmarried partner, whether of the same or opposite sex. These employers include nearly 300 Fortune 500 companies, along with city, county, and state agencies.

Why do a growing number of employers offer benefits to domestic partners? One reason is simple fairness. Many employers believe that offering benefits to their employees' legally married partners, but not to nonlegal married partners, discriminates on the basis of sexual orientation and/or marital status. Because same-sex couples cannot legally marry in most states, their partners have traditionally been excluded from receiving benefits on the grounds that they are not part of an employee's legal family.

A second reason is competition in today's labor market. To attract and retain a high-quality, diverse workforce, employers must offer a comprehensive benefit package. Offering domestic partner benefits is simply a sound business practice.

Several states have passed or are considering laws that establish domestic partnerships for committed same-sex couples. These laws provide all of the same state-granted privileges, immunities, rights, benefits, and responsibilities for same-sex couples entering a domestic partnership that are granted to married couples. Other states, under pressure from conservatives, are restricting these benefits, at least for state employees. Regardless of state policy, however, unmarried persons are ineligible for specific federal benefits such as filing joint tax returns and cannot receive Social Security as a spouse. This example shows that our laws and definition of what constitutes a family can be powerfully felt at the personal level.

Sources: Employee Benefit Research Institute. February 2009; Human Rights Campaign, 2009, 2012.

WHAT DO YOU THINK?

1. Should an employer's domestic partner benefits cover both homosexual and heterosexual relationships? Why or why not?
2. Should we leave it to employers or to the state or federal government to decide whether to offer domestic partner benefits?

1.2 Describe the functions of families

Question That Matters

1.3 What are the functions that families provide?

marriage: An institutional arrangement between persons to publicly recognize social and intimate bonds.

In thinking about your family of orientation, how did your own family fulfill these functions? For example, how did your family socialize you and teach you about the culture you live in? How did your family care for, love, and nurture you? What type of identity and social position did your family give you?

The Functions of Families

Why do people marry? Why do we live in families? Whereas some functions of marriage and families might differ from one society to another, what is more remarkable is how *similar* these are across time and place. All societies have **marriage**, an institutional arrangement between persons to publicly recognize social and intimate bonds. There are clear norms that specify who is eligible to be married, to whom and how many people an individual can marry, what the marriage ceremony should be like, and how married persons should behave. Anthropologist William Stephens (1963) provided a broad definition of *marriage:* (1) it is a socially legitimate sexual union; (2) begun with a public announcement; (3) undertaken with some idea of permanence; and (4) assumed with a more or less explicit marriage contract that spells out reciprocal obligations between spouses, and between spouses and their children. Marriages and families in all cultures include such functions as

- *Regulation of Sexual Behavior:* Every culture, including your own, regulates sexual behavior, including who can have sex with whom and under what circumstances they can do so. One virtually universal regulation is the *incest taboo* that forbids sexual activity (and marriage) among close family members. The definition of a *close family member* differs, but includes at least parents and their children, and siblings. The incest taboo reduces the chance of inherited genetic abnormalities, and it also forges broader alliances by requiring marriage outside of the inner family circle.

- *Reproducing and Socializing Children:* Each society must produce new members and ensure **socialization**, teaching children the rules, expectations, and culture of that society. Societies generally prefer that reproduction occur within an established family, rather than randomly among unrelated partners so that birth parents will be responsible for socializing children.

- *Property and Inheritance:* For much of human history, when people were nomadic hunters and gatherers, families owned little or nothing of their own, and so had nothing to pass down or to inherit. However, the invention of agriculture made it possible for people to own property, or to obtain a surplus beyond what they needed for survival. Thus, it became important to identify heirs. Monogamy ensured that men would know who their heirs were; without monogamy, paternity was uncertain (Engels, 1902, original 1884).

- *Economic Cooperation:* A family is the group responsible for providing its members with food, shelter, clothing, and other basic necessities. Family members work with each other to provide these necessities. Often there is a gendered division of labor, although what constitutes *male tasks* and *female tasks* varies from one society to the next.

- *Social Placement, Status, and Roles:* Families give their members a social identity and position. Members find their place in the complex web of *statuses* (the positions that people occupy in a group or in a society) and *roles* (the behaviors associated with those positions). For example, families give us our initial social class position, provide us with a religious affiliation, and give us a racial and an ethnic identity.

- *Care, Warmth, Protection, and Intimacy:* Humans need far more than food, shelter, and clothing to survive. Families are intended to provide the emotional care needed to survive and thrive. Although romantic love might not be a basis for marriage in many societies, spouses are expected to care for and protect each other, and to love and nurture their children.

Most of us have lived in some sort of family, so we naturally think of ourselves as "experts" on the topic; yet our personal experiences are part of a larger picture. Although all of us experience family life as individuals, we can't fully understand this experience without appreciating the environment in which it takes place. The remainder of this chapter introduces the three key themes that are the focus of this text.

socialization: The process by which people learn the rules, expectations, and culture of society.

👁 **Watch** on **MySocLab**
Video: *Families: The Basics*

Families have many functions in society. One of the universal functions of families is to care for and nurture the children.

Theme 1: Linking the Micro-Level and Macro-Level Perspectives on Families

First, the best way to truly understand families is to link two perspectives: the "micro-level" and the "macro-level." Although it's easy to think of our relationships solely in personal terms, they're actually shaped in large part by **social structure**, the patterns of social organization that guide our interactions with others. Let's discuss this topic further.

We live in a society with hundreds of millions of other people, most of whom also have families. Most of the time, we focus on the uniqueness of our own

1.3 Recognize the link between micro-level and macro-level perspectives on families

Questions That Matter

1.4 What is the difference between a *micro-level* and a *macro-level* perspective for the study of families?

1.5 What is *social structure,* and why is it important?

social structure: A stable framework of social relationships that guides our interactions with others.

micro-level: Focus on the individual and his or her interactions in specific settings.

relationships: "I love him because . . ." "We get along so well because . . ." "I chose to marry her because . . ." "We decided not to have children because . . . ." Many people focus primarily on this **micro-level** perspective, concentrating exclusively on their individual interactions in specific settings. People who use this perspective focus on individual uniqueness, personal decision making, and the interactions between small groups of people in specific situations. For example, if you were taking a micro-level perspective on family problems, you might conclude that divorce could be reduced by teaching couples better communication skills, that violence can be controlled by learning to manage anger more effectively, or that stressed families balancing the demands of work and family just need to learn to manage their time better. In other words, a micro-level perspective emphasizes the importance of relationship dynamics, including personal choices or constraints, but doesn't place those family dynamics into their social context.

Although each relationship is certainly unique, families also behave in remarkably predictable ways. For example, if your female cousin told you that she is getting married next year, could you guess the color of her wedding dress? Of course, her dress could be any color of the rainbow, or even black with pink stripes! However, you would probably guess that her dress will be white.

Our relationships are fairly predictable because they operate within the larger social structure. One important theme you will find throughout this text is that *elements of social structure shape our daily experiences, privileges, and constraints.* The personal choices that we make—such as whom we marry; whether we have children and, if so, how many; how we divide household labor; what type of job we get; or the childcare we arrange—are all affected by social structure.

macro-level: Focus on the interconnectedness of marriage, families, and intimate relationships with the rest of society.

A **macro-level** perspective examines how marriage, families, and intimate relationships are interconnected with the rest of society and its institutions. Families are not isolated entities. Realizing how social, cultural, economic, and political forces influence families helps us understand our supposedly "personal" choices. Dating, marriage, divorce, domestic violence, work–family stress, and teen pregnancy are social processes rooted in social structure. To understand these processes, we must examine the organization of that social structure.

Family as a Social Institution

social institution: A major sphere of social life, with a set of beliefs and rules that is organized to meet basic human needs.

Because families and close relationships fulfill many of our personal needs, it's easy to forget that families are also a **social institution**: a major sphere of social life, with a set of beliefs and rules organized to meet basic human needs. Therefore, in addition to discussing *your* specific family, throughout this text we'll discuss the social context of families. Families are a social institution in much the same way that political, economic, religious, healthcare, and educational systems are social institutions. In early human civilizations, the family was the center of most activities. Within families, people learned and practiced religion, educated their young, and took care of the sick. Over time, other institutions took on many of these functions. Today, people worship in churches, educate children in schools, and go to hospitals when they are sick.

People still want to marry, despite a high divorce rate in the United States. Most individuals agree on some fundamental expectations between a husband and a wife, such as marital fidelity. For example, a 2011 Gallup Poll, based on a large representative sample of adults, found that more than 90 percent of Americans believe it is morally wrong for married men or women to have an affair (Gallup Poll, June 2, 2011).

Like other social institutions, families can't be understood without examining how they influence and are influenced by social institutions. Religious customs, the type of economy, the structure of education, and the political system all shape family patterns, as do our attitudes, behaviors, and opportunities. For example, until recently in Afghanistan, the Taliban did not allow girls to go to school or women to work outside the home. Women had virtually no power inside or outside the family; today, although there have been improvements, women and girls continue to face major constraints on their lives (Oxfam International, 2011; Revolutionary Association of the Women of Afghanistan, 2013; Trust in Education, 2013).

Social Status and Families

In addition to social institutions, another aspect of social structure is **status**, or the social position(s) we occupy. You hold many statuses; you may be a daughter or son, a student, an employee, a friend, a roommate, or a parent, to name just a few. A **master status** is a status that tends to dominate the others. Most of us hold several master statuses, each with a set of privileges or constraints. Sex, race, ethnicity, and social class represent some of the major organizing constructs in our society, as we shall see in Chapter 2. For example, when the Pew Research Center interviewed second-generation Hispanics and Asians about their views of success, nearly three-quarters of both groups believed that "most people can get ahead if they work hard." In contrast, only 58 percent of the full adult population felt that way (Pew Research Center, February 7, 2013b). Why do you think there is such a large racial and ethnic difference in something as fundamental as what it takes to succeed? Are Asians and Hispanics just more positive by nature, or could there be some structural reasons for their views, such as witnessing their parents' assimilation?

How do micro-level and macro-level perspectives together shed light on families? The feature box "Tying It All Together" shows the interrelationship between these perspectives. Next, you'll read about one detailed example of how macro-level issues can influence our personal choices—unemployment and marriage rates—and throughout this text you'll see many more ways that micro-level and macro-level issues are linked.

status: The social position that a person occupies.

master status: The major defining status or statuses that a person occupies.

TYING IT ALL TOGETHER — The Interrelationship of Micro-Level and Macro-Level Factors

What do we mean by *micro-level* and *macro-level factors or perspectives?* Both are important for understanding marriage, families, and intimate relationships. At a micro-level, the focus is on the individual and his or her social interactions. Opportunities, choices, and constraints are made or experienced by the individual, without much thought given to the social and cultural context in which that person lives. In contrast, a macro-level understanding shows us that our personal relationships are interconnected with the rest of society. Social structure influences the opportunities, choices, and constraints that we experience in everywhere in life, including in intimate relationships.

MICRO-LEVEL FACTORS

The focus is on the individual and his or her social interactions:

- Personal choices
- Behaviors
- Feelings
- Communication
- Decisions
- Constraints
- Values

MACRO-LEVEL FACTORS

The focus is on the way our personal relationships interconnect with the rest of society, the recognition that our social structure influences our marriages and families:

- Culture
- History
- Power and inequality
- Social institutions, including the economy, political system, or dominant religion
- Social status, including sex, race, ethnicity, and social class
- Social movements and social change

WHAT DO YOU THINK?

1. Can you think of three ways in which our culture has shaped your personal attitudes or values about specific family or intimate relationships?
2. How would a social institution such as the dominant religion affect you personally if you do not practice that religion? For example, how would Christianity affect you if you are Jewish?

An Example of the Interrelationship of Macro-Level and Micro-Level Perspectives: Unemployment and Marriage Rates

Many people are concerned about the number of single-parent households headed by women. People often wonder why these women keep having children outside of the institution of marriage. Terry Lynn is one of these women, and if you look closer, you can see that her life choices are grounded in a social context.

Terry Lynn is a single mother who has never married and is raising a 6-year-old daughter alone, with the temporary help of cash welfare assistance (Seccombe, 2014). She is a shy young woman, yet at the same time, she's eager to tell her story. Terry Lynn works part-time at a bowling alley, a good job considering her weak reading and writing skills. She takes the bus to work, and various shifts sometimes keep her at work well into the night. She is savvy about the additional help she needs to support her child, and therefore deliberately keeps her employment hours below a certain threshold so that she and her daughter will continue to qualify for Medicaid, the government-sponsored health insurance program. Her employer doesn't offer health insurance, and even at the age of 24, Terry Lynn knows that providing coverage for her daughter is vital. She and her daughter live with a sister in a cramped, rundown, two-bedroom apartment in an unfashionable part of town. The furniture is second hand, and the couch is threadbare. Nonetheless, Terry Lynn is proud of herself and her daughter for "making it" on their own. You may wonder where the child's father is. He comes around now and then, she says, usually when he wants money or sex from her. Does Terry Lynn ever plan to marry him? Her answer is a definite "No."

Single-parent households have been blamed extensively for a wide variety of social ills. They are far more likely than other families to be poor (DeNavas-Walt, Proctor, & Smith, 2012). Why are so many women, especially poor and low-income women like Terry Lynn, having children without marrying their children's fathers?

We might be tempted to look at micro-level factors and ask what is happening within intimate relationships, specifically the personal aspects of these relationships, including the couples' values, choices, and communication. Certainly, these are important; but many people have found that poor women seem to value marriage quite highly. In fact, if anything, perhaps they value it *too* highly. They believe that their own relationships will never meet the "gold standard" they have set for themselves, such as a partner with a steady job, the chance to own their own home, and a reasonably lavish wedding ceremony. Because of this, they shy away from marriage (Edin & Kefalas, 2005; Seccombe, 2015).

Therefore, we must look at macro-level factors to explain why poor women are often hesitant to marry their partners. William Julius Wilson has suggested that the high unemployment rate of inner-city urban dwellers contributes to their low marriage rate. In his well-known books, *The Truly Disadvantaged* (1987) and *When Work Disappears* (1996), Wilson pointed out that many poor women see marriage to inner-city men as risky because the men can't support families on their meager wages (Wilson, 1987; 1996). Furthermore, as factories and businesses move out to the suburbs or overseas, unemployment and poverty rates escalate. Consequently, there is a shortage of employed men whom these women see as good marriage prospects. Wilson shows us that our changing economy (macro-level factor) has a significant effect on individual relationship choices (micro-level factor).

In addition to high unemployment, or perhaps interrelated with it, are many other reasons why poor women may have trouble finding a suitable mate. For example, homicide, violence, drug addiction, and incarceration

Why do you think that people rush to micro-level explanations and interpretations of family life, and forget to think about the macro-level? Can you give some examples of specific issues when you have done this?

have all taken a tremendous toll on young Black men. In Terry Lynn's case, the father of her child was unemployed and has been in and out of jail, so she didn't see him as a reliable "good catch." Although she cared for him, why would she want to marry him?

Many poor women share these concerns regardless of race or ethnic background (Edin & Kefalas, 2005; Seccombe, 2014). Clearly, the "choices" that people make in their personal relationships occur in conjunction with other larger developments in society, such as economic conditions, crime rates, immigration policies, technological advances, changes in women's opportunities, new conceptions of fatherhood, and a wide variety of social and political movements.

Although macro-level forces that may seem outside of our immediate control shape our personal micro-level interactions, we aren't passive recipients of these forces. **Human agency** is the ability of human beings to create viable lives, even when constrained or limited by social forces (Baca Zinn, Eitzen, & Wells, 2010). Rich, poor, male, female, young, or old—we all actively direct our lives, even though powerful social forces help shape our opportunities. We do have free choice, but we need to be aware of the ways that social structure influences our lives and choices.

human agency: The ability of human beings to create viable lives even when they are constrained or limited by social forces.

Theme 2: Families Are Always Changing

1.4 Assess the ways that families are always changing

A second theme you will see throughout this text is that *families are not monolithic or static, but instead are ever-changing*. People have constructed families to meet their needs; therefore, change should be anticipated and not feared. To illustrate this concept, let's first see how families are arranged throughout the world in terms of patterns of authority, rules of descent, and patterns of residence. Second, let's examine the changes in marriage and family patterns in China, a country in the midst of rapid economic and social transformation. Third, let's review marriage and family patterns in U.S. history. Taken together, these examples illustrate the second theme of this text: that the singular, monolithic family structure is largely a myth; *families have always been, and always will be, changing*.

Questions That Matter

1.6 What types of marriage and kinship patterns exist around the world?

1.7 How would we characterize the changes in China's families and family policy in recent generations?

1.8 How have families changed throughout history, and what are the macro-level factors that have contributed to that change?

Marriage Patterns

How do you imagine a marriage? Like many people, you probably assume that a marriage consists of only two people, a marriage pattern called **monogamy**. Monogamy is found widely, although not exclusively, throughout the world.

Other societies practice **polygamy**, which allows either a husband or wife to have more than one spouse at a time. There are two types of polygamy. The more common type is **polygyny**, in which a husband can have more than one wife (Henrich, Boyd, & Richerson, 2012; Omariba & Boyle, 2007). Although illegal in the United States, there may be 30,000 to 50,000 Americans who currently practice polygyny, primarily in the western states (Anderson, 2010). Altman and Ginat (1996) found that, on average, polygamous families in the United States contained 4 wives and 27 children.

Polygyny is legal in several regions of the world today, including parts of Africa, the Middle East, and South America, and is often supported by religious custom. Researchers Charles Welch and Paul Glick examined 15 African countries and found that between one in five and one in three married men had more than one wife. Obviously, not all men can have more than one wife, given existing sex ratios. Welch and Glick found that those who practiced polygyny tended to have two, or occasionally three, wives (Welch & Glick, 1981). Having numerous wives is a sign of family wealth, education, and other dimensions of high

monogamy: Marriage between one man and one woman.

polygamy: A system that allows for more than one spouse at a time (gender unspecified).

polygyny: A marriage pattern in which husbands can have more than one wife.

👁 **Watch** on **MySocLab**
Video: *Families: Sociology in Focus*

Although polygamy is illegal in the United States, thousands of families practice a specific type—polygyny, with one man married to multiple women.

status. Men use it as a way to increase fertility within a family, because having more than one wife increases the number of children born within the family.

The second type of polygamy is **polyandry**, in which one wife is married to multiple husbands (Monger, 2004; Stone, 2006). This type of marriage pattern is rare, and more likely to occur in societies that experience harsh environmental conditions with widespread poverty, such as among nomadic Tibetans in Nepal or in parts of rural northern China or India. Multiple husbands are often brothers or otherwise related to one another, and the marriage occurs to provide economic advantages. Brothers may live together as adults to share resources, and children are more likely to survive if they have the contribution of many fathers. Often, there are fewer women in these societies to marry because of female infanticide, as the birth of an infant girl may be seen as burdensome to families.

Patterns of Authority

In countries that practice **patriarchy** ("rule of the father"), men are assumed to have a natural right to be in positions of authority over women. In such a society, patriarchy is manifested and upheld in legal, educational, religious, economic, and other social institutions. The legal system may prevent women from voting; the educational system may provide an unequal education for girls or even refuse to offer them any formal education at all; and religious institutions may attribute male dominance to "God's will." Patriarchy is widespread throughout the world. The opposite of patriarchy is **matriarchy**, in which social power and authority is vested in women. However, this is what is known as a *theoretical alternative,* because no historical cases of true matriarchies are known.

Between these two extremes are authority patterns that could best be described as approaching **egalitarian**. In these societies, the expectation is that power and authority are equally vested in both men and women. Although the United States and many other developed countries are headed in this direction, it would be wrong to assume that all vestiges of patriarchy have been eliminated, as you'll see in Chapter 2.

Patterns of Descent

Where did you get your last name? How is property passed down from one generation to another? Whom do you consider to be your legal relatives? Developed nations most commonly use a **bilateral** pattern of descent, in which descent can be traced through both male and female sides of the family. For example, in the United States it's widely recognized that both your mother's parents *and* your father's parents are related to you—you have, potentially, two sets of grandparents.

In a **patrilineal** pattern, lineage is traced exclusively (or at least primarily) through the man's family line. If you lived in a patrilineal society, your father's relatives are recognized as your kin, but only minimal connections with your mother's side of the family are noted. Even though the United States uses a primarily bilateral model in establishing descent, traces of patrilineal descent still exist: (1) last names almost always reflect the father's lineage rather than the mother's, and (2) sons are sometimes given their father's first names as well and are then referred to as "Jr." or by a number (III, IV). Notice that there is no

polyandry: The marriage pattern in which wives are allowed to have more than one husband.

patriarchy: A form of social organization in which the norm or expectation is that men have a natural right to be in positions of authority over women.

matriarchy: A form of social organization in which the norm or expectation is that the power and authority in society would be vested in women.

egalitarian: The expectation that power and authority are equally vested in men and women.

bilateral: Descent that can be traced through both male and female sides of the family.

patrilineal: A descent pattern where lineage is traced exclusively (or at least primarily) through the man's family line.

semantic equivalent for girls; they are not referred to as "Maria Gonzales, Jr." or as "Emma Smith III."

Finally, a few societies, including some Native American tribes, can be characterized as having **matrilineal** descent patterns because the lineage is more closely aligned with women's families than with men's families. This pattern is not the mirror opposite of a patrilineal pattern, however. In a matrilineal descent pattern, women pass their lineage on through their brothers or other male family members.

matrilineal: A descent pattern where lineage is traced exclusively or primarily within women's families.

Residence Patterns

With whom do you expect to live with after you marry? In industrial societies like the United States, most couples plan to live separately from either set of parents, a **neolocal** residence pattern. Families in other parts of the world practice **patrilocal** residence, meaning that the couple is expected to live with the husband's family. Less common is a **matrilocal** pattern, in which the newly married couple routinely lives with the wife's family.

These different marriage and family patterns, summarized in Table 1.1 (p. 13), have real consequences for the way we experience family life, including whom and how we marry, where we should live, who should have power, and how we inherit and trace our lineage.

How do these marriage and family patterns begin, and how do they change? A look at modern-day China shows the influence of a changing society.

neolocal: The expectation that a newly married couple establishes a residence and lives there independently.

patrilocal: The expectation that a newly married couple will live with the husband's family.

matrilocal: The expectation that a newly married couple will live with the wife's family.

Families in Transition: China

Yue Jiang Wang, who is 60 and lives in the largely rural Yunnan Province of China, is perplexed by young people today. He believes they want too much freedom, and with that freedom will come too many costly mistakes. "They even want to choose their own spouses," he sighs. Jiang married his wife Chang Mei Lin when he was 17 and she was 16. Their marriage was arranged by their parents, with the help of a matchmaker. Together they had seven children—three boys and four girls. Jiang met Mei Lin for the first time during their wedding ceremony. Their marriage began with "respect," but Jiang believes that they grew to love one another.

Jiang is confused by many aspects of life he observes in today's China, a country that has undergone many revolutionary changes in the past few decades. The new market-based economy is developing rapidly, education levels are rising, and cars and the infrastructure they require are altering the rural landscape dramatically. All these changes have affected many traditional beliefs, including those surrounding women's roles, marriage, and children.

Jiang and Mei Lin married in 1959, and a study conducted of people just like Mei Lin— women who married in China between 1933 and 1987—found that more than 70 percent had had no other boyfriends and more than 90 percent had not

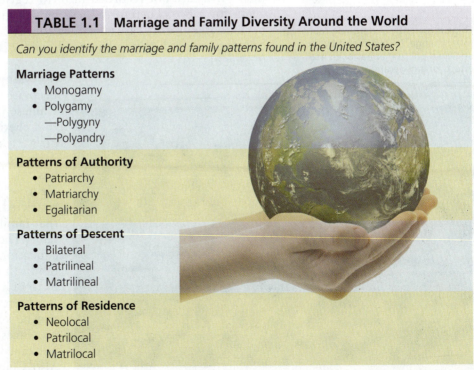

TABLE 1.1	Marriage and Family Diversity Around the World

Can you identify the marriage and family patterns found in the United States?

Marriage Patterns
- Monogamy
- Polygamy
  —Polygyny
  —Polyandry

Patterns of Authority
- Patriarchy
- Matriarchy
- Egalitarian

Patterns of Descent
- Bilateral
- Patrilineal
- Matrilineal

Patterns of Residence
- Neolocal
- Patrilocal
- Matrilocal

considered marrying anyone besides their husbands (Xu & Whyte, 1990). Today, many Chinese men and women, especially those from urban areas, date and socialize with many partners before they marry, and they're sexually active and cohabit (Chu & Yu, 2009; Wang & Davidson, 2006). They want to choose their own mates. They're likely to meet their spouse at school, at work, through a mutual friend, or even through the Internet, rather than through parents, relatives, or matchmakers.

Yet, despite these new freedoms to choose their own mates, couples in China still can't marry freely. The central government requires people who plan to marry to apply for permission and to register officially on a waiting list with the local government. The government regulates when a couple can marry because it's one way to regulate births. China had a large and exploding population, and beginning in the late 1970s, the government decided to control the number of births so that the country would be able to feed and care for all its members. Until the policy was liberalized in late 2013, most families were permitted to have only one child. Now, if both husband and wife are single children themselves, they will be permitted to have two children. When a couple wants to have children, they must again ask the government for permission to do so. A couple can't simply "get pregnant" without facing grave consequences, such as a heavy fine or strong encouragement to have an abortion (Waldmeir, 2013; Wang, Cai, & Gu, 2012).

The one-child policy has greatly increased the standard of living of the Chinese people. The population has been reduced by at least 300 million people—the size of the entire U.S. population—compared to what it would have been without the policy (Rosenberg, 2009). Chinese families can offer their single child the best of everything: the best education, their undivided attention, a more spacious house, and more disposable income.

Unfortunately, the one-child policy has also had many horrific side effects. Millions of baby girls have virtually disappeared. In a patriarchal country where people value boys more because they carry on the family lineage and take care of aging parents, and girls are considered an economic liability, should we be surprised that if couples are allowed only one child, they prefer a boy? Female fetuses have been aborted, and baby girls have been killed or abandoned. Other girls are kept hidden by their parents, and their births are not recorded in birth registries so that their parents can try again for a boy. Therefore, these hidden girls are ineligible for government benefits like health care or education. As a result, sex ratios in China are becoming exceedingly imbalanced, with 120 young boys for every 100 girls (Chi et al., 2013).

China is currently undergoing rapid social change, fueled in part by the one-child policy that has been in effect for a generation.

Many people around the world have become alarmed by this situation, as have Chinese government officials. In a country that cherishes family, the disappearance of girls is seen as a failure of what was intended to be a policy to strengthen families. As a result, the Chinese have banned elective amniocentesis tests and have restricted the use of ultrasound scanners so that families cannot determine the sex of a fetus. They have also implemented a mass education effort to promote the idea that the birth of a girl is "just as good" as the birth of a boy (Zhu, Li, & Hesketh, 2009).

There is some evidence that their efforts may be working. A survey conducted in three provinces shows that son preference has weakened considerably (Chi et al., 2013). Also, China may have fewer abandoned girls available for adoption. In 2012, 2,696 Chinese-born children (mostly girls) were adopted in the United States, down from a high of 7,900 in 2005 (U.S. Department of State, 2013).

Meanwhile, Jiang and Mei Lin, who had an arranged marriage and seven children many years ago, are proud that their children heed the government's call to have only one child. They remain, however, quite confused about many other decisions of their children, including their move to urban areas, their daughters' desire to go to college, their plans to share housekeeping and childcare with spouses, and their use of new gadgets and technology.

History of Family Life in the United States

To further understand how families are continually changing, one only need look at families throughout our own history. But how do we learn about families in earlier times, if no one is alive today to tell us about them? The feature box *Why Do Research? How to Study Families from the Past* (p. 15) gives us some clues about how historians can learn about some of the dynamics of these early families.

FAMILY LIFE IN COLONIAL AMERICA: EUROPEAN COLONISTS   Family historians have shown that families were the cornerstone of colonial society (Coontz, 2005b; Demos, 1970; Laslett, 1971; Mintz, 2004). They were the primary social institution, helping early immigrants adapt to life in the New World. Families acted as

- *Businesses*. Families were the central focus of economic production. Each household was nearly self-sufficient, and men, women, and children worked together to meet their material needs, including producing food, clothing, furniture, and household goods.

- *Schools*. Formal schooling conducted away from home was extremely rare. *taught by parents* Instead, parents educated their children, teaching them how to read and

---

Why Do Research?   How to Study Families from the Past

Piecing together the history of family life has become an active topic of research. Drawing on a variety of historical documents, including diaries; letters; birth, marriage, and death registries; and immigration records, historians attempt to weave together a social history of the United States to reveal the daily lives, customs, and lifestyles of ordinary citizens. This is a radical departure from the work of most historians who focus on events such as wars, economic downturns, or other large-scale social events. Because the field of social history is relatively new, and many historical documents have been lost or are unavailable, significant gaps exist in our understanding of history, especially about the dynamics of early minority families.

Historians and family scholars get creative as they piece together the past. Historical records can provide an aggregate record about immigration trends, age at first marriage, or the average length of time between marriage and first birth. Slave auctions, ledgers, and other transactions help us understand what—and who—was being bought and sold. Diaries and letters can reveal what was on the minds of ordinary people, including how they saw the world and how they expressed their views. Newspapers and magazines can reveal fads, fash-

ions, and the mood of the era. All of these records can provide insightful clues into the lives of ordinary people.

Finally, many scholars rely on *family reconstitution,* in which attempts are made to compile all available information about significant family events and everyday life. Members of each generation who are still alive are interviewed in depth, and they are asked to reconstruct their family history. Recreating the past is not easy. Historical researchers work as detectives and try to obtain the greatest number of sources possible as they reconstruct the past. Sometimes numerous sources are available, but unfortunately, sometimes only a few clues remain.

WHAT DO YOU THINK?

1. Think about your own family's history. How far back does your information reliably go? Who are the oldest members of your family? Could you conduct a family reconstitution?
2. If your books, magazines, computer, or other important artifacts were saved in a time capsule, what would someone a hundred years from now learn about you? About your lifestyle? About your relationships?

write, as well as the vocational and technical skills necessary to become productive adults.

- *Churches.* Families worshiped and prayed together in their homes because churches were usually far away. Parents and children read the Bible together, one of the few books and sources of moral instruction readily available.

- *Correctional institutions.* Jails were rare in colonial times, and therefore courts sentenced criminals and so-called idle people to live with more respected families in the community. These families were considered the best setting not only to impose discipline, but also to encourage reform.

- *Health and social welfare institutions.* Because there were no hospitals and few doctors during this period, families—and women in particular—took on the role of caring for the sick and infirm. Families also took care of the aging, the homeless, and orphans (Demos, 1970).

nuclear family: A family composed of adults and their children.

extended family: A family composed of parents, children, and other relatives such as grandparents.

Most people in colonial America lived in **nuclear families** composed of adults and their children. **Extended families**, including grandparents or other relatives, were the exception. Because couples tended to be relatively older at first marriage and people didn't live very long, older adults may have died before their grandchildren were born.

Families were large by today's standards, often containing six or more children. Siblings could be as much as 25 years apart in age. Husbands or wives may have married two or even three times because people died young (Laslett, 1971). Children often had stepsiblings or half-siblings. Some households also included servants or slaves, who were sometimes counted as household family members in statistical records.

Marriage and family were central events in people's lives. Although marriages were often arranged to further business or financial interests, husbands and wives considered themselves a team and anticipated that love and affection would develop between them. However, a wife was considered her husband's helpmate, but not his equal. The husband was the head of the family, and it was his wife's duty to obey him. Women had crucial economic roles inside and outside the family, including cooking, sewing, cleaning, gardening, and certain farm chores, and they produced many goods for the family. They raised and cared for many children. Husbands did the planting and harvesting, but women also helped at crucial times of the agricultural year.

Parents tended to be very strict with their children. They believed that children were born with "original sin" and needed firm discipline and severe religious training to break their innate rebellion and selfishness, and to ensure that children would grow up to be productive members of society. Excessive tenderness, they felt, could spoil the child. Children were treated as miniature adults; there was no concept of adolescence, as there is today. As soon as children were old enough to work on the family farm or in the household, they were put to work.

COLONIAL AMERICA: AFRICAN AMERICANS AND SLAVERY The first Africans forcefully brought over to the colonies were indentured servants, and after serving a specified amount of time they were considered "free" and able to marry and purchase their own land. But by the late 17th century, the slave trade was well underway, with a million Africans captured and brought to the American colonies against their will. Some prominent Americans, including Thomas Jefferson, primary author of the Declaration of Independence and the third U.S. President, publicly denounced slavery but supported it privately. In addition to owning slaves, it is now generally agreed that he fathered children with a slave named Sally Hemings (Gordon-Reed, 2008).

For years, slavery was used to explain the strong-female family patterns among contemporary Blacks; however, today, instead of seeing slave families as incomplete or emasculated, historians are noting the resiliency of slave families

(Sudarkasa, 1999; Wilkinson, 1997). African family ties were strong, and relationships created by "blood" were considered more important than those created by marriage (Gutman, 1976; Sudarkasa, 1999).

By the early 1800s, the United States prohibited the importation of new slaves, and owners began to recognize the value of encouraging family relationships and childbearing among the slaves they already owned. Some relationships were forced for "breeding" purposes; at other times, real love developed between slaves. Yet slave marriages were fragile; one study conducted in several southern states revealed that more than one-third of slave marriages were terminated by selling off either the husband or wife to another party elsewhere (Gutman, 1976). Even when slavery tore apart families, kinship bonds persisted. Children were often named after lost relatives as a way to preserve family ties.

Prior to the Civil War, there were approximately 150,000 free African Americans living in southern states, and another 100,000 living in the north (Mintz & Kellogg, 1989). Yet, even "free" African Americans weren't necessarily allowed to vote, attend White schools and churches, or be hired for jobs. Consequently, many free African Americans were poor, unemployed, and barely literate. Moreover, free women outnumbered free men in urban areas. Together, high poverty rates and the gender imbalance among free African Americans made it challenging for them to marry and raise children. It's therefore unsurprising that many children were reared in female-headed households. One study indicated that when property holdings, a key measure of income, were held constant, the higher incidence of one-parent families among African Americans largely disappeared (Mintz & Kellogg, 1989).

INDUSTRIALIZATION, URBANIZATION, AND IMMIGRATION Family life in the United States changed considerably in the 19th and early 20th centuries because of three primary factors. First, *industrialization* transformed the economy from a system based on small family farms to one of large urban industries. "Work" became something that people did away from the home. Increasingly more goods and services were produced for profit outside the home, and families purchased these with wages they earned at outside jobs.

Second, people started moving from rural areas and farms to urban areas in search of jobs, a process known as *urbanization*. This process tore extended families apart, as the vast distances between farm and city made frequent contact impossible.

Third, the large waves of *immigration*, in which people from Europe and Asia came to the United States with the hopes of a better life, provided the cheap labor that fueled this industrialization. Between 1830 and 1930, more than 30 million immigrants came to the United States from all over the world, including western Europe, the Slavic countries, and China. In packinghouses, steel mills, textile mills, coal mines, and a host of other industrial settings, nearly half the workers were immigrants to the United States (Steinberg, 1981).

THE POOR AND WORKING CLASSES
Most immigrants were poor, or nearly so. Doris Weatherford, in her book *Foreign and Female: Immigrant Women in America, 1840–1930* (1986), and Upton Sinclair's *The Jungle* (1906) describe the appalling conditions in which many immigrant families lived and worked. Housing was crowded, substandard, and

Immigrants to the United States in the 19th century were often poor and worked in the dangerous and dirty factories that characterized the Industrial Revolution.

often lacked appropriate sanitation facilities. Raw sewage was strewn about, causing rampant epidemics in immigrant neighborhoods. Early industrial working conditions were exceedingly dangerous, unsanitary, and inhumane, and many workers died or became disabled or disfigured. There were few safety mechanisms in place, the lighting and ventilation systems were woefully inadequate, and people routinely did hard manual labor for as many as 80 hours a week.

The strain of family life under these abysmal working and living conditions was severe and took its toll. Alcoholism, violence, crime, and other social problems stemming from demoralization plagued many families. Yet immigrants continued to crowd cities in search of work because they hoped it would eventually lead to a better life for their children.

MIDDLE AND UPPER CLASSES   In the middle and upper classes, ideally the husband was the breadwinner while the wife reared the children and took care of the home. Children were no longer seen simply as miniature adults, perhaps because middle- and upper-class families no longer relied on their labor. Instead, children were seen as innocents who could be molded into good or bad citizens, a view that emphasized the important role that mothers played at home (Degler, 1980). Experts elevated women's childrearing responsibilities and frowned on women working outside the home, because this was seen as taking women away from their primary, natural, and most important work—motherhood.

THE RISE OF THE "MODERN" FAMILY—THE TWENTIETH CENTURY   The early to mid-1900s saw two World Wars, a Depression, and the relative affluence of the 1950s and 1960s, all of which had an impact on families. Families faced new and daunting hardships during the Depression with increased unemployment, poverty, and homelessness. The World Wars separated families, and many men were injured or killed on the battlefield. World War II ushered women into the labor market as never before; their employment was deemed a "patriotic duty." After World War II and throughout the 1950s and early 1960s, women were encouraged to give up their wartime jobs to men returning from the battlefield, and many female workers were fired if they failed to resign voluntarily.

At the same time, technological innovations increased at a rapid pace. The popularity of the automobile changed the ways families traveled and increased their mobility. New suburban residential patterns and migration to the cities in search of work increased travel and commuting time and decreased the amount of time fathers spent with their families. Kitchen appliances were designed to reduce the amount of time women spent on domestic labor.

companionate family: A marriage based on mutual affection, sexual attraction, compatibility, and personal happiness.

A **companionate family** emerged, one based on mutual affection, sexual attraction, compatibility, and personal happiness. Young adults freely dated without chaperones, and placed greater emphasis on romantic love and attraction in their search for mates as compared to their parents and grandparents.

In her influential book *The Feminine Mystique* (Friedan, 1963), Betty Friedan documents a push toward domesticity during this period. Interviews with female college students revealed that their primary reason for attending college was to find a suitable husband rather than a career. College women who were unattached by their senior year thought they had failed in their ultimate mission—to get their "MRS. Degree." Friedan's content analyses of women's magazines found that few women had jobs or careers; in fact, those who did were often portrayed as cold, aloof, and unfeminine. The "normal" or "natural" role for women was portrayed as a wife and helpmate to her husband, and eventually as a mother to a large number of children.

During this period, the average age at first marriage dropped to an all-time low since records had been kept—barely 19 for women and 20 for men—and the birth rate exploded. To keep up with the move toward domesticity, the federal government underwrote the construction of homes in the suburbs, undertook massive highway construction projects that enabled long commutes from home to work, and subsidized low-interest mortgage loans with minimal down payments for veterans. Families, growing in size, craved the spaciousness and privacy of the new suburbs where they could have their own yards instead of community parks for their children. In the suburbs, women cared for their children in isolation, volunteered in their children's schools and within the community, and chauffeured their children to various lessons and events. Television programs, women's magazines, and other media sources glorified the new domesticity, but in reality, this cultural image was not attainable for many families. Working-class and poor women, including many minority women, often worked full- or part-time because their husbands didn't earn enough to support the family. Nonetheless, this cultural image was a powerful one.

Families Today

As we've seen from our look at family history, families are never isolated from outside events and the social structure in which they live. For example, the economy greatly affects family lifestyles, opportunities, and constraints. Over the past few decades, the U.S. economy has shifted from relatively high-paying manufacturing jobs to lower-paying jobs in the service sector, making it very difficult to support a family on one income; therefore, growing numbers of married women with children have returned to the labor market.

We also see evidence of increasing social inequality, and this, too, affects families. The rich have made tremendous gains during the past few decades, whereas the middle- and lower-income classes have experienced stagnation or a decline in real earnings when adjusted for inflation (Greenhouse, 2013). Middle-class families felt the squeeze of the recession most severely, and their recovery is coming more slowly than it has for the wealthy (Mishel & Finio, 2013). Although the economic forecast looks rosier than it did just a few years ago, unemployment still hovers around 7 percent at the end of 2013 (Bureau of Labor Statistics, November 20, 2013), and home foreclosures remains a problem (Christie, 2012).

Many workers are finding that temporary jobs with few benefits are the best available (Olson, 2011). Between one-third and one-half of workers have evening or weekend shifts, or they have rotating schedules, which can wreak havoc on families and childcare arrangements (Gornick, Presser, & Ratzdorf, 2009; Presser, 2003; Presser & Ward, 2011). Among couples with children, the risk of divorce increases up to six times when one spouse works between midnight and 8 a.m., as compared to working daytime hours. Both mothers and children whose mothers have nonstandard schedules are at great risk for depression, delinquency, or aggressive behaviors (Institute for Work & Health, 2010; Presser, 2003).

Many modern families have noticed that their purchasing power has steadily declined because their incomes have failed to keep up with inflation, a problem especially true for the lowest-income workers. The minimum wage doesn't allow parents to support their children adequately. Half of workers making the federal minimum wage are adults age 25 and older, often working in the service industry doing food preparation or serving (Bureau of Labor Statistics, March 2, 2012). Figure 1.1 illustrates the erosion in the value of the minimum wage, which is why some members of Congress propose raising it from $7.25 to $9.00 per hour (Mishel, 2013). In the late 1960s, the minimum wage equaled about one-half of the average hourly wage; today, the minimum wage is only 37 percent of the average hourly wage. This implies that the minimum wage hasn't kept pace with rising wages

📖 **Read** on **MySocLab**
Document: *Beyond the Nuclear Family: The Increasing Importance of Multigenerational Bonds*

📖 **Read** on **MySocLab**
Document: *Why American Families Need the Census*

Many middle-class families have fallen on hard times during the current recession. Unemployment hovers around 8 percent, causing many families to lose their homes in foreclosure.

FORECLOSURE

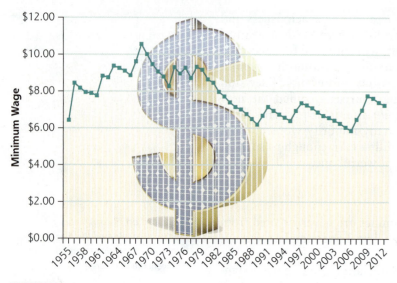

FIGURE 1.1

Inflation-Adjusted Value of the Minimum Wage, 1955–2012, in 2012 Dollars

The real value of the minimum wage declined until 2007, when the minimum wage was raised. However, its real value is starting to decline once again.
Source: Based on Infoplease.com, 2012.

*I*n your conversations with your grandparents or other older adults about the "good old days," what stories have you heard about family life? What information have you obtained about dating, marriage, or raising children? How is it similar or different from what you have learned in the history portion of this chapter?

1.5 Summarize the importance of social science theory and research

Questions That Matter

1.9 How does social science research help us understand families?

1.10 What methods do family scholars use to study families?

1.11 How can theory help us understand families and family research?

1.12 Are Americans rejecting marriage and families?

more generally. Not surprisingly, a small family trying to live on a minimum wage of $7.25, which translates to an annual salary of $14,500, is considered to be well below the poverty line (DeNavas-Walt, Proctor, & Smith, 2012).

In addition to lower real incomes, housing costs remain unaffordable for many people hoping to buy their first home. The average price of a single-family home in June 2009 was $173,600 (National Association of Realtors, 2013), a slight increase since the height of the recession. Many Americans are still forced to rent. Nationally, a modest two-bedroom apartment averages $900 a month, according to estimates from the Department of Housing and Urban Development (HUD). In fact, about 12 million households pay more than half of their income in housing (HUD, 2013a). Affordable housing is a serious problem for millions: a family with one full-time worker earning minimum wage can't afford to pay the fair market rate for an apartment anywhere in the United States. So, how do families cope with high housing costs? People who struggle to pay for housing are likely to reduce their spending on food, transportation, clothing, and other necessities (HUD, 2013b). Others who struggle with high housing costs become homeless. About 630,000 to 750,000 Americans are homeless on any given night, and 3.5 million are estimated to be homeless at some point over the course of a year (National Alliance to End Homelessness, 2013; National Coalition for the Homeless, 2009).

Because of these increased expenses, many families today not only work longer hours, but also have both spouses employed full-time outside the home. Unfortunately, many still find themselves in alarming debt, as credit cards such as Visa, MasterCard, or American Express are tempting to people with economic difficulties.

In this brief review of historical and cross-cultural differences in family life, you can see that marriage, families, and close relationships are constructed by humans, and therefore their structures are not monolithic. Families are always changing and adapting to a wide variety of historical and cultural traditions.

What do American families look like today? The feature box "Diversity in Families: Profile of U.S. Families" draws on the U.S. Census as well as other government information to present key demographic facts about families today—at least as families are defined by the government.

Theme 3: The Importance of Social Science Theory and Research

A third theme of this text is *an appreciation for the role that social science theory and research play in helping people understand families and close relationships.* Think for a moment about how you know what you know about families. We all have opinions about families based on our own experience or on information filtered through the mass media, our peers, our parents, religious teachings, or laws. Because virtually all of us were raised in families, we may feel that we are experts on the subject. In other words, we often just rely on our "common sense," a combination of political, legal, social, economic, and religious norms!

What do families look like today? Let's examine some key statistics from the U.S. Census Bureau, Current Population Reports, and other governmental sources that we discuss in more detail throughout the text. First, however, be aware that government statistics have some limitations. For example, they use catchall categories like "Hispanic" or "Asian," but these groups are far from homogeneous. Although Cuban Americans, Mexican Americans, and Puerto Ricans share a common language, their cultures are significantly different. Nonetheless, government statistics, although imperfect, offer an important source of demographic information about our population.

1. Both men and women are postponing marriage. Because of expanding opportunities and changing norms, women now marry at an average age of 25 years, compared to 21 years in 1970. Men now marry at an average age of 27 years, compared to 23 years in 1970.

2. Family size is shrinking. It's likely that nearly one in five women of childbearing age today will not have children, some by choice, and some because of infertility. Those who do have children are more likely to opt for just one or two.

3. The divorce rate has declined in recent decades. In the 1960s, the divorce rate began to rise rapidly, peaking around 1980, but since then it has steadily declined.

4. Single-parent households have been growing, particularly among men. Since 1970, there has been a 300 percent increase in single-parent households headed by mothers and a 500 percent increase in those headed by fathers. Today, about one-quarter of White families are headed by one parent, as are more than half of Black families and one-third of Hispanic families.

5. Mothers are increasingly likely to be employed outside the home. Today, this figure includes nearly two-thirds of mothers.

6. Hispanic groups are now the largest minority in the United States, at about 16 percent of the population. Because the birthrate and rate of immigration are higher among Hispanics than among other groups, their presence in the United States will continue to grow at a fast rate. By 2050, about 30 percent of all Americans will likely be of Hispanic descent.

7. The teenage birthrate has declined significantly since 1990. The birthrate among teenagers has declined by about 20 percent since that time. This decline is occurring among all racial and ethnic groups, although it has fluctuated in recent years.

8. Unmarried couples living together is common. The number of unmarried couples has almost doubled since 2000

Hispanics are now the largest minority group in the United States. By the year 2050, they may make up nearly one-third of the population. How will this change American culture?

to nearly 7 million today. This trend is found among all age groups, including the elderly.

9. The percentage of people living in poverty has fluctuated in conjunction with economic trends and is now rising. Poverty rates among families, single adults, and children were down in the 1990s; however, since then, poverty rates have risen. Today, about 14 percent of Americans live in poverty, including more than 20 percent of children.

10. The elderly population has been increasing almost four times as fast as the population as a whole. In 1900, only a small portion of people—one in 25—were age 65 or older. This has certainly changed. Moreover, people age 85 and older—referred to as the *oldest old*—are the fastest growing elderly cohort in the United States.

WHAT DO YOU THINK?

1. What other changes do you see occurring in families? Do you think these changes are for the better or for the worse? Why?

2. Do you think that any of these trends will be reversed over the next decade? If so, what will cause them to be reversed?

However, a scientific perspective can provide a more objective window on the world because common sense differs from one place to another, and from one point in time to another. The norms that underlie so-called common sense can also change. Instead, social science research can inform us about the structure of families, the experiences people have within them, and the meanings that they attach to their relationships. Research offers a firmer basis on which to form opinions and choose our values. After all, common sense allowed men to beat their wives throughout most of our history, because women were considered inferior. Today it's against the law in the United States (and many other countries) for husbands to beat their wives (and vice versa).

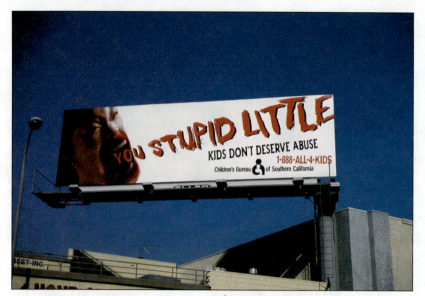

Social science research can tell us a lot about social problems, including how to create programs and policies to best serve vulnerable people.

empirical approach: An approach that answers questions through a systematic collection and analysis of data.

However, violence among intimates isn't illegal in many parts of the world. In certain countries, both husbands and wives believe that violence can be justified, and it's the husband's prerogative to beat his wife. A World Health Organization study of 24,000 women in ten countries found that the prevalence of physical and/or sexual violence by a partner varied from 15 percent in urban Japan to 71 percent in rural Ethiopia, with most areas being in the 30 percent to 60 percent range (World Health Organization, 2009).

If so-called common sense is subject to historical and cultural whims, then what can we depend on to help us understand family dynamics? Sociologists and other family scientists use an **empirical approach**, which answers questions through a systematic collection and analysis of data. Uncovering patterns of family dynamics can be extremely important for building stronger families.

The goals of family research can (e.g., in the case of violence among intimates)

- *describe* some phenomenon (e.g., how many women have been physically assaulted by someone close to them; how this compares to the number of men who are assaulted by their partners each year), or

- *examine the factors that predict or are associated with* some phenomenon (e.g., what factors are associated with violence among intimates; what factors predict whether a victim will report the assault to the police), or

- *explain the cause-and-effect relationships* or provide insight into why certain events do or do not occur (e.g., the relationship between alcohol and violence among intimates; the relationship between attitudes of male dominance and domestic violence), or

- *examine the meanings and interpretations* of some phenomenon (e.g., how abused women and men interpret the reasons for the assault, what the label "victim" means, and how that meaning might differ for women and men)

Because of research, we know that violence among intimates is a serious and pervasive social problem. Nearly one in four women in the United States report being physically assaulted by someone close to them (National Coalition Against Domestic Violence, 2011). How can social science research help women who are battered by their partners? Family scholars conduct basic and applied research to understand the phenomenon, striving to reveal information about the incidence, predictors, social factors associated with violence, or the experience of violence that psychologists, social workers, and politicians could use to develop programs to prevent violence, assist victims, and treat the perpetrators. Violence among intimates is a social problem, not simply an individual one, and research can uncover the social patterns that underlie it.

How Do We Know What We Know? Methods of Social Research

Family scientists use a number of different methods to collect and analyze data systematically. Provided here is a brief introduction to six primary ways of collecting data, and Table 1.2 (p. 23) summarizes these methods. Throughout this text, you will see these research methods in action.

TABLE 1.2 Six Research Methods: A Summary

Family researchers use a variety of methods to learn about families and close relationships.

Method	Application	Advantages	Limitations
Survey	For gathering information about issues that are not directly observed, such as values, opinions, and other self-reports. Can be administered by mail, telephone, or in person. Useful for descriptive or explanatory purposes; can generate quantitative or qualitative data.	Sampling methods can allow researcher to generalize findings to a larger population. Can provide open-ended questions or a fixed response.	Surveys must be carefully prepared to avoid bias. A potential for a low return or response rate. Can be expensive and time-consuming. Self-reports may be biased.
In-depth Interview	For obtaining information about issues that are not directly observed, such as values, opinions, and other self-reports. Useful for getting in-depth information about a topic. Conducted in person, conversation is usually audiotaped and later transcribed. Generates qualitative data.	Can provide detailed and high-quality data. Interviewer can probe or ask follow-up questions for clarification or to encourage the respondent to elaborate. Can establish genuine rapport with respondent.	Expensive and time-consuming to conduct and transcribe. Self-reports may be biased. Respondent may feel uncomfortable revealing personal information.
Experiment	For explanatory research that examines cause-and-effect relationship among variables. Several types: Classical Experimental Design and Quasi-experimental Designs based on degree of controlling the environment. Generates quantitative data.	Provides greatest opportunity to assess cause and effect. Research design is relatively easy to replicate.	The setting may have an artificial quality. Unless experimental and control groups are randomly assigned or matched on all relevant variables and the environment is carefully controlled, bias may result.
Focus Group	For obtaining information from small groups of people who are brought together to discuss a particular topic. Often exploratory in nature. Particularly useful for studying public perceptions. Facilitator may ask only a few questions; goal is to get group to interact with one another. Generates qualitative data.	Group interaction may produce more valuable insights than individual surveys or in-depth interviews. Research can obtain data quickly and inexpensively. Good at eliciting unanticipated information.	Setting is contrived. Some people may feel uncomfortable speaking in a group, and others may dominate.
Observational Study	For exploratory and descriptive study of people in a natural setting. Researcher can be a participant or nonparticipant. Generates qualitative data.	Allows study of real behavior in a natural setting. Does not rely on self-reports. Researchers can often ask questions and take notes. Usually inexpensive.	Can be time-consuming. Could be ethical issues involved in certain types of observation studies (i.e., observing without consent). Researcher must balance roles of participant and observer. Replication of research is difficult.
Secondary Analysis	For exploratory, descriptive, or explanatory research with data that were collected for some other purpose. Diverse. Can be large data sources based on national samples (e.g., U.S. Census) or can be historical documents or records. Generates quantitative or qualitative data, depending on the source of data used.	Saves the expense and time of original data collection. Can be longitudinal, with data collected at more than one point in time. Good for analyzing national attitudes or trends. Makes historical research possible.	Because data were collected for another purpose, the researcher has no control over what variables were included or excluded. Researcher has no control over sampling or other biases in the data.

survey: A form of research that gathers information about attitudes or behaviors through the answers that people give to questions.

random sample: A sample in which every "person of interest" has an equal chance of being selected into your research study.

A **survey** is used to gather information about attitudes or behaviors through the answers that people give to questions. You've probably completed many surveys throughout your life. They're a popular research method because they can cover most topics from politics to sexuality to consumer marketing. If used correctly, a survey can produce results that can be generalized to the population.

A **random sample** is the key to being able to generalize your survey findings. A random sample allows every "person of interest" an equal chance of being selected for your research study. For example, let's say we wanted to survey registered voters to see how they felt about same-sex marriage. If we put every registered voter's name "in a hat" (or more likely, enter it into a computer program), and randomly chose 1,500 names, we could say that we had a representative sample. Or, let's say we wanted to survey college seniors at your university about their experiences with cohabitation. We could easily get a list of college seniors from the administration and randomly select 150 of them to survey.

However, in many contexts, finding a complete list of everyone of interest is impossible. Suppose that we wanted to survey people who have had a same-sex experience, or men who plan to remain virgins until married, or teenagers who don't get along with their parents. Where would we find a complete list of persons of interest for these surveys? Sometimes, we need to use other sampling strategies. For example, perhaps I can identify a young man who plans to remain a virgin until marriage, and he can introduce me to others who share this value, who then each introduce me to even more people. This is called a *snowball sample* as the list grows larger.

Surveys can be performed in a number of ways, including *mail surveys,* which are self-administered questions that are mailed to respondents. A mail survey may be appropriate if the number of questions is short and the questions themselves are simple, such as, "How many children do you have?" or, "Do you smoke more than one cigarette a day?" However, if the questions require too much detail, respondents are unlikely to complete the survey on their own and simply throw it away.

With a telephone survey, an interviewer calls respondents and asks them the questions over the telephone. These are becoming increasingly popular, but many people find them annoying and hang up immediately. However, if the interviewer can keep the person on the line, telephone surveys can be a quick and effective means of gathering information.

In-person surveys are done in a conversational setting. The interviewer asks a series of questions that the respondent answers. Because they're sitting down together, the interviewer may be free to probe further or clarify anything that may be confusing to the respondent. This type of survey can work very well unless the topic is extremely sensitive and embarrassing, such as surveys on sexuality, for which the respondent may want a bit more privacy.

in-depth interview: A research method that allows an interviewer to obtain detailed responses to questions.

In-depth interviews are also conducted in person, and allow an interviewer to obtain detailed responses to questions such as, "How does your family cope when there is not enough food to eat?" or, "What does it mean to you to be a father?" Sometimes the questions follow a set pattern and every respondent is asked the same questions in the same order. Other in-depth interviews follow a different approach, where every interview is a conversation. The basic issues are covered, but much of the interview is emergent. The interviewer, with permission, records the interview, and later transcribes it verbatim.

experiment: A controlled method for determining cause and effect.

An **experiment** is a controlled method for determining cause and effect. It's often used in evaluation research or psychological research, which may ask such questions as, "Does abstinence-based sex education reduce teenage sexual activity?" or, "Does premarital counseling reduce the likelihood of divorce?"

There are many different types of experimental designs. The classical experimental design randomly divides individuals into two groups: an experimental group and a control group. The researchers might administer a pre-test to each group to ensure that the groups are similar and to use the information as a baseline to assess any future changes. Then, the researchers introduce a stimulus to the experimental group, such as the abstinence-based sex education program or the premarital counseling program. The control group does not receive the stimulus. Then, the two groups are compared again, referred to as the *post-test*. If there is a difference in the two groups, it's assumed that it was caused by the stimulus. We can say that the stimulus caused the effect. Experiments work well for certain types of questions, but not for all.

A **focus group** obtains information from a small group of people who are brought together to discuss a particular topic. It's a group interview and works well when a researcher is looking for exploratory information. The moderator may have only a few questions. The goal is to get the group members to interact, brainstorm, and exchange ideas with one another: "What types of responses have you had to your interracial relationship?" or, "Have you found online dating to be a worthwhile experience?" The researcher may then use ideas generated in focus groups to develop other types of research plans.

focus group: A small group interview of people who are brought together to discuss a particular topic.

Observational studies go to the natural setting and observe people in action. A researcher may observe children in a daycare center to answer the question, "How do four-year-old boys and girls express gender?" Or a researcher may visit nursing homes to answer the question, "How do nursing home staff treat people with Alzheimer's disease?" Researchers can be *participant observers*, meaning that they actively participate in the group they are studying. They may even go undercover and pretend to be a staff member while watching others in the nursing home, or they may take a teacher's aide job to watch the children more thoroughly. Other researchers are *non-participants*, in which case the researcher may simply stand by, watch, and take notes. These non-participant researchers may observe children through a two-way mirror, or they may walk around the nursing home, jotting down their observations.

observational study: A research method that goes into the natural setting and observes people in action.

Finally, many researchers rely on **secondary analysis**. This means that the data were collected for some other purpose, but still prove useful to the researcher. These can be large sources of data from the U.S. Census Bureau or the U.S. Department of Justice to answer questions across the population such as, "How many single-parent households are poor?" or, "What were the racial and ethnic backgrounds of crime victims last year?" We can also conduct secondary analyses using other, smaller sources of data. The hallmark is that you're using data collected by someone else for a different purpose. Although this is the least expensive method, it often means you must compromise your study because the original researchers may not have collected the data in exactly the same way you would have.

secondary analysis: A research method in which the data were collected for some other purpose but still are useful to the researcher.

As you can see from these various research methods, some researchers focus on **quantitative research**, where the focus is on data that can be measured numerically, such as "28 percent of college seniors regret the choice of their major" (by the way, I just made that up). Examples of quantitative research might be found in surveys, experiments, or doing a secondary analysis on available statistics from a government agency or some other source. Others use **qualitative research** and focus on narrative description with words rather than numbers to analyze patterns and their underlying meanings. "How do college seniors feel toward their chosen major? Several themes emerged. . . ." Examples of qualitative research methods include in-depth interviews, focus groups, observation studies, or conducting a secondary analysis using narrative documents (such as letters or diaries).

quantitative research: Research that focuses on data that can be measured numerically.

qualitative research: Narrative description with words rather than numbers to analyze patterns and their underlying meanings.

None of these research methods is inherently better or worse than the others. The method used depends on the research questions raised. For example, if we want to better understand what family life was like in the 19th century, we wouldn't conduct a survey. How would people who are alive today best inform us of what happened 200 years ago? The best method would be to conduct a secondary analysis of documents written during that time period. Diaries, letters, or other lengthy correspondence between people of that time period could help us understand the common everyday experiences between families. Historical records could give us a picture of immigration trends, age at first marriage, or the average length of time between marriage and first birth.

However, if we're trying to assess attitudes or opinions about people today, perhaps a survey or in-depth interviews would be best. If we want to ask the same questions of everyone and offer a standard set of answers from which they can choose from, such as "How many children do you personally want to have? Would you say it is zero, one, two, three, four, or five or more?" then a survey might be best. We can easily quantify the information and present it with statistics. We could look at multiple factors, such as how the number of children desired affects the likelihood of attending graduate school, and how that might differ for men and women. Or, if we're interested in broader questions and want each person in our study to elaborate on their answers in his or her own way, such as, "How did you decide on the number of children that you would like to have?" or "How do you think children may affect your career plans?" we would likely use in-depth interviews, which yield qualitative data.

Theories: Helping Us Make Sense of the World

theory: A general framework, explanation, or tool used to understand and describe the real world.

Research is guided by **theory**, which is a general framework, explanation, or tool used to understand and describe the real world (Smith & Hamon, 2012). Theories are important both before and after data have been collected because they help us decide what topics to research, what questions to try to answer, how best to answer them, and how to interpret the research results. Before collecting data, theories can help us frame the question. When data have been collected and patterns emerge, theories can help us make sense of what was found.

There are many theoretical perspectives that make different assumptions about the nature of society. Table 1.3 summarizes the most common theories for

Watch on MySocLab
Video: *Sociological Theory and Research: The Basics*

TABLE 1.3	**Summary of Family Theories**

Theories range from macro-level to micro-level.

LEVEL OF ANALYSIS				
MACRO	Structural Functionalism	⟷	The family as an institution and how it functions to maintain its own needs and those of society.
	Conflict	⟷	Social inequality results in unequal resources resulting in inevitable conflict.
	Feminism	⟷	Investigation of family life as experienced by those with minority status, especially women.
	Biosocial	⟷	The reciprocal roles of nature and environment in shaping family behavior.
	Social Exchange	⟷	Family life as a rational exchange designed to maximize rewards and contain costs.
	Symbolic Interaction	⟷	Family interaction governed by symbolic communication that defines reality.
MICRO	Developmental Theory	⟷	Family life predicted by passage through normative stages and the accomplishment of corresponding tasks.
	Family Systems	⟷	Circular interactions among the system members resulting in functional or dysfunctional outcomes.
	Stress	⟷	Analysis of the process of experiencing and resolving stressful life events.

Source: Based on Smith, Hamon, Ingoldsby, & Miller, 2008.

studying families. Some theories are more macro in nature, and attempt to understand societal patterns; these include structural functionalism theory, conflict theory, and feminist theory. Other theories are more micro in nature, such as social exchange theory, symbolic interaction theory, developmental theory, and systems theory, and focus on personal dynamics and face-to-face interaction.

◉ Watch on MySocLab
Video: *Sociological Theory and Research: The Big Picture*

STRUCTURAL FUNCTIONALISM The **structural functionalism theory** (often shortened to *functionalism*) attempts to determine the structure, systems, functions, and equilibrium of social institutions—in this case, the family. A popular theory in the 1940s and 1950s, the focus is on how the family is organized, how it interacts with other social systems, the functions that the family serves, and how it is a stabilizing force in a culture (Parsons, 1937). For example, Parsons and Bales (1955) focused on the division of labor in families, noting the ways in which separate spheres for men and women contributed to the stability and functionality of families. The expressive roles and tasks fell to women, whereas the instrumental roles fell to men, which contributed to smooth family functioning. Functionalists rarely note the tensions, conflicts, or the political ideologies behind their ideas, which may explain why it has fallen out of favor in recent decades among sociologists.

structural functionalism theory: A theory that attempts to determine the structure, systems, functions, and equilibrium of social institutions.

CONFLICT THEORY **Conflict theory** emphasizes issues surrounding social inequality, power, conflict, and social change; in this case, how these factors influence or are played out in families. Those who follow the writings of Karl Marx, a 19th-century philosopher, focus on the consequences of capitalism for families, such as the tensions and inequality generated by the distribution of wealth and power associated with capitalism (Marx & Engels, 1971, original 1867). Other conflict theorists focus on a broader array of issues surrounding conflict, inequality, or power differentials. For example, a conflict theorist might ask why virtually all elderly persons, regardless of income, receive government-subsidized health care that covers many of their health care needs (Medicare) when there is no similar program for children. Is this difference in treatment because the elderly represent both a large special interest group and a powerful voting block, whereas children as a group are virtually powerless?

conflict theory: A theory that emphasizes issues surrounding social inequality, power, conflict, and social change.

FEMINIST THEORY **Feminist theory** is related to conflict theory, but the difference between the two is that gender is seen as the central concept for explaining family structure and family dynamics (Osmond & Thorne, 1993). It focuses on the inequality and power imbalances between men and women and analyzes "women's subordination for the purpose of figuring out how to change it" (Gordon, 1979, p. 107). It recognizes that *gender* is a far more important organizing concept than is *sex* because the former represents a powerful set of relations that are fraught with power and inequality. For example, research indicates that women do more household labor than men even when both partners are employed full-time. Feminist theorists see the gendered division of household labor as a result of power imbalances between men and women that are embedded in larger society and have virtually taken on a life of their own. This is an example of *doing gender* when gender differences become embedded in our culture (West & Zimmerman, 1987). We discuss this further in Chapter 10.

feminist theory: A theory in which gender is seen as the central concept for explaining family structure and family dynamics.

SOCIAL EXCHANGE THEORY **Social exchange theory** draws on a model of human behavior used by many economists. It assumes that individuals are rational beings, and their behavior reflects decisions evaluated on the basis of costs—both direct and opportunity costs—and benefits (Becker, 1981; Nye, 1979). Exchange theorists might suggest that a particular type of family structure or dynamic is the result of rational decisions based on evaluating the social, economic, and emotional costs and benefits compared to the alternatives.

social exchange theory: A theory that draws on a model of human behavior used by many economists. It assumes that individuals are rational beings, and their behavior reflects decisions evaluated on the basis of costs—both direct and opportunity costs—and benefits.

SYMBOLIC INTERACTION THEORY   Symbolic interaction theory emphasizes the symbols we use in everyday interaction—words, gestures, appearances—and how these are interpreted by others (Mead, 1935). Our interactions with others are based on how we interpret these symbols. Some symbols are obvious—an engagement ring, a kiss, a smile. We know how to interpret these symbols. Others are less obvious and may be more confusing to interpret, thereby causing tension or conflict in a relationship. For example, we have a general agreement about what a "mother" is supposed to do, but what is the role of a "stepmother"?

DEVELOPMENTAL THEORY   Developmental theory suggests that families (and individual family members) go through distinct stages over time, with each stage having its own set of tasks, roles, and responsibilities. These developmental changes include (1) getting married; (2) having children; (3) experiencing the preschool years; (4) experiencing the school-age years; (5) living with teenagers; (6) launching one's children into adulthood; (7) being a middle-age parent; and (8) aging (Duvall & Miller, 1985). Early development theorists claimed that the stages were inevitable and occurred in a relatively linear fashion, although most now recognize that people might move in unpredictable ways. For example, some families never have children. Other families have children later in life, so that parents may face tasks associated with middle age (such as saving for retirement) before children are launched. Developmental theory uses both micro and macro approaches to describe and explain family relationships and stages (Rodgers & White, 1993).

A related perspective, called the life course perspective, examines how the lives of individuals change as they pass through events, with the recognition that many changes are socially produced and shared among a cohort of people (Elder, 1998; Schaie & Elder, 2005). For example, sociologist Glen Elder's longitudinal study followed a cohort of American children through the Great Depression and afterward to see how a historical event of such large proportions affected them (Elder, 1999).

SYSTEMS THEORY   A system is more than the sum of its parts. Likewise, **systems theory** proposes that a *family system*—the family members and the roles that they play—is larger than the sum of its individual members (Broderick & Smith, 1979). Collectively it becomes a system, but it also includes subsystems within it, such as the married couple subsystem, the sibling subsystem, or the parent–child subsystem. All family systems and subsystems create boundaries between them and the environment with varying degrees of permeability. They also create *rules of transformation* so that families function smoothly and everyone knows what to expect from another member. All systems tend toward equilibrium so that families work toward a balancing point in their relationship, and they maintain this equilibrium by feedback or control. Therefore, systems theory is particularly useful in studying how the family (or subsystems within the family) communicate with one another and the rippling effects of that communication.

Throughout this text you'll read about and analyze the results of many scientific research studies and see how theory informs our research. These studies are important, because they show us relevant facts and meanings associated with families and close relationships. Understanding these facts and meanings helps shape our choices and our values. Next, let's look at a detailed example of how research can inform our values about families.

Family Decline or Not? What Does the Research Reveal?

Today, some people are concerned that the family is in trouble (National Marriage Project, 2012), citing "the neglect of marriage," "lack of commitment by men," "loss of child centeredness," "the rise in cohabitation," and "fatherless families." Popular television shows, newspapers, and magazines bombard us with stories about the demise of the family. We hear that in the "good old days," there were fewer problems; life was easier, family bonds were stronger, families had more authority to fulfill their functions, and people were generally happier. People who believe that families are being threatened worry that (1) Americans are rejecting traditional marriage and family life; (2) family members are not adhering to roles within families; and (3) many social and moral problems result from the changes in families.

In contrast to this pessimistic perspective, others remind us that these golden years of the past never really existed. They argue that families have always faced challenges, including desertion, poverty, children born out of wedlock, alcoholism, unemployment, violence, and child abuse (Abramovitz, 1996; Coontz, 1997, 2000). Yet, despite these recurring problems, attempts to strengthen families through improved social services and financial assistance have been met with resistance. Providing families with services such as adequate child care, educational opportunities, jobs, health care, and housing is at odds with the emphasis in the United States on so-called rugged individualism. Instead, we are a nation that encourages all of our citizens to "pull themselves up by their own bootstraps."

Which view is correct? To answer this question, we return to the third theme of this text: Rather than relying on common sense or personal experience alone to inform us about families, we should examine the information that research can provide. For example, you shouldn't make sweeping statements that divorce is good or bad for children, that women on welfare neglect or don't neglect their children, that teenage pregnancy is increasing or decreasing, or that lesbians or gay men make bad or good parents on the basis of your personal opinion without looking at what research reveals about these issues. You may find that your own opinions are confirmed—or, conversely, that they're clearly refuted.

Are We Rejecting Marriage and Family Relationships? Attitudes

Studies looking at attitudes toward family life over the course of several decades show both change and consistency over time. A national Gallup Poll reveals a long-term trend toward endorsing sex and gender equality and a greater tolerance for different types of families and lifestyles, including same-sex marriage (Gallup, December 17, 2012; Pew Research Center, February 7, 2013). Nonetheless, there is also a continued emphasis on and commitment to marriage, children, and family life. Both younger and older Americans devote or plan to devote much of their lives to children and spouses. They see marriage as a lifetime commitment that shouldn't be terminated except under extreme conditions, and they view both marriage and having children as highly fulfilling. There is no evidence that this commitment has eroded over the past several decades.

Researchers from the University of Michigan collected data from high school seniors since the mid-1970s and the results indicate very little, if any, decline in the way young people value marriage and family in the last generation (National Marriage Project, 2012). Figure 1.2 reports the percentage of high school

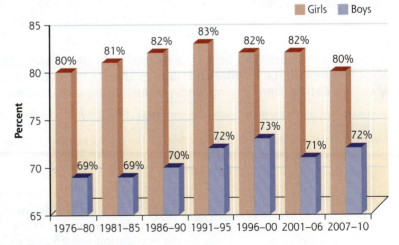

FIGURE 1.2

High School Seniors Who Said Having a Good Marriage and Family Life Is "Extremely Important"

Both young men and women believe in the importance of a good marriage and family life, and opinions haven't changed much since the mid-1970s.
Source: The National Marriage Project, The State of Our Unions: Marriage in America 2012.

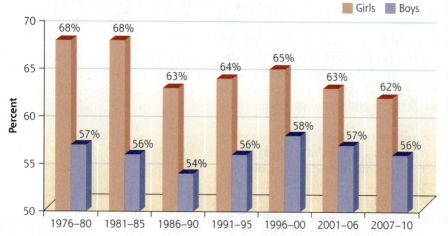

FIGURE 1.3

High School Seniors Who Expected to Marry, or Were Married, Who Said It Is "Very Likely" They Will Stay Married to the Same Person for Life, by Period

Attitudes toward the permanence of marriage among young men and women have changed very little since the mid-1970s.
Source: The National Marriage Project, The State of Our Unions: Marriage in America 2012.

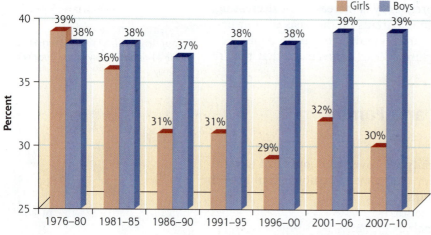

FIGURE 1.4

High School Seniors Who Said They Agreed or Mostly Agreed That Most People Will Have Fuller and Happier Lives If They Choose Legal Marriage Rather than Staying Single or Just Living with Someone

Young women today see more options for themselves than did young women more than 30 years ago.
Source: The National Marriage Project, The State of Our Unions: Marriage in America 2012.

seniors over time who said that having a good marriage and family life is "Extremely Important." Most young men and women strongly believe in the importance of a good marriage and family life. It appears that the opinions of young men and women in recent years are no different from those who graduated between 1986 and 1990.

The majority of high school seniors also agree that it's "Very Likely" that they will stay married to the same person for life, as Figure 1.3 shows. Young women are more likely than their male counterparts to agree with this statement, and students' attitudes have changed little over time.

Figure 1.4 reports the percentage of high school seniors who said they agreed, or mostly agreed, that "Most people will have fuller or happier lives if they choose legal marriage rather than staying single or just living with someone." Again, the researchers compared the answers across different cohorts of high school seniors. Despite the fact that young people value marriage and family life for themselves and hope to stay married forever, they are also becoming more tolerant of other lifestyle options. Interestingly, young men are somewhat more likely than young women to believe that most people will have happier lives if they choose legal marriage. Young women in particular increasingly recognize that cohabitation and singlehood could indeed be viable options for people, even if they themselves would prefer to marry.

Are We Rejecting Marriage and Family Relationships? Behaviors

Data from the U.S. Census Bureau show that the percentage of people who are currently married has declined. But is it fair to assume that we're rejecting marriage and family relationships? Figure 1.5 (p. 32) shows the marital status of the population age 15 and older by gender for the years 1970 and 2012. First, note that the percentage of people older than 15 who had "Never Married" has risen for both men and women since the 1980s. However, this increase is primarily the result of the *delayed age at marriage*, not an increased likelihood of remaining single over the life course. Women now marry at an average age of 25 and men marry around age 27, compared to 21 and 23, respectively, in 1970. In fact, the percentage of people age 65 and over who report never

The holidays are coming up and I've made my usual plans to drive down from Boston to see my family in Maryland. I haven't seen my parents, kid sisters, and grandma for about six months, so it will be great to see them all again. That is, until they start up on the "single thing."

What is it with the older generations, anyway? I'm 31, and they act like my life is nothing without a husband and kids. Last time I saw my mom she actually cried, and told me that if I don't hurry and get married, no one will be left for me. I'm too picky, she said. Another time she suggested that my eggs were "drying up" and I was sentencing myself to a life without children. My dad isn't much better, and grandma just smirks.

What they don't seem to understand is that I like being single right now. I have a great job in publishing, and enjoy the perks

An increasing number of people in their 20s and 30s are single, using this opportunity to focus on their work, education, and their social life, but this does not mean that they will never marry.

of a pretty good salary, a wonderful loft in a cool part of town, lots of travel, and the freedom to take some terrific vacations. Last year, I went to Morocco and Egypt with a friend for three weeks. I'm not sure I could swing any of this with a husband and kids.

Of course, this doesn't mean that I never want to get married, or never want to have a baby. Okay, I admit that sometimes I'm lonely. Sometimes I do wonder if "he" is out there for me. I'm just not in any rush. I've had a few serious boyfriends. In college I even lived with my boyfriend for a couple of years, but then we split. He moved for a job and I left for graduate school, and we just realized we were going in different directions emotionally as well as geographically.

Right now I feel like I have a lot of friends, male and female, and we enjoy hanging out on weekends—you know, going out for dinner and drinks, sailing, or going to the latest gallery opening. I'm also training for a half-marathon, and have a good group of folks for my long run on Sundays.

My parents get none of this. "Hurry up, hurry up," they say. It bothers me because, sure, I want to get married, someday, just not yet.

—Mariah, Age 31

WHAT DO YOU THINK?

1. What age do you think is ideal to marry? The average age for first marriage is increasing. Do you think delaying marriage is good or bad for society?
2. Is the pressure to marry and have children the same for men and women? Would Mariah have received more or less pressure if she were a man? Explain your answer.

marrying is actually lower than it was in 1970. In other words, *people are still marrying, but marrying later*. So, although the statistics may first look like a rejection of marriage, a closer look reveals that this isn't the case, as shown in the feature box "My Family: Not Married—Yet."

Figure 1.5 also reveals that between 1970 and 2013, the number of people who claimed to be currently divorced or separated more than doubled for both men and women. Divorce was rising in the 1970s for many reasons that we explore in Chapter 12. However, the divorce rate began to level off in the early 1980s and has declined significantly since then (Centers for Disease Control and Prevention [CDC], February 19, 2013). In other words, *divorce is declining, not increasing*. If you consider the fact that most divorced people eventually remarry, it's difficult to make the argument that Americans are rejecting marriage and family life.

Other national data show that an increasing number of adults don't have children. Today, about 18 percent of women approaching the end of their childbearing years are childfree, double the rate of only a generation ago (Livingston & Cohn, 2010; Martinez, Daniels, & Chandra, 2012). Although you might conclude that our society is deciding against having children, it's important to understand that about half of childfree women ages 40–44 are *involuntarily* childfree, and assisted reproductive technology is big business these days (CDC, February 13, 2013).

FIGURE 1.5

Marital Status of the Population 15 Years and Over, by Sex: 1970 and 2013

Although it seems that fewer people are married and more people never marry, this reflects a delay in the age at marriage, not a rejection of marriage itself.
Source: U.S. Census Bureau, November 2013.

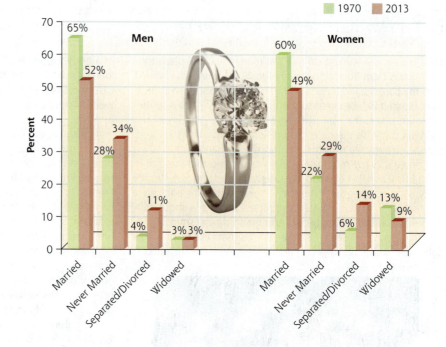

Watch on **MySocLab**
Video: *Arlene Skolnick: Newest Debate in Family Studies*

***W**hat are some common-sense assumptions about the family? Can you think of examples of family issues that you assumed to be true, but then you later learned the facts that showed you were wrong? How did you respond to this new information? Did you welcome, deny, or accept it immediately?*

Nonetheless, it remains that more women today than a generation ago choose to forgo parenthood. But let's ask ourselves, is that such a bad thing? In the past, many women who didn't want children were pressured to have them anyway. In other words, although fewer people are having children, we really don't know *whether the percentage of people who don't want children has increased or remained the same.*

Finally, some people consider the rise in the number of single-parent households to be a cause for concern. Single-parent households, which are about 30 percent of all families (Lofquist, Lugaila, O'Connell, & Feliz, 2012), have been blamed for a variety of family problems, including poverty, delinquency, teen pregnancy, and school dropouts. Most single-parent households are headed by single mothers; however, the composition of single-mother families is beginning to change. They are increasingly made up of older, more highly educated women, whereas the number of births by teenagers has been declining significantly, and has now reached an all-time low since data collection began in the 1940s (Hamilton & Ventura, 2012). In addition, the number of single-mother households has not increased appreciably since the mid-1990s; rather, it's the number of *single-father* families that is on the rise.

Let's pause to consider why so many single-parent households are vulnerable to a variety of social problems. Most studies do not find that it's single parenthood *per se* that accounts for these problems. Rather, other issues *associated* with single parenthood seem to be responsible, such as an increased likelihood of poverty. Almost a third of single, female-headed households are poor, compared to only about 13 percent of all families (DeNavas-Walt, Proctor, & Smith, 2013). In other words, single parenthood may make poverty more likely to occur, but if we could do something to help fight poverty as a society, then many social problems could be reduced.

An international comparison may shed some light on what could be done to eliminate poverty and improve outcomes for children who grow up in single-parent households (Ermisch, Jäntti, & Smeeding, 2012; Garfinkel, Rainwater, & Smeeding, 2010; Warner, 2005). For example, Houseknecht and Sastry (1996) examined the relationship between the decline of traditional families and the well-being of children in Sweden, the United States, the former West Germany, and Italy. *Family decline* was measured by such factors as the divorce rate, the rate of nonmarital births, and the percentage of mothers with young children in the labor force. *Child well-being* was measured by the percentage of children in poverty, deaths of infants from abuse, and juvenile delinquency rates. The researchers found that children seemed to fare best in both Italy and Sweden. But interestingly, Italy had low levels of family decline, whereas Sweden had significantly higher levels. Thus, it appears that changes in family structure don't necessarily have negative effects on children.

Why did Italy, with low levels of family decline, and Sweden, with high levels, both report high levels of child well-being? The researchers argued that both countries have many social policies and programs designed to help children and their families to keep them out of poverty, such as universal health insurance, subsidized childcare, a dependent child grant from the government, expanded paid maternity leaves, and many other programs that help families stay strong. From this, they concluded that *poor child outcomes result from weak social policies that don't provide the support that our naturally evolving family structure requires.* In other words, poor child outcomes don't simply happen because of change *per se*, and they aren't inevitable.

Bringing It Full Circle

In the beginning of this chapter, we introduced you to several groups of people and for each group posed the question, "Are they a family?" With the new information presented in this chapter, you now know how important the answer to this question can be. Our definitions of family and our views about family relationships reflect both micro-level and macro-level factors. Micro-level factors include issues of personal choice and interpersonal dynamics. Macro-level factors include broader social structures, such as social institutions and the statuses of sex, race and ethnicity, class, and sexual orientation. Rather than relying on common sense, personal opinion, or "It has always been that way . . . ," family scientists are interested in systematically uncovering the patterns of our relationships and answering intriguing questions using social science research methods.

Armed with your new information about families, reflect on the opening vignette.

- Do you think that all of the individuals, couples, and groups introduced are a family? Why or why not?

- Which are more accepted as families in our society, and why? Which are less accepted?

- Choose one of the families in the opening vignette, and explain how both micro-level and macro-level factors shape how society views this family type and influences their family patterns and interactions.

- What questions do you have about the families in the opening vignette, and how could social science research help answer these questions?

CHAPTER REVIEW

LO1.1 Identify the different definitions of "family" and their implications

1.1 How does this text define *family*, and how does it differ from a legal perspective?

This text defines a family more broadly than the federal government. *Family* is a relationship by blood, marriage, or affection, that may cooperate economically, may care for any children, and may consider their core identity to be intimately connected to the group. Thus, this definition may include unmarried homosexual or heterosexual partners.

1.2 Why is the definition of family so important?

How our society defines a family has important consequences for many different rights, privileges, and responsibilities. Only married persons are eligible for federal benefits, such as Social Security benefits or the ability to file taxes jointly. These decisions involve billions of dollars in employer and government benefits and affect millions of adults and children each year.

LO1.2 Describe the functions of families

1.3 What are the functions that families provide?

Families provide many functions, including marriage; regulation of sexual behavior; reproducing and socializing children; property and inheritance; economic cooperation; social placement, status, and roles; and care, warmth, protection, and intimacy.

LO1.3 Recognize the link between micro-level and macro-level perspectives on families

1.4 What is the difference between a *micro-level* and a *macro-level* perspective for the study of families?

People often think of our relationships solely in personal terms, which is a micro-level perspective, but relationships are also shaped by the social structure. Our attitudes and behaviors, likes and dislikes, aren't completely random, but are formed by many social forces. A macro-level perspective examines the ways in which marriage, families, and intimate relationships are interconnected with the rest of society and its institutions.

1.5 What is *social structure*, and why is it important?

Social structure refers to the patterns of social organization that guide our interactions with others. Part of this social organization includes our social institutions and social statuses. Social structures shape our daily experiences, privileges, and constraints.

LO1.4 Assess the ways that families are always changing

1.6 What types of marriage and kinship patterns exist around the world?

Marriage patterns include *monogamy* (including serial monogamy) and two types of *polygamy* (polygyny and polyandry). Patterns of authority include *patriarchy*, *egalitarian*, and (theoretically, at least) matriarchy. Patterns of descent include *bilateral*, *patrilineal*, and *matrilineal*, and residential patterns include *neolocal*, *patrilocal*, and *matrilocal*.

1.7 How would we characterize the changes in China's families and family policy in recent generations?

Interrelated with the changes in China's economy, China's families have moved from a large amount of parental involvement and supervision to greater individual freedom of choice. However, the Chinese people must adhere to strict governmental rules regulating marriage and fertility. Couples must request permission both to marry and to have a child. Families are generally only allowed one child.

1.8 How have families changed throughout history, and what macro-level factors that have contributed to that change?

Families evolved from being largely economic units to being based on mutual affection, sexual attraction, compatibility, and personal happiness. Several macro-level factors contributed to these changes, including urbanization, industrialization, immigration, social events such as wars and the Great Depression, and the rise of new technologies.

LO1.5 Summarize the importance of social science theory and research

1.9 How does social science research help us understand families?

An empirical approach can describe some phenomenon, examine the factors that predict or are associated with some phenomenon, explain cause-and-effect relationships, or provide insight into why certain events do or do not occur.

1.10 What methods do family scholars use to study families?

Many different methods are used to study families. Depending on the research question, studies can be based on surveys, in-depth interviews, experiments, observation, focus groups, or the analysis of secondary data.

1.11 How can theory help us understand families and family research?

Research is guided by *theory,* which is a general framework, explanation, or tool used to understand and describe the real world. Theories are important both before and after data have been collected because they help us decide what topics to research, what questions to try to answer, how best to answer them, and how to interpret the research results. Before collecting data, theories can help us frame the question. When data have been collected and patterns emerge, theories help us make sense of what was found.

1.12 Are Americans rejecting marriage and families?

Families are changing, but there is little evidence that Americans are rejecting marriage and families. If we look at both attitudes and behaviors, we can see that most Americans do marry and do have children. However, the age at marriage has risen, and more women are remaining childfree.

KEY TERMS

bilateral
companionate family
conflict theory
developmental theory
egalitarian
empirical approach
experiment
extended family
family
family of orientation
family of procreation
feminist theory
fictive kin
focus group
human agency
in-depth interview

marriage
master status
matriarchy
matrilineal
matrilocal
macro-level
micro-level
monogamy
neolocal
nuclear family
observational study
patriarchy
patrilineal
patrilocal
polyandry
polygamy

polygyny
qualitative research
quantitative research
random sample
secondary analysis
social exchange theory
social institution
social structure
socialization
status
structural functionalism theory
survey
symbolic interaction theory
systems theory
theory

2

Social Status: Sex, Gender, Race, Ethnicity, and Social Class

((• **Listen** to Chapter 2 on **MySocLab**

LEARNING OBJECTIVES

2.1 Summarize the link between private experiences and social structure

2.2 Explain the importance of sex, gender, and patriarchy to families

2.3 Describe the importance of race and ethnicity to families

2.4 Identify the importance of social class to families

2.5 Discuss how poverty affects families

2.6 Analyze the intersections of sex, gender, race, ethnicity, and class

What are the long-term effects of growing up in poverty?

Poverty involves more than just the absence of money. It can affect the way you see yourself, and how you are able to negotiate the broader world. Becca's story provides a close-up glimpse of what it is like to be poor.

Today, Becca is a vibrant thirty-something-year-old mother on the path to success. But her life has had more than its share of dark periods and eroded self-esteem. Becca was born into poverty and raised in the dismal housing projects of an urban city. Her mother was mentally ill, bounced from boyfriend to boyfriend, and could not care for either herself or Becca properly. Becca was left mostly on her own, unsupervised, dodging the addiction and violence that consumed her family. Becca loved school and did well; school was her refuge. There she was safe, loved, and well cared for. She graduated from high school with honors, despite her personal turmoil, and soon left for a prestigious university that she paid for herself with grants, loans, and her own hard work. She carried the baggage of her past with her to college, a place where she didn't feel comfortable. She felt different from other students, and was certain they wouldn't understand where she came from. She isolated herself and had few friends, further eroding her self-esteem. This distress caused her to make poor choices, including becoming too dependent on a man who took advantage of her—a pattern that she would repeat for several years. She became pregnant, and wanting a better life for her son, she gave him up for adoption. Given the situation, she believed this was best for all involved. Her decision, however, infuriated her family, and they disowned her for it. By this time Becca hit bottom—she dropped out of school, had nowhere to live, and was homeless from ages 19 to 23, moving from shelter to shelter. Looking for love and some semblance of security she again found a boyfriend, but he too was abusive. Together they lived under a bridge, begging for spare change from those passing by. Although she felt that she was giving up her pride, she says that part of living in poverty is blocking out how others might judge you. You must learn to block out others' harsh judgments. Becca became pregnant again, and this time was determined to provide a good life for her child, a daughter she named Taylor. The next few years offered a story of hope and renewal as she struggled to leave her alcoholic abusive partner, find housing for herself and Taylor—who has special needs and developmental delays—and continue with school. These paths are not easy for a person in poverty, because the American social service system is cumbersome and difficult to navigate. For example, most landlords will not take her Section 8 subsidized housing voucher, but how can a poor person amass first and last month's rent? Yet, despite the numerous obstacles in her path, Becca is searching for and finding her way.

👁 **Watch** on **MySocLab**
Video: *Raising Children in Poverty: Becca*

As this story illustrates, our choices—even personal ones—do not exist in a vacuum. Sex, race, ethnicity, and social class affect a wide variety of opportunities, privileges, constraints, and choices available to us. This chapter introduces the importance of sex and gender, race, ethnicity, and social class for our family relationships. Why a separate chapter? Shouldn't coverage in the subsequent chapters—dating, intimacy, marriage, children, divorce—suffice? You'll learn the particulars in later chapters, but here we introduce these signature concepts, provide useful definitions, and illustrate their importance in our lives. This chapter reveals the linkages between our micro-level private experiences and the macro-level social structure in which we live.

social stratification: The hierarchical ranking of categories of people within society.

The Link between Private Experiences and Social Structure

Sex, race, ethnicity, and social class are social statuses that, alone and together, have a strong influence on us throughout our lives (Bakanic, 2008; Hurst, 2013). They're also dimensions of **social stratification**, or the hierarchical ranking of categories of people within society. Not all these categories are treated equally. For example, some people have more, less, or at least different opportunities because of their sex, race, social class, or any combination of these. Yet, we generally hesitate to acknowledge the stratification of our society. In this chapter, I encourage you to look further at the link between private experience and social structure. Do our statuses, such as being male or female, really influence our lives, or have things changed? Because we tend to associate with other people who are similar to us, we sometimes don't understand the real power of social structure.

"Why can't we all just be equal?" students have asked. Shouldn't we just pretend that race and ethnicity, and the differences we experience because of them, do not exist in our society? Likewise, aren't we all really middle class? Aren't men and women really equals now? These questions ignore the fact that women and men, Whites and minorities, and the rich and the poor can have quite different experiences. For example, low-income families have significant difficulties finding even something as basic as housing. The median wage needed to pay for a two-bedroom rental unit is about $17 per hour, more than double the minimum wage and far more than many families earn. In seven states—Hawaii, California, Massachusetts, New Jersey, New York, Connecticut, and Maryland—along with the District of Columbia, the average wage needed for a two-bedroom unit is over $20 per hour (Wardrip, Pelletiere, & Crowley, 2009). The lack of affordable housing forces many families to live in either dilapidated dwellings without appropriate ventilation or heat, or in dangerous neighborhoods that are unsafe for children, or to be homeless.

sociological imagination: The recognition that our personal experiences are, in large part, shaped by forces within the larger society.

Acknowledging differences allows us to recognize how our private lives and family relationships are affected by what is happening in society. This is called the **sociological imagination** (Mills, 1959), and certain categories of people are more likely to experience certain events than are others. It's not simply a coincidence, for example, that Whites are more likely to marry than are Blacks, that persons with lower incomes are more likely to divorce, that Hispanics have more children than do other groups, that racial or ethnic minority members have significantly higher unemployment rates, or that women are more likely to experience sexual harassment on the job than are men. These patterns are shaped by social and cultural forces, rather than by individual whim or random events.

But haven't things really changed for the better, you ask? Isn't our society more progressive now? Sure, there have been many social changes during the

TABLE 2.1	Race-based and Sex-based Charges of Discrimination		
Charges of race and sex discrimination have increased.			
	FY 2000	**FY 2005**	**FY 2012**
Race-based	28,945	26,740	33,512
Sex-based	25,194	23,094	30,356

Source: U.S. Equal Employment Opportunity Commission, 2012.

past decades, but let's not exaggerate the *degree* of social change. For example, in fiscal year 2012, the U.S. Equal Employment Opportunity Commission (EEOC) received more than 30,000 sex discrimination charges, as shown in Table 2.1 (U.S. EEOC, 2012). Likewise, the EEOC received more than 33,000 charges of racial or ethnic discrimination (U.S. EEOC, 2012). These charges represent an increase of more than 20 percent since 2005.

Despite reports of discrimination, some students are reluctant to acknowledge sex, race, or ethnicity as organizing constructs in our society. They may agree that men and women differ in sexuality and reproductive roles, but they are less likely to believe that their personal relationships, goals, aspirations, expectations for marriage, job prospects and pay, and current and future roles are considerably shaped by their sex. However, economic data reveal that women still earn only 83 percent of men's earnings, even when both work full-time (U.S. Bureau of Labor Statistics, October, 2012). It's easy to make the claim that "Things have changed for the better," but social science research can reveal important trends and patterns.

Quite naturally, we tend to spend time with others most like us—people who live in the same neighborhoods, go to the same churches and schools, and share the same interests as we do. For example, many neighborhoods remain racially segregated (CensusScope, 2010). In Chicago, Illinois, Whites live in neighborhoods that average 80 percent White, despite being only 60 percent of the population. Blacks live in neighborhoods averaging 75 percent Black, yet they make up only 20 percent of the population in Chicago. As you might expect, people in the same neighborhood who attend the same schools and churches are likely to be of the same social class and share similar values.

Lack of contact with people different from ourselves can foster misconceptions. The poor, for example, are often denigrated by the middle class and blamed for their own economic circumstances. Welfare recipients in particular are criticized for living off the "public dole," despite the fact that most of them are children (Lindsey, 2011). Yet, many college students also live off the "public dole"; the tuition at public state universities does not cover the real costs of a college education. Taxpayers, including people who have no college-age children, make up much of the difference.

Considering the ways in which race and ethnicity, sex and gender, and social class shape our lives allows us to make rational choices about ourselves and our relationships with others. Acknowledging differences does not have to make us feel superior or inferior; rather, it can help us better recognize the ways in which our society both empowers and constrains us. These privileges and constraints follow us as we mature and develop intimate relationships.

Throughout this text, you'll see many ways that these statuses shape our marriages and families, including how we develop intimacy, our marriage and partnering patterns, how we raise children, issues surrounding aging, and how we face challenges and transitions such as a divorce or remarriage. This chapter introduces and defines these signature concepts so that you can better understand the social context in which we live and how this context influences our relationships.

Do you think that the increase in charges of sex, racial, and ethnic discrimination represents an increase in incidents of discrimination? Or do you think that women and minorities are now more comfortable identifying when they have been discriminated against?

Sex, Gender, and Patriarchy

Most of us would be shocked if someone suggested women should no longer vote or be allowed to drive a car, should eat only after the men in their families had finished their meal, and should be under the authority of men at all times. But people hold these beliefs in many countries around the world. For example, women in Saudi Arabia are separated from men in public. They must also obtain permission from a male guardian—a father, husband, brother, or son—to work, travel, study, marry, or even access health care (Pew Research Center, 2008). Some say that Saudi Arabia is creating a form of *gender apartheid* because of its plans to build an industrial city populated exclusively by female workers. The all-female city is expected to provide Saudi women with 5,000 work and career opportunities, while maintaining complete sex segregation (Crimi, 2012).

Who we are—men or women—profoundly affects our experiences within our relationships and families, even here in the United States. As you'll see in subsequent chapters:

- Girls and boys are treated differently by their parents, and parents hold different expectations for them.
- Males begin sexual relationships earlier than do females and have a larger number of sexual partners.
- Although women are more likely to graduate from college than are men, they are less likely to have careers and they earn less money.
- Wives are more likely than their husbands to do most of the housework and childcare.
- Husbands are more likely to be responsible for supporting the family financially.
- If a couple divorces, the man is more likely to remarry.
- Wives are more likely to be widowed than are their husbands.

Biological sex differences are important, but so is the way that men and women are *treated* within their culture. **Sex** refers to biological differences between men and women and their role in reproduction. One is a *man* or a *woman*. **Gender** describes the culturally and socially created differences that we see in the meanings, beliefs, and practices associated with *femininity* and *masculinity*. Gender tells us what men and women are supposed to be like. Gendered expectations vary considerably, as we shall see.

sex: Biological differences between men and women, and their role in reproduction.

gender: Culturally and socially constructed differences between males and females found in the meanings, beliefs, and practices associated with "femininity" and "masculinity."

Sex and Gender Differences

A popular Mother Goose nursery rhyme goes:

What are little boys made of, made of?
What are little boys made of?
Frogs and snails
And puppy-dog tails,
That's what little boys are made of.
What are little girls made of, made of?
What are little girls made of?
Sugar and spice
And all things nice,
That's what little girls are made of.

Poems, nursery rhymes, and songs often accentuate the traditional differences between men and women. Historically, people have viewed masculinity and femininity as a set of different, or even opposite, traits (Lindsey, 2011). Men are often considered to be naturally more aggressive, strong, and independent, whereas women may be considered to be more emotional, nurturing, and sensitive.

Researchers note some very important biological differences between men and women beyond those needed for reproduction. For example, males are diagnosed with a wider variety of physical illnesses despite being stronger, more active, and more aggressive on average (National Center for Health Statistics, 2011). In contrast, females are more likely to be diagnosed with emotional illnesses such as depression. Certainly, I don't want to overgeneralize here, because many men suffer from depression and many women deal with physical illness; however, we are talking about averages. Scientists tend to be interested in typical behaviors rather than exceptions.

On average, males and females also solve intellectual problems differently. Although no overall differences in intelligence are found (according to IQ tests), men tend to perform better on certain types of mathematical reasoning tests, and women outperform men in the precision with which they perform certain manual tasks. Women also tend to excel on tests measuring recall or matching.

Cognitive sex differences appear in very young children, and are evident among other types of animals used in research, even rats. What accounts for these sex differences? Research is still in its infancy because of the complexity of sex differences, but studies in the past few decades suggest that the size, shape, and use of the brain may differ somewhat between men and women in regions involved in language, memory, emotion, vision, hearing, and navigation (Becker, Berkley, Geary, Hampson, Herman, & Young, 2008). Women also seem to use more parts of their brain at once (ask your parents who was a better multitasker, your mom or your dad). Hormonal differences may be the cause of some of the dissimilarity, as women have higher levels of estrogen and progesterone, and men have higher levels of testosterone (Hines, 2005; McCarthy, Arnold, Ball, Blaustein, & De Vries, 2012; Onion, 2005). Exposure to different hormones begins in our mother's womb and may help explain the way the brain is "wired."

It's intriguing to think about how men and women are different and whether these differences are innate and biological, or whether we learn them in the social environment. How much is fixed, and how much is flexible? We may never have definitive answers, but we do know that social and cultural factors, alongside biology, are very powerful (Etaugh & Bridges, 2013; Helgeson, 2012; Renzetti, Curran, & Maier, 2012). And interestingly, what one culture defines as feminine behavior, another may see as quite masculine. Thus, gender is *socially constructed*, meaning that the culture creates it.

Gender Learning

We learn expected gender behavior through a process called **gender socialization,** which teaches us the cultural norms associated with being male or female. It may be a conscious effort, as in a parent scolding a young son for showing his emotions—"Big boys don't cry"—or less consciously, as in a parent buying a doll for a daughter and a truck for a son. Gender socialization also occurs in our social structure; both religious institutions and the mass media, for example, teach us about what it means to be male or female.

gender socialization: Teaching the cultural norms associated with being male or female.

Gender socialization also has an important *evaluative component*. We learn that many traits associated with men or boys are considered "better" than the ones associated with women or girls. Here are two examples: When I ask my female students to raise their hands if they were considered "tomboys" when growing up, the hands eagerly and proudly shoot up. When I ask the male students how many were "sissies" as children, the class breaks into laughter. In other words, women have no trouble identifying with traditionally defined masculine behavior, but men are embarrassed to identify with that which is traditionally feminine. When I ask my female students to raise their hands if they have cried (with visible tears) during the past week, about half raise their hands. When I then ask my male students the same question, again

weak = feminine

TABLE 2.2	Agents of Socialization and How They Work
Gender socialization has many sources.	
Parents	Differential treatment becomes a self-fulfilling prophecy
Toys	Books show boys as leading characters and girls in stereotypical roles; toys are sex-typed
Schools	Hidden curriculum encourages sex-typed behavior and teaches girls to fear academic success
Peers	Same-sex play reinforces different interaction styles that carry over into adulthood
Mass Media	Television, music videos, and video games tend to focus on boys and present girls in stereotypical ways

agents of socialization: The primary groups responsible for gender socialization.

hidden curriculum: Gender socialization, which is taught informally in school.

Read on **MySocLab**
Document: *Too Many Women in College?*

I hear mostly laughter. No man wants to admit to being seen as "weak," which is, in turn, seen as feminine.

Agents of socialization are the social groups responsible for gender socialization and include parents, schools, toys, peers, and the mass media, as shown in Table 2.2.

PARENTS Parents provide the first exposure to a particular culture, and consciously or not, they may treat their sons and daughters differently (Endendijk, Groeneveld, van Berkel, Hallers-Haalboom, Mesman, & Bakermans-Kranenburg, 2013; Lindsey, Cremeens, & Caldera, 2010). They hold baby girls more gently and cuddle them more than boys. Parents of infant girls describe their children as more dainty and delicate than do parents of infant boys, and the choice of dress usually reflects this (Leaper & Friedman, 2006). Differential treatment continues throughout childhood. "Don't get dirty," a parent may say to a daughter as she goes outside to play, whereas her brother goes unnoticed. When people are treated differently, it can become a self-fulfilling prophecy that goes beyond any true biological differences. Solely on the basis of sex, parents may assign rules, toys, expected behavior, chores, hobbies, and a multitude of other cultural values or artifacts differently (Raffaelli & Ontai, 2004). When girls and boys are treated differently, not surprisingly they become more different.

SCHOOLS From daycare through high school, schools present a **hidden curriculum** that informally teaches girls to value compliance (Orenstein, 1994). School textbooks and readers often have stories of boys or men as main characters, relegating girls and women to the sidelines or showing them in a limited number of roles or occupations (Etaugh & Bridges, 2013). Even college textbooks often reveal gender stereotyping (Yanowitz & Weathers, 2004). A decade ago, girls excelled over boys during grade school, but the situation reversed in middle and high school. A 2006 study involving 518 boys and girls from fifth to seventh grades found that girls were more successful than boys in the younger grades in math and on math achievement tests, but these differences tended to disappear among the older children. One study found that girls began to lose their academic confidence as they became teens (Kenney-Benson, Pomerantz, Ryan, & Patrick, 2006).

However, it appears that today many girls and young women have a strong achievement ethic, are doing well in school, and are surpassing boys and young men. More young women apply to, attend, and graduate from college now than young men. Fifty-seven percent of bachelor's degrees are awarded to women, up from only about a third in 1970 (Fry & Cohn, 2010; U.S. Department of Education, 2012). And more than half (53 percent) of doctorates are now awarded to women, as shown in Figure 2.1. Many college majors, however, remain sex-typed. Students in nursing, elementary

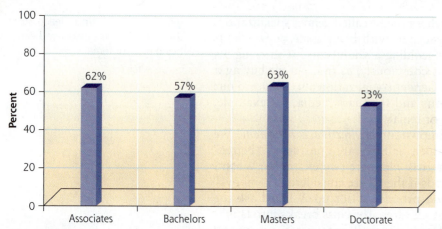

FIGURE 2.1
Percentage of Degrees Conferred to Females, 2009–2010

Women now earn more than half of college degrees, including at the most advanced levels.
Source: National Center for Education Statistics, 2012.

1970

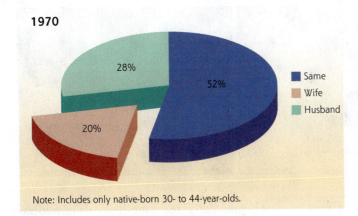

28%

52%

20%

- Same
- Wife
- Husband

Note: Includes only native-born 30- to 44-year-olds.

2007

19%

28%

53%

- Same
- Wife
- Husband

Note: Includes only native-born 30- to 44-year-olds.

FIGURE 2.2
Who Has More Education: Husbands or Wives?

Married women now have more education than their husbands.
Source: Fry & Cohn, 2010.

education, and social work are overwhelmingly female, whereas students in engineering and computer science are primarily male. Nonetheless, among married couples under age 45 (born in the United States), wives are now likely to have more education than their husbands, as shown in Figure 2.2 (Fry & Cohn, 2010).

TOYS Children's toys, books, and games also reflect our gendered culture and teach children important cultural messages about what it means to be a boy, girl, man, or woman (Diekman & Murnen, 2004). If you visit any children's toy store, or even the Disney Store website (Auster & Mansbach, 2012), you'll see that pink aisles specialize in "girl toys" (dolls and their accessories, arts and crafts, domestic toys), whereas other aisles are for "boy toys" (war games, sport accessories, action figures). Boys' favorite toys are manipulation-based, whereas girls' favorites are dolls (Cherney & London, 2006). Even a toy as gender-neutral as a bicycle takes on gender significance by its color; bicycles for boys are *not* painted pink with white wheels! A review of 455 toy commercials on Nickelodeon, a popular children's network, showed a high degree of gender-role stereotyping (Kahlenberg & Hein, 2010).

Video games are an increasing part of children's and teen's entertainment, and consumers spent almost $25 billion on games, hardware, and accessories (Entertainment Software Association, 2012). Women and girls are portrayed much less frequently than are men and boys, and when included, are often shown in subordinate or hypersexualized ways (see Near, 2013, for a review). In videos with ratings of *Teen* or *Mature*, women's bodies are most often artificially thin with exaggerated breasts. They often wear revealing clothing. They are also considerably more attractive than most of the male characters.

Children's books also reveal marked gender stereotypes. For example, a content analysis of the best-selling and award-winning children's books published from 1999 to 2001 found that stories were nearly twice as likely to feature males as characters. When girls and women were portrayed, they were more than three times as likely to be shown as nurturing or caring for others as compared to boys and men. Female characters were more likely to be found indoors, whereas males were more likely to be outdoors. Males were found in a range of 32 different jobs, as compared to 12 for females. Of 23 female adult characters shown with an occupation, 21 had stereotypically feminine occupations. More recent reviews of children's books show marked improvement (Adams, Walker, & O'Connell, 2011); however, the stereotypes remain, even in children's coloring books (Fitzpatrick & McPherson, 2010).

PEERS The influence of peer groups begins early, reaching its peak in adolescence. Psychologist Eleanor Maccoby found that children between the ages of 2 and 3 tend to sort themselves into same-sex play groups when given the opportunity to do so (Maccoby, 1998), and are more social with children of the same sex. She also noted that when girls were playing with other girls, they were as active as were boys playing with other boys. However, when girls were playing with boys, they frequently stood back and let the boys dominate the toys or games. Maccoby speculated that boys' rougher play and greater focus on competition was unattractive to girls, and girls responded by pulling back rather than by trying to exert their own play style. These different interaction styles tend to carry over into adulthood: boys' groups reinforce a more competitive, dominance-oriented style of interaction, which becomes adult male communication patterns that include greater interrupting, contradicting, or boasting. Girls' cooperative groups reinforce a style that contributes to adult female communication patterns including expressing agreement and acknowledging the comments of others, and asking questions rather than making bold pronouncements.

THE MEDIA The mass media, including film, television, radio, and the Internet, represent an increasingly important mechanism for socializing children. Boys and men remain at the center of most programming. Even among the top-grossing G-rated family films, girl characters are outnumbered by boys three-to-one, a ratio that's existed since the end of World War II. For decades, male characters have dominated nearly three-quarters of speaking parts in children's entertainment, and 83 percent of film and TV narrators are male. From 2006 to 2009, not one female character was depicted in G-rated family films in the field of medical science, as a business leader, in law, or in politics. In these films, 80.5 percent of all working characters are male and 19.5 percent are female, a striking contrast to real world statistics, where women make up 50 percent of the workforce (Smith, Choueiti, Prescott, & Pieper, 2012). Some suggest that these absences teach children to accept the stereotypes represented. What they see affects their attitudes toward male and female values in our society (Geena Davis Institute on Gender in the Media, 2012).

A study of morning commercials showed that half of the commercials aimed at girls spoke about physical attractiveness, whereas none of the commercials aimed at boys referenced attractiveness (National Institute on Media and the Family, 2009). Incidentally, females are less likely than males to be shown eating, not an insignificant finding given the high rates of eating disorders among girls and women (National Institute of Mental Health, 2009).

Think about the influence these agents of socialization had upon your own childhood. Which ones had the most influence on your gender?

How Do Race, Ethnicity, and Class Shape Gender Socialization?

We must remember that people's experiences differ widely, because the intersections of gender, race, ethnicity, and class are complex. However, it does appear there are significant class, racial, and ethnic variations in how boys and girls are socialized (Brown, Linver, & Evans, 2010; Helgeson, 2012; Hill, 2002, 2005; Wallace, 2007). For example, Hill's (2002) in-depth interviews with a small sample of 35 Black parents examined the extent to which parents think gender influenced the ways in which they socialize and treat their children. All parents expressed some belief in gender equality, but middle-class Black parents expressed the strongest support.

In another example, Black women and girls are found to be more satisfied with their body types than are their White counterparts (Bailey, 2008). Blacks have a more flexible standard of attractiveness, believing that curves and a fuller body are more desirable than supermodel thinness. Black girls are more likely than White girls to say that they are beautiful, that they like their bodies, and that they like themselves the way they are (Bailey, 2008).

Gender's Influence on Our Family and Close Relationships: Division of Household Labor

Although gender is forged into all aspects of social life, it is particularly evident within families and close relationships. A striking example is how work chores are divided in the home, which you will read about in depth in Chapter 10. Cooking, cleaning, grocery shopping, yard work, and laundry are critical functions and take up a lot of time when a family has children. Household labor has been traditionally defined as "women's work" and was not seriously studied 20 or 30 years ago. Yet, a poll by the Pew Research Center (2007) reveals many people are adamant that sharing household chores is "very important for a successful marriage." This sentiment is growing, as shown in Figure 2.3. In fact, there was very little change between 1990 and 2007 in the factors that people consider important for a happy marriage, except for sharing chores! The only other change was the decline in the percentage of people who believe children are very important for marital success.

We now know that women average about twice the amount of time on household tasks that men do (Galinsky, Aumann, & Bond, 2009; Foster & Kreisler, 2012); a smaller difference occurs with childcare (Finley, Mira, & Schwartz, 2008). These differences continue to hold when the wife is employed full-time or when both partners are retired, and they occur at all income levels. In fact, marriage has been shown to increase women's time spent in housework, whereas it reduces men's time (Gantert, 2008).

One explanation for why women do a disproportionate share of household labor is that society has defined such work as simply part of being a woman (Lachance-Grzela & Bouchard, 2010). We often view gender as a reasonable and legitimate basis for distributing rights and responsibilities. We define housework as a part of women's "essential nature," whereas a man's "essential nature" is *not* to engage in it (West & Zimmerman, 1987). In other words, studying housework gives us insight into power and equity in intimate relationships (Davis & Greenstein, 2013).

※ Explore on MySocLab
Activity: *Domestic Life: A Battle of the Sexes?*

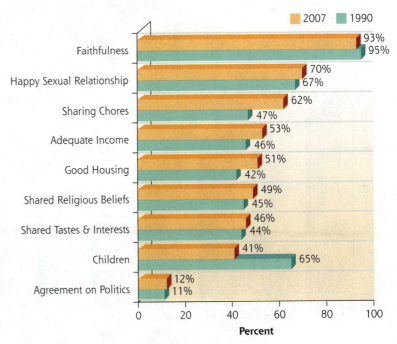

FIGURE 2.3
Percent Saying Each Characteristic Is Very Important for a Successful Marriage

Increasingly, people value the sharing of chores.
Source: Pew Hispanic Center & Kaiser Family Foundation, 2004.

Male Privilege: Patriarchy

Patriarchy, introduced in Chapter 1, is found in a wide variety of social institutions, including legal, educational, religious, and economic ones. Traditional religious texts are filled with passages demeaning women, although their interpretations may be softened in modern-day texts.

> *Let the woman learn in silence with all subjection. But I suffer a woman not to teach, nor to usurp authority over the man, but to be in silence. For Adam was formed first, then Eve. And Adam was not deceived, but the woman being deceived was in the transgression. Notwithstanding she shall be saved in childbearing, if they continue in faith and charity and holiness in sobriety.*
>
> The Official King James Bible Online. 2014. Retrieved 23 February 2014 (www.kingjamesbibleonline.org/1-Timothy-Chapter-2/).

Patriarchy is widespread and found in every society to some degree. As women improve their economic status, male–female relationships tend to become more egalitarian. Nonetheless, as we'll see shortly, clear patterns of male dominance continue to exist even in the United States.

However, let's first consider an example of patriarchy found in other parts of the world—female genital cutting. It's often easier to identify patriarchy and social inequality elsewhere than it is within our own culture.

FEMALE GENITAL MUTILATION *Female circumcision, female genital cutting, or female genital mutilation* is commonly practiced in more than two dozen countries in Africa, the Middle East, and among some immigrant communities in North America and Europe (World Health Organization, 2011). In one form, *clitoridectomy,* the clitoris is clipped—or literally cut out of—the body. In the more extreme form, *infibulation,* a girl's entire external genital area is removed, including the vaginal lips, and the outer portion of the vagina is stitched together, leaving only a miniscule opening for menstrual blood and urine to escape. The girl's knees are bound together for several weeks for the incision to heal. Both procedures are excruciatingly painful, have many serious side effects, and eliminate women's ability to experience sexual pleasure. This procedure has no known health benefits.

Between 130 million and 140 million girls and women today have had their genitals cut or mutilated, and the practice appears to be spreading (World Health Organization, 2011). Even those women who privately oppose it undergo the procedure and intend to continue it with their daughters. They believe that failure to do so will make their daughters "different" or "promiscuous," and perhaps unmarriageable as a result (Yount, 2002). Figure 2.4 shows the prevalence of female genital mutilation among seven African countries. You can see that in Somalia, nearly every woman, young or old, has undergone this procedure (World Health Organization, 2011).

Why is female genital mutilation so widespread, and why has it continued for so many years? It is deeply rooted in the patriarchal traditions of societies where it is found. Although no religion formally endorses female

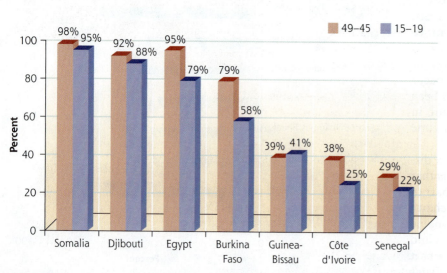

FIGURE 2.4

Prevalence of female genital mutilation in oldest and youngest age groups

Female genital mutilation is common in many parts of Africa.
Source: Reproduced, with permission of World Health Organization, 2011.

genital mutilation, it is widespread because of customs demanding that women be virgins at the time of marriage and remaining sexually faithful thereafter. Removing the clitoris, the source of a woman's sexual pleasure, ensures she will not experience orgasm, and therefore will be less likely to have sexual relations outside of marriage. Among women whose entire external genital area has been removed, the opening that remains is so small that penetration cannot occur without tearing or ripping. Female genital mutilation persists because women's status is low and their options in society are few. Marriage and motherhood are the primary ways in which a woman receives recognition. Virginity is highly valued, and this procedure helps ensure that she won't have sex before marriage, thus bringing the family honor, and aiding the search for a suitable mate.

In more than 200 years of history, the United States has yet to elect a female President or Vice President. Is this just a coincidence, or does it reflect patriarchy? Will it change in the 2016 election?

DOES PATRIARCHY EXIST IN THE UNITED STATES? After reading the previous example about female genital mutilation, it's easy to say, "Whew, I'm glad I live in the United States." However, the United States has its own set of patriarchal norms and customs. Do any come to mind? How many U.S. presidents have been women? Vice presidents? Senators? How many heads of Fortune 500 companies are women? How does women's pay compare to that of men? How do standards of beauty vary for men and women—some with potentially painful or dangerous repercussions (think of cosmetic surgery, breast implants, waxing, or even high-heeled shoes)? Over 15 million cosmetic surgery procedures were performed in the United States in 2013 (American Society of Plastic Surgeons, 2014). Nine out of ten of all cosmetic surgery procedures are performed on women and 4 percent are performed on teenagers. Table 2.3 lists the top five surgical cosmetic procedures in 2013 (American Society of Plastic Surgeons, 2014). These procedures should be cause for concern, as these surgeries are not risk-free, and can have both short- and long-term side effects. Some suggest that women who have cosmetic surgery have internalized the media messages about the body image of the "ideal" woman, and are dissatisfied with their own bodies (Markey & Markey, 2009).

TABLE 2.3	Top Five Surgical Cosmetic Procedures, 2013
Why is breast augmentation the most frequently performed surgical procedure? How would a feminist theorist explain this?	
Breast augmentation	290,000
Nose reshaping	221,000
Eyelid surgery	216,000
Liposuction	200,000
Facelift	133,000

Source: American Society of Plastic Surgeons, 2014.

Let's look at an example that probably affects all of you—where did you get your *last name*? Most children carry their father's last name. When women marry, they usually take their husband's last name (Jayson, 2005; Lockwood, Burton, & Boersma, 2011). Based on almost 7,000 wedding announcements published in *The New York Times*, only about 17 percent of women kept their own names, down from 23 percent in 1990 (Jayson, 2005). Women who keep their own last names are more likely to have graduated from more prestigious colleges, have more advanced degrees, marry later, hold more feminist attitudes, and have greater career commitment (Hoffnung, 2006).

Why do most women change their last names when they marry? The reasons are summarized in the *Tying It All Together* box (p. 49). There are many micro-level reasons, for example, "It's easier this way." But let's think of the macro-level reasons. The changing of women's names is a carryover from older patriarchal and patrilineal customs dictating that, on marriage, the wife became the legal property of her husband. Last names clarified paternity so that a man could be certain of passing his property on to his heirs. These continuing

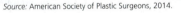

✳ **Explore** on **MySocLab**
Activity: *The Laboring Family: Negotiating Gender Roles*

In the United States, you can really have any name you want. When you marry, you can keep the one your parents gave you, you can take your partner's name, you can hyphenate your name with that of your partner, or you can even invent one of your own. Given all these different options, have you noticed a pattern? Women usually take their partner's name or use a hyphen with both names. In contrast, men usually keep their own names, and rarely even hyphen their name with their partner's. What's behind this? At first glance, our choice of names seems personal, and we therefore draw on micro-level explanations—"Oh, it's easier that way." Yet, why is it only "easier" for women, but not for men? There must be more going on to explain our choice of last name, and we must look for macro-level explanations to see the whole story.

MICRO-LEVEL EXPLANATIONS

- "It's easier this way."
- "It helps make us a family to have the same last name."
- "Why burden children with parents who have different last names from one another, or a long hyphenated name?"

- "It works out better this way for the children's school and medical records."

MACRO-LEVEL EXPLANATIONS

- It is a carryover from patriarchal and patrilineal customs in which, when they marry, the wife became the legal property of her husband.
- Last names clarify paternity.
- It demonstrates that women have found a husband to avoid the stigma associated with being unmarried.

WHAT DO YOU THINK?

1. What do you plan to do with your last name if you marry, and why?
2. Why do you think that fewer women retain their last name when they marry despite greater equality nowadays? Do names no longer reflect patriarchy or paternity? What do they represent?

Read on MySocLab
Document: *Night to His Day: The Social Construction of Gender*

patriarchal traditions tell us something about women's roles in society and about male privilege.

Dr. Ben Barres, a neurobiologist and professor at Stanford University, has something to say about male privilege. Barres has the unique experience of living as both a woman and a man. He was born a woman, but from an early age felt that he was really a man trapped in a woman's body. As an adult, Barres had a sex change operation, and has now lived as a man for more than a decade. What did he learn from this experience? He is adamant that women and men are treated very differently, and that women are routinely discriminated against in ways that most of us are unaware of. As a man, Barres believes he is afforded more respect than when he was a woman, is thought to be more intelligent, has greater access to other physician and science colleagues, and is interrupted less in conversation. For example, after giving a lecture, he overheard a colleague say, "Ben Barres gave a great seminar today, but then his work is much better than his sister's," unknowingly referring to him prior to his sex change operation (*Science Daily*, 2006; Vedantam, 2006).

Sex and gender are firmly rooted in our social structure and affect a wide variety of opportunities, privileges, constraints, and choices available to us as we form families and intimate relationships. The task here has been to introduce these concepts.

In addition to sex and gender, race, ethnicity, and social class are also important parts of our social structure and shape our relationships. Although many Whites have the luxury of rarely thinking about racial or ethnic issues and many Americans believe that we live in a middle-class society, I want to impart a greater sensitivity toward how and why these statuses shape the structure of, and interactions within relationships. I introduce them here so that you'll have a fuller understanding when they are revisited in later chapters.

How would your life be different if you were of the opposite sex? Assume you were raised in the same family, went to the same schools, and lived in the same neighborhood. Think about the ways in which your experiences, opportunities, or choices might be different or similar.

Race and Ethnicity

Like sex and gender, *race* and *ethnicity* are also statuses that deeply influence our relationships and families. We see many examples of this throughout this text, including:

- Blacks are more likely than Whites to live in extended families.
- Hispanics have the largest number of children, whereas Asian Americans are most likely to be childfree.
- Blacks are less likely than other groups to remarry.
- Teenage pregnancy and birth rates are declining among all racial groups, but the declines have been the largest among Blacks.
- Whites are least likely to live in poverty, whereas Native Americans are most likely to do so.
- Hispanics, in particular Mexican Americans, are least likely to have health insurance.
- Asian Americans are the least likely to divorce.
- Blacks begin sexual activity earlier than other groups.

Let's first step back and ask ourselves: What is race? What is ethnicity? Why are these concepts so important for understanding family patterns, interactions, and dynamics?

The Population Is Growing More Diverse

Race, ethnicity, and *minority* are often-used terms (Farley, 2012; Parrillo, 2012; Schaefer, 2013). But do we know what they really mean? Theoretically, **race** is a category describing people who share real or perceived physical traits that society deems socially significant, such as skin color. Nineteenth-century biologists created a three-part classification of races: Caucasian, individuals with relatively light skin; Negroid, individuals with darker skin and characteristics such as coarse curly hair and full lips; and Mongoloid, individuals with yellow or brown skin and folds on their eyelids (Simpson & Yinger, 1985). However, over the past half century or so, because of tremendous growth in our knowledge of genetics, race has ceased to be a useful construct (Lewontin, 2006). An increasing number of people are biracial, further leading most social scientists to suggest that narrow conceptions of race are not particularly accurate, nor are they a useful way to understand differences.

Ethnicity, or shared cultural characteristics such as language, place of origin, dress, food, religion, and other values, is a far more useful concept. Ethnicity represents culture, whereas race attempts to represent biological heritage (which is increasingly mixed). People who share specific cultural features are members of an **ethnic group.** There are many different ethnic groups in the United States, such as Hispanic or Chinese, and hundreds of ethnic groups around the world. Even Caucasians may identify themselves as members of ethnic groups, such as Polish, German, or Italian, if they share interrelated cultural characteristics with others.

Usually when we talk about **minority groups,** we aren't really referring to the size of the group, but rather, to a category of people with less power than the dominant group and who may be subject to unequal treatment. Members of a minority

2.3 Describe the importance of race and ethnicity to families

Questions That Matter

2.5 What is the difference between *race* and *ethnicity,* and which term is generally more useful?

2.6 What is the difference between *individual* and *institutional discrimination*?

2.7 Is the United States becoming more diverse?

Read on MySocLabDocument: *Our Mothers' Grief: Racial-Ethnic Women and the Maintenance of Families*

race: A category describing people who share real or perceived physical traits that society deems socially significant, such as skin color.

ethnicity: Shared cultural characteristics, such as language, place of origin, dress, food, religion, and other values.

ethnic group: A group of people who share specific cultural features.

minority group: A category of people who have less power than the dominant group, and who are subject to unequal treatment.

Ethnicity is a more useful concept than race because it reflects cultural traditions such as language, food, and celebrations.

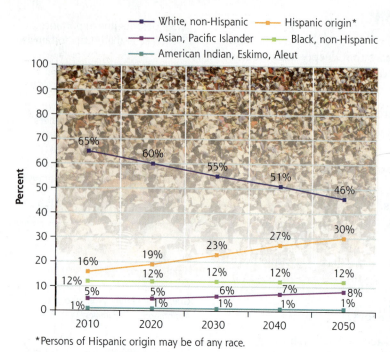

Legend:
- White, non-Hispanic
- Hispanic origin*
- Asian, Pacific Islander
- Black, non-Hispanic
- American Indian, Eskimo, Aleut

*Persons of Hispanic origin may be of any race.

FIGURE 2.5

Resident Population by Race and Hispanic Origin Status—Projections: 2010 to 2050

Hispanics are the fastest-growing portion of the U.S. population.
Source: U.S. Census Bureau Population Division, 2009.

group tend to earn less money and have less representation in politics and other social disadvantages. Most people agree that women and people of color are members of minority groups; however, other ethnic groups, such as Irish Americans, are probably not. In some cases, minority groups may actually represent the statistical majority, as is the case for Blacks in South Africa, or for women in most societies around the world.

The United States is a nation with many minority groups, and is becoming even more diverse, as shown in Figure 2.5 (U.S. Census Bureau Population Division, 2009). About one person in three is a member of a minority group, and in Hawaii, New Mexico, California, Texas, and the District of Columbia, minorities outnumber non-Hispanic Whites. By 2050, minority groups are likely to make up about 54 percent of the U.S. population. The largest increases will occur among Hispanics. I use the term *Hispanic* rather than *Latino* here because, among those with a preference, *Hispanic* is the preferred term (Suro, 2006). Hispanic groups, now 16 percent of the population, are expected to nearly double to 30 percent by the year 2050. Asians are expected to increase to 8 percent of the population. The percentage of Blacks and American Indians (Native Americans)/Alaska Natives are expected to stabilize at 13 percent and 1 percent of the population, respectively.

Throughout its history, people have immigrated to the United States. Some came willingly, fleeing persecution or seeking better opportunities, whereas others were coerced or brought as slaves or indentured servants. Together, these immigrants joined the Native Americans and Mexicans who were already living here and flourishing with many different cultures and languages. Today, about 13 percent of our population, or approximately 40 million people, immigrated to the United States as either children or adults (Motel & Patten, 2013). Today, they are likely to come from Mexico and Latin America rather than Europe, as was the case for much of our history (Department of Homeland Security, 2012). There are also an estimated 11.1 million undocumented migrants in the United States (in 2011), a significant decline from the peak of 12 million in 2007 (Passel & Cohn, 2012).

Minority groups are sometimes devalued and treated with suspicion and contempt by other members of society. The next section discusses these forms of treatment.

Prejudice and Discrimination: Pervasive Problems

Let's say you are a manager for a medium-size company and you want to hire someone for a job. You receive four interesting applications from the following people: Emily, Greg, Lakisha, and Jamal. Who are you going to contact for an interview?

Researchers at the University of Chicago submitted fictitious resumes to more than 1,000 ads in Boston and Chicago newspapers. Resumes were randomly assigned Black- or White-sounding names, but other aspects of their resumes were similar. Those resumes with White-sounding names received 50 percent more telephone calls for interviews. This racial gap was found across different occupations, industries, and employer size (Bertrand & Mullainathan, 2004).

However, we also know that many jobs are never posted in newspaper want ads, but are advertised informally through "word of mouth" or through social networking connections. These connections, referred to as **social capital**, can be a valuable source of information about job leads. A study using a nationally representative survey found that minorities and women have much less social capital than do White men, and therefore miss many employment opportunities (McDonald, Lin, & Ao, 2009).

Prejudice is a negative attitude about members of selected racial and ethnic groups. Prejudice often forms from **stereotypes**, or an oversimplified set of beliefs about a group of people. For example, the stereotype that Black teenage girls are always having babies outside marriage, that Mexican Americans do not want to learn English, that Whites get all the breaks in life, and that Jews are stingy represent widespread stereotypes prevalent in the United States.

Discrimination is a behavior that has harmful effects, such as refusing to hire or promote someone because of his or her race or ethnicity. Discrimination remains widespread in the United States today, as noted by the EEOC (U.S. EEOC, 2012). A number of studies by scholar Ian Ayres found overwhelming evidence that in a variety of markets, Blacks and females are often at a disadvantage. For example, when Ayres sent people out posing as potential buyers to more than 200 car dealerships in Chicago, he found that dealers regularly charged Blacks and women more than they charged White men. In another social experiment, he found that minority male defendants are frequently required to post higher bail bonds than their White counterparts. Given these differences in treatment, should we be surprised to find that only 61 percent of Blacks believe that relations between Whites and Blacks are "very good" or "somewhat good," compared to 70 percent of Whites? It's important to note that prior to President Obama's election, the gap between Blacks and Whites was 20 percentage points (Gallup News Service, 2013).

We tend to think of discrimination occurring at the *micro*, or individual, level. For example, the Collins family doesn't want to sell their home to the Juarez family, who are Mexican, so they have their realtor falsely tell the Juarez family that they already have a buyer. This form of discrimination, called **individual discrimination**, is widespread and problematic, although generally illegal. However, we should also recognize that another form of discrimination exists at the macro level: **institutional discrimination**, which occurs when social institutions, such as the government, religious groups, and schools, create policies and practices that systematically disadvantage certain groups. Often, such discrimination is unintentional and might not be readily apparent to everyone. Institutional discrimination is difficult to eradicate because the policies and practices are woven into the fabric of our culture as "the way we always do things." No one individual or group can be held accountable for these discriminatory policies and practices, and they aren't questioned by most people.

For example, students are routinely taught that Christopher Columbus "discovered" America and opened the New World to Western civilization. Every year in the United States, we celebrate Columbus Day in his honor. Yet this "truth" is really a social construction. Many Native American groups had been living rich and meaningful lives in this region long before Columbus and his associates sailed across the Atlantic Ocean from Europe. How might a young Native

social capital: Social networking connections, which can be a valuable source of information, such as a resource for job leads.

prejudice: A negative attitude about members of selected racial and ethnic groups.

stereotypes: Oversimplified sets of beliefs about a group of people.

discrimination: Behaviors, actions, or practices based on racial or ethnic preferences that have harmful impacts.

individual discrimination: One person exhibiting a negative behavior towards another person.

institutional discrimination: Social institutions, such as the government, religion, and education, create policies and practices that are systematically disadvantageous to certain groups.

We like to believe that things have changed, but prejudice and discrimination are still a part of American culture. How do minority parents prepare their children?

American feel about the celebration of European conquest and a decimation of her people? That might be her "truth."

It's important to recognize the diversity of experiences in the United States. Next, we briefly highlight some of its largest racial and ethnic groups—Hispanic, Black, Asian, and Native American/Alaska Native—so that we can better understand their marriage and family histories and current experiences in upcoming chapters.

Hispanic Families

The label *Hispanic* contains so many diverse ethnic groups that it may not make much sense to combine them into one category. Mexican Americans, Puerto Ricans, and Cuban Americans have little in common ethnically, except that they can trace their ancestry to Latin America or Spain. Their food, clothing, socioeconomic status, and even their language differ from one another. Yet the U.S. Census Bureau and other organizations often place these groups together for statistical purposes. As a group, Hispanics make up about 16 percent of the U.S. population, and are the largest and fastest growing minority group (Motel & Patten, 2013).

In the past, the growth in the Hispanic population was fueled primarily by immigration, but today only 11 percent of Hispanic children are first-generation (i.e., were born elsewhere and immigrated here; Fry & Passel, 2009). Instead, today's rapid growth of the Hispanic population is because of a high birth rate. Hispanic women have the highest fertility rate among all racial and ethnic groups at about 76 births per 1,000 women, compared to a national average of 63 births per 1,000 women (Hamilton, Martin, & Ventura, October 3, 2012). In other words, the population is now expanding not only because of immigration, but because of the increase in the number of children born to those immigrants.

This change poses many new and intriguing questions for the Hispanic population. How will the lives of the second generation differ from those of their parents? How are families changing? Does the second generation do better economically? Do they retain their Spanish language and Hispanic culture? How is the second generation changing the dominant U.S. culture?

Differences among first- and second- or third-generation Hispanics are very pronounced, and the future of U.S.-born children of Hispanic immigrants looks bright (Motel & Patten, 2013; Pew Research Center, February 7, 2013). Their earnings, college graduation rates, and rates of home ownership surpass those of their immigrant parents, and closely approximate the national average; in fact, second-generation Hispanics are more likely to be college graduates than are other Americans combined, as shown in Figure 2.6. Many see English as their primary language. Second- and third-generation Hispanics are also more likely to hold mainstream U.S. values than the more conservative and traditional values of their parents. For example, they're more likely to support a woman's right to choose an abortion, to see divorce as an acceptable solution to an unhappy marriage, and to believe that undocumented immigration hurts the economy.

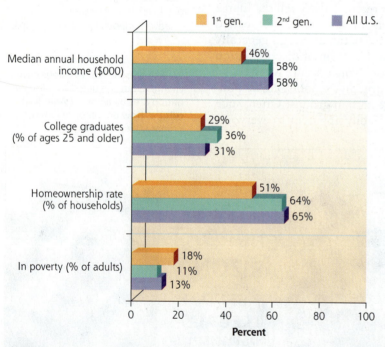

FIGURE 2.6

Comparing First Generation Immigrants, the Second Generation, and All U.S. Adults

Second-generation children from immigrant parents have assimilated well into American culture.
Source: Pew Research Center, February 7, 2013.

Second- and third-generation Hispanics are assimilating and may blend in more easily with Whites. However, many new Hispanics are still immigrating legally and illegally, so that assimilation may not be very visible to the casual observer.

Nonetheless, many second-generation Hispanics report personal experience with discrimination; in fact, they're more likely than their parents to believe that they have been discriminated against. Their incomes are still significantly below those of Whites, and many don't have health insurance (DeNavas-Walt, Proctor, & Smith, 2013).

Black Families

Blacks, made up primarily of African Americans, make up about 13 percent of the U.S. population. On average, Black families tend to be somewhat larger than those of Whites. Although married Black couples have a similar number of children to their married White counterparts (about two per family), Black female-headed households have more children than do their White counterparts (U.S. Census Bureau, September 13, 2012).

Read on MySocLab
Document: *African American Families: A Legacy of Vulnerability and Resistance*

Black families are also larger because they more likely contain extended family members, including grandparents, aunts, and uncles (Taylor et al., 2010). More than one in five Black children lives in an extended family, a rate nearly double that for Whites. Extended families can provide critical resources to family members, such as the ability to pool finances or share childcare. Yet, in the United States, where independence is highly valued, extended families are often denigrated as inferior or lacking in some way. However, extended families offer considerable strengths, and Blacks (and other minority groups) are more likely than Whites at all income levels to live in extended families, in part because they have a rich cultural heritage of drawing on and sharing aid with other family members (Hill, 2005).

Black families are also more likely than any other racial or ethnic group to be headed by females. Forty-eight percent of Black children live with single mothers, compared with 16 percent of White children, 25 percent of Hispanic children, and 13 percent of Asian children. Few children live with single fathers (about 4–5 percent), and the differences across racial and ethnic groups are small. Single-parent families have been maligned and referred to as *broken homes*. They are disadvantaged financially, and are overrepresented among those living in poverty; 31 percent of female-headed households are impoverished, compared to only 6 percent of married-couple families (DeNavas-Walt, Proctor, & Smith, 2013). But the problem with such a sweeping generalization is that there are different types of single-parent families with different circumstances—the situation of a pregnant teenager vastly differs from that of a 40-year-old single professional woman with children. And the number (and proportion) of teenage pregnancies is down (Hamilton, Martin, & Ventura, October 3, 2012).

Asian American Families

The term *Asian* or *Asian American* is a catchall for many different groups who had their origins with the early peoples of the Far East, Southeast Asia, or the Indian subcontinent. Often combined with these diverse groups are Pacific Islanders who have origins in Hawaii, Guam, Samoa, or other Pacific Islands. As is the case with Hispanics, these groups represent great diversity with respect to food, culture, language, and socioeconomic conditions. They came to the United States for different reasons, at different time periods, and had different opportunities for assimilation. Some, like Japanese or Chinese Americans, may have been in the United States for generations, whereas others, such as the Vietnamese or Cambodians, may have arrived as refugees from the Vietnam conflict in

TABLE 2.4 Educational Attainment by Race and Ethnicity: Ages 25 and Older

Asian Americans are more likely than other groups to go to college and earn an advanced degree.

	High School Graduate or More	Some College or More	Bachelor's Degree or More	Advanced Degree
White (Non-Hispanic)	90%	62%	34%	12%
Black	82%	51%	21%	8%
Asian	89%	69%	51%	20%
Hispanic	62%	35%	15%	4%

Source: U.S. Census Bureau, January 7, 2013.

the 1970s (Reeves & Bennett, 2003). It may make little sense to combine these groups, but, nonetheless, for statistical purposes most government agencies combine these groups into one large category labeled *Asian American.*

Asian Americans have been sometimes nicknamed a *model minority* because their families tend to be stable, their parents are highly educated and work in professional jobs, and they have the highest family incomes of any group, surpassing those of Whites. Although the rate of high school graduation is similar to other racial or ethnic groups, a much higher number of Asian Americans go to college and graduate, and then go on to graduate or professional school, as shown in Table 2.4 (U.S. Census Bureau, January 7, 2013). Asian American families also have the lowest rate of divorce, and their children are more likely to reside in married-couple households than are any other racial or ethnic group (DeNavas-Walt, Proctor, & Smith, 2013).

Many important factors help to explain why Asian American families are considered to be so successful (Farley, 2012; Schaefer, 2013). Many who came to the U.S. were from privileged social classes in their countries of origin; they were professionals with college degrees, and often had considerable wealth to invest in their employment or educational opportunities in the United States. Certainly, this is not the case for all Asian Americans, as some recent immigrants fleeing Vietnam, Cambodia, and Laos, for example, were from poor rural villages.

There are very few Asian Americans on television, and of these, they tend to play roles of well-educated professionals, illustrating their "model minority" status, such as B.D. Wong's role in *Law & Order: Special Victims Unit.*

Perhaps even more important is the long-standing emphasis on education, learning, and family primacy that characterizes Asian cultures. Individuality is deemphasized, and family well-being is of primary concern. Parents invest heavily in their children's education, and the children tend to take their studies seriously because they believe that their success bestows honor on the entire family.

Despite their overall positive record, it's important to recognize the diversity within Asian Americans (Zhou & Bankston, 2006). Not all Asian American families are doing well on social and economic indicators. In particular, some of the more recent immigrants lack the resources of other Asian Americans, and therefore have low incomes and high rates of poverty. For example, immigrants from Vietnam, Cambodia, and Laos have high poverty rates and have

Research on immigrant families often finds a generational gap between children who acculturate, or adapt, faster to the new society than slower-changing parents. My interviews with second-generation Asian Americans suggest another acculturation divide also occurs in many immigrant families.

The Study Unfolds: When I chose to study college-age children of Korean and Vietnamese immigrants, there was little research that captured the family lives of most of my students who are second-generation Asian Americans. I set out to do such a study so that these students would no longer be invisible in our course materials. Many students on my campus eagerly volunteered to participate, from whom I collected face-to-face interviews, asking them to describe their subjective experiences growing up in immigrant families, with a focus on their relationships with parents and siblings. More specific research questions emerged over the course of collecting the first 73 interviews (Pyke, 2000).

As expected, respondents often described acculturation gaps with parents who were more likely than their children to maintain traditional ethnic practices and experience difficulty learning English. I was intrigued, however, when several respondents described deep acculturative differences with a sibling. To learn more, I embarked on a new study of families with acculturative divides between siblings. I gathered a sample of 32 college-age Korean and Vietnamese Americans who had at least one sibling they regard as more ethnically traditional or more assimilated ("Americanized") than themselves. Respondents ranged in age from 18 to 26 and averaged 21 years; they were born in the United States or immigrated at an average of 5 years. Of the 32 respondents, 15 were the oldest sibling, 7 the youngest, and 10 had at least an older and younger sibling. During the face-to-face interviews, I asked them to describe the nature of their acculturation differences with their siblings, relationships with their parents and between their siblings and parents, and how they and their siblings were raised.

More Traditional Older Siblings: In 28 of the 32 families I studied, the more traditional sibling was older than the assimilated sibling, and typically the first-born child. I wondered if perhaps older siblings had spent more time in the parents' homeland prior to immigration and thus had more contact with the ethnic culture. However, on comparing the length of time siblings spent in the United States, I found little difference—both spent most, if not all, of their childhood in

the United States. Instead, it appears the practice in many Asian families of affording greater power and responsibility to the eldest child contributes to a sibling acculturative divide.

Asian Family Structure: Older siblings in the families studied commonly assisted parents with English translation, financial matters, household tasks, and caring for younger siblings. They were often expected to also care for and live with their parents as they aged. Parents closely monitored their older children in preparing them to serve as role models and disciplinarians to their younger siblings, and socialized them with greater intensity to the ethnic beliefs and practices they were expected to pass on. They tended to be more lax with and interacted less frequently with their younger children, who were under the care of older siblings. Older siblings thus interacted more with their parents and had a greater need to maintain fluency in their ethnic language, while younger siblings, who were assigned fewer responsibilities, were freer to assimilate. Indeed, many younger siblings could not speak Korean or Vietnamese well and depended on older siblings to translate conversations with their parents. As one respondent said, "My sister is kind of the connection, the middle person, between me and my parents. She kind of holds us together."

The big acculturative gap in these families was not between parents and children. Rather, the more ethnic older siblings and parents stood on one side of the acculturative divide, and the younger, more assimilated siblings on the other. Some assimilated children felt like outsiders in their family, like one young woman who said, "I know if I . . . tried to sit and talk with [my parents and sister], it wouldn't work. I wouldn't fit in."

WHAT DO YOU THINK?

1. Immigrant parents sometimes complain that American society influences their children to let go of ethnic beliefs and practices and become Americanized. How does the family structure of Asian immigrant families encourage younger siblings to adopt more Americanized ways?

2. This study finds that immigrant parents get much assistance from older children who maintain ethnic practices. In what ways might immigrant parents also derive benefits from having younger children who are more Americanized?

Source: Pyke, 2000; 2005.

among the highest rates of welfare use in the United States (Huang, 2002). Other families struggle with acculturation, with children adapting to the culture faster than parents, or even other siblings, as revealed in the feature box *Why Do Research? The Challenge of Acculturation* (Pyke, 2000, 2005).

Native American and Alaska Native Families

Native Americans and Alaska Natives make up about 1.5 percent of the U.S. population, at about 5.2 million people (Norris, Vines, & Hoeffel, 2012). They have origins with many of the early peoples of North, Central, and South

America who maintain tribal affiliation or community attachment. Three-quarters identify themselves as belonging to a specific tribe; Cherokee is the largest with nearly 900,000 members. Yup'ik is the largest Alaska Native tribe, with nearly 34,000 members. About one-third live on designated American Indian Areas, which include reservations and off-reservation land trusts; 2 percent live in Alaska Native Village Statistical Areas; and nearly two-thirds live outside tribal areas (Ogunwole, 2006). The largest concentration of Native Americans and Alaska Natives is in the western United States. Among places of 100,000 or more population in 2010, Anchorage, Alaska, had the greatest proportion (12 percent) of American Indians and Alaska Natives alone or in combination. Other places with large proportions of American Indians and Alaska Natives were Tulsa, Oklahoma (9 percent); Norman, Oklahoma (8 percent); Oklahoma City, Oklahoma (6 percent); and Billings, Montana (6 percent) (Norris, Vines, & Hoeffel, 2012).

About three-quarters of Native American and Alaska Native households are family households, which is significantly higher than for other racial or ethnic groups. About a third of the Native American and Alaska Native population is under age 18, compared to 26 percent in the total population, and the median age is seven years younger, revealing their higher than average birth rates (U.S. Census Bureau, December 16, 2009).

Extended families are the cornerstone of Native American family life, and children enjoy close relationships with their grandparents, particularly grandmothers. More than half of Native Americans and Alaska Natives live with their grandchildren (U.S. Census Bureau, 2006). Relatives share a strong ethic of social, emotional, and financial support, and relationships are less rigid than in other groups—aunts and uncles often refer to their nieces and nephews as "daughters" or "sons" and families may live together temporarily or permanently. Fifty-six percent of Native Americans or Alaska Natives age 30 and older live with their grandchildren (U.S. Census Bureau, October 15, 2009). They provide hands-on care to children and families, which is particularly helpful to the 28 percent of single-parent families—twice the national average. Kinship is also an important component of political organization because of the ties it establishes to a specific tribe.

Native American and Alaska Native elders have traditionally held high status in their families and communities, reinforcing their cultural identity. Although the value of this to younger generations has waxed and waned, there has been a resurgence in recognizing the importance of Native American and Alaska Native spirituality, language, values, food, and cultural traditions. Eighteen percent report speaking a language other than English "very well," compared to only 10 percent of the general population (Ogunwole, 2006). Eighty percent of parents in Anchorage, Alaska want their children in an Alaska Native language immersion program, and 85 percent want to learn along with their children (Alaska Native Heritage Center, 2011).

Native American families do face many challenges. Infant mortality rates are comparatively high and life expectancy is low. Unemployment and poverty rates are high, and many live in substandard housing (U.S. Census Bureau, December 16, 2009). For example, between 10 percent and 20 percent of housing on reservations lacks basic indoor plumbing. Smoking and alcoholism rates are high among Native Americans and Alaska Natives, as are violence and suicide (National Center for Health Statistics, 2009). About one in three American Indian or Alaska Native women have been raped or experienced an attempted rape (Williams, May 22, 2012). Despite these difficulties, tribal leaders have implemented

extended families: Families that include not only parents and children, but also other family members, such as grandparents, uncles, aunts, or cousins.

All people have a racial and ethnic background, although Whites have the privilege of rarely thinking about this. How might these differences influence the Pitt-Jolie family?

numerous strategies to improve social and economic conditions. For example, highly profitable (and controversial) gambling establishments fund critically needed education programs and social services, create jobs, and provide individual tribal members with cash stipends that have improved their economic circumstances considerably.

Interracial and Interethnic Families

So far, we have discussed race and ethnicity as though they are discrete categories, but millions of people in the United States have a clear and unequivocal connection to two or more racial or ethnic groups. As taboos against interracial or interethnic marriage begin to break down, the growth in the number of children with multiple races or ethnicities is inevitable.

Parents of multiracial or multiethnic children continue to face issues that other parents don't experience (Smith & Hattery, 2009). For example, when both parents are White, despite good intentions, they may know very little about how prejudice and discrimination really operate, or how it feels to be discriminated against. But in a multiracial or multiethnic family, the White parent must address these issues head on because his or her spouse and children may likely have been affected by prejudice and discrimination (Rockquemore & Laszloffy, 2005). Recent books speak to these issues and the challenges of forming a multiracial identity, including President Barack Obama's *Dreams from My Father: A Story of Race and Inheritance* (Obama, 2007). Table 2.5 reviews some important tips to parents raising children in an interracial or interethnic family.

We all have a race and an ethnicity, whether we think a great deal or only rarely about these aspects of ourselves. Each group has a rich history and culture and draws on them in meaningful ways to create relevant family structures and relationships. We will see more specific examples of this throughout the following chapters. However, there is another important aspect of our lives worthy of discussion here because it also powerfully shapes our families and intimate relationships. We now turn to a discussion of social class.

Describe your racial or ethnic background. Can you provide some examples of the ways in which your background has influenced your life? Why do you think that Whites have the privilege of rarely thinking about race or ethnic issues?

TABLE 2.5   **Tips for Interracial or Interethnic Families**

Identify yourselves. All people are a combination of many identity facets: race, gender, national origin, religion, sexual preference, personality, style, their position in any given relationship, etc. You may choose not to use race as your primary identifying factor, or your family's mixed heritage may be a great source of pride. Help children see that who they are is much more than their race and encourage them to cherish every aspect of who they are.

Explore and honor your family's multiple heritages and cultures. Celebrate holidays, foods, and customs from all of your backgrounds, and try others that interest you. If you and your partner or spouse speak different languages, speak both of them regularly in your home.

Educate your children about the negative comments and racial barriers they will most certainly have to face. Acknowledge that these times can be terribly difficult and frustrating. Help your children prepare how to respond. Encourage them to share your feelings with you. Share experiences you've had and how you dealt with them. Role play.

Help your children develop resilient self-esteem. Praise their efforts, their good choices and their character traits that you love. Help them learn to value what makes them who they are so that they love themselves and can spring back more easily from adversity they will face.

Honor diversity in others. Learn about other cultures and races. Study other countries together and watch travel shows and specials on PBS. Check out picture books and National Geographic from your library. Help your children learn about the diversity of the world they live in and teach them to respect those that are different from them—and to honor the things they have in common.

Consider living in a diverse community. The lessons above may be easier for your children to learn in a place where race isn't the primary identifier of people. You'll also likely have an easier time finding multicultural events and activities, books, and other resources your family can enjoy.

Source: The Learning Community, 2011. "Tips for Parents: Interracial Families." Retrieved 6 December 2013. (www.thelearningcommunity.us/resources-by-format/tips-for-parents/diverse-families/interracial-families.aspx)

Read on **MySocLab**
Document: *Social Class Matters*

social class: A social position based primarily on income and wealth, but occupational prestige and educational level may be relevant as well.

socioeconomic status (SES): Some combination of education, occupation, and income.

Social Class

While social class is less visible than race, ethnicity, or sex, we are probably all aware that social class can have a significant impact on our lives. Class is an important focus of such well-known novels as *The Great Gatsby* (Fitzgerald, 1925, reprinted 1999), which focused on the lives of the wealthy, or *The Grapes of Wrath* (Steinbeck, 1939, reprinted 2002), which portrayed the desperate lives of sharecroppers from Oklahoma who migrated to California to escape the ravages of the Dust Bowl.

Today, we are bombarded by images of the rich and famous cavorting in Hollywood, and by the poor in the most desperate of situations. The gap between the rich and poor continues to widen, and New Mexico, Arizona, California, and Georgia can "boast" the greatest inequality (Center on Budget and Policy Priorities, November 15, 2012). Yet, in the United States social class is often downplayed or denied (Lareau & Conley, 2008), but you know that where you come from matters. Social class is not just about money; it encompasses an entire way of seeing and experiencing the world (Doob, 2013; Eitzen & Smith, 2009; Hurst, 2013; Weininger & Lareau, 2009). Social class shapes your worldview and influences those so-called personal choices you make. Think back to Becca in the opening vignette. How do you think that poverty influenced her sense of self and her self-esteem? And didn't these, in turn, affect some of her choices?

Approaches to Measuring Social Class

Social class is an abstract concept compared to sex, race, or ethnicity because we cannot always identify social classes or who are members of these classes. Social classes are based most obviously on income and wealth, but also on other resources, such as educational level and occupational prestige. Social class boundaries in the United States are theoretically open, so people who gain schooling, skills, or income may experience a change in their social class position; however, there is much less movement across social classes than people imagine (Doob, 2013; Hurst, 2013; Lareau & Conley, 2008).

Today, researchers usually define *class* as some combination of education, occupation, and income, and we sometimes call this combination **socioeconomic status**, or **SES**. Dennis Gilbert and Joseph A. Kahl (1993) developed a widely used model of social class based on SES that includes six categories: (1) the upper class; (2) the upper middle class; (3) the middle class; (4) the working class; (5) the working poor; and (6) the underclass.

THE UPPER CLASS The upper class is the wealthiest and most powerful social class in the United States and consists of only about 3 percent to 5 percent of the population. Although few in number, its members have a tremendous influence on the economy and the rest of society, often sitting on boards of major corporations or being active in politics. They may have very high incomes of more than $1 million per year. However, more important than income, the upper class sustains substantial wealth.

Some upper-class families, nicknamed *Old Money* or *Bluebloods,* have been wealthy for generations, such as the Kennedys, Bushes, and Hiltons. They may belong to the exclusive *Social Register,* an annual listing of elites that has been published since the late 1800s, and may prefer to socialize only with their peers. There is very little mixing with other social classes; private schools and the Debutante Ball, which brings unmarried young men and women together to meet each other, carefully control socializing.

Other members of the upper class, sometimes nicknamed *New Money,* have acquired their great wealth within one generation and therefore lack the prestige of the Bluebloods. The media mogul Oprah Winfrey and Microsoft founder Bill

Gates are examples, and many people see them as having fulfilled the "American dream."

THE UPPER MIDDLE CLASS   Approximately 15 percent to 20 percent of the U.S. population is categorized as *upper middle class*. Members of the upper middle class tend to be highly educated professionals, including physicians, dentists, lawyers, college professors, and business executives. Household income may be in the range of $100,000 to $200,000, possibly more if both people in a couple are employed. These families generally have accumulated some wealth, have nice homes in well-respected neighborhoods, and play important roles in local political affairs. They strongly value education, and a large majority of their children go on to college and graduate school, often at private institutions.

THE MIDDLE CLASS   Most people say they are *middle class*, but this is not exactly true. With incomes of about $40,000 to $100,000 a year, only 40 percent are really middle class. The median household income is little more than $50,000 for all households, $74,000 for married couples, and $34,000 for female-headed households (DeNavas-Walt, Proctor, & Smith, 2013).

The middle class have a distinctive set of values, and prioritize security at home and at work as being very important (Lopez-Calva, Rigolini, & Torche, 2012; Taylor et al., 2008). College is valued by the middle class, and many work in white-collar jobs that require a college degree, such as teaching, nursing, or business, whereas others may be in highly skilled blue-collar jobs, such as electronics or construction. Traditionally, middle-class jobs have been secure and provided a variety of opportunities for advancement; however, with corporate downsizing and a generally rising cost of living, many middle-class families find their lifestyles tenuous. For example, many young middle-class families have difficulty purchasing their first home, and older middle-class families find that saving for both retirement and their children's college stretches their budget beyond its means.

THE WORKING CLASS   The term *working class* is somewhat misleading, because just about all adults work; therefore, some people refer to this group as the *lower middle class*. They earn less than middle-class families, approximately $20,000 to $40,000. About 20 percent of the U.S. population falls into this group. Jobs may include factory and custodial work and semiskilled labor. Members of the working class report less satisfaction in their jobs than do those in higher social classes, as their jobs are often more routine and require following specific directions rather than exercising creativity (Kohn, 1977, 2006). Family members face insecurity (Yates, 2009); they must plan carefully to pay their monthly bills on time, as unexpected doctor bills or car repair bills can wreak havoc on the family budget. Working-class families tend to live in modest neighborhoods, and many cannot afford to buy their own home. They may have financial difficulty helping their children attend college.

THE WORKING POOR   The working poor, making up about 15 percent of the population, are employed in minimum- or near-minimum-wage jobs, such as service work in the fast-food or retail industry (Ehrenreich, 2001; Shipler, 2004). Their wages hover near or only slightly above the poverty line, up to about $20,000 a year. Many workers receive no fringe benefits such as health insurance or sick pay, and they may have nonstandard schedules—switching between evening and day shifts, for instance (Presser, 2003; Seccombe, 2014). The working poor are very vulnerable, and unemployment is not uncommon. They live month-to-month and are unable to save money for the unforeseen, yet sometimes inevitable, emergency. Single mothers and their children are overrepresented among the working poor.

THE UNDERCLASS This group, perhaps 3 percent to 5 percent of the population, is extremely poor and often unemployed (Gilbert & Kahl, 1993). There are many reasons people may become destitute (Jasinski, Wesely, Wright, & Mustaine, 2010; Liebow, 1995). Some members cannot work because of disability, mental problems, or age; others face difficult employment prospects because they lack education and job skills. Many reside in the inner cities, where job prospects are few because factories and businesses have moved across town or overseas. Some receive assistance from governmental programs such as homeless shelters. Some beg for spare change or hold up a "Will work for food" sign. Their circumstances are bleak and may be exacerbated by racial or ethnic discrimination. Sociologist William Julius Wilson (Wilson, 1987) refers to these individuals as a *truly disadvantaged underclass.*

How Does Social Class Affect Our Family and Close Relationships?

Watch on MySocLab
Video: *Susan Ostrander: Understanding Social Class*

Just as with sex, race, and ethnicity, social class influences many aspects of family life. As we'll see throughout this text, social class influences the following:

- our *likelihood of being born* in the first place, because birth rates are higher in lower classes
- our *health,* including our chances of surviving the first year of life, and our overall life expectancy, which is dramatically lower among lower-income groups
- our *gender expectations,* with egalitarian roles more likely in the middle- and upper-middle-class groups, whereas upper and lower classes are more polarized
- the *values our parents socialize in us,* with working-class parents more likely to value conformity and obedience to authority, whereas middle- and upper-middle-class parents tend to value creativity and self-direction in their children
- our likelihood of *attending and graduating from college,* with only part of the difference being the result of finances per se, and much of the remainder the result of the different value afforded to college education among classes
- our *dating and premarital sexual expectations* and behavior, with teen girls from poorer households more likely to experience a nonmarital pregnancy and to have a child outside marriage
- our *likelihood of marriage and age at first marriage,* with upper-middle-class women less likely to marry than other groups, and marrying at later ages
- our *hobbies and pastimes,* with income shaping the way in which we view leisure and the opportunities we have to participate in leisure activities
- the types of *stresses we experience and coping mechanisms we use,* with wealthier individuals having a wider range of coping strategies, such as travel, shopping, or access to athletic clubs, whereas lower-income individuals may resort to more immediate gratification, such as smoking or overeating

Consider the following two profiles, shown in the *Diversity in Families* feature box. Can you see how social class influenced the life courses of these two young men?

SOCIAL MOBILITY AND THE LACK OF IT Tommy Johnson and Randall Simmons, as shown in the *Diversity in Families* box, are two young men who live in large metropolitan areas and could not lead more different lives. Although both work long hours and are highly motivated, the social class in which each

How does a macro-level issue such as family income affect our micro-level choices and experiences? Let's take a look at the profiles of Tommy Johnson and Randall Simmons.

PROFILE 1

Name: Tommy Johnson

Age: 29

Father's Occupation: Janitor

Mother's Occupation: Nurse's Aide

Community when Growing Up: Miami, Florida

Principal Caretakers when a Child: Grandmother, Neighbor, Older Sister

Education: Large public elementary and secondary schools in inner-city Miami. Emphasis on rote learning of basic skills. Security guards patrolled school. Occasional church camp during the summer. Classmates included sons and daughters of domestics, sales clerks, factory workers, service workers.

Family Activities When a Child: Church, television, visiting family members.

First Job: Age 16, short-order cook at a fast-food restaurant in Miami.

Hobbies: Working on cars

College: Attended nearby community college. Quit after two semesters to take a full-time job.

First Full-time Job: Age 19. Sales clerk at auto parts store in Miami.

Current Position: Muffler installer at a national chain shop devoted to installing mufflers and brakes. Has been with the company for three years. Works Tuesday through Saturday, with occasional overtime. Annual earnings approximate $29,000 a year.

Marital Status: Married at age 20. Wife is employed part-time, 20 hours per week as a sales clerk in a discount department store. Annual earnings approximately $9,000 a year. Three children ages 7, 5, and 2.

Family Activities: Bowling, church, watching television, city league baseball, visiting relatives

Current Residence: Owns a small three-bedroom mobile home in a trailer park in a lower-income Miami suburb. Comfortably furnished with older and well-worn furniture and appliances. Has two cars, a Ford Escort and a minivan, both over seven years old.

Goals: To someday manage his own auto parts store, send children to vocational college to learn a "good trade," and be a good father and provider to his family.

PROFILE 2

Name: Randall Simmons

Age: 29

Father's Occupation: Real Estate Attorney

Mother's Occupation: Homemaker and Community Volunteer

Principal Caretakers when a Child: Mother and governess

Community when Growing Up: Beverly Hills, California

Education: Private elementary and secondary schools devoted to liberal and creative arts. Small student–teacher ratio. Supplemental tutoring in French, piano, clarinet. Fellow students are the sons and daughters of business leaders, physicians, investment bankers, and ambassadors. Spent summers in camps devoted to educational enrichment, including athletics and horseback riding.

Family Activities as a Child: Riding horses, theater, summer vacations in Europe, winter vacations at a condo in the Caribbean. Parents made generous donations to the performing arts community, and were granted season tickets for the family to music and dance events at the community theater.

Hobbies: Riding horses (owns two horses, boarded approximately 35 miles from home), golf, gourmet cooking

College Attended: Bachelor of Arts degree in small, elite private college. Active in a campus fraternity and the college debate team. Attended law school at Harvard University, where father and uncle are alumni.

First Full-time Job: Age 26. Attorney in large and prestigious law firm in West Los Angeles.

Current Job and Earnings: Attorney in the same law firm. Works approximately 50 hours per week. Annual salary approximates $200,000 a year. Also receives dividends of $150,000 a year from stocks and trust funds established by his wife's parents.

Marital Status: Married at age 27. Wife is a community volunteer. She has a Bachelor of Arts degree in Music from the same college as Randall. No children, but would like to have a baby within two or three years. Ideal family size is three children.

Family Activities: International travel, theater, riding horses, golf at the country club

Current Residence: 3,000-square-foot home in Pacific Palisades area of Los Angeles, located five blocks from a private beach on the Pacific Ocean. Parents helped with the down payment. Interior was professionally designed and furnished. Family has two cars, a late-model BMW and a new Mercedes Benz.

Goals: To make partner in law firm where he is currently employed within next 5 to 7 years.

WHAT DO YOU THINK?

1. How does your life compare to those of Tommy Johnson and Randall Simmons? Whose life is closer to yours? Can you think of ways in which income has specifically shaped your personal choices and behaviors?
2. In a country as "free" and open as the United States, why does income still shape our choices and behaviors?

There are two very different Americas—one for the wealthy and one for the poor. Think about the different opportunities, challenges, and constraints that children in each group face.

social mobility: Movement from one social class to another.

was born has substantially shaped opportunities, goals, and achievements. Although theoretically people in the United States can be anything they want to be, in reality, there is little upward **social mobility,** or movement from one social class to another. People usually live out their lives in the same social class in which they are born because of the norms they learn and the constraints and privileges they experience (Hurst, 2013).

If Randall had been born poor, his likelihood of going to law school would certainly be diminished. He would be more likely to have attended poorly funded and inferior public elementary and secondary schools. Chances are, Randall would have met few people who went to college, and even fewer people who went to law school—he would not have considered law school to be a real opportunity.

But let's take this example further. Had Randall been born an upper-class *female*, her life would probably also be different. Her family may have steered her to other, more "feminine" pursuits associated with the upper class instead of law. Perhaps she would be the non-employed wife of a lawyer, rather than a lawyer herself. Or perhaps she would be an elementary school teacher at a private school, earning about 15 percent of Randall's salary. What if Randall had been born the daughter of farm workers? What would her options probably look like as a working-class Hispanic girl?

Why would Randall's chances of being a successful lawyer be so different given these various scenarios? With financial aid available to all students, we must look beyond sheer financial considerations. Many women, ethnic and racial minority groups, and those within the lower social classes are discouraged from attaining these goals by family, peers, and school counselors. For example, women may actively (or more subtly) be discouraged from graduate or professional school because of fears that a career will interfere with their ability to raise a family. When we add racial discrimination or social class barriers such as having fewer role models or inadequate preparation at poor secondary schools, it's not surprising that entering classes in professional schools tend to reflect the background of Randall Simmons rather than that of Tommy Johnson (Eitzen & Smith, 2009; Lareau, 2003; Lareau & Conley, 2008).

Let's now look at the bottom of the social class scale—poverty. Poverty touches the lives of millions of adults and children, all with serious consequences.

Identify what social class you were born into—what evidence do you have to help you decide? How has your social class shaped your world-view, your opportunities, your choices, and your constraints? In what social class do you think you will be for most of your adulthood? If these classes are different, how will this mobility be possible?

Poverty

Dee is a single mother who left an abusive marriage to begin anew with her 11-year-old daughter. She works the evening shift to support the two of them while her daughter stays home alone. Kate was a middle-class woman who left her husband after his infidelity. She now lives in a small, seedy apartment, trying to support herself and her two young children on a low-paying job without child support. Robert and Maria are a happily married couple who face a crisis because Robert's serious illness caused him to lose his job, cutting off the primary source of support for them and their four children. What do these three families have in common? They're all poor (Seccombe, 2007).

Poverty comes in many shapes, sizes, and colors—big families, small families, two-parent families, single-parent families, White families, and minority families—all have the potential to slip into poverty for a month, a year, or a lifetime (Edin & Kissane, 2010). In fact, by age 65, more than half of us will likely have spent at least one year of our adulthood in poverty (Rank, 2009).

The Social Security Administration established the official *poverty threshold* (sometimes called the *poverty line*) in 1964 as a way to measure the number of people living in poverty (Orshansky, 1965). Survey data in the early 1960s indicated that families spent approximately one-third of their income on food. Therefore, the poverty line was calculated from the estimated annual costs of a minimal food budget designed by the U.S. Department of Agriculture (USDA), which we then multiply by three. This food budget parallels the current "Thrifty Food Plan," the least expensive food plan developed by the USDA (USDA, February 2012). It allows a family of four with two children under age 12 only $147 a week for food. Compare this to the $241 allowed weekly for this same family under the "moderate plan" or $292 allowed weekly under the "liberal plan" (Center for Nutrition Policy and Promotion, 2012). The Thrifty Plan is far below the amount most middle-class families spend on food. Individuals or families with annual incomes below this established threshold of "food costs multiplied by three" are counted as "poor." The poverty threshold varies by family size (and a few other features), and is revised yearly based on inflationary changes in the Consumer Price Index. In 2012, the average poverty thresholds were $17,916 for a family of three and $23,021 for a family of four (DeNavas-Walt, Proctor, & Smith, 2013), as shown in Table 2.6. Poverty guidelines in Alaska and Hawaii were slightly higher.

The quick budgeting exercise shown in the *Policy and You: From Macro to Micro* boxed feature (p. 66) asks you to think about how much money it really takes to live. It shows that the poverty thresholds are inadequate to meet basic needs.

Who Is Poor?

About 47 million people, or 15 percent of the U.S. population, lived in poverty in 2012. Twenty-two percent of children—more than one in five—live in poverty (DeNavas-Walt, Proctor, & Smith, 2013). Table 2.7 shows which groups of people are most likely to be poor.

Consequences of Poverty

Poor families face a higher degree of stress, disorganization, and other problems in their lives. Poverty is difficult

TABLE 2.6	Average Poverty Thresholds by Size of Family (2012)
Do you think a family could easily live on a poverty-level budget?	
Persons in Family	**Poverty Threshold**
1	$11,720
2	14,937
3	18,284
4	23,492
5	27,827
6	31,471
7	35,743
8	39,688
9+	47,297

Source: DeNavas-Walt, Proctor, & Smith, 2013.

People and Families in Poverty by Selected Characteristics, 2012

...ren, Blacks, Hispanics, and female-headed ...useholds are most vulnerable.

Total U.S. Population	15%
Age	
Children Under 18	22%
18–64	14%
65+	9%
Race	
White (Non-Hispanic)	10%
Black	27%
Asian and Pacific Islander	12%
Hispanic	25%
Family Type	
Married Couple	6%
Female-Headed	31%
Male-Headed	16%

Source: DeNavas-Walt, Proctor, & Smith, 2013.

food insecurity: A lack of available nourishing food on a regular basis

for everyone, but weighs especially heavily on children's physical, social, and emotional health (National Center for Health Statistics, December 2012). For this reason, let's first look at the consequences of poverty on children.

Poor children exhibit more antisocial behavior and are more likely to drop out of school or become teenage parents, are more likely to suffer from depression, and are in poorer health (Bloom, Cohen, & Freeman, 2012). Naturally, not all poor children suffer these outcomes; many poor children are the models of success. However, they're more likely than other children to face a host of serious challenges. How does poverty exert its influence? Figure 2.7 (p. 65) summarizes the pathways through which poverty hurts children (Seccombe, 2007). Poverty contributes to

- inadequate health and nutrition
- lower-quality home environment
- parental stress and mental health problems
- fewer resources for learning
- housing problems
- poor-quality neighborhoods

INADEQUATE HEALTH AND NUTRITION Research is clear about the relationship between poverty and health. Poverty puts the health of children at risk in many ways, including the likelihood of having low birth weight, which in turn increases chances of serious chronic and acute illness, along with emotional and behavioral problems (Bloom, Cohen, & Freeman, 2012; Federal Interagency Forum on Child and Family Statistics, 2012). Poor children also may receive inadequate food and nutrition. At some point, nearly 15 percent of households experienced **food insecurity,** defined by the USDA as not having enough nourishing food available on a regular basis (Coleman-Jensen, Nord, Andrews, & Carlson, 2012). Twenty-one percent of households with children are food insecure. Children suffer the immediate pain of hunger and the longer-term consequences of malnutrition. They run the risk of more frequent colds, ear infections, and other infectious diseases; impaired brain function; stunted growth; and are more vulnerable to lead and other environmental toxins.

QUALITY OF THE HOME ENVIRONMENT Warm and loving relationships with parents, in conjunction with rich opportunities for learning, help children thrive. The Home Observation of the Measurement of the Environment (HOME) is a widely used interview and observation tool assessing parent–child interaction. HOME shows that poverty has a significant negative effect on the quality and stimulation of the home environment (Crosnoe, 2010; Yeung, Linver, & Brooks-Gunn, 2002). One study of the linguistic capabilities of young children found that poor children on welfare who were between the ages of 13 and 36 months hear only half as many words per hour as the average working-class child, and less than one-third the average of a typical child in a professional family (Children's Defense Fund, 2005). Obviously, parents cannot teach their children what they themselves do not know. There are other differences as well. For example, poor parents are less nurturing and more authoritarian, and they use more inconsistent and harsh physical discipline.

PARENTAL STRESS AND MENTAL HEALTH What else about an impoverished family environment increases the likelihood of negative outcomes for children? Parents who are living in poverty face a high level of stress, depression, and mental health problems related to their situation. For example, high levels of male unemployment are significantly associated with child abuse and deprivation. Although child abuse occurs in many different type of households, poor children have a higher probability of being abused, neglected, and more severely injured by abuse than do children in more affluent households (Cancian, Slack, & Yang, 2010; National Center for Health Statistics, 2012).

FEWER RESOURCES FOR LEARNING On average, poor children have fewer resources for learning in the home, including books and educational toys. Therefore, high-quality childcare and preschool programs become very important to helping them overcome the disadvantages in their home environment. Unfortunately, childcare and preschool are very expensive, as you will see in Chapter 10, and fewer subsidized spots are available. Full-time childcare can easily cost more than $10,000 per year for each child (Childcare Aware of America, 2012; National Association of Child Care Resource & Referral Agencies, 2011). Consequently, many poor children start school academically behind their peers, a disadvantage that often continues throughout life. Generally, poor children receive lower grades and lower scores on standardized tests, they are less likely to finish high school, and are less likely to attend or graduate from college than are other children (Federal Interagency Forum on Child and Family Statistics, 2012).

HOUSING PROBLEMS According to the Department of Housing and Urban Development, the 2013 fair market rent for a two-bedroom apartment is $925 in Phoenix, $966 in Chicago, and $1,122 in Miami (U.S. Department of Housing and Urban Development, 2013). Poor families cannot afford to pay this rent, and so they often live in housing that may lack proper cooking, heating, or sanitation facilities. Some poor families are homeless, and a survey of 25 U.S. cities found that most of these cities reported a rise in homelessness (U.S. Conference of Mayors, December 2012).

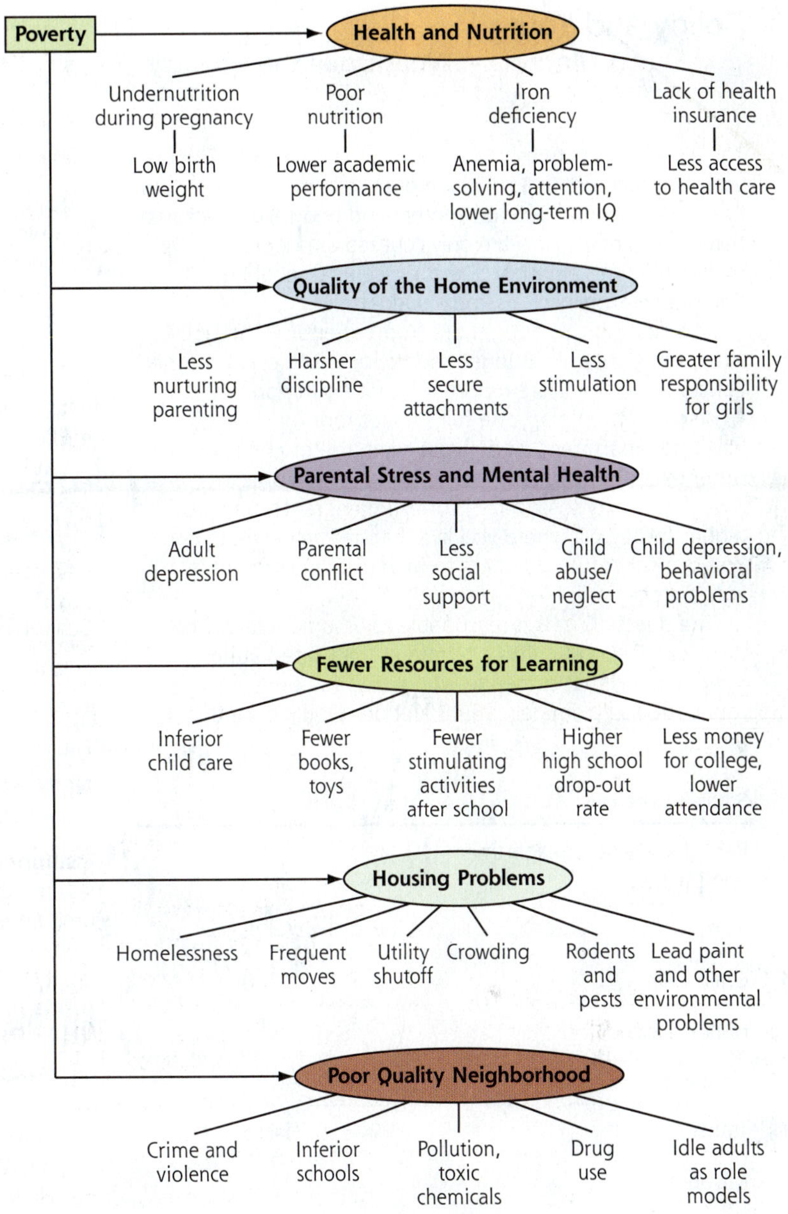

POOR-QUALITY NEIGHBORHOODS Poor children are increasingly isolated from the non-poor in their communities and live in inner cities where violence, crime, truancy, loitering, and a sense of despair predominate (Massey & Denton, 1993; O'Hare, 1995; Wilkenfeld, Moore, & Lippman, 2008). Guns kill more than 1,500 children and teens each year, and homicide is the third leading cause of death among children ages 1 to 4, the fifth leading cause among children ages 5 to 14, and the second leading cause among teens ages 15 to 19. It is the leading cause of death among young Blacks ages 15 to 34 (Children's Defense Fund, 2009; Nationwide Children's Hospital, 2013).

FIGURE 2.7

Pathways from Poverty to Adverse Child Outcomes

Poverty has many adverse effects on children.
Sources: Adapted from Children's Defense Fund 1994; Brooks-Gunn and Duncan 1997, from Seccombe, Families in Poverty, 1e. © 2007. Allyn & Bacon.

The 2011 poverty threshold for a family of three is $17,916 a year, which comes to $1,493 a month. This means that a family of three people—a single mother and two children, or two parents and one child—are only counted as poor if they live on less than this amount. Does this seem reasonable? Let's find out by examining a sample budget.

The costs in this budget are from reports by the USDA, HUD, the Center on Budget and Policy Priorities, and other consumer expenditure reports estimating the price of a "low-cost" food plan, the fair market rent for a two-bedroom apartment, and a cost estimate for childcare and other expenditures. The cost of living varies somewhat from one community to another; for example, rents may be higher (or lower) where you live than in the estimate here. You can substitute numbers from your own community if you prefer.

The question is: Is it reasonable to assume a family of three can live on $1,493 a month in the United States? Keep in mind that someone who works full-time, year round, at approximately $8.48 an hour would earn this amount.

Sample Expenses

Rent (two-bedroom apartment and utilities):	$800
Food:	$425
Child Care:	$620
Health Care:	$65
Clothing:	$60
Transportation:	$416
Miscellaneous:	$100
TOTAL:	**$2,486/month, or $29,832/ year before taxes**

Already we have gone over budget. How can we cut back?

- Find a cheaper apartment, or one in a less desirable part of town? Don't forget that children live here.
- Lower the utility bill by keeping the house colder? This is one reason why poor children are sick more often.
- Eliminate the telephone? This could be dangerous in an emergency.
- Cut back on toiletries? Toilet paper, shampoo, and tampons are basic needs.
- Eliminate car maintenance? How will the family get to work, school, or run errands? A bus system may not be available or feasible with children.

We are over budget and we have not yet included other basic needs for this family:

School Supplies:	$25
Health Insurance:	$300
Entertainment:	$100
Laundry:	$25
NEW TOTAL:	**$2,936/month, or $35,232/ year before taxes**

Assumption Even this revised budget assumes the family already has an established household. There is no money included to buy furniture, a car, or household items like towels or dishes. In other words, even $2,936 a month is unrealistically low. As you can see, the poverty line is an inadequate measure of poverty.

WHAT DO YOU THINK?

1. If the poverty line is as inadequate as it appears, why doesn't the federal government increase it to a more realistic level? What should the poverty line be based on? What are the implications of changing it?
2. How can a family make ends meet if a parent earns poverty-level wages?

Source: Adapted and updated from Seccombe, 2007.

The effects of poverty on the lives of children are clear; however, the potentially harmful health effects of poverty on adults are also numerous. For example, poor adults have significantly higher morbidity (sickness) and lower life expectancy than other adults (National Center for Health Statistics, 2012). They are more likely to work in dangerous occupations and live in unsafe neighborhoods, and their homes are more likely to be located near toxic sites.

One issue with far-reaching consequences for families is that poor men and women are less likely to marry (Edin & Kefalas, 2005; White & Rogers, 2000). Poverty undermines economic security and makes men less attractive marriage partners. For example, Wilson suggests that the key factor in explaining the falling marriage rate among inner-city Blacks is their declining employment opportunities as jobs move to the suburbs or overseas (Wilson, 1987, 1996).

Why does poverty persist? Do your reasons tend to focus more on micro or macro explanations? What kinds of programs do you think are really needed to end poverty? What are you doing today to ensure that you are not poor in the future? Do you feel that you can avoid poverty?

Poverty also undermines marital stability and leads to greater marital conflict; it increases stress or depression, which can then lead to anger, resentment, and hostility between partners, and difficulties among children (Conger & Conger, 2008; Cui, Donnellan, & Conger, 2007; Scaramella, Neppl, Ontai, & Conger, 2008).

The Intersections of Sex, Gender, Race, Ethnicity, and Class

2.6 Analyze the intersections of sex, gender, race, ethnicity, and class

Question That Matters

2.13 Why are the intersections of sex, gender, race, ethnicity, and class important?

It is important to remember that we are each made up of many characteristics. We aren't simply male or female, Asian American or Hispanic, rich or poor. Our statuses intersect with one another (Dill & Zambrana, 2009; Lobo, Talbot, & Morris, 2010; Segal & Martinez, 2007). For example, a person may be a White working-class female, a Japanese American upper-class male, a Cuban middle-class male, a White upper-class female, or any number of other racial, ethnic, gender, sex, and class combinations. We have multiple statuses, and they all interact to shape our lives. We may be gay or lesbian. We may also be elderly. We may have a developmental disability. We are made up of all these statuses and more.

A study by family scholar Charlotte Olsen (1996) analyzed the opinions of Black adolescent women about how their gender, race, and class related to their lives. Their lives reflected the fact that they were not simply "Black" or "women," but reflected the unique experiences associated with these multiple statuses. These young women, although acutely aware of times they had been discriminated against based on race, also believed they had experienced male domination and saw both as potential obstacles to achieving their own life goals. They reported many instances of prejudice and discrimination because of both their race and their sex. These included challenges associated with employment and in finding a college-educated, middle-class Black husband, because far fewer Black men finish high school or go to college than do Black women. Thus, race, class, and sex are interwoven, and together they shape the nuances of our lives (Dill & Zambrana, 2009; Doob, 2013).

Bringing It Full Circle

Sex and gender, race and ethnicity, and social class, individually and together, shape a constellation of privileges and constraints that can affect our goals, opportunities, and choices. This chapter introduces these critical concepts. Throughout the remainder of the text, you'll see how they influence the family structure we are born into, the way our parents raise us, our choices and opportunities in intimate relationships, how we parent, and how we age. These statuses shape both us and the way others respond to us. As we saw in the opening vignette, Becca, a young woman born into poverty, violence, and addiction, is trying to beat the odds. She shows us vividly that social and emotional obstacles are real, but that we can also react to these obstacles. We are not simply passive recipients of our social structure.

Now that you have finished the chapter and have a greater understanding of these concepts, let's reflect on a few questions:

- What are some of the likely consequences of Becca's impoverished childhood? How did her childhood affect her adulthood?

- How do gender, race, ethnicity, and social class interact to influence Becca's situation?
- What pathways from poverty do you see in Becca's story?
- What are you doing today to ensure that you will never be homeless? Can you guarantee it?

On MySocLab

 Study and **Review** on MySocLab

CHAPTER REVIEW

LO2.1 Summarize the link between private experiences and social structure

2.1 Why are gender, race and ethnicity, and social class important?

These three social positions, referred to as *statuses*, have a strong influence throughout our lives. They represent significant categories that shape our world-view, including our opportunities, constraints, or privileges.

LO2.2 Explain the importance of sex, gender, and patriarchy to families

2.2 What is the difference between *sex* and *gender*?

Sex refers to biological differences between men and women and their role in reproduction, whereas *gender* is the culturally and socially constructed differences between males and females found in the meanings, beliefs, and practices associated with "femininity" and "masculinity."

2.3 How do we learn our gendered expectations?

We learn gendered expectations through a process of gender socialization. Important agents of socialization include our parents, our teachers, toys, peers, and the media.

2.4 What is *patriarchy,* and why is it important to the study of gender?

Patriarchy is a form of social organization in which the expectation is that men have a natural right to be in control of women. Patriarchy is manifested and up-held in a wide variety of social institutions, including those in legal, educational, religious, and economic arenas. Vestiges are found in virtually every society.

LO2.3 Describe the importance of race and ethnicity to families

2.5 What is the difference between *race* and *ethnicity,* and which term is generally more useful?

Race is a biological concept. *Ethnicity* is far more useful, because it focuses on shared cultural characteristics, such as language, place of origin, dress, food, religion, and other values. Ethnicity represents culture, whereas race attempts to represent biological heritage (much of which has become mixed over the years).

2.6 What is the difference between *individual* and *institutional discrimination*?

Individual discrimination is a micro-level phenomenon that occurs when one person exhibits a negative behavior toward another individual. *Institutional discrimination* is a macro-level phenomenon that occurs when social institutions, such as the government, religious groups, and schools, create policies and practices that systematically disadvantage certain groups. These are woven into the fabric of our culture so deeply that many people do not even notice them.

2.7 Is the United States becoming more diverse?

Yes. By the year 2050, projections are that minority groups will make up more than half the U.S. population. The largest increase is expected to be among Hispanic groups.

LO2.4 Identify the importance of social class to families

2.8 How many social classes are there?

There is no exact way to measure social class. A common typology compares and contrasts six categories: upper, upper middle, middle, working class, working poor, and the underclass.

2.9 How does social class affect our lives?

Social class affects our lives in many ways, includ-ing our likelihood of being born; our health status and gender expectations; the values our parents hold for us; the likelihood of our attending and graduat-ing from college; our dating and nonmarital sexual behavior; our likelihood of and age at marriage; our income and consumption patterns; our hobbies; and stress and coping mechanisms.

LO2.5 Discuss how poverty affects families

2.10 How is poverty calculated?

Poverty is calculated on the basis of the cost of a very low food budget developed by the USDA. This budget is then multiplied by three.

2.11 Who is most likely to be poor?

About 15 percent of the U.S. population lived in poverty in 2012, an increase of roughly 2.5 percent since 2007 (almost 9 million additional Americans over this period). Almost 22 percent of children—more than one child in five—live in poverty.

2.12 What are the consequences of poverty?

There are many social and health consequences for both adults and children, most of which are negative.

For example, impoverished children suffer far more health risks from infancy on, including higher rates of infant mortality. They are also more likely to suffer from depression, have behavioral problems, and do poorly in school.

LO2.6 Analyze the intersections of sex, gender, race, ethnicity, and class

2.13 Why are the intersections of sex, gender, race, ethnicity, and class important?

We all have a race, ethnicity, sex, and social class, and these master statuses operate both individually and together. A person is not simply a man or a woman, but, for example, a poor White woman, or a middle-class Black man, or a wealthy Asian American. Together, these statuses interact to shape our experiences.

KEY TERMS

agents of socialization	hidden curriculum	social capital
discrimination	individual discrimination	social class
ethnicity	institutional discrimination	social mobility
ethnic group	minority group	social stratification
extended families	poverty guidelines	socioeconomic status (SES)
food insecurity	prejudice	sociological imagination
gender	race	stereotypes
gender socialization	sex	

3

Building Relationships

((· **Listen** to Chapter 3 on **MySocLab**

Ask your grandmother if she considered living with your grandfather before they were married, and you're likely to receive a rather surprised glare. Things have certainly changed.

Meet Meghan and Jonothan, who goes by the nickname Jono, a couple living together before marriage.

Meghan and Jono are among the nearly 7 million couples who cohabit. They are bright, well educated, madly in love, and as your grandmother might say, "living in sin." In your grandmother's day, people met, dated, got engaged, and then married quickly. Men and women—especially women—were expected to be virgins on their wedding day, so a four-year courtship was not very realistic.

Today, the progression toward marriage is quite different. Courtships often last much longer, as people do not seem to be in any particular hurry to marry. Instead of marrying first and then going to college, getting a job, saving money, buying a house, or having a baby, couples now expect to do many or even all of these things before marriage. Today's couples cohabit, and they do so for many reasons: as a prelude to marriage, as a relationship instead of marriage, and as another form of "going steady."

Meghan and Jono, both age 30, have been happily together for four years, the last two of which they have been cohabiting. She is in her final year of a nurse practitioner program, while he works full-time at a biotech company managing its lab. They met at a summer barbeque and quickly became very close. Fifty years ago, they would probably have become engaged and married within a short period. But today, what's the rush?

Like many other couples today, Meghan and Jono think of moving in together as normative: It's what you do when you're in love with someone. It's what all your friends are doing. It's how you take your relationship to the "next level." They had no specific plans to marry when they moved in together. As Meghan says, "I think I wanted to move in after about a year of being together, and it just seemed like the next step. We were really happy together and we had a really good thing going on. I had been in a probably four- or five-roommate situation for a long time and it was getting old. It was a great opportunity to get out of that and move in."

In addition to their friends, Meghan's parents cohabited, as did her aunts, uncles, and siblings, so her parents had no problem with their decision to move in together. Jono's parents were a bit more reserved at first, but they have come around and accepted the situation.

"We're happy right now and we don't really need to get married for any particular reason."

👁 **Watch** on **MySocLab**
Video: *Cohabitation: Meghan and Jono*

Would Meghan and Jono ever consider marriage? Yes, but it's on the back burner. After two years of living together, they both now feel that they will eventually marry, but only when they're ready. As Jono explains, "All of our friends are getting married and everyone's asking us 'Are you going to get married? When are you going to get married?' So, it's definitely something we're starting to talk about. We're thinking, the timing has to be right, and we have to just feel good about it and know that we're secure in our lives with our careers and financially everything is set before we go there. Because we're happy right now and we don't really need to get married for any particular reason."

Relationships like this one begin and end every day. Quite naturally, Meghan and Jono believe that they have a relationship that is special, even magical. Yet, their relationship has followed a fairly predictable pattern—singlehood, dating, cohabitation, and possibly marriage—a pattern that has certainly shifted over time and varies from culture to culture. There is no one right way to build a relationship. The pattern popular in your parents' generation was different from their parents' generation, which also probably created considerable angst back then.

This chapter looks at where we've been and where we're going with respect to the processes by which we develop relationships with others. We begin our discussion with singlehood, and then move to friendships, dating, and end with cohabitation. The goal of this chapter is to show you how many of our personal choices are shaped by macro-level social and cultural factors, including the choices we make as we build our relationships.

3.1 Analyze singlehood

Questions That Matter

3.1 How many people are single?
3.2 What does it mean to be *single*?

👁 **Watch** on **MySocLab**
Video: *Just Like You Imagined: A Look at the Lives of Young People's Relationships*

Singlehood

We may all be born single, but very few of us remain that way forever. Only about 4 percent of people never marry—a number that has remained stable for generations (U.S. Census Bureau, November 22, 2013). However, what is different today is the large and growing number of people who delay marriage, who prefer to cohabit instead of marrying, or who are divorced. Consequently, many people spend considerable amounts of time being single, but it's unfair to assume that they have no close personal relationships.

How Many Stay Single? It Depends on How You Define It

Although *single* can mean different things to different people, the U.S. Census Bureau assigns people to one of several specific groups: *Never Married, Married, Separated, Divorced,* and *Widowed.* Can you see a problem with this classification? It ignores the *social* meaning of being single. People like Jono and Meghan, who live together, are classified as "Never Married," implying that they're single even though they have a committed partner. Divorced and widowed persons, who are single, are not classified as such. In other words, these categories can be quite misleading.

Figure 3.1 shows the percentage of people who (1) never married and (2) who are *single*—defined as being unmarried for whatever reason. Note that there's little difference between the two groups when people are young. After all, what's the likelihood that a 17-year-old would be widowed or divorced? For young people,

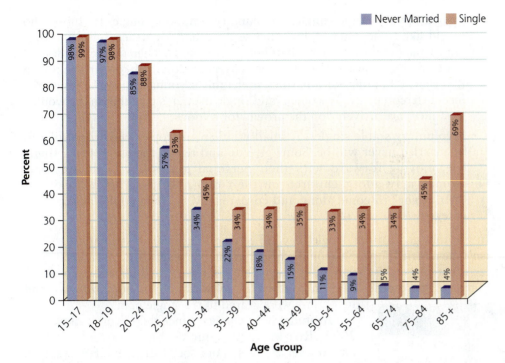

Never Married ■ **Single** ■

FIGURE 3.1

Percentage *Never Married* versus Percentage *Single* (Defined as *Unmarried for any Reason*), Ages 15 to 85+, 2012

Never married and *single* are not the same thing. Young people are most likely to have never married and to be currently single, whereas older people may have married in the past, but are often single as a result of widowhood.

Source: U.S. Census Bureau, February 25, 2009.

being *never married* and being *single* mean about the same thing. However, this begins to change in our 20s, as we gain more life experiences. In our 20s, 30s, and 40s, many people get divorced (see Chapter 12). As we continue to age into our 60s, 70s, 80s, and beyond, many of us will be widowed (see Chapter 14). Therefore, we are single again, even though the label of "Never Married" no longer applies.

What Does It Mean to Be Single? A Useful Typology

There are all kinds of single people. You may be single. A Catholic priest is single. A lesbian in a committed relationship living in Texas is single. My 10-year-old daughter is single. If we want to broaden our understanding of singles, we should ask two critical questions: (1) Is it voluntary; and (2) is it temporary? Together, these two dimensions yield four very different groups of singles (Stein, 1976, 1981):

- **Voluntary temporary singles.** Many so-called single people are really just delaying marriage. They may be pursuing higher education or establishing themselves in a career. However, this group is interested in marrying someday and will marry sometime in the future. A large majority of people fit into this category.

- **Voluntary stable singles.** Voluntary stable singles want to be single, and want to be so for life. Catholic priests and nuns, for example, take a vow of celibacy. In most states, same-sex couples cannot legally marry, and therefore could be categorized as voluntary stable singles. Other people could marry but choose not to, including those who are committed to cohabitation or who want to remain single for other personal reasons.

*I*f you are a single person now, which of the four categories of singles best describes you? Could you imagine a scenario in which you became a part of another category? For example, let's say you consider yourself a "voluntary temporary single," but over the course of your life you became an "involuntary stable single." How would you cope with such a change?

voluntary temporary singles: Unmarried adults who may be delaying marriage while pursuing education or establishing a career.

voluntary stable singles: Unmarried adults desiring a single (unmarried) lifestyle.

involuntary temporary singles:
Singles actively searching for a mate but unable to find a suitable one.

- **Involuntary temporary singles.** Involuntary temporary singles are those who would like to be married, but can't seem to find a partner. Television programs and other media are full of images of single women (and men) desperate to find a spouse. Older women may be nicknamed *cougars*, implying that they're hunting for a partner, preferably a younger man. Although the media stereotype single women (and single men), it's true that many women (and men) are actively "on the prowl" for a spouse.

involuntary stable singles:
Unmarried adults who can expect to be single for life even though they may not want to be.

- **Involuntary stable singles.** A small number of people who would like to be married never will be. Some give up and resign themselves to a single life, moving forward with their personal goals. For example, some women may adopt children on their own, deciding not to wait for "Mr. Right" to come along and co-parent. Very few people fall into this category.

In previous generations, singles beyond a "certain age" were stigmatized. "Why isn't she married?" people would whisper among themselves. Women in particular experienced close scrutiny, as few viable options existed for them outside of marriage and motherhood. In contrast, many social clubs, organizations, and magazines were geared to the single man.

What are the stereotypes surrounding older single women? Either they are "old maids" or "cougars" on the hunt, like Courteney Cox's character on *Cougar Town*. How do these stereotypes differ from those of single older men?

Attitudes have changed since then (Koropeckyj-Cox, 2005; Roark, 2009). Our changing attitudes reflect macro-level changes in our social structure. For example, many of us may have parents who are single (maybe they have never married, are cohabiting, or are divorced). And, because people tend to marry later, we come across single adults all the time.

In addition to the aforementioned typology, it's important to remember that singlehood, like most everything else, may be experienced differently depending on a person's sex, race, ethnicity, social class, age, or other dimensions. For example, a 30-year old single Hispanic man with only a high school diploma may have a completely different experience of singlehood than a 30-year-old college-educated White woman because of cultural expectations and economic opportunities. In other words, both macro-level social and cultural contexts interact to shape our individual, personal experiences.

Whether single or not, we all know the importance of connecting with others. Being single hardly means we're all alone. One critical dimension of connecting and building relationships is through our friendships.

3.2 Discuss issues surrounding friendships

Questions That Matter

3.3 Why is friendship important in our lives?

3.4 How do friendships differ by sex, race, ethnicity, or social class?

3.5 Can men and women ever really be "just friends"?

Friendships

Some of our most important and intimate relationships are with our friends. Even the youngest of children are ready to socialize (Dewar, 2009). Friendships not only provide companionship, but they're also good for our health, according to a review of nearly 150 scientific research studies (Holt-Lundstad, Smith, & Layton, 2010). Having close friends that you can confide in may help you live longer. Friendships have been shown to lower blood pressure, heart rates, and cholesterol levels. One longitudinal study followed 61 women with advanced ovarian cancer and found that those with weaker friendships had higher levels of a particular protein linked to more aggressive cancers and that also inhibited the effectiveness of chemotherapy. Women with stronger, more extensive supportive networks fared considerably better (Costanzo, Lutgendorf, Sood, Anderson, Sorosky, & Lubaroff, 2005). Friendships perform a myriad of duties: they support us, help us build communities, enhance our self-esteem, and teach us about ourselves and others (Rawlins, 2008; Wissink, Dekovic, & Mejier, 2009).

Being Friends: Sex Differences

> One of the things I really like about my girlfriends is that they love me no matter what. I can cry to them, and pour out my heart when I'm feeling depressed, and they always do their best to cheer me up.
>
> **—Sophia, age 25**

> One of the things that I really like about my friends is that they are always there for me no matter what. When I need to play some basketball to let off steam, or when I'm bored and want to go hang out, I can count on them.
>
> **—Xavier, age 25**

Researchers looking at same-sex friendships have compared the quality and quantity of men's and women's attachments. Men and women have about the same number of friends, but men's friendships appear less personal or intimate than women's (Flood, 2008; Hall, 2010). Women are more verbal and self-disclosing with their friends, and are more likely to have their feelings of friendship returned (I like her, and she likes me) (Vaquera & Kao, 2008). Men spend time with other men engaging in activities. Because of cultural prescriptions about appropriate behavior for men, along with the fear of homosexuality that exists in our culture, men create close connections to other men through side-by-side physical activity. Instead of talking, as women do, men play sports and show signs of intimacy through back-slapping or "high-fives" (Kiesling, 2005).

A study of adolescents found several important differences in same-sex friendships (Johnson, 2004). The subjects included 95 eighth-graders, 54 tenth-graders, 55 twelfth-graders, and 66 first-year university students, and both experimental and survey methods were used. Male adolescents reported knowing their friends longer than did females. Female adolescents reported spending more time with their friends, as well as experiencing more closeness and commitment in their friendships, than did males. This research tells us that males and females both consider their friendships important, but they experience friendships in ways that are aligned with gendered norms. They enjoy their friendships, but expect different things out of them. Females expect greater closeness, commitment, and intimacy.

Men and women tend to have about the same number of friends, but they relate to their friends differently. Women's friendships tend to be more intimate and personal.

Being Friends: Social Class and Race/Ethnicity

Friendships appear to differ across social classes (Walker, 1999). Members of the working class tend to have friendships that last longer than middle-class friendships. Walker found that working-class persons were more likely to have grown up in the same neighborhood and to continue living there as adults. The longevity of the friendships allowed more opportunity to become intimate and share more about themselves. Friendships among people in the middle class appeared to be of shorter duration. Occupations in the middle and upper middle classes often require geographic mobility. Although friendships can be maintained over time, they're more likely to continue over the telephone or through the mail (or email), unlike friendships among the working class.

Another structural difference Walker noted is that working-class persons experienced more crises in their lives. Unemployment, substance abuse, and family health problems were more frequent. Crises among those in the middle class were less severe on average, and not as long. Intimacy in friendships often occurs by sharing problems.

The family is an important means of social support to ward off stress and depression, but so are friends (McAdoo, 2006). A recent qualitative longitudinal study examined how friendships patterns differ for Black, Latino, and Asian American adolescents (Way, Gingold, Rotenberg, & Kuriakose, 2005). These authors argue that Hispanic and Black adolescents establish and maintain friendships for a longer time, and that Asian American adolescents are the least likely to form close friendships because they're discouraged by their parents from spending time with friends outside school. If both Black and Hispanic youth maintain their friendships for a long time, this is likely to improve their chances of strengthening friendship ties, and thus improve the chances of reciprocal friendships.

Clyde Franklin's (1992) early work on friendship among Black men also suggests that racial and ethnic, as well as social class, differences shape social relationships among men. "Because working-class black males experience greater isolation from mainstream society than upwardly mobile black men, they may not internalize the same taboos against male same-sex friendships, which result in non-self-disclosure, competitiveness, and nonvulnerability" (Franklin, 1992, p. 207). Franklin found that working-class Black men expressed strong sentiments about their friends because they trusted them. They shared experiences, including being Black in a society with a long history of racism. Like Walker, Franklin suggests that upwardly mobile people are more temporary to a specific geographic area, and in their striving to succeed in life, have a more competitive relationship with others, including their friends.

Friendships between Women and Men: Just Friends?

Can men and women ever really be "just friends"? Friendship certainly is a good basis for a romantic relationship. But friendships *independent* of romance are sometimes suspect. Some people are concerned that men and women can never be "just friends." They assume that spending too much time together is bound to result in intimacy or sexual relations, or that misperceptions of sexual and romantic interests are bound to happen (Koenig, Kirkpatrick, & Ketelaar, 2007).

Historically, **cross-sex friendships**, a strictly platonic friendship between a man and a woman, have been rare, and they have been studied even more rarely because they were believed to be part of the developmental process of romantic engagement (friends become lovers or lovers later become friends). Some people also viewed cross-sex friendships as threatening to the heterosexual social order (Monsour, 2002).

cross-sex friendship: A friendship between a man and a woman that is strictly platonic.

Today, cross-sex friendships are far more common than they were in your parents' or grandparents' generation (Bleske-Rechek, Somers, Micke, Erickson, Matteson, Stocco, Schumacher, & Ritchie, 2012; Guerrero & Mongeau, 2008). Opportunities for women and men to meet are increasing in the workplace, schools, and in the community. Many women and men find they share mutual interests and enjoy similar activities. Cross-sex friendships can provide valuable insights into how the other sex thinks, feels, and behaves.

Nonetheless, cross-sex friendships can contain elements of tension and are not always easy to maintain (Bleske-Rechek et al., 2012). A study of more than 100 university students and over 300 adults ages 27 to 55 found that cross-sex friends face a challenge of addressing sexuality in their relationship. Many men and women in the study experienced some degree of romantic attraction toward their cross-sex friends. The magnitude of that attraction was stronger for men than for women. These feelings of attraction to a cross-sex friend were associated with lower levels of satisfaction with one's romantic relationship, and caused some jealousy with their romantic partner. Further, participants of varying ages experienced feelings of jealousy.

The boxed feature *Why Do Research?* reveals that people can create a set of stories to help them maintain their cross-sex friendships.

Can women and men ever really be just friends? Do you have any cross-sex friendships? If so, what kinds of challenges do you experience, if any? How are these friendships different from same-sex friendships? If you do not have any cross-sex friendships, do you know why?

Why Do Research? "Just Friends"

Like many people today, you probably have some opposite-sex friends who are just that—friends. Cross-sex friendships have some unique advantages, but also some potential challenges (Bleske-Rechek, 2008). A study by Vickie Harvey (2003) examined how people interpret the romantic challenges that cross-sex friendships can face.

Harvey asked 120 students enrolled in communication classes at two universities to keep a journal discussing the aspects of a cross-sex friendship. The journal entries were to answer three types of questions. The first type was questions about the friendship's emotional nature, such as, "What kinds of things do you typically do when you are together?" and "Is this an intimate relationship in terms of sharing experiences and confiding in each other?" The second type of question concerned the friendship's romantic nature, such as, "If ever, discuss the times when you felt you would like the friendship to become a romantic relationship," and "How do you communicate affection for each other?" The third type were audience-related questions, such as, "How do you manage your public image as one of friends rather than as dating partners?" and "How have the reactions of other people affected your friendship?" Harvey collected the journals several times from the students over a 16-week period.

Cross-sex friendships have few guidelines and people are charting new territory, so they create myths to maintain these types of friendships as platonic rather than romantic. Harvey found the students' myths included the following themes (the answers are not mutually exclusive, and therefore add up to more than 100 percent):

- *I'm not attracted to my friend*. Sixty-five percent of students acknowledged they had sent or received mixed messages about attraction.

- *We can remain just friends*. Forty-seven percent of the friends felt attracted to the other person at the beginning of the relationship when the other person assumed they were going to be just friends and struggled to remain so.
- *I could be attracted that way*. Thirty-two percent of the students reported their friend was attracted to them, but they did not feel the same way.
- *I don't discount my feelings*. Thirty percent reported they do not communicate their romantic interests in the other person because it has caused discomfort in the past, or they fear it will in the future.
- *Kissing doesn't count*. Twenty-six percent of the friendships included some romantic or sexual behavior, but it was considered only an extension of the friendship itself.
- *If we've been romantically involved, we can't be friends*. Nine percent of the students reported being romantically involved with their friend at some point and were now struggling to build a friendship.

Harvey's study, like others (Bleske-Rechek, 2008), reveals that cross-sex friendships are created and maintained without a clear set of guidelines, and the friends struggle to define and sustain these relationships.

WHAT DO YOU THINK?

1. Can you describe one of your closest cross-sex friendships? Do any of these myth constructions fit your situation?
2. Do you think men and women can be just friends? Why or why not? What micro- and macro-level factors help explain why cross-sex friendships are more common today than in the past?

Sources: Bleske-Rechek, 2008; Rawlins, 2008; Harvey, 2003.

Friendships are important to our social, physical, and mental well-being. All friendships are valuable, but some do cross into new territory. We may see these friends in a new light and want to spend increasing amounts of time with them. They pique our romantic and sexual interests. Call it what you wish—"hanging out," "dating," or "going out"—but in our society, pairing up is how we acquire our mates.

3.3 Identify the influences on dating, courtship, and mate selection

Questions That Matter

3.6 How have the purpose and structure of dating changed over time?

3.7 How have macro-level factors shaped our micro-level choices with respect to dating?

3.8 What are some contemporary trends in dating?

Dating, Courtship, and Mate Selection

How do we decide who marries whom in our society? In some cultures, it's easy—fathers or parents (often with the help of matchmakers) choose the mates for their children. However, most people in the United States want to choose their own mates, and dating is the mechanism for finding a mate in Western culture. Dating serves many functions. It

- provides fun and recreation
- offers companionship
- allows intimacy
- confers social status
- assists in mate selection

We generally assume in our "free" society that dating reflects our personal choices—*who, how,* or *why* we date is of our choosing. This reflects a micro-level orientation. Yet, we see in the next section that our personal choices do not exist in a vacuum; they are embedded in macro-level historical, social, and cultural factors (Regan, 2008).

A Look at History: Macro-Level Influences on Our Micro-Level Choices

In the past the ultimate goal of dating was to eventually select a mate, but today we don't usually think of dating as being so narrowly focused. Meeting others and socializing can be fun in and of itself. Yet although we think of dating as a micro-level personal experience (e.g., "I hang out with whomever I like") it's also shaped by larger, macro-level structural conditions in society. Throughout the past 200 years, U.S. society has changed substantially, and along with those changes have come new ways of meeting and getting to know one another, falling in love, and selecting a mate. Let's look at some of these social and economic changes throughout our history (Calhoun, 2009).

COURTSHIP IN EARLY AMERICA During colonial times, interactions between unmarried individuals of the opposite sex were highly supervised. This isn't surprising when we consider the organization of social life prior to 1800 in the United States. Social life centered on family and community, and the primary economic activity was agriculture. Therefore, opportunities for interaction occurred either at public social gatherings or in the homes of families. At social gatherings, parents could influence who their daughters and sons met, and who might be later invited to their homes for a visit. The "date" was conducted in the parents' home. This practice was referred to as **calling**, as in, "Jed is going to come calling next week." Because distances between communities were often great and transportation was slow, it was not uncommon for the young man to spend days and nights at the home of the young woman's family.

Some people might believe that because women and their families could control who was allowed to call, women held more power in the development of romantic relationships than men. However, this is not really the case (Cott, 1978).

calling: A dating practice of the 18th and 19th centuries in which a young man would visit a young woman in her parents' home.

Women were influenced not only by their parents, who had an incentive to encourage contacts with only certain men, but also by the men themselves, who were responsible for initiating contact. Women had to sit and wait to be called on and hope for the best. Because there were so few opportunities for women outside of marriage and motherhood, they knew that marriage was a necessity.

INDUSTRIALIZATION, CONSUMERISM, AND THE EMERGENCE OF DATING Rapid industrialization in the mid-19th century resulted in rural to urban migration and the shifting of work from the farm to the factory. This change brought with it a higher standard of living and a cash economy that allowed people to save money for discretionary purposes. As automobiles became more affordable and popular in the 20th century, young couples had both a means of transportation and a place for intimacy. Likewise, urbanization brought with it a new set of social activities in places such as theaters or dance halls where young people could congregate.

Dating was a relatively new concept in the early 20th century, emerging alongside the new view of adolescence.

Many other social changes also occurred in the early part of the past century that influenced interactions among unmarried young people. For example, labor laws limited the hours teenagers could work, and mandatory education required that they spend time in school. These two changes resulted in a period termed **adolescence**—a new developmental period between childhood and adulthood. Public schools were coeducational, which created an environment for adolescent girls and boys to interact socially. As relationships developed, couples could spend time together, away from parental supervision, at the movies or a dance club. Dating shifted focus from the family to the peer group.

We also see that young men and women played different roles in dating. Generally, it was the young man who initiated, planned, and paid for the date. It was the young woman's responsibility to control the man's behavior, specifically his sexual advances, within the relationship.

The first major study of dating in college was conducted by Willard Waller in the 1930s at Penn State University (Waller, 1937). He found that, among the students, young men and women were rated in terms of their dating value; Waller's article was called "The Rating and Dating Complex." Men were at the top of the list if they had access to automobiles, could dance well, and had a lot of money. Women were held in higher regard if they dressed well, had good conversation skills, and were considered popular. Waller found that the goal was to be rated as high as possible, which would bring an enhanced reputation and the ability to get the most and the "best" dates. We can see how ideas about sex and gender (e.g., women should be pretty; men should have money) were important components of the dating scene. Waller's research also compared the level of emotional attachment between dating partners. Waller coined the term **principle of least interest**, referring to the idea that unequal emotional involvement between romantic partners has implications for the quality and stability of relationships.

Read on **MySocLab**
Document: *Egalitarian Daters/ Traditionalist Dates*

adolescence: The period of life that occurs between childhood and adulthood.

principle of least interest: The idea that unequal emotional involvement between romantic partners has implications for the quality and stability of relationships.

Macro Influences Today: Sex and Gender, Race and Ethnicity, Social Class, Sexual Orientation

Many macro-level influences have shaped dating and the choices we make. The 1970s ushered in many political movements, including a resurgence of the women's

Read on **MySocLab**
Document: *The Balance of Power in Dating*

movement, and dating became less formal. The passage of the Education Amendments of 1972 and the famous Title IX, which included mandates that girls be allowed access to sports in ways comparable to boys, resulted in increased coeducational experiences. Sex segregation in the curriculum also declined. Colleges offered coed dormitories, increasing opportunities for social interaction. In the workforce, the opportunities for women and men to engage in similar types of occupations or jobs and to work together have also increased.

Perhaps one of the biggest changes in dating over the past generation is that it's becoming more distinct from mate selection—dating may lead to partnering or marriage, but it may not, and so we enjoy it for its own sake. Rather than the pairing up of the past, dating today often involves simply "hanging out" or "getting together" with larger groups of people. There is less pressure to be paired off and more emphasis on group friendship, although obviously many people do pair off and eventually become partners.

GENDER AND DATING   Despite the increased informality of dating, researchers have found many young adults still behave in relatively traditional ways. Women and men often follow **dating scripts**, or sets of expectations about how to behave. The following scripts may sound old-fashioned, but do you see anything familiar in them? Women's dating scripts include waiting to be asked for a date, buying a new outfit, waiting for the date to arrive, eating lightly while out, going to the bathroom to primp, and calling a friend afterward to discuss the date. Men's scripts include asking someone for a date, preparing the car, getting money, planning the date, picking up the date, opening doors for her, paying the bill, and walking her to the door when returning home. Both men and women have generally agreed to these gendered scripts. In other words, although attitudes about relationships have become less traditional and more egalitarian, these attitudes haven't been fully translated into behavior.

> **dating script:** A set of expectations around dating that differ somewhat for men and women.

It's not surprising that these scripts are still with us when we look at how the mass media presents ideas about dating. The Internet, television shows, books, music, and movies all perpetuate the idea that men and women approach dating in different ways.

Other rituals also reveal the ways in which dating is gendered. For example, how can we tell when a couple is dating exclusively? Your parents or grandparents may have known such rituals as getting pinned, exchanging ID bracelets, or wearing a boyfriend's class ring or a promise ring. These actions were especially important because they revealed to others that the young woman was in a relationship and had been chosen. Again, not that much has changed in this dating ritual. Exclusive relationships today are reinforced by the multi-million-dollar business of marketing engagement rings (Gona & Merry, 2007). About 75 percent of all first-time brides wear engagement rings at an average price of $4,600, which represents a 20 percent drop since the peak of the recession (Barlette, 2012; Jaeger, 2011). Notice that only women wear engagement rings, and they're usually purchased by the man. The diamond industry claims this is a good financial investment for the couple, but fails to mention that this habit reflects the patriarchal idea of male ownership of women. It signals "Hands off—she's taken" to the larger society. It appears that despite the greater informality of dating, gendered norms persist.

Have you noticed that men don't wear engagement rings? Why do you think this is?

DIFFERENCES AND SIMILARITIES IN DATING PRACTICES: SOCIAL CLASS, RACE, ETHNICITY, AND SEXUAL IDENTITY

Dating takes different forms and has different objectives across different social groups (see Sassler, 2010, for a review). Those who study the upper socioeconomic classes believe the wealthy control dating opportunities to maintain their distinctive place in society (Kendall, 2002). Private schools, private clubs, and gated communities are examples of the ways wealthy people segregate themselves by social class. Upper-class families also make sure their children fall in love with the "right" kind of people. Debutante balls, private schools, and social clubs serve as mechanisms to introduce young people to appropriate dating partners (Domhoff, 2010).

Dating ideals also reflect distinctive subcultures within racial or ethnic groups (Jackson, Kleiner, Geist, & Cebulko, 2011). One example is the *quinceañera*, a coming-out party for young Hispanic women (Quinceanera. com, 2012), as described in the feature box *Diversity in Families: I Am 15 and a Woman Today!* A *quinceañera* is held at the time of a young woman's fifteenth birthday and includes a Catholic mass followed by a party. It is a festive event for both family and friends at which the young woman wears a special gown and a tiara, and gets to feel like a princess for a day. It's expected that she can begin dating after this celebration. Young Hispanic men are not given a *quinceañera* as this event is designed to signal the young woman's availability in Hispanic culture.

Some groups, including lesbians, gays, bisexuals, and transgender (LGBT) individuals, may have a more difficult time meeting others because of the stigma still attached to these groups. In a general social setting, it's difficult to determine who may be LGBT, because most people are heterosexual. The slang term *gaydar* refers to being able to identify LGBT others. As one woman says, "Some

DIVERSITY IN FAMILIES   I Am 15 and a Woman Today!

A *quinceañera* is a special celebration given for a Hispanic girl by her family to indicate that she is growing up and can now begin dating. How does this celebration reflect gendered cultural values?

Maria was dressed in a beautiful new floor-length pastel gown, her hair swept up on top of her head, her rhinestone necklace and bracelet glittering in place around her neck and wrist. Her mother and godmother, beaming with pride, helped her with the final touch, placing the tiara on her head. Maria picked up her bouquet, ready to greet the 14 friends she had chosen for her court, other girls in their ball gowns, and boys in their tuxedos. Today was her special day—her *quinceañera*.

The passage from childhood to adulthood is a significant transition in many cultures. In Mexico, Puerto Rico, Cuba, and Central and South America, a girl's fifteenth birthday is the time for celebrating her journey into womanhood. The *quinceañera* is her coming-out party—she is presented to her peers and their families as a young woman approaching marriageable age.

The most important part of the celebration is the thanksgiving Mass (*Misa de acción de gracias*). The young woman takes a prominent place at the foot of the altar, kneeling on a special pillow personalized with her name, and after the Mass leaves her bouquet on the altar to honor the Virgin Mary. Afterward, the party can begin, with food, drink, music, and dancing—few details are spared for this festive occasion. It is held in a banquet hall or home, depending on the size of the party and the economic means of the family. It resembles a wedding reception, with its formal invitations, guest book, photo album, gifts, cake and cake server set, and champagne glasses. The young woman's guests will toast her, offering their congratulations and best wishes for her future. The party also includes other traditions unique to the *quinceañera*, such as the Changing of the Shoes, in which the father ceremoniously changes the girl's shoes from flats to high heels, symbolic of her changing from a girl into a young woman.

The origins of the *quinceañera* celebration are unclear but it may come from the early Aztecs. Today among all social classes, it's a girl's rite of passage that celebrates families and elevates traditional womanhood.

WHAT DO YOU THINK?

1. Why do you think that girls have a *quinceañera* celebration, but boys do not? How does this celebration reflect ideas about sex and gender in Hispanic culture?
2. How would you feel about having a *quinceañera* celebration or attending one? What macro-level and micro-level factors have shaped your opinions of this celebration?

Sources: Loeffler, 2008; Palfrey, 1997; Quinceañera-Boutique.com, n.d.

Read on MySocLab
Document: *Exiles from Kinship*

people have nearly infallible gaydar. I would rate my gaydar as 'fair' and I have embarrassed myself a few times." Public spaces created for LGBT individuals are limited, and many date by going to personal residences of friends or to gay-friendly bars and restaurants. In addition, because of potential discrimination at work, many gays and lesbians choose to stay closeted about their sexual identity and dating relationships to protect their jobs.

LGBT individuals share many similarities with heterosexuals in their relationships (Kurdek, 2006, 2007, 2009; Liu, Reczek, & Brown, 2013). Those relationships last longest when the partners have a sense of greater equity. Research also suggests sex differences are similar to those among straight women and men. Gay men tend to have shorter relationships with more partners, whereas lesbians tend more toward monogamy. Straight men are also more likely than straight women to have more partners and to have more than one partner at a time.

A recent study (Liu, Reczek, & Brown, 2013) asked same-sex couples who were living together about their health status, and compared their responses to those of heterosexual couples who were married or living together, as well as to people who were divorced, widowed or had never married. People in same-sex relationships reported better health than those who were single, but the same-sex partners reported poorer health than heterosexual married couples.

Clearly, relationships take place within a social context. How we date and become partnered are shaped by important macro-level historical, cultural, social, and economic conditions. How are men and women viewed in society, and what types of opportunities do they have? What are the existing economic conditions? What types of technologies are available? What is the support for LGBT persons in the community? All these factors, and the ways in which they vary, influence the micro-level choices in selecting our mates.

A Micro View: Who Do We Date and Where Do We Meet?

Most people do not often focus on the broader, macro-level factors that shape who and how we date. We tend to take them for granted and focus instead on the here and now. Let's examine dating from this micro-level perspective. What are some contemporary dating trends?

DATING TRENDS Dating is viewed as a major developmental marker for teenagers. Nonetheless, twelfth-grade students are less likely to date than they were in 1991, as shown in Figure 3.2. The percentage who claimed they never dated jumped from 12 percent in 1991 to 21 percent in 2000, and then to 30 percent in 2010 (Bachman, Johnston, & O'Malley, 1993, 2001, 2011). Those who claimed they date frequently (defined as more than once a week) declined significantly, from 34 percent in 1991, to 28 percent in 2000, to only 21 percent in 2010. These differences could reflect the changing definition of dating itself; for instance, is "hanging out" with a group of people considered to be a date? A generation or two ago, this situation might have been considered "double dating," but what do teens and young adults think today? How about texting or emailing—is that a date (Pascoe, 2009)? Young people spend many hours socializing with others electronically, as shown in Table 3.1. For example, a national study found that 33 percent of high school seniors spend 20 hours or

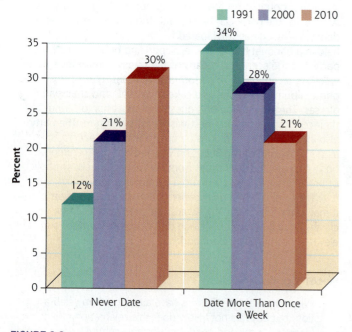

FIGURE 3.2

Percentage of Twelfth-Grade Students Who Never Date or Who Date Frequently (More than Once a Week), 1991, 2000, 2010.

Fewer high school seniors say that they go out on dates, or go out on dates frequently.

Source: Based on Bachman, Johnston, & O'Malley, 1993, 2001, 2011.

TABLE 3.1	Not Counting Work for School/Job, about How Many Hours Per Week Do You Spend. . . .	
Young people spend many hours per week using electronic devices, especially for texting.		
On the internet emailing, instant messaging, gaming, shopping, searching, downloading music, etc.		
None		7%
up to 5		50%
6–9		16%
10–19		13%
20+		15%
Playing electronic games on a computer, TV, phone, or other device		
None		15%
up to 5		48%
6–9		13%
10–19		9%
20+		15%
Texting on a cell phone		
None		8%
up to 5		37%
6–9		12%
10–19		10%
20+		33%
Talking on a cell phone		
None		10%
up to 5		65%
6–9		10%
10–19		6%
20+		10%

Source: Bachman, Johnston, & O'Malley, 2011.

homogamous relationships: Relationships in which we spend most of our time with people who are very similar to ourselves.

Online dating services are a big business, with more than 1,400 different dating sites available.

more every week texting friends (Bachman, Johnston, & O'Malley, 2011).

Older people also date. Given that many people marry later today than in the past and many couples divorce, should we be surprised? A survey of more than 3,000 people ages 57 to 85 found that 14 percent of all singles were in a dating relationship, especially men, and that daters were more likely to be college educated, had greater assets, and were in better health than non-daters (Brown & Shinohara, 2013).

WHO DO WE DATE?   Relationships, including romantic ones, tend to be **homogamous**; we spend most of our time with people who look like us, act like us, and think like us. The majority of partners in both long-term and short-term relationships are similar with respect to

- race and ethnicity
- social class

propinquity: Geographic closeness.

✳ **Explore** on **MySocLab**
Activity: *Fishing for a Mate? Eligibility Characteristics in Alaska*

pool of eligibles: The group from which we are likely to choose our mates.

- education
- age
- religion (Blackwell & Lichter, 2004; Wellner, 2005)

One reason for homogamy is **propinquity**, or geographic closeness. We tend to date (and eventually marry) people with whom we interact, and we're likely to interact with people who live in our neighborhoods and attend the same schools, churches, or other institutions. We share common interests: eating at the same restaurants, going to the same churches, and enjoying the same neighborhood activities. A wealthy young man from a rich and privileged family who went to elite schools may have a difficult time understanding the life of someone from the working class, as shown in the profiles of Randall Simmons and Tommy Johnson, introduced in Chapter 2. Likewise, a devout Muslim woman may have very little in common with, and thus not be particularly attracted to, a man actively committed to a Christian faith.

Another reason for homogamy is that parents may exert pressure on children to marry within their race. For example, although interracial marriages have now increased to about 7 percent of all couples and about 15 percent of *new* marriages (Lofquist, Lugaila, O'Connell, & Feliz, 2012; Wang, 2012), parents and other older relatives may not approve of them. Figure 3.3 reveals 83 percent of people now believe that it's all right for Blacks and Whites to date each other. However, large differences in opinion exist by age. Among young adults ages 18 to 29, 93 percent approve; among adults ages 65 and older, only 67 percent approve.

Nonetheless, some people do date (and marry) outside their demographic categories. Why do these people defy tradition? One explanation is the size of the **pool of eligibles**, or the group from which you're likely to choose a mate. We tend to choose partners from a certain "pool" of people. Among Whites, the number of unmarried men and women is roughly equal across age groups. For other races, the pool is more limited. For example, eligible Black women far outnumber eligible Black men. Reasons for the skewed sex ratio include higher rates of crime and incarceration, crime victimization, and deaths from illness among Black men. One in every 15 Black men is incarcerated, as compared to 1 in 36 Hispanic men, or 1 in 106 White men (Kerby, 2012). Unemployment is also higher among Blacks than Whites, and wages are lower. These realities result in fewer opportunities for Black women to date or marry Black men (Edin & Kefalas, 2005).

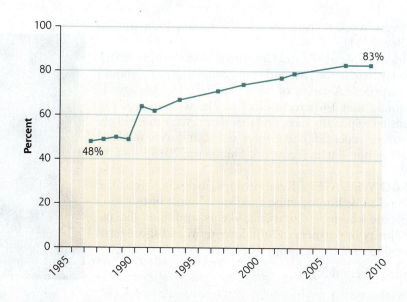

FIGURE 3.3

Acceptance of Blacks and Whites Dating Each Other, 1987–2009.

The public is more accepting of interracial marriage than they were a generation ago.
Source: Wang, 2012.

WHERE DO WE MEET?   As you may guess, most people meet each other the old-fashioned way: through friends, at work, or at school. However, now many people also meet online (Finkel, Eastwick, Karney, Reis, & Sprecher, 2012; Hertlein, 2012; Rosenfeld & Thomas, 2012). Through the 1980s and into the 1990s, there was a stigma associated with personal advertisements and online dating. It was often seen as a last resort, the route of the desperate, and people were generally embarrassed about using these sources. Only 1 percent of adults admitted that they used online dating services in 1990. Today, however, online dating has shed that stigma and entered the mainstream, possibly for several reasons: More people socialize on media than ever before; why should dating be any different? Another reason is that people now marry later than they did in the past; therefore, they are single and presumably dating for longer periods. It becomes more difficult to find partners through friends as we finish college, become consumed with jobs, and watch others around us marrying.

Therefore, online dating services and websites have become an increasingly popular way to look for romantic partners. *Online Dating Magazine* (2013) estimates that there are approximately 2,500 online dating sites in the United States and more than 5,000 worldwide. Fewer than 25 online dating sites in the United States are considered "major" sites, with more than 1 million current, active members. The largest online dating sites in the United States are Match .com, which consists of a supermarket of online profiles, and eHarmony.com, which uses compatibility mathematical algorithms. Today, smartphone apps continue to expand the reach of online programs. Overall, the online dating industry is estimated to be worth more than $1.5 billion annually. Millions of people pay premium monthly prices to use the service to find dates or a potential relationship. For example, monthly prices for the major online dating services range from $40 to $60.

What's the current allure of online Internet dating? Many Internet users agree that it helps people find a better match because one can meet the profiles of a larger number of people quickly, and assess basic compatibility. However, online daters themselves are divided about whether this is the easiest and most efficient method of dating. First, there is no compelling evidence that the mathematical algorithms improve the chances of finding a compatible partner (Finkel, Eastwick, Karney, Reis, & Sprecher, 2012). Second, reducing people to a profile may miss the true essence of a person's character. For example, in constructing profiles, women focus on their looks and sociability, whereas men focus on their financial and occupational successes (McWilliams & Barrett, 2012). Finally, some see it as potentially dangerous and are wary of the risks of other people misrepresenting themselves (e.g., by claiming they are single when they are really married) or trying to obtain personal information. Nonetheless, equal numbers of online daters report positive and negative experiences (Madden & Lenhart, 2006).

Oddly enough, despite the popularity of online dating, little research has been done on the topic by family scholars. Only 79 of more than 11,000 articles published between 1996 and 2010 in couple and family therapy journals were devoted to technology (Blumer, Hertlein, Smith, & Allen, 2012). Yet, technology has redefined the rules for dating and intimacy. For example, participation in online communications can enhance intimacy and feelings of closeness because of the frequency of online interaction and the fewer inhibitions that people feel online.

As you can see, macro-level factors (e.g., technology) can shape our personal micro-level choices about whom we date and why we choose to do so. These can be summed up in the boxed feature *Tying It All Together: Factors That Shape Dating*. Some dating relationships become exclusive with a greater degree of commitment. Some people go on to marry, whereas others decide to cohabit. The next section examines these cohabiting relationships.

*T*alk with your parents or someone from a previous generation about how they dated. Do you see a difference from your own style? Do you think recent changes in our patterns of dating, with an emphasis on informality, are a good thing or a bad thing for developing intimacy? Why or why not?

Watch on **MySocLab**
Video: *Online Dating*

Listen on **MySocLab**
Audio: *NPR: The Personal Dating Coach*

Watch on **MySocLab**
Video: *Pepper Schwartz: Internet Dating*

cohabitation: An arrangement in which two people live together without being married.

It would seem that deciding who you spend time with and who you become intimate with are very personal issues. Why would you say that you're dating a certain person? Your answers may include reasons like, "He's cute." "She's smart." "I like his smile." "She's kind." But there's more to your reasons than this as shown below.

MACRO-LEVEL FACTORS

- Cultural norms surrounding mate selection (Do you choose, or do your parents choose for you?)
- Technology
- Urbanization
- Development of an adolescent subculture
- Social and political movements
- Dating scripts based on sex

- Racial/ethnic cultural differences
- Economic considerations

MICRO-LEVEL FACTORS

- Personal whims
- Friends, connections, and ways to meet new people
- Propinquity
- Size of your pool of eligible people

WHAT DO YOU THINK?

1. Can you see how any of these macro- and micro-level factors have operated in your own life?
2. Why do you think that most people just see the micro-level side of dating?

3.4 Describe heterosexual cohabitation

Questions That Matter

3.9 How common is cohabitation?

3.10 How have attitudes regarding cohabitation changed over time?

3.11 How does cohabitation affect marriage?

3.12 What are the effects of cohabitation on children?

The late 1960s and early 1970s were a period of great social change, including the so-called sexual revolution.

Heterosexual Cohabitation

It's tempting to think that this generation invented **cohabitation**, or living with your romantic and sexual partner without being married, but this isn't the case. In the mid-1800s, we may have spoken little of cohabitation, but it was a fact of life for many people, especially in rural areas. As a predominantly rural nation, people were isolated from one another. A couple may have wanted to marry, but perhaps a minister was unavailable, or perhaps the couple was waiting until family could arrive for the wedding. Cohabitation was usually considered a temporary state until the couple could marry, and therefore others in the community generally treated them as a married couple (Cott, 2002).

However, as the United States began to develop and urbanize, these reasons for cohabitation became much less relevant. Distances were not so vast between communities, and methods of transportation improved. Consequently, cohabitation became less common in the early part of the 20th century. People who lived together without being married were considered sinful, deviant, or were branded as uncouth.

The attitude toward cohabitation changed again in the late 1960s and 1970s, when young people revolted against established norms and institutions (Popenoe, 2008). This was a period of new freedoms for a large baby-boom youth cohort—the "sexual revolution" and the availability of reliable birth control, and the "women's movement" with increasing numbers of women experiencing expanded access to education and the workplace. People no longer felt the need to marry young, and the average age at first marriage increased by several years. Divorce laws also changed, making it easier for married couples to divorce because of "irreconcilable differences," further increasing the number of single adults. These macro-level changes may have led people to ask, why not just live together?

Today, about 8 million U.S. households are maintained by heterosexual cohabiting couples like Meghan and Jono from the opening vignette (U.S. Census Bureau, November 22, 2013). Figure 3.4 shows that this is more than double the number from 2000. It seems that today everyone knows someone who has, or is currently, cohabitating, because it's a typical pathway to marriage.

People cohabit for many reasons, including convenience, economic considerations, as a way to assess compatibility for marriage, as a substitute for marriage, or as a way to avoid the expectations of marriage (Lofquist, Lugaila, O'Connell, & Feliz, 2012). In fact, unlike in the past, marriage may not be in the couple's future plans. Cohabitation may be an extension of dating, or it may be an alternative to marriage itself (Sassler, 2010). A primary challenge of characterizing cohabitations is that partners may have differing motivations, their motivations may shift over time, their intentions to marry may be strong or non-existent, or they may even disagree about whether they are in fact cohabiting (Seltzer, 2004). Let's say that you maintain an apartment with a friend, but you spend six nights a week at your boyfriend's or girlfriend's place. Most of your clothes are stored there and you have designated closet space and dresser drawers in the bedroom, which you share. You cook, do laundry, and grocery shop with your boyfriend or girlfriend. Are you living together? Some say yes; others say no, because you maintain a separate apartment, even though you are rarely there. Because of these large differences, most research on cohabitation now goes beyond simple dichotomies of cohabiting versus not cohabiting, and instead looks at cohabitation more holistically, such as including marital intentions or length of time spent cohabiting with a partner (Kuperberg, 2012).

Who Cohabits?

People who cohabit span all ages, races, and ethnic groups, and are found within all social classes. A nationwide study found that 44 percent of adults say they have cohabited, currently or in the past. Among persons ages 30 to 49, more than half have cohabited (Pew Research Center, 2012). In fact, today, most people who marry begin their union by cohabiting. Figure 3.5 compares those who have cohabited with those who haven't. As you can see, cohabitation has become so common that differences between groups are not very large. Overall, women, the elderly, Hispanics, and those who are currently married with young children are the least likely to have cohabited (Pew Research Center, 2012).

Some people argue that cohabitation and marriage have become indistinguishable in many respects; however, this isn't really the case (Fry & Cohn, 2011). How

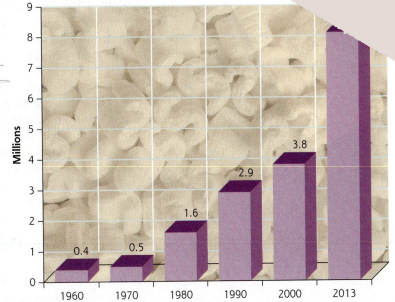

FIGURE 3.4

Number of Cohabiting Couples of the Opposite Sex, 1960–2013.

Cohabitation has skyrocketed and is becoming increasingly normative.
Source: U.S. Census Bureau, November, 2013.

FIGURE 3.5

Percent Saying Yes to "Have You Ever Lived with a Partner without Being Married?"

Almost one-half of adults have cohabited, including almost one of every five people older than 65.
Source: Pew Research Center, 2012.
Note: Hispanics are of any race. Whites and Blacks include only non-Hispanics.

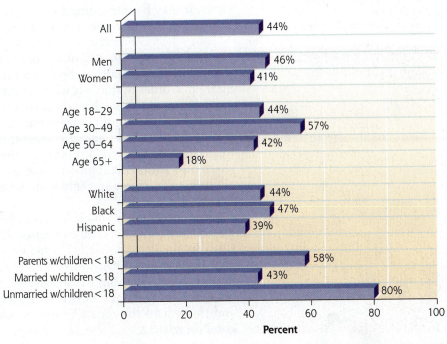

do cohabiters differ from married couples? Cohabiters tend to be more politically liberal, have more non-traditional ideas about gender, and are more likely to share housework and breadwinning responsibilities than are married couples (Fry & Cohn, 2011; Kreider & Elliott, 2009; Lofquist, Lugaila, O'Connell, & Feliz, 2012). Interestingly, a study conducted in 27 countries found that, in most countries, cohabiters were less happy than their married counterparts. However, this difference in happiness was affected by the gendered expectations found among the countries. In countries such as Denmark or Sweden, in which equal rights for women are the expectation, cohabiters were equally likely as married people to be happy. However, in countries like Brazil, with very traditional gender beliefs, the happiness gap between the married and the cohabiting was quite large (Lee & Ono, 2012). In addition, compared to their married counterparts, cohabiting men and women

- are younger
- have less education and are less likely to have graduated from college without a college degree
- have lower household incomes, but those with a college degree have comparable incomes; however, cohabiters are far more likely to live in poverty
- are somewhat less likely to have children residing with them, although the differences aren't large
- are nearly three times as likely to have a female partner who is six or more years older than the male partner, who earns more, and who is more highly educated
- are nearly twice as likely as married couples to be interracial, particularly with one Black and one White partner.

((• Listen on MySocLab
Audio: *State Law Prohibiting Unmarried Cohabitation Challenged*

Attitudes toward Cohabitation: Is It Still "Living in Sin"?

Along with changing behavior toward cohabitation, there's now a greater acceptance of cohabitation, as shown by the attitude of Meghan and Jono's parents at the beginning of this chapter. Before we look at the national trends, ask yourself how you feel about cohabitation. The boxed feature *Getting to Know Yourself: How Do You Feel about Cohabitation?* provides a short inventory of your views. It may be interesting to share these views with your partner, friends, or classmates. How are you similar? How are you different?

Now let's consider national trends of attitudes toward cohabitation. In a national survey, high school seniors were asked whether they agreed with the statement, "It is usually a good idea for a couple to live together before getting married in order to find out whether they really get along." Attitudes are considerably more favorable than those of a generation ago, with 69 percent of young men and 63 percent of young women agreeing that cohabitation is a good idea, compared to only 45 and 33 percent, respectively, in the late 1970s (National Marriage Project, 2012). Likewise, the General Social Survey, a large survey based on a nationally representative sample of adults, reports that 44 percent of adults agree or agree strongly with the statement, "Living together is an acceptable option."

But "acceptable" doesn't necessarily mean that cohabitation is seen as a "good" thing (Pew Research Center, 2012). Figure 3.6 shows the results of a study by the Pew Research Center, which conducts research on many political and social values. This study found that overall, 9 percent of adults see cohabitation as a good thing for society, 46 percent believe that it makes no difference, and 43 percent feel it is bad for society. Men, Hispanics, young adults, and those who live in the West are most likely to consider cohabitation as good for society.

Please answer how you feel regarding each statement. Your answers can include:

1 = Strongly Agree 2 = Agree 3 = Neither Agree nor Disagree 4 = Disagree 5 = Strongly Disagree

	SA	A	N	D	SD
1. Living together without being married is immoral.	1	2	3	4	5
2. Cohabitation is a good way to have a trial marriage.	1	2	3	4	5
3. I have many friends who cohabit and I am comfortable with it.	1	2	3	4	5
4. I have cohabited before, and would never do it again.	1	2	3	4	5
5. It's a good idea for a couple who intends to marry to live together first.	1	2	3	4	5
6. It is all right for a couple to live together without intending to get married.	1	2	3	4	5
7. Cohabitation is harmful to children.	1	2	3	4	5
8. I currently live with someone.	1	2	3	4	5
9. My family strongly disapproves of cohabitation.	1	2	3	4	5
10. Living together without getting married causes a lot of problems in society.	1	2	3	4	5

Scoring: First, transpose the answer categories of questions 2, 3, 5, 6, 8, and 9 so that Strongly Disagree is now worth 1 point, Strongly Agree is worth 2 points, etc. Keep questions 1, 4, 7, and 10 as is. Now, count up your points for each question. In general, the lower the score, the more negative you feel about cohabitation; the higher the score, the more positive you feel about cohabitation.

WHAT DO YOU THINK?

1. Do you think your attitudes differ significantly from your partner, friends, or classmates who might take this inventory? In what ways?
2. Can you identify any micro-level or macro-level factors that have shaped your views?

Another study of 1,036 young adult college students suggests that the endorsement of cohabitation is strongly associated with permissive attitudes toward sex. Young adults who held positive attitudes toward marriage were less likely to endorse cohabitation where the couple did not have marital plans. Results suggest that different background and individual factors predict whether young adults believe cohabitation is beneficial and if they endorse cohabitation based on the marital plans of the partners (Willoughby & Carroll, 2012).

There is also some evidence that men and women see cohabitation a bit differently. Although both endorse it, there are differences in how they characterize its drawbacks. Men are more concerned about their loss of freedom, whereas women are more likely to express concerns over delays in marriage. Overall, it seems that gendered cultural norms governing intimate relationships extend to cohabiting unions as well (Huang, Smock, Manning, & Bergstrom-Lynch, 2011).

Demographer Judith Seltzer (2004) noted three important demographic issues about cohabitation that still seem relevant today. First, although the majority of marriages today begin by cohabitation, cohabiting unions are less likely to be a prelude to marriage now than they were in past decades. Second, cohabiting couples are more likely to be parents. One or both may have a child from a previous union, or the couple may have a child together. Third, single women who become pregnant are about as likely to cohabit today as they are to marry the child's father.

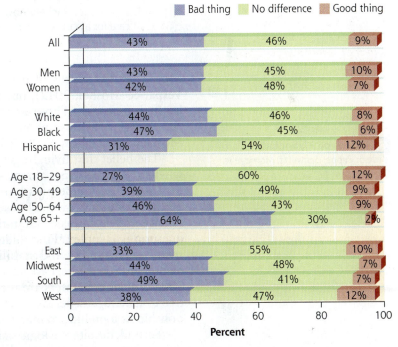

FIGURE 3.6

Percent Saying Unmarried Couples Living Together is a . . .

Most adults do not see cohabitation as a "bad thing for society," but at the same time, not very many say it's a "good thing."
Source: Pew Research Center, 2012.

Some people voice grave concern over these issues. They may believe it's wrong for people to engage in sexual relationships outside of marriage, or they believe that living together isn't a good way to start a healthy marriage. In particular, some people voice concern that cohabitation is harmful for children (National Marriage Project, 2012; Popenoe, 2008). David Popenoe, a leader of the National Marriage Project, says:

> In the final analysis, the issue of cohabitation comes down to a conflict between adult desires and children's need. It seems a tragedy that, with all the opportunities that modernity has brought to adults, it may also be bringing a progressive diminution to our concern for the needs of children—and thus for the many generations to come. (Popenoe, 2008)

Do these concerns have a strong basis in reality? The next section examines the research on cohabitation, marriage, and children.

Cohabitation and Marriage

Rachel and Adam, both just out of college and beginning their careers, have been together for over a year. While in college, they each had their own apartments that they shared with roommates; however, over time, they spent increasing numbers of days and nights at one another's places. Occasionally, Rachel's roommate would complain, "Geez, he's practically living here," and she let Rachel know that she did not care for a part-time third roommate (Adam) who was not paying rent. So, Rachel and Adam decided that once they were out of college and had more money of their own, they would get their own place. Why not, they asked? They would no longer be subject to the complaints of other roommates, it made good financial sense, and it would be a good way to test if they were compatible for marriage, although they had no specific plans to marry.

Watch on **MySocLab**
Video: *Pepper Schwartz: Marriage vs. Cohabitation*

More than two-thirds of marriages begin with cohabitation (Copen, Daniels, Vespa, & Mosher, 2012), but that doesn't necessarily mean that cohabitation leads to marriage. Those are two different issues. In fact, only about half of cohabiting relationships end up in marriage within three years (Goodwin, Mosher, & Chandra, 2010). The others either break up or continue cohabiting.

The belief that living together before marriage is a useful way "to find out whether you really get along," and thus avoid a bad marriage and an eventual divorce, is now widespread among young people (National Marriage Project, 2012). Cohabitation may ease roommate problems, and it may make good financial sense, but is cohabitation a good test for marriage? The answer to that question is complex. First, older cohabiters report significantly higher levels of relationship quality and stability than do younger cohabiters, although older persons are less likely to have plans to marry their partners (King & Scott, 2005). Older cohabiters are more likely to view their relationship as an alternative to marriage, whereas younger cohabiters are more likely to view their relationship as a prelude to marriage.

Second, despite the logic that living together prior to marriage gives partners the opportunity to test the relationship and therefore, to decrease their chances of divorce, people who cohabit, may actually be *more* likely to have unhappy marriages and to divorce (Copen, Daniels, Vespa, & Mosher, 2012; Tach & Halpern-Meekin, 2009). However, recent research suggests that the association between cohabitation and divorce for first marriages may have weakened somewhat among younger couples (Copen, Daniels, Vespa, & Mosher, 2012; Manning & Cohen, 2012). Cohabitation after a divorce is associated with reduced marital satisfaction in the remarriage and a higher rate of subsequent divorce (Xu, Hudspeth, & Bartkowski, 2006).

Two primary reasons explain the positive relationship between cohabitation and divorce. First, a **selection effect** may operate (Copen, Daniels, Vespa, & Mosher, 2012; Lichter & Qian, 2008; Kulu & Boyle, 2010). The type of person who cohabits may be the same type of person who would willingly end an unhappy marriage. For example, someone who values personal freedom may be both more likely to cohabit and also more likely to divorce. Or, a less religious person may be more likely to cohabit and also more likely to end an unhappy marriage. In other words, it's not the case that cohabitation *causes* the divorce, *per se*. Rather, the relationship between cohabitation and divorce is **spurious**, meaning that both cohabitation and divorce are really caused by a third factor—in these examples, the high value placed on personal freedom, or weaker ties to religion.

selection effect: An explanation for the fact that people who cohabit tend to be the same ones who later divorce.

The second reason may be causal—perhaps something about the cohabitation experience weakens a relationship and makes it more prone to divorce. Attitudes and behaviors developed through cohabitation may be at odds with long-term marriage. For example, couples who cohabit are more likely to maintain financial independence and keep their own separate checking accounts (Eggebeen, 2005), possibly emphasizing the couple's degree of separateness and undermining a feeling of unity. It is possible that cohabiting couples are living more like singles, with less of an emphasis on permanence, and therefore aren't really "testing" the relationship as if it were marriage. Consequently, when they do marry, the social expectations that come along with being a husband, wife, son-in-law, and daughter-in-law remain new and uncharted territory. Is the relationship between cohabitation and divorce only spurious, or does cohabitation really cause divorce? It's likely that both operate to some degree (Rhoads, Stanley, & Markman, 2009), but selection effects seem to receive the most support (Tach & Halpern-Meekin, 2009).

spurious: When a relationship between two variables is actually caused by a third variable.

Why are there racial and ethnic differences in the relationship between cohabitation and divorce? Researchers Phillips and Sweeney (2005) speculate that it may be because Whites are more likely to characterize their relationship as trial marriages, whereas cohabitation for Blacks and Mexican Americans is more likely to function as a substitute for, or a precursor to, marriage. They suggest that more research is needed to truly understand the meanings of cohabitation across different racial and ethnic groups.

We do know that cohabiting relationships, just like all relationships, don't always end easily, nor are they free of problems. For example, after dissolution, the economic standing of formerly cohabiting women declines precipitously compared to that of men, leaving a substantial portion of women in poverty (Avellar & Smock, 2005). This problem is particularly pronounced for Black and Hispanic women. The economic inequality among men and women is primarily the result of women having custody of children (33 percent of formerly cohabiting women have children living with them, compared to 3 percent of men), and the lower earnings of women. Women can't maintain the same standard of living as men after their relationship ends, and nearly one-third of them become impoverished (Avellar & Smock, 2005).

Cohabitation and Children

About 40 percent of cohabiting couples have children under the age of 18 residing in the home, born to one or both partners, which is about the same percentage of married couples who have children in the home (Lofquist, Lugaila, O'Connell, & Feliz, 2012). Most often, the children are from one partner's previous union, but today, many cohabiting couples have at least one child together. Let's meet one of these children in the boxed feature *My Family: My Mom, Her Boyfriend, and Me.*

What effects does living in a cohabiting family have on children? It's not easy to answer this question. Whether cohabitation is good or bad for children largely depends on what alternatives exist, such as living with a single mother, living with a mother and her unmarried partner, living with a mother and her new spouse (stepfather), living with two cohabiting biological parents, or living with two married biological parents. Children can potentially benefit from living

My mom and dad divorced when I was seven. I have quite a few early memories of my dad, mostly positive. I remember how he used to sing a little wake-up song for me every morning, and he often made me oatmeal before going to school. However, I also remember that he and my mom would argue a lot, and most of those fights ended with him leaving and slamming the back door behind him.

One day, when he was making my oatmeal, he told me that he was going to go live somewhere else. I didn't really know what that meant, but I didn't feel good about it. He didn't say anything else. Later that day, after school, my mom told me more. They both loved me, she said, but couldn't live together, and my dad was going to move to a different town to find a new job. I didn't see my dad for almost four months after that, and I was devastated. Finally, he reappeared, and from then on I would say that I saw him about once a month. I rarely went to his house. He usually just came to see me for the day, or even for just a few hours. So, my life basically just revolved around my mom and me. Sometimes I felt lonely, but my mom and I got really close. In some ways she seemed like a big sister, and we talked about a lot of private things.

My mom dated a little bit, which was very weird for me. But then, when I was about eleven, she met Jack, and he started coming over all the time. He was okay—kind of funny, and nice, but it bugged me having him there all the time. After awhile my mom said that we were going to move and live together at Jack's house. I wasn't happy at all because this meant that I had to switch schools. But they told me what a cool room I was going to have, and they would now have the money to do fun things, like to go to Disney World.

Jack was nice and all, and my mom really liked him, but it was weird at first. He started acting like he was my dad or something, you know, telling me what to do, or when my bedtime would be. I already have a dad, you know? But, I did like him coming to the school's open house with my mom, and he would sometimes come with my mom to my soccer games on Saturday. I liked that, but I was always embarrassed about what to call him. Dad? No way. Jack? I was afraid my friends would stare at me. My mother's boyfriend? How embarrassing! So, I didn't really ever call him anything. I wonder if he noticed.

One of the challenges of cohabiting families is that they are not very stable, which can be detrimental to children's social and emotional well-being.

We all lived together for years, but then, he and my mom started arguing about things. After a while they seemed to argue about everything. So, when I was 14 my mom and I moved out and got our own apartment. It was small compared to Jack's place, and not nearly as nice, but luckily I didn't have to switch schools again. My mom was sad at first, and moped around a lot, but is doing just fine now. You know, the odd thing is, although we lived together for about three years, I never saw Jack again. Poof, he just vanished.

—Ella, age 19

WHAT DO YOU THINK?

1. What are some of the challenges and opportunities that Ella faced when her mother cohabited with Jack? Do you think the cohabitation was good, bad, or neutral for Ella?
2. What advice would you offer a parent who wants to cohabit on how to make it easier for the child?

with a cohabiting partner when resources are shared with family members. For example, a study by sociologists Manning and Brown (2006) found that between 7 percent and 9 percent of children of cohabiting relationships faced *high risk* (defined as experiencing poverty, food insecurity, and housing insecurity), compared to 13 percent of children living with a single mother. However, just to make a complete comparison, only 2 percent of children in married biological or married stepparent families faced this risk.

In general, children receive most support and do best when they're raised in households with two married biological parents (Goodman & Greaves, 2010; Osborne, Manning, & Smock, 2007). On average, children in two-parent biological families have better academic, psychological, and social outcomes. These children have greater family incomes, experience fewer transitions in their lives, and have more involvement with their fathers. In particular,

- Cohabiting biological fathers spend less time in activities with their children than do married fathers, although they tend to spend more time with and are more supportive of their children than unmarried fathers who don't live with their children (even when still romantically involved with the children's mother).

- Male cohabiting partners spend less time in children's organized activities, such as school and community activities, than do married stepfathers or biological fathers.

- Children who live with their mother and her unmarried partner have poorer school performance and exhibit more behavioral problems than do children who live solely with a single mother, with a mother and stepfather, or with two biological parents.

- Cohabiting families spend their money differently than do married-parent families, divorced single-parent families, or never-married single-parent families. For example, compared to married families, cohabiting families spend a greater amount of money on alcohol and tobacco and a smaller amount of money on education (DeLeire & Kalil, 2005).

Some of these differences may be because of the different motivations for cohabitation (e.g., some have marriage plans and some don't). Cohabitation relationships are not homogeneous (Poortman & Mills, 2012). Differences may also be because of the vagueness of the cohabiting partner's role in childrearing. For example, is a male cohabiting partner supposed to be a father-surrogate, a special adult male in the child's life, or simply the mother's boyfriend? Few norms surround the role of cohabiting partner, and families are largely left on their own to negotiate this social terrain.

These differences may also result from differing characteristics of cohabiting and married couples, such as lower education levels of cohabiting parents (Faban, 2013; Goodman & Greaves, 2010). For example, a longitudinal study of 19,000 newborns in the UK, with subsequent interviews when the child was 9 months old, 3 years old, and 5 years old, suggests that we must look at multiple factors when we assess how children fare in cohabiting versus married-couple households. The researchers found that by the time children were age 3, statistically significant differences had already emerged in child outcomes between children born to married parents and those born to cohabiting parents. On average, children born to married parents display better social and emotional development and stronger cognitive development than children born to cohabiting parents. However, the gap in cognitive development was greatly reduced after differences in parents' education, occupation, income, and housing tenure were controlled for. This suggests that the lower cognitive development of children born to cohabiting parents compared with children born to married parents is largely accounted for by their parents' lower education and income, and not by their parents' unmarried state, *per se* (Goodman & Greaves, 2010).

However, let's not overgeneralize the strength of two-parent biological families; some married-couple households are unhappy or fraught with conflict, while many cohabiting families are warm and loving. Moreover, not all families can be constructed with two married parents. Rather than embrace only one type of family structure as "best" and others as "less than," a strengths perspective allows us to see the value of many different family forms and encourage their strengths while minimizing their challenges.

How do your parents feel about cohabitation? If you were to tell them that you and your boyfriend/girlfriend were going to move in together, what would they say? Are there certain contexts in which they would likely approve or disapprove? Do their opinions matter to you?

3.5 Discuss gay and lesbian intimate relationships

Question That Matters

3.13 What are some differences and similarities between homosexual and heterosexual couples?

Gay and Lesbian Intimate Relationships

Throughout the world, there are differing personal opinions and governmental policies surrounding gay and lesbian intimate relationships. In some countries, same-sex couples are freely allowed to wed and adopt children. In other countries, there are serious legal penalties for persons engaging in consensual sex between adults of the same sex. Today, the United States falls somewhere between these two views. Although sex between consenting adults of the same sex is no longer illegal, in 1996 the U.S. Congress passed a federal law, the Defense of Marriage Act (DOMA), which had two main goals: (1) to define *marriage* as a "legal union of one man and one woman as husband and wife"; and (2) to allow each state to deny constitutional marital rights between persons of the same sex that have been recognized in another state. Former President Bush emphasized, "I strongly believe that marriage should be defined as between a man and a woman. I am troubled by activist judges who are defining marriage." As a presidential candidate, President Obama said he would work to repeal DOMA (Wilson, 2009). In June 2013, the U.S. Supreme Court declared that Section 3 of DOMA was unconstitutional, which meant that same-sex couples could no longer be denied federal marriage benefits, such as receiving social security survivor benefits or filing joint tax returns. In the meantime, a number of states have independently legalized same-sex marriage. A study of same-sex couples and their views of marriage found that a large majority of participants reported a positive attitude toward the legalization of same-sex marriage. It also found that gay men expressed a lower desire to marry than did lesbian participants (Baiocco, Argalia, & Laghi, 2012).

Commitment and Cohabitation

Despite popular stereotypes that homosexuals, particularly gay men, have frequent sex with multiple partners, in reality, many gays and lesbians lead quiet and unassuming lives in committed monogamous relationships (Biblarz & Savci, 2010; Peplau & Beals, 2004). Estimating the number of same-sex couples is difficult; many fear identification because of discrimination or abuse. With this

Many gays and lesbians are in long-term committed relationships, despite our stereotypes to the contrary.

caveat in mind, the American Psychological Association suggests that between 40 percent and 60 percent of gay men and between 45 percent and 80 percent of lesbians are currently involved in a committed relationship. In addition, between 18 percent and 28 percent of gay couples and 8 percent to 21 percent of lesbian couples have lived together 10 years or more (American Psychological Association, 2009; Kurdek, 2004). Another source of data is the U.S. Census Bureau, which began to compile data on unmarried same-sex households in 2000. The Census Bureau showed 358,000 same-sex unmarried partner households in 2000, increasing to 646,000 in 2010 (Lofquist, Lugaila, O'Connell, & Feliz, 2012). In 2000, same-sex unmarried partner households accounted for 0.3 percent of all households, doubling in proportion to 0.6 percent of all households in 2010. Regionally, same-sex unmarried partner households were most common in the West (0.7 percent) and least common in the Midwest (0.4 percent). Of all areas, Washington, DC, had the highest percentage of same-sex unmarried partner households (1.8 percent).

Similarities and Differences

We know that many gays and lesbians live together in committed and loving relationships despite the fact that they cannot marry in most states. This leads researchers to wonder if same-sex couples differ significantly from heterosexual couples, or whether gay relationships are structured differently from lesbian relationships.

DIFFERENCES BETWEEN SAME-SEX AND HETEROSEXUAL COUPLES   To compare different types of relationships, the late family scholar Lawrence Kurdek collected data over time from gay, lesbian, and heterosexual married couples and compared many aspects of their relationships (Kurdek, 2006, 2007, 2009). He looked at relationship quality, level of commitment, level of satisfaction with the relationship, social support from family and friends, conflict and its resolution, and equality. He controlled for important sociodemographic variables (e.g., age, time living together, whether the couple had children) so that any findings could be attributed to sexual orientation rather than to other factors.

Kurdek found very few differences between same-sex couples and heterosexual couples, and most differences he did find were very small. For example, both gay and lesbian couples were more comfortable with closeness compared to their married counterparts, were more open with their partner, and were more autonomous in the relationship. Lesbians, in particular, reported greater levels of equality in their relationship and higher satisfaction. Gays and lesbians also reported receiving less support from family members than did the married couples, although lesbians reported greater support from friends. Overall, on three-quarters of the indicators, no significant differences emerged between same-sex and heterosexual married couples. It would seem then that heterosexual and same-sex couples are more alike than they are different.

The husband and wife research team of psychologists John and Julie Gottman (Gottman Relationship Institute, 2013) report similar findings: Their 12-year study shows few if any critical differences between same-sex and heterosexual couples. What they did find is that same-sex couples are more upbeat in the face of conflict. Compared to straight couples, gay and lesbian couples use more affection and humor when they bring up a disagreement, and partners are more positive in how they receive it. Gay and lesbian couples are also more likely to remain positive after a disagreement. The Gottmans found that same-sex couples use fewer controlling and hostile emotional tactics and display less belligerence, domineering, and fear with each other than straight couples do. In an argument, same-sex couples take things less personally. In straight couples, it's easier to hurt a partner with a negative comment than it is to make one's partner feel good with a positive comment. This appears to be reversed in same-sex couples (Gottman Relationship Institute, 2013).

DIFFERENCES BETWEEN LESBIAN AND GAY COUPLES   Using the same set of variables from gay, lesbian, and married couples, Kurdek assessed how gay and lesbian couples differ from one another (Kurdek, 2003). He found even fewer differences between gay and lesbian couples than he did when he compared them to heterosexual married couples. There were virtually no differences between the two groups in the predictors of relationship quality, social support, and the likelihood of dissolution. The most significant results emerged in the relationship-related attitudinal questions, where there were differences in three of the eight variables. Lesbian couples reported stronger liking, trust, and equality than did gay couples. Again, it appears that differences among committed couples are generally minimal, whether gay, lesbian, or married heterosexual.

*D*o you know any gay or lesbian couples? If so, how are their relationships similar to or different from the heterosexual couples you know? Since they probably had few role models to observe how gays or lesbians behave in committed relationships, where or how did they learn about what it means to be a couple?

Bringing It Full Circle

This chapter explored how we build loving and intimate relationships. It discussed our lives as singles and the friendships that we share. It then turned to a discussion of the changing nature of courtship, dating, and mate selection. The opening vignette focused on cohabitation, and the way in which it has become increasingly normative, and a normal, natural part of building a relationship—it may or may not lead to marriage. At first glance, this vignette seems to be the personal story of Meghan and Jono and the choices they made; however, there is far more to the story than personal choice because many macro-level factors are at play. Did you notice that neither Meghan nor Jono feels stigmatized for being single at age 30, reflecting macro-level changes in the age at first marriage? We also saw that their cohabitation had an air of informality, a result of women's increasing social and economic opportunities that, in turn, offer more chances for men and women to meet and socialize. Finally, 50 years ago, their cohabitation would have likely been a scandal. Today, because of many social movements, cohabitation has become an increasingly common feature of romantic relationships. As you can see, both micro- and macro-level factors can help us understand how we build relationships.

Now that you see things in a new light, let's review the information throughout the chapter in the opening vignette to see how it might relate to your life:

- How are dating and courtship today different from your parents' generation? How about your grandparents' generation? Can you think of specific ways that things have changed in your own family?

- What are your views of cohabitation? Would you cohabit, as Meghan and Jono do, or have you already? Why or why not?

- What evidence have you seen that cohabitation is becoming increasingly common, or even expected? Do you think there may be racial, ethnic, or social class differences in the way that cohabitation is viewed? Why or why not?

On MySocLab

 Study and Review on MySocLab

CHAPTER REVIEW

LO3.1 Analyze singlehood

3.1 How many people are single?

It depends on what you mean by single. Do you mean never married? Or do you mean currently unmarried, which includes people who are also widowed or divorced? The difference between these two ways of defining *single* can yield very different results.

3.2 What does it mean to be *single*?

Single means different things to different people. It can include the never married, divorced, and widowed people who are not in a committed relationship or cohabiting. If we want to broaden our understanding of singles, we can ask two critical questions: (1) Is it voluntary; and (2) Is it a temporary situation? Together these two dimensions yield four very different groups of singles: voluntary temporary singles, voluntary stable singles, involuntary temporary singles, and involuntary stable singles.

LO3.2 Discuss issues surrounding friendships

3.3 Why is friendship important in our lives?

Close friendships provide companionship, support, self-esteem, and teach us about ourselves and others. Some of our most important and intimate relationships are with our friends. Friends are also good for your physical and mental health. Having close friends who you can confide in has been shown to lower blood pressure, heart rate, and cholesterol level.

3.4 How do friendships differ by sex, race, ethnicity, or social class?

Our social statuses shape the types of our friendships. For example, although men and women have about the same number of friends, women's friendships are usually more personal or intimate in nature. We also find that friendships among lower-income and minority groups tend to be longer-lasting and more intimate.

3.5 Can men and women ever really be "just friends"?

Historically, cross-sex friendships that were strictly platonic were rare and believed to be part of the developmental process of romantic engagement (friends become lovers or lovers later become friends). Today, cross-sex friendships are far more common than they were in your parents' or grandparents' generation. They are highly valued, but can contain some tensions as well.

LO3.3 Identify the influences on dating, courtship, and mate selection

3.6 How has the purpose and structure of dating changed over time?

One of the primary goals of dating is mate selection. In the past, dating was more formal. A young gentleman "called" on a woman and remained under the watchful eye of her parents. With the rise of an adolescent subculture, where young men and women have more opportunities at school or work to interact with less supervision, they are now more able to date and socialize independently.

3.7 How have macro-level factors shaped our micro-level choices with respect to dating?

In the realm of dating, many macro-level factors influence our personal choices. Examples of these factors include women's status in society, the rise of an adolescent subculture, technology (e.g., the automobile), and economic considerations.

3.8 What are some contemporary trends in dating?

Many people do not even use the term *date* today. High school seniors, for example, are far less likely than just a generation ago to say that they date. Today, dating is often conducted in informal groups, with the possibility of gradually pairing off. Many couples cohabit, with or without discussing marriage.

LO3.4 Describe heterosexual cohabitation

3.9 How common is cohabitation?

The number of people who cohabit has increased dramatically over the past few decades. In 1970, there were only about 500,000 couples cohabiting; by 2008, there were nearly 7 million.

3.10 How have attitudes regarding cohabitation changed over time?

Our society began to view cohabitation more favorably beginning in the 1960s and 1970s. Today most of us know people who have cohabited and we consider it an acceptable lifestyle. However, few people say that cohabitation has been "good" for our society—most say that it either has made no difference or that it is actually bad for society.

3.11 How does cohabitation affect marriage?

Many cohabiting relationships do not lead to marriage; about half of cohabiting relationships break up in less than a year, and less than 10 percent last 5 years or more. Among those cohabiting couples who do marry, they have a greater chance of divorcing than do couples who did not cohabit. However, this may be a selection effect, or it may be a spurious relationship.

3.12 What are the effects of cohabitation on children?

Deciding whether cohabitation is good or bad for children largely depends on what alternatives exist. Cohabitation can be both good and bad, depending on the family make-up. Generally speaking, children do best when they live with two biological parents, but of course there are exceptions to this.

LO3.5 Discuss gay and lesbian intimate relationships

3.13 What are some differences and similarities between homosexual and heterosexual couples?

There are very few differences between homosexual and heterosexual couples, and the differences found seem to be rather small. In sum, these groups are far more alike than they are different.

KEY TERMS

adolescence	homogamous relationships	propinquity
calling	involuntary stable singles	selection effect
cohabitation	involuntary temporary singles	spurious
cross-sex friendships	pool of eligibles	voluntary stable singles
dating script	principle of least interest	voluntary temporary singles

Love and Loving Relationships

((• Listen to Chapter 4 on **MySocLab**

Would you consider allowing your mother to choose your marriage partner? In the United States, most young people would say, "No thanks."

However, arranged marriages are common in other parts of the world and most young adults would not have it any other way.

Rati and Subas are an educated and attractive young couple from Nepal, married here in the United States four years ago. What distinguishes them from other young couples is that their marriage was arranged. As Rati, the young woman, gratefully says, "I never had the thought that I would find my own partner because even though it was risky, I wanted to be on the safer side and have my parents make the major decision for me because their support has always worked. So in the big step of my life, I just let my parents decide."

"I wanted to be on the safer side and have my parents make the major decision for me because their support has always worked."

👁 **Watch** on **MySocLab**
Video: *Arranged Marriage: Rati and Subas*

In an arranged marriage, instead of the couple getting together and interacting with each other, parents or other family members bring a proposal to either the groom or the bride. In Rati and Subas' case, Rati's mother set up the meeting. She met Subas for an hour or so, and asked him a series of questions about himself, his occupation, and his family. She thought he might be an excellent match for her daughter. Rati said that her mother did not push her, but simply encouraged her to think about Subas as a possible husband. Rati and Subas met briefly on a few occasions, always supervised by others, and quickly agreed to be married.

"In our culture, you don't have to appeal to each other before you get married," Rati explains. "You get married and start to get to know one another, and then you'll develop feelings."

Rati boarded a plane in Nepal for the United States, where Subas was living. She had never been to the United States before, or had even been on an airplane, so she was nervous. But when she saw him at the airport ready and waiting to greet her, she immediately felt comfortable. It was then, she says, that she started developing feelings for him.

Subas takes his role as a husband very seriously. He believes that it is his job to take care of his wife emotionally, financially, and socially. He has introduced Rati to American culture and has taught her how to cope with life in an American city. Rati thinks he is an excellent husband. Subas and Rati have been married for four years, are very happy, and hope to have children soon. They both agree that their arranged marriage now "is like a love marriage."

When we think about love, we usually see it as a micro-level phenomenon—full of warmth, intimacy, and passion. We care deeply about someone, and he or she in turn cares deeply about us. We *feel* love on this level, and we like it. However, our feelings don't exist in a vacuum. The way we experience love is also shaped by the macro-level social context in which we live. First, love is related to culture. In the United States, for example, the focus is on romantic love. In other cultures, this type of passion may be thought of as foolish. Love alone is a poor reason for marriage because it's too fragile, and possibly too fleeting (Allendorf, 2013; Griffith, 2006). Instead, like Rati and Subas, many young people in these cultures opt for an arranged marriage.

Second, people have been socialized to see and experience love differently depending on their sex, social class, race, and ethnicity. The meanings attached to love and how we express them differ; for example, women often express their love with words, whereas men may express their love more with actions.

Third, love is also related to the relationship between the people who love, including parents and children, friends, and romantic partners. These relationships are profoundly different from one another, but contain an emotion that we all call *love*. What is love, then, that it can encompass so many different relationships and distinct feelings within those relationships?

This chapter addresses some of the complexities of the meanings and experiences of love. First, however, let's try to define this ideal that we all seem to seek.

love: A strong affection for one another arising out of kinship or personal ties; attraction based on sexual desire; and affection based on admiration, benevolence, or common interests.

4.1 Define love

Question That Matters

4.1 What do we mean by the term *love*?

Love is based on mutual affection and emotion. When we love someone, we feel something stronger toward him or her than we do toward others.

What Is Love?

The topic of love is everywhere, and is deeply fascinating, but providing a definition of *love* for all of our different types of relationships is complicated (Felmlee & Sprecher, 2006; Fehr, Sprecher, & Underwood, 2009). It's hard to imagine that the way we feel about our lovers, fathers, best friends, and daughters can be generalized to a "one-size-fits-all" definition.

The Merriam-Webster dictionary defines **love** as (1) a strong affection for one another arising out of kinship or personal ties; (2) attraction based on sexual desire; and (3) affection based on admiration, benevolence, or common interests (Merriam-Webster Online, 2013). We may speak of the love a parent feels for a child, the love a child feels for a sibling, the love between two friends, or the love experienced by romantic partners. Let's discuss a few components of this definition. First: Love is an enduring bond between two or more people. Loving relationships are those we intend to be long-lasting. Second: Love is based on affection and emotion. When we love another person, we feel something stronger toward him or her than we do towards others. In romantic partners, these feelings are usually sexual. Third: Love includes a feeling of obligation toward another. When you love someone, you want to take care of that person and help him or her when he or she needs it, both physically and emotionally.

People who study love approach the concept in a variety of ways. Some focus on our first description for love—a strong affection for one another arising out of kinship or personal ties. This refers to a bond or sense of attachment. How do we come to attach ourselves to others, and what are these different types of attachments? Psychologists believe that we observe a biological component of bonding in early infancy, when dependent infants become attached to their primary caregivers (usually their mothers). As we discuss in the next section, psychologists think that this initial bonding, or *attachment*, then shapes the way we construct all other attachments throughout our lives, including those of romantic relationships.

Do you think it's possible to study love scientifically? Recalling what you learned in Chapter 1 about research methods, which approach, if any, might work best, and why? Which approach, if any, might be inappropriate, and why?

Love as Attachment

Humans are social beings and need interaction with others to survive. This notion forms the basis of **attachment theory** (Bowlby, 1969; Kriss, Steele, & Steele, 2012), which asserts that the way infants form attachments early in life affects their relationships later in life.

Attachment in Children

In the beginning, infants and children stay close to their parents or caregivers because they must for survival. They're completely dependent on others for their physical and emotional care. Attachment theorists suggest these early attachments infants make with their primary caregiver have implications for the way they make attachments to others throughout life.

How important are bonds and secure attachment early in life? You may have heard stories of children growing up in orphanages or children living in abusive families who have been denied opportunities to form secure and loving bonds with consistent caregivers. If a child's needs are frequently ignored or the child is repeatedly given a harsh or inappropriate response, he or she may fail to develop a sense of trust. This lack of trust can lead to further problems in personal development and in social relationships (Fearon, Bakermans-Kranenburg, IJzendoorn, Lapsley & Roisman, 2010; Mooney, 2009). Children with insecure attachment patterns have difficulty forming close and intimate relationships, possibly throughout their lives, unless they receive help (Kochanska & Kim, 2013; Lee, 2003).

One of the first case studies of the damage inadequate attachment can cause is the study of Anna, a girl born in the 1930s who lived her early life tied to a chair, alone in a room (Davis, 1940, 1947; Macionis, 2013). A social worker was called to a rural farmhouse to investigate a complaint about possible child abuse. In the house, she was greeted gruffly by an elderly man and his obviously mentally challenged adult daughter. The daughter was dependent on her elderly father for help, but she showed no outward signs of abuse—so why was the social worker called? The answer was soon revealed. A noise, a search of the farmhouse, and there, in a dimly lit second-floor attic, was a girl about 8 years old wedged into a chair with her arms tied. The girl was thin, dirty, and in diapers. She sat listlessly and stared into space. As the social worker approached her, speaking softly and kindly, the girl showed no sign of outward communication, such as eye contact or speech.

The social worker learned the little girl was called "Anna." Her mother had become pregnant out of wedlock as a young woman, and Anna's grandfather was so enraged about the pregnancy that at first he refused to allow the baby in the house. Anna was initially cared for elsewhere, but her mother could not afford this care and brought Anna home to the farmhouse. The little girl was shut away, with only enough food and water to keep her alive. She stayed in the attic for years until found by the social worker.

When sociologist Kingsley Davis heard of the child, he went to see her immediately. Although Anna was 8, she had the mental development of a 2-year-old. She did not talk or even smile. Anna's deprivation and trauma were so

4.2 Explain love as attachment

Questions That Matter

4.2 How do we first learn to love?

4.3 What are the three primary attachment styles?

4.4 Does our attachment in infancy affect us as adults?

attachment theory: A theory postulating that the way in which infants form attachments early in life affects relationships throughout later life.

⊙ **Watch** on **MySocLab**
Video: *Attachment in Infants*

Infants whose emotional needs are frequently ignored by their primary caregiver experience considerable stress, resulting in insecure attachments.

secure attachment: An attachment type where infants feel safe when their mothers are out of sight.

anxious-ambivalent attachment: An attachment type where infants become nervous when their parent leaves the room and can show rejection when the parent returns.

avoidant attachment: An attachment type where infants show little attachment to their primary parent.

severe that they left her nearly devoid of human qualities. Davis visited her again after Anna had been in the care of social workers for 10 days, and he found considerable improvement. Anna was somewhat responsive and even smiled. Over the next year, she learned to walk and to feed herself, but it took her nearly 2 years to begin to speak. Her years of isolation had done tremendous damage, but just how much of it was permanent we will never know; tragically, she died of a blood disorder at the age of 10.

What is attachment, and why is it so important? Psychologist Mary Ainsworth and her colleagues studied early interactions between infants and their mothers to answer these questions (Ainsworth, Blehar, Waters, & Wall, 1978). Using experiments to assess infants' reactions when their mothers were temporarily removed from their sight, they found three basic patterns of reactions, reflecting the quality of the infants' attachments with their mothers. About two-thirds of the infants had **secure attachments**, in which they felt safe when their mothers were out of sight. These attachments reflected children's confidence in knowing their mothers would be available when needed, an assurance that came from mothers having been warm, responsive, and consistently available to infants over time. In other relationships, mothers were less predictably warm and responsive to their infants, resulting in stress among the infants who, in turn, developed insecure attachments. Some of these infants were characterized as **anxious-ambivalent**; they became nervous when their mothers left and then showed rejection of their mothers when they returned. An equal number of infants were characterized as **avoidant**, showing little attachment to their mothers at all. Ainsworth and her colleagues found that these mothers neglected the physical and emotional needs of their infants, and therefore the infants had no expectation that the mothers would be there for comfort.

Adult Romantic Attachments

Elicia and Damien met while working as counselors at a summer camp sponsored by their church. Elicia liked Damien immediately. They struck up a close friendship, but the rules at the camp prohibited them from developing much intimacy. Nonetheless, they spent a lot of time together and genuinely enjoyed one another's company. Elicia told Damien that she was in love with him and asked Damien if he felt the same way. Damien felt flustered by her question, and told her that he liked her, but that he really did not know her well enough to think about being in love. This answer made Elicia insecure, and she panicked for fear that he would not want to see her when the summer ended and they went back to college. Elicia decided that she would try even harder to make Damien love her.

> *. . . she panicked for fear that he would not want to see her when the summer ended and they went back to college.*

Can our relationships as infants affect our relationships twenty, thirty, or forty years later? Infants and children develop a history of attachment that researchers and psychologists refer to as a *working model* (Cassidy, 2000). This history influences our friendships (Dwyer, Fredstrom, Rubin, Booth-LaForce, Rose-Krasnor, & Burgess, 2010) and adult relationships, for better or worse (Fletcher, Simpson, Campbell, & Overall, 2013; Obegi & Berant, 2009; Shaver & Mikulincer, 2009). Adult romantic relationships exhibit three distinct types of bonds, corresponding to the infant attachments described here (Mikulincer

& Shaver, 2007; Shaver & Mikulincer, 2009). The three types, with some representative characterizing statements, are:

1. Secure attachments
   —*I find it relatively easy to get close to others.*
   —*I am usually comfortable depending on others and having them depend on me.*
   —*I generally don't worry about being abandoned.*

2. Anxious–ambivalent attachments
   —*Other people don't seem to want to get as close as I do, and it scares them away.*
   —*I often worry that my partner doesn't really love me or won't want to stay with me.*
   —*I tend to get close to a partner very quickly, usually before they do.*

3. Avoidant attachments
   —*I am just not that comfortable being close to someone.*
   —*It's difficult to trust people completely, and I'd rather not become too dependent on them.*
   —*Other people seem to want me to be more intimate and personal than I feel comfortable being, and that makes me nervous.*

Elicia, introduced in the story on page 102, demonstrates an anxious-ambivalent set of attachments. She wants to get close to Damien very quickly, and is worried that he doesn't love her or will abandon her after their summer camp experience.

As individuals create new relationships and romantic partnerships, they rely in part on earlier relationships to give them clues about what to expect from others. For example, a seven-year longitudinal survey following 112 adolescents as they entered adulthood found that individuals with secure working models experienced low stress in their relationships with parents, peers, and romantic partners and turned to their social network when they needed any help with their relationships. In contrast, those adolescents with more anxious working models experienced high relationship stress, especially with their parents, and used less effective coping mechanisms (Seiffge-Krenke, 2006).

Attachment reveals itself in other ways. A survey based on 53 couples (heterosexual and same-sex couples) who had been together for at least two years examined how the combination of attachment styles related to their conflict and communication patterns. Secure-secure couples reported the most mutually constructive communication (Domingue & Mollen, 2009). Researchers also note that securely attached adults tend to be more comfortable with their sexuality (Feeney & Noller, 2004). They're less likely to have casual sexual partners, one-night stands, or sex outside their primary relationships, and are less likely to use sex to avoid negative emotions or to bolster self-esteem (Cooper, Pioli, Levitt, Talley, Micheas, & Collins, 2006; Stefanou & McCabe, 2012).

Critique of Attachment Theory

Although attachment theory can provide important insights into our marital and family relationships, some researchers question the degree to which we should apply research on infant attachments to explain the complexities of adult romantic attachments. First, for infants, attachment depends on receiving protection and comfort from another. However, in adult romantic relationships, both partners take the role of caregiver. At times, one partner can be stressed and in need of comfort, whereas at other times the other partner is in need. From a structural functionalist theoretical perspective, introduced in Chapter 1, this mutual dependency provides the stabilizing bond in marriage (Nock, 1998).

Can you identify the attachment model you had as a child? If so, can you point to specific instances where it has influenced your adult relationships? Was this attachment a positive or a negative experience?

Second, among adults, the love relationship is sexual, which further distinguishes it from infant attachment. Third, both positive and negative events happening in later childhood or adulthood, such as special mentoring, a parental divorce, or a sexual assault, can also shape attachment style (Hollist & Miller, 2005). Given these cautions, a review of a decade of theory and research on attachment concludes that studies in infant attachment cannot fully explain the dynamic nature of love in relationships over time (Fraley & Shaver, 2000).

Writings on love show it to be a complex and multidimensional concept. We next examine a broad sweep of history to highlight some of the more powerful images of love that provide the source of our ideals that continue to influence us today.

4.3 Identify images of love in history

Question That Matters

4.5 Have meanings of love changed over time?

Throughout history, there has been a high value on women's virginity. Chastity belts like this one helped to ensure that unmarried women would remain virgins.

Images of Love in History

Love and marriage—most people assume they go together "like a horse and carriage," as in the words of a popular song. In fact, the assumption that love and marriage go together is a relatively recent phenomenon (Coontz, 2005b; Maynes & Waltner, 2012). The way you view love is quite different from the way your great-grandparents probably viewed love.

Some of the earliest stories of love come from ancient Greek and Roman mythology. The mythological figures of Venus, the Roman goddess of love, and her son Cupid (the Greek version is the goddess Aphrodite and her son Eros) are familiar to us. The writings of the Greek philosopher Plato were infused with notions of love. Most classical stories of love were about passion and adoration, but they did not connect these romantic feelings to marriage. Greek men often kept their wives locked in their homes while they entertained prostitutes (Pomeroy, 1975). Marriage was more mundane and used for the purpose of reproduction. In fact, Plato wrote of the highest form of love as something that existed only between men—homosexual relationships were the only way to experience true love and romance (Dover, 1978). Women were not considered suitable partners for men's true love because they were thought to be intellectually inferior.

Early Christianity also didn't associate love with marriage. People—from nobles to peasants—married for practical or economic reasons, or because they couldn't control their sexual desires (Searle, 1988). Erotic sexuality was considered immoral. Ideally, men and women were to deny all desire in order to obtain holiness (Queen & Habenstein, 1967). Protective devices like chastity belts helped ensure that unmarried women would remain virgins; if a woman lost her virginity, she was thought to be unmarriageable and useless (Williams, 1993). Although marriage was seen as the route for those who couldn't control their desires of the flesh, even sex in marriage was suspect (Hendrick & Hendrick, 1992). Newly married couples could be barred from church for a period of time, followed by a set penance. Men who had sex with their wives were required to bathe before entering church (Williams, 1993).

In the 12th century, during the Middle Ages, we begin to see some precursors to our own ideas about love—passion, desire, romance, intensity, idolizing the other, and jealousy (Collins, 1986). This was a period of time when society was highly stratified—most people were peasants, but families with successful warriors gradually established a system of hereditary knighthood. These knights, particularly minstrel knights called *troubadours,* focused on the lord and especially on his lady, offering gifts, writing poetry, and singing romantic songs of adoration for the beautiful—yet unattainable—woman (Dickens, 1977). We call this courtly love (from which the term *courtship* is derived) because it was primarily engaged in by members of the royal court. As another sign of loyalty, the knights would sometimes wear an item belonging to the lord's wife, such as a scarf, into battle. These early forms of romantic love, as part of the concept of chivalry, placed women in a position of being idolized and adored.

A famous example of a relationship stirred by romantic courtly love is described in the legend of King Arthur, where his Queen Guinevere fell in love with Sir Lancelot. Many "illicit" romances among the ruling class were fueled by the quest for courtly love. In fact, one of the key characteristics of courtly love was that it was unattainable (de Rougemont, 1956). Poets wrote of passionate love for a woman who was unattainable because she was married to the lord. Yet, during the Middle Ages, most people were peasants and didn't have time for the rituals, rules, secrecy, and intensity of courtly love. Therefore, love was a phenomenon experienced primarily among the ruling class—the members of the courts across Europe (Alchin, n.d.).

By the 18th and early 19th centuries, ideas about romance expanded through the population, with an eye toward the marital relationship. People grew to value similarities between partners, sexual expression, and the emotional side of love. This *romantic love ideal* includes five core beliefs: (1) love at first sight; (2) there is one "true love" for each person; (3) love conquers all; (4) the beloved is (nearly) perfect; and (5) we should marry for love (Lantz, Keyes, & Schultz, 1975).

However, the Victorian period of the 19th century and the accompanying Industrial Revolution changed much of this romantic love ideal (Cott, 1978). As discussed in Chapter 1, people relocated from rural to urban areas to take paid work in shops and factories. As men were spending less time in the home, women became the heads of household and spent an increased amount of time caring for the needs of men and children. Along with these changes in gendered expectations, a new view emerged about men and women that historians call *the ideology of separate spheres*. The partnership orientation between married couples began to break down. Women were seen as childlike, delicate, and less intelligent than men, in need of their protection (Cott, 1978; Haller, 1972). This 19th-century popular view, evident in magazines, political speeches, and religious sermons across the United States, claimed that men were better suited for the harsh, difficult world of the new economy, whereas women were best suited for the work of caregiving. This separate-spheres idea perpetuated the view that love was defined by what women did in the home.

This change led to the **feminization of love** in the 19th century (Cancian, 1987). Marriage manuals, popular magazines, and other writings noted a lack of intimacy between partners, as their lives were increasingly dissimilar. Women were thought to have little or no sexual desire. The purpose of sexual behavior was to reproduce, and therefore the only acceptable behavior was heterosexual vaginal intercourse, because only that behavior could result in conception. Thus, sexuality was tied to the family, which was seen as a system of marriage, kinship, and inheritance (Foucault, 1978).

By the early 20th century, numerous social and political changes occurred in the United States that encouraged new constructions of love and sexuality. Love and sexuality were not just important intimate bonds between husbands and wives, but were considered *mandatory* to a good relationship (Coontz, 2005b; D'Emilio & Freedman, 1998). Marriage manuals during this era reveal a preoccupation with romantic love and sexual compatibility among partners. Sexual expression was no longer just a component of love, but the very basis of love itself. Falling *out* of love, or failing to experience sexual gratification, became defined as marital problems in need of help (Firestone, Firestone, & Catlett, 2008).

This brings us to our modern concept of love. In our culture, love has something to do with just about everything. "All you need is love," or so say the lyrics of the popular song by the Beatles.

courtly love: A poetic style of the Middle Ages when poets or troubadours would write songs of unrequited love and present them at the court of their aristocratic/royal masters.

feminization of love: The process beginning in the 19th century in which love became associated with the private work of women in the home, namely, nurturing and caring for family members.

Think back to your oldest relatives that you have known or have heard about. Do you think they equated marriage with love? Would you guess that they thought about love the same way you did when they were your age?

Question That Matters

4.6 What is the difference between romance and companionate love?

romantic love: A type of love characterized by passion, melodrama, and excitement, and that receives a lot of media attention.

👁 **Watch** on **MySocLab**
Video: *Relationships and Love*

Contemporary Ideas about Love

How do we think about love today? Romantic love seems to get the most attention, but companionate love seems to last the longest.

Romance, Romance, and More Romance

We can easily see vestiges of courtly love in today's **romantic love** (Hatfield, Bensman, & Rapson, 2012). It's a passionate, melodramatic, and exciting experience for all concerned. A look at fairy tales, movies, books, magazines, and television programs reveal countless images of beautiful "ladies" saved by strong "troubadour" knights. Think of the classic movies *Cinderella*, *Gone with the Wind*, *Titanic*, and many of today's reality dating shows. Women bring their beauty to these relationships, get the attention of men through flirting, and win them over by being coy. Yet, this romantic "script" has a downside, because it places women on a pedestal, promotes chivalry, and diminishes women to trophy status. This isn't real.

However, for most of us, romance also feels good, and we take it very seriously (Boer, 2013; Sternberg & Sternberg, 2008; Tennov, 1999). Although other cultures may see romantic love as rather silly, we consider it the most basic prerequisite for dating, cohabiting, and getting married. In fact, when romantic love no longer exists, many people end their marriages.

When in the throes of romantic love, partners find it difficult to concentrate fully on study or work—they long for their partner. They care so passionately for one another that they may ignore their other friends and responsibilities, living in a two-person world (Hatfield, 1988; Sternberg & Sternberg, 2008). But let's pause and ask ourselves: Does romantic love really last? Couples in long-term loving relationships do continue to mention the importance of romance (Acevedo & Aron, 2009; Graham, 2011; Masuda, 2003). However, long-term couples tend to focus on a deeper attachment that may not include physical passion. In fact, one researcher sought to conceptualize love by asking a group of people to list its various features or attributes freely (Fehr, 1988, 1993). After a long list of features was generated, a second group of people ranked them, and they're shown in Table 4.1. Note that romance isn't even on the list of the top 12 features of love. This research was originally conducted in the 1980s, but do you think the list would be any different today?

TABLE 4.1	Top Twelve Features of Love
Do you see anything missing? What happened to romance?	
1. Trust	
2. Care	
3. Honesty	
4. Friendship	
5. Respect	
6. Desire to promote the well-being of the other	
7. Loyalty	
8. Commitment	
9. Accepting the other without wanting to change the other	
10. Support	
11. Desire to be in the other's company	
12. Consideration of and interest in the other	

Source: Fehr, 1988.

Companionate Love

Over time, the intensity of romantic love can begin to fade as people get to know one another. What may have seemed cute about someone at the beginning of a relationship can be downright annoying a few years later. Although people who are newly in love think this type of relationship will last forever, long-term love is deep, meaningful, and gratifying to those lucky enough to have it. **Companionate love** is based on strong commitment and trust that the other person will genuinely "be there" for you, no matter what. It grows over time as partners come to know and understand one another. They have learned one another's strengths, weaknesses, and quirks, and appreciate the feeling of connectedness and support they share (Knobloch-Fedders & Knudson, 2009).

companionate love: A type of love that grows over time, based on strong commitment, friendship, and trust.

Companionate love can also contain romance, but the emphasis is on companionship. It's based on strong commitment and trust that grows over time.

We consider romantic love to be the most basic prerequisite for marriage, even though other cultures see our preoccupation with romantic love as silly.

Long-term loving couples have a shared history, a sense of community, and likely have children together who solidify a strong family bond. Moreover, a long-term relationship needn't kill romantic love. In fact, romantic love, without the early obsession that so often goes with it, can make long-term relationships stronger and more rewarding (Acevedo & Aron, 2009).

If you are (or have been) in a loving relationship, would you guess that your relationship leans toward being more romantic or more companionate? The boxed feature *Getting to Know Yourself* gives you the opportunity to assess

GETTING TO KNOW YOURSELF — Is Your Loving Relationship More Romantic or Companionate?

If you're in (or have been in) a loving relationship, let's see if it leaned more toward a passionate romance or comfortable companionship. Answer each question about this relationship honestly. Your answers can include:

1 = Yes, almost always; 2 = Sometimes; 3 = No, not really

____ **1.** I feel included in my partner's life.
____ **2.** We are very good friends, and I expect that we always will be.
____ **3.** Our sex life is intense, satisfying, and very important to us.
____ **4.** We were attracted to each other immediately when we met—love at first sight.
____ **5.** I believe that my partner sees me as a best friend.
____ **6.** I like to spend all my free time with my partner.
____ **7.** Sometimes I get so excited about being in love with my partner that I cannot sleep.
____ **8.** My partner admires me.
____ **9.** My partner and I touch each other a lot.
____ **10.** I like to know where my partner is all the time, so we call, text, or email each other several times a day.
____ **11.** I get butterflies in my stomach when I think of my partner.

____ **12.** I'm not really sure when our friendship turned to love.
____ **13.** We have shared goals and future plans.
____ **14.** My partner will always "be there" for me when I have difficult times.
____ **15.** My partner and I spend a lot of time gazing into one another's eyes.

There is naturally some overlap between romantic and companionate relationships. However, in general, questions 3, 4, 6, 7, 9, 10, 11, and 15 lean toward the romantic, and questions 1, 2, 5, 8, 12, 13, and 14 lean toward the companionate. Were you more likely to score 1s or 2s on one set of traits versus the other?

WHAT DO YOU THINK?

1. Do you think that you and your partner would answer these questions in the same way? How might gendered expectations, which you learned about in Chapter 2, influence the way people answer this quiz?
2. Do you think these answers might vary across social classes, or among persons of different races or ethnicities? Why or why not?

your relationship. Keep in mind that romantic and companionate relationships are not actually *dichotomies*; romantic relations certainly contain companionship, whereas companionate relationships contain romance. The difference is on the emphasis within each.

4.5 Classify theoretical perspectives on love

Question That Matters

4.7 What do biological, micro-level, and macro-level perspectives teach us about love?

Theoretical Perspectives on Love

If you've ever been in love, do you ever wonder why you fell in love with that *particular* person, given the thousands of people you can expect to meet in your life? Next, we discuss the different conceptions about love, how and why people fall in love, how love develops, and the different types of love that people experience. The theories fall into three categories: (1) biological perspectives, (2) micro-level perspectives, and (3) macro-level perspectives. Remember, there's no single *right* perspective. Each looks at different issues, and together they give us a broad picture of love.

Biological and Chemical Perspectives on Love

Many researchers are turning to biology to help us understand the role that love plays in our lives.

sociobiology: An evolutionary theory that all humans have an instinctive impulse to pass on their genetic material.

SOCIOBIOLOGY   **Sociobiology** is the study of how biology shapes our social life. Sociobiologists would argue that attraction and love are evolutionary processes that assist humans in passing on their genetic material and drawing them into long-term relationships to raise a child. When a woman bears a child, it's clear she is the biological mother (except in recent cases of surrogacy, as discussed in Chapter 8). There is little certainty, however, who is the biological father, and sociobiologists claim that this has led men and women to approach love and desire in different ways (Buss, 2012; Duntley & Buss, 2008). Historically, men may look to establish more than one romantic attachment because having multiple partners increases the odds of becoming a parent. Yet because women know their biological offspring, they're more selective about entering a relationship. Sociobiologists point to this as an evolutionary process that over the centuries has produced the behavioral patterns of dating and sexual relationships we observe today (Thornhill & Gangestad, 2008).

Sociobiology also suggests that biology holds a clue to the *type* of people to whom men and women are attracted. Women tend to seek out older, larger men, who have a higher status than they do so that the men can support and protect them when they're physically restricted through pregnancy, childbirth, and the child-rearing years. Men's attraction, however, tends toward younger women who are the most fertile. Interestingly, these age and status patterns persist today. Buss's research (1989) from more than 10,000 people spanning 33 countries found that men across cultures were more likely to value physical attractiveness and youthfulness in their potential mates, whereas good financial prospects appealed to women.

biochemical perspective of love: Theories that suggest humans are attracted to certain types of people, at which point the brain releases natural chemicals that give us a "rush" we experience as sexual attraction.

BIOCHEMICAL APPROACHES TO LOVE   A related approach that looks at biological and chemical factors to explain love is called a **biochemical perspective**. When we establish eye contact with, touch, or smell the scent of a person with features we see as desirable, our brain releases a flood of natural amphetamines, such as dopamine, norepinephrine, and phenylethylamine (PEA), to the nerves and blood stream and give us the rush we know as *sexual attraction*. These chemicals result in heavy breathing, flushed skin, dilated pupils, sweating, and stomach "butterflies," along with feelings of elation and euphoria. Biologists also point to another set of chemicals that help to maintain relationships after the initial excitement lessens. A new group of endorphins, chemically similar to morphine, help calm us and reduce anxiety.

Biochemical research on love is still in its infancy, but many interesting research projects point to the importance of biochemical influences on love (Fisher, 2010; Ortigue, Bianchi-Demicheli, Patel, Frum, & Lewis, 2010; Pfaff & Fisher, 2012; Siegel, 2012). For example, using a functional magnetic resonance imaging (fMRI) machine on her subjects, Fisher found that the brain creates dramatic surges of norepinephrine, dopamine, and serotonin that fuel such feelings as passion, obsession, joy, and jealousy (Fisher, 2004). Ortigue and her colleagues (2010) found that when a person falls in love, 12 areas of the brain work in tandem to release euphoria-inducing chemicals such as dopamine, oxytocin, adrenaline, and vasopressin. The love feeling also affects sophisticated cognitive functions, such as mental representation, metaphors, and body image. The study also showed different parts of the brain are used in loving situations. For example, unconditional love, such as that between a mother and a child, is sparked by the common and different brain areas, including the middle of the brain. Passionate love is sparked by the reward part of the brain, and also associative cognitive brain areas that have higher-order cognitive functions, such as body image. These findings call into question our use of a heart as the symbol of love. Perhaps we should be using a picture of a brain!

Before concluding that love is *all* a product of biochemical forces, however, let's look at other factors that help explain the meaning and experience of love.

Micro-Level Perspectives on Love

A micro-level perspective focuses on the interpersonal nature of love. Several theorists can help us understand the different styles of love, its components, and the stages in the development of love.

STERNBERG'S TRIANGULAR THEORY OF LOVE A second approach explores the many multidimensional components of love. Robert **Sternberg's triangular theory of love** (1986, 1988) suggests that love has three components: *passion*, *intimacy*, and *commitment*, which he views as a triangle, as shown in Figure 4.1. *Passion* encompasses feelings of physical attraction, romance, and sexual arousal. Of the three components, passion is the most intense, but it peaks rather quickly, and can give way to a companionate love that is characterized by a calm, stable, and comfortable sense of attachment. *Intimacy* encompasses feelings of closeness and bonding, and includes such things as self-disclosure, respect, trust, and warmth. *Commitment* represents both the short-term decision to love one another and the longer-term commitment to continue that love. It includes such feelings as loyalty, faithfulness, dedication, and devotion.

Sternberg argues that individuals can place different emphases on these three elements of love throughout their lives, and love is a process that undergoes change. When couples are complementary in these dimensions—when they want the same degrees of intimacy, passion, and commitment at the same time—relationships are stable and the couple is considered perfectly matched. Couples who vary just a little on these three dimensions may still be considered a close match. However, as individuals become more different from one another, their relationship becomes less stable.

Sternberg's triangular theory of love: A theory that sees love as having three elements: intimacy, passion, and commitment.

Intimacy

Sternberg's Triangular Theory of Love

Passion

Commitment

FIGURE 4.1
Sternberg's Triangle Theory of Love

Robert Sternberg conceptualized love as a process with three interconnected components: passion, intimacy, and commitment. We place different emphases on these three elements throughout our lives because love is a process that undergoes change.

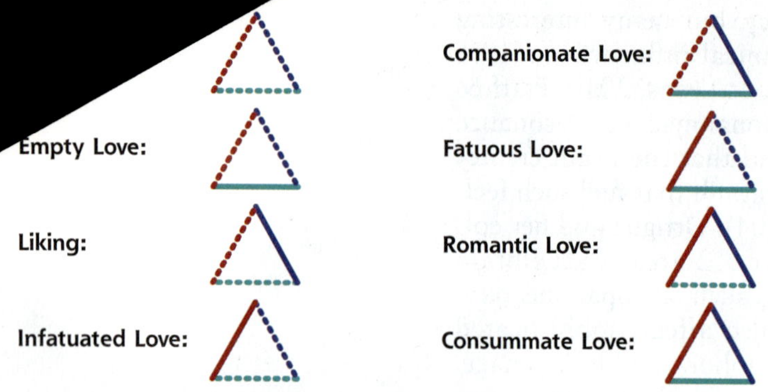

FIGURE 4.2
Sternberg's Love Types

Sternberg proposed eight types of love based on the combination of passion, intimacy, and commitment.

Watch on **MySocLab**
Video: *Robert Sternberg: Triangular Theory of Love*

Lee's styles of love: A categorization of six types of love that describe how couples are attracted to one another.

TABLE 4.2	Lee's Six Styles of Love

Based on a review of thousands of works of fiction and non-fiction across the centuries dealing with love, and interviews in the United States and Canada, Lee came up with six different styles of love.

	Characteristics
Eros	Passionate, strong physical attraction
Storge	Companionate, mutual love, respect, trust
Pragma	Practical, sensible
Ludus	Playful, carefree, casual
Agape	Altruistic, kind, patient
Mania	Obsessive, possessive, intense

Sources: Lee, 1973, 1974, 1988.

Sternberg also suggests that various combinations of intimacy, passion, and commitment breed different kinds of love, as shown in Figure 4.2:

- *Nonlove:* Many relationships really have no love in them. There's little or no intimacy, passion, or commitment.
- *Empty Love:* Sometimes people remain together solely because of a commitment—perhaps they stay together "for the sake of the children" or because they are also business partners and ending the relationship would be too complicated. These relationships are void of passion and intimacy.
- *Liking:* These relationships are intimate, such as good friendships, but typically there is no passion or commitment.
- *Infatuated Love:* We see these types of relationships on television or among movie stars—the relationship is full of passion, but when that passion ends, little intimacy or commitment remains.
- *Companionate Love:* These relationships characterize long-term couples; the passion may have waned, but the couples share intimacy and a commitment to one another.
- *Fatuous Love:* Passion and commitment are the elements of this type of love; people may marry (or cohabit) very early on, but without developing real intimacy.
- *Romantic Love:* These relationships are intense and full of passion and intimacy; however, they typically lack a degree of commitment, and the focus is on physical and sexual attraction.
- *Consummate Love:* When the relationship contains all three components, Sternberg calls this *consummate love*—it's all that love can be.

JOHN LEE'S STYLES OF LOVE Canadian sociologist John Lee reviewed thousands of works of fiction and nonfiction across the centuries dealing with love (1973, 1974, 1988). From his review of the literature and input from young heterosexual men and women living in Canada and Great Britain, he developed a six-category classification scheme on various styles of love, as shown in Table 4.2. **Lee's styles of love** are distinct from one another, yet relationships can also be characterized by having more than one style.

- *Eros. Eros,* the root word of *erotic,* derives its name from that of the Greek god Eros, son of Aphrodite. It describes love that is passionate, all-consuming, and highly sexual. Erotic lovers have a highly powerful physical and sexual attraction to one another, often to the exclusion of anything or anyone else. This type of love is most often presented in movies, television, and popular culture.
- *Storge. Storge* (pronounced *STOR-gay*) represents a love that develops slowly with the passage of time. A couple may begin as friends, and over time, the relationship moves forward in its degree of commitment and intimacy. This kind of love lacks the extreme highs and lows of other types, but the couple enjoys shared activities and mutual interests. It's a comfortable love, with mutual trust, compatibility, and respect.
- *Pragma. Pragma* is a rational, down-to-earth (pragmatic) style of love based on practical considerations.

Pragmatic lovers may actually have a checklist of traits they are looking for in a partner, such as their level of education, earnings, and religious or political views. Being compatible on key issues is important for those in Pragma relationships. These couples constantly evaluate the practical aspects of their relationship, and if the relationship doesn't work, they can make mid-course corrections.

- *Ludus.* Ludus is a playful, carefree type of love. Ludic lovers aren't possessive, and are more focused on fun and games than on commitment. They aren't possessive or jealous, and may have a number of sexual relationships at one time. They aren't jealous, however, because they believe sex is for fun rather than intimacy.

- *Agape.* Agape (pronounced *ah-GAH-pay*) is self-sacrificing, altruistic, kind, and patient. Partners are completely selfless, giving without any thought of getting something in return. The partners' first goal is to help one another, without thought to themselves. Lee's research produced no true examples of an Agape lover.

- *Mania.* Manic relationships are characterized by possessiveness, dependency, and jealousy. Partners are very demanding, have a high level of anxiety about their partner, and obsess over the other's whereabouts at all times. Spending time apart is painful and can produce considerable anxiety. Manic lovers have a high need for attention and affection, likely a result of their low self-esteem, as shown in the feature box *My Family: "Living in Mania."*

Naturally, the types of love we experience will develop and change over a lifetime. Singles are more likely to hold Manic and Ludic love attitudes than married adults, whose relationships are more likely to be represented by Storge. But few, if

MY FAMILY   Living in Mania

The relationship began quite nicely. We were introduced by some mutual friends, and the four of us would go out partying on the weekends. Jay was so attentive to me, always calling or texting to see if I was okay, happy, and asking me questions about myself, although in retrospect I think he knew many of the answers before I told him. That should have been a clue—how did he know so much about me—but what do they say, love is blind? At first I really liked all the attention; I was looking to have a lot of fun.

When did I realize that something wasn't right? My girlfriends made fun of him for calling and texting so often. They thought his 5–10 messages a day were crazy—"Romeo" they would call him. But I didn't really see a problem until he wanted me to quit hanging around them and to spend all my time with him. He didn't even want me to study much—I remember he got really mad and yelled at me because I didn't acknowledge his messages for six hours when I was at the library studying for my Calculus midterm. He seemed to be jealous of anything and everything that took my attention off of him, even for an hour.

I began to feel really smothered, and told him that I needed more space—that maybe we should see less of each other. He was just like a puppy dog, dragging around, looking weepy, and telling me he was lonely and couldn't live without me. He seemed so anxious and afraid to be alone. Then he decided that I must have met another guy, which was not the case, and he really lost it, begging me to take him back. Wow, I've never

Manic relationships are characterized by possessiveness, dependency, and jealousy.

met anyone like this before. I feel badly that I hurt him, but his intensity is way too much for me.

—Sylvia, Age 24

WHAT DO YOU THINK?

1. What clues did you see indicating Jay has a manic style of love? What would you guess Sylvia's preferred style to be?
2. How might Jay's early attachment experiences contribute to his style of love? What would you guess to be Sylvia's early attachment experience?

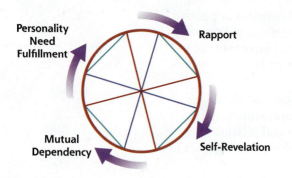

FIGURE 4.3
Reiss's Wheel Theory of Love

Ira Reiss described love as an ongoing process that unfolds in four stages. Similar to a rolling wheel, the stages may be experienced many times, going forward and backward.

Reiss's wheel theory of love: A developmental theory that shows relationships moving from the establishment of rapport, to self-revelation, mutual dependence, and finally, need fulfillment.

any, relationships are characterized in terms of only one type of love. The six types might be useful to help us understand how couples come together, and which couples may be the most, and the least, likely to have long-term relationships. Some researchers feel the styles match up with the categories of attachment we discussed earlier. For example, Agape and Storge are more secure types of love, while Mania is more anxious-ambivalent, and Ludus is closest to avoidant (Hendrick & Hendrick, 1992).

REISS'S WHEEL THEORY OF LOVE   Ira Reiss's work examines the various stages in which love develops and is called **Reiss's wheel theory of love** (1960). He describes four stages of love: building rapport, self-revelation, mutual dependency, and personality need fulfilment, as shown in Figure 4.3:

- In the beginning, people meet and establish *rapport* with one another. We're most likely to meet those who live near us, share our interests, and engage in the same activities that we like. As a result, we're also likely to share cultural, social, political, or religious values.

- After rapport is established, couples may move to a second stage of *self-revelation*. We become closer, more at ease, and begin to disclose more about ourselves. Over time, our sharing becomes more personal, and we talk about our intimate thoughts, fears, and insecurities.

- As our relationship becomes more intimate, we may move to a third stage called *mutual dependence*. In this stage, we open ourselves up even more and begin to depend on our partner, as they do on us.

- As couples become dependent upon each other, they may move to the final stage of *personality need fulfilment*. In this stage, the couple's lives become intertwined; they may make decisions together, and they support one another's ambitions and goals.

Using an analogy to spokes on a wheel, these four stages may keep turning to develop into a deep and lasting relationship. The wheel can turn quickly or slowly, and it may move forward or backward or even stop at any stage. As we learn more about our partners, we may discover that we're incompatible in some way and so we end the relationship (Perillous & Buss, 2008) or step back a stage in its development.

Lee, Sternberg, and Reiss examine the micro-level factors associated with love—different types, how love develops, and how we experience love. Love is a personal emotion, but to understand how it develops and is experienced fully, we must continue our review of the research and examine our social environment.

Macro-Level Perspectives on Love

Love is more than just a personal emotion; it is also rooted in macro-level factors related to culture and social structure. For example, race, class, and sex all help to influence our ideas about and experiences with love. Love also has important implications for how societies are structured, as shown in the *Diversity in Families* feature box. In Iraq, among many other countries, a common pattern is for cousins to marry one another so that the family lineage can be kept intact. But for this to work, Iraqis must find a way to control or prevent their kin from falling in love with a stranger. How do they do this?

CONTROLLING THE DEVELOPMENT OF LOVE   Many societies, both in the past and today, feel that love can be dangerous and must be monitored or

Shada cannot remember the first time she saw the man who would one day be her husband because she was a newborn at the time and he was only a toddler. However, she clearly remembers when she knew she would marry him. Her uncle walked over from his house next door one hot afternoon nine years ago, and proposed that she marry his son Rahim. She was surprised by his request, but right away knew it was a wise choice. They were both in their early twenties, and agreed it was time to marry. There was no question that the marriage should take place among family members. "It is safer to marry a cousin than a stranger" according to Shada.

Shada lives in Iraq, where nearly half of marriages are between first or second cousins. This fact of marriage is one of the most important and least understood differences between Iraq and the United States. Family bonds in Iraq are extraordinarily strong, and these complicate virtually everything Americans have tried to do in Iraq, from finding Saddam Hussein to improving women's status to creating a liberal democracy. Most Americans do not understand what a different world Iraq is because of these cousin marriages. Their world is divided into two groups: kin and strangers. Strangers are suspect.

What Americans would view as nepotism—favouring family members—Iraq sees as a moral duty. The idea that Iraq's leaders put family relationships and obligations above public service receives a nod and smile from Shada's uncle and now father-in-law, Hakim, the patriarch in charge of the entire clan's farm on the Tigris River south of Baghdad. "In this country, whoever is in power will bring his relatives in from the village and give them important positions," Hakim said, sitting in the garden surrounded by some of his 21 children and 83 grandchildren. "That is what Saddam did. . . ."

Saddam Hussein fit the Iraq pattern well. He married a first cousin who grew up in the same house as he did, and he ordered most of his children to marry their cousins. Unlike Saddam, Hakim said he never forced any of his children to marry anyone, but more than half of them chose to wed cousins. In his role as patriarch, he was often the one who suggested the match, as he did with his son Rahim nine years ago. His sons appreciate the wisdom offered by their father. "My father said that I was old enough to get married, and I agreed," Rahim recalled. "He and my mother recommended Shada, and I respected their wishes. It was my desire, too. We knew each other, and it a good match. It was much simpler to marry within the family."

After the wedding, Shada moved next door to the home of Rahim, Hakim, and their family. Moving in with the in-laws might be an American bride's nightmare, but it is common and expected in Iraq. In fact, Shada said her toughest adjustment occurred five years later, when she and her husband moved to their own home. Patriarch Hakim decided that the couple were ready to live by themselves in a new home he provided just behind his own. "I didn't like moving into my own home. I felt a little lonely at first without the family right here," Shada said. Her husband Rahim also felt lonely in the new house separated from his family, even by only yards. When told that American newlyweds usually live in their own home many miles from their parents, he expressed pity for American parents and children living so far apart. "Families should be

Nearly half of marriages in Iraq are between first or second cousins. Iraqis put family first—nepotism is a moral duty. As Shada said, "It is safer to marry a cousin than a stranger."

together. That's the natural way." he said. "It's cruel to keep children and parents apart from each other."

Hakim also thinks it is cruel, and does not understand how the elderly in the United States cope in their homes alone. He sees his children daily, and cannot imagine even a week without them. However, a few of his daughters have married men outside the family—men who are clearly seen as outsiders by the rest of the clan. These daughters moved into other patriarchal clans, but the rest of the children live close by, or with him.

Rahim and two other sons live on the farm with him, helping to supervise the harvesting of the crops they grow. The other three sons and one daughter have moved 11 miles away to Baghdad. Eleven miles seems like a very long way to Hakim, but his children come back often for meals, advice, or help. During the war, most of the clan returned and took refuge with their family at the farm. "Family are the only people you can really trust," said one of the older sons.

If we look around the world today, how common is it to marry a cousin? Cousin marriage was once the norm throughout the world, but the Roman Catholic Church discouraged it. Theologians such as St. Augustine and St. Thomas argued that the practice promoted family loyalties at the expense of universal love and social harmony. Eliminating it was seen as a way to reduce clan warfare and promote loyalty to larger social institutions such as the church. In time cousin marriages became taboo in Europe.

However, marriage among cousins continues to persist in some parts of the world. In the Middle East close-knit cousins like Shada and Rahim often marry. In other regions, woman commonly marry a cousin who is outside her social group, such

controlling the development of love: A macro-level perspective on love suggesting that all societies control or channel love.

controlled by parents or by society at large (Goode, 1959). Love, for example, has the ability to break up families, destroy communities, topple governments, and even cause wars. Sociologist William Goode claims that all societies, even our own in modern times, **control the development of love** to some degree through at least one of the following mechanisms:

- *Child Marriage:* One way to control love is to have a child married or betrothed before feelings of love for another person can even develop. Marriage might even occur prior to puberty.

- *Kinship Rules:* Another way to control love is to clearly define and restrict the set of eligible people that young people can and cannot marry, such as a cousin. As shown in the *Diversity in Families* box, this mechanism is widely practiced in Iraq, and has important political and economic consequences.

- *Isolation of Young People:* A third way to control love is by segregating young people from one another. Boys and girls may go to different schools. Men and women may attend different religious services. Males and females are kept strictly segregated and isolated to eliminate opportunities for interaction.

- *Close Supervision:* Short of isolation, some cultures watch over children and young adults very carefully, especially their girls and women. In many cultures, a high value is placed on female virginity; therefore, girls and women are highly supervised whenever they are in public to keep them at a safe distance from men.

- *Formally Free:* This mechanism of controlling love is found in our society today. Young people are considered free to choose their own mates based on love and attraction; however, their social environments can still be manipulated by their parents, such as sending children to private schools or living in a certain neighborhood to channel the influence of peers.

Read on **MySocLab**
Document: *Sometimes the Perfect Mate Is Someone You Hardly Know*

A MODERN-DAY EXAMPLE: INDIA Although people in the United States think of romantic love as a basis for partnering and marriage, in other countries people find their mates for different reasons: bringing families together, economic considerations, or other motivations (Leeder, 2004; Medora, 2003). Love may be a part of the equation (Allendorf, 2013), or develop after the marriage, as shown in the opening vignette with Rati and Subas, both from Nepal. Another good example is found in modern-day India.

In India, parents play an important part in whom their children marry (Griffith, 2006). Many marriages are arranged by parents, and the children may know little or nothing about their future mate. These marriages have nothing to do with love in the way we think of love. However, that doesn't mean this marriages are not happy.

Listen on **MySocLab**
Audio: *NPR: Arranged Marriages*

It is important to remember that an arranged marriage is not necessarily a forced one (Mines & Lamb, 2010). In other Indian families, children have greater choice, and work together with their parents to find the best mate. For example, the parents may screen a list of possible suitors. "Arranged marriages . . . remove so much of the anxiety about 'is this the right person?'" according to Dr. Willoughby, a professor who studies arranged marriages. "Arranged marriages start cold and heat up and boil over time as the couple grows. Non-arranged marriages are expected to start out boiling hot but many find that this heat dissipates and we're left with a relationship that's cold" (Lee, 2013).

Most Indians would find our belief in dating and romance as odd as we might find their idea of arranged marriage. They would suggest that we're too focused on passionate love, and on fun and games, to the detriment of building a solid and lasting relationship. "I want an arranged marriage," said a 22-year-old college student who considers himself a connoisseur of Western culture, including National Basketball Association games. A survey of 15- to 34-year-olds living in Delhi, Mumbai, Kanpur, and Lucknow found that 65 percent said that they would obey their elders "even if it hurts." More than two-thirds of urban college students preferred to have their parents arrange their marriage. "Any girl I could find for myself would not be as good as the one my parents will find," says a 19-year-old college student (Derne, 2003). In 2009, a survey conducted by a matchmaking service reports that more than half of the respondents preferred arranged marriages, whereas just 18 percent favored the love marriage option that we are more comfortable with (Megala, 2012).

Love isn't a foreign idea to Indians. They simply have a different conception of it, influenced heavily by Hinduism, the caste system, and other norms of Indian culture. They hold that much of a person's life is predetermined by his or her karma. Marriage is out of the hands of the couple, and few would attempt to change fate. Some educated professionals prefer to choose their own mates, but for the most part, Indians anticipate that their parents will select their marriage partner for them.

Commonly, before two people from India can consider marriage, both sets of parents consult a matchmaker or an astrologer to examine their zodiac signs to determine the couple's compatibility. The astrologer helps determine whether the young man and woman are a proper match. If they're deemed to be a good match, then families can begin to discuss issues surrounding the dowry.

Despite their lower status in India's patriarchal society, women are important because of their fertility; large families and especially a large number of sons are still considered highly desirable by most Indians. Therefore, families spend considerable time negotiating a **dowry**, the financial gift given to a woman's prospective in-laws by her parents. The woman is generally not involved in the negotiations. Parents spend considerable amounts on the dowry, depending on their caste or class standing, and may be left impoverished or in substantial debt as a result.

Child marriage was outlawed in 1978 in India; however, it is still the practice in many parts of the country. Almost half of girls in India are married before their eighteenth birthday (International Center for Research on Women, 2012). Child marriages free a family from the obligations of supporting a girl, who is viewed as destined to leave the family anyway. In the eyes of the parents, it also decreases her likelihood of engaging in premarital sex or being exploited sexually, which would reduce her status.

Throughout the text thus far we've discussed the importance of how macro-level social forces shape our personal experiences. In this chapter, we see that love—what it means, its importance, and how it's achieved—varies considerably over time and place. The feature box *Tying It All Together: Factors That Shape Attraction and the Development of Love* summarizes the contributions of different perspectives on love.

Arranged marriages are common in India and in many other parts of the world, including among the well educated and the wealthy. Adult children believe that something as important as selecting a spouse is too important to be left up to chance.

dowry: A financial gift given to a woman's prospective in-laws by her parents.

What do you think might be some of the benefits of an arranged marriage? Answer the question from a parent's perspective and then from a child's perspective. Do the benefits differ from these two perspectives? Explain.

The development and experience of love takes many perspectives. These speak to biological and biochemical issues, micro-level dimensions such as relationship stages or choices, and macro-level factors such as the ways that love is controlled and channeled for mate selection.

Biological Theories	Basic Assumptions or Arguments
Sociobiology	• All humans have the instinct to pass on their genes.
Biochemical Perspective	• Men prefer younger and more physically attractive women. • Women prefer men who are more financially secure. • Attraction emits dopamine, norepinephrine, and phenylethylamine (PEA), which give us the rush we know as sexual attraction. • Another set of chemicals helps to maintain relationships by calming us and reducing anxiety.
Micro-level Theories	
Sternberg's Triangle Theory of Love	• Love has three primary dimensions: intimacy, passion, and commitment. • The weight of each dimension can vary and depends on the needs of the couple and the stage of their relationship.
Lee's Styles of Love	• There are six distinct styles of love: Eros, Storge, Ludus, Pragma, Agape, and Mania. • Relationships can be characterized by more than one style of love.
Reiss's Wheel Theory of Love	• Relationships develop in stages of rapport, self-revelation, mutual dependence, and need fulfillment. • Couples can move both forward and backward through the stages.
Macro-level Theories	
Social Structure and Control of Love	• Marriage has broad and important social, economic, and political implications, and children should not make their own decisions about who they marry. • Love is channeled in a number of ways, from "child marriages" to being "formally free."

4.6 Discuss how we experience love

How We Experience Love

Questions That Matter

4.8 Are women more interested in love than men?

4.9 What is the importance of same-sex love?

4.10 What is *unrequited love*?

Ryan and Kim were living in the dorms when they met in the dining hall one evening. The room was crowded with students trying to get a quick bite before studying or going to their social engagements for the evening. There was an empty seat next to Ryan, so Kim said rather matter-of-factly, "Okay if I join you?" They struck up a conversation, and quickly discovered they shared many interests, including their love of basketball, playing the violin, and travel. They laughed together as they shared some of their craziest travel stories. The next evening Ryan looked for Kim in the crowd of students in the dining hall, hoping to find a pal to go together to the basketball game. They spotted each other, and so began their friendship sharing conversation and laughs during meals, sporting events, and study breaks. As the semester went on, they found themselves spending more time together, and their conversations became more disclosing and personal; there was discussion of an alcoholic father, an assault during high school, their most embarrassing moments. Their relationship grew intense, passionate, sexual, and romantic. Ryan sent flowers when Kim received an "A" on a History exam. Kim would invite Ryan to stay the night when roommates were out of town. After many months, both expressed that they were in love.

> As the semester went on, they found themselves spending more time together, and their conversations became more disclosing and personal. . . .

Here is a simple story about a young couple falling in love while they are away at school. But the story takes on more complexity when we add contextual material to the story. What if Ryan and Kim are high school students living away at boarding school? What if they're both males? What if they're "returning students" both 40 years old? What if they're of different racial or ethnic groups? What if Ryan's romantic feelings are not reciprocated? Let's look at a number of these aspects associated with experiencing love.

Sex, Gender, and Love

If we're to believe popular culture, women are more interested in love than are men. However, surveys show that men, in fact, are more likely than women to be in or looking for committed relationships (Madden & Lenhart, 2006; Madden & Rainie, 2006), and they report falling in love sooner and with more people than do women (Covel, 2003). Seventy-seven percent of men and 68 percent of women reported they're in love with someone right now (Saad, 2004). More than twice as many men (24 percent) as women (11 percent) say they've been in love five or more times since turning 18.

We also note that men are more preoccupied with love. Table 4.3 reveals that single men are two and a half times more likely than single women to report that they're looking for a partner.

If men actually fall in love more quickly than do women and are more focused on love, why does cultural rhetoric claim the opposite is true—that women are the ones obsessed with love? There may be several reasons for this myth. In reviewing the different styles of love, one study found that, in general, men were more *ludic* (carefree), whereas women tend to lean toward *storge* (comfortable and compatible) and *pragma* (rational) (Hendrick & Hendrick, 1992). Not surprisingly then, some women are concerned that men are "afraid of commitment," or "commitment phobic" (Gerson, 2009; Whitehead & Popenoe, 2002).

Another reason we assume that women are more loving has to do with the different ways that men and women express love and our belief that women's expressions of this emotion are somehow innately better. This is referred to as the feminization of love (Cancian, 1987). The problem isn't that men don't express love, but they often don't get credit for it because women ignore or minimize masculine-type expressions. Thus, the man who is a good provider, who takes his daughter to soccer, and who folds the laundry may be showing as much love as the woman who says "I love you" regularly. He may think that "actions speak louder than words," but his female partner is waiting for the words, and miscommunication can result.

Men and women fall in love for many of the same reasons—similar values, emotional maturity, dependability—but men are more likely than women to fall in love for reasons related to physical attractiveness (Eastwick, Eagly, Finkel, & Johnson, 2011; Eastwick & Finkel, 2008). Women are more cautious about love, taking longer and using a wider variety of factors in deciding whether they are in love. These factors include physical attractiveness and similarity in values and other traits, but also ambition, industriousness, and financial prospects.

Reasons for falling in love appear to be associated with the ways that sex and gender are defined in our society. For most of history, women have been financially dependent on men in marriage; therefore, it made good sense to closely examine a man's economic prospects before choosing a mate. But as the context changes, so do the reasons for choosing a mate. Since the 1970s, more married women are working outside the home and their financial dependence

TABLE 4.3 Single Men, Single Women, and Their Relationship Interests

Men appear to be more interested in love and a committed relationship than do women.

	All Singles	Men	Women
In a Committed Relationship	46%	30%	23%
Not in a Committed Relationship and Not Looking for a Partner	55%	42%	65%
Not in a Committed Relationship and Looking for a Partner	18%	23%	9%
Don't Know or Refused to Answer	3%	5%	3%

Source: Madden, Mary, & Rainie, 2006.

Listen on **MySocLab**
Audio: *NPR: Ideas About Love in Our Culture*

on men in marriage has declined (U.S. Bureau of Labor Statistics, February 2013). Therefore, with less *need* for a husband as a provider, women focus on other qualities for their intimate relationships.

Same-Sex Love

We love many people of the same sex: our parents, other relatives, friends, and if you are gay or lesbian, your partner. As we discussed in Chapter 3, friendships are a valuable part of our lives. For most of history, friendships were almost exclusively between two men or two women (Caine, 2010; Schweitzer, 2006); cross-sex friendships were thought to be threatening. Moreover, husbands and wives may have been partners, but they tended to work in different "spheres" and their same-sex friendships reflected the different worlds they inhabited. One interesting study of friendships between women from 1760 to 1880 focused on letters written between friends (Smith-Rosenberg, 1975). These letters may reveal the lives only of literate, middle-class women, but they show that women developed strong bonds with other women. The letters express love and tenderness and frequently describe a physical and emotional longing for the other. Some of these may have been *romantic friendships*. Same-sex friendships were not seen as threatening, and terms such as *homosexual* were not really part of the vocabulary (Spenser, 1995).

Today, men and women can openly admit that their same-sex friends aren't just friends but lovers or partners. The foci of this chapter—how we define love, the importance of attachment, theoretical perspectives, and the experiences of love—are generally the same for same-sex couples as they are for heterosexual couples. Most gay, lesbian, and straight people want to be emotionally close to someone, share romance and companionship, and have a deep trusting relationship (Biblarz & Savci, 2010; Clarke, 2010). Perhaps the primary difference has to do with the prejudice and discrimination gays and lesbians experience on a regular basis. In many places around the country, same-sex couples are not free to show affection in public or acknowledge their love out of fear of being ostracized, attacked, or even killed (Gold & Drucker, 2008; Shepard, 2009). These issues are explored further in Chapter 5.

Unrequited Love

Have you ever felt that you loved a person, but he or she didn't love you? Or that someone loved you, but you didn't feel the same way? This is referred to as **unrequited love**—one person's feelings are not reciprocated by the other (Merriam-Webster Online, 2013). Popular songs are full of examples of unrequited love, especially in country and western music. Unrequited love can occur any time during the process of a relationship. Sometimes it occurs in the beginning—one person is simply not interested in the other, and doesn't find him or her particularly attractive or interesting. Unrequited love can also occur as a relationship is being formed. Perhaps the motivations for the relationship are different—one is looking for a hook-up, whereas the other is looking for a lasting relationship. And finally, unrequited love can also occur in an established relationship. Couples break up or divorce, sometimes after many years of being together. Unrequited love can be a gut-wrenching, sad, and painful experience. Yet, the difficult fact is that we can't control other people's feelings (Herbenick, 2009).

unrequited love: When one person's feelings are not reciprocated by the other person in the relationship.

In your experience with love, does it seem that men and women want the same thing from love? Do they express love differently? What macro-level factors contribute to the way we express love?

Unrequited love is when the feelings of love of one person are not reciprocated. In this case, her messages are ignored.

The Downside to Relationships and Love

Falling in love is a powerful emotion. For the most part, it feels wonderful, but there are a few "downsides" to relationships and love. One of these is jealousy.

Jealousy

4.7 Summarize the downside to relationships and love

Questions That Matter

4.11 Is jealousy always irrational?

4.12 What is *stalking*, and how serious is this problem?

4.13 Why are breakups so difficult?

"We dated for three years—I devoted three years of my life to her trying to make her happy. I thought she was happy, I thought we were a good team. But then, out of the blue, she tells me that she wants to go out with a guy she works with. Who in the hell is this guy? He's younger than she is, and doesn't even earn that much money. Why on earth would she want to go out with him? She must be crazy. Really crazy. I'm so angry!"

... out of the blue, she tells me that she wants to go out with a guy she works with.

This man is experiencing an emotion we've probably all felt at one time or another when threatened by the loss of an important relationship—that of jealousy (Fisher, 2009; Shackleford, Voracek, Schmitt, Buss, Weekes-Shackleford, & Michalski, 2004). He feels threatened, angry, sad, and resentful that a rival is competing for his girlfriend. He tries to make himself feel better by criticizing his girlfriend and his rival.

Jealousy can be rational, based on some real rival threat, as in the case above, or it can be irrational, based on a perceived threat that isn't real (Buunk, Massar, & Dijkstra, 2007). People can feel jealous for many reasons; men are more likely to focus on physical aspects of the threat, feeling jealous that their partner will be sexual with someone else, for example, whereas women more often focus on the emotional aspects, feeling jealous that their partner loves someone else (Groothof, Dijkstra, & Barelds, 2010; Rutley, 2001). Men and women show their jealousy in different ways, consistent with the way they've been socialized, as we see in Chapter 3. Men are more likely to deny their jealous feelings, whereas women are more likely to acknowledge them.

Jealousy, especially if irrational, can come about from our own insecurities about our relationships and ourselves. It can be responsible for some very bad behavior, including physical or emotional abuse, as we see in Chapter 11. How then can you deal constructively with jealousy?

- Make some agreements with your partner that you can both feel comfortable with about how you'll behave.

- Try not to be too hard on yourself for feeling jealous. Jealousy can be a natural emotion; the trick is to be in control of your feelings rather than the other way around.

- Identify and isolate the specific reason for your jealousy. Is it something your partner is actually doing, or is it something you feel he or she *might* do? Once you know why you are jealous, you have a better idea how to deal with it.

- Tell your partner your feelings in a calm, nonthreatening, and constructive manner; then, listen to what he or she has to say in return. Communication is a two-way process. If you calmly discuss your feelings, you may find your partner can empathize and offer some measure of help.

Cyberstalking or *electronic monitoring* is a growing form of stalking and can take a heavy personal toll on its victims.

Test Your Technology IQ

This woman just:

A. RSVP'd an invitation to her grandmother's birthday celebration.

B. Arranged to meet her friend for a movie.

C. Confirmed tomorrow's lunch with a business associate.

D. **Unknowingly informed her stalker exactly where she'll be this week.**

Stalkers install spyware and other unwanted technologies on computers to capture information that can put victims at risk.

Stalking is a crime. If you or someone you know is a victim of stalking, **we can help.**

Stalking resource center
www.ncvc.org/src

THE NATIONAL CENTER FOR
Victims of Crime
1-800-FYI-CALL

This document was developed under grant number 2004-WT-AX-K050 from the Office on Violence Against Women (OVW) of the U.S. Department of Justice. The opinions and views expressed in this document are those of the author(s) and do not necessarily represent the official position or policies of the Office on Violence Against Women of the U.S. Department of Justice.

- Depending on the cause of your jealousy, if you can't negotiate a solution to the problem, or if you or your partner continually create situations that aggravate jealousy, you may need to find a counselor to help you resolve the problem (Sorgen, 2008).

Controlling Behavior

There are other types of controlling behavior besides jealousy. **Stalking** is a pattern of repeated and unwanted attention, harassment, contact, or any other course of conduct directed at a specific person that would cause a reasonable person to feel fear. Stalking can include:

- Repeated, unwanted, intrusive, and frightening communications from the perpetrator by phone, mail, and/or email.
- Repeatedly leaving or sending victim unwanted items, presents, or flowers.
- Following or lying in wait for the victim at places such as home, school, work, or recreation place.
- Making direct or indirect threats to harm the victim, the victim's children, relatives, friends, or pets.
- Damaging or threatening to damage the victim's property.
- Harassing victim through the internet.
- Posting information or spreading rumors about the victim on the internet, in a public place, or by word of mouth.
- Obtaining personal information about the victim by accessing public records, using Internet search services; hiring private investigators; going through the victim's garbage; following the victim; or contacting victim's friends, family, work, or neighbors. (Stalking Resource Center, 2013)

The federal government and all 50 states have laws criminalizing stalking, but it occurs frequently nonetheless—about 3.3 million adults are stalked each year (Catalano, 2012a). The U.S. Department of Justice conducted a study of stalking and measured the following stalking behaviors: (1) making unwanted phone calls; (2) sending unsolicited or unwanted letters or emails; (3) following or spying; (4) showing up at places without a legitimate reason; (5) waiting at places for the victim; (6) leaving unwanted items, presents, or flowers; and (7) posting information or spreading rumors about the victim on the internet, in a public place, or by word of mouth. The study found that during a 12-month period, 1.5 percent of persons age 18 and older were victims of stalking, and it was highest for those who were divorced or separated (3.3 percent). Nearly seven in ten stalking victims knew their offender in some way. The type of stalking that occurred is reported in Table 4.4. As you can see, the percentages add up to more than 100 percent because many cases involve multiple forms of stalking (Catalano, 2012a). About three-quarters of victims are women, and about two-thirds of stalkers are men, but plenty of cases arise in which women are stalking men or other women, and men are stalking other men. Victims are most often ex-girlfriends, ex-boyfriends, or ex-spouses, but they can also be friends, roommates, neighbors, work colleagues, relatives, or even strangers.

TABLE 4.4	Nature of Stalking Behaviors Experienced by Victims (3,424,100)	
With more than 3 million known incidents of stalking, many victims report being stalked in multiple ways.		
		Victims
Unwanted phone calls and messages		66%
Unwanted letters and email		31%
Spreading rumors		36%
Following or spying		34%
Showing up at places		31%
Waiting for victim		29%
Leaving unwanted presents		12%

Note: Responses sum to more than 100% because multiple responses were permitted.
Source: Baum, Catalano, Rand, & Rose, 2009.

Another relatively new but very dangerous type of stalking is **cyberstalking** (or **electronic monitoring**), which involves stalking contact using electronic technology (Stalking Resource Center, 2013). As shown in Table 4.5, 26 percent of stalking victims reported that some form of cyberstalking or electronic monitoring was used on them. Most commonly, this took the form of unwanted email—82 percent of those who reported being victims of this form of cyberstalking reported unwanted emails, but they were also victims of instant messaging, blogs or bulletin boards, Internet sites about them, and chat-room conversations. Those who had been stalked by electronic monitoring were most likely victims of video or digital cameras, listening devices/bugs, computer spyware, or even GPS tracking devices (Catalano, 2012a).

Stalking takes a heavy personal toll on its victims (Baum, Catalano, Rand, & Rose, 2009; Stalking Resource Center, 2013). They fear not knowing what will happen next, and worry that the stalking will never stop. Many suffer anxiety, insomnia, and severe depression. One in eight victims loses time from work because of the stalking, and one in seven feels forced to move for their safety.

TABLE 4.5	Involvement of Cyberstalking or Electronic Monitoring in Stalking

Cyberstalking and electronic monitoring are increasing. Sending unwanted emails is a form of stalking.

	Victims
Any type of cyberstalking or electronic monitoring	26%
Cyberstalking	22%
Percentage of cyberstalking involving	
Email	83%
Instant messenger	35%
Blogs or bulletin boards	12%
Internet sites about victim	9%
Chat rooms	4%
Electronic monitoring	8%
Percent of electronic monitoring involving	
Computer spyware	34%
Video/digital cameras	46%
Listening devices/bugs	42%
Global Positioning System (GPS)	11%

Note: Responses sum to more than 100% because multiple responses were permitted.
Source: Baum, Catalano, Rand, & Rose, 2009.

cyberstalking (or electronic monitoring): Stalking contact using electronic technology.

Breaking Up Is Hard to Do

A third possible downside to love is breaking up. When we're in love, we think it will last forever. However, nothing about love is guaranteed, and most dating relationships break up within a few years (Regan, 2003). Some break up and renew again (and possibly break up again) (Dailey, Rossetto, Pfiester, & Surra, 2009).

Sociologist Diane Vaughan (1986) developed a *theory of uncoupling*, suggesting that there is a specific *turning point* in the dynamics of ending a relationship, where one partner knows the relationship is over, yet continues it for an extended period of time, possibly even years. The initiator has time to mull things over and to visualize a life apart from their partner. The other person must then deal with the aftermath. As a result, Vaughan suggests that getting out of a relationship includes a redefinition of oneself at several levels: in the private thoughts of the individual, between partners, and in the larger social context in which the relationship exists. The uncoupling is complete when the partners see themselves and are seen by others as separate and independent of each other; that is, when being partners is no longer a major source of identity.

Just like meeting a partner, breaking up with a partner is influenced by a host of macro-level and micro-level factors. On the micro-level, partners may stop communicating, discover different values or interests, or clash over differences in personalities. On the macro-level, socioeconomic conditions that affect employment or income may introduce friction into the relationship.

Given the significance that romantic partners have on each other's lives, the loss of a relationship is among the most distressing events we can experience as adults (Lewandowski, Aron, Bassis, & Kunak, 2006; Sbarra, 2006). Partners develop shared friends, activities, goals, and memories. They even have overlapping self-concepts, and are more likely to spontaneously use first-person-plural pronouns, such as *we, our,* and *us.* After a breakup, this self-concept can become unclear, generating considerable emotional distress (Slotter, Gardner, & Finkel, 2010).

Research has found that some couples break off relationships for the same reasons they were attracted to each other in the first place (Felmlee, 2001). Based on a sample of 125 undergraduates, some individuals were attracted to people who were "nice" or "considerate," but later these nice people were criticized as being unwilling to open up and be honest. Other undergraduates were attracted to people with "strong" personalities, only to feel later that these people were "stubborn." Many other changes in the evaluation of people's personalities occurred as well: What started out as "funny" later was seen as "flaky," "exciting" became "scary," and what was considered "successful" became "workaholic" (Felmlee, 2001).

Other research goes back to the pioneering work of Waller's (1937) principle of least interest, introduced in Chapter 3, and examines the consequences of unequal emotional involvement in romantic relationships. One study of 101 dating couples (college students) followed the relationships for more than 3 years to determine the frequency and effects of unequal involvement (Sprecher, Christopher, & Cate, 2006). The researchers found that in 75 percent of the couples, at least one partner said that one partner was more emotionally involved in the relationship than the other partner. In 56 percent of the couples, both partners acknowledged that one person in the relationship was more involved than the other. They also found that the person who was least involved had more control over the relationship and whether it continued. The person who "loved the least" was also less satisfied in the relationship. Finally, relationships with unequal emotional involvement were more likely to break up over the course of the 3-year study than were relationships based on more equal attachment (Sprecher, Christopher, & Cate, 2006).

Another theme in the research on love focuses on the individual benefits of romantic relationships. In Chapter 7, we see that marriage brings some adults greater happiness and better health. Yet oddly, research on romantic attachments, at least during adolescence, finds just the opposite (Joyner & Udry, 2000). Using a survey tracking almost 8,000 seventh through twelfth graders for one year, the study found that those who entered into romantic relationships were more likely to experience an increase in depression compared to those who didn't enter relationships. Adolescent girls, in particular, were more likely to become unhappy over time when they were involved romantically, and both boys and girls in romantic relationships had more alcohol and delinquency problems.

What do you think is responsible for the relationship between teenage romantic relationships and depression (and delinquency)? Is it a selection effect, or do teenage romantic relationships cause these negative outcomes? Can you draw from your own experiences?

Why would adolescent romance seem to have such negative consequences? It isn't clear if romantic relationships are causing the problem, or whether those with problems are more likely to get involved in relationships—a selection effect. One finding from this study is that over time, those who enter romantic relationships tend to do more poorly in their schoolwork and experience problems with their parents. Romance includes a lot of emotional work, both positive and negative, which can affect the time and energy available for other relationships (Joyner & Udry, 2000).

Yet it's also possible that adolescents who have problems at school or at home seek out romantic relationships, and therefore are already more likely to be depressed and unhappy. Another study looked at the associations between relationships and depression among more than 300 adolescents and found that girls who engaged in sexual activity in short-term romantic relationships that were low in intimacy had a high frequency of depression, but that boys didn't experience a high frequency of depression. In contrast, involvement in stable romantic relationships wasn't associated with depression for either boys or girls (Shulman, Walsh, Weisman, & Schelyer, 2009).

A basic reality of most relationships is that they eventually come to an end. One study found that nearly half of respondents said they've broken up with a partner at least twice, and almost one-quarter say that they've been "dumped" six to ten times. We usually feel very bad after a breakup. Men tend to feel worse, and, probably related to that, they resume dating more quickly than women (Fetto, 2003; Zinczenko, 2007). Nonetheless, recall that one of the positive functions of dating is to weed out unsuitable prospective mates. Breaking up allows us to open up to a larger group of people so we can make a more suitable and confident choice before we marry.

Bringing It Full Circle

The way people think about and experience love is very much shaped by the structure of society, its norms, values, and customs. Our culture glorifies romantic love, but ask people who are in a long-term loving relationship and they'll tell you that love is about more than romance, and includes companionship, commitment, caring, and a sense of shared history. Rati and Subas, our married couple from Nepal in the opening vignette, understand this perfectly well. Romantic love, if it develops at all, is last on the list, not first, in establishing a loving, long-term commitment. Many different theoretical perspectives help us understand love in all its forms. Taken together, these biochemical, micro-level, and macro-level perspectives shed light on why and how we love.

Now let's reflect on what you've learned from this chapter to answer the following questions:

- William Goode suggested that cultures try to control love in one of a number of ways. The arranged marriage of Subas and Rati, introduced in the opening vignette, would fall into which category? Into which category do love and marriage in the United States fall?

- Using Sternberg's triangle theory of love and Lee's styles of love, which styles best describe the relationship of Subas and Rati? How does this compare with the loving relationships you've experienced?

- Put yourself in Rati's position—she had never been to the United States before marrying Subas. Can you guess what she thinks of our cultural ideals about love?

On MySocLab

 ✓ **Study and Review on MySocLab**

CHAPTER REVIEW

LO4.1 Define love

4.1 What do we mean by the term *love*?

Love is (1) a strong affection for another arising out of kinship or personal ties; (2) an attraction based on sexual desire; and (3) an affection based on admiration, benevolence, or common interests. We may be speaking of the love a parent feels for a child, the love a child feels for a sibling, the love between two friends, or the love experienced by romantic partners.

LO4.2 Explain love as attachment

4.2 How do we first learn to love?

Psychologists suggest our first relationships in life, those with our primary guardian, shape the way we approach relationships with others.

4.3 What are the three primary attachment styles?

Secure attachments reflect children's confidence in knowing their mothers (or caregivers) are warm, consistently available to them. *Anxious-attachment* occurs when the mother is less warm and responsive to her infant. These relationships result in stress among infants in turn, tend to develop insecure attachments. *Avoidant attachments* show little attachment by infants to their mothers. Avoidant infants may have been neglected by their mothers in terms of their physical and emotional needs, and therefore had no expectation the mothers would be there for comfort.

4.4 Does our attachment in infancy affect us as adults?

Yes, our attachment history can influence our friendships and intimate adult relationships throughout our lives, for better or worse. People with secure attachments may find it relatively easy to get close to others and don't worry about depending on others or fearing abandonment. People with anxious-ambivalent attachments may act needy and tend to get close too quickly or worry that their partner doesn't care for them. Those with avoidant attachments may not be comfortable with closeness and intimacy.

LO4.3 Identify images of love in history

4.5 Have meanings of love changed over time?

The ways we define and experience love depend on *whom* we love, *where*, and *when*. For instance, love has been constructed as occurring only between men in ancient Greece, as a sexual flirtation between men and women who cannot be together in the Middle Ages (courtly love), and as a feminine quality allowing the care of family members during the mid-19th century (feminization of love).

LO4.4 Describe contemporary ideas about love

4.6 What is the difference between *romance* and *companionate love*?

A look at fairy tales, movies, books, magazines, and television programs reveals countless stories of romantic love, which is full of passion and excitement. We consider it the most basic prerequisite for dating, cohabiting, and getting married. Yet, over time, the intensity of romantic love can begin to fade as people get to know one another. Companionate love is based on strong commitment and trust that the other person will genuinely "be there" for you, no matter what. It grows over time, as partners come to know and understand one another.

LO4.5 Classify theoretical perspectives on love

4.7 What do biological, micro-level, and macro-level perspectives teach us about love?

Biological perspectives such as sociobiology and biochemistry look at evolutionary properties of love and chemicals or hormones released during attraction; micro-level perspectives, such as the work by Steinberg,

Lee, and Reiss, focus on the development or the experiences of love; and macro-level perspectives, such as the work by Goode, focus on the way that our social structure controls love.

LO4.6 Discuss how we experience love

4.8 Are women more interested in love than men?

The short answer is "No." Men, in fact, are more likely than women to be in or looking for committed relationships, and they report falling in love sooner and with more people than do women. More men than women reported they are in love with someone "right now," and twice as many men as women say they have been in love five or more times since turning 18.

4.9 What is the importance of same-sex love?

Men and women's same-sex friendships have been an important source of love and affection, fostered by the fact that their lives have been segregated through most of history. Some of these same-sex friendships may have included a romantic and sexual component, but these were rarely discussed publicly. Today, gays and lesbians are freer to acknowledge their romantic partners; however, many heterosexual people remain uncomfortable with their public displays of affection, sometimes even resorting to violence over it.

4.10 What is *unrequited love*?

Unrequited love is when a person's feelings of love for someone are not reciprocated. It can occur any time in the process of a relationship: in the beginning, when one person is simply not interested in the other; as a relationship is being formed when the people have different intentions; and in a long-term relationship.

LO4.7 Summarize the downside to relationships and love

4.11 Is jealousy always irrational?

Jealousy occurs when we feel threatened by the loss of an important relationship. Jealousy can be rational, based on some real rival threat, or it can be irrational, based on a perceived threat that's not real.

4.12 What is *stalking*, and how serious is this problem?

Stalking is conduct directed at a specific person that would cause a reasonable person to be fearful, and can include making unwanted telephone calls; sending unsolicited or unwanted letters or emails; following or spying on the victim; showing up at places without a legitimate reason; waiting at places for the victim; leaving unwanted items, presents, or flowers; and posting information or spreading rumors about the victim on the Internet, in a public place, or by word of mouth. About 3.4 million adults are stalked each year, increasingly through cyberstalking.

4.13 Why are breakups so difficult?

Breakups can occur at any stage of the relationship. Partners develop shared friends, activities, goals, and memories. They even have overlapping self-concepts, and are more likely to spontaneously use first-person-plural pronouns, such as *we, our,* and *us.* After a breakup, this self-concept can become unclear, contributing to considerable emotional distress.

KEY TERMS

anxious/ambivalent attachment
attachment theory
avoidant attachment
biochemical perspective of love
companionate love
controlling the development of love
courtly love

cyberstalking (or electronic monitoring)
dowry
feminization of love
Lee's styles of love
love
Reiss's wheel theory of love
romantic love

secure attachment
sociobiology
stalking
Sternberg's triangular theory of love
unrequited love

LEARNING OBJECTIVES

5.1 Identify historical and cultural influences on sexuality

5.2 Recognize how biology and culture shape our sexual selves

5.3 Compare and contrast sexual scripts

5.4 Explain the double standard

5.5 Summarize the study of human sexuality

5.6 Explain sexual expression throughout our lives

5.7 Discuss sexual satisfaction in committed relationships

5.8 Identify sex as a social problem

Sex may be biological, but it occurs in a social context.

Chris and Kayla offer a glimpse of the social context of sexuality among young, unmarried adults.

Out of the blue, ask your parents or grandparents about the "double standard." Even if you provide no context, they will know exactly what you're talking about: that it's more acceptable in our society for boys and men to engage in non-marital sex than it is for girls and women.

But that was then, and this is now. Does the double standard still exist? What is the social context of sexuality for young people today, and how is it different from in the past? I posed these questions to two young adults: Chris, a 23-year-old male graduate student studying physical therapy, and Kayla, a 26-year-old administrative assistant.

Both Chris and Kayla note the acceptance of casual sex, often called *hook-ups* today. People meet one another on social networking websites and through friends, but bars are a primary venue for casual hook-ups. Although men and women in earlier generations also engaged in non-marital sex, it was more likely to occur within a committed relationship. Sure, some had so-called one-night stands, but rarely did women talk about these casual encounters with the openness that surrounds today's hook-ups. As Kayla told me, "I've had experience when I was hooking up with a friend of a friend and we both just said, 'This is fun, we like each other's company, and it doesn't have to be any more than that.' We were both very clear from the start. As long as those expectations don't change, I think that it could be great."

But, the more things change, the more they also stay the same. According to Chris, the double standard is alive and well. First, he acknowledges that despite its shallowness, men still rank a woman's attractiveness as her most important attribute, at least initially—is she "hot" or not? Kayla, in contrast, refers to a man's sense of humor as "always the best part."

Chris also says that women who have casual sex are looked at more negatively than men who have multiple partners: "I think there is a double standard between men who have slept with tons of women and women who have slept with tons of men. For women, it's a lot more negative. It's 'She's a whore, she's sexually promiscuous, she doesn't think highly of herself, or she doesn't have a lot of confidence.' For a guy it's almost like 'He's awesome, he's the man,' and you think 'This guy must just know everything.'"

Kayla sees things somewhat differently and feels that gender stereotypes are becoming less important. "There is still some stigma attached to women who have multiple casual sexual partners, but I also believe that there is a— maybe a less harsh stigma, but a stigma as well attached to men who have multiple casual sexual partners." What do you think?

According to Chris, the double standard is alive and well.

◉ **Watch** on **MySocLab**
Video: *Perspectives on Sexual Identity and Behavior: Kayla and Chris*

exuality is a universal human experience. Even young children are keenly interested in their genitals and feelings of arousal (Thigpen, 2009). We know that sexuality has a biological basis, but we also think of sexuality as a highly personal matter. Our sexuality is so intimate that it's an integral part of our own identity—our feelings of *who* we are. We may have particular sexual preferences and personal desires. However, sex is more than just biological or personal; it's also *social*. We cannot understand sexuality until we look at macro-level factors. In previous chapters, we have stressed how human behavior varies around the world or at different times in history. We've emphasized how your membership in certain groups, such as your sex, race, or social class, shapes who you are, the values you hold, and the opportunities and constraints you encounter. These factors influence the realm of sexuality as well (Hock, 2012; Stombler, Baunach, Burgess, Donnelly, Simonds, & Windsor, 2010). This chapter shows you how the biological, personal, and social factors are intertwined in our sexuality.

You may vividly remember the first time you heard about how babies were "made." But learning about sex means more than just discovering its mechanics. It includes learning the *who, what, where, when, how,* and *why* of sexual behavior. With whom do we have sex? What is appropriate sexual behavior? Where do we have sex? When do we have sex? How do we have sex? Why do we have sex?

The answers to these questions say a lot about how sex is accepted and practiced in a particular culture, and in a particular historical period (Rathus,

Images of sexuality are found in all types of media, including those that are readily available to children. Parents say that they are very concerned about the messages their children are receiving.

Nevid, & Fichner-Rathus, 2014). For example, in your grandparents' era, sex was largely hidden from public discussion. Today, discussions of sex are very public, as Kayla and Chris show us in the opening vignette. Media depictions of sex are as close as the magazines in the checkout line at the grocery store. Mainstream women's and girls' magazines such as *Cosmopolitan, Redbook,* and *Seventeen* use sex to sell copies. *Sports Illustrated*'s annual swimsuit edition, featuring bikini-clad women in provocative poses, sells twice as many copies as any other issue. Television, radio, film, and the Internet also use sex to entertain and to increase their profits. Verbal and visual references to sexual activity bombard us with images of what it means to be sexual in mainstream U.S. culture. Forty percent of programming on the Cartoon Network, a television cable network watched by children of all ages, contains either sexual depictions or references (Parents Television Council, 2011).

5.1 Identify historical and cultural influences on sexuality

Questions That Matter

5.1 Is sexuality purely biological?

5.2 How do macro-level factors influence sexuality?

Overview of Historical and Cultural Influences on Sexuality

Sexuality may be a universal and natural physiological experience, but sexual attitudes and behaviors can be quite different across cultures. For example, among the Mangaia people of Polynesia, both girls and boys are expected to have a high level of sexual desire in early adolescence. At the age of 13 or 14, boys are given explicit instruction through personal experience with an older female teacher in how to please a girl through kissing, fondling, oral sex, and are taught specific techniques for giving her multiple orgasms. It's critical that a boy quickly learn these techniques. Soon he will begin sexual relations with a girl his own age, and if he fails to satisfy her, she will likely publicly denounce him and his lack of sexual skill (Strong, DeVault, Sayad, & Yarber, 2002).

In contrast to the Mangaia, the Dani of New Guinea show little interest in sex beyond what is needed for reproduction. Sexual intercourse is performed quickly and female orgasm is virtually unheard of. After childbirth, mothers and fathers abstain from sex for five years. Sexual affairs are rare or nonexistent. These examples from two different cultures illustrate that many aspects of sex are far from innate.

We can also see differences *within* our own culture, including across historical periods, between racial and ethnic groups, social classes, and between women and men. For example, our images of early American sexuality are of prim and proper Puritans and sexually repressed Victorians. Religious and medical authorities of the time did not believe that women experienced sexual desires; those women who did were considered dangerous or evil (Ehrenreich & English, 1989).

Myths and stereotypes surrounded males as well. People believed sexual intercourse drained a man of his natural vitality, and therefore engaging in it too frequently—more than once a month—was not recommended. **Masturbation**—the rubbing, fondling, and stimulating of one's own genitals and other body parts—was considered perverse or dangerous for men, and virtually unheard of among women. The Reverend Sylvester Graham (1794–1851) preached that the loss of even an ounce of semen was equal to the loss of several ounces of blood (Bullough, 1976). Each time a man ejaculated, he was thought to be risking his physical health. Graham encouraged men to control their sexual feelings by adopting a diet based on whole-grain flour. His name is still identified with a cracker he developed in the 1830s to help men control their sexual urges—the Graham cracker!

The 20th century witnessed a number of new social trends that began to shape sexual behavior, marriage, and family life (Weis, 1998). Industrialization and the growth in jobs encouraged men and women to move away from their extended families in rural areas. In urban areas, away from their traditions, they experienced greater independence and opportunities. The growth in public schools allowed young men and women to spend time together with less parental supervision, and led to the creation of a new adolescent subculture. More women worked outside the home, which, together with required schooling, increased opportunities for both sexes to meet, interact, and socialize. The employment of women also increased a family's standard of living, and gave rise to a growing middle class that could afford some of the latest technologies, such as an automobile or telephone. These technologies increased opportunities for freedom and privacy for young people.

All of these changes led many people to question existing ideas about sexuality, and the traditional values began to give way to a search for personal fulfillment and satisfaction. Both men and women began to view sexual gratification as a right, and the availability of birth control offered women and men a degree of control over their lives that had been largely unavailable. Marriage was increasingly connected to romance as husbands and wives were seen as companions attending to each other's physical, emotional, and sexual needs.

Today, our culture addresses sexuality more openly than a few generations ago. At the turn of the 20th century, it was illegal to provide unmarried people with information about birth control, whereas today, many unmarried teenagers already know about and have used various methods of preventing pregnancy. Most American adults today approve of non-marital sex (Newport & Himelfarb, May 20, 2013). In fact, Americans now have more sexual partners over the lifespan, begin sexual activity at an earlier age, and are less likely to view sexual activity solely as an act of procreation. If pregnancy occurs, marriage is only one of several options available. Most Americans believe it's morally acceptable to have a baby outside marriage, and 53 percent believe abortion should be legal in all or most circumstances (Newport & Himelfarb, May 20, 2013; Morin, 2011; Pew Research Center for the People & the Press, August 22, 2012).

masturbation: Sexually stimulating one's own body.

Watch on **MySocLab**
Video: *Sexual Attitudes in the United States*

menarche: A woman's first menstrual period.

We're single for longer periods of time, thereby increasing our likelihood of having non-marital sex. Biology is interwoven with these social and cultural conditions. In 1890, the average age at menarche, or a woman's first menstrual period, was 15–17 years, and the average age of marriage for women was 22 years. Today, the average age at menarche is around 12 years, and the average age of marriage for women is almost 27 years, resulting in at least eight more years as an unmarried yet physically mature woman (Cohn, February 13, 2013). This provides a larger window of opportunity for young women and men to explore their sexuality.

Some people, however, are concerned that the age of physical development and menarche has decreased to a point at which children are not yet equipped emotionally to handle these changes. For example, as shown in the *Why Do Research?*

Why Do Research?

Researchers Note Earlier Onset of Puberty in U.S. Girls

The definition of *normal development* for U.S. girls is changing, and this vividly illustrates how the biological and social aspects of sexuality are intertwined. Girls' childhoods are growing shorter, with developmental milestones occurring at earlier ages. While the typical 8-year-old U.S. girl is enjoying third grade, practicing her cursive writing, and jumping rope on the playground, increasingly more of these young girls are also experiencing the process of becoming women.

Researchers are noting that signs of pubertal development can be seen in girls as young as 7 or 8. The blossoming of breast buds is the first sign of pubertal development in girls. Breast bud development used to be considered average between the ages of 10 and 12 years old, but now girls are experiencing this development change at an earlier age. In a study of 17,000 girls in North Carolina, almost 50 percent of Black and 15 percent of White girls showed breast buds by age 8.

The onset of *menarche,* or first menstruation, is also experienced at a younger age than in years past. Between 1890 and today, the average age of menarche has decreased from an average of 15–17 to about 12 now. What is behind the trend of earlier pubertal development among girls?

Explanations have included growth hormones in our foods, better sanitation, easier access to good nutrition, and public health interventions that reduced the spread of disease. As the health of females improved, the chemical signals within the body began to initiate the process of puberty sooner because the body was better equipped to reproduce at earlier ages. In many ways, puberty has traditionally been a sign of good health and wealth, although early puberty does carry some health risks—longer exposure to estrogen over a lifetime may contribute to breast cancer, other forms of cancers, or other problems.

But why else should we be concerned? The combination of an 8- or 9-year-old girl with breast buds, along with societal messages telling young girls to dress and act sexy, may be dangerous for a young girl whose emotional and mental development has not caught up with her physical maturation. Sexy clothing and makeup are now heavily marketed to a new group called *tweens,* children between the broad ages of 7 and 12. In fact, sales of thong underwear to tweens have quadrupled since 2000. Young girls are increasingly sexualized, and they feel social pressure from their peers to look, act, and *be* sexy. Even their immature genitals are sexualized: many

The marketing industry has been accused of sexualizing young children, especially girls, as young as seven or eight.

adult women have taken to waxing to remove their pubic hair to more closely resemble a prepubescent girl.

Although many young girls are biologically capable of having babies, they are still children themselves and need time to grow into adult women.

WHAT DO YOU THINK?

1. Compare and contrast the biological, micro-level, and macro-level factors associated with early pubertal development. Do you think these differ for boys and girls?
2. Have you seen evidence of the sexualization of tweens? What do you think are some of the consequences of this sexualization?

Written by Nicole K. Smith

Sources: Brink, 2008; Levin & Kilbourne, 2008.

feature box, some girls are experiencing breast development as young as eight. What are the implications of this early physical change? One implication is that businesses now heavily market sexually suggestive clothing and makeup to *tweens*—girls between the ages of 7 and 12. This marketing sexualizes young children in new and disturbing ways. For example, a recent report from the Parents Television Council found that teenage girls are more likely than older women to be depicted in sexual situations on prime time television, including implied nudity and sexual gestures such as suggestive dancing, erotic kissing, erotic touching, or implied intercourse (Parents Television Council, 2010).

*B*ecause sexual attitudes and behaviors seem to change over time, do you think those of the next generation will be different from your own? If yes, in what ways? If not, why not?

Our Sexual Selves: Biology and Culture Intertwined

Sex is biological, personal, and social. Let's begin our discussion of sexuality with the biological basics of who we are and show how biology and our social environment are intertwined to shape our personal identities, attitudes, and behaviors.

Sex and Gender

Recall from Chapter 2 that our definition of *sex* refers to biological differences and our role in reproduction. Typically, people think of two sexes based on genitalia: male and female. But the categories are not always that obvious.

Some people are born **intersexed,** a term used for a variety of conditions in which a person has a reproductive or sexual anatomy that doesn't fit the typical definitions of what is considered female or male (Haas, 2010). For example, a person might be born with a female appearance, but have mostly male genitalia. Or a person may be born with genitals in between the usual male and female types—a girl may have a noticeably large clitoris or lack a vaginal opening, or a boy may be born with a notably small penis or a divided scrotum formed more like labia.

How common are these differences? It depends on the condition. A variation that is so atypical as to require surgery occurs only in about 1 or 2 in 1,000 births. However, many other people are born with subtler forms of sex anatomy variations (American Psychological Association, 2013; Intersex Society of North America, 2008).

In contrast to sex, recall that **gender** refers to the culturally and socially constructed differences between the meanings, beliefs, and practices associated with femininity and masculinity (Lindsey, 2011). Gender is social in nature and consists of learned attitudes and behaviors, not biological or physical qualities. We are *born* male or female, but we *learn* the cultural and socially prescribed traits associated with masculine or feminine patterns of behavior.

Not everyone fits so neatly into his or her prescribed category; sometimes a person's identity does not conform to his or her biological anatomy. **Transgender** individuals manifest characteristics, behaviors, or self-expressions associated typically with the other gender (American Psychological Association, 2013b; PFLAG, 2013). A man may feel as relaxed, comfortable, and normal engaging in feminine traits such as wearing certain clothing (dresses), following particular grooming practices (painting nails), or having typically feminine hobbies, as he does in engaging in masculine ones, or even more so. Transgender women are not usually as obvious to us because we allow women more leeway to behave in traditionally masculine ways, such as wearing men's clothing or acting aggressively.

5.2 Recognize how biology and culture shape our sexual selves

Questions That Matter

5.3 What is the difference between *sex* and *gender*?

5.4 Do sex and gender go together?

5.5 What do we mean by *sexual orientation*?

 Read on **MySocLab**
Document: *The Five Sexes: Why Male and Female Are Not Enough*

intersexed: Those born with genitalia that do not clearly identify them as unambiguously male or female.

transgender: When a person feels as comfortable, if not more so, in expressing gendered traits that are associated with the other sex.

Transgender issues have been largely ignored, but this is beginning to change (Pfeffer, 2010). It's not known how many transgender men and women exist because of the long-held stigma associated with being transgender. The American Psychological Association estimates that 2–3 percent of biological males may engage in cross-dressing, at least occasionally (American Psychological Association, 2013b).

Some transgender individuals harbor a deep sense of discomfort about their sex and wish to live fully as members of the other sex. Usually referred to as **transsexuals**, these individuals may have sex reassignment surgery and hormone treatments, either male-to-female or female-to-male. Current estimates of the prevalence of transsexualism are about 1 in 10,000 for biological males and 1 in 30,000 for biological females (APA Task Force on Gender Identity and Gender Variance, 2009). Reassignment surgery is expensive, costing up to $50,000, and the preparation is time-consuming and emotionally difficult. It's estimated that 100 to 500 sex reassignment surgeries are conducted each year in the United States, and two to five times this many worldwide. Perhaps 25,000 U.S. adults have undergone sex reassignment surgery (Encyclopedia of Surgery, 2009).

Sexual Orientation

Another aspect of who we are concerns our **sexual orientation**, which refers to an enduring pattern of romantic, emotional, and sexual partners we choose. It involves a person's *identity*, or how one sees oneself.

Although we now understand that sexual orientation ranges along a continuum, with many people somewhere in the middle (Kinsey, Pomeroy, & Martin, 1953), for ease of discussion many people still talk about sexual orientation in terms of discrete categories. A **heterosexual** identity, sometimes called *straight*, refers to an attraction and preference for developing romantic, emotional, and sexual relationships with the other sex (i.e., a man and a woman). A **homosexual** identity refers to attraction and preference for relationships with members of one's own sex (i.e., two men or two women). Homosexual men may be referred to as *gay males* or just *gay*. Homosexual women are often called *lesbians*. The term **bisexual** refers to an orientation in which a person is attracted to both males and females (engaging in both heterosexual and homosexual partner choice) (Rathus, Nevid, & Fichner-Rathus, 2014).

Counting the number of persons who are gay, lesbian, and bisexual is challenging. One reason is that having a gay or lesbian *identity* can be a very different thing from having a gay or lesbian *experience* (Ward, 2010). Some people have had a gay or lesbian experience, or many experiences, yet still think of themselves as heterosexual (Vrangalova & Savin-Williams, 2010). The number of people who self-identify as gay or lesbian is quite a bit smaller. When researchers asked in one survey, "Do you think of yourself as heterosexual, homosexual, bisexual, or something else?" about 3 percent of men and slightly less than 2 percent of women claimed either a homosexual or bisexual self-concept (Vrangalova & Savin-Williams, 2010). In a recent Gallup poll, 3.4 percent of adults claimed to identify as lesbian, gay, bisexual or transgender (Gallup.com, 2012). Yet, the likelihood of having a same-sex sexual *experience* may be two or three times higher (McCabe, Brewster, & Tillman, 2011), and the number of people with same-sex *interests* is higher still (Vrangalova & Savin-Williams, 2010). One study of teenagers and young adults ages 15 to 21 found that 10.5 percent of women and 3.7 percent of men reported having a same-sex sexual experience (McCabe, Brewster, & Tillman, 2011). Another study of young adults ages 19 to 26 found that 25 percent of women and 10 percent of men reported having some homosexual experience, interest, or identity (Pedersen & Kristiansen, 2008). Thus, the number of persons who identify themselves as homosexual or

---

transsexual: An individual who undergoes sex reassignment surgery and hormone treatments.

sexual orientation: The sexual and romantic pattern of partners of choice.

heterosexual: Having an attraction and preference for developing romantic and sexual relationships with the opposite sex.

homosexual: Having an attraction and preference for relationships with members of one's own sex.

bisexual: An orientation in which a person is attracted to both males and females.

bisexual is significantly smaller than the number of persons who have had, or have considered having, a same-sex sexual experience.

WHAT DETERMINES SEXUAL ORIENTATION?   How do we come to have a specific sexual orientation? Are we the way we are because of biology, or because of social and environmental factors? Is our sexual orientation a choice? The question of what causes sexual orientation is an intriguing one that we cannot yet definitively answer. However, scientists are coming to the conclusion that a complex set of biological (genetics and hormones) and social factors shape who we are. In other words, sexual orientation is not really a choice (American Psychological Association, 2013c).

There are probably many reasons for a person's sexual orientation and these reasons may differ for different people, but emerging evidence suggests the biological components are far greater than we once imagined. Psychologists, psychiatrists, and other mental health professionals generally agree that homosexuality is not an illness, mental disorder, or emotional problem. In 1973, the American Psychiatric Association removed homosexuality from the official manual that lists mental and emotional disorders. Two years later, the American Psychological Association passed a resolution supporting the removal (Conger, 1975).

For most people, sexual orientation is shaped at an early age (American Psychological Association, 2013c). One study of college students found that 17 percent of gay and bisexual men and 11 percent of lesbian and bisexual women reported knowing they were gay or bisexual as early as grade school (Elliott, Brantley, & Johnson, 1997).

Research that focuses on siblings, especially twins, can demystify the causes of sexual orientation (Burri, Cherkas, Spector, & Rahman, 2011). One study set out to determine whether identical twins, who share all their genetic material, were more likely to be gay or lesbian than other siblings. The researchers considered three types of sibling pairs *in which one was known to be gay or lesbian*: (1) identical twins, who share all their genetic material; (2) fraternal twins, who share half their genetic material; and (3) adopted siblings, who share no genetic material. The researchers found that 52 percent of the male identical twin pairs and 48 percent of the identical female twin pairs were both homosexual, compared to only 22 percent of male fraternal twins and 16 percent of female fraternal twins. Adopted siblings were least likely to both be homosexual (11 percent and 6 percent for male and female adopted siblings, respectively) (Bailey & Pillard, 1991; Bailey, Pillard, Neale, & Agyei, 1993). These results suggest that homosexuality may contain an important biological component.

Another study examined the relationship between the sexual orientation of 55 gay or bisexual fathers and their 82 adult sons at least 17 years of age (Bailey, Bobrow, Wolfe, & Mikach, 1995). More than 90 percent of the sons were heterosexual. Furthermore, gay and heterosexual sons did not differ on potentially relevant variables, such as the length of time they had lived with their fathers. Thus, the researchers question environmental influences and suggest that they do not appear as important as previously assumed.

Some researchers suggest homosexuality is more common on the maternal side, fueling a discussion that homosexuality may be "passed" through women (Hamer & Copeland, 1994). Other researchers have noted that there may be structural differences in the brains of heterosexuals and homosexuals (BBC, 2008; LeVay, 1991; Schmid, 2005). Gay men's brains respond differently from those of heterosexual men's in some ways, and actually operate more like women's brains (Schmid, 2005).

What explains our sexual orientation? Although the answers are not completely known, most scientists think that biology can give us important clues.

Scientists interpret these results with caution. Even if we could directly link specific genes or brain processes to sexual orientation, our behavior is also shaped and molded by our cultural and historical context.

ATTITUDES TOWARD LGBT Attitudes toward lesbians, gays, bisexuals, and transgender persons (LGBT) differ around the world. For example, in many countries in the Middle East and Africa, homosexuality is against the law and carries harsh penalties, such as imprisonment or even death. For example, in the African countries of Malawi and Kenya, homosexuality is punishable by up to 14 years in prison, and a lawmaker with the governing party in Uganda recently proposed executing people who are gay (Bearak, 2010; Gettleman, 2010). The *New York Times* recently reported that police broke up a same-sex wedding in Kenya; not only were they concerned about its illegality, but they were afraid that an angry mob would stone the couple to death (Gettleman, 2010).

In the United States, many people still disapprove of homosexuality, but attitudes are becoming more accepting. In 2013, according to a Gallup Poll, 59 percent of Americans believed homosexuality was "morally acceptable"—as shown in Figure 5.1 (May 20, 2013). In particular, Blacks, older persons, those with less education, conservative Republicans, and those persons who attend church more often were more likely to believe that homosexuality was morally unacceptable or to hold other negative attitudes (Vincent, Peterson, & Parrott, 2009). Polls assessing support for same-sex marriage also show that most people now approve (*Washington Post/ABC News*, March 18, 2013).

What are your attitudes toward homosexuality? The *Getting to Know Yourself* feature box offers a self-assessment survey that measures your thoughts, feelings,

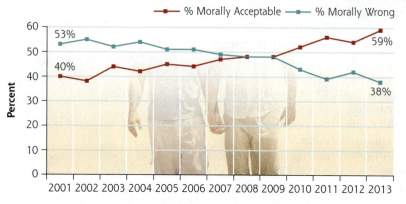

FIGURE 5.1

Perceptions of the Morality of Homosexual Relations

Attitudes are changing: More people now believe that same-sex relationships are morally acceptable rather than morally wrong.
Source: Gallup Poll, May 20, 2013.

GETTING TO KNOW YOURSELF · Weigh Your Attitudes and Beliefs about Homosexuality

Answer the following questions truthfully. For the sake of ease, *gay* refers to both homosexual men and homosexual women.

1 = Strongly Agree; 2 = Agree; 3 = Neither Agree nor Disagree; 4 = Disagree; 5 = Strongly Disagree

_____ 1. I worry that gay people will try to seduce me.
_____ 2. Gay people are immoral.
_____ 3. Homosexuality is acceptable to me.
_____ 4. I would not be good friends with someone if I knew he or she was gay.
_____ 5. I think gay people should not be teachers.
_____ 6. I usually laugh at derogatory gay jokes.
_____ 7. Marriage between gays is acceptable.
_____ 8. It does not matter to me whether my friends are gay or straight.
_____ 9. I make jokes about gay people.
_____ 10. Gay people demand too many rights.
_____ 11. Organizations that promote gay rights are important and necessary.
_____ 12. I have called a gay person a name out loud to their face, like *queer*.

_____ 13. I have damaged property of a gay person, such as scratching their car.
_____ 14. I would feel uncomfortable having a gay roommate.
_____ 15. Homosexual behavior should be against the law.
_____ 16. It would bother me to see gays kissing.
_____ 17. I have never met anyone who is gay.

First, transpose the answer categories of questions 3, 7, 8, and 11, so that Strongly Disagree is now worth 1 point, Strongly Agree is worth 2 points, and so on. Now, count up your points for each question. In general, the lower the score, the greater the negative attitudes and beliefs about homosexuals; the higher the score, the more positive.

WHAT DO YOU THINK?

1. Do you think average scores of men and women differ? Why or why not? How about Whites, Blacks, Hispanics, Asian Americans, Native Americans, and other minority groups?
2. Can you identify any micro-level or macro-level factors that have shaped your views?

and behaviors regarding homosexuality. How do you compare with your friends or others in class?

Some people experience very strong negative feelings toward homosexuality, called **homophobia (or anti-gay prejudice)**, a display of which can take many forms, including using derogatory names, making disparaging jokes, discriminating, or even causing violence (Pascoe, 2007). Much media attention was given to the plight of Matthew Shepard, a young gay man in Wyoming who was tied to a fence, pistol-whipped, and left to die in 1998 (Shepard, 2009). This horrendous crime outraged the public and led some state legislatures to add violence against gays and lesbians to their hate crime statutes. The U.S. Justice Department claims that, of all hate and bias crimes reported to the FBI, about 20 percent involve sexual orientation (Federal Bureau of Investigation, 2012).

Anti-gay prejudice adversely affects both homosexuals and heterosexuals. It creates fear, anxiety, misunderstanding, and hatred. Heterosexuals, for example, may restrict their same-sex friendships, or heterosexual males may act hyper-masculine for fear they may be mistaken for gay men. The delay in our country's response to the HIV/AIDS epidemic has been attributed to anti-gay prejudice. In his best-selling book, *And the Band Played On: Politics, People, and the AIDS Epidemic*, Randy Shilts (1987) illustrated the ways in which the labeling of HIV/AIDS as the "gay" disease kept the government from acting as quickly or thoroughly as if another, more acceptable group had initially contracted the disease.

In summary, understanding our sexual selves leads us to examine closely our sex, our gender, and our sexual orientation, as shown in Table 5.1. For many, these three components operate together in predictable ways: If you're a woman, you behave in ways our culture considers feminine, and you're romantically and sexually attracted to men. Likewise, if you're a man, you act in ways deemed masculine, and you're attracted to women. However, as we've learned in this section, sex, gender, and sexual orientation are separate and distinct components and don't always operate in a predictable fashion.

We've seen some influences of biology in shaping who we are—our sex and our sexual orientation. Yet, our sexual attitudes and many of our sexual behaviors are learned. From where do we learn them?

TABLE 5.1	Sex, Gender, and Sexual Orientation	
Sex, gender, *and* sexual orientation *are three distinct components of our identity. Often they go together in a predictable fashion, but because they are distinct, they can also be mixed. What are the possibilities?*		
Sex:	Male	Female
Gender:	Masculine	Feminine
Sexual Orientation:	Heterosexual	Homosexual

- A heterosexual feminine man
- A homosexual feminine man
- A heterosexual masculine man
- A homosexual masculine man
- A heterosexual feminine woman
- A homosexual feminine woman
- A heterosexual masculine woman
- A homosexual masculine woman

homophobia (or anti-gay prejudice): Having very strong negative feelings toward homosexuality.

Do you know anyone (including yourself) whose sex, gender, and sexual orientation do not conform to traditional expectations? For example, do you know anyone who is transgender, intersexed, or gay or lesbian? What have been some of their (your) experiences with respect to intimate relationships or with discrimination?

Sexual Scripts

We like to think that our sexual attitudes are distinctly our own and our behavior represents uniquely individual likes and dislikes. Yet, even these personal aspects of our lives are highly shaped by social and cultural factors. Our sexual attitudes and behaviors are organized and directed through **sexual scripts**, which are the norms or rules regarding sexual behavior. They govern the *who, what, where, when, how,* and *why* we have sex. For example, our culture prohibits sex with animals, children, and, unless you live in a few selected counties in Nevada, someone to whom you have paid money. It doesn't prohibit sex among unmarried people or those of different religious faiths, races, or ethnic backgrounds. As a society, we've decided that a married person should only have sex with his or her spouse. We've decided that sex can be enjoyed for pleasure rather than just for reproduction. Other cultures see things differently. Sexual scripts act as a

5.3 Compare and contrast sexual scripts

Question That Matters

5.6 What are *sexual scripts,* and where do we learn them?

sexual scripts: The norms or rules regarding sexual behavior.

blueprint, informing us what is expected and appropriate, and what is considered inappropriate or taboo regarding our sexuality (Masters, Casey, Wells, & Morrison, 2012).

We learn our sexual scripts from at least three different sources (Laumann, Gagnon, Michael, & Michaels, 1994):

- The culture in which we live, including our parents, our friends, the mass media, and the dominant religion practiced.
- The interpersonal communication between us and our partner as we begin, and attend to, our personal relationship.
- Our personal views of sex, based on feelings, desires, and fantasies.

In other words, we must look beyond biology to explain our sexual rules and behaviors.

5.4 Explain the double standard

Question That Matters

5.7 Are sexual scripts different for men and women?

double standard: The idea that men have been allowed far more permissiveness in sexual behavior than women.

Gender and Sexual Scripts: The Double Standard

Traditionally, men are granted far more leeway in sexual behavior than are women, a situation called the **double standard** (Fasula, Carry, & Miller, 2014; Masters, Casey, Wells, & Morrison, 2013). Men are expected to be assertive in seeking sexual behavior, to always be ready for sex, and to have more sexual partners. They are rewarded socially for "scoring." Boys who deviate in any way from traditional masculinity are stigmatized as being gay (Risman & Seale, 2010). Women, in contrast, are to walk a fine line by being "sexy," yet not "too sexy." They must make themselves desirable and attractive to the attention of men, but by becoming too desirable or attractive they risk being labeled "easy," "cheap," or a "slut." They must be careful to appear interested, but not too interested, in sex.

Content analyses of adolescents' top 25 primetime network programs, including four top reality shows, *Jersey Shore, Real World, Teen Mom 2,* and *16 and Pregnant,* revealed that sexual scripts are highly gendered. The data showed a high degree of disrespect for both sexes, and was particularly apparent when referring to females (Kim, Sorsoli, Collins, Zylbergold, Schooler, & Tolman, 2007; Parents Television Council, 2012). For example, so-called reality shows that appeal to adolescents offer a disturbingly unrealistic portrayal of "reality" with harsh, demeaning, degrading, and sexualized dialogue. Although young women were routinely the recipients of denigrating language, they were also more likely than young men to be negative to themselves and to other women. The data revealed that across all shows, only 24 percent of what females said about themselves was positive. Similarly, only 21 percent of language about or directed at females (including female to female or male to female) was positive. The terms used to refer to women included:

Atomic bomb, bitch, cock blocker, cunt, dick, dirt bag, dog, drunk, DTF (down to f**k), flavor, good time, gremlin, grenade, landmine, loser, parasite, psycho, slut, stage-5 clinger, stalker, clown, toad, turd, whore, knuckleheads, player, porn star.

In contrast, terms used to describe males tended to be viewed by males as much more complimentary or flattering (or at least less disrespectful) (Parents Television Council, 2012). They included:

Big man, dawg, superhero, pimp, DTF (down-to-f**k), gangsta, holiday, MacGyver, winner, badass, caveman, knucklehead, monster, psycho.

Have you seen any evidence that the double standard still exists?

The portrayals of boys and men showed a clear message: accumulating sexual experience is an important, desirable, and even necessary component of masculinity. Boys and men should attain sexual experience by whatever means available, including possibly force or deceit. Television images of girls and women in these top primetime shows were more conflicted: girls and women walk a precarious line between making themselves sexually available and being appropriately demure. Feminine courtship strategies encouraged girls and women to seduce boys and men by exploiting their bodies and dressing in tight, revealing clothing, even though these same behaviors were then devalued and seen as a sign of their sexual indiscretion.

Girls and women faced a challenge: how to conform to pervasive conventions of sexuality and be sexually available, while trying to control boys and men's "uncontrollable" sexual desire. In other words, these images give young viewers information about how girls, women, boys, and men are supposed to think, feel, and behave in romantic and sexual situations (Kim, Sorsoli, Collins, Zylbergold, Schooler, & Tolman, 2007).

But these television shows are extreme, you may argue. Yes, however, sociologist Michael Kimmel has studied gender for decades, especially masculinity, and he has concluded that the double standard persists in everyday relationships as well. Perhaps his interview with "Ted," a 21-year-old college student, sums it up best:

When I've just got laid, the first thing I think about—really, I shouldn't be telling you this, but really it's the very first thing, before I've even like "finished"—is that I can't wait to tell my crew who I just did. Like I say to myself, "Omigod, they're not going to believe that I just did Kristy. . . . Like I just know what will happen. They'll all be high-fiving me and shit. And Kristy? Uh well, she'll probably ask me not to tell anyone, you know, to protect her reputation an all. But, like, yeah, right. I'm still gonna tell my boys." (Kimmel, 2008, p. 206)

Interestingly, both men and women uphold the double standard: Even women perceive other women more negatively if they have sex in an uncommitted rather than a committed relationship. People of all ages, including pre-adolescent boys and girls, middle and high schoolers, college students, and adults commonly use harsher terms to refer to sexually active girls than they do to their male counterparts (Bogle, 2008; Kreager & Staff, 2009; Reid, Elliott, & Webber, 2011).

Peggy Orenstein, in her book *School Girls,* found that the fear of being labeled a slut in middle school affects how girls see themselves and directly influences how they relate to both other girls and to boys. She describes one interview with Evie, a typical middle-school girl obsessed with pointing out the girls at school who are "sluts." Evie is learning the rules, or scripts, about sexuality. She explains to Orenstein in her middle-school language that sex "ruins" girls but enhances boys; that boys have far fewer constraints than do girls; and that sexual behavior for girls is controllable, but for boys it's inevitable and excusable: "Boys only think with their dicks" (Orenstein, 1994, p. 58). Girls who fail to follow the scripts are shunned. If they dare to complain about the scripts, or confront a boy who is pressuring them for sex, *their* reputations are on the line. "The thing is, we don't have control," Evie explains. "He could just say that we were asking for it or that we wanted it. Then everyone will think we're sluts" (Orenstein, 1994, p. 64).

Another study based on extensive interviews with teenage girls found that girls genuinely wrestled with their sexuality. In *Dilemmas of Desire* (2005), author Deborah Tolman describes how girls eagerly wanted to be desired by boys, but at the same time, they disassociated from their own bodies and did not seem to express any real sexual feelings themselves. They were content simply to be "objects of desire." Sex was something that just happened to them, and was not something they felt that they owned.

((⦿ **Listen** on **MySocLab**
Audio: *NPR: Absent Dads Impact Daughters' Sexual Behavior*

Components of the Male and Female Sexual Scripts

Let's examine male and female sexual scripts in our society. First, what are some components of the *male* sexual script? Keep in mind that these features are certainly modified in a relationship where people are able to break free from cultural stereotypes and experience true intimacy. Nonetheless, the male script, which will look familiar to you, emphasizes sex over intimacy:

- *A man's looks are relatively unimportant, but his status is enhanced if he's with a beautiful woman.* A woman is a trophy, and the more attractive the trophy, the more of a man he's perceived to be.

- *The man always wants sex and is ready for it.* It doesn't matter much what else is going on or what his feelings are toward a potential partner. A man is like a machine and can be "turned on" immediately.

Males and females have different scripts in our society. What does this photograph from a scene of the sitcom *The Big Bang Theory* tell you about their sexual scripts?

- *A man is in charge.* He's the initiator, the leader, and knows more about sex than his partner does. He wouldn't feel comfortable asking his partner what she really likes.

- *All physical contact leads to sex.* Because a man is a machine, ideally any physical contact should lead to sexual intercourse. Touching, caressing, and kissing are not pleasurable ends in themselves.

- *A man cannot easily stop himself once he gets turned on.* Men have greater sexual needs than women do, and they may not be able to stop once aroused, regardless of whether a man's partner asks him to stop.

- *Sex equals intercourse.* The focus of sex is on stimulating the penis. It is hoped that this will be satisfactory to his partner.

- *Sexual intercourse always leads to orgasm.* According to the male sexual script, the purpose of intercourse is for the male to have an orgasm. If one doesn't occur, the act is incomplete or a failure. However, it's less important that a female has an orgasm.

In contrast, what are some components of the *female* sexual script? Again, these features may be modified in relationships in which people can truly be themselves and move away from rigid scripts. For women, we can see that the sexual script emphasizes feelings over sex:

- *Women should make themselves sexually attractive to men to get their attention, but they should not make themselves too attractive.* Women should dress "a certain way" so that they'll gain the attention of men, but they also run the risk of gaining too much attention. It's up to women to sort out the appropriate type of dress, makeup, and demeanor to attract the right amount of male attention.

- *Women's genitals are mysterious.* Many girls and women know little about their bodies. They've been taught not to touch or explore them, and many have never even used a mirror to look at them. What they do know comes from media images that tell them that their genitals have an odor, which must be controlled. Consequently, many women are very uncomfortable with their bodies.

- *Women should not know too much about sex or be too experienced.* Women walk a fine line today—they must not appear too uptight about sex, but they must not feel too comfortable with it either. Women shouldn't be "too experienced," however it's quantified, because they run the risk of being labeled a "slut" or a "whore."

- *Good girls don't plan in advance to have sex or initiate it.* To plan in advance (and take appropriate precautions) may look to her partner as though she's too experienced or likes sex too much. She can't take the lead or she may risk her reputation.

- *Women shouldn't talk about sex.* Many women can't talk about sex because they're not expected to be very knowledgeable or to feel very comfortable with it. Women may feel more comfortable *having* sex than having a simple conversation about it with their partner.

- *A man should know how to please a woman.* Although he may be primarily focused on his penis and his own orgasm, a woman feels it's his job to know how to arouse her. He's supposed to know what she wants, even if she doesn't want (or doesn't know how) to tell him.

*H*ow would a conflict theorist analyze the difference between male and female scripts? How does that compare to a functional theorist?

- *Sexual intercourse is supposed to lead to orgasm and other stimulation should be unnecessary.* Studies indicate that between one-third and one-half of women don't have an orgasm in sexual intercourse; they need additional oral or manual stimulation of the clitoris. Nonetheless, many women believe that something is wrong with them if sexual intercourse itself doesn't produce an orgasm.

The double standard is found throughout the world, in both developed and developing nations. Sometimes it even lays the foundation for government social policy. The *Diversity in Families* feature box illustrates how the double sexual standard has affected government policy in Japan. Although the Japanese government took many decades to approve birth control pills to prevent pregnancy, the government offered no delays when it came to approving Viagra to help men with impotence. Many Japanese found this a flagrant example of sexism.

DIVERSITY IN FAMILIES
Quick Passage of Viagra in Japan Reignites the Birth Control Debate

Masako, a 32-year-old mother of two, was frustrated by the lack of reliable birth control available in Tokyo. Why was she concerned? In Japan, birth control pills were under government review for decades. Meanwhile, the Japanese government took only six months to approve the impotence treatment drug Viagra. This left many people asking why women's need for the birth control pill was less important than men's desire for Viagra.

Advocates of the birth control pill claimed that approval would serve more people and be of greater benefit than Viagra. Women's groups and the media accused the Japanese government of sexism. "When old guys want something, they get it. But when women want something, nothing happens. . . . Japan is still a male-dominated society," says Midori Ashida, who heads a Tokyo-based group that lobbied for acceptance of the birth control pill.

Advocates of the birth control pill finally met with success. Within a few months after the public outcry over the approval of Viagra, the Japanese government decided to allow limited sale of the birth control pill. However, it requires a doctor's prescription and is not covered by public health insurance.

The Health Ministry says the main reason the pill spent so long in review is that the government had concerns about possible side effects. However, more than 300 million women around the world already use birth control pills, and recent studies show few, if any, long-term ill effects.

The Japanese government also claimed to be concerned that acceptance of the birth control pill would cut into the use of condoms and contribute to the spread of HIV/AIDS. Others cited fears about the destruction of moral values. However, the government did not seem concerned with the possible side effects of Viagra for HIV/AIDS transmission, or for declining morality.

Why was Viagra approved so quickly? Takaichi Hirota, a spokesman for Pfizer (which makes the drug), believes the reason is that the company provided hard data on the drug. Others believe the quick passage of Viagra and the slow passage of the birth control pill were more likely related to the Japanese government's goal of raising the nation's rapidly declining birthrate. It is at an all-time low of 1.39 births per woman, and government officials are worried this will increase the proportion of elderly in the population and create a serious financial problem for Japan in the coming decades. Others see it as a vivid example of the sexual double standard in action.

WHAT DO YOU THINK?

1. If you were living in Japan, what would your reaction have been to the quick approval of Viagra, while approval of birth control pills was stalled?
2. What social and cultural factors do you think may account for these policy decisions?

Sources: Hayashi, 2009; Kageyama, 1999; Parker, 1999.

The Double Standard in Current Sexual Behavior

Given the strong gendered sexual scripts in our society, it isn't surprising that researchers continue to find significant differences between men and women in their sexual behavior (Fryar, Hirsch, Porter, Kottiri, Brody, & Louis, 2007; Langer, Arnedt, & Sussman, 2004). An *ABC News* survey (Langer, Arnedt, & Sussman, 2004) of adults showed that men think about sex more often than women (70 percent of men vs. 34 percent of women reported "thinking about sex every day"); more often enjoy sex "a great deal" (83 percent vs. 59 percent); have visited a sex website more often (34 percent vs. 10 percent); and have more sexual partners. Regardless of actual behavior, men and women have different *ideal* numbers of lifetime sex partners; if there were no risks or limitations on sexual activity, men say about 13 partners would be an "ideal number," whereas women report 5 partners would be "ideal" (Fenigstein & Preston, 2007).

The double standard permeates all aspects of society and illustrates important ideas about women, men, and how they should relate to one another (Fasula, Carry, & Miller, 2012). It contributes to a number of problems: It fosters a lack of knowledge about women's bodies and the mistaken idea that women have less important sexual needs; it perpetuates the notion that male sexuality should be the normative baseline for eroticism and sexual activity; and it objectifies women by keeping them as the "objects of desire." Here's an example of a problem exacerbated by this double standard: the lack of knowledge about women's bodies.

Example of the Double Standard: Confusion over the Source of Women's Pleasure

Sexual intercourse is often viewed as the ultimate sexual act; it's sometimes referred to as *having sex,* as though other sexual activities are preliminaries or foreplay. Although this makes sense from a procreative standpoint—because sexual intercourse is needed to make babies—it doesn't make sense to the many women who are more likely to have orgasms from manual or oral stimulation than from sexual intercourse itself.

To reach orgasm, many women need additional clitoral stimulation beyond that which is provided in sexual intercourse (Richters, de Visser, Rissel, & Smith, 2006). For example, as shown in Figure 5.2, a study based on a representative sample of more than 19,000 Australians between the ages of 16 and 59 found that half of women didn't have an orgasm during their most recent sexual encounter if they had only vaginal intercourse. However, if manual or oral stimulation was included, the odds of women having an orgasm significantly increased. In fact, orgasm was most likely if the sexual encounter didn't contain intercourse at all!

This seems to confirm what some people have long suspected. *The Hite Report,* a non-representative sample but based on information from more than 3,000 women, found that only 26 percent reported experiencing orgasm regularly during intercourse (Hite, 1977).

Yet, women felt so much pressure from their partners to have an orgasm during intercourse that the majority of women reported faking them (Langer, Arnedt, & Sussman, 2004; Muehlenhard & Shippee, 2009). A recent study from *The Journal of Sexual Medicine* found that 85 percent of men said their partners had an orgasm during the most recent sex act, whereas 64 percent of women reported they actually did (Herbenick, Reece, Schick, Sanders, Dodge, & Fortenberry, 2010). "There's this massive gap between men's perception and women's reality," says Debby Herbenick, co-author of the research and associate director at the Center for Sexual Health Promotion at Indiana University. "It shows a lack of communication between partners, either by women faking it, or by men not asking or noticing if their partner [climaxed]" (cited in Hutchinson, October 4, 2010).

Historically, sexologists have often been confused over women's sexuality and the real source of women's pleasure. They've debated between vaginal and

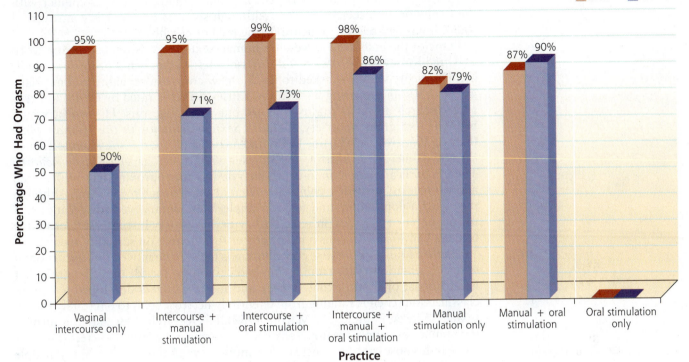

FIGURE 5.2

Likelihood of Having an Orgasm by Different Sexual Activities

Despite the simultaneous orgasms often depicted in the media, sexual intercourse alone doesn't seem to "do it" for many women. *Source:* Richters, de Visser, Rissel, & Smith, 2006.

clitoral orgasms. Women who didn't have orgasms in intercourse were thought to have a *female sexual dysfunction* requiring treatment. Although recent sex researchers have tried to clear up this confusion, even today, people seem fairly ignorant about female anatomy, orgasm, and sexual response. If half to three-quarters of women need clitoral stimulation to have an orgasm, why is stimulation often not considered a normal part of sex?

Research now shows us that the clitoris is, in many ways, the female counter-part of the penis. Both organs receive and transmit sexual sensations. However, in sexual intercourse, whereas the penis receives direct stimulation, the clitoris may be stimulated only indirectly. And while the penis is directly involved in reproduction, the clitoris is unique in serving no known purpose but pro-viding sexual pleasure. It's ironic that many cultures, both past and present, have viewed women as unresponsive to sexual stimulation, when it's women, not men, who possess a sexual organ apparently devoted solely to providing pleasurable sensations. The double standard is powerful!

*H*ow did you learn your sexual script? Can you think of people or events that shaped your script? Have you ever violated your sexual script? What were the consequences of that violation?

Studying Human Sexuality

5.5 Summarize the study of human sexuality

Throughout this text, we've shown the importance of research and described how research is conducted, but you might think that something as personal as sexuality is too difficult to study. Will people really participate in experiments, respond to surveys, participate in lengthy interviews, or subject themselves to observation about sex? Next, let's focus on some of the key pioneers in sex research—**sexology**—and learn about the research methods they used in their work.

Question That Matters

5.8 What are some important studies that have been done on human sexuality?

sexology: A field composed of a multidisciplinary group of clinicians, researchers, and educators who study sexuality.

Early Pioneers

Sigmund Freud (1856–1939) focused much of his work on the study of the psy-chosexual development of children and how it affected adult life and mental condition. Freud believed we're all born with biologically based sex drives. These drives must be channeled through socially approved outlets, he believed;

otherwise, the individual experiences internal conflict, as well as conflict with the family or with society at large. Although some of his work is controversial today, it has had a large influence on the field of psychology.

One of the first large surveys on human sexuality was the pioneering work of Alfred Kinsey (1894–1956) and his associates. Kinsey was a professor at Indiana University who was asked to teach a new course in sexuality and marriage in the 1930s. In preparing his lectures, Kinsey was frustrated by the lack of reliable research about sexuality and set out to change this. His work, which brought him great notoriety, includes *Sexual Behavior in the Human Male* (Kinsey, Pomeroy, & Martin, 1948) and *Sexual Behavior in the Human Female* (Kinsey, Pomeroy, & Martin, 1953), otherwise known as *The Kinsey Reports*. These reports are based on in-depth interviews with approximately 11,000 men and women and provide a complete sexual history of each respondent. Although they used a nonrandom and biased sample, these data served for decades as a major source of statistics on sexual behavior. The Kinsey Institute, still located at Indiana University, remains a major center for research on sexuality today.

Perhaps Kinsey's greatest contribution is the way he moved the discussion of sexual orientation away from a simple dichotomy—the idea that you're either heterosexual or homosexual. Kinsey and his researchers developed a 7-point classification scheme, ranging from 0 (entirely heterosexual) to 6 (entirely homosexual) (Kinsey, Pomeroy, & Martin, 1953). His research showed that a surprising number of people are not really 0's or 6's—meaning entirely heterosexual or entirely homosexual, but instead are more toward the middle. Many people reported that they had some homosexual experiences, although they continued to think of themselves as heterosexual. Kinsey's work revealed that sexual identity is conceptually distinct from sexual behavior.

The groundbreaking research of William Masters and Virginia Johnson in the 1960s addressed several features of sexuality, including the physiology of human sexual response, a greater understanding of women's sexuality, and the treatment of sexual dysfunction. Rather than relying on Kinsey's survey methods, Masters and Johnson adopted observational designs within a laboratory setting (Maier, 2009). They used sophisticated instruments to measure the physiological responses of nearly 700 individuals during sexual activity. The married couples engaged in intercourse and other forms of mutual stimulation. The unmarried subjects participated in studies that didn't require intercourse, such as masturbation. The participants experienced more than 10,000 orgasms in these controlled laboratory experiments! The findings were published in their book *Human Sexual Response* (Masters & Johnson, 1966).

In particular, Masters and Johnson are known for their understanding of the sexual response cycle, which they divided into four states—(1) desire; (2) excitement; (3) orgasm; and (4) resolution—and they found that men and women experience these states in a similar fashion. Their work enlightened us about the source of women's pleasure—the clitoris—and debunked previous myths that some women have orgasms originating in their vaginas. They taught us that, sexually, men and women are far more alike than different.

More Contemporary Research in Human Sexuality

The field of sexology is now well developed, and a number of more recent studies offer important information about contemporary sexuality in the United States. In 1992, the National Opinion Research Center and the University of Chicago conducted a large research project based on face-to-face interviews with a random sample of 3,432 U.S. adults ages 18 through 59. The results are reported in *The Social Organization of Sexuality: Sexual Practices in the United States* (Laumann, Gagnon, Michael, & Michaels, 1994) and *Sex in America: A Definitive Survey* (Michael, Gagnon, Laumann, & Kolata, 1994). The respondents were selected using the same sophisticated sampling techniques as in other social and political research, and 80 percent of those contacted agreed to participate, ensuring findings that are far more representative and generalizable to the adult population than previous research. Their study focused on a wide variety of attitudes and behaviors—marital, non-marital, heterosexual, and homosexual—and examined differences by age, racial, ethnic, gender, and class subgroups. Although the sample omitted participants age 60 and older, and therefore doesn't tell us about the sexual activities of the elderly, it nonetheless gave us the first truly scientific study of sex among a representative sample of younger adults in the United States.

Several other excellent and more recent sources of data about human sexuality use surveys. For example, the *Youth Risk Behavior Survey* (YRBS), conducted every other year for the Centers for Disease Control and Prevention (CDC), measures the prevalence of many health-risk behaviors, including sexual behavior, contraceptive use, risking sexually transmitted diseases, and unintended pregnancy among 14,000 students in grades 9–12. The *National Health and Nutrition Examination Survey* (NHANES) is about the sexual behavior of more than 6,000 adults ages 20 through 59 (Fryar, Hirsch, Porter, Kottiri, Brody, & Louis, 2007). The survey collects data by way of an audio computer-assisted self-interview, which allows respondents to answer questions about sensitive issues in complete privacy. The *National Survey of Family Growth* (NSFG) is another contemporary survey, based on personal interviews conducted in the homes of a national sample of women ages 15 through 44. Its main purpose is to provide reliable national data on marriage, divorce, contraception, infertility, and the health of women and infants in the United States. The Kinsey Institute, described earlier, remains a source of research on sexuality, and recently conducted the National Survey on Sexual Health and Behavior (NSSHB). Public opinion polls such as *Gallup, NBC News,* and *ABC News* also conduct surveys with representative samples of U.S. adults or teens.

All together, these sources reveal important trends regarding sexual behaviors and their changes over time. Let's now turn to some of these trends.

Popular magazines are consumed with sex—what you and others are or should be doing. Do you think they present a realistic image about sexuality?

Sexual Expression throughout Our Lives

When you're next at your neighborhood grocery store, look at the magazine covers on display. What titles do you read? Here are some examples:

"The Sex Skill Men Adore"

"You've Cheated, Should You Tell?"

"Faking Orgasms: Will He Really Know?"

"Love Your Breasts, Even If They Are Small"

"10 Sex Tips That Will Drive Him Wild"

"New Places to Make It"

Sex! Everybody seems to be doing it. Or are they? What are they doing, with whom are they doing it, and why? The vast majority of adults are monogamous and happy, expressing a desire for emotional commitment and a satisfaction with their sex lives. But what *are* we doing? Table 5.2, based on an *ABC News* poll, gives some interesting clues (Langer, Arnedt, & Sussman, 2004). Having sex outdoors, discussing fantasies, and faking orgasms are high on the list.

Once considered taboo, **oral sex,** oral stimulation of the genitals, has become nearly as common as intercourse among heterosexual, White, young, and more highly educated samples, including adolescents and college students (Chambers, 2007; Halpern-Felsher, Cornell, Kropp, & Tschann, 2005; Prinstein, Meade, &

5.6 Explain sexual expression throughout our lives

Questions That Matter

5.9 When do we become sexual?

5.10 How big a social problem is teenage pregnancy?

5.11 How prevalent is non-marital sex among young adults?

oral sex: The oral stimulation of the genitals.

TABLE 5.2 Americans' Sexual Behavior (Percentage)

What are Americans up to? More than half have had sex outdoors or discussed fantasies; nearly half of women report that they have faked orgasms.

Sex outdoors	57%
Discuss fantasies	51%
Faked orgasm (women)	48%
Sexually adventurous	42%
First-date sex	29%
Paid for sex (men)	15%
Paid for sex (single men, 30+)	30%
Cheated	16%
Threesome	14%
Sex at work	12%

Source: ABC News (http://abcnews.go.com/Primetime/PollVault/story?id=156921).

TABLE 5.3 Number of Sex Partners (Percentage)

Men have a greater number of sex partners in their lifetimes.

	All	Men	Women
One	19%	12%	25%
2–4	25%	16%	33%
5–10	28%	26%	29%
11–20	12%	18%	6%
21+	12%	20%	4%
Mean	13%	20%	6%
Median	5%	8%	3%

Source: ABC News (http://abcnews.go.com/Primetime/PollVault/story?id=156921).

cunnilingus: The oral stimulation of the woman's genitals by her partner.

fellatio: The oral stimulation of the man's genitals by his partner.

Cohen, 2003). Whites are more likely to engage in and receive oral sex, both **cunnilingus**, oral stimulation of the woman's genitals by her partner, and **fellatio**, oral stimulation of the man's genitals by his partner, than are Blacks and Hispanics (Sterk-Elifson, 1994).

Table 5.3 reveals the number of sexual partners U.S. adults have had, according to a survey by *ABC News* (Langer, Arnedt, & Sussman, 2004). Women report a mean (average) number of 6 sex partners in their lifetimes; men report an average of 20. However, these data are highly skewed because a few men report a very large number of partners. A better gauge is the median, or the midpoint between the high and low. Using this measure, we find that women have a median of three sexual partners, whereas men have eight.

Blacks report the greatest number of sexual partners. For example, 46 percent of Black men have had 15 or more sexual partners, compared to 27 percent of Whites, and 20 percent of Mexican Americans. In contrast, only 6 percent of Black men claim to have had no more than one sexual partner, compared to 17 percent of White men and 24 percent of Mexican American men (Fryar, Hirsch, Porter, Kottiri, Brody, & Louis, 2007). Although persons with lower incomes and less education begin sexual activity at a younger age, there is little difference in the number of sexual partners across income and education levels (Fryar, Hirsch, Porter, Kottiri, Brody, & Louis, 2007).

Next, let's turn to a discussion of sexual expression throughout our lives, from when we are infants until our old age. We tend to think that only young adults are sexually active. We don't like to acknowledge that our parents are sexual, and are even less inclined to think about our grandparents as sexual beings, or your seven-year-old kid sister. But in reality, we are sexual throughout our lives.

Childhood

We know that we become sexual very early in our lives—even infants have been observed to stimulate themselves. We don't just become sexual when we reach puberty (Rathus, Nevid, & Fichner-Rathus, 2014). Newborns have the physiological changes associated with sexual response. Boys as young as a few days can have erections, and girls secrete vaginal lubrication. Young infants and toddlers fondle their genitals for the pleasure it provides.

During early childhood (2 to 6 years), children develop a sense of who they are as girls or as boys and have a good understanding of gendered behavior. They're curious about their bodies and the bodies of others, perhaps even playing "doctor" as a way to explore the genitals of others.

In middle childhood (7 to 11 years), children experiment with masturbation. During the late part of this period, many children will develop their first "crush" or have their first sexual fantasies.

Adolescence (12 to 21 years) is a period when children sexually mature. Increased estrogen causes girls' breasts and sexual organs to grow, and the average age of menarche is now about 12 years. Among boys, the increased androgen sex hormones, testosterone in particular, cause hair growth, voice changes, and growth in size of sexual organs. By the end of middle school or the beginning of high school, most boys and girls have experienced the physiological changes necessary to begin sexual activity. Some do begin sexual activity at this time, although U.S. culture largely frowns on it.

Teenage Sexuality, Pregnancy, and Motherhood

Jake and Lianne met six months ago at a party given by a mutual friend who was celebrating a milestone birthday. It was a warm summer night, and the air, the music, and the drinks were richly intoxicating. He first noticed her hair: long, silky, and nearly jet black. She first noticed his eyes, piercing and blue.

> **"What began as a casual encounter—a little flirting, a sensuous smile, and a few laughs—has since evolved into much more."**

"Who is that?" they both asked themselves. Jake had to find out, and made his move. What began as a casual encounter—a little flirting, a sensuous smile, and a few laughs—has since evolved into much more. They began having a sexual relationship within a month. Jake and Lianne are 15.

Many American adolescents are sexually active, as shown in Figures 5.3 and 5.4. A large study conducted by the CDC with 14,000 students in grades 9 through 12 shows that 46 percent of girls and 49 percent of boys have had sexual intercourse (Kann, Lowry, Eaton, & Wachsler, 2012). About one-third of high school boys and girls have a current sexual partner, and about one-half of females, and two-thirds of males say they didn't use a condom during their last sexual intercourse.

Black teens are more likely to be sexually active than are Hispanics or Whites. Sixty percent of Black students in grades 9 through 12 have had sexual intercourse, compared with 49 percent of Hispanics and 44 percent of Whites. Blacks are also more likely to report being currently sexually active. Reasons for racial and ethnic differences include environmental and socioeconomic issues; for example, Blacks are more likely to have lower incomes and live in poorer neighborhoods, and thus are less likely to be enrolled in supervised after-school programs (Eaton et al., 2008).

By the end of high school, nearly two-thirds of young men and women have had intercourse. However, it's important to note that fewer teens, particularly males, are having sexual intercourse than was the case in the recent past. For example, according to the National Survey of Family Growth, 60 percent of never-married 15- to 19-year-old males reported having sexual intercourse in 1988, dropping to less than half of males in 2010.

However, unlike sexual intercourse, the percentage of teens engaging in oral sex is increasing (Chambers, 2007; *NBC News/People Magazine*, 2005; Herbenick, Reece, Schick, Sanders, Dodge, & Fortenberry, 2010). Research from

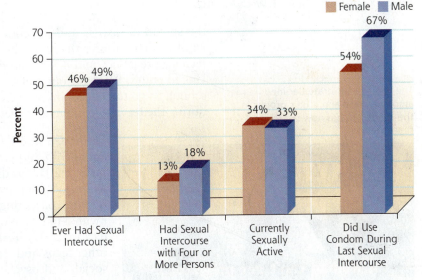

FIGURE 5.3
Teenage Sexual Behaviors, Grades 9-12, by Sex, 2011

About half of high school students in grades 9 through 12 have had sexual intercourse, and about one-third are currently sexually active.
Source: Kann, Lowry, Eaton, & Wechsler, 2012.

((**Listen** on **MySocLab**
Audio: *NPR: 20 Percent of Young Teens Sexually Active*

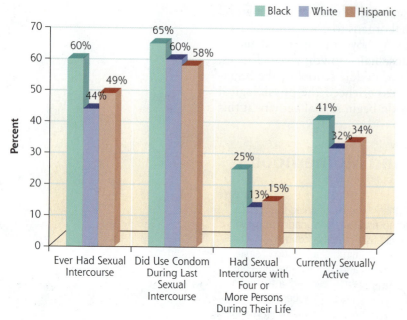

Legend: Black | White | Hispanic

FIGURE 5.4

Teenage Sexual Behaviors, Grades 9–12, by Race/Ethnicity, 2011

Black high school students are more sexually active than Hispanics or Whites.
Source: Kann, Lowry, Eaton, & Wechsler, 2012.

The teenage birthrate declined among all race and ethnic groups in the 1990s, but has now started to fluctuate.

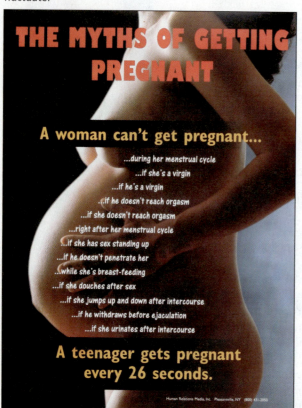

the Kinsey Institute shows that about 18 percent of 16- to 17-year-old males and 22 percent of 16- to 17-year-old females performed oral sex with another sex partner (Herbenick, Reece, Schick, Sanders, Dodge, & Fortenberry, 2010). Interestingly, nearly half of young teens don't believe oral sex is "as big a deal" as intercourse and they don't see it as spoiling virginity, although fewer girls feel this way than do boys. Indeed, over one-quarter of adolescents reported oral sex wasn't even sex.

Teenagers engage in sex for a variety of reasons and in a variety of contexts. Some are in monogamous long-term relationships and see sexuality as a mechanism for expressing their love. Others are in short-term relationships, and some aren't in relationships at all, but engage in sex with friends or even strangers for physical gratification, peer pressure, or a desire to be popular.

Most parents are concerned about teenage sexual activity. They worry that their teens aren't mature enough to handle sexuality. They fear exploitation of young teenage girls by older boys or men. They're concerned about the spread of disease and infection. They also worry about teenage pregnancy. Unlike other cultures that consider it "normal" for teenage girls to have babies, teenage pregnancy and motherhood are considered major social problems in the United States. We want our teens to have a carefree adolescence—to finish high school, to go to college or complete other training, and to work. Having a baby during the teenage years makes these things difficult to accomplish.

TEENAGE PREGNANCY AND MOTHERHOOD Nonetheless, about 330,000 teenagers between the ages of 15 and 19 gave birth in 2011, as did almost 4,000 girls age 10 to 14 (Hamilton, Martin, & Ventura, October 2012). The negative consequences of early parenting in the United States have been well documented (CDC, November 21, 2012; The Annie E. Casey Foundation, 2009). Teenage parents are disadvantaged compared to other teens and they're generally unprepared for the financial, social, and psychological challenges of raising children. Teenage mothers are more likely to die in childbirth than are older mothers; their infants are more likely to be of low birth weight and die within the first month of life. Further, teenage mothers are more likely to drop out of school than are other teens, are considerably poorer, and are more likely to receive welfare. Adolescent mothers are also less knowledgeable about child development, less prepared for childrearing, and more likely to be depressed than are other mothers.

The good news is that the number of births among teenagers has been declining over the past twenty years, and reached an all-time low by 2011. In 1991, there were 62 births per 1,000 women age 15 to 19. However, by 2011, the rate had declined to only 31 per 1,000 women ages 15 to 19—a reduction of 50 percent. This impressive decline is found among both older and younger teens and among all racial and ethnic groups, as shown in Figure 5.5 (Hamilton, Martin, & Ventura, April 2012).

There is no single explanation as to why the teenage birthrate has declined so sharply. Teens may be waiting to have sex until they are older, and are having sex less frequently. Perhaps the biggest change is that those teens who are sexually active are more likely to use birth control than in the past, condoms in particular (Santelli, Orr, Lindberg, & Diaz, 2009).

Non-Marital Sex and Young Adults

Although our society largely frowns on teenage sexuality, people are far more accepting of non-marital sex (often referred to as *premarital sex*) among young adults. Fifty-nine percent of adults reported that premarital sex is only "sometimes or not at all wrong," according to a 2007 nationwide study based on more than 2,000 adults. There is, however, a generational gap in these views: 70 percent of people ages 18–24 believe that premarital sex is only sometimes or not at all wrong, but only 40 percent of people age 65 and older agree with that sentiment (Pew Research Center, 2007). And it's likely that attitudes have become more permissive since 2007.

As with teenagers, premarital sex among young adults takes place for a variety of reasons and in a variety of contexts. By age 25, 88 percent of women and 89 percent of men have engaged in premarital sex (Finer, 2007). Note this is higher than the number of people who believe that premarital sex isn't wrong. Again, some young adults have done so within the confines of a committed relationship; others have engaged in more casual sexual encounters. As shown in Chapter 3, dating has evolved from more formal to more informal interactions in recent years, and therefore not surprisingly, sexual relationships have followed suit and sometimes become more casual as well.

HOOKING UP One type of casual sexual experience has received widespread attention—**hooking up,** or the casual sexual interactions among people without any expectations of commitment. On college campuses, in dorms, fraternities, and sororities, "hooking up" parties are common that give young adults the opportunities to engage in sexual acts that may include anything from only kissing to mutual masturbation, oral sex, or sexual intercourse (Armstrong, England, & Fogarty, 2010; Bogle, 2008; Joshi, Peter, & Valkenburg, 2013; Lewis, Atkins, Blayney, Dent, & Kaysen, 2013). These sexual encounters are an outgrowth of how young people socialize today. Instead of socializing in dating pairs, young people today socialize in groups. Male–female relations are more casual, sometimes leading to sexual activity among friends or acquaintances. Whereas earlier generations saw dating as the beginning of an intimate relationship, with possible sex to follow, many young people today have sex first and then possibly date afterward (Bogle, 2008). Common media portrayals of hookups both reflect and create these trends (Joshi, Peter, & Valkenburg, 2013).

How common is the practice of hooking up? Some suggest that it's very common (Bradshaw, Kahn, & Saville, 2010). One study of more than 600 students at a university on the West Coast found that 40 percent of students reported that they've hooked up (England & Thomas, 2007). Another study of 404 students enrolled in an introductory psychology course in a large Southern university noted that 52 percent of males and 36 percent of females reported having engaged

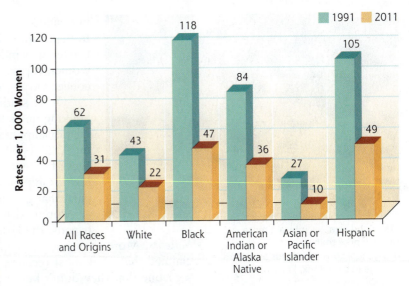

FIGURE 5.5

Birthrates for Women Ages 15–19 Years, by Race/Ethnicity, United States, 1991–2011

Teenage birth rates have declined among all groups since 1991, especially among Black teens.
Source: Hamilton, Martin, & Ventura, 2012.

Listen on **MySocLab**
Audio: *NPR: Teen Pregnancy*

hooking up: Sexual interactions without commitment or even affection for one another.

Males and females interact more casually now than they did in previous generations. This leads some to engage in casual sex, known today as *hook-ups*.

in casual sexual relationships (Grello, Welsh, & Harper, 2006). In-depth interviews with 50 students at Stanford and Indiana Universities indicate that about three-quarters of both men and women reported at least one hookup by their senior year in college (Armstrong, England, & Fogarty, 2010).

Other studies suggest that college students aren't actually hooking up as frequently as one might think, and that romantic relationships are still the most common context for sexual behavior. A survey of nearly 500 college freshman women between the ages of 18 and 21 reveals that romantic sex with a boyfriend or relationship partner was twice as common as hookup sex for this particular group of students (Fielder, Cary, & Cary, 2012).

Potential hookup partners range from strangers to good friends, the latter of which may be referred to as *friends with benefits*. More than one-third of respondents in the Southern university study claimed that their most recent casual sexual encounter was with a stranger or someone that they didn't know well. The West Coast study found that half of the surveyed students had hooked up five or more times; a third said that they had hooked up more than 10 times. Although about a third reported that their hookup didn't go any further than kissing and non-genital touching, nearly half reported that their hookup included either oral sex or sexual intercourse. Alcohol is a big part of hooking up; it decreases inhibitions and encourages people to feel freer to do things they might not otherwise (Grello, Welsh, & Harper, 2006).

The trouble is, hooking up doesn't offer very good sex, at least from a woman's perspective. In a large study of nearly 13,000 undergraduate college students at 17 different universities and 50 in-depth qualitative interviews, only 19 percent of the women reported having an orgasm from a hookup. Women often complain about the sex being very one-sided: "He did that thing where . . . they put their hand on the top of your head . . . and I hate that! . . . Especially 'cause there was no effort made to, like, return that favor!" (Armstrong, England, & Fogarty, 2010, p. 371).

The researchers noted that when a woman received oral sex, her odds of orgasm improved somewhat to about 25 percent. However, women are far less likely than are men to receive oral sex in a hookup (Armstrong, England, & Fogarty, 2010).

Many women, it turns out, fake orgasm for several reasons—to make that person feel good, to make them "feel like they've done their job." But some women fake orgasms just to get the sex over with, "just really to end it," because they are "like, bored with it." Trish, a college senior says:

> He was like, trying too hard to make me come. And there was, like no way it was going to happen. I felt so bad for him. I mean, I had gone down on him and he came already, and he was, like, trying to be a good sport about it, but really. . . . So I just faked it, and he felt good and I felt relieved. (Kimmel, 2008, p. 210)

One study from a midsize university in the Southeast interviewed men and women about their preferences and found that in most situations women preferred dating over hooking up, whereas the opposite was true for men—they preferred hooking up over dating (Bradshaw, Kahn, & Saville, 2010). Perhaps this is because women are far more likely to have an orgasm in a sexual relationship with a steady dating partner than they are in a casual hookup (Armstrong, England, & Fogarty, 2010). Men are more attentive to their partner's needs in a relationship, and men and women communicate about their bodies and their sexual desires:

> Now that I'm in a relationship, I think [her orgasm is] actually pretty important. More important than in a hookup. Because you have more invested in that person. You know, when you have sex, it's more a reciprocal thing. When it's a hookup you feel less investment.
> [In my relationship] she comes every time and that's because I know what she likes and I make sure she does. And if I have to go down on her

for a longer period of time, I'll do that. I've a pretty good idea of what she likes and it's been partly through trial and error, partly through explicit instruction. (Armstrong, England, & Fogarty, 2010, p. 371)

But women aren't the only ones who may prefer dating over hookups. Although men are often portrayed as happy beneficiaries of casual sex, many men, like many women, yearn for a greater emotional connection (Epstein, Calzo, Smiler, & Ward, 2009). In fact, engaging in casual sex is negatively associated with psychological well-being. That is, among both women and men, people who engage in casual sex are more likely to report symptoms of psychological distress or depression (Beramin, Zamboanga, Schwartz, Donnellan, Hudson, Weisskirch, Kim, Agocha, Whitbourne, & Caraway, 2014).

Gay and Lesbian Sexual Relationships

Gay men and lesbians are so often only defined by their sexuality that it's easy to get the mistaken impression that all they ever do is have sex! However, we know that all people—gay, lesbian, heterosexual, and bisexual—lead busy lives, and while sex is important, other things can also take center stage such as work, school, children, and life's daily routine (Peplau & Beals, 2004). Certainly, love, intimacy, and sexual relationships are important to most of us, regardless of sexual orientation. The late researcher Lawrence Kurdek collected extensive information over time to determine how same-sex relationships differ from, or are similar to, heterosexual relationships (Kurdek, 2006, 2008, 2009). Overall, he, like other researchers, found that the similarities between the relationships far outweigh the differences (Gottman, 2013). All people value love and commitment, and hope for a good relationship with open and strong communication. Likewise, gays and lesbians engage in the same sexual behaviors as heterosexuals—for example, kissing, caressing, and oral sex—with the exception of penile–vaginal intercourse, and respondents report no differences in sexual satisfaction.

A few differences between same-sex and heterosexual relationships have been noted by researchers John Gottman, a renowned couples therapist who was then at the University of Washington, and Robert Levenson, a psychology professor at the University of California, Berkeley, closely evaluated 40 same-sex couples and 40 straight married couples, noting similarities and differences. The psychologists concluded that gays and lesbians are nicer than straight people during arguments with partners: they're significantly less belligerent, less domineering, and less fearful. Same-sex couples also use humor more often when arguing. The authors concluded that "heterosexual relationships may have a great deal to learn from homosexual relationships" (cited in Cloud, 2008). But Gottman and Levenson also found that when gay men initiate difficult discussions with their partners, the partners have more difficulty making up than do straight or lesbian couples.

Nonetheless, research comparing gay and lesbian relationships does reveal some notable differences. First, although most gays and lesbians value monogamous intimate relationships, gay men are more accepting of non-monogamous relationships than are lesbians or heterosexuals, and, on average, they have more casual sex (Christopher & Sprecher, 2000). Gendered expectations may play a part here, as men have been socialized to initiate sex. Second, lesbians may engage in sex less frequently than gay men or heterosexual women, although this may be a function of the way that *sex* is defined and tabulated (sometimes *sex* is defined as *sexual intercourse*). Third, although both lesbians and gay men link sex with intimacy, lesbians are more likely to emphasize this than are gay men.

Sex in Marriage

Sex in marriage is often the butt of jokes: "Sex in marriage? Now that's an oxymoron." A review of television primetime shows in the early 1990s revealed that

TABLE 5.4 Percentage of Married Men (M) and Women (W) Reporting Frequency of Vaginal Sex

The frequency of vaginal sex declines with age for both men and women.

Age	18–24		25–29		30–39		40–49		50–59		60–69	
	M	W	M	W	M	W	M	W	M	W	M	W
Not in the past year	4	12	2	4	5	7	9	8	21	22	34	38
A few times a year to monthly	13	15	9	12	16	16	16	22	25	24	21	20
A few times a month to weekly	17	15	46	48	47	50	51	47	38	36	35	36
2–3 times per week	46	35	37	35	27	22	20	21	15	17	10	6
4 or more times a week	35	24	6	2	6	5	4	3	1	1	0	0

Source: Kinsey Institute, 2012.

less than one in ten sex scenes shown were between married couples (Hanson & Knopes, 1993). Instead, there were six times as many scenes of non-marital sex. In fact, extramarital sex was portrayed four times as often as sex in marriage. For some reason, the topic of sex in marriage doesn't seem to be very interesting to most people.

However, most married people are indeed sexually active, and report being quite satisfied with the sexual aspects of their relationship. As one woman said, "As I'm growing older and my husband's growing older, and we're monogamous, it's so pleasant to have one other person that you trust completely. It's a treasure."

How frequently do married couples have sexual relations? As Table 5.4 suggests, it depends on their ages (cited in The Kinsey Institute, 2012). Younger couples engage in sex more often; older couples less often. For example, about 40 percent of married couples between the ages of 25 and 29 have vaginal sex at least two to three times a week, whereas only about 17 percent of couples between the ages of 50 and 59 are sexually active that frequently.

Most married couples don't consider the decline in frequency of sex to be a major problem. They attribute it to a lack of time or energy because of work and family demands, and to becoming more "accustomed" to one another. A study by the American Association of Retired Persons (AARP) reports that, among men and women ages 45 through 49 who have a regular sex partner (presumably a spouse, but could be otherwise), 65 percent of men and 61 percent of women report that their sex lives are extremely or very physically pleasurable, and 69 percent of men and 62 percent of women report that their sex lives are extremely or very emotionally satisfying. There was little variation across racial or ethnic groups (AARP, May 2005).

EXTRAMARITAL SEX Despite the pleasure and intimacy that sex provides to married couples, some married persons have engaged in **extramarital sex**, defined as sex while married with someone who isn't your spouse. Other terms commonly used are *affair, adultery, infidelity,* or *being unfaithful.* Americans frown on extramarital sex, with 78 percent saying that it is always wrong, and another 15 percent saying that it's almost always wrong. Only 2 percent believe that it's not wrong at all (General Social Survey, 2009; Sides, 2011). Two-thirds of Americans say that they wouldn't forgive their spouse for having an affair, and two-thirds would also seek a divorce (Jones, 2008).

However, as we all know, there are *beliefs*, and there are *behaviors*, and these don't always correspond. The best estimates are that about 3 percent to 4 percent of currently married people have a sexual partner besides their spouse in a given year, and about 15 percent of women and 22 percent of men have had a sexual partner other than their spouse at some time while married (Smith, 2006).

Men are somewhat more likely to have extramarital sex, and the longer they live, the more likely they are to do so. According to the National Health and

extramarital sex: Sex, while married, with someone other than your spouse.

📖 **Read** on **MySocLab**
Document: *Sexual Infidelity Among Married and Cohabiting Americans*

Social Life Survey, based on a representative sample of American adults, 37 percent of men ages 50 through 59 have had extramarital sex, compared with just 7 percent of men ages 18 through 29. The men's percentages went up steadily in each age range, whereas for women, differences across age groups weren't as large. About 20 percent of older women reported having an affair, but in all other age ranges, infidelity hovered between 11 and 15 percent (Downs, 2003). There are many reasons for extramarital sex, including sexual curiosity, a lost sense of fun and excitement in the marriage, an inability to communicate one's own needs and desires, sexual addiction, or boredom with marriage or life in general.

For those involved, especially the spouse of the person who had an affair, feelings of betrayal, hurt, and anger are common (Baucom, Snyder, & Gordon, 2009). Extramarital affairs can also hurt an entire family, including children who are usually incapable of understanding the situation or what led to it, and have little say in how their parents will deal with the aftermath. They may even hurt the person who has the affair; researchers note a correlation between extramarital sex and heart disease (Coffey, 2012). As the family systems theory introduced in Chapter 1 reminds us, family members are inextricably linked, and what happens between two members is likely to influence the whole group (Smith & Hamon, 2012).

⦿ **Watch** on **MySocLab**
Video: *Marriage and Cheaters*

✳ **Explore** on **MySocLab**
Activity: *Behind Closed Doors: Adultery, Attitudes, and Behaviors*

Sex and the Elderly

My husband and I probably enjoy sex more today than we did when we were younger. All of our children are now grown up and out of the house, which I'm sure helps our sense of privacy and stress. I don't have to worry about getting pregnant anymore because I'm way past that stage. Also, our sex seems more affectionate now, if that's possible—what I mean is that the goal isn't just on having your own orgasm, but really relaxing and pleasing the other person. Our sense of love and commitment after all these years really shines through. Seriously, I think sex is better now.

"Seriously, I think sex is better now."

—Carmen, age 62

A common misperception about the elderly is that they're no longer sexually active. In the college classroom, any discussion of the sexuality of the elderly is largely met with snickers or looks of disbelief. In response, I ask students, "Well, at what age do you plan to give up sex?" Then, I hear gasps of astonishment.

Sexuality remains an essential element of the lives of the elderly (DeLamater & Sill, 2010; Karraker & DeLamater, 2013; Lodge & Umberson, 2012). The vast majority of elders have a positive view of sexual relationships, and if married or partnered, it's quite likely that they're still sexually active. A large national survey on sexuality provides us with important data to remind us that the elderly remain sexual beings. Figure 5.6 indicates the frequency in which older men and women report having vaginal sex, by whether they are single, partnered, or married. As you can see, 13 percent of single men, 63 percent of partnered men, and 20 percent of married men who are age 70 and older have sex at least a few times a month.

Another study based on a random sample of more than 3,000 adults ages 57 through 85 reported similar conclusions (Lindau, Schumm, Laumann, Levinson, O'Muircheartaigh, & Waite, 2007). Although the likelihood of sexual activity does decline with age, 39 percent of men ages 75 through 85 were still sexually active, as are 17 percent of women. A primary reason that the figures are not higher than this is simply that no partner is available; rates of widowhood are high.

It appears that it's time to debunk the myth that the elderly are asexual!

People often assume that the elderly are not sexually active, but that could not be further from the truth.

FIGURE 5.6

Percent of Men and Women Age 70+ Who Report Having Sex At Least a Few Times Per Month

Many elderly remain sexually active, especially if they are married or partnered.
Source: Kinsey Institute, 2007.

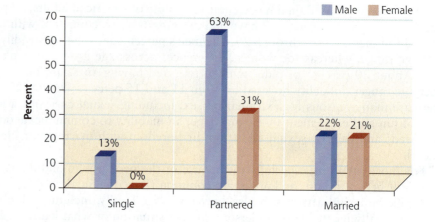

5.7 Discuss sexual satisfaction in committed relationships

Questions That Matter

5.12 What are some common sexual trends in marriage?

5.13 Do people remain sexual throughout their lives?

👁 **Watch** on **MySocLab**
Video: *The Monster: Relationships and Communication*

*W*hy do you think that people find it hard to believe that the elderly are sexual? Where did these attitudes come from? Do you think these attitudes are found throughout the world? Why or why not?

Sexual Satisfaction in Committed Relationships

How important is sex in a committed and loving relationship? For most men and women, there is a positive relationship between sexual satisfaction and overall relationship satisfaction, commitment, and stability regardless of whether we're talking about heterosexual, gay, or lesbian relationships (Harvey, Wenzel, & Sprecher, 2004; Schwartz, 2007). Both the quality and quantity of sex in a committed relationship is associated with feelings of love for one's spouse or partner.

A study of a random sample of the adult U.S. population (Schwartz, 2007) found that a large majority of married individuals reported feeling extremely or very satisfied in their sexual relationship and reported having feelings of love and intimacy after engaging in sexual behaviors. However, it appears that the relationship between sexual satisfaction and the quality of the overall relationship is somewhat stronger for men than for women. Although men are more likely to feel that a poor sex life undermines the entire relationship, women are more likely to feel that a relationship can still be good even if the sex life isn't so great.

Other differences between men and women exist as well, related to the gendered nature of our sexual scripts (Byers, 2005). For example, among women, increased relationship satisfaction leads to increased sexual satisfaction, but among men, increased sexual satisfaction leads to increased relationship satisfaction. Why the difference? Men's sexual scripts focus on sexual behavior first, relationships second; while women are encouraged to think of the relationship first. Good communication is important to all aspects of a couple's relationship; their sex life is no exception. Open communication isn't always easy, but it significantly contributes to both relationship and sexual satisfaction, and brings couples closer together. It's important that each partner feels comfortable expressing his or her sexual needs, wants, and desires. Openness, honesty, respect, and integrity are critical in strong intimate relationships (American Psychological Association, 2005). And as discussed in the section on hooking up, women are more likely to experience orgasm in committed relationships where they feel more comfortable communicating with their partner than in quick, casual sexual encounters (Armstrong, England, & Fogarty, 2010).

An important theme in this chapter is that our sexual norms, attitudes, and behaviors are influenced by the social world in which we live and the human groups to which we belong. In other words, micro-level factors and macro-level factors intertwine with biology to influence how we engage sexually with others. Using teenage sexuality as an example, the *Tying It All Together* feature box summarizes the importance of these dual factors.

Why are so many teenagers sexually active? It's easy to just say, "Because they want to be." Although that may be true to some extent, the reason is far more complex. To really understand teenage sexuality, we must look at a number of different micro- and macro-level factors.

MICRO-LEVEL FACTORS INFLUENCING TEENAGE SEXUALITY

- Sexual desire
- Love, or the desire to please a partner
- Wanting to have a baby
- Manipulation
- Lack of information about how pregnancy is prevented

MACRO-LEVEL FACTORS INFLUENCING TEENAGE SEXUALITY

- Sexual attitudes and behaviors differ across cultures (the United States has the highest rate of teenage pregnancy of any developed country)
- Sexual attitudes and behaviors change over time (the teenage pregnancy rate has declined significantly since 1990)
- Social institutions channel and direct sexuality (the United States defines teenage pregnancy and births as problematic and tries to reduce them through sex education programs in the schools, yet at the same time our economic system sexualizes teens and children)

Sex as a Social Problem: Sexually Transmitted Infections

Millions of Americans currently have at least one sexually transmitted infection (STI), and an additional 20 million people become infected each year (CDC, February 2013). STIs include chlamydia, genital human papillomavirus (HPV), herpes, trichomoniasis, gonorrhea, syphilis, pelvic inflammatory disease (PID), and HIV/AIDS. About one in four girls between the ages of 14 and 19 in the United States is infected with at least one of the most common sexually transmitted diseases.

Although people might be inclined to think of STIs as personal problems, they affect large numbers of people and are social problems. Our ideas about family privacy and personal shame tend to exacerbate our misunderstanding of STIs, allowing them to spread at alarming rates and inhibiting effective treatment.

Despite the fact that STIs are widespread and can strike people of any age, sex, or sexual orientation, most people remain unaware of the risks and consequences of all but the most publicized—HIV and AIDS. However, other STIs are far more prevalent in the population. Genital HPV is estimated to be the most common STI, with at least 50 percent of sexually active men and women acquiring genital HPV infection at some point in their lives. Chlamydia is the most commonly reported STI, with millions of people infected, and more than 1.4 million new cases a year; however, even more go undiagnosed (CDC, February 11, 2013).

Although STIs like chlamydia and genital HPV are widespread across all racial and ethnic groups, average STI rates tend to be higher among Blacks than Whites. We can attribute some of this difference to differences in risky behaviors (i.e., beginning sexual intercourse at an earlier age, having multiple partners, engaging in unprotected intercourse, having a higher level of drug use) and social conditions like poverty and limited access to health care. However, part of the disparity is because Blacks are more likely to seek health care in public clinics, which report STIs more thoroughly than do private providers (CDC, November 13, 2009). Consequently, the statistics may actually underreport the rates among Whites.

According to the CDC, abstaining from sex, reducing the number of sexual partners, and consistently and correctly using condoms are all effective STI prevention strategies. Safe, effective vaccines are also available for some STIs. The CDC recommends that all individuals who are sexually active—particularly young people—should have STI screening and prompt treatment to protect a person's health and prevent transmission to others (CDC, February 2013).

5.8   Identify sex as a social problem

Questions That Matter

5.14 What is the most common sexually transmitted infection (STI)?

5.15 Hasn't the issue of HIV and AIDS been resolved by now?

How should education about STIs be targeted to young people to be most effective?

Watch on **MySocLab**
Video: *Nightmare on AIDS Street: Taking an HIV Test*

Genital HPV

Genital HPV is the most common STI in the United States, with about 80 million Americans currently infected, and another 14 million people becoming newly infected each year (CDC, February 2013). There are more than 40 different types of genital HPV infections, but in all cases, the virus infects the skin and mucous membranes. You can't see HPV symptoms; therefore, most people who become infected aren't even aware they contracted the disease.

Fortunately, most people with HPV don't develop symptoms or health problems. In 90 percent of cases, the body's immune system clears the HPV infection naturally within two years. Although there is no treatment for the virus itself, there are treatments for the serious diseases that HPV can cause, including genital warts, cervical, and other cancers. About 12,000 women develop cervical cancer each year (CDC, March 18, 2013). It can also cause cancers of the vulva, vagina, anus, and penis, which usually aren't detected until they are quite advanced.

How can genital HPV be prevented? One method is to avoid having sex with an infected person; however, most people don't know that they're infected, making this method extremely unreliable. Condoms may lower the risk; however, a condom may not fully cover the infected area. According to the CDC, HPV vaccines are recommended for 11- or 12-year-old boys and girls. HPV vaccines are safe and effective, and can protect males and females against some of the most common types of HPV that can lead to disease and cancer. HPV vaccines are given in three shots over six months; it's important to get all three doses to get the best protection. Boys and girls at ages 11 or 12 are most likely to have the best protection provided by HPV vaccines, and their immune response to vaccine is better than for older women and men (CDC, March 18, 2013).

HIV and AIDS

Acquired immunodeficiency syndrome (AIDS) is caused by infection with the human immunodeficiency virus (HIV) and passed from one person to another through blood-to-blood transmission; through sexual contact; and through pregnancy, delivery, or breastfeeding. HIV and AIDS receive more media attention than any other STI because they are so deadly, and because of the political implications surrounding their discovery and treatment (they were originally labeled a "gay" disease).

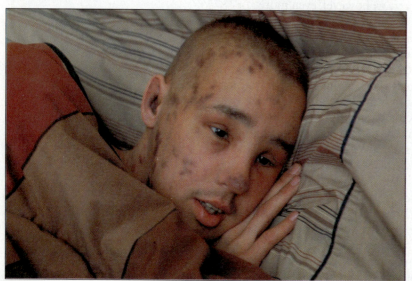

More than 1.1 million people in the United States have HIV/AIDS, about half with full-blown AIDS. No cure has yet been found, and many will die as a result.

HISTORY AND DEVELOPMENT In the early 1980s, physicians in a number of U.S. cities began to notice that numerous cases of rare diseases were occurring among otherwise strong and healthy men. Kaposi's sarcoma, a type of cancer of the blood vessels, and *Pneumocystis carinii* pneumonia, a usually mild lung infection, had become deadly diseases in the gay male population because of a breakdown in the immune system. It was given the name AIDS even before the virus responsible (HIV) was discovered.

At first AIDS seemed to be confined to few groups: gay men, people with hemophilia, and Haitians. Some have argued that because the disease seemed not to run through the entire population, but through groups that faced stigma and discrimination, the government was slow to act

(Shilts, 1987). As Pat Buchanan, a conservative leader and former U.S. presidential hopeful, said, "The poor homosexuals—they have declared war upon nature and now nature is exacting an awful retribution" (Strong, DeVault, Sayad, & Yarber, 2002).

Scientists identified a type of chimpanzee in West Africa as the source of HIV infection in humans. The virus most likely jumped to humans when they hunted these chimpanzees for meat and came into contact with their infected blood. Over several years, the virus slowly spread across Africa and later into other parts of the world. Since then, HIV/AIDS has become one of the greatest public health challenges both nationally and globally (CDC, April 11, 2012). Throughout the world, tens of millions of people have died, including about 636,000 in the United States (CDC, February 27, 2013).

CURRENT STATUS More than 1.1 million persons live with HIV/AIDS in the United States, including 200,000 who are unaware of their infection. Since the beginning of the 21st century, the number of people living with HIV has increased, whereas the annual number of new infections has remained relatively stable at about 50,000 per year (CDC, February 27, 2013). Three-quarters of new HIV/AIDS diagnoses are males, who are most likely to get HIV/AIDS through male-to-male sexual contact. In 2010, there were nearly 20,000 new HIV infections among men who have sex with men, a significant 12 percent increase from 2008. In contrast, females are most likely to contract the disease through heterosexual contact, as shown in Figure 5.7 (CDC, February 28, 2013).

Minority groups have been particularly hard-hit by HIV/AIDS. For example, Blacks make up only 12 percent of the U.S. population, but they represent 44 percent of newly reported HIV/AIDS cases; Hispanics represent 16 percent of the population, but account for 21 percent of the new AIDS cases reported (CDC, February 27, 2013). To be particularly effective in minority communities, the CDC recommends that prevention programs be culturally sensitive. Although race and ethnicity alone are not risk factors for HIV/AIDS, underlying social and economic conditions such as higher rates of poverty, substance abuse, limited access to health care, cultural diversity, and language barriers may increase the risk of infection. Moreover, some Black and Hispanic men are in denial; because Black and Hispanic men who have sex with other men tend to identify themselves as heterosexual, they may not relate to prevention messages geared towards men who identify as homosexual (CDC, March 20, 2013).

The number of AIDS deaths has decreased slightly, and the number of persons living with HIV/AIDS has increased because of promising HIV treatments that have slowed the progression from HIV to AIDS. Nonetheless, there remains no known cure, and about 19,000 men and women will likely die this year in the United States alone (CDC, February 28, 2013).

As devastating as HIV/AIDS is in the United States, the picture here is dwarfed by that in other parts of the world, where 34 million people are infected and 2.5 million new infections occurred in 2011 (UNAIDS, November 2012a). Particularly hard hit is sub-Saharan Africa; with slightly more than 10 percent of the world's population, it's home to more than 69 percent of persons with

Males

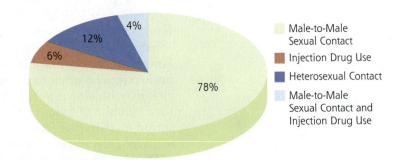

Other categories total less than 1%.

Females

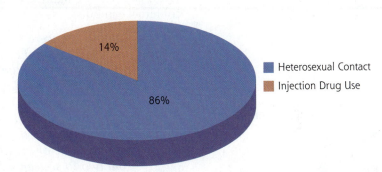

Other categories total less than 1%.

FIGURE 5.7

Transmission Categories of Adults and Adolescents with HIV/AIDS Diagnosed During 2011

Most males contract HIV through male-to-male sexual contact, whereas most females contract HIV through heterosexual contact. *Source:* Centers for Disease Control and Prevention, February 28, 2013.

Watch on MySocLab
Video: *AIDS in Black America*

HIV (UNAIDS, November 2012b). Five percent of the adult population in sub-Saharan Africa is infected, and the number is increasing.

Unlike the United States, where most HIV/AIDS victims are men who have sex with other men, heterosexual women and girls are most vulnerable in sub-Saharan Africa. Fifty-eight percent of those with HIV are women and girls. Power imbalances make it difficult for women to protect themselves from their husbands, who often have multiple sex partners. Moreover, young women and girls may become infected through "survival sex"—having sex with older men for a promise of food or shelter. Men seek out young girls because of the widespread myth that sex with a virgin can cure HIV. The United Nations insists that increasing the status of women and girls is a primary strategy for fighting HIV/AIDS throughout the world (UNAIDS, November 2012b).

Meanwhile, HIV/AIDS is wreaking havoc on families. More than 17 million children have been orphaned in sub-Saharan Africa alone because of AIDS. These children are fighting to survive, according to Stephen Lewis, at the ICASA conference in 2003:

> [I]n Zambia, we were taken to a village where the orphan population was described as out of control. As a vivid example of that, we entered a home and encountered the following: to the immediate left of the door sat the 84-year-old patriarch, entirely blind. Inside the hut sat his two wives, visibly frail, one 76, and the other 78. Between them they had given birth to nine children; eight were now dead and the ninth, alas, was clearly dying. On the floor of the hut, jammed together with barely room to move or breathe, were 32 orphaned children ranging in age from two to sixteen. . . . It is now commonplace that grandmothers are caregivers for orphans. (UN Secretary-General's envoy for HIV/AIDS in Africa, Stephen Lewis (2003), Opening Address of the XIIIth International Conference on AIDS and STIs in Africa.The full speech is available at this link: http://data.unaids.org/media/Speeches01/lewis_speech_icasa_21sep03_en.doc)

How has the world changed because of HIV/AIDS? How have relationships and families changed? On a micro-level, how do you think HIV/AIDS has affected your intimate relationships?

Many children are now cared for by aging and frail grandparents, while others are left to fend for themselves, as described in the feature box *My Family: Apiwe*.

Bringing It Full Circle

What could be more personal than sex? And yet, what seems to command as much public attention? Television shows, blogs, magazines, and other media blare out their entertainment, opinions, and advice. They offer us a definition of normalcy—*who* we should have sex with, *what* we should do, *where* we should have sex, *how often* we should have sex, and *why* we should have sex. They influence Chris and Kayla, and they influence you. These sexual scripts are rooted in macro-level social, cultural, and historical arrangements. Based on what you have learned in this chapter, let's go back to the opening vignette and answer a few questions about our sexual scripts and the double standard:

- Chris believes that a double standard still exists, but Kayla has her doubts. Are your views more similar to Chris's or to Kayla's? In general, do you think that men and women see the double standard differently?

- What experience, if any, do you have with a double standard? What consequences have you experienced?

- If you wanted to research the double standard, which research method introduced in Chapter 1 would you use, and why?

MY FAMILY   Apiwe

Apiwe is already a well-known thief in her community. She mostly steals food from gardens or from the local stores. Sometimes when people catch her they give her a good beating—many of them are hungry too—but Apiwe is lucky today. "Shoo, get away," said the farmer's wife, calling her a foul name, and chasing her with a broom, yet letting Apiwe keep what she has taken. All in all, it was a good day, and she and her sister will have food to eat tonight.

Apiwe is 12 years old and is responsible for the complete care of herself and her 7-year-old sister. They are two of the 14 million children who have been orphaned by AIDS in sub-Saharan Africa, and they are testimony to the devastation that HIV/AIDS is causing in this part of the world. They live in their parents' house, a one-room shack that was rickety in the best of times, but is decaying further from lack of care. Apiwe misses her parents and does not really understand how they got "that" disease—the disease everyone whispers about. Her father died first, several years ago, withering away slowly and painfully. Her mother soon fell weak, and Apiwe quit school to care for her until she died last year. "That disease" is highly stigmatized and no one talks about why they died. Apiwe has no place to go for answers to her questions.

The number of children orphaned by AIDS is increasing at an unprecedented rate, as shown in Figure 5.8. Without AIDS, the percentage of children who are orphans would be expected to decline in number because of general improvements in health, but AIDS has changed all this. As more parents develop AIDS and die, the number of orphans will continue to rise rapidly.

Apiwe and her sister live in a resource-poor environment made even more perilous by the death of their parents. Basic needs like schooling, food, shelter, clothing, and healthcare have disappeared. The sisters beg on the streets, hoping for a coin here and there, and steal food when they can. Some days are more successful than others.

Five percent of adults in sub-Saharan Africa have HIV/AIDS—that is 1 out of every 20 adults. When they die, they leave behind their children.

A "nice" older man has been paying attention to Apiwe lately. Apiwe thinks that he must be rich because he gives her two shiny coins every time he comes by. He has even invited her to his house, offering to "take care of her," he says with a sly grin. Apiwe does not want to go to his house. The man says her sister cannot come, and Apiwe will not leave her alone. Besides, she has an idea of what the man will do to her, and she does not want to make a baby. But some days, when she and her sister are really hungry, she wonders whether it would be so bad. Yes, there would be one more mouth to feed, but maybe this man would help all of them.

WHAT DO YOU THINK?

1. What type of stigma do Apiwe and her sister face? What types of dangers may lay ahead for them?
2. What can be done to help Apiwe, her sister, and the millions of other AIDS orphans? To what degree is the United States helping with this crisis?

Figure 5.8 Data:

Year	Millions of Children Under Age 18
1990	0.6
1995	3.0
2000	8.5
2005	12.3
2012	17.8

Note: Estimate of children who lost at least one parent to an AIDS-related cause.

FIGURE 5.8
Increase in Children Orphaned by AIDS in Sub-Saharan Africa, 1990–2012

The number of AIDS orphans in sub-Saharan Africa is skyrocketing, increasing from 8.5 million to more than 17 million in just 11 years.
Source: United Nations Children's Fund & UNAIDS, 2006; UNAIDS, 2012b.

Sources: Based on AVERT.ORG, December 22, 2009; UNAIDS and World Health Organization, 2009.

✓ **Study** and **Review** on MySocLab

ER REVIEW

.1 Identify historical and cultural influences on sexuality

5.1 Is sexuality purely biological?

Sexuality contains biological, personal, and social components. We cannot understand sex apart from our membership in human groups.

5.2 How do macro-level factors influence sexuality?

Human behavior, including norms surrounding sexuality, varies around the world and at different points in history. Your sex, race, and social class also shape your sexual values, behaviors, opportunities, and constraints.

LO5.2 Recognize how biology and culture shape our sexual selves

5.3 What is the difference between *sex* and *gender*?

Sex refers to the biological differences and our role in reproduction, whereas *gender* refers to culturally and socially constructed differences associated with masculinity or femininity.

5.4 Do sex and gender go together?

What we define as feminine and masculine can vary dramatically from one culture to the next or from one historical period to the next. Also, some people are transgender: their physical sex and their gendered feelings do not match in the predicted fashion.

5.5 What do we mean by *sexual orientation*?

Sexual orientation refers to the sexual and romantic partner of choice. Kinsey's early work showed that sexual orientation exists on a continuum from completely heterosexual to completely homosexual. Although the number of people who are exclusively homosexual is small, many people lie somewhere in between these two polar points. Individuals who are bisexual are attracted to both males and females.

LO5.3 Compare and contrast sexual scripts

5.6 What are *sexual scripts*, and where do we learn them?

Sexual scripts are the norms regarding sexual behavior. They act as a blueprint, informing us what is expected and appropriate, and what is considered inappropriate or taboo. We learn our sexual scripts from the culture in which we live, including our parents, our friends, the mass media, and the dominant religion, as well as the

interpersonal communication between us and our partner as we begin, and attend to, our personal relationship.

LO5.4 Explain the double standard

5.7 Are sexual scripts different for men and women?

Yes. We refer to this difference as the *double standard*. Men are allowed far more latitude in sexual behavior than are women. Men are expected to be assertive in seeking sexual behavior, to be always ready for sex, and to have more sexual partners; they are rewarded socially for "scoring." Women, in contrast, are to walk a fine line between being "sexy," and yet not "too sexy." They must be careful to appear interested, but not too interested, in sex.

LO5.5 Summarize the study of human sexuality

5.8 What are some important studies that have been done on human sexuality?

A number of excellent studies of human sexuality give us keen insights into values and sexual behaviors, including Freud's work in the late 19th century, Kinsey's work in the 1940s and 1950s, Masters and Johnson's work in the 1970s, and more recently, work by organizations such as the CDC, other large national studies, and popular media polls. The most useful studies rely on large and representative samples.

LO5.6 Explain sexual expression throughout our lives

5.9 When do we become sexual?

We know that we become sexual very early in our lives—even infants have been observed to stimulate themselves. Newborns have the physiological changes associated with sexual response.

5.10 How big a social problem is teenage pregnancy?

Hundreds of thousands of teenagers have babies every year. However, there is much good news. The teen pregnancy, abortion, and birthrates are at their lowest points since they were first measured in the early 1970s. Declines are seen among both younger and older teens, and across all racial and ethnic groups.

5.11 How prevalent is non-marital sex among young adults?

Non-marital (or premarital) sex among young adults takes place for a variety of reasons and in a variety

158   PART 2   The Foundations of Relationships

of contexts. By age 25, 88 percent of women and 89 percent of men have engaged in non-marital sex. Some young adults engage in casual sex, or *hooking up*. Studies of college students reveal that somewhere between 30 percent and 50 percent report having engaged in hook-ups.

LO5.7 **Discuss sexual satisfaction in committed relationships**

5.12 What are some common sexual trends in marriage?

It may be the butt of jokes, but apparently most married people are sexually active on a regular basis and are happy with the frequency of sex and its intimacy.

5.13 Do people remain sexual throughout their lives?

Yes. If your grandparents are married or partnered, it's likely that they have remained sexually active. For example, one survey reports that 13 percen[t] men, 63 percent of partnered men, and 20 p[ercent of] married men age 70 and older have sex at leas[t] times a month.

LO5.8 **Identify sex as a social problem**

5.14 What is the most common sexually transmitted infection (STI)?

Genital human papillomavirus (HPV) is the most common STI, with about 80 million currently affected and more than 14 million new cases a year; however, chlamydia is the disease most often reported.

5.15 Hasn't the issue of HIV and AIDS been resolved by now?

Unfortunately, no. In the United States alone, there are about 50,000 new cases every year. HIV and AIDS are particularly devastating in sub-Saharan Africa.

KEY TERMS

bisexual	homophobia (or anti-gay prejudice)	oral sex
cunnilingus	homosexual	sexology
double standard	hooking up	sexual orientation
extramarital sex	intersexed	sexual scripts
fellatio	masturbation	transgender
heterosexual	menarche	transsexual

Communication, Conflict, and Power in Our Relationships

((◦ **Listen** to Chapter 6 on **MySocLab**

LEARNING OBJECTIVES

6.1 Identify the importance of communication

6.2 Recognize the cultural context of communication

6.3 Compare and contrast types of communication

6.4 Analyze sex differences in communication

6.5 Identify communication to keep your relationship strong

6.6 Describe conflict, communication, and problem solving

6.7 Compare and contrast power, control, and decision making

Think about the communication style you have in your current (or most recent) relationship. An answer of T (True) indicates that item usually applies to your relationship, (S) if it sometimes applies, and F (False) if it rarely or never applies. Consult the scoring key after you finish to get an assessment of your communication patterns.

1. Disagreements almost never occur in our relationship.   T   S   F

2. We consider ourselves to be best friends.   T   S   F

3. When we get angry, at least one of us uses profanity.   T   S   F

4. At least one of us tends to keep feelings bottled up inside until we cannot take it anymore.   T   S   F

5. We both feel free to talk about anything with each other.   T   S   F

6. I can trust my partner with my sensitive feelings, and he or she trusts me.   T   S   F

7. When we argue, someone ends up with hurt feelings.   T   S   F

8. We try to be truthful and honest with each other.   T   S   F

9. We mutually express our love for one another.   T   S   F

10. It is easy for us to forgive if we offend one another.   T   S   F

11. My partner always interrupts me, or complains that I interrupt.   T   S   F

12. We often blame and accuse one another.   T   S   F

13. There is give-and-take in our interactions.   T   S   F

14. At least one of us really hates conflict.   T   S   F

15. One of us inevitably gets his or her way even at the other's expense.   T   S   F

16. We are very competitive with one another.   T   S   F

SCORING KEY

First, give yourself 2 points for each statement that you answered this way: 1=F; 2=T; 3=F; 4=F; 5=T; 6=T; 7=F; 8=T; 9=T; 10=T; 11=F; 12=F; 13=T; 14=F; 15=F; 16=F.

Second, give yourself 1 point for each S answer.

Then, total your points. The higher the score, the better the communication.

WHAT DO YOU THINK?

1. Look at the items you missed and discuss them with your partner. Would improvement in these areas enhance the overall communication in the relationship?
2. Do the findings from this assessment accurately reflect you, your expectations, and your experiences? Why or why not?

Race, Ethnicity, and Communication

Because we're more likely to interact with people who are like ourselves, it's not surprising that members of a particular social class, race, or ethnic group develop their own ways of communicating through words, gestures, or expressions (Allen, 2004). For example, linguists have documented substantial differences between Standard American English (SAE), variants of which are spoken by whites and some blacks in the United States, and African American English (AAE), variants of which are spoken by many blacks, especially in the South. These linguistic differences include actual words, syntax, acoustics, and rules for subject–verb agreement (Clopper & Pisoni, 2004). Listeners can identify a speaker's race from his or her speech, even if only hearing short snippets of speech (Grogger, 2011), and this identification has been used to discriminate against blacks. For example, a study that asked black- and white-sounding telephone callers to enquire about an advertised apartment for rent found that black-sounding callers were more likely than white-sounding callers to be told the apartment was already rented (Massey & Lundy, 2001).

Racial differences in speech patterns also help explain the gap in wages between blacks and whites (Grogger, 2011; Stepanikova, Zhang, Wieland, Eleazer, & Stewart, 2012). Audio data from a random sample of 402 black and white respondents from the National Longitudinal Survey of Youth were used to

Read on **MySocLab**
Document: *Use of Black English and Racial Discrimination in Urban Housing Markets (Massey)*

There are significant racial, ethnic, and social class differences in speech patterns and nonverbal communication.

📖 **Read** on **MySocLab**
Document: *Talking Past Each Other: Black and White Languages of Race*

assess the relationship between the sound of a respondent's speech and his or her wages. Participants were recruited to listen to the audio excerpts and provide their perceptions of a number of speaker characteristics, including his or her race. Nearly 84 percent of the white speakers were accurately identified by the listeners, as were about 77 percent of the black speakers. The study found that blacks with racially distinct speech earned lower wages than did whites. However, blacks who didn't use racially distinct speech had wages equal to those of whites. The wage gap persisted even when taking skill level, education, family structure, and income into account (Grogger, 2011). The results show that speech patterns are highly correlated with wages among young black workers.

Nonverbal messages also differ across racial and ethnic groups. Roberto, for example, is referred for special education testing by his fourth-grade teacher because he seems inattentive in class and barely makes eye contact with her when she speaks (McGee, 2008). She assumes that Roberto is "tuned out." However, Roberto is only being respectful, because many children from Latin American, Native American, and Asian cultures avoid making eye contact with authority figures. Thus, to stare at a teacher could be construed as a sign of disrespect, or of "showing off."

Social Class and Communication

The pioneering work of Basil Bernstein and William Labov on social class and linguistics also showed substantial differences in how language is used by different groups (Bernstein, 1960, 1973; Labov, 1966, 1972). For example, members of the working class tend to speak less SAE, use more words of simple coordination such as *like* or *but,* and use fewer pronouns compared to the middle and upper-middle classes (Macaulay, 2005; Wardhaugh, 2010). The *Diversity in Families* feature box describes a young working-class woman's realization that she spoke differently from her college peers. Although some sociolinguists question the utility of traditional conceptualizations of social class (Mallinson & Dodsworth, 2009), it's widely recognized that people with different levels of income, education, and occupational prestige communicate in different ways. At the same time, groups sometimes "break code"—they know what SAE is and can weave in and out of it when it suits their interests (Bernstein, 1973). Even President Obama has given speeches with two different linguistic styles: one for a mostly upper-middle-class white audience in which he closely followed SAE, and one for an audience comprised of black working-class "brothers," in which his accent, word choice, and tone all differed.

Cultural Differences

Culture is another macro-level factor that shapes our communication. In the early part of the 20th century, anthropologist Edward Sapir and his student Benjamin Whorf noticed that language shapes our culture, and at the same time, our culture shapes our language. This is known as the **Sapir–Whorf hypothesis** (Sapir, 1949). These anthropologists studied the language patterns of several different cultural groups and found, for example, that Hopi Native Americans use one word for every creature that flies, except for birds. That may

Sapir–Whorf hypothesis: The concept that language shapes our culture, and at the same time, our culture shapes our language.

Okay, here's the deal: I'm a working class girl done good. Please allow me to rephrase that. I would like to share that I am a highly successful woman who has roots in the working class. Do you see the difference in these two ways of speaking? My words, syntax, tones, even gestures change depending on the group I'm with. It hasn't always been that way.

I was raised in a working class family with notoriously bad grammar. Around them parts we said "ain't," as in "I ain't hungry no more," and "fixin'," as in "Hey Janey, you fixin' to get to the store soon?" We all spoke this way in my family, as did many people within my community, so I really wasn't aware that my grammar was incorrect. I don't even remember my teachers calling me on it.

Things changed drastically when I went to college. Because I did well in high school, I had the fortunate opportunity to attend a prestigious college in the Northeast. I would like to say that I loved the experience, but the culture shock was so overwhelming that I might as well have landed on Mars. In particular, I noticed that people did not speak the same way I did. They didn't have my accent, they used different words, and they used those words in a different pattern. I immediately felt inadequate.

One incident stands out in particular: In one of my math classes I wanted to ask the professor to expand upon his explanation, so I simply asked "How come?" He stared at me. "How come?" he repeated. Then he said it again more loudly than the first, "HOW COME?" The class snickered. At first I didn't catch what they were laughing about. But then it came to me, "I mean, why?" I gulped. Later that day I withdrew from the class.

That same day I also went to the English department and asked the secretary if the department offered any English tutors "for, you know, people who talk different." She was a sweet lady, "Oh, you mean for people who have English as a second language? Sure honey, let me get you a list." I didn't dare tell her that I was looking for a tutor for me. But I contacted the first name on the list, Darcy, and I am forever grateful. She taught me to speak "Standard American English," as she called it. We met weekly for an entire year, and I practiced almost daily. The drills included verbal and nonverbal communication, as well as the written word.

I can now easily pass as an upper-middle-class student at my college. I know how to "talk the talk." However, when I go back home to see my mama and pa, I'm just one of the working class girls done good.

By the way, I think I'll stop by to see my old math professor just to say "Hey."

—Janey, Age 20

WHAT DO YOU THINK?

1. What is it about social class that contributes to different speech patterns? Can you think of specific issues that would cause these differences?
2. Why is an upper-middle-class speech pattern, Standard American English, more valued than other speech patterns? How would a conflict theorist answer this?

seem odd to modern-day English speakers, but for the Hopi, flying creatures occupy a single category.

Likewise, Native Alaskan groups have many different words for *snow*. Given that their culture revolves around snow, this makes good sense. After all, snow can be soft, crunchy, wet, melting, or powdery, to name just a few descriptors, and how Native Alaskan groups are able to use this snow depends on the type. In comparison, residents of Miami, Florida, probably have few words in their repertoire for snow because it's not a meaningful part of their everyday lives.

Let's think about the Sapir–Whorf hypothesis in your world today. Our technology-driven culture has provided many new words—chances are, words like *cell phone, texting,* and even *PC* were not a part of the everyday vocabulary of your parents. And our language also shapes our culture. New words like *Attention Deficit Disorder* or *gifted* have created new dimensions of our culture, with the fields of medicine and special education to go along with these labels. We used to label these people as *disruptive* or *smart,* but now we have words that help shape our culture's collective worldview (Beebe, Beebe, & Redmond, 2014).

Understanding how language influences, and is influenced by, culture is critical in our global world (Asante, Miike, & Yin, 2007; Lustig & Koester, 2013). Success at interpersonal relationships on the job, in our social life, and in personal relationships depends on our ability to communicate with those who may have a different cultural orientation. We must understand how cultures differ and how these differences influence our forms and styles of communication. Communication experts have discovered at least six cultural orientations. Keep in mind, however, that differences in each of these dimensions exist on a continuum rather than in discrete categories as presented later (Beebe, Beebe, & Redmond, 2014; Hall, 1976; Hofstede & Hofstede, 2004; Lustig & Koester, 2013):

A collectivist culture focuses on the needs of the group over the needs of the individual. China is an example of a culture with a collectivist orientation.

- *Individualist versus Collectivist Cultures:* An *individualist culture,* such as those found in the United States, Australia, and the Netherlands, values personal achievement and independence. The general belief is that people are responsible for themselves and should receive little help from outside sources, such as the government. In contrast, a *collectivist culture,* such as those found in China, Guatemala, and Pakistan, focuses more on the needs of the group—the family, the community, or the society. The goals of the group supersede the goals of the individual. The potential for miscommunication between people of these two types of cultures is great because of the differing emphasis on individualism.

- *High- versus Low-context Cultures:* In *high-context cultures,* emphasis is placed on indirect and nonverbal communication. Communication is based on the context of the individual. High-context cultures are also collectivist cultures, such as Latin America or Japan, where people may want to get to know one another well before engaging in any transactions. People tend to use more "feeling" in their expressions. In contrast, in a low-context culture like the United States or Germany, communication is more direct; because people don't know each other well, more emphasis is placed on formal transactions and everything must be explained explicitly. This directness may be perceived as being rude by someone from a high-context culture.

- *Masculine versus Feminine Cultures:* Some cultures emphasize stereotypical male values of achievement, assertiveness, and material success, whereas others emphasize traits that have been more traditionally aligned with the feminine, including caring for others, modesty, and enhancing overall quality of life. In masculine cultures, such as Japan, Austria, and Mexico, gender stereotypes tend to be more rigid and women have less power in society. Feminine cultures, such as Sweden and Norway, are more likely to see compromise and negotiation as useful communication tools, whereas masculine cultures may see these tools as signs of weakness.

- *Centralized versus Decentralized Power:* In some cultures power is *centralized,* or in the hands of a few. There is usually a great distance between those few who have power and the masses that do not; for example, India, the Philippines, and Brazil. In cultures with a more decentralized power structure, such as Denmark and New Zealand, power is more evenly distributed and average people have a chance to participate. These differences also affect our worldview and our communication styles. If you're from a culture in which power is shared, you may feel comfortable complaining to your boss about your workload, talking with your professor about the "C–" you received on the last test, or telling your parents that you and your partner are going to cohabit. These conversations would be more difficult to have if you are from a culture with a centralized power.

- *High versus Low Ambiguity:* Tolerance for ambiguity is another cultural trait that is highly variable. Some cultures, such as Greece, Portugal, or Serbia, don't tolerate ambiguity well, and their members may experience anxiety about the future. These cultures tend to create clear-cut rules for behavior and communication. In contrast, people living in cultures that tolerate high levels of ambiguity, such as Hong Kong, Malaysia, and Sweden, are generally comfortable with unknown situations. They minimize the importance of strict rules governing relationships and communication.

- *Short-term versus Long-term Time Orientation:* How a culture uses and values time is critical to understanding its worldview and patterns of communication. Cultures that focus on the long term, such as many Asian cultures, emphasize the future and tend to value traits like thrift, deferred gratification, and perseverance. Other cultures, such as Nigeria, the Czech Republic, and Pakistan, think in the short term. These cultures are more interested in spending rather than saving, place greater emphasis on social status, and look for quick results from their efforts.

These six cultural orientations provide a framework for the ways in which our culture influences us and shapes our thinking about the world. Thus, communication takes place within our cultural experiences.

Types of Communication

We participate in many different kinds of everyday communication. In this section, you are introduced to several types, including listening, verbal communication, nonverbal communication, electronic written communication, and disclosure.

Are You Listening to Me?

Many students have taken a speech class in college, but how many have had a class on listening? Learning how to listen well is an acquired skill, and one that's very important for effective communication (DeVito, 2014; Nadig, 2013). **Listening** is more complex than just hearing; it's the process of giving thoughtful attention to what we hear. Listening requires us to use more than just our ears. In fact, the Chinese character for the word *listening* includes the character for ears, eyes, and heart, as shown in Figure 6.1, because the Chinese believe that really listening involves all three structures.

Listening is a collection of skills that involves several components, as shown in Figure 6.2 (DeVito, 2014). First, you must receive, or hear, the message. You note not only what is said, but what is missing. Second, understanding occurs when you decode what the speaker is saying. You grasp both the words and the tone that accompanies the words, such as anger, joy, or boredom. Third, messages that you receive and understand must be retained for some period of time. Fourth, you evaluate the messages that you hear by asking yourself: Why are they saying this? Do I agree? What do I think? Finally, you respond to what has been said. Your responses can happen while the other person is speaking by nodding your head, saying "uh-huh," or it may be after they've finished. Note that the listening process is circular and continues in a loop—often within a split second. However, listening can also go wrong at any of these five stages.

At the heart of most communication problems is poor listening—not poor hearing, but not really focusing on and understanding what the other person is saying (Lane, 2010). For example, if a friend vents her frustration about a partner, a poor listener may interrupt, change the subject, or share one's own views about that person, *"Oh, I agree that Devan doesn't seem to get it. Do you know what he said to me? You won't believe it. . . ."* The listener might even wander off the topic to talk about her own partner, *"Oh yeah, you know what my boyfriend does? It drives me crazy. . . ."* This person is not truly listening to the friend. A good listener focuses on what the person is saying, and isn't distracted in any manner or thinking of his or her own response. A good listener listens to both the content and the feelings that are associated with that content (Kelly, 2008).

Have you ever traveled to another country? Or do you know another culture well through conversations with a close friend, or from reading or watching television? Can you identify where this culture is along these six dimensions? Does the orientation of this culture differ from the one in which you were raised? Can you see how this might affect communication with people from this culture?

listening: The process of giving thoughtful attention to what we hear.

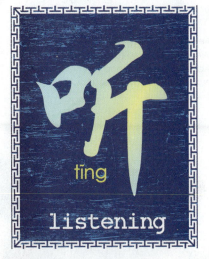

FIGURE 6.1
The Chinese Character for *Listening*

Listening is a key concept in communication, in any language.

Receiving
Hearing
Attending

Understanding
Learning
Deciphering
meaning

Responding
Answering
Giving feedback

Remembering
Recalling
Retaining

Evaluating
Judging
Criticizing

FIGURE 6.2
Five-Stage Model of the Listening Process

Good listening is a collection of skills and occurs in a circular fashion.
Source: Devito, 2014a, b.

active listening: Extremely attentive listening, where the listener has good eye contact and body language, and encourages the other person to continue talking.

verbal communication: The spoken exchange of thoughts, feelings, or other messages.

We all know how to listen, right? Actually, being a good listener is more difficult than it sounds.

One type of listening is referred to as **active listening** (Perkins & Fogarty, 2005). This occurs when you're extremely attentive, with good eye contact and body language, and encourage the other person to continue talking. As an active listener, you may also paraphrase what the person is saying, or ask for clarification or further details. Some examples of sentences that indicate active listening include:

"You seem to be frustrated about that. Is that because . . . ?"

"Tell me what happened next."

"How did that make you feel?"

"What do you think we should do?"

Active listening involves asking good questions, listening non-judgmentally, empathizing, and paraphrasing (Perkins & Fogarty, 2005). As summed up by Beebe, Beebe, and Redmond (2014), a good listener (1) stops; (2) looks; (3) listens; (4) asks questions; and (5) reflects by paraphrasing.

Verbal Communication: It's All Your Fault

Verbal communication is the spoken exchange of thoughts, feelings, or other messages (DeVito, 2014; Dunn & Goodnight, 2014). This type of communication includes the content of the words themselves, and the tone and the expression used. Were the words said in a playful bantering tone, in a heated exchange, or with an aggressive stance? One study compared three groups—happily married couples, couples seeking marriage therapy, and couples in the process of divorce—and found happily married couples showed more effective verbal communication skills in their daily lives than did the other two groups (Smith, Heaven, & Ciarrochi, 2008).

Words are symbols that represent something else. The word *dog,* for example, triggers an image of a four-legged animal. However, drawing on symbolic interaction theory, introduced in Chapter 1, we know that people attach meaning through their experiences and interactions with others. The word *dog* may conjure up a furry friend curled up on your bed, or a growling creature with sharp fangs. We can't be in charge of the meanings that people derive from our messages; therefore, we must communicate as clearly as possible.

Words have the power to create monumental misunderstandings as well as deeply felt connections (Kopecky & Powers, 2002). Some specific barriers to understanding verbal communication include the following (Beebe, Beebe, & Redmond, 2014):

- *Bypassing:* It's easy to misunderstand what someone is saying when one word has several meanings. The English language can be quite imprecise. The 500 or so words used most often in daily conversation have more than 14,000 different dictionary definitions. If someone says that they "love" you, what does that really mean?

- *Lack of precision:* We've all heard people mistake one word or phrase for another (e.g., "prescription" for "proscription"; "literally" for "figuratively"; "I could care less" for "I couldn't care less"). Sometimes this is humorous, as are using words out of context, or putting words in the wrong order. Consider these statements by former President George W. Bush:

"I know how hard it is to put food on your family." "For every fatal shooting there are roughly three nonfatal shootings. And folks, this is unacceptable in America."

"I have opinions of my own, strong opinions, but I don't always agree with them." (About.com, 2013)

Watch on MySocLab
Video: *The Role of Humor*

Whether funny or not, incorrect or unclear language can easily foster miscommunication.

- *Overgeneralizing:* Some people have a tendency to make sweeping generalizations, such as *"You always forget to unload the dishwasher," "You are never ready on time," "Why do you always drink too much when we have dinner at the Smiths' house?"* These statements imply that evidence has been collected to reach a definitive conclusion, when in reality this is probably not the case.

- *Static evaluation:* Think back to a time in your life when you did something silly or embarrassing. Don't you hate to be reminded of it? After all, the event may have occurred ten years ago and you've changed since then. Yet, some people continue to make statements that don't allow for change such as, *"You've always been the wild one in the family, haven't you?" "You're pregnant? Why, I thought you didn't want children."*

- *Polarization:* Some people speak in extremes, or see the world in black and white terms such as, *"It's all your fault,"* or *"I didn't do it."* If you ignore the middle ground on issues, your language probably doesn't reflect reality.

- *Biased language:* Using words that reflect biases about race, ethnicity, sex, sexual orientation, religious faith, or other cultures can also foster miscommunication and conflict. Many people find this type of language offensive. (Ivy & Backlund, 2008)

How can we improve our verbal communication in intimate relationships? In addition to paying attention to the barriers described earlier, we can create a supportive environment for speaking and listening. For more than three decades, communication researcher Jack Gibb studied groups of people in conversation, and noted that some exchanges created a supportive environment, whereas others created a more defensive one (Gibb, 1961). There are several ways to make the environment more of a true supportive dialogue rather than a debate shrouded in defensiveness (Beebe, Beebe, & Redmond, 2014):

How often do you hear biased language, such as a racist or sexist joke, or the use of disparaging terms? Do you find this language offensive? What do you do when you hear it?

- *Describe your own feelings rather than evaluate the behavior of others.* Few of us like to be judged or evaluated. It creates an environment of defensiveness, which makes good communication difficult. One way to avoid evaluating others is to focus on your own feelings, using "I" words. For example, instead of saying, *"Why are you always home late from work?"* you can rephrase the question as an "I" statement, *"I find it hard to manage the kids when you come home late."*

- *Solve problems rather than try to control others.* We don't like to be judged, and we also don't like to feel that another person is controlling us. Open-ended questions such as, *"What should we do?"* create a more supportive

environment than a judgmental statement such as, *"This is why you're wrong."*

- *Be genuine rather than manipulative.* Being a genuine person means that you strive to be yourself and that you take an honest interest in others. In contrast, a manipulative person has hidden agendas and focuses primarily on his or her own needs and desires. Those who strive to be more genuine in their interactions with others promote a more positive communication environment.

- *Empathize rather than remain detached.* Empathy, the ability to understand the feelings of others and predict their emotional responses, is a critical component of a supportive communication environment.

- *Be flexible rather than rigid.* We all have opinions, but when we express them in a rigid fashion it creates an environment that curtails rather than encourages communication. No one wants to hear you say to them, *"I know I'm right,"* even if this is a true statement. Another way of voicing your opinion could be, *"The way I see it is . . ."* or *"Here's one way to look at the problem. . . ."*

- *Present yourself as equal rather than superior.* We can antagonize others when we act as though we're superior to them. The statement *"Listen to me because I have a lot more experience than you do,"* might work if you're talking to a child (or it might not), but your partner will probably not appreciate it. When we communicate as equals, it creates a more supportive environment, *"We each bring our own perspective, and here's mine."*

These tactics can move us towards the goal of creating a supportive rather than a defensive communication environment. But as you know, not all communication is expressed through words as our nonverbal behavior can also reveal our feelings.

nonverbal communication:
Communicating without words, by using gestures, expressions, and body language.

Nonverbal messages can be easily understood. What does this man's smile really mean? Is he happy? Surprised? Upset?

Nonverbal Communication: What Exactly Does That Smile Mean?

An awkward silence; a smile; eye contact; holding hands; a grimace; an erect posture; a squint; aggressive hand gestures; rolling the eyes—these are all forms of **nonverbal communication**, or ways we communicate without words (Seiler, Beall, & Mazer, 2014). We use nonverbal messages all the time to convey attitudes and express emotions, from love and affection to contempt and disdain, although we may not be conscious of these messages. In fact, we may use nonverbal messages more often than verbal messages when we want to discuss the state of our feelings within the relationship (Koerner & Fitzpatrick, 2002). For example, if a partner feels jealous of the attention given to another person, he or she is likely to communicate this nonverbally—rolling the eyes, being silent, or pulling away from touch—rather than saying, *"You know, I feel insecure when you talk with Pat at parties because I worry that you're rejecting me."*

In face-to-face communication we blend verbal and nonverbal messages to best convey our meanings (DeVito, 2014). Nonverbal messages may accentuate or complement our spoken words. When we meet someone for the first time, we might not only say, *"It's nice to meet you,"* but we'll say it with eye contact and a smile. But what if our verbal and nonverbal messages aren't in agreement? For example, you may see your ex-boyfriend or ex-girlfriend while running errands and say with a grimace, *"Nice to see you."*

We've all heard the phrase "Actions speak louder than words." It means that nonverbal communication is often more believable than verbal communication when the two conflict. People trust what they see more than what they hear. Nonverbal communication is more difficult to falsify. Research shows that people who are lying tend to have reduced eye contact, pauses in their conversation, slower speech, a higher pitch to their voice, and more deliberate pronunciation and articulation of words (Porter & ten Brinke, 2008, 2010; Zuckerman, DePaulo, & Rosenthal, 1981).

One problem with nonverbal messages is that they're easily misunderstood. We have dictionaries to help us interpret words, but what do we use for help with interpreting gestures, posture, or expressions? Does the furrowed brow mean a person is deep in thought, or expressing disapproval? Does that smile represent happiness or nervousness? Is someone yawning from boredom or from sleepiness? Does that deliberate pronunciation and articulation mean that someone is lying, or just trying to be clear?

The potential for misinterpretation is made even greater by cultural differences. Figure 6.3 shows how specific hand gestures have significantly different meanings from one country to another. What is a sign of support or friendliness in one place may be a crude or vulgar gesture elsewhere!

Another example of nonverbal messages is the degree of *personal space* we're comfortable with when interacting with the world. Although we're not always conscious of how much space we need, researchers have analyzed the comfort level of Americans in different situations (Hall, 1966). In intimate relationships, our comfort zone of communication is between actual touch and 18 inches. In other social relationships, such as classmates working on a group project, the comfort zone is between 18 inches and 4 feet. In communication of a non-personal nature, such as a business meeting or an interaction with a sales clerk, the comfort zone is about 4 to 12 feet. Yet these distances vary among different racial or ethnic groups in the United States. For example, Hispanics in casual conversation stand or sit much closer to each other than do whites (Kaleidoscope, 2003). Therefore, in a conversation between a white person and a Hispanic person, we may find the Hispanic person moving closer to talk, while the white person backs away because the closeness feels awkward.

Eye contact is another example of a nonverbal message. In the United States, direct eye contact is considered polite and shows interest in another person and his or her conversation. However, in many other parts of the world, eye contact has a different meaning. In particular, eye contact between men and women is a sign of sexual suggestiveness and invitation.

OK sign
France: you're a zero; **Japan:** please give me coins; **Brazil:** an obscene gesture; **Mediterranean countries:** an obscene gesture

Thumb and forefinger
Most countries: money; **France:** something is perfect; **Mediterranean:** a vulgar gesture

Thumbs up
Australia: up yours; **Germany:** the number one; **Japan:** the number five; **Saudi Arabia:** I'm winning; **Ghana:** an insult; **Malaysia:** the thumb is used to point rather than the index finger

Open palm
Greece: an insult dating to ancient times; **West Africa:** "You have five fathers," an insult akin to calling someone a bastard

FIGURE 6.3

Hand Gestures in Different Cultures

Gestures are a very important component in communication, but they can mean different things across cultures.

Something as simple as eye contact has very different meanings across cultures. In the United States, making eye contact is a form of politeness, but in many other regions of the world it is considered rude or even sexually suggestive.

Written Electronic Communication

Increasingly, people "talk" to each other electronically; in other words, they really don't talk at all, they write. Unlike the days when we relied solely on the U.S. Postal Service to relay our messages, electronic messaging is instantaneous, which

TABLE 6.1 Electronic Shorthand

We communicate through words and symbols, and these are continually changing as our culture changes. If you read a text written in the 18th century, you will see that word use, grammar, and spelling have changed significantly since then. For example, we no longer say thou *or* thee.

Our reliance on electronic forms of communication is also changing our words, grammar, and spelling, as these examples reveal:

Acronyms:		Emoticons:	
2G2B4G	Too good to be forgotten	:-*	kiss on the cheek
2more	Tomorrow	:-@	screaming
9	Parent watching	I-o	yawning
AATK	Always at the keyboard	'-)	winking
BWL	Bursting with laughter	:-}	embarrassed
CM	Call me	%)	confused
ILY	I love you		
M4C	Meet for coffee		
GMAB	Give me a break		
OMG	Oh my god		
THX	Thanks		
Y	Why?		
P-ZA	Pizza		

Our electronic media allows us to share information right as it is happening. We can live in the moment and share it with others.

has changed the way we communicate. As of late 2013, more than a billion people use Facebook, and about 700 million people log in every day (Bort, 2013). College students are required to have email accounts, so electronic messaging has become a requisite part of student life.

Electronic communication is now how many of us communicate daily. How has our increased reliance on the electronic written word changed communication? Linguist Naomi Baron suggests many changes have already or will occur in our society (2008):

- *Informality is the new norm.* We write more informally, are less concerned about grammar and punctuation, and are more likely to use slang or abbreviations for words, as shown in Table 6.1. We may become increasingly uncertain about how we use words, so we may make up our own language rules.

- *Our writing influences our speech.* The way we communicate electronically influences how we communicate face-to-face. We use more abbreviations in our speech patterns, and are less concerned about grammar. We even have new meanings for old words like *cookie*, *worm*, and *spam*.

- *We have volume control over our messages.* We can see who is contacting us and can better screen our communications: we decide when, where, and even if we'll receive messages, unlike the past when we answered a ringing telephone without knowing who was on the other end.

- *We have more relationships with less depth.* We communicate with more people, but we do so only very briefly, and we know less about each of them. In the past, you may have spoken by telephone a couple of times a day or written one or two letters a week; you may now send over a dozen electronic messages in a single morning.

- *We can live in the moment.* Unlike in the past when a letter or telephone call usually involved a synopsis of what *had* happened, communication today can be more of a running discourse. We can actually live in the other person's moment and "hear" the information as it is unfolds.

Electronic communication is likely to be a growing part of our culture, influencing how we communicate, access, and share information. Unfortunately, it also opens up a new way of miscommunication.

Sex Differences in Communication

Do men and women communicate differently? Much media attention has been devoted to the idea that women and men have different communication patterns and are prone to miscommunication. Popular self-help books such as *Men are from Mars, Women are from Venus* (Gray, 1992) have widespread appeal because people are concerned about communication and genuinely would like to improve their communication skills.

Communication researchers have challenged many of Gray's assertions that men and women are really so different as to occupy different communication "planets" (Edwards & Hamilton, 2004; Wood, 2002). One of these challenges is revealed in the feature box *Why Do Research?* (p. 176). It describes a research study designed to investigate the stereotype that women talk more than men.

Linguists, however, have noted a number of sex differences in communication (Ivy, 2012; Wood, 2013). One sex difference involves the way we self-disclose information. Women tend to be more verbal in disclosing their feelings about the relationship; men tend toward more physical displays. Yet, the woman may complain that she wants more than just the presence of her partner in her life; she would like more regular verbal displays of affection from him: *"Tell me you love me,"* she says. *"I'm here, aren't I?"* he responds.

This sex difference in communication can lead to a misunderstanding between partners. Both styles are self-disclosing, but they don't always give the other credit, given their different styles. It may be the *perception* of disclosure that makes the difference in the quality of marriages (Richman & Rosenfeld, 1995; Uebelacker, Courtnage, & Whisman, 2003). Women don't see as much communication disclosure from their partners as they would like, which partly explains why women show lower rates of satisfaction in marriage than men do.

There are many other sex differences in communication as well, both verbal and nonverbal, as shown in Table 6.2 (Cameron, 1998; Tannen, 1990, 1994; Trenholm, 2014). What are some of these differences?

How might social class influence our different forms of communication? For example, are the poor as likely to have computers, Internet access, and cell phones? Likewise, how might social class affect verbal and nonverbal communication? If you think that there might be differences, what accounts for these differences? Money? Culture? Or something else?

✳ **Explore** on **MySocLab**
Activity: *Family Communication in the Digital Age*

6.4 Analyze sex differences in communication

Question That Matters

6.10 How do men's and women's communication styles differ?

📖 **Read** on **MySocLab**
Document: *Sex and Temperament in Three Tribes*

Jamal and Renée get lost driving to visit friends in another part of the city. Seeing they may be late, Renée suggests that they stop and ask for directions, but Jamal refuses. He's uncomfortable asking for help and believes there's no guarantee a stranger will give accurate information.

"He is certain that he can find the way himself and would rather just drive around until he does so."

He's certain that he can find the way himself and would rather just drive around until he does so. This doesn't make sense at all to Renée, who is getting angry. She isn't embarrassed about asking for directions and believes that anyone who is lost should ask for help.

What causes these sex differences in communication? Linguist Deborah Tannen, who has extensively studied sex and gender differences in communication, believes that men and women grow up in different cultures (1990, 1994). *Women's culture* stresses intimacy and connection with others, whereas *men's culture* values autonomy and individual achievement. These different perspectives influence men's and women's topics of conversation, communication styles, and interpretations of one another's messages. Throughout their lives, men and women learn how to use behavior in line with their gender identities. Men learn that being competitive and strong is a way of expressing masculinity. Women learn that stressing connection and feelings is feminine. This explains why many men don't seem to mind driving around when lost, rather than asking for directions, which might reveal weakness (Trenholm, 2014).

TABLE 6.2	Conclusions Drawn from Research on Sex Differences in Communication

It's not really correct to say that women talk more than men; it's much more complicated than that.

Quantity of Talk: Who Talks the Most
- In task-oriented cross-sex groups, men talk more than women
- In friendly same-sex pairs, women prefer to spend time talking; men prefer to share activities like sports or hobbies

Topics of Talk: What Do Men and Women Talk about?
- Women talk more about private matters, such as family, relationship problems, other women or men, clothing, and feelings
- Men talk more about public matters, such as sports, money, and news, and they tell more jokes

Vocabulary: Do Men and Women Use Different Words?
- Women more often use weak expletives (e.g., "Oh dear" or "oh my"), whereas men more often use stronger expletives, including obscenities
- Women use more color detail terms than men (e.g., "mauve," "teal")

Grammatical Constructions: Do Men's and Women's Syntax Differ?
- Women use more qualifiers (e.g., "somewhat," "kind of," "I guess")
- Women use more disclaimers (e.g., "I'm no expert, but . . .," "Don't get mad, but . . .")
- Women are more likely to use polite forms of conversation (e.g., "May I please have . . .," "I'm sorry about that . . .")

Taking Turns: Who Controls Interaction?
- In cross-sex pairs, men interrupt women more than women interrupt men.
- Women ask more questions and men make more statements during conversation
- Men successfully initiate topics more often than do women

Sources: Trenholm, 2014; Arliss, 1991.

You know the stereotype: Women talk more than men. But is it true? Whether women really do talk more than men is an *empirical question,* meaning that it's a question that can be answered using scientific research methods. "No one knows where this belief even came from, but it's been reported for years," says psychologist James Pennebaker, from the University of Texas at Austin.

To answer this question, a group of psychologists from the Universities of Arizona, Texas, and St. Louis set out to listen to men and women, and count their words. The researchers placed microphones on 396 college students ages 17 through 29 from the United States and Mexico, for periods ranging from two to ten days. The researchers sampled their conversations and calculated how many words they used in the course of a day. The electronically activated recorder unobtrusively records snippets of conversation during a person's daily routine. The small device, the size of a cell phone, turns itself on every 12 minutes and records whatever it hears for 30 seconds. This digital technology is a far better approach than relying on the self-reported data from surveys that were done in the past.

The researchers then transcribed the recordings of the students, and calculated the words used per day. Any guesses on what they found? Men averaged 15,669 words per day, whereas women used 16,215, which is such a small difference that it's not statistically significant. In other words, men and women use about the same amount of words. It's time to put to rest the myth that women have the gift of gab!

Who talks more, men or women? Any guesses?

WHAT DO YOU THINK?

1. Why did the stereotype that women talk more than men begin, and why does the myth persist?
2. If men and women talk about the same amount, do they talk about the same kinds of things?

Sources: Brizendine, 2006; Mehl, Vazire, Ramirez-Esparza, Slatcher, & Pennebaker, 2007.

Women's Patterns

Women are more likely to use conversation as a way to establish and maintain relationships. They tend to use communication for the purpose of connecting and relating to other people, whereas men tend to approach communication as an exchange of information.

Compared to men, women tend to smile more often, express a wider range of emotions through facial expressions and nonverbal behavior, and maintain more eye contact with others (Ivy, 2012). When they speak, women use more qualifying, tentative statements, such as *"I think I would like to do this"* or *"It sort of seems like you would rather not do that."* These qualifiers weaken the message and add an element of uncertainty. Women are also more polite in tone, ask a greater number of questions, and are more likely to show interest and concern, using phrases such as *"Oh, really?"* or *"I know what you mean."* Women also offer more personal details and disclosures while referring to their feelings, *"I felt so good when . . ."* or *"Wasn't it depressing when . . . ?"* These phrases serve to maintain and perpetuate conversations, fostering closeness and understanding. However, they also reflect the gendered patterns in our society—women are taught not to be too pushy, to be kind and accommodating, and to cooperate and build consensus.

Women and men also use their bodies differently when they communicate. For example, when talking with others, women are more likely to prefer side-by-side interactions than the more confrontational face-to-face style of interaction of men. Women also occupy less personal space than men.

Men and women communicate verbally and nonverbally in different ways. One important difference is the way they use their bodies. Men are more likely to spread out their arms and legs and take up greater personal space than do women.

Men's Patterns

Men tend to approach communication from a content orientation. They talk when they have something to say or need to receive or give information (Beebe, Beebe, & Redmond, 2014). Compared to women, men's nonverbal communication and speech are more direct and assertive. Their speech is more instrumental and less likely to convey feelings or emotions. Men's speech tends to be more authoritative and absolute, *"I'll give you three reasons why it won't work . . . ,"* rather than women's more tentative style, *"I'm not sure this will work. . . ."* Communication experts have noticed that in most mixed-sex contexts men tend to dominate the conversation, speak more frequently and for longer periods of time, speak on topics of their interest, and interrupt more frequently (West & Zimmerman, 1983; Tannen, 1994).

Men tend to spread their bodies out and occupy more personal space around them than do women, and are more likely than women to talk face-to-face. They use more gestures, for example, "talking with their hands," whereas women rest their hands on the arm of a chair while seated. Men are also more likely to touch others, especially women, when talking with them (Beebe, Beebe, & Redmond, 2014).

Why Do Women and Men Communicate Differently?

Given these distinctive styles of communication, it's easy to see why men and women often miscommunicate. What accounts for these differences? Are they biological, or are they social in origin?

This question cannot yet be definitively answered, but it's likely a combination of both factors. We've learned that males and females are socialized differently, but we've also learned of important brain differences. Women tested in such diverse countries as Japan, England, the Czech Republic, Nepal, and the United States use more words correctly, use better grammar and pronunciation, and in other ways, excel at verbal communication compared to men (Fisher, 2000). Certain regions of the prefrontal brain area are activated differently during language tasks performed by women and men. At least one study showed that both the left and right hemispheres of the prefrontal area were activated in women as they performed language tasks, whereas only the left hemisphere was activated in men. This suggests that it's easier for women, biologically, to articulate words (Baron-Cohen, 2003). And in the event of a stroke, men's verbal abilities are more likely to be impaired because women's right-hemisphere language areas take over some functions if the left-hemisphere language areas are damaged.

Now that you've learned about sex differences in communication, use this information to analyze your own communication style. Think about same-sex and cross-sex communication with friends, partners, family members, and even strangers or acquaintances. What kinds of patterns do you see? Where did you learn your communication style?

self-disclosure: Telling a person something private about yourself that he or she would not otherwise know.

6.5 Identify communication to keep your relationship strong

Question That Matters

6.11 How does self-disclosure benefit intimate relationships?

Communicating to Keep Your Relationships Strong: Self-Disclosure

One of the primary ways we can use communication to help create satisfying marriages and intimate relationships is through self-disclosure, or telling your partner something private about yourself that he or she wouldn't otherwise

TABLE 6.3   The Windows on Myself

A useful way of thinking about self-disclosure distinguishes how much information you know about yourself, how much others know about you, and how much you're willing to disclose.

	Known to Self	Unknown to Self
Known to Others	**Open Window Pane** Known to self and others	**Blind Window Pane** Blind to self, seen by others
Unknown to Others	**Hidden Window Pane** Open to self, hidden from others	**Unknown Window Pane** Unknown to self and others

Sources: Luft, 1969 (cited in Borchers, 1999); Luft & Ingram, 1955.

know (Galvin, Bylund, & Brommel, 2012). Self-disclosure can range from insignificant or superficial topics, such as "My favorite color is orange," to information that can be extremely personal and significant, such as sexual fantasies or childhood traumas. We have various layers of information about ourselves, and when we develop intimacy with another person, we allow that person to penetrate through the superficial layers to the core of deeply personal topics.

However, it's important to acknowledge that engaging in self-disclosure doesn't guarantee the success of a relationship (Lane, 2010). Disclosing disturbing information may even contribute to the demise of a relationship, because the other partner may be very uncomfortable hearing this type of information, such as *"Honey, I've been having an affair for the past three years."*

A useful way of viewing self-disclosure is shown in the so-called Johari window in Table 6.3. The *Johari window* distinguishes how much information you know about yourself, how much others know about you, and how much you're willing to disclose.

As you can see, the *Open Window Pane* includes information that is clearly visible or known, such as your physical appearance or where you live. The *Blind Pane* includes information others can see in you, but you can't see in yourself. You might think you're a talented manager, yet others think you exhibit weak leadership skills. The *Hidden Pane* contains information you wish to keep private, such as your fantasies. The *Unknown Pane* includes everything neither you nor others know about you. For example, you may have hidden artistic talents you haven't explored. Through self-disclosure, we open and close the windowpanes so we may become more intimate with others (Luft, 1969).

However, for self-disclosure to benefit a relationship, there must be reciprocity and support (Galvin, Bylund, & Brommel, 2012), a tenet of the social exchange perspective introduced in Chapter 1. That is, both partners should feel free to be honest with each other and supportive of the feelings being shared. Disclosing feelings can be risky, because not all feelings are positive; but if partners support each other in sharing both the good and the bad, trust can develop. Lack of support, or a negative response to self-disclosure, can be detrimental to the quality of a relationship.

Watch on MySocLab
Video: *ABC Nightline: Military Families*

Given what you've learned about sex differences in general and sex differences in communication, do you think there are also differences in men's and women's methods of self-disclosure? What evidence can you provide for your answer?

Conflict, Communication, and Problem Solving

The potential for conflict is inherent in any relationship (Nadig, 2013). You and a friend may disagree over what movie to watch; you and your partner may have different views of where to go on vacation; you and your fiancé may

6.6 Describe conflict, communication, and problem solving

Question That Matters

6.12 What are four types of conflict?

disagree about your type of wedding; you and your spouse may have different spending habits; and you and your child may disagree over whether fast food is a healthy meal choice.

Conflict occurs when members of the group disagree over two or more options to make a decision, solve a problem, or achieve a goal (Beebe & Masterson, 2012). It applies to all types of relationships, including friendships, romantic relationships, other family relationships, and even work-related relationships. Individuals who are involved in conflict have some degree of dependence on the other person—why would we need to resolve a disagreement if we didn't affect one another? Conflict can result from differences between group members in personality, perception, information, tolerance for risk, and power or influence.

Culture also influences the issues that people fight about and how people experience conflict. For example, a woman in the United States who loses her virginity prior to marriage probably faces little parental conflict, but a woman in Saudi Arabia would face the wrath of her angry parents. Conversely, an American man who engages in extramarital sex is likely to cause more conflict in his marriage than a married man living in Spain. In cultures that have a more collectivist orientation, conflict is likely to involve breaking the group rules or norms in some way. On a recent trip to Tokyo, I was advised to always stand to the right on escalators. To stand to the left or in the middle of an escalator is considered very rude and could cause tension or conflict. In more individualist cultures like the United States, conflict is more likely to arise because of a transgression or perceived transgression on an individual. *You* didn't do something for *me*, and that made me angry.

Conflict, *per se*, is not unhealthy. In fact, people in stable, romantic relationships experience conflict about twice a week (Lloyd, 1987). The question is not how can you avoid conflict, but how can you best manage the inevitable conflict that occurs in any relationship?

Types of Conflict

There are many different types of conflict, and some are easier or more difficult to resolve than others. Figure 6.4 illustrates four types of conflict: pseudoconflict, content conflict, value conflict, and ego conflict; we discuss each next (Lane, 2010; Miller & Steinberg, 1975).

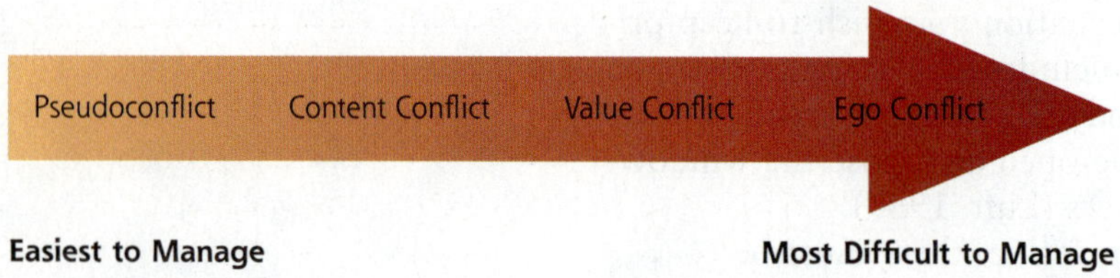

Pseudoconflict   Content Conflict   Value Conflict   Ego Conflict

Easiest to Manage   **Most Difficult to Manage**

FIGURE 6.4
Types of Conflict

Not all conflict is the same; this typology suggests four distinct types.

Pseudoconflict occurs when we falsely perceive that our partner is interfering with our goals or has incompatible goals. This type of conflict is relatively easy to resolve once we realize that we actually don't disagree with one another. For example, suppose a friend teases you about a new item of clothing that you were wearing. You may become upset because you believe that this person's goal is to embarrass you, but perhaps their goal is only to acknowledge that you have something new.

Content conflict occurs when we disagree about information. This type of conflict can also be easy to resolve if the correct information is readily available. For example, suppose you believe the party begins at 8:00 PM, but your partner believes that it begins at 9:00 PM. How to resolve this disagreement? Find a credible source with the information—simply look at the invitation, or contact the host for the correct time.

Value conflict is more difficult to resolve because it results from differing opinions on subjects that relate to personal values and to issues of right or wrong. You may try to bring someone around to your way of thinking, which may or may not work. For example, suppose you want to adopt a baby from Ethiopia because you're concerned about the growing number of children orphaned by AIDS, but your partner isn't at all comfortable adopting a child.

Whereas you want to save the world one child at a time, your partner doesn't share your sentiment. Can this conflict be resolved?

Finally, **ego conflict** may be among the most difficult type of conflict to resolve because it arises when individuals believe they must win at all costs to save face. The issue under discussion almost becomes secondary because the ego becomes involved and the real goal is simply to win. Perhaps in the midst of a conflict your partner told you, *"You're being ridiculous."* You may then find yourself becoming defensive and trying to prove your worth, even after the original source of the conflict is long forgotten.

How we deal with a conflict depends on the type of conflict, how much concern we have for the relationship, and our own personal conflict styles. These styles include avoiding, accommodating, competing, compromising, and collaborating, as shown in Table 6.4 (Lane, 2010).

- *Avoiding* occurs when we remove ourselves from the conflict psychologically or physically. We may deny the existence of the conflict, refuse to discuss the issue, or walk away. This type of response can be labeled "lose–lose" because neither partner really accomplishes his or her goals. In fact, because the conflict is avoided, it may resurface later, and the tension may even increase.

ego conflict: A type of conflict where individuals believe they must win at all costs to save face.

TABLE 6.4	Personal Conflict Styles			
Researchers identify five conflict styles that show how much concern we have for our communication partner and how much concern we have for obtaining our own goals.				
Style	**Approach**	**Example**	**Advantages**	**Disadvantages**
Avoiding	Lose–Lose	"Just leave me alone."	Can reduce intense emotions; can be effective when used with unimportant issues	Increased relational tension and difficulty solving a dispute; may influence us to perceive a conflict as more serious than warranted
Accommodating	Lose–Win	"Whatever you say."	Can be effective when used with unimportant issues and when we give in for "social credit"	May lead to poor decision making; possibly being taken advantage of
Competing	Win–Lose	"It's my way or the highway!"	Can be effective in emergency situations and if an issue is critical to our own or our partner's well-being	Damage to a relationship
Compromising	Lose–Lose	"I'll do some of this if you do some of that."	Can be effective when we don't have the time to engage in a collaborative conflict style or when the use of other conflict styles are not successful.	Lose a portion of what we desire; may accept a less effective solution to bring about the compromise; feeling dissatisfied with the solution
Collaborating	Win–Win	"Let's work on finding the best solution for both of us."	Goals of both self and other are achieved	Takes time and knowledge of win–win conflict resolution methods

Source: Lane, 2010.

- *Accommodating* is a strategy that entails satisfying our partner's needs at the expense of our own goals, and can therefore be labeled "lose–win." The accommodating partner chooses to lose and let the other partner win. Accommodating the other partner may be an effective strategy some of the time, but habitual accommodation signals a potential imbalance in the relationship.
- *Competing* is the opposite strategy: We attempt to meet our own goals without concerns for our partner's needs. We may use any tactic available to us, possibly even verbal attacks, lies, or threats. This has been called "win–lose" because we try to meet our own goals no matter what the cost is to our partner.
- *Compromising* occurs when both partners give up part of what they want to achieve partial satisfaction in meeting their goals. Both partners may walk away from the conflict feeling the resolution is not particularly satisfying; hence, it is called "lose–lose." However, compromising may work best when other styles are not successful.
- *Collaborating* is used when we attempt to satisfy both our own needs and those of our partner. This style is labeled "win–win" because the goals of both partners are attained. Using this style, conflict can actually strengthen a relationship.

Intimacy, Communication, and Conflict

Research on communication in relationships has focused primarily on its ability to help reduce conflict and improve problem solving. The way couples communicate about their differences has real implications for happiness and stability. Conflict in any marriage or personal relationship is normal and expected. The key is *how* we communicate and deal with conflict.

regulating couples: Couples who use communication to promote closeness and intimacy.

non-regulated couples: Couples who have many negative communication exchanges.

John Gottman presents how couples communicate and resolve their differences in his extensive body of work, including his book *Why Marriages Succeed or Fail* (1994). He distinguishes between **regulating couples,** who generally use communication to promote closeness and intimacy and use constructive comments even during arguments, and **non-regulated couples,** who have far more negative exchanges. Non-regulated couples may use the following techniques:

- *Contempt:* An attitude of feeling superior to your spouse, such as rolling your eyes while he or she is talking.
- *Defensiveness:* An effort to defend yourself and your position when you feel attacked in an argument.
- *Criticism:* Includes making negative evaluations of your spouse's behavior or feelings.
- *Stonewalling:* A type of withdrawal technique in which some people show how they refuse to listen to their spouse.
- *Belligerence:* A challenging behavior meant to establish power in the marital relationship (Gottman, 1994).

Gottman's research suggests there may be a pattern to conflict. He and his colleagues observed 130 couples at the beginning of their marriages, and then followed them for six years (Gottman, Coan, Carrere, & Swanson, 1998). At the end of six years there had been 17 divorces, and the communication patterns of those who divorced were different from those who had remained married. In particular, there seemed to be an initiation of conflict by the wife, perhaps as a result of something in the relationship she didn't like or didn't believe was fair. This was followed by the husband's refusal to accept input from his wife. The wife then reciprocated with negativity, and the husband made little or no effort to lower the negativity of his wife. The couples who finished the study in happy, stable marriages, however, had more positive exchanges, expressing humor, affection, and interest.

Growing up I watched my parents argue a lot. Often the subject of their arguments were trivial—who gets to watch what television show; what to have for dinner; whose job it is to fold the laundry; and things of that nature—definitely not earth-shattering. But their fights followed a common pattern. My mom would say something really direct, often in an accusatory tone, and my father would ignore her. She would say something like, "I'm choosing the television show tonight because you always choose it." "I'm making tacos for dinner because I'm tired of all the hamburgers you make." "It's your turn to do the laundry because I always do it." My dad, in turn, would just ignore her, and flip on the show he wanted to watch, or just let the clothes pile up. My mom would then say something again about it, and then he would get defensive, "You're crazy, I do so much around here. You don't know the half of all I do." Blah-blah-blah.

Their arguments would escalate from there, sometimes lasting an hour or two. I remember my brother and me sitting in our rooms thinking, "Geez, the laundry could have been done by now," or "The TV show is long over so would you quit arguing?" or "We've lost our appetite and don't want tacos or hamburgers."

One night, after a really heated argument, again probably over something stupid, my dad yelled, "I'm leaving!" and grabbed his coat and ran out the door. He was gone for two days, without a word. My brother and I were only about eight and ten at the time, and we were scared. My mom didn't say anything, but apparently she was scared too. Despite all the arguing, I guess she really loved my dad, and was worried that he was going to leave us for good.

When he came back home, I remember her crying, and then he started crying too. They decided that they were going to see a marriage counselor to help them work on communicating better. I don't know exactly what they did in therapy, but whatever it was, it seemed to work.

In looking back over the years, I can see that my mom had a point: to be honest, my dad did hog the television, didn't do his share of the housework, and well, he did always cook the same thing when it was his night in the kitchen. But she approached it all wrong and therefore didn't get the results she was looking for. He responded in a way that made things even worse by ignoring her, then getting defensive when she repeated herself. He didn't get the result he was looking for either. In therapy they learned how to talk things over when they disagreed about something, without yelling, accusing, or being defensive. Whew, life at home became a lot more peaceful after that.

—Geraldo, Age 24

WHAT DO YOU THINK?

1. Do you think that Geraldo's parents were a *regulated* or an *unregulated* couple, according to Gottman? Which techniques did they use in their disagreements?
2. How did their pattern of conflict compare to the other couples that Gottman studied?

These research results shouldn't be interpreted to mean wives start all the arguments in marriage! Rather, women are more likely to verbalize their feelings—one study of nearly 4,000 men and women found that 32 percent of men compared to 23 percent of women say they bottle up their feelings in a spat (Parker-Pope, 2007). Instead, Gottman's work suggests both husbands and wives can improve their communication styles to reduce the level of negativity, and hence, reduce the likelihood of unhappiness and divorce. Wives can think of better ways to communicate that soften the initiation of conflict, and husbands can learn to accept input from their wives and reduce their own negative comments. In other words, husbands can learn to share power with their wives in their marital relationships.

Try to identify the pattern of conflict in the feature box *My Family: How My Parents Dealt with Conflict.*

We all have our own patterns for dealing with conflict. Chances are we use different communication styles at different times. Think about your current or a recent intimate relationship. What types of conflicts did you tend to have, and what types of patterns of resolving conflict emerged?

Power, Control, and Decision Making

Keesha gets a promotion at work, but accepting it means that she and her family will have to relocate. Her husband, Clay, doesn't want to move.
Jody wants to take a vacation with her girlfriend to Hawai'i, but her husband thinks it's inappropriate for a married woman to go on a vacation without her husband.

Lee wants to put the family's tax refund toward the purchase of a new car, but Masako wants to use it to visit her grandmother in Japan.
Emma is tired of doing much of the housework, but she's afraid to discuss the issue with her partner.

6.7 Compare and contrast power, control, and decision making

Question That Matters

6.13 What theories explain the distribution of power and decision making in relationships?

Intimate partner power involves decision making, the division of household labor, and a sense of entitlement.

power: The ability to exercise your will.

personal power: The degree of autonomy a person has to exercise his or her will.

social power: The ability to exercise your will over another person.

intimate partner power: A type of power that involves decision making among intimate partners, their division of labor, and their sense of entitlement.

Each of these situations is related to the balance of power in the relationship. Even in the best of marriages and intimate relationships, partners may still have different attitudes, interests, or goals that require negotiation and compromise. Micro-level decisions about who does the household chores, what types of jobs spouses take, or how families spend their leisure time all must be negotiated.

Power is the ability to exercise your will. There are many different types of power. **Personal power** is the degree of autonomy a person has to exercise his or her will. It includes the ability to make choices about yourself; for example, "Should I go to graduate school?" "Should I adopt a cat?"

A second type is **social power**, or the ability to exercise your will over another person. This kind of power can be found in many different arenas, including that of work, home, or social settings. When your boss tells you that a specific report is due immediately, you know to make it a priority. Failing to do so may cost you your job.

The third type of power is **intimate partner power** (sometimes known as *conjugal power*). This type of power involves decision making among intimate partners, their division of labor, and their sense of entitlement. Who gets to make the major decisions? Who does the housework? And who is allowed to complain? Most marriages may not include overt opposition—"We're doing it this way or else . . ."—but differences of opinion can be strong. Are the outcomes of negotiation random, or do some spouses have an edge in getting an outcome that is to their advantage?

Intimate partner power is a complex phenomenon. For example, true equity and the *perception* of equity are not necessarily the same thing. Does my husband have more power than me if he works outside the home to earn money and I stay home and do housework and take care of the children? What if he makes the major purchasing decisions, whereas I make the day-to-day decisions around the house, and we both believe this arrangement to be fair?

Early social scientists acknowledged that power is not a one-dimensional concept. There are at least six sources of power, and each can bring a different aspect to the relationship:

- *Coercive power* is based on the ability to achieve your will by force, either psychological or physical. Spanking a child and withholding a child's food are examples of coercive power.

- *Reward power* comes from the ability to offer material or nonmaterial benefit to achieve your goal. Offering your teenage son a chance to go to a concert if he gets all "As" on his report card is an example of reward power.

- *Expert power* stems from a person's special knowledge or ability. Your doctor has the power to tell you to have a colonoscopy, even though you may find it to be an uncomfortable procedure.

- *Informational power* comes from the information that a person may use to persuade another to do something he or she wouldn't otherwise do. A woman might be able to persuade her partner to wear a condom when they have sexual intercourse, not because the man wants to, but because she informs him of what might happen otherwise—pregnancy or a possible sexually transmitted infection.

- *Referent power* stems from the emotional identification of the less dominant person towards the more dominant person. A wife might attend the football game with her husband not because she likes football, but because he wants her to go, and satisfying his desires are important to her.

- *Legitimate power* is based on a person's claim of authority or the right to exercise his or her will. For example, fundamentalist Christians may take the biblical passage literally that men are the head of the household just like Jesus Christ is the head of the Church.

Theories of Power

Sociologists and other family scientists have been studying marital power for years and can explain it with several theoretical approaches (Blood & Wolfe, 1960; Cancian, 1987; Cohen & Durst, 2001; Fenstermaker Berk, 1985; Thompson & Walker, 1989; Waller, 1937; West & Zimmerman, 1987).

RESOURCE THEORY   One of the first major studies about marital power, conducted by Blood and Wolfe (1960), reported that the socioeconomic status of a spouse is influential in making family decisions. **Resource theory** suggests that the spouse with the more prestigious or higher-paying job can use that advantage to generate more power in the relationship, and thereby influence decision making. As women entering the workforce have increased their economic resources, so too has their power increased in relationships. In marriages where the occupational prestige, education, and income of spouses are more equal, resource theory suggests the relative power of each will be more equal as well.

> **resource theory:** A theory of power that suggests that the spouse with the more prestigious or higher-paying job can use that advantage to generate more power in the relationship and thereby influence decision making.

A problem with resource theory, however, is that reality doesn't reflect this pattern. No matter what their occupational status is relative to that of their wives, husbands continue to have more power in marriage even if they're unemployed (Cohen & Durst, 2001; Thompson & Walker, 1989). Regardless of socioeconomic status, men have been more successful in bargaining to avoid tasks such as housework that offer no pay, carry minimal social prestige, and aren't generally thought of as fun.

PRINCIPLE OF LEAST INTEREST   Another explanation of marital power draws on the principle of least interest, introduced in Chapter 3 (Waller, 1937). Recall that this perspective acknowledges that power comes from sources other than socioeconomic status. Instead, the partner with the least commitment to the relationship has the most power. The spouse who loves or needs less, or who is more willing to end the relationship, can use his or her lack of interest as a bargaining tool to exert dominance and power. The spouse who believes that he or she has more to lose may be willing to acquiesce to the other spouse.

RELATIVE LOVE AND NEED THEORY   Like resource theory and the principle of least interest, the **relative love and need theory** suggests that each partner brings resources to the relationship. However, a strictly micro-level analysis of who contributes what doesn't allow for the understanding of more macro-level factors that contribute to the interpretation of the exchange. One of these factors is the way that love itself is defined and interpreted, as shown in Chapter 4. Love has been "feminized" according to Francesca Cancian; women are socialized to become more relationship oriented, to need love, and to express their feelings of affection, whereas men are socialized differently (1987). As Cancian notes, "Men's dependence on close relationships remains covert and repressed, whereas women's dependence is overt and exaggerated" (p. 258). Men dominate women in marriage and intimate relationships because they hold at bay the expressions such as talking, caressing, and disclosing that our society, and women in particular, have come to define as *love*.

> **relative love and need theory:** A theory of power that looks at the way that love itself is feminized, defined, and interpreted.

DOING GENDER   Another macro-level factor that can influence the nature of power in intimate relationships is the way that sex and gender are conceptualized in our society, and the fact that these conceptualizations affect nearly every aspect of our lives. This perspective, called **doing gender**, suggests that we take power differentials among men and women for granted and continue to reproduce them simply because they're so ingrained (Fenstermaker Berk, 1985; West & Zimmerman, 1987). "Doing gender" reflects the fact that our culture has traditionally placed a higher value on the traditional activities of men, including their employment, while devaluing those of women. We often fall into traditional roles without even realizing it. For example, as shown in Chapter 10,

> **doing gender:** A theory of power that suggests that we take power differentials between men and women for granted and continue to reproduce them.

We make decisions in our relationships every day. What types of decisions do we make, and how do we make them? Sometimes decisions are made, or differences are negotiated, on the basis of whim, but both micro-level and macro-level factors influence our day-to-day decisions. Following are some micro-level examples of decisions we may make, and the macro-level sources of the power that influences these decisions.

DAY-TO-DAY DECISIONS

- Who is taking the children to daycare?
- What type of new car should we buy?
- Our son Johnny is sick; who will stay home from work to care for him?
- What shall we have for dinner?
- Should we move for that new job?
- Planning ahead, where should we take our vacation this summer?

MICRO-LEVEL FACTORS THAT INFLUENCE THESE DECISIONS

- *Relative resources:* People who have the most prestigious job have the most power in the relationship to make the decisions that favor them (e.g., minimize their household responsibilities; maximize their larger decisions).

- *Principle of least interest:* The partner with the least to lose has the most power, and can avoid doing those tasks that he or she is less interested in.

MACRO-LEVEL FACTORS THAT INFLUENCE THESE DECISIONS

- *Relative love and need theory:* Definition of love has been "feminized," and women have been socialized to believe that they want or need love more than men do.
- *Doing gender:* Power differentials are so ingrained in our culture based on sex and gender that we don't even think about them (e.g., men maximize their traditional breadwinner or household chores, while women do the remainder).

WHAT DO YOU THINK?

1. Thinking about your parents' relationship, can you see any of these theories of power in operation? Do you think they would agree or disagree with your assessment?
2. Do you think the relevance of these theories differs for social groups in our society, such as among racial or ethnic groups, or by sexual orientation, or by age? Why or why not?

women do most of the housework because it's been culturally defined as "women's work." It's easier (and takes less effort) to fall back on traditional cultural definitions than it is to make up our own.

These five perspectives help us explain power, control, and decision making in intimate relationships. They're summarized in the feature box *Tying It All Together: Factors That Shape Power*, and illustrate ways in which personal, micro-level family decisions may reflect macro-level structural forces, such as gendered norms or other types of resources.

Power and Control in Gay and Lesbian Relationships

Reflecting on the relationship of your parents (or other close relatives), how is power distributed between them? Who makes the decisions? Can you identify which theory most closely explains their distribution of power and decision making?

Power operates in same-sex relationships as well as in heterosexual ones. Couples face many of the same issues regardless of sexual orientation, including who makes decisions about major lifestyle issues, how money is spent, how children are raised, and who contributes what to the division of household labor (Biblarz & Savci, 2010; Goldberg & Perry-Jenkins, 2007; Kurdek, 1994; Powell, Bolzendahl, Geist, & Steelman, 2010).

Researchers have also noted a few differences, however, that may be rooted in gendered expectation, or from learning to live in a society in which same-sex relationships are often disvalued. John Gottman and colleagues conducted a 12-year study of same-sex couples to learn more about them (The Gottman Institute, 2013). Again, Gottman found similarities, but he also noted that compared to heterosexual couples, same-sex couples are more upbeat in the face of conflict. They use fewer controlling, hostile, and emotional tactics and communication; they're less apt to take their argument personally; and they show lower levels of physiological arousal (i.e., are less likely to have the jitters, sweaty palms, or elevated heart rate).

Philip Blumstein and Pepper Schwartz (1983) headed an important study with more than 12,000 couples, including heterosexual married couples, cohabiting heterosexual couples, gay couples, and lesbian couples to look at power (and other issues) in their relationships. They highlight several important conclusions:

- The principle of least interest operates in all groups.
- Money is a major determinant of power, as resource theory would suggest, except within lesbian relationships.
- Sex is the most significant determinant of the allocation of power in a relationship.
- Heterosexual couples tended to be the least egalitarian, while gay and lesbian couples were the most. However, even in gay male relationships the influence of gendered expectations was apparent: gay men tended to be more competitive and therefore, more aware of differences in socioeconomic status, whereas lesbians were more likely to hold values of cooperation and sharing.

A study of black and Hispanic lesbian families with children suggests that power may operate somewhat differently than among white lesbian families, although further research is needed on this vastly understudied topic (Moore, 2004). Based on information gathered from 125 black American, Caribbean, and Hispanic lesbians from in-depth interviews, focus groups, and mail surveys, the study shows that the division of household labor is often not shared equally, and the distribution of power is not closely aligned with who brings in the most money, as resource theory suggests. Instead, regardless of financial contribution, the balance of power in these families lies with the person who organizes the household, and that person is usually the biological mother. The biological mother is at the center of power, not the breadwinner.

Bringing It Full Circle

We may have been communicating since infancy, but as the opening vignette reveals, it sometimes seems amazing that we understand others, or are understood by others, at all. This chapter has shown you the importance of good communication for relationships, and revealed some of the challenges of achieving it. Many types of communication exist, including verbal, nonverbal, and electronic methods, each with its unique aspects. But regardless of the type, all communication exists within a social context. Communication both shapes our culture and is shaped by it. Statuses such as sex, race, ethnicity, and class also contribute to different patterns of word choice, syntax, gestures, and other aspects of verbal and nonverbal communication. These macro-level factors can also determine how power and decision making are distributed within intimate relationships. Given what you've learned in this chapter, let's revisit the opening vignette that focused on sex differences in communication:

- In what ways do men and women communicate differently?
- Do you think the participants in our vignettes exaggerate these differences?
- How do you think that other statuses, such as race, ethnicity, and social class, interact with sex to influence communication?
- What theoretical perspectives introduced in Chapter 1 are useful in explaining sex differences in communication?

CHAPTER REVIEW

LO6.1 Identify the importance of communication

6.1 What are four general concepts that summarize communication?

First, communication is a transaction; all human behavior is a continuous exchange, and partners are simultaneously senders and receivers of messages. Second, communication is a process; it's dynamic and always changing, and culture, race, ethnicity, and sex are critical. Third, communication includes the co-construction of meanings; each partner speaks a language and interprets meaning in a way acquired from his or her family of orientation. Fourth, communication uses symbols; to construct meanings or definitions, we rely on symbols that can be verbal, like words, or nonverbal, like gestures.

LO6.2 Recognize the cultural context of communication

6.2 How does communication vary across racial and ethnic groups, and among social classes?

Members of different social classes or racial or ethnic groups develop their own ways of communication through words, gestures, or expressions. For example, linguists have documented substantial differences between Standard American English and African American English, variants of which are spoken by many blacks. These linguistic differences include actual words, syntax, acoustics, and rules for subject–verb agreement.

6.3 What is the *Sapir–Whorf hypothesis*?

Linguists have noted vast cultural differences in language patterns. The Sapir–Whorf hypothesis suggests that language shapes our culture, and at the same time, our culture shapes our language.

6.4 What are the six dimensions of culture that can affect communication styles?

These six dimensions are (1) individualist versus collectivist cultures; (2) high-context versus low-context cultures; (3) masculine versus feminine cultures; (4) centralized versus decentralized power; (5) high versus low ambiguity; and (6) short-term versus long-term time orientation.

LO6.3 Compare and contrast types of communication

6.5 What are the components of listening?

First, you must receive, or hear, the message. Second, you must understand, or when necessary, decode what the speaker is saying. Third, messages that you receive and understand must be retained for some period of time. Fourth, you evaluate the messages that you hear. Finally, you respond. The listening process is circular and continues in a loop—often in a split second.

6.6 What are some barriers to verbal communication?

Bypassing: misunderstanding what someone is saying when one word has several meanings; *lack of precision:* mistaking one word for another, or using incorrect or unclear language; *overgeneralizing:* making sweeping generalizations; *static evaluation:* making statements that don't allow for change; *polarization:* speaking in extremes; and *biased language:* using words that reflect biases toward other groups.

6.7 How can we improve our verbal communication?

Describe your own feelings rather than evaluate the behavior of others; solve problems rather than try to control others; be genuine rather than manipulative; empathize rather than remain detached; be flexible rather than rigid; and finally, present yourself as equal rather than superior.

6.8 What do we mean by the phrase "Actions speak louder than words"?

It means that nonverbal communication is often more believable than verbal communication when the two conflict. Nonverbal communication is more difficult to falsify.

6.9 How are electronic means of communication changing the face of communication?

There are five main ways that electronic communication is changing the way we communicate: (1) We write more informally; (2) our writing influences our speech, we use more abbreviations in our speech patterns, and are less concerned about grammar; (3) we have control over our messages because we can see who is contacting us, and therefore we can better screen our communications; (4) we have more relationships, but with less depth; and (5) we can live in the moment and our communication today can be more of a running discourse.

LO6.4 Analyze sex differences in communication

6.10 How do men's and women's communication styles differ?

Without overgeneralizing, many differences have been noted. For example, compared to men, women tend to smile more often, express a wider range of emotions through facial expressions and nonverbal behavior, and maintain more eye contact. When they speak, women use more qualifying and tentative statements that weaken the message and add an element of uncertainty. Women are more polite in tone, ask a greater number of questions, and are more likely to show interest and concern. Women also offer more personal details and disclosures.

LO6.5 Identify communication to keep your relationship strong

6.11 How does self-disclosure benefit intimate relationships?

When we develop intimacy with another person, we allow that person to penetrate through the superficial layers to the core of deeply personal topics—this is *self-disclosure*. However, it's important to acknowledge that engaging in self-disclosure doesn't guarantee the success of a relationship, because some types of self-disclosure can threaten the relationship.

LO6.6 Describe conflict, communication, and problem solving

6.12 What are four types of conflict?

Pseudoconflict occurs when we falsely perceive that our partner is interfering with our goals or has incompatible goals. *Content conflict* occurs when we disagree about information. *Value conflict* results from differing opinions on subjects that relate to personal values and issues of right or wrong. *Ego conflict* arises when individuals believe they must win at all costs to save face.

LO6.7 Compare and contrast power, control, and decision making

6.13 What theories explain the distribution of power and decision making in relationships?

Resource theory suggests that the spouse with the more prestigious or higher-paying job can use that advantage to generate more power in the relationship and thereby influence decision making. The *principle of least interest* acknowledges that power comes from other sources than just socioeconomic status, including having less investment in the relationship. The *relative love and need theory* is a macro-level perspective that looks at the way that love itself has been defined and interpreted as feminine. The *doing gender* perspective suggests that we take power differentials among men and women for granted and continue to reproduce them simply because they are so ingrained in us.

KEY TERMS

active listening	listening	relative love and need theory
communication	non-regulated couples	resource theory
conflict	non-verbal communication	Sapir–Whorf hypothesis
content conflict	personal power	self-disclosure
doing gender	power	social power
ego conflict	pseudoconflict	value conflict
intimate partner power	regulating couples	verbal communication

CHAPTER

7

Marriage

((• Listen to Chapter 7 on MySocLab

What are the ingredients for a happy and sustaining marriage? While every marriage is different, that of Scherazade and Roderick provides us with some important clues.

They show us that a good marriage is the result of shared values, commitment, and communication.

Scherazade and Roderick, married for 13 years, are a very happy couple in love with life, each other, and their family. They met 14 years ago when they were tenants in the same apartment building. Given their hectic but exciting schedules in which 80-hour workweeks were the norm, they agree that it was a good thing that they shared a roof because otherwise, they would never have had the time to meet!

But meet they did and quickly fell in love. Scherazade describes herself as ambitious and playful, a global citizen, and as someone who wants a full life. She wanted a partner who could keep up with her and share a lot of things—not only what she currently likes, but introduce her to new things as well. Roderick explains that he was looking for someone who shared his values: spirituality, family, and the desire to explore the world.

Scherazade and Roderick's marriage is one of complete partnership.

👁 **Watch** on **MySocLab**
Video: *Marriage: Scherazade and Roderick*

Their marriage is one of complete partnership. They speak of taking turns with their careers; first, Roderick finished his medical residency, then Scherazade fulfilled her dream of doing international work in Africa. Roderick then completed his master's degree in public health, and afterward Scherazade started a nonprofit organization. Roderick began a consulting practice and then they had a baby, and are currently expecting their second child. Now, Roderick and Scherazade work only 4 days a week so that they can spend alternate days with their 18-month-old son, Arshan, who is the light of their lives. "He just reminds us of playing, laughing, and being spontaneous— things that are a really big part of who I am, and he also reminds us to put these things back into our lives because I had gotten away from them," Scherazade says.

"Life is really busy right now. We just have all kinds of things happening, all at the same time," Roderick says, but neither of them would trade their lives for anything else. How do they maintain the intimacy of their relationship? As Scherazade explains, "Maintaining that same level, or more, of passion, romance, and excitement is a challenge when you have everything else going on, but we definitely pay attention to it because it's something we value." Consequently, they schedule a date night weekly, and after their son goes to bed each night, they make time to talk and share their feelings and ideas.

Their shared values, commitment, and communication are clear. As Roderick says, reflecting on their family's past and future, "We've had a very rich and exciting life, and now we have the opportunity to make it rich and exciting with children. So, we have ideas of living overseas and having them learn other languages and seeing what it's like to be in a different part of the world—the idea of having them grow up as global citizens. I think that is going to be fun and exciting and a new way to grow our family." Scherazade nods in agreement.

👁 **Watch** on **MySocLab**
Video: *Families: The Big Picture*

More than 2 million women and men say their wedding vows each year as they move their relationships toward what they hope will be a lifetime commitment (Centers for Disease Control and Prevention, February 19, 2013). Nearly ninety-five percent of Americans marry at least once in their lives (U.S. Census Bureau, November 2012). Most adults who divorce eventually remarry. They all want a relationship full of passion, love, and sexual energy, and a spouse who is kind, attentive, and compassionate—a best friend. They expect marriage to ward off loneliness and be a safe haven in an increasingly impersonal world. This is a tall order to fill, especially over the course of 50 to 60 years!

However, for many married couples, such as Scherazade and Roderick, marriage seems to work. Whereas overall only about one quarter of unmarried U.S. adults consider themselves "very happy," 43 percent of married persons do (Taylor, Funk, & Craighill, 2006). Regardless of race, ethnicity, sex, or social class, most adults place marriage at the top of their priority list. Among high school seniors, 80 percent of young women and 72 percent of young men say having a good marriage and family life is "extremely" important to them (National Marriage Project, 2012).

In this chapter, we explore two sides of marriage. Most of us see the micro-level aspects of marriage; this is a personal relationship full of fun and hard work. However, marriage is also a macro-level social institution with rules, rights, and responsibilities, some determined at the state or federal level. For example, you aren't free to marry just anyone. Laws in all states say you can't marry your sibling or your 12-year-old neighbor; in most states you can't marry your first cousin. And as of June 2013, in only nine states and the District of Columbia can you marry someone of the same sex (Stark, 2013). States also establish the rules for both marriage and its dissolution. Why is the government so involved in your personal relationships? Because society views marriage as a stabilizing force and the government views marriage as its business. Here, **marriage** is defined as *a legally and socially recognized relationship that includes sexual, economic, and social rights and responsibilities for partners.*

marriage: A legally and socially recognized relationship that includes sexual, economic, and social rights and responsibilities for partners.

7.1 Discuss the universal nature of marriage

Questions That Matter

7.1 Is marriage found in every society?

7.2 Is marriage a personal relationship or a social institution?

Marriage: Here, There, and Everywhere

We find marriage in every human society. As an institutional arrangement for publicly recognizing social and intimate bonds, it's an important factor in ensuring the success of a society. For example, because marriage is closely connected with the socialization of children, it can also serve as a way of ensuring intergenerational continuity (Farrell, 1999). Cultural norms and sanctions, often codified into laws, specify who is eligible to be married, to whom, what the marriage ceremony should consist of, and what behavior is expected of married men and women.

Marriage is a deeply meaningful micro-level personal relationship *and* an important macro-level social institution. It's likely to shape many aspects of our personal lives—where and with whom we live, with whom we have sex, our economic well-being, how much personal power we have, and our relationship to society.

In today's mainstream American culture, we marry for love; most of us believe love is the priority for a good marriage. If we fall out of love, we may even end the marriage. In other countries, love is considered among the worst reasons to marry (Leeder, 2004). Instead, marriage in these countries is about forging new bonds among extended families, creating and raising children, or continuing family lineage. For example, extraordinarily strong family bonds influence all aspects of Iraqi society because to Iraqi people, the world is divided between strangers and kin. Through your kin, you receive financial and emotional support, job opportunities, and social position, far too much to risk with a stranger. In Iraq, it's quite common and much safer to marry a first cousin (Tierney, 2003). In parts of Africa, young teenage girls are married to older men whom they have never met. As one 14-year-old girl living in a poor area of rural Kenya speculates about the 27-year-old man her parents have chosen for her:

📖 **Read** on **MySocLab**
Document: *What Is Marriage for?*

> I wonder whether he already has other wives. Will we live together, or will he live away from the family to work in the city? Does he have a job? I probably will not continue in school or have a job. Instead, I will be having and taking care of children. . . . I wonder if he could have AIDS? If I become infected, who will care for our children? Will they have it? My mind is in a whirl of questions; I am excited, happy, nervous, and concerned (Wilson, Ngige, & Trollinger, 2003).

📖 **Read** on **MySocLab**
Document: *Mate Selection and Marriage Around the World*

Parents are deeply involved in choosing their children's mates in many parts of the world. As you learned in Chapter 4, the majority of marriages in India are arranged (India Today, 2013). A survey of 15- to 34-year-olds living in Delhi found 65 percent said they would obey their parents' choice. *"Any girl I could find for myself would not be as good as the one my parents will find,"* says a 19-year-old college student (Derne, 2003).

Because families, communities, and the state all have an interest in marriage, they also have a hand in controlling whom people

All societies mark the beginning of marriage with some type of publicly recorded ceremony, although features of the ceremony can be quite different.

marry. They do so by channeling and restricting interactions (and the development of love) among young people in ways that are specific to different cultures. Here's a review of some of these strategies that were introduced in Chapter 4 (Goode, 1959):

- *Child marriage*—having the child betrothed or married prior to puberty, before feelings of romantic love are likely to develop.
- *Kinship rules*—adopting specific kinship rules so there's little choice as to whom to marry.
- *Segregation*—separating men and women so there's little or no chance for interaction.
- *Close supervision*—short of isolation, strictly supervising and chaperoning of young people.
- *Relative freedom*—managing the social environment of young people through schools, neighborhoods, churches, and other organizations.

All societies mark the beginning of marriage with some type of publicly recorded ceremony. In some cultures, weddings are highly festive with a party-like atmosphere and plenty of food, drink, and dancing. Weddings and wedding receptions in the United States are big business, and cost an average of $25,631 (The Wedding Report, 2013). Many parents can't afford this high cost, but lavish weddings are so much a part of American culture that two-thirds of brides and grooms pay the costs themselves rather than opt for simplicity (Lin, 2010). Other cultures have weddings that are somber, and which may be an avenue for grieving the loss of a child. Some cultures include both men and women in the wedding or the reception, or both, whereas in other cultures, such as where Islam is practiced, men and women are strictly segregated. The women party together in one room, while the men party together in another.

What components of the wedding ceremony (or the reception) are unique to American culture? How do these components contribute to the high costs of weddings in our society? How do you think wedding guests would feel if some of these components were eliminated?

7.2 Identify marriage patterns in U.S. history

Question That Matters

7.3 How has marriage changed over time?

(((Listen on MySocLab
Audio: *NPR: History of U.S. Marriage*

Marriage in U.S. History

In the prevailing Judeo–Christian model of marriage, husband and wife "shall be one flesh" and man shall be the "head" of his wife, as Jesus Christ was the head of the Church. We can see these themes in the story of marriage throughout U.S. history.

Colonial America: Marriage and the Formation of a Nation

The founders of the U.S. government established marriage as a free-choice, heterosexual union that put husbands at the head of the household. Husbands were required to support their wives and children, and to represent them legally. The marriage "union" literally meant the husband and wife were "one," and that "one" was the husband. Wives didn't have the right to vote, own property, or enter into any legal agreements without the consent of their husbands. Because they didn't hold independent legal status, wives also couldn't be tried for a crime. Their husbands, as their freely chosen representatives, would represent them and ensure their protection.

Early Native Americans held different ideas about marriage from the colonists. The Iroquois allowed polygamy and followed matrilineal descent and patterns of matrilocal residence. As you recall from Chapter 1, this means that the kinship was drawn from the mother's lines, and the family tended to live with or near her family. Because women were the primary farmers while men were migratory hunters, it made sense that families should organize themselves around the more geographically settled wives (Brown, 1975). Some Native American groups were also known to permit premarital sex, divorce, and remarriage. This posed a challenge to early European settlers, who considered premarital sex immoral and promiscuous behavior, and divorce as sinful. As Native Americans were forced into treaties and resettlement, government officials tried to impose Christian forms of marriage on them by offering land for relinquishing their tribal affiliations and practices (Cott, 2000).

Because the early U.S. government did not establish a national church and instead formalized the separation of church and state, states were left to regulate marriage and family relationships. In a vast and growing nation, state laws about marriage varied, and many of these differences persist today.

Redefining Marriage in the 19th Century

The institution of marriage faced many challenges throughout the 19th century. A draft of the Thirteenth Amendment, intended to eliminate slavery, included the phrase "All persons are equal before the law, so that no person can hold another as a slave." Senators worried that such language could threaten the power of men as heads of household—some might argue that wives were not unlike slaves, given that they had no independent rights to vote or own property, even though they entered marriage voluntarily. The phrase was deleted from the Amendment, and "Neither slavery nor involuntary servitude . . . shall exist within the United States" was substituted (Cott, 2000).

The first wave of the women's movement began with women working for the emancipation of slaves, as some noticed that *their* equal rights had been passed over with the adoption of the Thirteenth Amendment. The first Women's Rights Convention was held in 1848 in Seneca Falls, New York, where a group of women, including Susan B. Anthony, Elizabeth Cady Stanton, and Lucretia Mott, formed their own constitution demanding equal civil rights for all citizens, regardless of sex. They urged a marriage standard of equal partnership and greater social, economic, and legal opportunities for women.

Marriage was also challenged by those who resisted monogamy. Mormons in the Utah Territory permitted polygamy, arguing that monogamous marriage could isolate couples from the broader community or leave some women without husbands, threatening the cohesion of society. Other alternative groups, such as the Oneida Community, sprang up in the Midwest and Northeast and allowed polygamy or group marriages using the same arguments.

Marriage after the Industrial Revolution

The Industrial Revolution not only carved separate spheres of work for men and women; it also moved families from farms and small communities to cities in search of work, weakening the community's influence on the married couple and bringing a more personal focus to marriage based on companionship. Responsibilities of spouses were still largely differentiated and complementary; men worked outside the home while women took care of the children and the home itself. Other social changes influenced marriage as well including:

- *The changing experiences of youth.* As we learned in Chapter 3, relationships between young men and women underwent significant changes at the turn of

For most of history a person moved quickly from childhood to adulthood. But today people spend longer in school and are financially dependent for more years, and therefore, delay marriage. *How I Met Your Mother* is one of many television shows that depict this trend. When people do marry, they have high expectations for affection, intimacy, and friendship.

the 20th century. Because young people spent increasing time in school, away from parents, there was more opportunity for personal growth and the development of romantic relationships (Coontz, 1992). This focus carried forward into marriage. Couples made decisions about marriage based more on love and less on the economic aspects of earlier generations.

• *A sexual revolution.* We often think of the "sexual revolution" occurring during the 1960s among college students. However, most historical research shows that non-marital sex has been far more common throughout U.S. history than some have assumed. The early 1900s, for instance, ushered in a greater amount of leisure time away from parents, an emphasis on romantic love, opportunities for privacy in new places like the automobile, and the availability of birth control.

• *Changing life-course patterns.* For most of U.S. history, a person moved quickly from childhood to adulthood. By the 20th century, more young people were deciding to attend college, and were financially dependent for more years, which often delayed marriage and parenthood. When they did marry, couples placed greater demands on marriage for affection, intimacy, and friendship. Over the past several decades, marriage has also changed from a model in which the man earns the income while the woman stays home with the children to one of interdependence and symmetry (Fry & Cohn, 2010). Increasingly, partners negotiate their obligations, and both men and women are expected to earn income *and* take care of children.

*M*arriage has moved from an institution based primarily on practical considerations to one based primarily on mutual happiness and fulfillment. Overall, do you believe this is a good thing? Can you think of specific ways that this shift has been good for marriage, and some specific ways that it has been bad for marriage?

For more than 250 years, the concept of marriage in the United States has taken a number of turns. Today, the focus of marriage is on love, rather than economic considerations or bearing and raising children, as shown in Table 7.1 (Wang & Taylor, March 9, 2011. p. 29).

Yet, despite today's greater emphasis on marriage as a satisfying rather than just a practical relationship, marriage rates seem to be declining and people are delaying marriage. What's happening to the institution of marriage?

TABLE 7.1	Percentage of Persons Ages 18–29 Saying This Is a "Very Important" Reason to Marry
Love is still the most important reason to marry, even among young adults.	
Love	88%
Making a lifelong commitment	76%
Companionship	71%
Having children	49%
Financial stability	27%

Source: Wang and Taylor, March 9, 2011.

What Is Happening to Marriage Today?

According to the **marital decline perspective**, the institution of marriage is increasingly threatened by the hedonistic pursuit of personal happiness at the expense of long-term commitment (Morin, 2011; Murray, 2012; National Marriage Project, 2012; Stanton, 2005). Proponents of this perspective point to high divorce rates and the increase in cohabitation and childbearing outside marriage as evidence of a collapse in the values associated with marriage. They suggest that a decline in marriage has caused many other social problems, including poverty, violence, and teenage delinquency.

In contrast, the **marital resilience perspective** believes that marriages are overall no weaker than in the past. Marriage has always had its share of problems, such as violence or desertion. People today actually may enter into marriage more intelligently, because they're less likely to marry for purely economic reasons or to avoid the stigma of singlehood. Proponents of this perspective suggest the real threats to marriage are social problems such as poverty, discrimination, poor schools, or the lack of social services that families need to remain strong and resilient (Amato, 2004; Coontz, 2006; Furstenberg, 2007). They conclude that marriage and family disorganization *result* from these social problems, rather than *cause* them (Furstenberg, 2007).

Regardless of your perspective, marriage in the United States is indeed changing (Amato, Booth, Johnson, & Rogers, 2007). We take a closer look at these changes in the next section.

Marriage Rates

Less than five percent of Americans remain single their whole lives, a relatively constant figure during our nation's history. Most people want to marry and eventually do so. The U.S. Census Bureau reported that in 2013, 52 percent of men and 49 percent of women ages 15 and older were currently married, as shown in Figure 7.1 (U.S. Census Bureau, November 2012). Because these cross-sectional data represent a moment in time, it doesn't mean that all the others *won't* marry. It only means that when the U.S. Census Bureau tabulated the marital status of the population, about half the population age 15 and older were married, and the remainder were either widowed, divorced, separated, or hadn't yet married.

We can see a decline in marriage rates—a snapshot of who is married and who isn't reveals that fewer people are currently married today than in the past. As shown in Figure 7.2, 55 percent of non-Hispanic Whites age 15 and older were married in 2013, compared to 60 percent in 1995. Among Hispanics in 2013, 45 percent were married, down from 54 percent in 1995. The low rates of marriage are particularly noteworthy among Blacks; in 2013, only 32 percent of Blacks were married, according to the U.S. Census Bureau, down from 40 percent in 1995 (U.S. Census Bureau, November 22, 2013).

Sometimes these results across race are misinterpreted to mean that Blacks do not value marriage; however, this isn't necessarily true (Edin & Kefalas, 2005; Seccombe, 2014). Many macro-level structural factors affect whether we marry. One such factor is the high unemployment rate among Blacks. Black men and

7.3 Recognize the changing nature of marriage today

Questions That Matter

7.4 How does the marital decline perspective compare with the marital resilience perspective?

7.5 How do we explain the decline in marriage rates?

7.6 How do Americans feel about same-sex marriage?

7.7 In what ways are attitudes toward marriage changing?

marital decline perspective: The view that the institution of marriage is increasingly threatened by hedonistic pursuits of personal happiness at the expense of long-term commitment.

marital resilience perspective: The view that overall, marriage is no weaker than in the past, but that all families need an increase in structural supports to thrive.

👁 **Watch** on **MySocLab**
Video: *Arlene Skolnick: Idealized Family*

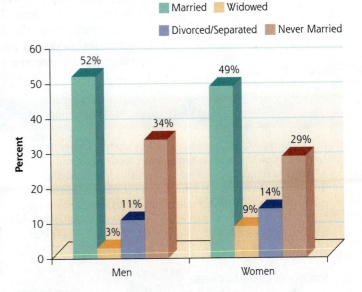

FIGURE 7.1

Marital Status of Population 15 Years and Older by Sex, 2013

More than half of the population ages 15 and older are currently married. The others are divorced, widowed, or have never married. *Source:* U.S. Census Bureau, November 22, 2013.

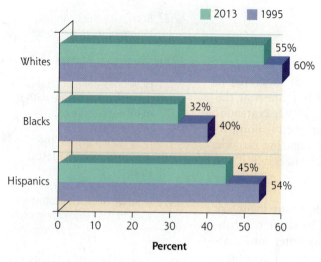

FIGURE 7.2

Percent Married, 15 Years and Older, by Race/Ethnicity, 1995–2013

Only one-third of Blacks ages 15 and older are married, but this does not imply that Blacks do not value marriage.
Source: Saluter, 1996; U.S. Census Bureau, November 22, 2013.

Explore on **MySocLab**
Activity: *Decades in Review: Marital Status Change in Columbus, Ohio*

women are more likely than Whites to believe that economic security prior to marriage is important (Edin & Kefalas, 2005; Gibson-Davis, Edin, & McLanahan, 2005). Black men with stable employment were twice as likely to be married as Black men with sporadic work lives (Tucker, 2000). Low-income minority groups have a strong desire to marry but set very high standards for marriage that they often can't meet. They want employment, a secure home, and an expensive wedding; "I want a yard with grass, plus, I want a nice wedding" (Edin & Kefalas, 2005, p. 47). Marriage is a sign of prestige: it comes *after* a certain level of attainment. Yet, these goals are difficult to obtain on low-wage work; therefore, many Blacks put off or forgo marriage. In other words, macro-level factors, such as economic conditions, can shape our micro-level choices, such as whether we choose to marry.

A second macro-level reason for lower marriage rates in the U.S., particularly among Blacks, is a skewed sex ratio in some Black communities, which makes it difficult for women to find marriage partners. For example, the rate of incarceration among Blacks is six times that of Whites (Wagner, 2012). Even though the number of Blacks in prison declined by nearly 18,500 since 2000, Black men are 30 times as likely to be in jail as Black women, skewing the sex ratio for available mates.

These are only two challenges facing Black marriages, but there are many others. The high school dropout rate among Blacks is considerably higher than for Whites, which makes it more challenging for educated Black women to find partners (National Center for Education Statistics, 2012). Perhaps, it isn't surprising that young Black people are significantly more likely to assume that they will never marry (Crissey, 2005). In other words, macro-level factors shape our opportunities and constraints.

Blacks who *do* marry are a select group; they're more likely to have stable jobs; they report more traditional attitudes about marriage, cohabitation, and premarital sex than Whites; and they're more religious (Brown, Orbuch, & Bauermeister, 2008; Wilcox & Wolfinger, 2007). In other words, despite the structural odds against marriage for this group, they believe so strongly in marriage that they're able to beat those odds.

TYING IT ALL TOGETHER | What Explains Blacks' Lower Rate of Marriage?

In the United States, Blacks are far less likely to marry than are Whites. A snapshot in time reveals that only about 33 percent of Blacks were married in 2009, compared to 56 percent of Whites. Certainly more people postpone marriage; this partially accounts for why so few people today fall into the category of "married." However, several macro-level factors operate that influence our micro-level personal choices and values.

MICRO-LEVEL FACTORS

- "I haven't yet met the right person . . ."
- "I don't want to get married . . ."
- "I like being single . . ."
- "I don't want to get married yet . . ."
- "I don't think I will ever get married. . . ."

MACRO-LEVEL FACTORS

- Economic considerations: unstable work, low pay
- Imbalanced sex ratio
- Racism
- Levels of education

WHAT DO YOU THINK?

1. Can you think of specific ways that the macro-level factors might shape the micro-level choices about marriage?
2. Do you think these macro-level factors operate differently across different racial and ethnic groups? In other words, how might they operate differently for Hispanics, or what other macro-level factors might be uniquely pertinent for Hispanics? Asian Americans? Native Americans? Whites?

As the number of years between reaching adulthood and marriage increases for all racial and ethnic groups, so does the opportunity for non-marital sex and cohabitation. Rising rates of singlehood, cohabitation, non-marital sex, and non-marital childbearing are all seen as challenges to the institution of marriage. Nonetheless, most U.S. adults want to marry, and most eventually do. In fact, the likelihood of never having married by age 65 hasn't changed in more than 100 years. Instead, the two primary reasons for the cross-sectional decline in the percentage of the population who is married at any given time is that (1) people are more likely to divorce—the percentage of persons divorced or separated in 2012 was more than twice that in 1970 (although most divorced people eventually remarry); and (2) people are delaying marriage until later in life. In other words, these people do eventually marry (sometimes even a second or third time), but because they marry when they are older, cross-sectional data portray a large number of unmarried individuals.

Blacks have lower rates of marriage than do other groups, but it's not because they don't value marriage; actually, they value it very highly. Many don't want to marry until important markers are in place, such as a good job or a nice house, or money for a wedding.

Watch on **MySocLab**
Video: *Susan Ferguson: Never Married*

Delayed Marriage

Thais is 26, has a master's degree in education, is a teacher, and writes dramatic movie scripts in the evening. She is also developing a nonprofit tutoring organization so that she can someday have her own business.

She is happy, and has a plan for where she is going over the next several years. It isn't down the aisle. "I don't see myself getting married until, maybe, when I'm over thirty. Well over thirty." (Malernee, 2006)

Ask your grandparents or any other older person about the 1950s (and early 1960s), and they'll likely tell you that they married when they were about 20 or 21. During this period, there was a near-feverish push to get married and have a family. One psychiatrist wrote in 1953 that "a girl who hasn't a man in sight by the time she is 20 is not altogether wrong in feeling that she may never get married," and therefore, young women set their sights on finding a husband early (Coontz, 2007). Betty Friedan chronicled the emphasis on domesticity in her best-selling classic, *The Feminine Mystique* (1963). Even if your grandmother went to college, she understood that even more important than earning her BA degree was obtaining her "MRS" degree. Television shows, radio, and magazines seemed to glorify being a wife and mother to the exclusion of all other choices. The cheerful housewife was portrayed in her immaculate dress, wearing heels and a necklace of pearls, happily cooking dinner for her husband and many children. Consequently, as shown in Figure 7.3, age at marriage dropped to an

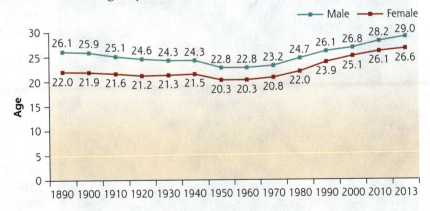

FIGURE 7.3
Median Age at First Marriage, 15 Years and Older, By Sex, 1890–2013

The average age at which we marry has been increasing since 1960 for both men and women.
Source: U.S. Census Bureau, November, 2013.

all-time low during the 1950s, to 20 years for women (with the greatest number marrying at 18) and 23 for men.

Since that period, the age at first marriage has been steadily increasing, particularly over the past few decades. Today, the average age for first marriage is nearly 27 for women and 29 for men (U.S. Census Bureau, November 26, 2013); for those persons with advanced degrees, the age is even higher. The reasons for this increase include changes in occupational and educational opportunities—especially for women, broader cultural shifts in values associated with marriage and singlehood, and structural changes in the economy. Women and men are remaining unmarried not because marriage is less appealing, but because it's becoming more appealing to wait. Marriage has shifted from being the cornerstone to the capstone of adult life. It used to be considered the foundation on which young adults built their prospects for future prosperity and happiness. Today, marriage often comes only *after* partners have moved toward financial and psychological independence—after school is completed, a house is purchased, or a good job is found. It's not hard to understand this mindset, especially given the recent shaky economy, and the fact that many of today's young adults are children of divorce and express worry about divorce themselves. They view marriage as something that shouldn't be undertaken without both security and a suitable exit strategy (Hymowitz, Carroll, Wilcox, & Kaye, 2013).

What are the societal consequences of large numbers of people waiting until their late twenties to marry? In terms of benefits, first, women enjoy an annual income premium if they wait until 30 or later to marry. For college-educated women in their mid-thirties, this premium amounts to $18,152. Second, delayed marriage may have helped to bring down the divorce rate in the U.S. since the early 1980s because couples who marry in their early twenties and especially their teens are more likely to divorce than couples who marry later (Hymowitz, Carroll, Wilcox, & Kaye, 2013). However, some people also note that although the age at marriage has increased, the age at which young women have babies hasn't increased accordingly. By age 25, 44 percent of women have had a baby, whereas only 38 percent have married. Many people are concerned by this (Hymowitz, Carroll, Wilcox, & Kay, 2013; Morin, 2011).

Homogamous versus Heterogamous Marriages

People tend to marry others who look like them and have similar backgrounds, making **homogamous marriages**. A 70-year-old man marrying a 28-year-old woman or a woman on welfare marrying a millionaire may make gossip magazine headlines, but these types of relationships are rare. Still, our society has become more tolerant of **heterogamous marriages**, in which spouses don't share certain social characteristics, such as race, ethnicity, religion, education, age, or social class.

This section discusses three ways in which marriages are becoming more heterogamous in our society: (1) interracial/interethnic marriages; (2) marriages between different social classes; and (3) interfaith marriages.

INTERRACIAL AND INTERETHNIC MARRIAGES Marriage across racial and ethnic lines continues to grow in the United States. The share of new marriages between spouses of different races or ethnicities increased to 15.1 percent, and the share of all current marriages that are either interracial or interethnic has reached an all-time high of 8.4 percent, as shown in Figure 7.4

homogamous marriage: A type of marriage in which spouses share certain social characteristics such as race, ethnicity, religion, education, age, and social class.

heterogamous marriage: A type of marriage in which spouses don't share certain social characteristics such as race, ethnicity, religion, education, age, and social class.

In heterogamous marriages, spouses are significantly different from one another on a critical dimension, such as age, religion, race or ethnic background, or social class.

(Pew Research Center, 2013a). Asians are most likely to marry someone of a different race or ethnicity, and Whites were least likely (Passel & Cohn, 2010).

Interracial marriage, or marrying someone of a different race, once was illegal in the United States. During the 19th century, concerned by the impending emancipation of slaves, states created **antimiscegenation laws** forbidding interracial marriage, mainly to prevent marriage between Whites and those considered non-White, especially Blacks. Marriages between different non-White races, such as between a Black and an Asian, were generally not prohibited. The laws were meant to maintain the power and privilege of Whites and uphold popular beliefs about racial separation, difference, and purity (Lee & Edmonston, 2005). It wasn't until 1967 that the U.S. Supreme Court struck down such laws in *Loving v. Virginia*. Alabama was the last state to formally repeal its antimiscegenation law through a state constitutional amendment in 2000.

Interethnic marriages, with partners from different cultural or ethnic backgrounds, are more common than interracial marriages. Partners in interethnic marriages must be sensitive to cultural differences and the social and political forces that have created or perpetuated them. For example, a study about marriage between Western women and Palestinian men living in Palestinian cities on the West Bank found that patriarchy and East–West power relations and stereotypes affect the relationships. One man describes the importance of compromise:

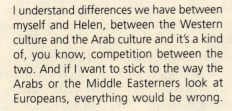

I understand differences we have between myself and Helen, between the Western culture and the Arab culture and it's a kind of, you know, competition between the two. And if I want to stick to the way the Arabs or the Middle Easterners look at Europeans, everything would be wrong. Just take women's lives, the way it is open in the West, the way women have rights, freedom, all this. It's different here and we have to accept these differences and take steps towards each other. (Roer-Strier & Ben Ezra, 2006, p. 49)

Attitudes toward interracial and interethnic relationships have become more favorable in the past 30 or 40 years (Pew Research Center, January 8, 2013; Rosenfeld, 2008). Nearly two-thirds of Americans (63 percent) say they "would be fine" if a family member were to marry someone outside their own racial or ethnic group. More than four in ten Americans (43 percent) say that more people of different races marrying each other has been a change for the better in our society, whereas only about one in ten think it is a change for the worse. Minorities, younger persons, and those who are more educated, liberal, and live in the Eastern or Western states tend to think more positively about intermarriage (Pew Research Center, January 8, 2013).

Despite potential challenges, partners in one study of interracial relationships reported significantly higher relationship satisfaction than those in same-race relationships (Troy, Lewis-Smith, & Laurenceau, 2006). A second study found no differences between interracial and same-race relationships in relationship quality, conflict patterns, coping style, and attachment. These studies cast doubt on the idea that interracial relationships are burdened with more problems, or break down in the face of challenges more often than do more homogamous relationships (Troy, Lewis-Smith, & Laurenceau, 2006).

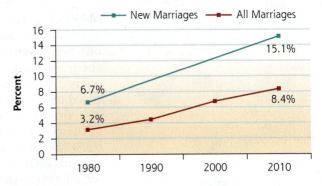

FIGURE 7.4

Percent of Marriages Involving Spouses of a Different Race or Ethnicity From Each Other

Interracial marriage has increased nearly threefold over recent decades.
Source: Pew Research Center, 2013a.

interracial marriage: A type of marriage in which spouses come from different racial groups.

antimiscegenation laws: Laws forbidding interracial marriage, which existed at the state level until 1967.

interethnic marriage: A type of marriage in which spouses come from different countries or have different cultural, religious, or ethnic backgrounds.

📖 **Read** on **MySocLab**
Document: *Breaking the Last Taboo: Interracial Marriage in America*

MARRIAGE ACROSS SOCIAL-CLASS BOUNDARIES The extent of opportunities to meet and marry others outside your social position influences the rate of heterogamous marriages. Certainly, people are free to marry anyone they choose—rich or poor. The idea of marrying across class lines is a common theme in U.S. movies, but the movie-going public tends to marry within its own social class.

For example, a common way to meet a spouse is through college. Many of the very rich attend elite private colleges and universities to make connections for some of the best jobs; however, being accepted into these colleges depends on far more than just grades. Most have *legacy preferences*—programs for admitting children of alumni—that account for 10 percent to 15 percent of the composition of every incoming class (Economist.com, 2004). The incoming classes aren't particularly diverse; these schools perpetuate a way for the elite to meet other elites. Middle- and working-class students tend to go to state-funded universities and meet other middle- and working-class students.

Moreover, some boundaries in the socioeconomic hierarchy are difficult to cross. In terms of occupations, someone who works with his or her hands—for example, in construction—is less likely to marry someone who works with ideas—for example, a college professor. With respect to education, intermarriage is also less likely between those with and those without a college education. The reason is that occupation and education serve as both indicators of preferences and tastes *and* predictors of economic success, and thus people choose spouses with whom they have things in common.

Marriages that cross class boundaries may not present as obvious a set of challenges as those that cross the lines of race or nationality. But people who marry across class lines may also be moving outside their comfort zones, into the uncharted territory of partners with a different level of wealth and education, and often, a different set of assumptions about things like manners, food, child-rearing, gift-giving, and how to spend vacations. In cross-class marriages, one partner usually has more money, more options and, almost inevitably, more power in the relationship (Lewin, 2005b).

We don't know how many interclass marriages exist. If we can use education as a proxy for class, they seem to be declining. Even as more people marry across racial and religious lines, fewer are choosing partners with a different level of education. In the past, most of those marriages involved men marrying less-educated women. However, today, that pattern has flipped, so that the majority involve women marrying less-educated men. This may be because the changes in education levels outlined previously—young women now have more education that do young men. However, this combination—higher educated wife and lower educated husband—is the marital pattern most likely to end in divorce (Lewin, 2005b).

INTERFAITH MARRIAGES Marrying someone of a different religious faith is less frowned on in society than marrying across other groups because faith is generally not as visible as race, age, or social class. Nonetheless, interfaith marriages can still face challenges.

Religion is important to many people. Seventy-one percent of U.S. adults are "absolutely certain" there is a God, and 58 percent claim their religion is very important in their lives (Pew Research Center, June 23, 2008; July 19, 2012). Religions provide beliefs about what is right and wrong, and different religions approach certain topics very differently, such as women's and men's roles in marriage, divorce, abortion, or how to raise children—all issues that may require considerable negotiation and compromise in a marriage. Therefore, it isn't surprising that couples who hold similar religious beliefs and participate jointly in religious practice have, on average, happier and more satisfying marriages than those who don't (Curtis & Ellison, 2002; Myers,

2006; Vaaler, Ellison, & Powers, 2009). Shared religion can increase family cohesiveness and provide a unified approach to resolving marital and family issues. One study looked at the risk of divorce among a nationwide sample of 2,979 first-time married couples. It noted that *although each partner's religious attendance* contributed to whether a couple divorced, *the risk of divorce was lower if husbands had conservative theological beliefs and when both partners belonged to mainline Protestant denominations. Conversely, the risk of divorce was* higher *if husbands attended services more frequently than their wives and if wives were more theologically conservative than their husbands* (Vaaler, Ellison, & Powers, 2009).

There are many different types of interfaith marriages, including

- a spouse who follows a specific religion and a spouse who follows a non-theistic ethical system (say, Judaism and Humanism)
- spouses of two religions that are totally different (such as Christianity and Buddhism)
- spouses of two religions that have at least some points of similarity (two Abrahamic religions that share Abraham as a Patriarch, including Christianity and Islam)
- spouses from different major divisions within the same religion (Roman Catholicism and Protestantism)
- spouses from different sects of the same religion (Evangelical and mainline Christian)
- spouses from different traditions within the same sects of the same religion (two conservative denominations such as Southern Baptist and Assemblies of God)

To make the marriage combination even more complex, one spouse could be an atheist. The degree of complexity in interfaith marriages largely depends on (1) the degree of difference between the partners' faiths and (2) how religious the partners actually are. A marriage between a devout Mormon and a committed Muslim would likely face far more differences and potential clashes of faith than would a marriage between two Protestant denominations, despite the fact that both religions are misunderstood by a substantial number of Americans (Pew Forum on Religion & Public Life, December 14, 2012). More than half of U.S. adults say they don't know very much or anything about Muslims or Mormons; yet, 70 percent say the Muslim religion and 62 percent say the Mormon religion is "a lot different" from their own religion, and more than one-quarter have an unfavorable attitude toward these two groups (Pew Research Center, September 25, 2007).

Overall, rates of intermarriage based on race, ethnicity, class, and religious differences have increased, both in the United States and in other developed nations. The mainstream U.S. view is that we're free to choose whom we marry, and the decision to marry should be based on love. At the same time, marriages don't exist in a vacuum. Prejudice still exists in U.S. society, and there are still consequences for those who marry someone significantly different from themselves. Macro-level factors continue to shape our micro-level choices.

Same-Sex Marriage

Another change in marriage is the legalization of same-sex marriage in Connecticut, Iowa, Maine, Maryland, Massachusetts, New Hampshire, New York, Vermont, Washington, and the District of Columbia. California allowed same-sex marriage until ballot measures overturned the decisions. One of the most important policy issues of the day, same-sex marriage is also among the most controversial.

Watch on **MySocLab**
Video: *Reaction to Gay Marriage Ban*

> Jack Baker, a lawyer, and Mike McConnell, a librarian who has been Jack's partner since 1967, are old-fashioned romantics in the Midwestern tradition. Each believes the other is his soul mate, his "better half," the one person whose love makes his own life complete. Once you have found your soul mate, Baker and McConnell agree, you ought to commit your lives to one another. The institution within which you should do that—for spiritual, personal, and even civic reasons—is marriage, which they idealize as potentially perfect. Anything else is a cheap imitation. (Eskridge & Spedale, 2006, p. 1)

Why are gays and lesbians demanding the right to marry? Because marriage matters (Waite & Gallagher, 2000). At least 1,400 documented legal rights associated with marriage aren't guaranteed to cohabiting couples, including joint parenting and adoption laws, tax savings, immigration and residency, insurance benefits, crime victims' recovery benefits, and the right to make end-of-life decisions. Some of these rights are given to members of **civil unions**, a public policy designed to extend some benefits to partners who aren't legally married, but as shown in Table 7.2, civil unions don't provide the same degree of protection as marriage. For example, partners in civil unions can't file joint federal tax returns.

civil union: A public policy designed to extend some benefits to partners who are not legally married.

TABLE 7.2   The Benefits of Marriage versus Civil Unions

Marriage confers many benefits on a couple that civil unions do not.

	Married Couples	Unmarried Couples	Civil Unions
Portability of rights	Union automatically recognized in all 50 states.	Can register as domestic partners in some states.	Usually only recognized in the state that approves them. But recently in New York, a civil union from Vermont was recognized in a wrongful-death suit.
Gifts and property transfers	May make unlimited transfers and gifts to each other.	Any gift or transfer worth more than $10,000 in a year requires filing a federal gift tax return.	Same as unmarried couples—larger gifts and transfers are subject to federal tax.
Income tax status	"Married filing jointly" generally works to the advantage of couples when one earns much more than the other, but creates a penalty when their incomes are similar.	Unmarried couples cannot file jointly, although an adult with custody of a child can file as "head of household."	A couple can file only state tax returns jointly; federal returns are filed individually.
Child or spousal support	Criminal penalties are imposed on spouses who abandon a child or a spouse.	Unmarried partners have no legal obligation to support their partners or their partner's children.	In state where the union is granted, the courts can impose penalties on a partner who abandons a child or a spouse.
Medical decisions	A spouse or family member may make decisions for an incompetent or disabled person unless contrary written instructions exist.	A health-care proxy, prepared before a problem occurs, can designate anyone, including a partner, to make decisions.	Partners in the state where the union was granted can make health decisions, but in other states, that authority may not be recognized.
Immigration	U.S. citizens and legal permanent residents can sponsor their spouses and other immediate family members for immigration purposes.	Not allowed to sponsor a partner or other immediate family members.	Not allowed to sponsor a partner or other immediate family members.

Source: Pew Research Center for the People & the Press and the Pew Forum on Religion & Public Life, October 9, 2009.

"Our marriage is even more precious to us because we had to work so hard for it."

Gina and Heidi, both 43, are the picture of domesticity. Together since 1990, they live and raise children together, and are upstanding members of their community, volunteering for such projects as adult literacy, fair housing, and mentoring a high school student. Gina works as a classroom aide for students with disabilities, and Heidi is an executive director of an

emergency food pantry. They never intended to be in the limelight. Yet Gina and Heidi made history—they were among the plaintiffs in the Massachusetts lawsuit against the State Department of Public Health after being denied a marriage license, which led to the legalization of same-sex marriage in 2004. With their sons by their side and 100 family members and friends in attendance, they were legally married in May 2004.

Why was it so important for Gina and Heidi to marry? Their answer resembles that of any couple in love, "The most important reason we wanted to get married is that we love each other, and we wanted to be responsible for and to each other," said Gina. She continued, "No one knows Heidi as I do—what her fears are, her hopes, her dreams. I know what she wants if she is unable to make decisions for herself. I know what she wants for our children. And she knows those things about me. Marriage makes us feel secure in our relationship and ensures that those wishes will be respected. It is a public statement of our love and commitment."

How do they address the concerns of others that somehow their marriage devalues traditional marriage? Gina continues, "Some people think that we are not honoring marriage by pursuing the lawsuit. But the complete opposite is true, because we saw marriage as a way to protect our family and to stand up and have our community recognize us as a serious relationship." They do not see themselves as dishonoring marriage, but rather, as asking to be a part of something that they honor so deeply. Heidi adds, "I don't think we ever take our marriage for granted."

Massachusetts was the first state to allow same-sex marriage. In 2004, a lesbian couple filed a lawsuit in Massachusetts, claiming they, too, had a right to marry. Since then, many other states have allowed same-sex marriage, allowing many same-sex couples (like the one shown here) to marry.

WHAT DO YOU THINK?

1. People may think same-sex marriage devalues traditional marriage. What is your opinion on the issue? How did you form this opinion?
2. Can you think of any issue that you would be willing to fight for in the courts?

Sources: WorldNetDaily, 2003; Redbook, June 2008; Gay & Lesbian Advocates & Defenders, 2008.

Vermont is credited as the leader of the same-sex marriage movement in the United States for its adoption of a civil union bill in 2000, which moved the debate to a new level. However, Massachusetts was the first state to actually allow same-sex marriage. How did that law come about? In 2004, a lesbian couple filed a lawsuit in Massachusetts, claiming they, too, had a right to marry. Massachusetts courts sided with them and ruled that only full, equal marriage rights for gay couples, rather than civil unions, are constitutional. "The history of our nation has demonstrated that separate is seldom, if ever equal," one Justice claimed, evoking similarities to Blacks' struggle for equality (Peter, 2004, p. 1). The lesbian couple is introduced in the *Diversity in Families* box.

Advocates see same-sex marriage as a civil rights issue, akin to equal rights for women, minorities, or the disabled. The Court's ruling repeatedly invoked the words "respect and dignity" and framed the marriage question as one that deeply affected not just couples, but also their children.

The opinions of opponents vary, but many feel same-sex marriage is immoral and violates God's teaching. Others believe marriage has always been defined as

*W*hat do you think about these various changes in marriage laws? Which ones do you think are good ideas, and which do you see as potentially problematic, and why?

between a man and a woman, and changing the definition cheapens its fundamental meaning. Others say homosexuality is unnatural, and states shouldn't sanction homosexual relationships or raising children in a homosexual household (Family Focus, 2008). Some opponents of same-sex marriage support civil unions or domestic partnerships for gays and lesbians, but shut the door on legal marriage. Former President Bush was an outspoken opponent of same-sex marriage and supported a national ban against it,

If we're to prevent the meaning of marriage from being changed forever, our nation must enact a constitutional amendment to protect marriage in America. Decisive and democratic action is needed because attempts to redefine marriage in a single state or city could have serious consequences throughout the country. (The White House, 2004, p. 1)

Although a national ban never materialized, many states have passed laws prohibiting same-sex marriage. President Obama is slowly warming up to same-sex marriage.

Public support for same-sex marriage is growing rapidly, as shown in Figure 7.5. Overall, more U.S. adults now support same-sex marriage than oppose it. As you can see in Table 7.3, women, Whites, those unaffiliated with a religion, the young, and Democrats are most likely to support same-sex marriage (Pew Research Center's Religion and Public Life Project, March 2014).

When you think about marriage, do you think about it as a micro-level personal relationship, or as a macro-level social institution? What are your reasons for your views?

Changing Attitudes about Marriage

Americans are shifting the way they think about marriage and intimate relationships, which, in turn, changes the nature of marriage in our country. As you learned in Chapter 3, we are becoming more tolerant of non-marital sex, cohabitation, and non-marital childbearing, and we are witnessing a change in attitudes about the gendered division of labor (Morin, 2011; National Marriage Project, 2012). In the opening vignette of this chapter, the depiction of Roderick and Scherazade show that breadwinning and domestic labor are increasingly shared by married couples.

One area that has *not* changed much, however, is the value associated

Percent opposing allowing gays and lesbians to marry legally
Percent favoring allowing gays and lesbians to marry legally

FIGURE 7.5
Changing Attitudes about Same-Sex Marriage

Opinions have changed—more Americans now support same-sex marriage than oppose it.
Source: Based on Pew Research Center's Religion and Public Life Project, March 2014; Craighill & Clement, March 5, 2014.

TABLE 7.3	Percentage Who Support Same-Sex Marriage

People with no specific religious affiliation, younger persons, and those who claim to be Democrats are more likely to support legalizing same-sex marriage.

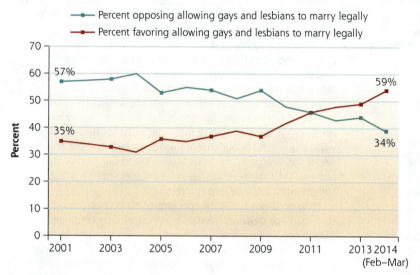

	Favor
Total	54%
Unaffiliated	77%
White Mainline Protestants	62%
Black Protestants	43%
White Evangelical Protestants	23%
Born 1981 to 1995	68%
Born 1965–1980	55%
Born 1946–1964	48%
Born 1920–1945	38%
Democrats	69%
Republicans	39%
Have a Gay or Lesbian Friend, Relative, or Colleague	66%
Do Not have a Gay or Lesbian Friend, Relative, or Colleague	29%

Sources: Based on Pew Research Center's Religion and Public Life Project, March 2014; Kiley, 2014; Clawson, 2014; Marriage Equality USA, 2014.

with marriage. Most people want to marry and view a "good" marriage as an important life goal. They believe marriage is a lifetime commitment and shouldn't be terminated except under extreme circumstances. Nonetheless, most people believe there are other legitimate paths to happiness as well. This may explain why belief in a "decline" in the value of marriage is a misinterpretation: people do want a happy marriage, but they are also tolerant of different lifestyles.

ATTITUDES ABOUT NON-MARITAL SEX U.S. attitudes toward non-marital sex have shifted strongly, as noted in Chapter 5 (Pew Research Center, July 1, 2007). In 1970, about half of survey respondents believed non-marital sex was "almost always" or "always" wrong. Most people, especially younger generations, now believe non-marital sex is not wrong, and most have engaged in it (Axinn & Thornton, 2000; Carter, 2006). Therefore, people no longer need to turn exclusively to marriage early in life to fulfill their sexual needs.

ATTITUDES ABOUT COHABITATION With millions of cohabiting couples, almost all of us know someone who has or is currently cohabiting (National Marriage Project, 2012; U.S. Census Bureau, November 2012). Marriage may or may not be a part of the couple's future plans. Today, people of all ages are more likely than in the past to approve of living together (Manning, Longmore, & Giordano, 2007; Morin, 2011). More than half of high school seniors agree it's a "good idea for a couple to live together before getting married in order to find out if they really get along" (National Marriage Project, 2012). Young people may be including cohabitation in their life trajectories, but rarely do they see it as a substitute for marriage (Manning, Longmore, & Giordano, 2007).

ATTITUDES ABOUT NON-MARITAL CHILDBEARING About 20 years ago, Murphy Brown, a television character who epitomized the single professional woman of the time, shocked viewers by choosing to have, and raise, a baby outside marriage. Then-U.S. Vice President Dan Quayle condemned the controversial television show, saying Murphy Brown was mocking the role of fathers and glorifying single motherhood. What do today's Americans think about single women having children?

Overall, most people don't think positively about single motherhood. Although people are more tolerant than they were in the past, 69 percent of adults still believe that single women having children "is a bad thing for society" (Morin, 2011). Men and Whites are far more disapproving than are women or minorities. Interestingly, age makes little difference: 65 percent of adults ages 18–29 think that single women having children is bad for society, as do 68 percent of adults ages 50–64 (Pew Research Center, July 1, 2007).

Although many Americans don't think single motherhood is a good idea, most don't have a problem with unmarried couples having children. The same survey by the Pew Research Center found that only about 43 percent of adults reported that it was "a bad thing for society, while most thought it was either a good thing, or didn't make much difference" (Morin, 2011, p. 12).

ATTITUDES ABOUT SHARED BREADWINNING

Tran and Lan Li Li have been married for 9 years and have two young sons, ages 6 and 7. Tran is an architect and Lan Li Li works as a librarian for the county courthouse. They always knew they would both work while raising their children and never seriously considered otherwise. Tran is happy to share the responsibility of earning an income, "Of course Li Li works, this isn't the 1950s here. Besides, a family cannot really make it on one income anyway. I really wouldn't want all that responsibility on my shoulders. Sure, we scramble in the morning to get everyone ready for school and work, but Li Li and I do it together."

> They always knew they would both work while raising their children and never seriously considered otherwise.

How do your attitudes about marriage differ from those of your parents? What do you think accounts for these changes? Can you identify any macro-level factors? What do your parents think of your attitudes toward marriage?

More married women are working outside the home than ever before. They work for many reasons: as the sole provider, to share the bread-winning role, for supplemental income, or for the fun of it. In previous generations, women often quit work when they married, or at least when they had children. Marriage meant a complementary division of labor: husbands earned the family income and wives stayed at home and raised the children.

Today, women make up nearly half the labor market, are outpacing men in education, and most U.S. adults believe both spouses should work outside the home (Pew Research Center, November 18, 2010). In fact, nearly one-quarter of wives earn more than their spouse (Fry & Cohn, 2010). "There are fewer Cinderella marriages these days. Men are less interested in rescuing a woman from poverty. They want to find someone who will pull her weight," says Dr. Stephanie Coontz, author of several books on families, including *Marriage, a History* (Coontz, 2006, cited in Paul, 2006). The man who is a physician, lawyer, or business executive is more likely to marry his peer than his nurse, legal secretary, or office assistant. This change has significantly reshaped marriage as an institution to include the allocation of power, decision making, and household labor.

ATTITUDES ABOUT THE DIVISION OF HOUSEHOLD LABOR

If men now want a woman who will "pull her weight financially," then, when both partners work, who should be responsible for cooking, cleaning, yard maintenance, and taking care of the children? As we see in Chapter 10, housework and child-care are still primarily done by women, even when women work outside the home (Bianchi & Milkie, 2010; Krantz-Kent, 2009; Schiebinger & Gilmartin, 2010; Wright, Bianchi, & Hunt, 2013). Nonetheless, the time men spend on domestic tasks is increasing (Galinsky, Aumann, & Bond, 2009). Younger men and women, in particular, believe housework should be shared and are learning to negotiate these important tasks.

In summary, attitudes about marriage and sexual relations have changed considerably over the past several decades. U.S. adults are now more accepting of non-marital sex, cohabitation, having children outside marriage, and less traditional domestic practices. But despite views that challenge traditional notions of marriage, most people continue to endorse marriage, want to marry, and eventually do. Marriage still holds a special place in people's lives. Their expectations have changed, but they still believe marriage is a good thing. What benefits accrue from marriage?

Although women still do more domestic labor than do men, things are changing, especially among the young, as shown here.

marriage premium: The concept that married people are happier, healthier, and financially better off than those who aren't married.

7.4 Describe the "marriage premium"

Questions That Matter

7.8 What is the *marriage premium*?

7.9 What is a *selection effect*?

The Marriage Premium: Happiness, Health, and Economic Security

Arguments in favor of marriage include a **marriage premium**, meaning that married people are happier, healthier, and financially better off than those who aren't, including cohabiters (Addo & Lichter, 2013; Carr & Springer, 2010; DeNavas-Walt, Proctor, & Smith, 2012; McFarland, Hayward, & Brown, 2013). But does marriage *cause* people to be happier, healthier, and have a better economic situation? Or, in a **selection effect**, are people who are happier, healthier, and wealthier more likely to marry in the first place? Marriage is likely both a cause and a consequence of happiness, health, and stronger finances for the married couple. Yet, there's no denying that marriage seems to protect people and confers on them many real and important benefits (DeNavas-Walt, Proctor, & Smith, 2012; Manzoli, Villari, Pirone, & Boccia, 2007).

selection effect: The hypothesis that people who marry may be different from those who don't marry; for example, they may be happier, healthier, and have more money.

Psychological Well-Being and Happiness

Married people are more likely to say that they're "very happy" with life in general than are unmarried people (43 percent vs. 24 percent, respectively) (Taylor, Funk, & Craighill, 2006). This has been a consistent research finding over many years, for men as well as women, for young and old, although the marriage gap in happiness isn't quite as great among the elderly. At the other end of the spectrum, married people are the least likely to say they're unhappy with their lives. Married people also benefit in other dimensions of psychological well-being, including having lower rates of depression, higher levels of self-esteem, closer personal relationships with others, a stronger sense of personal growth, and feelings of being more in control of one's life (Fagan, 2009; Frech & Williams, 2007). Although some of the difference may be because of a selection effect—happy people are more likely to marry in the first place—researchers are quick to point out that marriage affords a number of protections such as social support and companionship that can significantly boost psychological well-being. People with depression may get the biggest boost of all from marriage, as shown in the *Why Do Research?* feature box.

Why Do Research?   Marriage Is Good Medicine for Those with Depression

Marriage, at least a good marriage, seems to boost levels of happiness, but what happens if you experience depression prior to getting married? Do people with depression also benefit from marriage? A research team from Ohio State University, Drs. Frech and Williams, pondered that question, and hypothesized that people who have depression would have worse marital quality and would therefore, experience fewer benefits from marriage, but that isn't what they found.

The researchers used data from the National Survey of Families and Households, a large, nationally representative sample that included more than 3,000 unmarried adults under age 55. After following their sample for 5 years, they identified

people who married during that period and asked questions about the quality of their marriage and their psychological well-being.

What they found surprised them: Although marriage seems to provide benefits, it provides even greater psychological benefits to persons with depression than it does to the rest of the population. When they compared *all* the people who married with *all* the people who didn't marry during this period, they found that those who married were somewhat less likely to have depression than those who were unmarried. However, among the subgroup of persons with depression, the benefits of marriage were even greater, and they scored even lower on the depression scale. The study did find that persons with depression have marriages with greater conflict and report being less happy in their marriages; nonetheless, apparently being in even a less-than-perfect marriage considerably increased their level of happiness. The researchers speculate that marriage might provide the companionship that singles with depression typically lack in their lives.

Unmarried people, on average, have higher rates of depression, lower levels of self-esteem, more distant personal relationships with others, a weaker sense of personal growth, and feelings of being less in control of one's life.

WHAT DO YOU THINK?

1. Do you think the benefits of marriage might differ for men with depression and women with depression? Would the benefits differ for Blacks, Whites, Asians, Hispanics, or Native Americans? Why or why not?
2. Think about what you learned in Chapter 3 about cohabitation. Why do you think cohabitation doesn't lower depression or increase happiness in the same way marriage does?

Sources: Frech & Williams, 2007; Health Behavior News Service, 2007.

Health

Watch on MySocLab
Video: *Is Marriage Good for Your Health?*

Married people, men in particular, are healthier than unmarried people (Hughes & Waite, 2009; National Center for Health Statistics, 2012; Schoenborn & Adams, 2010). They live longer and are less likely to die from the leading causes of death (i.e., coronary heart disease, stroke, pneumonia, cancer, cirrhosis, automobile accidents, murder, and suicide) (Manzoli, Villari, Pilone, & Boccia, 2007). Married men and women are less likely to smoke, drink heavily (women only), and use illegal drugs than their unmarried (or previously married) counterparts (Green, Doherty, Fothergill, & Ensminger, 2012). Married persons are less likely to have depression or anxiety than the unmarried, and have better health habits, are more likely to have health insurance, and to receive more regular health care (National Center for Health Statistics, 2012).

Why do these health differences exist between married and unmarried people? It's generally thought marriage confers a health advantage by offering social support and decreased isolation, an incentive to behave in healthier ways, and an increased income for the couple (Carr & Springer, 2010). However, researchers have found that it's not any marriage that's associated with better health, but a *satisfying* marriage (Parker-Pope, 2010; Partenheimer, 2003). In a study of nearly 500 middle-age women over a 13-year period, researchers found happy marriages were associated with good health, but unhappy marriages were linked to more depression, hostility, and anger—all risk factors for coronary heart disease and other health problems.

Economic Security

People who are married have more money and accumulate greater assets than those who are single or divorced, regardless of race or ethnic background (DeNavas-Walt, Proctor, & Smith, 2012). In particular, married men have higher earnings than their unmarried counterparts—by at least 12 percent. What accounts for this **wage premium** associated with marriage? The premium may be attributed to at least three factors: (1) married men may work harder, knowing they're supporting others; (2) employers may discriminate in favor of "family men," whom they see as stable and good workers; and (3) wives still have most of the responsibility for housework and childcare, freeing men to focus on paid work. Women receive financial gains from marriage as well, although not necessarily in terms of their own earnings. They benefit indirectly because of the addition of their husbands' income and greater earning power to the household. Spouses pool their resources together and therefore have higher incomes, are more likely to have savings and assets, and health insurance and retirement benefits through employers.

wage premium: Generally, married men earn more than their unmarried counterparts, particularly married men with stay-at-home wives.

It appears that a happy marriage conveys many important health and economic benefits, and being married is considered a positive ideal in the U.S. But again, is there a marriage premium in operation, or is it a selection effect? Even though both factors likely contribute—that is, marriage is both a cause and a consequence of happiness, health, and stronger finances—there is no denying that marriage seems to protect people and confer on them many real and important benefits (Manzoli, Villari, Pilone, & Boccia, 2007).

Listen on MySocLab
Audio: *NPR: Keeping a Marriage Solid When Money Is Tight*

One way in which marriage confers benefits is by producing **social capital**—goods and services that are by-products of social relationships, such as connections, social support, information, and financial help. Marriage, through its obligations and bonds, is an important source of social capital. These social obligations and bonds exist not only between the married partners, but also between the couple and their extended families, and between the couple and their community.

social capital: The goods and services that are by-products of social relationships, including connections, social support, information, or financial help.

Do these benefits accrue to cohabiting couples as well? The answers to this question are not completely clear, but a recent study using a large and representative sample suggests that similarities in well-being

*T*hink about yourself, or someone close to you who is married. What specific types of social capital are received in this marriage? How might this social capital be different from that received by a cohabiting couple or a single person?

between married people and cohabiters may be more striking than the differences (Musick & Bumpass, 2012). For example, they found that the married fared better in health than cohabiters, but the opposite was true of happiness and self-esteem. They suggest that the formal nature of marriage and the package of entitlements that go with it, such as health insurance for spouses, could explain the better health of the married.

Does Marriage Benefit Everyone Equally?

Marriage may confer considerable benefits on the married couple, but we may not have the entire picture if the only comparison made is between married and unmarried people. Another important point to consider is whether marriage benefits all married people equally. The answer is complex, but we're beginning to see that macro-level social factors such as sex, race, and ethnicity influence the benefits we receive from marriage.

"His" and "Her" Marriage

In her classic study of marriage, Jessie Bernard (1972) argued that two types of marriages exist in American society: "his" and "her." Based on data she collected in the 1960s, Bernard argued that marriage benefited men more than women. But much has changed since then, hasn't it?

Yet, people continue to talk about "his" and "her" marriages (Waller & McLanahan, 2005), because in some ways men do benefit from marriage more than women. Married women are less happy and experience more depression and distress than do married men. The physical health benefits of marriage are also substantial for men, but less so for women. Marriage reduces men's more risky behaviors—married men are less likely to drink, take drugs, smoke, get into fights, or drink and drive than are unmarried men, whereas marriage brings more modest changes in women's risky behavior (Duncan, Wilkerson, & England, 2006). Married men are also the group most likely to say that someone (their wives) monitors their health (makes doctor's appointments, follows up on health concerns, and so on).

There also appears to be a growing happiness gap between married men and women. In the early 1970s, married women reported being slightly happier than men, but today that result has been reversed—married men are happier than married women (52 percent vs. 47 percent, respectively), reporting that they're "highly satisfied" with their lives (Hymowitz, Carroll, Wilcox, & Kaye, 2013). One likely explanation is that women now have a much longer to-do list than they once did and they often feel rushed and stressed (Parker, 2009). It's not enough to take care of the children and keep a clean house; now women are expected to manage an exciting career, too. As one student explained, her mother's goals in life "were to have a beautiful garden, a well-kept house, and well-adjusted children who did well in school. I sort of want all those things too, but I also want to have a great career and have an impact on the broader world" (Leonhardt, 2007, p. 1).

Although most women today are pleased to have a wide range of opportunities, they also do the majority of the housework and childcare, as we see in Chapter 10. With limited availability of part-time work, flexible workplaces, subsidized childcare, and family leaves or other family programs, it's no wonder that some parents, mothers in particular, find that juggling all these competing demands detracts from their sense of happiness. In fact, because of the lack of social supports, some mothers are deciding to remain at home rather than try to maintain their careers (Parker, 2009; Stone, 2008).

7.5 Identify whether marriage benefits everyone equally

Question That Matters

7.10 Does marriage benefit everyone equally?

Read on MySocLab
Document: *Men and Women: Together and Apart in Later Years*

Race, Ethnicity, and the Benefits of Marriage

We've learned that some racial and ethnic groups are less likely to marry than others. The highest rate of marriage is among Whites; the lowest among Blacks (U.S. Census Bureau, November 2012). However, minority groups believe in marriage at least as strongly as Whites do (Edin & Kefalas, 2005; Gibson-Davis, Edin, & McLanahan, 2005; Seccombe, 2014).

The benefits of marriage can also be quite different across racial and ethnic groups. For example, the economic benefits accrued by married couples largely depend on wages, and most minority groups earn significantly less than Whites. The median annual income is about $69,000 for Asians, $57,000 for Whites, $39,000 for Hispanics, and $33,000 for Blacks (DeNavas-Walt, Proctor, & Smith, 2013). Likewise, only about 7 percent of White families and 9 percent of Asian families lived in poverty, compared to 26 percent of Black and 25 percent of Hispanic families. Although Black and Hispanic married couples can pool their incomes and increase their economic standing, marriage doesn't necessarily provide the same income security that it does for Whites or Asian-Americans.

As another example, African Americans tend to report lower marital quality than do Whites, Hispanics, or even other Blacks, such as Black couples from the Caribbean (Bryant, Taylor, Lincoln, Chatters, & Jackson, 2008; Roebuck & Brown, 2007). Although the reasons for this are unclear, one suggestion is that a selection effect again operates: they have such high expectations for the rewards of marriage that they're disappointed when these expectations aren't completely met. They've set high standards that should be in place before marrying (e.g., financial stability), and these standards persist throughout marriage. When difficulties arise, they're then more likely to view their relationship negatively (Fagan, 2009; Gibson-Davis, Edin, & McLanahan, 2005).

7.6 Discuss marital satisfaction and success

Question That Matters

7.11 What factors are associated with marital satisfaction and success?

Marital Satisfaction and Success

We can define a *successful marriage* in a number of ways. One dimension of success is *stability*, or the likelihood that a couple remains married and doesn't divorce. Staying together, as we've seen, benefits couples in terms of health and wealth. A second dimension is the *quality* of the relationship. Are both partners happy or satisfied with their relationship? Do they see their relationship as fair? Although stability and quality are correlated with one another, they aren't the same thing; stable or enduring marriages may not necessarily be happy relationships.

Types of Marriages

Until the 1960s, most marriages were defined as *happy* as long as they didn't end in divorce. This, however, doesn't make sense, because it's likely that some very unhappy people stay married for one reason or another—children, jobs, religious beliefs, or a lack of alternatives. Recognizing the inadequacy of this definition, Cuber and Haroff (1965) developed a typology of different marriage styles by studying 400 marriages. The partners ranged between the ages of 35 and 55 and most had been married for many years. The researchers found several different types of long-term marriages, and although couples may have no intention of ever divorcing, *happy* can mean very different things to different people:

conflict-habituated marriage: A type of marriage that includes frequent conflict, although it may be enduring.

devitalized marriage: An enduring marriage that exists without much passion.

- **Conflict-habituated marriage:** This type of marriage is filled with tension and verbal and perhaps, physical, conflict, but the partners don't feel these are reasons to divorce. They believe fighting is a normal part of marriage and is an acceptable way to communicate and solve problems.

- **Devitalized marriage:** Although the couple may have been in love when they married, their relationship now exists without much passion. They spend time together, but from obligation or habit (for their children, jobs, or community) rather than for the joy of being together.

- **Passive-congenial marriage:** These partners may have married with low expectations of the intimacy marriage would provide, and their expectations have remained low. There is little conflict in these marriages but also little excitement; however, excitement was never expected.

- **Vital marriage:** The lives of the partners are intertwined in this type of marriage. Both physical and emotional intimacies are important to them, and they work hard at communication and compromise so their relationship continues to be satisfying and enjoyable.

Conflict-habituated marriages are filled with tension and conflict. Partners believe that fighting is a normal part of marriage and is an acceptable way to communicate and solve problems.

- **Total marriage:** As in vital marriages, these partners have considerable energy invested in each other and their marriage is a priority. They share additional facets of their lives, however; perhaps they own a business together, have the same friends, or spend time on the same hobbies. They have few independent interests.

These different concepts reveal that marriage can be enduring without necessarily being particularly happy—or at least happy by traditional standards. Cuber and Haroff (1965) found 80 percent of the relationships in the study were in one of the first three categories. These marriages may come up short of conventional definitions of "happy," but the spouses consider them "good enough" with no real reason to end them.

Measuring Marital Satisfaction

Just as there are many different types of marriages, there are many different ways to measure satisfaction in marriage. These range from detailed evaluations about the relationship and interaction patterns to a single-item measure such as, "Would you say you are very happy, somewhat happy, somewhat unhappy, or very unhappy with your marriage?" Studies may also be cross-sectional (a snapshot in time) or longitudinal (following people over time to better capture the dynamic nature of marriage). Because of these different ways of measuring marital satisfaction, we shouldn't be surprised to find that research has produced some mixed results on what makes a satisfying and enduring marriage.

Nonetheless, one recent poll found that 75 percent said they're happy with their marriage at least three-quarters of the time. About 15 percent said they're happy at least half the time. Just 5 percent said they're never happy in their marriages (Kimball, 2013). Another survey reported that 64 percent of men and 60 percent of women said their marriages are "very happy" (Popenoe, 2007). Longitudinal data allow us to see the changing level of satisfaction with marriage over the life course as people experience the initial year of marriage, have children, raise teenagers, launch children into adulthood, or retire from work (Glenn, 1998; VanLaningham, Johnson, & Amato, 2001). Most marriages start out quite happy, but satisfaction begins to decline early. As the marriage continues, many transitions foster the decline in satisfaction—children are born and therefore responsibilities increase and bills may mount. The couples' relationship may become more routine and utilitarian. However, as a couple ages and children grow up and leave home, marital satisfaction rises again, although it doesn't approach the high level at the beginning of the marriage.

passive–congenial marriage: An enduring marriage that includes little conflict but also little excitement.

vital marriage: A type of marriage in which the lives of partners are intertwined; physical and emotional intimacy are important, and both work hard at communication and compromise so their relationship continues to be satisfying and enjoyable.

total marriage: A type of marriage in which spouses share many facets of their lives such as a business they own, friends, or hobbies with few independent interests.

What Makes a Successful Marriage?

Unfortunately, there's no guaranteed 12-step program for how to have a happy marriage. A study asked more than 2,000 adults to evaluate the importance of several factors to marital success, and as you can see in Figure 7.6, "Faithfulness" was most likely to be rated as "very important for a successful marriage." Next came a happy sexual relationship, followed by sharing household chores (Pew Research Center, July 1, 2007).

Underlying Figure 7.6 are some interesting differences by race and ethnicity. Whites stand apart because, other than "Faithfulness," they're less likely to rate various components of marital success as very important. For example, they're less likely to rate having a happy sexual relationship, sharing household chores, having an adequate income, having good housing, sharing religious beliefs, having similar tastes and interests, having children, and agreeing on political issues as very important. Blacks and Hispanics are remarkably similar in their evaluation of a successful marriage with two exceptions: Blacks are most likely to rate good housing as very important, and Hispanics are most likely to rate having children similarly.

Other factors associated with happy and successful marriages include the backgrounds and characteristics people bring to marriage, the transitions they experience, and the way couples communicate and spend time together. Some of the factors people bring to relationships include the following:

- *Type of relationship with parents:* The relationship children have with their parents influences the relationship they develop with their spouses. Recall the discussion of attachments in Chapter 4—the type of attachment formed

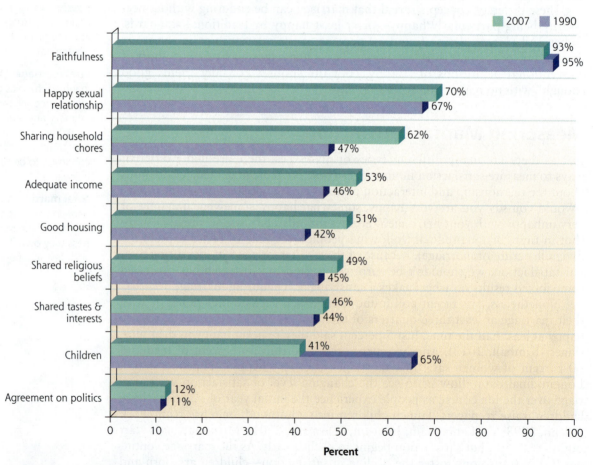

FIGURE 7.6

Percentage Saying Each Is Important to a Successful Marriage

Children are considered much less important to a successful marriage than in the past.
Source: Pew Research Center, July 1, 2007.

between parents and their children carries forward into the children's relationships with others later in life. Marital quality is enhanced when spouses recall having secure attachments rather than avoidant or anxious attachment styles with their parents.

- *Quality and stability of parents' marriage:* Individuals whose parents have happy and stable marriages are more likely to have happy and enduring marriages themselves. Adult children model their own parents' behavior, both positive and negative. Parents who have strong communication skills, who value commitment in their marriage, or who believe physical or verbal abuse is an appropriate way to settle an argument, model these behaviors for their own children.

- *Shared values, goals, and characteristics:* Spouses with similar values and goals—like shared views about spending, child-rearing, religion, or the integration of work and family—are more likely to have happy and enduring marriages. Similar personality traits are important as well (Partenheimer, 2005). One study found that people are attracted to mates with similar values, but once in a committed relationship and dealing with the challenges of daily life, personality factors, such as degree of extroversion or introversion, or the degree to which a person is fearful or secure, become at least as or even more important (Shanhong & Klohnen, 2005).

What makes a happy marriage? One factor is shared religious faith and practice.

📖 **Read** on **MySocLab**
Document: *Religion and the Domestication of Man*

- *Religious faith and practice:* People who are more religious, regardless of their age, sex, income, or the age at which they married, report higher levels of marital satisfaction and commitment to their partners, and fewer negative interactions (Pew Forum on Religion & Public Life, June 2009). For example, one survey found that, among people who attend religious service at least once per week, 73 percent report being very happy with their marriages, compared to 52 percent of persons who never or almost never attend service (Johnson, Stanley, Glenn, Amato, Nock, Markman, & Dion, 2002). Couples who are religious are also less likely to think of divorce as an option to deal with an unhappy relationship (Proulx, Helms, & Buehler, 2007).

- *Frequency and satisfaction with sexual relationship:* Sexual activity obviously influences the quality of the relationship. Couples who report having regular or frequent sex, and who report enjoying their sex life, are more likely to evaluate their marriages as satisfying (AARP, 2005; Goodwin, 2009; Holmberg, Blair, & Phillips, 2010). For example, a study of women in both heterosexual and lesbian long-term relationships found that sexual satisfaction was linked to stronger relationship well-being and mental health for both types of couples (Holmberg, Blair, & Phillips, 2010).

- *Satisfaction with gender relations and the division of household labor:* Couples who have more egalitarian attitudes about sex and gender, especially men, tend to report greater satisfaction with their marriages (Helms, Proulx, Klute, McHale, & Crouter, 2006; Kaufman & Taniguchi, 2006). Marital satisfaction is higher among couples who share housework. When women perceive that the division of housework or childcare is unfair and they feel as if they're doing more than they should, conflict increases and their marital satisfaction declines (Weigel, 2007).

The *My Family* feature box tells the story of one couple's long-lasting marriage. How many of the factors just discussed can you identify in their marriage?

No one knows exactly why some marriages end after one year and why others last for more than sixty years. Having shared values and similar interests is certainly a good start.

Who would have thought that a blind date would lead to 66 years of marriage? Introduced in 1946 while Bill was in the U.S. Navy stationed in Portland, Bill and Bernadine simply planned to go on a "double date" to a friend's party. "Come on," Bernadine's twin sister said, "we'll meet them there. It'll be fun." No one had marriage on their mind that evening.

But fate has a way of intervening. *"We danced, and talked; he's quiet so I kept asking him questions. I thought he was so cute, and I liked him, but he was a sailor, and I thought, 'Oh well, here today, gone tomorrow.'"*

Eighteen-year-old Bernadine and 19-year-old Bill, just out of high school, decidedly hit it off. He remained stationed in Portland, and became a regular sight in the Polish, working-class neighborhood as he walked the three-mile route from the Navy base to Bernadine's family's house in inner Portland. They played cards with Bernadine's older sisters and their husbands, took the bus to the movies, shared family meals, and he helped her widowed mother with repairs around the house. Bill became well known in her tight-knit ethnic neighborhood. He was neither Polish nor Catholic, which were two potential strikes against him, but he won over Bernadine, her family, the Polish community, and eventually the parish priest who married them. Bernadine's priest first tried to talk her out of marriage because Bill wasn't Catholic. *"I cried and told the priest, 'He's a good man and I'm going to marry him.' Then, after spending some time with Bill, he agreed with me. So then the advice was 'The man is the boss of the family.'"*

Like others of that era, Bernadine and Bill married young. Within 9 months of their first date they were engaged, and 9 months after their engagement they wed in the neighborhood Polish Catholic church in January 1948, after World War II had ended. And like other young couples in their generation, they had children quickly. Bernadine had two children by the time she was 21, and four children by 27. Not long after they married, Bill converted to Catholicism, which is an important bond they continue to share today.

Today, 66 years later, with four children, eight grandchildren, and four great-grandchildren, they remain happily married. Like all families, they've weathered a few storms. *"Sure, we've had our disagreements. Who hasn't?"* Bernadine says. *"Marriage isn't healthy unless you have a few scrapes. You have to let it out and talk about it. But we get along and like the same things. Not everything of course—I'm not into fishing,"* she laughs, knowing that she loves to eat what Bill catches. *"We enjoy our own company."*

Would she still say that the man is the boss of the family? *"Well, not exactly,"* she winked.

WHAT DO YOU THINK?

1. Have marriage and its expectations changed over the course of the last 66 years?
2. Have you known anyone who has been married this long? Do you know the secrets to their longevity?

👁 **Watch on MySocLab**
Video: *Leroy and Geneva*

7.7 Summarize the marriage movement and covenant marriage

Question That Matters

7.12 What is the *marriage movement*?

The Marriage Movement and Covenant Marriage

Concerned about the challenges of creating and maintaining successful marriages today, some government officials, marriage and family therapists, and religious leaders have created a **marriage movement** that aims to influence public policy to promote and strengthen traditional two-parent marriage. The movement contains a broad agenda, including

- reducing unmarried pregnancy
- increasing the likelihood that unmarried couples expecting a baby will marry before the child's birth
- reducing or preventing excessive conflict among married couples
- reducing divorce
- protecting the boundaries of marriage by distinguishing it from other family and friendship units, including cohabiting ones
- transmitting and reinforcing shared norms of responsible marital behavior such as encouraging permanence, fidelity, financial responsibility, and mutual support
- communicating the benefits of and preference for marriage as the ideal family form, particularly to young people (The Marriage Movement, 2004)

The marriage movement believes the decline of traditional marriage is responsible for many social problems that cost taxpayers, such as poverty, crime, and delinquency. As a solution, they suggest that the government should use taxpayer money to promote traditional marriage. The movement was further advanced by former President George W. Bush, who pledged $1.5 billion to a "Healthy Marriage Initiative" during his presidency to impart the values, attitudes, and skills to encourage unmarried couples to enter marriage and married couples to maintain their vows. Much of that money was taken from cash welfare programs for low-income single parents, and shifted to marriage education programs.

marriage movement: The activities of some religious and government leaders, as well as marriage and family therapists, who hope to influence public policy to promote and strengthen traditional marriage.

Watch on **MySocLab**
Video: *PBS FRONTLINE: Let's Get Married*

Policy and You: From Macro to Micro — Covenant Marriage

When Samantha and Joey married 6 years ago, they chose to have a covenant marriage—a special type of marriage that requires premarital counseling and makes it much more difficult to get a divorce—one that reflects their deep commitment to each other and their Christian faith. *"We believe that God designed marriage as a covenant, and our commitment to one another goes far beyond traditional marriage vows,"* said Samantha.

Covenant marriage is only available in a few states, and even within those states, the number of couples who choose a covenant marriage is quite small; for example, only 5 percent of couples in Louisiana opt for covenant marriage. This didn't deter Samantha and Joey, who believe that covenant marriage has given them a degree of security and certainty that only strengthens their bond, *"We know life's every day challenges won't do us in because divorce just isn't an option for us. We rely on our faith, on God, and one another for things to work."*
The specific components of covenant marriage include:

- Some type of marriage preparation
- A full disclosure of all information that could reasonably affect the decision to marry
- An oath of lifelong commitment to marriage
- Acceptance of limited grounds for divorce, such as abuse, adultery, addiction, felony imprisonment, or separation for 2 years
- Marital counseling if problems threaten the marriage

Court clerks who issue marriage licenses in the three states that offer covenant marriage are supposed to tell couples about the option as they apply for their licenses. Few couples elect covenant marriage and those who have done so tend to be more religious and more politically conservative than average. A study of attitudes about covenant marriage reveals that some parts of covenant marriage are more popular than others. For example, whereas a majority of those surveyed agreed it's a good idea for couples to get counseling before marriage and be willing to seek it if trouble arises, less popular were waiting periods or other restricting mechanisms for divorce.

Covenant marriage provides a clear example of the interplay between macro- and micro-level factors in marriage. Our personal choices depend on the laws and policies available to us.

WHAT DO YOU THINK?

1. If you lived in a state that allowed for covenant marriage, would you consider it? Why or why not?
2. Do you think that covenant marriage appeals more to couples who are religious?

Source: From Brown, 2008; Hawkins, Nock, Wilson, Sanchez, & Wright, 2002; Nock, Wright, & Sanchez, 1999.

covenant marriage: A type of voluntarily chosen marriage available in three states that restricts access to divorce, requires premarital counseling, and imposes other rules and regulations.

The marriage movement has been widely criticized, however, as ill-conceived, ineffectual, anti-gay, and a means for using public money to empower and fund religious organizations (Furstenberg, 2007). Moreover, critics believe that many social problems result from the lack of social and government support for families in all their forms, rather than from the decline of traditional marriage *per se* (Coontz, 2006; Mintz, 2003; Furstenberg, 2007). "Fixing" marriages and families, the critics say, should focus on appreciating *all* family forms by providing the assistance they need, such as a living wage, health insurance, and subsidized childcare.

Although many supporters of the marriage movement come from religious communities, the initiative has also produced political change. In three states—Arizona, Arkansas, and Louisiana—**covenant marriage** is now legal. This type of marriage is different from standard marriage in that it specifies a unique set of legal standards in addition to those already in place in state law (Covenant Marriage Movement, 2013; Nock, Sanchez, & Wright, 2008). As shown in the feature box *From Macro to Micro: Covenant Marriage*, the standards are designed to increase the level of commitment couples make to each other at the time of marriage and reduce the likelihood of divorce (Brown, 2008; Covenant Marriage Movement, 2008).

*G*iven the health and economic benefits of marriage, do you believe that the government should be involved in promoting marriage? Why or why not?

Finally, let's look at another way that marriage is changing: many husbands and wives are moving toward peer relationships, rather than living in "separate spheres." This means that husbands and wives are increasingly likely to share breadwinning and domestic roles.

7.8 Define peer marriage

Question That Matters

7.13 What is a *peer marriage*?

Peer Marriage

Sociologist Pepper Schwartz was particularly intrigued by what she has termed **peer marriages,** or relationships in which spouses consider themselves to have equal status or standing in the relationship, sharing breadwinning, housework, and childrearing roles (1994; 2001). Schwartz interviewed 57 couples that tried to maintain no less than a 60–40 split on housework, childcare, and financial decision making and compared them with other couples considered "near-peers" or "traditionals." The near-peers believed in equality, but the husband participated in less than 40 percent of domestic tasks. The traditionals were those in which males held more power and authority in the relationship, and both spouses were satisfied with this arrangement.

peer marriage: A type of marriage in which couples consider themselves to have equal status or standing in the relationship.

Schwartz found that peer marriages took a lot of work on the part of both the wife and the husband. Both spouses were likely to have been raised with more traditional notions of sex and gender, and friends, family, and employers continued to reinforce this socialization. Yet the couples had a strong desire to have an egalitarian marriage, and were often willing to forgo the husband's career advancement and income so he could maintain equal involvement at home and his wife could share breadwinning (and domestic chores) with him. Schwartz found these couples needed to continually monitor their behavior and regularly check in with each other to maintain balance.

Schwartz published her work in the early 1990s, and in many ways it's easier to have a peer marriage today. Married couples are becoming increasingly homogamous, with spouses having similar levels of education, occupational status, and income. More husbands want to share the breadwinning role, and, as feminist Gloria Steinem once said, "more women are becoming the men we want to marry" (Paul, 2006, p. 1). Domestic labor and childcare, too, are more widely shared, as we discuss in Chapter 10.

But these progressive shifts have been accompanied by another development: the growing gap between rich and poor families in the United States. Husbands and wives have moved closer together on measures of education and income, but the divide between well-educated, high-earning couples and less-privileged counterparts has grown. This raises a challenging point (Paul, 2006): Are we achieving more egalitarian marriages at a cost of egalitarian society? Again, we can see how the micro-level and macro aspects of marriage and intimacy are intertwined; what occurs in the larger society shapes our intimate relationships.

7.2 Is marriage a personal relationship, a social institution?

It's both. Naturally, it's two people, but two people can marry, and afterwards us afterward

LO7

Bringing It Full Circle

More than 2 million women and men each year say wedding vows; a formal start to what they hope will be a lifetime commitment that remains full of passion, love, and sexual energy. However, marriage isn't just a personal relationship, but a social institution as well. All societies have marriage, but in each, it's unique because of cultural circumstances and social structure. We've also learned that marriage in the United States is changing. Fewer people are married at any given moment today, yet most people want to marry, and eventually most do. Marriage confers health, psychological well-being, and economic benefits, but staying married takes work, including strong communication skills. These include listening and self-disclosure, and we've learned that there are important sex differences in these communication skills. When we say our wedding vows, we probably give little credence to issues about communication or even power differentials in relationships—the love we feel is paramount on our mind. Yet, learning to live together constitutes more than just micro-level individual aspects of our relationships, but reflects broader macro-level influences as well. Let's review what we've learned as we return to the opening vignette describing the marriage of Scherazade and Roderick:

- Speculate on the ways that the marriage premium may be operating in Scherazade and Roderick's relationship.

- In thinking about the factors that contribute to successful marriages, which of these factors do Scherazade and Roderick display? Which ones aren't evident in the interview?

- Do you think that Scherazade and Roderick have a peer marriage? What evidence supports your answer? What do you think are the pros and cons of a peer marriage in our society? What cultural values make a peer marriage possible, or unlikely?

On MySocLab

 **Study and Review on MySocLab**

CHAPTER REVIEW

LO7.1 Discuss the universal nature of marriage

7.1 Is marriage found in every society?

Yes, but its structure may be very different. In mainstream U.S. culture, for example, we have a relatively free mate-selection choice, and we marry for love. Other societies may think these are poor ways to structure a lasting or satisfying marriage.

relationship or a social

...s a personal relationship between ...te laws and regulations tell us who ...how we marry, and what's expected of ...ds.

...2   Identify marriage patterns in U.S. history

7.3   How has marriage changed over time?

In colonial America, marriage was established as a monogamous relationship, entered into freely, with the husband as the head of the household. Today, marital relationships are more symmetrical than those of previous generations, with wives providing a greater share of the family income and husbands providing more domestic labor.

LO7.3   Recognize the changing nature of marriage today

7.4   How does the marital decline perspective compare with the marital resilience perspective?

These are the two primary perspectives from which to view marriage today. The marital decline perspective suggests that the value society places on marriage is declining. The marital resilience perspective suggests that marriages have always faced challenges—the real threats to marriage are social problems such as poverty, discrimination, poor schools, and the lack of social services that families need to remain strong and resilient.

7.5   How do we explain the decline in marriage rates?

Although the number of people who are married at any given time has declined, the main reason for the decline is that more people are delaying marriage and more are divorcing, although divorced people usually remarry.

7.6   How do Americans feel about same-sex marriage?

Attitudes toward same-sex marriage have become more accepting over time, and now more people support than oppose same-sex marriage.

7.7   In what ways are attitudes toward marriage changing?

Americans are shifting the way we think about marriage and intimate relationships, and, naturally, this changes the nature of marriage. We are becoming more tolerant of non-marital sex, cohabitation, and non-marital child-bearing, and we are witnessing a change in attitudes about the gendered division of labor. One area that has *not* changed much, however, is the value associated with marriage.

LO7.4   Describe the "marriage premium"

7.8   What is the *marriage premium*?

The marriage premium explains the observation that married people live longer and are happier, healthier, and financially better off than their unmarried counterparts, including cohabiters. Although we can attribute much of this difference to marriage *per se*, it's also likely that people who are happier, healthier, and have more money are more likely to marry in the first place.

7.9   What is a *selection effect*?

We know that married people tend to be happier, healthier, and better off financially. However, does marriage provide these advantages, or do happier, healthier, and wealthier people self-select into marriage? The selection effect suggests that people who marry may be different from those who don't; for example, they may be innately happier, healthier, and have more money.

LO7.5   Identify whether marriage benefits everyone equally

7.10   Does marriage benefit everyone equally?

In general, men benefit more from marriage than women, partly because men are more likely to change their behavior significantly when married, including taking fewer risks. There are racial and ethnic differences in the marriage premium as well, especially in terms of economic well-being.

LO7.6   Discuss marital satisfaction and success

7.11   What factors are associated with marital satisfaction and success?

Although there is no clear formula for a happy marriage, people bring a number of personal background factors and characteristics to marriage, such as their parents' attachment style; whether their parents divorced; the degree to which they share values, goals, interests, and religious faith with their spouse; and their degree of satisfaction with the gendered division of labor. The way couples communicate and spend time together also affects marital satisfaction and success.

LO7.7   Summarize the marriage movement and covenant marriage

7.12   What is the *marriage movement*?

The marriage movement believes the decline of traditional marriage is responsible for many social problems that place a large burden on taxpayers, such as poverty, crime, and delinquency. As a solution, they suggest the government should use taxpayer money to promote traditional marriage. The movement is controversial, and tends to be supported more fully by those who are religious and politically conservative.

LO7.8 Define peer marriage

7.13 What is a *peer marriage*?

Peer marriages involve relationships in which spouses consider themselves to have equal status or standing in the relationship, and equally and fairly share breadwinning, housework, and childrearing roles.

KEY TERMS

antimiscegenation laws
civil union
conflict-habituated marriage
covenant marriage
devitalized marriage
heterogamous marriage
homogamous marriage

interethnic marriage
interracial marriage
marital decline perspective
marital resilience perspective
marriage
marriage movement
marriage premium

passive-congenial marriage
peer marriage
selection effect
social capital
total marriage
vital marriage
wage premium

LEARNING OBJECTIVES

8.1 Interpret population and fertility trends worldwide

8.2 Explain fertility in the United States

8.3 Compare and contrast the costs and rewards of raising children

8.4 Discuss the trend of remaining childfree

8.5 Recognize the interconnection of micro and macro factors influencing childbirth

8.6 Describe adoption as another path to parenthood

8.7 Analyze the transition to parenthood

Tracey and Juan, a happily married couple, wanted children, but couldn't have them. Having no success with infertility treatments, they turned to adoption.

Seeing themselves as members of a global community, they adopted two children from Colombia.

Tracey and Juan dreamed about the time they would be parents. However, like growing numbers of couples they struggled with infertility, and underwent painful and invasive treatments to increase their odds of becoming pregnant. Still having no success, they began to expand their thinking about the issue: Why not adopt? After all, many children are in need of a loving home.

Thousands of American children need families, but that number is small compared to the number of children around the world who need families. Choose any region: China, Eastern Europe, India, Haiti, Africa, or South America, and you'll find parents who are living in the vise-like grips of poverty, succumbing to AIDS, adhering to government policies allowing only one child, or are caught in the ravages of war and unable to take care of their children. Tracey and Juan looked to the world and found their children in Colombia.

👁 **Watch** on **MySocLab**
Video: *Adoption: Tracey and Juan*

Nearly 8,900 children were adopted internationally in 2012; 194 of these children were from Colombia. For Tracey and Juan, it is a natural fit because Juan is originally from Colombia, still has family there, and speaks fluent Spanish. They could teach their children about their native culture, and provide some continuity in their children's lives.

Juan's family in Bogotá steered them to a reputable orphanage from where they first adopted Cassandra. They know very little about Cassandra's birth mother other than that she was very young, poor, had little education, and was overwhelmed caring for multiple children. She surrendered Cassandra to the orphanage at birth; Cassandra was only 2 months old when she joined Juan and Tracey.

Several years later, they adopted John. His story is different; his mother was older, a high-school graduate, and she had only one other child besides John. She vacillated about what to do. She gave him to the orphanage to raise, but didn't immediately relinquish her parental rights. He finally joined Tracey and Juan's family when he was 4 months old.

How has Tracey and Juan's family fared since the adoptions? The children are bright, happy, well adjusted, and display no particular issues associated with spending their first months in an orphanage. The research supports their experience: children adopted young usually adjust very quickly to their new family. Tracey and Juan have also adjusted quickly to their new roles; they see themselves as parents, not simply as "adoptive parents." They treat adoption as a natural part of their family: *"From our standpoint, there is no difference. You give the same amount of love, the same amount of care, the same amount of everything that you would give any child. If there is any difference, it is that these are wanted children, and I know not all biological children are as wanted or as welcome. Our children were anticipated, waited for, and there were great strides taken to get them here. So if there's any significant difference in being adopted, it's that they were truly wanted, and that makes all the difference in the world."*

Most, but not all, adults become parents. How does the process of deciding if, when, and how we will be parents unfold? What kinds of decisions do we make along the way? What types of changes does parenting bring to our lives? This chapter focuses on the decisions surrounding fertility, infertility, and the life-changing process of becoming a parent. You will see that the transition to parenting can be <u>surprisingly challenging</u>, yet tremendously rewarding.

Fundamental changes are occurring today with the value associated with having children. As educational and economic opportunities for young women continue to expand, coupled with the increasing availability of relatively effective birth control and a growing acceptance of singlehood, cohabitation, and divorce, women and men are having fewer children than ever before. People are having children when they are older, and a growing number don't have children at all either by choice or because of infertility, as in the opening vignette with Juan and Tracey.

But before we discuss micro-level issues regarding becoming a parent, let's first look at the larger picture. What are some population and fertility trends around the world? An examination of these worldwide trends sets the stage for what is happening here in the United States.

👁 **Watch** on MySocLab
Video: *Families: Slideshow*

8.1 Interpret population and fertility trends worldwide

Question That Matters

8.1 What are population and fertility trends worldwide?

Population and Fertility Trends Worldwide

The world's population is growing rapidly, but this hasn't always been the case. The population didn't reach 1 billion people until about the year 1800. However, it increased to 1.6 billion only 100 years later. The world's population is a little more than 7 billion in 2013, and is projected to be 9.2 to 9.6 billion by 2050 (Population Reference Bureau, 2013a; Worldwatch Institute, 2013). If the concept of a billion is difficult to comprehend, consider the following:

- If you were 1 billion seconds old, you would be 31.7 years old.
- The circumference of the Earth is 25,000 miles. If you circled the Earth 40,000 times, you would have traveled 1 billion miles.

In some countries, such as Mexico, the size of the population could double in less than 35 years. In others, such as Japan, the population is not expected to double for nearly 500 years (Bremner, Haub, Lee, Mather, & Zuehlke, 2009). Why such a large difference between countries? Population change is linked to many important macro-level issues that affect families, including economic opportunities or constraints, geography, food production and distribution policies, health threats, infant mortality and life expectancy, status of women, and overall quality of life.

Fertility and Mortality Rates: The Keys to Understanding Population Growth

Population statistics such as these reflect two important trends that occur at opposite ends of the lifespan. First, they represent **fertility rates,** which can be reported in different ways to yield somewhat different information:

- *Total fertility rate:* Average number of children born to a woman during her lifetime. This is a direct measure of the level of fertility because it refers to births per woman. This indicator shows the potential for population change in the country. A rate of two children per woman is considered the replacement rate for a population, resulting in relative stability in terms of total numbers. Rates more than two children indicate populations growing in size. This measure allows for useful historical and international comparisons.

- *General fertility rate:* Number of children born per 1,000 women ages 15 through 44 (some countries use 49 as the cut-off age). This refined method allows us to make international or historical comparisons because it relates birth to the age and sex group likely to give birth.

- *Crude fertility rate:* The number of children born per 1,000 population. Note that this doesn't account for the age of the population. Obviously, if the average age of the population is young (e.g., Kenya), there will be more children born than if the average age of the population is old (e.g., Japan).

Globally, the *total fertility rate* (or average number of children born per woman) fell from 5.0 to about 2.5 between 1950 and 2012; however, the fertility rate in developing nations far exceeds the rate in developed nations. In Niger, for example, an average woman bears 7.1 children, whereas in Taiwan she has only 1.1 (Population Reference Bureau, 2013b). In many developing nations, less than a third of married women use contraceptives, including 27 percent in Pakistan and 32 percent in Haiti (Population Reference Bureau, 2013b). Contraceptive use is hindered by such obstacles as inadequate funds for supplies and a lack of comprehensive programs to educate women and their partners on their options. Also, large families are often valued as a means of social security. In reality, large numbers of children are likely to keep families impoverished.

In addition to fertility rates, population statistics also reflect a country's **mortality rates,** or death rates. Countries with high fertility rates (many births) also tend to have high mortality rates (many deaths) because of a lack of medical care and family planning services (e.g., most of Africa). Conversely, countries with the lowest fertility rates also tend to have low mortality rates (e.g., the United States, Canada, Western Europe) (Population Reference Bureau, 2013a).

However, in recent years we observe an important change: Those high mortality rates have begun to decline in the developing world. What has happened in these countries to decrease mortality? More people have benefited from improved vaccinations, sanitation, and modern medicines, and have learned new ways to combat the spread of disease. This is very good news, but these factors also exacerbate population growth because fewer people are now dying. Therefore, when we speak of a population explosion in developing nations, the cause is not just too

fertility rate: A measure reported as: (1) average number of children born to a woman during her lifetime; (2) number of children born per 1,000 women ages 15–44 (some other countries use 49 as the cut-off age); or (3) number of children born per 1,000 population.

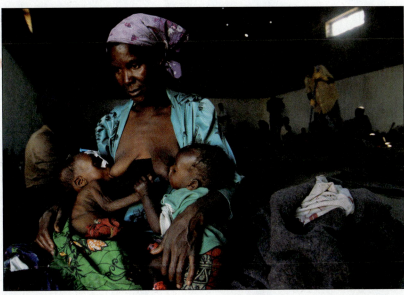

Population trends reflect both fertility (birth) rates and mortality (death) rates. Countries that have high fertility rates tend also to have high mortality rates.

mortality rate (or death rate): A measure of the number of deaths in a population.

If the world's population reaches 8 billion by 2025—in your lifetime—what kind of social, environmental, and economic changes do you think will take place? How will these changes affect families? Will all these changes be bad for families, or will any be good?

many babies being born (and, in fact, most such countries have actually reduced their fertility rates). The cause of spiraling population growth is also declining death rates, especially among infants and children.

The United States is a developed nation with great wealth. It's easy to assume that our fertility patterns don't reflect these kinds of macro-level influences, but that would be incorrect.

Fertility in the United States

Pronatalism

A strong incentive toward having babies exists in just about every part of the world. Although each culture has its own values associated with childbearing and encourages fertility in its own unique way, pronatalism—a cultural value that encourages childbearing—is found virtually everywhere. In the United States, pronatalist values suggest that having children is a normal and natural part of a happy life, and that those who voluntarily remain childfree are selfish, immature, lonely, unfulfilled, insensitive, and more likely to have mental problems than parents are. About 40 percent of adults in one national survey thought it's "better to have a child than to remain childless" (Koropeckyj-Cox & Pendell, 2007b), and another national survey found that 41 percent of adults believed that having children was important for a successful marriage (Livingston & Cohn, 2010). Older adults, men, and persons with lower levels of education were most likely to agree with pronatalist statements. Pronatalism is not just supported by your own parents and grandparents who may be pushing you to have a child; it's also supported by social institutions and policies here and around the world. For example, the Christian Bible exhorts us to "be fruitful and multiply."

Historical Fluctuation

We can observe many interesting patterns within U.S. fertility rates. One is the degree of fluctuation, as shown in Figure 8.1 (Hamilton, Martin, & Ventura, 2012; Martin, Hamilton, Ventura, Osterman, Wilson, & Mathews, 2012). The U.S. birthrate shows remarkable highs and lows, often occurring in quick succession. In 1920, which was a period of relative affluence and limited birth control, the U.S. *general fertility rate* (defined as live births per 1,000 women ages 15–44) hovered around 118 per 1,000 women. Yet, only 15 years later the fertility rate plummeted, bottoming out in 1935 at 77 per 1,000 women. Why would such a steep decline occur in such a short amount of time? Birth control measures were still fairly limited in the 1930s, so this can't be the primary factor.

Such a sharp decline suggests that fertility rates are far more than simply biological phenomena. Personal choices are influenced by macro-level structural conditions and social trends. During the 1930s, the United States fell into a deep economic depression. Because of the dire consequences of this Great Depression,

FIGURE 8.1

Fertility Rates per 1,000 Women Ages 15–44, 1920–2012

Fertility rates were low during the Great Depression, high after World War II, and then declined sharply in the 1960s.
Source: Hamilton, Martin, & Ventura, 2012; Martin, Hamilton, Ventura, Osterman, Wilson, & Mathews, 2012.

fewer people were marrying, others were marrying later, and many families split up to pursue employment. Not surprisingly, the birthrate declined accordingly.

However, a decade later, as the Depression was ending and the United States moved into and out of World War II, the birthrate rose to a level not seen for decades. By 1960, the fertility rate increased to 118 per 1,000 women ages 15 through 44, a period that has since been described as the *Baby Boom*. A look at macro-level economic trends helps explain this growth: The United States experienced a degree of affluence after the war; therefore, couples married younger and the number of employed married women working outside the home declined. Women were encouraged to find fulfillment as shown in a content analysis of the articles and advertisements in "women's magazines" (Friedan, 1963). Family, and particularly motherhood, became a primary cultural goal.

Yet, by the middle of the 1960s, the fertility rate began to drop significantly once again. This period is sometimes called the Baby Bust, and rates have fluctuated very little since then (Hamilton, Martin, & Ventura, 2012). Many macro-level reasons explain this rapid decline in fertility rates. One demographic explanation is that the number of women of childbearing age was lower in the 1970s as a result of the declining birthrates during the Great Depression, which generally translates into fewer children being born. Other reasons for the decline in fertility rates are more social in origin and represent changing attitudes about women's social and family roles. More women began going to college, including graduate and professional schools, and gained employment in new fields. Likewise, the number of married women employed outside the home increased. Women saw that additional options were available to them, so many chose to delay childbearing or not to have children at all.

Today's fertility rates differ across racial and ethnic groups in the United States, as illustrated in Figure 8.2 (Hamilton, Martin, & Ventura, 2012). American Indian/Alaska Natives have the fewest children on average (47 births per 1,000 women ages 15–44, respectively); Hispanics have the highest fertility rate at nearly 74 births per 1,000 women. Again, these differences likely reflect macro-level issues, including cultural and economic considerations. For example, Hispanics are more likely to be Roman Catholic, and the church frowns upon the use of birth control. Hispanics also celebrate large families more so than do other groups.

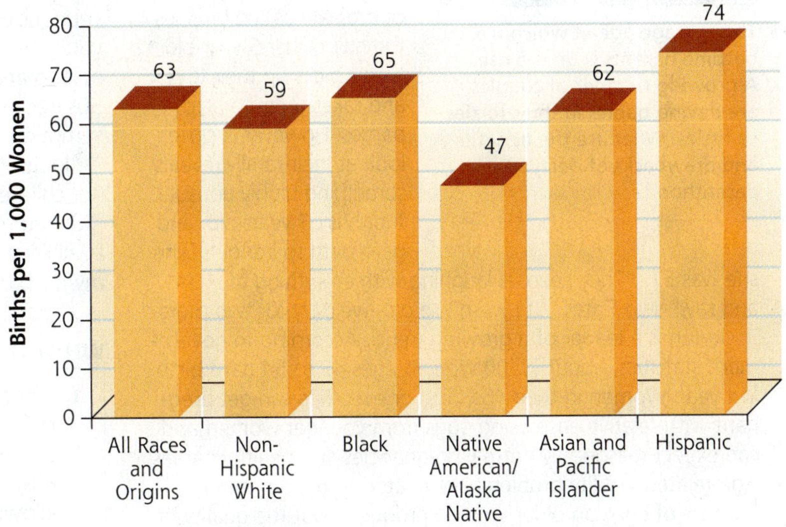

FIGURE 8.2

Fertility Rate by Race and Ethnicity, 2012

Hispanic groups have the highest fertility rates, and non-Hispanic Whites have the lowest.
Source: Hamilton, Martin, & Ventura, 2012.

Delayed Parenthood

Another interesting and more recent pattern is that women and men are delaying the age at which they have their first child. In 1970, the average age at which women had their first birth was around 21, but today it's 25.4 years (Martin, Hamilton, Ventura, Osterman, Wilson, & Matthews, 2012). The average age varies across racial and ethnic groups, with Asian women likely to have their first baby around age 29, whereas Native American women are around age 22. This overall change from 21 to 25.4 may not sound like a huge increase, but it's more important than you may realize. Perhaps another way of seeing the change is this: About 27 percent of women ages 30 through 34 don't have children today, compared to only 16 percent of women in the same age group in 1976 (U.S. Census Bureau, September 9, 2008). (The Census Bureau doesn't

The average age at which we become parents is on the rise. A growing number of couples are having babies in their forties or fifties. What are the benefits and drawbacks of delayed parenthood?

Much public concern exists about teenagers being too young to have a baby, but when is a person *too old* to have a baby? Biology used to answer that question, at least for women. With the onset of perimenopause, few women conceive naturally after their early 40s. But modern technology has changed this, and with the help of donor eggs, women can now have children considerably later in life.

At first glance, Judith Cates' life seems the picture of ordinary as she brushes the hair of her 5-year-old twins, picks up their toys, and takes them to pizza parties. However, a closer look at their family reveals something highly unusual. Judith is 63 years old, and gave birth to her girls when she was 57. "They keep us laughing with everything they do and say," said Cates. "If I wasn't so old, we'd try for two more."

Judith is a leader of a growing trend. According to government statistics, about 7,500 women ages 45 to 54 gave birth last year. Women in their 40s, 50s, or even 60s can get pregnant with relative ease using eggs from younger women and can expect reasonably normal pregnancies and healthy babies. Age-related fertility problems are related to the declining number of eggs an older woman produces, not the quality or condition of her uterus. Researchers tracked the fates of 77 women ages 50 to 63 who underwent in-vitro fertilization with donor eggs over a 10-year period. The women received, on average, three to four embryos each. Forty-two of the 77 women had live births—including three who each had two consecutive births—for a total of 45 births producing 61 babies (31 single children, 12 sets of twins, and 2 sets of triplets), all of them healthy. Some complications such as pregnancy-related high blood pressure do increase with age, but there's no definitive medical reason for excluding these women from attempting pregnancy on the basis of age alone.

Helping women in their 50s become pregnant has been controversial. The ethics committee of the American Society of Reproductive Medicine has concluded that the practice is not unethical, but should be discouraged. Others have echoed that view, warning against widely promoting the practice. "Just because you can do something doesn't mean you should," said Robert Stillman, medical director of the Shady Grove Fertility Reproductive Science Center in Rockville, Maryland. The Center has refused to treat women older than 50, the average age of menopause. However, there are no restrictions on men's ages for fertility treatment.

Furthering the debate is the research that shows that older women and men often make excellent parents. Brian Powell, a sociology professor at Indiana University, noted in a study of 30,000 households that people who had children in their 40s were better off financially, spent more time with their children, and had a closer connection to their children's friends than younger parents. He summarized his research with, "The older you were as a parent, the better off the child." Powell was not able to analyze the results of parents who had children in their 50s because statistically there are so few of them, but the presumption is that the findings would be consistent.

Judith Cates doesn't worry about her age difference with her children or worry that she will die when they are young. "My mom lived to be 83. It was a wonderful life. I pray to God I will live to her age and have that much time with my girls and my husband. That's something nobody knows," Cates replied.

WHAT DO YOU THINK?

1. Some people claim that it is unethical or inappropriate to help women in their 50s or 60s have babies. What arguments can you make for and against a 50- to 60-year-old woman having a successful pregnancy by allowing her to use donor eggs? Do you think that these people would make the same argument against men in their 50s or 60s fathering babies? Why or why not?

2. A number of famous older men in recent years have fathered children while in their 50s and 60s, including Paul McCartney, Michael Douglas, Hugh Hefner, and Larry King. Have they (or their younger wives) experienced stigma because of their age? What if the reverse occurred—a 55-year-old woman had a baby with her 35-year-old husband? Is there a double standard?

Sources: Hamilton, Martin, & Ventura, 2012; Hefling, 2004; Weiss, 2002.

keep equivalent data on men.) It's likely that many of these women will eventually have one or more children; they're simply postponing the age at which they have them.

Delayed parenthood is, again, more than just a biological phenomenon. The reasons for later parenthood are often social in nature (e.g., women wanting to pursue education or careers; the rise in the number of second marriages). In other countries, including the Netherlands, Japan, and Switzerland, the average age of a first-time mother is over 29 (Vienna Institute of Demography, 2008).

A small but growing number of women are having their first child in their late 40s or even 50s. According to national government statistics, 571 women older than age of 50 gave birth in 2010 (Martin, Hamilton, Ventura, Osterman, Wilson, & Mathews, 2012). This delayed fertility takes on an interesting twist depending on the sex of the parent, as shown in the *Diversity in Families* feature box (p. 226). Although most people aren't particularly concerned when a man becomes a father at age 50, the sentiment seems to be quite different if a woman wants to become a mother at the same age.

This section has shown that more than just personal choice affects how many babies are born. Now that we've explored the "big picture," let's look specifically at people who have children. In the next section, we examine the costs and rewards associated with children.

__W__hat fertility trends do you expect in the next few decades? For example, do you think that the age at which women have babies will rise, decline, or stay about the same as it is today? What about the number of children? If you expect to see some changes, can you explain why they will occur?

The Costs and Rewards of Raising Children

8.3	Compare and contrast the costs and rewards of raising children

Questions That Matter

8.5 What are some of the costs associated with having children?

8.6 What are some of the benefits associated with having children?

There are two contrasting pictures of how children affect the lives of adults. One picture is very positive, emphasizing the emotional rewards. The other picture, in contrast, negatively emphasizes the emotional or financial costs. For many people, reality is a complex mixture of these pictures (Umberson, Pudrovska, & Reczek, 2010). Let's first discuss the costs of raising children.

Economic and Opportunity Costs

Raising children is costly in more than just economic terms. Parents experience more stress, have lower psychological well-being, and face greater declines in intimacy with their partner, compared to those couples without children (Doss, Rhoades, Stanley, & Markham, 2009; Evenson & Simon, 2006; Gorchoff, John, & Helson, 2008). And then, there's the economic cost.

Economists often talk about **direct financial costs** (i.e., out-of-pocket expenses for things such as food, clothing, housing, and education) and **opportunity costs** (e.g., lost opportunities for income by working only part-time or not at all because of children). In many developing nations, children are a valuable source of labor. However, in developed nations like the United States, the cost of children is an important explanation of the decline in fertility rates. The U.S. Department of Agriculture estimates that it will cost middle-income families $301,970 for food, clothing, shelter, and other goods and services for a child born in 2012 until his or her 18th birthday (Lino, 2013). Remember, this is only *one* child. And it doesn't include college tuition, room, and board, which averages about $16,000 at a *public* university during the academic year (U.S. Department of Education, National Center for Education Statistics, 2012).

What exactly costs so much money? Figure 8.3 shows the average expenses for a typical American two-parent family with two children (estimates are for the youngest child). Housing is the largest category of costs, at roughly 30 percent (Lino, 2013).

With a financial picture such as this, one might wonder why anyone would want children at all! What are the rewards of being a parent?

direct financial costs: Out-of-pocket expenses for things such as food, clothing, housing, and education.

opportunity costs: Lost opportunities for income by working only part-time or not at all because of children.

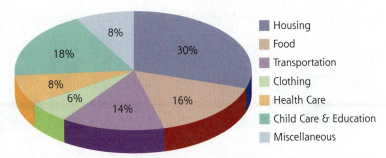

Housing
Food
Transportation
Clothing
Health Care
Child Care & Education
Miscellaneous

FIGURE 8.3

Expenditure Shares on a Child from Birth through Age 17 as a Percentage of Total Child Rearing Expenditures, 2012

Families spend approximately half of their expenses associated with children on two items: housing and food. *Source:* Lino, 2013.

The Rewards of Parenting

Perhaps one reason studies conclude that the costs outweigh the rewards of parenthood is that the rewards are subjective and more difficult to measure. The

Watch on **MySocLab**

Video: *Florence Denmark: Multiple Roles of Women*

emotional feelings of love and devotion toward children are harder to quantify. Children can bring tremendous joy and purpose into the lives of their parents. A nationwide Gallup Poll asked parents about what they gained the most from having children. Common responses included "Children bring love and affection"; "It is a pleasure to watch them grow"; "They bring joy, happiness, and fun"; "They create a sense of family"; and "They bring fulfillment and a sense of satisfaction" (Gallup, 2001). Many parents feel a great deal of satisfaction and pride in seeing their child's accomplishments—excelling in the school spelling bee, singing in the choir, giving a first violin recital, scoring a first goal on the soccer pitch—and parents do take some measure of credit for their child's success.

A study by the Pew Charitable Trust asked people where they find the most fulfillment in their lives. Eighty-five percent of parents said the relationship with their minor children was most fulfilling, whereas only 23 percent with jobs or careers evaluated those as most fulfilling (Pew Research Center, July 1, 2007).

Another area of parental reward that has received attention is the degree to which children connect parents socially with others. Research shows that parents are more socially integrated than are adults without children (Gallagher & Gerstel, 2001; Nomaguchi & Milkie, 2003). Children provide parents with opportunities to interact in new ways with relatives, neighbors, and friends. Children also provide parental links to social institutions such as churches or schools, thereby providing further opportunities to develop relationships.

*W*hat do you think are the costs and benefits of having children for you personally? Do you think differences exist across sex, social class, racial, or ethnic groups in perceived costs and benefits? If so, can you explain why?

In weighing the costs and rewards, a record number of adults are deciding that the costs associated with children outweigh the rewards; others are finding that they can't become pregnant. The next section reviews what we know about those adults who remain childfree.

8.4 Discuss the trend of remaining childfree

Questions That Matter

8.7 How serious a problem is infertility?

8.8 Why are more couples choosing to remain childfree today?

Remaining Childfree

According to U.S. Census Bureau data, about 16 percent of women between the ages of 40 and 44 do not have children (Figure 8.4) (Livingston & Cohn, 2010; Martinez, Daniels, & Chandra, April 12, 2012). It's possible that a few of these women may have children during this period, or even after age 44, but most won't. At first glance, the high number of childfree women seems a radical societal change that our country isn't completely comfortable with (Livingston & Cohn, 2010). A look through history, however, reveals other time periods with similar or even higher rates of childlessness. For example, recall from earlier in the chapter that during the Great Depression of the 1930s, about 25 percent of women in their childbearing years didn't have children, many by choice (Grabill, Kiser, & Whelpton, 1958).

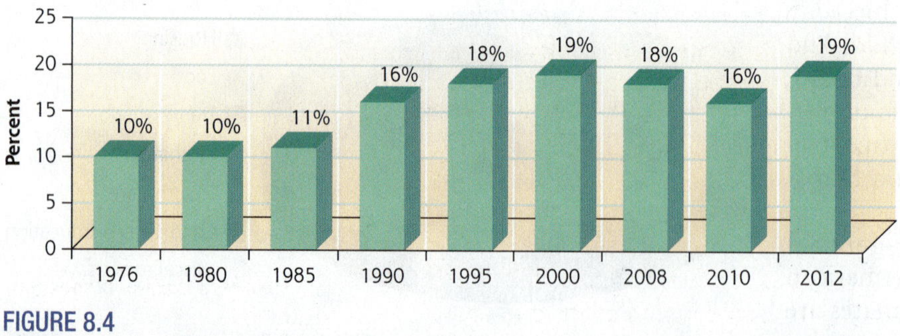

Who's most likely to be childfree today? Women who don't have children are a diverse group; yet, overall they tend to be among the most highly educated, having completed college or graduate school (Koropeckyj-Cox & Call, 2007; Livingston & Cohn, 2010). However, this is beginning to change a bit—although the likelihood of remaining childfree is rising among all women, the rate is dropping among those with advanced degrees. In the early 1990s, about one-third of women ages 40 through 44 with doctoral or other professional degrees didn't have children; today, that figure has dropped to just under one-quarter. The childfree women tend to live in central cities and metropolitan areas. Blacks and Whites are most likely to be childfree; Hispanics are least likely (Dye, 2008).

FIGURE 8.4

Percentage of Women Age 40–44 Who Do Not Have Children, 1976–2012

One in six women between the ages of 40 and 44 do not have children. Although some of these women may have children eventually, most will not. *Sources:* Livingston & Cohn, 2010; Martinez, Daniels, & Chandra, 2012.

People have different reasons for remaining childfree (Koropeckyj-Cox, 2002). Some are childfree because of longstanding infertility or postponed childbearing until age-related infertility prohibited it; others chose to remain childfree voluntarily. Let's look at these different childfree groups.

Infertility

Not all individuals without children are childfree by choice. For many people—more than 7 million—the dream of having a child is not easily realized, as shown by Tracey and Juan in the opening vignette. **Infertility** is the inability to get pregnant after 1 year of trying (Centers for Disease Control and Prevention [CDC], February 12, 2013). It's a medical problem that affects about 12 percent of adults of childbearing age in the United States and occurs in all income groups and racial and ethnic categories. It affects men and women equally; roughly 30 percent of infertility difficulties can be attributed to a problem with the woman, 30 percent with the man, and in the remaining cases, it results from problems with both partners or from indeterminate causes (Resolve: The National Infertility Association, 2013). Infertility services include medical tests to diagnose infertility, medical advice, and treatments to help a woman become pregnant, and services other than routine prenatal care to prevent miscarriage.

MEDICAL TREATMENT   Many treatment options are available to women and men trying to conceive a child from hormone treatments, sperm treatments and insemination, to more advanced technologies such as in vitro fertilization (IVF) (with or without egg or sperm donation, or both) and surrogacy. **Assisted reproductive technology (ART)** includes all fertility treatments in which both egg and sperm are handled. IVF is by far the most common form of ART, making up about 99 percent of procedures. During IVF, a woman uses ovulation-stimulating drugs to produce an excess number of eggs. These eggs are then surgically removed and fertilized in a dish with sperm. If fertilization takes place, the physician implants the embryo(s) into the woman's uterus. Sometimes eggs from a donor are used instead of those from the woman herself.

IVF was first performed successfully in 1978 and resulted in the birth of Louise Brown on July 25, 1978. The world reacted as if she, and IVF, were a creation of science fiction. Children born from IVF were referred to as *test tube babies*. However, given the widespread desire among infertile couples to have children and advancing ART technologies, much has changed.

Approximately 138,000 ART cycles were conducted in 2010, including about 12 percent that used embryos from donor eggs. Between one-quarter and one-third of these cycles resulted in a birth—in other words, it averages about three or four attempts to have a successful birth (CDC, January 6, 2012). Success rates, however, differ by a woman's age, as shown in Table 8.1, whether the embryos were fresh or frozen, and whether they belonged to the woman herself or were from a donor. This procedure can be extremely expensive, costing more than $12,000 per cycle. Many insurance companies only partially cover costs, and some insurers won't cover ART at all (American Society for Reproductive Medicine, 2013).

Many issues surrounding ART are controversial. For example, how many embryos can or should be implanted at one time? No U.S. laws address this question, but the American Society for Reproductive Medicine recommends implantation of no more than two embryos. However, some doctors implant more, either because of parental wishes or to increase the clinic's "success rate." This can result in multiple births, occurring in about one-quarter of ART treatments, which can endanger the lives of both mother and embryos (CDC, January 6, 2012). In some cases, doctors implant a very large number of embryos, sometimes resulting in shocking numbers of fetuses. Couples must then resort to selective abortion to increase the odds that at least one or two babies will survive, or take their chances with multiple births. This was the case with Nadya Suleman, the so-called Octomom, who bore eight children from fertility treatments (after already having six older children).

assisted reproductive technology (ART): All fertility treatments in which either egg or sperm (or both) are handled.

👁 **Watch** on **MySocLab**
Video: *New Reproductive Technologies and Family*

TABLE 8.1 Pregnancy Success Rates

As women age, in vitro fertilization is less effective.

Type of Cycle	Age of Women					
Fresh Embryos from Non-donor Eggs	**< 35**	**35–37**	**38–40**	**41–42**	**43–44**	**> 44**
Number of cycles	41,744	21,369	21,741	10,122	4,501	1,347
Percentage of cycles resulting in pregnancies	48	39	30	20	11	3
Percentage of cycles resulting in live births	42	32	22	12	5	1
Average number of embryos transferred	2.0	2.2	2.6	3.0	3.2	2.7
Percentage of pregnancies with twins	33	27	22	15	8	2
Percentage of pregnancies with triplets or more	2.6	3.1	3.7	3.0	0.6	2.3
Frozen Embryos from Non-donor Eggs	**< 35**	**35–37**	**38–40**	**41–42**	**43–44**	**> 44**
Number of transfers	12,631	6,195	4,682	1,591	710	432
Percentage of transfers resulting in live births	38	35	28	22	17	13
Average number of embryos transferred	2.0	1.9	2.1	2.2	2.2	2.0

Source: Centers for Disease Control and Prevention, April 4, 2013.

Another controversial issue is what happens to unused embryos. Should they be destroyed? Should they be donated to science? Should they be given or sold to other infertile couples? These are important ethical questions for which our society is only beginning to explore the answers.

surrogacy: The act of giving birth to a child for another person or a couple who then adopts or takes legal custody of the child.

Many assisted reproduction technology (ART) procedures are controversial. For example, how many embryos should be implanted at one time? Nadya Suleman bore eight children, after already having six others.

SURROGACY   Because of the high risk of ART failure and its controversies, or repeated miscarriages, some people instead turn to **surrogacy,** which involves a relationship in which one woman gives birth to a child for another person or a couple who then adopts or takes legal custody of the child. One woman acts as a surrogate, or replacement mother for another woman, sometimes called the *intended mother,* who either cannot produce fertile eggs or cannot carry a full-term pregnancy.

Surrogate mothering can be accomplished in many ways. Most often, the husband's sperm is implanted in the surrogate by a procedure called *artificial insemination.* In this case, the surrogate mother is both the genetic mother and the birth (or gestational) mother of the child. This method is sometimes called **traditional surrogacy.** At other times, when the intended mother can produce fertile eggs but can't carry a child to term, the intended mother's egg is removed, combined with the husband's or another man's sperm in IVF, and implanted in the surrogate mother. This method is called **gestational surrogacy.**

The issue of surrogate motherhood came to national attention during the 1980s with the *Baby M* case. In 1984, a New Jersey couple, William and Elizabeth Stern, contracted to pay Mary Beth Whitehead $10,000 to be artificially inseminated with William Stern's sperm and carry the fetus to term. Whitehead decided to keep the baby after it was born, refused to receive the

Some people turn to surrogacy to help them have a child—a woman gives birth to a child for another person or a couple who then adopts or takes legal custody of the child.

I love being pregnant. I feel one with nature and I feel closer to God when I'm carrying a baby. I love the high with all those rushing hormones. But I don't really want to raise another child because I already have three and that's about all my husband and I can afford.

I'm built to have babies. I'm tall, relatively slim, but I have wonderfully wide hips—"birthing hips" I like to call them. The births of all three of my own children were pretty easy—well, I don't know if "easy" is the right word, but it's part of the pregnancy process and I love it.

I first started to think about surrogacy when my cousin couldn't carry a baby to term—she has had a total of six miscarriages. I am a religious person, and when I began to investigate what my faith would have to say about surrogacy I was pleasantly surprised. In the 16th chapter of Genesis, the infertile Sarah gives her servant Hagar to her husband Abraham, to bear a child for them. Later, Jacob fathers children by the maids of his wives Leah and Rachel, who raise them as their own.

So I went to my cousin and suggested that I could carry the baby for her, using her own egg and her husband's own sperm. At first she was unsure, but it only took them a week to decide,

yes, let's do it! I did not charge them anything of course, but they did give me $5,000 to help cover some medical expenses and to pay for a housekeeper so I could rest a little more. Everything worked out well, and their son Ben is now 7 years old. I don't feel like his mother at all, just a special cousin.

But then I got to thinking—why not do this again for someone else? To be honest, I could use a little money. And if I can earn some money while helping someone else have a baby, why not? What job would be better for me? So I contacted an agency and they did a number of psychological and physical tests. I passed with flying colors and then put together a portfolio so prospective families could learn more about me.

Over the last four years I have been a surrogate twice. I was paid about $30,000 by each of the families. The money has helped our family purchase day-to-day things. There is always some unexpected expense raising my three! And we were able to treat our children to a first-class trip to Disney World as well.

Some people wonder, isn't it hard to give up the baby to someone else after I have carried it for nine months and given birth? No, not really. My family feels complete, so I don't really long for another baby to raise. Besides, at this point I have never used my own eggs, so the baby isn't really related to me genetically anyway. But, don't get me wrong. I have continued to have a relationship with each family and have been invited to baptisms and a few other family events. I have a special relationship with each of the babies I carried and birthed, but I just don't think of myself as their mother.

—Terri, Age 35

WHAT DO YOU THINK?

1. Could you envision being a surrogate mother, or a partner to a surrogate mother? Could you easily give up the baby? If you are male, how would you feel watching your spouse/partner's belly grow as she is carrying another couple's child?
2. Terri began as an altruistic surrogate, but her last two experiences were commercial surrogacy. Did you feel uncomfortable reading this narrative when she discussed financial issues?

$10,000 payment, and fled to Florida. In July 1985, the police arrested Whitehead and returned the baby to the Sterns.

We don't know precisely how many people turn to surrogacy because it's unregulated. The CDC and the Society for Assisted Reproductive Technology (SART) only record data from gestational surrogacy, not from traditional surrogacy. In 2010, SART member clinics reported 2652 gestational carrier cycles resulting in the births of 1353 babies, about 2.4 percent of the babies reported born from ART that year (American Society for Reproductive Medicine, April 12, 2012). This represents a small but rapidly growing form of ART (Council for Responsible Genetics, 2010).

Why would anyone want to be a surrogate mother? Who would carry a baby to term, only to hand him or her over to someone else moments after birth? Surrogacy arrangements are categorized as either commercial or altruistic. In *commercial surrogacy*, the surrogate is paid a fee plus any expenses incurred in her pregnancy. In *altruistic surrogacy*, the surrogate is paid only for expenses incurred or isn't paid at all. The feature box *My Family: Why I Became a Surrogate Mother* tells the story of a woman who chose to be a surrogate.

traditional surrogacy: A type of surrogacy where the man's sperm is implanted in the surrogate through artificial insemination.

gestational surrogacy: A type of surrogacy where the intended mother's egg is combined with the man's sperm and implanted in the surrogate through in vitro fertilization.

Surrogacy, too, isn't without ethical considerations (Caplan, 2013; Deonandan, 2012; Hall, Bobinski, & Orentlicher, 2008). It challenges our most basic ideas about motherhood. States have conflicting statutes regarding surrogacy; some pose restrictions such as requiring at least one parent to have a genetic link to the child (Saul, 2009). Surrogacy also raises concerns about "renting out bodies" and the potential for exploiting low-income women. Rumors circulate about the wealthy who hire surrogates simply to avoid stretchmarks or the "hassle" of pregnancy (Ali & Kelley, 2008). In some countries such as India, surrogate motherhood for wealthy Americans is becoming a big business. It's been nicknamed *reproductive tourism*—poor women "rent their wombs" to the wealthy. One Indian surrogate said that with a $4,000 debt and an alcoholic husband, she had first considered selling a kidney, but decided that the $7,000 surrogacy fee was the better option (Deonandan, 2012).

THE HIDDEN EMOTIONS OF INFERTILITY In addition to its financial costs, infertility can also be emotionally and physically exhausting. Infertility involves many losses for individuals, their loved ones, and society as a whole (Resolve: The National Infertility Association, 2013), including the

- Loss of the pregnancy and birth experience
- Loss of a genetic legacy and loss for future contributing citizens of the next generation
- Loss of the parenting experience
- Loss of a grandparenting relationship
- Loss of feelings of self-worth
- Loss of stability in family and personal relationships
- Loss of work productivity
- Loss of a sense of spirituality and sense of hope for the future

Infertility can erode a person's self-esteem. Suddenly your life, which may have been well planned and successful up to this period, seems out of control. Not only is the physical body not responding as expected, but it feels as if your entire life is "on hold" or that you are being "left out" (McQuillan, Greil, Shreffler, Wonch-Hill, Gentzler, & Hathcoat, 2012). Facing the disappointment of not becoming pregnant month after month can lead to depression. Studies have shown that infertility depression levels can rival those of cancer (Resolve: The National Infertility Association, 2013). Because infertility often involves major personal life issues and decisions, it's often experienced as a private matter and isn't ordinarily discussed in public forums. The personal nature of the infertility experience contributes to the failure of society to recognize infertility as a disease, thus creating a lack of sound knowledge about the issue.

Voluntarily Childfree

> As a child, I usually preferred the company of adults, or at least older kids. As a teen I never wanted to babysit—boring! Today, I am much more interested in my career, travel, and hanging out with my boyfriend. Don't get me wrong—I'm a caring person. I volunteer for Meals on Wheels twice a month, and I am involved in a number of social issues in my community. It's just that, well, I don't want to have kids. My boyfriend is okay with that. I think he could go either way, but said the decision is up to me.
>
> —**Janine, age 27**

Nearly 19 percent of women ages 40 through 44 don't have children (Livingston, 2014). The decision not to have children is usually made not just

Having babies is part biology and part choice, but even our so-called choices exist in a social context. Let's examine the macro- and micro-level influences on fertility.

MACRO-LEVEL FACTORS

- Pronatalist cultural views
- Dominant religion
- Cultural considerations: Are children a benefit or liability?
- Education and employment opportunities for women
- Level of technology to combat infertility

MICRO-LEVEL FACTORS

- Biological considerations: Is the couple capable of reproducing?
- Perceived psychological benefits and costs associated with children
- Pressure from family or friends
- Personal desire for children
- Economic situation
- Willingness to adopt

once, but many times, as people undergo a *process* of deciding about children. They might think about whether to have children while in their twenties, like Janine, then revisit the issue in their thirties, and again in their forties.

Women usually have firmer opinions than men about forgoing parenthood, despite our thinking to the contrary (Koropeckyj-Cox & Pendell, 2007a, 2007b; Koropeckyj-Cox, Romano, & Moras, 2007). It's men rather than women who are more likely to report "It is better for a person to have a child than to go through life childless." Men are more likely than women to want to have children, and look less favorably on people who are childfree.

Common concerns that childfree people express are: "Will I regret my decision? Will I be lonely in my old age?" Research studies have examined the lives of older childfree people to answer these questions, and most studies conclude that they aren't particularly disadvantaged. For example, older childfree adults have similar or lower rates of depression than do other older people (Bures, Koropeckyj-Cox, & Loree, 2009). They may have fewer relationships with friends or extended family, but they have strong ties to their partners (Zhang & Hayward, 2001). Older childfree adults may be more isolated than couples with children, and are more likely to live alone or in an institution, but their finances are generally better (Plotnick, 2009). However, it's important to distinguish between those individuals who are voluntarily childfree and those who are involuntarily without children, as their experiences are likely to differ.

Thus far, a number of macro-level and micro-level factors that might account for fertility rates have been discussed. The number of children born isn't just related to personal choices. Our social structure also shapes our interest in parenting and ability to be parents, as summarized in the feature box *Tying It All Together: Factors That Influence Fertility*.

Explore on **MySocLab**
Activity: *Becoming Parents (or Not)*

Do you plan to have children? Why or why not? If your answer is "No," what kind of pronatalist sentiment have you experienced, or do you believe you will experience in the future? If you do want children, how do you think you would react if you found out that you or your partner can't get pregnant? How far would you go to have a baby?

The Interconnection of Micro and Macro: Childbirth

8.5 Recognize the interconnection of micro and macro factors influencing childbirth

Question That Matters

8.9 How has childbirth changed and become medicalized in the United States?

Although infertility and voluntary childlessness are on the rise, most women do become pregnant and have a child. The biological processes involved in these events are the same everywhere. Women get pregnant the same way in Bangladesh as they do in England, and babies are born the same way in Nigeria as they are in Canada.

Nonetheless, it would be a mistake to assume that pregnancy and childbirth are simply biological processes. We make many micro-level choices along the way about how a baby is conceived, the experience of pregnancy, the process of giving birth, and the experiences we have as new parents. Yet, many macro-level social factors are intertwined with these micro-level choices and experiences. For example, historical, cultural, and social norms influence who should or shouldn't get pregnant (ideal age, or importance of marital status); who should impregnate a woman (the qualifications necessary for a spouse or partner); conditions and habits of the pregnant woman (what foods or beverages to be consumed or avoided); the degree of medical intervention appropriate to deliver a baby (whether a baby is born in a hospital or at home); and what a baby is fed (breast milk or formula). How we conceive children, give birth to them, and care for them are choices highly influenced by structural conditions, historical period, and social and cultural norms.

Childbirth throughout History: Toward Medicalization

Children are born every minute in all parts of the world. However, what may be considered normal, healthy, and appropriate childbirth practices in one culture or historical period may be viewed as dangerous or barbaric in another (Epstein, 2010). Even something as routine as the position in which a woman gives birth—lying on her back or squatting—reflects how norms are woven into social structure (van Teijlingen, Louis, McCaffery, & Porter, 2004). As feminist theorists point out, the medical establishment, the economic system, the political culture, and the degree of technological sophistication all play a role in defining an event as intimate as a woman giving birth.

Until the 19th century, childbirth was considered largely "women's business," attended to by mothers, sisters, friends, and a midwife, if one were available (Cassidy, 2007). Doctors were generally absent, because childbirth was not considered a medical event. Midwives believed that for most women, childbirth is a normal part of life, and that their job was to help women do what they innately know.

By the middle of the 19th century, physicians seeking to develop the medical specialization of obstetrics worked to eliminate midwives (Dawley, 2003; Sullivan & Weitz, 1988). To achieve their professional dominance, physicians began claiming that childbirth was inherently dangerous and required medical assistance, and that midwives were inadequately trained to deal with the complex nature of delivering babies. Their desire to eliminate midwives had more to do with professional turf battles and less to do with the safety of birth itself.

As providers shifted, so did the role of women in childbirth (Wagner, 2008). Instead of being largely in control, women surrendered to the power and authority of male doctors. Wealthy women were the first to flock to male doctors for childbirth, lured by the promise of new technology and painkillers. Thus, childbirth became a medical event in which drugs and technological intervention became routine—the **medicalization of childbirth.** In the early 1900s, the German method of *twilight sleep* was introduced in the United States—a combination of morphine for pain relief and other drugs that caused women to have no memories of giving birth (Cassidy, 2007). Because it was difficult to apply technology to childbirth in the home, childbirth was moved to a hospital setting. In 1900, physicians in hospitals were attending approximately one-half of all births in the United States, largely along social class lines. But by 1970, virtually all births occurred in hospitals (Dawley, 2003; Rooks, 1997). With this change of venue, childbirth had shifted from a normal, home-based event to a hospital-based and sickness-oriented model (McCool & Simeone, 2002; Rothman, 1991).

In hospitals throughout most of the 20th century, women routinely had their pubic areas shaved, were strapped down on their backs to cold metal labor and delivery tables with their feet in stirrups (a painful and unnatural position), were given drugs that fogged the mind of mother and baby, and were given enemas to empty the bowels (which often empty on their own in the early stages of labor). They were hooked up to IVs and external fetal heart monitors that limit a laboring woman's mobility (which can increase her pain), and were given episiotomies (cutting through the perineum toward the anus to enlarge the vaginal

medicalization of childbirth: The belief that childbirth is a medical event in need of drugs and technological intervention.

opening). Husbands and partners were barred from the birth event. This was the dominant birth paradigm throughout most of the 20th century, but it started to change slowly in the 1980s as more women began to ask for alternatives.

Childbirth Today: A More Natural Approach or Not?

By the 1980s, many Americans questioned whether hospitalization and such intense technological intervention were always needed to deliver healthy babies. Books circulated advocating more natural methods, arguing that although medical technology can indeed save lives, it isn't without emotional, financial, and physical costs. A low-technology approach could have equally favorable results as a high-technology approach for low-risk women (e.g., women who aren't diabetic, not having twins, or are without other identified fetal or maternal health problems) (Davidson, 2002). New alternatives to pain management came into vogue—breathing and stretching exercises were presented as more natural approaches.

Birth settings also began to change. Families demanded that hospital policies and the hospital environment change so that a mother's needs would have a greater focus. Most hospitals responded by making their birthing rooms more personal and cozy. A woman could now write her own birth plan, labor in water, and be free to use alternative positions for delivery. However, hospitals still largely treat childbirth as a medical event, and compared to other birth settings, use far more technology—technology that many claim is invasive without producing better results (Block, 2008; Wagner, 2008).

Some women choose to give birth outside of hospitals. **Birth centers** are freestanding facilities, usually with close access to, but not affiliated with, a hospital. Birth centers usually present a homelike setting, and offer clients a greater degree of autonomy to decide the conditions surrounding the birth while at the same time offering a degree of medical security appealing to many couples. However, insurance companies are less likely to cover births in a birthing center as compared to those in a hospital.

A small number of women opt for home births, attended by trained midwives or naturopathic physicians. One study found that 91 percent of women who had a baby at home said they would prefer to have their next baby at home. Among those who had experienced both a home birth and a hospital birth, 76 percent preferred the home birth, citing factors such as safety, avoiding medical interventions common in hospital births, previously negative hospital experiences, more control, and a comfortable and familiar home environment (Boucher, Bennett, McFarlin, & Freeze, 2009). With skilled attendants present, women with low-risk pregnancies have outcomes just as safe at home as in hospitals (de Jonge, van der Goes, Ravelli, Amelink-Verburg, Mol, Nijhuis, Bennebroek, & Buitendijk, 2009; NHS Knowledge Service, 2009; Stapleton, Osborne, & Illuzzi, 2013).

Yet at the same time, elements of the medicalization of childbirth may be as strong as ever. The rate of caesarean delivery increased to about 33 percent of all U.S. births, rising more than 50 percent in the past decade alone (Martin, Hamilton, Ventura, Osterman, Wilson, & Matthews, 2012). This is the highest rate ever recorded anywhere in the world. Caesarean section (C-section) operations are the leading operation performed in the United States. Some hospitals require a C-section for

birth centers: Freestanding facilities (usually with close access to, but not affiliated with, a hospital) where childbirth is approached as a normal, healthy process.

Childbirth has become a highly medicalized event, usually occurring in hospitals surrounded by high technology. About one-third of births are by C-section. This doesn't improve birth outcomes, so some people are reconsidering a more natural approach to birth, including home births.

subsequent births if the first baby was delivered by caesarean, citing a higher risk of uterine rupture, although the risk may be only 1 percent (Cohen, 2009). The World Health Organization (WHO) argues that many C-sections performed in the United States are medically unnecessary, potentially dangerous, and don't improve our infant or maternal mortality statistics, which are among the worst in the developed world (Population Reference Bureau, 2013). In fact, an increasing number of C-sections are actually "elective" surgery (American Congress on Obstetricians and Gynecologists, 2013; Waknine, 2013), arranged for the convenience of the mother or the physician:

> *Courtney Mizel Green describes herself as a "total type-A personality and meticulous planner." So when it came to the birth of her first child, the Los Angeles lawyer was not willing to simply wait for nature to take its unpredictable course. Instead she decided to schedule a C-section for her baby's delivery. "I liked the idea of knowing what day and time my baby would arrive so I could schedule my parents to be here, a baby nurse, and furniture delivery," says Green. (Korn, 2010, p. 2)*

Elective C-sections are problematic. First, they can be dangerous, increasing the risk of injury and trauma for both mother and child (abcnews.go.com, January 7, 2009). A study in the *New England Journal of Medicine* found that 36 percent of women having elective C-sections scheduled their delivery before the recommended 39 weeks, making babies more likely to visit the intensive care unit, have infections, and develop respiratory distress (Tita et al., for the Eunice Shriver NICHD Maternal–Fetal Medicine Units Network, 2009).

Second, organizations such as Lamaze International, the American College of Nurse–Midwives, and the International Cesarean Network argue that birth is a natural physiological process that should be allowed to unfold naturally unless there is a strong medical reason for surgical intervention. Some critics even question how many so-called elective C-sections are really "convenience surgeries" pushed by medical professionals who don't want their vacations or weekends interrupted by a spontaneous delivery (Cosentino, 2006).

Most adults become parents, but there are other paths to becoming a parent besides childbirth. Some people become parents through adoption, the different contexts of which we discuss next.

If any of your friends or members of your family had children recently, what type of birth did they have? Was it at home, in a birthing center, or in a hospital? Did they choose a more natural method, or one that used more technology? If you plan to have children, what type of birth would you like to have (or like your partner to have)?

8.6 Describe adoption as another path to parenthood

Questions That Matter

8.10 What is the difference between *open* and *closed* adoptions?

8.11 What are some of the social contexts of adoption?

Other Paths to Parenthood: Adoption

Adoption is a mechanism by which adults legalize their parental relationship to non-biological children (Jones, 2008). It provides parents to infants who are relinquished at birth, and parents for older children whose birth parents have died or had their parental rights revoked. It offers both individuals and couples a way to add children to their families when they can't conceive or carry a pregnancy because of infertility. It provides an avenue for humanitarian assistance by offering a home to a child without one. It also provides a legal relationship between an adult and a non-biological child for whom the adult is already caring, such as a stepchild or the child of a gay or lesbian partner.

Adoption touches the lives of many people. About 135,000 infants and children are adopted every year (Child Welfare Information Gateway, 2011). Although only about 4 percent of Americans are adopted, one survey based on a representative nationwide sample of 1,416 adults found that 64 percent reported a direct personal experience with adoption. They, a family member, or a close friend was adopted, had adopted a child, or had relinquished a child for adoption (National Adoption Information Clearinghouse, 2002).

Despite its prevalence, little attention is paid to adoption in current college texts that focus on family issues (Fisher, 2003). The feature box *Why Do Research? Teaching about Adoption* describes a content analysis of 21 family texts and 16 undergraduate readers, and reveals how adoption is portrayed.

Texts about marriages and families like this one are designed to give students the knowledge base and tools to better understand family types, processes, and interactions. The texts recognize diversity and multiple paths to building families. One such path is adoption. How do these texts cover this type of family?

Let's pause for a moment and think how best to answer this research question. With a survey? With an experiment? Perhaps the best way to address how marriage and family texts cover adoption is to look through the texts themselves. A **content analysis** closely and systematically examines the content of materials—in this case, college texts. A researcher can count up pages or words devoted to the topic of adoption to see how much coverage a text gives to the topic, or can tabulate the type of comments that are made about adoption.

One such study looked at marriage and family books, both texts and readers that were published between 1998 and 2001 (Fisher, 2003). Fisher found that 4 of the 21 texts reviewed (19 percent) and 3 of the 16 readers reviewed (19 percent) offered no coverage of adoption. Among those books that did discuss adoption, the texts devoted an average of 2.4 pages, and the readers devoted few more.

Moreover, as shown in Table 8.2, Fisher found that the negative points made about adoption far outnumbered the positive points. Books tended to comment on potential problems, such as the behavioral and psychological problems among adoptees; the unavailability of healthy children; the high costs of adoption; legal problems; the stigma surrounding adoption; the ideological or ethical problems associated with adoption; the long waits; or the unknowns about the child's genetic background or physical or emotional treatment. Although these problems may exist, Fisher notes that the many positive aspects of adoption were far less likely to be discussed in these books, such as the changes in public policy that have made adoption less difficult and less expensive; the benefits of adoption for adopted children and adoptive parents; the decline in stigma toward adoption; the more open and less secretive process of adoption; the humanitarian reasons that many adoptive parents offer for adopting; and the fact that despite the risks, most adoptions work out very well.

TABLE 8.2   **Number of Positive and Negative Points Made about Adoption, by Type of Work**

Coverage of adoption in college textbooks has tended to overemphasize the negative and de-emphasize the positive.

Type of Book	Positive	Negative
Texts (n = 21)	38	57
Readers (n = 16)	10	37
All books (N = 37)	48	94

Source: Fisher, 2003.

WHAT DO YOU THINK?

1. Why do you think that adoption is given so little attention in marriage and family texts? Is it simply an oversight, or is it because of the stigma once attached to adoption?
2. Content analysis is a useful research method for answering certain types of questions. What other research questions about marriages and families would lend themselves well to content analysis?

Source: Fisher, 2003.

Closed and Open Adoptions

While the practice of adoption has probably been around forever, the recent history of adoption in the United States can be tracked to the 1850s. Massachusetts passed the first "modern" adoption law that recognized adoption as a social and legal process based on child welfare (as opposed to adult interests). The 1850s also began the era of the orphan trains that relocated children from New York to live with families throughout the United States and Canada (Child Welfare Information Gateway, 2013; National Orphan Train Complex, 2013).

Adoption was once stigmatized and often kept secret. In the past, most adoptions were **closed adoptions,** meaning that when an infant or very young child was adopted, all information about the birth parents remained sealed. The sealed records prevented the adoptee and the biological parents from knowing or discovering anything about each other, which at the time was thought to be in the best interest of everyone concerned.

Today, although closed adoptions still exist, **open adoptions,** which includes the sharing of information among the birth mother, the adoptee, and the adoptive parents, are more common. Semi-open and open adoptions can have many

content analysis: A research method that systematically examines the content of materials.

closed adoption: An adoption where identifying information is sealed and unavailable to all parties.

open adoption: A type of adoption that involves direct contact between the biological and adoptive parents.

advantages for the child, birth mother, and adoptive parents (Silber, 2013) and can take many forms along a continuum. An open adoption can mean as little as a birth parent providing basic information to the adoptee, or it can mean as much as a birth parent remaining actively involved in the child's life.

Public and Private Adoptions

Public adoptions occur through licensed public agencies that specialize in placing children in adoptive families. **Private adoptions** are arranged directly between adoptive parents and the biological birth mother, usually with the assistance of an attorney. In a private adoption, the attorney may contact social workers, other attorneys, or doctors, or place a notice in a newspaper looking for a woman who intends to relinquish her child. Although "baby selling" is prohibited, the adopting couple will likely pay the birth mother's medical fees and often her living and other miscellaneous expenses. Private adoptions tend to be more expensive than public adoptions; however, they're more common because they're likely to result in the adoptive family obtaining an infant. Children in public adoptions are often older or have special needs.

Transracial Adoptions

Three-quarters of adoptive U.S. parents are White, yet nearly two-thirds of adopted children are of an ethnic or racial minority, including Black (23 percent), Asian (15 percent), Hispanic (15 percent), and Other (9 percent) (Vandivere, Malm, & Radel, 2009). This raises a controversial issue: Is it appropriate to place minority children with White families (Simon & Roorda, 2000, 2009)? In the 1970s, the Association of Black Social Workers and Native American activists strongly objected to placing Black and Native American children with White families, suggesting that transracial adoptions amounted to cultural genocide. Immediately afterward, the number of transracial adoptions declined, but then rose again due in large part to the number of international adoptions. Today, there is less stigma surrounding transracial adoptions.

Given the large number of transracial adoptions, it's important to assess the impact on a child who is raised by parents of a different race or ethnic group. *Cultural socialization* involves teaching children about their cultural heritage and can instill a sense of identity and pride. It teaches children about religious traditions, introduces them to specific types of foods, cultural holidays, languages, or dialects, and imparts a set of values associated with a larger group identity.

Cultural socialization has been associated with positive psychological outcomes including higher self-esteem among children and greater well-being among adults (Tessler & Gamache, 2009; Thomas & Tessler, 2007; Toomey & Umaña-Taylor, 2012; Vonk, Lee, & Crolley-Simic, 2010). For example, Tessler and Gamache (2009) examined the feelings and identity of girls from China adopted into non-Chinese families throughout the U.S. and found cultural socialization to be a source of empowerment for them.

Single-Parent Adoptions

Heather, who is 42, was married once when she was very young. That marriage ended in divorce, and she has yet to find "Mr. Right." Yet, Heather is very eager to have children. After mulling over her idea for several years, she finally went ahead and decided to adopt a child on her own. Last summer she became the mother of 18-month old Mateo, a biracial child whose mother lives in another part of the state. It is an open adoption, and Heather looks forward to having Mateo's birth mother and his two biological sisters involved in their lives.

A generation ago, if a single woman presented herself to an adoption agency to apply for an adoption, she would probably have been turned away. It was highly unusual (and in some states, illegal) for a single person to adopt a child. Much has changed in 30 years; today, single women are actively involved in adoption. Among adopters, 17 percent of women, and 6 percent of men, have never been married (Jones, 2008). In particular, single women and men tend to adopt children who are older, are racial or ethnic minorities, are from foster care, have special health care needs, or are from other countries, although some countries, such as China, have recently imposed quotas or restrictions on single-parent adoptions. Single men often have difficulty adopting children. Despite the growing recognition of men as nurturers, there is still suspicion that a single man could not be sensitive to a child's needs and concern about what type of man would want to raise a child alone.

Adoptions by Gays and Lesbians

Gay men and lesbians have always adopted, although in the past, they usually hid their sexual orientation. Today, just as gays and lesbians are becoming more visible in all other aspects of American society, they're being considered more seriously as potential adoptive parents. In 2010, Florida, the final holdout, lifted its ban against gays and lesbians adopting children. Yet, only some states allow for same-sex *couples* to adopt jointly. Other states allow for one partner to first adopt the child, and then for the other partner to apply for a second-parent adoption. These second-parent adoptions create a second legally recognized parent for the adoptive child. These two methods are the only way for same-sex couples to both become legal parents of their children (Johnson, 2008). Yet, in some states, the law is either unclear or contradictory from one region to another.

Concerns are frequently raised surrounding gay and lesbian adoption, many of which are based on stereotypes or myths about sexual orientation or homosexuality. What are these concerns, and what do research findings suggest? (Biblarz & Stacey, 2010; Crowl, Ahn, & Baker, 2008).

A common way for same-sex couples to have children is through adoption. On October 22, 2010, Florida, the final holdout, lifted its ban against gays and lesbians adopting.

- *Homosexual parents will molest their children.* No scientific research suggests a significant link between homosexuality and pedophilia. One study looked at 269 cases of child sexual abuse, and found only two cases in which the offenders were gay or lesbian. Indeed, the study found that a child's risk of being molested by his or her parent's (or other relative's) *heterosexual* partner was more than 100 times greater than being molested by someone identified as homosexual (Jenny, Roesler, & Poyer, 1994).

- *Children raised in homosexual households will become gay.* Stacey and Biblarz found that children of gay and lesbian parents are no more likely to identify themselves as gay, lesbian, or bisexual than the children of heterosexual parents. However, they are more likely to consider or experiment with same-sex relationships during young adulthood (2001).

- *Children raised in gay or lesbian households will suffer from depression or mental health problems.* Research reveals that children of same-sex parents show either no difference from those of heterosexual parents, or show a reduction in levels of anxiety, depression, or behavior problems (Biblarz & Stacey, 2010; Stacey & Biblarz, 2001). These children also score as high or higher on social performance, self-esteem, secure attachments, and affection and concern for younger children.

- *Children raised in gay or lesbian households will be teased and harassed.* Children of gay and lesbian parents *are* vulnerable to teasing and harassment,

Pretend that you are in a grocery store when your 5-year-old adopted daughter asks you, "Mommy/Daddy, you know that woman whose tummy I came out of? Why didn't she want to keep me?" How would you respond, right there, to your daughter's effort to understand her adoption?

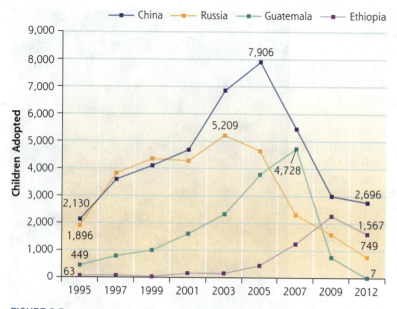

FIGURE 8.5

Trends in International Adoption, 1995–2012

The number of international adoptions has declined significantly since its peak in 2005.
Source: U.S. Department of State, January 2013.

About 13,000 children were adopted from outside the United States in 2009, a significant decline from just a few years earlier. People adopt for many reasons, including humanitarian ones, and the need is great. These young children live in an orphanage in Haiti.

particularly as they approach adolescence. Courts have often viewed the stigma surrounding gay and lesbian parenting as possibly damaging to a child's self-esteem, and therefore side with the heterosexual parent in custody disputes. However, gay and lesbian parents are generally aware of this stigma and its effects, and go to great lengths to prepare and support their children. Although children of gays and lesbians do report teasing because of their parents' sexual orientation, their self-esteem levels are no lower than those of children of heterosexual parents (Garner, 2005; Huggins, 1989; Snow, 2004).

The leading medical society of pediatricians, the 65,000-member American Academy of Pediatrics, endorses the legal rights of homosexuals to adopt a partner's child, saying "Children deserve to know their relationships with both parents are stable and legally recognized" (Hall, 2002, p. 339).

International Adoptions

The number of Americans who are adopting children from other countries has declined sharply over the past few years. American parents adopted 8,600 foreign-born children in 2012, down from about 23,000 in 2004 (U.S. Department of State, 2013; U.S. Department of State, January 2013). New standards have made adoption more difficult, including the Hague Adoption Convention, which adds many new regulations and restrictions designed to ensure that inter-country adoptions are in the best interest of the child. Figure 8.5 shows how many children have been adopted in the United States over the past 10 years from China, Russia, Guatemala, and Ethiopia, the top four countries for international adoptions (U.S. Department of State, 2013).

Political decisions or social problems often produce orphans who need families. For example, adoptions from China are in response to the strict one-child policy enforced by the Chinese government, and adoptions in Russia are in response to the extreme poverty following the transition to a market economy (Tarmann, 2003). New on the list of popular countries for adoption is Ethiopia—families are concerned about the rising number of AIDS orphans, and are offering homes to children who have lost their parents. There were 1,567 U.S. adoptions of Ethiopian children in 2012, up from only 165 in 2003 (U.S. Department of State, 2013).

The primary reason that Americans turn to international adoptions is the declining availability of U.S.-born children available for adoption. Unmarried American mothers are no longer a common source of children available for adoption. There are several reasons for this, including a lower teenage pregnancy rate compared to the 1990s, the increasing use of contraceptives, fewer women putting their children up for adoption, the availability of legal abortion, and the declining stigma of unwed motherhood. Prospective parents are also looking internationally because adopting within the United States is slow, costly, and often has stricter guidelines, such as age restrictions. There is also usually a more clear-cut termination of birth parents' rights in international adoptions that appeals to many people. Finally, some people adopt internationally for humanitarian reasons or because they have a personal interest or stake in that part of the world.

Children adopted internationally are usually not available for adoption until they're at least 6 months to 1 year old, and in the case of Eastern Europe, sometimes considerably older. Children are likely to have spent all or most of their infancy in orphanages, and therefore may have been exposed to some degree of biological and social risks. The severity of these potential risks depends on their country of origin, the age at which the child was adopted, and the length of time in the orphanage. Risks may include infectious diseases, which could result in other deficits in cognitive, social, and physical well-being. However, these risks are still small, especially if children are adopted young, as shown in the opening vignette. Most children, including Cassandra and John, do very well when placed with an adoptive family, and within a year very few children continue to display atypical behavior or socio-emotional problems (Beverly, McGuinness, & Blanton, 2008; Johnson, 2009; Le Mare, Audet, & Kurytnik, 2007; Tan & Yang, 2005). In other words, adopted children usually thrive with their new families.

Most adopted children do well when placed with a loving adopted family. This photo was taken less than a week after returning from China with Yue Linwang. Today, Olivia Lin is a thriving second grader who, like her big sister, loves school, riding her bike, eating pizza, playing the violin, and learning how to speak Mandarin.

The Transition to Parenthood

The birth of a child is one of the most significant events in life. People plan in anticipation, yet the transition to parenthood can be surprisingly difficult (Keizer & Schenk, 2012; Pinquart & Teubert, 2010; Umberson, Pudrovska, & Reczek, 2010). In the past, when extended families were more common, grandparents, aunts, and uncles all could help teach new parents how to parent a child. For example, they could help a woman learn to breastfeed, which doesn't necessarily come naturally to either mother or baby. They could offer sage advice about dealing with a colicky baby, and they could teach a parent how to hold or swaddle the child, how to get the baby to sleep through the night, or even how to change a diaper correctly. These things aren't innate within most adults—they must be learned.

How do new parents learn these parenting skills today when the extended family may not live close by? Many new and expecting parents turn to advice books, such as the best-selling *What to Expect When You're Expecting* (Murkoff & Mazel, 2008), the book by Dr. Sears that emphasizes attachment parenting (2001), or the book by Le Leche League International advocating breastfeeding, *The Womanly Art of Breastfeeding* (2004). Although they can help to calm the nerves of many new parents, these books aren't without their critics. Some believe that they do more harm than good by promoting their own opinions as a gold standard (e.g., a woman *must* breastfeed; a baby *must* co-sleep with parents; a baby *must* not be allowed to cry, or else the child will grow up emotionally disadvantaged in some critical way). The more likely truth is that there are many ways of raising healthy, happy, and well-adjusted children.

8.7 Analyze the transition to parenthood

Questions That Matter

8.12 Why is the transition to parenthood challenging for new mothers and fathers?

8.13 How do other countries help to make the transition to parenting easier?

Read on MySocLab
Document: *Thinking about the Baby: Gender and Divisions of Infant Care*

Why Is the Transition So Challenging?

New parents are often shocked by the amount of work involved in caring for an infant (Cockrell, O'Neill, & Stone, 2008; Gottman & Gottman, 2008; Springer, 2013; Walzer, 1998). When a baby arrives, everything changes. Parents are no longer free to do as they please, but must instead adapt to the constant care of a new

The transition to parenthood can be surprisingly stressful. Few people are prepared for the high demands made on their time, sleep, and relationships with their spouse or partner.

and vulnerable infant. This is exceedingly difficult, and is made even more challenging by the fact that most new parents are sleep-deprived. Newborns have no sense of day or night; their cycles of crying, feeding, wetting, and sleeping go on around the clock. As a result, 40 percent to 70 percent of couples experience stress, conflict, and a decline in marital satisfaction during this time, all of which affect their baby's care (Gottman & Gottman, 2008).

As one new father said, *"I mean, if I'm watching him during the day—she's at work—forget about doing anything. It's constant attention. You can't read, you can't study, you can't paint, you can't do anything. You really got to sit there and watch him"* (Walzer, 1998, p. 24).

Sociologist Alice Rossi suggested why the transition to parenthood can be so challenging, comparing the adoption of the parent role to that of other adult roles such as becoming a spouse. Rossi (1968) explains:

- *Pronatalist sentiment may pressure people to become parents* even though they may not really want to or be ready to parent. Yet, once a baby is born, there is no chance to change one's mind about parenthood.

- *Most parents have little or no experience in childcare.* They must quickly learn how to care for a completely dependent human being.

- *Becoming a parent is an abrupt change,* unlike other adult roles. Expecting a baby is not the same thing as having one. New parents are suddenly on duty 24 hours a day, 7 days a week.

- *The transition to parenthood necessitates complex changes in the couple's relationship.* Activities become more instrumental, and the division of labor becomes more gender-based. Most of the workload and lifestyle changes fall on the woman.

The transition to parenthood also changes the couple's relationship, and not always for the better. Marital satisfaction often declines (Dew & Wilcox, 2011; Keizer & Schenk, 2012). Quality time for just the two of them declines and the workload increases, sometimes leading to feelings of unfairness (Dew & Wilcox, 2011).

However, not all parents find the transition to parenthood so stressful. It's important to look at the social context of parenting, because many factors can mediate the challenges faced by new parents (Perry-Jenkins & Claxton, 2011), including the baby's temperament, the parents' expectations about their baby, the support and assistance they receive from kin, their marital adjustment and communication skills, the father's parenting and household involvement, the work hours and demands of the parents, the couple's expectations for shared leisure, whether the baby was planned, and the baby's sex (Belsky & Rovine, 1990; Keizer & Schenk, 2012; Mulsow, Caldera, Pursley, Reifman, & Huston, 2002; Simpson, Rholes, Campbell, Tran, & Wilson, 2003). For example, if a couple who enjoys their peace and quiet has an active, fussy baby who needs little sleep, and this couple doesn't have family around to help, especially while the father travels away from home on business, you can guess that the transition to parenthood will be a challenge. In contrast, a couple who has a so-called easy baby who cries or fusses little, who has flexible work schedules or family leave, and has family around to help will probably have an easier time adjusting to parenthood.

Sex Differences in the Transition to Parenthood

Few could disagree that women and men have different experiences as they transition into parenthood. Nonetheless, we know far more about how women are changed by becoming parents than we know about men.

TABLE 8.3	Time Spent in the Parenting of Infants Younger Than Age 1 (in hours and minutes)		
Mothers spend far more time caring for infants than do fathers, both on weekdays and weekends.			
	Partnered Mothers	**Partnered Fathers**	
Total Childcare Weekdays	**11:05**	**5:01**	
Solo Childcare	8:08	2:06	
Primary Childcare (other parent helped)	3:15	1:25	
Total Childcare Weekends	**11:58**	**9:31**	
Solo Childcare	5:50	3:11	
Primary Childcare (other parent helped)	3:19	1:52	

Source: Drago, 2009.

In most families, babies spend considerably more time with their mothers than their fathers, as shown in Table 8.3 (Drago, 2009). Women retain most of the childcare responsibilities, and this is particularly true with an infant who may be nursing. With more than half of mothers with children under the age of 1 in the labor force, work–family stress is a serious problem for many women, as you will see in Chapter 10.

Yet, as sociologist Susan Walzer explains, the transition to parenthood is far more than the logistics of juggling work and family. Her study of 25 couples who recently had a baby revealed that our image of what it takes to be a "good" mother or a "good" father is socially constructed and inextricably linked with our views about gender. Parenthood is a vivid example of "doing gender." Walzer writes:

> *"Mother" and "father" are social categories that existed before the individuals I interviewed became parents—or were born. These social categories have particular meanings attached to them—meanings that are socializing influences on new parents and that are institutionalized in cultural imagery associated with motherhood and fatherhood. New parents are channeled toward differentiation by social arrangements, and especially by cultural imagery that constructs what it means to be a "good" mother or father, wife or husband, woman or man. (Walzer, 1998, p. 7)*

These images set up a difficult situation for women because the image of a "good mother" is one who is always there and available for her child, yet the image of a "good woman" is to work and have a career. Balancing these two cultural images that are at odds with each other can be difficult. Men don't face this contradiction in roles. An employed father who has minimal caregiving tasks may still be perceived as a "good father." If a mother works outside the home, she and her husband usually frame her employment as something that should only minimally interfere with her mothering role.

Walzer suggests that mothers and fathers think about babies in different ways, and they analyze their thoughts so that they fit the culturally appropriate image of "good" mothers and fathers. Mothers are expected to expend considerably more mental energy on their babies than are fathers. For example, mothers worry more about their babies (and they worry about the way they are perceived by others), they buy and read the self-help books, they process the information and then translate it for their husbands or partners, and they manage and orchestrate childcare and the division of household labor.

What Can Help the Transition to Parenthood?

The transition to parenthood is a challenge for most families and is exacerbated by family policies that fail to recognize the structural pressures associated with a

In Detroit, Michigan, Rhea, a first-time mother, is trying to get used to the thought of putting her 6-week-old son in daycare so she can get back to work. *"It's hard to imagine leaving him for 9 hours a day with a stranger, but I need the money,"* she laments. Across the border in Toronto, Canada, Kim is back at work after 14 months of paid maternity leave. *"It was terrific,"* she says. *"I was still making enough money to get by while I was at home with Ethan."* Across the ocean in Sweden, Nils is looking forward to sharing 16 months of parental leave at 80 percent pay with his girlfriend, whose baby will be born any day: *"It's great that we both have the time to bond with him."*

The United States has the least generous maternity and family leave policy of any developed nation. Other countries promote integration of work and family because they believe it's a benefit to everyone—child, parents, employer, and the society at large.

Longer leaves after childbirth are associated with better maternal and child health, lower stress, and greater well-being. Women are likely to breastfeed for longer periods if they have extended leave benefits. Employers themselves also benefit from longer parental leave; women are more likely to return to work after their leave expires, rather than feel forced to quit. It's also more cost-effective to develop a well-planned parental leave policy than it is to rehire and retrain new employees.

What type of leave policies exists in the United States? Congress passed the **Family Medical Leave Act (FMLA)** in 1993, which requires employers with more than 50 employees to provide 12 weeks of *unpaid* leave to eligible employees (both men and women) to care for themselves or their immediate families with specified medical conditions, including care of a newborn. Employees must have worked for the employer at least 1 year or 1,250 hours to be eligible for FMLA. Employers in small firms aren't required by law to offer leaves.

Yet, in reality, few people can afford to take unpaid leave. Therefore, many new mothers come back to work shortly after their short-term disability, vacation, or sick pay—if they have any—has been exhausted, often within a few short weeks.

In contrast to the United States, here are some examples of family support available in other countries:

- Japan offers 14 weeks of paid leave at 60 percent of salary.
- Denmark offers 18 weeks of paid maternity leave at 90 percent of salary.
- Spain offers 16 weeks of leave at 100 percent of salary.
- Switzerland provides 98 days at 80 percent of salary.

Parental leave is also more generous in poor or developing nations than it is in the United States. Even in Bangladesh, one of the poorest nations on Earth, women who work in *qualifying jobs* receive 12 weeks of maternity leave paid at 100 percent of salary. Mexico also offers 12 weeks of maternity leave at 100 percent of salary. In Iran, women receive 67

The United States is unique in that it offers no national paid maternity (or paternity) policy for new families. Most other peer nations offer new parents many months, or even years, off to relax and enjoy their new baby.

percent of their salary for 90 days. (Granted, many women in poor nations don't work in qualifying jobs because they work as maids, in the fields, or in the underground economy.)

However, the United States is one of two countries that don't guarantee paid leave at all for any of its workers. (Australia also does not, although it does provide 1 year of unpaid leave.) A recent report from the Families and Work Institute found that 16 percent of large firms in the United States with more than 100 workers provide full pay during a maternity leave (usually 6 weeks); however, this is down from 27 percent in 1998 (Galinsky, Bond, & Sakai, 2008). If Americans have paid for optional short-term disability insurance with their employer, they can receive a partial salary for 6 weeks of leave. Yet, because the leave is "disability-related," it wouldn't provide any pay for fathers, or for mothers of children who are adopted. Is this the best our government can do?

WHAT DO YOU THINK?

1. It took the United States until 1993 to pass the Family Medical Leave Act (FMLA), which provides only unpaid leave to certain qualified workers. Why do you think it took this long, and why is the FMLA less generous than the leave policies of other countries? Who would oppose the FMLA, and why? Who would support it, and why?
2. Do you think both males and females should be offered leave? Should it be paid for both? Why or why not?

Source: Brown, 2009; Galinsky, Bond, & Sakai, 2008; United Nations Statistics Division, 2005, Table 5c.

new baby. One such pressure involves time, including the ability to take time off from work after a baby is born. The feature box *From Macro to Micro: Maternity and Paternity Leaves* compares the leave policies in different countries, and as you will see, the United States isn't highly ranked. Because many women have no paid maternity leave, more than half of women return to work within 5 months of giving birth (Laughlin, 2011).

Family leaves aren't the only things that can help new families. In her book, *Perfect Madness: Motherhood in the Age of Anxiety* (2005), Judith Warner describes the generous assistance available to her as a new mother living in France, and presents a jolting contrast after she returns to the United States:

> *I was living in France, a country that has an astounding array of benefits for families—and for mothers in particular. When my children were born, I stayed in the hospital for five comfortable days. I found a nanny through a free, community-based referral service, then employed her, legally and full-time, for a cost to me of about $10,500 a year, after tax breaks. My elder daughter, from the time she was eighteen months, attended excellent part-time preschools, where she painted and played with modeling clay and ate cookies and napped for about $150 per month—the top end of the fee scale. She could have started public school at age three, and could have opted to stay until 5 P.M. daily. My friends who were covered by the French social security system (which I did not pay into), had even greater benefits: at least four months of paid maternity leave, the right to stop working for up to three years and have jobs held for them, cash grants after their second children were born starting at about $105 per month.*
>
> *And that was just the beginning. There was more: a culture. An atmosphere. A set of deeply held attitudes toward motherhood—toward adult womanhood—that had the effect of allowing me to have two children, work in an office, work out in a gym, and go out to dinner at night and away for a short vacation with my husband without ever hearing, without ever thinking, the word "guilt." (Warner, 2005, pp. 9–10)*

What is the impact of this collectivist orientation? French parents receive a great deal of government assistance when they have a baby. This assistance begins early in the child's life, made possible by three types of parent leaves: 16 weeks of paid maternity leave for the mother for the first child (longer leaves are available for subsequent births); 11 days of paid paternity leave for the father; and up to 3 years of unpaid leave for either parent with their job guaranteed (provided they've been on the job for at least 1 year) (Social Security Administration, August 2012).

Family Medical Leave Act (FMLA): An act that requires employers with more than 50 employees to provide 12 weeks of *unpaid* leave to eligible employees (both men and women) to care for themselves or their immediate families with specified medical conditions.

Read on **MySocLab**
Document: *The Rhetoric and Reality of "Opting Out"*

*I*f you have a child, do you think your transition to parenthood will be easier, more difficult, or about the same as it was for your parents? What types of macro-level changes would you like to see to help people transition more easily to parenthood? Do you think people who don't have children should pay to help those who do (through their taxes)? Why or why not?

Bringing It Full Circle

We began this chapter by meeting Tracey and Juan, the couple who adopted two children from Colombia. Families are created in many ways, and adoption itself touches the lives of people both in the United States and around the world. This chapter reveals that micro-level personal issues such as *whether, when, who,* and *how* to have a baby represent a complex intertwining of biological and macro-level structural and social forces. Cultural values such as pronatalism shape our attitudes and behaviors. Political, religious, economic, health care, and other social institutions also shape family life and policies about fertility, infertility, pregnancy, adoption, childbirth, and the transition to parenthood—dimensions of family life that many see as extremely personal. Reflecting on what you've learned in this chapter, let's revisit the opening vignette with Juan and Tracey:

- Were the adoptions of Juan and Tracey's children private or public? Open or closed?

- What are some issues facing adopted children and their families that other families don't face? Think of the different contexts of adoption, including international adoption, transracial adoption, adoption by gays and lesbians, single-parent adoption, and closed versus open adoption.

- What transitions to parenthood might Tracey and Juan face, if they are typical parents? Would any of their transitions be different because their children are adopted?

- How do both macro-level and micro-level factors influence fertility patterns across cultures and across generations in your own family?

On MySocLab

 Study and Review on MySocLab

CHAPTER REVIEW

LO8.1 Interpret population and fertility trends worldwide

8.1 What are population and fertility trends worldwide?

The world's population could reach almost 10 billion by 2050. Population growth occurs unevenly. Less developed countries have about 81 percent of the world's population, and in some countries, the population may double in less than a generation. This is related to both birthrates and death rates.

LO8.2 Explain fertility in the United States

8.2 What factors have influenced fertility rates in the United States over the past century?

Fertility rates have fluctuated throughout history. Trends are influenced by macro-level structural conditions, such as affluence, depression, war, and increasing opportunities for women.

8.3 What is *pronatalism*?

Pronatalism is a cultural value that encourages childbearing. In the United States, pronatalism is manifested in the values that having children is a normal, natural part of a happy life, and that those who voluntarily

remain childfree are selfish, immature, lonely, unfulfilled, insensitive, and more likely to have mental problems than parents. It's also supported by social institutions and policies around the world.

8.4 What are current trends showing about the age at which people have children?

Most people have children, but they have them later in life. The average age for women is now 25.4 years, up from 21.4 years in 1970. Here's another way of understanding this trend: about 27 percent of women ages 30 through 34 don't have children today, compared to only 16 percent of women ages 30 through 34 in 1976.

LO8.3 Compare and contrast the costs and rewards of raising children

8.5 What are some of the costs associated with having children?

Economists talk about *direct financial costs* (i.e., out-of-pocket expenses for food, clothing, housing, and education), which now amount to about $234,900 until a child's 18th birthday, and *opportunity costs* (i.e., lost opportunities for income by working only part-time, or not at all because of children).

8.6 What are some of the benefits associated with having children?

The emotional feelings of love and devotion may be more difficult to quantify; however, children can bring tremendous joy and purpose into people's lives. Parents love their children, take pride in them, and have fun with them. Children also connect parents socially with others.

LO8.4 Discuss the trend of remaining childfree

8.7 How serious a problem is infertility?

Not all people who are childfree are so by choice. Infertility is the inability to get pregnant after one year of trying. It's a medical problem affecting approximately 12 percent of adults of childbearing age in the United States. It occurs in all income groups and racial and ethnic categories, and affects men and women equally.

8.8 Why are more couples choosing to remain childfree today?

With new educational and employment opportunities available to women, a growing number of couples opt to forgo parenthood. The decision not to have children is usually not made once, but many times, as people undergo a *process* of deciding about children. They might think about whether to have children while in their twenties, revisit the issue in their thirties, and again in their forties. Women usually have firmer opinions than men about forgoing parenthood because their lives would be most changed by parenthood.

LO8.5 Recognize the interconnection of micro and macro factors influencing childbirth

8.9 How has childbirth changed and become medicalized in the United States?

Until the 19th century, childbirth was "women's business," attended by midwives. To achieve their professional dominance, physicians began to claim that childbirth was inherently dangerous, required medical assistance, and that midwives were inadequately trained to deal with the complex nature of delivering babies. Women began to have their children in hospitals instead of at home, and birth was shaped by the latest technology. After a movement toward more holistic childbirth, the United States began to see an increase in elective caesarean births.

LO8.6 Describe adoption as another path to parenthood

8.10 What is the difference between *open* and *closed* adoptions?

In an *open adoption*, information is shared between birth mothers, the adoptee, and the adoptive parents to varying degrees. In a *closed adoption*, popular in the past, all information about the birth parents is legally sealed.

8.11 What are some of the social contexts of adoption?

Many types of families adopt children, and each has its own unique reasons. For example, there are transracial adoptions, single-parent adoptions, adoptions by gays and lesbians, and international adoptions (in which the family usually has a different race or ethnic background from the adoptees).

LO8.7 Analyze the transition to parenthood

8.12 Why is the transition to parenthood so challenging for new mothers and fathers?

Most new parents are shocked by the amount of work involved in caring for a new baby. This is because of many factors: Pronatalist sentiment may pressure people to become parents even though they may not really want to or be ready to parent; most parents have little or no experience in childcare; and becoming a parent is an abrupt change, unlike other adult roles. Expecting a baby is not the same thing as having one. New parents are suddenly on duty 24 hours a day, 7 days a week; and the transition to parenthood necessitates complex changes in the couple's relationship.

8.13 How do other countries help to make the transition to parenting easier?

Other countries offer more extensive maternity and paternity leaves than does the United States. Longer leaves are associated with better maternal and infant health and well-being, and they're also good for business. In addition to leaves, many countries offer services to meet the needs of new parents. These services, along with personal social support, can make the transition to parenting smoother.

KEY TERMS

assisted reproductive technology (ART)
birth centers
closed adoption
content analysis
cultural socialization
direct financial costs
Family Medical Leave Act (FMLA)

fertility rate
gestational surrogacy
infertility
medicalization of childbirth
mortality rate (or death rate)
open adoption
opportunity costs

private adoption
pronatalism
public adoption
surrogacy
traditional surrogacy

Raising Children

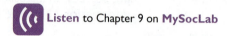
Listen to Chapter 9 on **MySocLab**

What's it like to raise children? There's no simple answer to that question. Many aspects of parenting are similar across parenting contexts.

Yet there are unique differences as well. Meet Karen and Betsy, a same-sex couple raising their two children.

Karen and Betsy, who live in Massachusetts, have been together for 13 years. In 2005, they married after Massachusetts became one of only a handful of states that allow same-sex couples to legally wed. Karen and Betsy spoke early on about wanting children, and today they are proud parents of Henry, who is 8 years old, and Jayla, who is almost 4. Henry is Karen's biological son. Henry's father doesn't live close by, but still plays a role in his life. Jayla is adopted, and joined their family just shy of her first birthday.

Karen and Betsy would tell you that in many ways raising children with two moms is no different from raising children in any other type of family. They worry about their children's health, safety, and happiness. However, a closer look reveals that Karen and Betsy have to address issues that other families take for granted.

● **Watch** on **MySocLab**
Video: *Same Sex Parents Raising Children: Karen and Betsy*

For example, whereas most parents simply move to any community convenient to work or school, Karen and Betsy had to make a concerted effort to find a community where other same-sex families lived, where the local public school reflected this diversity, and the community as a whole was inclusive. They wanted their children to grow up in an environment in which families like theirs are seen as normal. Karen and Betsy found such a community. Their children have grown up with other families with two moms, attend synagogue with other same-sex families, and attend a school with many families just like theirs.

Nonetheless, challenges remain. There have been some uncomfortable moments at Henry's school around Mother's and Father's days. Not all teachers recognize that such holidays or practices can be stressful to children and their parents. A preschool director insisted on having moms and dads visit the school on separate nights instead of just having one "parent night." If they can anticipate events or occasions, Karen and Betsy make a point of talking to the school administrators in advance. In other words, they must always be on guard, even in their relatively supportive environment.

At age 8, Henry, who until now never thought much about having two moms, is beginning to ask questions about their family. He's not so sure he likes being different. Karen and Betsy are aware he is experiencing a sense of loss, but they reassure him that there are many types of families and that he's very lucky to have two parents who love him dearly. Meanwhile, always aware of his needs, they've begun to add more male role models in his life. A high-school boy who is a friend of the family picks him up from school once a week to hang out with him. Like all good parents, Karen and Betsy want to surround their children with love, support, and self-confidence.

Being a parent is sure to be a labor of love, but it's also an emotional rollercoaster. Parents have to care for, nurture, and socialize their children. Some parents also have to teach their children about (and shield them from) the harsh realities of prejudice and discrimination.

In this chapter, we explore many important issues about raising children. It's essential to remember that the journey is a two-way street: parents influence their children, but children also influence their parents. In particular, we'll see that all parenting (and being parented) takes place in a social context.

Read on MySocLab
Document: *Parents' Socialization of Children*

9.1 Recognize the diversity in parenting historically and cross culturally

Questions That Matter

9.1 Are there cross-cultural differences in parenting practices?

9.2 How has parenting changed over time?

9.3 What are some current trends in parenting found throughout the world?

Definitions of *good parenting* differ across cultures. In some cultures, parents would never think of putting their children in strollers, or having their babies sleep in cribs. Instead they strap their children to their backs, and sleeping together is routine.

Parenting: It's Not the Same Everywhere

We know what parents are supposed to do: care for, nurture, and socialize their children, right? Yes, but it's not that simple. These interactions between parents and children also occur within a broader social and cultural environment. Economic conditions, region of the country (whether it's urban or rural), cultural and religious traditions, gendered norms, job opportunities, and level of technology are just a few of the macro-level factors that set the stage for micro-level family interactions. For example, a couple living in an environment where reliable birth control isn't readily accessible will have significantly more children than a couple with regular access to contraceptives. In much of the world—Africa, for example—families commonly have six, seven, eight, or even more children (Population Reference Bureau, 2013a). Think about how parenting in these families differs from parenting in the United States, where having only one or two children is the norm. Technology and its access—in this case, birth control—matter.

Most people become parents, but *how* we parent our children and what we consider *good parenting* differs among cultures and across different times in history. In some countries, parents (usually the mother) literally wear their children for a few years. They strap them to their backs and work, play, cook, and do errands without a second thought. Think for a moment about parenting in the United States. Women usually give birth in hospitals away from family and friends, and this isolation sets the stage for our parenting. Our babies sleep in separate beds called *cribs*; they sleep in separate rooms away from their parents; and many are fed from bottles rather than their mother's breasts (Centers for Disease Control and Prevention [CDC], January 22, 2013). We place our children in strollers instead of carrying them close to our bodies. Within 3 months after giving birth, 28 percent of new mothers return to work (Laughlin, 2011), primarily because the United States has no mandated paid maternity leave. In contrast, in the United Kingdom, only 7 percent of new mothers return to work in 3 months.

As shown in Chapter 8, parents in many countries have an extensive array of maternity, paternity, and other benefits that allow them to stay at home while their children are young without losing their jobs, seniority, or pay. In fact, families often receive a cash benefit from the government to help with the costs of raising

As April 15th approaches and American families with children fill out their tax returns, they will find some financial relief in the form of newly expanded child tax credits ($1,000 per child). Although many families are delighted to have these expanded credits, how does the United States compare to other countries with respect to the financial help we give families?

Unfortunately, the United States is one of the few industrialized nations that doesn't provide families with child or family allowances. Eighty-eight countries provide cash benefits to families with children to help with the costs of raising their children. These are universal benefits, available to all families, regardless of income. The rationale is that all members of society benefit by having healthy, happy, and well-educated children, and therefore all members of society should share in the costs.

Many European countries began offering family allowances as early as the beginning of the 20th century. In Canada, family allowances were considered the first real social welfare program. In some countries, family allowances may be supplemented by many other cash programs or tax credits, including birth grants, school grants, childrearing or childcare allowances, adoption benefits, special supplements for single parents, guaranteed minimum child support benefits, and allowances for adult dependents and disabled children. By providing these cash benefits, governments are directly helping families with the costs of raising children and indirectly helping lower the rate of child poverty.

Does the United States provide any similar program? Not exactly, but the United States does provide several tax benefits to families with children, particularly to low-income families. For example, low-income working families could apply for the refundable Earned Income Tax Credit (EITC) as long as their income was under $35,463 in tax year 2009 (with one qualifying child). The EITC is designed to partially offset taxes that low-income persons would otherwise pay, thereby serving as an inducement to work. Tax credits for families adopting a child, paying for a child's education, and for the costs of a child in eligible childcare are also available. All of these are designed to help low- and middle-income families, and all phase out as a family's income rises.

The problem is that applying for tax benefits can be confusing because it requires that a family be savvy enough to understand the tax system, available programs, and their eligibility requirements and ceilings. The net effect is that those American families who most need assistance are the least likely to apply for, or even be aware of, the benefits.

For example, the Internal Revenue Service acknowledges that 25 percent of those eligible for the EITC don't receive this tax credit. Even when people do receive assistance, it arrives just on an annual, rather than on a regular monthly, basis. Given that poverty rates are significantly higher in the United States than in other developed nations, it might be worth taking a look at family allowances to determine how they could offset poverty for millions of families.

WHAT DO YOU THINK?

1. Why do you think that most Americans have never even heard of *family allowances*?
2. Do you think that family allowances help families by offering financial assistance to parents raising their children, or do they hurt families by creating dependency on the government?

Sources: Kamerman & Gatenio, 2002; Internal Revenue Service, April 13, 2009; Social Security Administration, 2013; The Canadian Encyclopedia, 2010.

---

children. This benefit, known as a **family allowance** (or a **child allowance**), is available to all families—rich and poor—and is described in the feature box *Policy and You: From Macro to Micro*.

What's the *best* way to raise children? This question is difficult to answer, because there may not really be one correct way. Although we have a strong sense of right and wrong, many of our childrearing rules are based on cultural and historical preferences rather than fact. Our way of doing things today is virtually unheard of in many parts of the world. In other countries, parents and young children sleep together, children breastfeed for a few years, are carried by their parents in a sling, and mother and child are never separated for 40 hours a week (Han, Ruhm, & Waldfogel, 2009; Karraker, 2008; Waldfogel, 2006).

Our guidelines for good parenting have changed throughout the years, and what we think of as good parenting today was not always seen that way (Mintz, 2004). For example, compared to today's parents, parents in colonial America tended to be strict, emotionally distant, and expected unqualified obedience from their children. Some of this detachment may have been the result of the high infant and child mortality rates during this period; parents were cautious about becoming too close with their children (Corsaro, 1997). Children were also thought to be born with "original sin," and therefore needed firm discipline and severe religious training to discourage their innate rebellion and selfishness,

family allowance (or child allowance): A cash benefit to families provided by the government to help offset the costs of raising children.

📖 **Read** on **MySocLab**
Document: *Breastfeed at Your Own Risk*

👁 **Watch** on **MySocLab**
Video: *Kathleen Gerson: Parental Choices*

and to keep them from literally going to Hell. Excessive tenderness from the parents was thought likely to spoil the child.

Children were treated as miniature adults in many ways (Mintz, 2004). There was little concept of adolescence, as there is today. As soon as children were old enough to labor on the family farm or in the household, they were put to work to help support the family.

During the Industrial Revolution, many families needed their children to work in the growing number of dangerous and dirty factories and other industries.

There were, of course, differences by race, ethnicity, social class, sex, and religious orientation (Mintz, 2004). For example, Quaker families tended to be more emotionally attached to their children than were Puritans. Wealthy families tended to be more indulgent with their children than poorer families. Slave families faced the psychological burden of worrying about when and where their children might be sold. Boys were seen as belonging under the tutelage of a father, whereas a girl's training was the domain of the mother and included many domestic tasks, such as cooking, cleaning, and sewing.

With industrialization, urbanization, and immigration during the 19th and early 20th centuries came sweeping changes in society (Handel, Cahill, & Elkin, 2007). Families moved from farms to cities in search of jobs, and record numbers of immigrants came from Europe in the hope of a better life. This period produced two views of childhood: the *protected child* among wealthy families, who was given education and leisure; and the *useful child,* whose labor was needed by poor and working-class families to make ends meet (Mintz, 2004). Although a protected childhood was the cultural ideal for which most people strived, few families could attain this ideal for their children. Most families needed their children to earn a wage in the growing number of dangerous and dirty factories and other industries, as well as to cook, clean, and take care of younger siblings at home.

During the Progressive Era of the early 1900s, people became concerned about the increasing exploitation of children (Stern & Axinn, 2012; Day & Schiele, 2013). Social reformers noted that there were few, if any, child labor laws, and many children toiled for 10 hours a day, 7 days a week, and never completed school. Because of the reformers' determination, many laws were finally passed protecting all workers, children in particular. With these workplace protections in place, the concept of childhood expanded to include a period that we now know as *adolescence.*

This brief historical review reveals some of the macro-level aspects that influenced how we personally experienced families. Economic considerations and the need for child labor, dominant religious paradigms, the degree of industrialization and urbanization, slavery laws, and views about men and women all came together to shape our context of parenting.

Cultural and historical differences make us wonder: Is parenting so different everywhere that we can find no common ground? This section of the chapter began by noting that the primary job of parents is to care for, nurture, and socialize children. Such parental responsibilities for children are found everywhere. Yet, there are other, newer themes beginning to emerge in the area of parenting. In looking at the evolution of childrearing, family scholars note at least three trends that exist in varying degrees in both industrial and nonindustrial societies today (Adams, 2004; Adams & Trost, 2004):

- *First, although parents are central to childrearing, other people and social institutions are becoming increasingly involved in raising children.* These include grandparents and other relatives, daycare settings, governmental agencies, schools, and factories. Related to this is the rising tide of women's employment outside the home. Even in historically poor and patriarchal countries such as Bangladesh, increases in women's employment are profoundly changing the nature of families, the distribution of spousal power, and the care of children (Ahmed & Bould, 2004).

- *Second, parents around the world increasingly encourage permissiveness and child independence.* There has been a decline in the value placed on obedience to parental authority, and more emphasis is now placed on independence and personal responsibility. Certainly, not all cultures meet these changes with unabashed enthusiasm, but worldwide trends persist nonetheless (Adams, 2004; Adams & Trost, 2004).

- *Third, in most societies in the world, a higher value is placed on boys than on girls.* The traditional preference for sons is based on family inheritance and the need for sons to care for aging parents. These values are very strong in countries such as China, Kenya, and India, but a preference for males is found in other countries as well (Banister, 2009; Barot, 2012). For example, a study conducted in India by the International Center for Research on Women showed that 46 percent of women said that they want more sons than daughters. Only 3 percent of women reported wanting more daughters than sons, and the remainder said that they wanted an equal number of sons and daughters or had no preference (Pande & Malhotra, 2006).

Next, let's explore some dimensions of parenting. First, we focus on the process by which we learn about the rules of our culture and what's expected of us at different stages of our lives.

✳ **Explore** on **MySocLab**
Activity: *Parenthood in the Twin Cities*

*I*f you've had the opportunity to travel to other countries, compare and contrast the parenting there with what you're familiar with in the United States. If you witnessed any differences, what types of macro-level factors may contribute to those differences?

Socialization: Learning to Be Human

Socialization refers to the lifelong process by which we acquire the knowledge, cultural values, and skills needed to function as human beings and participate in society. Socialization is unique to humans because children are helpless at birth and have few instincts compared to other mammals. Although the debate about how much of "human nature" is biological and how much is social has not yet been definitely settled (and perhaps never will be), we do know that socialization is a powerfully complex process that imparts the qualities and cultural traits we think of as "human" (Aronson, Wilson, & Akert, 2012; Baron & Branscombe, 2012).

Theoretical Approaches to How Children Develop

Social psychologists have elaborated on many theories to explain child development and the process of socialization (Aronson, Wilson, & Akert, 2012; Feldman, 2010; Maccoby, 2007). We discuss four prominent social psychologists—Sigmund Freud, Jean Piaget, Charles Horton Cooley, and George Herbert Mead—and their works next.

SIGMUND FREUD AND THE PSYCHOANALYTIC PERSPECTIVE Sigmund Freud (1856–1939) lived in an era when biological explanations of human behavior were prevalent. He proposed that human behavior and personality originate from unconscious forces within individuals: the id, ego, and superego. The **id** is the part of the personality that includes biological drives and needs for immediate gratification. It's present at birth and readily visible in young children; however, this aspect of personality continues throughout our lives. The **ego** is the rational component of personality that attempts to balance the need for

9.2 Explain the socialization process

Questions That Matter

9.4 What are some well-known theories of human development and socialization?
9.5 Who socializes our children?
9.6 How does socialization differ by social class, race and ethnicity, and gender?

socialization: The lifelong process by which we acquire the cultural values and skills needed to function as human beings and participate in society.

id: According to Freud, the part of the personality that includes biological drives and needs for immediate gratification.

ego: According to Freud, the rational component of personality that attempts to balance the need for immediate gratification with the demands of society.

superego: According to Freud, this is our conscience, which draws upon our cultural values and norms to help us understand why we can't have everything we want.

sensorimotor stage: Piaget's first stage of cognitive development (from birth to age 2) in which infants and toddlers understand the world primarily through touch, sucking, listening, and looking.

preoperational thought: Piaget's second stage of cognitive development, occurring from ages 2 through 7, as the child learns language, symbolic play, and symbolic drawing, but does not grasp abstract concepts.

concrete operational thought: Piaget's third stage of cognitive development, which occurs between the ages of 7 and 12, when children begin to see the causal connections in their surroundings, and can manipulate categories, classification systems, and hierarchies in groups.

formal operational thought: Piaget's fourth stage of cognitive development, beginning at adolescence and continuing through adulthood, in which children develop capacities for abstract thought and can conceptualize more complex issues or rules that can be used for problem solving.

looking-glass self: Cooley's suggestion that we come to see ourselves as others perceive and respond to us.

role taking: According to Mead, the process of mentally assuming the role of another person to understand the world from their point of view and to anticipate their response to us.

social learning theory: Developed by Alfred Bandura, the theory that behavior is learned through modeling and reinforcement.

immediate gratification with the demands of society. It arises as we become aware that we can't have all that we desire and that our needs must be balanced with the demands of society. The **superego** is our conscience, which draws on our cultural values and norms to help us understand why we can't have everything we want.

JEAN PIAGET AND COGNITIVE DEVELOPMENT

Jean Piaget (1896–1980) was a Swiss psychologist whose research focused on how people think and understand. He was particularly interested in how children come to understand the world and make meaning of their experiences. He identified four stages of cognitive development that are rooted in biology and based on age. The first stage, which occurs in the first 2 years of life, is called the **sensorimotor stage.** Infants and toddlers understand the world primarily through touch, sucking, listening, and looking. A child begins to organize and exercise some control over his or her life. The second stage, **preoperational thought,** occurs from ages 2 through 7 as the child learns language, symbolic play, and symbolic drawing. They don't yet grasp abstract concepts, and their knowledge is tied to their own perceptions. The third stage, **concrete operational thought,** occurs between the ages of 7 and 12. During this period, children begin to see the causal connections in their surroundings and can manipulate categories, classification systems, and hierarchies in groups. The final stage of cognitive development is **formal operational thought,** which begins in adolescence and continues through adulthood. During this stage, children develop capacities for abstract thought, and can conceptualize more complex issues or rules that can be used for problem solving.

CHARLES HORTON COOLEY AND GEORGE HERBERT MEAD: THE SELF

Charles Horton Cooley (1864–1929) and George Herbert Mead (1863–1931) turned attention to a sociological perspective by proposing that an individual can't form a self-concept without social contact with others. They rejected or minimized Freud's claim of biological drives and Piaget's assertion that individuals develop chronologically as they age. Instead, they believed that human behavior and our self-identity are shaped by interactions with others and the meanings we attach to those interactions. Cooley suggested that we come to see ourselves as others perceive and respond to us, a process he described as the **looking-glass self.** For example, we see ourselves as thin or heavy, intelligent or less intelligent, attractive or unattractive, and trustworthy or irresponsible based on the way that other people perceive and respond to us.

Mead extended Cooley's sociological insight in several ways, including the view that social experience includes symbolic interaction. This was introduced in Chapter 1—we interact not just with words, but also with important symbols and meanings, such as eye contact or a wave of the hand. Mead also elaborated on Cooley's work by focusing on **role taking,** which is the process of mentally assuming the role of another person to understand the world from his or her point of view and to anticipate his or her response to us. Role taking helps us become self-reflective. Mead suggests that the self is divided into two components—the *I* and the *me*. The *I* is the subjective element of the self and represents spontaneity and interaction that we initiate. The *me* is the objective element of self, reflecting the internalized perceptions of others toward us. Both the *I* and the *me* are needed to form the social self. In other words, the feedback loop is critical—we initiate behavior that is ultimately guided by the ways that others see us.

SOCIAL LEARNING THEORY

Social learning theory, developed by Alfred Bandura (1973; 1977; 1997), expanded on the idea that children learn by reinforcement. Bandura believes that children also learn by watching and imitating others. As he has argued, "Learning would be exceedingly laborious, not to mention hazardous, if people had to rely solely on the efforts of their own actions to inform them what to do. Fortunately, most human behavior is learned observationally through modeling" (Bandura, 1977, p. 22). In his famous "Bobo doll" studies, the child participants observed an adult acting violently toward a doll. When the children were later allowed to play in a room with the doll, they began to imitate the aggressive actions they had previously observed. The children received no encouragement or incentives to beat up the doll; they were simply imitating the behavior they observed. Therefore, when parents smile, hug, or hit their children, it's a powerful socialization process that sets an example for how children choose to interact with other people.

📖 Read on MySocLab
Document: *The Looking Glass Self* (Cooley)

Who Teaches Our Children? Agents of Socialization

Chapter 2 introduced the various ways individuals, groups, or institutions—collectively referred to as *agents of socialization*—teach children about the norms and values of their particular culture. We briefly review these agents of socialization:

👁 Watch on MySocLab
Video: *Melissa Milkie: The Looking Glass Self*

- *Family members, especially parents*, have the greatest impact on socializing children because they provide the first exposure to a particular culture. Parents provide children with a place to live, food to eat, clothes to wear, vocabulary to learn, and medical care when sick, thus introducing the child to values and customs. They also pass on to the child his or her socioeconomic status and social position in terms of race, ethnicity, and religion.

- *Schools and childcare* enlarge children's worlds by introducing them to people and settings different from those of their immediate family. Schools organize and teach children a wide range of knowledge, skills, and customs, including the political ideology of the society.

- By the time they enter school, children are able to form *peer group* relationships without the direct supervision of family members and other adults. Peers usually reward conformity rather than deviations, so children learn to look, dress, talk, and act like others in their group. For example, young people learn which specific clothing styles are popular and which aren't.

- *Toys and games* also reflect our culture and teach children important messages about what it means to be a member of society. For example, as shown in Chapter 2, toys and games tell children about what it means to be a boy, girl, man, or woman in our culture.

- *The mass media*, including television and the Internet, are increasingly important mechanisms for socializing children. Ninety-seven percent of households have at least one television, and more than 80 percent have two or more (Stelter, 2011). In 1984, only 8 percent of Americans had a computer in their home. By 2011, 77 percent owned a computer, including 83 percent of households with children between the ages of 3 and 17, as shown in Table 9.1 (File, 2013). Low-income families and those with less education are less likely to have computers in their home (Newburger, 1997; U.S Census Bureau, July 2012).

Children imitate those around them, including family, peers, and who they see in the mass media.

In other words, socialization teaches children about the culture in which they live, but the socialization process isn't completely uniform. Macro-level factors shape our families, the schools we attend, the peers we come to know, our toys and games, and our exposure to mass media.

Next, we look at how a few of these macro-level factors influence the socialization process.

TABLE 9.1 Who Lives in a Home with at Least One Computer?

Most households now have computers, especially those that are wealthier or with higher levels of education. However, only about half of poor households or those with the least levels of education have a computer in the home.

Total	77%
Age	
3–17	83%
18–34	83%
35–44	86%
45–64	82%
65 and older	62%
Sex of householder	
Male	81%
Female	80%
Race and Ethnic Origin	
White, not Hispanic	85%
Black	68%
Asian	89%
Hispanic	68%
Household Income	
Less than $25,000	57%
$25,000–49,999	76%
$50,000–$99,999	92%
$100,000–$149,999	96%
$150,000 or more	96%
Education	
Less than High School Graduate	51%
High School or GED	71%
Some College or Associate's Degree	83%
Bachelor's Degree or Higher	93%

Source: U.S. Census Bureau, 2012.

Socialization and Social Class

Watch on MySocLab
Video: *Socialization: The Big Picture*

Your social class position has had a large effect on the ways you've been socialized and has helped shape who and what you are (Conger, Conger, & Martin, 2010; Crompton, 2006). First, social class affects how much money parents have to spend on their children. This in turn affects where they live; the quality of schools they attend; the types of neighbors and friends they have; the type of clothing they wear; and the types and amount of toys, hobbies, and enrichment activities, such as music lessons or sports. Participation in these programs costs money, may require parental involvement, and may necessitate significant preparation time, all of which low-income families may have little of or even lack completely (Weininger & Lareau, 2009). Yet, these programs can boost academic achievement and social development (Davies & Peltz, 2012; Gardner, Roth, & Brooks-Gunn, 2008; Society for Research in Child Development, 2008).

However, social class affects more than just material goods; it also affects the values, norms, and expectations that parents have for their children (Lareau, 2003; Seccombe, 2014). It's possible that the lower participation rates of low-income families also represent a different set of core values. Research studies have generally noted the following differences:

- When parents are asked to choose from a list of childhood traits they consider most desirable for their children, lower-income parents tend to choose traits such as obedience, conformity, staying out of trouble, and keeping neat and clean. In contrast, higher-income parents tend to choose traits such as creativity, ambition, independence, curiosity, and good judgment (Kohn, 1977; 2006).

- Lower-income parents tend to be more controlling, authoritarian, arbitrary in their discipline, and apt to use physical punishment, whereas higher-income parents tend to be more democratic and are more receptive to their children's opinions (Berlin, Ispa, Fine, Malone, Brooks-Gunn, Brady-Smith, Ayoub, & Bai, 2009; Lareau, 2003).

- Higher-income parents tend to show more warmth and affection to their children, talk to them more, and use more complex language than do parents from lower-income families (Berns, 2001; Ispa, Fine, Halgunseth, Harper, Robinson, Boyce, Brooks-Gunn, & Brady-Smith, 2004).

Sociologist Melvin Kohn suggested that parents value traits in their children that reflect the parents' world, particularly their world of work (1977). Lower-income parents tend to emphasize conformity and related traits because these traits will be useful in the working-class jobs their children are likely to hold in the future. For example, success on an assembly line requires obedience and conformity, not creativity, ambition, or curiosity. Those latter characteristics could actually sabotage good job performance. In contrast, higher-income parents are likely to have jobs that entail working with people or ideas, and involve self-direction and creativity. Higher-income parents value these characteristics and socialize their children to have them.

Therefore, it's likely that class differences in socialization reflect not only simple economic resources, but also the core values of parents as they prepare their children for their likely roles in society. We learn these values in our family of orientation, and we then reproduce these values in our families of procreation (Crompton, 2006).

To illustrate the power of social class, let's examine the work of sociologist Annette Lareau, who studied 88 families of school-age children (Lareau, 2003; Weininger & Lareau, 2009). She spent time with these families during meals, on trips to school and extra-curricular events, and on errands and appointments, visiting them about twenty different times over the course of her research. Lareau found strong social class differences in the ways parents interacted with their children. For example, middle-class parents enrolled their children in organized activities that they believed transmitted important life skills. They disciplined their children by talking with them; they valued creativity and independent thought. As one middle-class father told her,

> of the things I think is important is just exposure. The more I can expose children to, with a watchful eye and supervision, the more creative they can be in their own thinking. The more options they will be able to see for themselves, the more they get a sense of improved self-esteem, self-worth, and self-confidence. I think it is something they will carry over into adulthood. (Weininger & Lareau, 2009, pp. 688–689)

In contrast, children from working-class and low-income families engaged in fewer organized activities and were far more likely to spend their free time with their family and neighborhood friends. Working-class parents were more likely to see themselves as authority figures, and to issue directives rather than to try negotiating with their children. One mother spoke for many when she explained to her daughter why she must do something, "Because I said so and I'm your mother" (Weininger & Lareau, 2009, p. 690). Lareau also found that working-class parents were more likely to discipline their children with physical punishment and spanking.

Despite these differences, let's be careful not to overgeneralize. Weininger and Lareau also found that middle-class parents routinely exercised subtle forms of control while attempting to instill self-direction in their children, whereas working-class and low-income parents tended to give children considerable autonomy in certain parts of daily life (Weininger & Lareau, 2009). Because working-class parents generally don't view life as a series of "teachable moments," they're less likely to try to manipulate or hover over their children. For example, one young girl, Katie, typically comes home after school, fixes a snack, and then decides by herself what to do for the rest of the afternoon. Sometimes she rides her bike; other times she watches television or plays with her younger brother or cousin. She has long stretches of unstructured leisure time and the choice to fill it spontaneously however she chooses. In contrast, her middle-class peers are given a structured menu of activities from which to choose.

Socialization, Race, and Ethnicity

As shown in Chapter 2, the United States is becoming more ethnically and racially diverse, creating a great need for sensitivity to values and customs that may differ among groups. The following story illustrates the importance of cultural values:

When Luana came to school with an unusual smear of dirt on her right arm, the teacher paid little attention. "Kids will be kids," she thought, aware that children often get dirty when they play. But the smudge on Luana's arm remained day after day, and on the fourth day her teacher told her to go and wash herself. Luana, usually a shy and quiet child, argued with her teacher, but the teacher told her not to argue and to do what she was told. Luana sulked, but did as the teacher asked. The next week Luana's parents took her out of school to attend her grandmother's funeral. Almost two weeks passed, and Luana had not yet returned to school, so the principal paid a visit to her home. There, Luana's mother firmly told him that Luana would never return to school because the teacher caused the grandmother's death. Since we are one with nature, an illness indicates that we are out of balance, her mother explained. When someone is sick, each family member uses oil to place soil on the body. The soil from Mother Earth shows that the family begs for balance. When the teacher made Luana wash her arm, our oneness with nature was broken. The teacher caused her death.

> "Since we are one with nature, an illness indicates that we are out of balance."

Racial and ethnic families may differ from the majority culture in terms of how they practice religion or medicine, the primacy of their family ties and sense of family obligation, their gendered patterns of behavior, their emphasis on time and promptness, the degree of hierarchy and authority in their relationships, how strict parents are with their children, their views on the roles of the elderly, the importance placed on group cooperation or individual achievement, and the way they interact, nurture, and discipline their children (McLoyd, Cauce, Takeuchi, & Wilson, 2000). For example, the Japanese have more traditional views of gender than do most Americans. Because middle-class jobs often require very long hours, often extending well into the night, few Japanese mothers work outside the home. Japanese women do the majority of housework and childcare. Japanese fathers, especially those who work at large corporations, are largely absent from the domestic world (Ishii-Kuntz, 2008, 2013; Ishii-Kuntz, Makino, Kato, & Tsuchiya, 2004). When fathers are engaged with their children, it's most often in "fun" activities like eating, rather than in more mundane activities such as food preparation or cleanup. On a recent visit to Tokyo, I gave a lecture at a large university, and the female graduate students were shocked to learn that I have children and a career, and wondered how American women manage to have both.

One important difference between the socialization practices of White and minority parents is that the latter must teach their children about the importance of race, ethnicity, prejudice, and discrimination, as they provide their children with the coping skills necessary to develop and maintain a strong and healthy self-image (Barr & Neville, 2008; Bentley, Adams, & Stevenson, 2009; Knight, Berkel, Umaña-Taylor, Gonzales, Ettekal, Jacionis, & Boyd, 2011; Tamis-LeMonda, Way, Hughes, Yoshikawa, Kalman, & Niwa, 2008; Umaña-Taylor, Zeiders, & Updegraff, 2013). Known as familial **racial** (or **ethnic**) **socialization,** parents' communication is important in shaping children's attitudes, beliefs, and self-efficacy in dealing with racial and ethnic experiences. Racial or ethnic socialization can instill a sense of identity, pride, and enculturation. Parents teach their children about religious traditions, cook specific types of foods, speak a particular language or dialect, and impart a set of values associated with their group identity. The feature box *Why Do Research?* reveals the importance of this socialization experience (Umaña-Taylor, Alfaro, Bámaca, & Guimond, 2009).

Racial and ethnic socialization also includes teaching the hard truths about racial and ethnic oppression in our society and provides children with the coping skills necessary to develop and maintain a strong and healthy self-image (Knight, Berkel, Umaña-Taylor, Gonzales, Ettekal, Jacionis, & Boyd, 2011; Umaña-Taylor, Zeiders, & Updegraff, 2013). When parents see instances of unfair treatment of their children, they become even more protective, and step up their cautions and warnings to them about racial and ethnic issues and relationships (Hughes & Johnson, 2001). This supportive parenting has been shown to reduce the harmful effects of racism, including anger, hostility, and aggressive behavior. For example, a study of more than 300 Black adolescent males found that those with supportive parents were less likely to respond with anger or hostility to perceived discrimination, and when angered, were less likely to behave aggressively (Simons, Simons, Burt, Drummund, Stewart, Brody, Gibbons, & Cutrona, 2006).

racial (or ethnic) socialization: Teaching minority children about prejudice, discrimination, and the coping skills necessary to develop and maintain a strong and healthy self-image.

Socialization and Gender

Chapter 2 identified many ways in which gender is constructed by families, social institutions (e.g., schools), and cultural artifacts (e.g., toys). Although there is no definitive answer as to how much of our gendered self is related to biology, most scientists suggest that gender differences probably are the result of biology and the social environment (Sax, 2005). Children learn about what it means to be a girl or a boy in a particular culture in a particular time first by the images, words, play, and rituals of their parents. Comments such as "Big boys don't cry," "You throw like a girl," "Let's play dress-up," "You're my little tomboy," "Help your mother with the dishes," and "Help your dad take out the trash," all teach us about how masculinity and femininity are defined across cultures and across different periods in history.

Parents are a major force in shaping the gendered attitudes of their children. One such gendered attitude is that boys tend to evaluate themselves as more intelligent than girls evaluate themselves. A recent study based on nearly 500 eleventh and twelfth graders looked at whether boys' greater confidence is a result of actual sex differences in intelligence, or whether it may be the result of sex-typed parental perceptions of their children's intelligence (Steinmayr & Spinath, 2009). All students were assessed for verbal, numerical, figural, and reasoning intelligence; no differences were found. Yet the students' parents rated boys' numerical, figural, and reasoning intelligence higher than that of the girls.

Watch on MySocLab Video: *Gender and Socialization*

The Importance of Ethnic Socialization for Hispanic Adolescents' Sense of Cultural Identity

The meanings that people make of their race, ethnicity, or culture are referred to as *cultural orientation,* which includes the degree to which individuals (1) adhere to the values and behaviors of mainstream culture (i.e., *acculturation*); (2) adhere to the values and behaviors of the native culture (i.e., *enculturation*); and (3) explore and define their identity with respect to the native culture (i.e., *ethnic identity*). This study examines the importance of ethnic socialization to the enculturation and ethnic identity of adolescents. The researchers also wondered whether ethnic socialization had different effects on adolescent boys and girls.

Hispanic students were recruited from five high schools with small Hispanic populations (only 8–16 percent), with an equal number of adolescent boys and girls participating. The study was longitudinal, meaning that the students were followed over time, in this case over the course of four years. Each student completed a 45-minute survey every year, and was paid for their participation. About 20 percent of the students dropped out over the course of the four-year study—they may have graduated, transferred schools, or were otherwise unavailable or unwilling to participate, but 80 percent were followed over the full four years.

The researchers asked students a wide variety of questions in their surveys to identify (1) their generational status; (2) the degree of ethnic socialization they experienced; (3) the depth of their enculturation; and (4) their ethnic identity. With respect to their generational status, adolescents reported the country of birth for themselves, each parent, and each grandparent to produce an account of their generational status in the United States. With respect to ethnic socialization, students responded to a series of statements such as, "My family teaches me about our family's ethnic/cultural background," and "Our home is decorated with things that reflect my ethnic/cultural background." Enculturation was measured by students' fluency in reading, writing, and understanding Spanish, and students were asked about how frequently they used Spanish electronic media. Level of enculturation was also determined by a series of questions about traditional values, such as, "The family should consult close relatives (uncles and aunts) concerning its important decisions." Finally, with respect to ethnic identity, students were asked a series of questions that assessed the degree to which adolescents have explored and resolved what their ethnic identity means to them, such as "I have attended events that have helped me learn more about my ethnicity," and "I have a clear sense of what my ethnicity means to me."

Minority parents must teach their children about the importance of race, ethnicity, prejudice, and discrimination, while providing the skills necessary to instill pride and maintain a strong and healthy self-image.

Using sophisticated statistical techniques, the researchers concluded that generational status is an important predictor of ethnic socialization and Spanish fluency. The longer a family has lived in the United States, the less likely are parents to partake in ethnic socialization or to teach their children Spanish. Second, ethnic socialization is an important predictor of ethnic identity for both adolescent boys and girls. Students whose parents deliberately taught them about their ethnicity and culture were more likely to be interested in, explore, and feel comfortable with their ethnic heritage. Third, they found that adolescent girls experience more overt ethnic socialization than do adolescent boys. Parents assume that adolescent girls will be the carrier of the culture, and spend more time overtly teaching them about Hispanic issues. Taken together, this research identifies the central importance that families play in racial and ethnic socialization.

WHAT DO YOU THINK?

1. What do you think are the methodological strengths and weaknesses of this study? Think about things like the research method used (see Chapter 1, pp. 22–26).
2. Do you think these findings would hold true for other racial or ethnic groups? Why or why not?

Sources: Umaña-Taylor, Alfaro, Bámaca, & Guimond, 2009; Umaña-Taylor, Yazedjian, & Bámaca-Gomez, 2004.

Think about your social class, racial or ethnic background, or your sex, and reflect on specific ways that these statuses have shaped the way you were socialized by your parents. Of these three statuses, which had the most powerful influence on your socialization, and why?

Parents also shape gendered attitudes of their children by their own behavior. For example, a longitudinal study that followed children for 30 years found that sons who grew up in a household in which their mothers stayed home while their fathers worked outside the home held more traditional gendered views as adults than did sons with dual-earner parents (Cunningham-Burley, 2001). Likewise, sons who saw their fathers doing stereotypical female labor in the home (e.g., washing dishes, cooking) were more likely to engage in those types of tasks as an adult than were other sons.

Parents have many different ways or styles of socializing their children. Let's explore these parenting styles in the next section.

Parenting Styles

Question That Matters

9.7 What are three different parenting styles?

My daughter Ramona came home with a "C–" in algebra on her report card. I know that Ramona is capable of doing much better than this. Yes, I realize that her algebra homework takes extra time to understand and do correctly, and I am going to help her make the time in her busy day to devote to algebra. She will have to postpone one of her extracurricular activities until her grade improves. I will let her choose which one to postpone, and then we can assess the situation after her next report card.

My son Derek came home with a "C–" in algebra on his report card. I know that the subject is hard for Derek and he can't really help his poor grade. I don't want him to feel badly about it; I certainly don't want it to erode his self-esteem. I think we will all go out to dinner tonight and have fun, and try to forget about his "C–," after all, it's only a grade, isn't it? I'm sure he is doing his best.

My daughter Rebecca came home with a "C–" in algebra on her report card. What in the hell is that all about? That's it! She's grounded for a month. No child of mine is going to be a "C–" student. She can just get over herself. "Rebecca, come here right now because you have some explaining to do, do you hear me?"

In the mid-1960s, researchers began to study parenting practices systematically. After careful observation and analysis of many different parents with their children, Diana Baumrind (1966; 1968) identified three general styles of parenting—a typology that remains widely used today. One style is reflected in the quote of Ramona's parent and is referred to as an **authoritative parenting style**. Parents are demanding and maintain high levels of control over their children, but they're also warm and receptive. These parents try to guide their children with compassion while also setting limits on their behavior. Children are expected to follow the house rules, but at the same time, parents are flexible, caring, and responsive.

In contrast, the quote of Derek's parent exhibits a **permissive parenting style**. Parents who adopt this style may be very nurturing, caring, and responsive to their children. They communicate well with their children, but they are, however, quite lenient. They put few controls or demands on their children and don't hold them accountable for their actions.

Finally, the quote of Rebecca's parent illustrates an **authoritarian parenting style**. In this style, parents are strict, punitive, less communicative, and offer less warmth and support. These parents love their children, but tend toward rigidity. They expect complete obedience as there is little room for compromise, and they offer little real communication with their children. These parents may also be more likely to use *corporal punishment* (spanking and physical discipline), an issue covered more fully in Chapter 11. Between 1986 and 2010, the proportion of women who agreed or strongly agreed that it's sometimes necessary to give a child a "good, hard spanking" dropped from 82 percent to 64 percent. Among men over the same period, this proportion fell from 84 percent to 75 percent (Child Trends, 2012).

Can you guess which type of parenting style yields the best results? Both boys and girls tend to perform better in school and are more socially competent when raised by authoritative parents as compared to the other two types (Bradley, 2006; Larzelere, Morris, & Harrist, 2012). Children raised by authoritarian parents were more often fearful, and children raised by permissive parents were more likely to be aggressive and impulsive (Baumrind, 1966; 1968). In sum, developmental psychologists believe that the authoritative parenting style best predicts outcomes in children thought to be most desirable (Cheah, Leung, Tahseen, & Schultz, 2009; Dumas, Lawford, Tieu, & Pratt, 2009).

Let's now look at specific aspects of parenting—the identities of parents and their specific activities–and see how these identities and activities differ for fathers and mothers.

authoritative parenting style: A parenting style that is demanding and maintains high levels of control over the children, but is also warm and receptive.

permissive parenting style: A parenting style that places few controls or demands on the child.

authoritarian parenting style: A parenting style that is strict, punitive, and not very warm.

Which parenting style did your parents have? Did the style differ between your mother and father? How does their parenting style influence you today?

👁 **Watch** on **MySocLab**
Video: *ABC Nightline: The Mommy Mystique*

Mothering

Mother and *father* are nouns—these words identify biological lineage. But they also indicate legal and social ties, which aren't always the same as biological lineage. For example, an adopted child may think of someone as *Mom* even though the child has no biological connection to her. In addition, this child may have no real connection at all to the person who gave birth to her. Does the word *mother* describe the relationship between a child and the partner of her lesbian mother? Both women may see themselves as mothers, although the law may only recognize one of them. And just to make things more confusing, when a surrogate gives birth, who is the mother—the woman giving birth, or the woman who hired the surrogate? We can see from these examples that the seemingly simple nouns *mother* and *father* aren't always so simple. They're both biological and social statuses.

But what do we mean when we say *mothering* or *fathering*? These terms are even more complex. They represent both an identity and a specific set of tasks.

Mothering as an Identity

What is *mothering*? Most people think it's the emotional and physical work involved with caring for children, but mothering takes place within specific historical and cultural contexts, and is framed by structures of gender, race, and class. The expectations associated with mothering are socially constructed—they're never static, but are continually changing. What is seen as good or appropriate mothering in one place and time may be perceived quite differently elsewhere. Anthropological literature provides many examples of the variability in mothering, suggesting that it's primarily Western societies in which women (and their partners) raise children in isolation. Anthropologists illustrate other models that draw on an extended circle of family, including older siblings, grandmothers, grandfathers, aunts, uncles, and cousins.

In the United States, motherhood is a powerful identity, more powerful than either marital status or occupation. Women with children report experiencing greater meaning in their lives than do childfree women (Ross & Van Willigen, 1996). Ironically, however, they also report greater distress or depression than do childfree women (Doss, Rhoades, Stanley, & Markman, 2009), although this may depend on the age of the child (Nomaguchi, 2012a). This is because of the stresses associated with the extensive and ongoing emotional work; the increased household labor; the reduction in finances (e.g., a mother quitting work or working only part-time); the increased financial needs that accompany children; and the lack of social support and government assistance they receive for their mothering tasks.

Compared to other developed nations, American mothering is more intense and fraught with anxiety (Warner, 2005). In her book *Perfect Madness: Motherhood in the Age of Anxiety*, Judith Warner describes the "mess" that accompanies American motherhood—the unending anxiety about whether American women are perfect mothers wreaks havoc on their emotional well-being. Women in other countries are less likely to fret about the pros and cons of combining work with employment, or to debate whether young children benefit from childcare or should stay at home. They're more able to relax and feel confident in their abilities as mothers. Much of this confidence comes from knowing that they're not mothering alone, but that they have a cadre of social and health professionals, midwives, physicians, nannies, and professional childcare providers, available at government expense, ready to help them and their children, as described in Chapter 8.

Mothering as an Activity

Mothering can bring tremendous personal satisfaction and growth, and boundless love. Most women want to become mothers; however, mothering, especially in the United States, isn't without personal, financial, and social costs.

Mothers in the United States are typically more involved with their children than are fathers. Mothers do the majority of socialization, hands-on care, emotional work, discipline, transporting, and management (e.g., remembering to make the twice-yearly dental appointment) (Parker & Wang, 2013; Poortman & van der Lippe, 2009). Mothers spend twice the amount of time per week caring for children as do fathers, on average.

How does employment affect the time a woman has to spend mothering? Employment slightly reduces the amount of time she spends with her children; however, it doesn't increase the amount of time a father spends with his children (Parker & Wang, 2013).

Nonetheless, many employed mothers feel guilty about the time they spend away from home. There is a cultural contradiction: Even though most mothers work outside the home, they must deal with critical judgments for doing so. Yet, if a mother stays at home, she pays the price of being treated as an outsider to the larger world. As one woman laments:

Did your mother work or stay home when you were a child? How did this arrangement affect you? What arrangement would you like to have if you have children, and why?

> I felt really torn between what I wanted to do. Like a gut-wrenching decision. Like, what's more important? Of course your kids are important, but you know, there's so many outside pressures for women to work. Every ad you see in magazines or on television shows this working woman who's coming home with a briefcase and their kids are all dressed and clean. It's such a lie. I don't know of anybody who lives like that (Hays, 2001, p. 317).

It's no wonder that many women, especially women with children, are tired. A recent Gallup poll asked men and women if they felt "well-rested" yesterday (Gallup Inc., 2010). Thirty-three percent of women said "no," in comparison to only 26 percent of the men. Likewise, 34 percent of adults who had at least one child in the household did not feel well rested, as compared to only 27 percent of childfree adults. But how do mothers with children and fathers with children compare to one another? The gap continues to grow, as shown in Figure 9.1.

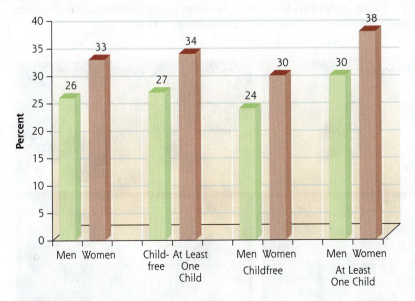

FIGURE 9.1

Percentage of Respondents Saying They "Did Not Feel Well-Rested Yesterday", by Sex, and Whether They Have a Child in the Home

Women are more likely than men to say that they're not well rested. Why do you think this is the case?
Source: Gallup Inc., 2010. All rights reserved. The content is used with permission: however, Gallup retains all rights to republication.

Question That Matters

9.9 How have fathers' roles changed in recent years?

👁 **Watch** on **MySocLab**
Video: *Alford Young: Parenting*

📖 **Read** on **MySocLab**
Document: *Fathering: Paradoxes, Contradictions, and Dilemmas*

Fathering

What about fathers? What are their identities, and what activities do they engage in? How are these identities and activities different from those of mothers?

Fathering as an Identity

Despite the popular stereotype of fathers as only "breadwinners," fathers have played other social roles throughout history, including moral overseer, nurturer, and a gender model for their sons (LaRossa, 2011; Marsiglio & Roy, 2012). However, specific details about the hands-on role they've had with their children aren't as well-known. Sociologist Jessie Bernard (1973) traced the historical development of and the changes in male roles in U.S. families. She observed that the Industrial Revolution in the mid-19th century transformed men's roles into that of the "good provider," in which the focus shifted to primarily their breadwinning capabilities (Bernard, 1973). Instead of participating in the more nurturing and caretaking aspects of family life, as they had done in the past, fathers were removed physically and emotionally from the work done at home. Being a good provider became the dominant concept of male identity. Moreover, having an employed wife was indicative of the father's failure to provide for his family, and threatened to undermine his position as "head of the household."

This model continued until the 1970s and 1980s, when the women's movement and other social movements ushered in ideological changes about men's and women's positions and roles within the family. As more married women with children sought employment, families began to restructure themselves. Men are now becoming more involved in domestic life and caring for their children, and many are relieved that they no longer have the economic burden of being the sole breadwinner.

Since about the late 1980s, there has been an explosion in research on fathering: What do fathers do with their children, what are the outcomes, and what are the meanings associated with being a father? Culturally, most of us now believe that a father should be engaged with his children, and recognize him as an important nurturing figure in the family (Marsiglio & Roy, 2013; Nielsen, 2012). Many programs have been developed to promote and encourage this relationship (see National Fatherhood Initiative, 2013).

Most people want to have children; however, *mothering* and *fathering* are really quite different roles and responsibilities. Mothers tend to spend far more time on their child's physical care, while fathers spend more time in play.

Fathering as an Activity

How involved are fathers in their children's lives? We know that mothers perform the majority of parenting tasks; however, fathers do play an important role, and their involvement is increasing, as shown in Table 9.2 (Parker & Wang, 2013). A generation ago, fathers spent only about 2.5 hours a week in direct childcare; today, that figure has nearly tripled to 7 hours a week (Bianchi, Robinson, & Milkie, 2006; Parker & Wang, 2013). Fathers are also now more likely than mothers to say that they spend "too little" time with their children, as shown in Figure 9.2.

Let's meet one of these "new" fathers, Cade, in the feature box *My Family: What I Like about Being a Dad . . . and What I Don't.*

The amount of time spent with children tends to decline as the child ages. Fathers with children ages 2 and younger spend most of their time playing with children. As the child ages, fathers spend a greater portion of time on caregiving activities such as personal care or making meals; however, caregiving tasks still primarily fall to the mother.

Those fathers who were raised by their biological fathers, have higher levels of education, who have employed partners, and who have more egalitarian views about gender, are more involved with their children—both sons and daughters—than are fathers with more traditional gender ideologies (Bulanda, 2004; Yoshida, 2012). Involved fathers take pride and pleasure in their participation, although they may try to justify why their participation is less than that of their wives, as these two men do (Gerson, 2001, p. 335):

TABLE 9.2	Hours Spent on Childcare per Week	
Fathers' involvement with their children has grown significantly.		
	Fathers	**Mothers**
1965	2.5	10.2
1975	2.6	8.6
1985	2.6	8.4
1995	4.2	9.6
2005	6.8	13.6
2011	7.3	13.5

Source: Parker & Wang, 2013.

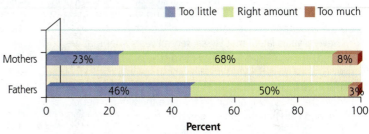

FIGURE 9.2

Time with Children Too Much or Too Little? (Percent)

Fathers are now more likely than mothers to say they spend "too little" time with their children.
Source: Parker & Wang, 2013.

> I guess we both have to do some sacrificing; that's basically what it is to be a parent. It's probably not going to be fifty-fifty. . . . I think the mother would have a tendency to do a little more. But even sixty-forty is pretty good compared to the average.
>
> **— William**

> I wish I did more, but our time reference is quite different. I'll say, "Okay, I'll do that, but let me do this first." But she will frequently get frustrated and just not be able to stand the thought that it's not done, and then go ahead and do it.
>
> **—Sam**

How does involvement on the part of fathers affect their children? Father's involvement can enhance children's social, emotional, and cognitive well-being (Bronte-Tinkew, Carrano, Horowitz, & Kinukawa, 2008; National Fatherhood Initiative, 2013; Solomon-Fears, Falk, & Fernandes-Alcantara, 2013). In a survey analysis of nearly 100 studies on parent–child relationships, the degree of *father love* (measured by children's perceptions of paternal acceptance/rejection and affection/indifference) was as important as the degree of "mother love" in predicting the social, emotional, and cognitive development and functioning of children and young adults (Horn & Sylvester, 2006; Rohner & Veneziano, 2001).

Many children don't live with their fathers because of divorce, separation, or because their parents were never married. Nearly one-half of U.S. children will experience living without a biological father for some period of their childhood. Some of these children see their fathers regularly, whereas others see their fathers sporadically or infrequently. Boys generally have more frequent contact with

Read on **MySocLab**
Document: *Dilemmas of Involved Fatherhood*

Read on **MySocLab**
Document: *Life Without Father: What Happens to the Children?*

I've always assumed I would have a few kids. While I've never been obsessed about it, I just figured that when I met the right person, we would get married and have two or three kids soon there after. I had to confront that image head-on when I was in a serious relationship after college. Amari was clear—she didn't want children. Not now, not ever. I didn't understand her decision at first—she spoke of how they would limit her career options, she would have to do most of the work, and she didn't really enjoy the company of children. Now, I'm a pretty enlightened guy, so I thought I could convince her that her number one and two concerns just really weren't issues. But my rational reasoning fell on deaf ears. So, I then considered forgoing kids for her sake. But that didn't last. We finally had to acknowledge that there really is no way to compromise on the issue, and so we ended our relationship.

Several years later I met Elyssa, several years after that we married, and voilà, today we have two fabulous kids. Nathan is now 6, and Liza is 5. What do I like about being a dad? I feel like I now have a greater purpose in life than just focusing on myself. I know that these two are going to make the world a better place, and I am here to show them how to do it. Also, they're fun. I get a kick out of their silly antics. We love to work on model airplanes in the living room, eat ice cream for breakfast on Saturdays, and play on the swings at the park. They make me feel like I'm a kid again. I took Nathan canoeing last month, and I'm really looking forward to him getting a little older so we can do more things like that together. Elyssa and I also have a strong bond as parents, and I feel confident that it will never be broken.

Now that I've said all this, let me tell you that being a dad can also be a real drag. Okay, while I'm glad to focus on someone other than just myself, it would be nice to focus on me once in a while! Remember sleeping in late on Saturdays? Forget it. Liza is up every day at 6:00, and Nathan is up soon after. Elyssa usually gets up with them, but sometimes she's just so darn tired that I do it. And the house is usually a mess, with toys everywhere, dirty laundry piled up, and dishes in the sink. Speaking of which, the amount of housework that needs to be done is just ridiculous. I feel like I'm always cooking, cleaning, and soothing somebody, but to be honest, Elyssa is far more involved in it than I am. One more thing, and this is a big one—our sex life has taken a turn for the worse. We're both so busy with work and kids that we almost have to pencil it in on the calendar—well, that's her excuse anyway. And, I never thought I'd be doing *date night*—an evening planned way in advance—there just isn't any spontaneity when you have to line up a teenage babysitter.

So, while I'm really glad I'm a dad, it is not all a party, believe me. It's hard work. But would I have it any other way? Not on your life.

—Cade, Age 34

WHAT DO YOU THINK?

1. If you only read Cade's viewpoint, can you describe his family relationships? Look for clues throughout his story. What type of marriage do you think he has? Is he an involved parent? Describe the division of labor.
2. What macro-level factors affect Cade's experiences? Can you see macro-level influences with both Amari and Elyssa?

Listen on **MySocLab**
Audio: *NPR: Fathers Taking More Active Role in Raising Children*

*T*hink about your own father. To what degree was he involved in your life? What changes or similarities would you like to make in fatherhood for your own children, if you have them?

their nonresident biological father than do girls, at least with respect to overnight visits, sports, and movies (King, Harris, & Heard, 2004; Mitchell, Booth, & King, 2009). Racial and ethnic differences exist as well in specific activities (e.g., staying overnight, playing sports, going to religious services, talking about dating); however, no one racial or ethnic group stands out as being significantly higher or lower on father involvement (King, Harris, & Heard, 2004).

Thus far we've discussed the identities and activities of parents, but what about those of children? They aren't passive recipients of their parents' behaviors because they, too, shape parent–child relationships. Socialization, mothering, and fathering occur in *interaction* with children. Children aren't only influenced by their parents, but also influence them.

9.6 Identify how children influence their parents

Question That Matters

9.10 How do children influence their parents?

How Do Children Influence Their Parents?

From infancy to adulthood, children are actively engaged with their parents and help influence their own family experience and the behaviors, attitudes, and well-being of their parents (Kalmijn & Graaf, 2012; Warner, 2006). Parents don't simply socialize children; children also influence this socialization through their own temperament, cognitive abilities, health and well-being, and sex. Systems theory, introduced in Chapter 1, is useful here because it reminds us that families aren't just one unit, but are made up of many different subsystems (Broderick & Smith, 1979), and each subsystem operates to influence the whole. Parents influence children, and children influence their parents in the following ways:

- *Temperament.* "Oh, he's an easy baby," we hear a new parent say. "She was such a difficult child," we hear another parent report. What do they mean by their children being *easy* or *difficult*? All people have a certain behavioral style known as *temperament* (Gartstein & Rothbart, 2009; Rothbart & Sheese, 2007). Behavioral differences are present from birth, and they influence how babies and, later, children behave toward others and how, in turn, they're affected by their environment. Temperament assessments often look at nine characteristics: activity level, regularity, adaptability, approach to novelty, emotional intensity, quality of mood, sensory sensitivity, distractibility, and persistence (Temperament.com, 2013; Thomas & Chess, 1957). A child who is often fussy; cries a lot; is highly sensitive to light, sounds, or scratchy clothing; doesn't respond well to change; and is very active is more difficult to parent than is the child who is usually in a good mood and smiles a lot, doesn't often cry, sleeps on a fairly regular schedule, and adapts well to transitions. Therefore, the "easy" child may give and receive lots of attention and affection, but the "difficult" child may receive less nurturance and affection, especially if the fit between child and parent temperament is poor (Bornstein, 2002). Temperament affects the views that parents have of the child and the views they have of themselves as parents.

- *Cognitive abilities.* Earlier, you were introduced to Piaget's work on the different stages of cognitive development. A child's stage of development has an important influence on how the parents socialize and interact with that child. For example, an infant or toddler in the sensorimotor stage understands the world primarily through touch, sucking, listening, and looking. A parent wouldn't assume that their infant or toddler had capacities for abstract thought or could conceptualize more complex issues or rules for problem solving. Children go through these stages at approximately the same age.

Children's temperament, cognitive stages and intellectual abilities, health, and sex all work together to shape the parenting experience. This intelligent young man, Sameer Mishra, 13, is embraced by his father, while his sister watches, after winning the Scripps National Spelling Bee in Washington, DC. Mishra correctly spelled *guerdon,* meaning something one has earned or gained, to win the competition.

However, other cognitive abilities, such as intelligence quotient (IQ), are far more variable, and also greatly influence how parents interact with and socialize their children (Kaufman, 2009). There are many arguments that IQ tests are culturally biased or ignore creativity or practical intelligence (Kaufman, 2009; Murdoch, 2007). Most researchers are aware that biases in test questions are possible and have made serious attempts to overcome them. They also are quick to acknowledge that IQ tests measure only one part of intelligence—cognitive abilities—and shouldn't be interpreted to reflect global intelligence (Fletcher-Janzen, 2009). Nonetheless, if an IQ of 100 is average, what do we make of a child who scores 135 and is in the 99th percentile? This means that if 100 children were in the room, he or she would have scored higher on cognitive abilities than the other children. This child is as far from average as is the child who scored a 65—someone who is in the range of mental retardation or otherwise has such low cognitive abilities that they're in the first percentile, the lowest score in the room. The cognitive skills that children bring to a family can greatly affect the ways that parents and children interact, including the types of conversations they have, the games they can play, the chores children are given to do, the type of discipline used, and overall expectations for the child and his or her place within the family and society.

- *Health and well-being.* Today, pregnancy, childbirth, and infancy are relatively safe, with only 6 babies out of 1,000 live births failing to survive the first year of life in the United States (Central Intelligence Agency, 2013). Immunizations and access to health care have improved children's chances of staying healthy and surviving to adulthood. Nonetheless, not all children are healthy. Asthma, chronic ear infections, lead paint poisoning, attention deficit disorder, diabetes, and disabilities are just some of the many ailments that millions of children suffer. Not surprisingly, parents of children with chronic conditions or disabilities must prepare their children for a unique set of challenges. For example, 6 million children alone have asthma, and there is no known cure (National Heart, Lung, and Blood Institute, 2009). Parents must actively monitor their children, teach them about the factors that trigger their asthma, and develop a treatment plan for them, such as how to use an inhaler properly.

Parents face many stressors. The feature box *Diversity in Families*: *Sara and Jake: Living Disability* reveals the struggles that families of severely

DIVERSITY IN FAMILIES   Sarah and Jake: Living Disability

I met Sarah several years ago when I was interviewing families for a research project about the health of low-income families and whether they were able to get the health insurance and health care they need. I will always remember her. Before undertaking the "business" of the interview, it was clearly important to Sarah that I meet her son Jake. She carefully and lovingly presented Jake, an 8-year-old, who was lying on a blanket on the floor of her cramped living room, wearing nothing but a diaper. His skin was pale, as though he had never been exposed to sunlight. Although he's the size of a typical third grader, in all other respects, Jake is like an infant. He has severe cerebral palsy and developmental disabilities, which may have been caused by complications during Sarah's pregnancy and his birth. He was not breathing at birth, but was successfully revived; nonetheless, he suffered brain damage because of oxygen deprivation.

Sarah described for me what their lives have been like since Jake's birth:

He's 8 years old and he doesn't talk. He makes sounds, more or less to indicate what he needs. He's in a wheelchair because he doesn't walk. So it's basically like having a 3-month-old child that cries whenever it needs anything, and as a mom you do the same thing that any mother would. You go down a checklist: you've just eaten; you've just had your diaper changed, so it's a matter of a guessing game of what he needs or wants. His favorite sound is "uh," which sometimes means he wants a drink of water. But "uh" also means he can't reach his toy, or "uh" means you're watching TV and not feeding me.

My child is 8 years old and the plain fact is, he's 8 years old and he can't do anything for himself except play with his toys and his newspaper. If I set him here on the

floor he stays in this vicinity—he falls over on his side, he rolls on his tummy, he turns himself around a little, but he's subject to this part of the house because that's where I put him. Other than crying, I could leave him here all day long if I so desired and that would just have to work because there is nothing he could do about it. Not that I would, and let me tell you, that boy's got a great set of lungs.

Sarah went on to tell me of the difficulties raising Jake. She can take nothing for granted:

You can't have somebody come over and babysit at your house for five dollars. You're not talking about a kid who can say, "I'm tired, I want to go to bed," or "Can we watch a movie?" or "I'm hungry now." My fear of having any other sort of daycare take care of him is because of the fact that he doesn't complain about things. Does that mean he's going to sit in the corner for an hour and a half? There's no way of knowing, and in this day and age, God knows, he can't tell me if someone is doing anything unmentionable to him. I just pray to God every time he leaves the house that the person I'm sending him to school with is dependable and not some weirdo.

WHAT DO YOU THINK?

1. In what ways do you think Jake's disability has affected Sarah's role as a mother?
2. How is Sarah's mothering—both the identity and the activity—similar to and different from other mothers who do not have a child with a disability?

Source: Seccombe & Hoffman, 2007.

disabled children face every single day, including finding adequate childcare (Lee, Chen, Wang, & Chen, 2007), organizing critical social and health services (Seccombe & Hoffman, 2007), coping with the stigma attached to the condition, and managing the guilt that parents often feel when they see their child suffer.

- *Sex.* As you may recall, *sex* refers to biological categories—being female or male. But how does a child's sex affect parenting? First, parents react differently to sons and daughters. For example, parents are more verbal with daughters and more physical with sons, even when children are infants (Nokoff & Fausto-Sterling, 2008; Sax, 2005). Second, the amount of time that parents spend with sons and daughters, especially the father's time, differs (Lundberg, McLanahan, & Rose, 2007; Mammen, 2009). Fathers spend more time with sons than they do with daughters and are more willing to be involved in the care of even young infants if they have a son (Yoshida, 2012). Moreover, fathers who have all sons spend more time with them than do those fathers who have all daughters. In fact, fathers of boys are willing to reduce their own leisure time so that they'll have additional time to devote to their sons. Finally, a child's sex also influences the parents' relationship with one another, increasing the quality and stability of their marriage. Parents report more satisfaction with their relationship after the birth of a son and are more likely to marry, if they haven't done so already (Raley & Bianchi, 2006). Likewise, married couples are less likely to divorce if they have sons than if they have daughters (Dahl & Moretti, 2008). These research findings reveal that a child's sex influences the parent–child relationship in many ways.

Changing family demographics have created new social contexts for raising children, including with teen parents, single parents, gay and lesbian parents, and even with grandparents. The next section reveals unique challenges and strengths of a number of different contexts.

If you have siblings, think about the ways that each of them influenced your parents, their interactions with your parents, and the socialization process. Was their temperament, cognitive abilities, health, or sex a factor at all? Compare and contrast your siblings' experiences to your relationship with your parents. Are there any differences?

Parenting and Family Contexts

The traditional family has given way to a variety of different family arrangements. Growing numbers of singles, gays and lesbians, grandparents, stepparents, cohabiting couples, and extended families have altered the social context of parenting and have fueled new debates over parental rights and responsibilities. We explore several of these contexts next.

Teen Parents

As discussed in Chapter 5, fewer teens are becoming parents. Hispanics have the highest birth rates, but they also show the largest recent decline in birth rates. Nonetheless, about 330,000 teenagers gave birth in 2011 (Hamilton, Martin, & Ventura, October 2012), and our society is still very concerned about these numbers because of the difficulties teen mothers, fathers, and their children face.

What can be done to help reduce the number of teen pregnancies? In its annual report *Kids Count*, The Annie E. Casey Foundation makes the following recommendations (The Annie E. Casey Foundation, 2009):

- *Reinvigorate prevention efforts, intensifying the focus on underlying causes.* Most prevention efforts focus on young people's decision-making and behavior, but ignore broader macro-level social and environmental factors. Yet, the rates of teen pregnancy and childbearing are affected by race and ethnicity, family income, single parenthood, unemployment, neighborhood

9.7 Discuss different types of parenting contexts

Questions That Matter

9.11 What can be done to reduce the number of teen pregnancies?

9.12 Why should we be careful not to overgeneralize single parents?

9.13 How distinctive are gay and lesbian parents from heterosexual parents?

9.14 What are the unique strengths and challenges of grandparents raising grandchildren?

effects, and exposure to media (Advocates for Youth, 2009). Prevention efforts should be research-based, carefully targeted to those teens at greatest risk, and should consider protective factors such as social support networks as well as risk factors.

- *Help parents succeed in their role as sex educators.* Teen boys and girls who have strong emotional attachments to their parents and are closely supervised by them are much less likely to become sexually active; when those teens do become sexually active, they are more likely to use contraceptives. Prevention efforts should build and sustain ongoing parental involvement in all pregnancy prevention programs, and parents should be given the tools to talk to their children effectively and confidently.

About 400,000 U.S. teens give birth each year. In our culture, this is considered problematic because teens have not finished their education, have few job skills, and are not socially and emotionally well equipped to be parents.

- *Broaden the scope of pregnancy prevention efforts.* When prevention efforts are focused too narrowly, they miss critical opportunities to reach teens. For example, programs and policies aimed at preventing teen pregnancy should focus on both males and females, because young men are also at risk for poor outcomes when they create unwanted pregnancies. Programs that focus on a wide spectrum of risk-taking behaviors, not just sex, are important because teens who drink or use drugs are more likely to have sex, to begin having sex at a younger age, and to forgo using contraceptives.

- *Provide accurate, clear, consistent, and ongoing information about how to reduce risk-taking behavior.* There is a large and growing body of research on effective sex education; the best programs focus less on reproductive biology and more on teaching adolescents correct information about pregnancy and prevention, and giving them the skills they need to handle relationships, resist peer pressure, negotiate difficult situations, and make good decisions. Teens are eager for this information and want their parents to be involved.

- *Create a community-wide plan for teen pregnancy prevention, including adolescent reproductive health services.* Although most Americans want teens to refrain from having sex, most say that sexually active teenagers should have access to contraception. Reproductive health services should be located at sites that are accessible to teens and be low-cost or free, but community-wide plans should also address factors such as sex abuse and coercive sex, which play a greater role in teen pregnancy than has been commonly recognized.

- *Give young people a credible vision of a positive future.* Young people should be given opportunities to imagine a broad range of experiences and options that are open to them if they delay childbearing and parenting. This may involve developing teen programs that show clear connections and pathways to college or jobs that give them hope and a reason to stay in school. It may also involve developing mentoring programs for at-risk youth that provide a rich combination of education, support services, service learning, employment opportunities, and a caring adult willing to listen and help.

An extensive plan such as this one outlined by The Annie E. Casey Foundation could reduce our teenage birthrate even further.

Single Parents

Single-parent families are often seen as problematic and have even been referred to in the past as *broken homes*. Today, many people take exception to this negative term.

👁 **Watch** on **MySocLab**
Video: *ABC Nightline: Single Mothers*

The vast majority of single-parent families are single-mother families, and the terms are often used interchangeably—if you say *single parent* people typically think of *single mother*. These kinds of families have been maligned for causing juvenile delinquency, poverty, and a host of other social problems. The difficulty with such a generalization is that (1) there are different kinds of single-parent families with different kinds of circumstances (e.g., a teenage mother vs. a 40-year-old female executive); (2) there are different paths to becoming a single parent with varying consequences (i.e., never marrying, divorce, and widowhood); (3) the cause-and-effect relationship is unclear (i.e., does poverty cause single parenthood, or does single parenthood cause poverty?); and (4) single parenthood is less problematic in other industrialized nations because they have many social supports that are notably lacking in the United States (e.g., a higher minimum wage, nationalized health care, and childcare assistance).

Nonetheless, the number of single parents has risen in recent generations, as shown in Figure 9.3. In 1950, only 6 percent of households with children were maintained by a mother; now it's 24 percent. Only 1 percent of households in 1950 were maintained by single fathers, but that number has increased to 4 percent (U.S. Census Bureau, 2012; Kreider & Elliott, 2009). Yet, the total number of single-mother and single-father families has been relatively stable since the mid-1990s.

As Figure 9.4 reveals, Black children are far more likely to live with a single parent than are other racial or ethnic groups. Two-thirds of Black children live with a single parent, as compared to just 17 percent of Asian/Pacific Islander children (Annie E. Casey Foundation, 2013).

The route to single parenthood can take many different paths. Some women have babies outside of marriage; other people become single parents because of a divorce; still others may be widowed. We can make some generalizations about single parents—they're more likely to be impoverished and on food stamps, they're less likely to own a home, and they have lower levels of education (File, 2013; Kreider & Ellis, 2011). Yet, we should be cautious with these generalizations because the different routes to single parenthood produce different results.

For example, 15 percent of single mothers have a bachelor's degree or higher. Much of the scrutiny and concern surrounding single-parent families is targeted toward *young* women having babies outside of marriage. But the rise in single-parent families is largely the result of the rise in *older* unmarried women who are having babies, often by choice. Unmarried women in their thirties or forties offer a substantially different portrait of single parenthood than teens do. A

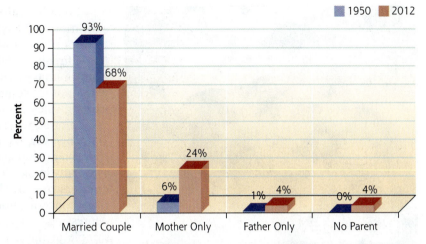

FIGURE 9.3

Family Households with Children Under 18, by Type, 1950 and 2012

In recent decades, the percentage of families with young children that are headed by mothers alone has increased fourfold.
Sources: U.S. Census Bureau, 2012; Kreider & Elliott, 2009.

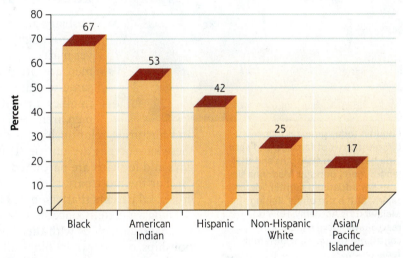

FIGURE 9.4

Percent of Children Living with a Single Parent by Race/Ethnicity, 2011

Two-thirds of Black children in the United States live with a single parent.
Source: Annie E. Casey Foundation, 2013.

📖 Read on **MySocLab**
Document: *Unmarried with Children*

📖 Read on **MySocLab**
Document: *Where's Papa?: Disappearing Dads Are Destroying Our Future*

Children today grow up in many different types of families, and each type has its own strengths and challenges. Here, pop star Madonna sits with her adopted daughter, Mercy James, at the site of her Raising Malawi Girls Academy. How do macro-level social conditions contribute to our many different family forms?

woman in her thirties or forties is likely to have completed her education and have a job, perhaps even a well-paying career.

Another important distinction is that, in some cases, what might first be viewed as a "single-parent" household isn't really a single household at all. The single parent may be cohabiting with another adult. The parents' partner in these families plays varying roles. Some have close, parent-like relationships with the children, whereas others are more distant.

However, some people remain concerned that so many children are being raised without a father present in the home, especially in light of the poor economic circumstances of single mothers overall (National Marriage Project, 2013). Despite these concerns, not all the news about single-parent families is depressing. For example, one study based on a representative sample in the United States found that children from single-parent families report that they talk to their mothers more often than do children in two-parent families. After a divorce, mothers and their children often report greater equality, intimacy, and companionship (Arditti & Madden-Derdich, 1997; McLanahan & Sandefur, 1994).

Lesbian and Gay Parents

Lesbians and gay men are still fighting for a basic human right: to be recognized and accepted as families. Because they can't yet marry in most states, the relationships of lesbians and gay men are often trivialized. The small amount of research on same-sex families tends to focus on lesbian families rather than families formed by gay males, enforcing the stereotype that gay men aren't interested in committed relationships with partners and nurturing relationships with children (Biblarz & Stacey, 2010). However, these stereotypes are untrue (Kurdek, 2008). As discussed in Chapter 3, many gays and lesbians are partnered, and some are raising children.

For the most part, same-sex parents have a great deal in common with heterosexual parents (Patterson & Hastings, 2007), as Karen and Betsy reveal in the opening vignette. Concerns that children growing up in gay or lesbian families will have difficulties with their own sexual identity, have difficulty in social relationships, or suffer psychologically have been largely unfounded. Instead, research studies find little or no significant difference in psychological well-being, performance in school, substance abuse, delinquency, or early sexual experiences (Biblarz & Savci, 2010; Biblarz & Stacey, 2010; Potter, 2012). Children growing up with same-sex parents are somewhat more likely to have had a homosexual experience or to envision that they could have one in the future, but as adults, they're no more likely than others to adopt a gay, lesbian, or bisexual identity.

There are many pathways for lesbians and gay men to become parents, including adoption and artificial insemination with a known or unknown sperm donor. However, most lesbian and gay families are formed as stepfamilies, in which the children were conceived in an earlier heterosexual relationship by one of the partners (Allen, 1997). Although most aspects of raising children are similar regardless of parents' sexual orientation (e.g., the daily tasks of getting children to school on time, taking children to soccer practice, getting involved in the PTA), several specific features can affect the dynamics of lesbians and gays raising children (Biblarz & Savci, 2010; Biblarz & Stacey, 2010; Spock, 2004; Stacey & Biblarz, 2001):

- *Because lesbians and gay men are stigmatized for having children, the decision to parent is generally a deliberate choice that reflects a strong commitment to raising children.* Studies tend to show either no difference among homosexuals and heterosexuals in their fitness to parent, or that lesbian mothers and gay fathers may have an edge. For example, lesbian mothers exhibit more parenting skills and awareness of child development than heterosexual couples, and there is greater similarity between partners' parenting skills. Likewise, compared to heterosexual fathers, gay fathers go to greater lengths to promote their children's cognitive skills, are more responsive to their children's needs, and are more involved in activities with children. Lesbian and gay couples also tend to have a more egalitarian division of household labor than do heterosexual couples, and this is reflected in their joint division of childcare.

- *Lesbian and gay families are more likely to be affected by loss.* Lacking institutional constraints and support such as legalized marriage, lesbian and gay relationships are somewhat more likely to dissolve than are heterosexual ones. Yet because lesbians and gay men can't legally marry in most states, their trauma may not be publicly recognized or as easily supported. Our society acknowledges the tremendous disruption caused by a divorce; however, a breakup may be trivialized. Lesbian and gay families may experience other losses as well. Lesbian and gay stepfamilies are created following a divorce (as are heterosexual stepfamilies), and children experience a loss of family members. Likewise, the HIV and AIDS epidemic has touched many lives, especially those in the gay male community.

- *Lesbian and gay families must cope with homophobia and discrimination.* Homosexuality is stigmatized, and living openly as a family leaves them vulnerable to ridicule or discrimination. Although you've learned that attitudes are becoming more tolerant, many people still condemn homosexual relationships as unnatural or immoral. Violence against gays and lesbians is a possibility (Shepard, 2009). Just as racial and ethnic minorities must teach their children about racism, gay and lesbian parents must teach their children that some people have disparaging feelings toward them as well.

- *Lesbians and gay men often have a close network of friends whom they regard as an extended family who provide emotional and social support.* Social support is crucial from family and friends as a way to ward off oppression and to create a safe and supportive environment for lesbians, gay men, and their children. They often have developed a close network of people who form a sort of extended family, or fictive kin, as introduced in Chapter 1. They are there to celebrate birthdays; participate in commitment ceremonies; babysit when needed; and in countless ways offer the love and support that are needed to keep a household and a family running smoothly. In fact, fictive kin are often more reliable and consistent in their support than biological families (Demo & Allen, 1996). Parents and families respond in a variety of ways, and organizations such as Parents, Families, and Friends of Lesbians and Gays (PFLAG) provide education, advocacy, and support to those in need.

Do you see any of these features in Karen and Betsy's family from the opening vignette?

Watch on MySocLab
Video: *Same Sex Marriages and Families*

Grandparents Raising Grandchildren

Grandparents have an important role in providing care for children (Dunifon & Bajracharya, 2012; Luo, LaPierre, Hughes, & Waite, 2012). In some cases, children live with their grandparents full-time and grandparents are significant or even sole caretakers. The U.S. Census Bureau estimates that almost 8 million children lived with their grandparents in their grandparents' own home (Kreider & Ellis, 2011). Sometimes the child's parent(s) also lives with the grandparent, and may live together to share expenses or provide social support to a frail grandparent or to a young family, but the greatest growth has occurred among children living with grandparents on their own without a parent present.

Where are these children's parents? Mothers and fathers may be absent for many reasons, including incarceration, drug or alcohol problems, physical or mental illnesses, employment difficulties, child abuse or neglect, desertion, or even death. When parents are unable or unwilling to care for their children, grandparents often step in. Most arrangements are done privately, but in about one in six cases, child welfare agencies have intervened on behalf of the child. One study of 129 grandparents raising their grandchildren examined the situations that led to grandparents taking over their grandchildren's care and found multiple problems (Sands & Goldberg-Glen, 2000). The most commonly reported problem was substance abuse, but the parent's inability to care for the child, neglect, and psychological and financial problems were also cited as factors. Many of these problems are long-term issues for families. When the grandparents first began to care for their grandchildren, only one-third expected to be the caregiver until the grandchild grew up. However, at the time of the study's interview, more than three-quarters of grandparents had come to believe that they would be the caregivers.

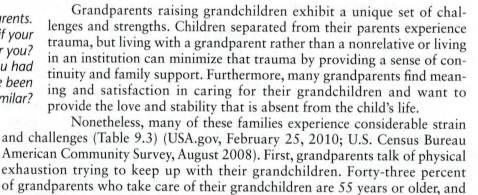

Shane and Ricky came to live with me when they were 4 and 5 years old. Geez, what did I know about babies? It's been years since I had mine. But that mother of theirs was just awful to them. I think she even burned them with her cigarettes. And my son, Chris, well, he's so messed up with drugs. He's never even around. He just lives for meth. So, what could I do? I really have no choice. I love my grandsons and want to give them a better life.

—Barbara, age 61

*T*hink about your own grandparents. Would you have lived with them if your parents were unable to care for you? What would your life be like if you had lived with them? How would it have been different or similar?

Grandparents raising grandchildren exhibit a unique set of challenges and strengths. Children separated from their parents experience trauma, but living with a grandparent rather than a nonrelative or living in an institution can minimize that trauma by providing a sense of continuity and family support. Furthermore, many grandparents find meaning and satisfaction in caring for their grandchildren and want to provide the love and stability that is absent from the child's life.

Nonetheless, many of these families experience considerable strain and challenges (Table 9.3) (USA.gov, February 25, 2010; U.S. Census Bureau American Community Survey, August 2008). First, grandparents talk of physical exhaustion trying to keep up with their grandchildren. Forty-three percent of grandparents who take care of their grandchildren are 55 years or older, and 15 percent are 65 or older. More than half are single grandparents, yet many are caring for young children who require considerable energy. Second, the grandparents often have physical or mental health problems, which could make caring for a child difficult. Third, many of these families are poor, have difficulty paying housing bills, or on public assistance (Kreider & Ellis, 2011).

Despite these challenges, a growing number of grandparents continue to assume the responsibilities of caring for their grandchildren. As Barbara said, "I really have no choice." Out of love and out of duty, grandparents step in when parents fall short of their own responsibilities.

Parents usually see themselves as having the most important role in their child's socialization. However,

About 3 million children live solely with their grandparents—their own parents are not in the home. Parents are absent for many reasons, often because of neglect, abuse, incarceration, or drug addiction.

TABLE 9.3 Demographics and Hardships for Children Living with Grandparents (n = 771)

Can you identify the hardships that many grandparents and grandchildren face?

Caregiver	
Under 45 years	12%
45 to 54 years	44%
55 to 64 years	28%
65+ years	15%
Married	48%
In fair or poor health or has a limiting condition	54%
Symptoms suggesting poor mental health	32%
Poor	37%
Low income (200% of poverty line)	66%
For Low-Income Families	
Crowding or difficulty paying housing bills	31%
Food insecurity	48%
Receiving food stamps	43%
Child	
≤5 years	29%
6 to 11 years	41%
12 to 17 years	30%
High levels of behavioral or emotional problems (ages 6–17)	9%
In fair or poor health or has a limiting condition	19%
Low levels of school engagement (ages 6–17)	26%

Source: Demographics and Hardships for Children Living with Grandparents from Urban Institute Calculations. 1999 National Survey of America's Families. Urban Institute.

TYING IT ALL TOGETHER Factors That Shape Parent–Child Interaction

Parenting takes place in a particular social context, and this affects the ways that parents socialize and interact with their children. Let's look at the macro-level influences and micro-level influences on this endearing intimate relationship.

MACRO-LEVEL FACTORS

- Cross-cultural traditions
- Level of technology
- Economic considerations
- Social class, race and ethnicity, and sex
- Level and types of discrimination
- Types of programs and policies aimed at helping vulnerable families

MICRO-LEVEL FACTORS

- Parenting style
- Personal characteristics of child
- Personal characteristics of parent

WHAT DO YOU THINK?

1. Which theories introduced in Chapter 1 do you see as particularly useful for explaining parent–child interaction?
2. Do you think these micro- and macro-level factors differ for mothers and for fathers, given their different parenting identities and activities?

---

our look at parenting reveals that the parent–child relationship doesn't exist in a vacuum. This chapter has shown you that many micro-level and macro-level factors shape parent–child relationships, and these are summarized in the feature box *Tying It All Together: Factors That Shape Parent–Child Interaction.*

Bringing It Full Circle

This chapter has shown us the social context of raising children. Most parents are so busy with day-to-day activities that they rarely notice the way that social and cultural forces shape how we care for, nurture, and socialize our children. You've learned that parents are only one agent of socialization, although an important one. Schools, peers, and the media also shape who and what we are. All of these socialization influences, including parents, are shaped by macro-level social factors.

Let's review what we've learned as we reflect on Karen and Betsy in the opening vignette, and apply this information to our own lives.

- How is parenting in same-sex families similar to, and different from, parenting in heterosexual two-parent families?

- Do agents of socialization operate differently for Karen and Betsy's children compared to children in other parenting contexts?

- Should they talk to their children about the prejudice and discrimination leveled at same-sex families? How is this different from or similar to racial/ethnic socialization?

- If you decide to have children, what's likely to be your parenting context? What do you think will happen if that context suddenly changes? How will you and your children cope?

 Watch on **MySocLab**
Video: *Susan Ferguson: Family and Work*

On MySocLab

✓ **Study** and **Review** on MySocLab

CHAPTER REVIEW

LO9.1 Recognize the diversity in parenting historically and cross culturally

9.1 Are there differences in parenting practices cross-culturally?

Parents take care of, nurture, and socialize their children, but these interactions between parents and children take place within a broader social and cultural environment. Economic conditions, region of the country, whether it is urban or rural, cultural and religious traditions, gendered norms, job opportunities, and level of technology are just a few of the macro-level factors that set the stage for micro-level family interactions.

9.2 How has parenting changed over time?

Definitions of good parenting fluctuate greatly. For example, parents in colonial America tended to be strict, emotionally distant, and expected unqualified obedience from their children. The Industrial Revolution produced two views of childhood: the *protected child*, whose family wealth offered education and leisure; and the *useful child,* whose labor was needed by their poor and working-class families to make ends meet.

9.3 What are some current trends in parenting found throughout the world?

Three trends are emerging: (1) Although parents are central to childrearing, there are other influences as well, including other people (e.g., babysitters, grandparents) and social institutions (e.g., schools, daycare centers); (2) parents increasingly encourage permissiveness and child independence; and (3) a higher value is placed on boys than on girls in most societies.

LO9.2 Explain the socialization process

9.4 What are some well-known theories of human development and socialization?

Sigmund Freud believed that human behavior and personality originate from unconscious forces within individuals. Jean Piaget was interested in how children come to understand the world and make meaning of their experiences, and identified four stages of cognitive development. Charles Horton Cooley and George Herbert Mead believed that a person cannot form a self-concept without social contact and social experience with others—they learn to see themselves as others see them. Alfred Bandura claimed that children not only learn by reinforcement, but that children also learn by watching and imitating others.

9.5 Who socializes our children?

There are many agents of socialization, including parents, peers, toys, schools, and the media.

9.6 How does socialization differ by social class, race and ethnicity, and gender?

Social class affects not only how much money parents have to spend, but it also shapes values, norms, and expectations that parents have for their children. For example, working-class children are more likely socialized to be obedient and to conform. Racial and ethnic groups may have different cultural traditions, language, or food. One important difference between the socialization practices of White and minority parents is that the latter must teach their children about the importance of race, ethnicity, prejudice, and discrimination. Parents are very influential in teaching children about how masculinity and femininity are defined, and what appropriate roles are for girls and boys.

LO9.3 Compare and contrast parenting styles

9.7 What are three different parenting styles?

An *authoritative* parenting style is one in which parents are demanding and maintain high levels of control over their children, but they are also warm and receptive. Parents who have a *permissive* parenting style may be very nurturing, caring, and responsive to their children; however, they put few controls or demands on the children. Parents who practice an *authoritarian* parenting style tend to be strict, punitive, less communicative, and offer less warmth and support to their children.

LO9.4 Discuss what it means to be a mother

9.8 What does it mean to be a *mother,* and how does that role differ from a *father*?

Mother and *father* are roles involving both an identity and specific actions. Mothers report experiencing greater meaning in their lives compared to childfree women, but also report more distress and depression.

Compared to fathers, mothers typically do more emotional labor and childcare.

LO9.5 Discuss what it means to be a father

9.9 How have fathers' roles changed in recent years?

Fathers' roles also involve both an identity and specific activities. Compared to fathers of the past, today's fathers see themselves as more than just breadwinners. They are far more likely to be involved in the emotional and physical care of their children. Fathers' involvement can enhance the social, emotional, and cognitive well-being of their children.

LO9.6 Identify how children influence their parents

9.10 How do children influence their parents?

Parent–child interaction is a two-way street, and children can influence their parents through their own temperament, cognitive abilities, health and well-being, and sex.

LO9.7 Discuss different types of parenting contexts

9.11 What can be done to reduce the number of teen pregnancies?

Prevention efforts focus on such things as reinvigorating these efforts; intensifying the focus on underlying causes of teen pregnancy; helping parents succeed in their role as sex educators; broadening the scope of pregnancy prevention efforts; providing accurate, clear, consistent, and ongoing information about how to reduce risk-taking behavior; creating community-wide plans for teen pregnancy prevention, including adolescent reproductive health services; and giving young people a credible vision of a positive future.

9.12 Why should we be careful not to overgeneralize single parents?

There are different kinds of single-parent families with different kinds of circumstances (e.g., a teenage mother vs. a 40-year-old female executive); there are different paths to becoming a single parent with varying consequences (i.e., never marrying, divorce, and widowhood); the cause-and-effect relationship is unclear (i.e., does poverty cause single parenthood, or does single parenthood cause poverty?); and single parenthood is less problematic in other industrialized nations because of a wide array of social supports lacking in the United States.

9.13 How distinctive are gay and lesbian parents from heterosexual parents?

In most ways, there are very few differences. Research studies find no significant differences in psychological well-being, performance in school, substance abuse, delinquency, or early sexual experiences. Children growing up with gay or lesbian parents were more likely to have had a homosexual experience or to envision that they could have one in the future, but as adults, they were no more likely than others to have adopted a gay, lesbian, or bisexual identity.

9.14 What are the unique strengths and challenges of grandparents raising grandchildren?

Grandparents step in to raise their grandchildren because mothers and fathers may be absent as a result of incarceration, drug or alcohol abuse, physical or mental illness, employment difficulties, child abuse or neglect, desertion, or even death. Children separated from their parents experience trauma, but living with a grandparent can minimize that trauma by providing a sense of continuity and family support. Many grandparents find meaning in caring for their grandchild, but it's often not without emotional and financial cost.

KEY TERMS

authoritarian parenting style
authoritative parenting style
concrete operational thought
ego
family allowance (or child allowance)
formal operational thought

id
looking-glass self
permissive parenting style
preoperational thought
racial (or ethnic) socialization
role taking

sensorimotor stage
social learning theory
socialization
superego

Families and the Work They Do

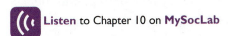

((• **Listen** to Chapter 10 on **MySocLab**

Chris and Lisa are like many other professional couples struggling to balance their work and family time.

As you read their story, ask yourself what could be done to make their lives—and the lives of millions of others—easier.

 **Watch** on **MySocLab**
Video: *Balancing Work and Family Life: Lisa and Chris*

Most young adults say that they would like to marry, have children, and work at an interesting job. Is it possible to really "have it all"—an exciting career, a happy relationship, and the joy of parenthood? Ask Chris and Lisa. They're about as close to having it all as you can get, but they're also acutely aware of the stresses associated with their delicate balancing act.

Chris is the Chief Operating Officer for the Transit Authority of a large city. Lisa is a research administrator on the medical campus of a university. Both jobs are rewarding and very demanding. A 40-hour workweek easily spills over into evenings and weekends—there are always e-mails to answer, phone calls to make, and catching up on paperwork—often resulting in a 50- or even 60-hour workweek. Although they're unhappy about how work encroaches on their private life, they believe there is little they can do about it. They might not be aware that the United States is among those countries with the longest workweek and the least amount of vacation. The time they do have available is devoted to their delightful son, Christopher, who is now 2 years old.

Like most people, Lisa had minimal maternity leave and had to resume working 5 weeks after giving birth. "I was not happy about it," she said, but given that the United States has no national maternity policy, what choice did she have? She and Chris also began the overwhelming task of finding quality childcare for young Christopher. Luckily, her mother lives nearby and was able to help care for Christopher. When he reached 8 months of age, Lisa and Chris decided to give her mother a break and enroll Christopher in a daycare facility for a few days each week. Finding quality care, however, wasn't easy. There were few openings, many didn't meet their quality standards, and those that did were surprisingly expensive. Again, unlike other countries, the United States generally doesn't help families with childcare costs, which are considered largely a personal responsibility.

A lengthy search finally led to an ideal childcare situation in which little Christopher thrives. Nonetheless, the beginning was daunting, with their son screaming in fear as Lisa walked out the center's door. Wracked with "mother guilt," Lisa wondered if she did the right thing. Is her son suffering? However, like virtually every child who has a rough beginning, he is now happy and enjoys his time at his home daycare.

Yet even after getting past this hurdle, Lisa and Chris still don't have an easy time. Both talk of wanting more time with their son, being sleep-deprived, having little time to themselves or for one another, feeling stressed, constantly rushing around, and feeling guilty. What would relieve some of these burdens? Given the dearth of policies in the United States to help working families, they look to individual solutions, such as working fewer hours, or starting their own business.

This chapter examines the work that families do inside and outside the home, and how these domains interact and influence one another. We used to think of work as something that was done *outside* the home. Home and work were separate spheres and largely segregated—men went off to work, women stayed at home. Today, we recognize that work and family aren't separate domains, but are in fact highly interrelated. Several important issues speak to the overlap of these concepts.

First, a majority of mothers now work outside the home, including mothers with preschool-age children. Women and men no longer live in separate spheres. Both are involved in work inside and outside the home, and dual-worker or dual-career families are the norm rather than the exception (Gibbs, 2013).

Second, the organization of work done inside the home has a tremendous influence on the work done outside the home. Issues such as how childcare, housework, or emotional labor is divided between partners influence stress level, which in turn can affect worker productivity, absenteeism, and retention (Parker, 2009). For example, how do parents negotiate who leaves work early to pick up a sick child from school? Who will routinely arrive at work a few minutes late to drop off a child at school?

Third, specific work policies have the ability to reduce work-family tensions and conflicts that parents experience—for example, the degree to which work policies allow for part-time or flexible work options, as well as offer health insurance, sick pay, parental leaves, and other important family-friendly fringe benefits (Hostetler, Desrochers, Kopko, & Moen, 2012; Jung Jang, Zippay, & Park, 2012). Yet today, families feel more economic pressure than ever. Work encroaches on home life for a growing number of families as the number of single-parent and dual-earner households continues to rise, hours on the job increase, and job benefits erode. Employment hasn't kept pace with the changing nature of the workforce by offering a family-friendly environment. Despite these problems, most adults want to have children; they aren't willing to sacrifice having children for the sake of work. Children can bring great joy to adults, enriching their lives in many ways. This chapter examines key issues and challenges in the work that families do both inside and outside the home.

Every culture—in both developed and developing nations—must find ways to combine work and family.

10.1 Assess the changing dynamics of the workplace

Questions That Matter

10.1 What is the history of work in early America?

10.2 How has participation in the women's labor force changed in the past century?

10.3 How have increased technology and globalization contributed to a changing occupational structure?

The Changing Dynamics of the Workplace

The context of work and family life has changed considerably over the course of U.S. history. Let's briefly review some of these work and family life changes.

Early America

In early colonial America, most families worked closely with the land. Their lives revolved around the seasonal work necessary for farming and ranching.

The labor of men, women, and children was needed, and was considered invaluable to the success of the family enterprise. Men and women usually had different tasks, with men involved in the more physical agricultural work while women and children did the cooking, cleaning, weaving, and tending of small animals. However, at several crucial times of the year associated with planting and harvesting, the labor of all family members was needed in the fields. In other words, although sex may have been a central construct in the division of labor, the line between men and women's work often shifted.

In the 19th century, the U.S. economy was evolving from an emphasis on agriculture to an emphasis on industrialization. During this century, work was done away from home and people were paid wages for this labor. There was considerable movement to urban areas in search of jobs, and over time, many small family farms could not support themselves and folded. An urban middle class emerged, with men going off to work outside the home and women doing the unpaid work within. Increasingly more goods and services were produced for profit outside the home, and families purchased these with the wages they earned at jobs in factories and other places of work. An ideology emerged asserting that the man was supposed to earn the money and the woman was supposed to nurture her husband and family (Kimmel, 2006).

Women of the 19th century were consumers rather than producers of goods and services, yet the new industries needed expanding numbers of laborers so, in addition to recruiting men, young, poor, minority, and immigrant women and children were hired. By 1890, 17 percent of women were in the labor force, most of whom were unmarried and without children (Coontz, 2000). Much of the work in these factories was dangerous and dirty, as there were minimal occupational safety standards compared to today. Thus, women's roles became increasingly intertwined with class and race: poor or minority women *had* to work, whereas White middle-class women could enjoy "true" womanhood far away from the dangerous and unsafe world of work.

There have been short-term shifts in this ideology. For example, during World War II, because of a (male) labor shortage, entering into paid employment was seen as women's patriotic duty. Businesses and governments even helped create and pay for childcare so that mothers could more easily work outside the home. Once the war ended, women were fired or encouraged to quit their jobs. They were asked to return home to their role as wives and mothers and to focus on more domestic activities. The childcare facilities were closed.

Trends in Child Labor

American children have often performed paid and unpaid labor, including indentured servitude. As industrialization took hold, and families moved from farms into urban areas in search of work, poor children often toiled beside their parents in dangerous factories, textile mills, canneries, and mines (Child Labor Public Education Project, 2011). Poor families needed the labor of all members to earn enough for even minimal food, shelter, and clothing. In fact, children were often preferred as laborers because they were seen as less expensive, less likely to strike, and more docile. Thousands of children were employed in dismal working conditions doing hard labor for only a fraction of the wages paid to men or women. Opposition to child labor soon began to grow in the northern states. The first state child labor law in Massachusetts was passed in 1836 and required children under age 15 working in factories to attend school at least 3 months per year. In 1892, the Democratic Party platform voted to

During World War II, when many men were off to war, women were encouraged to take their jobs. Paid employment was seen as a woman's patriotic duty.

ban factory employment for children under age 15. Many factories moved south to avoid the growing protection of young workers in the north. By the early decades of the 20th century, the number of child laborers in the United States had peaked, and then began to decline as the labor and reform movements became more outspoken about the plight of many young workers. New protection laws were passed during this era, and by 1938 a minimum age of employment and maximum hours of work for children were regulated by federal law for the first time.

One important aspect of the changing dynamic of the workplace is the surge of women into the paid labor market in recent decades. There's been a cultural shift in opportunities for women in work, education, and family life. Unlike in the past, many women now work because they *want* to work. For many others, though, the *need* and *want* to work are virtually indistinguishable. In the next section, we explore how macroeconomic, occupational, and cultural values have influenced the participation of women in the labor force.

◉ **Watch** on **MySocLab**
Video: *Families: Social Inequalities*

Women's Labor Force Participation

You can really see how women's opportunities have changed by looking at my family. My grandmother, who never worked outside the home, is pretty adamant that mothers should not be working. She talks about that a lot, and is pretty worried about the state of families today. Meanwhile, my mom thinks it's okay for mothers to work as long as their children are in school. That's what she did—she waited until my brother and I were in first and third grade. Today, I feel differently. I'm planning to go to medical school, and I just assume that I'll be working when I have my children. I think women can have a fulfilling career and have children at the same time.
—**Abby, Age 22**

> **"My grandmother, who never worked outside the home, is pretty adamant that mothers should not be working."**

◉ **Watch** on **MySocLab**
Video: *Stages of Family Life: Arlene Skolnick: Working Women*

◉ **Watch** on **MySocLab**
Video: *ABC 20/20: Working Moms*

For most of the 20th century, most married women with children didn't work outside the home. Even as recently as 1975, only 55 percent of mothers with children under age 18 worked, and only a third of women with children under age 3 worked outside the home, as shown in Figure 10.1 (Bureau of Labor Statistics, February 2013). However, a large cultural shift was underway. Today, the majority of mothers are employed, regardless of the age of their children. The change during this period likely reflects increasing job and educational opportunities for women, the popularity of feminist ideas of social and economic equality promoted by the women's movement, and changes in the economy. Women work for a variety of reasons: to put food on the table, to provide housing, to pay for vacations, or for personal fulfillment. Today, it's common for mothers to work outside the home, although the number has remained relatively stable since 2000 and doesn't appear to be growing.

Mothers with older children are more likely to work than are mothers with younger children, regardless of marital status, race, or ethnicity.

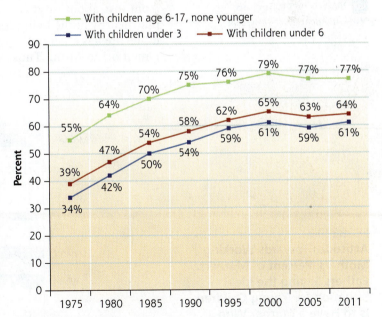

FIGURE 10.1

Employment Status of Mothers 1975–2011, by Age of Youngest Child

There has been a large shift since the mid-1970s in the likelihood of mothers working outside the home.
Source: Bureau of Labor Statistics, February 2013.

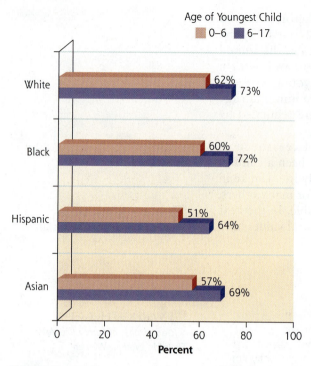

FIGURE 10.2
Mothers' Employment by Age of Youngest Child and Race/Ethnicity

Regardless of race or ethnicity, mothers' employment is influenced by the age of their youngest child.
Source: Gibbs, 2013.

👁 **Watch on MySocLab**
Video: *Arlene Skolnick: Recent Research*

Figure 10.2 shows the percentage of mothers who are employed, by the age of their youngest child, and their race or ethnicity. It shows that White and Black mothers are most likely to be employed, including when their children are young, and Hispanic mothers are least likely to be employed (see Gibbs, 2013).

Yet, despite the fact that most families have a mother who is employed, *attitudes* toward working mothers are more mixed than one might imagine. Figure 10.3 shows that only a small percentage believe that the ideal situation for young children is to have a mother who works full-time. Most suggest that part-time or no outside work at all is optimal. Blacks are most likely to say that full-time employment is ideal. What might be a macro-level reason for this?

Next, let's take a look at both the recent changes that have occurred in the economy and with employment, and examine the consequences of these changes on families. In particular, we examine technological changes and global competition. How have these factors affected families?

The Changing Occupational Structure

American industries have undergone rapid restructuring in the past few decades in response to technological changes and global competition. First, the widespread use of personal computers (virtually unheard of 30 years ago), cell phones, fax machines, and pagers has changed the way we do business and how we conduct our personal lives. We regularly buy e-tickets for our flights, order groceries over the Internet, check our e-mail on our cell phones, and text our friends to see what's on the agenda for the weekend. Many companies also use these technologies to conduct business. Increasingly more people can do their work from just about anywhere, including the dining room table as their children play nearby in the living room. Work now has entered our home. Likewise, our home life has entered the work arena: when we are "at work," we send a quick e-mail off to Mom. Thus, for many people, the boundaries between work and

FIGURE 10.3
Attitudes Towards Working Mothers. Percent of Mothers/Fathers Saying the Ideal Situation for Young Children Is to Have a Mother Who Works Full Time, Part Time, or Not at All

Despite the fact that most mothers work outside the home, not everyone thinks it's a good idea.
Source: Parker & Wang, 2013.

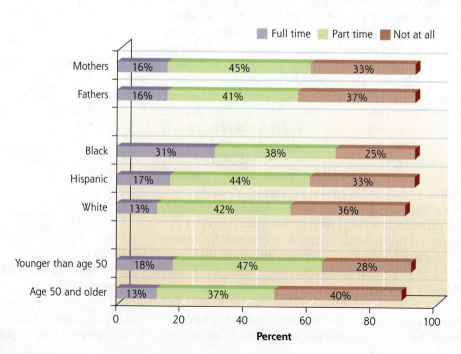

family are becoming blurred. Sometimes there are benefits to this arrangement; maybe you can reduce your childcare costs if you can do some of your work at home. However, for others, the development of technology over the past few decades has increased their level of stress.

Second, many jobs are being outsourced to other countries, especially India, Indonesia, and China as companies search for cheaper labor costs and fewer governmental restrictions (Galinsky, Aumann, & Bond, 2009; Statistics Brain, 2013; Whoriskey, 2009). Manufacturing, service, and sales jobs are now increasingly shipped overseas. Are you experiencing problems with your computer? When you telephone a call center for help, it's likely that a computer technician in India will answer the telephone.

The occupational structure is changing as many jobs are being outsourced to other countries because of cheaper labor costs or fewer labor or environmental protections.

Consumers appreciate the 24/7 availability and we benefit from the lower cost of goods and services, but this outsourcing has contributed to widespread job loss in the United States. In particular, the number of workers in U.S. manufacturing has declined considerably over the past few decades. These disappearing jobs tended to pay relatively high wages because of union protections. Instead, the U.S. economy has experienced an increase of jobs in the service sector, particularly in semi-skilled or unskilled positions characterized by job insecurity and low wages. The number of sales clerks, waiters, and food-service workers expanded quickly during this period.

These transformations have caused some major changes in how families conduct their work both inside and outside the home. Together with technology and globalization, many of today's working-class and middle-class families are facing a severe economic recession. Let's examine the current economic climate in the United States so that we can better understand the modern relationship between work and family.

How do you think your life has been affected by the changes in the labor force participation of women, new technologies, and globalization? Have these changes been good or bad for you? Are they good or bad for society? Why is it that sometimes what is good for you is at odds with what is good for society (and vice versa)?

👁 **Watch** on **MySocLab**
Video: *Margaret Andersen: Work and Family*

Life in a Recession

The recession that began in the late 2000s has caused financial hardship for many working-class and middle-class families in the United States. The civilian labor force shrunk by well over 1 million workers between 2008 and 2009 alone. The proportion of workers who worked full-time, year round in 2009 was 64.8 percent, down from 68.4 percent in 2007, whereas the number of involuntary part-time workers (people whose work hours were reduced or who cannot find a full-time job) rose (Bureau of Labor Statistics, 2009a; 2010b).

Unemployment and Families

The U.S. unemployment rate averaged 7.0 percent at the end of 2013, representing a steady decline since the height of the recession in 2009 (9.9 percent) as shown in Table 10.1 (Bureau of Labor Statistics, December 22, 2013). The unemployment rate is highest among Blacks and lowest among Asian Americans (Bureau of Labor Statistics, 2013a, 2013b).

What these unemployment figures mean is that many breadwinners lost their jobs (or worry that they will) or had their income reduced, contributing to the rise in home foreclosures, personal bankruptcies, and the number of families

10.2 Describe aspects of life in a recession

Questions That Matter

10.4 How has the rise in unemployment affected families?

10.5 How has the current recession contributed to unstable wages, working conditions, and a disposable workforce?

10.6 How serious a threat is losing health insurance?

TABLE 10.1	Unemployment Rates, November
The unemployment rate peaked in 2010 at the height of the recession, but has been going down since then.	
2007	4.7%
2008	6.8%
2009	9.9%
2010	9.8%
2011	8.6%
2012	7.8%
2013	7.0%

Source: Bureau of Labor Statistics, December 22, 2013.

who cannot access the health care system because they have lost their health insurance. Let's look at some of these financial problems and related issues in more depth.

What does it feel like to look for work week after week and find no job offers? When even the lowest-tier jobs in our economy have stiff competition, many people who would like to work feel psychologically wounded by the lack of employment opportunities. A Gallup poll based on a nationally representative sample found that people who have been unemployed for more than 6 months are far more likely than those who are employed to feel stress, sadness, and worry (Marlar, 2010). Unemployment also affects personal relationships. For example, high unemployment tends to lower marriage rates—people are less likely to marry if they or their potential partner can't find a job (Edin & Kafalas, 2005; Wilson, 1987, 1996). Other periods of high unemployment, such as the Great Depression, led to fewer children being born, as discussed in Chapter 8. The stress associated with unemployment can also endanger relationships, contribute to domestic violence, and harm children's social well-being (Aubry, Tefft, & Kingsbury, 2006). For example, a study based on 4,476 school-age children in 2,569 families across the United States found that when fathers are involuntarily unemployed, children have a greater likelihood of repeating a grade or getting suspended from school (Kalil & Ziol-Guest, 2007; Luo, 2009). We can see that these macro-level factors affect how we experience relationships.

Unstable Wages and Working Conditions

Some families earn just the minimum wage or wages only slightly above it. The federal minimum wage in the United States, at $7.25 per hour in 2014, doesn't enable even a small family to rise out of poverty. Working 40 hours per week at $7.25 an hour yields $290 a week, and $15,080 a year before taxes. And people working at minimum wage still pay taxes. So how does a person pay for rent, utilities, food, clothing, and other incidentals on the federal minimum wage? Because this rate is so low, 18 states have adopted state minimum wages that are higher than the federal wage. Washington and Oregon have the highest state minimum wages in the nation at $9.19 and $8.95 an hour, respectively (Wage and Hour Division, January 1, 2013). President Obama has called on Congress to raise the federal minimum wage to $9 an hour and to adjust it automatically for inflation, but as this book goes to press, there has been no movement (Lowrey, 2013).

About 3.6 million hourly workers earn the minimum wage or even less. Half of these persons are age 25 or older. These low-wage workers are distributed evenly across racial and ethnic groups (except for Asians, who are more likely to have higher wages). Women are more likely to earn minimum wage (or less) than are men, and it's likely that many of these women are supporting children as well as themselves (Bureau of Labor Statistics, March 25, 2013).

Recognizing that the minimum wage is too low to support a family, the concept of paying a **living wage** is taking hold. A living wage ordinance ties the "minimum" wage of a community to the price of housing in the area, according to an index from the U.S. Department of Housing and Urban Development. Housing should constitute no more than 30 percent of a person's income, and the living wage is indexed accordingly. This usually results in

More than 2 million people in the United States earn only minimum wage for their labor, not enough to support even a small family.

a wage ranging from 150 percent to 200 percent above the poverty line, depending on the affordability of housing in the area. So, for example, the living wage in Tucson, Arizona, would be $10.21, whereas it would be $21.83 in Boston, Massachusetts, and only $6.90 in Macon, Georgia, which is actually less than the federal minimum wage (Universal Living Wage Campaign, 2013).

PART-TIME, NONSTANDARD, AND TEMPORARY WORK In addition to pay, another concern is that many new jobs associated with economic restructuring are part-time, sub-contracted, temporary in nature, or have only evening hours. Some offer irregular work schedules. Employees working in these types of jobs, referred to as **nonstandard work schedules,** represent the fastest-growing category of U.S. workers (Gornick, Presser, & Ratzdorf, 2009; Presser, Gornick, & Parashar, 2008). Since 1982, temporary employment has increased several hundred percent. In other words, millions of women and men begin the workday not knowing if, and for how long, their jobs are likely to continue. There is also a growing trend towards jobs that require weekend, evening, or variable non-fixed schedules, particularly those found in the lower-paying service sector.

Some part-time and contingency workers prefer this arrangement, especially highly paid professionals who value their freedom and independence on the job, or mothers with young children who would prefer to work only sporadically, or parents who are trying to work opposite shifts to minimize the need for childcare arrangements (Jung Jang, Zippay, & Park, 2012; Täht & Mills, 2012). However, most American families prefer the assurance of a steady job with prearranged hours and an established pay scale with fringe benefits. Families with non standard work schedules may find it difficult to organize childcare, as most childcare centers are only open between 7 A.M. and 6 P.M. Furthermore, childcare centers usually require a regular paid commitment to a particular schedule, such as a Monday through Friday schedule, or a Monday, Wednesday, Friday schedule. When a parent works full-time one week, 3 days the next week, and 4 half-days the next, it wreaks havoc on childcare arrangements, children's academic achievement, and many other dimensions of family life (Han & Fox, 2011). It also affects the degree to which family, friends, and neighbors are able to provide childcare. All of this, in turn, creates tremendous stress for families (Davis, Goodman, Pirretti, & Almeida, 2008; Perry-Jenkins, Goldberg, Pierce, & Sayer, 2007).

Most women don't work these schedules out of personal inclination, but because these are the required working conditions of their jobs as cashiers, maids, nursing aides, cooks, or waitresses. Moreover, these occupations are likely to grow in the future.

Rhonda is one of many people who are looking for a good job with good pay (Seccombe, 2014). She has a high school diploma, but doesn't have a college degree. She is a single mother, and wants to raise her young son Bobby without relying on government assistance. Rhonda wants a permanent full-time job, but she has been stymied by the tremendous growth in part-time, temporary positions, she explains (Seccombe, 2014, p. 177):

Hopefully I can get me a job. A permanent job. My sister's trying to get me a job where she works. I put my application in last week. And it would be a permanent job. When you go through those agencies, it's just temporary work. It's just whenever they need you, and it's unfair too. Every job I've found is through this temporary agency, like Manpower, but it's only temporary. And they cut my check and my food stamps, and when my job ends, it's like you're stuck again. So I'm trying to find a permanent steady job. But it's hard around here. I've been out looking for work, and hoping that something comes through.

Rhonda may be surprised to learn that temporary agencies are doing very well in this recessionary economy. Manpower is one of the largest private employers in the United States, ranked 129 in the Fortune 500 list of large companies, and has revenues around $21 billion worldwide. They serve more than 400,000 employer clients, and have placed 12 million workers in more than 80 countries and territories (Manpower Group, 2013).

DISPOSABLE WORKFORCE   Turnover rates among workers in many low-tier jobs are high because they are the expendable workforce that consists of workers in the service industry, in clerical fields, and on assembly lines performing routine tasks. To the management of these industries, people in these largely unskilled or semi-skilled jobs are interchangeable. A high turnover rate isn't a problem for management, and in fact, it may even be considered desirable so that health insurance premiums and payments of other benefits can be avoided. These disposable workers generally earn less than those on the regular payroll, and must live with the uncertainty that their jobs may permanently end today when they clock out at 5:00 P.M. Their anxiety level about their employment is high, and for many, unemployment insurance is not an option.

Eliza, a single mother of four children, epitomizes the plight of many people who are looking for work, but are at the mercy of employers that don't see providing stable employment, reliable and sufficient work hours, and benefits for their employees as a priority. Eager to work, Eliza was delighted to find a job in a fast-food restaurant. She told the management that she was looking for 30 to 40 hours of employment per week. Knowing of her desire to work, the restaurant hired her, but instead of meeting her needs, her boss routinely asks Eliza to leave work early, unpaid, during the slow periods. She was hired to fill an organizational need, and released as soon as their need for her labor lessened. Because Eliza's income was so much less than she anticipated when being hired, she found that the job did not pay her bills. In addition, Eliza felt that the long commute wasn't worth her while, so she quit, returning to welfare (Seccombe, 2014, p. 178). She explained:

That's something I need is a job. I've been looking. I just can't find the right one. I used to work at [fast food industry], but I wasn't making much money. By the time I caught the city bus, went out there, by the time I got to my kids, I spent all the money that they gave me. I liked the job, but it was just that I had to pay 75 cents to get to work, and paid 75 cents to get back. If I missed the bus I had to give somebody $3.00 or $4.00 to take me. And they wouldn't give me enough hours. I told them when they gave me this job that I needed at least 30–40 hours a week. I just can't afford to work less. But I was wasting my time going out there. I had to be at work by 11 o'clock, but they would send me home by 2 o'clock. I didn't even get 20 hours a week. You hear what I'm saying? Ten or 12, maybe. I think what they were doing was hiring you for the busy hour, and once the busy hour passed, you was sent out of there. I had to quit because it was costing me too much to go way over there.

In other words, Eliza, a struggling single mother who is trying to work hard to support her children, was thwarted by the uncertainty associated with being part of a *disposable workforce*.

The Threat of Losing Health Insurance

In 2010, sweeping reforms to the U.S. health care system under the Affordable Care Act were passed by Congress and signed into law by President Obama. Many of these reforms are being implemented slowly from 2010 through 2014. Briefly, the new legislation makes the following changes (Kaiser Family Foundation, April 2013):

- Most individuals are required to have health insurance by 2014.
- Individuals without access to affordable employer coverage will be able to purchase coverage through a health insurance exchange with credits available

to make coverage more affordable to some people. Small businesses will be able to purchase coverage through a separate exchange.

- Employers will be required to pay penalties for employees who receive credits.

- New regulations will be imposed on health plans that will prevent health insurers from denying coverage to people for any reason, or for charging higher premiums based on health status or sex.

- Medicaid will be expanded to 133 percent of the federal poverty level (for individuals under age 65, roughly $15,000 for an individual and $30,000 for a family of four in 2012).

This health care legislation was hotly contested by many groups, vehemently supported by some, and criticized by others who said it didn't go far enough. Why was this proposed legislation so controversial?

Many Americans have difficulties getting the health care they need when they are ill because they are without health insurance. Unfortunately, by 2009, the year prior to the passage of the Affordable Care Act, about 50 million Americans had no health insurance (Commonwealth Fund Commission on a High Performance Health System, 2009; DeNavas-Walt, Proctor, & Smith, 2010). The number of uninsured would continue to rise if the system wasn't reformed substantially.

The uninsured delay or forgo needed health care because they can't afford it (Panchal, Rae, & Claxton, 2012). As a result, they experience unnecessary suffering and even death. How can this problem exist in a country as wealthy as the United States?

The brief answer to this question is that the United States has traditionally had a *fee-for-service* health care system; in other words, if you get sick or injured, you must *pay* to go to the doctor. Other countries "roll" the price of health care into their taxes so that there is little or no additional cost when their citizens are sick or injured and seek medical help.

During World War II, when wage freezes were in effect, some large U.S. companies decided to offer health insurance as a fringe benefit. Insurance was cheap to purchase because health care costs were relatively inexpensive and few drugs were available. People appreciated the fact that they didn't have to pay taxes on health insurance, unlike income. Over time, most large U.S. businesses began to offer health insurance to their workers and their families. To compete for labor, medium-size and small businesses decided to get into the insurance act as well (Blumenthal, 2006).

By the 1950 and 1960s, Americans began to equate health insurance with employment—you get a job and health insurance is part of the benefits package. We tend to forget that this connection began through a simple historical accident (i.e., wage freezes), and we also tend to forget that no other industrialized nation has tied health insurance to employment. In all other developed nations, access to healthcare is a guaranteed right of citizenship, much like education or access to police protection.

However, by the 1970s and 1980s, U.S. health care costs began to rise substantially. Offering health insurance to workers and their families became an expensive benefit, not a cheap one. Small businesses were the first to complain about the increasing costs of health care. Soon medium-size and large businesses began to feel the financial strain as well. Today, companies of all sizes are completely dropping health insurance coverage, asking workers to pay more of the insurance plan costs or to be on the job for 6 months or a year before becoming eligible for insurance, or are covering workers but not their families. Only about 55 percent of Americans receive health insurance from an employer (Kaiser Family Foundation, December 2012). Among those people working in smaller firms, the figure is even less. Clearly, there has been an erosion of the connection between health insurance and employment that was so embedded in our collective consciousness.

TABLE 10.2	Average Cost of Health Insurance Premiums, for Single and Family Coverage, by Region of Country, 2012	
Health insurance is very expensive.		
	Single Coverage	**Family Coverage**
Total	$5,615	$15,745
Northeast	$5,964	$17,099
Midwest	$5,501	$15,388
South	$5,445	$14,988
West	$5,715	$16,198

Source: Kaiser Family Foundation, December 2012.

Medicaid: The federal-state health care program for eligible poor of all ages.

Medicare: The federal health care program for the elderly.

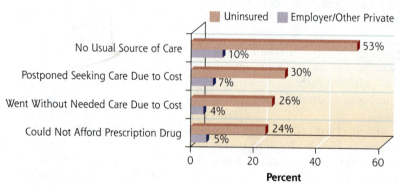

FIGURE 10.4

Barriers to Health Care among Nonelderly Adults by Insurance Status, 2011

People without insurance face multiple barriers to getting health care.
Source: Kaiser Family Foundation, September 2012.

Do you know anyone who has suffered economically during the recession? What happened to them? Did they lose their job, have their pay reduced, or lose their health insurance? How did they cope and how are they coping now?

10.3 Recognize family work at home

Questions That Matter

10.7 What does research have to say about who is doing the housework and childcare?

10.8 What are three common explanations for the gendered division of labor?

Why not just purchase the insurance yourself if you can't get it from an employer? Many can't afford the high costs, as the average price of family health coverage is almost $16,000 a year, as shown in Table 10.2 (Kaiser Family Foundation, December 2012.). Also, many people are turned down by health insurance companies because of a pre-existing condition, a problem that the Affordable Care Act addresses. Moreover, most Americans don't qualify for **Medicaid** (the federal-state health care program for the eligible poor) or **Medicare** (the federal health care program for the elderly) because they don't meet the economic or age requirements.

By 2012, about 48 million people were left with no health insurance, a slight decline since the Affordable Care Act was passed, although most features did not come into effect until 2014 (DeNavas-Walt, Proctor, & Smith, 2013). The consequences of being without this insurance can be devastating, as shown in Figure 10.4 and the feature box *My Family: "It's Not What We Had Planned for Our Family"* on p. 291. Compared to those with employer-sponsored or other private health insurance, the uninsured are five times more likely to be without a usual source of health care, are four times more likely to postpone seeking health care because of the cost, are six times more likely to go without needed care, and are five times more likely to say that they couldn't afford their prescription medications (Kaiser Commission on Medicaid and the Uninsured, September 2012).

We've discussed how the changing occupational structure and our current economy—including health care—touch the lives of families directly every day. However, these macro-level factors *indirectly* influence families as well, for example, by encouraging women to join the labor force. Unlike a generation or two ago, many more women now feel that they *must* work to make ends meet for their families. Alone or together with their partners, women in the workforce provide an important financial resource for the family.

Given that most parents—fathers and mothers—work outside the home now whether because of need, choice, or some combination thereof, we must ask ourselves how this has changed the nature of work done *inside* the home. How has the context of housework and childcare changed? Who is doing what chores? What new challenges, opportunities, and stressors does this bring?

Family Work at Home

The family work that feeds, clothes, shelters, and cares for both adults and children is just as important to the maintenance of society as the work that occurs in the labor market (Coltrane, 2000). Unfortunately, household labor and childcare have traditionally been considered "women's work," and therefore weren't considered worthy of scientific study until about 30 years ago. Since then, a tremendous amount of research has examined who does what in the home, under

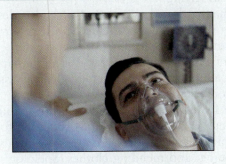

Roberto and Maria virtually grew up together in the same working-class neighborhood. They came from modest means, but both grew up surrounded by parents and family who loved and cared for them. Although they had known each other all of their lives, they began to see something special in each other during high school, and married a few years later.

Before marriage, both had gone to a community college near their home, but Roberto dropped out after a year for a full-time job in construction. Maria received a degree in cosmetology and then began work in a hair salon. Together they earned "good money," saved what they could, and soon were able to buy a small but cozy home in the neighborhood in which they grew up. Next, they decided to save money so that they could begin a family. They didn't care about fancy cars or extravagant vacations; a stable home and family life were what mattered most to this couple.

Maria had their first child a few years later when she was 25 and they named him Adrian. She quit her job immediately; their plan was for Roberto to be the breadwinner and Maria to stay at home with their children. Two years later Sarah was born. Three years after that their twins, Levi and Jake, were born, and their family now felt complete.

Life was good for this family. Roberto's earnings fluctuated somewhat month to month, but he usually earned about $4,000 a month, which was enough to support the growing family on a frugal budget. Their family life was stable and predictable.

Stable and predictable, that is, until the recession occurred. In an effort to reduce costs, Roberto's employer laid off a few of the most newly hired workers. Luckily, Roberto had some seniority, and wasn't personally affected. However, as a second cost-saving measure, his insurance benefits were reduced, requiring Roberto to pay several hundred dollars extra per month to cover his family. Later, this health insurance coverage was eliminated completely. His boss apologized profusely to Roberto, but said that it was just too expensive for his company to purchase any longer.

That evening when Roberto told Maria that their health benefits were now gone, she felt a stab of terror. With four active kids still under the age of nine, someone always needed to go to the doctor. In the past year alone, Adrian broke his arm, Sarah needed stitches, and Levi had been to the doctor several times for recurring ear infections. "You just can't imagine the fear unless you've been in this situation. . . . We can get food from relatives, and they can help us with school clothes and this and that. But how are we supposed to pay for all those high-priced doctor bills?" Maria asked.

Maria's fears were quickly realized. She developed a bladder infection and was wracked with pain. She put off going to the doctor and tried home remedies instead until she could wait no longer. The doctor scolded her for waiting so long to come in, and sent her home with some medicine and a hefty bill. The next month Levi had another ear infection, and the doctor recommended extensive tests to determine the cause of his medical problems. Maria and Roberto wanted to know how much these tests were going to cost. Were they all necessary? Could we have a few tests now and a few tests next month? These medical tests for their son drove Roberto and Maria deeper in debt.

Life for the family continued in this pattern for a few years—forgoing routine medical care and postponing needed medical care until the ultimate crisis happened. Roberto suffered a burst appendix. Still, he tried to minimize his pain, fretting over how much a doctor's visit would cost. When he could stand the pain no longer, Maria drove him to the emergency room where he was immediately prepped for surgery. The surgery cost more than $19,000, and the delay in care almost cost Roberto his life.

Roberto's recovery was slow, and his construction job couldn't be held for him. Maria was forced to go back to work as a stylist, but given that she had no clientele, she worked at a drop-in salon. Her earnings barely lifted the family out of poverty. She found working at odds with her values and she dreams of being a stay-at-home mother. They had to borrow money from her parents to pay their mortgage so that they wouldn't lose the house. "Where would the six of us go, anyway?" Maria asked herself. They pieced together childcare as cheaply as they could—Monday with Roberto, Tuesday with Grandma, Wednesday with a babysitter, and who knows about Thursday and Friday?

As you can see, losing their health insurance has wreaked havoc on this family and their dreams for the future.

WHAT DO YOU THINK?

1. Why do you think our country links insurance with employment? What are the strengths and weaknesses of this approach?
2. Whose "fault" is it that Roberto and Maria lost their health insurance? Who can we blame? His employer? The insurance company? Our healthcare system? Do you think their situation is unique?

what circumstances and why, and how housework is embedded in complex social processes related to the social construction of gender.

The Division of Household Labor

How is **household labor** defined? This is an important question, because it may be defined differently from one context to another. Generally, it refers to "unpaid

household labor: In general, the unpaid work done to maintain family members and/or a home.

work that is done to maintain family members and/or a home" (Knodel, Loi, Jayakody, & Huy, 2004, p. 1). Household labor sometimes excludes childcare and other types of emotional labor and caregiving.

The number of studies on the topic has exploded over the past few decades. Household labor is researched in many different ways, including self-reports made by one partner (usually the woman) or both partners, or by time diaries that are kept over a specific period (Lam, McHale, & Crouter, 2012). Perhaps not surprisingly, there is often a discrepancy between partners in their assessments of how much time each spends on housework (Lee & Waite, 2005).

According to national surveys, the five most time-consuming household tasks are (1) meal preparation or cooking; (2) housecleaning; (3) shopping for groceries and household goods; (4) washing dishes and cleaning up after meals; and (5) laundry, including washing, ironing, and mending clothes. Sociologist Scott Coltrane refers to these tasks as **routine household labor,** because they are repetitive and less able to be postponed than are other tasks (Coltrane, 2000). Although some people enjoy some or all of these activities (Poortman & van der Lippe, 2009), many people say that they don't enjoy routine household labor, or don't enjoy a significant number of specific tasks because they are seen as boring (Kroska, 2003). Other tasks, called **occasional labor,** occur less frequently and have more flexibility in timing, such as gardening, paying bills, household repairs, or servicing the car.

routine household labor: Non-discretionary, routine tasks that can't be postponed, such as cooking, washing dishes, or cleaning.

occasional labor: Household tasks that are more time-flexible and discretionary, such as household repairs, yard care, or paying bills.

Who Does What? Housework

Regardless of the way that housework is defined or measured, research indicates that women do significantly more housework than do men. The size of men's and women's contributions vary across studies, but most find that women spend significantly more time on household tasks (Bureau of Labor Statistics, June 20, 2013; Parker & Wang, 2013). A large survey of how Americans use their time shows this sex difference in the amount of time devoted to housework, and is illustrated in Figure 10.5.

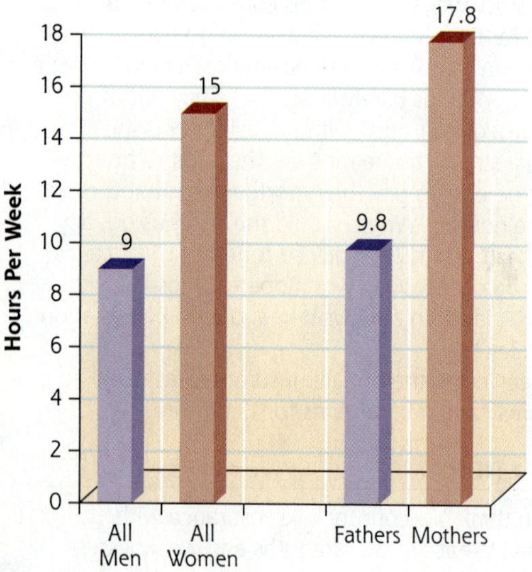

Women's work tends to be routine, which is usually nondiscretionary and repetitive. According to a study using the National Survey of Families and Households, based on a representative sample of Americans, the average married woman did about three times as much routine housework as the average married man (32 hours vs. 10 hours per week). With respect to occasional labor, which includes those tasks that tend to be more time-flexible and discretionary, married men performed 10 hours of housework per week whereas women performed about 6 hours. In total, women performed about twice as much housework as did men, and other studies show an even greater imbalance (Coltrane, 2000). Moreover, the tasks that women do tend to be inflexible about their timing. For example, women are more likely to be responsible for changing the baby's diaper, which must be changed *now,* or for fixing dinner, which must be prepared in the next *hour,* whereas men are more likely to do the yard work, which could be done any time this *week*. This difference alone can add to family stress.

The typical pattern in dual-earner families is presented in the book *The Second Shift* by sociologist Arlie Hochschild (1989). In her sample of 50 dual-earner couples, 20 percent equally shared the housework. In 70 percent of families, men did somewhere between one-third and one-half of the housework, and in 10 percent of families, men did less than one-third. Hochschild found that at the end of a long workday, women returned to do their "second shift"—their second job of housework and childcare, which included arranging, supervising, and planning, in addition to accomplishing actual tasks. For the most part, men just returned home to "help." She found that women on average work an extra 15 hours per week compared to men.

FIGURE 10.5

The Amount of Weekly Hours That Men and Women, Mothers and Fathers Spend on Housework, 2011

Women and mothers continue to spend more time on housework than do men and fathers.
Source: Parker & Wang, 2013.

Men's share of housework is on the rise, but the tasks remain gendered. Women tend to do the "routine labor," which is repetitive and cannot be delayed, while men tend to do the "occasional labor," which has greater flexibility on when tasks can be done.

Who Does What? Childcare

The research results of who does what with respect to childcare are not much different from who does the housework (Parker & Wang, 2013). Regardless of the employment status of parents, mothers spend more time with their children than do fathers. One study of more than 1,800 couples who completed time diaries revealed that when both partners are employed, 76 percent of the time spent on childcare is done by the mother. When the mother is not employed but the father is, she performs about 83 percent of childcare. If the father is not employed, but the mother is, she still spends more time on childcare than does the father, accounting for 53 percent of parental time (Pailhe & Solaz, 2008).

What, specifically, are mothers doing with their children? One study compared the time that mothers and fathers spend on various childrearing tasks: giving spiritual, emotional, social, moral, and physical guidance; helping with homework; providing companionship, advice, and mentoring; sharing leisure and activities; fostering independence, intelligence, and responsibility; providing care, protection, and discipline; and providing income (Finley, Mira, & Schwartz, 2008). The researchers found that mothers are more involved than fathers in all domains studied, with the exception of providing income. Mothers were rated as "often" or "always" involved in each domain, whereas fathers were rated as "sometimes involved" in each domain, except for providing income. Seven of the nine lowest-rated domains for fathers were in the expressive domain.

Fathers are willing to spend more time with their sons than with their daughters, and fathers are even willing to reduce their own private leisure to spend time with their sons (Mammen, 2009). Boys get more of their father's time than do their sisters, or do girls in all-female families. Girls with brothers receive more of fathers' time than do girls in all-female families, but this time is primarily spent watching television together.

Renegotiating Family Work

Despite the imbalance in the division of housework and childcare, it does appear that many families are renegotiating how family labor is performed. The amount of time both fathers and mothers are spending with their children has grown considerably since 1965, but father's time has increased threefold, from 2.5 hours per week to 7.3 hours per week (Parker & Wang, 2013). However, this still is much less than the amount of time mothers spend with their children, at 13.5 hours per week, as shown in Figure 10.6.

Men's time spent in housework and childcare is on the rise (Galinsky, Aumann, & Bond, 2009; Parker & Wang, 2013). However, despite these very

Watch on **MySocLab**
Video: *Kathleen Gerson: Work and Family Revolution*

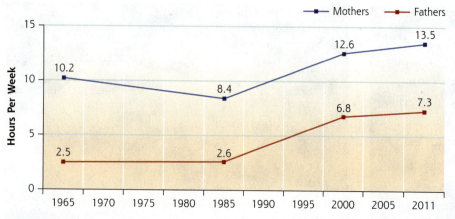

FIGURE 10.6

Parents' Childcare Time, 1965–2011 (hours per week)

In the past, fathers' participation in childcare was minimal; today, expectations have changed.

Source: Parker & Wang, 2013.

TABLE 10.3	Weekly Leisure Time of Mothers and Fathers (in hours)	
Fathers report an extra few hours of leisure per week compared to mothers.		
Married Fathers	27	
Married Mothers	24	
Cohabiting Fathers	33	
Cohabiting Mothers	29	
Single Fathers	31	
Single Mothers	27	

Source: Parker & Wang, 2013.

real changes, family work isn't shared equally. Consequently, fathers have more leisure time than do their wives, as shown in Table 10.3.

Not surprisingly, with the lack of leisure and high demands of children, home, and work, mothers experience more stress and burnout than do their husbands in the work–family balancing act (Parker, 2009; Roxburgh, 2012). This stress and burnout is significant, because it can lead to depression and marital instability. In particular, when women value equality in the home but end up doing the majority of household labor, their sense of fairness is violated and happiness with their marriage declines (Lavee & Katz, 2002). Men may compare how they contribute to household labor with how their fathers contributed, and believe that, "Wow, I'm doing a lot." Whereas many women compare the household contributions of their partners to what they are doing and think, "This isn't fair."

Children's Labor in the Home

How much, and under what conditions, do sons and daughters provide housework or childcare? What impact does their labor have on themselves and their families? Children perform household labor for many reasons. Some parents are attempting to socialize their children to future adult or parental roles (e.g., teaching a child how to use the vacuum or washing machine). Other parents simply need the extra assistance to keep up with housework and childcare demands (e.g., requiring a child to babysit a younger sibling after school).

One study of children and chores, which used both observational and survey methods, found that most children spent little time helping around the house and actually engaged in fewer tasks than what they reported in interviews. Within the context of children's minimal participation in household work, they also found that allowance was not an effective motivator. Although most children were aware that their working parents need help, in some families inconsistent and unclear expectations from parents negatively affected children's participation in household work (Klein, Graesch, & Izquierdo, 2009).

Among those who do chores, young children's housework is less gendered than that of adults or teens and may include picking up toys or making one's bed. On average, teenage girls do more housework than teenage boys. Girls tend to do more routine inside chores such as cleaning, cooking, or caring for siblings, whereas boys do occasional outside chores such as yard work (Antill, Goodnow, Russell, & Cotton, 1996). A longitudinal study that followed a group of boys through young adulthood found that boys who did more household chores as a child also did more of the routine housework as an adult (Anderson & Robson, 2006).

Children in two-parent, dual-earner families, and children of highly educated families tend to do less housework and childcare than do children in other family types. Lower-income families and single-parent families rely on children, especially daughters, to a considerable extent to help with numerous household tasks and to take care of younger siblings. These daughters have been nick-named *mini-moms* (Dodson & Dickert, 2004).

Explanations for the Gendered Division of Labor

Several theories explain the relationship between gender and the division of household labor, including (1) the time-availability perspective; (2) the relative resources perspective; and (3) the gender perspective.

TIME-AVAILABILITY PERSPECTIVE The **time-availability perspective** suggests that the division of labor is largely determined by (1) the need for household labor, such as the number of children in the home; and (2) each partner's avail-ability to perform household tasks, such as the number of hours spent in paid work (Shelton, 1992). Both husband and wife are expected to perform domestic work to the extent that other demands in their lives allow them. The partner who has the most time available because of fewer other commitments will spend more time on housework. However, because gendered family decision-making often determines the amount of time that men and women spend in paid work, it's unclear whether women do the majority of the housework because they spend fewer hours in paid labor or whether they spend fewer hours in paid labor because they have to do the majority of the housework (Evertsson & Nermo, 2004).

time-availability perspective: A perspective that suggests the divi-sion of labor is largely determined by (1) the need for household labor, such as the number of children in the home; and (2) each partner's availability to perform household tasks, such as the number of hours spent in paid work.

RELATIVE RESOURCES PERSPECTIVE The theory behind the **relative resources perspective** is based on the premise of *exchange theory* (Becker, 1981; Blood & Wolfe, 1960), which posits that the greater the relative amount or value of resources contributed by a partner, the greater is his or her power within the relationship. This power can then be translated into bargaining to avoid tasks such as housework that offer no pay and minimal social prestige (Bittman, England, Sayer, Folbre, & Matheson, 2003). However, working-class partners often provide relatively similar resources to the family, yet their roles are often highly segregated (Rubin, 1976). Resources are usually defined as monetary ones, but they can take other forms as well, such as occupational prestige, edu-cation level, or even good looks or an exceptionally charismatic personality.

relative resources perspective: The greater the relative amount or value of resources contributed by a partner, the greater is his or her power within the relationship, which can then be translated into bargaining to avoid tasks such as housework that offer no pay and minimal social prestige.

GENDER PERSPECTIVE ("DOING GENDER") The perspectives of time-avail-ability and relative resources are largely gender-neutral. However, some scholars suggest that gender itself is the ultimate explanatory variable, not how much time a partner has available or how many resources he or she brings to the rela-tionship. "Doing gender," introduced in Chapter 6, suggests that housework is so ingrained as "women's work" that it functions as an area in which gender is symbolically created and reproduced (Fenstermaker Berk, 1985; West & Zimmerman, 1987). Wives do the majority of housework because it's expected of them as women and they have heard these messages since childhood. Like-wise, men do less because housework isn't a part of their gendered identity. This is likely why many men and women feel that the division of household labor is fair even when it isn't split equally between partners. Gendered norms exert a powerful influence on what we see as normative. When we remember the house-hold tasks we may have done as children, most women report that they were involved in inside domestic labor, such as helping with cooking, cleaning, or tak-ing care of siblings, and men remember that they were more involved in outside labor, such as mowing the lawn. In other words, even girls do more routine labor, whereas boys do occasional labor. Moreover, which household task is more highly valued in our society? Typically, we pay more for someone to mow our lawn than to babysit our children. These gendered values are so ingrained that we rarely question this logic.

Families have a lot of work to do both inside and outside the home. How do they divide up household labor—both housework and childcare? There are many macro- and micro-level factors that influence how this work gets done.

MACRO-LEVEL FACTORS

- Sex
- Cultural attitudes toward gender
- Cultural expectations for mothers and fathers
- Historical period
- Value attributed to specific resources (e.g., money)
- Sex of children

MICRO-LEVEL FACTORS

- Personal inclination
- Employment status and number of hours worked

- Presence and age of children
- Comparison to others (e.g., fathers)

WHAT DO YOU THINK?

1. In looking back to how your parents negotiated the division of household labor, can you see any of these macro-level and micro-level factors in operation?
2. Do you think these macro-level and micro-level factors influence the division of household labor differently today than they did in your parents' generation? If you think they do operate differently, can you explain the difference and what caused it?

What was the division of household labor when you were a child? If you were in a two-parent household, were housework and childcare divided along gendered lines? Which theoretical perspective is most useful for understanding the pattern of household labor? How do you think you and your partner will structure household labor?

Clearly, who does what tasks in the home is usually not some random event. There are both micro-level and macro-level factors operating here, as shown in the feature box *Tying It All Together: Factors That Shape the Division of Household Labor*. Can you see how these factors operate in your own life?

You have learned that home and work were once considered separate spheres and were largely segregated by sex. Today, we recognize that work and family aren't separate, but are highly interrelated with one another (Voydanoff, 2008). Family members have work to do both inside and outside the home. The next section explores the delicate art of juggling this household work among them.

| 10.4 | Analyze the juggling of work and family |

Questions That Matter

10.9 What are three important concepts that help explain the causes of stress for adults when they combine work and family?

10.10 If balancing work and family can be stressful, why don't adults work part-time?

Juggling Work and Family Life

We often hear parents, especially women, say that they can "have it all," but combining work and family isn't easy, as Lisa and Chris show us in the opening vignette (Bianchi & Milkie, 2010). If you know someone who is combining work and family, compare their situation with Lara, an American mother living in Hungary, described in the feature box *Diversity in Families: Why We Choose to Live in Hungary*. Their experiences are likely as different as night and day. Yet, the balance between a happy work life and a happy home life are what we all strive for. Let's look further to better understand the tension between work and family, and perhaps learn how to minimize this tension. As the example from Hungary shows—in a nation not nearly as wealthy as the United States—balancing work and family doesn't have to be so difficult.

Conflict, Overload, and Spillover

Researchers have been studying the mutual influences of work and family (Goodman, Crouter, & The Family Life Project Key Investigators, 2009; Hostetler, Desrochers, Kopko, & Moen, 2012; Nomaguchi, 2012b; Voydanoff, 2008). From this research have come several important concepts that help us understand the reciprocal relationship between work and family life.

One such concept is **work–family conflict,** which is the tension people feel when the pressures from paid work and family roles are incompatible in some

work–family conflict: A form of tension under which people feel that the pressures from paid work and family roles are incompatible in some way.

way (Nomaguchi, 2009, 2012b; Stewart, 2013). The conflict can go both ways: work is made more difficult by participation in family roles (e.g., it's difficult to work the expected overtime at your job because you need to pick up your children from daycare), and participation in family roles is made more difficult by work (e.g., it's difficult to get to your son's soccer practice every Wednesday afternoon because it conflicts with the department meeting at work). People feel greater work–family conflict when (1) the demands of paid work and family responsibilities are higher; (2) the resources that help them manage those demands are fewer; or (3) the perceptions of demands they believe they must fulfill are higher (Voydanoff, 2004). Work–family conflict has increased for both men and women over the past few decades (Nomaguchi, 2009). In fact, now that fathers are doing more housework and childcare, 50 percent now say that they find it somewhat or very difficult to balance work and family (as compared to 56 percent of mothers) (Parker & Wang, 2013).

Another concept is **role overload**, which refers to feeling overwhelmed by many different commitments and not having enough time to meet each commitment effectively (Duxbury, Lyons, & Higgins, 2008; Pearson, 2008). Role overload can lead to stress and depression. A recent study of more than 700 randomly selected mothers found that those who felt the most overload among their work, parent, and spouse roles had lower levels of mental well-being than did women who perceived less role overload. *Perception* of overload is the key here. Simply working more hours didn't necessarily lead to more feelings of overload; in fact, women who worked *less than* 30 hours a week *or more than* 35 hours a week had the fewest feelings of role overload. What appears to make the difference in role overload is not how many hours are worked, but how much support is available. Mothers with higher incomes (who can, presumably, hire more help), higher marital quality, and higher-quality jobs were least likely to feel role overload (Glynn, Maclean, Forte, & Cohen, 2009).

Another related concept, **spillover**, refers to the negative (or sometimes positive) moods, experiences, and demands involved in one sphere that carry over, or "spill over," into the other sphere (Davis, Goodman, Pirretti, & Almeida, 2008; Okechukwu, Ayadi, Tamers, Sabbath, & Berkman, 2012). How do you purge the rushed and hectic mood at work when you now have to grocery shop with your toddler? How do you play with your children after work when your

Explore on **MySocLab**
Activity: Family vs. Job: Who Wins?

role overload: Feeling overwhelmed by many different commitments and not having enough time to meet each commitment effectively.

Listen on **MySocLab**
Audio: NPR: The Ethicist: Working Mothers and Overtime

spillover: An occurrence caused by the demands involved in one sphere of work carrying over into work in another sphere.

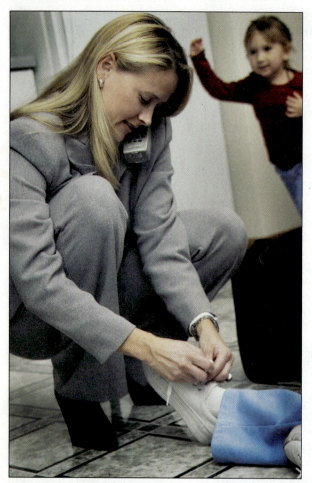

How do work and family influence one another? Social scientists talk about *work–family conflict, role overload,* and *spillover.*

boss is still sending you e-mails in the evening? With the creation of computers, cell phones, and other important technology, work increasingly encroaches on family time (Conley, 2009). Other people may be required to travel for their jobs away from their homes and families for periods of time. These different work demands mean that families have trouble finding quality time together.

Likewise, family demands can spill over into employment. Who takes care of the children on teachers' workdays at school? How do you face the day's challenges at work when your child has a fever of 101 degrees? Even if you can arrange for childcare when your child is ill, the stress at home can affect your work performance.

Spillover could also be positive (Poelmans, Stepanova, & Masuda, 2008). One study measured positive family-to-work spillover by asking 156 couples to respond to statements such as, "My family gives me ideas that can be used at work," or "My family helps me face challenges at work." The researchers found that in families with higher cohesion, such as feelings of togetherness and mutual support, both mothers and fathers expressed more positive family-to-work spillover. In particular, women who were satisfied with housework arrangements perceived more positive spillover, whereas satisfaction with their marital relationship increased men's positive spillover (Stevens, Minnotte, Mannon, & Kiger, 2007).

The relationship between work and family is gendered (Galinsky, Aumann, & Bond, 2009). Men receive pressure from their employers to fulfill work obligations and to ignore or minimize family obligations (Coltrane, 1997; Hertz & Marshall, 2001). The idea is to let someone else, presumably the wife, take time off from work when a child is sick or has to go to the dentist. Women get more pressure from home to fulfill home obligations at the cost of work obligations. Consequently, although men may miss more family functions (e.g., their child's violin recital or school play), men aren't necessarily penalized at work for having children in the same way that women are penalized (Stone, 2008). In fact, many employers see men with children as more stable and hardworking, as the term *family man* implies. However, having children doesn't have this same effect for women. There is no equivalent *family woman* term.

Most of the research on the interface of work and family has been conducted in Western countries; however, a study using data from the IBM Corporation in 48 countries reveals that significant work–family conflicts are experienced throughout much of the world (Hill, Yang, Hawkins, & Ferris, 2004). In particular, the concern is usually about how the conflict affects family life, not necessarily how it affects work; in other words, work was thought to be more detrimental to family than family was thought to be detrimental to work. The research found that having a spouse or intimate partner contributed to a reduced conflict for women in developed countries, but not for women in developing countries. They also found that responsibility for children contributed more than twice as much to conflict for women as it did for men, likely because women carry a larger share of childcare responsibilities.

What are the consequences of work–family conflict, role overload, and spillover? Stress is certainly one consequence (Bianchi & Milkie, 2010; Okechukwu, Ayadi, Tamers, Sabbath, & Berkman, 2012). Eighty-six percent of working mothers say that they sometimes or frequently experience stress in their lives, as compared to 44 percent of working fathers (Parker, 2009). Poor health is another consequence, as is unhappiness (Parker & Wang, 2013). The source of these problems is that parents believe that there isn't enough time to do it all and to

Watch on **MySocLab**
Video: *Stages of Family Life: Kathleen Gerson: Do Children Suffer When Mothers and Fathers Work?*

do it all well. In this next section, let's look at the time crunch that many parents experience.

The Time Crunch

What are the largest challenges that parents report facing today? Feeling rushed and not spending enough time with their children seems to be at the top of the list. A study from the Pew Research Center, which conducts regular surveys on social and demographic trends, found parents, especially mothers, are more likely to say that they "always feel rushed," in comparison to adults who do not have children under age 18 (Figure 10.7).

Finally, another study that used two different samples of U.S. adults found that nearly 50 percent of parents residing with their children believed that they spend too little time with them (Milkie, Mattingly, Nomaguchi, Bianchi, & Robinson, 2004). Parents find enjoyment in caring for their children, playing with them, and teaching them, and believe that spending time with their children is important for the child's sense of happiness and well-being. Several factors are associated with experiencing time deficits with children, including the amount of time in paid work, the age of the youngest child, and sex of the parent—parents who work longer hours, who have a younger child, and fathers are more likely to report feeling a time deficit. However, once the work hours are held constant, mothers actually feel more time deficits than fathers (Milkie, Mattingly, Nomaguchi, Bianchi, & Robinson, 2004).

Yet, despite their feelings to the contrary, parents actually spend *as much or even more time* with children than they did in the past (Bianchi, Robinson, & Milkie, 2006; Parker & Wang, 2013). Studies based on large and representative samples of parents in the United States find (1) the amount of time both mothers and fathers spend with children is on the rise, regardless of employment status; (2) mothers continue to spend significantly more time with their children than do fathers; and (3) unemployed mothers spend more time with their children than do employed mothers (Bianchi, Robinson, & Milkie, 2006; Kendig & Bianchi, 2008).

If parents spend more time with their children than they used to, why do parents report that they aren't involved enough? One reason is that expectations for parenting have changed (Layne, 2004). Parents, especially mothers, are expected to be far more involved in their children's lives than they were in the past—a trend that some suggest is actually detrimental to children (Honore, 2008; Sayer, Gauthier, & Furstenberg, 2004). Parents hover over their children, paying extremely close attention to their children's experiences and trying to ward off

Parents feel a time crunch and report wanting to spend more time with their children. Yet, interestingly, parents today actually spend as much or more time with their children than parents of the past.

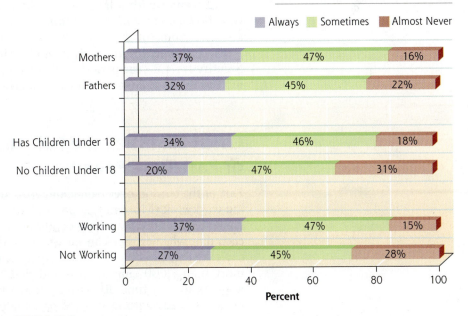

FIGURE 10.7
Percent Feeling Rushed

Parents, especially mothers, are more likely to say that they always feel rushed.
Source: Parker & Wang, 2013.

any problems before they emerge. This constant vigilance has given rise to a new nickname—*helicopter parents*. Parents drive their children from playdate to playdate; orchestrate their children's after-school activities; confront and blame teachers when their child performs poorly; and e-mail, text, or call their adult children daily when they're away at college. Some parents even run interference with their children's professors when they can't enroll in a preferred class or if they received a lower grade than expected. The availability of technology is often to blame for the explosion in helicopter parenting—cell phones have been called the world's longest umbilical cord (Briggs, 2006).

Perhaps another reason why parents feel that they aren't spending enough time with their children is frustration by their inability to respond spontaneously because of encroaching demands placed on them by their employers (Daly, 2001). As parents work more hours per week, and as work conditions and hours become less standardized, parents may find it difficult to meet their children's needs. They apparently continue to spend time with them, but it may be at greater personal cost, such as lack of leisure activities, exercise, or sleep (Nomaguchi & Bianchi, 2004; Pelham, 2010).

Consequently, by the late 2000s we began to see a growing number of mothers report that they would prefer to work part-time or not at all. In 1997, a third of working mothers said that they would prefer to work full-time, but by 2007 that figure had dropped to only 21 percent. Yet, by 2012, the figure has risen back to 37 percent, possibly reflecting the difficult economic times felt by many families during the recent recession. Yet, even so, the majority of working women continue to say that they would either prefer to work either part-time, or not at all, as shown in Table 10.4.

TABLE 10.4	The Preferred Work Status of Working Mothers		
Working mothers had a growing interest in part-time work until the recession hit. Interest in full-time work saw a big jump between 2007 and 2012.			
Would Prefer	**1997**	**2007**	**2012**
Full-time work	32%	21%	37%
Part-time work	48%	60%	50%
Not working	20%	19%	11%

Source: Parker & Wang, 2013.

If mothers would prefer to work part-time or not work outside the home at all, then why do they work full-time? Some reasons are financial, others might be related to the fear they would be unable to enter the job market later or would reenter with a large disadvantage compared to other workers. The feature box *Policy and You: From Macro to Micro: Fixing Social INsecurity* addresses some of these concerns and offers a proposal to help families have a parent at home. It's an innovative idea that would allow people to draw Social Security for a 3-year period while raising children rather than having the funds unavailable to them until they are elderly.

Catch 22: Inflexible Full-Time Work or Part-Time Penalty

Part of the tension over balancing work and family is because of an ever-increasing workweek (Morrissey, 2008) and a feeling that workers have little control or flexibility over their working conditions—when they work, how long they work each day, whether they can miss a day to take care of children, or whether they can take extended time off and reenter without penalty. For example, a study of more than 1,000 employers found that only 55 percent report allowing most workers to take time off during the workday to attend to important family or personal needs without loss of pay. Only 27 percent of employers allow their workers to periodically change their starting and quitting time within some range; most aren't given time off to care for sick children without losing pay (Matos & Galinsky, 2012). Meanwhile, work is demanding more time of its employees: the average American worked 48 more hours per year—6 extra days or more than a work week—than did Americans a generation ago (Morrissey, 2008).

Ask parents and many will tell you that they would like to take some time out from their jobs to devote more attention and energy to their young children. Parents, especially mothers, would like to work part-time or stay home altogether. What is preventing them? One factor is the well-founded anxiety about the career setbacks that such an arrangement would cause. Mothers want the continued rewards of work, but with scaled-down hours. For many families, however, the biggest barrier is practical: they simply cannot afford to reduce their work hours.

Here is a proposal to help families. Why not allow working parents to draw Social Security benefits for up to 3 years during their prime childrearing years? This would give them a choice about how much time to spend working and how much time to spend with their children. Those who elected to "borrow" on their Social Security would repay the system when they returned to work. For example, the government could increase the employee's share of the payroll taxes they pay when parents return to work, parents could defer their age of retirement with full Social Security benefits on a year-for-year basis, or parents could accept a reduced monthly benefit, as those who opt for early retirement do now.

How much of a difference would this make for parents trying to make ends meet? It would make a huge difference. Taxes and childcare costs take such a large portion out of parents' incomes that even modest Social Security benefits could largely replace the net income from an average job. For example, a parent earning a second salary of $30,000 (assuming the spouse also makes $30,000) would only net about $10,065 after taxes, childcare, and work expenses (see the following table).

Among parents taking advantage of an early option to access Social Security, most would probably stay at home during their children's earliest years. But the needs of children continue after early childhood. A fifth-grader struggling in school or a troubled teenager can also demand parental attention. This policy would let parents decide what makes sense for them and their families.

One issue that would need to be addressed is overcoming barriers to re-entering the workforce. Although common in other countries, it's probably unrealistic to ask employers to guarantee someone's job after a leave of a year or more. Continuation of health insurance would also need to be addressed. More fundamentally, we must change the national mindset, so that nurturing children is seen as a respectable and worthwhile accomplishment that strengthens, rather than interferes with, the worker's attachment to employment.

Net Income after Taxes, Childcare, and Work Expenses

Example: A two-earner couple, where each parent makes	$30,000
The second salary	$30,000
Subtract	
Social Security and Medicare taxes	2,295
Additional state and local taxes	1,500
Estimated additional federal income tax	6,180
Additional childcare (estimated at $120/week)*	6,240
Commuting cost ($25/week times 50)	1,250
Cost of work clothing and dry cleaning	870
Cost of restaurant meals on workdays ($25/week times 50)	1,250
Other (non-reimbursed expenses, paid help, meals out, etc.)	350
Net income	**$10,065**

The proposal offered here—allowing parents to draw Social Security at two points in their lives—could offer relief from the time crunch experienced by millions of Americans struggling to meet the dual demands of work and family. In the 20th century, we focused on meeting the needs of the elderly. Today, we recognize that compelling needs emerge earlier in our lives as we are raising our families. Yet, our policies have not adequately changed to compensate for the massive entry of women into paid employment. Our Social Security system has long been thought of as providing a measure of financial security in return for a lifetime of work. What could be a more vital contribution to the future of our country than raising children well?

WHAT DO YOU THINK?

1. Do you think a program that would allow parents to draw on Social Security as they raise their children would be popular among Americans? Why or why not? Would it be stigmatized as welfare?
2. What do you think might be some of the logistic barriers to adopting this type of program? Do you think the barriers (if any) are surmountable?

Sources: Official Journal of the European Communities, 1998; Parker, 2009; Rankin, 2002.

Because of the inflexibility of many workplaces, some parents have opted to reduce their work hours to part-time, or wish that they could (Parker, 2009; Parker & Wang, 2013); however, they generally pay a steep price for this added flexibility. Workers who go part-time or a non-standard (e.g., temporary, contract) route earn less pay than regular full-time workers, and are less likely to have health insurance, sick pay, or a pension.

These drawbacks to part-time work aren't found in many other countries. In 1997, the European Union (EU) drafted a Directive "to eliminate discrimination against part-time workers and improve the quality of part-time work" (Official Journal of the European Communities, 1998). The Directive prohibits employers from treating part-time workers less favorably than comparable full-time workers (unless they can demonstrate that the differential treatment is justified). It addresses issues of pay equity, Social Security, job benefits, training and promotion opportunities, and collective bargaining rights. How does this Directive actually work? Germany grants the right to work part-time in firms that have more than 15 workers; Belgium grants employees the right to work 80 percent time for 5 years; the UK allows employees the right to request flexible and part-time work to care for a child under the age of 6 or a disabled child under the age of 18, and Sweden allows parents to work 6 hours a day until their children turn 8 years old (Gornick, Heron, & Eisenbrey, 2007).

If you plan to have children, what would be the preferred work schedule for you and your spouse or partner? Do you think it will be possible, or easy, to have this schedule? What would facilitate or interfere with your preferred schedule?

Because the United States offers no options for part-time work, parents must scramble to find childcare for significant portions of each day. The next section examines childcare arrangements available in this country and some of the critical issues that affect the delicate balance of work and family life.

📖 **Read** on **MySocLab**
Document: *Caring for Our Young: Child Care in Europe and the United States*

daycare centers: Nonresidential facilities that provide childcare.

family childcare providers: Private homes other than the child's home where childcare is provided.

nannies/babysitters: Non-relatives that provide childcare in the home.

Who's Minding the Kids?

With increasing numbers of mothers turning to employment over the past several decades, many children are spending substantial amounts of time in the care of someone other than their parents (Laughlin, April 2013). In a typical week in 2011, about 12.5 million (61 percent) children under 5 years of age were in some type of regular childcare arrangement. Given these figures, is the quality of childcare and its high costs a private matter, or is it a public concern?

Childcare is a necessity for most families, but families are left on their own to find the highest-quality childcare they can afford. However, quality controls are limited and vary by state. For example, most childcare facilities aren't accredited (National Association of Child Care Resource & Referral Agencies, 2009). CPR and First Aid requirements vary substantially and are nonexistent in some states. Pay for childcare workers is low (median is around $9.50 per hour); few workers receive fringe benefits such as health insurance, sick pay, or vacation time; and turnover in these positions is high (Bureau of Labor Statistics, October 26, 2012).

Not all developed nations think of childcare as a private matter. Some see it as a public concern, and as a social good that can ultimately benefit everyone. What can other countries teach us about how to structure quality childcare and early education to the benefit of everyone? The feature box *Policy and You: From Macro to Micro: A Comparative Look at Early Childhood Education and Childcare Policies* shows what is possible.

Preschool-age Children

Who provides care for young children when parents are unavailable? Figure 10.8 answers this question using data from the Census Bureau. Some dual-earner families arrange working different shifts so that one parent can always be home with the children, and a few turn to other relatives, such as grandparents or aunts. Others use more formal arrangements, such as **daycare centers**, where care is provided in nonresidential facilities. Others rely on non-relatives, such as **family childcare providers**, where care is provided in a private home other than the child's home, or **nannies/babysitters**, where the child is cared for in the home by a non-relative. In fact, many parents, such as Lisa and Chris in the opening vignette, have multiple arrangements (e.g., with a grandparent on Tuesday and

A Comparative Look at Early Childhood Education and Childcare Policies

Early childhood education and care (ECEC) has become an important issue in many parts of the world because of the dramatic rise in labor force participation of mothers, the push for single mothers to work rather than receive public aid, and a growing interest in ensuring that all children begin elementary school with basic skills and are ready to learn. ECEC programs enhance and support children's cognitive, social, and emotional development. A review of a number of European countries shows that the availability, quality, and affordability of ECEC programs far exceed what is found in the United States.

What is so different in these countries? In several countries, access to ECEC is a statutory right. Although compulsory school begins at age 6 or 7, ECEC availability begins at age 1 in Denmark, Finland, and Sweden (after generous maternity and family leave benefits are exhausted), 2½ in Belgium, 3 in Italy and Germany, and 4 in Britain. Most countries have full coverage of 3- to 6-year-olds.

In contrast, in the United States there is no statutory entitlement until ages 5–7, depending on the state. Access to publicly funded ECEC programs is generally restricted to at-risk children, usually defined as poor or near-poor (e.g., the Head Start Program). The demand for these programs among vulnerable groups far outstrips their availability. Only New York and Georgia have developed universal pre-kindergarten programs for all 4-year-olds regardless of family income.

In most countries reviewed, governments pay the largest share of the costs, with parents covering only 25 percent to 30 percent. Countries may also make arrangements for sliding-scale payments for low-income families to help make programs affordable. Most countries require staff to complete at least 3 years of training at universities or other institutes of higher education. Their earnings are in accordance. In contrast, American parents pay an average of 70 percent of ECEC costs. Some of these costs can be recouped through tax benefits, but many low-income families find the tax system confusing and therefore, end up using informal or unregulated childcare. There is also no agreed-on set of staff qualifications. Their status and pay are low and turnover is high.

In the United States, families generally fend for themselves to find and pay for childcare. In other developed nations, high-quality childcare is readily available and the cost is subsidized by the government to make it more affordable to parents.

The United States is a national leader in research on child development, but hasn't developed the programs that research suggests are needed and which are increasingly available in other countries. In other words, the United States has not yet made the critical political commitment to early childhood education and care.

WHAT DO YOU THINK?

1. Why do you think the United States lags behind other European nations with respect to providing early childhood education and care? Is it related to cost, social views about working parents, stigma of ECEC, political issues, taxpayer revolts, or some other issue? Which groups might oppose ECEC, and why?
2. What will it take for our ECEC policies to become more responsive to working families?

Source: The Clearinghouse on International Developments in Child, Youth, & Family Policies, 2001, 2007, 2008.

Thursday, and a daycare center on Monday, Wednesday, Friday) to ensure that their children are well cared for and to minimize costs.

These differences reflect both personal inclinations (a micro-level issue) and the costs of childcare (a macro-level issue). Relative care and care provided by other families are usually the least expensive childcare options, or may even be free. However, for many people these aren't options, and they must pay for childcare. People without children often don't realize how expensive childcare can be. For example, in 2011 in 40 states and the District of Columbia, the average annual cost of *infant care* in a center exceeded 10 percent of the median household income for a two-parent family. In 2011 in 22 states and the District of Columbia (DC), the average annual cost of care for a *4-year-old* in a center exceeded 10 percent of the median household income for a two-parent family. Put another way, childcare costs often exceed college costs. In 2011 in 35 states and DC, the average annual cost for an infant in center-based care was higher than a year's tuition and fees at

early childhood education and care (ECEC): An international term for daycare, preschool, and other programs to ensure that all children begin elementary school with basic skills and are ready to learn.

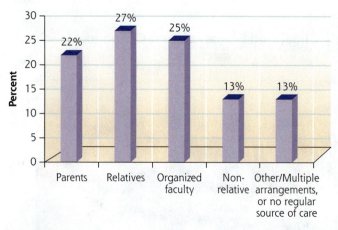

FIGURE 10.8

Primary Childcare Arrangements of Preschoolers with Employed Mothers, 2011

Almost half of all preschool-age children of employed mothers are cared for by either a parent or another relative.
Source: Laughlin, 2013.

TABLE 10.5	Range of Annual Childcare Costs for 2011			
Childcare is expensive, especially for an infant in a daycare center.				
	Average Annual Fees for Full-Time Childcare for			
	Daycare Center		**Family Home**	
	Infant	**4-Year-Old**	**Infant**	**4-Year-Old**
Massachusetts	$16,500	$12,200	$12,100	$11,300
Mississippi	$4,650	$3,900	$3,850	$3,600
New York	$13,650	$10,550	$10,200	$9,450
South Carolina	$5,850	$5,450	$4,550	$4,100

Source: National Association of Child Care Resource & Referral Agencies, 2011.

self-care: Children who are unsupervised and taking care of themselves.

a 4-year public college. Even the annual cost of care for a 4-year-old, which is less expensive than care for an infant, was higher than public college costs in 19 states and DC (ChildCare Aware of America, 2012). Family childcare providers are often the most economical option, as shown in Table 10.5; however, the quality of care that children receive in many childcare homes may be unknown if the home is unlicensed. Childcare centers tend to be the most expensive options and often place a greater emphasis on educational learning. Prices vary throughout the country, but clearly, the cost of childcare centers remains out of reach of many parents without some sort of public subsidy (especially when you consider that most people have two children, not just one).

School-Age Children

The costs of childcare may be reduced as children begin school, but parents who work full-time must look for childcare arrangements to supplement the school day. Most school-age children (5–14 years old) with employed parents are supervised before and after school by family, nannies/babysitters, or attend before- and after-school programs. However, largely because of cost, some school-age children are left unsupervised, called **self-care**. According to the U.S. Census Bureau, about 4 percent of elementary-school children ages 5 through 11 and 30 percent of middle-school children ages 12 through 14 take care of themselves after school on a regular basis (Laughlin, 2013).

Although self-care is certainly not always harmful (e.g., it may make a child more independent), there are also potential problems with unsupervised children (e.g., the risk of getting into trouble). However, most states have no legal age limits for when it's appropriate to leave a child alone (U.S. Department of Health & Human Services, 2006). Other states may have guidelines that are distributed to child protective services, often suggesting that a child should be at least 10 or 12 before being left alone for even short times, but also recognizing that the maturity level of children can differ. Child welfare workers therefore have some degree of discretion, but can declare a parent unfit if the child is left alone when deemed inappropriate.

Effects of Childcare on Children's Well-Being

One research article headline reads, "Study Finds That Child Care Does Impact Mother–Child Interaction" (American Psychological Association, 1999b). Another headline reads, "New Longitudinal Study Finds That Having a Working Mother Does No Significant Harm to Children" (American Psychological Association, 1999a). Which headline is correct? Both articles are reporting findings from studies using large, longitudinal, nationally representative samples. The first article uses data from the National Institute of Child Health and Human Development Study of Early Child Care, a longitudinal study of approximately 1,300 children. The second uses data from the National Longitudinal Survey of Youth, a survey of approximately 12,600 individuals. How can two good data sources yield opposite conclusions?

Determining the effects of mothers' employment and childcare on the well-being of children is a complex task. It's made more difficult by the use of different measures of well-being, the different types of childcare settings and their quality, the different types of relationships that mothers and children have (regardless of employment or childcare), the role of the father and other family members in childcare, the mother's physical and emotional health, the child's temperament, the age of the child, the mother's hours of work and other working conditions, and many other factors not yet identified. Because of all the confounding factors, it's not surprising that some studies report a negative association between mother's employment and cognitive and social outcomes, such as less attachment or a child's greater level of aggression (Belsky, Weinraub, Owen, & Kelly, 2001), whereas others find positive outcomes such as children's higher language and other academic skills, especially among poor children (Loeb, Bridges, Bassok, Fuller, & Rumberger, 2007).

A study that garnered tremendous media attention was led by Professor Jay Belsky, and found that children who were in childcare for more than 30 hours per week during the first 4 years of life were somewhat more likely to behave aggressively as compared to those who had been in childcare for less than 10 hours a week. This finding received widespread attention because no other issue is as fraught with worry as the choice of childcare. However, both groups of children exhibited levels of aggression that were well within the normal range. A follow-up study tracked the same children through early elementary school and found that by third grade, children who spent longer time in childcare had higher math and reading skills, and their greater likelihood of aggressive behavior had disappeared. However, it also found that children with longer time in childcare had poorer work habits and social skills, although again, the effects were very small and within the normal range (Lewin, 2005a).

It appears that the relationship between mother's employment and child well-being is somewhat mixed and contradictory, because the results from research are small and depend on many other factors. Perhaps the most important factor is the quality of care that the child experiences (National Institute of Child Health and Human Development, 1999, 2005; Vandell, Belsky, Burchinal, Steinberg, & Vandergrift, 2010). Children in poor-quality childcare have been found to be delayed in language and reading skills, display more aggression, demonstrate lower mathematical ability, have poorer attention skills, and have more behavioral problems than children in higher-quality care. In contrast, children who spend time in a higher-quality childcare setting are often at an advantage. One study of more than 1,300 children continued to follow them through their teenage years. The researchers found that those teens who had higher-quality childcare as children had higher cognitive–academic achievement and exhibited fewer behavioral problems. Yet, the researchers also found that more hours of non-relative care predicted greater risk-taking and impulsivity by the teenage years (Vandell, Belsky, Burchinal, Steinberg, & Vandergrift, 2010).

Do you remember spending time in childcare or after-school care? What did you think of your experience? How might parents' views differ from the views of the child, and why?

Bringing It Full Circle

All families do meaningful work inside or outside the home, but the changing nature of the economy and the occupational structure has altered the context and meaning of work for many families. More women work outside the home for pay. Globalization and expanding technology have blurred the lines between work and family. The current recession has resulted in a rise in temporary employment, non-standardized work schedules, and fewer union protections (e.g., fringe benefits, such as health insurance). These changes have critical implications for how families combine work and family. Many families now need two paychecks to make ends meet. No longer are work and family domains separate; instead, they interact and influence each other. Issues such as work–family conflicts, spillover, feelings of time deficits with children, negotiations over the division of household labor, and struggles to find suitable childcare are among the issues that most employed families face today, as shown by Lisa and Chris in the opening vignette. Using the information you've learned in this chapter, let's return to Lisa and Chris's story and answer a few questions:

- Can you provide any examples of conflict, overload, and spillover in the story of Lisa and Chris?
- What differences might you see between a professional couple, such as Lisa and Chris, and a working-class couple in their division of household labor or in how they juggle work and family?
- Why do Lisa and Chris feel such a time crunch, and what can be done about it? Can you think of both micro-level and macro-level causes and potential solutions?

On MySocLab

 **Study and Review on MySocLab**

CHAPTER REVIEW

LO10.1 Assess the changing dynamics of the workplace

10.1 What is the history of work in early America?

In early colonial America, most families worked closely with the land. By the 19th century, the U.S. economy was evolving from agriculture to industrialization. During this period, work was done outside the home and people were paid wages for their labor.

10.2 How has participation in the women's labor force changed in the past century?

For most of the 20th century, few married women with children worked outside the home. However, by 1980, we began to see an important cultural shift: the majority of mothers, whether married, single, or divorced, were now employed outside the home. This change likely reflected increasing job and educational opportunities for women, the acceptance of social and economic equality brought forth by the women's movement, and other changes in the economy.

10.3 How have increased technology and globalization contributed to a changing occupational structure?

First, the widespread use of technology such as personal computers, cell phones, fax machines, and pagers has changed both the way we do business and conduct our personal lives. Second, many jobs are being outsourced to other countries as companies search for less expensive labor and fewer governmental restrictions. Jobs in manufacturing, service, and sales are increasingly shipped to other countries.

LO10.2 Describe aspects of life in a recession

10.4 How has the rise in unemployment affected families?

The overall U.S. unemployment rate was 7.0 percent in November 2013 and higher for minority groups. Many people lost their jobs or had their income reduced, contributing to the rise in home foreclosures, bankruptcy, and the number of families who no longer have their health insurance.

10.5 How has the current recession contributed to unstable wages, working conditions, and a disposable workforce?

Millions of people earn only the minimum wage. Half are adults age 25 or older, most of them women. There has been a large increase in the number of people with non-standardized work schedules, meaning temporary work, weekend or evening shifts, or rotating schedules. This, along with low wages, makes family life difficult.

10.6 How serious a threat is losing health insurance?

Millions of Americans have no health insurance, a number that may decline somewhat after passage of the Affordable Care Act. Small firms are finding the cost of providing insurance to their workers prohibitive. Persons without insurance are more likely to delay or forgo needed health care because of the cost.

LO10.3 Recognize family work at home

10.7 What does research have to say about who is doing the housework and childcare?

Regardless of how housework is defined or measured, research indicates that women do significantly more housework and childcare than do men. However, men and women are renegotiating household labor, and men's participation, especially in childcare, has increased significantly.

10.8 What are three common explanations for the gendered division of labor?

The *time-availability perspective* suggests that the division of labor is largely determined by the need for household labor, such as the number of children in the home, and each partner's availability to perform household tasks, such as the number of hours spent in paid work. The *relative resources perspective* suggests that the greater the relative amount or value of resources contributed by a partner, the greater is his or her power within the relationship to avoid tasks such as housework that offer no pay and minimal social prestige. *"Doing gender"* suggests that housework is ingrained as "women's work." Wives do the majority of housework because it's expected of them as women and they have heard these messages since childhood.

LO10.4 Analyze the juggling of work and family

10.9 What are three important concepts that help explain the causes of stress for adults when they combine work and family?

First, *work–family conflict* is a form of tension in which people feel that the pressures from paid work and family roles are incompatible in some way. Second, *role overload* refers to feeling overwhelmed by many differ- ent commitments and not having enough time to meet each commitment effectively. Third, *spillover* occurs when negative (or sometimes positive) moods, experiences, and demands involved in either the work or family domain carry over or "spill over" into the other domain. Families also experience a time crunch, and wish they had more time to spend with their children.

10.10 If balancing work and family can be stressful, why don't adults work part-time?

Most adults would like to, but there are limited part-time options and part-time workers generally are paid a lower wage for this added flexibility. This, however, is not the case in many European countries.

LO10.5 Compare and contrast childcare arrangements

10.11 Who is taking care of preschool-age and school-age children while parents work?

Parents piece together childcare arrangements from a variety of sources, depending on their own inclinations and their financial situation. Some parents juggle work schedules so that one parent is always home, others rely on relatives, and others rely on childcare centers or family care. Others don't have a usual source of childcare, or they rely on different arrangements during the week.

10.12 What are the effects of childcare on child well-being?

The relationship between childcare and child well-being is somewhat mixed and contradictory because the results are small and depend on many other factors, especially the quality of the childcare.

10.13 What could the United States learn from other countries about early childhood education and childcare policies?

The United States views childcare as a private matter left up to parents, but many other developed nations view childcare as a public concern. Because it is seen as a social good that can ultimately benefit everyone, childcare is more available, affordable, and of higher quality in these countries.

KEY TERMS

daycare centers
"doing gender"
Early Childhood Education and Care (ECEC)
family childcare providers
household labor
living wage

Medicaid
Medicare
nannies/babysitters
nonstandard work schedules
occasional labor
relative resources perspective
role overload

routine household labor
self-care
spillover
time-availability perspective
work-family conflict

Family Stress and Crisis: Violence among Intimates

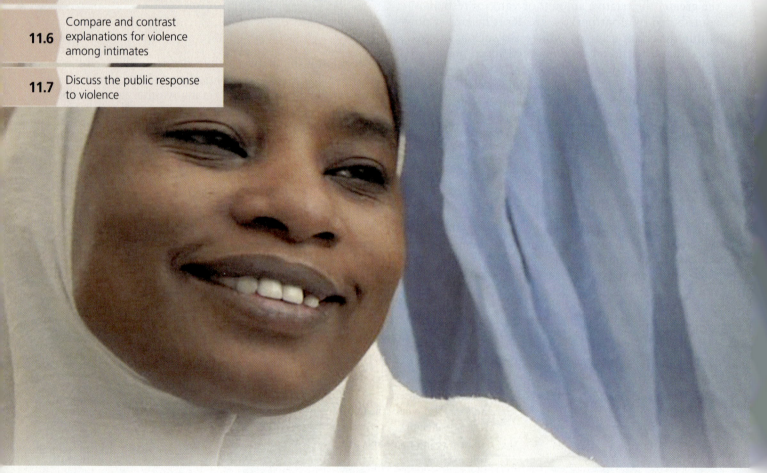

(((**Listen** to Chapter 11 on **MySocLab**

LEARNING OBJECTIVES

11.1 Describe the nature of stress and conflict

11.2 Identify why violence among intimates is a social problem

11.3 Explain intimate partner violence

11.4 Explain child abuse and neglect

11.5 Identify elder abuse

11.6 Compare and contrast explanations for violence among intimates

11.7 Discuss the public response to violence

Shannon's story began innocently enough, but quickly turned into a nightmare that would haunt her forever. She was repeatedly beaten, abused, and threatened with death by a boyfriend who held her in captivity. One night, in the midst of the terror, she fought back. But the story does not end there.

As a young woman, a naïve Shannon agreed to go on a date with a man who had tirelessly pursued her. They went dancing and the date seemed to go well. Yet, as they drove home, he viciously cursed at her, accusing her of staring at other men during their date. As she got out of the car, he hit her hard, then ran after her, choking her, saying that she belonged to him. She could not believe what was happening; the violence was unprovoked and seemed to come from nowhere.

Watch on **MySocLab**
Video: *Intimate Partner Violence: Shannon*

Later the young man repented, as batterers often do, and in an action that Shannon would forever regret, she went back to him. Eventually, they moved in together. Immediately, his home became a prison where she was locked inside. He controlled everything in the house, including her. The beatings began again. He hit her with bottles. He threw a pan of hot grease at her. He raped her. He pistol-whipped her. He threatened to kill her. The few times she did escape, he tracked her down and beat her even more.

One night, after a particularly violent episode of pistol-whipping and death threats, Shannon honestly believed he would kill her. He put his gun under the mattress, and told her to lie down. "I'm tired and can't go through this anymore," she told him. She grabbed the gun. He lunged after her and she shot him. After the first shot, he laughed, and she shot again, hitting him in the head. Shannon remembers, "It was like a horror movie."

Covered in blood, Shannon blacked out, but came to after police arrived. During this period—the 1980s—there was little support for battered women. No one had ever heard of Battered Women's Syndrome, no one connected repeated violence to Post-Traumatic Stress Syndrome, and no one thought of her actions as self-defense. Shannon was alone, without the support of society or of social services.

Shannon was charged with murder. Her defense attorney believed in her innocence, but knowing that the odds were against her, he encouraged her to accept a plea bargain of 15 years to life. Shannon was sent to Framingham Prison in Massachusetts, where she met other battered women with stories similar to hers, all who had been sentenced to jail because they fought back against their attacker—an intimate partner.

These women, recognized as heroines by many today, are known as the "Framingham Eight." Together, they petitioned the governor for early release, arguing that they all had acted in self-defense while fearing for their lives. Human rights organizations, such as Amnesty International, championed their rights. After weighing the evidence, William Weld, the Massachusetts governor at the time, agreed and commuted the sentences of the Framingham Eight. Still, by then Shannon had served 8 years behind bars.

Because of the Framingham Eight, people began to be aware of intimate partner violence. The Massachusetts governor's ruling also opened doors for other governors to review cases. Today, the terms *Battered Women's Syndrome*, *self-defense*, and *Post-Traumatic Stress Syndrome* are part of our vocabulary, thanks in part to Shannon's efforts.

Shannon's story reveals the darker side of family and intimate relationships. Her experience reminds us that for many people, families are not a haven of safety and security, but a place of pain and suffering. Fortunately, most families don't feel pain of this magnitude, but all families do experience some level of stress and face critical challenges. In this chapter, we explore the nature of family stress and crises to better understand how families deal with or adapt to them. We then look in depth at one crisis that is, unfortunately, all too common today: violence among intimates, including partners, children, and elderly parents. This chapter illustrates that family stress and crises occur in a social context. To better understand the complex web of causes, consequences, and solutions, we must look beyond individual personal experiences and see macro-level influences.

Watch on **MySocLab**
Video: *Claire Renzetti: Different Types of Partner Violence*

| **11.1** | Describe the nature of stress and conflict |

Questions That Matter

11.1 What is the difference between *family stress* and *family crisis*?

11.2 What are the *ABC-X* and *Double ABC-X* models of coping with a family crisis?

crisis: A critical change of events that disrupts the functioning of a person's life.

family stress: Tensions that test a family's emotional resources.

Listen on **MySocLab**
Audio: *NPR: Marital Stress*

acute stress: Short-term stress.

chronic stress: Long-term stress.

The Nature of Stress and Crisis

Family members usually fall into predictable and comfortable routines for everyday events like dividing household chores, taking vacations, and spending and saving money. A family crisis, whether positive or negative, can upset all of these routines. At one time or another, all families face a **crisis**, which is a critical change or event that disrupts the functioning of the lives of one or more family members. An unexpected job loss drastically alters spending and saving. The accompanying loss of health insurance may prevent the family from getting necessary health care. The arrival of a new baby may quickly change the division of household labor that a couple has developed over the years. We tend to think of crises as negative turning points, such as the death of a child or a divorce. However, some crises are positive in nature, such as an upcoming wedding or a new job.

Sometimes, a crisis occurs completely unexpectedly. A child is critically injured by a drunk driver; a wife tells her husband their marriage is over; a teenage girl learns she is pregnant. Other crises evolve more slowly from **family stress**, the tensions that occur either *within* the family (e.g., violence, alcoholism) or *outside* the family (e.g., coping with a hurricane or other natural disaster). Family stress differs from other types of personal stress because events that affect one member, such as an illness, may ripple through the entire family, as systems theory from Chapter 1 shows us.

Stress can be *normative*, such as adjusting to the family changes brought on by the arrival of a new baby, or *non-normative*, such as adjusting to the family changes brought on by caring for a child with a serious disability. Stresses may be **acute**, or short term, such as cramming for an exam, planning a wedding, or having a disagreement with your partner. Stresses can also be **chronic**, or long term, such as Shannon's experience living with an abusive partner, challenges associated with combining work and family, or living with a chronic illness like diabetes.

What do you think are the most common family stressors? Take a guess, and then check your answers with Table 11.1.

Responses to Stress

What are the stressors presently in your life? Managing your money? Studying for exams? Dealing with your parents? Combining school, work, and family? How do you cope with stress? Our bodies tend to have a fairly predictable pattern for coping with stress, including phases of alarm, resistance, and exhaustion known as **General Adaptation Syndrome (GAS)** (Selye, 1955; 1956):

- *Alarm Reaction:* In this first stage, the brain perceives a stressor and sends a message to the body, resulting in immediate changes in neurological and physiological states, so that the defensive forces of the body are mobilized for *fight or flight*. Our normal state of balance is upset as the body responds to a perceived threat. Our metabolism increases (to give us increased energy), and hormone levels rise (giving us a feeling of anxiety).

- *Resistance:* In this second stage, the body continues to battle the stressor by maintaining its elevated state of alert. If the stress continues, it can wreak havoc on the immune system. It's no coincidence that you are often sick during or immediately after finals week—your body weakens as it tries to fight off the stress of taking exams.

- *Exhaustion:* Chronic stress over long periods can be dangerous and can lead to depression, fatigue, frequent headaches, panic attacks, insomnia, and eating disorders. It can also result in heart disease, ulcers, or diabetes. The stressful situation itself must be controlled or alleviated for health to improve.

The Social Readjustment Rating Scale

Can we predict what types of stressors affect our health? Two physicians, Thomas Holmes and Richard Rahe, have quantified the impact of many life events on health and well-being (Holmes & Rahe, 1967). The result is known as the **Social Readjustment Rating Scale**. It assigns a certain point value to stressful events that may have occurred over the previous 12 months. For example, the death of a close friend is given a score of 37, whereas sex difficulties warrant a 39. The higher the total score, the greater the person's chance of becoming ill. Even positive events can be stressful and lead to illness, because they too require a reorganization of life patterns and a change in daily routines.

How valid are these scales? Another study by Rahe and colleagues asked 2,500 U.S. sailors to rate scores of life events over the previous 6 months and recorded details of their health during the following 6 months (Rahe, Mahan, & Arthur, 1970). The relationship they found between stress scale scores and illness was small but statistically significant, and supports the hypothesis that there is a link between life events and health.

Patterns of Family Crises

A family crisis often follows a reasonably predictable pattern with three distinct phases: (1) the *event* that causes the crisis; (2) the period of *disorganization* that

TABLE 11.1   The Ten Most Common Family Stressors

Money is the number one–cited family stressor.

1. Finances and budgeting
2. Children's behavior
3. Insufficient time as a "couple"
4. Lack of shared responsibility in family
5. Communication with children
6. Insufficient time for "me"
7. Guilt for not accomplishing more
8. Relationship with spouse
9. Insufficient family "play time"
10. Overscheduled family calendar

Source: Curran, 1985.

General Adaptation Syndrome (GAS): The predictable pattern one's body follows when coping with stress, which includes the alarm reaction, resistance, and exhaustion.

Social Readjustment Rating Scale: A scale of major life events over the past year, each of which is assigned a point value. The higher the score, the greater the chance of having a serious medical event.

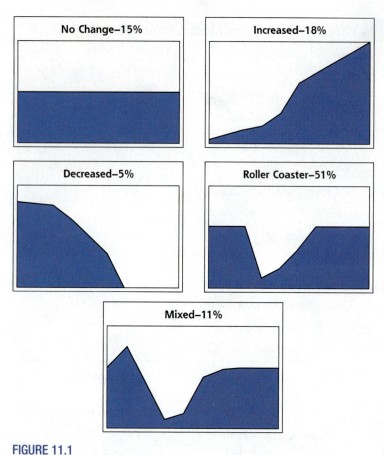

No Change–15%

Increased–18%

Decreased–5%

Roller Coaster–51%

Mixed–11%

FIGURE 11.1

Five Patterns of the Effects of Stress/Crises on Family Functioning

What happens after a family faces a stressful event or even a crisis? Five patterns have been identified; the most common is a rollercoaster effect, with a decline in functioning, followed by an increase in functioning, and then, finally stabilizing.
Source: Burr & Klein, 1994.

Read on MySocLab
Document: *How History and Sociology Can Help Today's Families*

follows; and (3) the *reorganization* that takes place afterward. Family members may return to functioning at a level similar to where they were just before the crisis; they may also be strengthened and become more effective as a family, or the crisis may weaken them.

Family researchers Wesley Burr and Shirley Klein (Figure 11.1) interviewed 51 families who had experienced a family crisis (1994), then asked the adults to draw a graph that illustrated how the crisis affected their overall family functioning over time, including such factors as marital satisfaction, communication, and family togetherness. Only 15 percent said the family didn't change; 51 percent fell into a roller-coaster pattern, with a decline of family functioning during the crisis, but rebounding after time had passed. For example, the Nguyen family grieved when their eldest son, Quyet, left for college. The house felt empty with Quyet's absence, and his siblings and parents really missed him, especially at the dinner table, where he often discussed the antics of his classmates during their high school senior year, or during high school baseball season when the family enjoyed watching Quyet play shortstop. It took the family many months to adjust to the loss of their cherished routines. However, in time they did adjust, and were able to return to their normal functioning.

Eighteen percent of families in the study claimed the crisis made the family stronger. For example, when one spouse has an extramarital sexual relationship, it can threaten the functioning of the entire family. Sometimes families are permanently injured; other times, however, families bounce back even stronger than before. Claire was devastated when she discovered that Peter had an affair with a colleague from work. She tried to ignore the signs, but finally confronted Peter and he confessed. He told Claire that he did not love his colleague and begged for her forgiveness. She didn't forgive him easily, but together they went to marriage counseling to see if their marriage could be saved. They discovered that they still loved each other and wanted to remain together. With hard work, they learned more effective ways of communicating, of coping with stress, and of developing intimacy. Peter and Claire's relationship was not only able to endure, but actually to blossom after this crisis.

Only 5 percent of families in the study said family functioning declined permanently and that marital satisfaction, communication, and family togetherness were never the same. Marty was offered a generous promotion at his job, but it required that he and his family move out of state. It was a tough decision, because his wife, Nikkonia, was very close with her mother who lived only a few miles away and enjoyed visiting with her every week. Nikkonia also had a job that she enjoyed, although she wasn't the family breadwinner, so neither she nor Marty believed that it was appropriate for him to turn down a dream promotion because of her job. Instead, Marty and Nikkonia sold their house, which they had lived in for 14 years, and bought a new one nearly 1,600 miles away where they had no family or friends, where the climate was considerably different, and where the subculture felt quite alienating. Marty worked very long hours and Nikkonia was extremely lonely. She complained about the snobbery of the neighbors, the poorly funded schools for the children, the lack of fellowship at church, her own lack of job opportunities, and the fact that her mother was growing old without her. Marty either ignored her concerns or lashed out in anger when she voiced them. Their relationship grew very tense and fraught with conflict. "Doesn't she see what a good move this is for our family?" he asked himself. "Doesn't he see what a bad move this is for our family?" she wondered. The conflict reached a point at which Nikkonia decided that she and their children were better off in her hometown without Marty. She took the children and left.

For many other families in their research study, the outcome was not as clear. The remainder said their family's response was mixed, which may be because of the stress not yet being fully resolved.

A family crisis can stem from a positive event as well as a negative one. This family may face a period of disorganization and reorganization as their child finishes high school and moves away to college.

Coping or Not: The ABC-X Models

Why are some families devastated by a crisis, whereas others bounce back stronger than before? Family scholar Reuben Hill proposed the **ABC-X model** to help us understand differences in family coping, as shown in Figure 11.2 (1958). A family crisis contains a number of elements, all of which affect how a family will fare. "A" factors are the *initial event* causing the crisis (e.g., graduation, extramarital affair, moving across the country). "B" factors are the *resources* a family has to meet the demands of the crisis (e.g., social support, money, religious faith, counseling). "C" factors are the *meanings families ascribe to the event* (e.g., human nature, a catastrophe, an opportunity, God's will). The outcome or "X" factors depend on the combination of ABC factors—the type of crisis itself, the resources of the family, and their perceptions of and meanings they associate with the crisis.

Here's an example of the ABC-X model. Josie and Luis faced a crisis that no family should have to experience: their oldest daughter was killed in a car accident (Factor A). They are part of a large extended family, and their siblings and cousins rallied around them in the months afterward, offering their love and support, and also provided instrumental care such as meals, childcare for their other children, and help running errands and general housekeeping (Factor B). How do you interpret or find meaning in a crisis of this magnitude? Armed with their Catholic faith, and with the help of their priest, Josie and Luis grew to believe that their daughter's life wasn't really cut short—she had actually accomplished all that God set out for her to do (Factor C). Together as a family they try to cope with their loss. Although they miss her every day, as they nurture one another, this crisis has helped the family grow closer (Factor X).

ABC-X Model: A model designed to help us understand the variation in the ways that families cope with stress and crisis.

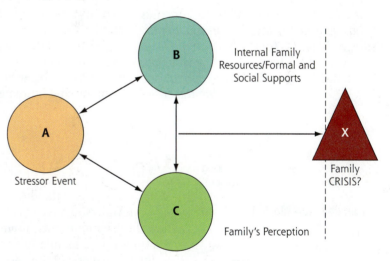

FIGURE 11.2
ABC-X Model of Family Stress and Crisis

The outcome of the crisis depends on the combination of ABC factors—the type of crisis itself, the resources the family has to deal with it, and their perceptions of and meanings they associate with it.
Source: Reuben, 1958.

Double ABC-X Model of Family Stress and Crisis: Pile-Up

The Double ABC-X model is designed to understand the effects of the accumulation of stresses and crises and how families adapt to them.
Source: McCubbin & Patterson, 1982.

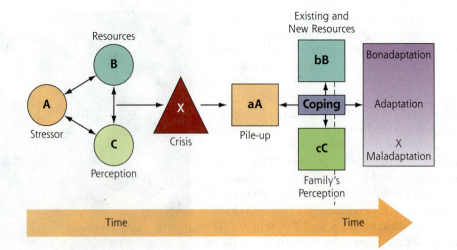

Double ABC-X Model: A model designed to help us understand the effects of the accumulation of stresses and crises and how families adapt to them.

Other researchers have expanded and built upon Hill's model (McCubbin & Patterson, 1982). For example, Figure 11.3 illustrates the **Double ABC-X model**. Do you ever notice that "When it rains, it pours"—in other words, stresses may accumulate? A single event may cause multiple effects, or many stresses may happen all at once. The Double ABC-X model is designed to understand the effects of the accumulation of stresses and crises and how families adapt to them. The *Double A Factor* refers not only to the initial event, but also to *family life changes and transitions* that take place because of it. The *Double B Factor* includes both the *resources the family already has* and the *new coping resources* the family obtains because of the stress or crisis. The *Double C Factor* takes into account not only the family's *perception of the stressor itself*, but also their *perceptions of the aftermath*. These two models reveal that it takes more than just events to devastate a family; the family's resources and perceptions are paramount.

*W*hat types of family stresses or crises has your family faced? Can you identify the A, B, and C Factors? Which model in Figure 11.1 best reflects the way your family functioned before, during, and after the crisis?

We could discuss many different types of family stress and crises. In the next section, let's examine one particular type of crisis in depth—violence among intimates, which is violence that occurs among family members and intimate partners.

Violence among Intimates

What do former talk show host Oprah Winfrey, singer Rihanna, and actress Pamela Anderson have in common? In addition to being celebrities, they all have had the frightening experience of being abused within their families or close relationships. Rihanna and Pamela Anderson were victims of violence by their intimate partners; Oprah Winfrey revealed that several members of her extended family sexually abused her as a child. We find violence in families to be particularly abhorrent because we like to idealize families as safe havens. Yet, for many people, especially women and girls, this is not the case.

Violence has touched the lives of millions of families, perhaps including your own family. Violence among intimates takes many forms, including intimate partner violence, child abuse, and elder abuse. As you'll see, violence is more than simply a personal problem. It involves far more than "He just has a bad temper." Violence among intimates is also a *social* problem. First, it affects large numbers of people. Second, violence is not completely random—we can detect particular patterns and risk factors for both victims and perpetrators. Third, the causes, consequences, and solutions of violence must address its macro-level dimensions, including social, cultural, and economic factors.

Intimate Partner Violence

11.3 Explain intimate partner violence

Intimate partner violence (IPV) refers to violence between those who are physically and sexually intimate, such as spouses or partners. The violence can encompass physical, economic, sexual, or psychological abuse, and many abusive situations include more than one type. In some countries, IPV is common and virtually accepted by both men and women. For example, a study conducted in the West African country of Liberia shows that gender norms and cultural beliefs reinforce widespread IPV, including physical, sexual, verbal, and economic abuse. Most women learn to accept it because there are few legal and financial supports, and men hold the balance of power (Allen & Dewitt, 2012). This may seem like something that would never happen here, but you were introduced to Shannon and her story of intimate abuse in the opening vignette. Her story may seem extreme—she actually killed her partner—but the abuse she faced is all too common in our society.

Questions That Matter

11.4 What is *intimate partner violence*?

11.5 What is the *Conflict Tactics Scale*?

11.6 What are the four different types of intimate partner violence?

11.7 Why do people stay in abusive relationships?

11.8 How does violence in gay and lesbian relationships compare to violence in heterosexual ones?

11.9 How common are rape and sexual assault?

How We Define and Measure Intimate Partner Violence?

Sociologist Murray Straus and his colleagues conducted some of the earliest nation-wide studies of spousal and partner abuse in the United States. They faced some ridicule at first—how are you going to get people to talk about hitting, slapping, or biting their partner? However, in 1975 and 1985, they interviewed more than 2,000 married or cohabiting adults with children ages 3 through 17, and from this information developed a conflict assessment tool that is still used today to measure intimate partner violence (Straus, Gelles, & Steinmetz, 1980). The **Conflict Tactics Scale (CTS)** asks people how they deal with disagreements in relationships:

Non-aggressive responses:

Discussed an issue calmly

Got information to back up your side of the issue

Brought in or tried to bring in someone to help settle the problem

Cried

Psychologically aggressive responses

Insulted or swore at him or her

Sulked or refused to talk about the issue

Stomped out of the room or house

Did or said something to spite him or her

Physically aggressive responses

Threatened to hit or throw something at him or her

Threw, smashed, hit, or kicked something

Threw something at him or her

Pushed, grabbed, or shoved him or her

Slapped him or her

Kicked, bit, or hit him or her with a fist

Hit or tried to hit him or her with something

Beat him or her up

Choked him or her

Threatened him or her with a knife

Used a knife

Violence between those who are physically and sexually intimate is referred to as *intimate partner violence,* and it can happen to any of us, even famous people. Chris Brown made headlines for his brutal attack on his then-girlfriend Rihanna.

Although the CTS isn't without flaws, it remains an important assessment tool because it acknowledges different and multiple forms of violence. It allows us to make comparisons across groups, and over time; for example, do men and women engage in different types of violence? Do physically aggressive responses also include psychologically aggressive ones? Do types of violence differ across income or education levels?

ARE MEN OR WOMEN MORE LIKELY TO BE VICTIMS? BIAS AND THE CTS

Who do you think is more likely to be a victim of violence by an intimate partner, a man or a woman? Studies using the CTS sometimes find that *men* are more likely to be victims of physical aggression than are women (Felson, 2006). This research finding may surprise you. However, on closer scrutiny, the finding is misleading.

The CTS is certainly a better way of measuring violence than a single-item question such as, "Have you ever been hit?" Yet, it's also somewhat problematic for at least three reasons (DeKeseredy & Schwartz, 1998; Fulfer, Tyler, Choi, Young, Verhulst, Kovach, & Dorsey, 2007; Kishor, 2005). First, men are less likely than women to remember their own acts of violence, and they may not perceive their acts as abusive.

Second, CTS respondents are asked to tell the researcher how they *responded to* a situation of conflict or disagreement. Yet, violence and abuse can take place without a preceding disagreement, and therefore the CTS may again underreport some violence.

Third, women are more likely to experience the most extreme forms of violence, some of which the CTS does not list, including severe beatings and even murder. Finally, the CTS doesn't include acts of sexual violence or aggression, which are far more likely to be perpetrated by men.

Consequently, more recent studies show that women are far more likely to be victims of intimate partner violence than are men. However, this does *not* mean that intimate partner violence against men is rare or inconsequential. Almost one-quarter of intimate partner homicides are committed against men, nearly 350 a year (U.S. Department of Justice, Bureau of Justice Statistics, 2007).

Frequency of Intimate Partner Violence

Until the 1970s, what we knew about spousal and partner abuse was based on small and non-representative samples from the isolated case files of social workers, psychologists, and police. These data can be very biased, because only certain types of abuse and abusers come to the attention of these professionals. However, since that time, family and social scientists have been using large and representative samples to understand how often spousal and partner violence occurs, who is likely to be a victim, and what are the causes and consequences.

Early surveys by Murray Straus and colleagues (Straus, Gelles, & Steinmetz, 1980) show an alarming rate of IPV in the United States, and more recent studies confirm this. There are two primary recent sources of data. First, the National Intimate Partner and Sexual Violence Survey is an ongoing, nationally representative random-digit-dial telephone survey that collects information about experiences of sexual violence, stalking, and intimate partner violence among non-institutionalized English and/or Spanish-speaking women and men ages 18 or older in the United States (Black, Basile, Breiding, Smith, Walters, Merrick, Chen, & Stevens, 2011). The survey provides detailed information on the magnitude and characteristics of these forms of violence for the nation and for individual states. Many of the data used in this chapter are from 2010, the first year of data collection, and are based on complete interviews with 16,507 adults (9,086 women and 7,421 men).

The second primary source of information about violence is the National Crime Victimization Survey, which collects information on nonfatal crimes both reported *and* not reported to the police. It's the largest data collection on criminal victimization independent of crimes reported by law enforcement agencies to the FBI's Uniform Crime Reporting program. During 2011, about 79,800 households and 143,120 persons were interviewed for the National Crime Victimization Survey (Bureau of Justice Statistics, October 17, 2012).

According to these two sources of information, somewhere between 1.4 and 4.3 million women are victims of IPV violence annually. The two surveys report different numbers, in part because one surveys the year 2009, whereas the other surveys the year 2011. According to Bureau of Justice Statistics, IPV may be declining (Catalano, 2012b). According to the National Crime Victimization Survey, which collects information on nonfatal crimes reported *and* not reported to the police, the overall rate of IPV has declined by 64 percent between 1994 and 2010. The decline was particularly large for Hispanics, dropping 78 percent during this period. The reason that I say that IPV *may* be declining is that, unfortunately, data for 2011 show a slight rise in the number of cases.

IPV also accounts for 12 million injuries and 2,000 deaths in the United States every year (Centers for Disease Control and Prevention [CDC], 2012a). Differences between women's and men's rates become greater as the seriousness of the assault increases. For example, women were two to three times more likely than men to report that an intimate partner threw something at them, or pushed, grabbed, or shoved them. However, women were 7 to 14 times more likely to report that they had been beaten up, choked, tied down, threatened with a gun, or had a gun used on them.

Figure 11.4 reveals the differences in the likelihood of IPV for men and women, and across most racial or ethnic groups, over the course of one's life (Black, Basile, Breiding, Smith, Walters, Merrick, Chen, & Stevens, 2011). We can see several important themes in the figure. First, well more than one of every three women is likely to be a victim of IPV over the course of her life, as is the case for more than one of every four men. Second, we see that women are more likely to be victims than are men, regardless of race or ethnic background. Third, we can see that multiracial women, American Indian/Alaska Native women, and Black women are particularly vulnerable.

Women are especially vulnerable when pregnant (Campbell, Glass, Sharps, Laughon, & Bloom, 2007; Datner, Wiebe, Brensinger, & Nelson, 2007; Samandari & Martin, 2010). A review of the literature reveals that intimate partners perpetrate one- to two-thirds of pregnancy-associated **femicides**, or killing of women, in the United States (Martin, Macy, Sullivan, & Magee, 2007).

Who is likely to be a victim? Who is likely to be a perpetrator? Several macro-level and micro-level characteristics increase the odds of being a victim or perpetrator, as shown in the *Tying It All Together* feature box. Keep in mind, however, that these are *risk* factors; these traits do *not* make violence inevitable (CDC, 2012a; Crandall, Nathens, Kernic, Holt, & Rivara, 2004).

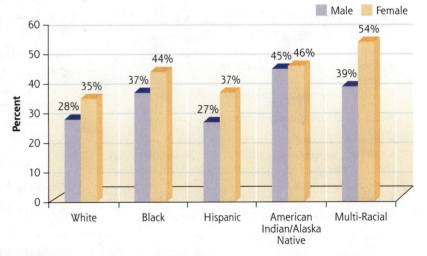

FIGURE 11.4

Lifetime Prevalence of Rape, Physical Violence, and/or Stalking By an Intimate Partner, 2010*

Both men and women can be victims of rape, violence, or stalking by an intimate partner, although women are more likely to be victims.
Source: Black, Basile, Breiding, Smith, Walters, Merrick, Chen, & Stevens, 2011.
*Asian total prevalence 20% (gender data not available).

femicide: The killing of women.

Types of Intimate Partner Violence

Relationship violence can take many forms. Family researcher and sociologist Michael Johnson has recently drawn attention to the importance of distinguishing

Many factors are associated with being a victim or a perpetrator of a crime. It's important to note that this doesn't mean that all of these factors are present; it simply means that they increase the likelihood of being a victim or a perpetrator. Some of these factors are micro-level factors that are experienced by the individual; others are macro-level factors that are embedded in our social structure. However, as you can see, these factors are interrelated.

RISK FACTORS FOR VICTIMIZATION

Persons at risk of being victims of violence may have one or more of the following characteristics:

Micro-level Individual Factors

- Prior history of intimate partner violence
- Female sex
- Youth
- Heavy alcohol and drug use
- High-risk sexual behavior
- Experience of witnessing or suffering violence as a child
- Unemployment
- For women, being American Indian/Alaska Native or Black

Micro-level Relationship Factors

- Income, educational, or job status disparities between the partners
- Dominance and control of the relationship by the other partner
- Verbal abuse, jealousy, or possessiveness by the other partner

Macro-level Community Factors

- Poverty and associated factors such as overcrowding
- Low social capital—lack of institutions, relationships, and norms that shape the quality and quantity of a community's social interactions
- Weak community sanctions against intimate partner violence (such as police being unwilling to intervene)

Macro-level Societal Factors

- Traditional gender norms that suggest, for instance, women should be submissive or stay home and not enter workforce
- Power differentials

RISK FACTORS FOR PERPETRATION

Persons at risk of perpetrating violence may have one or more of the following characteristics:

Micro-level Individual Factors

- Low self-esteem
- Low income
- Low academic achievement
- Aggressive or delinquent behavior as a youth
- Heavy alcohol and drug use
- Depression
- Anger and hostility
- Personality disorders
- Prior history of being physically abusive
- Few friends and isolation from other people
- Unemployment
- Emotional dependence and insecurity
- Belief in strict gender roles including male dominance and aggression
- Desire for power and control in relationships
- Experience being a victim of physical or psychological abuse (consistently one of the strongest predictors of perpetration)

Micro-level Relationship Factors

- Marital conflict—fights, tension, and other struggles
- Marital instability—divorces and separations
- Dominance and control of the relationship by the male
- Economic stress
- Unhealthy family relationships and interactions

Macro-level Community Factors

- Poverty and associated factors such as overcrowding
- Low social capital—lack of institutions, relationships, and norms that shape the quality and quantity of a community's social interactions
- Weak community sanctions against intimate partner violence (such as unwillingness of neighbors to intervene when they witness violence)

Macro-level Societal Factors

- Traditional gender norms that suggest, for instance, women should be submissive or stay home and not enter the workforce

WHAT DO YOU THINK?

1. To what degree do the risk factors for victims and perpetrators differ, and why do they do so?
2. Do you think these risk factors differ among heterosexual and same-sex couples? Why or why not?

Source: Centers for Disease Control and Prevention, October 21, 2008.

---

among types of violence, motives of perpetrators, social characteristics of both partners, and the cultural context in which violence occurs. Johnson has identified four patterns of violence that have now become a common way to conceptualize IPV (2008, 2009).

- *Common couple violence* arises out of a specific argument in which at least one partner lashes out physically. It's less frequent than other types of abuse and less likely to escalate or cause severe injury; yet, it's this type of violence that is usually captured in research studies.

- *Intimate terrorism* is physical, psychological, or sexual violence that is motivated by a desire to control the other partner. It's more likely than other types of violence to escalate over time and to cause serious injury and post-traumatic stress syndrome, as discussed in Shannon's story in the opening vignette. You can see that Shannon experienced intimate terrorism, which then turned into violent resistance, described next.

- *Violent resistance* is the non-legal term for self-defense. Research is scarce, but those who put up violent resistance are almost always women. It may indicate a woman will leave her abusive partner soon.

- *Mutual violent control* refers to a pattern of behavior in which both partners are controlling and violent and are battling for control.

This conceptualization reminds us that there are different motives, patterns, and consequences of IPV.

Stalking and Cyberstalking

As discussed in Chapter 4, stalking has received greater attention as a crime since California passed the first anti-stalking law in 1990. Stalking consists of obsessive contact or tracking of another person—attention that is unwanted and causes a reasonable person to be fearful. It touches the lives of about 5.2 million women and 1.4 million men annually (Black, Basile, Breiding, Smith, Walters, Merrick, Chen, & Stevens, 2011). Stalking is a combination of many unwanted acts that, by themselves, aren't necessarily abusive—such as sending flowers or gifts, calling on the telephone, or sending a text message—but when taken together in a context designed to harass and promote fear, these acts constitute a form of mental abuse. Stalking exists on a continuum. It may be so subtle that the victim may not even be aware it's happening or, in contrast, the perpetrator may purposefully try to instill terror in the victim (Logan & Walker, 2009). The range of stalking behaviors and the percentage of female stalking victims who report receiving such behaviors is reported in Figure 11.5. These data, taken from the annual National Intimate Partner and Sexual Violence Survey, define people as *stalking victims* if they experienced multiple stalking tactics or a single stalking tactic multiple times by the same perpetrator and felt very fearful, or believed that they or someone close to them would be harmed or killed as a result of the perpetrator's behavior.

Given the importance of computers, cell phones, text messages, social networking sites, and e-mail in our lives, some stalkers harass or threaten their victims electronically, known as **cyberstalking**. Repeated unwanted attention could come in the form of e-mail, texts, bulletin boards, blogs, chat rooms, or other types of media (Stalking Resource Center, 2012). One factor that distinguishes cyberstalking from other forms of stalking is ease; one can repeatedly threaten and harass a person by simply clicking a button on the computer. In fact, programs can be set up to send messages at random times when the sender isn't even physically present at the computer. Although the contact may be indirect, it can be threatening nonetheless.

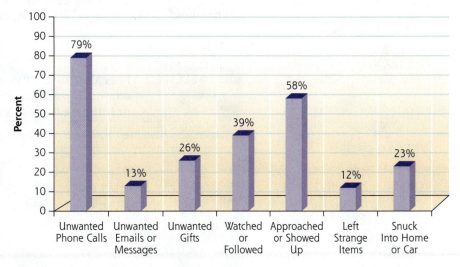

FIGURE 11.5

Lifetime Reports of Stalking among Female Victims by Type of Tactic Experienced (2010)

Unwanted phone calls or showing up unexpectedly are the most common forms of stalking. *Source:* Black, Basile, Breiding, Smith, Walters, Merrick, Chen, & Stevens, 2011.

Consequences of Intimate Partner Violence

IPV can have tragic results, both mentally and physically (Hegarty, O'Doherty, Chondros, Valpled, Taft, Astbury, Brown, Gold, Kaket, Feder, & Gunn, 2013; Lacey, McPherson, Samuel, Sears, & Head, 2013). In general, victims of repeated violence over time experience more serious consequences than victims of one-time incidents (CDC, 2012). Minor forms of bruises, scratches, and welts are most common, but broken bones, severe bruising, or head trauma are other consequences of violence.

Some consequences are not as visible, but just as real. The stress from IPV can wreak havoc on the immune and endocrine systems, causing conditions such as fibromyalgia, gynecological disorders, irritable bowel syndrome, or gastrointestinal problems (Black, 2011; Leserman & Drossman, 2007). As you can see in Table 11.2, the list of problems associated with IPV is quite diverse, and quite serious. The largest differences in prevalence of health outcomes between those with and without a violence history were observed for difficulty sleeping, activity limitations, chronic pain, and frequent headaches.

Because physical violence is typically accompanied by emotional or psychological abuse, many victims are depressed, have anxiety, have disturbed sleep, have low self-esteem, are socially isolated, and have thoughts of suicide (Afifi, MacMillan, Cox, Asmundson, Stein, & Sareen, 2009; CDC, September 26, 2012; Choudhary, Coben, & Bossarte, 2010). Victims of IPV are more likely to behave in unhealthy ways, such as engaging in high-risk sexual behavior (e.g., having unprotected sex, trading sex for food or money); using harmful substances (e.g., smoking cigarettes, using illicit drugs); or having unhealthy diet-related behaviors (e.g., binging and purging food).

Despite the clear need for mental health care, many women, especially minority women, often experience barriers to getting this care. Barriers include cultural or language differences, or lack of services and providers in poor or ethnic communities (Bryant-Davis, Chung, & Tillman, 2009; Rodriguez, Valentine, Son, & Muhammad, 2009; Weaver, 2009). Agencies specializing in the treatment of

TABLE 11.2	Prevalence of Physical and Mental Health Outcomes among Those Who Have Been Victims of Rape, Stalking, or Intimate Partner Violence, 2010	
Women who have been victimized have a wide variety of health problems.		
	With Victimization	**Without Victimization**
Asthma	24%	14%
Irritable Bowel Syndrome	12%	7%
Diabetes	13%	10%
High Blood Pressure	27%	28%
Frequent Headaches	29%	17%
Chronic Pain	30%	17%
Difficulty Sleeping	38%	21%
Activity Limitations	35%	20%
Poor Physical Health	6%	2%
Poor Mental Health	3%	1%

Source: Black, Basile, Breiding, Smith, Walters, Merrick, Chen, & Stevens, 2011.

domestic violence and sexual assault victims face challenges that make it difficult to provide the full scope of services needed. They may have funding difficulties, tension between grassroots versus professional service providers, or a lack of comprehensive services (Macy, Giattina, Parish, & Crosby, 2010).

In addition to the consequences to the individual, there are also societal consequences. In other words, you and I are affected by IPV even if we don't know anyone who is a victim or perpetrator (which is highly unlikely). Victims lose nearly 8 million days of paid work a year, the equivalent of more than 32,000 full-time jobs. Costs affiliated with IPV exceed $8 billion, most of which goes to medical and mental health care (CDC, 2003).

Coping with Violence: Leaving and Staying

People often ask why some victims seem to stay in abusive situations. Most of the concern focuses on women, because they're generally thought to be more vulnerable than men: the violence is often more extreme, they may be financially dependent, or they may have children. Lenore Walker (1979, 1993) suggests that women stay in abusive relationships because of a condition called **learned helplessness**. Because of repeated verbal and physical assaults, these women have developed low self-esteem, and believe that they can't control the abuse or the events around them. In essence, they have learned to feel helpless and have difficulty envisioning a way out of their situation.

The truth is, however, that most women don't stay in abusive situations—at least not indefinitely. A longitudinal study conducted over 30 months revealed that three-quarters of battered women had left the relationship or the abuse in their relationships had ended (Campbell, Rose, Kub, & Nedd, 1998).

Leaving is often a *process* rather than a single event (Kim & Gray, 2008). It may be difficult for some women to gather the courage and resources to leave immediately, especially if they believe the myths about IPV (e.g., "She was asking for it") or if she has little social support to help her (Shorey, Tirone, Nathanson, Handsel, & Rhatigan, 2013; Yamawaki, Ochoa-Ahipp, Pulsipher, Harlos, & Swindler, 2012). Recall the typology discussed by Johnson (2008, 2009). Men who engage in intimate terrorism use a wide range of control tactics that can cripple a victim's sense of command over her own life. What are some of these control tactics?

- *Blaming the victim:* "If you weren't so stupid, I wouldn't have to hit you." After hearing blaming comments often enough, some women begin to believe they must deserve the abuse and be unworthy of a positive and loving relationship.

- *Inducing shame:* Embarrassment and shame are common among abused women because they know many other women are not abused. They fear others will look down on them for provoking or tolerating abuse, or on their spouse/partner for being abusive. They may try to hide their bruises under makeup or clothing.

- *Lowering self-esteem:* "You're an idiot, and everybody thinks so." A victim's self-esteem can be eroded by repeated name-calling, mind games, and emotional and physical bashing. She may begin to think of herself as not worthy of better treatment.

- *Creating financial dependency:* Some women are particularly vulnerable because they are financially dependent on men. Perhaps they have children to support and lack specific job skills or recent employment experience. Some perpetrators foster this economic dependence by not allowing their partners to work; establish credit in their own name or have their names on checking, savings, or other accounts.

- *Isolating the victim:* Whether initiated by the abuser as a control tactic or by the victim out of shame, isolation cuts off the abused from family and

learned helplessness: The psychological condition of having low self-esteem, feeling helpless, and having no control, which is caused by repeated abuse.

friends. The abused may cease going to church, work, or school, thereby going without social support and having no one to turn to for a "check-in."

- *Threatening retaliation:* Fear of retaliation keeps some victims in abusive relationships. The perpetrator may have threatened the woman, her children, or even her pets, and because he has been abusive before, the threats are real.

- *Exploiting love and hope:* Many abused women harbor fantasies that their abuser will miraculously change. They don't want the relationship to end, just the abuse. They love their spouse/partner, and are told that if they just work harder in the relationship or external forces change (e.g., "If he can find a good job") the abuse will somehow stop.

- *Exploiting commitment to the relationship:* When we marry, we agree to take our partner "For better or worse, until death do us part." Although we take these vows seriously, most people would leave an out for domestic violence. Some people believe, however, that they must endure their marriage regardless of the costs. An abuser can exploit this commitment (e.g., "You can't leave; you promised you would stay").

- *Creating fear of abandonment:* Many people are afraid of being without a spouse or partner. They have low self-esteem and are unsure whether they can live alone and take care of themselves. Women have been socialized to derive much of their social status through their affiliations with men.

These factors can contribute to **Battered Women's Syndrome**, a now-recognized psychological condition to describe someone who has been the victim of consistent or severe domestic violence. It's often considered a subcategory of post-traumatic stress syndrome, and can be measured and treated by a trained mental health professional.

Violence in Gay and Lesbian Relationships

Until recently, we knew little about IPV among same-sex couples, probably for the same reason that we knew little about their relationships in general—the focus of study tends to be on majority groups—that is, heterosexuals (Kaschak, 2002; Ristock, 2009). A book about IPV published as recently as 2001, *Couples in Conflict* (Booth, Crouter, & Clements, 2001), includes 17 chapters on recognizing and responding to domestic violence, but includes no chapters specifically on violence in same-sex couples. Despite this omission, the rate of abuse in gay and lesbian relationships is similar to or even higher than that in heterosexual relationships, around 25 to 30 percent (Aardvarc.org, 2008; Burke, Jordan, & Owen, 2002). Like heterosexual couples, violence is usually not a single event, but represents a pattern in the relationship. Same-sex couples are not immune to violence, abuse, jealousy, or struggles over power and control.

Although similar in many respects, IPV in same-sex relationships is also distinctive in many ways as compared to heterosexual relationships (Center for American Progress, 2013).

- Gay or lesbian batterers threaten "outing" their victims to work colleagues, family, and friends. This threat is amplified by the sense of extreme isolation among gay and lesbian victims because some are still closeted from friends and family, have fewer civil rights protections, and lack access to the legal system.

- Lesbian and gay victims are more reluctant to report abuse to legal authorities. Survivors may not contact law enforcement agencies because doing so would force them to reveal their sexual orientation or gender identity.

- Gay and lesbian victims are also reluctant to seek help out of fear of showing a lack of solidarity among the gay and lesbian community. Similarly, many gay men and women hide their abuse out of a heightened fear that society will perceive same-sex relationships as inherently dysfunctional.

Battered Women's Syndrome: A recognized psychological condition, often a subcategory of post-traumatic stress syndrome, used to describe someone who has been the victim of consistent and/or severe domestic violence.

👁 **Watch** on **MySocLab**
Video: *Claire Renzetti: Gay Violence*

- Gay and lesbian victims are more likely to fight back than are heterosexual women. This can lead law enforcement to conclude that the fighting was mutual, overlooking the larger context of domestic violence and the history of power and control in the relationship.
- Abusers can threaten to take away the children from the victim. In some states, adoption laws don't allow same-sex parents to adopt each other's children. This can leave the victim with no legal rights should the couple separate. The abuser can easily use the children as leverage to prevent the victim from leaving or seeking help. Even when the victim is the legally recognized parent, an abuser may threaten to out the victim to social workers hostile to gays and lesbians, which may result in a loss of custody. In the worst cases, the children can even end up in the custody of the abuser.

Some people may dismiss IPV among same-sex couples as less serious—"Come on, shouldn't men be able to defend themselves from one another?" "How much harm can two women do?" "Why doesn't he just leave—what's stopping him?" (Cruz, 2003; Ristock, 2009). However, the violence that same-sex couples inflict can be substantial and no less serious than the violence inflicted by abusive heterosexual men or women on their partners. One study found 79 percent of gay male victims had suffered some physical injury, with 60 percent reporting bruises, 23 percent reporting head injuries and concussions, 13 percent reporting forced sex with the intention to infect the victim with HIV, 12 percent reporting broken bones, and 10 percent reporting burns (Merrill & Wolfe, 2000). Thus, the issue of IPV deserves the same attention in same-sex relationships as it does in heterosexual ones.

Watch on MySocLab
Video: *Claire Renzetti: Lesbian Violence*

Dating Violence

We think that forming relationships is about having fun, exploring your own identity, and getting to know someone else. At first glance, dating seems like the last place for violence to occur. Yet, young women ages 16 through 24 experience high rates of relationship violence (CDC, 2012b). Dating violence often starts out with teasing and name-calling, and young people assume this is a normal part of a relationship. However, these behaviors can escalate. Among adult victims of rape, physical violence, or stalking by an intimate partner, 22 percent of women and 15 percent of men first experience some form of partner violence between the ages of 11 and 17 (Black, Basile, Breiding, Smith, Walters, Merrick, Chen, & Stevens, 2011). About 9 percent of high school students and about one-third of unmarried adults under age 30 have experienced or used physical violence in a dating relationship in the previous 12 months. Others are victims of sexual assault or feel pushed into a sexual relationship before they are ready, as found in Alicia's dating violence story in the *My Family* feature box.

Many young women don't report violence to their parents, police, or other authority figures. They may be embarrassed, fear their parents' reaction, or worry that their partner will retaliate if they tell someone. Some women are overly dependent on their partners and fear they may never meet anyone else again (Few & Rosen, 2005).

How can we prevent dating violence? The CDC reminds us that the ultimate goal is to stop dating violence before it starts (2012b). The preteen and teen years are

Our culture fails to openly acknowledge the fact that young women between the ages of 16 and 24 face the highest rates of intimate partner violence.

In the following story, "Alicia" describes the pressure she felt to have a sexual relationship before she was ready. Note that the ending could go a number of different ways.

We met in chemistry, 4th period. He was one of the cutest boys in school and a star on our soccer team. Although he seemed pretty shy to our classmates, he would talk hours on end to me. He made me feel special and I began to feel very strongly towards him. One night we were in my parents' basement watching his favorite television show. We started French kissing and I felt so pretty and wanted. He leaned me back on the couch and put his hand up my skirt. I wasn't too sure I wanted to go further since we had only been dating for two weeks. I told him I wasn't ready and he got up and stormed out.

I was concerned I had done something wrong so I called him on his cell phone a few moments later. He didn't pick up. Later that night my cell phone rang and I rushed to it, hoping it was him. It was. He said that I act like a baby and that real women have sex. He called me a tease and told me that if I wanted to be his girl that I would have to have sex with him. My eyes started to fill with tears. I knew I wasn't ready.

When I first started high school I made a vow to myself that I'd wait until I was in a long-term committed monogamous relationship with someone whom I loved before I started having sex. But now I'm starting to question myself, and it makes me feel confused. I tell him that I'm scared and he calls me a "slut" for having him in my house when my parents weren't home. He says that I probably have all kinds of guys down there "just to tease them and kick them out." But I didn't kick him out, he just left! I'm starting to get really confused because just yesterday he was telling me how pretty and special I was. Now he's calling me names? What did I do to deserve this?

Maybe I should have just had sex with him. Maybe he is right. I tell him I have to go and I'll see him in school tomorrow. He asks me if he can come over again tomorrow and I say . . .

This story can end in many different ways, depending on whether this young woman knows she has a right to say and do what she wants.

He asks me if he can come over tomorrow and I say, "You said very nasty and untrue things about me because you were upset that I told you I wasn't ready. I do not want to be mistreated by someone I like and if you don't have enough respect for me to understand my decision to not have sex then I would rather we just be 'friends.'" He hung up the phone and we never spoke again. But I was okay with that. Four months later I met a boy at summer camp, who is supportive and willing to wait until I am ready. I am glad I decided to do better for myself.

WHAT DO YOU THINK?

1. Have you, or someone you know well, been in a similar situation? Did that story end differently or in a similar fashion? How do you think most of these stories end?
2. Have the pressures put on women to be sexual changed over the last few generations? Do you think women in your parents' generation felt these same pressures? Why or why not?

Source: Based on "My dating violence story from "Alicia" on MySistahs: a project of Advocates for Youth, 2008," in Advocates for Youth. 2009. Advocates for Youth, Washington, D.C.

Watch on MySocLab
Video: *Sexual Violence Billboards*

formative years; young people are learning the skills they need to form positive relations with others and learning what's acceptable and what isn't. Prevention programs targeted to this age group can be incorporated into the school curriculum, with an emphasis on changing social norms and improving problem-solving skills.

Rape and Sexual Assault

Rape is defined as any completed or attempted unwanted vaginal (for women), oral, or anal penetration through the use of physical force (such as being held down), or threats of physical harm. Rape is still rape if the victim was drunk, high, drugged, or passed out and unable to consent. Nearly 1 in 5 women in the United States have been raped in their lifetime, as compared to 1 in 71 men (Black, Basile, Breiding, Smith, Walters, Merrick, Chen, & Stevens, 2011).

Sexual assault may include rape, but it also includes other types of behavior, such as unwanted physical contact (e.g., grabbing or pinching a woman's breasts) or non-contact unwanted sexual experiences (e.g., flashing or masturbating in front of the victim). More than one woman in four has experienced unwanted sexual contact, as have one in nine men. Non-contacted unwanted sexual experiences have occurred to one in three women and one in eight men (Black, Basile, Breiding, Smith, Walters, Merrick, Chen, & Stevens, 2011).

The perpetrators tend to differ across these crimes, as shown in Figure 11.6. For example, rape is most likely committed by a current or former intimate partner or by an acquaintance. Unwanted sexual contact is most often committed by an acquaintance, whereas non-contact unwanted sexual experiences tend to be committed by strangers (Black, Basile, Breiding, Smith, Walters, Merrick, Chen, & Stevens, 2011).

These crimes are often not reported to the police (Tjaden & Thoennes, 2006). Most victims knew their attackers. According to the women surveyed, 30 percent of perpetrators were intimate partners, 24 percent were family members, and 20 percent were acquaintances. Among the men surveyed, 32 percent of perpetrators were acquaintances, 18 percent were family members, 18 percent were friends, and 16 percent were intimate partners.

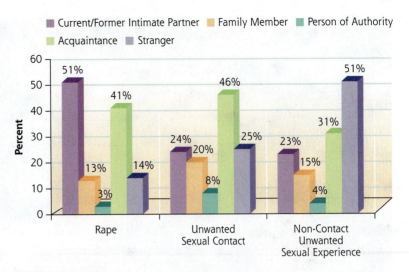

FIGURE 11.6

Lifetime Reports of Sexual Violence among Female Victims by Type of Perpetrator, 2010

Most rapes occur by a current or former intimate partner, but other forms of unwanted sexual contact are more likely to occur by an acquaintance or a stranger.
Source: Black, Basile, Breiding, Smith, Walters, Merrick, Chen, & Stevens, 2011.

RAPE ON COLLEGE CAMPUSES More than one-third of rape victims are between the ages of 18 and 24. Therefore, not surprisingly, college students are particularly vulnerable to rape and sexual assault. In a study of female undergraduates, 19 percent, or nearly one in five, experienced attempted or completed sexual assault since entering college. And many of the respondents in this study still had several years of college before them (CDC, 2012c).

Who is being raped, and who is doing the raping? Among college students, about 80 percent of victims and perpetrators know each other; they're intimate partners, "friends," roommates, acquaintances, and classmates. Women are raped by their study partner on the way to the library, by the guy they just met at the party in the dorm, by their roommate's brother, or even by their partner.

The work of Mary Koss and her colleagues (Koss & Cook, 1993; Koss, Gidycz, & Wisniewski, 1987) sheds interesting light on college-age perpetrators. In a survey of 32 college campuses, they found that although 12 percent of men had committed acts that would fit the legal definition of rape or attempted rape, only 1 percent thought their actions were criminal. Many made a distinction between "forcing a girl to have sex" and "rape," as though they're different, but the law, of course, makes no such distinction.

In another study, 521 college students completed a personality inventory and survey about sexual behavior, including whether they have committed rape or sexual assault (which includes unwanted sexual behavior other than rape). The researchers found that those men who had committed sexual assault (but not rape) had remarkably comparable personality profiles to non-perpetrators (Voller & Long, 2010). There was little or no difference in personality traits like agreeableness, conscientiousness, extraversion, warmth, excitement-seeking, altruism, competence, tenderness, or vulnerability. Men who rape, in contrast, had considerably different personality profiles in most of these areas. In other words, sexual assault perpetrators were more similar to non-perpetrators than to those who rape.

"DATE RAPE" DRUGS Alcohol or drugs are sometimes involved in a sexual assault (Roudsan, Leahy, & Walters, 2009). **Date rape drugs** such as gamma hydroxybutyrate (GHB), Rohypnol (popularly known as *roofies* or *roofenol*), or ketamine hydrochloride (Ketamine) can immobilize a person to facilitate an assault (U.S. Department of Health & Human Services, Office of Women's

date rape drugs: Drugs such as gamma hydroxybutyrate (GHB), Rohypnol (popularly known as *roofies* or *roofenol*), or ketamine hydrochloride (Ketamine) that are used to immobilize a person to facilitate an assault.

So-called date rape drugs can immobilize a person by causing a lack of muscle control, a feeling of extreme intoxication, or a loss of consciousness.

Health, July 16, 2012). The effects of these drugs cause people to be physically helpless, lose muscle control, feel very drunk, or lose consciousness. Victims of these drugs often can't remember what happened. The drugs usually have no color, smell, or taste and can be easily added to flavored drinks without the victim's knowledge. How can you protect yourself from these drugs?

- Do not accept drinks from other people.
- Open containers yourself.
- Keep your drink with you at all times, even when you go to the bathroom.
- Do not share drinks.
- Do not drink from punch bowls or other large, common, open containers. They may already have drugs in them.
- Do not drink anything that tastes or smells strange. Sometimes GHB tastes salty.
- Have a non-drinking friend with you to make sure nothing happens.
- If you think that you have been drugged and raped:

  - Go to the police station or hospital right away.
  - Get a urine test as soon as possible. The drugs leave your system quickly. Rohypnol stays in the body for several hours and can be detected in the urine up to 72 hours after taking it. GHB leaves the body in 12 hours.
  - Do not urinate before getting help.
  - Do not douche, bathe, or change clothes before getting help. These things may give evidence of the rape.
  - Feelings of shame, guilt, fear, and shock are normal. You can call a crisis center or a hotline to talk with a counselor. One national hotline is the National Sexual Assault Hotline at 1-800-656-HOPE (U.S. Department of Health & Human Services, Office of Women's Health, 2008).

*W*hat about a college environment makes rape and sexual assault so prevalent? What do you think is happening at your college? What can or should be done about it?

child abuse: An attack on a child that results in an injury and violates our social norms.

11.4 Explain child abuse and neglect

Questions That Matter

11.10 What forms does child abuse take?

11.11 What are the consequences of child abuse?

11.12 What is *trafficking,* and how common is it?

✳ **Explore** on MySocLab
Activity: *Violence over the Life Course*

Child Abuse and Neglect

Child abuse is an attack on a child that results in an injury and violates our social norms. Nearly 700,000 children were determined to be victims of abuse or neglect in 2011 (U.S. Department of Health & Human Services, Administration on Children, Youth, and Families, 2012). Tables 11.3 and 11.4 summarize information about these youngest victims of violence. Young children have high rates of victimization: about 27 percent of all abused children are under the age of 3. Victims are slightly more likely to be female, and Blacks are overrepresented among abuse victims, given their size in the population. The most common type of maltreatment is neglect.

More than 1,500 children died in 2011 as a result of abuse and neglect. More children under the age of 4 die from abuse and neglect than from falls, choking, drowning, fires, or motor vehicle accidents. Abuse occurs in all income, racial, religious, and ethnic groups, and in all types of communities (U.S. Department of Health & Human Services, Administration on Children, Youth, and Families, 2012).

Types of Child Abuse

There are several different types of child abuse, the most common of which are:

- *Neglect*, the failure to provide for the child's basic needs, is the most common form. Neglect can be physical, such as failing to provide adequate food, clothing, shelter, a safe environment, or medical care to a dependent child. Emotional or psychological neglect occurs when a parent or caretaker fails to meet a child's most basic need for love and affection, by being chronically cold and distant, or by allowing a child to witness spousal abuse or some other dysfunctional behavior in the family. An extreme form of neglect is outright abandonment.

- *Physical abuse*, such as hitting, shaking, burning, or kicking, inflicts physical injury and harm on a child. Among substantiated child abuse cases, about one-quarter included physical abuse. The most extreme cases may result in a child's death. One study of abused children admitted to a pediatric intensive care unit found the most common causes of death were skull fracture and internal bleeding (Irazuzta, McJunkin, Danadian, Arnold, & Zhang, 1997).

- *Sexual abuse* is inappropriate sexual behavior with a child for sexual gratification. It can include fondling a child's genitals, making the child fondle the perpetrator's genitals, and progressing to more intrusive sexual acts such as oral sex and vaginal or anal penetration. Sexual abuse also includes acts such as exhibition, Internet child pornography, or other ways of exploiting the child for sexual purposes.

- *Psychological or emotional maltreatment* can be verbal, mental, or psychological abuse that destroys a child's self-esteem. It often includes threatening, degrading, or humiliating the child and using extreme or bizarre forms of punishment, such as being confined to a dark room or tied to a chair for long periods of time. Emotional abuse probably occurs far more frequently than can be substantiated.

And as you might expect, multiple forms of abuse often occur simultaneously, as shown in Table 11.4.

TABLE 11.3	Prevalence of Rape by Race/Ethnicity, 2010
American Indians, Alaska Natives, and persons who are multiracial are most likely to be raped.	
Hispanic	15%
Black	22%
White	19%
Asian/Pacific Islander	*
American Indian/Alaska Native	27%
Multiracial	34%

*Unavailable.
Source: Black, Basile, Breiding, Smith, Walters, Merrick, Chen, & Stevens, 2011.

TABLE 11.4	The Most Common Types of Child Abuse
Neglect is by far the most common form of child abuse.	
Neglect	79%
Physical Abuse	18%
Sexual Abuse	9%
Other	10%
Psychological Maltreatment	9%
Medical Neglect	2%
Totals more than 100% because more than one category can be chosen.	

Source: U.S. Department of Health & Human Services, Administration on Children, Youth, & Families, 2012.

Is Corporal Punishment Child Abuse?

"I hit my daughter because she refused to eat her peas at dinner."

Is this child abuse? Does it matter whether the parent uses an open hand, a fist, or an object? Does it matter whether the blow leaves a welt? Does the reason for hitting the child make a difference? What about his or her age? Does it matter where the child was hit, or how often? What if we use the term *spank* instead of *hit*? What if we use the term *slapped*? How about *beat*?

Many adults believe it's appropriate to spank children as discipline, at least in certain contexts, whereas others vehemently disagree and consider spanking to be tantamount to child abuse and a violation of a child's human rights. The number of parents who approve of spanking is on the decline (Smith, 2012). A recent ABC News survey found that among parents with minor children at home, about half spank their children. There are big regional differences in spanking as well. Among Southerners, 62 percent of parents spank their kids, compared to 41 percent in the rest of the country.

Why Do Research?

What Do We Make of the Link between Spanking and Children's IQ?

Family violence research pioneer Murray Straus is at it again. For more than 30 years he's taught us about intimate partner violence and child abuse, and much of what we know today comes from his work. One of Dr. Straus's research interests is corporal punishment—spanking. He sees it as an insidious form of violence, one that most of us ignore, but that causes great harm to the spanked individual and the society at large that condones this type of violence. His continuing research has unearthed a startling new discovery: Children who are spanked have lower IQs than those who are not. Moreover, the difference is large enough to lower national IQ scores in countries where corporal punishment of children is routine.

This landmark study first examined the relationship between spanking and IQ in the United States, and then turned to see what the relationship looks like on a national basis. First, Dr. Straus and his colleague, Dr. Mallie Paschall, studied a nationally representative sample of 806 children in the United States ages 2 to 4 years, and a second representative sample of 704 children ages 5 to 9 years. Both groups were tested once and then retested 4 years later in a longitudinal research design. They found that the IQs of children ages 2 to 4 who were not spanked were 5 points higher 4 years later than the IQs of those children who were spanked. Likewise, the IQs of children ages 5 to 9 who were not spanked were nearly 3 points higher 4 years later than other children their age who were spanked. They also found that the more times a child was spanked, the more his or her IQ was affected. "How often parents spanked made a difference. The more spanking, the slower is the development of the child's mental ability. But even small amounts of spanking made a difference," Dr. Straus said.

Next, the researchers examined secondary data obtained from the International Dating Violence Study, which involved 17,404 college students at 68 universities in 32 countries. The study included two items about spanking, and respondents could Strongly Disagree, Disagree, Agree, or Strongly Agree with each one:

- I was spanked or hit a lot by my parents before age 12.
- When I was a teenager, I was hit a lot by my mother or father.

The researchers used the percentage of students who Agreed or Strongly Agreed to estimate the corporal punishment rate in each country. They then compared those rates to the national average IQ while controlling for many important variables, such as mother's education level or socioeconomic status. This statistical technique allows researchers to assure that any differences are likely to be the result of IQ, rather than the fact that some countries are poorer than others or that mothers in some countries may have lower educational levels than others.

The analysis showed that the countries with higher corporal punishment rates also had students with lower average IQs. The strongest association between spanking and IQ was found among those students whose parents continued to spank them into their teenage years. Why is this? First, Straus and Paschall speculate that corporal punishment is extremely stressful, even exhibiting similarities to post-traumatic stress symptoms, and these symptoms are associated with lower IQ. Second, a higher national level of economic development underlies both fewer parents using corporal punishment and a higher national IQ.

The researchers are glad to see a movement away from corporal punishment throughout the world, and hope that it may signal future gains in IQ scores. Twenty-four countries have banned corporal punishment, and there is evidence that attitudes favoring corporal punishment and actual use of corporal punishment have been declining even in nations that have not implemented the ban.

However, some researchers question the causal link that Straus and Paschall assert. For example, perhaps the relationship is spurious, meaning that there is another underlying issue that may affect both corporal punishment and IQ. For example, average education levels are rising, and better-educated parents use less corporal punishment and are more likely to engage in activities to increase children's IQ, such as reading to them regularly.

At this point, we don't have all the answers, but Straus, once again, brings to light the downside of personal violence.

WHAT DO YOU THINK?

1. Given what you have learned, what do you see as the pros and cons of spanking?
2. Why do you think that the United States is not among the countries that have banned spanking? What cultural norms are operating?

Sources: Kelly, 2009; Straus & Paschall, 2009.

Murray Straus, the pioneering domestic violence researcher previously introduced, argues that corporal punishment is detrimental to children, teaches them violent and abusive behavior, and legitimizes other forms of violence (Straus & Paschall, 2009; Straus, 2003). For example, being hit as a child is correlated with the frequency and intensity of acting out (Polaha, Larzelere, Shapiro, & Pettit, 2004; Turner & Muller, 2004). Interestingly, it's also linked to a lower IQ in children, as shown in the feature box *Why Do Research? What Do We Make of the Link between Spanking and Children's IQ?*

Spanked children are also more likely to suffer from depression (Christie-Mizell, Pryor, & Grossman, 2008). Adults who were hit as adolescents are more likely to hit their spouses and physically assault someone outside the family (Busby, Holman, & Walker, 2008). Even Dr. Phil, the famous sex and family advisor, opposes spanking (Dr.Phil.com, 2012), but not all parents agree with him.

Who Would Abuse Children?

Neglect, physical abuse, and sexual abuse are more clear-cut. Most people who abuse children are not strangers, but are family members—more than 80 percent, as shown in Figure 11.7 (U.S. Department of Health & Human Services, 2012). Mothers are more likely to abuse their children than are fathers, which isn't surprising, given that mothers spend more time with their children than fathers do. Why would someone who supposedly loves a child abuse that child? It's easy to attribute child abuse to mental disorder, but fewer than 10 percent of abusers suffer from mental illness.

People of all ages can abuse children; however, young parents are more likely to engage in abusive behaviors, in part because they have less knowledge about child development, unrealistic expectations about parenthood, and little preparation for its demands. It's fairly easy to have unrealistic expectations about parenthood and children. Parenting is hard work!

Single parents are also more likely to abuse their children than are married parents. Blacks are more likely to abuse their children than are Whites, Hispanics, or Asians (Table 11.5). Parents who earn less than $15,000 per year are 12 to 16 times more likely to physically abuse their children, 18 times more likely to sexually abuse them, and 44 times more likely to neglect them (U.S. Department of Health & Human Services, Administration on Children, Youth, and Families, 2012). The most common explanation is that low-income parents are under much stress and have lower levels of education, inadequate support systems, and higher rates of substance abuse. They're also more likely to be young and unmarried—other factors associated with child abuse.

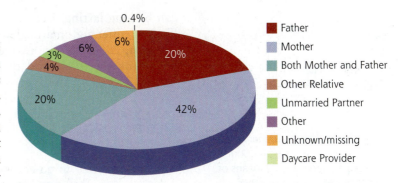

0.4%
6%
6%
3%
4%
20%
20%
42%

- ■ Father
- ■ Mother
- ■ Both Mother and Father
- ■ Other Relative
- ■ Unmarried Partner
- ■ Other
- ■ Unknown/missing
- ■ Daycare Provider

FIGURE 11.7
Perpetrator's Relationship to the Victim

Parents are the most common abusers of children.
Source: U.S. Department of Health and Human Services, 2012.

Child abuse can take many forms: neglect, physical, sexual, psychological, and emotional abuse. Most abusers are family members.

Consequences of Child Abuse

Abuse leaves approximately 18,000 children permanently disabled each year, and kills more than 1,500 children, most of whom are under the age of 3. Health consequences of child abuse can continue into adulthood, and may include such conditions as increased rates of gynecological problems, migraine headaches, obesity, digestive problems, asthma, and a host of other disorders (CDC, April 11, 2012; Perry, 2002).

More insidious are the long-term emotional scars left behind (Maas, Herrenkohl, & Sousa, 2008; Walsh, Dawson, & Mattingly, 2010). Abuse is trauma. For example, physically abused children tend to be more aggressive, be more likely get involved in delinquent activities, have difficulty in school, be involved in early sexual activity, and be associated with teen pregnancy. This doesn't mean, however, that all physically abused children have these outcomes. One study reviewed the findings of 21 published reports on child abuse to note any trends in children's behavior. They found that the number of abused children having difficulty in educational, behavioral, or emotional domains varied greatly, and a child might do poorly in one domain, but excel in another. About one in five abused children had difficulty and functioned poorly in all domains (Walsh, Dawson, & Mattingly, 2010). The emotional trauma

Read on MySocLab
Document: *Human Rights, Sex Trafficking, and Prostitution*

trafficking: The recruitment, transportation, transfer, harboring, or receipt of persons, by means of threat or use of force or other forms of coercion, of abduction, of fraud or deception, of the abuse of power or of a position of vulnerability, or of the giving or receiving of payments to achieve the consent of a person having control over another person, for the purpose of exploitation.

can be long lasting. Even as adults, children who have been abused are more likely to suffer nightmares, depression, panic disorders, and have suicidal thoughts (Hyman, 2000). It can also affect their relationship with their own children, increasing the likelihood of poor attachment, neglect, and abuse (Briere & Jordan, 2009).

Trafficking

I wasn't allowed to go anywhere, they locked us in. They didn't lock us in the house, they locked us in our room. The three of us in a size of room that's not enough for one person . . . I guess they rented us out, or landed us, or bought us? I don't understand what happened. They simply executed us physically, mentally and emotionally during that eight months while I was there. I still am afraid, what will happen if they find me, or when they leave jail. I can't go through that terror again, what I gone through while I was with them.

—"**Todor," labor trafficking survivor, in a statement submitted to sentencing judge (U.S. Department of State, June, 2012)**

TABLE 11.5	Rate per 1,000 Children of Child Abuse Victims by Race/Ethnicity
The highest victimization rates are among Blacks and American Indians/Alaska Natives.	
Black	14.2
American Indian/Alaska Native	12.4
Asian	1.7
Pacific Islander	8.7
Hispanic	8.4
White	8.0
Multiple Races	10.3

Source: U.S. Department of Health & Human Services, Administration on Children, Youth, & Families, 2012.

One extreme form of abuse is **trafficking**, which the United Nations defines as:

the recruitment, transportation, transfer, harboring, or receipt of persons, by means of threat or use of force or other forms of coercion, of abduction, of fraud or deception, of the abuse of power or of a position of vulnerability or of the giving or receiving of payments to achieve the consent of a person having control over another person, for the purpose of exploitation. Exploitation includes, at the minimum, the exploitation or the prostitution of others or other forms of sexual exploitation, forced labor or services, slavery, servitude, or the removal of organs. (United Nations Office on Drugs and Crime, 2013)

Trafficking victims can be girls, boys, women, and men, who are forced to work as housekeepers, prostitutes, in the fields, are forced into marriage, or recruited into armies (Table 11.6). The United Nations estimates that at least 21 million adults and children are in forced labor or sexual servitude at any given time (Polaris Project, 2013; U.S. Department of State, 2012). The best-selling book by Ishmael Beah, *A Long Way Gone: Memoirs of a Boy Soldier* (2007), reveals the horrors of child soldiers in Africa and other places. Separated from his family by violence, Ishmael was forced at age 13 to fight in a civil war in Sierra Leone. Injected with drugs from the government's troops, he recalls killing too many people to even count. His story is about tragedy, survival, and forgiveness.

TABLE 11.6	The Elements of Human Trafficking			
Human trafficking takes many forms.				
ACT	**MEANS**	**PURPOSE**		
Recruitment	Threat or use of force	Exploitation, including		
Transport	Coercion	Prostitution of others		
Transfer +	Abduction +	Sexual exploitation	=	**TRAFFICKING**
Harboring	Fraud	Forced labor		
Receipt of persons	Deception	Slavery or similar practices		
	Abuse of power or vulnerability	Removal of organs		
	Giving payments or benefits	Other types of exploitation		

Source: United Nations Office on Drugs and Crime, 2013.

SEX TRAFFICKING   Rania, in contrast, never wrote a book, but her story was discovered nonetheless. Years ago as a young Moroccan, she signed a contract that she couldn't read and set off to work as a cleaner in Cyprus. But when she arrived, a man told her that she was going to work in a cabaret, drink with the customers, and have sex with them when they wanted it. She refused and begged to be sent home, but she was told that she must repay her travel expenses. Rania was raped. She knew that if she returned home her strict Muslim brother would kill her for "having sex before marriage" and damaging her family's reputation. When she was finally able to flee, social workers took her to a government shelter for victims of sexual exploitation. While police investigated her case, she stayed in Cyprus and finally got her job as a cleaner (U.S. Department of State, 2009b).

Not only is human **sex trafficking** slavery, but it's also big business (Kristof & WuDunn, 2009). In fact, it's the fastest-growing business of organized crime and the third-largest criminal enterprise in the world. Most sex trafficking is international, with victims taken from such places as South and Southeast Asia, the former Soviet Union, Central and South America, and other less developed areas. They are then moved to more developed nations, including Asia, the Middle East, Western Europe, and North America, including the United States (Walker-Rodriguez & Hill, 2013). Victims of sex trafficking can include not only girls and women, but boys and men as well.

Sex trafficking results from a broad range of factors. Increasing poverty, inequality, and economic crises of the past few decades in many countries have placed tremendous stress on families. When these stressors are coupled with patriarchal norms in which women and girls are disvalued, some families sell their daughters to traffickers or put them in vulnerable positions as so-called domestic workers in far-off urban locations. Moreover, globalization has triggered an influx of money and goods, further aggravating disparities between rich and poor, and promoting new levels of consumerism. Around the world, young girls are sought out in the mistaken belief that they're unlikely to be HIV-positive.

Children who are trafficked into prostitution face many dangers (U.S. Department of State, 2012). In addition to injuries and disease associated with multiple sexual encounters, they become dangerously attached to pimps and brothel operators and financially indebted to them. Moreover, they may become addicted to drugs given to subdue them. If victims do manage to escape and return to their families, they may be rejected because of the stigma associated with prostitution (Kristof & WuDunn, 2009).

Elder Abuse

Abuse can happen at any age. Agnes, 85 years old, has arthritis and heart disease. When she lost her husband last year, she moved in with her 50-year-old daughter Emily and her family. The situation is difficult for all of them. Sometimes Emily feels she's at the end of her rope, caring for her mother, worrying about her college-age son, and fearing for her husband, who is about to be forced into early retirement. Emily has caught herself calling her mother names and accusing Agnes of ruining her life. Recently, she lost her temper and slapped her mother (American Psychological Association [APA], 2010).

What constitutes **elder abuse**? Generally accepted definitions include (1) *physical abuse*, the willful infliction of physical pain or injury, such as slapping or bruising; (2) *sexual abuse*, the infliction of non-consensual sexual contact of any kind; (3) *psychological or emotional abuse*, the infliction of

As many as 1.4 million girls, women, and boys are bought and sold every year across international borders for sexual purposes. Some are sold into prostitution by their parents or other relatives; others are tricked into thinking that they are leaving home for a good job. Macro-level factors such as poverty, patriarchal norms, and economic opportunities (or the lack thereof) contribute to sex trafficking.

How do the theories introduced in Chapter 1 inform your thinking about sex trafficking? Compare and contrast these theoretical perspectives.

sex trafficking: An industry in which children are coerced, kidnapped, sold, or deceived into sexual encounters.

11.5   Identify elder abuse

Question That Matters

11.13   What are some types of elder abuse?

elder abuse: Abuse of an elderly person that can include physical abuse, sexual abuse, psychological abuse, financial or material exploitation, and neglect.

mental or emotional anguish such as humiliating, intimidating, or threatening; (4) *financial or material exploitation*, the improper use of an older person's resources without his or her consent for someone else's benefit; and (5) *caregiver neglect*, the failure of a caregiver to provide goods or services necessary to avoid harm or mental anguish, such as abandonment or delay or denial of food, water, or needed medical services (Hildreth, Burke, & Glass, 2009).

Given these various types of abuse, which is most common? A team of researchers set out to answer that question and compiled a representative sample of 5,777 elders across the country (Acierno, Hernandez, Amstadter, Resnick, Steve, Muzzy, & Kilpatrick, 2010). They found that the prevalence of abuse over the previous year was 5.2 percent for financial abuse by a family member, 5.1 percent for neglect, 4.6 percent for emotional abuse, 1.6 percent for physical abuse, and 0.6 percent for sexual abuse. Although these figures themselves are alarming, 1 in 10 respondents reported emotional, physical, or sexual mistreatment or neglect in the previous year. In other words, the data reveal that elder abuse is unfortunately quite common, and that financial abuse and neglect are the most common forms.

A survey of State Adult Protective Services (APS), a rigorous national data source, found 565,000 reported and substantiated cases of abuse among persons ages 60 and over (National Center on Elder Abuse, 2006). Ninety percent of these cases occurred in a domestic setting, not in an institution such as a nursing home or hospital. Reports of elder abuse to adult protective services are on the rise, climbing to 20 percent over recent years. Because only about one-quarter of abuse cases are reported and substantiated by adult protective service agencies, it's likely that the true extent of elders who are abused each year may even exceed 2 million (APA, 2010).

Many of these elders, like Agnes, are frail, vulnerable, and dependent on others they trust for their physical or financial care (CDC, 2009b). They may be physically limited or immobile, have mental or memory problems, or both. Abuse can also cause further health problems. One study of 842 women ages 60 and older who were capable of completing a telephone survey found that abused women were significantly more likely to report more health conditions—including bone or joint problems, digestive problems, chronic pain, depression or anxiety, and high blood pressure—than women who had not been abused (Fisher & Regan, 2006).

Thinking about Agnes and her daughter Emily, discussed at the beginning of this section, would you say that this was an incident of elder abuse? If so, what type, and what should be done about it? Is this a personal problem or a social problem?

As discussed more fully in Chapter 14, caring for an elderly person can be very difficult, particularly when he or she is mentally or physically impaired, when the caregiver is ill-prepared for the task, or when needed resources are lacking (Lopez, Crespo, & Zarit, 2007; Raschick & Ingersoll-Dayton, 2004). Caregiver stress and frustration sometimes lead to abuse or willful neglect. Abusers tend to have more personal problems than do non-abusers, such as mental and emotional disorders, alcoholism, drug addiction, and financial difficulty.

11.6 Compare and contrast explanations for violence among intimates

Question That Matters

11.14 What theories do researchers use to explain violence?

Explanations for Violence among Intimates

A quick survey of your classmates would probably indicate that everyone abhors violence in family and intimate relationships. Then why is it so widespread in the United States and beyond? Two perspectives help us to explain violence among intimates. One focuses on micro-level individual causes, whereas the other examines macro-level societal and cultural factors that contribute to violence. In reality, both factors come into play to some degree.

Micro-Level Explanations

Focusing on the micro-level, two explanations for violence are often cited: (1) the intergenerational transmission of violence, and (2) the stress explanation.

THE INTERGENERATIONAL TRANSMISSION OF VIOLENCE The **intergenerational transmission of violence** perspective suggests that we learn norms and behaviors, including violence, by observing others. Our families of orientation are our primary source of early learning. Therefore, it makes sense that many adults who abuse their spouses, partners, or children learned this behavior in their own families. Perhaps they witnessed abusive or violent behavior between their own parents, or perhaps they were abused as young children.

Researchers have found a tendency toward an intergenerational transmission of violence—that violence is a cycle *potentially* passed down to dependents (Briere & Jordan, 2009; Busby, Holman, & Walker, 2008; Walker, Holman, & Busby, 2009). For example, Heyman and Slep found that the frequency of violence experienced as a child in the home predicted adult abuse (2002). They also found that children who lived with two abusive adults were more likely to abuse than those who lived with only one.

Likewise, a study based on 45,000 responses to the Web-based survey "Relationship Evaluation Questionnaire" (RELATE) found that 10 percent of couples without any reported violence in their family of orientation were violent in their current relationship, as compared to 32 percent of couples who reported that they had either witnessed or experienced violence in their home as children (Busby, Holman, & Walker, 2008). Although the sample is large, it is not based on a representative sample because people who completed RELATE may have been part of a class, workshop, or found the questionnaire on their own search of the Web. Nonetheless, it provides some degree of evidence of the intergenerational transmission of violence perspective.

However, it's also true that most people who witnessed or experienced abuse as children do *not* abuse others. An early study by Straus, Gelles, and Steinmetz reported a startling statistic—sons of the most violent parents are 1,000 times more likely to abuse their partners than the sons of non-violent parents, but this also translates into a rate of 20 percent (Straus, Gelles, & Steinmetz, 1980). That means that 80 percent of those sons witnessing the most extreme forms of violence do *not* abuse their own wives and partners.

The RELATE study found that more than two-thirds of people who witnessed or experienced violence as children were not in an abusive relationship (Busby, Holman, & Walker, 2008). Therefore, it's very important to note that the intergenerational transmission of violence refers to a greater *likelihood* of engaging in violence, but doesn't refer to determinism. Many persons who witnessed or experienced abuse as children grow up to be caring and supportive partners and parents without a hint of perpetuating domestic violence and abuse. Parents who are able to break the cycle of abuse realize that the abuse was wrong, perhaps through education, therapy, or a supportive partner, and they learn other ways to deal with their frustrations.

STRESS EXPLANATION Violent families often contain inordinate amounts of stress or crises. These can include unemployment, poor health, or financial difficulties. Families that experience a great deal of stress are more likely to abuse their partners and their children. Early research by Murray Straus (1980) used the Holmes and Rahe stress scale with more than 2,000 couples and assessed their level of violence using the Conflict Tactics Scale. He found that respondents who experienced none of the stresses in the Holmes and Rahe index had the lowest rate of violence. The likelihood of violence increased as the number of stresses experienced increased.

One micro-level explanation for violence among intimates suggests that we learn violent behavior by watching and imitating others, especially our families.

intergenerational transmission of violence: A cycle of violence passed down to dependents.

Alcohol and drug use can aggravate parental stress, decrease coping skills, and impair judgment. Sometimes specific traits of the child are associated with stress. For example, premature infants who require special care and who may cry harder and more frequently have an increased risk of abuse.

Most often, families are expected to learn how to manage and effectively deal with the stressors on their own. Few families seek outside support such as counseling or working with community agencies in dealing with the problems they face. If a family cannot cope adequately with the stress or crisis, the tensions sometimes push them toward violence.

Macro-Level Explanations

The two theories just discussed—the intergenerational transmission of violence and the stress explanation—help us understand why some people are violent, but they don't place individual actions into their social context. Murray Straus, in his 1980 study just described, also said that stress by itself doesn't necessarily lead to violence. He suggested that we look at social and cultural attitudes toward violence. Straus found that men who assaulted their partners were likely to believe that physical punishment of children and slapping a spouse were appropriate behaviors (Straus, 1980). Where do such attitudes come from?

At least three well-cited macro-level explanations are proposed for violence and abuse: (1) patriarchy; (2) cultural norms that support violence more generally; and (3) norms of family privacy.

PATRIARCHY Violence is more likely to occur in cultures when men are considered dominant and have control over women and children (Allen & Dewitt, 2012; Crittenden & Wright, 2013). Anthropologist Peggy Sanday (1981) has written about sexual aggression around the world. She finds that rape is not universal and is absent in some cultures. Other cultures tend to be more rape-prone—those that hold rigid gendered norms and in which women hold relatively low political and economic status.

In many cultures, violence against women actually has a wide degree of support. Using demographic and health surveys from seven countries—Armenia, Bangladesh, Cambodia, India, Kazakhstan, Nepal, and Turkey—one study estimated that the acceptance of beating one's wife ranged from a low of 29 percent in Nepal to a high of 57 percent in India (women only) and 56 percent in Turkey (men only) (Rani & Banu, 2009). In most of these countries, persons with lower incomes and education levels were more accepting of violence; however, so were younger persons. Many women supported wife beating. The authors concluded that an intergenerational transmission of patriarchal norms can influence both men and women's views (Rani & Banu, 2009).

Can you think of examples of patriarchy in the United States that would condone and perpetuate intimate partner violence? Can you think of examples in developing countries that would condone and perpetuate violence? How are these examples similar or different?

Studies conducted in Palestine show similar results (Dhaher, Mikolajczyk, Maxwell, & Krämer, 2010; Haj-Yahia, 2010). One study interviewed 450 women living in three West Bank cities to assess their attitudes toward wife beating. Overall, the women perceived violence against wives to be justified if a wife insults her husband (59 percent), if she disobeys her husband (49 percent), if she neglects her children (37 percent), if she goes out without telling her husband (25 percent), if she argues with her husband (11 percent), and if she burns the food (5 percent). Sixty-five percent of the women agreed with at least one reason for wife beating, and those with less education, who were employed, had more than one child, made few household decisions, and were married less than 10 years were most supportive overall (Dhaher, Mikolajczyk, Maxwell, & Krämer, 2010). Many Palestinian physicians also support moderate or severe violence against women, and one of the strongest predictors of their support of violence is their level of patriarchal attitudes (Haj-Yahia, 2010).

Although Japan is a modern developed nation, it's also one of the most patriarchal, and not surprisingly, also has high levels of violence against women (Nagae & Dancy, 2010). In-depth qualitative interviews with an admittedly small sample (11 women) indicate that physical, emotional, and even sexual abuse are systematic problems. Communication between spouses tended to be unilateral, with husbands dominating the conversation. The women identified the patriarchal society as a major contributor to violence (Nagae & Dancy, 2010).

But what's the prevalence of patriarchal attitudes in the United States? As you learned in Chapter 2, we also have vestiges of patriarchy. After all, not every American believes in equal rights, or that men and women should share the power and authority in intimate relationships or within society at large.

One macro-level theory to explain violence among intimates examines a culture's tolerance for violence in general. Those cultures that promote and celebrate violence in sports may also have higher rates of violence among intimates.

CULTURAL NORMS SUPPORT VIOLENCE A favorite American pastime is watching sports such as football, hockey, wrestling, or racecar driving—all extremely violent activities, but considered fun and entertaining. If we shove, tackle, or drive fast in some contexts, we're applauded and may gain social prestige or financial rewards. In other contexts, however, we're punished if we act in any of these ways. Your professor cannot shove you because you failed to read the assigned material. You cannot drive 90 miles an hour down the street just because you may find it thrilling. The difficulty lies in the fact that sometimes the lines get blurred between what is and isn't acceptable behavior. In U.S. culture, some types of violence are extremely public, readily available on television, and are condoned by the culture.

Violence in the family is no exception, because some dimensions of violence are also condoned by society. For example, most parents believe it's acceptable to hit their children when they are misbehaving, but where is the line between hitting and abuse? Not everyone agrees that a particular act is abusive. Because some forms of hitting are considered to be acceptable, it's unclear where the line is drawn. Therefore, it shouldn't be surprising that some people, in the heat of passion, push the boundaries beyond acceptable limits. To avoid the distinction between acceptable and non-acceptable family violence, 24 countries prohibit hitting children, including countries as diverse as Sweden and Romania (United Press International, 2010). The United Nations Committee on the Rights of Children has recommended that all countries prohibit spanking in the family and other social institutions (Vandivere, Tout, Capizzano, & Zaslow, 2003).

NORMS OF FAMILY PRIVACY We have all heard, "A man's home is his castle," "I didn't intervene because I knew they were married," "It's not really any of my business," suggesting that what goes on at home is a private affair. Families today are isolated like never before (Nock, 1998). Extended families are rare, and many families move hundreds or even thousands of miles away from their kin because of job or educational opportunities. We're not able to check in with one another as easily as we could have in the past.

Violence occurs in families that tend to be socially isolated (U.S. Department of Health & Human Services, Administration on Children, Youth, and Families, 2012). Family members may have little contact with others, have few friends, and belong to few community organizations. Sometimes the isolation occurs first, and sometimes they isolate themselves afterward to hide the abuse from

FIGURE 11.8
Power and Control Wheel

The Power and Control Wheel illustrates the methods by which batterers use power and control to abuse their victims.

Source: Domestic Abuse Intervention Project, www.theduluthmodel.org.

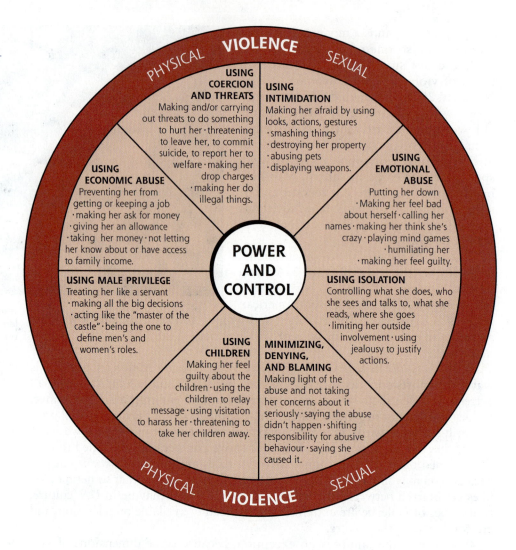

others. These families lack social support to help them with their stress and anger and the challenges of raising children. Moreover, some people believe that violence is a private matter between family members, and are hesitant to intervene when they suspect violence. Who helped Shannon through her repeated ordeals with her boyfriend? Our norms regarding family privacy are very strong (Berardo, 1998).

A Synthesis: Power and Control

Although micro-level and macro-level explanations focus on different factors that contribute to violence, a focus on power and control synthesizes elements of both levels of analysis. This perspective, which admittedly describes perpetrators as men and victims as women, suggests that men who assault their partners are exerting their domination, power, and control over women (Anderson, 2010; Vives-Cases, Gil-González, & Carasco-Portiño, 2009). Likewise, women who feel powerless within their relationships have higher rates of victimization (Filson, Ulloa, Runfola, & Hokoda, 2010). Batterers use threats and various forms of physical, sexual, and emotional abuse to exert their dominance and gain control in a relationship, perhaps making up for inadequacies they feel in other domains. The Power and Control Wheel in Figure 11.8 depicts behaviors and privileges that batterers use to dominate and control their partners or children.

If you look closely at the Power and Control Wheel, you can see a heterosexual bias—it reflects the power imbalances in male–female relationships

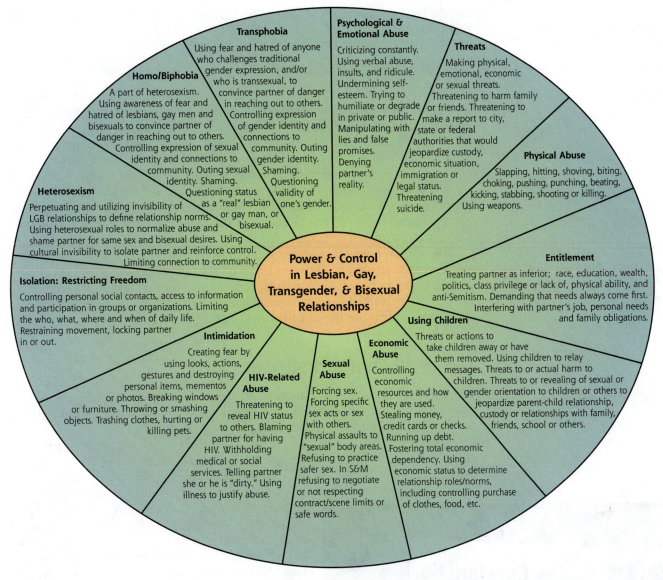

FIGURE 11.9
Power and Control Wheel in Lesbian, Gay, Transgender, and Bisexual (LGTB) Relationships

Power and control may operate somewhat differently in LGTB couples; there are additional ways perpetrators may try to control and intimidate their victims.
Source: Power and Control Wheel in Lesbian, Gay, Transgender, and Bisexual (LGTB) Relationships from Building Safer Communities for Lesbian, Gay, Transgender, Bisexual and HIV-Affected New Yorkers, 2003 New York City Gay & Lesbian Anti-Violence Project.

while ignoring the social and political context experienced by lesbians, gays, transgender persons, and bisexuals (LGTBs), such as homophobia or HIV-related abuse. Figure 11.9 illustrates a Power and Control Wheel that may more adequately reflect the realities for those who aren't heterosexual (New York City Gay & Lesbian Anti-Violence Project, 2003).

The Public's Response

Longstanding cultural attitudes, inadequate enforcement by law enforcement officials, and traditional ideas about sex and gender contribute to the public's uncertainty as to the causes and consequences of violence and what

11.7 Discuss the public response to violence

Question That Matters

11.15 How has the public responded to violence among intimates?

should be done about it (Mildorf, 2007). Let's look at a few public responses to violence.

Violence and the Law

Child advocates, feminists, family scholars, international human rights workers, and others have drawn attention to violence and abuse within families and intimate relationships. They advocate for change, including stricter penalties for abusers. Violence was long ignored by legislators and law enforcement officers in the United States, as it continues to be in many parts of the world. For example, until the 1990s, some states didn't recognize spousal rape as a crime; today, it's a crime in all 50 states and the District of Columbia, although differences in the treatment of spousal rape from that of non-spousal rape still remain, including more stringent reporting requirements or the requirement that the offender used force or threat of force.

There have been other recent legal gains as well, such as anti-stalking laws and the enforcement of restraining orders. Law enforcement officers now receive more training in how to deal with violence among intimates than they did in the past. They are trained to understand the law, but also to understand the dangers, family dynamics, the needs of victims, and resources in the community that could help.

((• Listen on MySocLab
Audio: *NPR: Ohio Marriage Law Hampers Efforts Against Domestic Abuse*

Domestic Violence Shelters

When fleeing an abusive situation, where can an abused person go? Some people have family or friends who can provide emotional support and temporary shelter. Others do not; to whom can they turn?

Kate is one of the "lucky" victims of intimate violence, enduring "only" weekend battering for years. The final straw was when her boyfriend attempted to set her house on fire one night after a particularly brutal argument; Kate and her two children could have perished. Instead, they smelled smoke, got out of the house just in time, and fled to her sister's house. Kate has many siblings, all of whom live close by, and they are protective of her and her children. They saw to it that her family had a safe place to stay, food to eat, and the necessary things to leave her boyfriend once and for all (Seccombe, 2014).

In contrast to Kate, Molly had no one to turn to in her time of need. She lived in an isolated, rural, mountainous area of West Virginia with her husband and three young sons, thirty miles from the nearest town. Molly's husband deliberately kept her isolated from family and friends. She couldn't work or leave the house without his permission, and he put a block on the telephone. He had been abusive to her for years, but when he began battering their oldest son who was only 6 years old, Molly knew she had to leave with her children.

But where could Molly and her sons go? She had heard about a domestic violence shelter in a distant community. One night, as her husband slept, Molly woke the boys, dressed them in multiple layers of clothing (since she knew that suitcases would be impossible to carry), and began the long trek down the mountain in the middle of the night. She rested briefly when her children were tired, then prodded them on again. Finally, she hitched a ride to the shelter from someone driving by in a pickup truck. The shelter was a lifesaver to Molly and her boys, but nonetheless, they lost everything they had ever owned (Seccombe, 2014).

Violence among intimates is against the law, and there are growing numbers of laws, policies, and programs to help victims and their families.

A **domestic violence shelter**, sometimes called a *battered women's shelter,* is a temporary safe house for women (with or without children) who are escaping an abusive relationship. Shelters began in the 1970s in response to two critical forces: (1) the research pointing to high numbers of women who were victims of violence and locked in relationships with their batterer, and (2) the resurgence of the women's movement that saw rape and battering as political and social issues. Shelter programs are premised on the idea that no one deserves to be beaten, and that battered women and their children need special resources to end the violence in their lives. They generally provide 24-hour hotlines, crisis intervention, and a place to stay on a temporary basis—a night, a week, or even months, depending on the demand for and supply of space. They may also offer legal advice, employment and job training assistance, and longer-term counseling. Unfortunately, shelters often face chronic funding challenges that limit their level of services (Macy, Giattina, Parish, & Crosby, 2010).

domestic violence shelter: A temporary safe house for a woman (with or without children) escaping an abusive relationship.

Treatment Programs for Abusers

Men and women who abuse others come from all walks of life. Intimate partner abusers tend to seek control of the thoughts, beliefs, and conduct of their partner, and punish their partner for resisting that control. They tend to minimize the seriousness of their violence, act impulsively, distrust others, control people and situations, and express feelings as anger. "If only you acted differently, I wouldn't have had to hit you," "You made me do it," "I can't control it," "You just bruise easily," "I'll never do it again," the batterer might say repeatedly to his victim. Intervention and treatment must get to the root of the battering, rather than just the symptoms (Alabama Coalition Against Domestic Violence, 2008).

Abusers can enter a treatment program voluntarily or be court-ordered to do so. There is no guarantee that the program will be successful, but most programs generally try to teach the abuser to be aware of his pattern of violence and to learn techniques for using nonviolent behavior such as relaxation techniques, exercise, or "time outs." One challenge of teaching anger management is that many abusers are actually quite good at managing their anger—they know not to explode in public, they know where not to leave bruises, and they know what to say afterward so that their partner will not leave them. Treatment programs might also include issues such as education about domestic violence, changing attitudes and beliefs about using violence in a relationship, and achieving equality in relationships. However, this too can be challenging because long-held beliefs can't be quickly or easily changed.

In the case of child abuse, intervention is first and foremost designed to protect the victims and then to assist and strengthen families. Child welfare agencies, health care workers, counselors, educators, legal counsel, and other professionals may be called on to provide counseling, temporary foster care, education programs, and family assessments. Children may be removed from the home and placed in temporary foster care. If a relative is available, the child may be released to their care.

Depending on the severity of the abuse and the court's decision, the parent may be arrested, incarcerated, or asked to complete a parent education class. A parent may be allowed only supervised visits over a period of time or none at all. Unfortunately, many government agencies who deal with child abuse are overburdened with high caseloads and few resources to do their work adequately. It's a difficult job, and given the concern that we express over child abuse, one cannot help but wonder why prevention, intervention, and treatment are not better funded.

Why do you think that domestic abuse shelters in the United States only serve women and their children, but not men?

Bringing It Full Circle

The focus on this chapter has been family stressors and crises, particularly highlighting the ways that they are rooted in macro-level social arrangements. To understand the causes and the consequences of these stressors, we must see beyond them as only individual micro-level experiences. We must see the connection between our personal experiences and the larger macro-level structural features of our society. Families may face many different types of crises. In this chapter, we've focused on one type of family crisis to provide an in-depth look—violence among intimates, which is violence that occurs among family members and intimate partners. Shannon, from the opening vignette, experienced repeated IPV. As you recall, she eventually killed her attacker in self-defense. In reflecting on what you've learned in this chapter, let's revisit Shannon's story to answer the following questions.

- In Shannon's situation, can you identify the A-factor—the event? The B-factor—the meaning assigned to the event? The C-factor—the resources available before, during, and after the event? What C-factors were absent?

- Of the four types of violence among intimates described in this chapter—common couple violence, intimate terrorism, violent resistance, and mutual violent control—which type do you think best describes Shannon's situation?

- What theory or theories do you think would be most helpful in explaining the violence that Shannon experienced?

On MySocLab

 Study and **Review** on MySocLab

CHAPTER REVIEW

LO11.1   Describe the nature of stress and conflict

11.1   What is the difference between *family stress* and *family crisis*?

Family stress includes tensions that test a family's emotional resources. They vary in type and degree, but are often a process rather than a single change of events. A *family crisis* is a critical change of events that disrupts the functioning of a person's life. It can be positive or negative, although we usually think of crises as negative.

11.2   What are the *ABC-X* and *Double ABC-X* models of coping with a family crisis?

The *ABC-X model* contains the stressor itself, resources available, and the perception of the stressors. The *Double ABC-X model* explains the effects of the accumulation of stresses and crises and how families adapt to

them. The *Double A Factor* refers not only to the initial event, but also to family life changes and transitions that take place because of it. The *Double B Factor* includes both the resources the family already has and the new coping resources the family obtains because of the stress or crisis. The *Double C factor* takes into account the family's perception of the stressor itself, but also their perceptions of the aftermath.

LO11.2   Identify why violence among intimates is a social problem

11.3   How is violence among intimates a social problem rather than just a personal issue?

Violence among intimates is a social problem because (1) it affects large numbers of people; (2) it is not completely random—there are specific risk factors and patterns; and (3) the causes, consequences, and solutions must address social, cultural, and economic factors.

LO11.3 Explain intimate partner violence

11.4 What is *intimate partner violence*?

Intimate partner violence (IPV) is the violence between those who are physically and sexually intimate, such as spouses or partners. The violence can encompass physical, economic, sexual, or psychological abuse. Many abusive situations include more than one type.

11.5 What is the *Conflict Tactics Scale*?

The *Conflict Tactics Scale* is an assessment tool that asks respondents how they deal with disagreements in intimate-partner relationships. It particularly focuses on violent behaviors.

11.6 What are the four different types of intimate partner violence?

To distinguish among types of violence, motives of perpetrators, social characteristics of both partners, and the cultural context in which violence occurs are considered. One typology describes common couple violence, intimate terrorism, violent resistance, and mutual violent control.

11.7 Why do people stay in abusive relationships?

Most don't stay in these relationships. Leaving is a process that doesn't occur all at once. It may be difficult for victims to find the courage or to orchestrate the logistics to leave the situation immediately.

11.8 How does violence in gay and lesbian relationships compare to violence in heterosexual ones?

Less attention has been paid to IPV among gay and lesbian couples, but the information we do have suggests that it's as common as, or more so than, among heterosexual couples.

11.9 How common is rape and sexual assault?

Nearly 1 in 5 women in the United States have been raped in their lifetime, as compared to 1 in 71 men.

LO11.4 Explain child abuse and neglect

11.10 What forms does child abuse take?

Child abuse is an attack on a child that results in an injury and violates our social norms. It takes many forms, including neglect, physical abuse, emotional maltreatment, and sexual abuse.

11.11 What are the consequences of child abuse?

Abuse touches the lives of many, and more than 1,500 children were killed by abuse in 2011. Health consequences that continue into adulthood for many victims can include increased rates of gynecological problems, migraine headaches, digestive problems, asthma, and a host of other disorders. Abuse is trauma, and can cause psychological and emotional problems as well, including aggression, delinquency, difficulty in school, and early sexual initiation.

11.12 What is *trafficking*, and how common is it?

The United Nations defines *trafficking* as follows:

> *the recruitment, transportation, transfer, harboring, or receipt of persons, by means of threat or use of force or other forms of coercion, of abduction, of fraud or deception, of the abuse of power or of a position of vulnerability or of the giving or receiving of payments to achieve the consent of a person having control over another person, for the purpose of exploitation. Exploitation includes, at the minimum, the exploitation or the prostitution of others or other forms of sexual exploitation, forced labor or services, slavery, servitude, or the removal of organs. (United Nations Office on Drugs and Crime, 2013)*

The United Nations estimates that there are at least 12 million adults and children forced into labor or sexual servitude at any given time.

LO11.5 Identify elder abuse

11.13 What are some types of elder abuse?

Elder abuse can include physical abuse, sexual abuse, psychological abuse, financial or material exploitation, or neglect, and affects the lives of about 2.1 million elderly each year.

LO11.6 Compare and contrast explanations for violence among intimates

11.14 What theories do researchers use to explain violence?

Researchers generally point to two lines of theoretical explanations. One focuses on macro-level factors, such as patriarchy, violent cultural norms, or norms of family privacy. Another explanation focuses on micro-level causes, including the intergenerational transmission of violence and stress.

LO11.7 Discuss the public response to violence

11.15 How has the public responded to violence among intimates?

In response to violence among intimates, new laws have been implemented, domestic violence shelters have been created, and treatment programs for abusers have been expanded to reduce violence.

KEY TERMS

ABC-X Model
acute stress
Battered Women's Syndrome
child abuse
chronic stress
Conflict Tactics Scale
crisis

date rape drugs
domestic violence shelter
Double ABC-X Model
elder abuse
family stress
femicide
General Adaptation Syndrome (GAS)

intergenerational transmission of violence
intimate partner violence
learned helplessness
sex trafficking
Social Readjustment Rating Scale
trafficking

The Process of Divorce

CHAPTER

12

Listen to Chapter 12 on **MySocLab**

What is divorce like through the eyes of a child? Unlike parents, children generally have little or no say in the matter.

The divorce is thrust on them, and they must learn to cope with it. As Melanie reveals, healing can be a very long process.

Melanie was ten years old when her parents divorced.

Watch on MySocLab
Video: *A Child's View of Divorce: Melanie*

As children, we rarely see our parents as people, they are just . . . well . . . parents. They aren't supposed to have personal problems. Yet one day, Melanie's parents sat down with her and her younger brother and told them that they were getting a divorce. Like other 10-year-olds who hear this news, the world that Melanie had known came screeching to a halt.

Melanie was flooded with emotion. Guilt. Fear. Anger. Embarrassment. Guilt—maybe it was her fault and she made them fight. Fear—she knew her life was going to change. Anger—how dare they do this to her! Embarrassment—no one else's parents are getting divorced, so why are hers?

After breaking the news, her dad first moved into the attic, and then eventually moved into his own place close by. Like other children of divorced parents, Melanie and her brother visited him one night a week and every other weekend. The visits were stressful and difficult for everyone. Her brother began wetting the bed. After some time and many complaints, the overnight visits ceased.

Melanie was angry with her mother for the divorce and even angrier when her mother began dating. Melanie hated the man and told her mother so, but her mother continued to date him. They eventually married. Melanie felt betrayed—if her mother really loved her, she would not stay with this man.

Concerned over Melanie's hostility, her mother sent Melanie and her brother to therapy to help them through the divorce. Melanie was so full of anger that she refused to speak in her therapy sessions for almost two years. She wanted to prove to her mother that therapy would not work and that the divorce could not be so easily "fixed."

Meanwhile, Melanie's father also remarried. Yet, despite her parents' remarriages, she harbored a secret hope that they would someday get back together. She even concocted ways to get them to meet. Melanie was devastated when her father and his new wife had a baby. She knew then that there was no chance her parents would ever reunite.

Today, Melanie is 25 years old. The passage of time has given her a new perspective, but it hasn't washed away the pain she vividly remembers. She sees how well her friends' families get along, and she feels jealous and sad that she isn't able to have this experience with her original family. But Melanie now acknowledges that perhaps the divorce was better than having her parents live together unhappily.

Melanie visits her parents regularly, but her father will occasionally say unkind things about her mother, and visits with her mother can also be tense. For many years, Melanie's mantra was "I won't get divorced, I won't get divorced." Today, she realizes that divorce sometimes happens, but she hopes that she will never put her own children through her experience.

If you're like many college students, you've seen divorce close up. Like Melanie, you may have watched your parents' marriage end, or perhaps you've experienced your own divorce or that of a sibling or friend. As family systems theory shows us, family relationships are interrelated, and therefore divorce requires that both children and adults in the family change their daily patterns, alter their dreams for the future, and start anew. When family relationships change, most people experience feelings of rejection, anger, hurt, betrayal, defeat, and fear. In this chapter, we explore the process of divorce. Although a judge can grant a divorce decree in minutes, divorce is a long-term process that begins years before and often continues years after the official decree.

Divorce in the United States

Divorce is a common occurrence in the United States. About one-third of people who have ever been married have also been divorced (Taylor, Funk, & Clark, 2007). In fact, the United States has one of the world's highest divorce rates—as Figure 12.1 shows, its rate is five times that of Mexico, twice that of China, and 40 percent to 50 percent higher than many other developed nations such as Japan or Germany. Only Russia's divorce rate is higher (United Nations Statistics Division, 2012).

Why do so many marriages in the United States end in divorce? This chapter addresses this vital question. But first, let's see how social scientists measure divorce; some measurements are more useful than others.

How Common Is Divorce? It Depends on How We Measure It

We often hear that "Half of all marriages end in divorce." But does this mean that half of all marriages that occurred last year ended in divorce? Of course not. Let's say that 100,000 couples married last year, and the courts granted 50,000 divorces. It appears that 50 percent of marriages ended in divorce. But this doesn't make sense, because this percentage measures the number of weddings that took place in only one year against the number of divorces among all weddings that have taken place over many years—10, 20, 30 years ago, or even longer.

What, then, is a better method of understanding the frequency of divorce? One method is to examine the rate of divorce per 1,000 people, which is called the **crude divorce rate**. In the United States in 2011, this rate was 3.6 divorces per 1,000 people, definitely not as sensational as

| 12.1 | Discuss divorce in the United States |

Questions That Matter

12.1 What is the best way to calculate the divorce rate?

12.2 Is the current rate of divorce in the United States increasing?

crude divorce rate: The number of divorces per 1,000 people in the population.

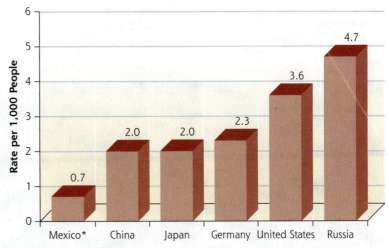

*Mexico Data from 2009.

FIGURE 12.1

Crude Divorce Rates per 1,000 Population for Selected Countries: 2010–2011

The United States and Russia have the highest divorce rates in the world. *Source:* United Nations, 2012.

the "50 percent" measure (Centers for Disease Control and Prevention [CDC], February 19, 2013). Because many different countries use this method, it makes international comparisons easier.

However, the crude divorce rate is problematic. Many people aren't married, so why should they be included in a divorce statistic? In determining the divorce rate, it makes more sense to focus on how many *married* people get divorces. Therefore, another method of measuring the frequency of divorce is the **refined divorce rate,** or the number of divorces that occur per 1,000 married women ages 15 and older. (Note: The measure is computed using women, but not men.) The refined divorce rate was 20.9 divorces per 1,000 married women (National Marriage Project, 2012), or about 2 percent a year, a much less sensational number than the familiar "Half of all marriages end in divorce," but considerably more accurate and useful.

The refined divorce rate provides a one-year snapshot of how many married women divorce. The other 979.1 out of 1,000 married women who didn't divorce in that year *could* get a divorce the following year, or the year after that, or 10 years later, of course. So even though a married woman had less than a 2 percent chance of divorcing in one year, she has a far greater chance of divorcing over the course of her married life. What is unknown is just how high her chances of a future divorce really are.

We don't know whether half of all current marriages will end in divorce because the divorce rate is always fluctuating. We do know, however, that the frequency of divorce is related to both micro-level choices and macro-level social factors, such as divorce laws, women's economic opportunities, and other norms. These factors have changed over time, as we see in the next section.

Historical Trends

Some people believe that divorce in the United States is a relatively new phenomenon, but people throughout our history have found ways to terminate marriages (Degler, 1980). Although legal divorce was rare and difficult to obtain before 1850, married couples in troubled relationships separated or deserted one another. Women in colonial America had few legal rights and their ability to initiate divorce was limited. Husbands were the head of the household, and they generally controlled the labor of children as well as that of their wives. An early study of marriage and divorce conducted in the mid-1800s examined 29 cases of divorce granted on the grounds of *cruelty* (Wright, 1889). In almost every case, the wife committed the cruelty by attempting to break out of her traditional subordinate role in one way or another. In half of these cases, the wife had refused to do domestic chores, such as keeping her husband's clothes in repair or cooking his meals.

Early feminists such as Susan B. Anthony, Elizabeth Cady Stanton, and Amelia Bloomer spoke out in favor of making divorce more available to women as a way of improving their rights and their position in marriage (Degler, 1980). By the mid-19th century, the divorce rate began to rise as it became easier for women to initiate and obtain a divorce. During the five years from 1872 to 1876, 63 percent of all divorces initiated and granted to women were on grounds such as cruelty, desertion, drunkenness, and neglect to provide for the family—each demonstrating failure on the husband's part to fulfill his role (Degler, 1980).

refined divorce rate: A measure of divorce based on the number of divorces that occur out of every 1,000 married women.

In the late 19th and early 20th centuries, the divorce rate rose; more women began filing for divorce because of their spouse's drinking, infidelity, or failure to support the family.

The divorce rate rose steadily between 1860 and 1940, though it dropped somewhat during the Great Depression of the 1930s. It's unlikely that marriages were happier during this extremely difficult period when as many as one in four workers lost their jobs. Instead, many unhappily married couples probably couldn't afford to divorce or they needed to keep the family together simply to survive.

After the Depression and World War II, the divorce rate rose quickly, and by 1946 it peaked at nearly 18 divorces per 1,000 married women. Why the surge in divorce? There are many reasons, including high rates of marriage during the 1940s, some of which may have been impulsive; stressors of war and reunification on relationships; increasing urbanization and geographic mobility that broke down traditional ties; and women's greater economic opportunities that allowed them to be more self-supporting.

Figure 12.2 illustrates the trends in the divorce rate between 1940 and 2011 (CDC, February 19, 2013). After the rush of divorces following World War II, the divorce rate dropped considerably to around 9 per 1,000 married women during the 1950s. Why was there a decline at this time? Domesticity was the cultural norm: women married younger, had more children than in previous decades, and were less likely to divorce. But in the late 1960s and 1970s, the divorce rate began to rise again, peaking at nearly 23 divorces per 1,000 married women around 1980. Since then, however, the divorce rate declined sharply, to less than 17 per 1,000 married women in 2009, but seemingly has risen in recent years to 20.9. I say *seemingly* because the method of calculation has changed. Calculations up to 2009 are based on National Center for Health Statistics data for the United States, but which excluded California, Georgia, Hawaii, Indiana, Louisiana, and Minnesota. The 2011 estimate is based on nationally representative data from the American Community Survey that includes these six states. Thus, the 2011 estimate isn't strictly comparable to estimates from earlier years. But the higher numbers could also reflect an improved economy—people who may have been postponing divorce due to the financial difficulties it would cause are now going through with it.

FIGURE 12.2
Crude and Refined Divorce Rates: 1940–2011

The divorce rate peaked in the late 1940s after World War II, and peaked again in 1980. Divorce declined significantly after 1980, but has recently increased sharply.
Sources: Centers for Disease Control and Prevention, February 19, 2013; National Marriage Project, 2012; Tejada-Vera and Sutton, 2010.

Do you think the divorce rate in the United States will stabilize, fall, or rise over the next decade? How will our changing demographic structure (e.g., an increase in the Hispanic population, delayed marriage and childbearing) and social trends (e.g., economic recession, greater equality between men and women) influence the divorce rate?

Why Do People Divorce?

If we were to ask a number of couples why they divorced, we would receive many different answers: "We fell out of love," "We grew apart," "We are just too different," "She met someone new," "He doesn't listen to me," or "We disagree about how to spend money." The explanations that people offer tend to focus on individual micro-level issues. Family scientists, however, try to look at the *patterns* associated with divorce to see the big picture. These patterns reveal that marriages end not only for individual reasons; something more is at work than simple incompatibility. Let's look at examples of critical micro-level and macro-level factors that influence the odds of divorce.

12.2 Analyze the macro- and micro-level reasons why people divorce

Questions That Matter

12.3 What kinds of micro-level factors influence divorce?

12.4 What kinds of macro-level factors influence divorce?

Micro-Level Factors

If we look at patterns of divorce, we can see that certain risk factors make divorce more likely (Amato, 2010). Naturally, this doesn't mean that all people with these risk factors will divorce; it just means that they have a greater chance of doing so.

intergenerational transmission of divorce: A pattern noted by researchers that people whose parents divorced are also more likely to divorce.

PARENTAL DIVORCE   People whose parents have divorced are also more likely to divorce themselves (Amato & Hohmann-Marriott, 2007; Morin, 2013; Sassler, Cunningham, & Lichter, 2009). This pattern is known as the **intergenerational transmission of divorce.** Parents serve as role models for their children; parents who remain married impart to their children a greater commitment to marriage. Adult children model their own parents' behaviors, including problematic traits such as poor communication skills. Children with divorced parents sometimes experience negative long-term consequences that continue into their own adulthood and can harm their marriages, such as emotional problems, anxiety, and depression (Cartwright, 2005). Children whose parents divorced tend to marry younger, have lower incomes, are more likely to be involved in a non-marital pregnancy, and are less likely to go to college, which puts them in several higher-risk categories for divorcing (McLanahan & Sandefur, 1994). Certainly not all children of divorced parents experience divorce themselves, but they do have a greater chance. One study looked at the quality of a *parent's remarriage* in predicting divorce (Yu & Adler-Baeder, 2007). More than 500 young adults completed a questionnaire regarding the quality of their parents' marital relationships and various aspects of their own committed relationships. Children whose parents had a higher-quality remarriage were less likely to divorce.

AGE AT MARRIAGE   Couples who marry at a young age are in one of the highest-risk categories for divorce (Lowenstein, 2005). Teenagers who marry are at particularly high risk because they tend to be poorly prepared for marriage and its responsibilities. Generally, teens aren't as mature as people in their twenties or thirties—they don't yet know what kind of adult they will be, or with what type of spouse they will be most compatible. Moreover, teen marriages are often precipitated by a premarital pregnancy, which increases the likelihood that the marriage will fail. Practically speaking, a teenage couple is also likely to struggle with a low income and an interrupted education, which also puts them in a higher-risk category.

One factor that predicts divorce is the sex of the children. Parents who have sons are less likely to divorce than are parents who have only daughters. Fathers tend to be more engaged with their children if they have sons.

PARENTAL STATUS   Couples who have children—particularly young children—or who have many children are less likely to divorce (Bramlett & Mosher, 2002; Hewitt, 2009). This, of course, says nothing about the quality of these marriages—a couple may stay in an unfulfilling marriage because they believe it's the appropriate thing to do for their children's sake. But regardless of marital quality, the fact remains that childfree married couples are more likely to divorce than couples with children because fewer barriers prevent them from leaving an unhappy marriage.

NON-MARITAL CHILDBEARING   Couples who bear or conceive children prior to marriage have higher divorce rates than do other couples. Pregnancy may encourage people to marry when they may not otherwise have chosen to do so. It may also cause them to marry before they're financially or emotionally ready. Pregnancy, caring for a newborn, and raising a child put additional stresses on a relationship. Couples who haven't had the opportunity to know themselves and their partner as a couple may have a difficult time making the transition to their roles as parents.

SEX OF CHILDREN   Couples who have sons are less likely to divorce than are couples who have daughters (Dahl & Moretti, 2003). Couples with sons are at lower risk for divorce because fathers in these families are more engaged with their children, and therefore mothers perceive the relationship as more equitable and stable (Mammen, 2009).

RACE AND ETHNICITY   Different racial or ethnic groups vary in their tendency to divorce, with Hispanic and Asian groups least likely to divorce and Blacks most likely to do so (Clarkwest, 2007). Social scientists generally offer a cultural explanation for this variation, focusing on the primacy of the family in Hispanic and Asian cultures, where the needs of the group outweigh the needs of the individual. Catholicism, which doesn't legally recognize divorce, is also a factor in Hispanic families. The higher divorce rate among Blacks may be related to the lack of jobs for urban Black males and high rates of unemployment or poverty.

EDUCATION   On average, people with lower levels of education are more likely to divorce than those with higher levels of education (Cohn, 2009; Jalovaara, 2003). However, the educational relationship is less clear for women than it is for men. Women with very high levels of education are also more likely to divorce, especially later in the marriage, because an advanced degree contributes to their ability to be economically independent and, therefore, leave an unhappy marriage.

INCOME   Divorce is more common among people with lower incomes than among those with higher incomes (Livingston, 2013; Taylor, Funk, & Clark, 2007). Financial and job-related stresses can contribute to marital problems. Although not all wealthy couples have happy marriages and not all couples with lower incomes are doomed to an unhappy or unstable union, unemployment, poverty, and financial strains decrease displays of affection, cause marital conflict, and even increase the likelihood of family violence and disruption.

DEGREE OF SIMILARITY BETWEEN SPOUSES   Spouses are less likely to divorce when they share characteristics such as age, religion, race, or ethnic group and are more likely to divorce when these characteristics differ (Bratter & King, 2008; Vaaler, Ellison, & Powers, 2009; Zhang & Van Hook, 2009). For example, a large study of more than 23,000 married couples found that interracial marriages faced a higher risk of divorce, especially marriages involving a Black husband and a White wife, or a Hispanic husband and a White wife (Zhang & Van Hook, 2009). Couples who differ from each other in some of these important ways may have different values, norms, or experiences. They may encounter additional stress from outsiders who disapprove of their marriage, which could lead to greater conflict and less social support.

THE COUPLE'S AGES   The likelihood of a couple divorcing rises during adulthood and then declines as the couple ages (Taylor, Funk, & Clark, 2007; U.S. Census Bureau, 2007). This decline may happen because unhappy couples divorce long before reaching middle or old age. Or, drawing on exchange theory, divorce may decline with age because unhappy older couples decide it is better to remain married than to divorce later in life. Dividing many years' worth of joint assets such as a home, retirement accounts, and savings can be problematic, and perhaps older couples see that the financial or emotional costs of divorce would outweigh its benefits.

Although individual micro-level reasons help us to understand why people divorce, they don't provide a complete picture because they miss the broad social context in which divorce occurs.

Macro-Structural Factors

Read on **MySocLab**
Document: *A Comparison of Civilian and Enlisted Divorce Rates During the Early All Volunteer Force Era*

Why did the divorce rate increase in the 1960s and 1970s? And why is the divorce rate declining today? Is it because married couples love each other more today? Probably not. Why is divorce in the United States still so common, but so rare in the Middle East? Do married couples there love each other more than we do? Divorce may have very little to do with micro-level issues such as "We fell out of love," or "We have irreconcilable differences." Many people stay in loveless marriages and consider irreconcilable differences irrelevant.

If we want to know why divorce occurs, instead of looking only at micro-level factors of the individual, we should also pay attention to cultural macro-level factors such as (1) the level of socioeconomic development; (2) the dominant religion practiced; (3) the divorce laws; (4) the status of women, including their employment situation; and (5) the general attitudes toward divorce.

LEVEL OF SOCIOECONOMIC DEVELOPMENT   Generally, less developed countries in Africa, Asia, Central and South America, and the Middle East have significantly lower divorce rates than do developed countries in North America and Europe (United Nations Statistics Division, 2012). Most people can't support themselves on their own in less developed countries, and families are of the utmost importance. Religious and cultural customs reinforce the family as the primary social institution. China, which has undergone rapid socioeconomic development since the early 1990s, has also seen a tremendous surge in its divorce rate, increasing more than 60 percent since 2000 (United Nations Statistics Division, 2012).

RELIGION   A second factor that influences the rate of divorce in a country is the level of religiosity and the most widely practiced religion of its citizens (Trent & South, 1989). Much of Central and South America is dominated by Roman Catholicism, which forbids divorce in all but the most extreme circumstances. In Italy and Ireland, the Catholic Church was influential in prohibiting divorce until the laws were overturned in the 1980s and 1990s, respectively. However, it's still not easy to divorce. In Ireland, for example, three conditions must be met before a divorce is granted: (1) At the date of the commencement of the proceedings, the spouses have lived apart for *four of the five previous years*; (2) there is no reasonable prospect of a reconciliation between the spouses; and (3) proper provision is or will be made for the spouse and dependent members of the family (DivorceInIreland.com/TheOptions.asp, accessed May 15, 2013).

DIVORCE LAWS   Divorce laws certainly help predict the likelihood of divorce, and they are quite different throughout the world (Kneip & Bauer, 2009). In many parts of the Middle East, men can divorce their wives for almost any reason, often by simply declaring "I divorce thee" (Human Rights Watch, 2004a). Women do not have the same prerogative. Only recently have Egyptian women been allowed to initiate divorce at all and the process remains highly discriminatory, as shown in the feature box *Diversity in Families: Patriarchy and Divorce in Egypt* (p. 351).

Although U.S. divorce laws may seem simple in comparison, it wasn't long ago that one of the marriage partners had to be the one "at fault" in a divorce proceeding. Common grounds for divorce included mental cruelty, adultery, or desertion. Beginning in the 1960s, states slowly began to amend their laws to reflect the concept of **no-fault divorce**. Now, a couple can go

no-fault divorce: A type of divorce, now prevalent in all 50 states, in which a divorcing couple can go before a judge without one party having to blame the other.

"The question of settling divorce should be in the hands of the wiser party, and that is men. Men are wise, which is why they do not have to go to court. Islamic law would consider the wise wife an exception, and you cannot generalize an exception."
— Ayman Amin Shash, chief judge, technical bureau of the National Center for Judicial Studies, Cairo; July 7, 2004

Egyptian men have a unilateral and unconditional right to divorce without resort to legal proceedings. They need only to renounce their wives, repeating three times that they are now divorced and registering the divorce within 30 days with a religious notary to make it official. A repudiated woman then has to observe a waiting period of up to one year in which she cannot marry another man just in case her former husband changes his mind. She will receive some compensation called *maintenance* during the waiting period, with consideration for the husband's means, the circumstances of the divorce, and the length of marriage.

In contrast to men, women have a much more difficult time initiating a divorce. To begin *fault-based* divorce proceedings, women, unlike men, must obtain legal counsel, provide evidence of harm, often through eyewitness testimony, and submit to compulsory mediation. There are only four grounds that a woman can use: (1) husband's illness, including mental illness, venereal disease, and impotence; (2) non-provision of maintenance or financial support; (3) absence or imprisonment; and (4) "injury," which includes a variety of forms of physical and mental harm.

Judges do not grant women fault-based divorce easily, and they often require substantial evidence of "harm." Judges tend to require a higher threshold of harm for poor or illiterate rural women on the assumption that physical abuse or polygyny, for example, is a natural part of their lives and does not necessarily warrant a divorce. Egypt's chief judicial inspector admitted, "What is harm for some women isn't harm for another. Some women accept beatings and insults as a joke, while others do not."

Beginning in 2000, Egyptian women were given a second option—the right to file for a no-fault divorce on the basis of "incompatibility." However, this requires that a woman forfeit her rights to alimony and she must repay her dowry. Given women's limited work experience and earning potential, the meager safety net provided by social services, and the high degree of patriarchy woven into Egypt's laws and policies, divorced women face very dim prospects. Therefore, this option is only available to women with significant financial resources or those who are most desperate for a divorce. As one man told his wife who wanted a "no-fault" divorce: "Leave the house if you want a divorce. Give up the house, the children, the furniture, and the clothing that

Only recently have women in Egypt been allowed to file for divorce, and the grounds for divorce remain strict compared to men who initiate divorce.

you're wearing. I will not give you anything. . . . You will go to your family's house and they'll bring you back to lick my shoes."

WHAT DO YOU THINK?

1. How do divorce laws reflect patriarchy? Do you think that Egypt is unique in its approach to divorce for women? Why or why not?
2. Do you think the changes made in 2000 to the divorce law help Egyptian women? Why or why not?

Source: Human Rights Watch, 2004b.

before a judge without the need to blame each other; instead, they can claim irreconcilable differences and state that they both wish to divorce. A no-fault law was first passed in Oklahoma in 1953 and then in Alaska in 1962, and no-fault divorce laws spread through the 50 states during the 1970s. By 1987, the final holdout state, Utah, enacted no-fault divorce legislation (Vlosky & Monroe, 2002).

A high number of divorces were granted immediately after the states' legislation was passed (Rodgers, Nakonezny, & Shull, 1997). A similar situation happened in Europe—the divorce rate rose substantially after the laws changed (Kneip & Bauer, 2009). This increase may indicate that there was a backlog of unhappy couples waiting until the legislation went into effect. Today, states vary somewhat in the details of their divorce laws (e.g., some states require waiting periods), but no-fault divorce is now available in all 50 states.

WOMEN'S STATUS AND EMPLOYMENT   Divorce laws tend to be more restrictive in patriarchal societies where women have fewer legal rights or economic opportunities (Amato, 1994; Greenstein & Davis, 2006). In many countries, laws regarding child custody and spousal support are designed to perpetuate patriarchy. In Iran, for example, wives are entitled to spousal support for only three months, despite the very limited economic opportunities available to women. Therefore, most divorced women in Iran return to their birth families, often in shame. In India, a divorced woman rarely receives any of the assets that she and her former husband have accumulated, for these are assumed to belong to her husband and his family. As these examples illustrate, in patriarchal societies divorce puts women at such an economic disadvantage that they often don't ask for a divorce.

Even in the United States, women have been economically dependent on men to support them for much of the country's history. This changed briefly during World War II, when many middle-class married women secured paid employment. Women's employment declined after the war, but began to rise again by the 1970s, when a large number of married women with children joined the workforce. This change in women's employment patterns enabled women to support themselves more easily and, therefore, end unhappy marriages. Women who are more self-sufficient, such as with above-average incomes or who earn more than half the household income, are more likely to divorce than are those who are economically dependent (Rogers, 2004; Teachman, 2010).

ATTITUDES TOWARD DIVORCE   In many parts of the world today, women who divorce are stigmatized. Until recently in the United States, in fact, the term *divorcée,* which applied only to women, had sexually suggestive connotations. Fifty years ago, a person who was known to have divorced—man or woman—would probably not have been elected to a major political office. Yet, by 1980, the fact that Ronald Reagan had a divorce in his past didn't prevent him from being elected President of the United States (Rothstein, 2001). By the 1992 presidential election, candidate Bob Dole's divorce was barely mentioned. Societal attitudes toward divorce changed as it became more common—both a cause and a consequence of an increasing divorce rate. Today, about two thirds of adults believe that divorce is "morally acceptable," and one-quarter say that it is "morally wrong" (the remainder say that "it depends") (Gallup, December 26, 2013).

As divorce became less stigmatized, unhappy couples considered it an appropriate way to end their relationship. Moreover, couples that contemplate marriage may have begun to see marriage as only semi-permanent, noting that they could opt out if it didn't work. One study based on a nationally representative sample of high school seniors found that only 56 percent of adolescent boys and 66 percent of adolescent girls claim, "It is 'very likely' that I will stay married to the same person for life" (National Marriage Project, 2012). Defining marriage as less than a permanent relationship supports a self-fulfilling prophecy; if partners enter marriage with the idea that it could easily be terminated, it's more likely that it will.

This attitude toward marriage doesn't necessarily mean that people take the events of marriage and divorce lightly. In fact, more people now oppose divorce and believe that it should be more difficult to obtain than people of a generation ago. Likewise, the Pew Research Center's 2007 study with a representative sample of adults across the United States found that 45 percent of adults ages 18 to 29 believe that divorce "should be avoided except in extreme situations," compared to only 32 percent of adults ages 65 and older (Pew Research Center, 2007). To repeat, it is *younger* adults, not older adults, who want divorce to be more restrictive, perhaps because many of them experienced divorce as children.

The researchers also found that Blacks were more likely than Whites or Hispanics to favor a more restrictive divorce, as shown in Figure 12.3. In fact, a fear of divorce keeps many low-income mothers from marrying in the first place (Edin & Kefalas, 2005). It thus appears that those people who are at a higher risk for divorce would like the divorce process to be more difficult.

Researchers Martin and Parashar (2006) compared data from the period 1974–2002 and also found that people have come to support more restrictive divorce laws in recent years. In particular, an intriguing change has occurred in attitudes toward divorce among *women*. In the past, researchers found that the more education women had, the more likely they were to support easier access to divorce. Attending college was thought to broaden women's perceptions and make them more open to lifestyles other than "married with children." In recent years, however, women with college degrees are the most likely to say that divorce should be more difficult to obtain, whereas women with less than a high school diploma hold the least restrictive views about divorce. What might explain this trend referred to as "the education crossover"?

Martin and Parashar (2006) suggest that women's attitudes are related to the expected *utility of divorce*. Women with less education (and who likely have lower incomes and less prestigious jobs) want to marry to increase their financial prospects, but they are faced with a pool of potentially risky marriage partners. If women are unsure about the economic prospects of their partners, they may want to keep divorce as an option. In contrast, women who have more education (and presumably higher incomes and jobs with more prestige) can be more selective about whom they marry. They can wait until they are confident they have found a relationship with long-term stability and are less likely to anticipate divorce. In other words, the researchers suggest that women who believe their options are more limited may want to keep divorce as a viable option, whereas women with greater earning potential are less likely to foresee the need for a divorce, and therefore think divorce should be more difficult to obtain.

As this research shows us, individual reasons are important in the decision to seek a divorce, but they can be greatly influenced by macro-level factors. Taken together, as shown in the *Tying It All Together* feature box, both micro-individual factors and macro-structural factors can provide us with a clearer picture of why people divorce.

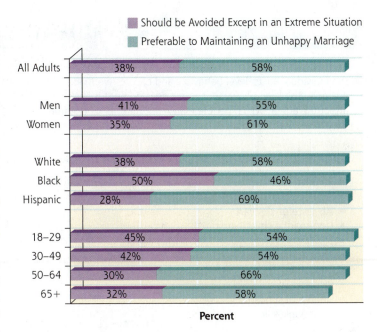

FIGURE 12.3

Views about Divorce, by Sex, Race/Ethnicity, and Age—"Which statement comes closer to your views about divorce"

Men, Blacks, and younger people are most likely to think that divorce should be avoided except in an extreme situation.
Source: Pew Research Center, July 1, 2007.

*L*et's consider your odds for divorce. Are they high or low? For example, did your parents divorce? Do you plan to have children? What do you think your income will be when you're finished with school? What are your attitudes toward divorce? What type of culture do you live in?

Why do people divorce? Many macro-level factors influence the individual micro-level behaviors and choices we make. For example, the level of socioeconomic development is likely to affect the age at which people marry, the number of children they have, and the couple's level of personal resources.

MICRO-LEVEL FACTORS ASSOCIATED WITH DIVORCE

- Parental divorce
- Age at marriage
- Absence of children
- Non-marital childbearing
- Sex of children
- Race and ethnicity
- Education
- Income
- Degree of similarity
- The couple's ages

MACRO-LEVEL FACTORS ASSOCIATED WITH DIVORCE

- Level of socioeconomic development
- Religion
- Divorce laws
- Women's status and employment
- Attitudes toward divorce

WHAT DO YOU THINK?

1. Identify a few different countries, and reflect on their macro-level factors associated with divorce. How do they differ from the United States?
2. Do you think that any micro-level factors associated with divorce operate differently across racial or ethnic groups?

12.3 Recognize how people experience divorce

Questions That Matter

12.5 What are the phases of a separation?

12.6 How is divorce experienced differently by women and men?

12.7 What are the stations of divorce?

12.8 What is *divorce mediation*?

Experiencing Divorce

My parents just divorced last year, but they've had a crummy marriage for years. I honestly don't know what took them so long to finally do it, to get a divorce. I've always hated it when they fought. Little things would set one of them off, and then they would both go ballistic. They would often pull me in the middle: "Matt, what do you think?" they would ask. Just leave me out of it.

—**Matt, Age 20**

Divorce is a *process* that is rarely quick or easy (Amato, 2007; Birditt, Brown, Orbuch, & McIlvane, 2010; Gregson & Ceynar, 2009; Symoens, Bastaits, Mortelmans, & Bracke, 2013; Wallerstein, 2007). Although a judge may grant the divorce decree in a matter of minutes, most couples have gone through a period of many years in which they have analyzed, redefined, and reorganized not only their relationship, but also nearly every aspect of their lives (Willén & Montgomery, 2006). This process may include many years of conflict, a separation to provide the emotional distance needed to work on resolving marital problems—sometimes followed by reconciliation, but perhaps finally ending in a divorce. In a study involving a national sample of more than 1,000 people interviewed several times between 1980 and 1992 (Amato & Rogers, 1997), researchers reported that marital problems identified in the first interview in 1980 predicted divorce up to 12 years later. In other words, couples who divorce tend to report problems in the marriage as early as 9 to 12 years before the actual divorce occurs.

A couple may choose to divorce for many reasons. One study conducted with more than 800 divorcing parents who had completed a mandated parenting class found that the most common reasons given for seeking a divorce were "growing apart" (55 percent) and "not being able to talk together" (53 percent) (Hawkins, Willoughby, & Doherty, 2012).

Women and men often provide different reasons for a divorce and experience the process and its aftermath differently. Although each may have difficult feelings including guilt, depression, embarrassment, failure, or low self-esteem, women and men experience divorce differently because of the different opportunities and constraints that society presents to each sex.

These differences are apparent even in the first stage in the process of divorce—voicing marital problems. Women report more marital problems than do their husbands, although interestingly, women tend to blame themselves for many of these problems (Amato & Rogers, 1997). This tendency may reflect women's subordinate position in many marriages; as a result, wives monitor and interpret their marriages more often than do husbands. Some of the biggest concerns between husbands and wives (and acknowledged by both) include the husband not spending enough time at home, his irritating habits, his use of alcohol or drugs, and his foolish spending of money. For wives, both acknowledged that her feelings are easily hurt. There were smaller perceived differences between the two sexes in who gets angry or jealous or who is domineering, critical, moody, and untalkative (Amato & Rogers, 1997). Nonetheless, despite the fact that women report more marital problems, they may not be more likely to initiate divorce (Hewitt, 2009).

The Phases of Separation

In the first phase of a marital separation, *pre-separation*, one or both partners begin to think about the benefits of a separation. They may first fantasize about leaving and being free of the responsibilities associated with marriage. But when they think about the logistics, people considering separation commonly experience anxiety, sadness, fear, anger, and loneliness at the same time. Couples in this stage may not fully reveal their intention to separate to friends and family. They may continue to attend family functions together or they may concoct a story to explain a partner's absence from events.

During the *early separation phase*, couples face a series of issues as they separate. Who will be the one to move out? How shall we work out financial matters, such as the house payment, the car payment, and other bills? How do we explain this decision to our children? How should parental responsibilities be divided? Should family, friends, and teachers be told of our intent, and if so, how? Couples may have conflicting feelings about both the separation and the possibility of divorce looming over the horizon.

In the *mid-separation phase*, the realities of daily living set in, such as maintaining two households, arranging visitation for the children, and living on a reduced income. Sometimes couples reconcile simply to avoid these pressures whether or not they have resolved the problems in the relationship. Unresolved problems may then resurface, causing another separation or leading directly to a divorce.

Finally, during the *late separation phase*, a couple must learn to live as two single people. They also must decide on their next step. Not all separated couples divorce; many continue to work on the problems they faced as a married couple and then reconcile successfully. Others remain separated indefinitely but do not divorce because of financial reasons or religious objections. They may file for a **legal separation**, a binding agreement signed by both spouses that provides details about child support. Others may decide that their marital problems can't be solved, and they therefore seek a divorce.

The Stations of Divorce

Divorce doesn't end a relationship between two people alone; it alters or even severs many personal and legal ties. Your divorce may signal the end of your relationships with other family members; with friends who find themselves taking sides; with neighbors whom you will rarely see now that you have moved

Divorce is usually a long process. Sometimes couples separate, reconcile, then separate again before they ultimately divorce.

legal separation: A binding agreement signed by both spouses that provides details about child support.

away; with community groups of which you are no longer a member or can no longer afford to join; or even with your children whom you may see infrequently. Bohannan (1971) refers to the emotional, legal, economic, co-parental, community, and psychic dimensions of divorce as the **stations of divorce.** They're interrelated, and taken together are an attempt to capture the complexity of the divorce experience. We discuss several of these dimensions next.

THE EMOTIONAL DIVORCE

Ending a marriage is extremely difficult emotionally. Divorced individuals, compared with those who are married, have more health problems, experience more depression and anxiety, and have a greater risk of mortality (Kamp Dush, 2013; Hughes & Waite, 2009; Symoens, Bastaits, Mortelmans, & Brache, 2013; Waite, Luo, & Lewin, 2009).

The emotional aspects of divorce begin long before any legal steps are taken, and may end long afterward. One or both partners may feel angry, resentful, sad, or rejected. Generally, one spouse initiates the breakup of the marriage (Hewitt, Western, & Baxter, 2006). Symbolic interaction theory reminds us here of how the interpretation we attach to events affects its meaning. Initiators have the advantage of preparing emotionally for the separation. A common pattern is that an initiator expresses general discontent at first, but without attributing it to the marriage *per se*. They may try to alter the relationship or their spouse's behavior by suggesting such remedies as a new job, having a baby, or some other substantial change to the nature of the relationship. They may even use the threat of leaving as a way to demand change. The other spouse's reaction—anger, resentment, sadness, resolve, or rejection—shapes his or her emotional response.

However, the labels of *initiator* versus *non-initiator* may really be accidental and random (Hopper, 1993). In fact, divorcing spouses sometimes disagree as to who the initiator actually was (Hewitt, Western, & Baxter, 2006; Sweeney, 2002). Hopper found that both spouses were generally aware that they had multiple marital problems, experienced discontent and contemplated divorce or separation, and were ambivalent about the best way to resolve their marital problems (1993).

Many factors influence how men and women experience a divorce, such as the degree of unhappiness and conflict they experience in the marriage, whether they have young children, their ages, and the amount of time they've been married. Men and women often have different emotional challenges following divorce (Blekesaune, 2008). As feminist theory reminds us, society offers men and women different opportunities and constraints that help explain our gendered experiences. For example, women are more likely than men to have financial problems after a divorce, as discussed later (Grall, 2011). In contrast, men often have a more difficult time emotionally after a divorce, and in some cases, this stress is so extreme that it can lead to increased illness or an early death. One reason for this emotional difficulty is that men tend to have a weaker network of supportive relationships (Chu, 2005). Men are also more dependent on marriage, and those who have been in more traditional marriages may find routine household tasks such as cooking, cleaning, and shopping to be daunting. Finally, most men lose custody of their children (Grall, 2011), and for many fathers, this loss in itself is a depressing proposition (Bokker, Farley, & Bailey, 2006; Hawthorne & Lennings, 2008).

In essence, perceived fairness seems to be key. One recent study of more than 700 couples who had been divorced for up to five years found that those people who initiated the divorce or felt they shared the initiation and those who felt that the division was fair and just had better mental health and less depression after the divorce. Interestingly, lengthy divorces or those riddled with conflict were not associated with depression per se (Symoens, Bastaits, Mortelmans, & Bracke, 2013).

LEGAL DIVORCE

A **legal divorce** terminates the marriage contract by a court order of the state. Partners are then legally free to conduct separate lives and to remarry. Although the legal proceedings themselves are very businesslike and may take only a few minutes to conduct, they mask the adversarial nature of most divorces. The couple must divide their assets and property, including their home, cars, savings, and retirement accounts. They must also divide their debts, including credit card debt or loans. If they have children, they must decide whom the children should live with and how often the children should visit the noncustodial parent. They also need a child support agreement.

Few couples can make these decisions easily, and therefore they turn to lawyers to help them. Hiring lawyers to oversee the division of assets and child visitation can cost an average of more than $15,000 (Meyer, 2013). Because a lawyer represents only his or her client's interests, which are not necessarily in the interests of all parties, both sides usually hire their own representation, increasing the drain on the couple's assets.

Some assets are difficult to divide easily. For example, suppose one spouse earned a college degree while the other worked full-time at a low-wage job to put his or her partner through school. How can the couple, or the court, divide this asset—the college degree—which translates into real future earning power? A court in Kentucky in 1979 had such a case before it: *Inman v. Inman*. The couple met while they were university undergraduates, and both intended to go to medical school. Mr. Inman attended medical school first while Ms. Inman supported him, with the understanding that after he received his medical degree, it would be her turn to attend medical school. Instead, the couple separated a year after Mr. Inman finished his studies. In court, Ms. Inman asked that she be awarded compensation for her husband's medical degree, arguing that she had paid for it in the anticipation of joint benefits, but because of the divorce, only Mr. Inman would reap the benefits. After hearing her argument, the court ordered the husband to reimburse her for the costs of his medical school, plus inflation and interest (Weitzman, 1985).

ECONOMIC DIVORCE

In one common stereotype of divorce, a wife runs off with most of the marital assets and takes her ex-husband "to the cleaners." What really happens to the financial well-being of men, women, and children after a divorce?

The economic fallout after a divorce is actually more painful to women and children than it is for men (Gadalla, 2009; Stirling & Aldrich, 2012). A study using a large and nationally representative sample compared men and women's incomes for up to five years during and after divorce or separation (Gadalla, 2008). It found a dramatic decline in women's income, but only a slight decline in men's income during the divorce year—1 in 5 women became impoverished, as compared to only 1 in 13 men. One year later, women's average income was 80 percent of men's, although women remained twice as likely as men to be impoverished. Four years after divorce, women's average income reached 85 percent of men's (Gadalla, 2008; 2009).

The U.S. Census Bureau reports similar findings, as shown in Table 12.1. An average married couple has an annual income of around $76,000, compared to $49,000 for a single male-headed family (no wife present) and only $34,000 for a single female-headed family (no husband present). Female-headed families are twice as likely as male-headed families, and five times as likely as married-couple families to live in poverty (DeNavas-Walt, Proctor, & Smith, 2013).

Why is there such a large income difference after a divorce? After a divorce, fathers become *single*, and mothers become *single parents* (Weitzman, 1985). A

📖 **Read** on **MySocLab**
Document: *Characteristics of Women with Children Who Divorce in Midlife Compared to Those Who Remain Married*

TABLE 12.1	Median Income and Percentage in Poverty by Family Type: 2011	
Married couple households are least likely to be in poverty, whereas single-parent households, especially single-mother households, have higher poverty rates.		
	Median Income	**Percentage in Poverty**
Married Couple Families	$74,130	6.2%
Male Householder, No Wife Present	$49,567	16.1%
Female Householder, No Husband Present	$33,637	31.2%

Source: DeNavas-Walt, Proctor, & Smith, 2013.

What happens to a family's standard of living after a divorce? During the divorce year, women and children's income declines significantly, whereas men experience only slight declines, on average. One in 5 women become impoverished, as compared to only 1 in 13 men.

alimony: Payment by one partner to the other to support the more dependent spouse for a period of time.

legal custody: A custody agreement in which one parent has the legal authority to make important decisions concerning the children after a divorce, such as where they will go to school, in what community or state they will reside, or who will be notified in case of a health emergency or school problem.

sole legal custody: A child custody arrangement in which legal custody is granted solely to the parent with whom the child lives.

joint legal custody: A custody agreement in which noncustodial parents (usually fathers) retain their legal rights with respect to their children.

woman's employment opportunities may be more restricted than those of her ex-husband because the demands of raising children may force her to alter her work schedule; reduce her ability to work overtime; and limit opportunities for the travel, relocation, and further training needed for advancement.

These constraints are further aggravated by the fact that many women have intermittent work histories because they may have decided—by mutual agreement—that the husband would support the family while the wife stayed at home to care for their children. In her book *Opting Out: Why Women Really Quit Careers and Head Home* (2007), author Pamela Stone found that even high-achieving and well-educated women have difficulty balancing work and family because of uncompromising workplaces with excessive hours and unrelenting demands. Women felt pushed out of their jobs by workplaces inhospitable to families.

Yet, after several years of unemployment, some women cannot easily re-enter the labor force. Their skills might be outdated and they can't command high salaries. Still, the law expects both parents to support their children, and mothers must become self-supporting relatively quickly. Some spouses may request **alimony**, a (generally temporary) payment by one partner to the other, usually a husband to a wife (Shehan, Berardo, Owens, & Berardo, 2002). Alimony is designed to support the more dependent spouse for a period of time (Ho & Sussman, 2008). The courts recognize that some people may need some short-term financial assistance, especially if they've been out of the labor market for a period of time while raising children.

However, the difficulty lies in the fact that there are no universal standards for alimony, as there is for child support. For example, a number of states, including Delaware, Illinois and Virginia, end alimony when the recipient cohabitates. Oklahoma is making it more difficult for an ex-spouse to share military retirement pay in a divorce settlement. Rhode Island mandates that alimony is to last for a "reasonable period of time" until the recipient becomes self-supporting, usually about five years. Massachusetts recently passed the Alimony Reform Act, which changes dramatically how maintenance payments are awarded. Along with implementing a formula for calculating alimony awards, the bill terminates alimony when the payer reaches retirement age and places a 12-year limit on payments. It also ends lifetime alimony—something most states have already eliminated or are trying to modify.

Because of all these issues, female-headed households in the United States are often on the economic margins (DeNavas-Walt, Proctor, & Smith, 2013). They would fare quite differently in many other developed nations, including most of Western Europe, where the government intervenes and assists divorced families to a greater extent than in the United States (Warner, 2005).

CO-PARENTAL DIVORCE When the divorcing couple has children, they must try to design and agree on parenting strategies. One crucial issue is the matter of custody. Who has the right to make important decisions about the children's lives, and where will the children live?

The person who has **legal custody** of the children has the legal authority to make important decisions concerning their welfare, such as where they will go to school, in what community or state they will reside, and who will be notified in case of a health emergency or school problem. Legal custody may have nothing to do with a child's living arrangement.

In the past, courts usually gave **sole legal custody** to the parent with whom the child lived, but this trend is changing. Under **joint legal custody**, non-custodial parents (usually fathers) retain their legal rights with respect to their children. One multi-year study of custody issues among 378 divorcing families (Wilcox,

Wolchik, & Braver, 1998) found that mothers were more likely to prefer joint legal custody, as opposed to sole maternal custody, when they were

- experiencing low levels of conflict with their ex-husband
- experiencing low levels of anger/hurt over the divorce
- experiencing fewer visitation problems
- perceiving the ex-husband as more competent as a parent
- experiencing little psychological distress
- receiving social support to maintain the father–child relationship

Fathers with joint legal custody pay more child support, spend more time with their children, and have more overnight visits with them (Seltzer, 1998).

Physical custody refers to the place where the children actually reside. Courts maintain that decisions about living arrangements should be based on the best interests of the child. Theoretically, these decisions should not discriminate against men or women in any systematic way. In more than 82 percent of divorces, however, mothers have **sole physical custody**, meaning that the child legally lives with the mother, and only "visits" the father (Grall, 2011).

Noncustodial fathers often have a poorer and more marginalized relationship with their children than do custodial fathers and their children face added risks (Hawthorne & Lennings, 2008; Peters & Ehrenberg, 2008; Stewart, 2010; Swiss & Le Bourdais, 2009). First, this may be the result of a selection effect: single fathers with custody (or married fathers) may value their relationship with their children more, which is why they sought custody (or remained married) in the first place. Second, the presence of children in the home allows the father a greater sense of control over the children's lives. Third, co-residence may also free the father from the aggravation associated with negotiating future visits. Fourth, living together may encourage fathers to become more involved in their children's lives. For example, a father is available to take his son or daughter to soccer practice and even coach the team.

Today, some families and courts are choosing **joint physical custody**, in which children spend a substantial portion of time in the homes of both parents, perhaps alternating weeks or days within a week (Nielsen, 2011; Spruijt & Duindam, 2010). Joint physical custody is widely supported, yet is also controversial. A survey of college students and other adults report that at least 80 percent believe in shared residential parenting after divorce (Braver, Ellman, Votruba, & Fabricius, 2011). Critics suggest that it disrupts children's routines and school schedules. They claim that it can exacerbate conflict between parents because no two parenting strategies are identical, and that it creates conflicting loyalties within children. However, supporters suggest that it lightens the economic and emotional responsibilities of single parenthood and that it provides men with the opportunity to care for and nurture their children on a routine basis, which is in the child's best interest.

Yet, because this arrangement requires a tremendous amount of cooperation, it tends to work best when both parents want it and are willing to work with one another to provide smooth transitions for the children. It generally works less well when the parents are in conflict, or when one parent believes that the arrangement was foisted on him or her. In fact, equal physical custody is almost never ordered by a judge if either parent objects. In many states, it's not even allowed unless both parents agree to it (Ellman, Kurtz, & Weithorn, 2010).

One review of many different studies that compared children living in sole custody or joint custody two-parent families found that children in joint custody arrangements tend to have less behavior and emotional problems, higher self-esteem, better family relations with their fathers and mothers, and often better school performance than children in sole custody arrangements (Bauserman, 2012; Nielsen, 2011). However, again, this may be the result, at least in part, of a selection effect—that is, couples with more amicable divorces and less overt

physical custody: A child custody arrangement that determines where the child will reside.

sole physical custody: A child custody arrangement in which the child legally lives with one parent and "visits" the other parent.

joint physical custody: A custody agreement in which children spend a substantial portion of time in the homes of both parents, perhaps alternating weeks or days within a week.

More than 200 children a day are kidnapped by a non-custodial parent, often for revenge or other self-serving reasons.

child snatching: The act of a non-custodial parent kidnapping his or her child.

conflict are more likely to choose (and be awarded) joint physical custody.

Some custody situations are contentious. Perhaps one of the most difficult situations to arise from this conflict has to do with a parent abducting a child. According to the U.S. Department of State, **child snatching** is an epidemic, with more than 200 children a day kidnapped by a noncustodial parent (Rigler & Wieder, 2007). Most of these children are under age 3 because they're easy to transport and are less able to complain or report the kidnapping to others.

When a parent kidnaps a child, the parent usually claims that he or she is acting in the best interest of the child; however, few cases actually involve saving the child from a harmful custodial parent. Far more often, child snatching is done for revenge or other self-serving reasons. Most cases of child snatching occur prior to the final court decree that outlines the economic and custody arrangements, and the children are held as pawns. "Searching parents worry and wonder, constantly tormented by this act. It is a revenge far sweeter and longer lived then a beating or even murder, for it never ends" (Rigler & Wieder, 2007).

THE COMMUNITY DIVORCE Marriage joins families and friendship networks; divorce breaks them apart, sometimes in a confusing or bitter fashion. Relationships between former in-laws or friends the couple shared can deteriorate or vanish altogether (Greif & Deal, 2012). Divorced people may feel uncomfortable with their old friends because they are uncertain of their allegiances. Also, their married friends may become reluctant to remain friends with a divorced person because he or she is seen as a threat to their own marriage. Community ties to teachers, neighbors, religious organizations, and children's recreation groups and sports teams can also sever if a parent and children move to a different, perhaps more affordable, neighborhood or school (Braver, Ellman, & Fabricius, 2003).

Divorce can also affect the extended family. One group that has sought legal protection and captured media attention in their quest to maintain ties with children is grandparents (Giles-Sims & Lockhart, 2005). Grandparents are important kin who provide unique benefits to children. Sometimes, grandchild/grandparent relationships are strengthened, as divorcing adults look to their own parents for financial help or childcare. However, in some divorces, the parent may choose to deny even visitation to former in-laws, their children's grandparents. A retired couple, Lola and Bill, lost touch for seven years with their two grandchildren after their daughter divorced her husband and he got custody. "When they came back to us, we had to mourn the children that we lost and we had to start from scratch," Lola said (Navarro, 2007). In her grief-filled years, Lola helped organize the National Committee of Grandparents for Children's Rights, an organization that lobbies for laws to protect children's rights to have contact with their grandparents following a divorce. The organization has had some success, and grandparents can pursue visitation rights in some cases; however, most grandparents are still at the mercy of the custodial parent, and some of the gains grandparents have made have been eroded in state courts on the grounds that grandparental rights' statutes violate parental rights.

THE PSYCHIC DIVORCE As time moves on, most people adjust to the separation and divorce (Gregson & Ceynar, 2009; Thomas & Ryan, 2008). There is no specific time frame for this adjustment, because some people take many months whereas others take many years. The *psychic divorce* refers to the process of

A Poppy in the Rain

Seven years ago in a light summer rain I got married in a meadow of wildflowers. The morning of the wedding, my soon-to-be husband and I went running with our friends, and called it the Dowry Dash. We talked about wearing our running shoes to the wedding, but our friends decided it wouldn't be a good idea, as it would be too easy to run away if one of us got the jitters.

People said rain at a wedding brings lasting happiness. They must be right, because I still feel happy. Today it's cool, gray and raining—just like our wedding day—with the tall grass and willows in the field behind our house generously soaked from the morning's shower.

Things change in seven years. Today I performed a ceremony to say goodbye to my soon-to-be ex-husband, to symbolically put the marriage behind me so I can start my new life. I found a tape of the music played during the wedding. I sat down on the floor and sorted through old photos from races and good times my husband and I had shared with our running friends.

Then I removed the photograph of my husband from the leather frame my sister gave me and replaced it with one of my dog, Joanie, sitting alone, looking windblown and happy. I called Joanie over to show her the picture that will now sit on my desk, and through tears, explained why this was so.

Afterwards I took her for a run in the rain, down to the field on a narrow path, through thick weeds and tiny yellow wildflowers, both of us getting wet from the light drizzle. We stopped momentarily by a ditch, watching the muddy water flow downstream. I imagined the water carrying away my pain, flushing me clean.

Rounding the curve, my eyes caught sight of a beautiful white poppy in the field, several yards off the path. It was the only flower out there in acres of high, green vegetation, and its white color stood out like a single cloud in a clear blue sky.

I ran over to it through the dripping grass, jumping over tall weeds, then bent down to take a closer look. I separated the delicate wet petals with my fingers.

The poppy reminded me of the calla lilies I carried in my wedding; still, it was different. This flower had a genuine, thorny, wild look—the way I've heard people describe me. A bright yellow display of anthers surrounded a five-sided centerpiece of deep maroon. It had a rough, spiky stem and leaves. The livery hairs on the stem gave it a mature, stalwart look.

Standing alone in the rain-soaked meadow, the poppy had been strong enough to weather the morning's downpour; its petal hadn't collapsed. As we ran further away, I could still see it, a brilliant white dot in the carpeted shades of green

The *psychic divorce* is the process of regaining autonomy, feeling whole again, and letting go.

and yellow framed by cottonwood and willow trees. Standing out there in the drenched field, the poppy looked happy—soft yet tough, determined to live among the thick stalks and grasses.

Later, when Joanie and I arrived home, I was still thinking about the flower. I stood on the back doorstep, watching the sun begin to break through the clouds. In the meadow 400 yards away, I could see the poppy, distinct and proud. It was looking upward at the broken sky, its arms outstretched in the rain, smiling confidently, happy to be alive.

WHAT DO YOU THINK?

1. Why are ceremonies and rituals so important?
2. What life changes tend to have rituals associated with them, and which ones don't? Why is that?

Source: Nitzky, 1998.

regaining psychological autonomy and beginning to feel whole and complete again as a single person. As people experience this phase of the divorce, ex-wives and ex-husbands must learn to distance themselves from the still-loved and still-hated aspects of the ex-spouse. Forgiveness is an important predictor of well-being (Rohde-Brown & Rudestam, 2011; Rye, Fleri, Moore, Worthington, Jr., Wade, Sandage, & Cook, 2012), but it often takes years to achieve (Yaben, 2009). The feature box *My Family: A Poppy in the Rain* examines one woman's "letting go" ceremony. It gave her the finality she needed to say goodbye to her ex-spouse.

A Helping Hand: Divorce Mediation

divorce mediation: A non-adversarial means of resolution, in which the divorcing couple, along with a third party, such as a therapist or trained mediator, negotiate the terms of their financial, custody, and visitation settlement.

Given that divorce touches so many aspects of our lives, how can a divorcing couple sort through all the decisions they must make? Many divorce settlements are reached through informal negotiation rather than through the courts (Lowenstein, 2009; Stoner, 2009). **Divorce mediation** is a non-adversarial means of resolution in which the divorcing couple, along with a third party, such as a therapist or trained mediator, negotiate the terms of their financial, custody, and visitation settlement (Katz, 2007). When couples decide to mediate, they choose to work as a team to resolve all of their divorce issues, avoiding the expensive and demoralizing court process that can exacerbate differences between the divorcing parties.

The couple and the mediator meet in a series of sessions, usually lasting one to two hours. In the first session, the couple and the mediator identify the issues that must be discussed, the order in which they will be addressed, and what information should be gathered and shared. Further meetings revolve around how to compromise on the various issues that were identified to best meet the needs of both parties and their children (Law and Mediation Offices of David L. Price, 2000).

How long mediation lasts really depends on how contentious the divorce is, whether the couple has children, and the size of their assets. Couples can be in mediation for a few weeks or even a few years. Once an agreement is reached by a mediating couple and filed with the court, it has the same force and effect as an order made by the court. Either party can go to the court and ask for its help in enforcing the agreement. An alternative option would be to return to mediation. Sometimes an amendment to the agreement, acceptable to both parties, solves the problem (Thomas, 2008).

Of all the dimensions of divorce— legal, economic, co-parental, community, and psychic—which do you think are most challenging to adults, and why? Which are most challenging to children, and why? Are these dimensions different?

Although mediation is a relatively new process that emerged only in the past few decades, couples who go through mediation are more likely to be happy with the process and results (Thomas, 2008), although men are more likely to experience initial reluctance than are women (Przybyla-Basista, 2008).

12.4 Summarize issues surrounding child support

Question That Matters

12.9 How common is child support and alimony?

child support order: A legal document delineating the amount and circumstances of the financial support of noncustodial children.

Divorce and Children: Child Support

Non-custodial parents have a legal responsibility to support their children. For much of U.S. history, these payments were arranged privately between former spouses; the noncustodial parent (usually the father) negotiated a **child support order** with the mother, a legal document delineating the amount and circumstances of the financial support of noncustodial children. Not surprisingly, the amount of these awards varied widely, even among similar types of families. In the past, the administrative authority for child support was left to the local courts, and an individual judge had the power to decide whether the noncustodial father should be required to pay and the amount of the payment. Enforcement was minimal; usually the burden of attempting to collect overdue payments was left to the mother.

Since then, the federal government has stepped up its efforts to improve the collection of child support payments. Congress passed laws to increase the proportion of children who were eligible for child support, to increase and standardize child support orders, and to improve collection rates (Garfinkel, Meyer, & McLanahan, 1998). Furthermore, strong child support enforcement

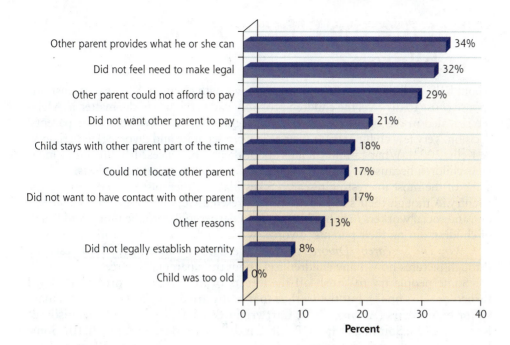

FIGURE 12.4
Reasons No Legal Child Support Agreement Established for Custodial Parents: 2010

Millions of parents have no legal child support agreement for any of the reasons shown.
Source: Grall, 2011.

increases fathers' involvement with their children (Nepomnyaschy & Garfinkel, 2007).

How successful have these governmental efforts been? Unfortunately, overall trends in child support haven't improved much. Only about half of custodial parents have a court order or some type of agreement to receive financial support from the noncustodial parent. When custodial parents without any agreements and those with informal agreements were asked why a formal legal agreement was not established, the two reasons most often cited were that they didn't feel the need to go to court to get legal agreements and that the non-custodial parent provided what he or she could afford, as shown in Figure 12.4 (Grall, 2011).

Of those custodial parents with an agreement in 2009, 29 percent still received no child support payment, and another 30 percent only received a partial payment, as shown in Table 12.2 (Grall, 2011). In 2009, the average amount of child support due was $5,955, but the average amount received was $3,634. This contributes to the low economic status of divorced women.

Fewer than half of children who are owed child support receive the full amount from their non-custodial parent. What, if anything, should the government do about fathers and mothers who don't pay their child support? How can the courts encourage them to make their payment, and what should be the consequences if they fail to pay?

TABLE 12.2	Child Support Receipt for Custodial Parents: 1993 and 2009	
Child support receipt has not improved over the years.		
	1993	**2009**
No Child Support Received	24%	29%
Received Any Child Support	76%	71%
Received Full Amount	37%	47%
Received Partial Payment	39%	30%
Average Child Support Due	$4,490	$5,955
Average Child Support Received	$2,920	$3,634

Source: Grall, 2011.

👁 **Watch** on **MySocLab**
Video: *Kathleen Gerson: Family Stability*

What Are the Effects of Divorce on Children?

About half of all divorce cases occur in families with children. Whereas at least one spouse *chose* to divorce, the children probably had no choice in the matter, as Melanie revealed in the opening vignette. These children must live with their parents' decision. Very few children want their parents to separate and divorce (Hetherington & Kelly, 2003). What can they tell us about their experiences? It's difficult to interview children because of a fear that an interview will have harmful effects. Perhaps some of the most interesting research takes place in therapists' offices around the country. Although their samples are not representative, therapists, family counselors, and social workers may be able to offer a deeper look into the minds and hearts of children during their parents' divorce. What do their stories reveal? The feature box *Why Do Research? Divorce through the Eyes of Children* (p. 365) describes through pictures how many children feel about their parents' divorce.

Some people try to brush off the effects of their parents' divorce ("Hey, I turned out just fine"), but the truth is that many are deeply affected, and remain so for many years (Amato, 2007; Cartwright & McDowell, 2008; Dennison & Koerner, 2008; South, 2013; Yu, Pettit, Landsford, Dodge, & Bates, 2010). Some factors that influence the consequences of divorce on children are micro-level ones, such as personal coping skills or their relationship with their (usually) noncustodial father; others are more macro in nature, such as their mother's economic situation. Because the interweaving of factors is complex, it may be helpful to distinguish between short-term and long-term effects.

Short-Term Effects

The first year or two after a divorce can be particularly difficult for both adults and children because of grief and the numerous transitions they face (Ricci, 2007). During this highly stressful time, parents may be distracted and preoccupied with their own grief and distress, thereby making it more difficult to be an effective parent (Taylor & Andrews, 2009). While in the midst of this crisis period, parents may not be able to offer the support, nurturing, and discipline that their children need. Some, in fact, turn to their children for comfort and support (Afifi, Afifi, & Coho, 2009; Koerner, Jacobs, & Raymond, 2004). Although this can, at times, lead to closer and more intimate relationships between parents and their children, sometimes it involves putting a child into an adult role that may be well beyond his or her years. The healthiest children are those with at least one parent who practiced an authoritative parenting style (Campana, Henderson, Stolberg, & Schum, 2008). Yet, divorcing parents sometimes minimize the effects of divorce on their children, especially those parents who initiated the divorce, and assume that their children are just fine (Moon, 2011).

Sometimes children's difficulties occur before as well as after the divorce. In one study that was based on a large and nationally representative sample, researchers examined children's academic performance and psychological well-being before and after their parents' divorce, and compared these results with their peers in families whose parents didn't divorce (Sun & Li, 2002). On average, children whose parents divorced had poorer academic performance and lower levels of psychological well-being both before and after the divorce as compared to the other children.

During this time, children are also grieving the loss of their intact family and dealing with new feelings and fears (Ricci, 2007). Young children in particular are egocentric, and may feel that they are responsible for their parents' conflict and divorce—that if they had just behaved better, their parents wouldn't have felt the need to separate. They may not have the maturity to describe the guilt and sadness they feel.

In the crisis period, children generally face a number of situations that they must learn to cope with, like Melanie, in the chapter-opening vignette. These may

Research is clear about the effects of divorce on children. Survey data tell us that for many children, divorce can be very unsettling. But what do children tell us about their experiences? It's difficult to interview children—human subjects committees closely safeguard children, worried that interviews may have harmful effects. Perhaps some of the most interesting research is done in the office of therapists around the country.

Although a far cry from representative samples, therapists and family counselors may be able to offer a deeper look into the minds and hearts of children during their parents' divorce. How do children really feel about their parents' divorce? These pictures represent a sample of the thousands of stories children tell to their therapists.

include (1) parental conflict; (2) the loss of a parent; (3) living with a reduced standard of living; and (4) adjusting to many transitions, possibly including a new home and a new school, or even a new stepfamily. If your parents divorced, consider how you experienced these issues and how you dealt with them.

PARENTAL CONFLICT   Sometimes parents involve children in their disputes by trying to use them as a weapon to hurt the ex-spouse, getting them to take sides in a dispute, or using them as a way to find out information. Parents may communicate their anger and hostility toward one another to their children, demeaning

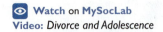

Watch on MySocLab
Video: *Divorce and Adolescence*

and ridiculing their ex-spouse. These situations cause children tremendous stress and lead to depression (Michael, Torres, & Seemann, 2007; Turunen, 2013). During and after a break-up, children have fewer health, emotional, and behavioral problems if their parents can cooperate or at least minimize overt conflict in front of them (Ahrons, 2005; Bing, Nelson, & Wesolowski, 2009).

LOSS OF A PARENT   During a separation and after a divorce, children most often live with their mothers and many children see their fathers only sporadically, if at all. Somewhere between 15 and 40 percent of children haven't seen their noncustodial parent over the course of a year; the figure is highest for children whose parents have never married, and somewhat lower for children whose parents have divorced (Koball & Principe, 2002). Yet the research continues to show that fathers are extremely important to their children's lives (Booth, Scott, & King, 2010; Hawkins, Amato, & King, 2007; Lundberg, McLanahan, & Rose, 2007). Children whose fathers are more involved in their lives are less likely to have behavioral problems, including delinquency and depression (Carlson, 2006). Fathers provide important social capital, in addition to love and material support. Moreover, noncustodial fathers who have frequent contact with their children during their younger years often have closer relationships with them as they mature into adulthood as well (Aquilino, 2006).

Why do so many noncustodial fathers fail to see their children regularly? The issue is more complex than you might think. Certainly many fathers *choose* to ignore their children, but the residential parent (generally the mother) is a gatekeeper (Trinder, 2008), and she may also interfere with the relationship between father and children in different ways:

- not supporting access
- not cooperating in arranging visits
- being inflexible about altering visitation schedules
- discouraging children from visiting (Pearson & Thoennes, 1998).

A REDUCED STANDARD OF LIVING   As we've discussed, the standard of living for mothers and their children often declines considerably after a divorce. Everyone in the family must adjust to a lower income. Certain types of clothing, outings, vacations, or other aspects of a family's lifestyle that were the norm before the divorce may no longer be possible. Given the severely limited budgets of most divorced families, consumption patterns must change drastically. Teenagers may need to work at after-school jobs to provide basic necessities for the family.

A divorce brings many transitions into the lives of children and their parents. Sometimes the family home is sold, which may require moving to a new neighborhood, attending a new school, and making new friends, leaving the familiar behind.

ADJUSTING TO TRANSITIONS   After a divorce, both children and adults must go through many transitions, and these transitions are often difficult for the child (Beck, Cooper, McLanahan, & Brooks-Gunn, 2010; Kelly, 2007; Sun & Li, 2009). The departure of one parent is likely to be only the first of many transitions to come. If the legal settlement requires that assets be divided, then the family's home may have to be sold, necessitating a move to a new house or apartment. For children, this may mean adjusting to new schools, new neighborhoods, and new friends, while leaving behind all that was familiar. Children must also adapt to a visitation schedule with the noncustodial parent and adjust to seeing that parent in unfamiliar surroundings. A study of college students found that about half of the students saw their parents' divorce coming, but for others it came as a shock. They reported that the divorce caused them particular difficulty over the holidays (Bulduc, Caron, & Logue, 2006).

Over time, both parents are likely to resume dating, and children will meet their parents' new partners. Cohabitation is increasingly common, so many children must also adapt to other adults moving in (and out) of the household. Finally, because most single parents eventually remarry, children will likely experience stepparent relationships. These issues are discussed more fully in Chapter 13.

Longer-Term Effects

Often, children continue to feel the effects of their parents' divorce for years after the actual divorce. Although most children adjust adequately over time to the transitions in their lives, some are plagued by depression or other behavioral problems. In the 1970s and early 1980s, Wallerstein and colleagues conducted a longitudinal study of 60 families in the San Francisco area who had experienced a divorce, interviewing them in depth, and following them for 25 years (Wallerstein, 1983; Wallerstein & Blakeslee, 1989). This is a small and non-representative sample, and we should therefore be careful about interpreting and generalizing the results; however, it's one of the few studies that followed people over many years and obtained detailed accounts of their experiences. Their findings are thought-provoking, if not definitive, and have set the stage for later research. The researchers found that many years following a divorce, more than one-third of the (now adult) children were still depressed and suffering from a number of behavioral problems related to the divorce.

Since the results of the Wallerstein study were published, other researchers have also found that parental divorce often has long-term effects for many children (Ängarne-Lindberg, Wadsby, & Berterö, 2009; Gahler & Garriga, 2012; Sun & Li, 2008a; Whitton, Rhoades, Stanley, & Markman, 2008). Children whose parents divorce are more likely to become pregnant or impregnate others prior to marriage, drop out of school, use alcohol or drugs, and be idle or unemployed. They're more likely to have behavioral problems, experience depression, and have overall poorer health. They also express some degree of anxiety about their own future marriages (Dennison & Koerner, 2008; Uphold-Carrier & Utz, 2012).

For example, one study based on representative samples containing more than 35,000 adults compared outcomes of children who grew up in single-mother families because of divorce or widowhood to children in families with two biological parents (Biblarz & Gottainer, 2000). They found that—even controlling for important background factors such as race, sex, mother's level of education, year, and age—children from single-mother homes produced by parental divorce were significantly less likely than those from families with two biological parents to complete high school, attend college (given high school completion), or graduate from college (given college entry). They also held occupations that are generally lower in status, and they had a lower level of psychological well-being. In contrast, children from widowed single-mother homes didn't differ significantly from families with two biological parents on any of these variables, except having slightly lower odds of completing high school.

More recently, another study of about 9,000 teens followed for 12 years into adulthood assessed the impact of their parents' divorce on their income and earnings (Sun & Li, 2008). Like others, this study also found that children whose parents divorced achieved, on average, lower educational credentials and lower incomes. Some of this difference may be explained by their own parents' lower levels of education and income as compared to others, but some difference remains, which the researchers attribute to divorce. In particular, they found that those children who were in unstable living situations after the divorce (e.g., first a single-parent household, then a stepparent household) seemed to fare worse than those children whose lives were more stable after the divorce.

AGE AND SEX OF THE CHILD The ages of children at the time of their parents' divorce and their sex seem to be important factors in understanding their adjustment. Divorce may be most difficult for school-age children, who may experience a greater number of transitions with school and friendships during their parents' changes from marriage to separation, divorce, cohabitation, and remarriage (Cavanagh & Huston, 2008). Boys may experience more difficulty than girls; they're more likely to do poorly in school, and are more likely to be aggressive, anxious, lonely and easily distracted in the classroom, particularly if they have little contact with their fathers (Cavanagh & Huston, 2008; UNH Cooperative Extension, 2006).

Others have found that the effects of divorce aren't very different for boys and girls (Schoppe-Sullivan, Schermerhorn, & Cummings, 2007). There might be a *sleeper effect* among girls, meaning that their behavioral problems are simply delayed until adolescence or adulthood. Some girls and young women whose parents had divorced seemed to have a lingering sadness about the divorce, and were hesitant and fearful of making a commitment themselves.

✳ **Explore** on **MySocLab**
Activity: *The Difficulty of Divorce*

A WORD OF CAUTION We should be aware of two points, however. First, these findings certainly don't mean that *all* children from divorced households experience these outcomes. Many children whose parents have divorced lead happy, well-adjusted, and successful lives (Harvey & Fine, 2004). You know many of these people; you may even *be* one of these people. The research indicates only that there is a correlation: Children whose parents have divorced are more likely to have these problems than are children from families in which parents haven't divorced. In fact, many of these negative outcomes are related to the higher rates of poverty among children growing up in divorced households and are far less likely to occur if the family has adequate financial resources.

The second point we should keep in mind is that it may be the transitions associated with divorce, rather than divorce itself, that are problematic for children (Amato, 2005; Cavanagh & Huston, 2008; Teachman, 2008). Changes associated with separation, divorce, cohabitation, and remarriage—such as moving, going to a new school, making new friends, losing pets, and having people move out of and into the household—can be stressful to children and weaken their sense of security.

If you had children and then later got divorced, how would you minimize the impact of divorce on your children? Think about both short-term and long-term effects.

Which Is Worse for Children—Divorce or Marital Conflict?

> At this point in life, I'm almost positive that I'll never get married. . . . I'm just so disillusioned by the whole concept. I don't think my parents' divorce has affected me negatively that much. Their marriage, however, has screwed me up more than I'll probably ever know. (Harvey & Fine, 2004, p. ix)

The question that people want the answer to is, "Are children better off when their parents remain unhappily married, or are they better off when their parents divorce?" The answer isn't simple, because it depends on many things, especially the *severity of the conflict* in the marriage.

Children don't fare well when there is tremendous conflict in their parents' marriage (Cummings, Schermerhorn, Goeke-Morey, & Cummings, 2006; Kaczynski, Lindahl, Malik, & Laurenceau, 2006; Michael, Torres, & Seemann, 2007). This is true regardless of whether parents divorce or remain married. In fact, many researchers suggest that it's the amount and intensity of conflict (e.g., violence, verbal abuse, spiteful behaviors) rather than a divorce *per se* that causes the most harm to children. For example, a longitudinal study, based on telephone and in-person interviews conducted in 1980 and then again in 1992, found that children in families with high marital conflict in 1980 actually were doing *better* in 1992 if their parents had divorced than if they had stayed together (Amato & Booth, 1997). They also found that children from low-conflict families were *worse* off if their parents had divorced. These findings suggest that the worst situations for children are to be in either (1) a high-conflict marriage that doesn't end in divorce or (2) a low-conflict marriage that does end in divorce. Other research tends to support this claim (Strohschein, 2005).

However, it's important to note that many—and perhaps most—couples who divorce don't experience extreme forms of conflict or distress (Amato & Hohmann-Marriott, 2007). Only one-quarter of parents in the study who divorced between 1980 and 1992 reported any sort of domestic violence or reported that they disagreed "often" or "very often" with their spouse. In fact, only 30 percent reported at least two serious quarrels during the previous month. Consequently, the researchers concluded that the majority of children whose parents divorced probably experienced relatively low conflict and therefore would have been better off if their parents had stayed together (Amato & Booth, 1997).

People wonder whether it is better for children if unhappy parents stay married or get divorced. Much of the answer depends on how much conflict there is in the home.

Should Divorce Be More Difficult to Obtain?

12.6 Analyze whether divorce should be made more difficult to obtain

Some people believe that divorce should be more difficult to obtain (Kapinus & Flowers, 2008; Martin & Parashar, 2006). What do you think about divorce? Take a look at the self-quiz in the *Getting to Know Yourself* feature box and compare your answers to those of your friends or partner.

Question That Matters

12.12 Are people happier when they divorce?

"Would I Be Happier?"

People who divorce do so because they believe they will be happier afterward. But this belief isn't necessarily valid (Amato & Hohmann-Marriott, 2007). A research team headed by Linda Waite of the University of Chicago used data collected by the National Survey of Families and Households (NSFH), based on a large nationally representative sample of adults in the United States (Waite & Gallagher, 2000). Out of more than 5,000 married adults, 645 reported being unhappily married. Waite's research focused on these unhappily married people, who were interviewed again five years later. By then, some had divorced. The researchers used detailed measures of psychological well-being to compare those who had stayed married to those who had divorced. Were the divorced people happier?

The study found that, on average, the people in the divorced group were no happier than those who remained married. First, divorce didn't reduce or eliminate feelings of depression, raise self-esteem, or increase a sense of mastery. This was the case regardless of income, race, sex, or age. Second, the researchers also found that two-thirds of those who stayed married over the five years reported that their marriages had improved. Interestingly, those who were in the least happy marriages at the time of the first interview reported the most dramatic turnaround.

Why didn't divorce make people happier? The study authors suggest that while divorce eliminates some stresses, it creates new ones as well that can have

The self-quiz below assesses your opinions about divorce and the difficulty or ease with which you believe it should be obtained. Please answer T if you think the statement is mostly true or if you mostly agree with it, and F if you think the statement is mostly false or if you mostly disagree with it. You may want to compare your answers to those of your partner, family members, friends, or classmates.

1. Marriage is forever and the bonds should never be broken.   T   F

2. I think no-fault divorce has been a good thing for our society because people should be allowed to get divorced if they are not happy.   T   F

3. I think divorce is harmful to many children.   T   F

4. My religion considers divorce to be a sin.   T   F

5. I think people who want a divorce should be required to see a counselor for several sessions before the divorce is granted.   T   F

6. Divorce should be more difficult to obtain if you have children.   T   F

7. I think divorce should be available to anyone based on irreconcilable differences.   T   F

8. I cannot imagine ever getting divorced.   T   F

9. Single parents can do just as good a job of raising children as can two-parent families.   T   F

10. Divorce is detrimental to our society.   T   F

SCORING

Give yourself 1 point for every T for questions 1, 3, 4, 5, 6, 8, and 10. Give yourself 1 point for every F for questions 2, 7, and 9. Add up your points. The higher your score, the more likely you think that divorce should be more difficult to obtain.

WHAT DO YOU THINK?

1. Can you identify any micro-level and macro-level factors that have influenced your opinions?
2. How do your answers compare to others? Are you surprised by the differences or similarities? Why or why not?

negative consequences. These include the reactions of children; potential disappointments and aggravations in custody, child support, and visitation orders; new financial stresses; or health problems.

To follow up on the finding that two-thirds of unhappy marriages had become happier five years later, the researchers also conducted focus group interviews with 55 formerly unhappy spouses who had turned their marriages around (Waite & Gallagher, 2000). Many of these couples had experienced periods of serious family problems in their marriage, including alcoholism, infidelity, verbal abuse, neglect, depression, illness, or work problems. Most of these couples didn't see divorce as a quick fix to their problems, and they had family and friends who encouraged them to stay married. Because of this, they invested great effort in overcoming or enduring problems in their relationships. Their stories fell into three broad types:

- *The marital endurance ethic:* Most commonly, couples reported that their marriages got happier not just because partners resolved problems, but because they stubbornly outlasted them. Over time, many of the sources of conflict ceased.

- *The marital work ethic:* Some spouses actively worked to solve problems, change their behavior, and improve their communication. They enlisted help or advice from others, including counselors or clergy. They may have rearranged their work or family schedules to attack the problem and to spend more time together.

- *The personal happiness ethic:* For these persons, the marriage problems did not diminish appreciably; however, they found alternative ways to improve their own happiness. They built a happy life despite an unhappy marriage.

Covenant Marriage

As you learned in Chapter 7, there is a growing marriage movement designed to promote and protect traditional marriage. Although much of this movement is rooted in religious communities, it has also produced political change (Maher, 2006). For example, Georgia now allows no-fault divorce only if both parties agree to the divorce and if no children are involved. Oklahoma spent $10 million on an initiative to reduce divorce by 30 percent by 2010. In three states—Arizona, Arkansas, and Louisiana—a covenant marriage is now legal. This type of marriage demands premarital counseling and an oath of lifelong commitment, and makes divorce more difficult to obtain by requiring counseling and offering only limited grounds for divorce, such as adultery, addiction, or imprisonment.

Many people support each of these ideals in principle. Nine in ten adults surveyed believe that partners should agree to seek counseling if they are unable to resolve problems. However, taken together, less than half of adults support covenant marriage. Moreover, only about 2 percent of new marriages in Louisiana, and even fewer in Arizona and Arkansas, are covenant marriages (Stritof & Stritof, 2006).

*P*rofessor Waite's research found that some people stay married despite being in an unhappy marriage because they find alternative ways to be happy; they build a happy life despite an unhappy marriage. What do you think of this approach? Could you ever see yourself in this situation? Why or why not?

The "Good Divorce"

12.7 Illustrate a "good divorce"

Question That Matters

12.13 What is meant by a *good divorce*?

My parents got divorced when I was twelve and my brother was eight. I felt sad at first, and a little embarrassed because my friends' parents all seemed happily married. But, you know, it was okay. We technically lived with my mom, but my dad was always there for us. We stayed with him a lot, whenever we wanted to. He still took my brother and me to our ball games and celebrated our birthdays at the house. I never heard my mom complain about child support, so I guess he paid everything he was supposed to. I don't really know; they didn't involve me in those kinds of things. I think he and my mom really tried hard to get along for our sake. And it seemed to work most of the time. My brother and I always felt loved and cared for.

—**Krish, Age 29**

Some couples have what has been nicknamed a *good divorce*, meaning they remain amicable, avoid serious conflict, work diligently to preserve family ties, and remain committed to their children's happiness and well-being.

Some couples part with respect and dignity, and work cooperatively to raise their children. For them, divorce represents a major change in family functioning, but not a devastating one (Ängarne-Lindberg, Wadsby, & Berterö, 2009; Hakvoort, Bos, Ban Balen, & Hermanns, 2011; McGene & King, 2012). For her book *The Good Divorce* (1994), family scholar Constance Ahrons interviewed nearly 100 divorcing couples over a five-year period in one region of Wisconsin to determine the ways in which they functioned after the divorce. She found that about half of the couples had a "good divorce," meaning they remained amicable toward one another, avoided serious conflict, and worked diligently to preserve family ties. They remained committed to their children and continued to be responsible for their children's emotional, economic, and physical well-being. Some even celebrated holidays together or went together on outings with their children. Ahrons used the term **binuclear families** to describe divorced parents who live in two households, but remain one family in spirit because of their children. Her respondents didn't always find it easy to remain on good terms, however, partly because there are so few role models of good behavior, as discussed in Chapter 13.

Years later, Ahrons interviewed the children of her divorced respondents to see how they fared (Ahrons, 2005). She located about 90 percent of the children, who were then in their 30s. About three-quarters of these adult children believed their parents' divorce was a good idea, and thought that they and their parents were better off for it. In particular, parents who

Have you ever known anyone who had a good divorce? What factors made this resolution possible for them? What factors seem to prevent other divorcing couples from having a good divorce?

binuclear family: A type of family consisting of divorced parents living in two separate households but remaining one family in spirit for the sake of the children.

made the effort to have a good divorce and maintain family bonds had children who felt stronger and more secure in their lives. Her results remind us that divorce doesn't have to be a devastating event for children.

A good divorce may not always be possible, but research suggests that it should be the model to strive for because children fare better after divorce when both parents remain involved in and committed to their lives (Gasper, Stolberg, Macie, & Williams, 2008).

Bringing It Full Circle

Divorce is common in American society, although the divorce rate has declined significantly over the past several decades. The fluctuating divorce rate has many macro-level and micro-level explanations, which are interrelated because macro-level factors shape our personal experiences and choices. As we saw in the opening vignette, conflict and divorce affect many relationships within the family, and families must sort through the emotional, legal, economic, co-parental, community, and psychic dimensions of separation and divorce. Children like Melanie are particularly affected by conflict and divorce, and they're more likely than other children to experience social and emotional challenges. Programs like mediation can offer a helping hand as couples move through the process of divorce. But, as we'll see in the next chapter, sometimes divorce doesn't just end a relationship. With high rates of remarriage, it can also mean the beginning of a new family unit. Let's return a moment to Melanie's experience with her parents' divorce in the opening vignette. With the information you've learned in this chapter, consider the following questions:

- How would you describe Melanie's experiences with the different stations of her parents' divorce: emotional, legal, economic, co-parental, community, and psychic?

- Because the research shows that children do better if they remain in close contact with their noncustodial parents, should children like Melanie be required to stay with their fathers even if they don't really want to?

- Do you think that Melanie's family had a good divorce? Explain your answer.

- If you or someone close to you divorced, how would you explain it to your child? Would you focus only on micro-level issues, or would any macro-level issues be relevant?

On MySocLab

✓ Study and Review on MySocLab

CHAPTER REVIEW

LO12.1 Discuss divorce in the United States

12.1 What is the best way to calculate the divorce rate?

Many different methods are used to calculate the divorce rate. Some of them are misleading. The two best methods are the *crude divorce rate* and *the refined divorce rate*.

12.2 Is the rate of divorce in the United States currently increasing?

No. Although the rate of divorce in the United States has varied over the years, it has been declining since 1980 with an upturn very recently, which may reflect an increase in divorce, or simply a change in reporting methods.

LO12.2 Analyze the macro- and micro-level reasons why people divorce

12.3 What kinds of micro-level factors influence divorce?

Micro-level factors associated with divorce include whether one's parents had divorced, age at marriage, the presence of children, non-marital childbearing, the sex of children, race and ethnic background, education, income, degree of similarity between spouses, and the age of the couple.

12.4 What kinds of macro-level factors influence divorce?

Macro-level factors associated with divorce include a country's level of socioeconomic development, the most widely practiced religion, divorce laws, the status of women, and the general attitudes toward divorce.

LO12.3 Recognize how people experience divorce

12.5 What are the phases of a separation?

In the first phase of a marital separation, *pre-separation*, one or both partners begin to think about the benefits of a separation. During the *early separation phase*, couples face a series of issues as they separate. Who will be the one to move out? How shall we work out financial matters, such as the house payment, the car payment, and other bills? In the *mid-separation phase*, the realities of daily living set in, such as maintaining two households, arranging visitation for the children, and living on a reduced income.

12.6 How is divorce experienced differently by women and men?

The different opportunities and constraints for men and women that are embedded in our culture can result in different experiences for men and women during a divorce. For example, women are more likely to report marital problems. They are also more likely to be impoverished after a divorce.

12.7 What are the *stations of divorce*?

The stations of divorce describe six important components of the divorce experience: the emotional, legal, economic, co-parental, community, and psychic divorce.

12.8 What is *divorce mediation*?

Divorce mediation is a non-adversarial means of resolution in which the divorcing couple, along with a third party, such as a therapist or trained mediator, negotiate the terms of their financial, custody, and visitation settlement. When couples decide to mediate, they choose to work as a team to resolve their divorce issues, avoiding the lengthy and often adversarial court process.

LO12.4 Summarize issues surrounding child support

12.9 How common is child support and alimony?

Most divorcing couples with children have a child support order that outlines the amount of monthly support, its duration, and other specific features of the arrangement. However, despite the order, many noncustodial parents fail to maintain their full payment on a regular basis. Alimony is a payment to the spouse.

LO12.5 Identify the effects of divorce on children

12.10 What are the short-term and long-term consequences of divorce for children?

A growing number of research studies suggest that divorce can be more harmful for children than previously thought. In the short term, children must learn to deal with parental conflict, the loss of a parent, a reduced standard of living, and adjusting to many transitions. Over the long term, many, but not all, children suffer emotionally, socially, and academically when their parents divorce.

12.11 Is it better for children if their parents stay in an unhappy marriage or get a divorce?

In marriages with a high degree of conflict, children may be better off if their parents divorce. In marriages with less conflict between spouses, which make up the majority of divorce situations, it may be better for the children if their parents stay married.

LO12.6 Analyze whether divorce should be made more difficult to obtain

12.12 Are people happier when they divorce?

One large study of unhappily married people followed them over five years and found that those who divorced were no happier than those who remained married. For example, divorce didn't reduce or eliminate feelings of depression, raise self-esteem, or increase a sense of mastery, regardless of income, race, sex, or age. The researchers also found that two-thirds of those who stayed married over the five years reported that their marriages had improved. Interestingly, those who were in the least happy marriages at the time of the first interview reported the most dramatic turnaround.

LO12.7 Illustrate a "good divorce"

12.13 What is meant by a *good divorce*?

Not all divorces represent the same degree of crisis and disorganization. For example, when both parents make a concerted effort to get along and co-parent, the negative effects of divorce can be reduced considerably or even eliminated.

KEY TERMS

alimony
binuclear family
child snatching
child support order
crude divorce rate
divorce mediation

intergenerational transmission of divorce
joint legal custody
joint physical custody
legal custody
legal divorce
legal separation

no-fault divorce
physical custody
refined divorce rate
sole legal custody
sole physical custody
stations of divorce

Family Life, Partnering, and Remarriage after Divorce

 Listen to Chapter 13 on **MySocLab**

We hear a lot about the negative aspects of "broken homes" or "wicked stepmothers."

But can't good things come of divorce, repartnering, and blending families?

Daneen and Jim each had two children from previous marriages when they married.

👁 **Watch** on **MySocLab**
Video: *Remarriage and Blending Families: Daneen and Jim*

Daneen and Jim show us what is possible after a divorce. They met, fell in love, and gave careful consideration to what the future could hold in store. Each had a son and daughter from a previous marriage. They wanted the best for their children and for themselves. After much thought, Jim and Daneen decided to marry when Daneen's children—Connor, 10, and Kate, 8—and Jim's children—Lindsay, 14, and Jamie, 10—were adolescents. Five years later, Daneen and Jim, as well as their four children, believe they have successfully blended their families. Both Daneen and Jim consider all the children to be "their own."

Their path to success wasn't completely smooth, however. It was a big adjustment for both families. For example, Jamie worried that this new woman and her family would take away his time with his father. His dad was his rock, especially because he rarely saw his own mother, who lives in another state. Jamie was very cautious, not ready to trust Daneen. It took some time, but the barriers are down now, and Daneen and Jamie are very close. She has become the mother that he never really had. Meanwhile, Daneen's own son Connor, whose father lives nearby, also had some difficulty adjusting to their blended family. He worried about his father's feelings, fearing that his father would be upset by his ex-wife getting remarried, but they too have worked through these concerns.

As a stepmom, Daneen feels that she always tries to treat the kids equally. Although Jamie and Lindsay sometimes tease her about being "stepmonster," Jamie maintains that Daneen is always fair. Daneen worried at first about how she would manage with a teenage stepdaughter, but she feels that she and Lindsay have really connected. And Kate, the youngest of the four children, adores her older stepsister. Kate is still working through some conflicted feelings for her stepfather Jim, however. Because she spent her early years without a father in the home, she can still put up a "wall" at times with Jim.

Despite some initial tensions, the four children have been able to bond. Being fairly close in age helps; in fact, Jamie's and Connor's birthdays are only 2 weeks apart. They share academic and athletic interests, although they have distinctive personalities. One important way that the children have bonded is through helping one another cope with some of the disappointments they each face with their noncustodial parents.

Jim and Daneen believe their children value the stability of their home life. Dinners together are an important ritual. Jim and Daneen place a high value on open communication, and will call family meetings as needed to sort things out. Blending two families takes work, but Jim, Daneen, Lindsay, Jamie, Connor, and Kate will all vouch that it is worth it.

After divorce, many relationships change. Severing a marriage allows each partner to go his or her own way and to begin anew. Their paths may involve a new job, different housing, a new network of friends, and finding a more compatible partner. And for better or worse, other family dynamics also change. For example, custodial parents and their children, especially their daughters, often become very close (Frank, 2008), while noncustodial parents and their children can sometimes drift apart (Krampe & Newton, 2012; Lin, 2008).

This chapter focuses on families after a divorce. It reveals how families reorganize themselves and highlights some of the challenges and strengths that this reorganization can bring. We will also explore issues surrounding repartnering and remarriage, as most divorced couples, like Daneen and Jim, cohabit or remarry. Often these couples have children, creating complex blended families with new sets of challenges and opportunities.

Being Single Again

Chapter 12 showed that divorce can be an emotionally complex and difficult experience. However, for most people, a divorce can also serve as a new beginning or a new "lease on life" that provides a second (or third or fourth) chance to develop intimate relationships and meaningful family ties. Whereas some family relationships are severed and others strained, other family relationships may blossom.

The Emotional Effects of Divorce

We learned in Chapter 12 that unhappily married people who divorce aren't always happier afterwards than those unhappily married couples who remain married. However, other surveys report that people who divorce are generally glad they took that step. This isn't a contradiction in terms; most people interviewed after their divorce have few regrets and say it was the right decision for them. This doesn't mean their lives are completely happy now, or that they initiated or even wanted the divorce at the time. Rather, reflecting back and weighing the pros and cons, most people decided divorce was the right decision. As one man said, "It was rough going at first when my wife left me. I thought that my world had come to an end. She took our daughter and moved to another town. It took about three years for me to feel like a real person again. Time heals. Overall, I think things have worked out for the best."

The divorce may not be completely behind them, however. Ten years after the break-up of their marriage, about half of women and one-third of men still feel anger toward their ex-spouse. Overall, people who remarry tend to be happier than people who remain unmarried after their divorce (Symoens, Bastaits, Mortelmans, & Bracke, 2013; Waite & Gallagher, 2000).

Relationships between Custodial Parents and Children

Over the long run, divorce often draws parents and their children closer together. Children in female-headed single-parent families report they talk to their mothers

13.1 Discuss key aspects of becoming single again after a divorce

Questions That Matter

13.1 What are some common feelings experienced by adults after a divorce?

13.2 What is the biggest issue facing women after a divorce?

13.3 What are some issues facing fathers after a divorce?

Divorce can be very difficult for children, but one of the upsides is that children and their custodial parent (usually a mother) often become closer as a result of the divorce.

more often than do children in two-parent families (Bulduc, Caron, & Logue, 2006; Frank, 2008). Although children of divorced parents are more likely to experience negative outcomes, as we saw in Chapter 12, it's also true that many children lead happy and well-adjusted lives. They continue to have warm relationships with one or both of their parents—more often with the custodial parent than with the noncustodial one (Frank, 2008; Lopez & Corona, 2012).

In fact, it's these positive relationships that help beat the odds against negative outcomes, such as dropping out of school or teen pregnancy. A primary factor in children's short-term and long-term adjustment to divorce is how effectively the custodial parent—usually the mother—functions as a parent (Hutchinson, Afifi, & Krause, 2007; Luedemann, Ehrenberg, & Hunter, 2006). The feature box *Why Do Research? When Is a Correlation Only a Correlation?* focuses on successful men raised by single mothers who have beaten the odds, including President Barack Obama. In other words, there may be a correlation between divorce and negative child outcomes, but we shouldn't overstate this. A correlation doesn't imply that all children from divorced families will experience negative outcomes, nor does it imply that divorce alone is the cause of any problems that do occur.

Oddly, however, the positive side of parent–child relationships after a divorce has rarely been studied. Instead, most researchers begin with a deficit model—that a home without two parents is somehow a "broken home."

Issues for Custodial Mothers: Downward Mobility

Often the first months or years after divorce are difficult because of a multitude of conflicting emotions: elation, anger, depression, and sadness. These emotions can be heightened by the significant financial losses that many families face. We see in Chapter 12 that divorce can often alter a family's standard of living, especially for mothers. Nearly one-third of custodial mothers receive some sort of public assistance (Grall, 2011), Supplemental Nutrition Assistance Program (SNAP), formerly the Food Stamp Program, in particular. Poverty and food insecurity are real problems that many single mothers face (DeNavas-Walt, Proctor, & Smith, 2013; Hernandez & Pressler, 2013). Middle-class and upper-middle-class women are more likely to achieve greater resiliency than poor or lower-middle-class women because they have greater personal resources, such as education and earning potential (Kjellstrand & Harper, 2012).

Most women are aware that their standard of living is likely to drop significantly after a divorce (Poortman & Seltzer, 2007). Using data on more than 5,000 parents collected for the National Survey of Families and Households, researchers found that 72 percent of mothers assumed that their standard of living would be worse or much worse after divorce, compared to 54 percent of fathers who thought their standard of living would be worse. Substantial differences were also found *within the same family*—more than twice as many mothers as fathers from the same family expected their standard of living to be worse (Poortman & Seltzer, 2007). Women in their 20s and 30s are more confident that they can maintain employment to provide sufficient income for their families, whereas older women are less confident about their earning capabilities (Arendell, 1986).

How do newly single mothers manage? Most drastically cut their expenses or move to cheaper housing so they can pay their monthly bills. Terry Arendell's qualitative study found that few women she interviewed had extra money left at

Conventional wisdom claims that the millions of boys who grow up without a father are at greater risk of problems, such as doing poorly in school, using drugs and alcohol, getting in trouble with the law, or becoming teen fathers. If this is so, then how do we account for the high-profile success of men like President Barack Obama, who was raised by a single mother and had virtually no relationship with his father? Or what about the success of eight-time Olympic gold medalist Michael Phelps, who also grew up in a fatherless household?

Research clearly shows a *correlation* between growing up with a single parent and negative social, educational, and emotional outcomes. This means that there is an association—children in single-parent households are more likely to have problems than those in two-parent households. Let's pause for a moment to reflect on the real meaning of this statement.

First, remember that a *correlation* does not mean that all children from single-parent households will have problems. There are many exceptions—happy, successful, and well-adjusted boys and girls can come from single-parent homes. With the right parenting style, social support, financial resources, and educational opportunities, children can overcome many obstacles. "What's important is not whether they are raised by one or two parents. It's how good is the relationship with the parent, how much support they're getting from that parent, and how harmonious is the environment," says University of Cambridge psychologist and fathering expert Michael Lamb (quoted in Jayson, 2008). "In the case of Obama, his mother was not particularly well off, though she was well-resourced intellectually and had been to college and had supportive parents," he continues.

Second, remember that a correlation does not necessarily mean that something *causes* something else. For example, a correlation between growing up in a single-parent household and doing poorly in school, or using alcohol or drugs, doesn't necessarily mean that single parenthood *per se* causes these negative outcomes. Another factor may be involved, such as family finances or level of education. Single mothers are more likely to have low incomes and less education, and it is these issues that often cause the difficulty for children.

If policymakers want to help children, it is crucial to determine the precise cause of the problems affecting them. If the negative child outcomes are not caused by single motherhood but by the social and economic challenges that often accompany single motherhood, then the solution is to address those social and economic challenges, a path many European countries are following. They have decided to actively invest in all families by providing more generous services, programs, and subsidies, including health insurance, childcare and education assistance, living wages, and other benefits. These services and benefits for families help alleviate their social and economic challenges.

Remember that growing up with single parents does not mean that one is doomed to a life full of problems. Although children in one-parent families may face higher odds of problems, many others grow up to be highly successful, including President Barack Obama.

What are the results of these European family policies? Single parenthood in European countries is less problematic and is not as highly correlated with poverty or negative child outcomes as in the United States. So, keep in mind that a correlation is really just a correlation. There are always exceptions, and a correlation does not imply causation.

WHAT DO YOU THINK?

1. Can you think of other family issues that you have learned about in this text in which people see a correlation, and incorrectly assume causality?
2. What changes are needed in our social and health policies to enhance the lives of children in single-parent families?

Sources: Jayson, 2008; Neuman, 2009.

the end of the month after paying for the minimum necessities (1986). Women of all ages and all income levels talked about the anxiety, depression, and despair associated with their financial difficulties after a divorce:

I've been living hand to mouth all these years, ever since the divorce. I have no savings account. The notion of having one is [as] foreign to me as insurance—there's no way I can afford insurance. I have an old pickup that I don't drive very often. In the summertime I don't wear pantyhose to work because I can cut costs there. Together the kids and I have had to struggle and struggle. Supposedly struggle builds character. Well, some things are not character building. There have been times when we've scoured the shag rug to see if we could find a coin to come up with enough to buy milk so we could have cold cereal for dinner. That's not character building.

> **"In the summertime I don't wear pantyhose to work because I can cut costs there."**

Custodial Fathers: A Growing Group

I thought, "Hey, she'll go in [into drug rehabilitation center], get cleaned up, and come and get these kids." But, no! [laughing] It did not happen that way at all. These kids have been living with me; they are my pride and joy and have been since '94, that's when they came to live with Daddy. But in the beginning I tell you, I did not want any part of it and they [Child Service Workers] had to practically threaten me to do it—they made me realize there was no other place for my kids to go, and my kids had been through a lot of bad things with their mother. I didn't know the extent of it until they was living with me. (Hamer & Marchioro, 2002, p. 121)

Listen on **MySocLab**
Audio: *NPR: Fathers Become Vocal on Parents' Rights*

About 83 percent of custodial parents are mothers, so naturally, this means that most children reside with their mothers after a divorce. However, this also means that some custodial parents are fathers—roughly 1 in 6, up from 1 in 10 a generation ago (Grall, 2011). Forty percent of custodial fathers live with only their children; the remaining live with a cohabiting partner or other adults, including family members or friends (Kreider & Ellis, 2011). The vast majority of custodial fathers are White (about 80 percent).

In the past, fathers usually could not obtain custody of their children unless the mother was proved to be unfit, didn't want the children, or there were other serious extenuating circumstances. Today, fathers may seek and gain custody for a wide variety of reasons, often through mutual agreement with the mother. Fathers may also step in because the mother is physically, emotionally, or financially unable to care for the children, or because they want to be the primary caretakers of their children. Moreover, fathers may seek and obtain custody at the request of their children.

Compared to two-parent families, single-father families have lower incomes, are twice as likely to be impoverished, have less education, and are more likely to live in rental housing than own their home. Although these households are more vulnerable than two-parent families, at least financially, they do have higher incomes than those headed by single mothers (Grall, 2011).

A study based on a representative sample of nearly 17,000 parents compared the amount of time that single and married parents spend caring for their children (Hook & Chalasani, 2008). They analyzed the total amount that parents spend caring for or interacting with children in a 24-hour period, and classified the care into one of three categories: (1) physical care and planning (e.g., organizing, looking after, waiting for, helping, teaching not related to education, traveling); (2) play and companionship (e.g., reading to or with, playing, talking

TABLE 13.1 Minutes Spent Caring for Children

First, single fathers spend more time than married fathers, but less time than single or married mothers, caring for very young children. Second, as children age, the amount of time single fathers spend with children, as compared to married or single mothers, is more comparable. Third, single fathers spend more time in direct physical care than do married fathers, but less time than single or married mothers.

	Total	Physical	Play	Achievement
Youngest Child, Ages 0–5				
Single fathers	127	78	45	4
Single mothers	142	102	34	6
Married fathers	106	59	43	4
Married mothers	150	101	44	5
Youngest Child, Ages 6–11				
Single fathers	73	47	15	11
Single mothers	80	53	14	13
Married fathers	54	29	16	9
Married mothers	72	49	12	12
Youngest Child, Ages 12–14				
Single fathers	43	23	10	10
Single mothers	46	29	10	7
Married fathers	24	15	5	4
Married mothers	35	22	6	7

Source: Hook & Chalasani, 2008.

More than 2 million fathers have custody of their children, sometimes by default, but increasingly by choice.

and listening, attending events); and (3) achievement-related activities (e.g., doing homework, attending school conferences, contacting with teachers, waiting associated with education). The results are found in Table 13.1. Several findings are apparent: First, single fathers spend more time than married fathers, but far less time than single or married mothers caring for very young children. Second, as children age, the amount of time single fathers spend with children is more comparable to mothers. Third, the types of activities in which parents engage with their children varies, with single fathers generally spending more time in direct physical care than do married fathers, but less time than single or married mothers.

In the feature box *Diversity in Families: "I'm Turning Out to Be a Darn Good Dad . . . ,"* meet Nick, a single father raising a daughter after his divorce.

Most studies of custodial fathers focus on the experience of White fathers who obtain custody following a divorce. One study by Hamer and Marchioro (2002) describes the circumstances in which low-income and working-class Black men come to gain custody of their children, how they transition to a full-time parent role, and what types of social support networks they use in parenting.

The researchers interviewed 24 men from an impoverished Midwestern urban area. They found the subjects generally became full-time fathers by default, often without any explicit discussion with the mother. Some mothers gradually withdrew from parenting by leaving their children progressively more with the father. Other mothers abruptly disengaged themselves from their children. Most

A growing number of fathers are asking for and being awarded custody of their children in the United States. Nick is one of these custodial fathers. Here is what he had to say about the situation:

It wasn't supposed to be this way, you know. Leah and I married right out of college, and we both assumed things would be great between us and that we would never have any major problems. It's not always easy to explain it to outsiders, but sometimes the best-laid plans just go up in smoke. Problems in our marriage began to surface within a couple of years, and we thought that maybe if we had a baby, things would be better. Clearly, having a baby is not the answer to marital problems! Don't get me wrong, I absolutely love my daughter, but she was not the glue to hold together an unhappy marriage. After seven years of marriage, when little Sabrina was four, Leah and I separated.

During the separation, we shared custody of Sabrina. She spent Sunday through Wednesday with me, and Thursday through Saturday with Leah. I rented a two-bedroom apartment and tried to fix Sabrina's room up like her old room, but most of her bedroom things were new and unfamiliar to her because Leah kept our condo. I have always been a pretty hands-on dad, but taking care of Sabrina full-time, for even four days a week, was definitely a new and often difficult experience. Waking her up in the morning, fixing her breakfast, helping her dress, taking her to preschool, picking her up at 5:00, cooking, cleaning, entertaining, teaching . . . it's hard. The handing-off process was usually awkward; Sabrina would cry for the parent she was saying goodbye to, and Leah and I would often argue about something.

After a year of separation, about the time Sabrina was ready to begin kindergarten, Leah and I decided to divorce. Leah told me that she didn't want custody. She said it was too tough, her job too demanding, and mothering was just too stressful. She asked for traditional visitation, which included every Wednesday after school, every other weekend, and four

weeks in the summer. I have to say I was shocked. Full custody isn't what I was envisioning, but I immediately said, "Deal." I cannot envision arguing about who has to take our daughter. I know we both love her, so I said, "Yes, I will have custody."

Leah gave us the condo, and through a mediator we worked out other aspects of the divorce agreement, including child support. That was a tough one—Leah didn't think she should pay anything because I earn a little more than she does, but the mediator really insisted. So, now she pays $400 a month, which I need because of afterschool care costs, health insurance, and a million and one other things that pop up monthly. Leah pays her child support every month, although not necessarily on time, which can irk me, and has been the cause of some big arguments. However, she has never missed any of her visitations, and from what I can tell, seems to be a good non-custodial mom to Sabrina.

I'm turning out to be a darn good dad, although I'm still not very good at fixing hair, buying "girlie" clothes or other things like that. Sabrina is almost nine now, and I'm hoping her mother will step in a little more, especially around adolescence. But, I've learned to be a great cook, an active soccer coach, and a happy PTA member. Who would have thought? It all comes down to this: I love that little girl. Being a single dad to Sabrina is definitely not easy, but I'm doing the best that I can.

—Nick, Age 34

WHAT DO YOU THINK?

1. Do you think single fathering compares to single mothering? Are the issues faced by single mothers and fathers similar or different?
2. Do you think the number of single-father families is on the rise? What micro-level and macro-level factors might explain the increase?

---

fathers were reluctant to accept their children, but did so because of pressure or because they assumed the situation would be only temporary.

The fathers' transition to full-time parenting was difficult for several reasons: First, they lacked confidence in their parenting abilities; second, they had little money and found it difficult to provide for their children; and third, they had to make drastic changes in their lifestyle and give up a degree of freedom.

Extended family members may ease these difficulties. Eight of the 24 fathers lived with other family members, usually parents or siblings. These fathers, along with those who lived independently, relied on family to help with babysitting, preparing children's meals, doing the laundry, and a multitude of parenting tasks. "If it weren't for my family, times would be very, very rough," says one dad (Hamer & Marchioro, 2002, p. 124). Custodial fathers tend to have closer ties with their parents than custodial mothers have with their parents, and they have more frequent contact with their parents (Hilton & Kopera-Frye, 2007). Custodial fathers also receive a broader range of support from extended kin than do custodial mothers. This help is likely related to their closer and more frequent contact, but it also may be related to a gender bias—people assume men need more help than women do with respect to parenting and other domestic tasks, and therefore are more likely to offer it.

Why do single fathers have closer ties and receive more assistance from their extended families than do single mothers? Are single fathers more likely to ask for help? Are family members more likely to offer help to single fathers than to single mothers? Why or why not?

Repartnering after a Divorce

13.2 Describe the process of repartnering after a divorce

Question That Matters

13.4 How common is cohabitation among divorced people?

There are many paths after a divorce. Some adults, feeling angry or betrayed, swear they will never marry again while others desperately look for mates to ward off loneliness or financial difficulties. A quick look at the status of adults ages 25 to 44 shows that a significant number are in a second or subsequent marriage or are cohabiting (Figure 13.1). Generally, finding a new partner after a divorce, or **repartnering,** is the most important factor in improving life satisfaction for both men and women (Shapiro, 1996). Women, in particular, gain financially from repartnering. In fact, on average, the financial gains women make from repartnering outweigh the benefits of reentering the labor force after divorce or increasing their working hours (Jansen, Mortelmans, & Snoeckx, 2009).

Dating Again

If the divorcing partners are young and were married only a short time, it may not be very difficult for them to begin dating. There are likely many single people in their "pool of eligibles," and many of their friends are probably single and can introduce them to potential partners.

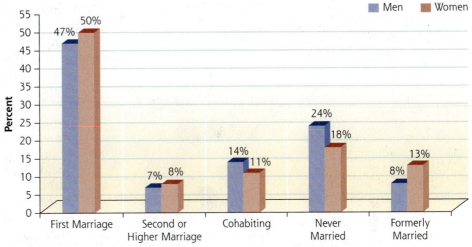

FIGURE 13.1

Current Marital Status among U.S. Adults Ages 25–44, 2006–2010

About 7 percent to 8 percent of adults ages 25 to 44 are currently in a second or subsequent marriage, but that does not mean that only 7 percent to 8 percent of people will ever be in a second or subsequent marriage.
Source: Copen, Daniels, Vespa, & Mosher, 2012.

In contrast, dating and courtship may be more difficult or awkward for people who are older and who have been married a long time because there are fewer potential dating partners, and they may be unaware of changing dating norms. Their concerns may include questions such as: Is it okay for a woman to initiate a date? Should we meet at the restaurant, or should one person pick up the other at home? Who pays for dinner? Who pays for the babysitter? What sexual expectations will there be? Am I supposed to like her children right away? Are my children supposed to like him right away?

Many older people complain that it's not as easy to find dating partners as when they were younger. Older women often find it difficult to meet men their age because men tend to date younger women (Ahrons, 2007; Calasanti & Kiecolt, 2007; Sassler, 2010). For example, a detailed study of dating relationships among older adults ages 57 to 85 found that 32 percent of single men ages 57 to 64 were in a dating relationship, as compared to only 18 percent of the single women (Brown & Shinohara, 2013). The researchers also found that people who are better educated, have more financial assets, and are more socially connected were more likely than their counterparts to date (Brown & Shinohara, 2013).

As shown in Chapter 3, the most common way to meet partners is through friends, but as we age, fewer of our friends are single or know others who are single. Consequently, online dating is popular. There are many online dating sites, and even special ones devoted to those ages 50 and older (OurTime.com, 2013). Forty-two percent of adults ages 50 to 64 know at least one person who has dated someone they met online, as do 24 percent of adults age 65, and most have relatively positive things to say about the experience (Smith & Duggan, October 21, 2013).

repartnering: The act of entering into a relationship after a divorce, which may lead to cohabitation or marriage.

👁 **Watch** on **MySocLab**
Video: *Love Again*

📖 **Read** on **MySocLab**
Document: *Transitions in Parental Repartnering after Divorce*

TABLE 13.2	Percentage of Cohabiting Couples Who Are Age 30 and Older	
Middle-age couples, many of whom have presumably been married before, are likely to cohabit.		
Age	**Male**	**Female**
30–40	27%	22%
41–64	35%	31%
65 and older	5%	3%

Source: U.S. Census Bureau, 2012c.

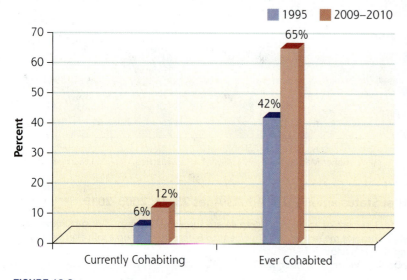

FIGURE 13.2

Percentage of Women Ages 40–44 Currently Cohabiting or Ever Cohabited

Cohabitation is becoming an increasingly common occurrence in the lives of adult women.
Source: Manning, 2013.

*H*ow do you think divorced parents with children should handle dating? What are some dilemmas you would face if in this situation, and how would you handle them? Do you think dating issues are different between mothers and fathers?

13.3 Explain the nature of remarriage

Questions That Matter

13.5 Which groups in the United States are more likely to remarry?

13.6 Why do men and women remarry at different rates?

13.7 How strong and stable are remarried relationships?

Cohabitation after a Divorce

As learned in Chapter 3, many people today live with a partner before marriage. However, cohabitation isn't just for the young; it's also becoming common among middle-age and older adults (Table 13.2; Manning, 2013; U.S. Census Bureau, 2012c; Vespa, Lewis, & Kreider, 2013). Figure 13.2 shows the increase in cohabitation among women ages 40 through 44 between 1995 and 2010 (Manning, 2013). In fact, the number of people ages 45 through 54 who are cohabiting (and presumably have been previously married) exceeds the number of people ages 15 through 24 who are cohabiting (and presumably have never been married) (U.S. Census Bureau, 2012c).

Divorced people who cohabit may view the arrangement as an extension of serious dating or as an alternative to marriage. Later-life cohabiting unions tend to be stable, and the majority remain intact over time (Vespa, 2013), although they may or may not lead to marriage. Remarriage rates decline substantially with age (Brown & Lin, 2013). This is why some researchers interested in relationships after divorce prefer to focus on *repartnering* rather than *remarriage* per se.

When a couple decides to cohabit or remarry, the decision often occurs quickly after the relationship begins, unlike first marriages in which the partners may have dated for years before making a commitment to marry (Wu & Schimmele, 2005). The relationship may progress quickly because divorced men and women believe they don't need as much time to get to know one another. They believe they've learned from past relationship mistakes, are more focused about what they are looking for in a partner, or are a better judge of character. Yet, Ganong and Coleman (1989) found that many couples preparing for remarriage fail to address critical issues: fewer than 25 percent discussed financial matters with their partner, and 13 percent discussed no substantive issues at all.

Remarriage

About 21 percent of all currently married men and women have been married at least twice. Of these, about 4 percent have been married three or more times. As shown in Figure 13.3, among all people ages 25 and older who have previously divorced, 52 percent of men and 44 percent of women have remarried (U.S. Census Bureau, 2008a). Others who do not remarry remain single for different reasons; perhaps they prefer a single lifestyle or haven't met the "right" person. Older persons may avoid marriage because of the potential loss of Social Security benefits, the challenges posed by merging households, or the lack of support of older children (Mahay & Lewin, 2007).

We often talk as though remarriage and the new family structures it creates are modern inventions; however, remarriage has always been a common feature of family life in the United States (Phillips, 1997). In early American history, life expectancy was considerably lower than it is today. Because it was difficult to maintain a household as a widow or widower, quick remarriage was common. If children were present, the remarriage substituted a new parent for the old one.

Nonetheless, it took until the 1970s for family scientists to begin to take a real interest in the subject of remarriage as a research topic. Today, most remarriages take place after divorce rather than widowhood. With divorce, the ex-spouse is still alive, perhaps living within the vicinity and exercising his or her parental rights. This provides many new situations that families did not face in the past when remarriage involved a widow or a widower.

U.S. Demographic Trends: Who Remarries, and When?

Most men and women remarry after a divorce, often relatively quickly, as compared to remarriage after a death of a spouse (Cruz, 2012; James & Shafer, 2012). More than one-third of women remarry within 3 years after a divorce, and about half are remarried within 5 years. By 10 years after a divorce, three-quarters of women have remarried (Bramlett & Mosher, 2002; Kreider, 2006). Younger women and higher-earning women are more likely to marry than are older women or those with lower incomes, although the effects of education levels are somewhat mixed.

Self-help books tend to advise people not to rush into a new relationship after one has ended, fearing that a relationship on the rebound will not be very stable. Although this sounds like common sense, it really is an empirical question, and research can help sort fact from fiction. One study (Wolfinger, 2006) decided to test the rebound effect—that is, the study asked whether relationships that began quickly after a divorce were more likely to break up than those that began at a later date. Using a large and nationally representative sample from the National Survey of Families and Households, Wolfinger measured the time between divorce and remarriage, then examined whether the length of this period predicted a subsequent divorce. He found no evidence of a rebound effect; those who remarried quickly were no more likely to divorce than were those who remarried after a longer period of time (Wolfinger, 2006).

RACIAL/ETHNIC DIFFERENCES IN REMARRIAGE
In the past, Whites were more likely to remarry than other racial or ethnic groups, but this is no longer the case (Bramlett & Mosher, 2002; Cruz, 2012). Figure 13.4 reveals the rate of remarriage by racial and ethnic group. Hispanics and Asian Americans are most likely to remarry, and this is the case for both women

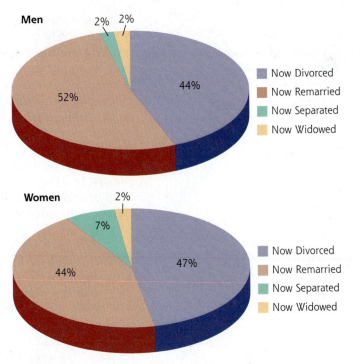

FIGURE 13.3

Current Marital Status for Men and Women Ages 25 and Older Who Were Previously Divorced

Among previously divorced adults age 25 and older, 52 percent of men and 44 percent of women have remarried.
Source: U.S. Census Bureau, 2008a.

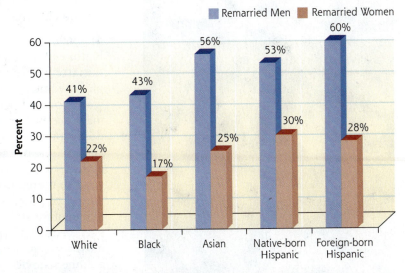

FIGURE 13.4

Remarriage Rates per 1,000 Men and Women by Race, Ethnicity, and Hispanic Nativity, 2010

Across all races and ethnicities, men are more likely to remarry than women.
Source: Cruz, 2012.

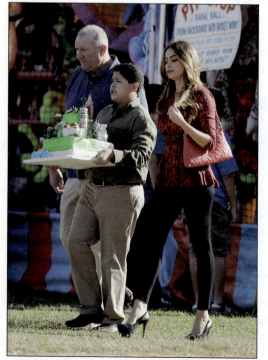
Listen on **MySocLab**
Audio: *NPR: Second Marriages*

and men. Culturally, both groups have a strong sense of family, and consequently are more likely to remarry and less likely to cohabit after a divorce.

Why are Black women less likely to remarry than other groups? The answer may be related to the reason they are less likely to marry in the first place. There is often a shortage of available marriageable Black men, particularly in inner-city urban areas (Edin & Kafalas, 2005; Wilson, 1987, 1993). With jobs moving to the suburbs from the urban areas, urban minority males face high rates of unemployment. Suburban jobs are often difficult to get to because public transportation is limited. Other Black men are in jail. Still others have low levels of education in comparison to Black females. Together with racism and discrimination, many minority males living in the inner cities experience poverty, and Harvard sociologist William Julius Wilson (1987) suggests these conditions significantly reduce the pool of men eligible for marriage.

SEX DIFFERENCES IN REMARRIAGE

Men are more likely to remarry than are women, and they do so more quickly (Ahrons, 2007; Cruz, 2012; Goodwin, Mosher, & Chandra, 2010). Men remarry on average within 3 years, compared to 5 years for women. But sex alone doesn't predict when or whether a person will remarry. For women, the likelihood of remarrying decreases substantially with age, especially if divorced when in their 40s or 50s. In contrast, age at divorce makes little difference for men. For example, James, who divorced when he was 30, is only slightly more likely to remarry within 5 years than is Lawrence, who divorced when he was 55. However, Karla, who also divorced at 30, is at least six times more likely to remarry than Renée, who divorced at 55. In fact, fewer than 7 percent of women who divorce between the ages of 50 and 59 remarry within 5 years, compared to 46 percent of men in that age group (Lampard & Peggs, 1999).

The reasons for these sex differences include both micro-level and macro-level factors. First, there is choice; some women don't want to remarry (Mahay & Lewin, 2007). If they can support themselves and their families easily enough, they might not feel the need to remarry. But for many other women who would like to remarry, cultural norms make it more difficult for them to find available spouses than men.

WHY DO MEN AND WOMEN REMARRY AT DIFFERENT RATES?

A number of reasons help explain why men are more likely to remarry, and to do so more quickly than are women:

- *Men tend to have more experience initiating contacts.* Men have a lifetime of socialization experiences that encourage them to be the initiator in personal relationships. Many women, particularly older women, have never asked a man out on a date. When they were younger, to do so was considered improper. Even today, many women are more comfortable in being "chosen" rather than doing the choosing themselves. In addition, men often have a larger circle of casual friends and acquaintances than do women, and they can draw on this circle to meet potential partners. Men are also more likely to have worked outside the home for a longer period of time, perhaps in managerial or professional positions that require skills in initiating and directing conversation. Moreover, because their incomes are considerably higher than those of most women, men typically have more money to treat someone to a dinner, movie, or some other type of date.

- *There is a double standard of aging.* People make different evaluations of the attractiveness of older men and older women. When men age they are considered to be "distinguished." Their graying hair, facial wrinkles, and weight gain is offset by their increased occupational prestige or financial assets. However, when women

Men are more likely to remarry after a divorce, and they do so more quickly. There are several reasons for this, including the cultural norm that allows men a wider range of dating partners. Older men can date women their own age, or women who are much younger, like Jay and Gloria in the sitcom *Modern Family*. Generally, the same latitude is not given to older women.

age they are typically considered less attractive, and therefore less desirable. For example, a study asked both elderly persons and college students to rate photographs of men and women at three different ages. Although both men and women were perceived to diminish in attractiveness as they aged, the decline for women was greater than that for men. Moreover, ratings of women's femininity decreased with age, whereas evaluations of men's masculinity were unaffected (Deuisch, Zelenski, & Clark, 1986). Susan Sontag labeled this concept the **double standard of aging** (1979).

double standard of aging: The view that women's attractiveness and femininity decline with age, but men's attractiveness and masculinity do not decline.

- *The pool of eligible partners is larger for men than it is for women because of cultural norms.* Women generally marry men who are older, or at least the same age. When a female is 23 and a male is 25, their age difference is not problematic because there are a near equal number of partners available to each of them, but imagine this same couple 30 years later. The female is now 53, and the male 55. Cultural norms allow men to choose partners from a wide age group, including women much younger than themselves. A 55-year-old man marrying a 35-year-old woman would generate little concern. However, although theoretically a 55-year-old woman could also marry a 35-year-old man, it would likely draw attention. In fact, many people would wonder what he sees in such an "old woman," or why she is "robbing the cradle."

Do you think the stigma surrounding older women dating younger men has changed in recent years? What evidence do you have to support your opinion?

- *Women are more likely to have children living with them.* Women who have custody of children are less likely to remarry than women who don't have children or don't have custody. One reason is that women may not have the time or financial resources to date. Some men are also hesitant to take on the financial and emotional responsibilities that come with a "ready-made" family. A third reason is that stepfamilies have a unique set of issues that can strain a relationship, as discussed in the next section. Some women may be hesitant or very cautious about remarrying and bringing a new person into these established family relationships. Finally, children may try to sabotage their mother's relationships out of fear or jealousy.

Power and Equity between Spouses

Remarried couples tend to perceive their new relationships as more equitable than their first marriages (Pyke, 1994; Pyke & Coltrane, 1996). Women often believe they have more power and autonomy regarding financial and other decisions. One study compared data from 111 remarried and first-married spouses and found that remarried spouses endorsed more autonomous standards in childrearing, friendships, and finances (Allen, Baucom, Burnett, Epstein, & Rankin-Esquer, 2001). Different reasons have been offered for this increased feeling of autonomy, power, and equity:

- Women have greater levels of financial resources in their second marriages than in their first
- Women seek more power because of specific experiences in their prior marriages
- Women concede more during marital conflicts than they did in their first marriages
- Remarried men and women have expanded their ideas about their roles in marriage (Coleman, Ganong, & Fine, 2000)

One area of interest is the division of household labor among remarried couples. One study analyzed a sample of 215 men and women who were in second marriages following a divorce and residing in Southern California (Pyke & Coltrane, 1996). The researchers used both interview and survey data to examine the marital processes underlying the division of household labor—to examine how the meanings associated with housework, paid work, and earnings affect the allocation of domestic labor. They suggest that not everyone values the equal sharing of tasks or women's financial contributions to the family in the same way. For example, in some families, men may view these contributions as threats rather than assets. Researchers Pyke and Coltrane found many people used housework experiences in their previous marriages as a point of reference for their new situation. For many women, this comparison tempered the feeling that housework should be shared and instead made them grateful that "he helps . . . ." Even an unequal division of domestic labor was at least less unequal than in the previous marriage.

One surprising finding, also related to using the previous marriage as a reference point, was that husbands who had extramarital affairs in their first marriage were less likely to share housework. Many used their fidelity in their second marriages to excuse them from participation in what they saw as mundane tasks. Hey, I'm not out carousing—she should be grateful!

Satisfaction and Stability of Remarriages

Reflecting on happiness in remarriage, we find second (and third) marriages report to be less happy and are more likely to end in divorce (Barna, 2008; Miricki, Chou, Elliott, & Schneider, 2013; Whitton, Stanley, Markman, & Johnson, 2013). This may indicate a selection bias—people who have divorced obviously consider divorce as an option to end an unhappy relationship. They also tend to more openly express criticism and anger than do couples in first marriages (although this isn't always a negative trait). They are also more prone to disagreements, in part because of tension between stepchildren and stepparents, or between stepparents on issues related to childrearing or discipline (Martin-Uzzi & Duval-Tsioles, 2013). In fact, both remarried men and women are more likely to be depressed than are first-married men and women, especially if stepchildren are involved (LaPierre, 2009; Schmeer & Kroeger, 2011; Shapiro & Stewart, 2011).

After 1 year of remarriage, the divorce rates of Whites, Blacks, and Hispanics are roughly the same, at about 5 or 6 percent; but over time, Blacks have the highest rate of re-divorce, followed by Whites, whereas Hispanics have the lowest rate of re-divorce. After 10 years of remarriage, 48 percent of Blacks, 39 percent of Whites, and 29 percent of Hispanics have divorced again (Bramlett & Mosher, 2002).

A second divorce is also more common among younger persons, those earning less income, and those who are not working. In addition, a second divorce is more common among persons with children from a previous relationship. Ten years into the second marriage, 43 percent of women who had two or more children at the time of the remarriage divorced again, as compared to 32 percent of women who were childfree.

The instability and fragile quality of a remarriage may reflect a problem in one or more of four areas critical to marital success (Ihinger-Tallman & Pasley, 1987):

- *Individuals may fail to make a real commitment to remarriage.* Having lived through at least one divorce, people may see that divorce is a remedy for an unhappy or unfulfilling marriage. Instead of making the necessary effort to resolve problems, they use divorce as the "easy way out" of what they perceive as a difficult situation.

- *The couple may fail to become a cohesive unit.* Developing bonds between adults with separate life histories and including other families may be difficult. Couples must learn to think of themselves as a "we," not simply an "I." There is bound to be conflict and confusion over new rules, new norms, and new ways of allocating assets. Children may—wittingly or unwittingly—pit one parent against the other: "But Mom said I could!" To avoid this dilemma, the new couple must make a concerted effort to work together to develop a unified set of household rules.

✳ **Explore** on **MySocLab**
Activity: *Married More than Once?*

- *Individuals may fail to communicate appropriately with one another.* Poor communication is a common problem, perhaps exacerbated by a previous marriage in which communication patterns were problematic. Learning how to communicate more effectively is difficult and time-consuming, but it's critical to break destructive old habits that interfere with the development of a strong family.

- *Remarried couples must deal with more boundary-maintenance issues than do couples in first marriages.* In addition to in-laws, there are also ex-spouses to contend with. This can be a source of tension if child custody, visitation, or child support disagreements continue for long periods and aren't resolved successfully. Furthermore, remarried families with children must establish new boundaries with one another—what are the new expectations among family members?

Remarriage among the Elderly

When older persons divorce, women do not have the odds in their favor for remarrying (Brown & Lin, 2013). Although more males than females are born, the sex ratio evens out when people are in their early 30s. After that, there are more females alive than there are males. For example, there are only about 90 men age 65 for every 100 women the same age, and the ratio declines significantly thereafter. Twenty years later, among persons ages 85 and older, there are only about 60 men for every 100 women (Howden & Meyer, 2011), and most of these men are already married. When we combine these imbalances with the double standard of aging and cultural norms (i.e., a 65-year-old man may marry a 45-year-old woman, but society may frown on the reverse), we can see that it makes it all the more challenging for older women to find partners.

Yet, many older adults do remarry, and a number of features can make such remarriages quite successful. First, elders usually don't have to worry about step-parenting issues to the same degree as younger remarried couples. Even if their adult children disapprove of the remarriage, the children are often living independently and aren't affected directly by the new union. Second, older adults may be financially established and therefore experience less stress and conflict over money. Finally, older adults may benefit from the wisdom that comes from a lifetime of experience and seek partners who offer comfort and companionship.

When older persons remarry, they have several factors working in their favor: usually no stepchildren are in the home; they may be financially established; and have the wisdom from a lifetime of experience, which helps them seek out people who will be good companions.

blended family (or reconstituted family): Another term for *stepfamily*; a family that may consist of stepparents, step-siblings, or half-siblings.

siblings: Children who share both biological parents.

Stepfamilies

Because many couples who remarry or cohabit also have children, let's now turn to the topic of stepfamilies, the feature of our opening vignette. Sometimes called **blended families** (or **reconstituted families**), *stepfamilies* are families in which one or both adult partners have at least one child either residing with them or elsewhere. Children living in stepfamilies can have one of many relationships: **siblings** (biologically related, or from the same parents); **step-siblings** (not biologically related, but their parents are married to each other); **half-siblings** (share one parent biologically); **mutual children** (child born to the remarried couple); **residential stepchildren** (live in the household with the remarried couple more than half of the time); and **non-residential stepchildren** (live in the household less than half the time) (National Stepfamily Resource Center, 2007).

Although we often talk about a stepfamily as though there were only one type, we know otherwise (Allan, Crow, & Hawker, 2010; Dupuis, 2007; Ganong & Coleman, 2004). Types of stepfamilies include the following:

- a child who lives with his or her married parent and stepparent
- children from a previous marriage who visit their remarried parent and stepparent

13.4 Summarize the unique aspects of stepfamilies

Questions That Matter

13.8 What are some common stereotypes of stepfamilies?

13.9 How do stepfamilies differ from biological families?

step-siblings: Children not biologically related but whose parents are married to one another.

half-sibling: A child who shares one biological parent with another child.

mutual child(ren): The child (or children) born to a couple that has remarried.

residential stepchild(ren): A child (or children) living in the household with a remarried couple more than half of the time.

nonresidential child(ren): A child (or children) living in the household of a divorced parent less than half of the time.

- an unmarried couple living together in which at least one of the partners has children from a previous relationship who live with or visit them
- a remarried couple in which both spouses bring children into the new marriage from the previous marriage
- a couple who not only bring children from a previous marriage, but also have a child or children of their own
- a married couple, both of whom have grown children from a previous marriage; the children may live in another state and have very little contact with the remarried couple

Stepfamilies are quite common. More than 5 million children (7.5 percent) live in stepfamilies (Lofquist, Lugaila, O'Connell, & Feliz, 2012), with about 1,300 forming every day (Stepfamily Foundation, 2013). More than 11 percent of fathers currently have stepchildren living with them, as do about 3 percent of mothers (Kreider & Ellis, 2011). These figures are relatively consistent for all racial and ethnic groups except Asians, who are least likely to live in stepfamilies, as shown in Table 13.3.

TABLE 13.3	Number of American Children Living in Blended Families by Child's Race and Ethnicity
Asian-Americans are least likely to live in stepfamilies.	
	Number
White, non-Hispanic	3,181,000
Black	679,000
Asian	65,000
Hispanic	1,159,000

Source: Kreider & Ellis, 2011.

Stepfamilies can have many positive attributes, and living in one can be an enriching experience, as Jim and Daneen in the opening vignette will tell you (Crohn, 2006; Stewart, 2007). For example, there is greater exposure to a wide variety of situations and lifestyles that can be beneficial to children in many ways. Children in stepfamilies also may benefit from living with an adult who is possibly more objective than their birth parent. For example, if a teacher sees problems with a young student, a biological parent may be defensive, whereas a stepparent may be able to observe the situation objectively. Children may also benefit from an increased standard of living made possible by two incomes, as well as their parents' greater happiness at being involved in a different relationship. Stepfamily adoptions are among the most common type of adoptions in the United States, a testament to the love and affection many stepparents and children feel toward one another (Child Welfare Information Gateway, 2008; Lamb, 2007). As one adopted son, now an adult, remembered:

> My dad adopted me when I was thirteen, after he and mom had been married for a year. I thought a lot about it that first year, "wow, he wants to be my dad!" That felt so great because my first dad—my biological dad—apparently didn't want much to do with me or my mom. He was rarely around. The formal adoption reminded me that I really was loved and someone actually wanted me to be their son, and I actually wanted someone to be my dad. It went both ways. We had a good relationship before the adoption, but the whole legal process allowed us to say it publicly.

Stereotypes of Stepfamilies: The Wicked Stepmother

Despite the prevalence of stepfamilies and the possible benefits of living in one, society's views of stepfamilies are remarkably negative. At best they are considered less than exemplary, and they're often stigmatized as damaging environments for children and adolescents (Claxton-Oldfield, 2008; Ganong &

Coleman, 1997; Weigel, 2008). For example, images of the "wicked stepmother" are rampant, from the plays of Shakespeare to the Cinderella figure in fairy tales, with connotations of cruelty, jealousy, and neglect (Whiting, Smith, Barnett, & Grafsky, 2007). Where did these stereotypes come from?

We can assume that these stereotypes are rooted in the stepfamilies of pre-Industrial society. Families needed the labor of two parents to provide food, shelter, and clothing for the family. When one spouse died—often the wife, given the dangers of childbearing—a husband had little choice but to remarry after a brief mourning period. Most people thought it would be very foolish, not to mention unmanly, for him to attempt to raise and provide for his children alone. Thus, the widower typically would remarry as soon as possible.

However, a father's remarriage choices were often limited. Women of his age were likely already to be married. Consequently, a second (or subsequent) wife may have been considerably younger than the man she married, perhaps by as much as 20 years; indeed, she could be the same age as some of his older children. The second wife was treated as a child rather than a spouse, given her age and the patriarchal norms of the time. She had little power in the relationship and little authority over children in the household, despite having to cook for them, clean up after them, and raise them. To gain some power, the stepmother would have a child or two of her own. Not surprisingly, she might favor her own biological children, further exacerbating strained stepfamily relationships and contributing to the stereotype of the "evil stepmother" (Mitterauer & Sieder, 1982).

The Unique Features of Stepfamilies

Stepfamilies are common, yet the expectations, obligations, and rules within them are ambiguous (Martin-Uzzi & Duval-Tsioles, 2013; Papernow, 2013; Schramm & Adler-Baeder, 2012; Stewart, 2007). More than a third of children born in the United States today will be in a stepfamily before reaching age 18 (Parke, 2007), and half will have a stepparent at some point in their lifetime (Stewart, 2007). Yet, no socially prescribed script explains how family members are expected to relate to one another. What names do children use for their stepparent? To what extent can stepparents discipline their stepchildren? How are stepparents and stepchildren supposed to feel about one another? Do stepparents and their stepchildren even count one another as part of their "family"? For example, your father's new wife is technically your stepmother, but what if you're grown and out of the house? Do you refer to her as "my dad's new wife," or as "my stepmother"? Do you count her children from her first marriage as your siblings? Who *is* part of your family, anyway (Suanet, van der Pas, & van Tilburg, 2013)?

Stepfamilies have unique features compared to families in which both biological parents reside (Allan, Crow, & Hawker, 2010; Gold & Adeyemi, 2013; National Stepfamily Resource Center, 2013; Stewart, 2007). These features include the following:

- *Stepfamilies come about because of a loss through death or divorce.* Children grieve over the loss of a parent, including the loss of stability; the loss of their fantasy about how they want life to be; and the loss of their old home, school, neighborhood, or friends. Adults grieve over similar things: the loss of a partner, the loss of their dreams about the way they thought marriage would be, and the losses that come with change.

- *The parent/child relationship has a longer history than the new couple's relationship.* This can make it challenging for the adults to see their relationship as a primary, long-term one. A new spouse can feel like an outsider. Sometimes the close relationships that develop between divorced parents and their children contribute to the difficulty the new spouse has in joining the family. This new person has not been a part of funny or tragic family memories, or a part of developing sentimental traditions. "Why do her

Read on MySocLab
Document: *Stepfamilies in the United States: A Reconsideration*

One of the tasks of a new stepfamily is to establish their own shared experiences, rituals, and traditions.

children expect to open their gifts on Christmas Eve instead of Christmas Day?" the new stepfather may ask himself. "Don't his children know the value of saying grace before meals?" the stepmother may wonder about her stepchildren who visit every other weekend. Remarried families have different histories, which accentuates the need for them to tolerate differences. In time, the family can develop meaningful and shared experiences and rituals.

- *A biological parent lives elsewhere.* Children usually continue to love their non-custodial parents and often long for their return. Children who do best after a divorce are those who have access to both parents. But how is that access facilitated? Can it be maintained? Even when fathers have no contact with children after a divorce or after an ex-spouse remarries, children hold on to their memories. Meanwhile, there is a new adult in the household. "Is he supposed to be my 'new dad'? I already have one," a child might wonder.

- *Children in stepfamilies hold membership in two households.* Living in two households can be an enriching experience. Theoretically, it can provide twice the love, twice the material goods, twice the number of family vacations, and twice the parental involvement in the child's schooling or other activities. However, it can also create confusion and conflict, including playing one parent off against another. "But Dad lets me stay up until 9:00 at his house, so why do I have to go to bed at 8:30 here?" a child might complain to her mother. Two households can also create loyalty conflicts. For example, suppose a son feels close and loving toward his new stepmother, but at the same time learns his biological mother doesn't like her. The child may feel pulled in two directions. To please Mom requires rebuffing the stepmother, but that would displease his father. It helps to have flexible family boundaries in stepfamilies so that children can more easily move from one household situation to another.

- *The model for step-parenting is ambiguous and poorly defined.* How do you stepparent? What authority does a stepparent have over his or her stepchildren? Biological parents have the opportunity to grow into parenting roles as their children grow; however, stepparents are often expected to adjust quickly (Chedekel & O'Connell, 2002). Biological parents have bonded with their children and are often more tolerant of their children's personalities and behaviors than someone who does not know them as well or have a sense of history with them. The reverse is also true: Children are bonded to (and thus often more tolerant of) their biological parents than they are to their stepparents. But roles and emotional bonds take time to develop. Stepfathers seem to be more satisfied with their family life if they adopt a father-like role (Marsiglio, 1992), whereas stepmothers are less likely to assume a mother-like role and instead act more like a friend (Church, 1999).

- *No legal relationship exists between stepparents and stepchildren.* The legal status of stepparents and the rights of parents are remarkably different. Legally, stepparents are largely invisible (Gold, 2009; Mason, Harrison-Jay, Svare, & Wolfinger, 2002). For example, biological parents have child support obligations, custody rights, and inheritance rights regardless of the social and emotional bonds between parent and child. In contrast, stepparents in most states have no obligation during the marriage to support their stepchildren. Without written authority, a stepparent cannot access school records or authorize emergency medical care. Stepparents also don't have any legal right to custody or even visitation if the marriage terminates through divorce or death. Moreover, in the case of divorce, they have no obligation to pay child support, regardless of whether their stepchildren have long depended on their income.

- *The children in stepfamilies have additional sets of relatives.* Living in a stepfamily offers the chance for many additional relationships, possibly including an extra set (or two) of grandparents, aunts and uncles, and cousins. The ties between these relatives can range from extremely close to none at all. The outcome of these relationships depends largely on the investment the "step-relatives" make (Cherlin & Furstenberg, 1994). The possibilities represent one of the exciting by-products of stepfamilies.

Because of these features, perhaps it isn't surprising that most adults who have step-relatives describe a stronger sense of obligation to their biological family members than they do their step-relatives (Becker, Salzburger, Lois, & Nauck, 2013; Henretta, Van Voorhis, & Soldo, 2013; Kalmun, 2013; Pew Research Center, 2011). A survey from the Pew Research Center based on a nationally representative sample of more than 2,500 adults asked them how obligated they would feel to provide assistance to family members who were dealing with a serious problem and needed either financial help or caregiving. The results are found in Figure 13.5 (Pew Research Center, 2011). Among adults who have both a living biological parent and a living stepparent, 85 percent say they would feel very obligated to help out their parent; in contrast, only 56 percent say they would feel that same sense

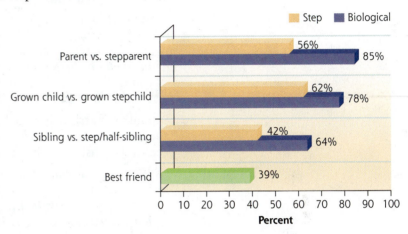

FIGURE 13.5

Percentage Who Feel Very Obligated to Family Members

People generally express a greater sense of obligation to their biological relatives than to their step-relatives.
Source: Pew Research Center, 2011.

of obligation toward a stepparent. Parents of grown children also feel the same way; whereas 78 percent say they would feel very obligated to help out a biological child, only 62 percent feel that way toward a stepchild. Siblings also have a different sense of obligation, with 64 percent saying they would feel very obligated to a sibling in serious trouble, but only 42 percent say they would feel very obligated to provide assistance to a step- or half-sibling.

Multiple Relationships and Dynamics

Remarriage may add new family members in all three generations: parents, children, and grandparents. Let's take a look at one example of multiple family relationships.

Kristin and Phil recently divorced after many years of marriage. They had two children together, Ella and Jake, who were ages 9 and 11, respectively, at the time of the divorce. Both children continued to live with Kristin, spending every other weekend, 4 weeks in the summer, and Thanksgiving and Spring Break with their father. Two years after the divorce, Phil married Bonnie, the custodial parent of a 12-year-old daughter, Jessie. The next year, Kristen remarried Rob, who had also been divorced and who has joint custody of two daughters, Peyton and Anna, ages 6 and 11. Within the next 4 years, Phil and Bonnie had two children of their own, a son and a daughter.

When Ella and Jake, the two biological children of our original couple, Kristen and Phil, are 15 and 17, their family looks like this: They have two biological parents, two stepparents, three stepsisters from two different families, a half-brother, and a half-sister. The extended family has also grown to include two sets of step-grandparents, two sets of biological grandparents, and an expanded network of aunts, uncles, and cousins.

Several components of these stepfamily relationships make them complex (Ahrons & Rodgers, 1987):

1. *Former spouse subsystem.* This relationship becomes more complicated as former spouses remarry or become involved in significant relationships. Tensions are more likely to arise if one of the former spouses marries quickly before other family relationships have been reorganized and stabilized. For the spouse who remains single, the remarriage may bring to light jealousy, old romantic feelings, or animosity. With respect to Phil's remarriage to Bonnie, Kristen said:

   When Phil told me he was getting married, I was upset, and reacted with a cutting comment, saying that I hoped she was better prepared for "his ways" than I was. But what I was really scared about was that he would be better with her than he was with me. What if he had really changed? This sounds awful, but I wanted his marriage to fail. Then I would know that I was right in divorcing him.

   Phil's remarriage initiated a critical set of changes for all participants. Even though Kristen and Phil had been divorced for 2 years, his remarriage caused their relationship to change even further. Phil anticipated many conflicts:

   When Bonnie and I decided to get married I felt guilty and I dreaded telling Kristen. When I did tell her she didn't say much, but I knew she was feeling upset. I wanted the kids to be part of our wedding but I knew Kristen was going to feel jealous and left out. I'd feel much better if she had someone else in her life. Bonnie's relationship with her ex-husband is nothing like my relationship with Kristen and she didn't understand my wanting to ease Kristen's pain by not flaunting my new life at her.

   Because of the children they had together, Kristen and Phil's lives are intertwined, yet Kristen must deal with a new set of loyalties—Phil's attachment to his new life with Bonnie and his role as a stepfather to her daughter, Jessie. It's difficult for Kristen to see that Bonnie's needs are important, or that Bonnie is a significant person to the children or to Phil. She had trouble recognizing Jessie as a part of the family. Six months after Phil's remarriage, Kristen summarized the new situation in this way:

   Things have changed a lot since Phil remarried and it has been frustrating. We used to try to be helpful with one another, but now he's less willing to accommodate when I need to change plans around the kids. He always has to check with Bonnie first. I really resent that—the kids should come first. I invited Phil to our daughter's birthday party but he couldn't come because of plans he had made with Bonnie and her child, Jessie. And now I feel uncomfortable calling him at home about anything because Bonnie usually answers the phone. I feel like she's listening the whole time and we cannot have any private conversations. Phil asked to take the kids on a week's vacation to visit Bonnie's parents over Spring Break. I know it's his time with the kids and all, but I think he should give them some special time and not make them spend it with Bonnie's family.

   Researchers find a pattern of deteriorating co-parental relations after remarriage, particularly if the ex-husband remarries and the ex-wife does not. The number and frequency of shared childrearing activities like birthday parties are highest when both partners are single and lowest when only the husband has remarried. Conversely, conflict is highest when only the husband has remarried, and lowest when both are single.

2. *Remarried couple subsystem.* Remarried couples overwhelmingly report being unprepared for remarried life, including the exchange of children, money, and decision making. When Phil and Bonnie married, they fantasized about their plans for blending their families, minimizing problems, and

remaining optimistic they could cope because of the love they share. But many problems created more stress than they had imagined. As Bonnie describes:

> When Phil and I decided to get married, I was surprised by his feelings about Kristen. He was very concerned about her feelings or whether she would be hurt. I didn't have any of those feelings about my ex, Tom. When Tom remarried last year it didn't make much difference in my life. He hadn't seen much of our daughter Jessie anyway and he just saw her less after he remarried. It was a relief not to have much to do with him. So, after living alone with Jessie for six years, I was really excited to have a family again and give her more of a dad.

> But it's not working out that way. Jessie is jealous of Phil. She is angry a lot about not having time alone with me and acts up. Her anger often ends up with Phil and me fighting a lot. Phil also feels badly about not spending enough time with his kids, and when the kids are altogether, it just seems to be everyone fighting over Phil. And I feel resentful at not having enough time alone with Phil. Between every other weekend with his kids and the long hours he works, we never seem to have time alone together. Last Saturday, the kids were out and we were finally spending an evening all alone. But just as I was putting dinner on the table, Kristen called about some problem. Phil and I then spent the next two hours talking about Kristen. It ended up spoiling our whole evening.

Bonnie's concerns are not unusual. Remarriage when children are present requires reorganization and realignment, and these are rarely simple or quick.

3. *Sibling subsystem.* The typically competitive struggles among siblings can become more heated in remarried families, because children must learn to share parental time, household space, and parental affection. Research suggests the transition to remarriage may, in fact, be more stressful to children than the transition to divorce, because the newly married parent is preoccupied with his or her new mate, and children may feel neglected in the transition (Stewart, 2005).

> Momma invited Daddy to come over to our house to help me celebrate my birthday, but he said he couldn't because he promised to take Jessie somewhere! I hate her!

How Similar Are the Expectations of Stepparents, Parents, and Stepchildren?

Do all members of a stepfamily see the role of the stepparent in the same way? To answer this question, family researchers Mark Fine, Larry Ganong, and Marilyn Coleman conducted a study of 40 families that surveyed each stepparent, biological parent, and one child between 10 and 19. One question asked respondents to describe the "ideal way" the stepparent should relate to stepchildren. Possible responses included "distant relative," "teacher," "friend," "stepparent," "acquaintance," "advisor," "boss," "parent," "uncle/aunt," and "enemy." Parents and stepparents were in general agreement—they most commonly identified "parent" as the ideal way stepparents should relate to stepchildren. The stepchildren, however, felt differently; they believed the role of "friend" was most appropriate. These different views can create tension in the home if clear expectations are not communicated among parents, stepparents, and stepchildren (Fine, Ganong, & Coleman, 1997).

Stepfamilies can be quite complex entities. To better understand why they are different and how to best live within them, we should be mindful of the associated macro-level and micro-level factors. Yes, stepfamilies do make up a set of personal relationships, but they're highly

Have you, or someone close to you, lived in a stepfamily? What were some of the specific micro-level factors and macro-level factors that shaped this experience? From your experience or from the experiences of someone close to you, what do you think are some of the biggest difficulties in living with a stepfamily? What are the best ways to help stepfamilies?

Why are stepfamilies so complex? Although some stepfamilies are characterized by loving relationships, others face many challenges as they try to define themselves and negotiate relationships. Many micro-level factors contribute to their complexity, owing to the personal nature of the relationships. However, macro-level social factors also shape stepfamily dynamics because societal norms and expectations are vague and inconsistent. Do we, as a society, define stepfamilies as true families?

MICRO-LEVEL FACTORS

- Multiple relationships and multiple dynamics are often conflicting
- Some stepfamily members may live with the new family while others do not
- Stepfamilies may be created from some type of loss
- Children may belong to two households
- New family members feel different degrees of affection and love toward each other

- Parents may not be equally committed to placing child(ren)'s needs first

MACRO-LEVEL FACTORS

- Expectations, obligations, and rules for stepfamily members are vague and confusing
- Stereotypes are negative, such as the "evil stepmother"
- Stepfamily members may each have different expectations
- Relationships between stepfamily members have little or no legal standing

WHAT DO YOU THINK?

1. How does American culture uniquely influence these macro- and micro-level factors associated with stepfamilies? How might these factors be different in developing nations, or are they different?
2. Why is the "evil stepmother" such a prevalent stereotype, when there is no real equivalent for stepfathers—or is there?

influenced by social norms—or in some ways, by the lack of social norms. The feature box *Tying It All Together* summarizes the micro-level and macro-level factors that shape stepfamily relationships in the United States today.

13.5 Identify ways to survive and thrive in stepfamilies

Questions That Matter

13.10 How do children fare in stepfamilies?
13.11 How do adults fare in stepfamilies?
13.12 How can stepfamilies be strengthened?

Surviving and Thriving in Stepfamilies

With so many different relationships, and with little guidance, many stepfamilies struggle to move beyond the obstacles. They usually make their way on their own, but sometimes stepfamilies need outside help (Higgenbotham, Skogrand, & Torres, 2010; Papernow, 2013). Let's look at how children and adults fare in stepfamilies. We first turn to the example of children in stepfamilies.

How Do Children Fare in Stepfamilies?

As described in Chapter 12, children from single-parent households face an increased chance of certain negative outcomes, but what about *after* their parents remarry? Although a few studies show that some aspects of children's circumstances improve in stepfamilies (Sweeney, Wang, & Videon, 2009; Wen, 2008), most find that many children in stepfamilies continue to have social, emotional, and behavioral difficulties, even those children who have been adopted by their stepparent (Brown, 2006; McLanahan & Sandefur, 1994; Stewart, 2010b).

Certainly not all stepchildren experience problems. Many stepchildren grow up feeling secure in happy homes made possible by their parent's remarriage. Among some minority groups, living in a stepfamily is often reported to have significantly positive effects on a child's well-being; for example, through increased income. Furthermore, high-quality relationships with stepfathers may have a positive effect on internalized problems, such as depression and low self-esteem, and on externalized problems, such as impulsivity and restlessness (White & Gilbreth, 2001).

Yet children living in stepfamilies, like children from single-parent homes, still tend to earn lower grades in school, complete fewer grades, and score lower on achievement tests as compared to children of two-parent biological families (Carlson, 2006; Fromby & Bosick, 2013; Ganong & Coleman, 2004; Turunen, 2013). Stepchildren also have higher rates of depression and emotional problems, particularly when there is conflict between the two households. They're more likely to exhibit behavioral problems, such as alcohol and drug abuse, teenage pregnancy or impregnating others, idleness, and arrest. Differences may not be large, but on average, many children in stepfamilies do face potential disadvantages.

EXPLANATIONS FOR ADDED RISK   Let's again be clear: most stepchildren do well in school and don't have emotional, behavioral, or delinquency problems; what we are discussing here is an increased chance of negative outcomes. One explanation points to *stress and instability*, suggesting repartnering and remarriage create many stressful transitions and potential conflicts for both adults (Cooper, McLanahan, Meadows, & Brooks-Gunn, 2009) and their children (Magnuson & Berger, 2009). Moving to a new residence, adapting to a parent's new partner, living with new family members, and settling into new routines could all contribute to poorer school performance, depression, early romance, and behavioral problems (Cavanagh, Crissey, & Raley, 2008; Cavanagh & Huston, 2006; Sweeney, 2010).

A second explanation focuses primarily on *social capital deprivation* (Shriner, Mullis, & Schlee, 2009), which suggests that children living in stepfamilies are disadvantaged because of their reduced levels of **social capital** (connections to other adults or institutions in the community) related to the divorce. Remarriage doesn't repair these deficits completely, perhaps because stepparents are expending resources on their own biological children from a prior union, or because they aren't fully invested in their stepchildren (McLanahan & Sandefur, 1994; Schwartz & Finley, 2006).

Children in stepfamilies also face added risk for academic, social, and emotional difficulties. Possible reasons include the many transitions the child has made, the reduced level of social capital the child has, and a compromised parent quality the child experiences—the parents may be so involved in their new relationships that they do not pay full attention to the needs of the child.

A third explanation suggests that *parenting quality* may be compromised as parents invest time and emotional energy in their new relationships rather than in childrearing. For example, parents may not spend as much time talking with their children, helping them with their homework, or monitoring their friends and activities as they did prior to the remarriage because they're preoccupied with their new partner (Stoll, Arnaut, Fromme, & Felker-Thayer, 2006; Sutherland, Altenhofen, & Biringen, 2012).

How Do Adults Fare in Stepfamilies?

Being in a new loving relationship can be exciting, but when children are involved, both men and women may need to make significant adjustments. For example, the privacy that newly partnered couples crave can be non-existent—married life might begin with a group of teenagers living with you! For non-custodial stepparents, the stepchildren may visit on a part-time basis—perhaps every other weekend and several weeks or months at a time in the summer. The presence of stepchildren invariably brings an ex-spouse into the picture. What potential tensions can arise with an "ex" or with your spouse's "ex"? The feature box *My Family: Journey to Healing* offers one woman's account of living in a stepfamily.

The situations of stepmothers and stepfathers are somewhat distinct from each other, and therefore, stepmothers and stepfathers face different issues

My husband and I divorced when our son, Alex was seven years old. At first I never wanted to marry again. But over time my feelings softened. When I realized that perhaps one day I would remarry, I felt that I would like to marry a man who already had children. I thought it would be nice for Alex to have a sibling, but I never thought about what it would mean to be a part of a step or blended family, and just how that would impact my life and Alex's.

Three years later I married a man who had two daughters. But that is not all. My new husband, William, also has an ex-wife, and ex-in-laws. The coming together of our family: my son, myself, my new husband, his daughters, his ex-wife, and her parents has been a very difficult task.

Forming a blended family has been tough on all of us. Part of the problem is that there are few, if any, guidelines to follow. What is a blended family supposed to be like? For example, we know how to behave and what is expected of us when we become in-laws. But we really do not know what our role is with our spouse's ex-spouse. There is no language for these new members of our extended family, no built-in expectations, nor do we think of them as friends. In fact, they may actually be seen as intruders, and having them in our lives can be an emotional roller coaster. This was the case with us.

My own story is probably similar to many other women who have married men who have previously been married and have children. It took over five years for the adults to come together and figure out our relationships. For years I was in the middle of an angry tug of war between William and Kelly [his ex] over the children, and there was very little peace. Williams's relationship with his Kelly held so much hostility and manipulation on her part, and he was unable to set boundaries for himself. It seemed that no matter what my husband and Kelly did, I had to enter into the picture, and would become angry and frustrated as well.

To be honest, I also felt incredibly jealous over the hold she still had on him. I kept these feelings to myself, but naturally they surfaced in other ways. I had no role model and I was very confused by all the emotions because of having his ex in my life. I think all three of us really had no idea of how to behave; for William and Kelly to be cordial ex-spouses who love their children and want what is best for them; for Kelly and myself, who had the awkward relationship of having been married to the same man; and even for myself and my husband on how to deal with his ex-wife. My ex-husband kept a low profile. Why couldn't she, I wondered?

There were no road maps to guide us, and the challenges between the three of us kept growing. I could no longer handle having Kelly call our home "to talk: because these conversations usually ended up in a heated argument. So I did

something really daring; I sent a letter to Kelly asking her not to call our home anymore.

About a year later I came to an important revelation: I can choose to be married to my husband, and if I do, then his ex-wife must be a part of the picture. I sent another letter, this time asking if we could put the past aside and to begin again. Our first meeting was awkward, but we all did our best because we were celebrating their daughter's middle school graduation. The whole family went, myself, my husband, all our children, Kelly, and her parents. Although we all try to maintain some distance, over the past two years we have shared several family events, including their children's birthdays. I feels so much happier and more at peace than ever before.

—Molly, Aged 37

WHAT DO YOU THINK?

1. If remarriage is so common, why are the ensuing relationships so awkward? Why do we not have a common understanding of language, behavior, expectations, and responsibilities?

2. What kinds of issues would cause such tension between the current and ex-wife? Are these issues similar to or different from the issues among current and ex-husbands? Do you think that her action was appropriate? Why or why not?

Source: Posner, 2002.

with their stepchildren. Can you make an educated guess as to how these might differ? Take the quiz in the *Getting to Know Yourself* feature box to assess your understanding of how the concept of stepmothering differs from that of stepfathering.

First, a stepmother is usually non-custodial—the children visit with their father and her. At best, the role of a stepmother is ambiguous and often

Many of you reading this text will someday become stepparents. Researchers have studied stepparent roles, expectations, and challenges, and have found interesting differences between stepmothers and stepfathers. Take the following test to assess how much you know about gender and stepparenting. For each of the following eight statements, answer whether you think the question is true or false.

_____ 1. If the new parent is a stepmother, the probability of the marriage surviving is reduced. *True False*

_____ 2. The role of the stepmother is considerably more difficult than that of the stepfather. *True False*

_____ 3. Stepmothers are less likely than stepfathers to achieve close ties with their stepchildren. *True False*

_____ 4. Because men do not have to deal with the myth of the "wicked stepfather," society is more supportive of their role and place in the home. *True False*

_____ 5. Regardless of a stepmother's parenting skills, her stepchildren are likely to regard her with suspicion and distrust. *True False*

_____ 6. Much of a child's anger and resentment toward his or her father is projected onto the stepmother. *True False*

_____ 7. Stepmother–stepdaughter relationships present the greatest problems. *True False*

_____ 8. Stepmothers are more likely to establish positive relationships with younger children regardless of the children's sex. *True False*

Answers: All of the statements are true.

WHAT DO YOU THINK?

1. How many of the eight statements did you guess correctly? Why did you answer the questions the way you did? From experience, media depictions, or general stereotypes?
2. Given what you know about gender in families and the difficulties stepfamilies face, can you analyze the macro-level and micro-level reasons why the stepmother role can be so challenging?

Source: Berke and Grant, 1981.

---

unrealistic (Cartwright, 2012; Deal & Petherbridge, 2009; Gosselin, 2010; Wenck & Hansen, 2009). A stepmother is often viewed as an outsider; she has little control over parenting practices during visitation and little say regarding financial obligations. This lack of control can generate a sense of powerlessness, anger, and resentment manifested in depression (Henry & McCue, 2009; Shapiro & Stewart, 2011). The stepmother may have to make financial adjustments and learn to accept that alimony and child support payments go toward maintaining her husband's previous wife and children from that union. Average child support payments are around $500 per month, but they can be significantly higher, depending on the husband's income and number of children he is supporting (Grall, 2011).

Stepfathers face a somewhat different set of issues because they're usually custodial stepparents—their stepchildren live with them full-time. Obviously, they must learn to get along with their wives' children, including the impact of his role on the mother and children, including loyalty issues, and the demands on the mother's attention (Cartwright, 2012). Moreover, because child support, even when given regularly, is not intended to cover the full costs of caring for the children, a stepfather may be challenged financially to support his stepchildren while also paying for his biological children. In addition, if his biological children now reside elsewhere with their own mother, the stepfather must also find ways to encourage his new partner to accept these children and minimize the problems that could arise from part-time residence or visitation.

Table 13.4 compares some of the classic complaints of stepmothers, stepfathers, and stepchildren (Stepfamily Foundation, 2005). If you've experienced one or more of these roles, do any of these complaints sound familiar? How are the concerns of stepmothers, stepfathers, and stepchildren similar to or different from one another? Can you think of creative ways to resolve some of these complaints?

TABLE 13.4   Classic Complaints of Stepmothers, Stepfathers, and Stepchildren

Living in a stepfamily brings out different concerns about different members.

The Stepmother

"Everyone in his life, his kids, his former wife, and his business, comes before me."

"I want a child of my own, and he's had enough."

"My money goes to support this family because his money goes to take care of her and them."

"His former wife never says 'thank you' for any of the things I do."

"The children treat me like the maid; I'm expected to do everything that their mother would do for them, but without the respect they would give to her. Even the cleaning lady gets more appreciation than I do."

"He believes that buying his children something, or entertaining, is fathering."

"His children say the meanest things to me, and my husband defends them and tells ME I'm overreacting."

"I think I'm becoming the 'cruel' stepmother."

"The worst of it is, when his children come over we have no sex life."

The Stepfather

"She always jumps to the kids' defense when I correct them. She's turning our boys into wimps."

"I give her kids the gift of my time and no one says 'thank you'."

"It's her house, the kids were there before me, and they let me know that."

"My wife treats me like an outsider when it comes to the kids."

"I buy the kids stuff and they hardly say 'thank you'."

"There is so much tension in the house when the children are here."

"I love her so much when we're alone and they're at their father's house."

"People write about the plight of the stepmother. What about the stepfather?"

"I feel like a third wheel when I'm with her and her kids."

"I must come first for this to work."

Stepchildren

"I want my old family back. I want things the way they were. I miss things the way they were—even though Mom and Dad fought."

"Nobody has enough time for me."

"I'm sad when Mom's sad, and I'm sad when Dad's sad, and they are both sad too much."

"Dad is busy with his new family."

"It's boring over at Dad's house."

"It's wonderful at Dad's house. I wish I could live with Dad."

"I miss my father."

"Dad and I have a great time, except for her."

"He gives more to her kids than to us."

"Mom is wonderful, but that boyfriend of hers is awful."

"We've been doing just fine without him. Why do we need him now?"

"They will never know how hard it is to visit Dad/Mom."

"They get upset when I tell them about the good time I had when I visit."

"Mom doesn't have enough money. I wish I could help her out."

Source: Lofas, 2005.

Strengthening Stepfamilies

How does a stepfamily forge a successful path? We do know that not all stepfamilies are successful—stepfamily difficulties are a key factor in the relatively high failure rate of remarriages. Yet, many other stepfamilies survive and thrive, and self-help books offer ways to help stepfamilies succeed (Papernow, 2013; Rosin, 2009).

Just like a *good divorce* (discussed in Chapter 12), there are *good stepfamilies*. Drawing on a strengths perspective, many ingredients of good stepfamilies (i.e., avoiding conflict, working well together, and being supportive of all members) are the same as those ingredients for a good divorce. First, open lines of communication are critical (Gosselin & David, 2007; Higginbotham, Skogrand, & Torres, 2010). Second, eliminating explicit criticism of the other parent or of stepparents is also important, as children benefit from a united and constructive family system. Third, stepparents must nurture and enrich the couple's relationship. Finally, keeping a support system of people who have had similar experiences can be crucial, because the norms for stepfamilies are vague and ambiguous. In fact, some stepfamilies participate in education groups and programs to learn about potential problems and how to avoid them. Do you see any of these features in Jim and Daneen's family in the opening vignette?

As the discussion of systems theory in Chapter 1 revealed, interventions aimed at the entire stepfamily, as opposed to just children or just adults, may prove particularly helpful. One study based on interviews with 40 families and 20 facilitators who participated in a stepfamily education program (Higgenbotham, Skogrand, & Torres, 2010) found that children benefited from the program by learning to express their feelings and further developing their relationship skills. They learned to see their situation as normal, and to accept social support from peers and others. Children also benefited from their parents' greater empathy, increased time spent with the family, and their parents' enhanced relationship skills.

Bringing It Full Circle

This chapter examines family relationships after divorce. We tend to view our experiences through an individual micro-level lens, but the aftermath of divorce and the beginning of new relationships are influenced by broader macro-level social forces as well. For example, most divorced persons remarry or repartner within 3 to 5 years after the divorce, but the likelihood varies by sex, race, and ethnic background. Repartnering and remarriage may involve the creation of a stepfamily with a unique set of characteristics, challenges, and opportunities. Although research tends to focus on the problems stepfamilies face, which can certainly be plenty, stepfamilies can also provide the love and stability that children crave. Given what you've learned in this chapter, let's return to the opening vignette to address a few questions.

- There are many different types of stepfamilies. What type does Jim and Daneen's family represent? How might the possible challenges and opportunities that stepfamilies face vary across different types of stepfamilies?

- Do you think the teasing term *stepmonster* would be used equally for a stepmother and stepfather? Why or why not?

- Drawing on the example of Jim and Daneen, how can stepfamilies achieve greater success for adults and children? Are the factors needed for success the same for parents and children?

On MySocLab

 **Study** and **Review** on MySocLab

CHAPTER REVIEW

LO13.1 Discuss key aspects of becoming single again after a divorce

13.1 What are some common feelings experienced by adults after a divorce?

Many studies show that custodial parents are often closer to their children and have a more peer-like relationship after divorce. People are also generally pleased after they divorce and feel that overall, they've made the right decision.

13.2 What is the biggest issue facing women after a divorce?

The first months or years after a divorce are a difficult time. One of the most pressing issues is the downward mobility that many women face. Most divorced women underestimate the amount of financial hardship that they and their children may confront.

13.3 What are some issues facing fathers after a divorce?

In the past, fathers usually could not obtain custody of their children unless the mother was proved to be unfit, did not want the children, or there were other extenuating circumstances. Today, fathers may seek and gain custody for a variety of reasons, often through mutual agreement with the mother. Compared to two-parent families, single-father families have lower incomes, are twice as likely to be impoverished, have less education, and are more likely to live in rental housing than in a home owned by the father. Although these households are more vulnerable than two-parent families, at least financially, they do have higher incomes than those headed by single mothers.

LO13.2 Describe the process of repartnering after a divorce

13.4 How common is cohabitation among divorced people?

Cohabitation isn't just for the young; it's also becoming increasingly common among previously married and middle-age adults. In fact, the number of people ages 45 through 54 who are cohabiting (and presumably have been previously married) is close to the number of people ages 15 through 24 who are cohabiting (and presumably have never been married). Cohabitation is quite common, and for some couples, it even replaces marriage altogether.

LO13.3 Explain the nature of remarriage

13.5 Which groups in the United States are more likely to remarry?

Nearly three-quarters of all people in the United States who divorce eventually remarry, and the average length of time between a divorce and remarriage is approximately 4 years. Some differences between groups do arise, however—Whites are more likely than minority groups to remarry, and men are more likely to do so than women.

13.6 Why do men and women remarry at different rates?

There are several reasons, including that men are able to initiate contact more easily; a double standard of aging that implies that older women are not as attractive as older men; the pool of eligible partners is larger for men; and women are more likely to have children living with them.

13.7 How strong and stable are remarried relationships?

Remarried relationships can be fragile. Typically, women feel that they have more power in their relationships regarding financial and other decisions. However, overall, subsequent marriages aren't necessarily happier than first marriages, and remarried couples are more likely to be depressed than are couples in their first marriage. The rate of divorce is higher among remarriages.

LO13.4 Summarize the unique aspects of stepfamilies

13.8 What are some common stereotypes of stepfamilies?

Our society's views of stepfamilies are quite negative. Stepfamilies are often stigmatized as harmful environments for children and adolescents. For example, images of the "wicked stepmother" are rampant, from the plays of Shakespeare to the fairy-tale figure of Cinderella, with connotations of cruelty, jealousy, and neglect.

13.9 How do stepfamilies differ from biological families?

Stepfamilies differ from biological families in some very critical ways: (1) they come about because of a loss; (2) the parent–child relationship has a longer history than the new couple's relationship; (3) there is a biological parent outside the stepfamily unit and an adult of the same sex as the absent parent in the household; (4) most children in stepfamilies hold membership in two households with two sets of rules; (5) models for stepparents are poorly defined; (6) no legal relationship exists between stepparents and stepchildren; and (7) children in stepfamilies have extra sets of relatives.

LO13.5 Identify ways to survive and thrive in stepfamilies

13.10 How do children fare in stepfamilies?

Many studies address this issue, focusing on the academic achievement, psychological well-being, and behavioral problems of children living in stepfamilies. Results of these studies usually indicate that, on average, children growing up in stepfamilies have an increased chance of negative outcomes compared to children growing up in biological two-parent households.

13.11 How do adults fare in stepfamilies?

Both husbands and wives must make substantial adjustments in stepfamilies, and the issues they face differ. For example, a stepmother is usually noncustodial and tends to be more of an outsider than a custodial stepfather. She has little control over parenting practices during periods of visitation or financial obligations, which can generate a sense of powerlessness, anger, and resentment that manifests in depression. She may have to make some financial adjustments and learn to accept that alimony and child support payments must go toward maintaining her husband's previous wife and children from that union. As for stepfathers, they must learn to get along with their wife's children, who likely reside with them. Moreover, the new husband probably financially supports his stepchildren through child support while also paying for his own children, if he has them. Finally, if he has children who now reside elsewhere with their own mother, the stepfather must also find ways to encourage his new partner to accept these children and minimize the problems that could arise from part-time residence or visitation.

13.12 How can stepfamilies be strengthened?

Many self-help books are available to help stepfamilies thrive. Some general tips include keeping open lines of communication; eliminating criticism of the ex-spouse; nurturing the couple's relationship; developing a support system; and participating in a formal stepfamily education program.

KEY TERMS

blended family (or reconstituted family)
double standard of aging
half-sibling
mutual child(ren)

nonresidential stepchild(ren)
reconstituted family
repartnering
residential stepchild(ren)

siblings
step-siblings

14

Families in Middle and Later Life

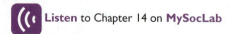

Listen to Chapter 14 on MySocLab

LEARNING OBJECTIVES

14.1	Explain the "demographic revolution"
14.2	Describe aging in historical perspective
14.3	Identify the transitions families experience
14.4	Summarize issues experienced by the aging couple
14.5	Discuss the grief process associated with widowhood
14.6	Analyze the role of grandparents in the lives of their grandchildren
14.7	Analyze the life stage of retirement
14.8	Discuss health issues of the elderly

"I am the mother that I wanted to be, but I am also the daughter I wanted to be."

Let's meet Amy. She is a 42-year-old woman who is a wife, mother, full-time hair stylist, and also a caregiver to her frail elderly mother.

Amy fits the description of someone in the *sandwich generation*— she is caring for two generations: her mother and her son. Amy often feels "sandwiched" in the middle.

For the last few years, Amy has been concerned about her mother, who, after 55 years of marriage, now lives alone since her husband died of a massive heart attack at the age of 80. Amy has seen her mother become isolated and depressed. Amy's mother has always been frail—she had polio as a child, and as an adult has battled breast cancer, arthritis, and diabetes. Amy knew that at some point she would be called on to care for her mother. That call came 6 weeks ago when her mother fell, fractured her hip, and because of the arthritis, needed a total hip replacement.

Despite working full-time and caring for a husband and their young son Michael, Amy spends at least 2 hours a day, 7 days a week caring for her frail mother, who is now in rehab. Amy loves her mother dearly, and feels that it is her duty to care for her because "She has always been there for me, so now I want to be there for her."

However, caring for two generations simultaneously is very stressful. On many days, Amy feels as though she is on a treadmill, going faster and faster, and trying to meet more and more demands. Her days consist of seeing her son off to the school bus, getting herself ready for work, and any break she has at work is devoted to caring for her mother. After a 10-hour day at work, Amy takes care of her own family, then visits her mother in the evening and does her chores such as laundry. The stress is getting to Amy, who says, "I have to put on a bright and happy face for my mother, a bright and happy face for Michael, and a bright and happy face for my clients. Sometimes I feel like, 'What about me?'"

At these times, Amy craves for a day off, but when she occasionally takes one, she is wracked with guilt. She wonders, "Am I selfish for wanting time with my own family? Am I letting my mother down? Being in the sandwich generation is really difficult on both ends. I'm squished in the middle having a young child and an aging mother." The bright spot is that her mother seems to enjoy the new company around her in the rehab center and appears to be less depressed. Amy is hopeful that her mother will agree to move to an assisted living facility after rehab, freeing up some of Amy's time for her son. Amy says, "In the future, I'd like to have my life back to what it was—concentrating on Michael. He's my number one priority."

"Sometimes I feel like, 'What about me?'"

◉ Watch on **MySocLab**
Video: *The Sandwich Generation: Amy*

C ouples who marry in their mid-20s can expect to live another 50 or 60 years. Newspapers are full of stories of couples celebrating their 50th wedding anniversaries; they are also full of obituaries, reporting deaths that leave widows and widowers behind.

What are some unique features of families as they mature? This chapter focuses on marital and family relationships when couples reach their middle and later years, exploring the many transitions they face at home, at work, and in their communities. Aging is far more than a biological process. The aging *experience* is largely social in nature, and is shaped by cultural and historical influences. As systems theory reminds us, the aging experience affects not only the couple, but the larger family system as well. For example, Amy will tell you that the changing circumstances of her aging mother touches the lives of her entire family.

◉ **Watch** on MySocLab
Video: *Aging and the Elderly: Sociology on the Job*

14.1 Explain the "demographic revolution"

Questions That Matter

14.1 What is a *demographic revolution*?
14.2 Which group of elders is increasing most rapidly?

The Demographic Revolution

Although we don't see people demonstrating in the streets, the United States is in the midst of a powerful revolution, destined to reshape the nation and the world—a *demographic* revolution (Figure 14.1). Only a century ago, birthrates were high and people didn't live very long; in 1900, very few—1 in 25, or only about 3 million people—were age 65 or older. Many younger people probably spent long portions of their lives rarely encountering an elderly person. But the elderly population has been increasing almost four times as fast as the population as a whole, and this group now constitutes 1 of every 8 people (Administration on Aging, 2012). In fact, elderly persons now outnumber teenagers in our country! In 2013, there were about 40 million people age 65 and older in the United States; by 2040, the number of seniors will nearly double, to almost 80 million—a huge increase in only 30 years (Administration on Aging, 2013). By then, 1 in 4 U.S. citizens could be 65 or older. By 2060, there may be 92 million seniors. Much of the population growth between 2010 and 2060 will occur as the people in the **baby boom generation** (those born after World War II through the early 1960s) are in their retirement years.

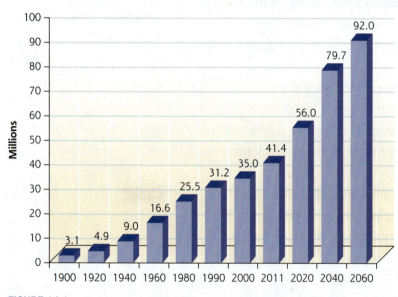

FIGURE 14.1
Number of Persons Age 65+, 1900–2060 (millions)

The number of elders is quickly rising as the baby boom generation grows older. The number of people age 65 and older will double between 2000 and 2030.
Source: Administration on Aging, 2013.

baby boom generation: People born in the years after World War II through the early 1960s.

life expectancy: The amount of time (in years) a person can expect to live from birth.

The *Oldest-Old* Are Increasing

Life expectancy, or the number of years a person born in a given year can expect to live, is on the rise. An American female born in 2009 can anticipate living 81 years, and a male 76 years (Central Intelligence Agency, 2013). This is a significant jump from a century earlier, as medical advances have eliminated or significantly reduced the occurrence of deadly infectious diseases such as influenza, smallpox, and measles.

As life expectancy increases, many people will live far longer than the so-called average. In fact, people ages 85 and older—referred to as the *oldest-old*—are the fastest-growing cohort in the United States. Today they number over 5 million, or only about 14 percent of all elders (U.S. Census Bureau,

2013c). However, because of the greater longevity of baby boomers, the number of the oldest-old is expected to jump to 19 million in 2050 (Table 14.1), making them about 25 percent of all elders.

Moreover, the number of persons living to be at least 100 years old is also growing rapidly. Even as recently as a generation ago, only very rarely did someone live to be 100. In 1990, there were only about 36,000 **centenarians** in the entire country. By 2050, the number of centenarians may exceed 1 million (Administration on Aging, 2009).

Who are these centenarians, and what are their lives like? Let's introduce you to one—my grandmother. She lived to be 108 (and a half) years old, and was doing quite well until the last year of her life; unfortunately, she passed away as this book was published. Look at the milestones of her life, shown in Table 14.2.

There were vast improvements in medical technology, drugs, and procedures during the 20th century, and people live considerably longer and are in better health as a result (Administration on Aging, 2013). Most elderly report being in excellent or good health; nonetheless, as more people live to the oldest ages, they will be diagnosed with many chronic conditions such as arthritis, osteoporosis, and senile dementia. People living with these and other conditions need assistance with cooking, cleaning, bathing, and home repair. Who will provide this care to an increasing number of elderly persons? More specifically, who will help *your* aging mother or father? Most elders don't really require the complete care provided in nursing homes. Usually, adult children in their 50s, 60s, or even 70s themselves provide the care their parents need, especially if they live nearby. Amy, the woman you met in the opening vignette to this chapter, is an example of one of these adult children.

TABLE 14.1	Population Projections for Persons Age 85 and Older (Millions)

More Americans are living longer than ever before.

Year	Population (Million)
2000	4.3
2012	5.0
2020	6.6
2030	8.7
2040	14.2
2050	19.0

Sources: Administration on Aging, February 4, 2010; U.S. Census Bureau, December 2, 2013c.

TABLE 14.2	Milestones in the Life of Blanche Seccombe

Believe it or not, my grandmother lived to be 108½.
She was born in 1901. Can you imagine the changes she witnessed during her life?

- William McKinley was President of the United States when she was born.
- Henry Ford showcased the first Model T for $950 when she was 7 years old.
- World War I began when she was 13 years old.
- Women did not receive the right to vote until she was 19 years old.
- She experienced the "Roaring Twenties" in her 20s.
- World War II, the deadliest war in history, began when she was 38 years old.
- *Brown v. Board of Education,* which integrated schools, was not settled until she was in her 50s.
- Medicare, the health insurance program for the elderly, was created when she was 64—just in time!
- Personal computers were not readily available until she was in her 80s.
- Cell phones were not commonplace until she was well into her 90s.
- The iPod swarmed the music market when she was nearly 100.

Elderly Women Outnumber Elderly Men

Because men have a lower life expectancy than women, we see more older women than older men. There are 77 men for every 100 women age 65 and older (Central Intelligence Agency, 2013). Among the oldest-old groups, however, the sex ratio is even more highly skewed—four times as many women as men are centenarians.

Living arrangements and marital status among the older population differ considerably between men and women as they age (U.S. Census Bureau, 2013c). As shown in Figure 14.2, most elderly men are married, which is not the case for elderly women. For example, three-quarters of men ages 75 to

centenarian: A person who lives to be at least 100 years old.

FIGURE 14.2

Percent of Older Men and Women Who Are Married or Widowed (2012)

As we age, the likelihood of being married decreases, especially for women, whereas the likelihood of being widowed increases.
Source: U.S. Census Bureau, 2013c.

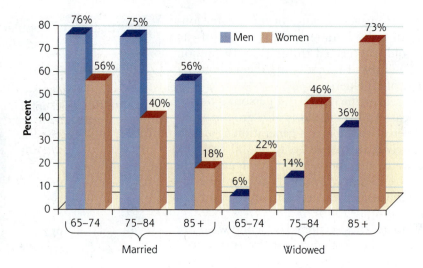

FIGURE 14.3

Living Arrangements of Men and Women Age 65+, 2012

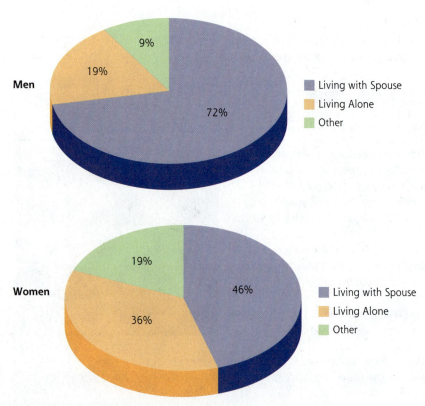

Most older men live with their spouses; most older women do not.
Sources: 2012 American Community Survey, U.S. Census Bureau, 2012; Medicare Current Beneficiary Survey, 2012.

What do these statistics about the elderly in the United States mean to you? How do you think this demographic revolution will affect you?

84 are married, as compared to only 40 percent of women that age. Among the oldest-old, more than half of men are married, compared to only 18 percent of women.

A consequence of the sex ratios and different rates of widowhood is that elderly women are far more likely than men to live alone (although not all widowed people live alone), as shown in Figure 14.3 (Administration on Aging, 2013). And differences in living arrangements grow even larger as people continue to age. These statistics also mask the diversity in living arrangements among persons of different racial and ethnic backgrounds. For example, Blacks are most likely to live alone; Asian Americans are least likely and often live in an extended family arrangement. People who live alone are more vulnerable to isolation and loneliness, and may face more social and health challenges; for example, they may be less likely to eat regular meals, or have access to transportation.

Although poverty rates are lower for the elderly on average than for other age groups (DeNavas-Walt, Proctor, & Smith, 2013), millions of elders still face financial difficulties. Despite Social Security, many don't have enough money to purchase good food or decent housing. About one-third of elderly households live on less than $35,000 a year (Administration on Aging, 2013). In particular, older minority women often have the lowest incomes.

How did we arrive at this point? In the next section, we take a look back through history.

Aging in Historical Perspective

14.2 Describe aging in historical perspective

Questions That Matter

14.3 In the past, were the elderly treated differently than they are today?

14.4 Why was Social Security created?

Perhaps you've heard about the "good old days" when families and communities treated the elderly with respect and showered them with power and prestige. Historians have now largely debunked this image as a myth. For example, many elders never retired—they had to continue to work at dangerous or dirty jobs to put food on the table and keep a roof over their heads. Only a small segment of the elderly population—some property-owning White males—experienced the status and prestige we generally associate with old age, whereas others were marginalized or considered outcasts in their own communities.

During the 17th and 18th centuries, most U.S. households consisted of nuclear families. Adult sons often continued to live at home until their fathers passed away, or until they received land as a wedding gift (Demos, 1986). Parents and their children did not live together, but they may have lived nearby, perhaps even on the same land. This family style has been called a *modified extended family system* (Greven, 1970).

Historians begin to see evidence of changing cultural ideals about aging in the 19th century as society moved from an agrarian to an industrial economy. Patriarchal power began to wane as increasingly more sons left their fathers' farms and moved to the city in search of work in the new factories. By the late 19th and early 20th centuries, only 12 percent to 18 percent of households contained extended family members outside the immediate nuclear family (Hareven, 1977). When extended families did live together, there was a reciprocal relationship between the generations—the elderly helped the younger members, and they, in turn, helped the elderly (Ruggles, 2011).

Over time, as these workers grew older in their factory jobs, they often found they couldn't keep up with younger workers who would eventually replace them. Old age was considered an economic liability (Farrell, 1999). Moreover, with families on the move, aging parents could not always rely on their children to take care of them when they became ill or frail. Poverty among the elderly was very high. Almshouses, which housed or provided charity to needy people, were increasingly made up of elderly persons with no money and no family members to turn to for help (Haber, 1983). People began to see old age as characterized by physical and mental decline, dependence, and weakness instead of as a natural process. During this period, geriatrics emerged as a branch of medicine focusing on medical symptoms of mental and physical decline (Hareven, 2000).

In the late 19th and early 20th centuries, few companies had private pensions for their retired employees, and the government didn't provide public pensions. Social Security didn't exist. Consequently, elderly persons who could still physically work usually continued to do so until the very end of their lives. In 1900, two-thirds of men older than 65 were employed, compared to only about 17 percent today (Taylor, Kochhar, Morin, Wang, Dockterman, & Medina, 2009). Many other developed nations had already created publicly funded programs that provided pensions for the elderly, including Germany in 1889, Great Britain in 1908, Sweden in 1913, Canada in 1927, and France in 1930 (Cockerham, 1997).

In the United States, bills for public pensions were introduced many times in the U.S. Congress between 1900 and 1935 with no success; however, during the Great Depression it became obvious that the elderly could not rely on jobs, private pensions, savings, or their families for financial support. By 1935, unemployment rates among those 65 and older were more than 50 percent (Hardy & Shuey, 2000), and a federal commission determined that

Today, the elderly have the lowest rates of poverty of any age group. However, for much of history the reverse was true. Social Security was created to help vulnerable elders.

Social Security: A federal government-sponsored cash assistance program for seniors (and survivors).

nearly half of all the elderly in the United States could not support themselves. Consequently, the **Social Security** Act was passed in 1935 as a response to the austere poverty that had enveloped many of our nation's elders. The federal government–sponsored cash assistance program for seniors (and survivors) is now seen as an earned right for this group, not as a form of welfare. Payments from Social Security have successfully reduced the percentage of seniors who are impoverished, and today the elderly are the age group *least* likely to live in poverty (DeNavas-Walt, Proctor, & Smith, 2013).

14.3 Identify the transitions families experience

Questions That Matter

14.5 What patterns are associated with adult children leaving their parents' home?

14.6 What type of relationships do parents have with their adult children after they finally leave home for good?

---

life-stage perspective: A perspective that claims development proceeds through a fairly set pattern of sequential stages that most people experience.

life-span perspective: A perspective that claims development is a lifelong process, is multidirectional, and consists of both positive and negative changes involving gains and losses.

life-course perspective: A perspective that sees age-related transitions as socially produced, socially recognized, and shared—a product of social structure, historical forces, and culture.

Family Transitions

During the course of a lifetime, families undergo a number of important transitions, such as the birth of children, raising and launching those children into adulthood, and the transition to grandparenthood. Chapter 1 introduced the developmental perspective (Duvall, 1977), which recognizes that families, like individuals, change over time and pass through a number of critical developmental stages. However, the timing of these experiences is dictated in part by cultural norms.

Several approaches elaborate on the developmental perspective and explain how people evolve and change over time. The three most common perspectives have similar names, but highlight different issues: (a) life stage; (b) life span; and (c) life course:

- The **life-stage perspective** contends that development proceeds through a fairly set pattern of sequential stages that most people experience. These are considered to be nearly universal and age-linked. Transition from one stage to the next depends on how successful a person was in the earlier stage.

- The **life-span perspective** proposes that development is a lifelong multidirectional process. Development consists of both positive and negative changes and always includes gains and losses. This perspective acknowledges a great deal of individual variability, because development depends on social and cultural conditions.

- The **life-course perspective** focuses on age-related transitions that are socially produced, socially recognized, and shared. Aging is a lifelong process influenced by social structure, historical forces, and culture. Glen Elder's (1998) work shows us how individuals change over time, how their transitions are connected to those of other family members, and how these changes reflect social and historical conditions, such as living through the Great Depression.

Children Leaving (and Returning) Home: Boomerangers

One transition families face is their grown children's departure from home. In the past, women's primary reason for leaving home was marriage; for men, it was marriage or the military. Few adults moved back into their parents' home once they had left. Today, however, young adults branch out on their own to attend school, to travel, to take a distant job, or simply to live on their own.

We also find that macro-level economic influences are causing many families to rethink their living arrangements (Fry, 2013; Parker, 2012). Housing costs, job opportunities, wages, and debt all influence their ability to live independently, and for many young adults, moving back home temporarily may make economic sense. In the peak of the recession, in 2007–2010, more than one-third of young adults were either unemployed or otherwise out of the workforce, the highest among this age group in nearly four decades

Explore on MySocLab
Activity: *What Do Older Families Look Like?*

(Pew Research Center, 2010a). Moreover, more than 8 out of 10 young adults carried debt. Their confidence in finding work began to erode (Taylor, Parker, Kochlar, Fry, Funk, Patten, & Motel, 2012).

Consequently, many young adults began to move back home with their parents to reduce expenses, pay off their debt, save money and look for work, as you can see in Figure 14.4. These adult children have been nicknamed the *boomerang generation* or simply *boomerangers* (Fredrix, 2008; Parker, 2012; Sukel, 2008; Wang & Morin, 2009). A survey of more than 800 of these boomerangers reveals that about half do pay some rent to their parents, and most help with other household expenses and share the household labor. The feature box *Diversity in Families: The Boomerang Generation* gives us a glimpse of this now-common family scenario.

Adult children who return home face both advantages and disadvantages, as do their parents (Parker, 2012; Ward & Spitze, 2007). About one-quarter of boomerangers say that moving home has been good for their relationship with their parents, another quarter say that it has been bad, and about half say that it has made no difference. Young adults may experience greater emotional and economic security living with their parents. If they have children of their own, they may benefit from having a grandparent participate in childcare. Likewise, older adults may benefit from having their adult children near them to provide assistance with such tasks as yard work,

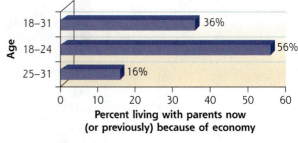

FIGURE 14.4
Young Adults Staying Close to Home

The recession brought many adult children back to their parents' home.
Source: Fry, August 1, 2013.

DIVERSITY IN FAMILIES   The "Boomerang Generation"

Children who move away to college often return to their parents' home afterwards while they look for a job. However, a growing number of adult children are moving home after job losses, accumulation of credit card debt, divorce, or the need to save for a down payment on a home.

Anna, age 27, lived on her own for many years until she lost her job and was unable to find another position. With mounting bills, she did what many other young adults are doing today, but what was rare a generation or two ago—she moved back in with mom and dad. By her own estimation, her parents spend about $1,000 a month helping her with her car payment and insurance, health insurance, and costs associated with going back to school, not to mention food and shelter. Her father is retired, her mother is nearly so, and they may not be able to support Anna much longer. *"It's kind of hitting me finally that I need to get out there and find a job,"* she said, *"even if it's just part-time just to help out however I can."*

People like Anna have been nicknamed the "boomerang generation." They move out, return home, then move out again, sometimes repeating the cycle many times. They find it difficult to maintain jobs, health insurance, and their lifestyles and come back home to their parents for financial help. Financial planners receive many calls from elderly parents asking for

advice. As one financial planner reports, parents *"jeopardize their financial freedom by continuing to subsidize their children. We have a hard time saying no as a culture to our children, and they keep asking for more."* Some delay or scale back their plans for retirement to help their adult children weather a financial or emotional crisis.

Not all parents are unhappy having their children come home again. Shirley, 80, is pleased to help out her "boomerang" daughter Jo Ann, a 52-year-old single parent who lost her job as an events planner at an upscale resort. Jo Ann struggled financially with several lower-paying jobs until Shirley invited her to move back home. *"I've got three kids and any of them can come home if they want,"* Shirley said. Meanwhile, Jo Ann is saving for a down payment on a house. While she loves her parents, she does feel somewhat embarrassed by her living arrangement, *"but you take humble steps in order to move forward."*

WHAT DO YOU THINK?

1. Should Jo Ann feel embarrassed by her living arrangement? Is there anything wrong with living with your parents into your adulthood? Why or why not?

2. How would your parents react if you wanted to move back home after college? How about after working for five years? How about after a divorce? Would their reactions vary according to the circumstances?

Source: Fredrix, Emily. 2008. "NOT-SUCH-BABY 'BOOMERANGS': Adults Returning to Nest Often Deplete Egg" Oakland Tribune (Oakland, CA), 22 March.

TABLE 14.3	Percentage of Households Experiencing Financial Distress, by Age Group

Many adult children rely on their parents for help during the recession, but many of their parents, who are likely in their 40s and 50s, are also affected by the recession.

Age	Percentage Experiencing Financial Distress
40–49	19%
50–59	16%
60–69	8%
70+	3%

Source: Mossaad, 2010.

cooking, or cleaning. Older adults may also appreciate having the additional interaction with their grandchildren.

Co-residence has some marked disadvantages, however. Older parents and adult children may regress to the roles they played when the children were teenagers. Parents may try to establish a curfew or establish rules governing their adult child's behavior. If the adult child has lived alone for a period of time, he or she is likely to resent these rules and see them as intrusions.

Having adult children who need assistance back in the home can alter the parents' lives considerably. The parents may not be able to retire as early as they wish; they may have to postpone plans to travel; they may need to reorganize their own finances to offer assistance to their children; they may need to rearrange furniture and space within the house; and they (primarily the mother) may find themselves doing the extra cooking and cleaning. Parents who had given thought to relocating to a new city or downsizing to a smaller house may have to postpone these plans (Bures, 2009). Children often return home when they have special needs and little or no money, and parents may feel obligated to help them out regardless of their own personal and financial situation. This isn't always easy; today, many older adults have also faced financial hardship because of the recession, as indicated in Table 14.3. They too may have had to reduce their spending, cope with unemployment, and face a loss of savings and assets (Mossaad, 2010; Soto, 2009).

Relationships between Adults and Their Elderly Parents

Overall, older parents and their adult children remain emotionally linked as children leave home (Umberson, Pudrovska, & Reczek, 2010). Both generations report strong feelings of connection to each other, although parents often have stronger feelings of attachment to their children than their children have to them. Generally, adult children and their parents want to get along, and therefore try to avoid those topics that cause tension in the relationship. However, parent–child relationships may contain elements of intimacy and conflict at the same time.

As adult children become partnered, cohabit, or marry, they're likely to see their parents less frequently than before (Bucx, van Wel, Knun, & Hagendoorn, 2008). However, as young adults have children of their own, they tend to see their parents more frequently again. This is consistent with the life course perspective (Elder, 1998), which suggests that family relationships change in response to the developmental transitions of family members.

Read on MySocLab
Document: *Intimacy at a Distance, Korean American Style: Invited Korean Elderly and Their Married Children*

Social exchange theory, introduced in Chapter 1, is a useful tool for thinking about the exchanges made between adult children and their aging parents. It focuses on the costs and benefits for different types of family interactions, including the exchange of aid, financial and otherwise. Although the scientific literature and popular press are full of articles about the help elderly parents will need from their adult children, in reality, many adult children receive substantial help from their aging parents. Until they are very old and frail, aging parents give far more assistance to their children than they receive from them (Dykstra & Komter, 2006; Fleck, 2009). Parents may lend money for a down payment on a new house or a new car; they may provide childcare to grandchildren; they may help pay a child or grandchild's college tuition; or they may provide extra cash in times of personal need, such as a family illness or a divorce. A nationwide study of 10,000 older adults between the ages of 48 and 70 asked about the degree to which they help their adult children (Fleck, 2009):

- 70 percent gave cash for day-to-day expenses
- 40 percent helped with mortgage or rent payments
- 24 percent provided money for health care
- 23 percent helped pay for daycare costs
- 21 percent provided funds for education

A study based on more than 14,000 parent–child dyads, found that those who lived at home with their parents for longer periods of time, had closer relationships to their parents than did other children, many years later into adulthood. Those who left home later lived closer to their parents, maintained more frequent contact, and were more likely to provide, as well as receive, intergenerational support. Other studies come to similar conclusions and find that financial assistance from parents is associated with closeness and intimacy (Johnson, 2013). In other words, living together in young adulthood tends to promote solidarity over the life course (Leopold, 2012).

Do your parents ever help you financially? It's likely they will at some point in your life. Adult children are almost four times more likely to receive financial assistance from their aging parents as they are to provide it to them, and almost twice as likely to receive practical and emotional help as they are to give it (Dykstra & Komter, 2006; Gallagher, 1994).

📖 **Read** on **MySocLab**
Document: *Women and Men in the Caregiving Role*

Adult Siblings

Deanne and Clay both live in a medium-size suburb outside of Los Angeles, California. They call each other weekly on the telephone and try to get together at each other's houses at least once or twice a month. Both are married—to someone else—but their spouses do not seem to mind the intimacy between them. In fact, the families seem to enjoy taking vacations together. Their children are roughly the same age, and even they see nothing wrong with the special relationship that seems to drive much of their families' leisure. They enjoy the barbeques, pool parties, and camping trips to the mountains, and see these as key events in their lives. But life is not all fun and games. Clay and his wife actually helped Deanne and her husband paint their home. Why would Clay and his wife offer such support? Deanne and Clay have known one another for all of their lives. They are sister and brother.

Although not all siblings may be as close as Deanne and Clay, most adults remain close to their siblings, and consider them an important source of love, support, aid, and companionship (Connidis & Campbell, 2001; Voorpostel & Bleiszner, 2008). The *Why Do Research?* feature box reveals that practical help and emotional support from siblings are common, and are also affected by the relationships that the siblings have with the parent.

What type of relationships do you have with your parents and your siblings, and how have these relationships changed as you have gotten older? How do you anticipate them changing further?

While growing up, most of you saw your siblings every day. Chances are you lived together, had at least dinner together, and even shared a bedroom or bathroom. As you grow older and move out of your parents' home, how do your relationships with your siblings change? Do you remain close—providing emotional or practical support—or do these relationships become distant?

An important study conducted in the Netherlands provides some insight into adult sibling relationships. The Netherlands Kinship Panel Study was conducted during 2002–2004, and focused on the topic of family solidarity. Interviewers conducted detailed face-to-face interviews with and administered survey questionnaires to over 8,000 persons between the ages of 18 and 80. Participants were asked to identify their living siblings and parents. For each participant, one sibling and one parent were randomly selected to join the study. In all, 2,731 siblings participated, as did 2,108 parents. These triads (i.e., original participant, sibling, and parent) are the center of the study.

The study found considerable closeness among adult siblings. Most reported that their relationship with a sibling was "good" or "very good" (as opposed to "not great" or "reasonable"). Thirty-three percent of the siblings reported *receiving* practical support from a sibling over the past three months with housework or odd jobs, and 35 percent reported *providing* such support. Emotional support was even more frequent: 94 percent of siblings claimed to have received

emotional support from a sibling over the past three months, and 93 percent had provided it. People seemed to report that the relationship was equal—they gave about as much as they received. Women were less likely to exchange practical support than were men; however, they were more likely to exchange emotional support, but only with sisters.

One would expect (i.e., hypothesize) that the amount of support given and received would depend on the quality of the sibling relationship; however, the researchers found the situation to be more complex. The quality of the bond with parents was *negatively related* to sibling support. That is, when a relationship with a parent was poorer, more support was exchanged between siblings. If the relationship with a parent was good, less support was exchanged among siblings. It appears that siblings compensate for a poor relationship with a parent by turning to each other.

WHAT DO YOU THINK?

1. Can you anticipate what type of relationship you might have with siblings, if you have them, in ten or twenty years?
2. This study was conducted in the Netherlands, yet was published in an American academic journal—can we generalize its findings to the United States? Why or why not?

Source: Voorpostel, Marieke, and Rosemary Bleiszner. 2008. "Intergenerational Solidarity and Support Between Adult Siblings." *Journal of Marriage and Family,* 70(1):157–67.

14.4 Summarize issues experienced by the aging couple

Questions That Matter

14.7 Are the elderly satisfied with their marriages?

14.8 What unique issues do lesbian-gay-bisexual-transgender (LGBT) elders face?

The Aging Couple

Most married older couples have a relationship that has endured over many years. Together they have faced life and its transitions: the birth of a child, the raising of children, job opportunities and disappointments, the effort to balance work and family, the departure of children from home, and then becoming a couple once again. Let's look at some of the issues couples experience together as they grow older.

Marital Satisfaction

We assume that marriage is an important buffer against loneliness and isolation in old age. But is that true for all married couples? Most older adults report being happy in their marriages, yet 20 percent to 25 percent experience moderate or strong social and emotional loneliness (Gierveld, van Groenou, Hoogendoorn, & Smit, 2008). Those who are most lonely tend to have a spouse with health problems, do not communicate frequently with their spouse, often disagree with their spouse, or evaluate their sex life as unpleasant.

How does the degree to which couples are satisfied with their spouses and their relationship change over the life course? One early study of 400 couples married in the 1930s looked at their marital satisfaction over a period of 20 years (Pineo, 1961). Each member of the couple evaluated the relationship soon after marriage, and then again 20 years later. Using a number of different measures, the study found that marital satisfaction for both partners had diminished over time.

More recent studies have usually been cross-sectional—that is, they look at one moment, like a snapshot in time—because it's very difficult to track couples for 20, 30, or 40 years. These cross-sectional studies generally report that the marital satisfaction of couples may instead be curvilinear, or shaped like the letter U. This means a marriage starts with a high level of satisfaction, begins to drop as couples have children, and then rises again when the children leave home (Morgan & Kunkel, 1998).

However, family researcher Norval Glenn examined several cohorts of families over a 10-year period, including couples who had married from the 1930s through the 1980s, and his work casts doubt on whether marital satisfaction actually rises after the children leave home (1998). Glenn found no evidence of the upturn; he suggested instead that variation in marital quality may simply be the result of *cohort differences*—that is, people of different *cohorts,* or ages, have different expectations about marriage. A couple who married many years ago may be more likely to emphasize duty and responsibility in marriage, and focus less on personal fulfillment. Therefore, they may rate their marriage as happier than that of a younger couple because their expectations are more easily met.

SEXUALITY   Despite common misperceptions, sexual desire and sexual activity remain essential elements of the lives of the elderly (Karraker & DeLamater, 2013; Kontula & Haavio-Mannila, 2009; Lodge & Umberson, 2012). As discussed in Chapter 5, a large majority of the elderly have a positive view of sexual relationships, and if married or partnered, will likely remain sexually active (Lindau, Schumm, Laumann, Levinson, O'Muircheartaigh, & Waite, 2007). Although the likelihood of sexual activity does decline with age, 39 percent of men ages 75 to 85 are still sexually active, as are 17 percent of women. Older men and women who experience a significant decline in sexual activity as a result of their own or their partner's poor health often find their situation depressing or frustrating (Hirayama & Walker, 2011; Karraker, DeLamater, & Schwartz, 2011; Syme, Klonoff, Mascera, & Brodine, 2012).

Although sexual relationships among the elderly are most often with life-long partners, this isn't always the case. Because of high rates of widowhood, some elderly persons are engaging in sexual relationships with new partners, yet practicing "safe sex" may be the furthest thing from their minds. They don't have to worry about pregnancy, and HIV/AIDS and many other sexually transmitted infections were not problems when they were younger. The *From Macro to Micro* feature box reveals new challenges some elders face as they remain sexually active, and the policies and programs to help them navigate this uncharted territory.

THE DIVISION OF HOUSEHOLD LABOR   As children leave home and parents retire, how do couples divide up household labor? As discussed in Chapter 10, women spend far more time on domestic tasks than do men, including when both work outside the home for pay (Bureau of Labor Statistics, October 22, 2012; Parker & Wang, 2013). Most studies show that the division of household labor changes little as a couple ages, and long-established patterns endure. Women continue to do the majority of housework.

What happens during the period after a husband retires and a wife is still working? Using a large nationally representative longitudinal sample of the elderly in which one spouse was employed at least 10 hours a week, Maximiliane Szinovacz examined how retirement changed a couple's allocation of domestic labor (2000). She found that retirees spend more time on housework than their employed counterparts, including tasks that were considered to be in their partner's domain. Retired husbands whose wives continue to work outside the home take on more responsibility; however, when the wife retires, she appears to take charge of "her" domain again. The division of household labor remains firmly entrenched within families.

Are your parents still married to one another? If so, what types of transitions have they endured together? Have these transitions been smooth or difficult, and why?

Jane Fowler may appear to be your typical grandmother. However, Jane is not typical as she has HIV. How did this come to be?

After 23 years of marriage, while in her late fifties, Jane and her husband decided to divorce. She had never pictured herself dating in her fifties, but she met a man in a similar situation, newly divorced and looking for a companion. On New Year's Eve the couple decided to have sex. Safe sex and condoms were the last things on their minds, especially since pregnancy was not a concern. Unfortunately, the risk of getting a sexually transmitted infection (STI) does not vanish just because you age. Sometime later, Jane found out she had acquired HIV. Now in her seventies, she travels to speak to other seniors and educate them on safe-sex practices and the risks of acquiring STIs, topics that many older people have never discussed.

As people age, their partners pass away or they divorce, leading many seniors to eventually reenter the dating scene. As it has likely been fifty years or more since they had to think about new relationships and new sex lives, safe-sex practices are anything but uppermost in their minds. In addition, the culture of sex has changed drastically in the last fifty years with the prevalence of STIs and the emergence of the HIV/AIDS epidemic. And innovations such as hormone replacement therapy for women and erectile dysfunction drugs for men allow for extended sex lives.

The older population is vulnerable because they are often overlooked when it comes to education and resources on safe-sex practices. Older men and women are also more likely to have a chronic illness and a depleted immune system, leaving them more vulnerable to an STI or HIV infection. Women are biologically more susceptible than men to becoming infected if exposed to an STI, because the vagina does not produce as much lubricant after menopause, causing more friction and vulnerability to infection during intercourse. STIs are also more likely to remain undetected in women. Few seniors get tested for HIV or STIs, so they may spread them without realizing they have a contagious disease.

Few elderly adults talk with their physicians about sexual health issues, and few physicians are likely to suspect HIV as a cause of illness in the older population. Cases such as Jane's are changing this situation.

In Arizona, a community center recruits volunteers to pass out condoms at popular events. Florida hosts safe-sex programs with health education; the Senior HIV Project works with seniors to train "safe-sexperts," who talk to their friends and neighbors about the importance of using condoms and getting tested for STIs. The University of Michigan has started an aging and intimacy clinic to address the concerns and questions of older adults in the community. Nancy Orel, a professor at Bowling Green State University, has students in her gerontology class speak with their grandparents about safe sex and STIs. She finds that once students get past the uncomfortable feelings, both they and their grandparents find they have much to learn from one another. Although a few programs are available to better inform older adults, many more resources are needed to target this overlooked population.

WHAT DO YOU THINK?

1. Would you feel comfortable talking with your grandparents about safe-sex practices? How could you present the subject to make it a good learning experience for both yourself and your grandparents?
2. What other resources could society provide to help inform older citizens of the risks of unprotected sex and acquiring STIs and HIV/AIDS?

Author: Nicole K. Smith
Source: Adapted from Huffstutter, P.J. 2007. "Experts: Elders Need Some Sex Education, Too." Los Angeles Times, 15 December.

Lesbian, Gay, Bisexual, and Transgender Elders

"I am in my 70s and I see the other gay women in my neighborhood who I grew up with and who have no Social Security benefits and I see how they have to live and it scares me."

—**Ira J., Harlem, NY (*The National Gay and Lesbian Taskforce, 2007*)**

When most people think of someone who is gay, lesbian, or transgender, chances are they do not think of a senior citizen. Nonetheless, somewhere between 1.4 and 3.8 million elderly are lesbian, gay, bisexual, or transgender (LGBT), a population that may number 7 million by 2030 (Grant, 2009). Most of these elderly are women. Although they face many of the same issues that other elders face, such as health problems or the need for reliable transportation or housing assistance, they also have unique concerns. For example, older gay men are aging in a context sharply shaped by HIV/AIDS (Rosenfeld, Bartlam, & Smith, 2013). Likewise, transgender older adults have significantly higher risk of poor health, disability, depressive symptoms, and stress, as compared with those who are not transgender (Fredriksen-Goldsen, Cook-Daniels, Kim, Erosheva, Emlet, Hoy-Ellis, Goldsen, & Muraco, 2013).

Most federal programs and laws treat same-sex couples different from married heterosexual couples (Grant, 2009; Human Rights Campaign, 2012):

Same-sex couples are not allowed to marry in most states, and are therefore disadvantaged with respect to Social Security, pension policies, and medical issues.

- Social Security pays survivor benefits to widows and widowers, but not to the surviving same-sex life partner of the deceased. This may cost LGBT elders $124 million a year in lost benefits.

- Married couples are eligible for Social Security spousal benefits, which can allow them to earn half their spouse's Social Security benefit if it's larger than their own. Unmarried partners in lifelong relationships aren't eligible for spousal benefits.

- Medicaid regulations protect the assets and homes of married spouses when the other spouse enters a nursing home or long-term care facility; no such protections are offered to same-sex partners.

- Tax laws and other regulations of 401(k)s and pensions discriminate against same-sex partners, costing the surviving partner in a same-sex relationship tens of thousands of dollars a year, and possibly more than $1 million over a lifetime. For example, if a person with a 401(k) pension plan dies, the money rolls over to a *legal spouse* without any tax penalty. However, because gays and lesbians cannot legally marry in most states, the surviving partner would have to pay a 20 percent federal tax.

The effect of this unequal treatment is striking. Assume Deborah dies at age 60 with $100,000 in her 401(k) account, which she leaves to her life partner, Ruth, also age 60. Ruth will receive the sum less taxes (at least $20,000), for a total of no more than $80,000. Ruth cannot roll the sum over into a tax-free IRA. If Ruth were a man—let's call him Rubin—as Deborah's widower, Rubin would receive the full $100,000 and be able to shield it from taxes until age 70½. In other words, the survivor of the legally married couple has a nest egg to invest that is roughly 20 percent larger than that of the surviving spouse in the same-sex couple. The nest egg can grow in a tax-deferred account until the maximum age of disbursement for the surviving spouse in a legally married couple. The surviving spouse of the same-sex couple, however, cannot roll the initial disbursement into an IRA (Cahill, South, & Spade, 2000).

Even basic rights such as hospital visitation or the right to die in the same nursing home as one's partner are regularly denied to same-sex couples. U.S. government policies affecting the aging population assume heterosexuality, close relationships with children, and extended families to provide basic needs as we age. These policies produce social, economic, and health consequences for LGBT elders (Grant, 2009; Hu, 2005; Human Rights Campaign, 2012). They may hide their sexual orientation from their health care and social service providers out of fear, further compromising their ability to get needed care and assistance. Several studies document widespread homophobia among those entrusted with the care of the elderly in the United States. Therefore, many LGBT seniors remain hidden, reinforcing isolation and forgoing services they may truly need. One study indicates that only 35 percent of older lesbian, bisexual, or transgender women are "out" to all of their healthcare providers, and 12 percent have no confidence that they will receive appropriate and unbiased treatment from medical personnel (MetLife, 2006).

Childfree Older Families

As discussed in Chapter 8, the number of couples without children is on the rise. About 10 percent of elders today don't have children (Kinsella & He, 2009), but nearly 20 percent of women ages 40 to 44 are childfree (Livingston & Cohn,

2010). What implication does this have for an aging population? One of the many benefits we assume will accrue from having children is that we will be happier in old age because children will provide social support, caregiving when we are frail, or financial help if we need it. But how do older childfree couples really fare?

Couples without children are as well adjusted in later life as those with children, and rely on their spouses, friends, and other kin for social support. Their finances are generally better (Plotnick, 2009), and they report being happy (or unhappy) as frequently as do those couples with children (Koropeckyj-Cox, 2008; Koropeckyj-Cox & Call, 2007; Koropeckyj-Cox, Pienta, & Brown, 2007). However, the childfree are more likely than other older adults to go to a nursing facility when their health deteriorates and they are unable to take care of themselves.

14.5 Discuss the grief process associated with widowhood

Question That Matters

14.9 Do men and women experience widowhood differently?

Widowhood

The death of a spouse stands as one of life's most stressful events (Holmes & Rahe, 1967). It means the loss of a companion and friend, perhaps the loss of income, and the ending of a familiar way of life. Many widowed men and women experience extreme sadness, weight loss, loneliness, insomnia, and depression. Widowhood can occur at any point in the life cycle, but because it's most likely to occur among the elderly, research tends to focus on that age group. Nonetheless, when people become widowed at a younger age, their difficulties may be exacerbated because death during young adulthood and middle age is so unexpected. Few of their friends are likely to be widowed, and they may stand alone from their peer group in an important way, as shown in the feature box *My Family: My Experience with Widowhood.*

More than 14 million persons are classified as *widowed* in the United States, and about three-quarters of widows are women (U.S. Census Bureau, 2012c). The number of persons who have *experienced* widowhood, however, is much larger, because many widowed people have remarried, and are therefore no longer classified as widows or widowers.

There are three primary reasons for the significantly higher rates of widowhood among women than men. First, mortality rates among females are lower than for males; therefore, they live to older ages. The life expectancy of females at age 65 exceeds that of males by nearly 7 years. Second, wives are typically a few years younger than their husbands and consequently, have a greater chance of outliving them. Third, widowed women are less likely to remarry than are widowed men. As discussed in Chapter 13, there is a lack of eligible men because our cultural norms encourage older men to date and marry younger women, but not the reverse (Berardo & Berardo, 2000).

We've all heard statements suggesting that an elderly person often dies soon after his or her spouse dies: "He just gave up"; "She died of sadness"; "He saw no reason to go on after Rose died." Is there really an increased probability of death among new widows and widowers? Two Harvard sociology professors decided to answer this question by following nearly 4,500 U.S. couples ages 67 and older for 5 years (Elwert & Christakis, 2006). They found that there seems to be some truth to the *widow effect,* because there is an increase in the likelihood of death after a spouse dies. The widow effect, however, doesn't occur equally among racial and ethnic groups. White men were 18 percent more likely to die shortly after their wives' deaths, and White women were 16 percent more likely to die shortly after their husbands' deaths. But among Blacks, a spouse's death had no effect on the mortality of the survivor.

Why would widowhood contribute to an early death for Whites, but not for Blacks? On marrying, Blacks and Whites appear to receive many of the same health, financial, and social benefits such as emotional support, caretaking when

At the age of ten, I lost my father to cancer. It was February of my fifth grade school year. Grief and sorrow smothered me, filling my chest with an aching heaviness that made breathing difficult. I doubted my ability to endure my endless sobbing, yet I also doubted my ability to stop. Nothing in my childhood had prepared me for such loss; no story books, classroom lesson plans, religious training, or parental advice.

The adults in my world did say "time heals all wounds." This brought me little solace at the time but proved true; my feelings of intense sorrow gradually subsided. I felt waves of deep sadness over my father's death until I was a young adult. When my daughter was born, I delighted in thinking she would never experience what had been the most painful occurrence of my childhood. My husband, who desired more time with his two sons from a previous marriage than shared parenting allowed him, delighted in "finally having a child I can raise from start to finish." Unfortunately, we were both wrong.

At the age of ten, my daughter lost her father to cancer. It too was February of her fifth grade school year. I drew on my experience with my father's death to console her. But she did not grieve as I had; she did not cry. Concerned she was not grieving "the right way," I took her to three therapists within two years of her father's passing. One after the other told me she was indeed grieving, in her own way, and adjusting well. The last therapist sternly demanded that I stop taking my daughter to therapists. Someday, she explained, my daughter might really need therapy but won't seek it if she believes it serves little purpose, which my dragging her from therapist to therapist seemed to be doing. So I stopped taking her to therapists. My daughter lives away at college now; a photo of her father sits on her dorm room desk. Periodically she feels deep waves of sadness over her father's passing which she soothes with old family videos, including an oral history I conducted with my husband before his death.

As for me, I was 41 when I lost my husband to cancer. It was February of my first year at a new university in a new town. An assistant professor of sociology, I was now a widow and a single parent of a 10-year-old child. How was I going to manage? Who was going to help me take care of my daughter? How was I going to write and publish so as to get tenure when grief filled my head with an unshakeable fog?

I looked around for someone who shared this experience to ask. I found no one. The only widows I encountered were much older, and did not share my career and parenting demands. The only single parents of young children I knew were not widows, nor were they assistant professors at research-intensive universities. As I tried to manage meetings and classes that sometimes ran into the dinner hour, I became angry with the insensitivity of my academic workplace to the difficulties of lone parenting. I felt I needed to be there for my daughter who had just lost her other parent. I was fortunate to be able to afford babysitters, and hired a patch work of college students to care for my daughter after school, serving as her

tutors, driving her to extra-curricular activities, and helping her to get dinner on days I taught late.

As a grieving widow, I felt oddly apart and disconnected from the world of the normal, in a parallel universe of muddled thinking, fragility, and tears. "I seemed to have crossed one of those legendary rivers that divide the living from the dead, entered a place in which I could be seen only by those who were themselves recently bereaved" (Didion, 2006:75). My grief made me aware of how truly vulnerable we all are; how little separates us from death. I taped to my computer a quote attributed to Ian Maclaren, "Let us be kind to one another, for most of us are fighting a hard battle." Everyday matters that seemed so important in normal times mattered far less to me now.

After the initial words and notes of sympathy in the days immediately following my husband's passing, my colleagues did not mention my loss again. Their talk centered on the university work I had so much difficulty concentrating on. In contemporary U.S. culture, we are not comfortable with death and tend to "treat mourning as morbid self-indulgence, and to give social admiration to the bereaved who hide their grief so fully that no one would guess anything happened" (Gorer, 1977, cited by Didion, 2006:60). I felt I had to hide my grief. I did not miss even one class in the days leading to my husband's death or immediately after. I knew I could not slow down my research productivity as I needed to get tenure or I would lose my job. And I was now the sole provider of my family.

I expected to experience a year of grief and mourning before rejoining the normal world. I was wrong. It took me well over three years; the fact that I expected it to be easier than it was only made it harder. I've learned to have patience with those enduring hardship and grief; we all experience traumas differently. Some might heal faster than others, or hide it better, but I know not to use them as a general standard of how long it takes to heal. We can help bereaved or traumatized co-workers, family members, friends, and acquaintances to cope by being patient and understanding when they are unable to perform at their usual level. Doing so will help them to heal.

I am now happily remarried and back in the world of the "normals" where I often have to remind myself not to put too much importance on minor matters, or forget how vulnerable we all are. The quote by Ian Maclaren is still taped to my computer.

WHAT DO YOU THINK?

1. How did the author's youthfulness affect her experience with widowhood?
2. Why do you think that people in our culture are so uncomfortable talking about death, loss, and mourning?

Reference: Didion, 2006.
Source: My Family: My Experience with Widowhood from Karen Pyke. Reprinted by permission of the author.

ill, and enhanced social support, so what could account for the widow effect? We do know that Blacks are almost twice as likely to live with other relatives (Pew Research Center, 2010c), are more active in religious groups, and when married are less likely to adhere to a traditional gendered division of labor, which may reduce dependence on a spouse. It seems that Blacks may somehow manage to extend the benefits of marriage into widowhood, and are therefore less likely than Whites to die soon after their spouse (Elwert & Christakis, 2006).

The Process of Grief and Bereavement

People handle their grief over the death of a loved one in a variety of ways. Some try to remain stoic, others cry out in despair. Some people fear death, whereas others, perhaps because of a strong religious faith, see death as part of a larger "master plan." Those widows and widowers in poor health at the time of widowhood had significantly higher risks of complicated grief and depression (Utz, Caserta, & Lund, 2012). The *Getting to Know Yourself* feature box offers the opportunity to assess your own attitudes toward death and offers some insights into your possible grieving process.

GETTING TO KNOW YOURSELF   **Death and Grief Assessment**

Answer the questions below as either true (T) or false (F) as they pertain to your life experiences. Keep in mind that there are no "right" or "wrong" answers. Wait until you have completed the assessment before you read the key.

1. Death scares me.   T   F
2. I rarely think about death.   T   F
3. I am afraid of dying in a painful manner.   T   F
4. I am troubled about the idea of life, death, and their overall purpose and meaning.   T   F
5. I rarely go to funerals, even if it is someone close to me who has died.   T   F
6. I am concerned about a nuclear holocaust.   T   F
7. We do not talk about death in my family.   T   F
8. I hate to look at either pictures of dead bodies or real dead bodies.   T   F
9. When people talk about death, I get real nervous.   T   F
10. I am concerned with how fast my life appears to be going.   T   F
11. I am horrified to fly in an airplane because of the possibility of a crash.   T   F
12. Life is too short.   T   F
13. I am afraid of contracting AIDS or some other disease.   T   F
14. Hospital treatments such as operations scare me.   T   F
15. Hearing about cancer, heart attacks, and strokes makes me feel uneasy.   T   F
16. In my family, we experience grief and deep feelings of loss when someone dies.   T   F
17. Grief can be felt in death and in other life events.   T   F
18. Each person grieves in his or her own way.   T   F
19. Children are capable of grieving.   T   F
20. The amount of time required for grieving varies from person to person.   T   F

21. Keeping busy is not the cure for grief.   T   F
22. Sometimes people grieve even if death has not occurred.   T   F
23. It is not very wise to tell a grieving person that you know how he or she feels.   T   F
24. Listening to a grieving person is a healthy form of support.   T   F
25. Unresolved childhood grieving may resurface later in life.   T   F
26. When others grieve, it is helpful to provide support in and around the house.   T   F
27. Religion and culture strongly influence how we grieve.   T   F
28. Shock and numbness are normal responses to grievers.   T   F
29. If you feel sad, it is okay to express it to those who are grieving.   T   F
30. Avoiding the grieving person is not a healthy approach.   T   F

Key: Give yourself 1 point for each False answer in items 1–15. Also give yourself 1 point for each True answer to items 16–30. The highest score you can earn is 30 points. The higher your score, the healthier and more knowledgeable you are about death, dying, and grief.

WHAT DO YOU THINK?

1. Do the findings from this assessment accurately reflect you, your expectations, and your life experience? Why or why not?
2. What have been your experiences with grief? How are they similar to or different from other people your age?

Source: Hammond, Ron J. and Barbara Bearnson. 2003a. "Death and Grief Assessment." pp. 125–26 in The Marriages and Families Activities Workbook. Wadsworth.

One of the more popular perspectives on death and dying is based on the work of Elizabeth Kübler-Ross (1969). Her work with 200 primarily middle-age cancer patients suggested five somewhat distinct stages that dying people and their loved ones experience. Although some critics say that not everyone experiences these stages, or necessarily in this order, Kübler-Ross's work is nonetheless useful. The five stages are

- **Denial:** Many people first refuse to believe that they or a loved one is dying. They may ask for additional medical tests, desire a second or third opinion, or in other ways deny that death is near.
- **Anger:** When coming to accept the truth, some people become angry. They may project this anger toward friends, family, people who are well, or medical personnel.
- **Bargaining:** The dying person or loved one may try to forestall death by striking a bargain with God (or a higher power).
- **Depression:** Depression may set in when the dying person or their loved ones realize they cannot win the fight against the illness or disease. They may be depressed over the symptoms of their condition (chronic pain) or effects of their treatment (hair loss from chemotherapy). As they plan for their future, the loss they face can feel overwhelming.
- **Acceptance:** Eventually, patients or loved ones may come to accept the approaching death. In this stage, they may reflect on their lives together.

These five stages are highly individualized; no two people pass through them at exactly the same pace, and many may go back and forth between stages before finally reaching acceptance of the inevitable.

Sex Differences in the Experience of Widowhood

Who do you think has a more difficult time adjusting to widowhood, men or women? Most research points to men's greater difficulty coping with widowhood (Bennett, Smith, & Hughes, 2005; Lee & DeMaris, 2007; Lee, Willets, & Seccombe, 1998). Men are generally more dependent on their spouse for social and emotional support. They're less likely to have close relationships with same-sex widowed friends (Felmlee & Muraco, 2009), are more likely to be older, may be in poor health, have fewer family ties, and are less proficient at domestic tasks.

Women are far more likely to be widowed than are men.

However, older women have largely been financially dependent on their husbands and when widowed may face substantial difficulties. First, their incomes and assets are significantly less than those of men's (DeNavas-Walt, Proctor, & Smith, 2013). Two-fifths of widows fall into poverty at some time during the 5 years after their husband's death, a higher proportion than widowed men or divorced women. The loss of income and assets is far greater for Black and Hispanic widows than for White widows (Angel, Jimenez, & Angel, 2007). We do know that widows who have worked tend to report less depression than those who have not worked (Pai & Barrett, 2007).

Second, widows may face the daunting practical problems of maintaining a house alone. A study of 201 widows drawn from public death records in a Midwestern metropolitan area found that their financial problems were not a primary cause of stress (although they were a major cause of stress for women getting divorced) (Miller, Smerglia, Gaudet, & Kitson, 1998). The researchers found that the lack of practical support, such as help with home repairs, significantly increased widows' stress.

Most of these studies, however, are cross-sectional research rather than longitudinal studies that follow people over time. Lee and DeMaris (2007) used longitudinal data from the National Survey of Families and Households to examine sex differences in psychological well-being before and after widowhood. They found that men whose wives died during the course of the study were already highly depressed at the first interview, even before their wives died. Apparently, the anticipation of their wife's death was depressing in and of itself. However, they found no such anticipatory effect of depression for wives.

What are some rituals that Americans use to mourn the dead? How might these be similar to or different from those used in other developed or developing countries?

14.6 Analyze the role of grandparents in the lives of their grandchildren

Question That Matters

14.10 What type of relationship do grandparents typically have with their grandchildren?

Grandparents and Their Grandchildren

Almost all parents eventually become grandparents. On average, first grandchildren are born when grandparents are in their late 40s or early 50s, although the age is increasing as young couples wait longer to have children. Some people may not become grandparents until their 70s. Compared with children in the past, children today are more likely to have all four grandparents alive when they are born, and most will continue to have at least two grandparents alive when they reach adulthood. Grandparents can play a number of different parts in the lives of their grandchildren, from occasional visitor, to custodial grandparents (Dunifon, 2013).

The role of grandparent has changed over the past century in several ways (Cherlin & Furstenberg, 1986; Kemp, 2007):

- Grandparenting has become a role distinct from parenting because grandparents are now less likely to have their own children still living in the home (except, of course, for the boomerangers).

- Grandparents are healthier and better educated, and have greater economic security, than in the past (Kinsella & He, 2009).

- Grandparents—and grandfathers in particular—are now more likely to recognize the importance of having direct emotional involvement with young children. Grandfathers have opportunities to participate in nurturing children that seemed unavailable to them as fathers or to grandfathers in the past (Cunningham-Burley, 2001).

- Grandparents and their grandchildren can more easily travel long distances and communicate by telephone or computer.

companionate grandparenting: A type of grandparenting where the grandparents and grandchildren enjoy recreational activities, occasional overnight stays, and even babysitting with an emphasis on fun and enjoyment.

Families are now able to construct their own conception of what it means to be a grandparent (Kemp, 2007; Walker, Manoogian-O'Dell, McGraw, & White, 2001). Relationships between grandparents and their grandchildren can take many forms, as shown in Table 14.4.

Most grandparents report that their relationships with their grandchildren are meaningful, fun, and pleasurable (AARP, September 2007; Reitzes & Mutran, 2004). In a national study of grandparents, Cherlin and Furstenberg (1986) found that more than half reported a **companionate grandparenting** relationship with their grandchildren, enjoying fun recreational activities, occasional

TABLE 14.4	Types of Grandparent–Grandchild Relationships
Family researchers classify grandparent–grandchild relationships into three broad types.	
Companionate	Grandparents and grandchildren have fun together, enjoy recreation together on a regular basis, and are important to each other's lives.
Remote	The grandparent–grandchild relationship is emotionally distant. Visits may be infrequent. Grandparents are only minimally involved in their grandchildren's lives.
Involved	Grandparents are highly involved in their grandchildren's lives. They may take care of their grandchildren on a regular basis, and perhaps even live together.

overnight stays, and even babysitting. Grandparents reported that they enjoy spending time with their grandchildren, but they are ready to leave the challenging parts of parenting to the parents themselves.

I love being a grandpa because I get to have all the fun. They love to spend the night and we have a party. I spoil them rotten. But afterwards, when I'm getting tired, my grandkids go back home. Their parents provide them with the routine and the discipline. I get the good part because I can enjoy myself without having much responsibility. (Henry, age 68)

Meanwhile, nearly one-third had **remote grandparenting,** or emotionally distant, relationships with their grandchildren, usually because they lived far away and did not, or could not, keep in regular touch. Another 15 percent had highly **involved grandparenting** relationships, with more frequent interaction, and sometimes even living together. Figure 14.5 shows the percentage of grandparents engaging in various activities with their children during the previous 12 months (Cherlin & Furstenberg, 1986).

Researchers also point to the changing relationship between grandparents and grandchildren. Cherlin and Furstenberg (1986) found a marked shift in the balance between respect and affection. They asked all respondents in a national survey, "Are you and the [study child] more friendly, less friendly, or about the same as your grandparents were with you?" Forty-eight percent reported that they were "more friendly," whereas only 9 percent said "less friendly." Similarly, 55 percent claimed that their relationship with the child was "closer" than their own relationship with their grandparents, and only 10 percent said that it was "not as close." When respondents were asked about respect, most reported no difference. However, 22 percent said they were more respectful of their grandparents, whereas only 2 percent believed their grandchildren showed them greater respect (Cherlin & Furstenberg, 1986).

remote grandparenting: A type of grandparenting in which the grandparents and grandchildren are emotionally or physically distant.

involved grandparenting: A type of grandparenting in which the grandparents and grandchildren have frequent interaction or possibly even live together.

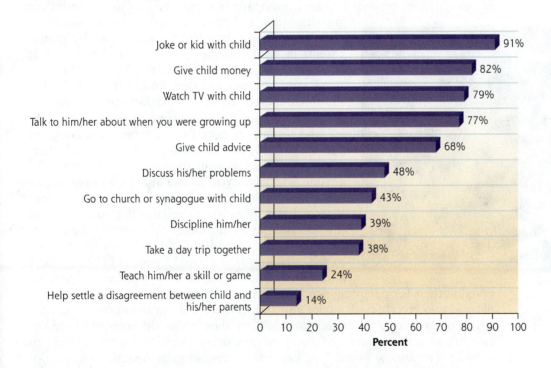

FIGURE 14.5

Percentage of Grandparents Engaging in Activities with Grandchild over Past 12 Months

Most grandparents have companionate relationships with their grandchildren and engage in a variety of fun and intimate activities.
Source: Cherlin & Furstenberg, 1986.

Grandmothers and Grandfathers: Same or Different?

Grandmothers and grandfathers have different parenting styles, and perhaps you noticed these differences when you were very young. Grandmothers are more likely to plan and orchestrate family activities, nurture their grandchildren, and assume caregiving responsibilities (Walker, Manoogian-O'Dell, McGraw, & White, 2001). This is consistent with their role at all ages of being the family *kinkeeper* and maintaining family contact (Fingerman, 2004). For example, it's usually the women in the family who are responsible for sending greeting cards on holidays and birthdays. **Kinkeeping,** the maintaining of ties among family members, carries over into the grandmother role as well.

In contrast, grandfathers are more likely to focus on practical issues, and spend more time exchanging help and services with their grandsons than with their granddaughters. One consequence of this difference in style is that family members generally feel greater obligation to and are closer to their grandmothers than to their grandfathers (Monserud, 2008). This may be the reason why grandmothers report greater satisfaction and overall meaning in grandparenthood than do grandfathers (Somary & Stricker, 1998). Another consequence is that children tend to feel closer to their grandparents (grandmother *and* grandfather) on their mother's side, rather than their father's side, especially when the mother reports having good relationships with her aging parents.

Racial and Ethnic Differences in Grandparenting Styles

We can observe different styles of grandparenting across racial and ethnic groups. For example, in minority families, grandparents are more likely to live with their grandchildren, and play a valued role in childrearing, often mimicking parent-like behavior, than are grandparents in White families (Dilworth-Anderson, 2001; Pew Research Center, 2010b, 2010c; Uttal, 1999).

A study by psychologist Andrea Hunter (1997) examined Black mothers' and fathers' reliance on grandmothers for parenting support. She used a sample of 487 parents ages 18 to 34 from the National Survey of Black Americans, and examined their responses to the following questions: (a) "Do you have anyone who gives you advice about child rearing or helps you with problems having to do with children? If yes, what is this advisor's relationship to you?"; and (b) "Do you have someone to count on to take care of the children? If yes, what is this person's relationship to you?" Hunter found that 57 percent of the mothers and 56 percent of the fathers reported relying on grandmothers for parenting support more often than on anyone else. Most people said they receive both advice and childcare from the grandmother.

Another study of Apache grandmothers shows how the roles of grandparents are socially constructed and can vary dramatically from one culture to another. The author noted four key differences between Apache and "Anglo-American" grandparenting styles (Bahr, 1994):

- *Obligation and responsibility:* An Anglo-American grandparent is a "spoiler" of grandchildren who may interact or give gifts, but who can also have meaningful relationships with grandchildren with only minimal obligation and responsibility. Among the Apache, particularly among grandmothers, grandparenting means heavy obligation and responsibility. The grandmother's role

kinkeeping: Maintaining ties among family members.

In many minority groups grandparents play a prominent role within families. They are often a "third parent."

**Read on MySocLab
Document:** *Growing Old in an Arab American Family*

is that of a parent substitute within the family. There is virtually no such thing as minimal involvement and responsibility.

- *Gender differences in grandparental role behavior:* In Anglo-American society, grandmothers are somewhat more important than grandfathers because they tend to have warmer and closer relationships with their own children as well as with their grandchildren. Among the Apache, the importance of grandmothers far exceeds the importance of grandfathers. Although Apache and Anglo-American patterns are similar, the magnitude of the difference between grandmothers and grandfathers is striking. This isn't only a function of grandmothers' greater longevity, but also of the cultural norm of their greater affinity with and responsibility to children.

- *Grandparents as part of a viable, functioning family network:* In Anglo-American families, kinship ties between parents, adult children, and grandchildren are valued, but households tend to be independent. They rarely share their homes and finances. In Apache families, not only are kinship ties valued, but households are also likely to be extended and often include cross-generational members like grandparents, aunts, uncles, or cousins. Family households have loose, permeable boundaries, and families are highly interdependent on other family members. This dependence is seen as a strength rather than as a weakness on the part of family members.

- *Economic security and economic responsibility:* Among Anglo Americans, grandparenthood and retirement are times of fairly secure economic status. Grandparents are likely to own their own homes and have accumulated savings. They generally aren't responsible for rearing or educating their grandchildren or for providing long-term support for their adult children. In contrast, in Apache families, being an elder and a grandparent is a time of heavy economic demand. Grandparents, including grandmothers, may be economically responsible for the support of their adult children and grandchildren. They may continue to work in the formal or informal sector of the economy so they can provide some or all the assistance to their often multi-generational family. Apache grandparents remain active and influential participants in community life.

Three theories explain why racial and ethnic minority families are more likely than White families to rely on grandparents (and other kin) to provide childcare for their grandchildren. The *cultural* explanation suggests that these practices are the product of different cultural experiences and adaptations (Uttal, 1999). The *structural* explanation conceives of childcare arrangements as an adaptation to structural constraints, such as racism or poverty (Goodman & Silverstein, 2002). The *integrative* explanation combines the other two explanations and suggests these arrangements are the result of the intersection of cultural values with structural constraints, operating alongside gendered expectations (Minkler & Fuller-Thomson, 2005).

Through in-depth interviews with seven Black mothers, seven Mexican-American mothers, and 17 Anglo-American mothers, Lynet Uttal found that the major difference among the groups was how the mothers *felt* about using kin for care (1999). Anglo-American mothers tended to feel that relying on grandparents and other kin was in some way inappropriate or problematic, whereas Black and Mexican-American mothers willingly accepted this help because they felt it was appropriate and acceptable (even if not necessarily ideal). Unlike the other groups, the Anglo-American mothers in Uttal's study were particularly concerned about being a burden or imposing.

Grandchildren and Grandparents Living Together

More than 7 million grandchildren live with their grandparents (Kreider & Ellis, 2011). Blacks, Hispanics, and Asians are most likely to co-reside, and Whites are least likely, as shown in Table 14.5.

How have your grandparents' social or cultural backgrounds affected their grandparenting? Can you pinpoint specific instances in which their social class, race, or ethnic background, for example, had an impact on their roles, values, or grandparenting style?

TABLE 14.5 Number and Percentage of Children Who Live with at Least One Grandparent

White children are least likely to live with a grandparent. Why is this? Economics? Culture?

	Number	Percentage
White, non-Hispanic	2,932,000	7%
Black	1,876,000	17%
Asian	380,000	15%
Hispanic (any race)	2,270,000	14%

Source: Kreider & Ellis, 2011.

We usually think of these as three-generational families—perhaps the adult child and grandchildren needed some financial help and therefore the family all lives together. Alternatively, perhaps an elderly grandparent was too frail to live independently, and therefore moved in with their adult child and grandchildren. However, another trend in co-residence has caught our attention: now about a quarter of these grandchildren live with their grandparent *without their parents present in the household* (Kreider & Ellis, 2011). Kids just live with their grandparents.

Where are these children's parents? Mothers and fathers are absent as a result of death; desertion; incarceration; drug problems; physical or mental illnesses, such as HIV/AIDS; unemployment; or child abuse; among other reasons. One study of 129 grandparents raising their grandchildren (Sands & Goldberg-Glen, 2000) examined the situations that precipitated this relationship and found multiple problems in the homes of the grandchildren's parents that led the grandparents to take over the care of their grandchildren. The most commonly reported problem was substance abuse, but the parents' inability to care for the child, neglect, and psychological and financial problems were also cited as factors. Many of these problems are long-term issues for families. When the grandparents in this study first began to take care of their grandchildren, only one-third expected to be the caregiver until the grandchild came of age. However, at the time of the interview, more than three-quarters of grandparents reported this expectation.

What are some characteristics of these intergenerational families maintained by the grandparents?

- They are usually headed by both grandparents or by only grandmothers—rarely are they headed by only grandfathers. The reason may be that women live longer and are more likely than men to assume a caregiving role.

- Most grandparents raising their grandchildren are younger than 65. Only one in five is 65 or older.

- Children in grandparent-maintained families are more likely to be Black, younger, and living in the South than are children in intergenerational families headed by their parents.

- Children in grandparent-maintained families are less likely than children in single-parent families to be poor (Kreider, 2008; Kreider & Ellis, 2011).

Grandparent caregivers face a number of problems and challenges (Harnett, Dawe, & Russell, 2012; MacNeil, Kosberg, Durkin, Dooley, DeCoster, & Williamson, 2010; Smith & Palmieri, 2007). Most are not particularly eager to take on the care of their grandchildren, but feel it's a "last resort" decision over which they have little choice. In addition to financial difficulties, grandparents may experience poor health, depression, and decreased life satisfaction (Cooney & Shin An, 2006; Leder, Grinstead, & Torres, 2007; Musil, Gordon, Warner, Zauszniewski, Standing, & Wykle, 2010; Smith & Palmieri, 2007). Sometimes, they must seek legal authority to make decisions on behalf of their children regarding the grandchildren's medical care, school enrollment, immunizations, and public assistance and other support services (Robinson-Dooley & Kropf, 2006); yet they step in because they know that their grandchild needs help and that they may be best able to provide it.

Watch on MySocLab
Video: *ABC Primetime: Grandmothers Raising Grandchildren*

Retirement

Work provides us with income, but for many of us, work is also an important part of our identity. "I *am* a professor . . . ," "I *am* a firefighter . . . ," "I *am* a doctor . . . ," is how we describe our work—we *are* the occupation. Consequently, retirement is an important transition not only because it reduces our income, but also because it alters a major part of the way we see ourselves (Ekerdt, 2009).

Still, many people eagerly await this change and see retirement as a legitimate, earned privilege. The median age at retirement fell from 69 years in 1950 to 62 in 1990, but has since risen to age 64 (Munnell, 2011). Many older persons continue to work, even into their 70s, as highlighted in Table 14.6 (Bureau of Labor Statistics, February 1, 2012).

The rise in the age of retirement is likely due to several factors, including the following:

- **Social Security:** Changes to Social Security have created many incentives to continue working and have made work more attractive relative to retirement. For example, the delayed retirement credit, which increases benefits for each year that claiming is delayed between the full retirement age and age 70, has also improved incentives to keep working.

- **Improved health and longevity:** Life expectancy for men at 65 has increased about 3.5 years since 1980, and much of the evidence suggests that people are healthier as well. The correlation between health and labor force activity is very strong.

- **Pension type:** The shift from defined benefit to 401(k) plans eliminated built-in incentives to retire. Studies show that workers covered by 401(k) plans retire a year or two later on average than similarly situated workers covered by a defined benefit plan.

- **Less physically demanding jobs:** With the shift away from manufacturing, jobs now involve more knowledge-based activities, which put less strain on older bodies.

- **Decline of retiree health insurance:** Combine the decline of employer-provided retiree health insurance with the rapid rise in health care costs, and workers have a strong incentive to keep working and maintain their employer's health coverage until they qualify for Medicare at 65.

- **Joint decision making:** More women are working; wives on average are 3 years younger than their husbands; and husbands and wives like to coordinate their retirement.

- **The recession of the 2000s.** Some elders sustained significant losses to their retirement funds, or were forced to take pay cuts during the recession, and now work longer to make up the difference (Munnell, 2011).

We also see that many older workers are now retiring in stages rather than all at once (Calvo, Haverstick, & Sass, 2009). This trend too has been exacerbated by the recession; more than a third of surveyed adults ages 62 and older (who have not retired) say they have delayed or will delay retirement because of the recession (Taylor, Kochhar, Morin, Wang, Dockterman, & Medina, 2009), and fewer Americans are confident that they will have the necessary money needed for retirement (Morin & Fry, 2012).

Question That Matters

14.11 How is retirement a *social construction*?

TABLE 14.6	Labor Force Participation among the Elderly, 1990–2020 (Projected)			
Because of reduced pensions and insufficient savings, people will postpone retirement and continue to work longer.				
	1990	**2000**	**2010**	**2020**
Age 60–64	45%	47%	55%	61%
Age 65–69	21%	25%	32%	38%
Age 70–74	11%	14%	18%	23%
Age 75+	4%	5%	7%	10%

Source: Bureau of Labor Statistics, February 1, 2012.

The Social Construction of Retirement

The notion of ending work at a specific age—retirement—is a social construction. Most people in the world today must work to support themselves (and sometimes other family members) and would never think to retire 20 or 30 years before they expected to die.

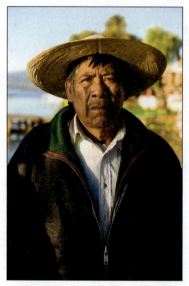

Americans think of 65 as the golden retirement age, but many cultures know no such thing as retirement. Individuals must work until they are no longer physically able.

Americans' ideas of retirement reflect more than just individual micro-level explanations such as, "I'm tired of my job," "I want to travel," "I think I'm too old to work," or even "I've saved enough money." It also reflects a convergence of macro-level public and private employment policies, the state of the economy, and other aspects of culture and society, as shown in the *Tying It All Together* feature box. People now rely heavily upon the Social Security program because employer-sponsored pensions or savings plans are more common, and because many employers are enticing older persons to exit the labor force.

For significant numbers of elderly to be able to withdraw from the labor force, four conditions must exist in a society (Morgan & Kunkel, 1998) that materialized in the United States after industrialization during the late 19th and 20th centuries. First, a society must produce an economic surplus large enough to support its non-employed members. Second, a mechanism must be in place to divert some of that surplus to the non-employed members, such as through a pension or government transfer program. Third, non-employed members should be viewed positively by the rest of society, and their activities or leisure must be seen as legitimate. Finally, non-employed members must have accumulated an acceptable number of years of productivity to warrant this support by the other members of society.

However, these conditions are now under threat. The cost of caring for the elderly—Social Security, health-care programs, and even private retirement plans—are consuming a greater share of our country's gross domestic product (GDP), as shown in Figure 14.6. People are rightly concerned that these programs as

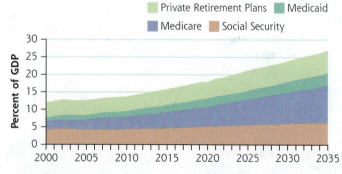

FIGURE 14.6

Care of the Elderly is an Increasing Share of the U.S. Gross Domestic Product (GDP)

The cost of elder care is consuming more and more of U.S. GDP.
Source: Schieber, 2008.

Work is a big part of our lives, yet the age at which we retire has been declining. What would motivate someone to retire?

A host of personal, micro-level reasons affect your ability to retire, such as whether you have enough money to retire or are tired of your job or career. But these reasons do not make up the whole picture. Many macro-level factors often influence the micro-level factors. For example, the creation of Social Security has given many elders the economic security to retire. Likewise, our culture's current view that elders deserve leisure has made it legitimate to simply be "tired of working."

MICRO-LEVEL FACTORS

- Tired of the job
- A desire to travel
- Feeling too old to work
- Feeling financially secure that one has enough money

MACRO-LEVEL FACTORS

- Society has an economic surplus that can support the nonemployed
- Pensions or government transfer programs are in place to divert the surplus to the unemployed members of society
- Other members of society believe elders' activities or leisure are legitimate
- Elders are seen as having earned the right to leisure

WHAT DO YOU THINK?

1. How might these micro- and macro-level factors operate differently for women and men?
2. What changes in these macro-level factors do you foresee in the near future?

configured are not sustainable as baby boomers age (Schieber, 2008). Furthermore, these programs for the elderly compete with funding for other groups; programs for children, for example, have received a declining proportion of federal spending (Uhlenberg, 2009).

Men, Women, and Retirement

Traditionally, retirement was seen as a transition important primarily to men because they were the primary breadwinners and were thought to derive more status and identity from their jobs than did women. Nonetheless, as more women enter the labor force, we must rethink our old conceptions (Duberley, Carmichael, & Szmigin, 2013). Today, with about half the workforce consisting of women and with the majority of men married to employed women, couples are forging new retirement paths. They not only face two retirements, but they must also coordinate their retirements and address whether to take up other paid work after they retire.

There is very little research that examines sex differences in the process of and satisfaction with retirement. One interesting study, drawing on resource theories and theories on the gendered division of labor introduced in Chapter 10, examines how preretirement resources relate to retirees' psychological well-being (Kubicek, Korunka, Raymo, & Hoonakker, 2011). The researchers hypothesized that possessing key resources prior to retirement as well as losing or gaining resources in the transition to retirement influence retirees' well-being. Furthermore, they suggest that these effects are partially conditioned by sex. Using a large sample that follows people over time, the study indicates that preretirement physical health, tenacity in goal pursuit, and flexibility in goal adjustment are beneficial for both men's and women's well-being. By contrast, financial assets and job dissatisfaction are more strongly related to men's psychological well-being in retirement. Friendships and social contacts prior to retirement are related to the well-being of women. Thus, the study underscores the importance of considering gendered resources in retirement research.

Read on **MySocLab**
Document: *A Gradual Goodbye: If People Are Living Longer, They Will Have to Work Longer Too*

How do you plan to save for your retirement years? Specifically, what do you need to do now (or soon) to retire "in the manner to which you would like to become accustomed?"

14.8 Discuss health issues of the elderly

Questions That Matter

14.12 What is *caregiving*?
14.13 What type of stresses do caregivers experience?

▶ **Watch** on **MySocLab**
Video: *Core Concepts: Physical Challenges of Living Longer*

gerontologists: Researchers studying issues affecting the elderly.

Activities of Daily Living (ADLs): General day-to-day activities such as cooking, cleaning, bathing, and home repair.

Health

Most elderly persons report their health is good or excellent. There's no denying, however, that as we age, our health is likely to decline in a number of ways. We're more likely to lose some of our vision and hearing; develop chronic conditions such as arthritis, heart disease, or diabetes; and suffer severe memory impairment (National Center for Health Statistics, 2010). We may need someone to help us with many things we used to do for ourselves: cooking, cleaning, home repairs, and perhaps even personal care. The health status of older adults is a result of many factors, including diet, exercise, and heredity; and structural factors, such as socioeconomic status, racism, and access to health care.

Activities of Daily Living

Gerontologists—researchers studying the elderly—measured the degree of physical impairment by using a common set of **activities of daily living (ADLs),** such as bathing, dressing, eating, getting into and out of bed, walking indoors, and using the toilet (Hooyman & Kiyak, 2011). By using a common set of measures, gerontologists can track the degree of impairment of elders and make some comparisons across different samples. Millions of elderly persons cannot perform at least one ADL by themselves. Millions more have trouble with most or all of them. Gerontologists estimate that the number of older persons needing significant care may increase dramatically over the next 50 years as the size of the oldest-old cohort increases: 14 million elders may need significant care by 2020, and 24 million by 2060.

Severe Memory Loss

I think there comes a point in everyone's life when we pause to reflect on the past, realize the present and look to the future. That happened for me at the age of 46. In the fall of that year I started to become forgetful—which was not like me at all. I had a very stressful job and worked long hours, so I blamed that for my forgetfulness. I couldn't remember things like my home phone number, my associates' names or on bad days, how to get home. I remember that many times I would stop at a gas station, and after filling my tank, not knowing whether I was going to work or coming home from work. I tried desperately to hide it and became pretty good at it! But one day in December, my husband and I were out shopping, and he went to a different department in the store.

"I would stop at a gas station, and after filling my tank, not knowing whether I was going to work or coming home from work."

The next thing I knew is that I couldn't remember where I was or how I had gotten there. It was time to fess up. I sought medical attention and after eight long months of testing, including all of the alphabet soup tests (EEG, EKG, MRI, etc.), blood work, spinal taps, B12 shots and neuropsychological testing, I was diagnosed with Alzheimer's disease. It was a relief to me because there was a name to it. Although it is an incurable disease, at least I knew what I was dealing with. My family, however, took a dimmer view. My husband likened it to the Titanic—that the ship was sinking, and he and my son were going to survive and I wasn't. My son reflected that it was like his mother was on death row, but innocent of the crime. (Alzheimer's Association, 2010, p. 1)

Perhaps one of the most difficult disabilities facing elders and those who care for them is severe memory loss, known as *dementia* (Alzheimer's Association, 2013a). Dementia is not a specific disease; it's an overall term that describes a wide range of symptoms associated with a decline in memory or other thinking skills severe enough to reduce a person's ability to perform everyday activities. Although symptoms of dementia can vary greatly, at least two of the following core mental functions must be significantly impaired to be considered dementia:

- Memory
- Communication and language
- Ability to focus and pay attention
- Reasoning and judgment
- Visual perception

People with dementia may have problems with short-term memory, keeping track of a purse or wallet, paying bills, planning and preparing meals, remembering appointments, or traveling out of the neighborhood.

People who suffer from memory loss don't necessarily have **Alzheimer's disease**, but it's by far the most common form of dementia, making up somewhere between 50 percent and 80 percent of dementia cases, and affecting more than 5 million persons. Alzheimer's disease is the sixth leading cause of death among persons ages 65 and older (Alzheimer's Association, 2013b). The disease starts subtly—a person may have difficulty remembering names or recent events. It progresses over the course of years, and later symptoms include impaired judgment; disorientation; confusion; behavior changes; lack of recognition of loved ones; and eventually, the inability to walk, speak, and even swallow. Alzheimer's disease is ultimately fatal. Given the changing demographics of our country and the increase in the size of the oldest-old cohort, we're likely to see a large increase in the number of people with Alzheimer's—10 million baby boomers are expected to eventually develop the disease.

Alzheimer's disease takes a large toll on the individual, the family, and the community. In 2012, 15.4 million caregivers provided more than 17.5 billion hours of unpaid care valued at $216 billion. It also takes a toll on our communities. In 2013, Alzheimer's cost the nation about $203 billion, as illustrated in Figure 14.7. This includes health care, long-term care, and hospice, and the amount is expected to rise to $1.2 trillion by 2050 as the number of Alzheimer's patients continues to grow (Alzheimer's Association, 2013b).

As Alzheimer's progresses, brain cells die and connections among cells are lost, causing cognitive symptoms to worsen. Although current medications can't stop the damage Alzheimer's causes to brain cells, they may help lessen or stabilize symptoms for a limited time by affecting certain chemicals involved in carrying messages among the brain's nerve cells. The U.S. Food and Drug Administration (FDA) approved two types of medicine to treat the cognitive symptoms (memory loss, confusion, and problems with thinking and reasoning) of Alzheimer's disease. Doctors sometimes prescribe both types of medications together. Some doctors also prescribe high doses of vitamin E for cognitive changes of Alzheimer's disease. Given the direct and indirect costs of Alzheimer's and other dementias, not to mention the cost in terms of families' heartache and despair, it's no wonder researchers are vigorously pursuing an agenda of prevention, treatment, and cure (Alzheimer's Association, 2013c).

Long-Term Care and Caregiving

It is clear that many elders are going to need long-term care for their chronic physical or mental conditions. Some will live for a decade or more without being able to perform

How would you cope if you realized, at around age 60, that you were becoming forgetful and were losing your memory? How would you react? What would you do?

Alzheimer's disease: The most common form of dementia; at present, it is incurable.

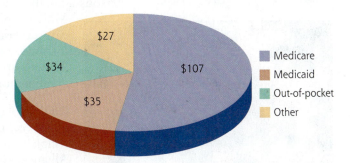

FIGURE 14.7

Cost of Alzheimer's Disease, 2013, United States (Billions)

Caring for persons with Alzheimer's is very expensive. Although Medicare and Medicaid cover much of it, some of the costs are born by the family themselves.
Source: Alzheimer's Association, 2013b.

The late U.S. President Ronald Reagan and British Prime Minister Margaret Thatcher are just two examples among the millions of elders who experience dementia, the most common of which is Alzheimer's Disease.

any of their ADLs. How do we care for the growing numbers of elderly who can no longer care for themselves?

FORMAL CARE   Some elderly persons rely on **formal care** provided by social service agencies on a paid or volunteer basis, such as paid visiting nurses, meals or housecleaning programs, a paid personal attendant, assisted living facilities, and nursing home care.

Others may need more in-depth care, and move into assisted living facilities. These vary in their scope: Some are little more than apartments for seniors with optional food and housekeeping services, whereas others provide more skilled nursing care. The price varies by what is included, but averages somewhere around $40,000 per year (MetLife Mature Market Institute, 2013). Assisted living facilities are a booming business, with more than 40,000 such facilities operating today, and many more slated for the future (Helpguide.org, 2010; Ortiz, 2012).

Nursing homes provide the most intensive level of care for people who can't be cared for at home and who have likely moved beyond what most assisted living centers can provide, but don't need the services of a hospital. Few elderly persons actually live in nursing homes, although that number rises with age.

Most people don't need the intense level of care, cannot afford such care (averaging about $80,000 per year [MetLife Mature Market Institute, 2013]), and would rather be cared for at home. More than 70 percent of nursing home residents are women, and the average age at admission is 80 years (Houser, 2007).

INFORMAL CARE   In contrast to formal care, most elders rely primarily on **informal care,** unpaid care by someone close to the care recipient, usually a wife, daughter, husband, or son (Family Caregiver Alliance, 2012; Fox & Brenner, 2012). Other relatives, such as nieces, siblings, grandchildren, or even friends or neighbors, also sometime serve as informal caregivers. About 70 million people (30 percent of the population) care for an aging adult, averaging nearly 20 hours per week. They provide a wide variety of hands-on care, such as cooking, cleaning, bathing, housekeeping, shopping, administering and managing medications, coordinating care with medical providers, and watching over the elderly to ensure their safety and well-being.

Many individuals who provide assistance and support to a loved one with chronic illness or disability don't identify themselves as "caregivers," but rather describe what they do in terms of their relationship with the other person: as a husband, wife, partner, daughter, daughter-in-law, son, grandson, niece, or close friend, for example.

A spouse is generally the first person in line to provide care if she or he is able. When a spouse is unavailable or unable to provide this level of care, adult children, usually daughters, daughters-in-law, or even granddaughters step in. The "typical" caregiving situation is a woman in her late 40s or early 50s caring for her elderly mother while also holding a full- or part-time job (Fox & Brenner, 2012). Some of these caregivers also have children to care for, as does Amy in the opening vignette, giving them the nickname the **sandwich generation** because they're members of the middle generation providing care to both a younger and an older generation. An estimated 83 percent of Americans say they would feel very obligated to provide assistance to their parent in a time of need. Those who take on this unpaid role risk the stress, physical strain, competing demands, and financial hardship of caregiving, and thus are vulnerable themselves. Family caregiving is now viewed as an important public health concern (Feinberg, Reinhard, Houser, & Choula, 2011).

Caring for elderly parents or a spouse can be a labor of love, but it's also time-intensive, potentially expensive, and often stressful (Boylstein & Hayes, 2012; Family Caregiver Alliance, 2012; Fox & Brenner, 2012). Most caregivers provide assistance 7 days a week with little help from formal services, as does

---

formal care: Care provided by social service agencies on a paid or volunteer basis.

informal care: Unpaid care by someone close to the care recipient.

Informal care refers to unpaid care that is provided by someone close to the recipient, such as a family member. If a spouse is unavailable, usually daughters or daughters-in-law step in to provide care.

sandwich generation: A generation of people who are in the middle of two living generations providing care to members of cohorts on both sides of them, parents and children.

Amy, introduced in the opening vignette. A recent national survey of more than 1,200 caregivers found that more than a third of caregivers provided all the help to the person they care for during the past 12 months and received no help from anyone else. Among caregivers who did receive some assistance, one-third said they provided most of the unpaid care (National Alliance for Caregiving and AARP, 2009). Because most female caregivers are employed, they have to make sacrifices at work to accommodate caregiving, including arriving late or leaving early, working fewer hours, taking a leave of absence, turning down a promotion, choosing early retirement, or giving up work completely—sacrifices that cost an average of hundreds of thousands in lost wages over a lifetime (National Alliance for Caregiving and AARP, 2009).

Caregivers often spend their own money to provide medicines, groceries, or other supplies to the person they're caring for. More than a third of Blacks report in the national survey that they spend between $101 and $500 of their own money every month to provide care, as compared to less than one-quarter of Whites. Not surprisingly, Blacks are more likely than Whites to say that caregiving creates a financial hardship for them (National Alliance for Caregiving and AARP, 2009).

Given these challenges, many people find caregiving to be highly stressful, as shown in Table 14.7. Thirty-one percent report that they find caregiving highly stressful, and another 22 percent report that it's moderately stressful. Likewise, 15 percent report experiencing a great deal of financial hardship, and another 15 percent report moderate hardship. Many caregivers say that caregiving has been hard on their health and emotional well-being, and decreases their time spent with friends or other family members (National Alliance for Caregiving and AARP, 2009). It's labor, but often it's a labor of love.

TABLE 14.7	Strain and Stress of Caregiving	
Many people find caregiving to be highly stressful or a financial hardship, although not all caregivers feel this way.		
Health of Caregiver		
Excellent or very good		57%
Average		26%
Fair or poor		17%
Impact of caregiving on health		
Made it better		8%
No impact		74%
Made it worse		17%
Emotional stress	**Scale**	
Very stressful	5	17%
	4	14%
Somewhat stressful	3	22%
	2	22%
Not at all stressful	1	25%
Financial hardship		
Great deal	5	9%
	4	6%
Somewhat of a hardship	3	15%
	2	19%
No hardship	1	51%

Source: National Alliance for Caregiving and AARP, November 2009.

Bringing It Full Circle

Our population is aging rapidly, with the number of elders increasing almost four times as fast as the population as a whole. Persons age 85 and older—referred to as the *oldest old*—represent the fastest-growing cohort in the United States. These demographic changes will have far-reaching consequences for family life in the future. For example, large numbers of elderly persons, especially women, are widowed; other women, such as Amy in the opening vignette, serve as family caregivers to frail parents or grandparents. How will our lives change as the number of elders grows? We'll likely see these types of issues take center stage,

Read on MySocLab
Document: *Facts and Fictions About an Aging America*

and our social and health policies must take our changing demographics and family structures into account. With the information that you've learned from this chapter, let's reflect on the opening vignette—the story of Amy who is caring for both a frail parent and her own young child.

- What stresses or strains are associated with caregiving, and how might these be affected by race, ethnicity, social class, and sex?
- What options does Amy have for reducing some of the stress in her life? What types of formal supports should be available to her? Why are they not available now, or are they?
- Reflecting on Amy's experience, how will you care for an aging parent who needs assistance? How will their needs, and your potential response to their needs, affect your work, family, and other dimensions of your life?

On MySocLab

 ✓ **Study** and **Review** on MySocLab

CHAPTER REVIEW

LO14.1 Explain the "demographic revolution"

14.1 What is a *demographic revolution*?

The *demographic revolution* refers to how the aging population is rapidly increasing today, and will continue to increase into the 21st century. Only a century ago, very few people—1 in 25—were age 65 or older; many younger people rarely met an elderly person. However, the elderly population has been increasing almost four times as fast as the population as a whole, and seniors now constitute one of every eight people. In 2040, one in four Americans could be age 65 or older as the baby boom generation ages.

14.2 Which group of elders is increasing most rapidly?

Persons age 85 and older—referred to as the *oldest-old*—are the fastest-growing cohort in the United States. In 2011, they numbered about 5 million, or 14 percent of all elders; however, they will increase to about 19 million in 2050. That would make the oldest-old about 25 percent of all elders and about 6 percent of the total population. And it's estimated that there may be 1 million persons age 100 and older. The oldest-old group is more likely to have health problems and need assistance; these individuals are also more likely to be female, widowed, live alone, and have financial difficulties.

LO14.2 Describe aging in historical perspective

14.3 In the past, were the elderly treated differently than they are today?

The "good old days" of the past are largely a myth. Rich, White, property-owning elderly men were generally treated with respect. However, poor or minority elders were often treated as outcasts. Industrialization decreased elders' status further because it was difficult for them to work in physically taxing and dangerous factories, yet most worked as long as they could because there were no pensions or Social Security.

14.4 Why was Social Security created?

With industrialization increasing, poverty was becoming more conspicuous. Elders were particularly vulnerable because few were covered by employer pensions, and they had a difficult time competing with younger men and women for jobs. During the Great Depression, many elders lost their jobs, and Social Security was created in 1935 to provide some degree of financial support on turning age 65.

LO14.3 Identify the transitions families experience

14.5 What patterns are associated with adult children leaving their parents' home?

Adult children used to leave home primarily for marriage or to join the military; now, they leave home for college or to take a job. These types of transitions are less final than those of the past and, therefore, children today are more likely to return to their parents' home for a period of time. The recession has also caused many adult children to move back home with their parents, often repeatedly, and they have been given the nickname *boomerangers*.

14.6 What type of relationships do parents have with their adult children after they finally leave home for good?

Most adult children receive substantial help from their older parents, with school, childcare, and mortgage assistance, until their parents are very old and frail. Most aging parents give far more assistance to their children than they receive from them.

LO14.4 Summarize issues experienced by the aging couple

14.7 Are the elderly satisfied with their marriages?

Most researchers have found that marriage begins with a high level of satisfaction, but the satisfaction begins to decline as couples have children, and then rises again when the children leave home. However, at least one researcher has found no evidence of the upturn; he suggested instead that variation in marital quality may simply be the result of cohort differences—people of different cohorts, or ages, have different expectations about marriage.

14.8 What unique issues do lesbian-gay-bisexual-transgender (LGBT) elders face?

Although LGBT elders face many of the same issues that other elders face, such as health problems or the need for reliable transportation or housing assistance, they also have many unique concerns. Most federal programs and laws treat same-sex couples differently from married heterosexual couples, including Social Security, which pays survivor benefits to widows and widowers, but not to the surviving same-sex life partner of someone who dies; Medicaid, which protects the assets and homes of married spouses when the other spouse enters a nursing home or long-term care facility, but offers no such protections to same-sex partners; or pensions, in which legal spouses avoid a tax penalty that same-sex partners must pay.

LO14.5 Discuss the grief process associated with widowhood

14.9 Do men and women experience widowhood differently?

Generally speaking, yes. Most widowers are females, who tend to have longer life expectancies, are generally several years younger than their husbands, and are less likely to remarry. They're also more likely than widowed men to live in poverty. Consequently, because of their greater number, there may be more avenues for social support.

LO14.6 Analyze the role of grandparents in the lives of their grandchildren

14.10 What type of relationship do grandparents typically have with their grandchildren?

Most report a *companionate relationship*, meaning that they enjoy recreational activities, occasional overnight stays, and have fun together. A growing number of grandparents are raising their grandchildren because of the parent's absence or unsuitability for parenthood.

LO14.7 Analyze the life stage of retirement

14.11 How is retirement a *social construction*?

Historically, and in many societies today, retirement as a concept has not existed—people had to work to support themselves and weren't exempt because of their age. Retirement is a relatively recent phenomenon. It's found in societies with an economic surplus, pensions, and/or government transfer; and a belief that elders' activities or leisure are legitimate and that they have an earned right to leisure. Moreover, retirement is seen and experienced differently by different groups in our society (i.e., men and women).

LO14.8 Discuss health issues of the elderly

14.12 What is *caregiving*?

The term *caregiving* is often used to refer to caring for a frail elderly person, although technically speaking, it can be done with any age group. In this chapter, caregiving refers primarily to *informal care,* which is unpaid care by someone close to the care recipient, usually a wife, daughter, husband, or son.

14.13 What type of stresses do caregivers experience?

Caring for elderly parents or a spouse can be a labor of love, but it's also time-intensive, potentially expensive, and often stressful. Most caregivers provide assistance 7 days a week with little help from formal services. Because most female caregivers are employed, they must make sacrifices at work to accommodate caregiving, including arriving late or leaving early, working fewer hours, taking a leave of absence, turning down a promotion, choosing early retirement, or giving up work completely. Many caregivers are also taking care of their own children, and are therefore nicknamed the *sandwich generation.*

KEY TERMS

Activities of Daily Living (ADLs)	formal care	life expectancy
Alzheimer's disease	gerontologists	life-stage perspective
baby boom generation	informal care	life-span perspective
centenarian	involved grandparenting	remote grandparenting
companionate grandparenting	kinkeeping	*sandwich generation*
dementia	life-course perspective	Social Security

Looking Ahead: Helping Families Flourish

(((**Listen** to Chapter 15 on **MySocLab**

LEARNING OBJECTIVES

15.1	Explain family resiliency
15.2	Classify types of family policies
15.3	Describe how our policies can foster family resilience
15.4	Identify specific policies and programs for children
15.5	Identify specific policies and programs for the elderly
15.6	Summarize what you have learned from this text

It's easy to be ethnocentric—to assume that your culture's way of doing things is the right way.

Yet, if we step back for a moment, we can see that other cultures have some pretty good ideas too.

The United States and France are two highly developed countries, but their governments' approaches to family policies are strikingly different. Sophie and Alain are teachers currently living in the United States, but who originally hail from France. As the parents of two young boys, they are in a unique position to compare the effects of social policies in each country on family life.

In France, Sophie tells us a woman is given 16 weeks of fully paid maternity leave, including 6 weeks prior to the child's birth and 10 weeks after. She was relieved to be able to stop teaching during her pregnancy; it reduced her stress, allowed her to rest, and helped her prepare mentally for the baby. She notices that American women have no such luxury.

In addition to the maternity leave, either parent can take up to 3 years leave from their job. Granted, they tell us, this is not on full salary, but a stipend is paid from the government each month. There is no such equivalent in the United States. Instead, Sophie and Alain see their American colleagues returning very soon after a baby is born because the family cannot afford to take unpaid leave or they fear that their jobs will be lost.

Even more incredible to Sophie and Alain is the high cost of childcare in the United States, which they say costs nearly a full teacher's salary. In France, State daycare is available and far less expensive. Most of their friends back in France use the State daycare. In fact, the demand is so high that in the larger cities you must put your name on a waiting list when you learn you are pregnant.

Sophie and Alain also describe the monthly stipend for each child that the French government pays. It is a valuable benefit because children are expensive. Meanwhile, most of their American colleagues are bewildered at the thought of the government paying parents to take care of their children.

They are also perplexed by our health-care system, which they say is expensive and quite uncoordinated. For example, Sophie has an eye condition requiring medication that is free in France, but costs them $50 every 3 weeks in the United States.

Information like this can leave us wondering whether they see any benefits from living in the United States. However, there is one issue in particular in which the United States shines, they say. They have been extremely impressed with the special education program for their youngest son, who was recently diagnosed with autism. They refer to France as being in the "Stone Age" with respect to special education, early intervention, or

👁 **Watch** on **MySocLab**
Video: *A Comparison of Family Policies: France and the United States: Sophie and Alain*

general assistance to the disabled or those with special needs. They believe their son is reaping benefits in the United States that are not available in their home country.

Families are of interest to just about everyone. Look no further than our popular culture represented in movies, television, or music, and you see that families and their relationships take center stage. Yet, in many ways, what could be more mundane—getting up in the morning, having breakfast, walking the kids to the school bus, going to work, making dinner, helping with homework, and putting the kids to bed at the end of a long day? Families can offer us the best times of our lives: falling in love, getting married, or the birth or adoption of a baby. Families can also offer us some of the worst times: conflict, betrayal, violence, and divorce. As discussed in previous chapters, relationships take place in a social context. This allows us to ask, what kind of world do we *want* for our children? This chapter looks to the future by examining the macro-level social policies and programs that can create a more compassionate environment for our families. What is it that families need to really flourish? Let's take a creative look at the many options and opportunities that could improve the health, security, and well-being of families, drawing from other countries as well as our own, as shown in the opening vignette with Alain and Sophie.

◉ **Watch** on **MySocLab**
Video: *Arlene Skolnick: Family Images*

15.1 Explain family resiliency

Questions That Matter

15.1 What is *family resilience*?
15.2 What are the components of family resilience?
15.3 What is missing from models of resilience?

What Do Families Need to Flourish?

Many aspects of family life, from communication to divorce, derive from macro-level changes in family demographics, needs, and functions. For example, as more women join the labor market, family members must find ways to meet both work and family demands. What resources are available to help them accomplish this balancing act? Or, as our country's demographics change, who will help care for a growing number of frail elders? Questions like these raise two interrelated points. First, *What do healthy families need to thrive*? Second, recognizing that many families face particular challenges—poverty, abuse, or neglect, for example—*What do challenged families need to become resilient*? As discussed in this chapter, families have surprisingly similar needs.

Family Resilience

Many adults and children do not have "picture-perfect" family lives (Miley, O'Melia, & DuBois, 2011). We've seen in earlier chapters that many people experience racism or sexism, grow up in impoverished environments, are torn by divorce, or are victims of intimate partner violence or child abuse. Yet, despite the toll these events can take, many adults and children overcome adversity and lead successful and well-adjusted lives. These individuals show **resilience**, derived from Latin roots meaning "to jump or bounce back" (Silliman, 1994). It's the capacity to rebound from adversity, misfortune, trauma, or other transitional crises and become strengthened and more resourceful (Walsh, 2006); it's a multi-faceted ability to thrive despite adversity (Benard & Truebridge, 2009; Pransky & McMillen, 2009).

The Kauai Longitudinal Study (Werner, 1994, 1995; Werner & Smith, 1989, 1992), based on 698 children born in 1955 on the island of Kauai in Hawaii, examined the long-term effects of growing up in high-risk environments. Most of these children were born to unskilled sugar plantation workers of Japanese, Filipino, Hawaiian, Portuguese, Polynesian, and mixed racial descent. Fifty-four percent lived in poverty. Approximately one-third (210) were considered high risk because of exposure to a combination of at least four individual, parental,

resilience: A multi-faceted ability to thrive despite adversity.

or household risk factors, such as having a serious health problem, familial alcoholism, violence, divorce, or mental illness in the family. The children were assessed from birth to ages 1, 2, 10, 18, and 32 years.

Two-thirds of those children who experienced four or more risk factors by age 2 developed learning or behavior problems by age 18. However, these children went on to become stable, confident, and productive adults, as rated on a variety of measures. In a later follow-up at age 40, all but two of the study participants were still successful. In fact, many had outperformed the children from low-risk families.

A key insight of this research is that we can develop resilience at any point in the life course. Among the two-thirds of high-risk children who had learning or behavioral problems at age 18, 50 percent of them did not exhibit these problems at age 30; instead, they had satisfying jobs and stable marriages, and in other measures were deemed successful by the research team. The researchers also noted that teenage delinquency isn't automatically a precursor to a life of crime. Meanwhile, a few individuals identified as resilient at age 18 in this study had developed significant problems by age 30.

The evidence shows us that many adults and children reared in poverty or with other disadvantages do overcome their adversities. What factors produce this resilience?

Individual, Family, and Community Factors

Individuals do not operate in isolation, but rather our lives are embedded within larger social systems (Bronfenbrenner, 1979). To understand resiliency, we must consider factors at a number of levels, including the following:

- Individual-level protective factors
- Family protective and recovery factors
- Community strengths (Benard & Truebridge, 2009; Sapienza & Masten, 2011; Walsh, 2006; 2012)

Individual-level protective factors include such micro-level traits as a positive self-concept, sociability, intelligence and scholastic competence, autonomy, high self-esteem, creativity, independence, good communication and problem-solving skills, humor, and good mental and physical health. For example, the resilient high-risk adolescents in the Kauai Longitudinal Study had developed a sense that obstacles weren't insurmountable, and they believed they had control over their fate. They had a high degree of self-esteem and self-efficacy, and many developed a special skill or hobby that was a source of pride.

Family protective factors are micro-level characteristics or dynamics that shape the family's ability to endure in the face of risk factors; they protect a family from crises and can include such family characteristics as warmth, affection, cohesion, and traditions. **Family recovery factors** assist families in bouncing back from a crisis situation (McCubbin, McCubbin, Thompson, Han, & Allen, 1997) and include commitment, communication, and emotional support for each other. However, if parents cannot provide a nurturing environment, other family members, such as siblings, grandparents, or aunts and uncles, may step in. Resilient families generally have reasonable and clear-cut expectations for their children. They participate in family celebrations, share spiritual connections, and have specific traditions and predictable

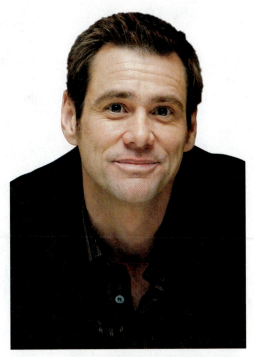

Some people, like Jim Carrey, are born into poverty, but become very successful despite the odds. What contributes to this resiliency?

Kurt Hummel's character in the television show *Glee* reminds us of the importance of family protective and recovery factors for building resilience. Here, Kurt received the support of his father after "coming out."

Answer the following questions as accurately as possible. You may do this for your family of origin or from your marriage or partnership.

1. I believe that my family is the best that it can be. Do you agree or disagree? (Circle one.)

1	2	3	4	5
Strongly Disagree	Disagree	Don't Know	Agree	Strongly Agree

2. My family often spends time together having fun.   T   F

3. My family often takes part in traditions.   T   F

4. My family members communicate well. We can talk about most things openly.   T   F

5. My family members express their feelings often.   T   F

6. My family members respect each other's feelings.   T   F

7. My family values working together and we often do.   T   F

8. My family shares the experience of religion and spirituality.   T   F

9. My family members enjoy each other's company.   T   F

10. Each member of my family is valued and important to other members.   T   F

11. When serious problems develop in my family we work them out eventually.   T   F

12. My family allows for each of us to be unique.   T   F

13. Every member of my family is committed to its well-being and success.   T   F

14. We often express appropriate physical affection in my family (hugs, kisses, etc.)   T   F

15. We can turn to one another when things get tough in my family.   T   F

16. We often express verbal affection in my family (love, praise, acceptance, etc.).   T   F

17. We often spend time together just taking it easy.   T   F

18. Each person in my family is allowed to suffer the consequences of his or her own actions.   T   F

19. In my family, we have favorite foods that we usually eat on holidays.   T   F

20. In my family, if things get too bad we will seek outside help.   T   F

21. In my family, we respect and maintain each other's boundaries.   T   F

22. In my family, everyone's input is considered when major decisions are made.   T   F

23. In my family, parents are clearly the leaders.   T   F

24. In my family, we give each other space when it is needed.   T   F

25. In my family, we have healthy relationships with extended family members.   T   F

26. In my family, adult children are allowed to make their own decisions.   T   F

27. In my family, everyone is supported in his or her interests.   T   F

28. In my family, we forgive each other when mistakes are made.   T   F

29. In my family, members listen to each other and are supportive.   T   F

SCORING

First, give yourself the number of points that corresponds to the answer you put for question 1 (i.e., if you put "4" for number 1, you get 4 points). Second, give yourself 1 point for each True answer in questions 2–29 (0 points for those questions you answered False). Third, add your points together. Scores can range from low of 1 to a high of 34. The higher your score, the stronger your family is, and the more likely your family is to have protective and recovery factors.

WHAT DO YOU THINK?

1. If you answered "False" to any of these questions, what, if anything, could be done to improve that area?

2. Are strong families perfect families? Might a strong family also have some weaknesses?

Source: Hammond & Bearnson, 2003b.

individual-level protective factors: Traits including a positive self-concept, sociability, intelligence and scholastic competence, autonomy, self-esteem, androgyny, good communication and problem-solving skills, humor, and good mental and physical health.

family protective factors: Family characteristics or dynamics that shape the family's ability to endure in the face of risk factors.

family recovery factors: Family characteristics or dynamics that assist families in bouncing back from a crisis situation.

routines. Moreover, resilient families generally share core values for financial management and the use of leisure time, even when money and time are in short supply. The *Getting to Know Yourself* feature box asks you to evaluate your family. Do you believe that you have a strong family that offers protective and recovery factors?

Macro-level **community factors,** such as social networks and religious and faith-based fellowships, also affect resilience (Miller, 2000; Silliman, 1998). Community institutions are important means of developing resilient youth and fostering resilience among adults. Researchers indicate several key community strengths (Blyth & Roelkepartian, 1993): First, a strong community has opportunities for participation in community life; extracurricular activities in school, religious youth groups, or other activities help bond youth to their schools, churches, or communities. In these settings, they can learn important skills, such as teamwork, group pride, or leadership. Adults also need opportunities to hone these skills. Second, a strong community should provide ways for members to contribute to the welfare of others (Blyth & Roelkepartian, 1993). Helping others can foster a sense of inner strength and self-esteem. Third, a strong community provides opportunities to connect with peers and other adults. Resilience is more likely when there is access to a role model, a friend, or a confidant. For youth, teachers may play a critical role in providing this type of social support. Finally, healthy communities have community facilities and events for youth. Education and youth activities should receive high priority in the community's budget, with a functioning committee focusing on youth issues.

community factors: Community features that help promote resilience, such as social networks and religious and faith-based fellowships.

What Is Missing? Macro-Level Factors

Strengthening families requires individuals, families, and communities to work together. But broader macro-level factors must also play a part—notably national and state policies (Seccombe, 2002). For example, how do we best help a woman who is battered by her husband or partner? Should we focus on getting her into therapy so that she can improve her self-esteem, which will eventually allow her to end the abusive relationship? This may be an important component of resilience, but it's not enough. Most battered women do not seek therapy because they don't have the time, money, or trust in therapists. Even when therapy is helpful, it occurs *after the fact*, when the psychological, physical, and emotional damage has already been done. Therefore, we must focus on the macro-level structural changes that could prevent violence in the first place, or at least minimize its chance of recurrence. These changes include passing and enforcing laws to prevent and protect women from violence, providing safe houses for their escape, and changing a culture that tolerates violence.

Sound economic and social policies and programs that are designed to strengthen all types of families, healthy as well as vulnerable, such as national health insurance, livable wages, and maternity leaves, can provide families and youth with the necessary tools to master resilience. They add an important level of strength above and beyond individual, family, and community factors. These micro-level and macro-level factors are summarized in the *Tying It All Together* feature box.

Strong community programs such as clubs and organizations can help children connect with peers and mentors to bolster self-esteem.

👁 **Watch** on **MySocLab**
Video: *Importance of Family Dinnertimes*

What type of micro-level individual or family resilience traits do you possess? How are these different from those you see in a close friend or partner? What avenues for resilience does your community offer?

TYING IT ALL TOGETHER — Factors That Influence Family Resilience

What factors are important for building strong families?
Strong families do not happen by accident. Their relative strength depends on what individuals bring to them, as well as the traits of the family as a whole. Macro-level factors in the social environment are also critical to building strong families, as families are embedded in broader social networks. Following are some of the micro-level and macro-level factors that work together to build family resilience.

MICRO-LEVEL FACTORS

- Individual-level protective factors include personality traits and disposition, such as self-confidence.
- Family protective factors, such as family warmth, include characteristics or dynamics that shape the family's ability to endure in the face of risk factors.

- Family recovery factors such as religious beliefs that assist families in "bouncing back" from a crisis.

MACRO-LEVEL FACTORS

- Community factors include adequate schools.
- Family policies and programs, such as Social Security or maternity leaves, offer assistance to help families thrive.

WHAT DO YOU THINK?

1. Can you identify the micro-level factors that you do and do not have that promote resilience?
2. What community factors are present and/or missing in your neighborhood that could help with resilience?

Let's return to the question: What do families need to thrive? Policy decisions—particularly at the national level—have the potential to improve our lives significantly.

Family Policy

The government regulates many aspects of families. For example, the government prohibits certain people from marrying each other, requires people who intend to marry to have a blood test, and requires two witnesses for a legal wedding ceremony. The government also touches the lives of families by an *absence* of certain policies. For example, U.S. adults have no guaranteed maternity leave, national health insurance, or subsidized childcare. These family policies reflect historical, cultural, political, and social factors in the United States, including norms that favor personal over collective responsibility. The United States has little in the way of a comprehensive and collective vision for families, unlike other developed nations (Dey & Wasoff, 2013; Warner, 2005; Zimmerman, 2001). The policies in place are selective in nature and are available only for a few, rather than being universal policies available to all citizens.

A "Selective" Approach to Family Benefits

The United States has a long history of rugged individualism and a general distrust of both government and governmental programs. U.S. policies reflect and promote the concept of self-sufficiency. Our culture expects people to be in charge of their own destinies and shows little tolerance for those who seem unwilling or unable to support themselves (Day & Schiele, 2013; Stern & Axinn, 2012). Borrowing from early English poor laws, our policies evolved over the 17th and 18th centuries to make clear distinctions between "worthy" needy people, who cannot support themselves through no fault of their own, and "unworthy" people, who (supposedly) have little or no desire to work and prefer to leech off the government.

Not surprisingly then, the United States has embraced a laissez-faire approach in which families are largely left to fend for themselves. Many of our social policies and programs tend to be **selective programs,** meaning that only certain people are eligible for government services. For example, only the elderly or certain categories of poor people qualify for governmental health insurance; it's not available to all citizens. Likewise, only low-income parents receive assistance with their childcare costs, rather than all parents regardless of income. Many policies and programs are **means-tested programs,** meaning that persons must meet an income requirement to qualify for benefits. These income thresholds are kept relatively low to limit the number of program users and thus control costs. However, police and fire protection and public education are available to all persons, regardless of income.

A Universal Approach to Family Benefits

When we compare U.S. social philosophy to that of most of Europe, Canada, and other developed nations, we see vastly different approaches, as Sophie and Alain explain in the opening vignette. Most developed nations take a universal approach consisting of an interrelated and coordinated set of proactive economic and social programs and policies to help strengthen all families. **Universal programs** are not means-tested; rather, they are available to everyone. For example, as shown in Table 15.1, in a recent review of 23 developed nations, the United States was the only country without universal health insurance coverage, paid maternal/parental leave at childbirth, or family allowance/child dependency grant, which offsets some of the costs of raising children (Social Security Administration, 2013).

Questions That Matter

15.4 What is the difference between the *universal approach* and the *selective approach* to family policies and programs?

15.5 How does family policy in the United States compare to other countries?

selective programs: Programs for which only a select group of people is eligible.

means-tested programs: Programs for which beneficiaries must meet some eligibility requirement to qualify.

universal programs: Programs to help strengthen all families without any eligibility requirement.

TABLE 15.1 Child Policies in Twenty-three Developed Countries Compared with the United States

The United States is the only developed country without universal health insurance/health care, paid maternal/paternal leave at childbirth, or a family allowance/child dependency grant for families.

Country	Universal Health Insurance/Health Care	Paid Maternal/ Paternal Leave at Childbirth	Family Allowance/ Child Dependency Grant
Australia	Yes	Yes	Yes
Austria	Yes	Yes	Yes
Belgium	Yes	Yes	Yes
Canada	Yes	Yes	Yes
Czech Republic	Yes	Yes	Yes
Denmark	Yes	Yes	Yes
Finland	Yes	Yes	Yes
France	Yes	Yes	Yes
Germany	Yes	Yes	Yes
Hungary	Yes	Yes	Yes
Iceland	Yes	Yes	Yes
Italy	Yes	Yes	Yes
Japan	Yes	Yes	Yes
Luxembourg	Yes	Yes	Yes
Netherlands	Yes	Yes	Yes
New Zealand	Yes	Yes	Yes
Norway	Yes	Yes	Yes
Poland	Yes	Yes	Yes
Portugal	Yes	Yes	Yes
Spain	Yes	Yes	Yes
Sweden	Yes	Yes	Yes
Switzerland	Yes	Yes	Yes
United Kingdom	Yes	Yes	Yes
United States	**No**	**No**	**No**

Source: Social Security Administration, 2013.

Although the United States thinks of health care and childcare in individualistic terms and expects parents to "figure them out" on their own, other countries have specific policies to ensure that all citizens receive these benefits. Yet, how do you arrange for a paid maternal leave after the birth of your child when an employer tells you that you will be fired if you don't return to work quickly? How do you go about finding a family allowance, when most people in the United States have never even heard of such a program? How do you secure comprehensive health insurance when your employer doesn't offer this option, and the cost of purchasing health insurance yourself exceeds your budget? President Obama asked this question, and has attempted to answer it through the passage of health care reform legislation, known as the Affordable Care Act.

Other countries have adopted programs of universal health care and childcare because their citizens believe poverty and inequality are caused by the structure of society, and therefore they look for structural, rather than individual, solutions. They fund safety net programs through **progressive taxation**—those who earn more pay a higher percentage of their income in taxes. U.S. citizens are more likely to equate poverty and its consequences with individual failure, immorality, lack of thrift, or laziness. For example, when asked "Why are there people in this country who live in need?" 39 percent of U.S. adults blamed personal laziness, compared to only 16 percent of Swedes and 15 percent of the French (Larsen, 2006). The Swedes, French, and many other people around the world believe families shouldn't be left to fend for themselves because they are the collective responsibility of all citizens. Therefore, they're willing to pay higher taxes than U.S. adults to ensure that all citizens are well cared for in their countries. How does this form of governmental policy work? In the feature box *My Family: What a Difference Location Can Make!*, the author describes the assistance

progressive taxation: A tax system under which those who earn more pay a higher percentage of their income in taxes than those who earn less.

Do you think that a more universal approach to social and health benefits will encourage people in the United States to become lazy and dependent on the government for help? Why or why not? Can you identify the factors that have shaped your values? Do you know of people who have very different values? Can you guess why they see the world as they do?

MY FAMILY   What a Difference Location Can Make!

Compare and contrast the French and American approaches to families.

I was living in France, a country that has an astounding array of benefits for families—and for mothers in particular. When my children were born, I stayed in the hospital for five comfortable days. I found a nanny through a free, community-based referral service, then employed her, legally and full-time, for a cost of about $10,500 a year, after tax breaks. My elder daughter, from the time she was 18 months, attended excellent part-time preschools, where she painted and played with modeling clay and ate cookies and napped for about $150 a month—the top end of the fee scale. She could have started public school at age three, and could have opted to stay until 5 P.M. daily. My friends who were covered by the French social security system (which I did not pay into), had even greater benefits: at least 4 months of paid maternity leave, the right to stop working for up to 3 years and have jobs held for them, cash grants after their second children were born, starting at about $105 per month.

And that was just the beginning. There was more, a culture. An atmosphere. A set of deeply held attitudes toward motherhood—toward adult womanhood—that had the effect of allowing me to have two children, work in an office, work out in a gym, and go out to dinner at night and away for a short vacation with my husband without ever hearing, without ever thinking, the word "guilt." (pp. 9–10)

. . . I know what had worked for me in France. It wasn't just that I had access to a slew of government-run or subsidized support services; it was also that I'd had a whole unofficial network of people to help and support me—materially and emotionally—as I navigated the new world of motherhood. There was the midwife who'd appeared as if by magic on day four in the hospital to offer tissues as I succumbed to the tears of the "baby blues," and who'd said matter of factly, "Everything is coming out now. Blood, milk, tears. You have to let it flow."

There was my local pharmacist who, unasked, filled my shopping bag with breast pads. The pediatrician who answered his own phone. The network of on-call doctors who made house calls at any time of the day or night. The public elementary school principal who gave us a personal tour of her school and encouraged us to call her if we had any questions. In short, an extended community of people who'd guaranteed that I was never, from the moment I became a mother onward, left to fend for myself alone (pp. 30–31).

—Warner, 2005

WHAT DO YOU THINK?

1. How does the experience of a new mother in France differ from that of a new mother in the United States? Which model do you prefer, and why?
2. Why do you think the experiences of mothers in these two countries are so different? What factors keep the United States from moving toward the French model?

Source: Warner, 2005.

available to her as a new mother living in France. Compare her story to that of a new mother living in the United States.

Building Resilience: General Policies and Programs to Support Families

This section contains several specific policies (among many possibilities) that, if enacted or expanded, could help all families thrive. In particular, they could strengthen vulnerable families and offer a genuine opportunity to develop resilience. We compare U.S. policies with those of other nations, examining what we can learn about strengthening families.

National Health Insurance

As discussed in Chapter 10, almost 50 million Americans have no health insurance, necessitating healthcare reform that passed in 2010 and is slowly being implemented (DeNavas-Walt, Proctor, & Smith, 2013). About 60 percent of Americans receive their health insurance from an employer, either as a worker or as a dependent of a worker (DeNavas-Walt, Proctor, & Smith, 2013).

Despite the current reforms to our healthcare system, the system remains highly unusual when compared to other countries. Linking health insurance to *employment* is virtually unheard of in other developed countries, as well as in many developing countries. Instead, they have **national health insurance**, which means that access to health care is considered a public right of all citizens. It is viewed as a public good, like education, police protection, and parks, and is therefore funded through taxes and general government revenues. Virtually no one is uninsured in these countries.

There are many different types of national health insurance systems; no two countries have identical systems. Americans often look to Canada to assess how their health care system performs, because Canadians changed from a system similar to that in the United States only about 40 years ago. Canadians spend about $5,000 per person on health care, compared to about $8,400 per person in the United States (Henry J. Kaiser Family Foundation, May 2012). Yet, perhaps surprisingly, the health outcomes of our neighbors to the north are better. They have a lower infant mortality rate and longer life expectancy than do U.S. adults (Central Intelligence Agency, 2013). They are more likely to get needed health care and less likely to go into debt for medical reasons. Canadians also like their health care system far more than Americans like theirs. Nonetheless, the Canadian system is far from perfect; wait times for certain procedures or the use of some types of technology can be long—far longer than in the United States (Schoen, Osborn, Doty, Bishop, Peugh, & Murukutla, 2007).

The United States is the only developed nation without some type of national health insurance that guarantees access to health care by right of citizenship. Because of this, our nation's health ranks low in the world. For example, as shown in Table 15.2, the United States has one of the highest maternal mortality rates of any developed nation because a large number of women fail to get prenatal care. They are without insurance and no doctor will see them. Approximately 24 of every 100,000 women die giving birth in the United States, much less than the 970 per 100,000 women who die in Sierra Leone, but many more than in at least 25 countries, including Italy, Ireland, Finland, the United Kingdom, Sweden, Switzerland, and Spain (Population Reference Bureau, 2011). Our maternal mortality rate is more than eight times that of Sweden, the country with the lowest rate. The 2010 Patient Protection and Affordable Care Act, which is being implemented over the course of several years, may eventually lower this as more people are insured, but the new legislation falls far short of guaranteed universal access.

15.3 Describe how our policies can foster family resilience

Question That Matters

15.6 What are some examples of policies or programs in the United States that help support families?

national health insurance: A health care system for all citizens that considers health care a public right.

Read on MySocLab
Document: *Health Care Reform - A Woman's Issue*

TABLE 15.2 A Comparison of Maternal Mortality (Deaths) per 100,000 Live Births

For every 100,000 live births, 24 women die in the United States, a far cry from Afghanistan, but a rate five times higher than Sweden or Denmark.

Sweden	5
Denmark	5
Japan	6
Canada	12
United Kingdom	12
New Zealand	14
United States	**24**
Saudi Arabia	24
Iran	30
China	38
Costa Rica	44
Cuba	53
Vietnam	56
Iraq	75
Mexico	85
Philippines	94
Bolivia	180
India	230
Nepal	380
Kenya	530
Rwanda	540
Sierra Leone	970
Afghanistan	1400

Source: Population Reference Bureau, 2011.

maternity (or family) leave: A paid and guaranteed leave from work to care for children, including after the birth of a child.

▶ **Watch** on **MySocLab**
Video: *Government, Business and Family Policy*

Maternity and Family Leaves

Another critically important way to invest in families is by providing paid **maternity (or family) leaves** at times of need, such as after the birth of a child. These are often called *maternity leaves,* but they could include paternity leaves as well.

Why are these leaves so important? Lengthy maternity leaves are associated with better maternal and child health, as well as lower family stress. Moreover, with extended leave benefits, women are likely to breastfeed for longer periods, which improves children's immunity and reduces their later risk of obesity. The benefit of longer parental leaves also extends to employers. Women are more likely to return to work after childbirth in those countries that have longer leaves. It's more cost-effective for a company to develop a well-planned parental leave policy than it is to rehire and retrain new employees.

Even fathers now want time off to help bond with and care for a newborn. One-third of fathers stay home more than 2 weeks, but generally they work in professional jobs with a higher degree of flexibility, and must use their vacation time or take unpaid leave (Oppenheimer, June 15, 2008). For example, Erich and Anna's daughter was born on Valentine's Day: "It was all the things they say: all the excitement, all the fear, all the anxiousness, and all the joy," says Erich, age 32 (Oppenheimer, June 15, 2008, p. A9). He used a week and a half of sick and vacation time from his job. Staying home any longer wasn't financially feasible, but he wanted to be involved. He scaled back his work to 4 days a week; Anna works 3 days as a community health nurse. "We're a little tighter financially than some parents, but the trade-offs are worth it," Erich says (Oppenheimer, June 15, 2008, p. A9). Erich and Anna are unique in that their employers offer the opportunity to work part-time; most U.S. employers don't provide this flexibility.

The United States has, by far, the least generous family leave policy of any nation, including poor and developing nations, as shown in Table 15.3. The Family Medical Leave Act of 1993, signed by President Clinton, requires employers with more than 50 employees to offer 12 weeks of *unpaid* leave for maternity or to care for a sick family member. Employers in small firms aren't required to offer even unpaid leaves; therefore, many women take only a brief leave from work after having a baby because they can't afford unpaid leave. They return to work soon after exhausting their short-term disability, vacation, or sick pay. Among women who worked during their pregnancy, 58 percent returned to work within 3 months after giving birth, and 72 percent returned within 6 months

(Johnson, 2008). Although some women may have returned to work quickly because they enjoyed their jobs, it's likely that finances were a primary reason for a quick return. Only one-third receive any paid leave from an employer, usually of short duration.

By way of contrast:

- France offers 16 weeks of paid maternity leave to women at 100 percent of their salary.

- In Denmark, women receive 52 weeks of paid maternity leave at 100 percent of their salary.

- Cuba offers women 18 weeks of leave at 100 percent of their salary.

- The United Kingdom allows maternity pay at 90 percent for 6 weeks, and a flat rate after that for up to 1 year.

- Brazil provides 120 days of maternity benefits at 100 percent of their salary (United Nations Statistics Division, 2011).

The United States is the only developed country that does not offer paid maternity leaves. Other countries know that maternity leaves are associated with better health and well-being for the entire family.

TABLE 15.3	A Comparison of Maternity Leave Benefits in Developed and Developing Nations	
Compare the United States with every other country listed. How do we measure up?		
	Length of Maternity Leave	**Percentage of Wages Paid in Covered Period**
Developing Nations		
Afghanistan	90 days	100%
Bangladesh	16 weeks	100%
Cuba	18 weeks	100%
Egypt	90 days	100%
Guatemala	84 days	100%
India	12 weeks	100%
Kenya	3 months	100%
Mozambique	60 days	100%
Republic of Korea	60 days	100%
Developed Nations		
Canada	17–18 weeks	55% for 15 weeks
Denmark	52 weeks	100%
Finland	105 days	80%
Ireland	28 weeks	80% or fixed rate
Italy	5 months	80%
Japan	14 weeks	67%
Netherlands	16 weeks	100%
Spain	16 weeks	100%
Sweden	480 days	80% for 390 days; flat rate afterward
Switzerland	98 days	80%
United Kingdom	52 weeks	90% for 6 weeks; flat rate afterward
United States	**12 weeks[a]**	**0%**

[a]Applies only to workers in companies with 50 or more workers.
Source: Adapted from United Nations Statistics Division, 2010.

Many countries around the world have been increasing the length of paid maternity leave since the early 2000s to give parents even more time with their babies (United Nations Statistics Division, 2011).

Leave is also far more generous in many poor or developing nations than it is in the United States. Even in Afghanistan, one of the poorest nations on Earth, the law entitles women in qualifying jobs up to 90 days of maternity leave paid at 100 percent of their salary. Of course, not all Afghan women receive this pay, as many of them work in the underground economy or in other jobs that do not qualify, but at least the law offers an element of protection for some that American women can only dream about.

Flexible Time and Place of Employment

The adoption of more flexible work environments could do much to enhance family life. Many parents report a high degree of tension in trying to balance work and family demands, including marital conflict, shorter periods spent breastfeeding infants, less involvement with their older children, and depression, as we discussed in Chapter 10. Flexibility in daily work hours, known as **flextime**, and in the location of work, **flexplace**, is high on the agenda of families and family scientists. One study of 3,200 workers at a major pharmaceutical company found that those with job flexibility were more likely to engage in healthful behaviors. They exercised more and attended more employer-sponsored health classes. They reported getting more sleep, and were more likely to describe themselves as living a healthful lifestyle (Parker-Pope, 2007).

About half of companies now offer flextime, according to a national study of nearly 3,000 employees, although only about one-quarter allow it on a daily basis (Bond, Galinsky, & Hill, 2004). Given the current recession, many employees believe it isn't available without repercussions for their careers (Blake, 2010; Clark, 2010). Corporate norms seem to dictate working longer hours than ever before, even for those employees with family responsibilities.

Flexplace, more often now referred to as **telecommuting**, involves maintaining a virtual office or working from home. Telecommuting is rising in popularity because of a growing concern about the automobile's effect on global warming, the rising price of gasoline, and the increasing numbers of parents combining work and family. More than 3.1 million people consider their home to be their primary place of work, a figure that is rising about 3 percent to 5 percent each year. However, millions more conduct some or much of their work at home (Gajendran & Harrison, 2007; Global Workplace Analytics, 2012).

What is the future potential for telecommuting? Research conducted and synthesized by Global Workplace Analytics (October 2012) shows us some interesting possibilities. They estimate that 64 million U.S employees hold a job that is compatible with at least part-time telework (approximately 50 percent of the workforce). They have found that 79 percent of U.S. workers say they would like to work from home at least part of the time. Taken together, this suggests that 50 million workers both could and want to telework.

More flexible work environments could benefit working parents by decreasing commuting time and the stresses associated with negotiating rush-hour traffic, and allowing them to synchronize work schedules with their children's activities and other family responsibilities. Flexible work environments may be ideal for the worker, but are they ideal for business? The analysis of more than 46 telecommuting studies published since the early 1990s and involving 12,833 employees reveals its overall beneficial effect, because the arrangement provides employees with more control—and thus more satisfaction with their work. Employees who were allowed to telecommute some or part of the time had less desire to leave the company and were given higher performance ratings by

Many parents appreciate flexible schedules and flexible workplaces so they can more easily combine work and family.

flextime: Flexibility in the daily hours of work.

flexplace: Flexibility in the location of work, including working from home.

telecommuting: Flexibility in the location of work, including working from home.

supervisors (Gajendran & Harrison, 2007). Likewise, Global Workplace Analytics (2012) reports that if those with compatible jobs and a desire to work from home did so just half the time (roughly the national average for those who do so regularly), the national savings would total more than $700 billion a year, including:

- A typical business would save $11,000 per person per year.
- The telecommuters would save between $2,000 and $7,000 a year.
- The oil savings would equal more than 37% of our Persian Gulf imports.
- The greenhouse gas reduction would be the equivalent of taking the entire New York State workforce permanently off the road.
- The Congressional Budget Office's estimate of the entire 5-year cost of implementing telework throughout government ($30 million) is less than a third of the cost of lost productivity from a single-day shutdown of federal offices in Washington DC because of snow ($100 million).

Nonetheless, given the current economic conditions, many workers are skittish about telecommuting, fearing that if they are out of sight, they may also be out of the boss's mind (Blake, 2010; Clark, 2010).

Living Wage

The federal minimum wage was increased in 2007 after being stagnant at $5.15 per hour for more than a decade (Table 15.4). The increase took place in three increments: $5.85 in 2007; $6.55 in 2008; and $7.25 per hour in 2009. Minimum wage rates are important, because many minimum-wage workers are adults and are parents. The average minimum-wage worker brings home almost half (48 percent) of his or her family's weekly earnings (Filion, 2009), yet the minimum wage remains inadequate to support a family. Many families earning the minimum wage are living below the poverty line and need programs such as food stamps, reduced-fee school lunch programs, and other benefits to make ends meet. A worker earning $7.25 per hour earns $290 a week, or $15,080 per year, a few thousand dollars below the poverty line for a family of three, as described in Chapter 2 (DeNavas-Walt, Proctor, & Smith, 2013).

In response to this concern, the living wage movement has gained a significant foothold in at least 60 local governments, including New York City, Baltimore, Portland (Oregon), Chicago, and Minneapolis (Fairris & Reich, 2005; Freeman, 2005; Thompson & Chapman, 2006). Recall from Chapter 10 that a **living wage** is pay that would support a decent standard of living. It means paying workers enough so that they can provide their families with food, shelter, clothing, energy, transportation, education, childcare, and health care. Generally speaking, this can't happen at federal or state minimum wage levels. Living wage proponents argue that (1) wages should be high enough to allow workers to meet basic needs; and (2) municipal governments should encourage or require living wages for their employees and contractors, rather than exacerbate the problems low-wage workers face by using public money to create jobs that keep people poor (Thompson & Chapman, 2006). A typical living wage ordinance requires contractors and businesses receiving governmental financial

TABLE 15.4	Characteristics of Workers Benefitted by Minimum Wage Increase to $7.25 in 2009

Millions of people earn only minimum wage, which increased nationally to $7.25 per hour in 2007. This increase especially benefitted women, parents, and older full-time workers.

Number of workers	5.3 million
Gender	
Male	39%
Female	61%
Family Status	
Parent	25%
Married Parent	15%
Unmarried Parent	9%
Age	
16–19	30%
20 and over	71%
Work Hours	
1–19	22%
20–34	36%
Full time (35 hours +)	43%

Source: Filion, 2009.

Listen on **MySocLab**
Audio: *NPR: Low-Wage America*

assistance to pay what is deemed a *livable wage* in that community, one that will ultimately decrease the number of people dependent on social programs. Usually these wages range from 150 percent to 225 percent of the current federal minimum wage. For example, effective July 1, 2009, the City of Los Angeles pays at least $10.70 per hour to those workers in covered contracts if they also receive health insurance, and $11.95 per hour to those workers who don't (City of Los Angeles, 2012), although this is still far below what is needed for a true living wage, estimated to be around $24 an hour for a family of one adult and one child (Living Wage Calculation, 2013). Living wage movements have expanded their goals to include vacation days, health insurance, and other benefits.

Critics of living wage legislation claim these laws actually harm those they are intended to help by reducing their work opportunities. As the price of labor increases, they say, a loss of jobs will result, and these workers will be even worse off. Consequently, wage subsidies are usually administered as federal tax credits. These credits shift much of the financial burden from the local governments to the federal government, which is better equipped to absorb these costs. An example of a wage subsidy, or tax credit for low-income persons, is the Earned Income Tax Credit (EITC).

Earned Income Tax Credit

Earned Income Tax Credit: A refundable federal tax credit for low-income working families that reduces the amount of taxes owed.

The **Earned Income Tax Credit** (EITC) is a refundable federal tax credit for low-income working families that can reduce the amount of taxes owed and result in a tax refund for those who qualify. In the 2012 tax year, working families with children that have annual incomes below about $36,900 to $50,300 (depending on marital status and the number of dependent children) could be eligible for the federal EITC. Also, working-poor people without children who have incomes below about $13,900 ($19,200 for a married couple) can receive a very small EITC (Center on Budget and Policy Priorities, February 1, 2013; Internal Revenue Service, 2013).

Roughly 27 million working families received the EITC during the tax season of 2012 (Marr, April 17, 2013). It's one of the country's largest sources of assistance for poor and low-income working families. Enacted in 1975 and expanded in the 1990s, and again in 2009, it helps millions of Americans—adults and children—avoid poverty each year, as illustrated in Figure 15.1 (Center on Budget and Policy Priorities, February 7, 2013). The EITC encourages employment because it offers a real supplement to wages for qualifying low-income workers, and makes it easier for families to transition from welfare into work. The boost in income provides a critical element of security for poor families. It can contribute to basic necessities, enable families to make special needed purchases, or build a savings cushion to offset a future job loss, illness, or another situation that can leave families vulnerable. Without the EITC, poverty rates among children would be about one-third higher than they are now. Research shows poor children who receive the EITC, as compared to poor children who do not, are healthier, have better school performance, and have higher earnings as adults—all this for only $3,000 per year (on average) (Marr, Charite, & Huang, 2013). Yet, millions of eligible Americans don't take their EITC, most likely because they're unaware that it's available to them.

The EITC receives enthusiastic bipartisan support because it encourages work and gives a helping hand to

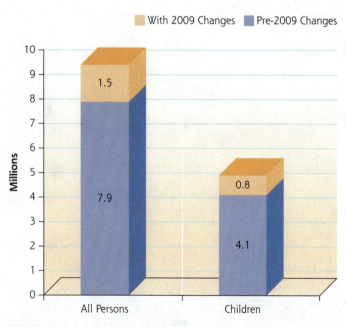

FIGURE 15.1

Earned Income Tax Credit and Child Tax Credit Lift Millions Out of Poverty (Millions)

The Earned Income Tax Credit and Child Tax Credit lift millions of people out of poverty each year.
Source: Center on Budget and Policy Priorities, February 7, 2013.

the lowest-income families. Yet at the same time, this benefit has had less impact than it could in the United States. The EITC is a once-a-year tax credit, unlike family allowances, which provide monthly support. Furthermore, the EITC offsets only *some* of the taxes the worker would pay, and doesn't really augment wages.

Welfare: Temporary Assistance for Needy Families

Welfare has been one of the most vexing social policy concerns in the United States. Its principal cash program, **Temporary Assistance for Needy Families (TANF)**, formerly called Aid to Families with Dependent Children (AFDC), has been accused of fostering long-term dependency, family breakups, and illegitimacy (Murray, 1988). Welfare recipients are stigmatized as lazy and unmotivated, looking for a free ride at the expense of the taxpayer (Seccombe, 2014).

Both Republicans and Democrats have tried to reconstruct welfare or end it completely. President Bill Clinton signed sweeping welfare reform legislation, which became federal law on July 1, 1997. Many details of welfare law were turned over to individual states, which set lifetime welfare payments at a maximum of 5 years and required the majority of adult recipients to work after 2 years.

Under TANF, the federal government provides a block grant to the states, which use these funds to operate their own programs. These programs are to assist in achieving the following four goals:

1. Provide assistance to needy families so that children may be cared for in their own homes or in the homes of relatives;

2. End the dependence of needy parents on government benefits by promoting job preparation, work, and marriage;

3. Prevent and reduce the incidence of out of wedlock pregnancies and establish annual numerical goals for preventing and reducing the incidence of these pregnancies; and

4. Encourage the formation and maintenance of two-parent families.

States have used their TANF funds for a variety of services and supports, including income assistance (including wage supplements for working-poor families), childcare, education and job training, transportation, aid to children at risk of abuse and neglect, and a variety of other services to help low-income families. Only a quarter of TANF money actually goes as cash to needy families (Schott, 2012).

Since the passage of welfare reform, many people have left welfare, usually for low-wage work. From 1994 to 2012, national caseloads fell by two-thirds, declining from 5 million to around 1.7 million families (Administration for Children & Families, 2013).

Although declining caseload numbers are often seen as a sign of success, families leaving welfare for work aren't necessarily better off financially (Schott & Pavetti, 2011; Seccombe & Hoffman, 2007; Trisi & Pavetti, 2012). Commonly, families have difficulty paying their rent or utilities, have experienced bouts of food insecurity (i.e., they didn't have money to purchase food for their family) or used a food bank, and many don't have reliable transportation, making it more difficult to work or take children to school. In the past, these vulnerable families could rely on TANF, but with the reforms of the 1990s, this is often no longer the case. As Figure 15.2 reveals, for

Temporary Assistance to Needy Families (TANF): The principal cash welfare program in the United States.

Read on **MySocLab** **Document:** *The Compassion Gap in American Poverty Policy*

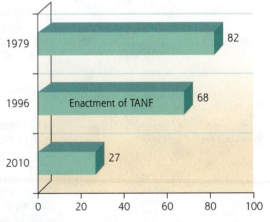

FIGURE 15.2

Number of Families Receiving Cash Welfare Benefits for Every 100 Families with Children in Poverty

TANF's role as a safety net has declined sharply over time. Most poor people received cash welfare benefits in 1979; today, however, because of changes, only about one-quarter of poor families receive cash benefits.
Source: Center on Budget and Policy Priorities, 2012.

every 100 families with children in poverty, only 27 of them even receive TANF benefits, a significant decline from when welfare was reformed. Are these children really better off?

Part of the reason that families leaving welfare sometimes fare poorly is that many face one or more significant barriers to securing employment (Bloom, Loprest, & Zedlewski, 2011). The most common work barriers TANF recipients face include low levels of education and a lack of work experience, mental and physical health challenges, and caring for a child with special needs. Other TANF recipients report domestic violence, and some have criminal records.

Statewide studies of families leaving welfare agree with national reports. For example, a study in Oregon that followed 552 former welfare recipients until 18 months after leaving TANF found that recipients' average income hovered near the poverty line, but their income rendered them ineligible for a number of important services (Seccombe & Hoffman, 2007). Forty percent had no health insurance, and 21 percent had at least one child uninsured. Thirty-two percent had cut or skipped meals entirely because of a lack of money, and 8 percent had cut or skipped their children's meals. Most reported outstanding debt, including 54 percent who had a medical debt averaging nearly $2,500, a sum nearly impossible to repay given their inadequate incomes.

The study included women like "Molly," who suffered a tubal pregnancy, yet tried to avoid seeking medical care because she had no insurance and no way to pay the medical bill. Finally, after enduring pain for nearly 2 weeks, she went to the emergency room of her local hospital and was immediately taken to surgery. Her fallopian tube was removed at a cost of $14,000. She discusses her debt:

> There's all these doctor's offices that I owe money to, and I had to set up payment plans with all of them. But, you know, it's like paying as much as rent every month to each doctor's office. I'm never going to come up with the money. I mean, I can try to make my payments, but it's never going to happen. I make eleven bucks an hour. I have to pay rent, gas, utilities, groceries, diapers, and, you know, daycare is way expensive. That's like 400 bucks a month, and now they want me to pay 400 bucks a month to different offices. And I'm like, dude, I'm not made of money. The next time something like that happens, I'm just going to dig a grave in the backyard. Fourteen grand's not worth it.
>
> **"It's like paying as much as rent every month to each doctor's office."**
>
> **—Molly (Seccombe & Hoffman, 2007, p. 4)**

Read on MySocLab Document: *If the French Can Do It, Why Can't We?*

Do you think the current economic recession has changed these policies and programs for families? For example, are any expanding or retracting? Why might this be the case?

Other countries have a different approach to helping poor families, as we saw in the opening vignette. For example, in her book *Saving Our Children from Poverty* (1996), economist Barbara Bergmann states that only one-quarter of single mothers in France receive welfare-type benefits, compared to two-thirds of single mothers in the United States. The reason is not that France is stingy toward its citizens, but that France has made a successful commitment to enhancing low-tier jobs so they pay a living wage, and the government doesn't automatically eliminate an array of benefits vital to a family's well-being. A single mother in France who moves from welfare to work retains approximately $6,000 in government cash and housing grants. She continues to receive health insurance and pays only a small amount for childcare, as do all French citizens. Therefore, even though France has an unemployment rate 50 percent higher than that in the United States, its poverty rate is considerably lower. In contrast, in the *Why Do Research? Surviving Welfare and Low-wage Work* feature box, researchers Katherine Edin and Laura Lein show us how nearly 400 low-income or welfare-reliant single mothers try to survive.

How do single mothers in the United States survive with meager welfare benefits and low-wage work? It is not easy, as a study of nearly 400 poor and low-income single mothers revealed. Researchers used both quantitative data, such as filling out budgets, and qualitative data based on in-depth interviews to determine how families on welfare and those who work in low-wage jobs make ends meet. Using multiple methods is rarely done because of the cost, time involved, and the fact that many researchers are experienced with only a single strategy for collecting data. Yet, using multiple methods allows us to obtain a better understanding of how poor and low-income families make ends meet. Here are a few excerpts that describe some of the strategies that low-income families use.

1. Contributions from family, friends, boyfriends:

"The kids give me a headache about clothes. Usually my mom, brother, or sister-in-law gives me money to buy them clothes. I can't afford it. I get clothes at church and other charitable clothes giveaways, or at garage sales."

"He [baby's father] sometimes gives me money. When I send her up there to his mother's house, he buys her Pampers and baby food, but all he puts into my hand is a $20 bill. I mean, what does he expect me to buy with $20? I can't even buy but two boxes of Pampers with $20. He's coming over here tonight to bring her back, and I said I needed $40 'cause she needs so many things right now. But I don't think he gonna bring it."

2. Reported work:

"Working overtime if I have to, anything to get a few extra dollars. I try to get to work one-half hour early, and leave one-half hour late, that's an extra five hours worth of pay each week! It comes in handy."

3. Unreported side jobs:

"I collect junk, trash pick—I'm the ultimate trash picker—and I go to garage sales. I have my friends picking up stuff in alleys and at garage sales for me too. They're all like, 'Oh, let's grab this for her!' whenever they see some old crap. Then on weekends, I'll get this friend of mine to help me load his pickup and we get a table at the flea market for about $50. Some weekends I'll make $200 or $300 on old junk I might have paid $20 total for, but that's not all the time."

4. Underground work:

"Some of our friends will sell drugs. I know some of my friends who have turned tricks. Usually, some people do it for their family, and some people do it for drugs. At one point I did sell drugs in order to keep my family [together]. When my husband left, and I had to make sure I could pay my bills. That's what I did."

5. Agency-based strategies:

"This morning I went to Catholic Charities and got a $20 voucher for the Market Basket [grocery store]. You can only go once a year. They're cutting back a lot of programs: no more emergency assistance, no more back payments in rent, no more rent assistance. These cuts will affect me a lot. I will have to dig deep. I don't know what I am going to do."

WHAT DO YOU THINK?

1. What might be some of the ethical issues involved in doing qualitative and quantitative research on poor and low-income families?
2. Did any of these survival strategies bother you personally? If so, why?

Source: Edin and Lein, 1997.

Child Tax Credit

Likewise, the Child Tax Credit (CTC) helps working families offset the cost of raising children. It is worth up to $1,000 per eligible child (under age 17 at the end of the tax year). Taxpayers eligible for the credit subtract it from the total amount of federal income taxes they would otherwise owe. For example, if a couple with two qualifying children would owe $4,600 in taxes without the credit, they would owe $2,600 in taxes with it, because the credit would reduce their tax bill by $1,000 for each child. The tax credit phases out for higher-income families, presumably because higher-income households are less in need of assistance to meet the costs of raising children. Couples with two children and income more than $110,000 (or $75,000 for single or head-of-household filers) receive a smaller CTC, and those with incomes more than $150,000 ($115,000 for singles and heads of household) receive no credit at all.

Question That Matters

15.7 What are some examples of policies or programs in the United States that help improve children's lives?

early childhood intervention: Attempts to maintain or improve the quality of life for young children.

📖 **Read** on **MySocLab**
Document: *The End of Welfare as We Know It*

Specific Policies and Programs for Children

Children depend on others to meet their basic needs of food, shelter, clothing, and love. What can we do to improve their circumstances, and therefore, improve their resilience and chance for a good and productive life?

Early Childhood Interventions

Early childhood interventions attempt to improve the quality of lives of children. Although most of the care young children receive comes from families, early childhood interventions are formal supports designed to augment this care. They can include (Children's Defense Fund, 2012):

- Public health and social welfare programs that provide prenatal care, immunizations, or food and nutritional supplements, including the feeding program Women, Infants, and Children (WIC);
- Childcare programs designed to ensure high-quality care, or to provide financial assistance to families needing childcare;
- Programs to promote early childhood development, such as parenting classes, Head Start, preschool, and kindergarten; and
- Income or other safety-net programs.

Researchers from RAND, a prominent research institute in California, conducted a project to determine whether early childhood intervention programs offer lasting success (Karoly, Kilburn, & Cannon, 2005). They examined 20 programs that provided three types of child development services, from the prenatal period to kindergarten: (1) parental education and home visiting; (2) early childhood education combined with parent education; and (3) early childhood education only. Of these 20 programs, 19 demonstrated favorable effects on child outcomes in at least one of the following domains: cognitive and academic achievement, behavioral and emotional competencies, educational progression and attainment, child maltreatment, health, delinquency and crime, social welfare program use, and labor market success. In other words, early childhood intervention programs *do* work. Moreover, many benefits can be translated into dollar figures and compared with program costs. For example, if children do better in school, less money will be spent on remedial or special education classes. Cost–benefit analyses estimate that for every dollar invested, the returns to society range from $1.80 to $7.07. In other words, early childhood education is cost-effective and pays important dividends for years to come (Karoly, Kilburn, & Cannon, 2005).

The *Policy and You: From Macro to Micro: Head Start Programs* feature box describes one well-known intervention program that combines early childhood education with parent education—Head Start. This program is designed to improve school readiness and basic cognitive skills for low-income preschool-age children, working with both the child and his or her family. This program currently serves nearly 1 million, yet funding falls far short and cannot cover all who qualify (Early Childhood Learning and Knowledge Center, May 2013).

Children's Health Insurance Program

Children are especially vulnerable to poor health and in need of preventive care; therefore, the Children's Health Insurance Program (CHIP; also sometimes known as State Children's Health Insurance Program, or SCHIP) was created in the 1990s to insure children in working families with incomes too high to qualify for Medicaid, but too low to afford private family coverage (Ross, Horn, & Marks, 2008). Congress created CHIP as a federal/state partnership similar to

Head Start began in 1965 as part of the War on Poverty program launched by President Lyndon B. Johnson. Nearly half the nation's poor people were children under age 12, and Head Start was developed to respond to the needs of poor children as early as possible. Research showed that early intervention through high-quality programs enhances children's physical, social, emotional, and cognitive development; enables parents to be better caregivers and teachers to their children; and helps parents meet their own goals, including economic independence.

Head Start was envisioned as a comprehensive program that would provide health and nutritional services to poor children while developing their cognitive skills and engaging parents as well. To improve school readiness, children may be taught the alphabet, numbers, colors, and shapes. They are monitored to keep them up to date on immunizations; testing is also available for hearing and vision. Many programs are integrated to include children with special physical or cognitive needs. Class size is limited to 17 to 20 children, with two teachers. Parents are encouraged to work as teacher's aides so they understand what their children are learning and help carry on that learning at home.

Head Start began by primarily serving 4-year-olds, who attend for one year before starting kindergarten. However, with the reauthorization of the program in 1994, Congress established a new program for pregnant women and low-income families with infants and toddlers called Early Head Start. Today, 46 percent of children attending Head Start are age 3 or younger. The Early Head Start program provides resources to community programs to address the needs of younger children and their families. Its goals are similar to those of Head Start—to demonstrate the impact of early, continuous, intensive, and comprehensive services to pregnant women and very young children and their families.

Measuring the program's actual success is not a simple matter. Head Start is said to save taxpayers' money because attendees are more likely to graduate from high school and get a job than their peers. However, its precise long-term benefits are difficult to gauge, and researchers disagree even about the short-term benefits. Nevertheless, one government publication states that, in the long term, $6 are saved for every $1 invested in the Head Start program. Other studies find that Head Start graduates are more likely than their peers to stay in the proper grade level for their age in elementary school. The price tag? Nearly $8 billion.

WHAT DO YOU THINK?

1. Draft an argument in favor of Head Start programs; then draft an argument against them. Be sure to include the bottom line: does it work? Is Head Start worth the money?
2. Why do you think so many poor children have deficits in their early education? Try to offer both micro-level and macro-level explanations.

Source: Adapted from Early Childhood Learning and Knowledge Center. April 2013.

Medicaid, with the goal of expanding health insurance to children. It's the single largest expansion of health insurance coverage for children since the initiation of Medicaid in the mid-1960s. Although eligibility criteria differ by state, 44 states and the District of Columbia now cover children living in households with incomes up to twice the poverty line (around $45,000 for a family of three) (Medicaid.gov, 2013). Despite this program, millions of needy families remain ineligible, aren't aware of CHIP, or otherwise don't or can't enroll in this program. More than 9 percent of all children, and 14 percent of children from poor households, are uninsured, as shown in Figure 15.3 (DeNavas-Walt, Proctor, & Smith, 2013).

If low-income and poor children are eligible for CHIP, then why are they not covered? First, it's possible that some families don't know of the program or can't access it for some reason—perhaps there are distance, language, or cultural barriers. Second, the program is underfunded and can't cover all eligible children. Third, applications are subject to bureaucratic rules, such as 90-day waiting periods, strict asset limits, or other regulations that limit their coverage. The result can be very disturbing, as shown in the Johnson household:

Thirteen-year-old Devante Johnson, of Houston, Texas, had advanced kidney cancer and could not afford to be without healthcare coverage. But last year, that is exactly what happened when Devante spent four desperate months uninsured while his mother tried to renew his Medicaid coverage. For years Devante and his two younger brothers were covered by Medicaid. Texas families who qualify for Medicaid or the Children's Health Insurance Program (CHIP) are required to renew their coverage every six months, and Devante's mother, Tamika, had tried to get a head start by sending in her paperwork two months before Medicaid was set to expire. The application sat for six weeks until it was processed and then transferred to CHIP because an employee believed their family no longer qualified for Medicaid. At that point, the paperwork got lost in the system. Tamika grew more and more desperate as she watched her son get worse. "I did everything I possibly could," Tamika said. "I would literally get off the phone in tears, crying because they [CHIP employees] frustrated me so much." For four months Devante went without health insurance as employees attempted to reinstate his coverage. As a result he could no longer receive regular treatment and had to rely on clinical trials for care. Meanwhile, his tumors grew. Time was running out. It wasn't until a state representative intervened that Devante's coverage was immediately reinstated. Two days later, Devante was able to start a promising new treatment. But it was too late. Devante Johnson died at the age of 14, from complications of the disease. (Children's Defense Fund, 2007, p. 13)

FIGURE 15.3
Uninsured Children by Poverty Status, Household Income, Age, Race and Hispanic Origin, and Nativity: 2011

Despite programs to help uninsured children, many remain uninsured, creating a need for health care reform.
Source: DeNavas-Walt, Proctor, & Smith, 2013.

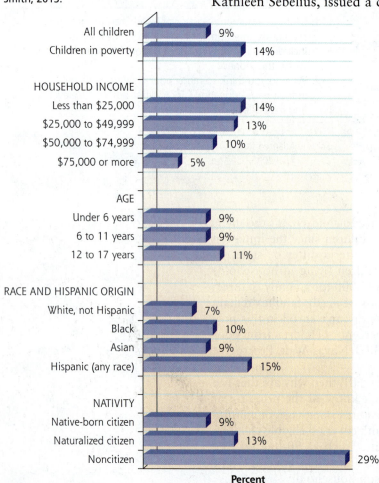

CHIP was reauthorized in 2009, with additional money targeted toward enrolling more eligible children and financial help to states to help them care for the additional children enrolled (Centers for Medicare and Medicaid Services, 2012). In early 2010, the U.S. Secretary of Health and Human Services, Kathleen Sebelius, issued a challenge to find and enroll approximately 5 million uninsured children eligible for Medicaid or CHIP. About 86 percent of eligible children are enrolled in either CHIP or Medicaid. Those children who are eligible but not enrolled are more likely to be teenagers, live with people other than their parents, and are American Indians or Alaska Natives (Kenney, Lynch, Huntress, Haley, & Anderson, 2012).

Child Support

The parents of 22 million children younger than 21 live apart from one another (Grall, 2011). Inadequate child support payments from the noncustodial parent have hurt many families. As discussed in Chapter 12, fewer than half of custodial parents receive the full amount of their court-ordered child support payment, and more than one-quarter receive nothing at all from their non-custodial parents. Although the average amount of child support due was $5,955, only $3,634 was received, shortchanging children out of more than $2,000 a year (Grall, 2011).

Defaulted or delinquent child support payments have been a long-standing problem. Since 1988, the government has made greater efforts to secure child support from the absent parent with passage of the Family Support Act, which includes withholding child support from the parent's wages, requiring states to adopt uniform standards for setting child support awards, and implementing computerized systems for locating delinquent parents. Some states take additional steps, such as intercepting tax returns, withdrawing funds from bank accounts, suspending drivers' licenses, or even sending nonpaying parents to jail. Despite these state efforts, compliance is still woefully inadequate. Consequently, child support enforcement was an important component of the welfare reform changes of 1996, and states must now comply with more rigorous federal guidelines to secure child support.

Will further enforcing child support orders really help children? For the millions of custodial parents who fail to receive the full amount of child support, and the millions of others without a child support agreement, rigorous collection could add several thousand dollars a year to their family income. Although this additional money would not bestow great wealth on these families, it would nonetheless make their lives far more comfortable and secure (especially given that child support payments are not taxed). About one-quarter of all custodial single parents live in poverty (Grall, 2011), and the addition of several thousand dollars a year could provide a possible financial safety net for their families.

Childcare Policies

As discussed in Chapter 10, childcare is expensive for families in the United States. Costs for full-time care can easily top $10,000 a year or more per child. Given that most families have more than one child, often spaced only a few years apart, childcare bills can easily exceed $20,000 per year. These costs are out of reach of many families. Although some subsidies are available to families leaving TANF for work, most people pay the cost of childcare themselves out of their own pockets. This imposes a considerable hardship on many families.

Watch on **MySocLab**
Video: *Day Care*

Families can offset some of the costs of childcare in two ways (Internal Revenue Service, 2011, 2013). One option is a childcare tax credit on the family's income tax form. Under current law, the Child and Dependent Care tax credit can cover between 20 percent and 35 percent of expenses to care for children younger than 13, depending on family income. The lower the family's income, the higher the allowable percentage. There is a dollar limit on the expenses toward which you can apply the credit: about $3,000 for the care of one child, $6,000 for two or more. Although this represents a real savings to families at tax time, it doesn't come close to covering the full costs of care.

As a second option, available only if provided by an employer, a family can set aside up to $5,000 in pre-tax dollars in a flexible spending plan for childcare (Internal Revenue Service, 2009). The family doesn't pay taxes on this set-aside amount, so in a 25 percent tax bracket, the family receives a 25 percent "bonus" ($1,250), which can be a real boon to many families. However, there are two problems with the flexible spending plan. First, given that most childcare costs far exceed $5,000, these savings, although helpful, are inadequate to meet the needs of most families. For example, if the real cost of childcare is $10,000, and by law the 25 percent tax benefit can be taken on only half that amount—$5,000—the real tax saving is reduced to 12.5 percent (half of 25 percent). Second, wealthier families in a higher tax bracket save more money than lower-income families in a lower income tax bracket. Therefore, this program is highly regressive: the wealthier end up getting a higher benefit than those families who need it the most.

How do other countries handle childcare issues, and what can the United States learn from them? In most of Europe, publicly funded childcare is readily available to everyone, often on a sliding scale based on income. In the United States, only 1 percent of children ages 2 and younger, and 14 percent of children ages 3 to school age, are in publicly funded childcare programs. Compare these statistics with Denmark, where 48 percent of children up to age 2, and 85 percent of children ages 3 to school age, are in publicly funded childcare. Or compare them with those of France and Belgium, where 20 percent of children to age 2 and 95 percent of children ages 3 and older are in publicly funded childcare. In the United States, parents bear most childcare costs themselves. Quality care is seen as a private good rather than a public one, even though as a society we benefit from having educated children who are well cared for.

France provides an example of what is possible (Bergmann, 1996; Warner, 2005). French parents at all income levels receive government assistance with childcare. Daycare centers for young children or smaller family childcare units are readily available, staffed by an educated and valued work force that is well paid and receives full benefits. Free public nursery schools are available for children ages 2½ to 6, and by the time they are 3 years old, virtually all French children attend them. There is also a well-coordinated before-school and after-school care program for a nominal fee. Because these programs are universal and available to all French citizens regardless of income, there is no stigma attached to using them. They are considered programs that all families may need, rich, poor, or in-between.

15.5 Identify specific policies and programs for the elderly

Question That Matters

15.8 What are some examples of policies or programs in the United States that help the elderly?

Specific Policies and Programs for the Elderly

As discussed in Chapter 14, both the number and the proportion of elderly persons are increasing substantially in the United States. We face new challenges in learning how best to deal with our changing demographic structure and care for the frailest members of our society. In the next section, we look at several policies related to the economic well-being and health of the elderly and compare U.S. policies to those of other nations.

Social Security and Economic Well-Being

Less than 9 percent of elders live in poverty, the lowest proportion of any age group (DeNavas-Walt, Proctor, & Smith, 2013). Yet to truly understand the economic well-being of the elderly, we must examine more than just the poverty line, because many elderly live only slightly above it. They aren't represented in the poverty statistics, but they are vulnerable nonetheless.

Moreover, subgroups of elderly differ substantially in their level of income and assets. Chances are an 80-year-old Black female who lives alone is significantly worse off than a 66-year-old married White male. Sex, race, ethnicity, and age interact to influence an individual's median income and likelihood of living in poverty. Sociologists refer to the notions of **cumulative advantage** and **cumulative disadvantage** to describe how early life choices influence status in later life. White males tend to have greater opportunities for financial success and can build on their successes to perpetuate their advantages into older age. Meanwhile, those who have faced early disadvantages carry these into old age, often resulting in poverty or near-poverty.

Have you, or someone close to you, used any of the programs or policies introduced in this chapter? Did the program(s) help, and if so how? If not, do you have any idea why not? What suggestions do you have to change the direction of our country's family policies? Can the efforts of one person affect social change?

cumulative advantage and disadvantage: Early life chances that influence status in later life.

Ideally, elders in the United States receive income from three primary sources: (1) retirement benefits from Social Security; (2) payments from private pensions; and (3) income from assets and personal savings. The Social Security Administration refers to these sources as a "three-legged stool"—all three "legs" are needed to provide support.

The United States is one of more than 150 countries that have some sort of financial program for elders, known here as Social Security and discussed in Chapter 14. Each program operates somewhat differently, but provides at least a minimal financial benefit for this group. Some serve virtually everyone above a certain age threshold, such as in the United States and United Kingdom, whereas others serve only people who meet an eligibility requirement. For example, in China, less than one-quarter of elders are covered; in Mexico, about one-third are covered (Social Security Administration, 2013).

The amount of money provided to the elderly also varies, and programs provide greater coverage to married couples than to singles. The difference in benefit size between married couples and singles is particularly acute in the United States, where elderly women who live alone are among the poorest in all developed countries; only in Australia are single elderly women worse off than in the United States. It appears that our "three-legged stool" may be adequate for married couples, but the cumulative disadvantage for single women, especially minority women, results in lower pay, less in savings and assets, and reduced Social Security benefits.

Health Policy

Health care is a rapidly growing segment of the U.S. economy, and the elderly use a sizable portion of healthcare services. Because most no longer work, how do they get their health insurance? Medicare is a federal health insurance program for people ages 65 and older (and some people younger than 65 with certain disabilities) (Medicare.gov, 2013). It was created in 1965 and today is virtually universal among the elderly in the United States. However, elders still pay a significant amount of money for health care; Medicare is *not* free health care.

Medicare really is made up of several distinct programs. Part A is *hospital insurance*. Most people receive Part A automatically when they turn 65 and don't have to pay monthly premiums. It covers overnight stays in hospitals, about 3 months in a skilled nursing facility, hospice care, and some home health care. The yearly *deductible* (the amount the recipient must pay before Medicare chips in) was almost $1,200 in 2013 (Medicare.gov, 2013).

Part B is sometimes called *supplemental insurance*. It's optional and for most people requires a $105 monthly premium (in 2013). Part B covers 80 percent of such costs as doctors' fees, outpatient hospital treatment, and lab services. The other 20 percent, referred to as a *co-payment*, is the part the elderly pay themselves. In addition to the monthly premium and co-payments, there is a yearly deductible (an initial uncovered outlay) of $155 (Medicare.gov, 2013). Part C includes care in health maintenance organizations, and Part D, created in 2006, covers some prescription drug costs.

Medicare has made health insurance far more affordable and available to elders. Because it's a universal program rather than means-tested (i.e., it's available to everyone rather than based on income), it has virtually no stigma attached. Yet, Medicare faces criticism. Given high deductibles, co-payments, and payments for non-covered expenses, most elderly persons with Medicare still spend thousands of dollars on medical care, averaging around $4,500 each year, as shown in Figure 15.4 (Henry J. Kaiser Family Foundation, November 14, 2012). Consequently, many elders have some form of additional insurance, a so-called *medigap policy* to augment their Medicare. The poorest elderly may qualify for Medicaid, the healthcare program designed to serve poor persons regardless of age.

In any case, our present healthcare system isn't designed to serve the elderly well. This is certainly not the fault of Medicare, but it does dampen the efficiency of the program. Elders commonly suffer from chronic conditions, such as arthritis and heart disease, that can be managed but not cured. Our healthcare system is geared instead to render acute care, such as surgical or high-tech treatments to fix short-term health problems. A healthcare system that focused more on maintaining health and well-being, rather than only on eliminating disease, would be more responsive to their needs.

Our changing demographic structure, outlined in Chapter 14, has repercussions for the Medicare program. Medicare is primarily funded through taxes—working people pay taxes today for programs used by the elderly today. There

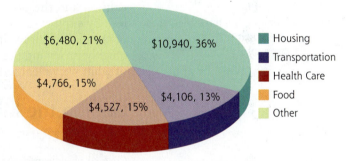

FIGURE 15.4
Distribution of Average Medicare Household Spending

The average elderly household that receives Medicare still pays about $4,500 annually for health care—Medicare isn't free.
Source: Henry J. Kaiser Family Foundation, November 14, 2012.

Read on **MySocLab**
Document: *The Medically Uninsured: Will They Always Be With Us?*

were approximately five workers for each beneficiary in 1960 and three in 2000, but there will be only 1.9 workers for each beneficiary by 2040 (De Lew, Greenbery, & Kinchen, 1992). Couple this with our rising overall healthcare costs, and it's easy to see a major financing disaster in the making. To avoid this, Congress will likely continue to increase the amount elders pay out-of-pocket by raising deductibles and co-payments, and possibly by covering fewer services. The goal is to keep Medicare solvent well into the future. We recognize that the health of our seniors is a social concern, not merely an individual problem.

Do you think that Medicare benefits will be available for you when you are elderly? What can be done now to make Medicare more solvent?

15.6 Summarize what you have learned from this text

Questions That Matter

15.9 What are some examples of family policies or programs that are still needed to support families?

15.10 What are the three themes of this text?

What Have We Learned?

This text has taken you on a path of personal self-discovery and greater societal awareness. It's covered the issues of love and dating, cohabitation and marriage, parenting, work, aging, divorce and remarriage, and family crises, and placed these within their social context. These processes don't exist randomly, but are shaped by our race, sex, social class, sexual orientation, historical period, our culture, and the dominant type of religion practiced in society, to name just a few. By exploring these social contexts, we've developed a greater understanding of familial relationships and the choices we make within them. Let's conclude by quickly reviewing the major themes of our investigation of families to remind us of what we've learned.

Linking the Micro-Level and Macro-Level Perspectives: Putting Our Choices in Social Context

One of the themes of this text has been to illustrate how our personal experiences, choices, and constraints are influenced by historical and cultural forces, social positions, and social institutions. Often, these factors are far beyond the control of any one individual. Families are not isolated entities. They're influenced by a wide variety of social issues, including the unemployment rate, racism, the quality of schools in the neighborhood, patriarchy, and crime rates. For example, the young man who drops out of high school is demonstrating more than just personal choice. Let's guess at macro-level factors that could be operating. He may be influenced by the larger social problem of school overcrowding. He may feel lost in the crowd, with little individual support or mentoring from teachers, parents, or peers. He may live in poverty. His parents may have a lower-than-average level of education. The *Diversity in Families: Moments in the Lives of Children* feature box reminds us that many family conditions are too common to be simply random, and invites us to speculate on how macro-level factors touch our personal lives (Children's Defense Fund, 2009).

We've also focused on the ways in which sex and gender, race and ethnicity, and social class—individually and in conjunction with one another—affect families. Seemingly personal choices, such as marrying, bearing children, divorcing, pursuing an education, finding a job, choosing a childcare program, caring for one's health, and maintaining one's well-being, are affected by these critical social statuses.

Linking micro-level perspectives and macro-level perspectives doesn't mean, however, that people have no choice. On the contrary, *people choose, cope with, adapt to, and change social structures, including marriage and families, to meet their needs.* The recognition that our personal experiences are influenced by the macro-level factors within the larger society can help us make the needed choices and changes in our lives. Human agency is the ability to create viable lives even when constrained by some of those macro-level forces.

42 seconds	a baby is born with no health insurance.
1 minute	a baby is born to a teen mother.
2 minutes	a baby is born at low birth weight.
4 minutes	a child is arrested for drug abuse.
7 minutes	a child is arrested for a violent crime.
18 minutes	a child dies before its first birthday.
45 minutes	a child or teen dies from an accident.
3 hours	a child or teen is killed by a firearm.
5 hours	a child or teen commits suicide.
6 hours	a child is killed by abuse or neglect.
15 hours	a woman dies from complications of childbirth or pregnancy.

Every—

1 second	a public school student is suspended.
11 seconds	a high school student drops out.
19 seconds	a child is arrested.
19 seconds	a baby is born to an unmarried mother.
20 seconds	a public school student is corporally punished.
32 seconds	a baby is born into poverty.
41 seconds	a child is confirmed as abused or neglected.

WHAT DO YOU THINK?

1. Why are these social problems so common in the United States? Are they randomly distributed through the population, or are certain groups more likely to experience them?
2. Can you think of ways these social problems could be reduced, if not eliminated? What programs and/or policies are needed? Why are they lacking?

Source: Children's Defense Fund, December 2009.

Families Change: Can We Return to the "Good Old Days"?

A second theme has been to show that families are not static, but change constantly. As you've learned, there are, have been, and will continue to be a multitude of family types, and these are influenced by many social, political, economic, historical, and cultural conditions. For example, even in the United States, families and intimate relationships are structured quite differently today than they were a generation ago. We've seen that dating is far more informal than in the past, non-marital sex is more common, people marry at older ages, more men and women are voluntarily childfree, family size is considerably smaller, more women work outside the home, and the division of household labor is more equitable. People may ask, "Are these societal changes good or bad?" There is no easy answer, because they reflect larger changes in our social structure, *and we couldn't return to the "good old days" even if we really wanted to.* For example, with the recent economic recession, more women *need* to work outside the home simply to make ends meet. The need to work, along with the increased levels of education required for that work, leads people to marry later (which, in turn, leads to increased non-marital sex), smaller family size, more women remaining childfree, and more egalitarian relationships.

Social Science Theory and Research: Can It Tell Me Right from Wrong?

A third theme of this text has been to show what roles theory and research can play in helping us understand families and relationships. Rather than relying on generalizations or inaccurate observations, social science research can provide a clearer picture of families and the relationships of their members. For example,

✳ **Explore** on **MySocLab**
Activity: *A Lot Can Change in 10 Years: 21st Century Families*

Does abortion kill? Social science cannot answer that question empirically. This information can then be used to guide our personal choices as well as public policy.

we can't assume that the poor routinely buy steak with food stamps just because we've always heard it is so, and we can't assume all partners have an equitable division of household labor just because our parents might have. Instead of relying on personal experience or what seems like common sense—often based on stereotypes or other fallacies—theory and observed data together can help us understand and interpret the occurrence of specific events, the conditions under which they occur, and the meanings people assign to them.

Information gleaned from social science research can be very liberating and can guide the way to understanding our "common-sense" world. Isn't it better to form opinions, have preferences, and meet our challenges head-on, armed with information obtained scientifically? *Nonetheless, despite our enthusiasm for empiricism, generally speaking, research can't always tell us what is right or wrong.* For example, researchers can't tell us whether abortion should be legal, nor under what conditions it should be illegal. However, findings from research can provide us with other important information that may help us answer these vexing questions. It can tell us how many abortions occurred last year, among what age groups, the percentage of unmarried women who had abortions, the level of support from their partner or parents, the percentage who would reportedly seek an illegal abortion if a legal abortion were unavailable, and the reported range of feelings from regret to relief that women feel after having an abortion. Data collected to address these types of questions can help guide discussions of abortion, inform personal choices, influence our values, and shape public policy.

Reflect on the information about families that you have learned in previous chapters of this text. Can you think of specific examples that represent each of these three themes? Which theme resonates with you the most, and why?

Bringing It Full Circle

What kind of family life do we want in the 21st century? How do we make our choices with our families? Families aren't socially isolated entities that can survive solely by their own effort; they're woven into a larger network that is part of a broader social system. Families can become resilient and flourish only when we provide the micro-level and macro-level support they need. Although micro-level individual and family strengths are invaluable and can help us make sound choices and community support is paramount, broad social and economic policies designed to help us care for one another must also be available. Our opening vignette with Alain and Sophie reveals the importance of these policies for building strong families. Let's review what you have learned in this chapter to answer the following questions:

- How do family policies and programs, or their absence, reflect social values? How do American values differ from those of France?

- Americans believe that strong family policies will actually weaken families by making members lazy and dependent on government programs or handouts. How do you think Sophie and Alain would respond to this argument?
- Of all the different programs and policies discussed in this chapter, which do you think would be most effective in helping to build stronger families?

On MySocLab

 **Study** and **Review** on MySocLab

CHAPTER REVIEW

LO15.1 Explain family resiliency

15.1 What is *family resilience*?

Family resilience is the multifaceted ability of a family to thrive despite adversity. It is the capacity to rebound from misfortune, trauma, or other transitional crises to become strengthened and more resourceful.

15.2 What are the components of family resilience?

Discussions of family resilience usually focus on (1) individual protective factors, including micro-level traits, such as a positive self-concept, sociability, intelligence and scholastic competence, autonomy, self-esteem, creativity, independence, good communication and problem-solving skills, humor, and good mental and physical health; (2) family protective factors, such as warmth, affection, and cohesion; (3) family recovery factors, including commitment, communication, and emotional support; and (4) community institutions, such as religious fellowships, clubs, and organizations.

15.3 What is missing from models of resilience?

Further consideration should be given to the importance of macro-level policies and programs to helping families flourish. Sound economic and social policies and programs that strengthen all families—healthy as well as vulnerable—can provide families and children with the necessary tools to increase resilience. They add an important level of strength above and beyond individual, family, and community factors.

LO15.2 Classify types of family policies

15.4 What is the difference between a *universal approach* and a *selective approach* to family policies and programs?

Most developed nations have an interrelated and coordinated set of proactive economic and social programs and policies to help strengthen all families, called a *universal approach*. These programs are available to everyone, regardless of income. In contrast, the United States has many policies and programs that use a *selective approach*, meaning that only certain people are eligible for government services, usually poor or low-income persons.

15.5 How does family policy in the United States compare to other countries?

Compared to many other countries, the United States lags behind in formulating a comprehensive family policy. For example, we are the only developed country without paid maternity leaves, family allowances, or national health insurance. Many other less-developed nations have these benefits as well.

LO15.3 Describe how our policies can foster family resilience

15.6 What are some examples of policies or programs in the United States that help support families?

The United States, although lacking the depth of family policy found in many developed nations, offers a number of programs that have been helpful to many, including the Earned Income Tax Credit (EITC), Temporary Assistance for Needy Families (TANF), living wages, and flexible time and place of employment.

LO15.4 Identify specific policies and programs for children

15.7 What are some examples of policies or programs in the United States that help improve children's lives?

Examples of programs and policies designed to help children include early child intervention, the Children's Health Insurance Program (CHIP), child support enforcement, and childcare policies.

LO15.5 Identify specific policies and programs for the elderly

15.8 What are some examples of policies or programs that help the elderly?

Social Security has improved the economic well-being of elders, and Medicare has helped elders obtain health care.

LO15.6 Summarize what you have learned from this text

15.9 What are some examples of policies or programs that are still needed to support families?

Examples include national health insurance, guaranteed and paid maternity leaves, living wages, further child support, and childcare assistance.

15.10 What are the three themes of this text?

First, micro-level and macro-level perspectives are linked and together provide the best appreciation of family and intimate relationships and the choices and constraints we face; second, families are not static, but are always changing and adapting to micro-level and macro-level forces; and third, social science theory and research can help us better understand families and intimate relationships.

KEY TERMS

community factors	flextime	selective programs
cumulative advantage and disadvantage	individual-level protective factors	telecommuting
early childhood interventions	maternity (or family) leave	Temporary Assistance to Needy Families (TANF)
Earned Income Tax Credit	means-tested programs	universal programs
family protective factors	national health insurance	
family recovery factors	progressive taxation	
flexplace	resilience	

Glossary

ABC-X Model A model designed to help us understand the variation in the ways that families cope with stress and crisis.

active listening Extremely attentive listening, where the listener has good eye contact and body language, and encourages the other person to continue talking.

Activities of Daily Living (ADLs) General day-to-day activities such as cooking, cleaning, bathing, and home repair.

acute stress Short-term stress.

adolescence The period of life that occurs between childhood and adulthood.

agents of socialization The primary groups responsible for gender socialization.

alimony Payment by one partner to the other to support the more dependent spouse for a period of time.

Alzheimer's disease The most common form of dementia; at present, it is incurable.

antimiscegenation laws Laws forbidding interracial marriage, which existed at the state level until 1967.

anxious/ambivalent attachment An attachment type where infants become nervous when their parent leaves the room and can show rejection when the parent returns.

assisted reproductive technology (ART) All fertility treatments in which either egg or sperm (or both) are handled.

attachment theory A theory postulating that the way in which infants form attachments early in life will affect relationships throughout later life.

authoritarian parenting style A parenting style that is strict, punitive, and not very warm.

authoritative parenting style A parenting style that is demanding and maintains high levels of control over the children, but is also warm and receptive.

avoidant attachment An attachment type where infants show little attachment to their primary parent.

baby boom generation People born in the years after World War II through the early 1960s.

Battered Women's Syndrome A recognized psychological condition, often a subcategory of post-traumatic stress syndrome, used to describe someone who has been the victim of consistent and/or severe domestic violence.

bilateral Descent that can be traced through both male and female sides of the family.

binuclear family A type of family consisting of divorced parents living in two separate households but remaining one family in spirit for the sake of the children.

biochemical perspective of love Theories that suggest humans are attracted to certain types of people, at which point the brain releases natural chemicals that give us a rush we experience as sexual attraction.

birth centers Freestanding facilities (usually with close access to, but not affiliated with, a hospital) where childbirth is approached as a normal, healthy process.

bisexual An orientation in which a person is attracted to both males and females.

blended family (or reconstituted family) Another term for stepfamily; a family that may consist of stepparents, stepsiblings, or half-siblings.

calling A dating practice of the 18th and 19th centuries in which a young man would visit a young woman in her parents' home.

centenarian A person who lives to be at least 100 years old.

child abuse An attack on a child that results in an injury and violates our social norms.

child snatching The act of a noncustodial parent kidnapping his or her child.

child support order A legal document delineating the amount and circumstances surrounding the financial support of noncustodial children.

chronic stress Long-term stress.

civil union A public policy designed to extend some benefits to partners who are not legally married.

closed adoption An adoption where identifying information is sealed and unavailable to all parties.

cohabitation An arrangement in which two people live together without being married.

communication An interactive process that uses symbols like words and gestures to both send and receive messages.

community factors Community features that help promote resilience, such as social networks and religious and faith-based fellowships.

companionate family A marriage based on mutual affection, sexual attraction, compatibility, and personal happiness.

companionate grandparenting A type of grandparenting where the grandparents and grandchildren enjoy recreational activities, occasional overnight stays, and even babysitting with an emphasis on fun and enjoyment.

companionate love A type of love that grows over time, based on strong commitment, friendship, and trust.

concrete operational thought Piaget's third stage of cognitive development, which occurs between the ages of 7 and 12, when children begin to see the causal connections in their surroundings, and can manipulate categories, classification systems, and hierarchies in groups.

conflict Disagreements over decision making, problem solving, or achieving goals, which can result from differences between group members in personality, perception, information, tolerance for risk, and power or influence.

conflict-habituated marriage A type of marriage that includes frequent conflict, although it may be enduring.

Conflict Tactics Scale A scale based on how people deal with disagreements in relationships.

conflict theory A theory that emphasizes issues surrounding social inequality, power, conflict, and social change.

content analysis A research method that systematically examines the content of materials.

content conflict A type of conflict where individuals disagree about information.

courtly love A poetic style of the Middle Ages when poets or troubadours would write songs of unrequited love and present them at the court of their aristocratic/royal masters.

covenant marriage A type of marriage available in three states that restricts access to divorce, requires premarital counseling, and imposes other rules and regulations.

crisis A critical change of events that disrupts the functioning of a person's life.

cross-sex friendship A friendship between a man and a woman that is strictly platonic.

crude divorce rate The number of divorces per 1,000 people in the population.

cultural socialization Parental practices that teach children about their racial/ethnic heritage and promote cultural practices and cultural pride.

cumulative advantage and disadvantage Early life chances that influence status in later life.

cunnilingus The oral stimulation of the woman's genitals by her partner.

cyberstalking (or electronic monitoring) Stalking contact using electronic technology.

date rape drugs Drugs such as gamma hydroxybutyrate (GHB), Rohypnol (popularly known as *roofies* or *roofenol*), or ketamine hydrochloride (Ketamine) that are used to immobilize a person to facilitate an assault.

dating script A set of expectations around dating that are somewhat different for men and women.

daycare centers Nonresidential facilities that provide child care.

dementia The loss of mental functions such as thinking, memory, and reasoning.

developmental theory A theory that suggests families, and individual family members, go through distinct stages over time, with each stage having its own set of tasks, roles, and responsibilities.

devitalized marriage An enduring marriage that exists without much passion.

direct financial costs Out-of-pocket expenses for things such as food, clothing, housing, and education.

discrimination Behaviors, actions, or practices based on racial or ethnic preferences that have harmful impacts.

divorce mediation A non-adversarial means of resolution, in which the divorcing couple, along with a third party, such as a therapist or trained mediator, negotiate the terms of their financial, custody, and visitation settlement.

"doing gender" A theory of power that suggests that we take power differentials among men and women for granted and continue to reproduce them; for example, housework is so ingrained as "women's work" that it functions as an area in which gender is symbolically created and reproduced.

domestic violence shelter A temporary safe house for a woman (with or without children) who is escaping an abusive relationship.

Double ABC-X Model A model designed to help us understand the effects of the accumulation of stresses and crises and how families adapt to them.

double standard The idea that men have been allowed far more permissiveness in sexual behavior than women.

double standard of aging The view that women's attractiveness and femininity decline with age, but men's attractiveness and masculinity do not decline.

dowry A financial gift given to a woman's prospective in-laws by her parents.

Early Childhood Education and Care (ECEC) An international term for daycare, preschool, and other programs to ensure that all children begin elementary school with basic skills and are ready to learn.

early childhood intervention Attempts to maintain or improve the quality of life for young children.

Earned Income Tax Credit A refundable federal tax credit for low-income working families that reduces the amount of taxes owed.

egalitarian The expectation that power and authority are vested in both men and women equally.

ego According to Freud, the rational component of personality that attempts to balance the need for immediate gratification with the demands of society.

ego conflict A type of conflict where individuals believe they must win at all costs to save face.

elder abuse Abuse of an elderly person that can include physical abuse, sexual abuse, psychological abuse, financial or material exploitation, and neglect.

empirical approach An approach that answers questions through a systematic collection and analysis of data.

ethnic group A group of people who share specific cultural features.

ethnicity Shared cultural characteristics, such as language, place of origin, dress, food, religion, and other values.

experiment A controlled method for determining cause and effect.

extended family A family composed of parents, children, and other relatives such as grandparents.

extramarital sex Sex, while married, with someone other than your spouse.

family A relationship by blood, marriage, or affection, in which members may cooperate economically, may care for children, and may consider their identity to be intimately connected to the larger group.

family allowance (or child allowance) A cash benefit to families provided by the government to help offset the costs of raising children.

family childcare providers Private homes other than the child's home where childcare is provided.

Family Medical Leave Act (FMLA) An act that requires employers with more than 50 employees to provide 12 weeks of unpaid leave to eligible employees (both men and women) to care for themselves or their immediate families with specified medical conditions.

family of orientation The family you are born into.

family of procreation The family you make through marriage, partnering, and/or parenthood.

family protective factors Family characteristics or dynamics that shape the family's ability to endure in the face of risk factors.

family recovery factors Family characteristics or dynamics that assist families in bouncing back from a crisis situation.

family stress Tensions that test a family's emotional resources.

fellatio The oral stimulation of the man's genitals by his partner.

femicide The killing of women.

feminization of love The process beginning in the 19th century in which love became associated with the private work of women in the home, namely, nurturing and caring for family members.

fertility rate A measure reported as: (1) average number of children born to a woman during her lifetime; (2) number of children born per 1,000 women ages 15–44 (some other countries use 49 as the cut-off age); or (3) number of children born per 1,000 population.

fictive kin Nonrelatives whose bonds are strong and intimate.

flexplace Flexibility in the location of work, including working from home.

flextime Flexibility in the daily hours of work.

focus group A small group interview of people who are brought together to discuss a particular topic.

food insecurity A lack of available nourishing food on a regular basis.

formal care Care provided by social service agencies on a paid or volunteer basis.

formal operational thought Piaget's fourth stage of cognitive development, beginning at adolescence and continuing through adulthood, in which children develop capacities for abstract thought and can conceptualize more complex issues or rules that can be used for problem solving.

gender Culturally and socially constructed differences between males and females found in the meanings, beliefs, and practices associated with "femininity" and "masculinity."

gender socialization Teaching the cultural norms associated with being male or female.

General Adaptation Syndrome (GAS) The predictable pattern one's body follows when coping with stress, which includes the alarm reaction, resistance, and exhaustion.

gerontologists Researchers studying issues affecting the elderly.

gestational surrogacy A type of surrogacy where the intended mother's egg is combined with the man's sperm and implanted in the surrogate through in vitro fertilization.

half-sibling A child who shares one biological parent with another child.

heterogamous marriage A type of marriage in which spouses do not share certain social characteristics such as race, ethnicity, religion, education, age, and social class.

heterosexual Having an attraction and preference for developing romantic and sexual relationships with the opposite sex.

hidden curriculum Gender socialization taught informally in school.

homogamous marriage A type of marriage in which spouses share certain social characteristics such as race, ethnicity, religion, education, age, and social class.

homogamous relationships Relationships in which we spend most of our time with people who are very similar to ourselves.

homophobia (or anti-gay prejudice) Having very strong negative feelings toward homosexuality.

homosexual Having an attraction and preference for relationships with members of one's own sex.

hooking up Sexual interactions without commitment or even affection for one another.

household labor In general, the unpaid work done to maintain family members and/or a home.

human agency The ability of human beings to create viable lives even when they are constrained or limited by social forces.

id According to Freud, the part of the personality that includes biological drives and needs for immediate gratification.

in-depth interview A research method that allows an interviewer to obtain detailed responses to questions.

individual discrimination One person exhibiting a negative behavior toward another person.

individual-level protective factors Traits including a positive self-concept, sociability, intelligence and scholastic competence, autonomy, self-esteem, androgyny, good communication and problem-solving skills, humor, and good mental and physical health.

infertility The state of being unable to produce offspring.

informal care Unpaid care by someone close to the care recipient.

institutional discrimination Social institutions such as the government, religion, and education create policies and practices that are systematically disadvantageous to certain groups.

interethnic marriage A type of marriage in which spouses come from different countries or have different cultural, religious, or ethnic backgrounds.

intergenerational transmission of divorce A pattern noted by researchers that people whose parents divorced are also more likely to divorce.

intergenerational transmission of violence A cycle of violence that is passed down to dependents.

interracial marriage A type of marriage in which spouses come from different racial groups.

intersexed Those born with genitalia that do not clearly identify them as unambiguously male or female.

intimate partner power A type of power that involves decision making among intimate partners, their division of labor, and their sense of entitlement.

intimate partner violence Violence between those who are physically and sexually intimate, such as spouses or partners. The violence can encompass physical, economic, sexual, or psychological abuse.

involuntary stable singles Unmarried adults who can expect to be single for life even though they may not want to be.

involuntary temporary singles Singles actively searching for a mate but unable to find a suitable one.

involved grandparenting A type of grandparenting in which the grandparents and grandchildren have frequent interaction or possibly even live together.

joint legal custody A custody agreement in which noncustodial parents (usually fathers) retain their legal rights with respect to their children.

joint physical custody A custody agreement in which children spend a substantial portion of time in the homes of both parents, perhaps alternating weeks or days within a week.

kinkeeping Maintaining ties among family members.

learned helplessness The psychological condition of having low self-esteem, feeling helpless, and having no control. and that is caused by repeated abuse.

Lee's styles of love A categorization of six types of love that describe how couples are attracted to one another.

legal custody A custody agreement where one parent has the legal authority to make important decisions concerning the children after a divorce, such as where they will go to school, in what community or state they will reside, or who will be notified in case of a health emergency or school problem.

legal divorce The termination of the marriage contract by a state court order.

legal separation A binding agreement signed by both spouses that provides details about child support.

life-course perspective A perspective that sees age-related transitions as socially produced, socially recognized, and shared—a product of social structure, historical forces, and culture.

life expectancy The amount of time (in years) a person can expect to live from birth.

life-span perspective A perspective that claims development is a lifelong process, is multidirectional, and consists of both positive and negative changes involving gains and losses.

life-stage perspective A perspective that claims development proceeds through a fairly set pattern of sequential stages that most people experience.

listening The process of giving thoughtful attention to what we hear.

living wage Wages that are above federal or state minimum wage levels, usually ranging from 100 percent to 130 percent of the poverty line.

looking-glass self Cooley's suggestion that we come to see ourselves as others perceive and respond to us.

love A strong affection for one another arising out of kinship or personal ties; attraction based on sexual desire; and affection based on admiration, benevolence, or common interests.

macro-level Focus on the interconnectedness of marriage, families, and intimate relationships with the rest of society.

marital decline perspective The view that the institution of marriage is increasingly being threatened by hedonistic pursuits of personal happiness at the expense of long-term commitment.

marital resilience perspective The view that overall, marriage is no weaker than in the past, but that all families need an increase in structural supports to thrive.

marriage An institutional arrangement between persons to publicly recognize social and intimate bonds.

marriage movement The activities of a group of some religious leaders, marriage and family therapists, and government leaders who hope to influence public policy to promote and strengthen traditional marriage.

marriage premium The concept that married people are happier, healthier, and financially better off than those who are not married.

master status The major defining status or statuses that a person occupies.

masturbation Sexually stimulating one's own body.

maternity (or family) leave A paid and guaranteed leave from work to care for children, including after the birth of a child.

matriarchy A form of social organization in which the norm or expectation is that the power and authority in society would be vested in women.

matrilineal A descent pattern where lineage is traced exclusively or primarily within women's families.

matrilocal The expectation that a newly married couple will live with the family of the wife.

means-tested programs Programs for which beneficiaries need to meet some eligibility requirement to qualify.

Medicaid The federal–state healthcare program for eligible poor of all ages.

medicalization of childbirth The belief that childbirth is a medical event in need of drugs and technological intervention.

Medicare A federal health insurance program for people age 65 and older (and some people with disabilities under age 65).

menarche A woman's first menstrual period.

micro-level Focus on the individual and his or her interactions in specific settings.

minority group A category of people who have less power than the dominant group, and who are subject to unequal treatment.

monogamy Marriage between one man and one woman.

mortality rate (or death rate) A measure of the number of deaths in a population.

mutual child(ren) The child (or children) born to a couple who have remarried.

nannies/babysitters Non-relatives who provide childcare in the home.

national health insurance A health care system for all citizens that considers health care a public right.

neolocal The expectation that a newly married couple will establish a residence and live there independently.

no-fault divorce A type of divorce, now prevalent in all 50 states, in which a divorcing couple can go before a judge without one party having to blame the other.

non-regulated couples Couples who have many negative communication exchanges.

nonresidential child(ren) A child (or children) living in the household of a divorced parent less than half of the time.

nonstandard work schedules Job schedules that are part-time, sub-contracted, temporary in nature, occur at night, or offer irregular work schedules.

non-verbal communication Communicating without words, by using gestures, expressions, and body language.

nuclear family A family composed of adults and their children.

observational study A research method that goes into the natural setting and observes people in action.

occasional labor Household tasks that are more time-flexible and more discretionary, such as household repairs, yard care, or paying bills.

open adoption A type of adoption that involves direct contact between the biological and adoptive parents.

opportunity costs Lost opportunities for income by working only part-time or not at all because of children.

oral sex Oral stimulation of the genitals.

passive–congenial marriage An enduring marriage that includes little conflict but also little excitement.

patriarchy A form of social organization in which the norm or expectation is that men have a natural right to be in positions of authority over women.

patrilineal A descent pattern where lineage is traced exclusively (or at least primarily) through the man's family line.

patrilocal The expectation that a newly married couple will live with the husband's family.

peer marriage A type of marriage in which couples consider themselves to have equal status or standing in the relationship.

permissive parenting style A parenting style that places few controls or demands on the child.

personal power The degree of autonomy a person has to exercise his or her will.

physical custody A child custody arrangement that decides where the child will reside.

polyandry The marriage pattern in which wives are allowed to have more than one husband.

polygamy A system that allows for more than one spouse at a time (gender unspecified).

polygyny The marriage pattern in which men can have more than one wife.

pool of eligibles The group from which we are likely to choose our mates.

poverty guidelines Guidelines established in 1964 as a way to measure the number of people living in poverty; based on a thrifty food budget, multiplied by three (sometimes called the *poverty line*).

power The ability to exercise your will.

prejudice A negative attitude about members of selected racial and ethnic groups.

preoperational thought Piaget's second stage of cognitive development, occurring from ages 2 through 7, as the child learns language, symbolic play, and symbolic drawing, but does not grasp abstract concepts.

principle of least interest The idea that unequal emotional involvement between romantic partners has implications for the quality and stability of relationships.

private adoption An adoption arranged directly between adoptive parents and the biological birth mother, usually with the assistance of an attorney.

progressive taxation A tax system under which those who earn more pay a higher percentage of their income in taxes than those who earn less.

pronatalism A cultural value that encourages childbearing.

propinquity Geographic closeness.

pseudoconflict Falsely perceiving that our partner is interfering with our goals or has incompatible goals.

public adoption An adoption that occurs through licensed public agencies.

qualitative research Narrative description with words rather than numbers to analyze patterns and their underlying meanings.

quantitative research Research that focuses on data that can be measured numerically.

race A category describing people who share real or perceived physical straits that society deems socially significant, such as skin color.

racial (or ethnic) socialization Teaching minority children about prejudice, discrimination, and the coping skills necessary to develop and maintain a strong and healthy self-image.

random sample A sample in which every "person of interest" has an equal chance of being selected into your research study.

reconstituted family *See* blended family.

refined divorce rate A measure of divorce based on the number of divorces that occur out of every 1,000 married women.

regulating couples Couples who use communication to promote closeness and intimacy.

Reiss's wheel theory of love A developmental theory that shows relationships moving from the establishment of rapport, to self-revelation, mutual dependence, and finally, need fulfillment.

relative love and need theory A theory of power that looks at the way that love itself is feminized, defined, and interpreted.

relative resources perspective The greater the relative amount or value of resources contributed by a partner, the greater is his or her power within the relationship, which can then be translated into bargaining to avoid tasks such as housework that offer no pay and minimal social prestige.

remote grandparenting A type of grandparenting in which the grandparents and grandchildren are emotionally or physically distant.

repartnering The act of entering into a relationship after a divorce, which may lead to cohabitation or marriage.

residential stepchild(ren) A child (or children) living in the household with a remarried couple more than half of the time.

resilience A multifaceted ability to thrive despite adversity.

resource theory A theory of power that suggests that the spouse with the more prestigious or higher paying job can use that advantage to generate more power in the relationship and thereby influence decision making.

role overload Feeling overwhelmed by many different commitments and not having enough time to meet each commitment effectively.

role taking According to Mead, the process of mentally assuming the role of another person to understand the world from their point of view and anticipating their response to us.

romantic love A type of love characterized by passion, melodrama, and excitement, and which receives a lot of media attention.

routine household labor Non-discretionary, routine tasks that cannot be postponed, such as cooking, washing dishes, or cleaning.

sandwich generation A generation of people who are in the middle of two living generations, providing care to members of cohorts on both sides of them, parents and children.

Sapir–Whorf hypothesis The concept that language shapes our culture, and at the same time, our culture shapes our language.

secondary analysis A research method in which the data were collected for some other purpose but still are useful to the researcher.

secure attachment An attachment type where infants feel safe when their mothers are out of sight.

selection effect (for cohabitation) An explanation for the fact that people who cohabit tend to be the same ones who later divorce.

selection effect (for marriage) The hypothesis that people who marry may be different from those who do not marry; for example, they may be happier, healthier, and have more money.

selective programs Programs for which only a select group of people are eligible.

self-care Children who are unsupervised and taking care of themselves.

self-disclosure Telling a person something private about yourself that he or she would not otherwise know.

sensorimotor stage Piaget's first stage of cognitive development (from birth to age 2) in which infants and toddlers understand the world primarily through touch, sucking, listening, and looking.

sex Biological differences between men and women, and their role in reproduction.

sex trafficking An industry in which children are coerced, kidnapped, sold, or deceived into sexual encounters.

sexology A field composed of a multidisciplinary group of clinicians, researchers, and educators who study sexuality.

sexual orientation The sexual and romantic pattern of partners of choice.

siblings Children who share both biological parents.

social capital The goods and services that are byproducts of social relationships, including connections, social support, information, or financial help.

social class A social position based primarily on income and wealth, but occupational prestige and educational level may be relevant as well.

social exchange theory Draws on a model of human behavior used by many economists. It assumes that individuals are rational beings, and their behavior reflects decisions evaluated based on costs—both direct and opportunity costs—and benefits.

social institution A major sphere of social life, with a set of beliefs and rules that is organized to meet basic human needs.

social learning theory Developed by Alfred Bandura, the theory that behavior is learned through modeling and reinforcement.

social mobility Movement from one social class to another.

social power The ability to exercise your will over another person.

Social Readjustment Rating Scale A scale of major life events over the previous year, each of which is assigned a point value. The higher the score, the greater the chance of having a serious medical event.

Social Security A federal government–sponsored cash assistance program for seniors (and survivors).

social stratification The hierarchical ranking of categories of people within society.

social structure A stable framework of social relationships that guides our interactions with others.

socialization The lifelong process by which we learn the cultural values, rules, expectations, and skills needed to function as human beings and participate in society.

sociobiology An evolutionary theory that all humans have an instinctive impulse to pass on their genetic material.

socioeconomic status (SES) Some combination of education, occupation, and income.

sociological imagination The recognition that our personal experiences are, in large part, shaped by forces within the larger society.

sole legal custody A child custody arrangement in which legal custody is granted solely to the parent with whom the child lives.

sole physical custody A child custody arrangement in which the child legally lives with one parent and "visits" the other parent.

spillover An occurrence caused by the demands involved in one sphere of work carrying over into work in another sphere.

spurious When a relationship between two variables is actually caused by a third variable.

stalking Conduct directed at a specific person that would cause a reasonable person to be fearful.

stations of divorce The interrelated emotional, legal, economic, co-parental, community, and psychic dimensions of divorce, which together attempt to capture the complexity of the divorce experience.

status The social position that a person occupies.

step-siblings Children not biologically related but whose parents are married to one another.

stereotypes Oversimplified sets of beliefs about a group of people.

Sternberg's triangular theory of love A theory that sees love as having three elements: intimacy, passion, and commitment.

structural functionalism theory A theory that attempts to determine the structure, systems, functions, and equilibrium of social institutions.

superego According to Freud, this is our conscience, which draws on our cultural values and norms to help us understand why we cannot have everything we want.

surrogacy The act of giving birth to a child for another person or a couple who then adopts or takes legal custody of the child.

survey A form of research that gathers information about attitudes or behaviors through the answers that people give to questions.

symbolic interaction theory A theory that emphasizes the symbols we use in everyday interaction—words, gestures, appearances—and how these are interpreted.

systems theory A theory that proposes that a family system—the family members and the roles that they play—is larger than the sum of its individual members.

telecommuting Flexibility in the location of work, including working from home.

Temporary Assistance to Needy Families (TANF) The principal cash welfare program in the United States.

theory A general framework, explanation, or tool used to understand and describe the real world.

time-availability perspective A perspective that suggests the division of labor is largely determined by (1) the need for household labor, such as the number of children in the home; and (2) each partner's availability to perform household tasks, such as the number of hours spent in paid work.

total marriage A type of marriage in which spouses share many facets of their lives, such as a business they own, friends, or hobbies, with few independent interests.

traditional surrogacy A type of surrogacy where the man's sperm is implanted in the surrogate through artificial insemination.

trafficking The recruitment, transportation, transfer, harboring, or receipt of persons, by means of threat or use of force or other forms of coercion, of abduction, of fraud or deception, of the abuse of power or of a position of vulnerability, or of the giving or receiving of payments to achieve the consent of a person having control over another person, for the purpose of exploitation.

transgender When a person feels as comfortable, if not more so, in expressing gendered traits that are associated with the other sex.

transsexual An individual who undergoes sex reassignment surgery and hormone treatments.

universal programs Programs to help strengthen all families without any eligibility requirement.

unrequited love When one person's feelings are not reciprocated by the other person in the relationship.

value conflict A type of conflict that results from differing opinions on subjects that relate to personal values and issues of right or wrong.

verbal communication The spoken exchange of thoughts, feelings, or other messages.

vital marriage A type of marriage in which the lives of partners are intertwined; physical and emotional intimacy are important, and both work hard at communication and compromise so their relationship continues to be satisfying and enjoyable.

voluntary stable singles Unmarried adults desiring a single (unmarried) lifestyle.

voluntary temporary singles Unmarried adults who may be delaying marriage while pursuing education or establishing a career.

wage premium Generally, married men earn more than their unmarried counterparts, particularly married men with stay-at-home wives.

work–family conflict A form of tension under which people feel that the pressures from paid work and family roles are incompatible in some way.

References

Aardvarc.org. 2008. "Domestic Violence in Gay and Lesbian Relationships." Retrieved 25 March 2010 (www.aardvarc.org/dv/gay.shtml).

AARP. 2005. *Sexuality at Midlife and Beyond: 2004 Update of Attitudes and Behaviors*. May. Washington, DC.

—. 2007. "Grandparents Devoted to Grandchildren, but Their Support Constrained by Concerns about Their Financial Futures, Questions about Grandkids' Money Values." Retrieved 26 April 2010 (www.aarpfinancial.com/content/AboutUs/news_template.cfm?).

abcnews.go.com. 2009. "Pros and Cons: Elective C-Section." (abcnews.go.com/Health/story?id=3291512).

About.com. 2013. "Bushisms." Retrieved 7 October 2013 (politicalhumor.about.com/library/blbushisms.htm).

Abramovitz, Mimi. 1996. *Regulating the Lives of Women: Social Welfare Policy from Colonial Times to the Present (Revised Edition)*. Boston, MA: South End Press.

Acevedo, Bianca P., and Arthur Aron. 2009. "Does a Long-Term Relationship Kill Romantic Love?" *Review of General Psychology* 13(1): 59–65.

Acierno, Ron, Melba A. Hernandez, Amanda B. Amstadter, Heidi S. Resnick, Kenneth Steve, Wendy Muzzy, and Dean G. Kilpatrick. 2010. "Prevalence and Correlates of Emotional, Physical, Sexual, and Financial Abuse and Potential Neglect in the United States: The National Elder Mistreatment Study." *American Journal of Public Health* 100(2): 292–297.

Adams, Bert N. 2004. "Families and Family Study in International Perspective." *Journal of Marriage and Family* 66(6): 1076–1088.

Adams, Bert N., and Jan Trost. (Eds.) 2004. *Handbook of World Families*. Thousand Oaks, CA: Sage.

Adams, Brooke. 2005. "Fundamentalists: Most Espouse Polygamy as a Tenet, but Fewer Actually Practice It as Their Lifestyle." *Salt Lake Tribune*, 11 August.

Adams, Matthew, Carl Walker, and Paul O'Connell. 2011. "Invisible or Involved Fathers? A Content Analysis of Representations of Parenting in Young Children's Picturebooks in the UK." *Sex Roles* 65(3–4): 259–270.

Addo, Fenaba R., and Daniel T. Lichter. 2013. "Marriage, Marital History, and Black–White Wealth Differentials among Older Women." *Journal of Marriage and Family* 75(2): 342–362.

Administration for Children & Families. 2010. "TANF: Total Number of Families (Fiscal Year 2009)." Retrieved 3 May 2010. U.S. Department of Health and Human Services (www.acf.hhs.gov/programs/ofa/data-reports/caseload/2009/2009_family_tan.htm).

Administration for Children & Families, Office of Head Start, U.S. Department of Health and Human Services. 2009. "Head Start Program Fact Sheet." Retrieved 3 May 2010 (www.acf.hhs.gov/programs/ohs/About/fy2008.html).

Administration for Children & Families, U.S. Department of Health and Human Services. 2009. "Office of Family Assistance (OFA)." Retrieved 17 June 2009 (www.acf.hhs.gov/opa/fact_sheets/tanf_factsheet.html).

—. 2013. "TANF: Total Number of Families. Fiscal and Calendar Year 2012" (www.acf.hhs.gov/sites/default/files/ofa/2012tfam_tan.pdf?nocache=1358959575).

Administration on Aging. 2009. "Fact for Features From the Census Bureau." Retrieved 23 April 2010 (www.aoa.gov/AoAroot/Aging_Statistics/Census_Population/Population/2001/factsforfeatures2001.aspx).

Administration on Aging, Administration for Community Living. 2013. "A Profile of Older Americans: 2012." Retrieved 28 May 2013 (www.aoa.gov/AoAroot/Aging_Statistics/Profile/2013/4.aspx).

Advocates for Youth. 2009. "The Facts: Adolescent Childbearing and Educational and Economic Attainment, 2009." Retrieved 1 December 2009 (www.advocatesforyouth.org/ PUBLICATIONS/factsheet/fsadlchd.htm).

Afifi, Tracie O., Harriet MacMillan, Brian J. Cox, Gordon J.G. Asmundson, Murray B. Stein, and Jitender Sareen. 2009. "Mental Health Correlates of Intimate Partner Violence in Marital Relationships in a Nationally Representative Sample of Males and Females." *Journal of Interpersonal Violence* 24(8): 1398–1417.

Afifi, Tamara D., Walid A. Afifi, and Amanda Coho. 2009. "Adolescents' Physiological Reactions to Their Parents' Negative Disclosures about the Other Parent in Divorced and Nondivorced Families." *Journal of Divorce & Remarriage* 50(8): 517–540.

Ahmed, Sania Sultan, and Sally Bould. 2004. "One Able Daughter Is Worth 10 Illiterate Sons: Reframing the Patriarchal Family." *Journal of Marriage and Family* 66(5): 1332–1341.

Ahrons, Constance R. 1994. *The Good Divorce: Keeping Your Family Together When Your Marriage Comes Apart*. New York, NY: HarperCollins.

—. 2005. *We're Still Family: What Grown Children Say about Their Parents' Divorce*. New York, NY: HarperCollins.

—. 2007. "Introduction to the Special Issue on Divorce and Its Aftermath." *Family Process* 46(1): 3–6.

Ahrons, Constance R., and Roy H. Rodgers. 1987. *Divorced Families: A Multidisciplinary Development View*. New York, NY: Norton.

Ainsworth, Mary D. Salter, Mary C. Blehar, Everett Waters, and Sally Wall. 1978. *Patterns of Attachment: A Psychological Study of the Strange Situation*. Hillsdale, NJ: Lawrence Erlbaum.

Alabama Coalition Against Domestic Violence. 2008. "Why Do Abusers Batter?" Retrieved 12 May 2008 (www.acadv.org/abusers.html).

Alaska Native Heritage Center. 2011. Education and Programs. Retrieved 6 December 2013 (www.alaskanative.net/en/main-nav/education-and-programs/language-project).

Alchin, Linda K. No date. "Courtly Love." The Middle Ages. Retrieved 24 January 2010 (www.middle-ages.org.uk/courtly-love.htm).

Ali, Lorraine. 2008. "True or False: Having Kids Makes You Happy." Retrieved 6 March 2010. Newsweek.com (www.newsweek.com/id/143792).

Ali, Lorraine, and Raina Kelley. 2008. "The Curious Lives of Surrogates." Retrieved 15 December 2009. Newsweek.com (www.newsweek.com/id/129594).

Allan, Graham, Graham Crow, and Sheila Hawker. 2010. *Stepfamilies: A Sociological Review*. New York, NY: Palgrave Macmillan.

Allen, Brenda J. 2004. *Differences Matter: Communicating Social Identity*. Long Grove, IL: Waveland Press.

Allen, Elizabeth Sandin, Donald H. Baucom, Charles K. Burnett, Norman Epstein, and Lynn Rankin-Esquer. 2001. "Decision-making Power, Autonomy, and Communication in Remarried Spouses Compared with First-married Spouses." *Family Relations* 50: 326–334.

Allen, Katherine. 1997. "Lesbian and Gay Families." In *Contemporary Parenting*, Terry Arendell, ed. Thousand Oaks, CA: Sage.

Allen, Mary, and Catherine DeWitt. 2012. "Intimate Partner Violence and Belief Systems in Liberia." *Journal of Interpersonal Violence* 27(17): 3514–3531.

Allendorf, Keera. 2013. "Schemas of Marital Change: From Arranged Marriages to Eloping for Love." *Journal of Marriage and Family* 75(2): 453–469.

Altman, Irwin, and Joseph Ginat. 1996. *Polygamous Families in Contemporary Society*. Cambridge, England: Cambridge University Press.

Alzheimer's Association. 2010. "Kris's Story." Retrieved 2 May 2010 (www.alz.org/living_with_alzheimers_8810.asp).

—. 2013a. "What Is Dementia?" Retrieved 29 May 2013 (www.alz.org/what-is-dementia.asp).

—. 2013b. "Alzheimer's Disease: Facts and Figures." Retrieved 29 May 2013 (www.alz.org/alzheimers_disease_facts_and_figures.asp).

—. 2013c. "Medications for Memory Loss." Retrieved 29 May 2013 (www.alz.org/alzheimers_disease_standard_prescriptions.asp).

Amato, Paul R. 1994. "The Impact of Divorce on Men and Women in India and the United States." *Journal of Comparative Family Studies* 25: 207–221.

—. 2004. "Tension between Institutional and Individual Views of Marriage." *Journal of Marriage and Family* 66 (6): 959–965.

—. 2005. "The Impact of Family Formation Change on the Cognitive, Social, and Emotional Well-being of the Next Generation." *Marriage and Child Well-being: The Future of Children* 15: 75–96.

—. 2007. "Divorce and the Well-being of Adults and Children." *National Council on Family Relations Report* 52(4): F3–F4, F18.

—. 2010. "Research on Divorce: Continuing Trends and New Developments." *Journal of Marriage and Family* 72: 650–666.

Amato, Paul R., and Alan Booth. 1997. *A Generation at Risk: Growing Up in an Era of Family Upheaval*. Cambridge, MA: Harvard University Press.

Amato, Paul R., and Bryndl Hohmann-Marriott. 2007. "A Comparison of High and Low-Distress Marriages That End in Divorce." *Journal of Marriage and Family* 69: 621–638.

Amato, Paul R., and Stacy J. Rogers. 1997. "A Longitudinal Study of Marital Problems and Subsequent Divorce." *Journal of Marriage and the Family* 59: 612–624.

Amato, Paul, Alan Booth, David Johnson, and Stacy Rogers. 2007. *Alone Together: How Marriage in America Is Changing*. Cambridge, MA: Harvard University Press.

American Congress of Obstetricians and Gynecologists. 2013. "Elimination of Non-medically Indicated (Elective) Deliveries before 39 Weeks Gestational Age." Retrieved 20 April 2013 (www.acog.org/About_ACOG/ACOG_Districts/District_II?Less_Than_39_Weeks_Deliveries).

American Psychological Association. 1999a. "New Longitudinal Study Finds That Having a Working Mother Does No Significant Harm to Children." Press Release for "Short-term and Long-term Effects of Early Parental Employment on Children of the National Longitudinal Survey of Youth," *Developmental Psychology* 35(2). Retrieved 27 July 2003.

—. 1999b. "Study Finds That Child Care Does Impact Mother–Child Interaction." Press Release for "Child Care and Mother–Child Interaction in the First 3 Years of Life," NICHD Early Child Care Research Network, *Developmental Psychology* 35(6). Retrieved 27 July 2003.

—. 2005. "Controlling Anger—Before It Controls You." Retrieved 6 May 2008 (www.apa.org/pubinfo/anger.html).

—. 2010. "Elder Abuse and Neglect: In Search of Solutions." APA Public Interest (www.apa.org/pi/aging/resources/guides/elder-abuse.aspx).

American Psychological Association. 2013a. "Answers to Your Questions about Individuals with Intersex Conditions." Retrieved 1 April 2013 (www.apa.org/topics/sexuality/intersex.aspx?item=2).

—. 2013b. "Answers to your Questions about Transgender People, Gender Identity, and Gender Expression." Retrieved 1 April 2013 (www.apa.org/topics/sexuality/transgender.aspx).

—. 2013c. "Sexual Orientation and Homosexuality." Retrieved 1 April 2013 (www.apa.org/helpcenter/sexual-orientation.aspx).

American Psychological Association, Task Force on Gender Identity and Gender Variance. 2009. *Report of the Task Force on Gender Identity and Gender Variance*. Washington, DC.

American Society for Reproductive Medicine. 2009. "Frequently Asked Questions about Infertility." Retrieved 15 December 2009 (www.asrm.org/Patients/faqs.html).

American Society of Plastic Surgeons. 2013. "News & Resources." Retrieved 3 March 2013 (www.plasticsurgery.org/news-and-resources.html).

American Society of Plastic Surgeons. 2014. "Top Five Cosmetic Surgical Procedures of 2013." (www.plasticsurgery.org/news/plastic-surgery-statistics/2013/top-five-cosmetic-surgery-procedures.html).

Anderson, Kristin L. 2010. "Conflict, Power, and Violence in Families." *Journal of Marriage and Family* 72(3): 726–742.

Anderson, Gillian, and Karen Robson. 2006. "Male Adolescents' Contributions to Household Labor as Predictors of Later-life Participation in Housework." *The Journal of Men's Studies* 14(1): 1060–1065.

Anderson, Scott. 2010. "The Polygamists." National Geographic.com. February. Retrieved 28 February 2013 (ngm.nationalgeographic.com/2010/02/polygamists/anderson-text).

Angel, Jacqueline, Maren A. Jimenez, and Ronald J. Angel. 2007. "The Economic Consequences of Widowhood for Older Minority Women." *The Gerontologist* 47: 224–234.

Ängarne-Lindberg, Teresia, Marie Wadsby, and Carina Berterö. 2009. "Young Adults with Childhood Experience of Divorce: Disappointment and Contentment." *Journal of Divorce & Remarriage* 50(3): 172–184.

Annie E. Casey Foundation. 2009. *KIDS COUNT Indicator Brief: Reducing the Teen Birth Rate.* July. Baltimore, MD. The Annie E. Casey Foundation, July.

—. 2013. "National Kids Count Program." Retrieved 24 April 2013 (datacenter.kidscount.org/data/acrossstates/Rankings.aspx?ind=107).

Antill, John K., Jacqueline Jarrett Goodnow, Graeme Russell, and Sandra Cotton. 1996. "The Influence of Parents and Family Context on Children's Involvement in Household Tasks." *Sex Roles* 34(3/4): 215–236.

Aquilino, William S. 2006. "The Noncustodial Father–child Relationship from Adolescence into Young Adulthood." *Journal of Marriage and Family* 68(4): 929–946.

Arditti, Joyce A., and Debra A. Madden-Derdich. 1997. "Joint and Sole Custody Mothers—Implications for Research and Practice." *Families in Society: The Journal of Contemporary Human Services* 78(1): 36–45.

Arendell, Terry. 1986. *Mothers and Divorce: Legal, Economic, and Social Dilemmas.* Berkeley, CA: University of California Press.

Arliss, Laurie P. 1991. *Gender Communication.* Englewood Cliffs, NJ: Prentice Hall.

Armstrong, Elizabeth A., Paula England, and Alison C.K. Fogarty. 2010. "Orgasm in College Hookups and Relationships." In *Families as They Really Are* (pp. 362–377); Barbara J. Risman, ed. New York, NY: W.W. Norton & Company.

Aronson, Elliot, Timothy D. Wilson, and Robin M. Akert. 2012. *Social Psychology,* 8th Ed. Boston, MA: Pearson.

Asante, Molefi K., Yoshitaka Miike, and Jing Yin. 2007. *The Global Intercultural Reader.* New York, NY: Routledge.

Ashford, Lori, and Donna Clifton. 2005. *Women of Our World.* Population Reference Bureau. February. Retrieved 14 April 2007 (www.prb.org/pdf05/womenofourworld2005.pdf).

Aubry, Tim, Bruce Tefft, and Nancy Kingsbury. 2006. "Behavioral and Psychological Consequences of Unemployment in Blue-Collar Couples." *Journal of Community Psychology* 18(2): 99–109.

Auster, Carol J., and Claire S. Mansbach. 2012. "The Gender Marketing of Toys: An Analysis of Color and Type of Toy on the Disney Store Website." *Sex Roles* 67(7–8): 375–388.

Axinn, William G., and Arland Thornton. 2000. "The Transformation in the Meaning of Marriage." In *The Ties That Bind: Perspectives on Marriage and Cohabitation* (pp. 147–165), Linda J. Waite, Christine Bachrach, Michelle J. Hindin, Elizabeth Thompson, and Arland Thornton, eds. New York, NY: Aldine de Gruyter.

Baca Zinn, Maxine, D. Stanley Eitzen, and Barbara Wells. 2010. *Diversity in Families,* 9th ed. Boston, MA: Pearson.

Bachman, Jerald G., Lloyd D. Johnston, and Patrick M. O'Malley. 1993. *Monitoring the Future: Questionnaire Responses From the Nation's High School Seniors,* 1991. Ann Arbor, MI: Institute for Social Research.

—. 2001. *Monitoring the Future: Questionnaire Responses From the Nation's High School Seniors,* 2000. Ann Arbor, MI: Institute for Social Research.

—. 2011. *Monitoring the Future: Questionnaire Responses From the Nation's High School Seniors,* 2010. Ann Arbor, MI: Institute for Social Research.

Bahr, Kathleen S. 1994. "The Strengths of Apache Grandmothers: Observations on Commitment, Culture and Caretaking." *Journal of Comparative Family Studies* 25: 233–248.

Bailey, Eric J. 2008. *Black America, Body Beautiful.* Westport, CT: Praeger Publishers.

Bailey, J. Michael, David Bobrow, Marilyn Wolfe, and Sarah Mikach. 1995. "Sexual Orientation of Adult Sons of Gay Fathers." *Developmental Psychology* 31: 124–129.

Bailey, J. Michael, and Richard C. Pillard. 1991. "A Genetic Study of Male Sexual Orientation." *Archives of General Psychiatry* 48: 1089–1096.

Bailey, J. Michael, Richard C. Pillard, Michael C. Neale, and Yvonne Agyei. 1993. "Heritable Factors Influence Sexual Orientation in Women." *Archives of General Psychiatry* 50: 217–223.

Bakanic, Von. 2008. *Prejudice: Attitudes about Race, Class, and Gender.* Upper Saddle River, NJ: Prentice Hall.

Bandura, Alfred. 1973. *Aggression: A Social Learning Analysis.* Englewood Cliffs, NJ: Prentice Hall.

—. 1977. *Social Learning Theory.* New York, NY: General Learning Press.

—. 1997. *Self-Efficacy: The Exercise of Control.* New York, NY: W.H. Freeman.

Banister, Judith. 2009. "Son Preference in Asia—Report of a Symposium." U.S. Census Bureau. Retrieved 4 March 2010 (www.census.gov/ipc/www/ebspr96a.html).

Barna, George. 2008. "New Marriage and Divorce Statistics." The Barna Group, Ltd. March. Retrieved 26 April 2010 (www.barna.org).

Baron, Naomi S. 2008. *Always On: Language in an Online and Mobile World.* New York, NY: Oxford University Press.

Baron, Robert A., and Nyla R. Branscombe. 2012. *Social Psychology.* Boston, MA: Pearson.

Baron-Cohen, Simon. 2003. *The Essential Difference: The Truth about the Male and the Female Brain.* New York, NY: Basic Books.

Barot, Sneha. 2012. "A Problem-and-Solution Mismatch: Son Preference and Sex-selective Abortion Bans." *Guttmacher Policy Review.* Spring. Retrieved 23 April 2013 (www.guttmacher.org/pubs/gpr/15/2/gpr150218.html).

Barr, Simone C., and Helen A. Neville. 2008. "Examination of the Link between Parental Racial Socialization Messages and Racial Ideology among Black College Students." *Journal of Black Psychology* 34(2): 131–155.

Baucom, Donald H., Douglas K. Snyder, and Kristina Coop Gordon. 2009. *Helping Couples Get Past the Affair.* New York, NY: Guilford Press.

Baum, Katrina, Shannan Catalano, Michael Rand, and Kristina Rose. 2009. *Stalking Victimization in the United*

States. Bureau of Justice Statistics No. NCJ 224527. January. Washington, DC: U.S. Department of Justice.

Baumrind, Diana. 1966. "Effects of Authoritative Parental Control on Child Behavior." *Child Development* 37(4): 887–907.

—. 1968. "Authoritarian versus Authoritative Parental Control." *Adolescence* 3: 255–272.

—. 2012. "A Meta-analysis of Parental Satisfaction, Adjustment, and Conflict in Joint Custody and Sole Custody Following Divorce." *Journal of Divorce & Remarriage* 53(6): 464–488.

BBC NEWS. 2008. "Scans See 'Gay Brain Differences.'" 16 June. Retrieved 1 April 2013 (news.bbc.co.uk/2/hi/health/7456588.stm).

Beah, Ismael. 2007. *A Long Way Gone*. New York, NY: Sarah Crichton Books.

Bearak, Barry. 2010. "Malawi: Prosecutors State Case Against Gay Couple." NYTimes.com. Retrieved 21 February 2010 (www.nytimes.com/2010/02/19/world/africa/19briefs-Malawi.html).

Beck, Audrey N., Carey E. Cooper, Sara McLanahan, and Jeanne Brooks-Gunn. 2010. "Partnership Transitions and Maternal Parenting." *Journal of Marriage and Family* 72(2): 219–233.

Becker, Gary S. 1981. *A Treatise on the Family*. Cambridge, MA: Harvard University Press.

Becker, Jill B., Karen J. Berkley, Nori Geary, Elizabeth Hampson, James P. Herman, and Elizabeth A. Young, eds. 2008. *Sex Differences in the Brain: From Genes to Behavior*. New York, NY: Oxford University Press.

Becker, Oliver Arránz, Veronika Salzburger, Nadia Loiz, and Bernhard Nauck. 2013. "What Narrows the Stepgap? Closeness between Parents and Adult (Step) Children in Germany." *Journal of Marriage and Family* 75(5): 1130–1148.

Beebe, Steven A., Susan J. Beebe, and Mark V. Redmond. 2014. *Interpersonal Communication Relating to Others, 7th Ed.* Boston, MA: Pearson.

Beebe, Steven A., and John T. Masterson. 2012. *Communicating in Small Groups: Principles and Practices, 10th ed.* Boston, MA: Pearson.

Belsky, Jay, and Michael Rovine. 1990. "Patterns of Marital Change Across the Transition to Parenthood: Pregnancy to Three Years Postpartum." *Journal of Marriage and the Family* 52: 5–19.

Belsky, Jay, Martha Weinraub, Margaret Owen, and Jean F. Kelly. 2001. "Quantity of Child Care and Problem Behavior." Presented at the Biennial Meeting of the Society for Research on Child Development, Minneapolis, MN.

Benard, Bonnie, and Sara L. Truebridge. 2009. "A Shift in Thinking: Influencing Social Workers' Beliefs About Individual and Family Resilience in an Effort to Enhance Well-Being and Success for All." Ch. 11 in *The Strengths Perspective in Social Work Practice, 5th Ed.*, Dennis Saleebey, ed. Boston, MA: Allyn & Bacon.

Bennett, Kate M., Philip T. Smith, and Georgina M. Hughes. 2005. "Coping, Depressive Feelings and Gender Differences in Late Life Widowhood." *Aging & Mental Health* 9(4): 348–353.

Bentley, Keisha C., Valerie N. Adams, and Howard C. Stevenson. 2009. "Racial Socialization: Roots, Processes, & Outcomes." In *Handbook of African American Psychology*, Helen A. Neville, Brendesha M. Tynes, and Shawn O. Utsey, eds. Thousand Oaks, CA: Sage.

Berardo, Felix M., 1998. "Family Privacy: Issues and Concepts." *Journal of Family Issues* 19(1): 4–19.

Berardo, Felix M., and Donna H. Berardo. 2000. Widowhood. In *Encyclopedia of Sociology, 2nd ed.* (pp. 3255–3261), Edgar F. Borgatta and Rhonda J.V. Montgomery, eds. New York, NY: Macmillian.

Bergmann, Barbara R. 1996. *Saving Our Children from Poverty: What the United States Can Learn from France*. New York, NY: Russell Sage Foundation.

Berke, Melvin R., and Joanne B. Grant. 1981. *Games Divorced People Play*. Englewood Cliffs, NJ: Prentice Hall.

Berlin, Lisa J., Jean M. Ispa, Mark A. Fine, Patrick S. Malone, Jeanne Brooks-Gunn, Christy Brady-Smith, Catherine Ayoub, and Yu Bai. 2009. "Correlates and Consequences of Spanking and Verbal Punishment for Low-income White, African American, and Mexican American Toddlers." *Child Development* 80(5): 1403–1420.

Bernard, Jessie. 1972. *The Future of Marriage*. New York, NY: World Pub.

—. 1973. *The Future of Marriage*. New York, NY: Bantam.

Berns, Roberta M. 2001. *Child, Family, School, Community: Socialization and Support, 5th ed.* New York, NY: Thomson Learning.

Bernstein, Basil. 1960. "Language and Social Class: A Research Note." *British Journal of Sociology (London)* 11(3): 271–276.

—. 1973. *Class, Codes, and Control, Vol. 1*. London: Routledge & Kegan Paul.

Bernstein, Jared, and Isaac Shapiro. August 30, 2006. "Nine Years of Neglect: Federal Minimum Wage Remains Unchanged for Ninth Straight Year, Falls to Lowest Level in More than Half a Century." Issue Brief #227. Economic Policy Institute.

Bertrand, Marianne, and Sendhil Mullainathan. 2004. "Are Emily and Greg More Employable Than Lakisha and Jamal? A Field Experiment on Labor Market Discrimination." *American Economic Review* 94 (September): 991–1013.

Beverly, Brenda, Teena M. McGuinness, and Debra J. Blanton. 2008. "Communication Challenges for Children Adopted from the Former Soviet Union." *Language, Speech, and Hearing Services in Schools* 39: 1–11.

Bianchi, Suzanne M., and Melissa A. Milkie. 2010. "Work and Family Research in the First Decade of the 21st Century." *Journal of Marriage and Family* 72(3): 705–725.

Bianchi, Suzanne, John P. Robinson, and Melissa A. Milkie. 2006. *Changing Rhythms of American Family Life*. New York, NY: Russell Sage Foundation.

Biblarz, Timothy J., and Greg Gottainer. 2000. "Family Structure and Children's Success: A Comparison of Widowed and Divorced Single-mother Families." *Journal of Marriage and the Family* 62: 533–548.

Biblarz, Timothy J., and Evren Savci. 2010. (Lesbian, Gay, Bisexual, and Transgender Families). *Journal of Marriage and Family* 72(3): 480–497.

Biblarz, Timothy J., and Judith Stacey. 2010. "How Does the Gender of Parents Matter?" *Journal of Marriage and Family* 72(1): 3–22.

Bing, Nicole M., W.M. Nelson, III, and Kelly L. Wesolowski. 2009. "Comparing the Effects of Amount of Conflict on Children's Adjustment Following Parental Divorce." *Journal of Divorce & Remarriage* 50(3): 159–171.

Birditt, Kira S., Edna Brown, Terri L. Orbuch, and Jessica M. McIlvane. 2010. "Marital Conflict Behaviors and Implications for Divorce Over 16 Years." *Journal of Marriage and Family* 72(5): 1188–1204.

Bittman, Michael, Paula England, Liana Sayer, Nancy Folbre, and George Matheson. 2003. "When Does Gender Trump Money? Bargaining and Time in Household Work." *American Journal of Sociology* 109: 186–214.

Black, Michele C. 2011. "Intimate Partner Violence and Adverse Health Consequences: Implications for Clinicians." *American Journal of Lifestyle Medicine* 5(5): 428–439.

Black, Michele C., Kathleen C. Basile, Matthew J. Breiding, Sharon G. Smith, Mikel L. Walters, Melissa T. Merrick, Jieru Chen, and Mark R. Stevens. 2011. *The National Intimate Partner and Sexual Violence Survey (NISVS): 2010 Summary Report*. Atlanta, GA: National Center for Injury Prevention and Control, Centers for Disease Control and Prevention.

Blake, John. 2010. "More Workers Are Choosing Fear Over Flex Time, Experts Say." CNN.com. Retrieved 3 May 2010 (www.cnn.com/2010/LIVING/worklife/03/29/flex.time/index.html).

Blekesaune, Morten. 2008. "Partnership Transitions and Mental Distress: Investigating Temporal Order." *Journal of Marriage and Family* 70(4): 879–890.

Bleske-Rechek, April. 2008. "*Attraction in Young Adults' and Middle-Aged Adults' Cross-Sex Friendships*." Presented at the 80th Annual Midwestern Psychological Association Conference, May 1-3, Chicago, IL.

Block, Jennifer. 2008. *Pushed: The Painful Truth about Childbirth and Modern Maternity Care*. Cambridge, MA: Da Capo Press.

Blood, Robert O., and Donald M. Wolfe. 1960. *Husbands and Wives: The Dynamics of Married Living*. New York, NY: Free Press.

Bloom, Barbara, Robin A. Cohen, and Gulnur Freeman. 2012. "Summary Health Statistics for U.S. Children: National Health Interview Survey, 2011." National Center for Health Statistics. *Vital Health Statistics* 10(254).

Bloom, Dan, Pamela J. Loprest, and Sheila R. Zedlewski. 2011. "TANF Recipients with Barriers to Employment." Washington, DC: Urban Institute.

Blumenthal, David. 2006. "Employer-sponsored Health Insurance in the United States—Origins and Implications." *New England Journal of Medicine* 355(1, 6 July): 82–88.

Blumer, Markie, Katherine Hertlein, Justin Smith, and Harrison Allen. 2013. "How Many Bytes Does It Take? A Content Analysis of Cyber Issues in Marriage/Couple and Family Therapy Journals." *Journal of Marital and Family Therapy,* 39(S3).

Blumstein, Phillip and Pepper Schwartz. 1983. *American Couples: Money, Work, Sex*. New York, NY: William Morrow.

Blyth, Dale A. and Eugene C. Roelkepartian. 1993. *Healthy Communities, Healthy Youth*. Minneapolis: Search Institute.

Boer, Peter. 2013. "The Research of Romance." *St. Albert Gazette*. 13 February. Retrieved 26 March 2013 (www.stalbertgazette.com/article/20130213/SAG0301/302139995/-1/sag03/the-research-of-romance).

Bogle, Kathleen A. 2008. *Hooking Up: Sex, Dating, and Relationships on Campus*. New York, NY: NYU Press.

Bohannan, Paul. 1971. "The Six Stations of Divorce." In *Divorce and After: An Analysis of the Emotional and Social Problems of Divorce*, Paul Bohannan, ed. New York, NY: Doubleday, pp. 32–62.

Bokker, Lon Paul, Roy C. Farley, and William Bailey. 2006. "The Relationship between Custodial Status and Emotional Well-being among Recently Divorced Fathers." *Journal of Divorce & Remarriage* 44(3–4): 83–98.

Bond, James T., Ellen Galinsky, and E. Jeffrey Hill. 2004. *When Work Works: Summary of Families and Work Institute Research Findings*. Families and Work Institute and IBM.

Booth, Alan, Ann C. Crouter, and Mari Clements. 2001. *Couples in Conflict*. Mahwah, NJ: Lawrence Erlbaum Associates.

Booth, Alan, Mindy E. Scott, and Valarie King. 2010. "Father Residence and Adolescent Problem Behavior: Are Youth Always Better Off in Two-parent Families?" *Journal of Family Issues* 31(5): 585–605.

Bornstein, Marc H. 2002. *Handbook of Parenting Vol. 4*. Philadelphia, PA: Lawrence Erlbaum Associates.

Boss, Pauline, William Doherty, Ralph LaRossa, Walter Schumm, and Suzanne Steinmetz, eds. 1993 (reprinted 2008). *Sourcebook of Family Theories and Methods: A Contextual Approach*. New York, NY: Plenum.

Boucher, Debora, Catherine Bennett, Barbara McFarlin, and Rixa Freeze. 2009. "Staying Home to Give Birth: Why Women in the United States Choose Home Birth." *Journal of Midwifery & Women's Health* 54(2): 119–126.

Bowlby, John. 1969. *Attachment and Loss*. New York, NY: Basic Books.

Boylstein, Craig and Jeanne Hayes. 2012. "Reconstructing Marital Closeness while Caring for a Spouse with Alzheimer's." *Journal of Family Issues* 33(5): 584–612.

Bradley, Nicki. 2006. "Authoritative Parenting: An Overview." In *Parenting Advice*. Families.com. Retrieved 29 November 2009 (Parenting.families.com/blog/authoritative-parenting-an-overview).

Bradshaw, Carolyn, Arnold S. Kahn, and Bryan K. Saville. 2010. "To Hook Up or Date: Which Gender Benefits?" *Sex Roles* 62(9–10): 661–669.

Bramlett, Matthew D., and William D. Mosher. 2002. "Cohabitation, Remarriage, Divorce, and Remarriage in the United States." National Center for Health Statistics. *Vital Health Statistics* 23(22).

Bratter, Jenifer L., and Rosalind B. King. 2008. "'But Will It Last?': Marital Instability among Interracial and Same-race Couples." *Family Relations* 57(2): 160–171.

Braver, Sanford L., Ira Mark Ellman, Ashley M. Votruba, and William V. Fabricius. 2011. "Lay Judgments about Child Custody after Divorce." *Psychology, Public Policy and Law* 17: 212–238.

Bremner, Jason, Carl Haub, Marlene Lee, Mark Mather, and Eric Zuehlke. 2009. *World Population Highlights Key Findings from PRB's 2009 World Population Data Sheet*. Population Bulletin No. 64(3). September. Washington, DC: Population Reference Bureau.

Briere, John, and Carol E. Jordan. 2009. "Childhood Maltreatment, Intervening Variables, and Adult Psychological Difficulties in Women." *Trauma, Violence, & Abuse* 10(4): 375–388.

Briggs, Sarah. 2006. "Confessions of a 'Helicopter Parent.'" Experience.com. Retrieved 5 January 2010 (www. experience.com/alumnus/channel?channel_id=parents_ survival_guide&page_id=helicopter_parents).

Brink, Susan. 2008. "Modern Puberty." *Los Angeles Times.* 21 January. Retrieved 22 March 2008 (articles.latimes. com/2008/jan/21/health/he-puberty21).

Brizendine, Louann. 2006. *The Female Brain*. New York, NY: Harmony.

Broderick, Carlfred, and James Smith. 1979. "The General Systems Approach to the Family." In *Contemporary Theories about the Family*, Wesley Burr, Reuben Hill, F. Ivan Nye, and Ira Reiss, eds. Englewood Cliffs, NJ: Prentice Hall, Vol. 2, pp. 112–129.

Bronfenbrenner, Urie. 1979. *The Ecology of Human Development*. Cambridge, MA: Harvard University Press.

Bronte-Tinkew, Jacinta, Jennifer Carrano, Allison Horowitz, and Akemi Kinukawa. 2008. "Involvement among Resident Fathers and Links to Infant Cognitive Outcomes." *Journal of Family Issues* 29: 1211–1244.

Brown, Edna, Terri L. Orbuch, and Jose A. Bauermeister. 2008. "Religiosity and Marital Stability among Black American and White American Couples." *Family Relations* 57: 186–197.

Brown, Heidi. 2009. "U.S. Maternity Leave Benefits Are Still Dismal." Forbes.com. Retrieved 16 December 2009 (www. forbes.com/2009/05/04/maternity-leave-laws-forbes- woman-wellbeing-pregnancy.html?feed=rss_news).

Brown, Judith K. 1975. "Iroquois Women: An Ethnohistoric Note." In *Toward an Anthropology of Women*, Rayna R. Reiter, ed. New York, NY: Monthly Review Press, pp. 235–251.

Brown, Mackenzie. 2008. "The State of Our Unions." *Redbook*. Retrieved 22 February 2010 (www.redbookmag. com/love-sex/advice/types-of-marriages?click=main_sr).

Brown, Susan L., and I-Fen Lin. 2013. "Age Variation in the Remarriage Rate, 1990–2011." FP-13-17. National Center for Family & Marriage Research. Retrieved 30 December 2013 (ncfmr.bgsu.edu/pdf/family_profiles/ file134878.pdf).

Brown, Tiffany L., Miriam R. Linver, and Melanie Evans. 2010. "The Role of Gender in the Racial and Ethnic Socialization of African American Adolescents." *Youth & Society* 41(3): 357–381.

Browne, Joy. 2006. *Dating for Dummies, 2nd ed.* Hoboken, NJ: Wiley.

Bryant, Chalandra M., Robert Joseph Taylor, Karen D. Lincoln, Linda M. Chatters, and James S. Jackson. 2008. "Marital Satisfaction among African Americans and Black Caribbeans: Findings from the National Survey of American Life." *Family Relations* 57: 239–53.

Bryant-Davis, Thema, Haewoon Chung, and Shaquila Tillman. 2009. "From the Margins to the Center." *Trauma, Violence, & Abuse* 10(4): 330–357.

Bucx, Freek, Frits van Wel, Trudie Knun, and Louk Hagendoorn. 2008. "Intergenerational Contact and the Life Course Status of Young Adult Children." *Journal of Marriage and Family* 70(1): 144–156.

Bulanda, Ronald E. 2004. "Paternal Involvement with Children: The Influence of Gender Ideologies." *Journal of Marriage and the Family* 66: 40–45.

Bulcroft, Kris A., and Richard A. Bulcroft. 1991. "The Nature and Functions of Dating in Later Life." *Research on Aging* 13: 244–260.

Bulduc, Jessica L., Sandra L. Caron, and Mary Ellen Logue. 2006. "The Effects of Parental Divorce on College Students." *Journal of Divorce & Remarriage* 46(3–4): 83–104.

Bullough, Vern L. 1976. *Sexual Variance in Society and History*. New York, NY: John Wiley & Sons.

Bureau of Justice Statistics. 2009. 8 December. "Prisoners in 2008." Retrieved 21 February 2010 (bjs.ojp.usdoj.gov/ index.cfm?ty=pbdetail&iid=17653).

—. 2012. "Violent Crime Rate Up 17 Percent, Property Crime Rate Up 11 Percent in 2011 According to the National Crime Victimization Survey." 17 October. Retrieved 6 May 2013 (bjs.gov/content/pub/press/cv11pr.cfm).

Bureau of Labor Statistics. 2008. "Married Parents' Use of Time Summary." 8 May. Retrieved 31 December 2009 (www.bls.gov/news.release/atus2.nr0.htm).

—. 2009a. "Child Care Workers." In *Occupational Outlook Handbook, 2010–2011 Edition*. Retrieved 9 March 2010 (www.bls.gov/ooh/Personal-Care-and-Service/Childcare- workers.htm).

—. 2009b. "Economic News Release: Employment Situation Summary." 9 January. Retrieved 9 November 2009 (www. bls.gov/news.release/empsit.nr0.htm).

—. 2009c. "The Employment Situation: June 2009" (Press Release). 2 July. Retrieved 3 August 2009 (www.bls. gov/news.release/archives/empsit_07022009.pdf).

—. 2009d. "Quarterly Census of Employment and Wages." September. Retrieved 9 November 2009 (www.bls.gov/cew/ cewbultn09.htm).

—. 2009e. "Women in the Labor Force: A Databook (2009 Edition)." September. Retrieved 28 December 2009 (www. bls.gov/cps/wlf-databook2009.htm).

—. 2010a. "Employment Situation Archived News Release." Retrieved 9 March 2010 (www.bls.gov/schedule/archives/ empsit_nr.htm).

—. 2010b. "Employment Situation News Release." Retrieved 5 March 2010 (www.bls.gov/news.release/ empsit.htm).

—. 2010c. "Regional and State Employment and Unemployment Summary." Economic News Release. 22 October. Retrieved 24 April 2011 (data.bls.gov/cgi-bin/ print.pl/news.release/laus.nr0.htm).

—. 2012. (2012a–2012d). "Employment Projections: Civilian Labor Force Participation Rates by Age, Sex, Race, and Ethnicity." 1 February. Retrieved 28 May 2013 (www.bls.gov/emp/ep_table_303.htm).

—. 2012. "Characteristics of Minimum Wage Workers: 2011." Labor Force Statistics from the Current Population Survey. 2 March. Retrieved 26 February 2013 (www.bls.gov/cps/minwage2011.htm).

—. 2012. "Highlights of Women's Earnings in 2011." Report 1038. 22 October. Washington, DC: U.S. Department of Labor.

—. 2012. "Childcare Workers; Occupational Outlook Handbook." 26 October. Retrieved 4 May 2013 (www.bls.gov/ooh/personal-care-and-service/childcare-workers.htm).

—. 2013. "Women in the Labor Force: A Databook." *BLS Reports.* February.

—. 2013 (2013a–2013j). "Employment Situation Summary." Economic News Release. 1 February. Retrieved 25 February 2013 (www.bls.gov/news.release/empsit.nr0.htm).

—. 2013. "Minimum Wage Workers Account for 4.7 Percent of Hourly Paid Workers in 2012." TED: The Editor's Desk. 25 March. Retrieved 2 May 2013 (www.bls.gov/opub/ted/2013/ted_20130325.htm).

—. 2013. "Table A-2. Employment Status of the Civilian Population by Race, Sex, and Age." Economic News Release. 5 April. Retrieved 2 May 2013 (www.bls.gov/news.release/empsit.t02.htm).

—. 2013. "Table A-3. Employment Status of the Hispanic or Latino Population by Sex, and Age." Economic News Release. 5 April. Retrieved 2 May 2013 (www.bls.gov/news.release/empsit.t03.htm).

—. 2013. "Women in the Labor Force: A Databook." Report 1040. BLS Reports. February. Retrieved 24 June 2013 (www.bls.gov/cps/wlf-databook2013.htm).

—. 2013. "Databases, Tables & Calculators by Subject: Labor Force Statistics from the Current Population Survey." 2 May. Retrieved 2 May 2013 (data.bls.gov/pdq/SurveyOutputServlet).

—. 2013. "Employment Situation Summary." Economic News Release. 3 May (www.bls.gov/news.release/archives/empsit_05032013.pdf).

—. 2013. "American Time Use Survey—2012 Results." 20 June. (www.bls.gov/news.release/pdf/atus.pdf).

—. 2013. "Consumer Price Index—October 2013." 20 November. (www.bls.gov/news.release/pdf/cpi.pdf)

Bures, Regina M. 2009. "Moving the Nest: The Impact of Coresidential Children on Mobility in Later Midlife." *Journal of Family Issues* 30(6): 837–851.

Bures, Regina M., Tanya Koropeckyj-Cox, and Michael Loree. 2009. "Childlessness, Parenthood, and Depressive Symptoms among Middle-aged and Older Adults." *Journal of Family Issues* 30(5): 670–87.

Burke, Tod, Michael L. Jordan, and Stephen S. Owen. 2002. "A Cross-national Comparison of Gay and Lesbian Domestic Violence." *Journal of Contemporary Criminal Justice* 18(3): 231–57.

Burr, Wesley R., and Shirley R. Klein. 1994. *Reexamining Family Stress: New Theory and Research.* Newbury Park, CA: Sage.

Burri, Andrea, Lynn Cherkas, Timothy Spector, and Qazi Rahman. 2011. "Genetics and Environmental Influences on Female Sexual Orientation, Childhood Gender Typicality, and Adult Gender Identity." *PLoS ONE* 6(7): e21982.

Busby, Dean M., Thomas B. Holman, and Eric Walker. 2008. "Pathways to Relationship Aggression between Adult Partners." *Family Relations* 57 (January): 72–83.

Buss, David M. 2012. *Evolutionary Psychology: The New Science of the Mind,* 4th ed. Boston, MA: Pearson.

Buss, David M. 1989. "Sex Differences in Human Mate Preferences: Evolutionary Hypotheses Tested in 37 Cultures." *Behavioral and Brain Sciences* 12: 1–49.

Buunk, Abraham P., Karlijn Massar, and Pieternel Dijkstra. 2007. "A Social Cognitive Evolutionary Approach to Jealousy : The Automatic Evaluation of One's Romantic Rivals." In Forgas, Joseph, Haselton, Martie, and Von Hippel, William (Eds.) *Evolution and the social mind: Evolutionary psychology and social cognition* (pp. 213–228). New York, NY: Psychology Press.

Cahill, Sean, Ken South, and Jane Spade. 2000. *Outing Age: Public Policy Issues Affecting Gay, Lesbian, Bisexual, and Transgender Elders.* The Policy Institute of the National Gay and Lesbian Task Force Foundation.

Caine, Barbara. 2010. *Friendship: A History (Critical Histories of Subjectivity and Culture).* London: Equinox Publishing.

Calasanti, Toni, and K. Jill Kiecolt. 2007. "Diversity among Late-life Couples." *Generations* 31: 10–17.

Calvo, Esteban, Kelly Haverstick, and Steven A. Sass. 2009. "Gradual Retirement, Sense of Control, and Retirees' Happiness." *Research on Aging* 31(1): 112–135.

Cameron, Deborah. 1998. "Gender, Language, and Discourse: A Review Essay." *Signs* 23(4): 945.

Campana, Kathryn L., Sandra Henderson, Arnold L. Stolberg, and Lisa Schum. 2008. "Paired Maternal and Paternal Parenting Styles, Child Custody, and Children's Emotional Adjustment to Divorce." *Journal of Divorce & Remarriage* 48(3/4): 1–20.

Campbell, Jacquelyn C., Nancy Glass, Phyllis W. Sharps, Kathryn Laughon, and Tina Bloom. 2007. "Intimate Partner Homicide." *Trauma, Violence, & Abuse* 8(3): 246–269.

Campbell, Jacquelyn C., Linda Rose, Joan Kub, and Daphne Nedd. 1998. "Voices of Strength and Resistance: A Contextual and Longitudinal Analysis of Women's Responses to Battering." *Journal of Interpersonal Violence* 13: 743–762.

The Canadian Encyclopedia. 2010. "Family Allowance." Retrieved 26 June 2010 (www.thecanadianencyclopedia.com/index.cfm?PgNm=TCE&Params=A1ARTA0002718).

Cancian, Francesca M. 1987. *Love in America: Gender and Self-development.* New York, NY: Cambridge University Press.

Cancian, Maria, Kristen Shook Slack, and Mi Youn Yang. 2010. "The Effect of Family Income on Risk of Child Maltreatment." Discussion Paper No. 1385-10. August. Madison, WI: Institute for Research on Poverty.

Caplan, Art. 2013. "$10,000 to Abort? Surrogacy Case Reveals Moral Holes, Bioethicist Says." NBCNews.com.

6 March. Retrieved 20 April 2013 (vitals.nbcnews. com/_news/2013/03/06/17213836-/10000-to-abort-surrogacy-case-reveals-moral-holes-bioethicist-says?life).

Carlson, Marcia J. 2006. "Family Structure, Father Involvement, and Adolescent Behavioral Outcomes." *Journal of Marriage and Family* 68(1): 137–154.

Carr, Deborah, and Kristen W. Springer. 2010. "Advances in Families and Health Research in the 21st Century." *Journal of Marriage and Family* 72(3): 743–761.

Carroll, Joseph. 2007. "Most Americans Approve of Interracial Marriages." Gallup Poll. Retrieved 21 February 2010 (www.gallup.com/search/default.aspx?q=interracial+marriage&s=p=1).

Carter, Wendy Y. 2006. "Attitudes toward Pre-marital Sex, Non-marital Childbearing, Cohabitation, and Marriage among Blacks and Whites" (NSFH Working Paper No. 61). Center for Demography and Ecology, University of Wisconsin–Madison. Retrieved 8 July 2006 (www.ssc.wisc.edu/cdc/nsfhwp/nsfh61.pdf).

Cartwright, Claire. 2005. "You Want to Know How It Affected Me? Young Adults' Perceptions of the Impact of Parental Divorce." *Journal of Divorce & Remarriage* 44(3/4): 125–143.

—. 2012. "The Challenges of Being a Mother in a Stepfamily." *Journal of Divorce & Remarriage* 53(6): 503–513.

Cartwright, Claire, and Heather McDowell. 2008. "Young Women's Life Stories and Accounts of Parental Divorce." *Journal of Divorce & Remarriage* 49(1–2): 56–77.

Cassidy, Jude. 2000. "Adult Romantic Attachments: A Developmental Perspective on Individual Differences." *Review of General Psychology* 4: 111–131.

Cassidy, Tina. 2007. *Birth: The Surprising History of How We Are Born.* New York, NY: Grove Press.

Catalano, Shannan. 2012. "Stalking Victims in the United States—Revised." NCJ 224527. September. Washington, DC: Bureau of Justice Statistics, U.S. Department of Justice.

Cavanagh, Shannon E., Crissey, Sarah R., & Raley, R. Kelly. 2008. "Family structure history and adolescent romantic relationships". *Journal of Marriage and Family* 70: 698–714.

Cavanagh, Shannon E., and Aletha C. Huston. 2008. "The Timing of Family Instability and Children's Social Development." *Journal of Marriage and Family* 70(5): 1258–1269.

CensusScope. 2010. "Segregation: Neighborhood Exposure by Race." 14 December. Retrieved 3 March 2013 (www.censusscope.org).

Center for American Progress. 2013. "Domestic Violence in the LGBT Community: A Fact Sheet." Retrieved 6 May 2013 (www.americanprogress.org/issues/lgbt/news/2011/06/14/9850/domestic-violence-in-the-lgbt-community).

Center on Budget and Policy Priorities. 2012. "Wide and Growing Income Gaps in Most States, New Report Finds Rich Pulling Away from Low- and Middle-Income Households." 15 November. Retrieved 4 March 2013 (www.cbpp.org/cms/index.cfm?fa=view&id=3861).

—. 2012. "The EITC: Our Strongest Tool for Boosting Single Mothers' Employment." 28 June. Retrieved 30 May 2013 (www.offthechartsblog.org/the-eitc-our-strongest-tool-for-boosting-single-mothers-employment).

—. 2013. 2013a–2013b. "Policy Basics: The Earned Income Tax Credit." 1 February. Retrieved 30 May 2013 (www.cbpp.org/cms/index.cfm?fa=view&id=2505).

—. 2013. "Working Family Tax Credits Deserve Bipartisan Praise—and Action." 7 February. Retrieved 30 May 2013 (www.offthechartsblog.org/working-family-tax-credits-deserve-bipartisan-praise-and-action).

Center for Nutrition Policy and Promotion. 2012. "Official USDA Food Plans: Cost of Food at Home at Four Levels." February. Washington, DC: U.S. Department of Agriculture.

Centers for Disease Control and Prevention. 2003. *Costs of Intimate Partner Violence Against Women in the United States.* Atlanta, GA: CDC, National Center for Injury Prevention and Control.

—. 2008b. "Intimate Partner Violence: Risk and Protective Factors." 21 October. Retrieved 12 July 2009 (www.cdc.gov/ViolencePrevention/intimatepartnerviolence/riskprotectivefactors.html).

—. 2009a. "Assisted Reproductive Technology (ART) Report: National Summary." Retrieved 15 December 2009 (apps.nccd.cdc.gov/ART/NSR.aspx?SelectedYear=2007).

—. 2009b. "Deaths among Persons with AIDS Through December 2006." Retrieved 21 February 2010 (www.cdc.gov/hiv/topics/surveillance/resources/reports/2009supp_vol14no3/default.htm).

—. 2009c. *Sexually Transmitted Disease Surveillance, 2008.* November. Atlanta, GA: U.S. Department of Health & Human Services.

—. 2012a. "Sexual Violence: Facts at a Glance." National Center for Injury Prevention and Control, Division of Violence Prevention.

—. 2012b. "Understanding Teen Dating Violence." National Center for Injury Prevention and Control, Division of Violence Prevention.

—. 2012c. "Understanding Intimate Partner Violence: Fact Sheet." National Center for Injury Prevention and Control, Division of Violence Prevention.

—. 2012. 2012d–2012f. "National ART Success Rates." 3 January. Retrieved 20 April 2013 (apps.nccd.cdc.gov/art/Apps/NationalSummaryReport.aspx).

—. 2012. "Basic Information about HIV and AIDS." 11 April. Retrieved 7 April 2013 (www.cdc.gov/hiv/topics/basic/index.htm).

—. 2012. "Intimate Partner Violence: Consequences." 26 September. Retrieved 6 May 2013 (www.cdc.gov/violenceprevention/intimatepartnerviolence/consequences.html).

—. 2013. 2013a–2013i. "Breastfeeding Report Card—United States, 2012." 22 January. Retrieved 23 April 2013 (www.cdc.gov/breastfeeding/data/reportcard.htm).

—. 2013. "Infertility FAQ's." 12 February. Retrieved 20 April 2013 (www.cdc.gov/reproductivehealth/infertility/index.htm).

—. 2013. "What Is Assisted Reproductive Technology?" Retrieved 13 February 2013 (www.cdc.gov/ART/index.htm).

—. 2013. "National Marriage and Divorce Rate Trends." Retrieved 19 February 2013 (www.cdc.gov/nchs/nvss/marriage_divorce_tables.htm).

—. 2013. "HIV in the United States: At a Glance." 27 February. National Center for HIV/AIDS, Viral Hepatitis, STD, and TB Prevention.

—. 2013. "HIV Surveillance—Epidemiology of HIV Infection (through 2011)." Retrieved 7 April 2013 (www.cdc.gov/hiv/topics/surveillance/resources/slides/general/index.htm).

—. 2013. "Genital HPV Infection—Fact Sheet." 18 March. Retrieved 7 April 2013 (www.cdc.gov/std/HPV/STDFact-HPV.htm).

—. 2013. "HIV among African Americans." 20 March. Retrieved 7 April 2013 (www.cdc.gov/hiv/topics/aa/index.htm).

—. 2013. "Incidence, Prevalence, and Cost of Sexually Transmitted Infections in the United States." February. National Center for HIV/AIDS, Viral Hepatitis, STD, and TB Prevention.

Centers for Medicare & Medicaid Services. 2012. "Medicare Current Beneficiary Survey." Retrieved 7 October 2013 (www.cms.gov/Research-Statistics-Data-and-Systems/Research/MCBS/index.html?redirect=/mcbs/).

Central Intelligence Agency. 2009. "Country Comparison: Infant Mortality Rate." November. Retrieved 5 November 2009 (www.cia.gov/library/publications/the-world-factbook/rankorder/2091rank.html).

—. 2013. "The World Factbook." Retrieved 23 April 2013 (www.cia.gov/library/publications/the-world-factbook/geos/us.html).

Chambers, Wendy C. 2007. "Oral Sex: Varied Behaviors and Perceptions in a College Population." *Journal of Sex Research* 44(1): 28–42.

Cheah, Charissa S.L., Christy Y.Y. Leung, Madiha Tahseen, and David Schultz. 2009. "Authoritative Parenting among Immigrant Chinese Mothers of Preschoolers." *Journal of Family Psychology* 23(3): 311–320.

Chedekel, David S., and Karen O'Connell. 2002. *The Blended Family Sourcebook: A Guide to Negotiating Change.* New York, NY: McGraw-Hill.

Cherlin, Andrew J., and Frank F. Furstenberg. 1986. *The New American Grandparent: A Place in the Family, A Life Apart.* New York, NY: Basic Books.

Cherney, Isabelle D., and Kamala London. 2006. "Gender-linked Differences in the Toys, Television Shows, Computer Games, and Outdoor Activities of 5- to 13-Year-Old Children." *Sex Roles* 54(9–10): 717–726.

Chi, Zhou, Zhou Xu Dong, Wang Xiao Lei, Zheng Wei Jun, Li Lu, and Therese Hesketh. 2013. "Changing Gender Preference in China Today: Implications for the Sex Ratio." *Indian Journal of Gender Studies* 20(1): 51–68.

ChildCare Aware of America. 2012. "Parents and the High Cost of Child Care." (childcareaware.org)

Child Labor Public Education Project. 2011. "Welcome to the Child Labor Public Education Project." Retrieved 1 May 2013 (www.continuetolearn.uiowa.edu/laborctr/child_labor).

ChildTrends. 2012. "Attitudes toward Spanking." Retrieved 23 April 2013 (www.childtrends.databank.org/?q=node/187).

Child Welfare Information Gateway. 2008. "Stepparent Adoption: Factsheet for Families." Retrieved 13 April 2010 (www.childwelfare.gov/pubs/f_step.cfm).

—. 2011. "How Many Children Were Adopted in 2007 and 2008?" Washington, DC: U.S. Department of Health and Human Services, Children's Bureau.

—. 2013. "History of Adoption Practices in the United States." Retrieved 20 April 2013 (www.childwelfare.gov/adoption/history.cfm).

Children's Defense Fund. 2005. "Defining Poverty and Why It Matters for Children." Retrieved 24 April 2006 (www.childrensdefensefund.org).

—. 2007. *2006 Annual Report.* Washington, DC.

—. 2009. "Moments in America for Children." Retrieved 3 May 2010 (www.childrensdefense.org/child-research-data-publications/moments-in-america-for-children.html).

—. 2012. *The State of America's Children® 2012 Handbook.* Washington, DC.

Choudhary, Ekta, Jeffrey Coben, and Robert M. Bossarte. 2010. "Adverse Health Outcomes, Perpetrator Characteristics, and Sexual Violence Victimization among U.S. Adult Males." *Journal of Interpersonal Violence* 25: 1523–1541.

—. 2012. "Foreclosures Climbed in January." *CNNMoney.* 16 February. Retrieved 25 February 2013 (money.cnn.com/2012/02/16/real_estate/foreclosures_homes/index.htm).

Christie-Mizell, C. André, Erin M. Pryor, and Elizabeth Grossman, R.B. 2008. "Child Depressive Symptoms, Spanking, and Emotional Support: Differences between African American and European American Youth." *Family Relations* 57 (July): 335–350.

Christopher, F. Scott, and Susan Sprecher. 2000. "Sexuality in Marriage, Dating, and Other Relationships: A Decade Review." *Journal of Marriage and the Family* 62(4): 999–1017.

Chu, Judy. 2005. "Adolescent Boys' Friendships and Peer Group Culture." *New Directions for Child and Adolescent Development* 2005(107): 7–22.

Church, Elizabeth. 1999. "Who Are the People in Your Family? Stepmothers' Diverse Notions of Kinship." *Journal of Divorce & Remarriage* 31: 83–105.

City of Los Angeles, Department of Public Works. 2012. "Current and Prior Living Wage Rates."

Clark, Josh. 2010. "Employees with Flex Time Put in More Hours." Retrieved 3 May 2010. Discovery News (News.discovery.com/human/telecommuting-productivity-flex-time.html).

Clarke, Cheril N. 2010. *Love and Marriage: The Gay and Lesbian Guide to Dating and Romance.* Dodi Press.

Clarkwest, Andrew. 2007. "Spousal Dissimilarity, Race, and Marital Dissolution." *Journal of Marriage and Family* 69(3): 639–653.

Claxton-Oldfield, Stephen. 2008. "Stereotypes of Stepfamilies and Stepfamily Members." In: *The International Handbook of Stepfamilies: Policy and Practice in Legal, Research, and Clinical Environments,* Jan Pryor, ed. Hoboken, NJ: John Wiley & Sons.

The Clearinghouse on International Developments in Child, Youth, & Family Policies. 2001. "New 12 Country Study Reveals Substantial Gaps in U.S. Early Childhood Education and Care Policies." Retrieved 28 July 2003. Columbia University (www.childpolicyintl.org/issuebrief/issuebrief1.htm).

—. 2005. "Section 1.2: Early Childhood Education and Care." Retrieved 17 January 2006. New York/Columbia University (www.childpolicyintl.org/ecec.html).

—. 2009. "France." Retrieved 8 August 2009 (www.childpolicyintl.org/countries/france.html).

Clopper, Cynthia G., and David B. Pisoni. 2004. "Some Acoustic Cues for the Perceptual Categorization of American English Regional Dialects." *Journal of Phonetics* 32: 111–140.

Cloud, John. 2008. "Are Gay Relationships Different?" *Time Magazine*. 17 January. Retrieved 5 April 2013 (www.time.com/time/magazine/article/0,9171,1704660,00.html).

Cockerham, William C. 1997. *This Aging Society*. Upper Saddle River, NJ: Prentice Hall.

Cockrell, Stacie, Cathy O'Neill, and Julia Stone. 2008. *Babyproofing Your Marriage: How to Laugh More and Argue Less as Your Family Grows*. New York, NY: HarperCollins.

Coffey, Rebecca. 2012. "Why Extramarital Sex Can Kill." *Scientific American*. Retrieved 5 April 2013 (www.scientificamerican.com/article.cfm?id=why-extramarital-sex-can-kill).

Cohen, Elizabeth. 2009. "Mom Won't Be Forced to Have C-Section." CNNhealth.com. Retrieved 2 March 2010 (www.cnn.com/2009/HEALTH/10/15/hospitals.ban.vbacs/index.html).

Cohen, Theodore, and John C. Durst. 2001. "Leaving Work and Staying Home: The Impact on Men of Terminating the Male Economic Provider Role." In *Men and Masculinity: A Text-Reader*, Theodore Cohen, ed. Belmont, CA: Wadsworth Publishing Co.

Cohn, D'Vera. 2009. "The States of Marriage and Divorce: Lots of Ex's Live in Texas." Pew Research Center. Retrieved 5 April 2010 (pewresearch.org/pubs/1380/marriage-and-divorce-by-state).

—. 2011. "Marriage Rate Declines and Marriage Age Rises." Pew Research Social & Demographic Trends. 14 December. Retrieved 1 April 2013 (www.pewsocialtrends.org/2011/12/14/marriage-rate-declines-and-marriage-age-rises).

Coleman, Marilyn, Lawrence H. Ganong, and Mark Fine. 2000. "Reinvestigating Remarriage: Another Decade of Progress." *Journal of Marriage and the Family* 62: 1288–1307.

Coleman-Jensen, Alisha, Mark Nord, Margaret Andrews, and Steven Carlson. 2012. "Household Food Security in the United States in 2011." ERR-141. September. Washington, DC: U.S. Department of Agriculture, Economic Research Service.

Collins, Randall. 1986. "Courtly Politics and the Status of Women, Ch. 12." pp. 297–322 in *Weberian Sociological Theory*. New York, NY: Cambridge University Press.

Coltrane, Scott. 1997. *Family Man: Fatherhood, Housework, and Gender Equity*. New York, NY: Oxford University Press.

—. 2000. "Research on Household Labor: Modeling and Measuring the Social Embeddedness of Routine Family Work." *Journal of Marriage and the Family* 62 (November): 1208–1233.

Commonwealth Fund Commission on a High Performance Health System. 2009. *The Path to a High Performance U.S. Health System: A 2020 Vision and the Policies to Pave the Way*. February. New York, NY: Commonwealth Fund.

Conger, John J. 1975. "Proceedings of the American Psychological Association, Incorporated, for the Year 1974: Minutes of the Annual Meeting of the Council of Representatives." *American Psychologist* 30: 620–651.

Conger, Rand D., and Katherine J. Conger. 2008. "Understanding the Processes Through Which Economic Hardship Influences Families and Children," pp. 64–81 in *Handbook of Families and Poverty*, D. Russell Crane and Timothy B. Heaton, eds. Thousand Oaks, CA: Sage.

Conger, Rand D., Katherine J. Conger, and Monica J. Martin. 2010. "Socioeconomic Status, Family Processes, and Individual Development." *Journal of Marriage and Family* 72(3): 685–704.

Conley, Dalton. 2009. *Elsewhere, U.S.A.: How We Got From the Company Man, Family Dinners, and the Affluent Society to the Home Office, BlackBerry Moms, and Economic Anxiety*. New York, NY: Pantheon.

Connidis, Ingrid A., and Lori D. Campbell. 2001. "Closeness, Confiding, and Contact among Siblings in Middle and Late Adulthood," pp. 149–155 in *Families in Later Life*, Alexis J. Walker, Margaret Manoogian-O'Dell, Lori McGraw, and Diana L.G. White, eds., Thousand Oaks, CA: Pine Forge Press.

Cooney, Teresa M., and Jeong Shin An. 2006. "Women in the Middle Generational Position and Grandmothers' Adjustment to Raising Grandchildren." *Journal of Women & Aging* 18(2): 3–24.

Coontz, Stephanie. 1992. *The Way We Never Were: American Families and the Nostalgia Trap*. New York, NY: Basic Books.

—. 1997. *The Way We Really Are: Coming to Terms with America's Changing Families*. New York, NY: Basic Books.

—. 2000. *The Way We Never Were: American Families and the Nostalgia Trap*. New York, NY: Basic Books.

—. 2005a. "Fact Sheet on Polygamy." Retrieved 26 October 2008. Polygamy.com (www.polygamy.com/articles/templates/?a=171&z=3).

—. 2005b. *Marriage, A History: From Obedience to Intimacy, or How Love Conquered Marriage*. New York, NY: Viking.

—. 2006. "Three 'Rules' That Don't Apply." *Newsweek*, 5 June, p. 49.

—. 2007. "The Paradoxical Origins of Modern Divorce." *Family Process* 46 (March): 7–16.

Cooper, Carey E., Sara S. McLanahan, Sarah O. Meadows, and Jeanne Brooks-Gunn. 2009. "Family Structure Transitions and Maternal Parenting Stress." *Journal of Marriage and Family* 71(3): 558–574.

Cooper, M. Lynne, Mark Pioli, Ash Levitt, Amelia E. Talley, Lada Micheas, and Nancy L. Collins. 2006. "Attachment Styles, Sex Motives, and Sexual Behavior: Evidence for Gender-Specific Expressions of Attachment Dynamics," pp. 243–74 in *Dynamics of Romantic Love: Attachment, Caregiving, and Sex*, Mario Mikulincer and Gail S. Goodman, eds. New York, NY: Guilford Press.

Copen, Casey E., Kimberly Daniels, Jonathan Vespa, and William D. Mosher. 2012. "First Marriages in the United

States: Data From the 2006-2010 National Survey of Family Growth." National Health Statistics Reports No. 49. 22 March. Washington, DC: National Center for Health Statistics.

Corsaro, William A. 1997. *A Sociology of Childhood.* Thousand Oaks, CA: Pine Forge Press.

Cosentino, Barbra Williams. 2006. "Elective Cesarean: Is It for You?" Babycenter. Retrieved 16 December 2009 (www.babycenter.com/0_elective-cesarean-is-it-for-you_1498696.bc).

Cott, Nancy F. 1978. "Passionlessness: An Interpretation of Victorian Sexual Ideology, 1790–1850." *Signs* 4: 219–236.

—. 2000. *Public Vows: A History of Marriage and the Nation.* Cambridge, MA: Harvard University Press.

Council for Responsible Genetics. 2010. "Surrogacy in America."

Covel, Simona. 2003. "The Heart Never Forgets." *American Demographics.* 1 July.

Covenant Marriage Movement. 2008. "Home Page." Retrieved 22 February 2010 (www.covenantmarriage.com/index.php).

—. 2013. "About the Covenant Marriage Movement." Retrieved 15 April 2013 (covenantmarriage.com/about-the-covenant-marriage-movement).

Craighill, Peyton M. and Clement, Scott, March 5, 2014. "Support for Same-Sex Marriage Hits New High: Half Say Constitution Guarentees Right." Washington Post. (www.washingtonpost.com/politics/support-for-same-sex-marriage-hits-new-high-half-say-constitution-guarantees-right/2014/03/04/f737e87e-a3e5-11e3-a5fa-55f0c77bf39c_story.html).

Crandall, Marie L., Avery B. Nathens, Mary A. Kernic, Victoria L. Holt, and Frederick P. Rivara. 2004. "Predicting Future Injury among Women in Abusive Relationships." *Trauma-Injury Infection and Critical Care* 56(4): 906–912.

Crimi, Frank. 2012. "Saudi Arabia's Gender Apartheid City." *FrontPage Magazine.* 15 August. Retrieved 3 March 2013 (frontpagemag.com).

Crissey, Sarah R. 2005. "Race/Ethnic Differences in the Marital Expectations of Adolescents: The Role of Romantic Relationships." *Journal of Marriage and Family* 67(3): 697–709.

Crohn, Helen M. 2006. "Five Styles of Positive Stepmothering from the Perspective of Young Adult Stepdaughters." *Journal of Divorce & Remarriage* 46(1): 119–134.

Crittenden, Courtney A., and Emily M. Wright. 2013. "Predicting Patriarchy: Using Individual and Contextual Factors to Examine Patriarchal Endorsement in Communities." *Journal of Interpersonal Violence* 28(6): 1267–1288.

Crompton, Rosemary. 2006. "Class and Family." *Sociological Review* 54(4): 658–677.

Crosnoe, Robert. 2010. "Family Socioeconomic Status and Consistent Environmental Stimulation in Early Childhood." *Child Development* 81(3): 972–987.

Crowl, Alicia, Soyeon Ahn, and Jean Baker. 2008. "A Meta-Analysis of Developmental Outcomes for Children of Same-sex and Heterosexual Parents." *Journal of GLBT Family Studies* 4(3): 385–407.

Cruz, J. Michael. 2003. "'Why Doesn't He Just Leave?': Gay Male Domestic Violence and the Reasons Victims Stay." *The Journal of Men's Studies* 11(3): 309–323.

Cruz, Julissa. 2012. "Remarriage Rate in the U.S., 2010." FP-12-14. National Center for Family & Marriage Research. Retrieved 30 December 2013 (ncfmr.bgsu.edu/pdf/family_profiles/file114853.pdf).

Cui, Ming, M. Brent Donnellan, and Rand D. Conger. 2007. "Reciprocal Influences between Parents' Marital Problems and Adolescent Internalizing and Externalizing Behavior." *Developmental Psychology* 43(6): 1544–1552.

Cummings, E. Mark, Alice C. Schermerhorn, Patrick T. Davies, Marcie C. Goeke-Morey, and Jennifer S. Cummings. 2006. "Interparental Discord and Child Adjustment: Prospective Investigations of Emotional Security as an Explanatory Mechanism." *Child Development* 77(1): 132–152.

Cunningham-Burley, Sarah. 2001. "The Experience of Grandfatherhood," pp. 92–96 in *Later Life: Connections and Transitions*, Alexis J. Walker, Margaret Manoogian-O'Dell, Lori McGraw, and Diana L. White, eds. Thousand Oaks, CA: Pine Forge Press.

Curran, Dolores. 1985. *Stress and the Healthy Family: How Healthy Families Handle the 10 Most Common Stresses.* New York, NY: Harper Collins.

Curtis, Kristen T., and Christopher G. Ellison. 2002. "Religious Heterogamy and Marital Conflict: Findings from the National Survey of Families and Households." *Journal of Family Issues* 23: 551–576.

D'Emilio, John, and Estelle B. Freedman. 1998. *Intimate Matters: A History of Sexuality in America.* New York, NY: Harper & Row.

Dahl, Gordon, and Enrico Moretti. 2003. "The Demand for Sons: Evidence From Divorce, Fertility, and Shotgun Marriage," National Bureau of Economic Research, September. Unpublished draft.

—. 2008. "The Demand for Sons." *Review of Economic Studies* 75(4): 1085–1120.

Dailey, Rene M., Kelly R. Rossetto, Abigail Pfiester, and Catherine A. Surra. 2009. "A Qualitative Analysis of On-Again/Off-Again Romantic Relationships: 'It's Up and Down, All Around.'" *Journal of Social and Personal Relationships* 26(4): 443–466.

Daly, Kerry J. 2001. "Deconstructing Family Time: From Ideology to Lived Experience." *Journal of Marriage and Family* 63: 283–294.

Datner, Elizabeth M. Douglas J. Wiebe, Colleen M. Brensinger, and Deborah B. Nelson. 2007. "Identifying Pregnant Women Experiencing Domestic Violence in an Urban Emergency Department." *Journal of Interpersonal Violence* 12(1): 124–135.

Davidson, Michele R. 2002. "Outcomes of High-Risk Women Cared for by Certified Nurse-Midwives." *Journal of Midwifery & Women's Health* 47(1): 46–49.

Davies, Susan C., and Lindsay J. Peltz. 2012. "At-risk Students in After-school Programs: Outcomes and Recommendations." *Principal Leadership.* October. Retrieved 23 April 2013 (www.nasponline.org/resources/principal/Student_Services_-_Oct_2012.pdf).

Davis, Kelly D., W. Benjamin Goodman, Amy E. Pirretti, and David M. Almeida. 2008. "Nonstandard Work Schedules, Perceived Family Well-Being, and Daily Stressors." *Journal of Marriage and Family* 70 (6): 991–1003.

Davis, Kingsley. 1940. "Extreme Social Isolation of a Child." *American Journal of Sociology* 45: 554–565.

—. 1947. "Final Note on a Case of Extreme Isolation." *American Journal of Sociology* 52: 432–437.

Davis, Shannon N., and Theodore N. Greenstein. 2013. "Why Study Housework? Cleaning as a Window into Power in Couples." *Journal of Family Theory and Review* 5: 63–71.

Dawley, Katy. 2003. "Origins of Nurse–Midwifery in the United States and Its Expansion in the 1940s." *Journal of Midwifery & Women's Health* 48(2): 86–95.

Day, Phyllis J., and Jerome Schiele. 2013. *A New History of Social Welfare, 7th ed.* Boston, MA: Pearson.

Deal, Ron L., and Laura Petherbridge. 2009. *The Smart Stepmom: Practical Steps to Help You Thrive.* Ada, MI: Bethany House.

Degler, Carl N. 1980. *At Odds: Women and the Family in America from the Revolution to the Present.* New York, NY: Oxford University Press.

de Jonge, Ank, Birgit van der Goes, Anita Ravelli, Marianne Amelink-Verburg, Ben Mol, Jan Nijhuis, Jack Bennebroek Gravenhorst, and Simone Buitendijk. 2009. "Perinatal Mortality and Morbidity in a Nationwide Cohort of 529688 Low-risk Planned Home and Hospital Births." *BCOG: An International Journal of Obstetrics & Gynaecology* 116(9): 1177–1184.

De Lew, Nancy, George Greenbery, and Kraig Kinchen. 1992. "A Layman's Guide to the U.S. Health Care System." *Health Care Financing Review* 14: 151–165.

DeKeseredy, Walter S., and Martin D. Schwartz. 1998. *Woman Abuse on Campus: Results from the Canadian National Survey.* Thousand Oaks, CA: Sage.

DeLamater, John J., and Morgan Sill. 2010. "Sexual Desire in Later Life." Chapter 6: Sexual Practices in *Sex Matters: The Sexuality and Society Reader, 3rd ed.*, Mindy Stombler, Dawn M. Baunach, Elisabeth O. Burgess, Denise J. Donnelly, Wendy O. Simonds, and Elroi J. Windsor, eds. Boston, MA: Pearson.

Demo, David H., and Katherine R. Allen. 1996. "Diversity within Lesbian and Gay Families: Challenges and Implications for Family Theory and Research." *Journal of Social and Personal Relationships* 13(3): 415–434.

Demos, John. 1970. *A Little Commonwealth: Family Life in Plymouth Colony.* New York, NY: Oxford University Press.

—. 1986. "The Rise and Fall of Adolescence." In *Past, Present, and Personal.* New York, NY: Oxford University Press.

DeNavas-Walt, Carmen, Bernadette D. Proctor, and Jessica C. Smith. 2010. "Income, Poverty, and Health Insurance Coverage in the United States: 2009." Current Population Reports. P60-238. Washington, DC: U.S. Census Bureau.

—. 2013. "Income, Poverty, and Health Insurance Coverage in the United States: 2011." Current Population Reports. P60-243. September. Washington, DC: U.S. Census Bureau.

Dennison, Renee Peltz, and Susan Silverberg Koerner. 2008. "A Look at Hopes and Worries about Marriage: The Views of Adolescents Following a Parental Divorce." *Journal of Divorce & Remarriage* 48(3–4): 91–107.

Deonandan, Raywat. 2012. "The Ethics of Surrogacy." *India Currents.* 3 February. Retrieved 20 April 2013 (www.indiacurrents.com/articles/2012/02/03/ethics-surrogacy).

Derne, Steve. 2003. "Arnold Schwarzenegger, Ally McBeal, and Arranged Marriages: Globalization's Effect on Ordinary People in India." *Contexts* 2(1): 12–18.

Reprinted, pp. 146–153 in *Globalization: The Transformation of Social Worlds*, D. Stanley Eitzen and Maxine Baca Zinn, eds. Belmont, CA: Wadsworth Publishing Co., 2006.

de Rougemont, Denis. 1956. *Love in the Western World.* New York, NY: Pantheon.

Deuisch, Francine M., Carla M. Zelenski, and Mary E. Clark. 1986. "Is There a Double Standard of Aging?" *Journal of Applied Social Psychology* 16(9): 771–85.

DeVito, Joseph A. 2014a. *Essentials of Human Communication, 8th ed.* Boston, MA: Pearson.

—. 2014b. *Interpersonal Messages; Communication and Relationship Skills, 3rd ed.* Boston, MA: Pearson.

Dew, Jeffrey, and W. Bradford Wilcox. 2011. "If Momma Ain't Happy: Explaining Declines in Marital Satisfaction among New Mothers." *Journal of Marriage and Family* 73(1): 1–12.

Dhaher, Enas A., Rafael T. Mikolaczyk, Annette E. Maxwell, and Alexander Krämer. 2010. "Attitudes toward Wife Beating among Palestinian Women of Reproductive Age from Three Cities in West Bank." *Journal of Interpersonal Violence* 25(3): 518–537.

Dickens, A.G. 1977. *The Courts of Europe: Politics, Patronage, and Royalty, 1400–1800.* New York, NY: McGraw-Hill.

Diekman, Amanda B. and Sarah K. Murnen. 2004. "Learning to Be Little Women and Little Men: The Inequitable Gender Equality of Nonsexist Children's Literature." *Sex Roles* 50(5/6): 373–385.

Dill, Bonnie Thornton, and Ruth Enid Zambrana. 2009. *Emerging Intersections: Race, Class, and Gender in Theory, Policy, and Practice.* New Brunswick, NJ: Rutgers University Press.

Dilworth-Anderson, Peggye. 2001. "Extended Kin Networks in Black Families," pp. 104–106 in *Families in Later Life: Connections and Transitions*, Alexis J. Walker, Margaret Manoogian-O'Dell, Lori A. McGraw and Diana L. White, eds. Thousand Oaks, CA: Pine.

DivorceInIreland.com. 2013. "Frequently Asked Questions." Retrieved 15 May 2013 (www.divorceinireland.com/faqs.asp).

Dodson, Lisa, and Jillian Dickert. 2004. "Girls' Family Labor in Low-income Households: A Decade of Qualitative Research." *Journal of Marriage and Family* 66: 318–332.

Domingue, Rachel, and Debra Mollen. 2009. "Attachment and Conflict Communication in Adult Romantic Relationships." *Journal of Social and Personal Relationships* 26(5): 678–696.

Doob, Christopher B. 2013. *Social Inequality and Social Stratification in U.S. Society.* Boston, MA: Pearson.

Doss, Brian D., Galena K. Rhoades, Scott M. Stanley, and Howard J. Markman. 2009. "The Effect of the Transition to Parenthood on Relationship Quality: An Eight-Year Prospective Study." *Journal of Personality and Social Psychology* 96: 601–619.

Dover, Kenneth J. 1978. *Greek Homosexuality.* Cambridge, MA: Harvard University Press.

Downs, Barbara. 2003. "Fertility of American Women: June 2002." Current Population Reports. P20-548. October. Washington DC: US Census Bureau.

Dr.Phil.com. 2012. "Parenting: To Spank or Not to Spank?" Retrieved 13 May 2013 (www.drphil.com/articles/article/48).

Drago, Robert. 2009. "The Parenting of Infants: A Time-use Study." *Monthly Labor Review* 132(10): 33–43.

Duberley, Joanne, Fiona Carmichael, and Isabelle Szmigin. 2013. "Exploring Women's Retirement: Continuity, Context, and Career Transition." *Gender, Work, & Organization.* Doi:10.1111.gwao.12013.

Dumas, Tara M., Heather Lawford, Thanh-Thanh Tieu, and Michael W. Pratt. 2009. "Positive Parenting in Adolescence and Its Relation to Low Point Narration and Identity Status in Emerging Adulthood: A Longitudinal Analysis." *Developmental Psychology* 45(6): 1531–1544.

Duncan, Greg J., Bessie Wilkerson, and Paula England. 2006. "Cleaning Up Their Act: The Effects of Marriage and Cohabitation on Licit and Illicit Drug Use." *Demography* 43(4): 691–710.

Dunifon, Rachel. 2013. "The Influence of Grandparents on the Lives of Children and Adolescents." *Child Development Perspectives* 7(1): 55–60.

Dunifon, Rachel, and Ashish Bajracharya. 2012. "The Role of Grandparents in the Lives of Youth." *Journal of Family Issues* 33(9): 1168–1194.

Dunn, Daniel M., and Lisa J. Goodnight. 2014. *Communication: Embracing Difference, 4th ed.* Boston, MA: Pearson.

Duntley, Joshua D., and David M. Buss. 2008. "Evolutionary Psychology Is a Meta-Theory for Psychology." *Psychological Inquiry* 19: 30–34.

Dupuis, Sara B. 2007. "Examining Remarriage: A Look at Issues Affecting Remarried Couples and the Implications Towards Therapeutic Techniques." *Journal of Divorce & Remarriage* 48(1–2): 91–104.

Duvall, Evelyn. 1977. *Marriage and Family Development.* Philadelphia, PA: Lippincott.

Duvall, Evelyn, and Brent Miller. 1985. *Marriage and Family Development, 6th ed.* New York, NY: Harper and Row.

Duxbury, Linda, Sean Lyons, and Christopher Higgins. 2008. "Too Much to Do, and Not Enough Time: An Examination of Role Overload," pp. 125–40 in *Handbook of Work–Family Integration: Research, Theory, and Best Practices*, Karen Korabik, Donna S. Lero, and Denise L. Whitehead, eds. Amsterdam: Elsevier.

Dwyer, Kathleen M., Bridget K. Fredstrom, Kenneth H. Rubin, Cathryn Booth-LaForce, Linda Rose-Krasnor, and Kim B. Burgess. 2010. "Attachment, Social Information Processing, and Friendship Quality of Early Adolescent Girls and Boys." *Journal of Social and Personal Relationships* 27(1): 91–116.

Dye, Jane Lawler. 2008. "Participation of Mothers in Government Assistance Programs: 2004." Current Population Reports. P70–116. May. Washington, DC: U.S. Census Bureau.

Dykstra, Pearl A., and Aafke E. Komter. 2006. "Structural Characteristics of Dutch Kin Networks," pp. 21–43 in *Family Solidarity in the Netherlands*, Pearl A. Dykstra, Matthijs Kalmijn, Trudee C. Knijn, Aafke E. Komter, Aart C. Liefbloer, and Clara H. Mulder, eds. Amsterdam: Dutch University Press.

Early Childhood Learning and Knowledge Center (ECLKC). 2013. "Head Start Program Facts Fiscal Year 2012." May. Retrieved 31 May 2013 (eclkc.ohs.acf.hhs.gov/hslc/mr/factsheets/2012-hs-program-factsheet.html).

Eastwick, Paul W., and Eli J. Finkel. 2008. "Sex Differences in Mate Preferences Revisited: Do People Know What They Initially Desire in a Romantic Partner?" *Journal of Personality and Social Psychology* 94(2): 245–264.

Eastwick, Paul W., Alice H. Eagly, Eli H. Finkel, and Sarah E. Johnson. 2011. "Implicit and Explicit Preferences for Physical Attractiveness in a Romantic Partner: A Double Dissociation in Predictive Validity." *Journal of Personality and Social Psychology* 101: 993–1011.

Eaton, Danice K., Laura Kann, Steve Kinchen, Shari Shanklin, James Ross, Joseph Hawkins, William A. Harris, Richard Lowry, Tim McManus, David Chyen, Connie Lim, Nancy D. Brener, and Howell Wechsler. 2008. *Youth Risk Behavior Surveillance—United States, 2007.* Technical Report No. Morbidity and Mortality Weekly Report, v. 57, no. SS-4. 8 August. Atlanta, GA: Centers for Disease Control and Prevention.

Economist.com. 2004. "Ever Higher Society, Ever Harder to Ascend." Retrieved 24 June 2006 (www.economist.com/world/na/PrinterFriendly.cfm?story_id=3518560).

Edin, Kathryn and Laura Lein. 1997. Making Ends Meet: How Single Mothers Survive Welfare and Low-wage Work. New York: Russell Sage Foundation.

Edin, Kathryn, and Maria Kefalas. 2005. *Promises I Can Keep: Why Poor Women Put Motherhood before Marriage.* Chicago, IL: University of Chicago Press.

Edin, Kathryn, and Rebecca Joyce Kissane. 2010. "Poverty and the American Family: A Decade in Review." *Journal of Marriage and Family* 72(3): 460–479.

Edwards, Renee, and Mark A. Hamilton. 2004. "You Need to Understand My Gender Role: An Empirical Test of Tannen's Model of Gender and Communication." *Sex Roles* 50(7/8): 491–504.

Ehrenreich, Barbara. 2001. *Nickel and Dimed: On (Not) Getting by in America.* New York, NY: Henry Holt and Co.

Ehrenreich, Barbara, and Deirdre English. 1989. *For Her Own Good: 150 Years of Experts' Advice to Women.* New York, NY: Anchor Books/Doubleday.

Eitzen, D. Stanley, and Kelly Eitzen Smith. 2009. *Experiencing Poverty: Voices from the Bottom.* Upper Saddle River, NJ: Prentice Hall.

Ekerdt, David J. 2009. "Frontiers of Research on Work and Retirement." *The Journals of Gerontology: Series B* 65B(1): 69–80.

Elder, Jr., Glen H. 1998. "The Life Course and Human Development." pp. 939–991 in *Handbook of Child Psychology*, vol. 1, 5th ed., Richard M. Lerner, ed. Theoretical Models of Human Development. New York, NY: Wiley.

—. 1999. *Children of the Great Depression: Social Change in Life Experience. 25th Anniversary Edition.* Boulder, CO: Westview Press (Originally published in 1974, University of Chicago Press).

Ellman, Ira Mark, Paul M. Kurtz, and Lois A. Weithorn. 2010. *Family Law; Cases, Texts, Problems, 5th ed.* Newark, NJ: Lexis Nexis.

Elwert, Felix, and Nicholas A. Christakis. 2006. "Widowhood and Race." *American Sociological Review* 71(1): 16–41.

Employee Benefit Research Institute. 2013. "Debt of the Elderly and Near Elderly, 1992–2010 and Employer and Worker Contributions to Health Reimbursement Arrangements and Health Savings Accounts, 2006–2012." *EBRI Notes*. February. Retrieved 25 February 2013 (www.ebri.org).

—. 2009. "Domestic Partner Benefits: Facts and Background." Retrieved 26 October 2009 (www.ebri.org/pdf/publications/facts/0209fact.pdf).

Encyclopedia of Surgery. 2009. "Sex Reassignment Surgery." Retrieved 21 February 2010 (www.surgeryencyclopedia.com/Pa-St/Sex-Reassignment-Surgery.html).

Endendijk, Joyce J., Marleen G. Groenveld, Sheila R. van Berkel, Elizabeth T. Hallers-Haalboom, Judi Mesman, and Marian J. Bakermans-Kranenburg. 2013. "Gender Stereotypes in the Family Context: Mothers, Fathers, and Siblings." *Sex Roles*. DOI: 10.1007/s11199-013-0265-4.

Engels, Friedrich. 1902, original 1884. *The Origin of the Family*. Chicago, IL: Charles H. Kerr and Co.

England, Paula, and Reuben Thomas. 2007. "The Decline of the Date and the Rise of the College Hook Up." In *Family in Transition*, Arlene S. Skolnick and Jerome H. Skolnick, eds. Boston, MA: Allyn & Bacon.

Entertainment Software Association. 2010. "Industry Facts." Retrieved 16 April 2010 (www.theesa.com/facts/index.asp).

Epstein, Randi Hutter. 2010. *Get Me Out: A History of Childbirth from the Garden of Eden to the Sperm Bank*. New York, NY: W.W. Norton and Company.

Epstein, Marina, Jerel P. Calzo, Andrew P. Smiler, and L. Monique Ward. 2009. "'Anything from Making Out to Having Sex': Men's Negotiations of Hooking Up and Friends with Benefits Scripts." *Journal of Sex Research* 46(5): 414–424.

Ermisch, John, Markus Jäntti, and Timothy M. Smeeding, eds. 2012. *From Parents to Children: The Intergenerational Transmission of Advantage*. New York, NY: Russell Sage Foundation.

Eskridge, Jr., William N., and Darren R. Spedale. 2006. *Gay Marriage: For Better or for Worse?* New York, NY: Oxford University Press.

Etaugh, Claire. 2003. "Witches, Mothers, & Others: Females in Children's Books." *Bradley University Hilltopics* (Peoria, IL), Winter, pp. 10–13.

Evenson, Ranae J., and Robin W. Simon. 2006. "Clarifying the Relationship between Parenthood and Depression." *Journal of Health and Social Behavior* 46: 341–358.

Evertsson, Marie, and Magnus Nermo. 2004. "Dependence within Families and the Division of Labor: Comparing Sweden and the United States." *Journal of Marriage and Family* 66(6): 1272–1286.

Facebook. 2013. "Key Facts." Retrieved 10 April 2013 (newsroom.fb.com/Key-Facts).

Fagan, Jay. 2013. "Effects of Divorce and Cohabitation Dissolution on Preschoolers' Literacy." *Journal of Family Issues* 34(4): 460–483.

Fairris, David, and Michael Reich. 2005. "The Impacts of Living Wage Policies: Introduction to the Special Issue." *Industrial Relations* 44(1): 1–13.

Families and Work Institute. 2004. *Workplace Flexibility: What Is It? Who Has It? Who Wants It? Does It Make a Difference?* New York, NY: Families and Work Institute.

Family Caregiver Alliance. 2012. "Fact Sheet: Selected Caregiver Statistics." November. Retrieved 29 May 2013 (www.caregiver.org/caregiver/jsp/content_node.jsp?nodeid=439&big_font=true).

Family Focus. 2008. "Same-sex 'Marriage' and Civil Unions." Retrieved 25 June 2008 (www.family.org/socialissues/A000000464.cfm).

Farley, John E. 2012. *Majority–Minority Relations, Census Update, 6th ed.* Boston, MA: Pearson.

Farrell, Betty G. 1999. *Family: The Making of an Idea, an Institution, and a Controversy in American Culture*. Boulder, CO: Westview Press.

Fasula, Amy M., Monique Carry, and Kim S. Miller. 2012. "A Multidimensional Framework for the Meanings of the Sexual Double Standard and its Application for the Sexual Health of Young Black Women in the U.S." *Journal of Sex Research* Retrieved 27 March 2013 (www.tandfonline.com/doi/full/10.1080/00224499.2012.716874).

Fearon, R. Pasco, Marian J. Bakermans-Kranenburg, Marinus H. Van IJzendoorn, Anne-Marie Lapsley, and Glenn I. Roisman. 2010. "The Significance of Insecure Attachment and Disorganization in the Development of Children's Externalizing Behavior: A Meta-Analytic Study." *Child Development* 81(2): 435–456.

Federal Interagency Forum on Child and Family Statistics. 2012. *America's Children: Key National Indicators of Well-being, 2012*. Washington, DC: U.S. Governmental Printing Office.

Feeney, Judith A., and Patricia Noller. 2004. "Attachment and Sexuality in Close Relationships." In *Handbook of Sexuality in Close Relationships*. Mahwah, NJ: Lawrence Erlbaum.

Fehr, Beverly. 1988. "Prototype Analysis of the Concepts of Love and Commitment." *Journal of Personality and Social Psychology* 55(4): 557–579.

—. 1993. "How Do I Love Thee? Let Me Consult My Prototype," pp. 87–120 in *Individuals in Relationships*, Stephen Duck, ed. Thousand Oaks, CA: Sage.

Fehr, Beverly, Susan Sprecher, and Lynn G. Underwood. 2009. *The Science of Compassionate Love: Research, Theory, and Practice*. Malden, MA: Wiley-Blackwell.

Feinberg, Lynn, Susan C. Reinhard, Ari Houser, and Rita Choula. 2011. "Valuing the Invaluable: 2011 Update. The Growing Contributions and Costs of Family Caregiving." Washington, DC: AARP Public Policy Institute.

Feldman, Robert S. 2010. *Child Development, 5th ed.* Upper Saddle River, NJ: Prentice Hall.

Felmlee, Diane H. 2001. "From Appealing to Appalling: Disenchantment with a Romantic Partner." *Sociological Perspectives* 44(3): 263–280.

Felmlee, Diane H., and Anna Muraco. 2009. "Gender and Friendship Norms among Other Adults." *Research on Aging* 31(3): 318–344.

Felmlee, Diane H., and Susan Sprecher. 2006. "Love: Psychological and Sociological Perspectives," pp. 389–409 in *Handbook of Sociology of Emotions*, Jan E. Stets and Jonathan H. Turner, eds. New York, NY: Springer.

Felson, Richard B. 2006. "Is Violence Against Women about Women or about Violence?" *Contexts* 5(2): 21–25.

Fenigstein, Allan, and Matthew Preston. 2007. "The Desired Number of Sexual Partners as a Function of Gender, Sexual Risks, and the Meaning of 'Ideal.'" *Journal of Sex Research* 44(1): 89–95.

Fenstermaker Berk, Sarah. 1985. *The Gender Factory: The Apportionment of Work in American Households*. New York, NY: Plenum Press.

Fetto, John. 2003. "Love Stinks." *American Demographics* 25: 10–11.

Few, April L., and Karen H. Rosen. 2005. "Victims of Chronic Dating Violence: How Women's Vulnerabilities Link to Their Decisions to Stay." *Family Relations* 54 (April): 265–279.

Fielder, Robyn L., Kate B. Carey, and Michael P. Carey. 2012. "Are Hookups Replacing Romantic Relationships? A Longitudinal Study of First-Year Female College Students." *Journal of Adolescent Health* Published online 29 October 2012.

Fields, Jason, and Lynne M. Casper. 2001. "America's Families and Living Arrangements: March 2000." Current Population Reports. P20-537. Washington DC: U.S. Census Bureau.

Filion, Kai. 2009. "Fact Sheet for 2009 Minimum Wage Increase—Minimum Wage Issue Guide." Economic Policy Institute. Retrieved 3 May 2010 (www.epi.org/publications/entry/mwig_fact_sheet).

Filson, Jennifer, Emilio Ulloa, Cristin Runfola, and Audrey Hokoda. 2010. "Does Powerlessness Explain the Relationship between Intimate Partner Violence and Depression?" *Journal of Interpersonal Violence* 25(3): 400–415.

Fine, Mark, Lawrence H. Ganong, and Marilyn Coleman. 1997. "Consistency in Perceptions of the Step-Parent Role among Step-Parents, Parents, and Stepchildren." *Journal of Social and Personal Relationships* 15: 810–828.

Finer, Lawrence B. 2007. "Trends in Premarital Sex in the United States, 1954–2003." *Public Health Reports* 122 (January–February): 73–78.

Fingerman, Karen L. 2004. "The Role of Offspring and In-Laws in Grandparents' Ties to Their Grandchildren." *Journal of Family Issues* 25(8): 1026–1049.

Finley, Gordon E., Sandra D. Mira, and Seth J. Schwartz. 2008. "Perceived Paternal and Maternal Involvement: Factor Structures, Mean Differences, and Paternal Roles." *Fathering* 6(1): 62–82.

Firestone, Robert W., Lisa A. Firestone, and Joyce Catlett. 2008. *Sex and Love in Intimate Relationships*. Washington, DC: APA Press.

Fisher, Allen P. 2003. "A Critique of the Portrayal of Adoption in College Textbooks and Readers on Families, 1998–2001." *Family Relations* 52: 154–160.

Fisher, Bonnie S., and Saundra L. Regan. 2006. "The Extent and Frequency of Abuse in the Lives of Older Women and Their Relationship with Health Outcomes." *The Gerontologist* 46: 200–209.

Fisher, Helen E. 2000. *The First Sex: The Natural Talents of Women and How They Are Changing the World*. New York, NY: Ballantine Books.

Fitzgerald, F. Scott. 1925 (Reprinted 1999). *The Great Gatsby*. New York, NY: Scribner.

Fitzpatrick, Laura. 2009. "A Brief History of China's One Child Policy." *Time Magazine*. 27 July. Retrieved 9 November 2009 (www.time.com/time/world/article/0,8599,1912861,00.html).

Fitzpatrick, Maureen J., and Barbara J. McPherson. 2010. "Coloring within the Lines: Gender Stereotypes in Contemporary Coloring Books." *Sex Roles* 62(1–2): 127–137.

Fleck, Carole. 2009. "Grandparents Help Out." AARP Bulletin Today. Retrieved 4 December 2009 (bulletin.aarp.org/yourmoney/personalfinance/articles/more_grandparents_giving_money_to_kids_.html).

Fletcher-Janzen, Elaine. 2009. "Intelligent Testing: Bridging the Gap between Classical and Romantic Science in Assessment," pp. 15–29 in *Intelligent Testing: Integrating Psychological Theory and Clinical Practice*, James C. Kaufman, ed. New York, NY: Cambridge University Press.

Fomby, Paula, and Stacey J. Bosick. 2013. "Family Instability and the Transition to Adulthood." *Journal of Marriage and Family* 75(5): 1266–1287.

Foster, Ann C., and Craig J. Kreisler. 2012. "Wife's Employment and Allocation of Resources in Families with Children." *Monthly Labor Review* September: 3–13.

Foucault, Michel. 1978. *The History of Sexuality: An Introduction (R. Hurley Translation)*. Harmondsworth: Penguin.

Fox, Susannah, and Joanna Brenner. 2012. "Family Caregivers Online." Pew Internet & Family Life Project. 12 July. Retrieved 29 May 2013 (pewinternet.org/Reports/2012/Caregivers-online.aspx).

Fraley, R. Chris, and Phillip R. Shaver. 2000. "Adult Romantic Attachment: Theoretical Developments, Emerging Controversies and Unanswered Questions." *Review of General Psychology* 4(2): 132–154.

Franklin II, Clyde W. 1992. "'Hey, Home—Yo, Bro.' Friendship Among Black Men." pp. 201–214 in Men's Friendships., Peter M. Nardi, ed. Newbury Park, CA: Sage.

Frank, Hallie. 2008. "The Influence of Divorce on the Relationship between Adult Parent–Child and Adult Sibling Relationships." *Journal of Divorce & Remarriage* 48(3–4): 21–32.

Frech, Adrianne, and Kristi Williams. 2007. "Depression and the Psychological Benefits of Entering Marriage." *Journal of Health and Social Behavior* 48(2): 149–163.

Fredriksen-Goldsen, Karen I., Loree Cook-Daniels, Hyun-Jun Kim, Elena A. Erosheva, Charles A. Emlet, Charles A. Hoy-Ellis, Jayn Goldsen, and Anna Muraco. 2013. "Physical and Mental Health of Transgender Older Adults: An At-risk and Underserved Population." *The Gerontologist*. doi:10.1093/geront/gnt021.

Fredrix, Emily. 2008. "Not-Such-Baby 'Boomerangs': Adults Returning to Nest Often Deplete." *Oakland Tribune* (Oakland, CA), 22 March.

Freeman, Richard. 2005. "Fighting for Other Folks' Wages: The Logic and Illogic of Living Wage Campaigns." *Industrial Relations* 44(1): 14–31.

Friedan, Betty. 1963. *The Feminine Mystique*. New York, NY: Dell.

Fry, Richard. 2013. "Young Adults after the Recession: Fewer Homes, Fewer Cars, Less Debt." Pew Research Social & Demographic Trends. 21 February. Retrieved 22 May 2013 (www.pewsocialtrends.org/2013/02/21/young-adults-after-the-recession-fewer-homes-fewer-cars-less-debt).

Fry, Richard, and D'Vera Cohn. 2011. "Living Together: The Economics of Cohabitation." June. Washington, DC: Pew Research Center.

—. 2010. "Women, Men and the New Economics of Marriage." Retrieved 20 January 2010 (pewsocialtrends.org/2010/01/19/women-men-and-the-new-economics-of-marriage/).

Fry, Richard, and Jeffrey S. Passel. 2009. "Latino Children: A Majority Are U.S.-Born Offspring of Immigrants." Pew Hispanic Center. Retrieved 20 January 2010 (pewhispanic.org/reports/report.php?ReportID=110).

Fryar, Cheryl D., Rosemarie Hirsch, Kathryn S. Porter, Benny Kottiri, Debra J. Brody, and Tatiana Louis. 2007. "Drug Use and Sexual Behaviors Reported by Adults: United States, 1999–2002." Centers for Disease Control and Prevention, 384. 28 June. Hyattsville, MD: National Center for Health Statistics.

Fulfer, Jamie L., Jillian J. Tyler, Natalie J.S. Choi, J.S., Jill A. Young, Steven J. Verhulst, Regina Kovach, and J. Kevin Dorsey. 2007. "Using Indirect Questions to Detect Intimate Partner Violence." *Journal of Interpersonal Violence* 22(2): 238–249.

Furstenberg, Frank F., Jr. 2007. "Should Government Promote Marriage?" *Journal of Policy Analysis and Management* 26(4): 956–960.

Gadalla, Tahany M. 2008. "Gender Differences in Poverty Rates after Marital Dissolution: A Longitudinal Study." *Journal of Divorce & Remarriage* 49(3/4): 225–238.

—. 2009. "Impact of Marital Dissolution on Men's and Women's Incomes: A Longitudinal Study." *Journal of Divorce & Remarriage* 50(1): 55–65.

Gajendran, Ravi, and David Harrison. 2007. "The Good, the Bad, and the Unknown about Telecommuting: Meta-Analysis of Psychological Mediators and Individual Consequences." *Journal of Applied Psychology* 92 (639–650): 1524–1541.

Galinsky, Ellen, Kerstin Aumann, and James T. Bond. 2009. *Times Are Changing: Gender and Generation at Work and at Home*. New York, NY: Families and Work Institute.

Galinsky, Ellen, James T. Bond, and Kelly Sakai. 2008. *2008 National Study of Employers*. New York, NY: Families and Work Institute.

Gallagher, Sally K. 1994. "Doing Their Share: Comparing Patterns of Help Given by Older and Younger Adults." *Journal of Marriage and the Family* 56: 567–578.

Gallagher, Sally K., and Naomi Gerstel. 2001. "Connections and Constraints: The Effects of Children on Caregiving." *Journal of Marriage and the Family* 63: 265–275.

Gallup News Service. 2013. "Race Relations." Retrieved 3 March 2013 (www.gallup.com/poll/1687/Race-Relations.aspx#1).

Gallup Poll. 2001. "What's the Best Arrangement for Today's Families?" (www.gallup.com/tuesdaybriefing.asp).

Gallup Poll. 2011. "Americans Morally OK with Divorce, but Not Affairs." 2 June. Retrieved 25 February 2013 (www.gallup.com/video/147878/Divorce-Morally-Acceptable-Americans-Affairs-Least.aspx).

—. 2012. "Americans' Views on Same-Sex Marriage and Marijuana. "17 December. Retrieved 25 February 2013 (www.gallup.com/video/159299/americans-views-sex-marriage-marijuana.aspx?version=print).

—. 2013. "Older Americans' Moral Attitudes Changing: Moral Acceptance of Teenage Sex among the Biggest Generational Divides." 20 May. Retrieved 8 June 2013 (www.gallup.com/poll/162881/older-americans-moral-attitudes-changing.aspx).

Galvin, Kathleen M., Carma L. Bylund, and Bernard J. Brommel. 2012. *Family Communication: Cohesion and Change, 8th ed*. Boston, MA: Pearson.

Ganong, Lawrence H., and Marilyn Coleman. 1989. "Preparing for Remarriage: Anticipating the Issues, Seeking Solutions." *Family Relations* 38: 28–33.

—. 1997. "How Society Views Stepfamilies." *Marriage and Family Review* 26: 85–106.

—. 2004. *Stepfamily Relationships: Development, Dynamics, and Interventions*. New York, NY: Kluwer Academic.

Gantert, Tom. 2008. "Having a Husband Adds Work, Study Says." *The Sunday Oregonian*, 6 April, p. A8.

Gardner, Margo, Jodie Roth, and Jeanne Brooks-Gunn. 2008. "Adolescents' Participation in Organized Activities and Developmental Success Two and Eight Years After High School: Do Sponsorship, Duration, and Intensity Matter?" *Developmental Psychology* 44(3): 814–830.

Garfinkel, Irwin, Lee Rainwater, and Timothy M. Smeeding. 2010. *Welfare and Welfare States: Is America a Laggard or Leader?* Oxford, UK: Oxford University Press.

Garfinkel, Irwin, Daniel R. Meyer, and Sara S. McLanahan. 1998. "A Brief History of Child Support Policies in the United States," pp. 14–30 in *Fathers Under Fire: The Revolution in Child Support Enforcement*, Irwin Garfinkel, Sara S. McLanahan, Daniel R. Meyer, and Judith A. Seltzer, eds. New York, NY: Russell Sage Foundation.

Garner, Abigail. 2005. *Families Like Mine: Children of Gay Parents Tell It Like It Is*. New York, NY: Harper Paperbacks.

Gartstein, Masha, and Mary K. Rothbart. 2009. "Temperament." In *Encyclopedia of Infant and Early Childhood Development*, Marshall Haith and Janette Benson, eds. Academic Press.

Gasper, Jill A.F., Arnold L. Stolberg, Katherine M. Macie, and Larry J. Williams. 2008. "Coparenting in Intact and Divorced Families: Its Impact on Young Adult Adjustment." *Journal of Divorce & Remarriage* 49(3–4, September): 272–290.

Gattai, Flavia Budini, and Tullia Musatti. 1999. "Grandmothers' Involvement in Grandchildren's Care: Attitudes, Feelings, and Emotions." *Family Relations* 48: 35–42.

Gay & Lesbian Advocates & Defenders. 2008. "Gina and Heidi Nortonsmith." Retrieved 3 July 2008 (www.glad.org/marriage/Goodridge/Gina&Heidi.shtml).

Geena Davis Institute on Gender in Media. 2012. "Research Informs and Empowers." Retrieved 3 March 2013 (www.seejane.org/research).

General Social Survey. 2009. *Dataset: General Social Surveys, 1972–2006 [Cumulative File] Characteristics Ascribed to Blacks [MRDF].* (www.norc.org/GSS+Website/Browse+GSS+Variables/Subject+Index/[producer]).

Gerson, Kathleen. 2001. "Dilemmas of Involved Fatherhood," pp. 324–339 in *Shifting the Center: Understanding Contemporary Families,* Susan J. Ferguson, ed. Mountain View, CA: Mayfield Publishing Company.

Gerson, Michael. 2009. "Today's Singles, Lost without a Courtship Narrative." Washingtonpost.com. Retrieved 4 February 2010 (www.washingtonpost.com/wp-dyn/content/article/2009/09/15/AR2009091502981.html).

Gettleman, Jeffrey. 2010. "Kenyan Police Disperse Gay Wedding." NYTimes.com. Retrieved 21 February 2010 (www.nytimes.com/2010/02/13/world/africa/13kenya.html).

Gibb, Jack R. 1961. "Defensive Communication." *Journal of Communication* 11: 141–148.

Gibbs, Larry. 2013. "Working Women with Children in the Household." National Center for Family & Marriage Research. FP-13-09.

Gibson-Davis, Christine M., Kathryn Edin, and Sara McLanahan. 2005. "High Hopes but Even Higher Expectations: The Retreat from Marriage among Low-Income Couples." *Journal of Marriage and Family* 67: 1301–1312.

Gierveld, Jenny de Jong, Marjolein Broese van Groenou, Adriaan W. Hoogendoorn, and Johannes H. Smit. 2008. "Quality of Marriages in Later Life and Emotional and Social Loneliness." *The Journals of Gerontology: Series B* 64B(4): 497–506.

Gilbert, Dennis, and Joseph A. Kahl. 1993. *The American Class Structure: A New Synthesis,* 4th ed. Belmont, CA: Wadsworth.

Giles-Sims, Jean, and Charles Lockhart. 2005. "Grandparents' Visitation Rights Using Culture to Explain Cross-state Variation." *Journal of Divorce & Remarriage* 44(3/4): 1–16.

Glenn, Norval D. 1998. "The Course of Marital Success and Failure in Five American 10-Year Marriage Cohorts." *Journal of Marriage and the Family* 60: 569–576.

Global Workplace Analytics. 2012. "Latest Telecommuting Statistics." Retrieved 30 May 2013 (www.globalworkplaceanalytics.com/telecommuting-statistics).

Glynn, Keva, Heather Maclean, Tonia Forte, and Marsha Cohen. 2009. "The Association between Role Overload and Women's Mental Health." *Journal of Women's Health (Larchmont)* 18(2): 217–223.

Gold, Joshua M. 2009. "Stepparents and the Law: Knowledge for Counselors, Guidelines for Family Members." *The Family Journal* 17(3): 272–276.

Gold, Joshua M., and Oluwatoyin Adeyemi. 2013. "Stepfathers and Noncustodial Fathers: Two Men, One Role." *The Family Journal* 21(1): 99–103.

Gold, Mitchell, and Mindy Drucker. 2008. *Crisis: 40 Stories Revealing the Personal, Social, and Religious Pain and Trauma of Growing Up Gay in America.* Austin, TX: Greenleaf Book Group, LLC.

Goldberg, Abbie E., and Maureen Perry-Jenkins. 2007. "The Division of Labor and Perceptions of Parental Roles: Lesbian Couples across the Transition to Parenthood." *Journal of Social and Personal Relationships* 24: 297–318.

Goode, William J. 1959. "The Theoretical Importance of Love." *American Sociological Review* 24: 38–47.

Goodman, Catherine Chase, and Merril Silverstein. 2002. "Grandmothers Raising Grandchildren: Family Structure and Well-being in Culturally Diverse Families." *The Gerontologist* 42(5): 676–689.

Goodman, W. Benjamin, Ann C. Crouter, and The Family Life Project Key Investigators. 2009. "Longitudinal Associations between Maternal Work Stress, Negative Work–Family Spillover, and Depressive Symptoms." *Family Relations* 58 (July): 245–258.

Goodwin, Paula Y., William D. Mosher, and Anjani Chandra. 2010. *Marriage and Cohabitation in the United States: A Statistical Portrait Based on Cycle 6 (2002) of the National Survey of Family Growth. Vital Health Statistics* 23 (28). National Center for Health Statistics.

Goodwin, Robin. 2009. *Changing Relations: Achieving Intimacy in a Time of Social Transition.* New York, NY: Cambridge University Press.

Gorchoff, Sara M., Oliver P. John, and Ravenna Helson. 2008. "Contextualing Change in Marital Satisfaction During Middle Age: An 18-Year Longitudinal Study." *Psychological Science* 19(11): 1194–1200.

Gordon, Linda. 1979. "The Struggle for Reproductive Freedom: Three Stages of Feminism," pp. 107–36 in *Capitalist Patriarchy and the Case for Socialist Feminism,* Zillah R. Eisenstein, ed. New York, NY: Monthly Review Press.

Gordon-Reed, Annette. 2008. *The Hemingses of Monticello: An American Family.* New York, NY: Norton.

Gornick, Janet C., Harriet B. Presser, and Caroline Ratzdorf. 2009. "Outside the 9-to-5." *The American Prospect* 20(5): 21–24.

Gosselin, Julie. 2010. "Individual and Family Factors Related to Psychosocial Adjustment in Stepmother Families with Adolescents." *Journal of Divorce & Remarriage* 51(2): 108–123.

Gosselin, Julie, and Hélène David. 2007. "Risk and Resilience Factors Linked with the Psychosocial Adjustment of Adolescents, Stepparents and Biological Parents." *Journal of Divorce & Remarriage* 48(1–2): 29–53.

Gottman, John M. 1994. *Why Marriages Succeed or Fail.* New York, NY: Simon & Schuster.

Gottman, John, and Julie Schwartz Gottman. 2008. *And Baby Makes Three: The Six-step Plan for Preserving Marital Intimacy and Rekindling Romance after Baby Arrives.* New York, NY: Three Rivers Press.

Gottman Relationship Institute. 2013. "Same-sex Couples." Retrieved 14 March 2013 (www.gottman.com/49850/Gay-Lesbian-Research.html).

Goyer, Amy. 2006. "Intergenerational Relationships: Grandparents Raising Grandchildren." AARP.org. Retrieved 29 October 2007 (www.aarp.org/research/international/perspectives/nov_05_grandparents.html).

Graham, James M. 2011. "Measuring Love in Romantic Relationships: A Meta-analysis." *Journal of Social and Personal Relationships* 28(6): 748–771.

Grall, Timothy S. 2011. *Custodial Mothers and Fathers and Their Child Support: 2009.* Current Population Reports. P60-240. December. Washington, DC: U.S. Census Bureau.

Grant, Jaime M. 2009. *Outing Age: Public Policy Issues Affecting Gay, Lesbian, Bisexual, and Transgender Elders.* National Gay and Lesbian Task Force Policy Institute.

Gray, John. 1992. *Men Are from Mars, Women Are from Venus: A Practical Guide for Improving Communication and Getting What You Want in Your Relationships.* New York, NY: Thorsons.

Grabill, Wilson H., Clyde V. Kiser, and Pascal K. Whelpton. 1958. *The Fertility of American Women.* New York, NY: Wiley & Sons.

Green, Kerry M., Elaine E. Doherty, Kate E. Fothergill, and Margaret E. Ensminger. 2012. "Marriage Trajectories and Health Risk Behaviors Throughout Adulthood among Urban African Americans." *Journal of Family Issues* 33(12): 1595–1618.

Greenberg, Kenneth. 2009. "Half of Americans Know Someone Who Has Dated a Person They Met Online, According to New Study from People Media." PRWeb.com. Retrieved 22 January 2010 (www.prweb.com/printer/2758114.htm).

Greenhouse, Steven. 2013. "Our Economic Pickle." NYTimes.com. 12 January. Retrieved 25 February 2013 (www.nytimes.com/2013/01/13/sunday-review/americas-productivity-climbs-but-wages-stagnate.html?_r=0&pagewanted=print).

Greenstein, Theodore N., and Shannon N. Davis. 2006. "Cross-national Variations in Divorce: Effects of Women's Power, Prestige and Dependence." *Journal of Comparative Family Studies* 37: 253–273.

Greif, Geoffrey L., and Kathleen Holtz Deal. 2012. "The Impact of Divorce on Friendships with Couples and Individuals." *Journal of Divorce & Remarriage* 53(6): 421–435.

Grello, Catherine M., Deborah P. Welsh, and Melinda S. Harper. 2006. "No Strings Attached: The Nature of Casual Sex in College Students." *The Journal of Sex Research* 43(3): 255–267.

Greven, Philip. 1970. *Four Generations: Population, Land, and Family in Colonial Andover, Massachusetts.* Ithaca: Cornell University Press.

Griffith, Wendy. 2006. "A Look at India's Arranged Marriages." CBN.com. Retrieved 24 July 2006 (www.cbn.com/cbnnews/news/050323c.aspx).

Grogger, Jeffrey. 2011. "Speech Patterns and Racial Wage Inequality." *Journal of Human Resources* 46: 1–25.

Groothof, Hinke A.K., Pieternel Dijkstra, and Dick P.H. Barelds. 2010. "Sex Differences in Jealousy: The Case of Internet Infidelity." *Journal of Social and Personal Relationships* 26(8): 1119–1129.

Gutman, Herbert. 1976. *The Black Family in Slavery and Freedom, 1750–1925.* New York, NY: Pantheon.

Haas, Kate. 2010. "Who Will Make Room for the Intersexed?" In *Sex Matters: The Sexuality and Society Reader, 3rd ed.,* Mindy Stombler, Dawn M. Baunach, Elisabeth O. Burgess, Denise J. Donnelly, Wendy O. Simonds, and Elroi J. Windsor, eds. New York, NY: Prentice Hall.

Haber, Carole. 1983. *Beyond Sixty-five: The Dilemma of Old Age in America's Past.* Cambridge, MA: Cambridge University Press.

Haj-Yahia, Muhammad M. 2010. "Palestinian Physicians' Misconceptions about and Approval of Wife Abuse." *Journal of Interpersonal Violence* 25(3): 416–442.

Hakvoort, Esther M., Henny M.W. Bos, Frank Van Balen, and Jo M.A. Hermanns. "Postdivorce Relationships in Families and Children's Psychosocial Adjustment." *Journal of Divorce & Remarriage* 52(2): 125–146.

Hall, Carl T. 2002. "Pediatricians Endorse Gay, Lesbian Adoption 'Children Deserve to Know Their Relationships with Both Parents Are Stable, Legally Recognized.'" *San Francisco Chronicle.* Retrieved 13 July 2006 (www.sfgate.com/cgi-bin/article.cgi?file=/chronicle/archive/2002/02/04/MN227427).

Hall, Edward T. 1966. *The Hidden Dimension.* Garden City, NY: Anchor Books/Doubleday.

—. 1976. *Beyond Culture.* Garden City, NY: Doubleday.

Hall, Mark A., Mary Anne Bobinski, and David Orentlicher. 2008. *Health Care Law and Ethics, 7th ed.* New York, NY: Aspen.

Haller, Jr., John S. 1972. "From Maidenhood to Menopause: Sex Education for Women in Victorian America." *Journal of Popular Culture* 6(1): 46–69.

Halpern-Felsher, Bonnie L., Jodi L. Cornell, Rhonda Y. Kropp, and Jeanne M. Tschann. 2005. "Oral versus Vaginal Sex among Adolescents: Perceptions, Attitudes, and Behavior." *Pediatrics* 115: 845–851.

Hamer, Dean, and Peter Copeland. 1994. *The Science of Desire.* New York, NY: Simon and Schuster.

Hamer, Jennifer, and Kathleen Marchioro. 2002. "Becoming Custodial Dads: Exploring Parenting among Low-Income and Working-Class African American Fathers." *Journal of Marriage and the Family* 64: 116–129.

Hamilton, Brady E., Joyce A. Martin, and Stephanie J. Ventura. 2009. "Births: Preliminary Data for 2007." Vol. 57, No. 12. Retrieved 18 August 2009. Hyattsville, MD/National Center for Health Statistics (www.cdc.gov/nchs/data/nvsr/nvsr57/nvsr57_12.pdf).

Hamilton, Brady E., Joyce A. Martin, and Stephanie J. Ventura. 2012. "Births: Preliminary Data for 2011." National Vital Statistics Reports Vol. 61, No. 5. 3 October. Hyattsville, MD/National Center for Health Statistics.

Hamilton, Brady E., Stephanie J. Ventura, Joyce A. Martin, and Paul D. Sutton. 2006. "Final Births for 2004." Retrieved 13 July 2006. Hyattsville, MD/National Center for Health Statistics (www.cdc.gov/nchs/products/pubs/pubd/hestats/finalbirths04/finalbirths04.htm).

Hamilton, Brady E. and Stephanie J. Ventura. 2012. "Birth Rates for U.S. Teenagers Reach Historic Lows for All Ages and Ethnic Groups." NCHS Data Brief No. 89. April. Washington, DC: National Center for Health Statistics.

Hammond, Ron J., and Barbara Bearnson. 2003a. "Death and Grief Assessment," pp. 125–126 in *The Marriages and Families Activities Workbook.* Belmont, CA: Wadsworth.

—. 2003b. *The Marriages and Families Activities Workbook*. Belmont, CA: Wadsworth/Cengage Learning.

Han, Wen-Jui, and Liana E. Fox. 2011. "Parental Work Schedules and Children's Cognitive Trajectories." *Journal of Marriage and Family* 73(5): 962–980.

Han, Wen-Jui, Ruhm, J. Christopher, and Jane Waldfogel. 2009. "Parental Leave Policies and Parents' Employment and Leave-taking." *Journal of Policy Analysis and Management* 28(1): 29–54.

Handel, Gerald, Spencer E. Cahill, and Frederick Elkin. 2007. *Children and Society: The Sociology of Children and Childhood Socialization*. New York, NY: Oxford University Press.

Hanson, Barbara, and Carol Knopes. 1993. "Prime Time Tuning Out Varied Cultures." *USA Today*, 6 July.

Hardy, Melissa A., and Kim Shuey. 2000. "Retirement," pp. 2401–2410 in *Encyclopedia of Sociology, 2nd ed.*, Edgar F. Borgatta and Rhonda J. Montgomery, eds. New York, NY: Macmillan.

Hareven, Tamara K. 1977. "The Historical Study of the Family in Urban Society." In *Family and Kin in American Urban Communities, 1780–1940*, Tamara K. Hareven, ed. New York, NY: Franklin and Watts.

—. 2000. *Families, History, and Social Change: Life Course; Cross-Cultural Perspectives*. Boulder, CO: Westview Press.

Harnett, Paul H., Sharon Dawe, and Melissa Russell. 2012. "An Investigation of the Needs of Grandparents Who Are Raising Grandchildren." *Child & Family Social Work* doi:10.1111/cfs.12036.

Harvey, John H., and Mark Fine. 2004. *Children of Divorce: Stories of Loss and Growth*. Mahwah, NJ: Lawrence Erlbaum Associates.

Harvey, John H., Amy Wenzel, and Susan Sprecher. 2004. *The Handbook of Sexuality in Close Relationships*. Oxford, England: Taylor & Francis.

Harvey, Vickie. 2003. "'We're Just Friends': Myth Construction As A Communication Strategy In Maintaining Cross-Sex Friendships." The Qualitative Report 8: 314–332.

Hatfield, Elaine. 1988. "Passionate and Companionate Love." In *The Psychology of Love*, Robert J. Sternberg and Michael L. Barnes, eds. New Haven, CT: Yale University Press.

Hatfield, Elaine, Lisamarie Bensman, and Richard L. Rapson. 2012. "A Brief History of Social Scientists' Attempts to Measure Passionate Love." *Journal of Social and Personal Relationships* 29(2): 143–164.

Hawkins, Alan J., Steven L. Nock, Julia C. Wilson, Laura Sanchez, and James D. Wright. 2002. "Attitudes about Covenant Marriage and Divorce: Policy Implications from a Three-Stage Comparison." *Family Relations* 51: 166–175.

Hawkins, Alan J., Brian J. Willoughby, and William J. Doherty. 2012. "Reasons for Divorce and Openness to Marital Reconciliation." *Journal of Divorce & Remarriage* 53(6): 453–463.

Hawkins, Daniel N., Paul R. Amato, and Valarie King. 2007. "Nonresident Father Involvement and Adolescent Well-being: Father Effects or Child Effects?" *American Sociological Review* 72(6): 990–1010.

Hawthorne, Bruce, and C.J. Lennings. 2008. "The Marginalization of Nonresident Fathers: Their Postdivorce Roles." *Journal of Divorce & Remarriage* 49(3/4): 191–209.

Hayashi, Aiko. 2009. "Japanese Women Shun the Pill." Associated Press. 11 February. Retrieved 24 April 2010 from CBSNews.com (www.cbsnews.com/2100-204_162-637523.html).

Hays, Sharon. 2001. "The Mommy Wars: Ambivalence, Ideological Work, and the Cultural Contradictions of Motherhood," pp. 305–23 in *Shifting the Center: Understanding Contemporary Families, 2nd ed.*, Susan J. Ferguson, ed., Mountain View, CA: Mayfield Publishing Company.

He, Wan, Manisha Sengupta, Victoria A. Velkoff, and Kimberly A. DeBarros. 2005. *65+ in the United States: 2005*. Current Population Reports: Special Studies. P23-209. December. Washington, DC: U.S. Census Bureau.

Health Behavior News Service. 2007. "Depressed People Gain More from Being Married." *Center for the Advancement of Health. Medical News Today*. 9 June. Retrieved 25 June 2008 (www.medicalnewstoday.com/articles/73661.php).

Hefling, Kimberly. 2004. "Benefits Cited as More US Women Over 40 Give Birth." The Associated Press. *The Oregonian*, 27 November, p. A-2.

Hegarty, Kelsey L., Lorna J. O'Doherty, Patty Chondros, Jodie Valpied, Angela J. Taft, Jill Astbury, Stephanie J. Brown, Lisa Gold, Ann Taket, Gene S. Feder, and Jane M. Gunn. 2013. "Effect of Type and Severity of Intimate Partner Violence on Women's Health and Service Use: Findings from a Primary Care Trial of Women Afraid of Their Partners." *Journal of Interpersonal Violence* 28(2): 273–294.

Helgeson, Vicki S. 2012. *Psychology of Gender, 4th ed.* Boston, MA: Pearson.

Helms, Heather M., Christine M. Proulx, Mary Maguire Klute, Susan M. McHale, and Ann M. Crouter. 2006. "Spouses' Gender-typed Attributes and Their Links with Marital Quality: A Pattern-analytic Approach." *Journal of Social and Personal Relationships* 23 (December): 843–864.

Helpguide.org. 2010. "Assisted Living Facilities for Seniors: Exploring Services and Options." Retrieved 26 April 2010 (Helpguide.org/elder/assisted_living_facilities.htm).

Hendrick, Susan S., and Clyde Hendrick. 1992. *Romantic Love*. Newbury Park, CA: Sage.

Henretta, John C., Matthew F. Van Voorhis, and Beth J. Soldo. 2013. "Parental Money Help to Children and Stepchildren." *Journal of Family Issues* (in press).

Henrich, Joseph, Robert Boyd, and Peter J. Richerson. 2012. "The Puzzle of Monogamous Marriage." *Philosophical Transactions of the Royal Society B: Biological Sciences*. 367(1589): 657–669.

The Henry J. Kaiser Family Foundation. 2012. "Health Care Costs: A Primer." May.

—. 2012. 2012a and 2012b. "Medicare at a Glance." 14 November. Retrieved 1 June 2013 (kff.org/medicare/fact-sheet/medicare-at-a-glance-fact-sheet).

—. 2012. "The Uninsured and the Difference Health Insurance Makes." 1 September. Retrieved 22 December 2013 (kff.org/health-reform/fact-sheet/the-uninsured-and-the-difference-health-insurance).

—. 2013. "Summary of the Affordable Care Act." 25 April. Retrieved 22 December 2013 (kff.org/health-reform/fact-sheet/summary-of-new-health-reform-law).

Henry, Pamela J., and James McCue. 2009. "The Experience of Nonresidential Stepmothers." *Journal of Divorce & Remarriage* 50(3): 185–205.

Herbenick, Debby. 2009. "Unrequited Love and Lust: When the One You Want Doesn't Want You Back." Retrieved 8 February 2010. *Psychology Today* (www.psychologytoday.com/blog/the-pleasures-sex/200911/unrequited-love-and-lust-when-the-one-you-want-doesn-t-want-you-back).

Herbenick, Debby, Michael Reece, Vanessa Schick, Stephanie A. Sanders, Brian Dodge, and J. Dennis Fortenberry. 2010. "Sexual Behavior in the United States: Results from a National Probability Sample of Men and Women Ages 14–94." *The Journal of Sexual Medicine* 7(s5): 255–265.

Hernandez, Daphne C., and Emily Pressler. 2013. "Maternal Union Transitions and Household Food Insecurity: Differences by Race and Ethnicity." *Journal of Family Issues* 34(3): 373–393.

Hertz, Rosanna, and Nancy L. Marshall. 2001. *Working Families: The Transformation of the American Home.* Berkeley, CA: University of California Press.

Heslin, Kevin C., Alison B. Hamilton, Trudy K. Singzon, James L. Smith, and Nancy Lois Ruth Anderson. 2011. "Alternative Families in Recovery: Fictive Kin Relationships among Residents of Sober Living Homes." *Qualitative Health Research* 21(4): 477–488.

Hetherington, E. Mavis and John Kelly. 2003. *For Better or Worse: Divorce Reconsidered.* New York, NY: W.W. Norton and Co.

Hewitt, Belinda. 2009. "Which Spouse Initiates Marital Separation When There Are Children Involved?" *Journal of Marriage and Family* 71(2): 362–372.

Hewitt, Belinda, Mark Western, and Janeen Baxter. 2006. "Who Decides? The Social Characteristics of Who Initiates Marital Separation." *Journal of Marriage and Family* 68: 1165–1177.

Heyman, Richard E., and Amy M. Smith Slep. 2002. "Do Child Abuse and Interparental Violence Lead to Adulthood Family Violence?" *Journal of Marriage and Family* 64: 864–870.

Higgenbotham, Brian, Linda Skogrand, and Eliza Torres. 2010. "Stepfamily Education: Perceived Benefits for Children." *Journal of Divorce & Remarriage* 51(1): 36–49.

Hildreth, Carolyn J., Alison E. Burke, and Richard M. Glass. 2009. "Elder Abuse." *Journal of the American Medical Association* 302(5): 588.

Hill, E. Jeffrey, Chongming Yang, Alan J. Hawkins, and Maria Ferris. 2004. "A Cross-cultural Test of the Work/Family Interface in 48 Countries." *Journal of Marriage and Family* 17: 1300–1316.

Hill, Reuben. 1958. "Generic Features of Families Under Stress." *Social Casework* 49: 139–150.

Hill, Shirley A. 2005. *Black Intimacies.* Lanham, MD: AltaMira Press.

—. 2002. "Teaching and Doing Gender in African American Families." *Sex Roles* 47(11/12): 493–506.

Hilton, Jeanne M., and Karen Kopera-Frye. 2007. "Differences in Resources Provided by Grandparents in Single and Married Parent Families." *Journal of Divorce & Remarriage* 47(1/2): 33–54.

Hines, Melissa. 2005. *Brain Gender.* New York, NY: Oxford University Press.

Hirayama, Ryo and Alexis J. Walker. 2011. "When a Partner Has a Sexual Problem: Gendered Implications for Psychological Well-being in Later Life." *The Journals of Gerontology Series B: Psychological Sciences and Social Sciences* 66B(6): 804–813.

Hite, Shere. 1977. *The Hite Report.* New York, NY: Dell.

Ho, Victoria M. and Stephanie A. Sussman. 2008. "Appellate Court Trends in Permanent Alimony for 'Gray Area' Divorces: 1997–2007." *Florida Bar Journal* 82 (4, April): 45.

Hochschild, Arlie. 1989. *The Second Shift: Working Parents and the Revolution at Home.* New York, NY: Viking.

Hock, Roger R. 2012. *Human Sexuality, 3rd ed.* Boston, MA: Pearson.

Hoffnung, Michele. 2006. "What's in a Name? Marital Name Choice Revisited." *Sex Roles* 55(11–12): 817–825.

Hofstede, Geert, and Gert-Jan Hofstede. 2004. *Cultures and Organizations: Software of the Mind.* New York, NY: McGraw-Hill.

Hollist, Cody S., and Miller, Richard B. 2005. "Perceptions of Attachment Style and Marital Quality in Midlife Marriage." *Family Relations* 54(1): 46–57.

Holmberg, Diane, Karen L. Blair, and Maggie Phillips. 2010. "Women's Sexual Satisfaction as a Predictor of Well-being in Same-sex versus Mixed-sex Relationships." *Journal of Sex Research* 47(1): 1–11.

Holmes, Thomas H., and Richard H. Rahe. 1967. "The Social Readjustment Rating Scale." *Journal of Psychosomatic Research* 11: 213–218.

Honore, Carl. 2008. *Under Pressure: Rescuing Our Children from the Culture of Hyperparenting.* London: Orion Publishing.

Hook, Jennifer L., and Satvika Chalasani. 2008. "Gendered Expectations? Reconsidering Single Fathers' Child-care Time." *Journal of Marriage and the Family* 70(4): 978–990.

Hooyman, Nancy, and H. Asuman Kiyak. 2011. *Social Gerontology: A Multidisciplinary Perspective, 9th ed.* Boston, MA: Pearson.

Hopper, Joseph. 1993. "The Rhetoric of Motives in Divorce." *Journal of Marriage and the Family* 55: 801–813.

Horn, Wade F., and Tom Sylvester. 2006. "Father Facts: Research Notes." National Fatherhood Initiative, Fatherhood Online. Retrieved 16 July 2006 (www.fatherhood.org/fatherfacts_rsh.asp).

Hostetler, Andrew J., Stephan Desrochers, Kimberly Kopko, and Phyllis Moen. 2012. "Marital and Family Satisfaction as a Function of Work-Family Demands and Community Resources: Individual- and Couple-level Analyses." 33(3): 316–340.

Houseknecht, Sharon K. and Jaya Sastry. 1996. "Family 'Decline' and Child Well-being: A Comparative

Assessment." *Journal of Marriage and the Family* 58: 726–739.

Houser, Ari N. 2007. "Long-Term Care Trends: Women and Long-Term Care Research Report." Retrieved 19 March 2008 (www.aarp.org/research/longtermcare/trends/fs77r_ltc.html).

Howden, Lindsay M., and Julie A. Meyer. 2011. "Age and Sex Composition: 2010." 2010 Census Briefs C2010BR-03. May. Washington, DC: U.S. Census Bureau.

Hu, Mandy. 2005. *Selling Us Short: How Social Security Privatization Will Affect Lesbian, Gay, Bisexual, and Transgender Americans*. Washington, DC: National Gay and Lesbian Task Force Policy Institute.

Huang, Grace S. 2002. "TANF Reauthorization and Its Effects on Asian and Pacific Islander Families" (Policy Paper). *Asian & Pacific Islander Institute on Domestic Violence*. October. Retrieved 28 August 2008 (www.apiahf. org/apidvinstitute/ResearchAndPolicy/Policypaper.htm).

Huggins, Sharon L. 1989. "A Comparative Study of Self-esteem of Adolescent Children of Divorced Lesbian Mothers and Divorced Heterosexual Mothers." *Journal of Homosexuality* 18(1/2): 123–135.

Hughes, Diane, and Deborah Johnson. 2001. "Correlates in Children's Experiences of Parents' Racial Socialization Behaviors."*Journal of Marriage and Family* 63(4): 981–995.

Hughes, Mary Elizabeth, and Linda J. Waite. 2009. "Marital Biography and Health at Mid-life." *Journal of Health and Social Behavior* 50(3): 344–358.

Human Rights Campaign. 2009a. "Parenting Laws: Joint Adoption." Retrieved 2 March 2010 (www.hrc.org/ state_laws).

—. 2009b. "Parenting Laws: Second Parent Adoption." Retrieved 2 March 2010 (www.hrc.org/state_laws).

—. 2012. "Rights and Protections Denied Same-sex Partners." Retrieved 28 May 2013 (preview.hrc.org/ issues/5478.htm).

—. 2013. Home Page. Retrieved 25 February 2013 (www. hrc.org).

Human Rights Watch. 2004a. "Divorced from Justice: Women's Unequal Access to Divorce in Egypt." Retrieved 8 April 2010 (hrw.org/reports/2004/egypt1204/index.htm).

—. 2004b. "Domestic Violence." Retrieved 19 July 2005 (hrw.org/women/domesticviolence.html).

Hunter, Andrea G. 1997. "Counting on Grandmothers: Black Mothers' and Fathers' Reliance on Grandmothers for Parenting Support."*Journal of Family Issues* 18: 251–269.

Hurst, Charles. 2013. *Social Inequality: Forms, Causes, and Consequences, 8th ed.* Boston, MA: Pearson.

Hutchinson, Courtney. 2010. "Faking It? New Sex Study May Rat You Out." ABCNews.go.com. 4 October. Retrieved 2 April 2013 (abcnews.go.com/Health/Sex/ sex-surveys-masturbation-sheets-america/ story?id=11776702#.UVtiLKKR_Tp).

Hutchinson, Susan L., Tamara Afifi, and Stephanie Krause. 2007. "The Family That Plays Together Fares Better." *Journal of Divorce & Remarriage* 46(3): 21–48.

Hyman, Batya. 2000. "The Economic Consequences of Child Sexual Abuse for Adult Lesbian Women." *Journal of Marriage and the Family* 62(1): 199–211.

Hymowitz, Kay, Jason S. Carroll, W. Bradford Wilcox, and Kelleen Kaye. 2013. *Knot Yet: The Benefits and Costs of Delayed Marriage in America*. The National Marriage Project at the University of Virginia, The National Campaign to Prevent Teen and Unplanned Pregnancy, and The Relate Institute.

Ihinger-Tallman, Marilyn, and Kay Pasley. 1987. *Remarriage*. Newbury Park, CA: Sage.

India Today. 2013. "Indians Swear by Arranged Marriages." 4 March. Retrieved 12 April 2013 (indiatoday.intoday.in/ story/indians-swear-by-arranged-marriages/1/252496. html).

Institute for Work & Health. 2010. "Scientific Symposium: The Health Effects of Shift Work: Summary Report." Retrieved 26 February 2013 (www.iwh.on.ca/shift-work-symposium).

Internal Revenue Service. 2009. "EITC Thresholds and Tax Law Updates." Retrieved 4 December 2009 (www.irs.gov/ indivduals/article/0,id=150513,00.html).

—. 2011. "Ten Things to Know about the Child and Dependent Care Credit." IRS Tax Tip 2011-46. 7 March. Retrieved 15 May 2013.

—. 2013. "Topic 602—Child and Dependent Care Credit." 17 January.

International Center for Research on Women. 2012. "Child Marriage Facts and Figures." Retrieved 26 March 2013 (www.icrw.org/child-marriage-facts-and-figures).

Intersex Society of North America. 2008. "How Common Is Intersex?" Retrieved 14 August 2009 (www.isna.org/faq/ frequency).

Irazuzta, Jose E., James E. McJunkin, Kapriel Danadian, Forest Arnold, and Jianliang Zhang. 1997. "Outcome and Cost of Child Abuse." *Child Abuse and Neglect* 21: 751–757.

—. 2008. *Sharing of Housework and Childcare in Contemporary Japan*. 19 September. Division for the Advancement of Women. New York, NY: United Nations.

—. 2013. "Work Environment and Japanese Fathers' Involvement in Child Care." *Journal of Family Issues* 34(2): 250–269.

Ishii-Kuntz, Masako, Katsuko Makino, Kuniko Kato, and Michiko Tsuchiya. 2004. "Japanese Fathers of Preschoolers and Their Involvement in Child Care." *Journal of Marriage and Family* 66 (August): 779–791.

Ispa, Jean M., Mark A. Fine, Linda C. Halgunseth, Scott Harper, JoAnn Robinson, Lisa Boyce, Jeanne Brooks-Gunn, and Christy Brady-Smith. 2004. "Maternal Intrusiveness, Maternal Warmth, and Mother–Toddler Relationship Outcomes: Variations across Low-income Ethnic and Acculturation Groups." *Child Development* 75(6): 1613–1631.

Ivy, Diana K. 2012. *GenderSpeak: Personal Effectiveness in Gender Communication, 5th ed.* Boston, MA: Pearson.

Jalovaara, Marika. 2003. "The Joint Effects of Marriage Partners' Socioeconomic Positions on the Risk of Divorce." *Demography* 40(1): 67–81.

James, Spencer L., and Kevin Shafer. 2012. "Temporal Differences in Remarriage Timing: Comparing Divorce and

Widowhood." *Journal of Divorce & Remarriage* 53(7): 543–558.

Jansen, Mieke, Dimitri Mortelmans, and Laurent Snoeckx. 2009. "Repartnering and (Re)Employment: Strategies to Cope with the Economic Consequences of Partnership Dissolutions." *Journal of Marriage and Family* 71(5): 1271–1293.

Jasinski, Jana L., Jennifer K. Wesely, James D. Wright, and Elizabeth E. Mustaine. 2010. *Hard Lives, Mean Streets: Violence in the Lives of Homeless Women*. Boston, MA: Northeastern.

Jayson, Sharon. 2005. "Hyphenated Names Less-and-Less Used." *USA Today*. 30 May. Retrieved 24 April 2006 (www.usatoday.com/life/2005-05-30-name-change_x.htm).

—. 2008. "Single Moms' Sons Can Succeed, New Research Shows." *USA Today*. 29 August. Indiana Mothers for Custodial Justice. Retrieved 18 April 2010 (imfcj.blogspot.com/2008/08/single-moms-sons-can-succeed-new.html).

Johnson, Christine A., Scott M. Stanley, Norval D. Glenn, Paul R. Amato, Steve L. Nock, Howard J. Markman, and M. Robin Dion. 2002. *Marriage in Oklahoma: 2001 Baseline Statewide Survey on Marriage and Divorce*. Bureau for Social Research. Stillwater, OK: Oklahoma State University.

Johnson, Michael P. 2008. *A Typology of Domestic Violence: Intimate Terrorism, Violent Resistance, and Situational Couple Violence*. Boston, MA: Northeastern University Press.

—. 2009. "Differentiating among Types of Domestic Violence: Implications for Healthy Marriages," pp. 281–297 in *Marriage and Families: Complexities and Perspectives*, H. Elizabeth Peters and Claire Kamp Dush, eds. New York, NY: Columbia University Press.

Johnson, Tallese D. 2008. "Maternity Leave and Employment Patterns of First-time Mothers: 1961–2003." Current Population Reports. P70-113. February. Washington, DC: U.S. Census Bureau.

Jones, Jo. 2008. *Adoption Experiences of Women and Men and Demand for Children to Adopt by Women 18–44 Years of Age in the United States, 2002*. Vital and Health Statistics No. Series 23, Number 27. August. Atlanta, GA: Centers for Disease Control and Prevention.

Joshi, Suchi Pradyumn, Jochen Peter, and Patti M. Valkenburg, 2013. "A Cross-cultural Content-analytic Comparison of the Hookup Culture in U.S. and Dutch Teen Girl Magazines." *Journal of Sex Research* Retrieved 27 March 2013 (www.tandfonline.com/doi/full/10.1080/00224499.2012.740521).

Joyner, Kara, and J. Richard Udry. 2000. "You Don't Bring Me Anything but Down: Adolescent Romance and Depression." *Journal of Health and Social Behavior* 41 (December): 369–391.

Jung Jang, Soo, Allison Zippay, and Rhokeun Park. 2012. "Family Roles as Moderators of the Relationship between Schedule Flexibility and Stress." *Journal of Marriage and Family* 74(4): 897–912.

Kaczynski, Karen J., Kristin M. Lindahl, Neena M. Malik, and Jean-Philippe Laurenceau. 2006. "Marital Conflict, Maternal and Paternal Parenting, and Child Adjustment: A Test of Mediation and Moderation." *Journal of Family Psychology* 20(2): 199–208.

Kageyama, Y. 1999. "A Tale of Two Drugs Irks Japan's Women." The Oregonian, 11 February: A–6.

Kahlenberg, Susan G., and Michelle M. Hein. 2010. "Progression on Nickelodeon? Gender-role Stereotypes in Toy Commercials." *Sex Roles*. 62(11–12): 830–847.

Kaiser Commission on Medicaid and the Uninsured. 2009. *The Uninsured: A Primer: Key Facts about Americans without Health Insurance*. Washington, DC: The Henry J. Kaiser Family Foundation.

Kaiser Commission on Medicaid and the Uninsured. 2012. "The Uninsured and the Difference Health Insurance Makes." 1 September. Retrieved 22 December 2013 (kff.org/health-reform/fact-sheet/the-uninsured-and-the-difference-health-insurance).

Kaiser Family Foundation and Health Research & Educational Trust. 2009. *Employer Health Benefits: 2009 Summary of Findings*.

Kaleidoscope. 2003. "Latinos/Hispanics." Retrieved 30 June 2008 (cnnc.uncg.edu/pdfs/latinoshispanics.pdf).

Kalil, Ariel, and Kathleen M. Ziol-Guest. 2008. "Parental Employment Circumstances and Children's Academic Progress." *Social Science Research* 37(2): 500–515.

Kallen, Craig G. 2008. "How to Save on the Cost of a Divorce." *Woman's Divorce*. Retrieved 23 December 2008 (www.womansdivorce.com/cost-of-a-divorce.html).

Kalmijn, Matthijs. 2013. "Adult Children's Relationships with Married Parents, Divorced Parents, and Stepparents: Biology, Marriage, and Residence?" *Journal of Marriage and Family* 75(5): 1181–1193.

Kalmijn, Matthijs, and Paul M. De Graaf. 2012. "Life Course Changes of Children and Well-being of Parents." *Journal of Marriage and Family* 74(2): 269–280.

Kamerman, Sheila, and Shirley Gatenio. 2002. "Tax Day: How Do America's Child Benefits Compare?" In *Issue Brief*. Retrieved 15 July 2002. Columbia University/The Clearinghouse on International Developments in Child, Youth, & Family Policies (www.childpolicyintl.org/issuebrief/issuebrief4.htm).

Kamp Dush, Claire M. "Marital and Cohabitation Dissolution and Parental Depressive Symptoms in Fragile Families." *Journal of Marriage and Family* 75(1): 91–109.

Kann, Laura, Richard Lowry, Danice Eaton, and Howell Wechsler. 2012. "Trends in HIV-Related Risk Behaviors among High School Students—United States, 1991–2011." *Morbidity and Mortality Weekly Report* 61(29): 556–560.

Kapinus, Carolyn A., and Daniel R. Flowers. 2008. "An Examination of Gender Differences in Attitudes toward Divorce." *Journal of Divorce & Remarriage* 49(3/4): 239–257.

Karoly, Lynn A., M. Rebecca Kilburn, and Jill S. Cannon. 2005. "Early Childhood Interventions: Proven Results, Future Promise." Retrieved 3 May 2010. Rand Corporation (www.rand.org/publications/MG/MG341).

Karraker, Amelia, and John DeLamater. 2013. "Past-year Sexual Inactivity among Older Married Persons and Their Partners." *Journal of Marriage and Family* 75(1): 142–163.

Karraker, Amelia, John DeLamater, and Christine R. Schwartz. 2011. "Sexual Frequency Decline from Midlife to Later Life." *The Journals of Gerontology Series B: Psychological Sciences and Social Sciences* 66B(4): 502–512.

Karraker, Meg Wilkes. 2008. *Global Families*. Boston, MA: Allyn & Bacon.

Kaschak, Ellyn. 2002. *Intimate Betrayal: Domestic Violence in Lesbian Relationships*. New York, NY: Routledge.

Katz, Elana. 2007. "A Family Therapy Perspective on Mediation." *Family Process* 46: 93–107.

Kaufman, Alan S. 2009. *IQ Testing 101*. New York, NY: Springer Publishing Co.

Kaufman, Gayle and Hiromi Taniguchi. 2006. "Gender and Marital Happiness in Later Life." *Journal of Family Issues* 27: 737–757.

Keizer, Renske and Niels Schenk. 2012. "Becoming a Parent and Relationship Satisfaction: A Longitudinal Dyadic Perspective." *Journal of Marriage and Family* 74(4): 759–773.

Kelly, Joan B. 2007. "Children's Living Arrangements Following Separation and Divorce: Insights from Empirical and Clinical Research." *Family Process* 46(1): 35–52.

Kelly, Melissa. 2008. "Active Listening: Steps and Instructions." About.com. Retrieved 28 September 2008 (712educators.About.com/cs/activelistening/a/activelistening_2.htm).

Kelly, Maura. 2009. "Women's Voluntary Childlessness: A Radical Rejection of Motherhood?" *WSQ: Women's Studies Quarterly* 37(3–4): 157–172.

Kemp, Candace L. 2007. "Grandparent–Grandchild Ties." *Journal of Family Issues* 28(7): 855–881.

Kendig, Sarah M., and Suzanne M. Bianchi. 2008. "Single, Cohabitating, and Married Mothers' Time with Children." *Journal of Marriage and Family* 70(5): 1228–1240.

Kenney-Benson, Gwen A., Eva M. Pomerantz, Allison M. Ryan, and Helen Patrick. 2006. "Sex Differences in Math Performance: The Role of Children's Approach to Schoolwork." *Developmental Psychology* 42(1): 11–26.

Kim, Janna L., C. Lynn Sorsoli, Katherine Collins, Bonnie A. Zylbergold, Deborah Schooler, and Deborah L. Tolman. 2007. "From Sex to Sexuality: Exposing the Heterosexual Script on Primetime Network Television." *The Journal of Sex Research* 44(2): 145–157.

Kim, Jinseok and Karen A. Gray. 2008. "Leave or Stay? Battered Women's Decision after Intimate Partner Violence." *Journal of Interpersonal Violence* 23(10): 1465–1482.

Kimball, Michele. 2013. "Poll: Most Marriages Are Happy." Divorce360.com. Retrieved 15 April 2013 (www.divorce360.com/divorce-articles/statistics/us/poll-most-marriages-are-happy.aspx?artid=268).

Kimmel, Michael S. 2008. *Guyland: The Perilous World in Which Boys Become Men*. New York, NY: Harper Collins.

—. 2006 *Manhood in America: A Cultural History, 2nd ed.* New York, NY: Oxford University Press.

King, Valarie, Kathleen Mullan Harris, and Holly E. Heard. 2004. "Racial and Ethnic Diversity in Nonresident Father Involvement." *Journal of Marriage and Family* 66(1): 1–21.

Kinsella, Kevin, and Wan He. 2009. *An Aging World: 2008.* U.S. Census Bureau, International Population Reports No. P95/09-1. Washington, DC: U.S. Government Printing Office.

Kinsey, Alfred, Wardell B. Pomeroy, and Clyde E. Martin. 1948. *Sexual Behavior in the Human Male*. Philadelphia, PA: Saunders.

—. 1953. *Sexual Behavior in the Human Female*. Philadelphia, PA: Saunders.

Kinsey Institute. 2012. "Frequently Asked Sexuality Questions to The Kinsey Institute." Retrieved 5 April 2013 (www.kinseyinstitute.org/resources/FAQ.html#relation).

Kishor, Sunita. 2005. "Domestic Violence Measurement in Demographic and Health Surveys: The History and the Challenges." UN Division for the Advancement of Women in collaboration with the Economic Commission for Europe and the World Health Organization (www.un.org/womenwatch/daw/egm/vaw-stat-2005/docs/expert-papers/Kishor.pdf).

Kjellstrand, Elizabeth K., and Melanie Harper. 2012. "Yes, She Can: An Examination of Resiliency Factors in Middle- and Upper-income Single Mothers." *Journal of Divorce & Remarriage* 53(4): 311–327.

Klein, Wendy, Anthony P. Graesch, and Carolina Izquierdo. 2009. "Children and Chores: A Mixed-Methods Study of Children's Household Work in Los Angeles Families." *Anthropology of Work Review* XXX(3): 98–109.

Kneip, Thorsten, and Gerrit Bauer. 2009. "Did Unilateral Divorce Laws Raise Divorce Rates in Western Europe?" *Journal of Marriage and Family* 71(3): 592–607.

Knight, George P., Cady Berkel, Adriana J. Umaña-Taylor, Nancy A. Gonzales, Idean Ettekal, Maryanne Jaconis, and Brenna M. Boyd. 2011. "The Familial Socialization of Culturally Related Values in Mexican American Families." *Journal of Marriage and Family* 73(5): 913–925.

Knobloch-Fedders, Lynne M., and Roger M. Knudson. 2009. "Marital Ideals of the Newly-Married: A Longitudinal Analysis." *Journal of Social and Personal Relationships* 26(2–3): 249–271.

Koball, Heather, and Desiree Principe. 2002. March. *Do Nonresident Fathers Who Pay Child Support Visit Their Children More?* New Federalism: National Survey of America's Families No. Series B, No. B-44. The Urban Institute.

Kochanska, Grazyna, and Sanghag Kim. 2012. "Early Attachment Organization with Both Parents and Future Behavior Problems: From Infancy to Middle Childhood." *Child Development* 84(1): 283–296.

Koerner, Ascan F., and Mary Anne Fitzpatrick. 2002. "Nonverbal Communication and Marital Adjustment and Satisfaction: The Role of Decoding Relationship Relevant and Relationship Irrelevant Affect." *Communication Monographs* 69: 33–51.

Koerner, Susan Silverberg, Stephanie L. Jacobs, and Meghan Raymond. 2004. "When Mothers Turn to Their Adolescent Daughters: Predicting Daughters' Vulnerability to Negative Adjustment Outcomes." *Family Relations* 49(3): 301–309.

Kohn, Melvin L. 1977. *Class and Conformity: A Study in Values, 2nd ed.* Chicago, IL: University of Chicago Press.

—. 2006. *Change and Stability: A Cross-National Analysis of Social Structure and Personality*. Boulder, CO: Paradigm Publishers.

Kontula, Osmo, and Elina Haavio-Mannila. 2009. "The Impact of Aging on Human Sexual Activity and Sexual Desire." *Journal of Sex Research* 46(1): 46–56.

Kopecky, Courtney C., and William G. Powers. 2002. "Relational Development and Self-Image Communication Accuracy." *Communication Research Reports* 19(3): 283–290.

Korn, Peter. 2010. "Natural Birth? Nope, C-Section Rates on Rise." Retrieved 2 March 2010 (www.portlandtribune.com/news/story.php?story_id=126644252863826200).

Koropeckyj-Cox, Tanya. 2002. "Beyond Parental Status: Psychological Well-being in Middle & Old Age." *Journal of Marriage and Family* 64: 957–971.

—. 2008. "Loneliness in Later Life," pp. 229–32 in *Encyclopedia of the Life Course and Human Development*, Deborah S. Carr and Amy M. Pienta, eds. Farmington Hills, MI: Thomson/Gale.

Koropeckyj-Cox, Tanya, and Vaughn Call. 2007. "Characteristics of Childless Older Persons and Parents: Cross-National Comparisons." *Journal of Family Issues* 28: 1362–1414.

Koropeckyj-Cox, Tanya, and Gretchen Pendell. 2007a. "Attitudes about Childlessness in the United States." *Journal of Family Issues* 28(8): 1054–1082.

—. 2007b. "The Gender Gap in Attitudes about Childlessness in the United States." *Journal of Marriage and Family* 69(4): 899–915.

Koropeckyj-Cox, Tanya, Amy Mehraban Pienta, and Tyson H. Brown. 2007. "Women of the 1950s and the 'Normative' Life Course: The Implications of Childlessness, Fertility Timing, and Marital Status for Psychosocial Well-being in Late Midlife." *International Journal of Aging and Human Development* 64: 299–330.

Koropeckyj-Cox, Tanya, Victor Romano, and Amanda Moras. 2007. "Through the Lenses of Gender, Race, and Class: Students' Perceptions of Childless/Childfree Individuals and Couples." *Sex Roles* 56(7–8): 415–428.

Koss, Mary P., and Sarah L. Cook. 1993. "Facing the Facts: Date and Acquaintance Rape Are Significant Problems for Women." In *Current Controversies in Family Violence*, Richard J. Gelles and Donileen R. Loseke, eds. Newbury Park, CA: Sage.

Koss, Mary P., Christine Gidycz, and Nadine Wisniewski. 1987. "The Scope of Rape: Incidence and Prevalence in a National Sample of Higher Education Students." *Journal of Consulting and Clinical Psychology* 55: 162–170.

Knodel, John, Vu Manh Loi, Rukmalie Jayakody, and Vu Tuan Huy. 2004 May. Gender Roles in the Family: Change and Stability in Vietnam. PSC Research Report 04-559. May. Ann Arbor, MI: Population Studies Center at the Institute for Social Research, University of Michigan.

Krantz-Kent, Rachel. 2009. "Measuring Time Spent in Unpaid Household Work: Results from the American Time Use Survey." *Monthly Labor Review* 132(7): 46–59.

Kreager, Derek A., and Jeremy Staff. 2009. "The Sexual Double Standard and Adolescent Peer Acceptance." *Social Psychology Quarterly* 72(2): 143–164.

Kreider, Rose M. 2008. "Improvements to Demographic Household Data in the Current Population Survey: 2007, Housing and Household Statistics Working Paper." Retrieved 24 May 2013 (www.census.gov/population/www/documentation/twps08/twps08.pdf).

Kreider, Rose M., and Diana B. Elliott. 2009. "America's Families and Living Arrangements: 2007." Current Population Reports. P20-561. September. Washington, DC: U.S. Census Bureau.

Kreider, Rose M., and Renee Ellis. 2011. "Living Arrangements of Children: 2009." Current Population Reports. P70-126. June. Washington, DC: U.S. Census Bureau.

Kriss, Alex, Howard Steele, and Miriam Steele. 2012. "Measuring Attachment and Reflective Functioning in Early Adolescence: An Introduction to the Friends and Family Interview." *Research in Psychotherapy: Psychopathology, Process and Outcome* 15(2): 87–95.

Kristof, Nicholas D., and Sheryl WuDunn. 2009. *Half the Sky: Turning Oppression into Opportunity for Women Worldwide*. New York, NY: Knopf.

Kroska, Amy. 2003. "Investigating Gender Differences in the Meaning of Household Chores and Child Care." *Journal of Marriage and Family* 65(2): 456–473.

Kubicek, Bettina, Christian Korunka, James M. Raymo, and Peter Hoonakker. 2011. "Psychological Well-being in Retirement: The Effects of Personal and Gendered Contextual Resources." *Journal of Occupational Health Psychology* 16(2): 230–246.

Kübler-Ross, Elisabeth. 1969. *On Death and Dying*. New York, NY: Macmillan.

Kurdek, Lawrence A. 1994. "Areas of Conflict for Gay, Lesbian, and Heterosexual Couples: What Couples Argue about Influences Relationship Satisfaction." *Journal of Marriage and the Family* 56: 923–934.

—. 2006. "Differences between Partners from Heterosexual, Gay, and Lesbian Cohabiting Couples." *Journal of Marriage and Family* 68(2): 509–528.

—. 2008. "Change in Relationship Quality for Partners from Lesbian, Gay Male, and Heterosexual Couples." *Journal of Family Psychology* 22(5): 701–711.

—. 2009. "Assessing the Health of a Dyadic Relationship in Heterosexual and Same-sex Partners." *Personal Relationships* 16: 117–127.

La Leche League International. 2004. *The Womanly Art of Breastfeeding, 7th rev. ed*. New York, NY: Plume Publishing.

Labov, William. 1972. *Language in the Inner City*. Philadelphia, PA: University of Pennsylvania Press.

Labov, William. 1966. *The Social Stratification of English in New York City*. Washington, DC: Center for Applied Linguistics.

Lacey, Krim K., Melnee Dilworth McPherson, Preethy S. Samuel, Karen Powell Sears, and Doreen Head. 2013. "The Impact of Different Types of Intimate Partner Violence on the Mental and Physical Health of Women in Different Ethnic Groups." *Journal of Interpersonal Violence* 28(2): 359–385.

Lachance-Grzela, Mylene, and Amanda G. Bouchard. 2010. "Why Do Women Do the Lion's Share of the Housework? A Decade of Research." *Sex Roles* 63(11–12): 767–780.

Lamb, Kathleen A. 2007. "'I Want to Be Just Like Their Real Dad.'" *Journal of Family Issues* 28(9): 1162–1188.

Lampard, Richard, and Kay Peggs. 1999. "Repartnering: The Relevance of Parenthood and Gender to Cohabitation and Remarriage among the Formerly Married." *The British Journal of Sociology* 50: 443–465.

Lane, Shelley D., Ruth Anna Abigail, and John Gooch. 2014. *Communication in a Civil Society.* Boston, MA: Pearson.

Lane, Shelley D. 2010. *Interpersonal Communication: Competence and Contexts*, 2e. (Table 11.2, p. 290). Boston, MA: Allyn & Bacon.

Langer, Gary, Cheryl Arnedt, and Dalia Sussman. 2004. "Primetime Live Poll: American Sex Survey." Retrieved 9 June 2007 (abcnews.go.com/print?id=156921).

Lantz, Herman, Jane Keyes, and Martin Schultz. 1975. "The Family in the Preindustrial Period: From Base Lines in History to Change." *American Sociological Review* 40(February): 21–36.

LaPierre, Tracey A. 2009. "Marital Status and Depressive Symptoms over Time: Age and Gender Variations." *Family Relations* 58(4): 404–416.

Lareau, Annette. 2003. *Unequal Childhoods: Class, Race, and Family Life.* Berkeley, CA: University of California Press.

Lareau, Annette, and Dalton Conley, eds. 2008. *Social Class: How Does It Work?* New York, NY: Sage.

LaRossa, Ralph. 2011. *Of War and Men: World War II in the Lives of Fathers and Their Families.* Chicago, IL: University of Chicago.

Larsen, Christian Albrekt. 2006. *The Institutional Logic of Welfare Attitudes: How Welfare Regimes Influence Public Support.* Hampshire, UK: Ashgate Publishing, Ltd.

Larzelere, Robert E., Amanda Sheffield Morris, and Amanda W. Harrist. 2012. *Authoritative Parenting: Synthesizing Nurturance and Discipline for Optimal Child Development.* Washington, DC: American Psychological Association.

Laslett, Peter. 1971. *The World We Have Lost.* New York, NY: Charles Scribner's Sons.

Laughlin, Lynda. 2013. "Who's Minding the Kids? Child Care Arrangements: Spring 2011." Household Economic Studies. P70-135. April. Washington, DC: U.S. Census Bureau.

—. 2011. "Maternity Leave and Employment Patterns of First-time Mothers: 1961–2008." Current Population Reports. P70-128. October. Washington, DC: U.S. Census Bureau.

Laughlin, Lynda, and Joseph Rukus. 2009. "Who's Minding the Kids in the Summer? Child Care Arrangements for Summer 2006." Presented at the Annual Meeting of the Population Association of America, April 30–May 2, 2009, Detroit, MI.

Laumann, Edward O., John H. Gagnon, Robert T. Michael, and Stuart Michaels. 1994. *The Social Organization of Sexuality: Sexual Practices in the United States.* Chicago, IL: University of Chicago Press.

Lavee, Yoav, and Ruth Katz. 2002. "Division of Labor, Perceived Fairness, and Marital Quality: The Effect of Gender Ideology." *Journal of Marriage and Family* 64: 27–39.

Law and Mediation Offices of David L. Price. 2000. "Frequently Asked Questions about Divorce Mediation." Retrieved 10 April 2010 (library.findlaw.com/2000/Aug/1/129039.html).

Layne, Linda L. 2004. *The Mommy Myth: The Idealization of Motherhood and How It Has Undermined All Women.* New York, NY: Free Press.

Le Mare, Lucy, Karyn Audet, and Karen Kurytnik. 2007. "A Longitudinal Study of Service Use in Families of Children Adopted from Romanian Orphanages." *International Journal of Behavioral Development* 31: 242–251.

Leaper, Campbell, and Carly K. Friedman. 2006. "The Socialization of Gender," pp. 561–587 in *The Handbook of Socialization: Theory and Research*, Joan E. Grusec, and Paul D. Hastings, eds. New York, NY: Guilford Press.

Learning Community. 2011. "Tips for Parents: Interracial Families." Retrieved 6 December 2013 (www.thelearningcommunity.us/ResourcesbyFormat/TipsforParents/DiverseFamilies/InterracialFamilies/tabid/466/Default.aspx).

Leder, Sharon, Linda N. Grinstead, and Elisa Torres. 2007. "Grandparents Raising Grandchildren: Stressors, Social Support, and Health Outcomes." *Journal of Family Nursing* 13(3): 333–352.

Lee, Gary R., Marion C. Willets, and Karen Seccombe. 1998. "Widowhood and Depression: Gender Differences." *Research on Aging* 20: 611–630.

Lee, Gary R., and Alfred DeMaris. 2007. "Widowhood, Gender, and Depression." *Research on Aging* 29(1): 56–72.

Lee, Ji Hyun. 2013. "Modern Lessons from Arranged Marriages." NYTimes.com. 18 January. Retrieved 26 March 2013 (www.nytimes.com/2013/01/20/fashion/weddings/parental-involvement-can-help-in-choosing-marriage-partners-experts-say.html?).

Lee, John A. 1973. *The Colors of Love: An Exploration of the Ways of Loving.* Ontario: New Press.

—. 1974. "The Styles of Loving." *Psychology Today*, October: 46–51.

—. 1988. "Love-Styles," pp. 38–67 in *The Psychology of Love*, Robert J. Sternberg and Michael L. Barnes, eds. New Haven, CT: Yale University Press.

Lee, Mei-Yin, Yueh-Chih Chen, Huei-Shyong Wang, and Duan-Rung Chen. 2007. "Parenting Stress and Related Factors in Parents of Children With Tourette Syndrome." *Journal of Nursing Research* 15(3): 165–174.

Lee, Sharon M., and Barry Edmonston. 2005. June. "New Marriages, New Families: U.S. Racial and Hispanic Intermarriage." *Population Bulletin.*

Lee, Vicki L. 2003. "Human Agency." Retrieved 17 June 2005 (www.actusinfo.org/pre-07/human-agency.html).

Lee, Yun-Suk, and Linda J. Waite. 2005. "Husbands' and Wives' Time Spent on Housework: A Comparison of Measures." *Journal of Marriage and Family* 67 (May): 328–336.

Leeder, Elaine. 2004. *The Family in Global Perspective: A Gendered Perspective.* Thousand Oaks, CA: Sage.

Leonhardt, David. 2007. "He's Happier, She's Less So." NYTimes.Com. 26 September. Retrieved 27 September 2007 (www.nytimes.com/2007/09/26/business/26leonhardt.html).

Leopold, Thomas. 2012. "The Legacy of Leaving Home: Long-term Effects of Coresidence on Parent–Child Relationships." *Journal of Marriage and Family* 74(3): 399–412.

Leserman, Jane, and Douglas A. Drossman. 2007. "Relationship of Abuse History to Functional Gastrointestinal Disorders and Symptoms." *Trauma, Violence, & Abuse* 8(3): 331–343.

LeVay, Simon. 1991. "A Difference in Hypothlamic Structure between Heterosexual and Homosexual Men." *Science* 253: 1034–1037.

Levin, Diane E., and Jean Kilbourne. 2008. *So Sexy So Soon: The New Sexualized Childhood and What Parents Can Do to Protect Their Kids.* New York, NY: Ballantine Books.

Lewandowski, Gary, Arthur Aron, Sharon Bassis, and Johnna Kunak. 2006. "Losing a Self-expanding Relationship: Implications for the Self-Concept." *Personal Relationships* 13(3): 317–331.

Lewin, Tamar. 2005a. "3 New Studies Assess Effects of Child Care." *NYTimes.com.* Retrieved 5 January 2010 (www.nytimes.com/2005/11/01/national/01child.html?_r=1&pagewanted=print).

Lewin, Tamar. 2005b. "When Richer Weds Poorer, Money Isn't the Only Difference." 19 May. *NYTimes.com.* Retrieved 15 April 2013 (www.nytimes.com/learning/teachers/featured_articles/20050519thursday.html).

Lewontin, Richard C. 2006. "Confusion about Human Races" (Web Forum Organized by the Social Science Research Council). Retrieved 18 August 2008 (Raceandgenomics.ssrc.org/Lewontin/printable.html).

Liebow, Elliot. 1995. *Tell Them Who I Am: The Lives of Homeless Women.* New York, NY: Penguin.

Lin, I.-Fen. 2008. "Consequences of Parental Divorce for Adult Children's Support of Their Frail Parents." *Journal of Marriage and Family* 70(1): 113–128.

Lindau, Stacy T., L. Philip Schumm, Edward O. Laumann, Wendy Levinson, Colm A. O'Muircheartaigh, and Linda J. Waite. 2007. "A Study of Sexuality and Health among Older Adults in the United States." *New England Journal of Medicine* 357 (23 August): 762–774.

Lindsey, Eric W., Penny R. Cremeens, and Yvonne M. Caldera. 2010. "Gender Differences in Mother–Toddler and Father–Toddler Verbal Initiations and Responses during a Caregiving and Play Context." *Sex Roles* 63(5): 399–411.

Lindsey, Linda. 2011. *Gender Roles: A Sociological Perspective,* 5th ed. Upper Saddle River, NJ: Prentice Hall.

Lino, Mark. 2013. "Expenditures on Children and Families, 2012." U.S. Department of Agriculture, Center for Nutrition Policy and Promotion. Miscellaneous Publication No. 1528-2012.

—. 2012. "Expenditures on Children and Families, 2011." U.S. Department of Agriculture, Center for Nutrition Policy and Promotion. Miscellaneous Publication No. 1528-2011.

Lino, Mark, and Andrea Carlson. 2009. *Expenditures on Children in Families, 2008.* Washington, DC: U.S. Department of Agriculture, Center for Nutrition Policy & Promotion, Publication No. 1528-2008.

Livingston, Gretchen and D'Vera Cohn. 2010. "Childlessness Up among All Women; Down among Women with Advanced Degrees." 25 June. Retrieved 19 February 2013 (www.pewsocialtrends.org/2010/06/25/childlessness-up-among-all-women-down-among-women-with-advanced-degrees).

Living Wage Calculation for Los Angeles County, California. 2013. Retrieved 30 May 2013 (livingwage.mit.edu/counties/06037).

Lloyd, Sally A. 1987. "Conflict in Premarital Relationships: Differential Perceptions of Males and Females." *Family Relations* 36(3): 290–294.

Lloyd, Sally A., April L. Few, and Katherine R. Allen. 2009. *Handbook of Feminist Family Studies.* Thousand Oaks, CA: Sage.

Lobo, Susan, Steve Talbot, and Traci L. Morris. 2010. *Native American Voices, 3rd ed.* Upper Saddle River, NJ: Prentice Hall.

Lockwood, Penelope, Caitlin Burton, and Katelyn Boersma. 2011. "Tampering with Tradition: Rationales Concerning Women's Married Names and Children's Surnames." *Sex Roles* 65(11–12): 827–839.

Lodge, Amy C., and Debra Umberson. 2012. "All Shook Up: Sexuality of Mid- to Later Life Married Couples." *Journal of Marriage and Family* 74(3): 428–443.

Loeb, Susanna, Margaret Bridges, Daphna Bassok, Bruce Fuller, and Russell W. Rumberger. 2007. "How Much Is Too Much? The Influence of Preschool Centers on Children's Social and Cognitive Development." *Economics of Education Review* 26(1): 52–66.

Loeffler, William. 2008. Different Cultures Have a Different Rite of Passage. Pittsburgh Tribune-Review, 13 July.

Lofas, Jeannette. 2005. "Classic Complaints: Normal for the Stepfamily." The Stepfamily Foundation, Inc. Retrieved 17 April 2010 (www.winningstepfamilies.com/ClassicStepfamilyComplaints.html).

Lofquist, Daphne, Terry Lugaila, Martin O'Connell, and Sarah Feliz. 2012. "Households and Families: 2010." 2010 Census Briefs. April. Washington, DC: U.S. Census Bureau.

Logan, T.K., and Robert Walker. 2009. "Partner Stalking." *Trauma, Violence, & Abuse* 10(3): 247–270.

Lopez, Javier, Maria Crespo, and Steven H. Zarit. 2007. "Assessment of the Efficacy of a Stress Management Program for Informal Caregivers of Dependent Older Adults." *The Gerontologist* 47: 205–214.

Lopez-Calva, Luis F., Jamele Rigolini, and Florencia Torche. 2011. "Is There Such Thing as Middle Class Values? Class Differences, Values and Political Orientations in Latin America." November. The World Bank. Policy Research Working Paper No. 5874. Retrieved 7 March 2013 (www-wds.worldbank.org/servlet/WDSContentServer/WDSP/IB/2011/11/08/000158349_20111108082238/Rendered/PDF/WPS5874.pdf).

Lowenstein, Ludwig F. 2005. "Causes and Associated Features of Divorce as Seen by Recent Research." *Journal of Divorce & Remarriage* 42(3/4): 153–171.

—. 2009. "Mediation with Separated Parents: Recent Research, 2002–2007." *Journal of Divorce & Remarriage* 50(4): 233–247.

Lowrey, Annie. 2013. "Raising Minimum Wage Would Ease Income Gap but Carries Political Risks." *NYTimes.com.*

13 February. Retrieved 2 May 2013 (www.nytimes.com/2013/02/13/us/politics/obama-pushes-for-increase-in-federal-minimum-wage.html?_r=0&pagewanted=print).

Luedemann, Marei B., Marion F. Ehrenberg, and Michael A. Hunter. 2006. "Mothers' Discussions with Daughters Following Divorce." *Journal of Divorce & Remarriage* 46(1): 29–55.

Luft, Joe. 1969. "Of Human Interaction." In *Palo Alto*. Cited by Tim Borchers, 1999, Allyn & Bacon. Retrieved 30 June 2008 (www.abacon.com/commstudies/interpersonal/indisclosure.html).

Luft, Joe, and Harry Ingram. 1955. *The Johari Window: A Graphic Model of Interpersonal Awareness.* Proceedings of the Western Training Laboratory in Group Development. Los Angeles, CA: UCLA.

Lundberg, Shelly, Sara McLanahan, and Elaina Rose. 2007. "Child Gender and Father Involvement in Fragile Families." *Demography* 44(118): 79–92.

Luo, Michael. 2009. "Job Woes Exacting a Toll on Family Life." *NYTimes.com*. 12 November. Retrieved 30 December 2009 (www,nytimes.com/2009/11/12/us/12families.html?_r=1&pagewanted=print).

Luo, Ye, Tracey A. LaPierre, Mary Elizabeth Hughes, and Linda J. Waite. 2012. "Grandparents Providing Care to Grandchildren: A Population-based Study of Continuity and Change." *Journal of Family Issues* 33(9): 1143–1167.

Lustig, Myron W., and Jolene Koester. 2010. *Intercultural Competence: Interpersonal Communication Across Culture, 7th ed.* Boston, MA: Pearson.

Maas, Carl, Todd I. Herrenkohl, and Cynthia Sousa. 2008. "Review of Research on Child Maltreatment and Violence in Youth."*Trauma, Violence, & Abuse* 9(1): 56–67.

Macaulay, Ronald K.S. 2005. *Talk That Counts: Age, Gender, and Social Class Differences in Discourse.* New York, NY: Oxford University Press.

Maccoby, Eleanor E. 1998. *The Two Sexes: Growing up Apart, Coming Together.* Cambridge, MA: Harvard University Press.

—. 2007. "Historical Overview of Socialization Research and Theory," pp. 13–41 in *Handbook of Socialization: Theory and Research*, Joan E. Grusec and Paul D. Hastings, eds. New York, NY: The Guilford Press.

Macionis, John. 2013. *Society: The Basics, 12th ed.* Boston, MA: Pearson.

MacNeil, Gordon, Jordan I. Kosberg, Daniel W. Durkin, W. Keith Dooley, Jamie DeCoster, and Gail M. Williamson. 2010. "Caregiver Mental Health and Potentially Harmful Caregiving Behavior: The Central Role of Caregiver Anger." *The Gerontologist* 50(1): 76–86.

Macy, Rebecca J., Mary C. Giattina, Susan L. Parish, and Carmen Crosby. 2010. "Domestic Violence and Sexual Assault Services: Historical Concerns and Contemporary Challenges." *Journal of Interpersonal Violence* 25: 3–32.

Madden, Mary, and Amanda Lenhart. 2006. *Online Dating: Americans Who Are Seeking Romance Use the Internet to Help Them in Their Search, But There Is Still Widespread Public Concern about the Safety of Online Dating.* 5 March. Washington DC: Pew Internet & American Life Project.

Madden, Mary, and Lee Rainie. 2006. *Not Looking for Love: The State of Romance in America.* Pew Internet & American Life Project (http://www.pewinternet.org/Reports/2006/Romance-in-America/Report/Romance-in-America.aspx).

Magnuson, Katherine, and Lawrence M. Berger. 2009. "Family Structure States and Transitions: Associations with Children's Well-being during Middle Childhood." *Journal of Marriage and Family* 71(3): 575–591.

Mahay, Jenna, and Alisa C. Lewin. 2007. (Age and the Desire to Marry). *Journal of Family Issues* 28(5): 706–723.

Maher, Bridget E. 2006. "Why Marriage Should Be Privileged in Public Policy." Retrieved 6 June 2006. Family Research Council (www.frc.org/index.cfm?i=IS03D1).

Maier, Thomas. 2009. *Masters of Sex: The Life and Times of William Masters and Virginia Johnson, the Couple Who Taught America to Love.* New York, NY: Basic Books.

Malernee, Jamie. 2006. "Twenty-somethings' View on Marriage, Family." *Connecticut Post*, 29 October, pp. C1, C6.

Mallinson, Christine, and Robin Dodsworth. 2009. "Revisiting the Need for New Approaches to Social Class in Variationist Sociolinguistics."*Sociolinguistic Studies* 3(2): 253–278.

Mammen, Kristin. 2009. "Fathers' Time Investments in Children: Do Sons Get More?" *Journal of Population Economics* 24(3): 839–871.

Manning, Wendy D. 2013. "Trends in Cohabitation: Over Twenty Years of Change, 1987–2010." FP-13-12. National Center for Family & Marriage Research. Retrieved 30 December 2013 (ncfmr.bgsu.edu/pdf/family_profiles/file130944.pdf).

Manning, Wendy D., Monica A. Longmore, and Peggy C. Giordano. 2007. "The Changing Institution of Marriage: Adolescents' Expectations to Cohabit and to Marry." *Journal of Marriage and Family* 69(3): 559–575.

ManpowerGroup. 2013. "About ManpowerGroup." Retrieved 1 May 2013 (www.manpower.com/About/About.cfm).

Manzoli, Lamberto, Paolo Villari, Giovanni M. Pirone, and Antonio Boccia. 2007. "Marital Status and Mortality in the Elderly: A Systematic Review and Meta-analysis." *Social Science and Medicine* 64: 77–94.

Markey, Charlotte N., and Patrick M. Markey. 2009. "Correlates of Young Women's Interest in Obtaining Cosmetic Surgery." *Sex Roles* 61(3–4): 158–166.

Marlar, Jenny. 2010. "Worry, Sadness, Stress Increase with Length of Unemployment." 8 June. Retrieved 2 May 2013 (www.gallup.com/poll/139604/worry-sadness-stress-increase-length-unemployment.aspx).

Marr, Chuck, Jimmy Charite, and Chye-Ching Huang. 2013. "Earned Income Tax Credit Promotes Work, Encourages Children's Success at School, Research Finds for Children, Research Indicates That Work, Income, and Health Benefits Extend into Adulthood." Center on Budget and Policy Priorities. 9 April. Retrieved 30 May 2013 (www.cbpp.org/cms/index.cfm?fa=view&id=3793).

Marriage Equality USA, 2014. "Polling Data and the Marriage Equality Movement." (www.marriageequality.org/polls-and-studies).

Marriage Movement. 2004. "Can Government Strengthen Marriage? Evidence from the Social Sciences." National

Fatherhood Initiative, Institute for Marriage and Public Policy, and Institute for American Values. Retrieved 5 July 2005 (www.marriagemovement.org/gov/gov_print.htm).

Marsiglio, William. 1992. "Stepfathers with Minor Children Living at Home: Parenting Perceptions and Relationship Quality." *Journal of Family Issues* 13: 195–214.

Marsiglio, William, and Kevin Roy. 2012. *Nurturing Dads: Social Initiatives for Contemporary Fatherhood.* New York, NY: Russell Sage Foundation.

—. 2013. "Fathers' Nurturance of Children Over the Life Course," pp. 353–376 in *Handbook of Marriage and the Family,* Gary Peterson and Kevin Bush, eds. New York, NY: Springer.

Martin, Joyce A., Brady E. Hamilton, Stephanie J. Ventura, Michelle J.K. Osterman, Elizabeth C. Wilson, and T.J. Mathews. 2012. *Births: Final Data for 2010.* National Vital Statistics Reports, Vol. 61, No. 1. 28 August.

Martin, Sandra L., Rebecca J. Macy, Kristen Sullivan, and Melissa L. Magee. 2007. "Pregnancy-Associated Violent Deaths." *Trauma, Violence, & Abuse* 8(2): 135–148.

Martin, Steven P., and Sangeeta Parashar. 2006. "Women's Changing Attitudes toward Divorce, 1974–2002: Evidence for an Educational Crossover." *Journal of Marriage and Family* 68(1): 29–40.

Martin-Uzzi, Michele, and Denise Duval-Tsioles. 2013. "The Experience of Remarried Couples in Blended Families." *Journal of Divorce & Remarriage* 54(1): 43–57.

Martinez, Gladys, Kimberly Daniels, and Anjani Chandra. 2012. "Fertility of Men and Women Aged 15–44 Years in the United States: National Survey of Family Growth, 2006–2010." National Health Statistics Reports No. 51. 12 April. Washington, DC: National Center for Health Statistics.

Marx, Karl, and Friedrich Engels. 1971, original 1867. *Manifesto of the Communist Party.* New York, NY: International Publishers (Original work published 1867).

Mason, Mary Ann, Sydney Harrison-Jay, Gloria Messick Svare, and Nicholas H. Wolfinger. 2002. "Stepparents: De Facto Parents or Legal Strangers?" *Journal of Family Issues* 23(4): 507–522.

Massey, Douglas S., and Nancy A. Denton. 1993. *American Apartheid: Segregation and the Making of the Underclass.* Cambridge, MA: Harvard University Press.

Massey, Douglas S., and Garvey Lundy. 2001. "Use of Black English and Racial Discrimination in Housing Markets." *Urban Affairs Review* 36(4): 452–469.

Masters, N. Tatiana, Erin Casey, Elizabeth A. Wells, and Diane M. Morrison. 2012. "Sexual Scripts among Young Heterosexually Active Men and Women: Continuity and Change." *Journal of Sex Research* Retrieved 27 March 2013 (www.tandfonline.com/doi/full/10.1080/00224499.2012.661102).

Masters, William H., and Virginia E. Johnson. 1966. *Human Sexual Response.* Boston, MA: Little, Brown and Company.

Masuda, Masahiro. 2003. "Meta-analyses of Love Scales: Do Various Love Scales Measure the Same Psychological Constructs?" *Japanese Psychological Research* 45: 25–37.

Matos, Kenneth, and Ellen Galinsky. 2012. "2012 National Study of Employers." New York, NY: Families and Work Institute.

Maynes, Mary Jo and Ann Waltner. 2012. *The Family: A World History.* New York, NY: Oxford University Press.

McCabe, Janice, Karin L. Brewster, and Kathryn Harker Tillman. 2011. "Patterns and Correlates of Same-sex Sexual Activity among U.S. Teenagers and Young Adults." *Perspectives on Sexual and Reproductive Health* 43: 142–151.

McCarthy, Margaret M., Arthur P. Arnold, Gregory F. Ball, Jeffrey D. Blaustein, and Geert J. De Vries. 2012. "Sex Differences in the Brain: The Not So Inconvenient Truth." *The Journal of Neuroscience* 32(7): 2241–2247.

McCool, William F., and Sara A Simeone. 2002. "Birth in the United States: An Overview of Trends Past and Present." *Nursing Clinics of North America* 37(4): 735–746.

McCubbin, Hamilton I., Marilyn A. McCubbin, Anne I. Thompson, Sae-Young Han, and Chad T. Allen. 1997. "Families Under Stress: What Makes Them Resilient." Commemorative Lecture. Washington, DC: AAFCS, 22 June.

McCubbin, Hamilton I. and Joan M. Patterson. 1982. "Family Adaptation to Crisis." In *Family Stress, Coping, and Social Support,* Hamilton I. McCubbin, A. Elizabeth Cauble and Joan M. Patterson, eds. Springfield, IL: Thomas.

McDonald, Steve, Nan Lin, and Dan Ao. 2009. "Networks of Opportunity: Gender, Race, and Job Leads." *Social Problems* 56(3): 385–402.

McFarland, Michael J., Mark D. Hayward, and Dustin Brown. 2013. "I've Got You Under My Skin: Marital Biography and Biological Risk." *Journal of Marriage and Family* 75(2): 363–380.

McGee, Karen. 2008. "How Cultural Differences May Affect Student Performance." GreatSchools Inc. Retrieved 7 October 2013 (www.greatschools.org/special-education/support/704-cultural-differences-student-performance.gs).

McGene, Juliana, and Valarie King. 2012. "Implications of New Marriages and Children for Coparenting in Nonresident Father Families." *Journal of Family Issues* 33(12): 1619–1641.

McLanahan, Sara, and Gary Sandefur. 1994. *Growing Up with a Single Parent: What Hurts, What Helps.* Cambridge, MA: Harvard University Press.

McLoyd, Vonnie C., Ana Mari Cauce, David Takeuchi, and Leon Wilson. 2000. "Marital Processes and Parental Socialization in Families of Color: A Decade Review of Research." *Journal of Marriage and the Family* 62(4): 1070–1093.

McQuillan, Julia, Arthur L. Greil, Karina M. Shreffler, Patricia A. Wonch-Hill, Kari C. Gentzler, and John D. Hathcoat. 2012. "Does the Reason Matter? Variations in Childlessness Concerns among U.S. Women." *Journal of Marriage and Family* 74(5): 1166–1181.

Mead, Margaret. 1935. *Sex and Temperament in Three Primitive Societies.* New York, NY: Morrow.

Medicaid.gov. 2013. "Children's Health Insurance Program (CHIP)." Retrieved 30 May 2013 (www.medicaid.gov/CHIP/CHIP-Program-Information.html).

Medicare.gov. 2013. Home page. Retrieved 1 June 2013 (medicare.gov).

Medora, Nilufer P. 2003. "Mate Selection in Contemporary India," pp. 209–30 in *Mate Selection across Cultures*, Raeann R. Hamon and Bron B. Ingoldsby, eds. Thousand Oaks, CA: Sage.

Mehl, M. R., Vazire, S., Ramirez-Esparza, N., Slatcher, R. B., & Pennebaker, J. W. (2007). *Are women really more talkative than men? Science*, 317, 82.

Megala. 2012. "Some Staggering Statistics about Arranged Marriages in India." Divorce India Organization. Retrieved 26 March 2013 (www.divorceindia.org/some-staggering-arranged-marriage-statistics-from-india/#).

Merriam-Webster Online. 2013. "Love." Retrieved 26 March 2013 (www.merriam-webster.com/dictionary/love).

Merrill, Gary S., and Valerie A. Wolfe. 2000. "Battered Gay Men: An Exploration of Abuse, Help Seeking, and Why They Stay." *Journal of Homosexuality* 39(2): 1–30.

MetLife Mature Market Institute. 2013. *Market Survey of Long-term Care Costs: The 2012 MetLife Market Survey of Nursing Home, Assisted Living, Adult Day Services, and Home Care Costs.*

MetLife. 2006. "Out and Aging: The MetLife Study of Lesbian and Gay Baby Boomers." *MetLife Mature Market Institute*, November. Retrieved 24 April 2013 (www.metlife.com/WPSAssets/15374435731164722885V1F OutandAging.pdf).

Meyer, Cathy. 2013. "How Much Will My Divorce Cost?" About.com. Retrieved 16 May 2013 (divorcesupport. about.com/od/financialissues/f/costofdivorce.htm).

Michael, Kerry C., Aurora Torres, and Eric A. Seemann. 2007. "Adolescents' Health Habits, Coping Styles and Self-Concept Are Predicted by Exposure to Interparental Conflict." *Journal of Divorce & Remarriage* 48(1–2): 155–174.

Michael, Robert T., John Gagnon, Edward O. Laumann, and Gina Kolata. 1994. *Sex in America: A Definitive Survey.* New York, NY: Little, Brown and Company.

Mikulincer, Mario, and Philip R. Shaver. 2007. *Attachment in Adulthood: Structure, Dynamics, and Change.* New York, NY: Guilford Press.

Mildorf, Jarmila. 2007. *Storying Domestic Violence: Constructions and Stereotypes of Abuse in the Discourse of General Practitioners.* Lincoln, NE: University of Nebraska Press.

Miley, Karla Krogsrud, Michael W. O'Melia, and Brenda L. DuBois. 2011. *Generalist Social Work Practice: An Empowering Approach*, 6th ed. Boston, MA: Allyn & Bacon.

Milkie, Melissa A., Marybeth J. Mattingly, Kei M. Nomaguchi, Suzanne M. Bianchi, and John P. Robinson. 2004. "The Time Squeeze: Parental Statuses and Feelings about Time with Children." *Journal of Marriage and Family* 66 (4): 739–761.

Miller, Gerald R., and Mark Steinberg. 1975. *Between People: A New Analysis of Interpersonal Communication.* Chicago, IL: Science Research Associates.

Miller, J. Elizabeth. 2000. "Religion and Families over the Life Course." In *Families across Time: A Life Course Perspective*, Sharon J. Price, Patrick McKenry, and Megan J. Murphy, eds. Los Angeles, CA: Roxbury.

Miller, Nancy B., Virginia L. Smerglia, D. Scott Gaudet, and Gay C. Kitson. 1998. "Stressful Life Events, Social Support, and the Distress of Widowed and Divorced Women." *Journal of Family Issues* 19: 181–203.

Mills, C. Wright. 1959. *The Sociological Imagination.* New York, NY: Oxford University Press.

Mines, Diane P., and Sarah E. Lamb. 2010. *Everyday Life in South Asia.* Bloomington, IN: Indiana University Press.

Minkler, Meredith, and Esme Fuller-Thomson. 2005. "African American Grandparents Raising Grandchildren: A National Study Using the Census 2000 American Community Survey." *Journal of Gerontology* 60B(2): S82–S92.

Mintz, Steven. 2003. "Introduction: The Contemporary Crisis of the Family." Council on Contemporary Families. Retrieved 5 July 2005 (www.contemporaryfamilies.org/public/fact1.php).

—. 2004. *Huck's Raft: A History of American Childhood.* Cambridge, MA: Belknap Press.

Mintz, Steven, and Susan Kellogg. 1989. *Domestic Revolution: A Social History of Family Life.* New York, NY: Free Press.

Mirecki, Rachel M., Jessica L. Chou, Michael Elliott, and Christine M. Schneider. 2013. "What Factors Influence Marital Satisfaction? Differences between First and Second Marriages." *Journal of Divorce & Remarriage* 54: 78–93.

Mishel, Lawrence. 2013. "Declining Value of the Federal Minimum Wage Is a Major Factor Driving Inequality." Issue Brief No. 351. 21 February. Washington, DC: Economic Policy Institute.

Mishel, Lawrence, and Nicholas Finio. 2013. "Earnings of the Top 1.0 Percent Rebound Strongly in the Recovery." Economic Policy Institute. Issue Brief No. 347. 23 January. Retrieved 25 February 2013 (www.epi.org/publication/ib347-earnings-top-one-percent-rebound-strongly).

Mitchell, Katherine Stamps, Alan Booth, and Valarie King. 2009. "Adolescents with Nonresident Fathers: Are Daughters More Disadvantaged than Sons?" *Journal of Marriage and Family* 71(3): 650–662.

Mitterauer, Michael, and Reinhard Sieder. 1982. *The European Family: Patriarchy to Partnership from the Middle Ages to Present.* Chicago, IL: University of Chicago Press.

Monger, George. 2004. *Marriage Customs of the World: From Henna to Honeymoons.* Santa Barbara, CA: ABC-CLIO.

Monserud, Maria A. 2008. "Intergenerational Relationships and Affectual Solidarity between Grandparents and Young Adults." *Journal of Marriage and Family* 70(1): 182–195.

Moon, Michelle. 2011. "The Effects of Divorce on Children: Married and Divorced Parents' Perspectives." *Journal of Divorce & Remarriage* 52(5): 344–349.

Mooney, Carol Garhart. 2009. *Theories of Attachment: An Introduction to Bowlby, Ainsworth, Gerber, Brazelton, Kennell, and Klaus.* St. Paul, MN: Redleaf Press.

Moore, Mignon R. 2004. "Who Wears the Pants? Sources of Power and Conflict in Black and Latina Lesbian Families." Presented at the Annual Meeting of the American Sociological Association, 14 August, San Francisco, CA.

Morgan, Leslie, and Suzanne Kunkel. 1998. *Aging: The Social Context*. Thousand Oaks, CA: Pine Forge Press.

Morin, Rich. 2011. "The Public Renders a Split Verdict on Changes in Family Structure." Pew Research Social & Demographic Trends. 16 February. Retrieved 1 April 2013 (www.pewsocialtrends.org/2011/02/16/the-public-renders-a-split-verdict-on-changes-in-family-structure/?src=family-interactive).

Mossaad, Nadwa. 2010. "The Impact of the Recession on Older Americans." Population Reference Bureau. Retrieved 23 April 2010 (www.prb.org/Articles/2010/recessionolderamericans.aspx).

Motel, Seth, and Eileen Patten. 2013. "Statistical Portrait of Hispanics in the United States, 2011." Pew Hispanic Center. 15 February. Retrieved 3 March 2013 (www.pewhispanic.org/2013/02/15/statistical-portrait-of-hispanics-in-the-united-states-2011).

Muehlenhard, Charlene L., and Sheena K. Shippee. 2009. "Men's and Women's Reports of Pretending Orgasm." *Journal of Sex Research* 25 (August): 1–16.

Mulsow, Miriam, Yvonne M. Caldera, Marta Pursley, Alan Reifman, and Aletha C. Huston. 2002. "Multilevel Factors Influencing Maternal Stress during the First Three Years." *Journal of Marriage and Family* 64(6): 944–956.

Munnell, Alicia H. 2011. "What Is the Average Retirement Age?" No. 11-11. August. Boston, MA: Center for Retirement Research at Boston College.

Murdoch, Stephen. 2007. *IQ: A Smart History of a Failed Idea*. Hoboken, NJ: John Wiley & Sons.

Murkoff, Heidi, and Sharon Mazel. 2008. *What to Expect When You're Expecting*, 4th ed. New York, NY: Workman Publishing.

Murray, Charles. 1988. *In Pursuit of Happiness and Good Government*. New York, NY: Simon and Schuster.

—. 2012. *Coming Apart: The State of White America, 1960–2010*. New York, NY: Crown Forum.

Musick, Kelly, and Larry Bumpass. 2012. "Reexamining the Case for Marriage: Union Formation and Changes in Well-being." *Journal of Marriage and Family* 74(1): 1–18.

Musil, Carol M., Nahida L. Gordon, Camille B. Warner, Jaclene A. Zauszniewski, Theresa Standing, and May Wykle. 2010. "Grandmothers and Caregiving to Grandchildren: Continuity, Change, and Outcomes over 24 Months." *The Gerontologist* 51(1): 86–100.

Myers, Scott M. 2006. "Religious Homogamy and Marital Quality: Historical and Generational Patterns, 1980–1997." *Journal of Marriage and Family* 68(2): 292–304.

Mysistahs.org. 2013. "Story on Dating Violence by Alicia." Advocates for Youth. Retrieved 22 December 2013 (ealert.mysistahs.org/features/datingviolence/story.htm).

Nagae, Miyoko, and Barbara L. Dancy. 2010. "Japanese Women's Perceptions of Intimate Partner Violence (IPV)." *Journal of Interpersonal Violence* 25(4): 753–766.

National Adoption Information Clearinghouse. 2002. "Single Parent Adoption: What You Need to Know." U.S. Department of Health & Human Services: Administration for Children & Families. Retrieved 11 June 2003 (www.calib.com/naic/pubs/factsheets.cfm).

National Alliance for Caregiving and AARP. 2009. *Caregiving in the U.S.: Executive Summary*. November.

National Alliance to End Homelessness. 2013. "Snapshot of Homelessness." Retrieved 26 February 2013 (www.endhomelessness.org/pages/snapshot_of_homelessness).

National Association of Child Care Resource & Referral Agencies. 2009a. "Parent's Perception of Child Care in the United States: NACCRRA's National Parent Poll, January 2009."

—. 2009b. "What Child Care Providers Earn." March. Retrieved 23 December 2009 (www.naccrra.org/randd/child-care-workforce/what-providers-earn).

—. 2011. *Child Care in America: 2011 State Fact Sheets*. July.

National Association of Realtors. 2013. "Research & Statistics." Retrieved 26 February 2013 (www.realtor.org/research-and-statistics).

National Center for Education Statistics. 2012. "The Condition of Education 2012." NCES 2012-045. Washington, DC: U.S. Department of Education.

National Center for Health Statistics. 2009. *Health, United States, 2008: With Chartbook*. Hyattsville, MD.

—. 2010. *Health, United States, 2009: With Special Feature on Medical Technology*. Hyattsville, MD.

—. 2012. *Health, United States, 2011: With Special Feature on Socioeconomic Status and Health*. Hyattsville, MD.

—. 2012. "Summary Health Statistics for U.S. Adults: National Health Interview Survey, 2011." Vital and Health Statistics, Series 10, No. 256. December. Hyattsville, MD.

National Center on Elder Abuse. 2006. *Fact Sheet: Abuse of Adults Aged 60+. 2004 Survey of Adult Protective Services*. Washington, DC.

National Coalition Against Domestic *Violence*. 2011. *Fact Sheets*. Retrieved 26 February 2013 (www.ncadv.org/resources/FactSheets.php).

National Coalition for the Homeless. 2009. "How Many People Experience Homelessness?" Retrieved 9 November 2009 (www.nationalhomeless.org/factsheets/How_Many.html).

National Fatherhood Initiative. 2013. "For The Media: Press Releases." Retrieved 24 April 2013 (www.fatherhood.org/media/press-releases).

National Gay and Lesbian Taskforce. 2007. "Lesbian, Bisexual, and Transgender Female Elders—Women's History Month 2007 Fact Sheet." Retrieved 2 May 2010 (www.thetaskforce.org/downloads/misc/LBTFemaleEldersFactSheet.pdf).

National Heart Lung and Blood Institute. 2009. "At-a-Glance: Asthma."

National Institute of Mental Health. 2009. "Eating Disorders." Retrieved 21 November 2009 (www.nimh.nih.gov/health/topics/eating-disorders/index.html).

National Institute on Media and the Family. 2009. "Fact Sheet: Media's Effect On Girls: Body Image and Gender Identity." Retrieved 16 April 2010 (www.mediafamily.org/facts/facts_mediaeffect.shtml).

National Marriage Project. 2009. "The State of Our Unions: Marriage in America 2009." December

(nationalmarriageproject.org/
wp-content/uploads/2009/12/SOOU2009.pdf).

—. 2012. "The State of Our Unions: Marriage in America 2012." Retrieved 19 February 2013 (www.stateofourunions.org/2012/SOOU2012.pdf).

National Orphan Train Complex. 2013. Home Page. Retrieved 22 April 2013 (orphantraindepot.org).

National Stepfamily Resource Center. 2007. "Frequently Asked Questions." Retrieved 28 September 2007 (www.stepfamiles.info/faqs/faqs.php).

—. 2008. "Home Page." Retrieved 4 September 2008 (www.stepfamilies.info/index.php).

—. 2013. "Home Page." Retrieved 28 December 2013 (www.stepfamilies.info/index.php).

Nationwide Children's Hospital. 2013. "Gun Safety." Retrieved 4 March 2013 (www.nationwidechildren's.org/cirp-gun-safety).

Navarro, Mireya. 2007. "My Child's Divorce Is My Pain." *The New York Times*, 2 September.

NBC News/People Magazine. 2005. "National Survey of Young Teens' Sexual Attitudes and Behaviors." Retrieved 21 June 2007 (www.msnbc.msn.com/id/6839072).

Near, Christopher E. 2013. "Selling Gender: Associations of Box Art Representation of Female Characters with Sales for Teen- and Mature-rated Video Games." *Sex Roles* 68(3–4): 252–269.

Nepomnyaschy, Lenna, and Irwin Garfinkel. 2007. "Child Support, Fatherhood, and Marriage: Findings from the First Five Years of the Fragile Families and Child Well-being Study." *Asian Social Work and Policy Review* 1(1): 1–20.

Neuman, Lawrence W. 2009. *Understanding Research*. Boston, MA: Pearson.

Newberger, Eric C. 1999. "Computer Use in the United States: October 1997." *Current Population Reports*. P20-522. Washington, DC: U.S. Census Bureau.

New York City Gay & Lesbian Anti-Violence Project. 2003. "Building Safer Communities for Lesbian, Gay, Transgender, Bisexual and HIV-Affected New Yorkers."

NHS Knowledge Service. 2009. "Home Birth 'Safe as in Hospital.'" Retrieved 16 December 2009 (www.nhs.uk/news/2009/04April/Pages/HomeBirthSafe.aspx).

NICHD Early Child Care Research Network. 1999. "Study Finds That Child Care Does Impact Mother–Child Interaction" (Press Release for "Child Care and Mother–Child Interaction in the First 3 Years of Life"), Developmental Psychology 35(6): 1399–1413)

—. 2005. "Duration and Developmental Timing of Poverty and Children's Cognitive and Social Development from Birth through Third Grade." *Child Development* 76(4): 795–810.

Nielsen, Linda. 2011. "Shared Parenting after Divorce: A Review of Shared Residential Parenting Research." *Journal of Divorce & Remarriage* 52: 586–609.

—. 2012. *Father-Daughter Relationships: Contemporary Research and Issues*. New York, NY: Routledge.

Nitzky, Alene. 1998. "A Poppy in the Rain." *Runner's World*, 9 April, pp. 22–23.

Nock, Steven L. 1998. *Marriage in Men's Lives*. New York, NY: Oxford University Press.

Nock, Steven L., Laura A. Sanchez, and James D. Wright. 2008. *Covenant Marriage: The Movement to Reclaim Tradition in America*. New Brunswick, NJ: Rutgers University Press.

Nock, Steven L., James D. Wright, and Laura A. Sanchez. 1999. "America's Divorce Problem." *Society* 36: 43–52.

Nokoff, Natalie, and Anne Fausto-Sterling. 2008. "Raising Gender." National Sexuality Resource Center. Retrieved 5 December 2009 (Nsrc.sfsu.edu/article/raising_gender).

Nomaguchi, Kei M. 2009. "Change in Work–Family Conflict among Employed Parents between 1977 and 1997." *Journal of Marriage and Family* 71: 15–32.

—. 2012a. "Parenthood and Psychological Well-being: Clarifying the Role of Child Age and Parent–Child Relationship Quality." *Social Science Research* 41: 489–498.

—. 2012b. "Marital Status, Gender, and Home-to-Job Conflict among Employed Parents." *Journal of Family Issues* 33(3): 271–294.

Nomaguchi, Kei M., and Suzanne M. Bianchi. 2004. "Exercise Time: Gender Differences in the Effects of Marriage, Parenthood, and Employment." *Journal of Marriage and Family* 66: 413–430.

Nomaguchi, Kei M., and Melissa A. Milkie. 2003. "Costs and Rewards of Children: The Effects of Becoming a Parent on Adults' Lives." *Journal of Marriage and Family* 65: 356–374.

Norris, Tina, Paula L. Vines, and Elizabeth M. Hoeffel. 2012. "The American Indian and Alaska Native Population: 2010." 2010 Census Brief. January. Washington, DC: U.S. Census Bureau.

Nye, F. Ivan. 1979. "Choice, Exchange, and the Family," pp. 1–41 in *Contemporary Theories about the Family*, Wesley Burr, Reuben Hill, F. Ivan Nye, and Ira Reiss, eds. New York, NY: Free Press.

O'Hare, William P. 1995. "3.9 Million U.S. Children in Distressed Neighborhoods." *Population Today* 22: 4–5.

Obama, Barack. 2007. *The Audacity of Hope: Thoughts on Reclaiming the American Dream*. New York, NY: Vintage Books.

Obegi, Joseph H., and Ety Berant, eds. 2009. *Attachment Theory and Research in Clinical Work with Adults*. New York, NY: Guilford Press.

Official Journal of the European Communities. 1998. "Council Directive 97/81/EC of 15 December 1997 Concerning the Framework Agreement on Part-Time Work Concluded by UNICE, CEEP and the ETUC." Retrieved 5 January 2010. Eur-Lex (eur-lex.europa.eu/LexUriServ/LexUriServ.do?uri=CELEX:31997L0081:EN:HTML).

Ogunwole, Stella U. 2006. *We the People: American Indians and Alaska Natives in the United States*. Technical Report No. CENSR-28. February. Washington DC: US Census Bureau.

Okechukwu, Cassandra A., Alison M. El Ayadi, Sara L. Tamers, Erika L. Sabbath, and Lisa Berkman. 2012. "Household Food Insufficiency, Financial Strain, Work–Family Spillover, and Depressive Symptoms in the Working Class: the Work, Family, and Health Network Study." *American Journal of Public Health* 102(1): 126–133.

Okun, Barbara F. 2002. *Effective Helping: Interviewing and Counseling Techniques,* 6th ed. Monterey, CA: Brooks/ Cole.

Olsen, Charlotte. 1996. "African American Adolescent Women. Perceptions of Gender, Race, and Class." *Marriage and Family Review* 24(1–2): 107–15.

Olson, Elizabeth G. 2011. "The Rise of the Permanently Temporary Worker." *CNNMoney.* 5 May. Retrieved 26 February 2013 (management.fortune.cnn.com/2011/05/05/ the-rise-of-the-permanently-temporary-worker).

Omariba, D. Walter Rasugu, and Michael H. Boyle. 2007. "Family Structure and Child Mortality in Sub-Saharan Africa: Cross-National Effects of Polygyny." *Journal of Marriage and Family* 69(3): 528–543.

Onion, Amanda. 2005. "Scientists Find Sex Differences in Brain." *ABC News: Technology & Science.* 19 January. Retrieved 23 June 2006 (abcnews.go.com/Technology/ Health/story?id=424260&page=1).

Oppenheimer, Laura. 2008. "Dads Get Off-the-Job Training." *The Oregonian* (Portland, OR), 15 June, pp. A1; A9.

Orenstein, Peggy. 1994. *School Girls.* New York, NY: Anchor Books.

Orshansky, Mollie. 1965. "Counting the Poor: Another Look at Poverty." *Social Security Bulletin* 28: 3–29.

Ortigue, Stephanie, Francesco Bianchi-Demicheli, Nisa Patel, Chris Frum, and James W. Lewis. 2010. "Neuroimaging of Love: fMRI Meta-analysis Evidence toward New Perspectives in Sexual Medicine." *The Journal of Sexual Medicine* 7(11): 3541–3552.

Ortiz, Jesse. 2012. "Assisted Living Facilities." SBDCNet. U.S. Small Business Administration. Retrieved 29 May 2013. (www.sbdcnet.org/small-business-research-reports/ assisted-living-facilities).

Osmond, Marie, and Barrie Thorne. 1993. "Feminist Theories: The Construction of Gender in Families and Society," pp. 591–622 in *Sourcebook of Family Theories and Methods: A Contextual Approach,* Pauline Boss, William Doherty, Ralph LaRossa, Walter Schumm, and Suzanne Steinmetz, eds. New York, NY: Plenum.

OurTime.com. 2013. Home page. Retrieved 29 December 2013 (www.ourtime.com).

Owen, Jesse, and Frank D. Fincham. 2011. "Effects of Gender and Psychological Factors on 'Friends with Benefits' Relationships among Young Adults." *Archives of Sexual Behavior* 40: 311–320.

Oxfam International. 2006. *Free, Quality Education for Every Afghan Child.* November.

—. 2011. "High Stakes: Girls' Education in Afghanistan." 24 February. Retrieved 25 February 2013 (www.oxfam.org/ en/policy/high-stakes-girls-education-afghanistan).

Pai, Manacy, and Anne E. Barrett. 2007. "Long-Term Payoffs of Work? Women's Past Involvement in Paid Work and Mental Health in Widowhood." *Research on Aging* 29(5): 436–456.

Pailhe, Ariane, and Anne Solaz. 2008. "Time with Children: Do Fathers and Mothers Replace Each Other When One Parent Is Unemployed?" *European Journal of Population* 24(2): 211–236.

Palfrey, Dale Hoyt. 1997. "La Quinceañera: An Hispanic Celebration of Budding Womanhood." Retrieved 24 April 2007 (www.mexconnect.com/mex_/travel/dpalfrey/ dpquince.html).

Panchal, Nirmita, Matthew Rae, and Gary Claxton. 2012. "Snapshots: A Comparison of the Availability and Cost of Coverage for Workers in Small Firms and Large Firms." The Henry J. Kaiser Family Foundation. 5 December. Retrieved 22 December 2013 (kff.org/private-insurance/ issue-brief/snapshots-a-comparison-of-the-availability-and- cost-of-coverage-for-workers-in-small-firms-and-large- firms).

Pande, Rohini P. and Anju Malhotra. 2006. *Son Preference and Daughter Neglect in India: What Happens to Living Girls?* Washington, DC: International Center for Research on Women.

Papernow, Patricia L. 2013. *Surviving and Thriving in Stepfamily Relationships: What Works and What Doesn't.* New York, NY: Routledge.

Parents Television Council. 2010. "Sexualized Teen Girls: Tinseltown's New Target. A Study of Teen Female Sexualization in Prime-time TV."

—. 2011. "Cartoons Are No Laughing Matter: Sex, Drugs, and Profanity on Primetime Animated Programs." Retrieved 1 April 2013 (www.parentstv.org/PTC/ publications/reports/animation/main.asp).

—. 2012. "Reality on MTV: Gender Portrayals on MTV Reality Programming."

Parke, Mary. 2007. "Are Married Parents Really Better for Children? What Research Says About the Effects of Family Structure on Child Well-being." In *Couples and Married Research and Policy Brief (May 2003).* Center for Law and Social Policy. Retrieved 14 April 2010 (www.clasp.org/admin/site/publications_states/files/0086. pdf).

Parker, Ginny. 1999. "Japan Approves Birth Control Pill." Associated Press. Retrieved 24 April 2007 (www. yorkweekly.com/1999news/6_2_w2.htm).

Parker, Kim. 2009. "The Harried Life of the Working Mother." Pew Research Center. Retrieved 25 October 2009 (pewsocialtrends.org/pubs/745/the-harried-life-of-the- working-mother).

—. 2012. "The Boomerang Generation: Feeling OK about Living with Mom and Dad." Pew Research Social & Demographic Trends. 15 March. Retrieved 22 May 2013 (www.pewsocialtrends.org/2012/03/15/the-boomerang- generation).

Parker, Kim, and Wendy Wang. 2013. "Modern Parenthood: Roles of Moms and Dads Converge as They Balance Work and Family." Pew Social & Demographic Trends. 14 March. Retrieved 29 June 2013 (www.pewsocialtrends. org/2013/03/14/modern-parenthood-roles-of-moms-and- dads-converge-as-they-balance-work-and-family).

Parker-Pope, Tara. 2007. "Does Flex Time Lead to Better Health?" NYTimes.com. 13 December. Retrieved 4 April 2009 (Well.blogs.nytimes.com/2007/12/13/does-flex-time- lead-to-better-health).

—. 2010. "Is Marriage Good for Your Health?" Retrieved 23 May 2010. NYTimes.com (www.nytimes.com/2010/04/18/ magazine/18marriage-t.html?pagewanted=print).

Parrillo, Vincent N. 2012. *Strangers to These Shores: Race and Ethnic Relations in the United States,* 10th ed. Boston, MA: Pearson.

Parsons, Talcott. 1937. *The Structure of Social Action.* New York, NY: McGraw-Hill.

Parsons, Talcott, and Robert F. Bales. 1955. *Family, Socialization, and the Interactions Process.* New York, NY: Free Press.

Partenheimer, David. 2003. "Race Has Powerful Effects on Children's Perceptions of Occupations, Study Finds" (Press Release). American Psychological Association. Retrieved 6 January 2004 (www.apa.org/releases/race_jobs.html).

—. 2005. "Do Opposites Attract or Do Birds of a Feather Flock Together?" (Press Release). American Psychological Association. Retrieved 21 June 2005 (www.apa.org/releases/attraction.html).

Pascoe, C.J. 2007. *Dude, You're a Fag: Masculinity and Sexuality in High School.* Berkeley, CA: University of California Press.

Passel, Jeffrey, and D'Vera Cohn. 2012. "Unauthorized Immigrants: 11.1 Million in 2011." Pew Hispanic Center. 6 December. Retrieved 3 March 2013 (www.pewhispanic.org/2012/12/06/unauthorized-immigrants-11-1-million-in-2011).

Patterson, Charlotte J., and Paul D. Hastings. 2007. "Socialization in the Context of Family Diversity," pp. 328–351 in *Handbook of Socialization: Theory and Research,* Joan E. Grusec and Paul D. Hastings, eds. New York, NY: The Guilford Press.

Paul, Annie Murphy. 2006. "The Real Marriage Penalty." *New York Times Magazine,* 19 November, pp. 22–23.

Pearson, Jessica and Nancy Thoennes. 1998. "Programs to Increase Fathers' Access to Their Children," pp. 220–252 in *Fathers Under Fire,* Irwin Garfinkel, Sara S. McLanahan, Daniel R. Meyer, and Judith A. Seltzer, eds. New York, NY: Russell Sage Foundation.

Pearson, Quinn M. 2008. "Role Overload, Job Satisfaction, Leisure Satisfaction, and Psychological Health among Employed Women." *Journal of Counseling & Development* 86(1): 57–63.

Pedersen, Willy, and Hans W. Kristiansen. 2008. "Homosexual Experience, Desire and Identity among Young Adults." *Journal of Homosexuality* 54(1–2): 68–102.

Pelham, Brett W. 2010. "Rest Eludes Nearly 30% of Americans." Gallup Poll. Retrieved 2 March 2010 (www.gallup.com/poll/125471/rest-eludes-nearly-americans.aspx?version=print).

Peplau, Letitia A., and Kristin P. Beals. 2004. "The Family Lives of Lesbians and Gay Men," pp. 233–248 in *Handbook of Family Communication,* Anita Vangelisti, ed. Mahwah, NJ: Lawrence Erlbaum Associates.

Perillous, Carin, and David M. Buss. 2008. "Breaking Up Romantic Relationships: Costs Experienced and Coping Strategies Deployed." *Evolutionary Psychology* 6: 164–181.

Perkins, Daniel F., and Kate Fogarty. 2005. "Active Listening: A Communication Tool." In *FCS2151, One of a Series of the Family, Youth, and Community Sciences Department, Florida Cooperative Extension Service, Institute of Food and Agricultural Sciences, University of Florida.* Retrieved 29 September 2008 (Edis.ifas.ufl.edu/he361).

Perry, Bruce D. 2002. "Childhood Experience and the Expression of Genetic Potential: What Childhood Neglect Tells Us about Nature and Nurture." *Brain and Mind* 3(1): 79–100.

Perry-Jenkins, Maureen, and Amy Claxton. 2011. The transition to parenthood and the reasons "Momma ain't happy." *Journal of Marriage and Family* 73(1): 23–28.

Perry-Jenkins, Maureen, Abbie E. Goldberg, Courtney P. Pierce, and Aline G. Sayer. 2007. "Shift Work, Role Overload, and the Transition to Parenthood." *Journal of Marriage and the Family* 69: 123–138.

Peter, Jennifer. 2004. "Gay Marriage in MA." *Nitecrawler,* 4 February. Retrieved 9 March 2004 (donfox.blogdns.org/archives/000531.html).

Peters, Brad, and Marion F. Ehrenberg. 2008. "The Influence of Parental Separation and Divorce on Father–Child Relationships." *Journal of Divorce & Remarriage* 49(1–2): 78–109.

Pew Forum on Religion & Public Life. 2013. "High Court to Hear Same-Sex Marriage Cases." 20 March. Retrieved 7 October 2013 (www.pewforum.org/2013/03/20/high-court-to-hear-same-sex-marriage-cases).

—. 2012. "Americans Learned Little about the Mormon Faith, but Some Attitudes Have Softened." 14 December. Retrieved 15 April 2013 (www.pewforum.org/Christian/Mormon/attitudes-toward-mormon-faith.aspx).

—. 2009. "Brides, Grooms Often Have Different Faiths." 4 June. Retrieved 18 May 2010 (pewforum.org/Brides-Grooms-Often-Have-Different-Faiths.aspx).

Pew Research Center for the People & the Press. 2009. "Majority Continues to Support Civil Unions." Retrieved 20 February 2010 (people-press.org/report/553/same-sex-marriage).

—. 2012. "The Complicated Business of Abortion." 22 August. Retrieved 1 April 2013 (www.people-press.org/2012/08/22/the-complicated-business-of-abortion).

—. 2013. "Growing Support for Gay Marriage: Changed Minds and Changing Demographics." 20 March. Retrieved 7 October 2013 (www.people-press.org/2013/03/20/growing-support-for-gay-marriage-changed-minds-and-changing-demographics).

Pew Research Center. 2007. "As Marriage and Parenthood Drift Apart, Public Is Concerned About Social Impact: Generation Gap in Values, Behaviors." 1 July 2007. Retrieved 8 August 2008 (pewresearch.org/pubs/526/marriage-parenthood).

—. 2007. "Public Expresses Mixed Views of Islam, Mormonism." 25 September. (www.pewtrusts.org/news_room_detail.aspx?id=42462)

—. 2008a. "Perpetual Minors: Human Rights Abuses Stemming from Male Guardianship and Sex Segregation in Saudi Arabia." In *Human Rights Watch.* Retrieved 5 May 2008 (www.hrw.org).

—. 2008b. "Religion in America: Non-Dogmatic, Diverse, and Politically Relevant." 23 June. Retrieved 24 June 2008 (pewresearch.org/pubs/876/religion-america-part-two).

—. 2010a. "Millennials: Confident. Connected. Open to Change." February 2010. (www.pewsocialtrends.org/files/2010/10/millennials-confident-connected-open-to-change.pdf).

—. 2010b. "The Return of the Multi-Generational Family Household." 18 March. Retrieved 4 April 2010 (pewresearch.org/pubs/1528/multi-generational-family-household).

—. 2010c. "The Decline of Marriage and Rise of New Families." Pew Research Social & Demographic Trends. 18 November. (www.pewtrusts.org/our_work_report_detail.aspx?id=61878)

—. 2011. "A Portrait of Stepfamilies." 13 January. Retrieved 20 May 2013 (www.pewsocialtrends.org/2011/01/13/a-portrait-of-stepfamilies).

—. 2012. "The Complicated Politics of Abortion." 22 August. Retrieved 1 April 2013 (www.people-press.org/2012/08/22/the-complicated-politics-of-abortion).

—. 2013a. "Intermarriage on the Rise in the U.S." 8 January. Retrieved 15 April 2013 (www.pewresearch.org/daily-number/intermarriage-on-the-rise-in-the-u-s).

—. 2013b. "Second-Generation Americans: A Portrait of the Adult Children of Immigrants." Pew Research Social & Demographic Trends. 7 February. Retrieved 3 March 2013 (www.pewsocialtrends.org/2013/02/07/second-generation-americans/).

—. 2013c. "Changing Attitudes on Gay Marriage." June 2013. (http://features.pewforum.org/same-sex-marriage-attitudes/).

Pfaff, Donald W., and Helen E. Fisher. 2012. "Generalized Brain Arousal Mechanisms and Other Biological, Environmental, and Psychological Mechanisms that Contribute to Libido," pp. 65–84 (Ch. 5) in *From the Couch to the Lab: Trends in Neuropsychoanalysis,* Fotopoulou, Aikaterini, Donald W. Pfaff, and Martin A. Conway, eds. Cambridge, MA: Cambridge University Press.

Pfeffer, Carla A. 2010. "'Women's Work?'" Women Partners of Transgender Men Doing Housework and Emotion Work." *Journal of Marriage and Family* 72(1): 165–183.

PFLAG. 2013. Home Page. Retrieved 1 April 2013 (community.pflag.org/Page.aspx?pid=194&srcid=-2).

Phillips, Roderick. 1997. "Stepfamilies from a Historical Perspective," pp. 5–18 in *Stepfamilies: History, Research and Policy,* Ira Levin and Marvin Sussman, eds. New York, NY: Haworth.

Pineo, Peter. 1961. "Disenchantment in the Later Years of Marriage." *Marriage and Family Living* 23: 3–11.

Pinquart, Martin, and Daniela Teubert. 2010. "A Meta-analytic Study of Couple Interventions during the Transition to Parenthood." *Family Relations* 59(3): 221–231.

Plotnick, Robert D. 2009. "Childlessness and Economic Well-being of Older Americans." *The Journals of Gerontology: Series B* 64B(6): 767–776.

Polaha, Jodi, Robert E. Larzelere, Steven K. Shapiro, and Gregory S. Pettit. 2004. "Physical Discipline and Child Behavior Problems: A Study of Ethnic Group Differences." *Parenting: Science and Practice* 4: 339–360.

Polaris Project. 2013. "Human Trafficking." Retrieved 14 May 2013 (www.polarisproject.org/human-trafficking).

Pomeroy, Sarah B. 1975. *Goddesses, Whores, Wives, and Slaves: Women in Classical Antiquity.* New York, NY: Schocken Books.

Poortman, Anne-Rigt, and Judith A. Seltzer. 2007. "Parents' Expectations about Childrearing after Divorce: Does Anticipating Difficulty Deter Divorce?" *Journal of Marriage and the Family* 69(1): 254–269.

Poortman, Anne-Rigt, and Tanja van der Lippe. 2009. "Attitudes toward Housework and Child Care and the Gendered Division of Labor." *Journal of Marriage and Family* 71(3): 526–541.

Popenoe, David. 2007. "Essay: The Future of Marriage in America." In *The State of Our Unions: The Social Health of Marriage in America.* New Brunswick, NJ: The National Marriage Project.

—. 2008. "Cohabitation, Marriage, and Child Well-being: A Cross-National Perspective" (The National Marriage Project). Retrieved 28 August 2008 (marriage.rutgers.edu/Publications/NMP2008CohabitationReport.pdf).

Population Reference Bureau. 2011. "The World's Women and Girls: 2011 Data Sheet." Retrieved 30 May 2013 (www.prb.org).

—. 2013a. "2012 World Population Data Sheet." Retrieved 20 April 2013 (www.prb.org).

—. 2013b. "DataFinder." Retrieved 20 April 2013 (www.prb.org).

Porter, Stephen, and Leanne ten Brinke. 2010. "The Truth about Lies: What Works in Detecting High-Stakes Deception?" *Legal and Criminological Psychology* 15(57–75).

Posner, Patti. 2002. "One Family's Journey to Healing." Stepfamily Network. Retrieved 14 April 2003 (www.stepfamily.net).

Potter, Daniel. 2012. "Same-Sex Parent Families and Children's Academic Achievement." *Journal of Marriage and Family* 74(3): 556–571.

Powell, Alvin. 2005. "A New Comfort Zone? Fewer Women Keeping Names on Marriage." *Harvard University Gazette.* Retrieved 10 July 2007 (www.news.harvard.edu/gazette/2004/08.26/11-namechange.html).

Powell, Brian, Catherine Bolzendahl, Claudia Geist, and Lala Carr Steelman. 2010. *Counted Out: Same-sex Relations and Americans' Definitions of Family.* New York, NY: Russell Sage.

Pransky, Jack, and Diane McMillen. 2009. "Exploring the True Nature of Resilience." Ch. 13 in *The Strengths Perspective in Social Work Practice,* 5th ed., Dennis Saleebey, ed. Boston, MA: Allyn & Bacon.

Presser, Harriet B. 2003. *Working in a 24/7 Economy: Challenges for American Families.* New York, NY: Russell Sage Foundation.

Presser, Harriet B., Janet C. Gornick, and Sangeeta Parashar. 2008. "Nonstandard Work Schedules in Twelve European Countries: A Gender Perspective." *Monthly Labor Review* 131(2): 83–103.

Presser, Harriet B., and Brian W. Ward. 2011. "Non-Standard Work Schedules over the Life Course: A First Look." *Monthly Labor Review* 134(7): 3–16.

Prinstein, Mitchell L., Christina S. Meade, and Geoffrey L. Cohen. 2003. "Adolescent Oral Sex, Peer Popularity, and Perceptions of Best Friends' Sexual Behavior." *Journal of Pediatric Psychology* 28: 243–249.

Proulx, Christine M., Heather M. Helms, and Cheryl Buehler. 2007. "Marital Quality and Personal Well-being: A

Meta-analysis." *Journal of Marriage and Family* 69(4): 576–593.

Przybyla-Basista, Hanna. 2008. "The Influence of Spouses Resistance on Their Decision to Enter into Divorce Mediation." *Journal of Divorce & Remarriage* 48(3–4): 67–89.

Pyke, Karen. 1994. "Women's Employment as a Gift of a Burden? Marital Power Across Marriage, Divorce, and Remarriage." *Gender & Society* 8: 73–91.

—. 2000. "'The Normal American Family' as an Interpretive Structure of Family Life among Grown Children of Korean and Vietnamese Immigrants." *Journal of Marriage and the Family* 62: 240–245.

—. 2005. "'Generational Deserters' and 'Black Sheep': Acculturative Differences among Siblings in Asian Immigrant Families." *Journal of Family Issues* 26(4): 491–517.

Pyke, Karen, and Scott Coltrane. 1996. "Entitlement, Obligation, and Gratitude in Family Work." *Journal of Family Issues* 17: 60–82.

Queen, Stuart A., and Robert W. Habenstein. 1967. *The Family in Various Cultures*. Philadelphia, PA: Lippincott.

Quinceañera.com. 2012. Home Page. Retrieved 10 March 2013 (quinceanera.com).

Raffaelli, Marcela, and Lenna L. Ontai. 2004. "Gender Socialization in Latino/a Families: Results from Two Retrospective Studies." *Sex Roles* 50(5–6): 287–299.

Rahe, Richard, Jack L. Mahan, Jr., and Ransom J. Arthur. 1970. "Prediction of Near-Future Health Change From Subjects' Preceding Life Changes." *Journal of Psychosomatic Research* 14(4): 401–406.

Raley, Sara, and Suzanne Bianchi. 2006. "Sons, Daughters, and Family Process: Does Gender of Children Matter?" *Annual Review of Sociology* 32: 401–421.

Rani, Manju, and Sekhar Banu. 2009. "Attitudes toward Wife Beating." *Journal of Interpersonal Violence* 24(8): 1371–1397.

Rankin, Nancy. 2002. "The Parent Vote," pp. 251–264 in *Taking Parenting Public*, Sylvia A. Hewlett, Nancy Rankin and Cornel West, eds. Lanham, MD: Rowman & Littlefield.

Raschick, Michael, and Berit Ingersoll-Dayton. 2004. "The Costs and Rewards of Caregiving among Aging Spouses and Adult Children." *Family Relations* 53: 317–325.

Rathus, Spencer A., Jeffrey S. Nevid, and Lois Fichner-Rathus. 2014. *Human Sexuality in a World of Diversity,* 9th ed. New York, NY: Prentice Hall.

Rawlins, WIilliam K. 2008. The Compass of Friendship. Newbury Park, CA: Sage.

Redbook. 2008. "Same-Sex Marriage." *www.Redbookmag.com,* June, pp. 162–164.

Reeves, Terrance, and Claudette Bennett. 2003. "The Asian and Pacific Islander Population in the United States: March 2002." Current Population Reports. P20-540. Washington, DC: U.S. Census Bureau.

Regan, Pamela C. 2008. *The Mating Game: A Primer on Love, Sex, and Marriage,* 2nd ed. Thousand Oaks, CA: Sage.

Reid, Julie A., Sinikka Elliott, and Gretchen R. Webber. 2011. "Casual Hookups to Formal Dates: Refining the Boundaries of the Sexual Double Standard." *Gender & Society* 25(5): 545–568.

Reiss, Ira L. 1960. "Toward a Sociology of the Heterosexual Love Relationship." *Marriage and Family Living* 22: 139–145.

Reitzes, Donald C. and Elizabeth J. Mutran. 2004. "The Transition to Retirement: Stages and Factors That Influence Retirement Adjustment." *International Journal of Aging and Human Development* 59(1): 63–84.

Remarriage.com. 2008. "Remarriage Issues: General Findings." Retrieved 4 September 2008 (www.remarriage.com/Remarriage-Factsw/Likelihood-of-Marriage.html).

Renzetti, Claire M., Daniel J. Curran, and Shana L. Maier. 2012. *Women, Men, and Society,* 6th ed. Boston, MA: Pearson.

Resolve: The National Infertility Association. 2008. "Frequently Asked Questions about Infertility." Retrieved 15 December 2009 (www.resolve.org/site/PageServer?pagename=lrn_wii_faq).

Revolutionary Association of the Women of Afghanistan (RAWA). 2013. Home Page. Retrieved 25 February 2013 (www.rawa.org/index.php).

Ricci, Isolina. 2007. "Divorce from the Kids' Point of View: From Damage Control to Empowerment." *National Council on Family Relations Report* 52(4): F11–F12; F19.

Richman, Jack M., and Lawrence B. Rosenfeld. 1995. "The Relationship of Marital Self-disclosure and Spouse Descriptions to Therapists' Evaluations of Problem Severity and Couple Commitment to Therapy." *Journal of Couples Therapy* 4: 119–131.

Richters, Juliet, Richard de Visser, Chris Rissel, and Anthony Smith. 2006. "Sexual Practices at Last Heterosexual Encounter and Occurrence of Orgasm in a National Survey." *The Journal of Sex Research* 43(3): 217–226.

Rigler, William, and Howard L. Wieder. 2007. "The Epidemic of Parental Child-snatching: An Overview; Attempts to Prevent Parental Child Abduction, Applicable United States Laws, and the Hague Convention." Retrieved 6 September 2007 (Travel.state.gov/family/abduction/resources/resources_545.html).

Risman, Barbara J., and Elizabeth Seale. 2010. "Betwixt and Be Tween: Gender Contradictions among Middle Schoolers," pp. 340–361 (Ch. 30) in *Families as They Really Are*, Barbara J. Risman, ed. New York, NY: W.W. Norton & Company.

Ristock, Janice. 2009. *Intimate Partner Violence in LGBTQ Lives*. New York, NY: Routledge.

Robinson-Dooley, Vanessa and Nancy P. Kropf. 2006. "Second Generation Parenting: Grandparents Who Receive TANF." *Journal of Intergenerational Relationships* 4(3): 49–62.

Rockquemore, Kerry Ann, and Tracey Laszloffy. 2005. *Raising Biracial Children*. Lanham, MD: AltaMira Press.

Rodgers, Joseph Lee, Paul A. Nakonezny, and Robert D. Shull. 1997. "Feedback: The Effect of No-Fault Divorce Legislation on Divorce Rates: A Response to a Reconsideration." *Journal of Marriage and the Family* 59: 1026–1030.

Rodgers, Roy H., and James M. White. 1993. "Family Development Theory," pp. 225–254 in *Sourcebook of*

Family Theories and Methods: A Contextual Approach, Pauline G. Boss, William J. Doherty, Ralph LaRossa, Walter R. Schumm and Suzanne K. Steinmetz, eds. New York, NY: Plenum Press.

Rodriguez, Michael, Jeanette M. Valentine, John B. Son, and Marjani Muhammad. 2009. "Intimate Partner Violence and Barriers to Mental Health Care for Ethnically Diverse Populations of Women." *Trauma, Violence, & Abuse* 10(4): 358–374.

Roebuck Bulanda, Jennifer, and Susan Brown. 2007. "Race–Ethnic Differences in Marital Quality and Divorce." *Social Service Review* 36: 945–967.

Roer-Strier, Dorit, and Dina Ben Ezra. 2006. "Intermarriages between Western Women and Palestinian Men: Multidirectional Adaptation Processes." *Journal of Marriage and Family* 68(1): 41–55.

Rogers, Stacy J. 2004. "Dollars, Dependency, and Divorce: Four Perspectives on the Role of Wives' Income." *Journal of Marriage and Family* 66 (1): 59–74.

Rohde-Brown, Juliet, and Kjell Erik Rudestam. 2011. "The Role of Forgiveness in Divorce Adjustment and the Impact of Affect." *Journal of Divorce & Remarriage* 52(2): 109–124.

Rohner, Ronald P., and Robert A. Veneziano. 2001. "The Importance of Father Love: History and Contemporary Evidence." *Review of General Psychology* 5(4): 382–405.

Rooks, Judith. 1997. *Midwifery and Childbirth in America.* Philadelphia, PA: Temple University Press.

Rosenberg, Matt. 2009. "China's One Child Policy." About.com. Retrieved 9 November 2009 (geography.About.com/od/populationgeography/a/onechild.htm).

Rosenfeld, Dana, Bernadette Bartlam, and Ruth D. Smith. 2012. "Out of the Closet and into the Trenches: Gay Male Baby Boomers, Aging, and HIV/AIDS." *The Gerontologist* 52(2): 255–264.

Rosenfeld, Michael J. 2008. *The Age of Independence: Interracial Unions, Same-sex Unions and the Changing American Family.* Cambridge, MA: Harvard University Press.

Rosin, Mark Bruce. 2009. *Stepfathering.* New York, NY: Simon and Schuster.

Ross, Catherine E., and Marieke Van Willigen. 1996. "Gender, Parenthood, and Anger." *Journal of Marriage and the Family* 58: 572–584.

Ross, Donna Cohen, Aleya Horn, and Caryn Marks. 2008. "Health Coverage for Children and Families in Medicaid and SCHIP: State Efforts Face New Hurdles: Executive Summary." Kaiser Commission on Medicaid and the Uninsured. Retrieved 15 July 2008 (www.kff.org/medicaid/upload/7740_ES.pdf).

Rossi, Alice S. 1968. "Transition to Motherhood." *Journal of Marriage and the Family* 30: 26–39.

Rothbart, Mary K., and Brad Sheese. 2007. "Temperament and Emotion Regulation," pp. 331–350 in *Handbook of Emotion Regulation*, James J. Gross, ed. New York, NY: Guilford Press.

Rothman, Barbara Katz. 1991. *In Labor: Women and Power in the Birthplace.* New York, NY: W.W. Norton and Co.

Rothstein, Donna S. 2001. "Youth Employment in the United States." *Monthly Labor Review* 124: 6–17.

Roudsan, Bahman S., Matthew M. Leahy, and Scott T. Walters. 2009. "Correlates of Dating Violence among Male and Female Heavy-drinking College Students." *Journal of Interpersonal Violence* 24(11): 1892–1905.

Roxburgh, Susan. 2012. "Parental Time Pressures and Depression among Married Dual-earner Parents." *Journal of Family Issues* 33(8): 1027–1053.

Rubin, Lillian B. 1976. *Worlds of Pain.* New York, NY: Basic Books.

Ruggles, Steven. 2011. "Intergenerational Coresidence and Family Transitions in the United States, 1850–1880." *Journal of Marriage and Family* 73(1): 136–148.

Rutley, Daniel. 2001. *Escaping Emotional Entrapment: Freedom from Negative Thinking and Unhealthy Emotions.* Lakeland, FL: Pax Publishing.

Rye, Mark S., Amanda M. Fleri, Crystal Dea Moore, Everett L. Worthington, Jr., Nathaniel G. Wade, Steven J. Sandage, and Kevin M. Cook. 2012. "Evaluation of an Intervention Designed to Help Divorced Parents Forgive Their Ex-Spouse." *Journal of Divorce & Remarriage* 53(3): 231–245.

Saad, Lydia. 2004. "Romance to Break Out Nationwide This Weekend." Gallup Poll. Retrieved 25 September 2008 (www.gallup.com/poll/10609/Romance-Break-Nationwide-Weekend.aspx).

—. 2009. "Republicans Move to the Right on Several Moral Issues." Gallup Poll. Retrieved 14 February 2010 (www.gallup.com/poll/118546/republicans-veer-right-several-moral-issues.aspx).

Saluter, Arlene. 1996. "Marital Status and Living Arrangements: March 1995 (Update)." Current Population Reports PPL-52. U.S. Census Bureau.

Samandari, Ghazeleh, and Sandra L. Martin. 2010. "Homicide among Pregnant and Postpartum Women in the United States: A Review of the Literature." *Trauma, Violence, & Abuse* 11(1): 42–54.

Sample, Neal. 1999. "What I Felt Like Being Adopted." Retrieved 6 July 2004 (www.stepfamilynetwork.net/Adoption.htm).

Sanday, Peggy Reeves. 1981. "The Socio-cultural Context of Rape: A Cross-cultural Study." *Journal of Social Issues* 37: 5–27.

Sands, Roberta G. and Robin S. Goldberg-Glen. 2000. "Factors Associated with Stress among Grandparents Raising Their Grandchildren." *Family Relations* 49: 97–105.

Santelli, John S., Mark Orr, Laura D. Lindberg, and Daniela C. Diaz. 2009. "Changing Behavioral Risk for Pregnancy among High School Students in the United States: 1991–2007." *Journal of Adolescent Health* 44(7): 25–32.

Sapienza, Julianna K., and Ann S. Masten. 2011. "Understanding and Promoting Resilience in Children and Youth." *Current Opinion in Psychiatry* 24(4): 267–273.

Sapir, Edward. 1949. *Selected Writings of Edward Sapir in Language, Culture, and Personality,* David G. Mandelbaum, ed. Berkeley, CA: University of California Press.

Sassler, Sharon. 2010. "Partnering across the Life Course: Sex, Relationships, and Mate Selection." *Journal of Marriage and Family* 72(3): 557–575.

Sassler, Sharon, Anna Cunningham, and Daniel T. Lichter. 2009. "Intergenerational Patterns of Union Formation and Relationship Quality." *Journal of Family Issues* 30(6): 757–786.

Saul, Stephanie. 2009. "Building a Baby, with Few Ground Rules." NYTimes.com. Retrieved 20 December 2009 (www.nytimes.com/2009/12/13/us/13surrogacy.html?_r=1&pagewanted=print).

Sax, Leonard. 2005. *Why Gender Matters: What Parents and Teachers Need to Know about the Emerging Science of Sex Differences.* New York, NY: Doubleday.

Sayer, Liana C., Anne H. Gauthier, and Frank F. Furstenberg, Jr. 2004. "Educational Differences in Parents' Time with Children: Cross-national Variations." *Journal of Marriage and Family* 66: 1152–1169.

Sbarra, David A. 2006. "Predicting the Onset of Emotional Recovery Following Nonmarital Relationship Dissolution: Survival Analyses of Sadness and Anger." *Personality and Social Psychology Bulletin* 32(3): 298–312.

Scaramella, Laura V., Tricia K. Neppl, Lenna L. Ontai, and Rand D. Conger. 2008. "Consequences of Socioeconomic Disadvantage across Three Generations." *Journal of Family Psychology* 22(5): 725–733.

Schaefer, Richard T. 2013. *Race and Ethnicity in the United States,* 7th ed. Boston, MA: Pearson.

Schaie, K. Warner, and Glen H. Elder, Jr. 2005. *Historical Influences on Lives and Aging.* New York, NY: Springer Publishing Co.

Schieber, Sylvester J. 2008. *Beyond the Golden Age of Retirement.* May. University of Michigan Retirement Research Center Policy Brief No. 6. (www.mrrc.isr.umich.edu/publications/policy/pdf/Schieber.pdf)

Schiebinger, Londa, and Shannon K. Gilmartin. 2010. "Housework Is an Academic Issue." Academe Online. Retrieved 21 November 2010 (www.aaup.org/AAUP/pubsres/academe/2010/JF/feat/schie.htm).

Schmeer, Kammi K., and Rhiannon A. Kroeger. 2011. "Union Type and Depressive Symptoms among Mexican Adults." *Journal of Family Issues* 32(12): 1597–1621.

Schmid, Randolph E. 2005. "Scent Studies Find Gay, Straight Divide." *The Oregonian* (Portland, OR), 10 May, A, p. 3.

Schoen, Cathy, Robin Osborn, Michelle M. Doty, Meghan Bishop, Jordon Peugh, and Nandita Murukutla. 2007. "Toward Higher-performance Health Systems: Adults' Health Care Experiences in Seven Countries, 2007." *Health Affairs* 26(6): w717–w734.

Schoenborn, Charlotte A., and Patricia F. Adams. 2010. "Health Behaviors of Adults: United States, 2005–2007." National Center for Health Statistics. *Vital Health Statistics* 10(245).

Schoppe-Sullivan, Sarah J., Alice C. Schermerhorn, and E. Mark Cummings. 2007. "Marital Conflict and Children's Adjustment: Evaluation of the Parenting Process Model." *Journal of Marriage and Family* 69(5): 1118–1134.

Schott, Liz. 2012. "Policy Basics: An Introduction to TANF." Center on Budget and Policy Priorities. 4 December. Retrieved 30 May 2013 (www.cbpp.org/cms/index.cfm?fa=view&id=936).

Schott, Liz, and LaDonna Pavetti. 2011. "Many States Cutting TANF Benefits Harshly Despite High Unemployment and Unprecedented Need." Center on Budget and Policy Priorities. 3 October. Retrieved 30 May 2013 (www.cbpp.org/cms/index.cfm?fa=view&id=3498).

Schramm, David G., and Francesca Adler-Baeder. 2012. "Marital Quality for Men and Women in Stepfamilies: Examining the Role of Economic Pressure, Common Stressors, and Stepfamily-specific Stressors." *Journal of Family Issues* 33: 1373–1397.

Schwartz, Karyn. 2007. "Spotlight on Uninsured Parents: How a Lack of Coverage Affects Parents and Their Families" (Kaiser Low-Income Coverage and Access Survey). *The Kaiser Commission on Medicaid and the Uninsured,* June. Menlo Park, CA: The Henry J. Kaiser Family Foundation.

Schwartz, Pepper. 1994. *Love between Equals: How Peer Marriage Really Works.* New York, NY: Free Press.

——. 2001. "Peer Marriage: What Does It Take to Create a Truly Egalitarian Relationship?" pp. 182–189 in *Families in Transition,* 11th ed., Arlene S. Skolnick and Jerome H. Skolnick, eds. Boston, MA: Allyn & Bacon.

Schwartz, Seth J., and Gordon E. Finley. 2006. "Father Involvement, Nurturant Fathering, and Young Adult Psychosocial Functioning." *Journal of Family Issues* 27(5): 712–731.

Schweitzer, Ivy. 2006. *Perfecting Friendship: Politics and Affiliation in Early American Literature.* Chapel Hill, NC: University of North Carolina Press.

Science Daily. 2006. "Transgender Experience Led Stanford Scientist to Critique Gender Difference." Retrieved 21 November 2006 (www.sciencedaily.com/releases/2006/07/060714174545.htm).

Scott, Megan K. 2009. "Multitaskers Say One Online Dating Site Won't Do." Fall River, MA: The Herald News. Retrieved 22 January 2010 (www.heraldnews.com/lifestyle/x545172880/Multitaskers-say-one-online-dating-site-wont-do).

Searle, Eleanor. 1988. *Predatory Kinship and the Creation of Norman Power, 840–1066.* Berkeley, CA: University of California Press.

Seccombe, Karen. 2002. "'Beating the Odds' versus 'Changing the Odds': Poverty, Resilience, and Family Policy." *Journal of Marriage and Family* 64: 384–394.

——. 2007. *Families in Poverty.* Boston, MA: Allyn & Bacon.

——. 2014. *So You Think I Drive a Cadillac? Welfare Recipients' Perspectives on the System and Its Reform,* 4th ed. Boston, MA: Pearson.

——. 2015. *Families and Their Social Worlds,* 3rd ed. Boston, MA: Pearson.

Seccombe, Karen, and Kim A. Hoffman. 2007. *Just Don't Get Sick: Access to Health Care in the Aftermath of Welfare Reform.* Piscataway, NJ: Rutgers University Press.

Segal, Marcia Texler, and Theresa A. Martinez, eds. 2007. *Intersections of Gender, Race, and Class: Readings for a Changing Landscape.* New York, NY: Oxford University Press.

Seiffge-Krenke, Inge. 2006. "Coping with Relationship Stressors: The Impact of Different Working Models of Attachment and Links to Adaptation." *Journal of Youth and Adolescence* 35(1): 24–38.

Seiler, William J., Melissa L. Beall, and Joseph Mazer. 2014. *Communication: Making Connection,* 9th ed. Boston, MA: Pearson.

Seltzer, Judith A. 1998. "Fathers by Law: Effects of Joint Legal Custody on Nonresidental Fathers' Involvement with Children."*Demography* 35: 135–146.

Selye, Hans. 1955. "Stress and Disease." *Scientific American* 122 (7 October): 625–631.

—. 1956. *The Stress of Life*. New York, NY: McGraw-Hill.

Shackleford, Todd K., Martin Voracek, David P. Schmitt, David M. Buss, Viviana A. Weekes-Shackleford, and Richard L. Michalski. 2004. "Romantic Jealousy in Early Adulthood and in Later Life." *Human Nature* 15: 283–300.

Shanhong, Luo, and Eva C. Klohnen. 2005. "Assortative Mating and Marital Quality in Newlyweds: A Couple-centered Approach."*Journal of Personality and Social Psychology* 88: 304–326.

Shapiro, Adam D. 1996. "Explaining Psychological Distress in a Sample of Remarried and Divorced Persons: The Influence of Economic Distress." *Journal of Family Issues* 17: 186–203.

Shaver, Philip R., and Mario Mikulincer. 2009. "Attachment Theory and Attachment Styles," pp. 62–81 in *Handbook of Individual Differences*, Mark R. Leary and Rick H. Hoyle, eds. New York, NY: Guilford Press.

Shehan, Constance L., Felix M. Berardo, Erica Owens, and Donna H. Berardo. 2002. "Alimony: An Anomaly in Family Social Science."*Family Relations* 51: 308–316.

Shelton, Beth Anne. 1992. *Women, Men and Time: Gender Differences in Paid Work, Housework, and Leisure*. Westport, CT: Greenwood.

Shepard, Judy. 2009. *The Meaning of Matthew: My Son's Murder in Laramie, and a World Transformed*. New York, NY: Hudson Street Press.

Shilts, Randy. 1987. *And The Band Played On: Politics, People, and the AIDS Epidemic*. New York, NY: St. Martins Press.

Shipler, David K. 2004. *The Working Poor: Invisible in America*. New York, NY: Vintage Books.

Shorey, Ryan C.,Vanessa Tirone, Alison M. Nathanson, Vanessa A. Handsel, and Deborah L. Rhatigan. 2013. "A Preliminary Investigation of the Influence of Subjective Norms and Relationship Commitment on Stages of Change in Female Intimate Partner Violence Victims." *Journal of Interpersonal Violence* 28(3): 621–642.

Shriner, Michael, Ronald L. Mullis, and Bethanne M. Schlee. 2009. "The Usefulness of Social Capital Theory for Understanding the Academic Improvement of Young Children in Stepfamilies over Two Points in Time." *Journal of Divorce & Remarriage* 50(7): 445–458.

Sides, John. 2011. "Americans Have Become More Opposed to Adultery. Why?" *The Monkey Cage*. 27 July. Retrieved 5 April 2013 (themonkeycage.org/2011/07/27/Americans-have-become-more-opposed-to-adultery-why).

Silber, Kathleen. 2013. "Benefits of Open Adoption." Independent Adoption Center. Retrieved 20 April 2013 (www.adoptionhelp.org/open-adoption/benefits).

Silliman, Ben. 1994. "1994 Resiliency Research Review: Conceptual & Research Foundations." Retrieved 16 June 2001 (www.cyfernet.org/research/resilreview.html).

—. 1998. "The Resiliency Paradigm: A Critical Tool for Practitioners." *Human Development and Family Life Bulletin* (Ohio State University, College of Human Ecology), Spring.

Simon, Rita J., and Rhonda M. Roorda. 2000. *In Their Own Voices: Transracial Adoptees Tell Their Stories*. New York, NY: Columbia University Press.

—. 2009. *In Their Siblings' Voices: White Non-adopted Siblings Talk about Their Experiences Being Raised with Black and Biracial Brothers and Sisters*. New York, NY: Columbia University Press.

Simons, Ronald L., Leslie G. Simons, Callie H. Burt, Holli Drummund, Eric Stewart, Gene H. Brody, Frederick X. Gibbons, and Carolyn Cutrona. 2006. "Supportive Parenting Moderates the Effect of Discrimination upon Anger, Hostile View of Relationships, and Violence among African American Boys." *Journal of Health and Social Behavior* 47(December): 373–389.

Simpson, George Eaton, and J. Milton Yinger. 1985. *Racial and Cultural Minorities: An Analysis of Prejudice and Discrimination,* 5th ed. New York, NY: Plenum.

Simpson, Jeffry A., W. Steven Rholes, Lorne Campbell, Sisi Tran, and Carol L. Wilson. 2003. "Adult Attachment, the Transition to Parenthood, and Depressive Symptoms." *Journal of Personality and Social Psychology* 84: 1172–1187.

Sinclair, Upton. 1906 (reprinted 2012). *The Jungle*. Hollywood, FL: Simon & Brown.

Slotter, Erica B., Wendi L. Gardner, and Eli J. Finkel. 2010. "Who Am I Without You? The Influence of Romantic Breakup on the Self-concept." *Personality and Social Psychology Bulletin* 36(2): 147–160.

Smith, Aaron, and Maeve Duggan. 2013. "Online Dating & Relationships." Pew Research Center's Internet & American Life Project. 21 October. Retrieved 30 December 2013 (pewinternet.org/Reports/2013/Online-Dating.aspx).

Smith, Brendan L. 2012. "The Case Against Spanking." American Psychological Association. April. Retrieved 10 April 2013 (www.apa.org/monitor/2012/04/spanking.aspx).

Smith, Earl, and Angela Hattery. 2009. *Interracial Relationships in the 21st Century*. Durham, NC: Carolina Academic Press.

Smith, Gregory C., and Patrick A. Palmieri. 2007. "Risk of Psychosocial Difficulties among Children Raised by Custodial Grandparents."*Psychiatric Services* 58 (October): 1303–1310.

Smith, Lynne, Patrick C.L. Heaven, and Joseph Ciarrochi. 2008. "Trait Emotional Intelligence, Conflict Communication Patterns, and Relationship Satisfaction." *Personality and Individual Differences* 44(6): 1314–1325.

Smith, Stacy L., Marc Choueiti, Ashley Prescott, and Katherine Pieper. 2012. "Gender Roles & Occupations: A Look at Character Attributes and Job-related Aspirations in Film and Television." Executive Report. Marina Del Rey, CA: Geena Davis Institute on Gender in Media.

Smith, Suzanne R., and Raeann R. Hamon. 2012. *Exploring Family Theories*, 3rd ed. New York, NY: Oxford University Press.

Smith, Suzanne R., Raeann R. Hamon, Bron B. Ingoldsby, and J. Elizabeth Miller, 2008. *Exploring Family Theories*, 2nd ed. New York, NY: Oxford University Press.

Smith, Tom W. 2006. *American Sexual Behavior: Trends, Socio-demographic Differences, and Risk Behavior.* National Opinion Research Center. General Social Survey Topical Report No. 25. March. Chicago, IL: University of Chicago.

Smith-Rosenberg, Carol. 1975. "The Female World of Love and Ritual: Relations between Women in Nineteenth-Century America." *Signs: A Journal of Women in Culture and Society* 1: 1–29.

Snow, Judith. 2004. *How It Feels to Have a Gay or Lesbian Parent: A Book by Kids for Kids of All Ages.* New York, NY: Routledge.

Social Security Administration. 2012. "Social Security Programs Throughout the World: Europe, 2012." Retrieved 22 April 2013 (www.ssa.gov/policy/docs/progdesc/ssptw/2012-2013/europe/index.html).

—. 2013. "Social Security Programs Throughout the World." Retrieved 29 May 2013 (www.socialsecurity.gov/policy/docs/progdesc/ssptw/index.html).

Society for Research in Child Development. 2008. *Improving After-school Programs in a Climate of Accountability.* Social Policy Report Brief No. 22 (2).

Solomon-Fears, Carmen, Gene Falk, and Adrienne L. Fernandes-Alcantara. 2013. "Child Well-being and Noncustodial Fathers." 12 February. Washington, DC: U.S. Congressional Research Service.

Somary, Karen, and George Stricker. 1998. "Becoming a Grandparent: A Longitudinal Study of Expectations and Early Experiences as a Function of Sex and Lineage." *The Gerontologist* 38: 53–61.

Sontag, Susan. 1979. "The Double Standard of Aging." In *Psychology of Women: Selected Readings*, Juanita H. Williams, ed. New York, NY: Norton.

Sorgen, Carol. 2008. "Seeing Green: All about Jealousy." WebMD. Retrieved 10 November 2008 (www.webmd.com/sex-relationships/guide/seeing-green-all-about-jealousy).

Soto, Mauricio. 2009. "How Is the Financial Crisis Affecting Retirement Savings?" Urban Institute. Retrieved 24 April 2010 (www.urban.org/publications/901206.html).

South, Andrea Lambert. 2013. "Perceptions of Romantic Relationships in Adult Children of Divorce." *Journal of Divorce & Remarriage* 54(2): 126–141.

Spenser, Colin. 1995. *Homosexuality in History.* New York, NY: Harcourt Brace & Company.

Spock, Benjamin, Dr. 2004. "Gay and Lesbian Parents" (Webpage). In *Dr. Spock.* Retrieved 25 May 2006 (www.drspock.com/article/0,1510,4028,00.html).

Sprecher, Susan, F. Scott Christopher, and Rodney Cate. 2006. "Sexuality in Close Relationships," pp. 462–482 in *Handbook on Personal Relationships,* Anita L. Vangelisti and Daniel Perlman, eds. New York, NY: Cambridge University Press.

Springer, Shauna. 2013. "The Joint (Ad) Ventures of Well-educated Couples." *Psychology Today.* Retrieved 22 April 2013 (www.psychologytoday.com/blog/the-joint-adventures-well-educated-couples/201301/marital-happiness-and-the-transition-parenthood).

Spruijt, Ed, and Vincent Duindam. 2010. "Joint Physical Custody in The Netherlands and the Well-being of Children." *Journal of Divorce & Remarriage* 51(1): 65–82.

Stacey, Judith, and Timothy J. Biblarz. 2001. "How Does the Sexual Orientation of Parents Matter?" *American Sociological Review* 66: 159–183.

Stalking Resource Center. 2012. "The Use of Technology to Stalk." Retrieved 6 May 2013 (www.victimsofcrime.org/our-programs/stalking-resource-center/stalking-information/the-use-of-technology-to-stalk#gps).

—. 2013. Home Page. Retrieved 26 March 2013 (www.victimsofcrime.org/our-programs/stalking-resource-center).

Stanton, Glenn T. 2005. "How Is Marriage Dying in Our Culture?" *CitizenLink.* Focus on the Family. Retrieved 30 June 2005 (www.family.org/cforum/fosi/marriage/facts/a0028319.cfm).

Stapleton, Susan Rutledge, Cara Osborne, and Jessica Illuzzi. 2013. "Outcomes of Care in Birth Centers: Demonstration of a Durable Model." *Journal of Midwifery & Women's Health* 58(1): 3–14.

Stark, Caitlin. 2013. "By the Numbers: Same-sex Marriage." 26 March. CNN Politics. Retrieved 12 April 2013 (www.cnn.com/2012/05/11/politics/btn-same-sex-marriage).

Statistics Brain. 2013. "Job Outsourcing Statistics." Retrieved 2 May 2013 (www.statisticbrain.com/outsourcing-statistics-by-country).

Stefanou, Christina, and Marita P. McCabe. 2012. "Adult Attachment and Sexual Functioning: A Review of Past Research." *The Journal of Sexual Medicine* 9: 2499–2507.

Steinbeck, John. 1939 (Reprinted 2002). *The Grapes of Wrath.* New York, NY: Penguin.

Steinberg, Stephen. 1981. *The Ethnic Myth: Race, Ethnicity, and Class in America.* Boston, MA: Beacon Press.

Steinmayr, Ricarda, and Birgit Spinath. 2009. "What Explains Boys' Stronger Confidence in Their Intelligence?" *Sex Roles* 61(9–10): 736–749.

Stelter, Brian. 2011. "Ownership of TV Sets Falls in U.S." NYTimes.com. 3 May. Retrieved 23 April 2013 (www.nytimes.com/2011/05/03/business/media/03television.html?_r=0).

Stepanikova, Irena, Qian Zhang, Darryl Wieland, Paul Eleazer, and Thomas Stewart. 2012. "Non-verbal Communication between Primary Care Physicians and Older Patients: How Does Race Matter?" *Journal of General Internal Medicine* 27(5): 576–581.

Stepfamily Foundation. 2005. "Classic Complaints in Stepfamilies." Retrieved 28 September 2007 (www.stepfamily.org/classic_complaints_in_stepfamilies.htm).

Stephens, William N. 1963. *The Family in Cross-cultural Perspective.* New York, NY: Holt, Rinehart, and Winston.

Sterk-Elifson, Claire. 1994. "Sexuality among African American Women," pp. 99–127 in *Sexuality across the Life Course,* Alice S. Rossi, ed. Chicago, IL: University of Chicago Press.

Stern, Mark J., and June J. Axinn. 2012. *Social Welfare: A History of the American Response to Need,* 8th ed. Boston, MA: Pearson.

Sternberg, Robert J. 1986. "A Triangular Theory of Love." *Psychological Review* 93(2): 119–135.

—. 1988. *The Triangle of Love.* New York, NY: Basic Books.

Sternberg, Robert J., and Karen Sternberg, eds. 2008. *The New Psychology of Love.* New Haven, CT: Yale University Press.

Stevens, Daphne Pedersen, Krista Lynn Minnotte, Susan E. Mannon, and Gary Kiger. 2007. "Examining the 'Neglected Side of the Work–Family Interface.'" *Journal of Family Issues* 28(2): 242–262.

Stewart, Lisa M. 2013. "Family Care Responsibilities and Employment: Exploring the Impact of Type of Family Care on Work–Family and Family–Work Conflict." *Journal of Family Issues* 34(1): 113–138.

Stewart, Susan D. 2005. "How the Birth of a Child Affects Involvement with Stepchildren." *Journal of Marriage and Family* 67(2): 461.

—. 2007. *Brave New Stepfamilies*. Thousand Oaks, CA: Sage.

—. 2010a. "Children with Nonresident Parents: Living Arrangements, Visitation, and Child Support." *Journal of Marriage and Family* 72(5): 1078–1091.

—. 2010b. "The Characteristics and Well-being of Adopted Stepchildren." *Family Relations* 59(5): 558–571.

Stoll, Barre M., Genevieve L. Arnaut, Donald K. Fromme, and Jennifer A. Felker-Thayer. 2006. "Adolescents in Stepfamilies." *Journal of Divorce & Remarriage* 44(1): 177–189.

Stombler, Mindy, Dawn M. Baunach, Elisabeth O. Burgess, Denise J. Donnelly, Wendy O. Simonds, and Elroi J. Windsor, eds. 2010. *Sex Matters: The Sexuality and Society Reader*, 3rd ed. New York, NY: Prentice Hall.

Stone, Linda. 2006. *Kinship and Gender,* 3rd ed. Boulder, CO: Westview Press.

Stone, Pamela. 2008. *Opting Out? Why Women Really Quit Careers and Head Home*. Berkeley, CA: University of California Press.

Stoner, Katherine. 2012. *Divorce without Court: A Guide to Mediation & Collaborative Divorce*. Berkeley, CA: Nolo.

Straus, Murray A. 1980. "Social Stress and Marital Violence in a National Sample of American Families." *Annals of the New York Academy of Sciences* 347: 229–250.

—. 2003. *The Primordial Violence: Corporal Punishment by Parents, Cognitive Development, and Crime*. Walnut Creek, CA: AltaMira Press.

Straus, Murray A., and Mallie J. Paschall. 2009. "Corporal Punishment by Mothers and Development of Children's Cognitive Ability: A Longitudinal Study of Two Nationally Representative Age Cohorts." *Journal of Aggression, Maltreatment & Trauma* 48: 459–483.

Straus, Murray A., Richard J. Gelles, and Suzanne K. Steinmetz. 1980. *Behind Closed Doors: Violence in the American Family*. New York, NY: Anchor Books.

Stritof, Sheri, and Bob Stritof. 2006. "Covenant Marriage Statistics." About.com. Retrieved 6 June 2006 (marriage.about.com/cs/covenantmarriage/a/covenant_3.htm).

Strohschein, Lisa. 2005. "Parental Divorce and Child Mental Health Trajectories." *Journal of Marriage and Family* 67(5): 1286–1300.

Strong, Bryan, Christine DeVault, Barbara W. Sayad, and William L. Yarber. 2002. *Human Sexuality: Diversity in Contemporary America,* 4th ed. Boston, MA: McGraw Hill.

Strong-Jekely, L. (2006). Letter to the Editor. Brain, Child, p. 2. Budapest, Hungary, Winter.

Suanet, Bianca, Suzan van der Pas, and Theo G. van Tilburg. 2013. "Who Is in the Stepfamily? Change in Stepparents'

Family Boundaries between 1992 and 2009." *Journal of Marriage and Family* 75(5): 1070–1083.

Sudarkasa, Niara. 1999. "Interpreting the African Heritage in Afro-American Family Organization," pp. 59–73 in *American Families: A Multicultural Reader*, Stephanie Coontz, Maya Parson, and Gabrielle Raley, eds. New York, NY: Routledge.

Sukel, Kayt. 2008. "The Unexpected Dependent: When Retirement Is Not for You Alone." AARP Bulletin Today. Retrieved 4 December 2009 (Bulletin.aarp.org/yourworld/family/articles/the_unexpected_dependent.html).

Sullivan, Deborah A., and Rose Weitz. 1988. *Labor Pains: Modern Midwives and Home Birth*. New Haven, CT: Yale University Press.

Sun, Yongmin, and Yuanzhang Li. 2002. "Child Well-being during Parents' Marital Disruption Process: A Pooled Time-series Analysis." *Journal of Marriage and the Family* 64: 472–488.

—. 2008. "Stable Postdivorce Family Structures during Late Adolescence and Socioeconomic Consequences in Adulthood." *Journal of Marriage and Family* 69: 742–762.

—. 2009. "Postdivorce Family Stability and Changes in Adolescents' Academic Performance." *Journal of Family Issues* 30(11): 1527–1555.

Suro, Roberto. 2006. "A Developing Identity: Hispanics in the United States." In *Carnegie Reporter*. Spring. New York, NY: Carnegie Foundation.

Sutherland, Katie E., Shannon Altenhofen, and Zeynep Biringen. 2012. "Emotional Availability during Mother–Child Interactions in Divorcing and Intact Married Families." *Journal of Divorce & Remarriage* 53(2): 126–141.

Sweeney, Megan M. 2010. "Remarriage and Stepfamilies: Strategic Sites for Family Scholarship in the 21st Century." *Journal of Marriage and Family* 72(3): 667–684.

Sweeney, Megan M., Hongbo Wang, and Tami Videon. 2009. "Reconsidering the Association between Stepfamilies and Adolescent Well-being," pp. 177–225 in *Marriage and Family: Perspectives and Complexities,* H. Elizabeth Peters and Claire M. Kamp Dush, eds. New York, NY: Columbia University Press.

Swiss, Liam, and Céline Le Bourdais. 2009. "Father–Child Contact after Separation." *Journal of Family Issues* 30(5): 623–652.

Syme, Maggie L., Elizabeth A. Klonoff, Caroline A. Macera, and Stephanie K. Brodine. 2012. "Predicting Sexual Decline and Dissatisfaction among Older Adults: The Role of Partnered and Individual Physical and Mental Health Factors." *The Journals of Gerontology Series B: Psychological Sciences and Social Sciences* 68(3): 323–332.

Symoens, Sara, Kim Bastaits, Dimitri Mortelmans, and Piet Bracke. 2013. "Breaking Up, Breaking Hearts? Characteristics of the Divorce Process and Well-being after Divorce." *Journal of Divorce & Remarriage* 54(3): 177–196.

Szinovacz, Maximiliane E. 2000. "Changes in Housework after Retirement: A Panel Analysis." *Journal of Marriage and the Family* 62: 78–92.

Täht, Kadri, and Melinda Mills. 2012. "Nonstandard Work Schedules, Couple Desynchronization, and Parent–Child Interaction: A Mixed-methods Analysis." *Journal of Family Issues* 33(8): 1054–1087.

Tamis-LeMonda, Catherine S., Niobe Way, Diane Hughes, Hiro Yoshikawa, Ronit Kahana Kalman, and Erika Y. Niwa. 2008. "Parents' Goals for Children: The Dynamic Co-existence of Individualism and Collectivism in Cultures and Individuals." *Social Development* 17: 183–209.

Tan, Tony Xing, and Yi Yang. 2005. "Language Development of Chinese Adoptees 18–35 Months Old." *Early Childhood Research Quarterly* 20: 57–68.

Tannen, Deborah. 1990. *You Just Don't Understand: Women and Men in Conversation.* New York, NY: Morrow.

—. 1994. *Gender and Discourse.* New York, NY: Oxford University Press.

Tarmann, Allison. 2003. "International Adoption Rate in U.S. Doubled in the U.S." Population Reference Bureau. Retrieved 14 April 2003 (www.prb.org/Template.cfm?Section=PRB&template=/ContentManagement/Content).

Taylor, Paul, Cary Funk, and April Clark. 2007. *Generation Gap in Values, Behaviors: As Marriage and Parenthood Drift Apart, Public Is Concerned about Social Impact.* 1 July. Washington, DC: Pew Research Center.

Taylor, Paul, Cary Funk, and Peyton Craighill. 2006. *Are We Happy Yet?* 13 February. Washington, DC: Pew Research Center.

Taylor, Paul, Jeffrey Passel, Richard Fry, Richard Morin, Wendy Wang, Gabriel Velasco, and Daniel Dockterman. 2010. "The Return of the Multi-generational Family Household." Pew Research Center. Retrieved 11 November 2010 (pewresearch.orgs/pubs/1528/multi-generational-family-household).

Taylor, Paul, Rakesh Kochhar, Rich Morin, Wendy Wang, Daniel Dockterman, and Jennifer Medina. 2009. *America's Changing Workforce: Recession Turns a Graying Office Grayer.* 3 September. Washington, DC: Pew Research Center.

Taylor, Paul, Rich Morin, D'Vera Cohn, Richard Fry, Rakesh Kochhar, and April Clark. 2008. *Inside the Middle Class: Bad Times Hit the Good Life.* 9 April. Washington, DC: Pew Research Center.

Taylor, Paul, Kim Parker, Rakesh Kochhar, Richard Fry, Cary Funk, Eileen Patten, and Seth Motel. 2012. *Young, Underemployed and Optimistic: Coming of Age, Slowly, in a Tough Economy.* Social & Demographic Trends. 9 February. Washington, DC: Pew Research Center.

Taylor, Raymond, and Beth Andrews. 2009. "Parental Depression in the Context of Divorce and the Impact of Children." *Journal of Divorce & Remarriage* 50(7): 472–480.

Teachman, Jay D. 2008. "The Living Arrangements of Children and Their Educational Well-being." *Journal of Family Issues* 29(6): 734–761.

—. 2010. "Wives' Economic Resources and Risk of Divorce." *Journal of Family Issues* 31(10): 1305–1323.

Tejada-Vera, Betzaida and Paul D. Sutton. 2009. *Births, Marriages, Divorces, and Deaths: Provisional Data for May 2009.* National Vital Statistics Reports, Vol. 58, No. 12. Hyattsville, MD: National Center for Health Statistics.

Temperament.com. 2009. "Temperament and Parenting: Temperament FAQs." Retrieved 5 December 2009 (www.temperament.com/temperament.comfaqs.html).

Tennov, Dorothy. 1999. *Love and Limerence: The Experience of Being in Love.* New York, NY: Scarborough Place.

Tessler, Richard, and Gail Gamache. 2009. "Bi-cultural Socialization and Ethnic Identity in Adolescence." *The Journal of Families with Children from China* 1(1): 22–23, 45–46.

Thigpen, Jeffry W. 2009. "Early Sexual Behavior in a Sample of Low-income, African American Children." *Journal of Sex Research* 46(1): 67–79.

Thomas, Alexander, and Stella Chess. 1957. "An Approach to the Study of Sources of Individual Difference in Child Behavior." *Journal of Clinical and Experimental Psychopathology* 18: 347–357.

Thomas, Joan C. 2008. "Divorce Mediation: Frequently Asked Questions." DivorceMag.com. Retrieved 10 March 2008 (www.divorcemag.com/articles/Mediation/mediation_faq.html).

Thomas, Kristy A., and Richard C. Tessler. 2007. "Bicultural Socialization among Adoptive Families: Where There Is a Will, There Is a Way." *Journal of Family Issues* 28: 1189–1219.

Thompson, Jeff, and Jeff Chapman. 2006. "The Economic Impact of Local Living Wages." Economic Policy Institute. Retrieved 8 September 2008 (www.epi.org/content.cfm/bp170).

Thompson, Linda, and Alexis J. Walker. 1989. "Gender in Families: Women and Men in Marriage, Work, and Parenthood." *Journal of Marriage and the Family* 51: 845–871.

Thornhill, Randy and Steven W. Gangestad. 2008. *The Evolutionary Biology of Human Female Sexuality.* New York, NY: Oxford University Press.

Tierney, John. 2003. "Iraqi Marriage Bedevils Americans." *New York Times* News Service. *The Oregonian,* 28 September, p. A-2.

Tita, Alan T. N., Mark B. Landon, Catherine Y. Spong, Yinglei Lai, Kenneth J. Leveno, Michael W. Varner, Atef H. Moawad, Steve N. Caritis, Paul J. Meis, Ronald J. Wapner, Yoram Sorokin, Menachem Miodovnik, Marshall Carpenter, Alan M. Peaceman, Mary J. O'Sullivan, Baha H. Sibai, Oded Langer, John M. Thorp, Susan M. Ramin, and Brian M. Mercer for the Eunice Shriver NICHD Maternal-Fetal Medicine Units Network. 2009. "Timing of Elective Repeat Cesarean Delivery at Term and Neonatal Outcomes." *New England Journal of Medicine* 360(2, 8 January): 111–120.

Tjaden, Patricia, and Nancy Thoennes. 1998. "Prevalence, Incidence, and Consequences of Violence against Women: Findings from the National Violence against Women Survey." November. National Institute of Justice and Centers for Disease Control and Prevention. Retrieved 22 December 2013 (www.ncjrs.gov/pdffiles/172837.pdf).

—. 2000 November. *Full Report of the Prevalence, Incidence, and Consequences of Violence against Women: Findings from the National Violence against Women Survey.*

Washington, DC: National Institute of Justice and Centers for Disease Control and Prevention.

—. 2006. "Extent, Nature, and Consequences of Rape Victimization: Findings from the National Violence against Women Survey" (Report NCJ 210346). National Institute of Justice. Retrieved 24 April 2007 (www.ncjrs.gov/pdffiles1/nij/210346.pdf).

Tolman, Deborah L. 2005. *Dilemmas of Desire: Teenage Girls Talk about Sexuality.* Cambridge, MA: Harvard University Press.

Toomey, Russell B., and Adriana J. Umaña-Taylor. 2012. "The Role of Ethnic Identity on Self-esteem for Ethnic Minority Youth." *The Prevention Researcher* 19(2): 13–16.

Trask, Bahira Sherif, and Raeann R. Hamon. 2007. *Cultural Diversity and Families.* Thousand Oaks, CA: Sage.

Trenholm, Sarah. 2014. *Thinking through Communication,* 7th ed. Boston, MA: Pearson.

Trent, Katherine, and Scott J. South. 1989. "Structural Determinants of the Divorce Rate: A Cross-societal Analysis." *Journal of Marriage and the Family* 51: 391–404.

Trinder, Liz. 2008. "Maternal Gate Closing and Gate Opening in Postdivorce Families." *Journal of Family Issues* 29(10): 1298–1324.

Trisi, Danilo, and LaDonna Pavetti. 2012. "TANF Weakening as a Safety Net for Poor Families." Center on Budget and Policy Priorities. 13 March. Retrieved 30 May 2013 (www.cbpp.org/cms/index.cfm?fa=view&id=3700).

Troy, Adam B., Jamie Lewis-Smith, and Jean-Philippe Laurenceau. 2006. "Interracial and Intraracial Romantic Relationships: The Search for Satisfaction, Conflict, and Attachment Style." *Journal of Social and Personal Relationships* 23(February): 65–80.

Trust in Education. 2013. Home Page. Retrieved 25 February 2013 (www.trustineducation.org).

Tucker, M. Belinda. 2000. "Marital Values and Expectations in Context: Results from a 21-City Survey," pp. 166–187 in *The Ties That Bind: Perspectives on Marriage and Cohabitation,* Linda J. Waite, Christine Bachrach, Michelle J. Hindin, Elizabeth Thomson, and Arland Thornton, eds. New York, NY: Aldine de Gruyter.

Turner, Heather A., and Paul A. Muller. 2004. "Long-term Effects of Child Corporal Punishment on Depressive Symptoms in Young Adults." *Journal of Family Issues* 25: 761–782.

Turner, Lynn H., and Richard L. West. 2013. *Perspectives on Family Communication,* 4th ed. New York, NY: McGraw-Hill.

Uebelacker, Lisa A., Emily S. Courtnage, and Mark A. Whisman. 2003. "Correlates of Depression and Marital Dissatisfaction: Perceptions of Marital Communication Style." *Journal of Social and Personal Relationships* 20 (December): 757–769.

Uhlenberg, Peter. 2009. "Children in an Aging Society." *The Journals of Gerontology: Series B* 64B(4): 489–496.

Umaña-Taylor, Adriana J., Edna C. Alfaro, Mayra Y. Bámaca, and Amy B. Guimond. 2009. "The Central Role of Familial Ethnic Socialization in Latino Adolescents' Cultural Orientation." *Journal of Marriage and Family* 71(1): 46–60.

Umaña-Taylor, Adriana J., Ani Yazedjian, and Mayra Y. Bámaca-Gómez. 2004. "Developing the Ethnic Identity Scale Using Eriksonian and Social Identity Perspectives." *Identity: An International Journal of Theory and Research* 4(1): 9–38.

Umaña-Taylor, Adriana J., Katharine H. Zeiders, and Kimberly A. Updegraff. 2013. "Family Ethnic Socialization and Ethnic Identity: A Family-Driven, Youth-Driven, or Reciprocal Process?" *Journal of Family Psychology* 27(1): 137–146.

Umberson, Debra, Tetyana Pudrovska, and Corinne Reczek. 2010. "Parenthood and Well-being over the Life Course." *Journal of Marriage and Family* 72(3): 612–629.

UNAIDS. 2012a. "Global AIDS Epidemic Facts and Figures: Fact Sheet." 20 November. Retrieved 7 April 2013 (www.unaids.org/en/resources/presscentre/factsheets).

UNAIDS. 2012b. "Sub-Saharan Africa: Fact Sheet." 20 November. Retrieved 7 April 2013 (www.unaids.org/en/resources/presscentre/factsheets).

United Nations Children's Fund and UNAIDS. 2006. "Africa's Orphaned and Vulnerable Generations: Children Affected by AIDS." Retrieved 7 October 2013 (www.unicef.org/publications/files/Africas_Orphaned_Generation_Executive_Summary_Eng.pdf).

United Nations Office on Drugs and Crime. 2013. "Human Trafficking." Retrieved 13 May 2013 (www.unodc.org/en/human-trafficking/what-is-human-trafficking.html?ref=menuside).

U.S. Census Bureau. 2006. "Current Population Survey, March and Annual Social and Economic Supplements, 2005 and Earlier, Table UC-1" (www.census.gov/population/socdemo/hh-fam/uc1.pdf).

—. 2007. "Families and Living Arrangements" (www.census.gov/population/www/socdemo/hh-fam/cps2007.html).

—. 2008a. "Marital Status of the Population 15 Years Old and over by Sex and Race: 1950 to Present." 27 August. (www.census.gov/population/www/socdemo/hh-fam/ms1.csv).

—. 2008b. "Table SF1. Percent Childless and Births Per 1,000 Women in the Last Year: Selected Years, 1976 to 2006." In *Fertility of American Women.* Retrieved 7 March 2010 (www.census.gov/population/www/socdemo/fertility.html).

—. 2008c. *American Community Survey: California S1002. Grandparents.* August.

—. 2009a. "Age and Sex in the United States: 2008." Retrieved 12 April 2010 (www.census.gov/population/www/socdemo/age/age_sex_2008.html).

—. 2009b. "The Older Population in the United States: 2008." Retrieved 23 April 2010 (www.census.gov/population/www/socdemo/age/older_2008.html).

—. 2009c. "America's Families and Living Arrangements: 2008." Retrieved 12 April 2010 (www.census.gov/population/www/socdemo/hh-fam/cps2008.html).

—. 2009d. "American Indian and Alaska Native Heritage Month: November 2009" (Press Release). Retrieved 20 January 2010 (www.census.gov/Press-Release/www/releases/archives/facts_for_features_special_editions/014346.html).

—. 2010a. "America's Families and Living Arrangements: 2009." 14 January. Retrieved 21 February 2010 (www.census.gov/population/www/socdemo/hh-fam/cps2009.html).

—. 2010b. "Labor Force, Employment, & Earnings: Labor Force Status." In *2010 Statistical Abstract*. Washington, DC.

—. 2012a. "Computer and Internet Use in the United States: 2010." Retrieved 23 April 2013 (www.census.gov/hhes/computer/publications/2010.html).

—. 2012b. "Race: The Black Alone Population in the United States: 2011." 13 September. Retrieved 3 March 2013 (www.census.gov/population/race/data/ppl-ba11.html).

—. 2012c. "America's Families and Living Arrangements: 2012." 28 November. Retrieved 13 February 2013 (www.census.gov/hhes/families/data/cps2012.html).

—. 2013. "Educational Attainment in the United States: 2012—Detailed Tables." 7 January. Retrieved 3 March 2013 (www.census.gov/hhes/socdemo/education/data/cps/2012/tables.html).

—. 2013. 2012 American Community Survey. Retrieved 7 October 2013 (www.census.gov/acs/www).

U.S. Conference of Mayors. 2012. *A Status Report on Hunger and Homelessness in America's Cities: A 25-City Survey*. December. Washington, DC.

U.S. Department of Health and Human Services, Administration for Children, Youth, and Families. 2006. "Children Home Alone and Babysitter Age Guidelines." Retrieved 17 July 2006 (www.nccic.org/poptopics/homealone.html).

—. 2012. "Child Maltreatment 2011." Retrieved 8 March 2013. Washington, DC: Government Printing Office (www.acf.hhs.gov/programs/cb/research-data-technology/statistics-research/child-maltreatment).

—. 2013. "America's Families and Living Arrangements: 2012." 22 November. Retrieved 25 November 2013 (www.census.gov/hhes/families/data/cps2013.html).

U.S. Department of Health and Human Services, Office of Women's Health. 2008. "Date Rape Drugs: Frequently Asked Questions." Retrieved 28 March 2010 (www.womenshealth.gov/faq/date-rape-drugs.cfm).

—. 2012. "Date Rape Drugs Fact Sheet." 16 July. Womenshealth.gov. Retrieved 10 May 2013 (www.womenshealth.gov/publications/our-publications/fact-sheet/date-rape-drugs.html).

U.S. Department of Housing & Urban Development. 2013a. "Affordable Housing." Retrieved 26 February 2013 (portal.hud.gov/hudportal/HUD?src=/program_offices/comm_planning/affordablehousing).

—. 2013b. "Final FY 2013 Fair Market Rent Documentation System." Retrieved 4 March 2013 (www.huduser.org/portal/datasets/fmr/fmrs/docsys.html&data=fmr13).

U.S. Department of Justice, Bureau of Justice Statistics. 2007. "Homicide Trends in the U.S.: Intimate Homicide." Retrieved 10 October 2008 (www.ojp.usdoj.gov/bjs/homicide/intimates.htm).

U.S. Department of State. 2009a. "Total Adoptions to the United States." Retrieved 9 November 2009 (Adoption.state.gov/news/total_chart.html?css=print).

—. 2009b. "Trafficking in Persons Report 2009." Retrieved 25 March 2010 (www.state.gov/g/tip/rls/tiprpt/2009).

—. 2012. "Trafficking in Persons Report." June. Retrieved 7 October 2013 (www.state.gov/documents/organization/192587.pdf).

—. 2013. *Intercountry Adoption*. Retrieved 25 February 2013 (adoption.state.gov).

U.S. Equal Employment Opportunity Commission. 2010. "Race-Based Charges FY1997–FY2009." Retrieved 18 January 2010 (www1.eeoc.gov//eeoc/statistics/enforcement/race.cfm?renderforprint=1).

—. 2012. "Charge Statistics FY 1997 through FY 2012." Retrieved 8 March 2013 (www.eeoc.gov/eeoc/statistics/enforcement/charges.cfm).

Umberson, Debra J., Tatyana Pudrovska, and Corinne Reczek. 2010. "Parenthood, Childlessness, and Well-Being: A Life Course Perspective." *Journal of Marriage and Family* 72: 621–629.

United Nations Statistics Division. 2005. "Table 5c—Maternity Leave Benefits." In *Statistics and Indicators on Women and Men*. Retrieved 14 January 2006 (unstats.un.org/unsd/demographic/products/indwm/ww2005/tab5c.htm).

—. 2010. "Statistics and Indicators on Women and Men: Table 5g. Maternity Leave Benefits." Retrieved 3 May 2010 (unstats.un.org/unsd/demographic/poducts/indwm/tab5g.htm).

—. 2011. "Statistical Products and Databases." December. Retrieved 29 May 2013 (unstats.un.org/unsd/demographic/products).

United Nations Office on Drugs and Crime (UNODC). 2013. *Trafficking in Persons: Global Patterns*. April.

United Press International, Inc. 2010. "24 Countries Have Banned All Spanking." 10 August. Retrieved 14 May 2013 (www.upi.com/Health_News/2010/08/10/24-countries-have-banned-all-spanking/UPI-13381281421948/print).

Universal Living Wage Campaign. 2013. "Sample Cities." Retrieved 2 May 2013 (www.universallivingwage.org).

University of New Hampshire Cooperative Extension. 2006. *The Effects of Divorce on Children*.

USA.gov. 2010. "Grandparents Raising Grandchildren." 25 February. Retrieved 4 May 2013 (www.usa.gov/Topics/Grandparents.shtml).

Uttal, Lynet. 1999. "Using Kin for Child Care: Embedment in the Socioeconomic Networks of Extended Families." *Journal of Marriage and the Family* 61: 845–857.

Utz, Rebecca L., Michael Caserta, and Dale Lund. 2012. "Grief, Depressive Symptoms, and Physical Health Among Recently Bereaved Spouses." *The Gerontologist* 52(4): 460–471.

Vaaler, Margaret L., Christopher G. Ellison, and Daniel A. Powers. 2009. "Religious Influences on the Risk of Marital Dissolution." *Journal of Marriage and Family* 71(4): 917–934.

van Teijlingen, Edwin, George Louis, Peter McCaffery, and Maureen Porter, eds. 2004. *Midwifery and the Medicalization of Childbirth: Comparative Perspectives*. Hauppage, NY: Nova Science Publisher.

Vandell, Deborah Lowe, Jay Belsky, Margaret Burchinal, Laurence Steinberg, Nathan Vandergrift, and the

NICHD Early Child Care Research Network. 2010. "Do Effects of Early Child Care Extend to Age 15 Years? Results from the NICHD Study of Early Child Care and Youth Development." *Child Development* 81(3): 737–756.

Vandivere, Sharon, Kathryn Tout, Jeffrey Capizzano, and Martha Zaslow. 2003. "Left Unsupervised: A Look at the Most Vulnerable Children." In *Child Trends Research Brief*. Retrieved 27 July 2003 (www.childtrends.org).

VanLaningham, Jody, David R. Johnson, and Paul R. Amato. 2001. "Marital Happiness, Marital Duration, and the U-Shaped Curve: Evidence from a Five-Wave Panel Study." *Social Forces* 78: 1313–1341.

Vaughan, Diane. 1986. *Uncoupling—Turning Points in Intimate Relationships*. New York, NY: Oxford University Press.

Vedantam, Shankar. 2006. "Male Scientist Writes of Life as Female Scientist." Retrieved 21 November 2006. washingtonpost.com (www.washingtonpost.com/wp-dyn/content/article/2006/07/12/AR2006071201883.html).

Vespa, Jonathan, Jamie M. Lewis, and Rose M. Kreider, 2013. "America's Families and Living Arrangements: 2012." August (www.census.gov/prod/2013pubs/p20-570.pdf).

Vienna Institute of Demography. 2008. "European Demographic Data Sheet 2008." Retrieved 16 December 2009 (www.oeaw.ac.at/vid/datasheet/download/sources_notes_datasheet2008.pdf).

Vincent, Wilson, John L. Peterson, and Dominic J. Parrott. 2009. "Differences in African American and White Women's Attitudes towards Lesbians and Gay Men." *Sex Roles* 61(9–10): 599–606.

Vives-Cases, Carmen, Diana Gil-González, and Mercedes Carasco-Portiño. 2009. "Verbal Marital Conflict and Male Domination in the Family as Risk Factors of Intimate Partner Violence." *Trauma, Violence, & Abuse* 10(2): 171–180.

Vlosky, Denise Ashbaugh, and Pamela A. Monroe. 2002. "The Effective Dates of No-Fault Divorce Laws in the 50 States." *Family Relations* 51: 317–324.

Voller, Emily K., and Patricia J. Long. 2010. "Sexual Assault and Rape Perpetration by College Men: The Role of the Big Five Personality Traits." *Journal of Interpersonal Violence* 25: 457–480.

Voorpostel, Marieke, and Rosemary Bleiszner. 2008. "Intergenerational Solidarity and Support between Adult Siblings." *Journal of Marriage and Family* 70(1): 157–167.

Voydanoff, Patricia. 2004. "Community as a Context for the Work–Family Interface." *Organizational Management Journal* 1(1): 49–54.

—. 2008. "A Conceptual Model of Work–Family Interface," pp. 37–56 in *Handbook of Work–Family Integration: Research, Theory, and Best Practices*, Karen Korabik, Donna S. Lero, and Denise L. Whitehead, eds. Burlington, MA: Elsevier.

Vrangalova, Zhana, and Ritch C. Savin-Williams. 2010. "Correlates of Same-sex Sexuality in Heterosexually Identified Young Adults." *Journal of Sex Research* 47(1): 92–102.

Wage and Hour Division, U.S. Department of Labor. 2013. "Minimum Wage Laws in the States—January 1, 2013." Retrieved 2 May 2013 (www.dol.gov/whd/minwage/america.htm#Washington).

Wagner, Marsden. 2008. *Born in the USA: How a Broken Maternity System Must Be Fixed to Put Women and Children First*. Berkeley, CA: University of California Press.

Wagner, Peter. 2012. "Incarceration Rates by Race & Ethnicity, 2010." Statistics as of June 30, 2010 and December 31, 2010 from *Correctional Population in the United States* and from U.S. Census Summary File 1. Retrieved 12 April 2013 (www.prisonpolicy.org/graphs/raceinc.html).

Waite, Linda J., and Maggie Gallagher. 2000. *The Case for Marriage: Why Married People Are Happier, Healthier, and Better Off Financially*. New York, NY: Doubleday.

Waite, Linda J., Ye Luo, and Alise C. Lewin. 2009. Marital Happiness and Marital Stability: Consequences for Psychological Well-being. *Social Science Research* 38: 201–212.

Waknine, Yael. 2013. "Guidelines Discourage Elective C-Sections, Early Deliveries." Medscape Multispecialty. (www.medscape.com/viewarticle/781281).

Waldfogel, Jane. 2006. *What Children Need*. Cambridge, MA: Harvard University Press.

Waldmeir, Patti. 2013. "China Counts Cost of One Child Policy." *Financial Times*. 1 February. Retrieved 25 February 2013 (www.ft.com/cms/s/0/f60a25c8-6c52-11e2-b73a-00144feab49a.html#axzz2LxFwu0Q9).

Walker, Alexis J. 1999. "Gender and Family Relationships," pp. 439–474 in *Handbook of Marriage and the Family*. Marvin B. Sussman, Susan K. Steinmetz, and Gary W. Peterson, eds. New York, NY: Plenum.

Walker, Alexis J., Margaret Manoogian-O'Dell, Lori A. McGraw, and Diana L.G. White. 2001. *Families in Later Life: Connections and Transitions*. Thousand Oaks, CA: Pine Forge Press.

Walker, Eric C., Thomas B. Holman, and Dean M. Busby. 2009. "Childhood Sexual Abuse, Other Childhood Factors, and Pathways to Survivors' Adult Relationship Quality." *Journal of Family Violence* 24(6): 397–406.

Walker, Lenore. 1993. "The Battered Woman Syndrome Is a Psychological Consequence of Abuse." In *Current Controversies in Family Violence*, Richard J. Gelles and Dorileen R. Loseke, eds. Newbury Park, CA: Sage.

Walker-Rodriguez, Amanda, and Rodney Hill. 2011. "Human Sex Trafficking." FBI Law Enforcement Bulletin. March. Retrieved 14 May 2013 (www.fbi.gov/stats-services/publications/law-enforcement-bulletin/march_2011/human_sex_trafficking).

Wallace, Danielle M. 2007. "'It's A M-A-N Thang': Black Male Gender Role Socialization and the Performance of Masculinity in Love Relationships." *The Journal of Pan African Studies* 1(7): 11–22.

Waller, Maureen, and Sara McLanahan. 2005. "'His' and 'Her' Marriage Expectations: Determinants and Consequences." *Journal of Marriage and Family* 67: 53–67.

Waller, Willard. 1937. "The Rating and Dating Complex." *American Sociological Review* 2: 727–734.

Wallerstein, Judith S. 1983. "Children of Divorce: The Psychological Tasks of the Child." *American Journal of Orthopsychiatry* 53: 230–243.

—. 2007. "Adult Children of Divorce Speak Out." *National Council on Family Relations Report* 52(4): F12–F13; F19.

Wallerstein, Judith S., and Sandra Blakeslee. 1989. *Second Chances: Men, Women and Children a Decade after Divorce*. New York, NY: Ticknor & Fields.

Walsh, Froma. 2006. *Strengthening Family Resilience*, 2nd ed. *(Guilford Family Therapy Series)*. New York, NY: Guilford Press.

—, ed. 2012. *Normal Family Processes: Growing Diversity and Complexity*. New York, NY: Guilford Press.

Walsh, Wendy A., Jean Dawson, and Marybeth J. Mattingly. 2010. "How Are We Measuring Resilience Following Childhood Maltreatment? Is the Research Adequate and Consistent? What Is the Impact on Research, Practice, and Policy?" *Trauma, Violence, & Abuse* 11(1): 27–41.

Walzer, Susan. 1998. *Thinking about the Baby: Gender and Transitions into Parenthood*. Philadelphia, PA: Temple University Press.

Wang, Bo, and Pamela Davidson. 2006. "Sex, Lies, and Videos in Rural China: A Qualitative Study of Women's Sexual Debut and Risky Sexual Behavior." *The Journal of Sex Research* 43(3): 227–235.

Wang, Feng, Yong Cai, and Baochang Gu. 2012. "Population, Policy, and Politics: How Will History Judge China's One-child Policy?" *Population and Development Review (Brookings)* 38(Suppl): 115–129.

Wang, Wendy, and Rich Morin. 2009. "Recession Brings Many Young Adults Back to the Nest." Pew Research Center. Retrieved 4 April 2010 (pewsocialtrends.org/pubs/748/recession-brings-many-young-adults-back-to-the-nest).

Ward, Jane. 2010. "Straight Dude Seeks Same: Mapping the Relationship between Sexual Identities, Practices, and Cultures." In *Sex Matters: The Sexuality and Society Reader*, 3rd ed., Mindy Stombler, Dawn M. Baunach, Elisabeth O. Burgess, Denise Donnelly, Wendy Simonds, and Elroi J. Windsor, eds. New York, NY: Prentice Hall.

Ward, Russell, and Glenna Spitze. 2007. "Nestleaving and Coresidence by Young Adult Children." *Research on Aging* 29(3): 257–277.

Wardhaugh, Ronald. 2010. *An Introduction to Sociolinguistics*. New York, NY: Wiley-Blackwell.

Wardrip, Keith E., Danilo Pelletiere, and Sheila Crowley. 2009. *Out of Reach 2009: Persistent Problems, New Challenges for Renters*. Washington, DC: National Low Income Housing Coalition.

Warner, Judith. 2005. *Perfect Madness: Motherhood in the Age of Anxiety*. New York, NY: Penguin Group USA.

Warner, Rebecca L. 2006. "Being a Good Parent," pp. 65–83 in *Couples, Kids and Family Life: Social Worlds From the Inside Out*, Jaber F. Gubrium and James A. Holstein, eds. New York, NY: Oxford University Press.

Weatherford, Doris. 1986. *Foreign and Female: Immigrant Women in America, 1840–1930*. New York, NY: Checkmark Books.

Weaver, Hilary N. 2009. "The Colonial Context of Violence." *Journal of Interpersonal Violence* 24(9): 1552–1563.

Wedding Report. 2013. "United States Complete Market Report." Retrieved 12 April 2013 (www.theweddingreport.com/wmdb/index.cfm?action-db.viewdetail&t=s&lc=00&setloc=y).

Weigel, Daniel J. 2007. "Parental Divorce and the Types of Commitment-related Messages People Gain from Their Families of Origin." *Journal of Divorce & Remarriage* 47(1/2): 15–32.

Weigel, Daniel J. 2008. "The Concept of Family: An Analysis of Laypeople's Views of Family." *Journal of Family Issues* 29(11): 1426–1447.

Weininger, Elliot B. and Annette Lareau. 2009. "Paradoxical Pathways: An Ethnographic Extension of Kohn's Findings on Class and Childrearing." *Journal of Marriage and Family* 71(3): 680–695.

Weis, David L. 1998. "Basic Sexological Premises." In *Sexuality in America: Understanding Our Sexual Values and Behavior*, Robert T. Francoeur, Patricia Barthalow, and David L. Weis, eds. New York, NY: Continuum.

Weiss, R. 2002. LA Times–Washington Post News Service. *The Oregonian*, 13 November, p. A-10.

Weitzman, Lenore J. 1985. *The Divorce Revolution: The Unexpected Consequences for Women and Their Children in America*. New York, NY: Free Press.

Welch, Charles E., III, and Paul C. Glick. 1981. "The Incidence of Polygamy in Contemporary Africa: A Research Note." *Journal of Marriage and the Family*, 43(1): 191–193.

Wellman, Barry, Aaron Smith, Amy Wells, and Tracy Kennedy. 2008. "Report: Families, Mobile, New Media Ecology–Networked Families." 19 October. The Pew Internet & American Life Project.

Wen, Ming. 2008. "Family Structure and Children's Health and Behavior." *Journal of Family Issues* 29(11): 1492–1519.

Wenck, Stan, and Connie J. Hansen. 2009. *Love Him, Love His Kids: The Stepmother's Guide to Surviving and Thriving in a Blended Family*. Cincinnati, OH: Adams Media.

Wang, Wendy, & Paul Taylor. 2011. "For Millennials, Parenthood Trumps Marriage." *Pew Research Social & Demographic Trends*. 9 March. Retrieved 4 January 2014 (www.pewsocialtrends.org/2011/03/09/for-millennials-parenthood-trumps-marriage/3/).

Werner, Emmy E. 1994. "Overcoming the Odds." *Developmental and Behavioral Pediatrics* 15: 131–136.

Werner, Emmy E., and Ruth S. Smith. 1989. *Vulnerable but Invincible: A Longitudinal Study of Resilient Children and Youth*. New York, NY: Adams, Bannister, Cox.

—. 1992. *Overcoming the Odds*. Ithaca, NY: Cornell University Press.

West, Candace, and Don H. Zimmerman. 1983. "Small Insults: A Study of Interruptions in Cross-sex Conversations between Unacquainted Persons." In *Language, Gender and Society*, Barrie Thorne, Cheris Kramarae, and Nancy Henley, eds. Cambridge House: Newbury House.

—. 1987. "Doing Gender." *Gender and Society* 1: 125–131.

West, Richard, and Lynn Turner. 2006. *Introducing Communication Theory: Analysis and Application with PowerWeb*. New York, NY: McGraw-Hill.

White House. 2004. "President Calls for Constitutional Amendment Protecting Marriage" (Press Release). Retrieved 7 October 2005 (www.whitehouse.gov/news/releases/2004/02/20040224-2.html).

White, Lynn, and Joan G. Gilbreth. 2001. "When Children Have Two Fathers: Effects of Relationships with Stepfathers and Noncustodial Fathers on Adolescent Outcomes." *Journal of Marriage and the Family* 63: 155–167.

White, Lynn, and Stacy J. Rogers. 2000. "Economic Circumstances and Family Outcomes: A Review of the 1990s." *Journal of Marriage and Family* 62(4): 1035–1051.

Whitehead, Barbara Dafoe, and David Popenoe. 2002. "Why Men Won't Commit." In *The State of Our Unions: The Social Health of Marriage in America*. The National Marriage Project.

Whitton, Sarah W., Galena K. Rhoades, Scott M. Stanley, and Howard J. Markman. 2008. "Effects of Parental Divorce on Marital Commitment and Confidence." *Journal of Family Psychology* 22(5): 789–793.

Whitton, Sarah W., Scott M. Stanley, Howard J. Markman, and Christine A. Johnson. 2013. "Attitudes toward Divorce, Commitment, and Divorce Proneness in First Marriages and Remarriages." *Journal of Marriage and Family* 75(2): 276–287.

Whoriskey, Peter. 2009. "GM to Build More Cars Overseas." Washingtonpost.com. Retrieved 9 March 2010 (extracted from cbsnews.com) (www.cbsnews.com/stories/2009/05/08/politics/washingtonpost/main5001058.shtml).

Wilcox, Kathryn, L., Sharlene A. Wolchik, and Sanford L. Braver. 1998. "Of Maternal Preference for Joint or Sole Legal Custody." *Family Relations* 47: 93–101.

Wilcox, W. Bradford, and Nicholas Wolfinger. 2007. "Then Comes Marriage? Religion, Race, and Marriage in Urban America." *Social Science Research* 36: 569–589.

Wilkenfeld, Britt, Kristin Anderson Moore, and Laura Lippman. 2008. "Neighborhood Support and Children's Connectedness" (Child Trends Fact Sheet). The Annie E. Casey Foundation.

Wilkinson, Doris Y. 1997. "American Families of African Descent." In *Families in Cultural Context: Strength and Challenges in Diversity*, Mary Kay DeGenova, ed. Mountain View, CA: Mayfield Publishing Company.

Willén, Helena, and Henry Montgomery. 2006. "From Marital Distress to Divorce: The Creation of New Identities for the Spouses." *Journal of Divorce & Remarriage* 45(1/2): 125–147.

Williams, Juanita H. 1993. "Sexuality in Marriage," pp. 93–122 in *Handbook of Human Sexuality*, Benjamin B. Wolman and John Money, eds. Northvale, NJ: Jason Aronson.

Williams, Timothy. 2012. "For Native American Women, Scourge of Rape, Rare Justice." *New York Times*. 22 May. Retrieved 4 March 2013 (www.nytimes.com/2012/05/23/us/native-americans-struggle-with-high-rate-of-rape.html?pagewanted=all&_r=0&pagewanted=print).

Wilson, Stephan M., Lucy W. Ngige, and Linda J. Trollinger. 2003. "Connecting Generations: Kamba and Maasai Paths to Marriage in Kenya," pp. 95–118 in *Male Selection Across Cultures*, Raeann R. Hamon and Bron B. Ingoldsby, eds. Thousand Oaks, CA: Sage.

Wilson, William J. 1987. *The Truly Disadvantaged: The Inner City, the Underclass, and Public Policy*. Chicago, IL: University of Chicago Press.

—. 1993. *The New Urban Poverty and the Problem of Race*. Ann Arbor, MI: University of Michigan.

—. 1996. *When Work Disappears: The World of the New Urban Poor*. New York, NY: Alfred A. Knopf.

Wolfinger, Nicholas H. 2006. *Understanding the Divorce Cycle: The Children of Divorce in Their Own Marriages*. New York, NY: Cambridge University Press.

Wood, Julia T. 2002. "A Critical Response to John Gray's Mars and Venus Portrayals of Men and Women." *The Southern Communications Journal* 67(2): 201–211.

World Health Organization. 2009. "Gender, Women, and Health: Sexual Violence." Retrieved 18 August 2009 (www.who.int/gender/violence/sexual_violence/en/index.html).

—. 2011. *An Update on WHO's Work on Female Genital Mutilation (FGM): Progress Report*, World Health Organization, 2011 (www.who.int/reproductivehealth/publications/fgm/rhr_11_18/en/).

Worldwatch Institute. 2013. "U.N. Raises 'Low' Population Projection in 2050." Retrieved 19 April 2013 (www.worldwatch.org/node/6038).

Wright, Carroll. 1889. *A Report on Marriage and Divorce in the United States 1867–1886*. Washington, DC: Bureau of Labor.

Wright, Vanessa R., Suzanne M. Bianchi, and Bijou R. Hunt. 2013. "Explaining Racial/Ethnic Variation in Partnered Women's and Men's Housework: Does One Size Fit All?" *Journal of Family Issues* 34(3): 394–427.

Wu, Zheng, and Christopher M. Schimmele. 2005. "Repartnering after First Union Disruption." *Journal of Marriage and Family* 67(1): 27–36.

Xu, Xiaohe, Clark D. Hudspeth, and John P. Bartkowski. 2006. "The Role of Cohabitation in Remarriage." *Journal of Marriage and Family* 68(2): 261–274.

Xu, Xiaohe, and Martin King Whyte. 1990. "Love Matches and Arranged Marriages: A Chinese Replication." *Journal of Marriage and the Family* 52: 709–722.

Yaben, Sagrario Yarnoz. 2009. "Forgiveness, Attachment, and Divorce." *Journal of Divorce & Remarriage* 50(4): 282–294.

Yamawaki, Niwako, Monica Ochoa-Shipp, Craig Pulsipher, Andrew Harlos, and Scott Swindler. 2012. "Perceptions of Domestic Violence: The Effects of Domestic Violence Myths, Victim's Relationship with Her Abuser, and the Decision to Return to Her Abuser." *Journal of Interpersonal Violence* 27(16): 3195–3212.

Yanowitz, Karen L., and Kevin J. Weathers. 2004. "Do Boys and Girls Act Differently in the Classroom? A Content Analysis of Student Characters in Educational Psychology Textbooks." *Sex Roles* 51: 1–2.

Yates, Michael D. 2009. *In and Out of the Working Class*. Winnipeg, MB: Arbeiter Ring.

Yeung, Wei-jun Jean, Miriam R. Linver, and Jeanne Brooks-Gunn. 2002. "How Money Matters for Young Children's Development: Parental Investment and Family Processes." *Child Development* 73: 1861–1879.

Yoshida, Akiko. 2012. "Dads Who Do Diapers: Factors Affecting Care of Young Children by Fathers." *Journal of Family Issues* 33(4): 451–477.

Yount, Kathryn M. 2002. "Like Mother, Like Daughter? Female Genital Cutting in Minia, Egypt." *Journal of Health and Social Behavior* 43(September): 336–358.

Yu, Tianyi, and Francesca Adler-Baeder. 2007. "The Intergenerational Transmission of Relationship Quality: The Effects of Parental Remarriage Quality on Young Adults' Relationships." *Journal of Divorce & Remarriage* 47(3/4): 87–102.

Yu, Tianyi, Gregory S. Pettit, Jennifer E. Lansford, Kenneth A. Dodge, and John E. Bates. 2010. "The Interactive Effects of Marital Conflict and Divorce on Parent–Adult Children's Relationships." *Journal of Marriage and Family* 72(2): 282–292.

Zhang, Yuanting, and Jennifer Van Hook. 2009. "Marital Dissolution among Interracial Couples." *Journal of Marriage and Family* 71(1): 95–107.

Zhang, Zhenmei, and Mark D. Hayward. 2001. "Childlessness and the Psychological Well-being of Older Persons." *Journals of Gerontology: Social Sciences* 56B: S311–S320.

Zhou, Min, and Carl L. Bankston, III. 2006. "Delinquency and Acculturation in the Twenty-first Century: A Decade's Change in a Vietnamese American Community," pp. 117–139 in *Immigration and Crime: Ethnicity, Race, and Violence*, Ramiro Martinez, Jr., and Abel Valenzuela, Jr., eds. New York, NY: New York University Press.

Zhu, Wei Xing, Li Lu, and Therese Hesketh. 2009. "China's Excess Males, Sex Selective Abortion, and One Child Policy: Analysis of Data From 2005 National Intercensus Survey." *British Medical Journal* 338(9 April): b1211.

Zimmerman, Shirley L. 2001. *Family Policy: Constructed Solutions to Family Problems*. Thousand Oaks, CA: Sage.

Zinczenko, David. 2007. "Who Handles Break-Ups Better?" In *Dave Zinczenko's Mysteries of the Sexes Explained*. Yahoo! Health. Retrieved 25 September 2008 (Health.yahoo.com/experts/menlovesex/29235/who-handles-break-ups-better).

Zuckerman, Miron, Bella M. DePaulo, and Robert Rosenthal. 1981. "Verbal and Nonverbal Communication of Deception." *Advances in Experimental Social Psychology* 14: 1–59.

Name Index

Subject Index

Photo Credits

CHAPTER 1: pp. 1, 2, and 33: Pearson; p. 5: left: Roxana Gonzalez/ Shutterstock, right: Doug Berry/Photodisc/Getty Images; p. 7: Andrew Holbrooke/Corbis; p. 12: Tom Green Defense Team/AP Images; p. 13: Maxim Pimenov/Fotolia; p. 14: Alain Le Garsmeur/Impact/HIP/The Image Works; p. 17: Library of Congress Prints and Photographs Division Washington, D.C[LC-DIG-nclc-01293]; p. 19: Jeff Greenberg/The Image Works; p. 20: 3desc/Fotolia; p. 21: Andy Dean Photography/Shutterstock; p. 22: Patrick Olear/PhotoEdit; p. 26: kurhan/Shutterstock; p. 31: Maskot/ Getty Images; p. 32: apttone/Fotolia

CHAPTER 2: pp. 36, 37, and 67: Pearson; p. 43: right: Rsinha/Shutterstock; p. 44: left: Beau Lark/Corbis; p. 44: right: STEVE LINDRIDGE/Alamy; p. 47: top: Larry W. Smith/epa/Corbis, bottom: EDHAR/Shutterstock; p. 49: ChinaFotoPress/Getty Images; p. 50: roza/Fotolia; p. 51: Kennel Krista/SIPA/SIPPL SIPA USA/AP Images; p. 54: top: hxdbzxy/ Shutterstock, bottom: Will Hart/NBC/Everett Collection; p. 56: epa/ Corbis Wire/Corbis; p. 62: right: Anton Vengo/SuperStock, left: allen russell/Alamy; p. 63: tethysimagingllc/Fotolia; p. 64: stoonn/Fotolia

CHAPTER 3: pp. 70, 71, and 95: Pearson; p. 74: Karen Neal/Disney ABC Television Group/Getty Images; p. 75: left: ©bikeriderlondon/Shutterstock. com, right: David R. Frazier/The Image Works; p. 79: ClassicStock/Corbis; p. 80: Jamie Grill/Getty Images; p. 81: John Corney/Flickr Open/Getty Images; p. 83: David J. Green-lifestyle themes/Alamy; p. 86: John Minihan/ Evening Standard/Getty Images; p. 88: top: Gertan/Fotolia; p. 92: Kellie L. Folkerts/Shutterstock; p. 94: Larry Busacca/Getty Images

CHAPTER 4: pp. 98, 99, and 123: Pearson; p. 100: Toshiko Takahashi/ Getty Images; p. 102: Poncho/Photonica/Getty Images; p. 104: Vasily Smirnov/Shutterstock; p. 106: klang/Fotolia; p. 107: right: Stephen Coburn/Shutterstock, left: Timothy Large/Shutterstock; p. 109: top: vgstudio/Shutterstock, bottom left: Jason Stitt/istockphoto/Thinkstock, bottom right: wxin/Shutterstock; p. 111: Jan Mammey/Getty Images; p. 113: Graeme Robertson/Getty Images; p. 115: Rhoda Sidney/The Image Works; p. 118: Tommy Kay/Corbis; p. 119: National Center for Victims of Crime; p. 120: George Allen Penton/Shutterstock; p. 121: alexey_boldin/Fotolia

CHAPTER 5: pp. 126, 127, and 156: Pearson; p. 128: CBS/ Everett Collection; p. 130: Digital Vision/Getty Images; p. 133: Lionel Hahn/ Abacausa/Newscom; p. 134: Arrow Studio/Fotolia LLC; p. 138: Cliff Lipson/CBS/Courtesy Everett Collection; p. 143: Spencer Grant/ PhotoEdit; p. 144: ducu59us/Shutterstock; p. 146: Bill Aron/PhotoEdit; p. 148: Fabrice Lerouge/Onoky/Getty images; p. 151: Esbin-Anderson/ The Image Works; p. 154: A. Ramey/PhotoEdit; p. 157: Lefty Shivambu/ Gallo Images/Getty Images

CHAPTER 6: pp. 160, 161, and 185: Pearson; p. 164: Greg Gayne/ © Fox/Courtesy: Everett Collection; p. 166: Lee Snider/The Image Works; p. 167: myfotolia88/Fotolia; p. 168: Tanya Constantine/Photodisc/Getty Images; p. 169: Mark Peterson/Corbis; p. 170: camrocker/Fotolia; p. 171: Robin Laurance/Alamy; p. 172: top: The Star-Ledger/Mitsu Yasukawa/ The Image Works, bottom: asb63/Fotolia; p. 174: Edyta Pawlowska/ Fotolia; p. 175: moodboard/Corbis; p. 176: Heidi Gutman/Disney ABC Television Group/ABC via Getty Images; p. 177: jose_arbelaez/Fotolia; p. 182: Diego Cervo/Shutterstock.com

CHAPTER 7: pp. 188, 189, and 217: Pearson; p. 191: left: Bill Lai/The Image Works, right: Louise Gubb/Corbis; p. 194: Cliff Lipson/CBS/Courtesy Everett Collection; p. 197: Richard Lord/The Image Works; p. 198: Bruce Glikas/ FilmMagic/Getty Images; p. 203: Jim West/The Image Works; p. 204: Lasse Kristensen/Shutterstock; p. 206: Maskot/Alamy; p. 207: David M. Grossman/The Image Works; p. 211: Monkey Business Images/Shutterstock; p. 213: SW Productions/Photodisc/Getty Images; p. 214: left and right: Supplied by Karen Seccombe

CHAPTER 8: pp. 220, 221, and 245: Pearson; p. 223: Louise Gubb/ Corbis News/Corbis; p. 226: Erin Moroney LaBelle/The Image Works; p. 230: Sebastien Micke/Paris Match/Getty Images; p. 231: Denise Hager, Catchlight Visual Services/Alamy; p. 235: Sally and Richard Greenhill/ Alamy; p. 237: Hong Vo/Shutterstock; p. 239: Kayte Deioma/PhotoEdit; p. 240: JACQUELINE PIETSCH/AFP/Getty Images; p. 241: Supplied by Karen Seccombe; p. 242: Kim Eriksen/zefa/Corbis; p. 243: Gresei/Fotolia; p. 244: FRANCIS DEAN/DEAN PICTURES/Newscom

CHAPTER 9: pp. 248, 249, and 276: Pearson; p. 250: Alison Wright/ Corbis; p. 252: Library of Congress Prints and Photographs Division Washington, D.C[LC-DIG-nclc-05129]; p. 255: Susanne Walstrom/Getty Images; p. 260: Edward Le Poulin/Corbis; p. 264: left: Kate Mitchell/ Corbis, right: BananaStock/Jupiter Images; p. 267: Mike Theiler/epa/ Corbis; p. 270: Rohit Seth/Fotolia; p. 272: MIKE HUTCHINGS/Reuters/ Corbis; p. 274: Jupiterimages/Photolibrary/Getty Images

CHAPTER 10: pp. 279, 280, and 305: Pearson; p. 281: Sean Sprague/The Image Works; p. 282: Library of Congress Prints and Photographs Division Washington, D.C[LC-USZC4-5603]; p. 285: Andrew Holbrooke/ Corbis; p. 286: Jim West/Alamy; p. 291: ERproductions Ltd/Blend Images/Getty Images; p. 293: left: Sonda Dawes/The Image Works, right: Don Mason/Corbis; p. 294: bottom: Ideenkoch/Fotolia; p. 298: VStock/ Alamy; p. 299: Golden Pixels LLC/Shutterstock; p. 303: Caro/Alamy

CHAPTER 11: pp. 308, 309, and 340: Pearson; p. 311: Gino Santa Maria/Fotolia; p. 313: Ariel Skelley/Blend Images/Getty Images; p. 315: Splash News/Newscom; p. 323: Pascal Broze/Onoky/Corbis; p. 326: Stockbroker/MBI/Alamy; p. 329: Pixel Memoirs/Shutterstock; p. 331: Mike Goldwater/Alamy; p. 333: Goodshoot/Jupiter Images; p. 335: Bill Olive/Getty Images; p. 338: James Shaffer/PhotoEdit

CHAPTER 12: pp. 343, 344, and 372: Pearson; p. 346: Stapleton Historical Collection/HIP/The Image Works; p. 348: Kablonk/SuperStock; p. 351: Zurijeta/Shutterstock; p. 355: Erik Isakson/Blend Images/Getty Images; p. 358: Jasper White/Photographer's Choice/Getty Images; p. 360: Bob Daemmrich/PhotoEdit; p. 361: karnizz/Fotolia; p. 365: top left: Claire Barnes, top right: Claire Barnes, bottom left: Claire Barnes, bottom right: Claire Barnes; p. 366: Tony Savino/The Image Works; p. 369: Tatyana Gladskih/ Fotolia; p. 371: iofoto/Shutterstock

CHAPTER 13: pp. 375, 376, and 401: Pearson; p. 378: Heather Weston/ Photolibrary/Getty Images; p. 379: Ho New/Reuters; p. 381: John Birdsall/The Image Works; p. 386: KVS/Andrade,PacificCoastNews/ Newscom; p. 389: Francis Dean/Dean Pictures/The Image Works; p. 392: Jupiterimages/Stockbyte /Getty Images; p. 397: Eric Audras/ PhotoAlto/Corbis; p. 398: Jupiterimages/Getty Images

CHAPTER 14: pp. 404, 405, and 433: Pearson; p. 407: top: Judy Ben Joud, 2008/Used under license from Shutterstock.com, bottom: Supplied by Karen Seccombe; p. 409: CORBIS; p. 411: Jupiterimages/Getty Images; p. 412: Paul Maguire/Fotolia; p. 417: Talmadge Heyward/ Queerstock, Inc./Alamy; p. 421: Leah Warkentin/Design Pics/Getty Images; p. 424: Billy E. Barnes/PhotoEdit; p. 426: michaeljung/Fotolia; p. 428: left: Glow Images/Getty Images, right: Frank and Helena/cultura/ Corbis; p. 431: Mary Anne Fackelman-White House via CNP/Newscom; p. 432: ALAN ODDIE/PhotoEdit

CHAPTER 15: pp. 436, 437, and 462: Pearson; p. 439: top: Armando Gallo/Retna Ltd./Corbis, bottom: Kevin Winter/Getty Images; p. 441: Jeff Greenberg/PhotoEdit; p. 444: F.LEPAGE/SIPA/Newscom; p. 447: Picture Partners/Alamy; p. 448: Oscar Abrahams/beyond/Corbis; p. 455: Bob Daemmrich/PhotoEdit; p. 461: Tom Grill/Tetra Images/Corbis; p. 462: FABIANO/SIPA/Newscom